Let's Go

ISRAEL & EGYPT

is the best book for anyone traveling on a budget. Here's why:

▓ No other guidebook has as many budget listings.

In Israel & Egypt we list over 4,500 budget travel bargains. We tell you the cheapest way to get around, and where to get an inexpensive and satisfying meal once you've arrived. We give hundreds of money-saving tips that anyone can use, plus invaluable advice on discounts and deals for students, children, families, and senior travelers.

▓ Let's Go researchers have to make it on their own.

Our Harvard-Radcliffe researcher-writers travel on budgets as tight as your own—no expense accounts, no free hotel rooms.

▓ Let's Go is completely revised each year.

We don't just update the prices, we go back to the place. If a charming café has become an overpriced tourist trap, we'll replace the listing with a new and better one.

▓ No other guidebook includes all this:

Honest, engaging coverage of both the cities and the countryside; up-to-the-minute prices, directions, addresses, phone numbers, and opening hours; in-depth essays on local culture, history, and politics; comprehensive listings on transportation between and within regions and cities; straight advice on work and study, budget accommodations, sights, nightlife, and food; detailed city and regional maps; and much more.

▓ Let's Go is for anyone who wants to see Israel & Egypt on a budget.

Books by Let's Go, Inc.

EUROPE

Let's Go: Europe

Let's Go: Austria & Switzerland

Let's Go: Britain & Ireland

Let's Go: Eastern Europe

Let's Go: France

Let's Go: Germany

Let's Go: Greece & Turkey

Let's Go: Ireland

Let's Go: Italy

Let's Go: London

Let's Go: Paris

Let's Go: Rome

Let's Go: Spain & Portugal

NORTH & CENTRAL AMERICA

Let's Go: USA & Canada

Let's Go: Alaska & The Pacific Northwest

Let's Go: California

Let's Go: New York City

Let's Go: Washington, D.C.

Let's Go: Mexico

MIDDLE EAST & ASIA

Let's Go: Israel & Egypt

Let's Go: Thailand

Let's Go

The Budget Guide to

ISRAEL &
EGYPT

1995

Haneen M. Rabie
Editor

Robert Tsai
Associate Editor

Michael L. Cisneros
Assistant Editor

Written by
Let's Go, Inc.
A subsidiary of
Harvard Student Agencies, Inc.

MACMILLAN

HELPING LET'S GO

If you have suggestions or corrections, or just want to share your discoveries, drop us a line. We read every piece of correspondence, whether a 10-page e-mail letter, a velveteen Elvis postcard, or, as in one case, a collage. All suggestions are passed along to our researcher-writers. Please note that mail received after May 5, 1995 will probably be too late for the 1996 book, but will be retained for the following edition.

Address mail to:

**Let's Go: Israel & Egypt
Let's Go, Inc.
1 Story Street
Cambridge, MA 02138
USA**

Or send e-mail to:

letsgo@delphi.com

In addition to the invaluable travel advice our readers share with us, many are kind enough to offer their services as researchers or editors. Unfortunately, the charter of Let's Go, Inc. and Harvard Student Agencies, Inc. enables us to employ only currently enrolled Harvard-Radcliffe students.

Published in Great Britain 1995 by Macmillan, Cavaye Place, London SW10 9PG.

10 9 8 7 6 5 4 3 2 1

Maps by David Lindroth, copyright © 1995, 1994, 1993, 1992, 1991, 1990, 1989, 1986 by St. Martin's Press, Inc.

Published in the United States of America by St. Martin's Press, Inc.

ISBN: 0 333 62227 8

Let's Go: Israel & Egypt is written by the Publishing Division of Let's Go, Inc., 1 Story Street, Cambridge, MA 02138.

Let's Go® is a registered trademark of Let's Go, Inc.
Printed in the U.S.A. on recycled paper with biodegradable soy ink.

About Let's Go

Back in 1960, a few students at Harvard University got together to produce a 20-page pamphlet offering a collection of tips on budget travel in Europe. For three years, Harvard Student Agencies, a student-run nonprofit corporation, had been doing a brisk business booking charter flights to Europe; this modest, mimeographed packet was offered to passengers as an extra. The following year, students traveling to Europe researched the first full-fledged edition of *Let's Go: Europe*, a pocket-sized book featuring advice on shoestring travel, irreverent write-ups of sights, and a decidedly youthful slant.

Throughout the 60s, the guides reflected the times: one section of the 1968 *Let's Go: Europe* talked about "Street Singing in Europe on No Dollars a Day." During the 70s, *Let's Go* gradually became a large-scale operation, adding regional European guides and expanding coverage into North Africa and Asia. The 80s saw the arrival of *Let's Go: USA & Canada* and *Let's Go: Mexico*, as well as regional North American guides; in the 90s we introduced five in-depth city guides to Paris, London, Rome, New York City, and Washington, DC. And as the budget travel world expands, so do we; the first edition of *Let's Go: Thailand* hit the shelves last year, and this year's edition adds coverage of Malaysia, Singapore, Tokyo, and Hong Kong.

This year we're proud to announce the birth of *Let's Go: Eastern Europe*—the most comprehensive guide to this renascent region, with more practical information and insider tips than any other. *Let's Go: Eastern Europe* brings our total number of titles, with their spirit of adventure and reputation for honesty, accuracy, and editorial integrity, to 21.

We've seen a lot in 35 years. *Let's Go: Europe* is now the world's #1 best selling international guide, translated into seven languages. And our guides are still researched, written, and produced entirely by students who know first-hand how to see the world on the cheap.

Every spring, we recruit over 100 researchers and 50 editors to write our books anew. Come summertime, after several months of training, researchers hit the road for seven weeks of exploration, from Bangkok to Budapest, Anchorage to Ankara. With pen and notebook in hand, a few changes of underwear stuffed in our backpacks, and a budget as tight as yours, we visit every *pensione*, *palapa*, pizzeria, café, club, campground, or castle we can find to make sure you'll get the most out of *your* trip.

We've put the best of our discoveries into the book you're now holding. A brand-new edition of each guide hits the shelves every year, only months after it is researched, so you know you're getting the most reliable, up-to-date, and comprehensive information available. The budget travel world is constantly changing, and where other guides quickly become obsolete, our annual research keeps you abreast of the very latest travel insights. And even as you read this, work on next year's editions is well underway.

At *Let's Go*, we think of budget travel not only as a means of cutting down on costs, but as a way of breaking down a few walls as well. Living cheap and simple on the road brings you closer to the real people and places you've been saving up to visit. This book will ease your anxieties and answer your questions about the basics—to help *you* get off the beaten track and explore. We encourage you to put *Let's Go* away now and then and strike out on your own. As any seasoned traveler will tell you, the best discoveries are often those you make yourself. If you find something worth sharing, drop us a line. We're at Let's Go, Inc., 1 Story Street, Cambridge, MA, 02138, USA (e-mail: letsgo@delphi.com).

Happy travels!

Want a more comfortable nonstop flight to Israel than on EL AL's new 747-400s?

Run for president and fly on Air Force One.

At EL AL, we're the first and only airline to fly 747-400s nonstop between New York and Tel Aviv. Complete with personal TV monitors for each and every seat. And in first class: a personal VCR for every seat, a video library, and sleeperette seats. An onboard jacuzzi?

You must be mixing us up with that other airplane.

The Airline of Israel.

Contents

Maps

Acknowledgments

Thanks to our wonderful R-W's, the U.S. Embassy in Syria for making Steven's gargantuan task easier, John's parents for tracking him down, Mrs. Montasser, Mike Farbiarz for his help with Hebrew, Edward McBride, and Alexis, Liz, Matt, and Pete.

Eternal gratitude to RT & MC. **Rob** made format perfect & typos nonexistent, plus PB& J. **Mike** rocked my world with "Points in Syria;" and his comments were hysterical. Thanks to **Mom** for pep-talks & Arabic spellings, **Dad** for knowing every fact extant, **Kareemie** for chatting up a storm, **Aseel** for Vietnamese food, **Setto,** & especially **Khalo Mohamed. Kevin Bensley** (my partner R-W), **Radi** and **Cynthia** for Amman info. & all-around coolity, **Nadim** for headers help, **Lisan** and **Ludz** for a roof over my head, **Scott, LM & LH,** belly dancers **AK & TB, LKA & KLM. —HMR**

I want to thank my family for supporting my decision to take this not-specifically-pre-medically-oriented, fun-because-of-Haneen-and-Mike, and different extra-curricular-activity-*cum*-job. Without Kullada, I would never have been introduced to the world and joy of last-minute-deadline publishing and editing. Special thanks to ex-roommate Dave and a few other *a capella* singers for re-introducing me to Jerusalem and beyond, and re-sparking my interest in this stuff. **—RT**

Thanks to: Haneen and Rob, for rocking much house and rendering me damn near superfluous; Eleni and Alp, for sharing; the Internet, for allowing me to bypass the State Department; Broadway, for the musical backdrop; Larry, Carlyle, John, Kathryn, Mary, R.I., and Such for coming to *Godot;* Dave, Benn, Jamie, Amy, Beth, John, Chrissi, Jim, and A.J. for being there, and giving me something to look forward to; and my family, for everything. Gotta find my corner of the sky. **—MLC**

STAFF

Editor	Haneen M. Rabie
Associate Editor	Robert Tsai
Assistant Editor	Michael L. Cisneros
Publishing Director	Pete Keith
Production Manager	Alexis G. Averbuck
Production Assistant	Elizabeth J. Stein
Financial Manager	Matt Heid
Assistant General Manager	Anne E. Chisholm
Sales Group Manager	Sherice R. Guillory
Sales Department Coordinator	Andrea N. Taylor
Sales Group Representatives	Eli K. Aheto
	Timur Okay Harry Hiçyılmaz
	Arzhang Kamerei
	Hollister Jane Leopold
	David L. Yuan
President	Lucienne D. Lester
General Manager	Richard M. Olken

Researcher-Writers

Barak Ben-Gal   *Sinai, Tel Aviv-Jaffa, Haifa, Dead Sea and Deserts*
Prolific with his pen, this native-Israeli-turned-Floridian spurted incredibly enthusiastic prose reveling in everything from Shopping, Walks, and Parks to the 300th tiny kibbutz museum to the Masada sound and light show. He mastered uncharted territory in the Sinai, thoroughly enjoying himself in the process. With the bargain-basement budget traveler in mind, Barak crafted an itinerary so frugal that he had money left over. After seven weeks of life-on-the-rough, his hard-earned shekels were spent on (what else?) a few nights in an Eilat five-star hotel (bathroom telephone included). Breaking Olympic speed records to find an open post office, Barak made sure his copy was never late, impeccably organized, and a breeze to edit.

John J. Bentley IV   *Cairo, Nile Valley, Oases, Red Sea Coast*
John left the *Let's Go* offices in May without a backward glance, and became completely immersed in his itinerary. So immersed, in fact, that we were hard-pressed to find him around mid-July. But John persevered, consulting antiquities authorities and experts on Islamic history and architecture. This Middle Eastern Studies major and resident Cairene added informative sections on Egypt's ethnic make-up, giving much-needed recognition to its Nubian population. His knowledge of Arabic allowed him to talk to locals, who gleefully detailed enough devious deeds to provide the book with lengthy warning sections. Finally, thanks to John, anyone in need of a Bloody Mary or a cold Stella in Egypt will know exactly where to go.

Caralee Caplan   *Haifa, Galilee, Golan, Jerusalem*
The first clue was Caralee's list of Jerusalem's Old City gates, replete with translations, transliterations, and spellings of the Arabic, English, and Hebrew names. Then there were the three ink colors: one for text, one for important marginalia, and one for funny stories like the time the famous Eli Avivi tried to pick her up. Incredibly organized, our diminutive Canuck mastered colloquial Arabic (using the language glossary in the back of this very book, we might add), added insights for women traveling alone, and introduced us to all-the-wine-you-can-drink at The Winery. Winning a tough biological war against the evils of illness, she triumphantly turned in her meticulous copy on time, with help from a familial entourage of co-R-W's.

Hashem E. E. Montasser   *Cairo, Mediterranean Coast, Oases, Suez Canal, Sinai*
Who but this Cairene could have squeezed every bit of transportation information Cairo had to offer out of its harried *service* drivers and tourism minsitry officials? Slaving friends and family members for wheels and phone hook-ups, Hash made Practical Information a strong point. Covering more ground than Odysseus, he repaired the Oases' negative image, write up obscure Sinai retreats, and gave you an insider's itinerary by transferring his social life onto the pages of this book (billiards, the Atlas Disco, My Queen, El Agami). He peppered his prose with exclamation points (some of which we kept), references to E.M. Forster, and Arabic spellings; and his phone calls kept his editor laughing hysterically all summer.

Steven Purvis-Smith   *West Bank, Jordan, Syria*
Where some cities require multiple R-Ws (Washington, D.C. alone had two), this man single-handedly covered two-and-a-half countries, one of which was written up from scratch. Getting in good with the U.S. Ambassador to Syria (and the Syrian Ambassador to Jordan) and milking the entire American expatriate population of the Middle East for information, Steve impressed us immensely with his energy, enthusiasm, and insight. We can even say his copy was fun to edit. Though efforts to meet Arafat fell flat, Steve did garner numerous invitations throughout his travels; his contact with locals added an invaluable dimension to the book. We frequently had reason to fear for his life, but neither stonings nor a certain taxi driver nor "gunfire" in Jerusalem that turned out to be firecrackers could faze this stalwart adventurer.

How To Use This Book

Look, we don't want to insult your intelligence by assuming that you don't know how to use a book; but the Man says we have to write this section. We'll just explain the logic behind the guide's construction, and leave the rest up to you. Think of us as caring parents: pointing you in the right direction; giving you all you need to make your journey; but, ultimately, letting you discover the world for yourself.

Even though *we* find it gripping, we don't expect you to read the whole book; we understand that not everyone will visit every country we cover. However, should you decide to undertake such an ambitious journey, we are prepared—and so are you. We organized the book geographically (not alphabetically, and not because we like Israel more than Syria), to make an excursion of any duration easy to plan.

Take the time to peruse **Essentials** and the introductions to the countries you will be visiting, *before* you go traveling. Then you'll know not only how to get there, but also what you'll need before you go, what you need to know while you're there, what "there" is like, who will be waiting for you, and how they got there.

Shortly after you arrive, you'll need some specifics about the unfamiliar cities and towns that will be your temporary homes. Each city's description elaborates on why it's there, so you'll know why *you're* there. Then comes the lowdown—how to get there, what to see, where to eat, and where to sleep. Sometimes bad things happen to good people; when they do, we'll tell you where to go. (Really.)

Getting tired of speaking English loudly, playing charades, and feeling like Tipper Gore at Lollapalooza? The **language glossary** will put useful words into your mouth. It includes greetings, numerals, directions, and emergency phrases in both Arabic and Hebrew. You'll feel less like a *khawaga*, and more like a *townie*.

Our book was written with the budget traveler in mind, but a special breed of budget traveler: the adventurer. If you choose to use *Let's Go* as your ultimate travel authority, never straying from our suggestions, then by all means do so: you certainly won't be the first, and you'll most likely have a great trip. But there's a whole world out there; use *Let's Go* as the raw material from which to create your own masterpiece. With some creativity, caution, and *chutzpah*, your visit to the Middle East will be infinitely more fulfilling.

A NOTE TO OUR READERS

The information for this book is gathered by *Let's Go*'s researchers during the late spring and summer months. Each listing is derived from the assigned researcher's opinion based upon his or her visit at a particular time. The opinions are expressed in a candid and forthright manner. Other travelers might disagree. Those traveling at a different time may have different experiences since prices, dates, hours, and conditions are always subject to change. You are urged to check beforehand to avoid inconvenience and surprises. Travel always involves a certain degree of risk, especially in low-cost areas. When traveling, especially on a budget, you should always take particular care to ensure your safety.

ESSENTIALS

The birthplace of the world's three major religions is now the place where the purveyors of these faiths quibble over everything from relevant dates and places to less relevant lightbulb-changing rights in the Church of the Holy Sepulchre; and where young states seemingly formed upon a Great Powers whim brew enough political, ethnic, religious, and economic complexities to keep the world's press corps in business until Judgment Day. The backdrop for today's tumult is the region's engrossing, centuries-long history of ancient civilizations and conquering empires.

Most people go to the Middle East seeking the monuments of pharaohs, the footsteps of Moses, Jesus, and Muhammad, or the paths of Crusaders and Ottoman Turks. Some go to experience current conflicts and political events, while others are on personal pilgrimages of cultural or religious significance. All may overlook the area's stunning natural life, including eerie deserts dotted with lush oases, groves of olive and citrus trees, and flamboyant underwater life. They may also be surprised to discover that real human lives are carried out amidst the relics of the past and the political play of the present. Interacting with locals will make your Middle Eastern voyage more than a survey course in history or an evening with CNN.

PLANNING YOUR TRIP

■■■ WHEN TO GO

Egypt's high and low seasons depend on the region: Cairo is a year-round mob scene, while summertime is partytime in Alexandria and on the Mediterranean and Red Sea beaches for Egyptians and foreign visitors alike. In the Sinai and Upper Egypt, reasonable temperatures make winter high season, especially for wealthier tourists; students revel in summertime bargains. North Americans and students favor summer for visiting **Israel, Jerusalem,** and the **West Bank;** Europeans prefer winter. **Jordan's** peak seasons are spring and autumn, and **Syria** receives visitors from neighboring countries and Europe in summer. If you can stand the climate, off-season travel means smaller crowds, lower prices, and greater local hospitality.

Arrange your itinerary with an awareness of **holidays.** In Muslim countries, many businesses are closed on Friday, the day of prayer. On holidays, they may close during the afternoon, but are generally open in the morning. The dates of these holidays are difficult to pin down ahead of time, as Islam is based on a lunar calendar. Approximate dates for 1995 follow: **Ras as-Sana** (May 31) is the Islamic New Year's Day, and **Mawlid an-Nabi** (Aug. 9) celebrates Muhammad's birthday. The most important event and the one most likely to inconvenience self-indulgent travelers is **Ramadan** (Feb. 1-Mar. 4), the annual month-long fast during which Muslims abstain from food and drink from dawn to sunset. During this time, most restaurants close up shop until sundown. Shops may open for a few hours in the morning and a short time after *iftar,* the breaking of the fast; government services are either closed or open only in the morning. It would be rude to eat in public at this time. The celebratory, three-day **Eid al-Fitr** feast marks the end of Ramadan. **Eid al-Adhah** (May 10), commemorates Abraham's intended sacrifice of his son Ishmael and coincides with the *hajj* to Mecca, the 5th pillar of Islam.

In Israel, most businesses close Friday afternoon for **Shabbat,** the Jewish sabbath, and reopen on Sunday. They also close for Jewish holy days, which begin at sunset on the previous day. 1995 dates follow: **Tu B'Shevat** (Jan. 16) is an ancient Arbor Day celebration. **Ta'anis Esther** and **Purim** (Mar. 5 and 6) commemorate the fast of

Esther (Esther 4:16) and celebrate the deliverance of the Jews from persecution. **Pesaḥ**, or Passover (Apr. 4-10), celebrates the flight of the Jews from slavery in Egypt. Observant Jews refrain from eating bread and pastries; products made with regular flour and leavening agents may be hard to come by in Jewish areas. **Lag Ba'Omer** (May 7), **Shavu'ot** (celebrating the giving of the Torah; May 24), **Tisha B'av** (Ninth of Av Fast; July 25) and **Rosh Ha-Shana** (the Jewish New Year; Sept. 25-26) are other holidays. **Yom Kippur** (Oct. 4) is the holiest day of the Jewish calendar; observant Jews fast in atonement for their sins and Israel shuts down entirely. **Sukkot** (Oct. 9-17), the festival of the harvest, commemorates the Israelites' wilderness wanderings; open-roofed shelters called *sukkot* are built. **Simḥat Torah** is celebrated Oct. 16-17, and **Hanukkah** (Dec. 18-25) marks the Festival of Lights, commemorating the resanctification of the Temple in Jerusalem in 164 BCE.

Christians in the region celebrate the holidays of their various denominations.

CLIMATE

In southern **Egypt**, summer temperatures often reach 49°C (120°F) and can push 54°C (129°F). Fortunately, it's dry; your body's cooling system should know what to do. Winter here is perfect. In Cairo, also dry, pollution can make summer afternoons uncomfortable. Alexandria is temperate year-round, but the humidity makes every day a bad hair day. The Red Sea Coast is comfortably warm in winter and hot but dry in summer; higher elevations in the Sinai can be tooth-chattering in winter.

In **Israel**, the coastal plain is a sweaty steambath in summer. Cacti love Eilat, the Jordan Valley, and the Dead Sea, where it's hot and dry (except on the humid Dead Sea) in summer and mild in winter. The Negev Desert is not as hot; it has cool summer nights perfect for camel cuddling, and the winter can even be called "cold."

Summer in **Jerusalem** is dry with cool evenings, but winter blows, rains, blusters, depresses, and occasionally snows. The landlocked, hilly **West Bank** is spared the summer humidity of the Mediterranean coast, but not the heat. Summer afternoons will send you seeking shelter in the *souq;* cool nights invite long walks. Winters are cold, rainy, and in the higher elevations occasionally snowy.

Most attractions in **Jordan** are in the mountain region, where summer days could melt a cheap wig but evenings are deliciously cool. Winters are cold, and frequent rain mangles traffic even further. Aqaba enjoys balmy winter weather.

Syria has a varied Mediterranean climate: semi-arid, with sunny days and cool nights. There are four distinct seasons.

Average daily **temperatures** (minimum-maximum):

	January	July
Aleppo	2-10°C (36-51°F)	21-34°C (70-94°F)
Alexandria	11-19°C (53-66°F)	23-30°C (73-86°F)
Amman	4-16°C (40-61°F)	18-32°C (65-90°F)
Aqaba	10-21°C (49-70°F)	25-40°C (77-103°F)
Aswan	10-25°C (49-77°F)	26-42°C (79-108°F)
Cairo	8-18°C (46-65°F)	21-36°C (70-97°F)
Damascus	2-12°C (36-53°F)	18-36°C (64-96°F)
Eilat	10-21°C (49-70°F)	25-40°C (77-103°F)
Haifa	8-17°C (46-63°F)	20-30°C (68-86°F)
Jericho	5-10°C (42-51°F)	18-38°C (64-99°F)
Jerusalem	6-11°C (43-53°F)	19-29°C (66-84°F)
Luxor	6-24°C (43-75°F)	23-42°C (73-108°F)
Nablus	7-12°C (45-54°F)	19-30°C (66-86°F)
Tel Aviv	9-18°C (49-65°F)	21-30°C (70-86°F)
Tiberias	9-18°C (48-65°F)	23-37°C (73-98°F)

■■■ USEFUL ADDRESSES

EMBASSIES AND CONSULATES

Egyptian Embassies: Australia: 1 Darwin Avenue, Yarralumla, Canberra ACT 2600 (tel. (06) 273 44 37 or 38; fax 273 42 79). **Canada:** 454 Laurier Ave. E, Ottawa, Ont. K1N 6R3 (tel. (613) 234-4931 or -4935; fax 234-9347). **U.K.:** 26 South St., London W1Y 6DD (tel. (0171) 499 24 01; fax 355 35 68). **U.S.:** 3521 International Court NW, Washington, DC 20008 (tel. (202) 966-6342; fax 244-4319).

Egyptian Consulates: Australia: 335 New South Head Rd., Double Bay, Sydney NSW 2028 (tel. (02) 362 34 83; fax 327 10 96); 124 Exhibition St. 9th floor, Melbourne, Victoria 3000 (tel. (03) 654 88 69; fax 650 83 62). **Canada:** 3754 Côtes-des-Neiges, Montreal, Que. H3H 1V6 (tel. (514) 937-7781 or -7782). **U.K.:** 2 Lowndes St., London W1Y 6DD (tel. (0171) 235 97 19 or 77). **U.S.:** 1110 Second Ave., New York, NY 10022 (tel. (212) 759-7120; fax 308-7643); 3001 Pacific Ave., San Francisco, CA 94115 (tel. (415) 346-9700; fax 346-9480); and offices in Chicago and Houston.

Israeli Embassies: Australia: 6 Turrana St., Yarralumla, Canberra ACT 2600 (tel. (06) 273 20 45; fax 273 42 73). **Canada:** 50 O'Connor St., Ottawa, Ont. K1P 6L2 (tel. (613) 567-6450; fax 237-8865). **New Zealand:** Williams City Center (13th level), Plimmer Steps, P.O. Box 2171, Wellington (tel. (4) 472 23 62; fax 499 06 32). **South Africa:** Pretoria Dashing Center, 339 Hilda St., Hatfield, P.O. Box 3726, Johannesburg (tel. (12) 421 22 22; fax 342 14 42). **U.K.:** 2 Palace Green, London W8 4QB (tel. (0171) 957 95 00; fax 957 95 55). **U.S.:** 3514 International Drive NW, Washington, DC 20008 (tel. (202) 364-5500; fax 364-5423).

Israeli Consulates: Australia: 37 York St. 6th floor, Sydney NSW 2000 (tel. (02) 264 79 33; fax 29 02 59). **Canada:** 180 Bloor St. W #700, Toronto, Ont. M5S 2V6 (tel. (416) 961-1126; fax 961-7737). **South Africa:** Church Square House 3rd floor, Corner Spien and Plein St., P.O. Box 180, Cape-Town (tel. (021) 45 72 07 or 15; fax 461 00 75). **U.S.:** 800 Second Ave., New York, NY 10017 (tel. (212) 351-5200; fax 490-9186); 6380 Wilshire Blvd. #1700, Los Angeles, CA 90048 (tel. (213) 651-5700; fax 651-3123). Other offices in San Francisco, Miami, Atlanta, Chicago, New Orleans, Boston, Philadelphia, and Houston.

Jordanian Embassies: Australia: 20 Roebuck St., Red Hill, Canberra ACT 2603 (tel. (06) 95 99 51). **Canada:** 100 Bronson Ave. #701, Ottawa, Ont. K1R 6G8 (tel. (613) 238-8090). **U.K.:** 6 Upper Philimore Gardens, London W8 7HB (tel. (0171) 937 36 85). **U.S.:** 3504 International Dr. NW, Washington, DC 20008 (tel. (202) 966-2664; fax 966-3110).

Jordanian Consulates: U.S.: 866 United Nations Plaza #552, New York, NY 10017 (tel. (212) 752-0135; fax 826-0830); P.O. Box 3727, Houston, TX 77253 (tel. (713) 224-2911).

Syrian Embassies: Australia: J1 Kerang Asem 1, Kuninga Raya, Jakarta, Indonesia. **U.K.:** 8 Belgrave Square, London, SW1 (tel. (0171) 245 90 12). **U.S.:** 2215 Wyoming Ave. NW, Washington, DC 20008 (tel. (202) 232-6313; fax 265-4585).

Syrian Consulates: Australia: 10 Belmore St., Arncliffe, NSW 2205. **U.S.:** 820 Second Ave., New York, NY 10017 (tel. (212) 661-1553).

TOURIST AND INFORMATION OFFICES

The agencies and offices below are usually quick to respond to queries, but contact them well in advance of your departure just in case.

Egyptian Tourist Authority: Canada: 1253 McGill College Ave. #250, Montreal, Que. H3B 2Y5 (tel. (514) 861-4606; fax 861-8071). **U.K.:** 168 Piccadilly, London W1 (tel. (0171) 493 52 82 or 83; fax 408 02 95). **U.S.:** 630 Fifth Ave. #1706, New York, NY 10111 (tel. (212) 332-2570; fax 956-6439); Wilshire San Vicente Plaza, 83-83 Wilshire Blvd. #215, Beverly Hills, CA 90211 (tel. (213) 653-8815; fax 653-8961); 645 N. Michigan Ave. #829, Chicago, IL 60611 (tel. (312) 280-4666; fax 280-4788).

Israel Government Tourist Office (IGTO): Canada: 180 Bloor St. W #700, Toronto, Ont. M5S 2V6 (tel. (416) 964-3784; fax 961-3962). **South Africa:** Nedbank

USEFUL ADDRESSES

Gardens 5th floor, 33 Bath Ave., Rosebank, P.O. Box 52560, Saxonwold 2132, Johannesburg (tel. (11) 788 17 00; fax 447 31 04). **U.K.:** 18 Great Marlborough St., London W1V 1AF (tel. (0171) 434 36 51; fax 437 05 27). **U.S.:** 350 Fifth Ave. 19th floor, New York, NY 10118 (tel. (212) 560-0600; fax 629-4368); 6380 Wilshire Blvd. #1700, Los Angeles, CA 90048 (tel. (213) 658-7462; fax 658-6543, ext. 245); other offices in Atlanta, Chicago, Dallas, and Miami.

Jordan Information Bureau: U.K.: 11/12 Buckingham Gate, London SW1E 6LB (tel. (0171) 630 92 77; fax 233 75 20). **U.S.:** 2319 Wyoming Ave. NW, Washington, DC 20008 (tel. (202) 265-1606; fax 667-0777).

Palestinian Embassies and Information Offices: Australia: P.O. Box 97, 109 Drummond St. 2nd floor, Carlton, Victoria 3053 (tel. (03) 347 42 72). **U.K.:** 4 Clareville Grove, London SW7 5AR (tel. (0171) 370 32 44). **U.S.:** 1730 K St. NW #703, Washington, DC 20006 (tel. (202) 785-8394).

BUDGET TRAVEL SERVICES

Common services include student rates on tickets, ID cards (see Student and Youth Identification, p. 11), tours, maps and guides, and travel gear.

Campus Travel, 52 Grosvenor Gardens, London SW1W 0AG (tel. (0171) 730 88 32; fax 730 57 39). Offers a bookings service via telephone: from London/Europe (0171) 730 34 02; North America (0171) 730 21 01; elsewhere (0171) 730 81 11.

Council on International Educational Exchange (CIEE), 205 E. 42nd St., New York, NY 10017 (tel. (212) 661-1414). Administers professional, work, volunteer, and academic programs around the world. Publications include the useful *Student Travels* (free, postage US$1) and *Going Places: The High School Student's Guide to Study, Travel and Adventure Abroad* (US$13.95, postage $1.50).

Council Travel, 205 E. 42nd St., New York, NY 10017 (tel. (212) 661-1450), a subsidiary of CIEE. Specializes in student and budget travel. 43 other offices in the U.S., Dusseldorf, London, and Paris.

Federation of International Youth Travel Organisations (FIYTO). Write to FIYTO Secretariat, 25H Bredgade, 1160 Copenhagen K, Denmark. This organization of youth and student travel services sponsors the GO 25 card.

International Student Exchange Flights (ISE), 5010 East Shea Blvd. #A104, Scottsdale, AZ 85254 (tel. (602) 951-1177). Write for a free catalog.

International Student Travel Confederation, Store Kongensgade 40H, 1264 Copenhagen K, Denmark (tel. (33) 93 93 03). The masterminds behind the ISIC. Affiliated with the International Student Rail Association (ISRA), Student Air Travel Association (SATA), ISIS Travel Insurance, and the International Association for Educational and Work Exchange Programmes (IAEWEP).

Israel Student Travel Association (ISSTA), 109 Ben-Yehuda St., Tel Aviv 63401 (tel. (03) 527 0111; fax 523 0698).

Let's Go Travel, Harvard Student Agencies, Inc., 53-A Church St., Cambridge, MA 02138 (tel. (800) 5-LETS-GO or (617) 495-9649). The world's largest student-run travel agency. Offers *Let's Go* guides, maps, flights, and travel gear. All items available by mail; see this book's color insert.

New Zealand Student Travel, Scripture Building, Dixon St., Wellington (tel. (04) 05 61). Handles ISTC affairs and issues ISIC cards.

STA Travel, 5900 Wilshire Blvd. #2110, Los Angeles, CA 90036 (tel. (800) 777-0112). Student/youth travel. Over 100 offices in London, the U.S., and Australia.

Travel CUTS, 187 College St., Toronto, Ont. M5T 1P7 (tel. (416) 798-CUTS; fax 979-8167). Canada's CIEE, with 40 offices in Canada, one in London.

Travel Management International (TMI), 39 JFK St. 3rd floor, Cambridge, MA 02138 (tel. (800) 245-3672). Specializes in airline tickets to the Middle East.

WST Charters, 65 Wigmore St., London W1H 9LG (tel. (0171) 224 05 04; fax 224 61 42). Specializes in flights and tours to Israel and Egypt.

PUBLICATIONS

The **U.S. Government Printing Office** publishes *Key Officers of Foreign Serving Posts,* a quarterly State Department publication that lists all U.S. embassies, consulates, consulates general, and missions abroad (US$2.75 for a single issue, $5.85 for

TOP 5 Ways to Save Money While Traveling

5. Ship yourself in a crate marked "Livestock." Remember to poke holes in the crate.

4. Board a train dressed as Elvis and sneer and say "The King rides for free."

3. Ask if you can walk through the Channel Tunnel.

2. Board the plane dressed as an airline pilot, nod to the flight attendants, and hide in the rest room until the plane lands.

1. Bring a balloon to the airline ticket counter, kneel, breathe in the helium, and ask for the kiddie fare.

But if you're serious about saving money while you're traveling abroad, just get an ISIC--the International Student Identity Card. Discounts for students on international airfares, hotels and motels, car rentals, international phone calls, financial services, and more.

International Student Identity Card
Carte Internationale d'étudiant/Carnet internacional de estudiante

GRAHAM
DONNA
10/29/70   7/5/94
USA
U OREGON
STUDENT

For more information:
In the United States:

 Council on International Educational Exchange
205 East 42nd St.
New York, NY 10017
1-800-GET-AN-ID
Available at Council Travel offices (see inside front cover)

In Canada:

 Travel CUTS
243 College Street,
Toronto, Ontario M5T 2Y1
(416) 977-3703
Available at Travel CUTS offices nationwide

a subscription). Also *Your Trip Abroad* ($1.25), *A Safe Trip Abroad* ($1), *Tips for Travelers to the Middle East and North Africa* ($1.25), and *Health Information for International Travel* ($5). Write to Superintendent of Documents, P.O. Box 371954, Pittsburgh, PA 15250-7954 (tel. (202) 783-3238; fax (202) 512-2250). If you have a fax, dial the **Bureau of Consular Affairs** at (202) 647-3000 and follow the voice instructions for up-to-date information on Middle East countries. By phone call (202) 647-5225. Also see Specific Concerns, p. 27.

> **Bon Voyage!,** 2069 W. Bullard Ave., Fresno, CA 93711-1200 (tel. (800) 995-9716; from abroad (209) 447-8441). Annual mail-order catalog offering an amazing range of products. Prices guaranteed; 30-day return.
>
> **The College Connection, Inc.,** 1295 Prospect St., La Jolla, CA 92031 (tel. (619) 551-9770; fax (619) 551-9987). Publishes *The Passport,* a booklet with tips on every aspect of travel and study abroad (distributed free of charge to universities).
>
> **Forsyth Travel Library,** P.O. Box 2975, Shawnee Mission, KS 66201 (tel. (800) 367-7984; fax (913) 384-3553). Maps, guidebooks, railpasses, timetables, travel gear, and youth hostel memberships.
>
> **Hippocrene Books, Inc.,** 171 Madison Ave., New York, NY 10016 (tel. (212) 685-4371; orders (718) 454-2366; fax (718) 454-1391). Catalog of travel reference books and guides, maps, and language dictionaries and instruction materials.
>
> **Hunter Publishing,** 300 Raritan Center Parkway, Edison, NJ 08818 (tel. (908) 225-1900; fax 417-0482). Catalog of travel books, guides, and maps.
>
> **Rand McNally Travel,** 150 S. Wacker Dr., Chicago, IL 60606 (tel. (800) 333-0136). Maps, maps, maps; can be mail ordered.
>
> **Specialty Travel Index,** 305 San Anselmo Ave., San Anselmo, CA 94960 (tel. (415) 459-4900; fax 459-4974). Extensive semi-annual listing of "off the beaten track" and specialty travel opportunities.
>
> **Wide World Books and Maps,** 1911 N. 45th St., Seattle, WA 98103 (tel. (206) 634-3453; fax (206) 634-0558). Wide selection of travel guides and literature, travel accessories, and maps. Knowledgeable staff.

HOSTEL ASSOCIATIONS

Hostelling International (HI) is the universal trademark adopted by the International Youth Hostel Federation (IYHF). More than 5000 hostels display the HI logo (a blue triangle) alongside the symbol of one of 70 national hostel associations. HI membership is almost never required in Egypt and Israel's HI hostels; it will get you a small discount. Despite the name, you need not be a youth; travelers over 25 pay a slight surcharge for a bed. Children under 12 may receive a discounted rate.

Most people get a membership card before they leave, since some hostels don't sell them on the spot. They are available from Council Travel and STA and from the hostelling organization of your own country. HI encourages visitors to make reservations ahead of time, a good policy to follow for Israel. Send a letter or postcard with the date and estimated time of your arrival, the number of nights you plan to stay, and the number of beds or private rooms you will need. Include a check for the first night and a SASE to receive confirmation. By phone or fax, give a credit card number and expiration date.

Most national branches sell ISICs, arrange student and charter flights, and sell travel equipment and literature on budget travel. For more on hostels, see the Accommodations section in each country.

> **An Óige (Irish Youth Hostel Association),** 61 Mountjoy Street, Dublin 7, Ireland (tel. (01) 830 4555; fax 830 5808). 1-yr. membership IR£7.50, under 18 IR£4, family IR£15.
>
> **Australian Youth Hostels Association (AYHA),** Level 3, 10 Mallett St., Camperdown, NSW 2050 (tel. (02) 565 16 99; fax 565 13 25). Fee AUS$40, renewal AUS$24 (under 18 fee and renewal both AUS$12).
>
> **Egyptian Youth Hostels Association,** 1 El-Ibrahimy St., Garden City, Cairo (tel. (02) 354 0527). Fee E£24.

DOCUMENTS & FORMALITIES

Hostel Association of South Africa, P.O. Box 4402, Cape-Town 8000 (tel. (21) 419 18 53).

Hostelling International (HI), 9 Guessens Rd., Welwyn Garden City, Herts AL8 6QW England (tel. (01707) 33 24 87).

Hostelling International-American Youth Hostels (HI-AYH), 733 15th St. NW #840, Washington, DC, 20005 (tel. (202) 783-6161; fax 783-6171). Regional offices across the U.S.; 1-yr. membership US$25 (under 18 US$10, over 54 US$15, family US$35).

Hostelling International-Canada (HI-Canada), 400-205 Catherine St., Ont. K2P 1C3 (tel. (613) 237-7884; fax 237-7868). 1-yr. membership CDN$26.75 (under 18 CDN$12.84). 2-yr. membership CDN$37.45.

Israel Youth Hostels Association, 3 Dorot Rishonim St., P.O. Box 1075, Jerusalem 91009 (tel. (02) 252 706; fax 250 676). Youth Travel Bureau organizes tours for individuals and groups to Israel, Sinai, and Cairo. Write for the pamphlet *Israel on the Youth Hostel Trail.*

Scottish Youth Hostels Association (SYHA), 7 Glebe Crescent, Stirling FK8 2JA, Scotland (tel. (01786) 45 11 81; fax 45 01 98).

Syrian Youth Hostels, 66 Saleh al Ali St., Damascus (tel. (11) 459 540).

Youth Hostel Association of England & Wales (YHA), Treveylan House, 8 St. Stephens Hill, St. Albans, Herts AL1 2DY (tel. (01727) 85 52 15) or 14 Southampton St., Convent Garden, London WC2E 7HY (tel. (0171) 836 10 36). £9, under 18 £3.

Youth Hostels Association of New Zealand (YHANZ), P.O. Box 436, 173 Gloucester St., Christchurch 1, New Zealand (tel. (3) 379 99 70; fax 365 44 76). Fees: adult NZ$34, youth (15-17) NZ$12, under 15 free.

Youth Hostel Association of Northern Ireland (YHANI), 22-32 Donegall Rd., Belfast BT12 5JN, Northern Ireland (tel. (232) 32 47 33; fax 43 96 99).

■■■ DOCUMENTS & FORMALITIES

File applications for all documents several weeks in advance of your planned departure date. Some offices suggest applying in the winter off-season (August-December) for speedier service. Before leaving, photocopy all important documents and credit cards and leave them with someone you can contact easily. Your passport number is especially important. Consulates recommend that you carry an expired passport or an official copy of your birth certificate in a separate part of your baggage.

When you travel, always carry two or more forms of identification, including at least one photo ID. Many places (especially banks) require several IDs for cashing traveler's checks. Also carry a half-dozen extra passport-size photos that you can attach to the various IDs and visas you may eventually acquire.

PASSPORTS

A valid passport is required to enter Egypt, Israel, Jordan, or Syria and to return to your own country. As a precaution against loss or theft, keep photocopies of the pages containing your photograph, passport number, identifying information, and visa stamps. Carry a copy *apart from your passport*, perhaps with a traveling companion, and leave a copy at home. Also see Border Crossings, p. 33.

If you do lose your passport, notify the local police and your embassy or consulate immediately. To speed up replacement, provide your photocopies and show identification and proof of citizenship. Any visas stamped into your old passport will be irretrievably lost. In an emergency ask for temporary traveling papers that will permit you to return to your home country.

Citizens applying for passports from overseas should send the passport application to the nearest embassy, high commission, or consulate authorized to issue passports.

Australia: You must apply in person at a passport office, a post office, or an Australian diplomatic mission overseas; an appointment may be necessary. A parent may file an application for an unmarried child under 18.

Canada: Applications are available at any post office and most travel agencies. Call (24 hrs.) (800) 567-6868 from Canada, 973-3251 from Metro Toronto, 283-2152 from Montreal, or write for *Bon Voyage, But ...*, from the Passport Office, Department of Foreign Affairs, Ottawa, Ont. K1A OG3.

Great Britain: Applications are available at post offices and at the passport offices in Liverpool, Newport, Peterborough, Glasgow, or Belfast. Extensions can be obtained abroad at the nearest British high commission or consulate.

Ireland: Applications are available at Garda stations, or by mail from the Department of Foreign Affairs, Passport Office, Setanta Centre, Molesworth St., Dublin 2 (tel. (01) 671 16 33).

New Zealand: Application forms must be obtained from your local Link Centre, travel agent, or New Zealand Representative; they must then be completed and mailed to the New Zealand Passport Office, Documents of National Identity Division, Department of Internal Affairs, Box 10-526, Wellington (tel. (04) 474 81 00).

South Africa: Applications are available at any Department of Home Affairs Office.

U.S.: Call your local post office for the passport office nearest you.

VISAS AND VISA EXTENSIONS

A **visa** is an endorsement that a foreign government stamps into a passport; it allows the bearer to stay in that country for a specified purpose and period of time. The **Center for International Business and Travel (CIBT),** 25 W. 43rd. St. #1420, New York, NY 10036 (tel. (800) 925-2428, (212) 575-2811 from NYC), secures visas for travel to and from all countries. If you lose your visa overseas (via a stolen passport, for example), you must get a new one immediately to prove that you are allowed to be there; in Egypt, you will not be permitted to leave the country without a valid Egyptian visa. For a new Egyptian visa, go to the nearest passport office. In Israel, Jordan, and Syria, go to your embassy or consulate.

> Until Syria and Israel formalize a peace treaty (which could be very soon), you will not be allowed to enter Syria if you have an Israeli stamp on your passport. See Border Crossings, p. 33.

Egyptian visas can be easily obtained at the airport in Cairo, with less ease at borders. If you want to obtain one in advance, apply by mail or in person at the nearest Egyptian embassy or consulate. Provide the application and (1) your passport, which must be valid at least six months from the date of issue of your visa; (2) a passport-sized photo; and (3) the fees in cash or a certified check (US$15 for U.S. citizens, more for others). If applying by mail, include a stamped, self-addressed, certified envelope and allow at least 10 days for delivery. If you apply in person the process takes one day. No visa is required for citizens of South Africa.

Visas are good for entry within six months of the date of issue, valid for one month, and easily extended (see below). An Egyptian visa does not permit the holder to work. When applying, you can request a **multiple-entry visa** for travel in and out of Egypt, allowing you to reenter any number of times while the visa is valid. Visits to Sinai from Israel or Jordan can be made on a two-week **Sinai-only visa,** available at borders; see Border Crossings, p. 34.

Israeli visitors' visas are free for Australian, British, Canadian, Irish, New Zealand, South African, and U.S. citizens at the point of entry if your passport is valid at least nine months beyond your time of arrival. These visas are valid for three months but are extendable (see below). **Study visas** can be obtained from an Israeli embassy or consulate prior to departure or from any Office of the Interior once in Israel. Show proof of acceptance at an educational institution, a medical statement, and two photos. For work in Israel, have your employer in Israel contact the Office of the Interior and arrange a **work visa** before you leave. Five-day **transit visas** are also available. They may be extended for another ten days upon arrival in Israel. Cruise ship passengers visiting Israel are issued **landing cards** allowing them to remain in the country as long as the ship is in port. No visa application is required. **Collective visas** are issued by Israeli embassies or consulates for groups of 5 to 50 people.

Jordanian visas may be obtained upon arrival at Queen Alia Airport in Amman, or in person or by mail from any Jordanian embassy or consulate (takes two days). Requirements include a valid passport, a completed application form with one photo, and a self-addressed stamped envelope. Visas cost JD20 for U.S. citizens, and at least that for other nationalities. A **group visa** can be issued for tours of 10 persons or more, provided all have valid American passports. These are valid for one month and can be renewed at any police station (see below).

Syrian visas must be obtained before arrival in the country. Applications are available from any Syrian embassy. Send your completed application, passport (without evidence of a trip to Israel), a signed photo, a self-addressed envelope stamped for US$2, and payment to the embassy. Six-month single-entry visas and three-month double-entry visas cost US$20; six-month multiple-entry visas cost US$40. They will return the passport with your tourist visa in it. You may also have luck applying at Syrian embassies in Egypt or Jordan (see Cairo and Amman: Practical Information, p. 79 and p. 425).

Visa extensions are normally granted for six months to one year in Egypt, Israel, Jordan, and Syria. Egyptian visa extensions are available in Cairo at the Mugamma' Building or at any passport office, Israeli visa extensions at offices of the Ministry of the Interior, Jordanian visa extensions at the Ministry of the Interior in Amman, and Syrian visa extensions at any immigration office. To get an Egyptian visa extension, you must show evidence of having changed at least US$200 into Egyptian pounds.

CUSTOMS

You and your luggage will be examined as you pass through customs—often with exasperating thoroughness. Certain items may have to be declared upon entry, like jewelry, computers, cameras, and sports equipment. These items can usually be brought in duty-free as long as you take them with you upon departure. See Once There: Entry sections for each country for specific declaration and duty information.

It is wise to make a list, including serial numbers, of valuables that you carry from home. If you register this list with customs before your departure and have an official stamp it, you will avoid import duty charges and ensure an easy passage home.

Returning to your home country, there are additional restrictions:

Australian travelers over age 18 may bring AUS$40 worth of goods, plus the following goods duty-free: 1L liquor, 250 cigarettes or 250g of tobacco products, and an additional allowance of AUS$400 (under 18, AUS$200) for other goods intended as gifts. Contact: Australian Customs Service, 5 Constitution Ave., Canberra, ACT 2601 (tel. (6) 275 62 55; fax 275 69 89).

British citizens are exempted for up to £36 worth of goods purchased outside the E.U., plus no more than 200 cigarettes, 100 cigarillos, 50 cigars, or 250kg tobacco; 2L still table wine; 1L alcohol over 22% by volume or an extra 2L wine; and 60mL perfume and 250mL toilet water. You must be over 17 to import liquor or tobacco. Contact: Her Majesty's Customs and Excise, Customs House, Heathrow Airport North, Hounslow, Middlesex, TW6 2LA (tel. (0181) 750 15 49; fax 910 37 65).

Canadian citizens who remain abroad for at least one week may bring back up to CDN$300 worth of goods duty-free once every calendar year; anything above that is taxed at 12%. Citizens of legal age may import in person up to 200 cigarettes, 50 cigars, 400g loose tobacco, 1.14L wine or alcohol, and 355mL beer, all counted in the CDN$300 allowance. Contact: Canadian Customs, 2265 St. Laurent Blvd., Ottawa, Ont., K1G 4K3 (tel. (800) 461-9999, outside Canada (613) 993-0534).

Irish citizens may return home with the equivalent of IR£34 in goods purchased outside the E.U., and no more than 200 cigarettes, 100 cigarillos, 50 cigars, or 250g tobacco; 1L liquor (exceeding 22% volume) or 2L wine (less than 22%); 2L still wine; and 50g perfume and 250mL toilet water. Contact: The Revenue Commissioners, Dublin Castle (tel. (01) 679 27 77; fax 671 20 21) or The Collector of Customs and Excise, The Custom House, Dublin 1.

New Zealand citizens may bring home up to NZ$700 worth of goods duty-free if they are intended for personal use or as gifts. You may also bring in 200 cigarettes,

250g tobacco, 50 cigars, or a combination not to exceed 250g; 4.5L beer or wine, 1.125L liquor, 250mL toilet water, and 50mL perfume. Consult *New Zealand Customs Guide for Travelers,* available at customs houses. Contact: New Zealand Customs, 50 Anzac Avenue, Box 29, Auckland (tel. (09) 377 35 20; fax 309 29 78).

South African citizens may import duty-free 400 cigarettes, 50 cigars, 250g tobacco, 2L wine, 1L spirits, 250mL toilet water, 50mL perfume, and other items up to a value of R500. Anything exceeding this amount is taxable. Golf clubs, firearms, and items shipped home from abroad are not duty-free for travelers who have been absent for less than six months. Contact: Commissioner for Customs and Excise, Private Bag X47, Pretoria, 0001. They distribute the pamphlet *South African Customs Information* for visitors and residents who travel abroad. South Africans in the U.S. should contact: South African Mission to the IMF/World Bank, 3201 New Mexico Ave. #380 NW, Washington, DC 20016 (tel. (202) 364-8320 or -8321; fax 364-6008).

U.S. residents returning from abroad must declare all merchandise acquired abroad. The first $400 worth of personal or household merchandise is duty free, including 100 cigars, 200 cigarettes, and 1L (33.8 fl. oz.) alcohol. This $400 exemption is good once every 30 days, provided you have been out of the country for at least 48 hours. The next $1000 worth of merchandise will be taxed at a flat rate of 10%. Beyond that, different duty rates apply. Certain items made in Egypt, Israel, and Jordan may be excluded from the U.S. customs tax under the Generalized System of Preferences (GSP), designed to build the economies of developing nations. Get the brochure *Know Before You Go* from the U.S. Customs Service, Box 7407, Washington, DC 20044 (tel. (202) 927-6724). Foreign nationals living in the U.S. have different regulations; ask for *Customs Hints for Visitors (Nonresidents)*.

STUDENT AND YOUTH IDENTIFICATION

The **International Student Identification Card (ISIC)** is the most widely accepted form of student ID, providing medical insurance up to US$3000 and US$100 a day for up to 60 days of in-hospital illness, accidental death or dismemberment benefits, emergency evacuation coverage, access to a toll-free Traveler's Assistance hotline whose multilingual staff can help in emergencies (from the U.S. call (800) 626-2427; from elsewhere call collect (713) 267-2525), and cover up to $10,000 for emergency medical evacuation. It can be obtained from many student travel offices (local and national), student unions, and YHAs.

The annual *International Student Identity Card Handbook,* available wherever you apply for the card (or write to CIEE for a copy), lists by country some of the available discounts. These include discounts at museums and archaeological sites, retail stores, on flights, trains, buses, and accommodations. There are no special ISIC discounts in Egypt; any student ID gets substantial discounts on museums, sights, and train fares. A proliferation of phony cards may lead airlines and some other services to demand a second proof of identity and student status. It is wise to carry your school ID or a stamped letter from the registrar attesting to your student status. Present the card wherever you go; ask for discounts even when none are advertised.

Applicants must be at least 12 years old and enrolled at a secondary or post-secondary school. Applications (in person or by mail to CIEE; see Budget Travel Services, p. 5) must include (1) current, dated proof of full-time student status (e.g., a letter on school stationery signed and sealed by the registrar or a transcript); (2) a 1½"x2" photo with your name printed and signed on the back; (3) proof of birthdate and nationality; (4) name and address of beneficiary (for insurance purposes); and (5) a certified check or money order for US$16.

ISICs, valid September 1 to December of the following year, are issued by Council Travel, Let's Go Travel, and USTN in the U.S.; Travel CUTS in Canada; and any organization in the International Student Travel Confederation (ISTC).

A new, US$17 **International Teacher Identity Card (ITIC)** provides identical discounts; but many establishments are still reluctant to honor it. The application process is roughly the same as for an ISIC; teachers must present an official document from their department chair or another school official.

DOCUMENTS & FORMALITIES

Don't forget to write.

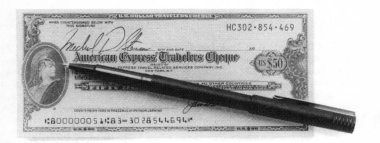

Now that you've said, "Let's go," it's time to say "Let's get American Express® Travelers Cheques." If they are lost or stolen, you can get a fast and full refund virtually anywhere you travel. So before you leave be sure and write.

The Federation of International Youth Travel Organisations (FIYTO) issues its own card to non-student travelers under 26. This **International Youth Discount Travel Card** (IYC or GO 25 Card) offers some of the same benefits as the ISIC; most organizations selling ISICs also sell IYCs. Get the free brochure when you purchase the card. In Israel, the card procures discounts on some Egged and Neot Ha-Kikar tours; Mano Seaways ferry travel between Israel, Egypt, Greece, and Italy; and numerous accommodations, restaurants, museums, etc. To apply, bring proof of birthdate (passport, valid driver's license, or copy of birth certificate) and a passport-sized photo. (Fee US$16, CDN$12, or £10.) Contact your local budget/student travel organization (see Budget Travel Services, p. 5).

INTERNATIONAL DRIVER'S LICENSE

An **International Driving Permit** is honored for driving in Egypt, Israel, Jordan, and Syria. Although other permits may be accepted, IDPs are useful in the event you get in an accident and the police do not speak English. They are available from any **American Automobile Association (AAA)** office with: completed application; two recent passport-sized photographs; valid U.S. driver's license; and US$10. Applicants must be 18 or older; the permit is processed and issued while you wait. Contact AAA Travel Agency Services Department, 1000 AAA Drive (mail stop 28), Heathrow, FL 32746-5080 (tel. (407) 444-4245; fax 444-7823).

If you hold a Canadian driver's license, you can obtain an IDP through any **Canadian Automobile Association (CAA)** office with CDN$10 and the same materials as above; CAA membership is not required. Contact CAA Toronto, 60 Commerce Valley Dr. East, Thornhill, Ont. L3T 7P9 (tel. (905) 771-3000; fax (905) 771-3046).

If you drive abroad you need insurance. In the Middle East, insurance is usually included in rental fees. For driving a private car, your insurance may extend overseas. An **International Insurance Certificate** or "green card" is needed to prove you have insurance. Applications are available at any AAA or CAA office. If leasing, get a green card from the dealer. Some travel agents offer the card as well.

■■■ MONEY MATTERS

See Money Matters sections for each country for more country-specific information.

CURRENCY AND EXCHANGE

The exchange rates valid at press time (Sept. 1994) are listed at the beginning of each country's section; however, rates fluctuate—often dramatically—so check them in the financial pages of a national newspaper when planning your trip. Before leaving home, buy enough currency to last the first 24-72 hours in the first country you will visit. This will save time at the airport and protect you if you arrive after banking hours or on a holiday or weekend.

Commissions can vary greatly; compare rates when exchanging money. Luxury hotels generally offer the worst rates. Try to exchange money in large sums (to minimize losses to commissions), but not so much that you'll have foreign currency left over. However, in a country with a high inflation rate, it is best to exchange money in small amounts. It might be a good idea for travelers of all nationalities to keep some U.S. dollars or German marks in case some booths refuse other forms of currency.

TRAVELER'S CHECKS

Traveler's checks are the safest way to hold money; if they get lost or stolen and you file a police report certifying this, you will get reimbursed by the checks' issuers. They can be purchased at many banks and should be signed at the time of purchase. Sometimes you will be charged a commission of 1-2%, sometimes a set fee, and sometimes, particularly if you are a customer of that bank, nothing at all.

The checks' serial numbers should be copied down and kept in a safe place separate from the checks themselves. Countersign the checks only when you're ready to use them and when the party accepting them is watching. Be sure to keep cash on hand in less touristy regions; smaller establishments may not accept traveler's checks. Finally, bring your passport whenever you plan to cash or spend the checks.

The smallest denomination is usually US$20 or equivalent. Get a few of these so that if you have to exchange money at a poor rate you won't lose too much.

Traveler's check companies offer a variety of services such as medical and legal referrals, emergency message relay, interpretation help, guaranteed hospital entry, and lost document assistance. Some companies also provide insurance coverage. In the Middle East, American Express is invaluable for its Client Letter Service; sometimes you have to have purchased checks to use it.

Listed below are some major traveler's check companies; to find the closest vendor of a particular brand, consult a telephone book or call a number listed below.

American Express (AmEx) (tel. (008) 25 19 02 in Australia (except Sydney); (0800) 44 10 68 in New Zealand; other South Pacific and Asian countries call Sydney collect at (612) 886 06 89; (800) 221-7282 in Canada and the U.S.; (177) 440 8694 in Israel; (0800) 52 13 13 in the U.K.; elsewhere call England collect 273) 57 16 00). The most widely recognized and easiest to replace if lost or stolen (with country-specific toll-free help lines). Checks are available in Canadian, English, U.S., and other currencies. There are several offices in Egypt, Israel (look for their affiliated company Meditrad), and Jordan (look for International Traders), and one in Syria (Damascus). Holders of AmEx Travelers' Cheques or credit cards can use most AmEx offices as a mailing address free of charge. The **Global Assist Hotline** (tel. (202) 783-7474, collect) offers emergency medical, legal, and financial services and advice. Consult *The American Express Traveler's Companion* (free for customers). Request the booklet well in advance; it is in high demand. Offices in Israel and Syria do not cash Travelers Cheques. The **American Automobile Association (AAA)** sells AmEx Cheques commission-free to its members.

Barclays Bank (tel. (800) 221-2426 in Canada and the U.S.; (202) 67 12 12 in the U.K.; elsewhere call New York collect (212) 858-8500). Sells Visa traveler's checks in British, Canadian, German, and U.S. currencies. There is a 1-3% commission depending on where the checks are purchased. They will cash Barclays-Visa or any other Visa brand traveler's checks for free.

Citicorp (tel. (800) 645-6556 in Canada and the U.S.; (0171) 982 40 40 in the U.K.; elsewhere call collect (813) 623-1709). Sells Visa traveler's checks in Australian, British, U.S., and other currencies. Commission is 1-2%. Buyers are automatically enrolled in Travel Assist Hotline (tel. (800) 523-1199) for 45 days after date of purchase. Provides English-speaking doctor, lawyer, and interpreter referrals.

MasterCard International (tel. (800) 223-9920 in North America, elsewhere call collect (44) (733) 502 995). Offers travelers checks in Australian, Canadian, English, U.S., and other currencies. Participating banks charge a 1-2% commission. Try buying at a Thomas Cook office for lower commissions.

Thomas Cook (tel. (800) 223-4030 in U.S. for orders, (800) 223-7373 for refunds; elsewhere call U.S. collect (212) 974-5696). Also sells MasterCard Traveler's Checks, with commissions ranging from 0-2%.

Any kind of Visa Traveler's Checks (Barclay's or Citicorp) can also be reported lost at the general Visa number: (800) 227-6811 in Canada and the U.S., (0171) 937 80 91 in the U.K., and collect from anywhere else at (212) 858-8500.

Refunds could involve some red tape and delay. To expedite the process, keep your receipt of purchase and the checks' serial numbers in a safe place separate from the checks themselves. Leave a list of check numbers with someone at home, and record check numbers as you cash them so that you can identify which checks are missing. Do not countersign checks until you cash them. Most importantly, keep a separate cache of cash and/or traveler's checks for emergencies.

CREDIT AND CASH CARDS

Credit cards are of limited day-to-day value in the Middle East—only places too expensive for the budget traveler will accept them. They are invaluable, however, if you need an instant cash advance. Both **Visa** (tel. (800) 336-8472) and **MasterCard** (tel. (800) 999-0454) give cash advances at affiliated banks (only likely to be found in capital cities). Also inquire about travel benefits (insurance, mail, etc.).

American Express (tel. (800) 528-4800) cashes personal checks of $1000-$5000 every seven days. In other words, you can draw on your bank account at home and write yourself a check. Call (800) 843-2273 to order a card, and (800) 528-4800 for general information and to report lost or stolen cards.

Cash cards may be the most convenient source for cash in Israel; there are now 220 Cirrus **automated teller machines (ATMs)** available at Bank Ha-Poalim branches; many of the machines are also in the PLUS network. Other ATMs in Israel give Visa and MasterCard cash advances. ATMs in Egypt and Jordan can be counted on your bodily appendages; credit-card affiliated banks are pretty much it. ATMs get the wholesale exchange rate, generally 5% better than the retail rate offered by most banks. Cirrus charges US$5 for each withdrawal outside the U.S. The Cirrus number is (800) 4-CIRRUS (424-7787). Call (800) 843-7587 to find a PLUS machine near you. AmEx plans to begin disbursing travelers checks from ATMs; inquire about this service before embarking.

SENDING MONEY

Try to avoid this horror. Carry a credit card or a separate stash of traveler's checks. Even a single US$50 bill can sustain you for quite some time in the Middle East.

If you run out of money on the road, money can be **wired** directly from bank to bank for about US$30 per US$1000, plus the commission charged by your home bank. Once you've found a bank that will accept a wire, write or telegram your home bank with your account number, the name and address of the bank to receive the wire, and a routing number. Also notify your bank of the form of ID that the second bank should accept before paying the money. Before you leave home, visit your bank to obtain a list of participating banks in the countries you will be visiting. You can also arrange in advance for your bank to send money from your account to foreign banks on specific dates. Remember that you will always need ID to pick up money that has been sent to you. **Bank drafts** or **international money orders** are cheaper but slower. As a last resort, **consulates** will wire home for you and deduct a fee from the money you receive.

With **American Express** you can write checks to yourself (see above). American Express Moneygram Service provides 10-minute, overnight, or 3-5 day delivery.

Bank of America (tel. (800) 346-7963) will send money to affiliated banks around the world. Someone brings cash, credit card, or cashier's check to the sending bank. You pick up the money (in US$) one to three working days later with an ID. There is a $37 flat fee for receiving incoming funds. The sending bank will also charge a fee (usually at least US$15, US$8.50 for BoA members).

Western Union (tel. (800) 325-6000 from North America, (448) 17 41 36 39 from Europe) is convenient for cabling money to Israel from the U.S. They do not serve Egypt or Jordan.

In dire emergencies, U.S. Citizens can have money sent abroad through the State Department **Citizens Emergency Center** (2201 C St. NW, Washington, DC 20520). Call (202) 647-5225 during business hours, (202) 647-4000 after hours. They will cable a modest amount of money to a foreign consular office, which disburses it according to instructions. Persons wishing to send money abroad through the State Department can cable money to them through Western Union (see above).

BARGAINING

As a general rule, the only places where prices are non-negotiable are restaurants and stores that are part of international chains, like Benetton or Stefanel. Even then, hell, give it a try. Prices quoted to tourists (especially the blond ones with accents) can be as high as ten times the "real" price (whatever that is), so don't be embarrassed to offer a fraction of the asking price. A good strategy is to offer what you want to pay even before inquiring about the price. Or ask the price in a somewhat blasé fashion, knit your brow, offer about half, and begin the bidding. You'd better be prepared to pay any price you offer; no backing off. If vendors decline your bid but call or chase after you, the haggling may continue in the street. In this case you've got them on the ropes. Yeah, boy. Knowing you will be staying at a hotel for several nights boosts your bargaining leverage; even starred hotels often strike deals.

■■■ KEEPING IN TOUCH

Mail can usually be sent internationally through **Poste Restante** (the international phrase for General Delivery). Address the envelope "Name, Poste Restante, City, Country." The mail will go to the central post office for that city. **AmEx** (see p. 14) offers its own mail-holding system, Client Letter Service (free for clients; buying a few AmEx Travelers' Cheques makes you a client). Check with AmEx for details.

International Express Mail Service (EMS) is operated by national postal services, providing 72-hour delivery at reasonable rates. It is available in most post offices in Israel and the West Bank and in at least one post office in each town in Egypt and Jordan. Syria does not participate in EMS. Private mail services are faster but much more expensive; try: **Airborne Express** (tel. (2) 693 15 66 in Australia, (800) 472-4900 in Canada and the U.S., (1) 844 41 83 in Ireland, (9) 275 80 34 in New Zealand, (11) 452 37 01 in South Africa, and (0181) 899 98 76 in the U.K.), **DHL** (tel. (2) 317 83 00 in Australia, (800) 225-5345 in Canada and the U.S., (353) 18 44 47 44 in Ireland, (9) 636 50 00 in New Zealand, (11) 921 36 00 in South Africa, and (0181) 890 93 93 in the U.K.), or **Federal Express** (tel. (2) 317 66 66 in Australia, (800) 238-5355 in Canada and the U.S., (1) 847 34 73 in Ireland, (9) 256 83 00 in New Zealand, (11) 921 75 00 in South Africa, and (0181) 844 23 44 in the U.K.).

Telephone communication is made much easier by **AT&T's USADirect** service, which allows you to call the U.S. from overseas and charge it to an AT&T Calling Card or any U.S. local phone company card. There is also a **World Connect** program for calling between two countries other than the U.S. Rates for USADirect and World Connect are constant throughout the day; they do not drop in the evenings. AT&T's customer service line in the U.S. is (800) 331-1140. In other countries, callers should dial the access code (call (800) 545-3117 for access code lists and other information) for the country they are in and ask for AT&T customer service. See the Keeping in Touch section for each country. **MCI** has a **WorldPhone** program similar to AT&T's World Connect; call (800) 444-3333 for more information.

See Keeping in Touch sections for each country for country-specific details.

■■■ PACKING

You lack the luxury of worrying about fashion. More important questions include, "How can I dress modestly but keep from sweating a hole into my clothing?" and "Can I carry this pack without sweating a hole in my clothing?" Pack lightly. Set out everything you think you'll need for your trip, eliminate half, and take more money.

Decide whether a backpack, light suitcase, or shoulder bag is most suitable for your travels. If you're planning on moving around a lot, a sturdy **backpack** is hard to beat. A small **daypack** is indispensable for flights, sight-seeing, and holding your valuables. On short trips, daypacks are especially useful for carrying your lunch, camera, canteen, notebook, whatever. To avoid theft, guard your money, passport, and other important articles in a **neck pouch** or **moneybelt.** "Fanny-packs" do not only look ridiculous, but they are also very visible—an invitation to theft. For added security, get a few combination locks for your bags (though these are hardly invulnerable); and label everything everywhere.

Natural fibers beat synthetics hands down in the heat. Dark colors hide dirt, but **light colors** deflect the sun. In Egypt, Jordan, the West Bank, Syria, and any holy site, both men and women should cover their knees and upper arms to avoid offending local rules of **modesty.** (See Travel Etiquette, p. 30.) Jeans are heavy and difficult to wash in the sink; take khakis or light cotton **trousers** instead. This doesn't mean you shouldn't bring **shorts;** you can wear them in tourist-frequented places. True, your tourist status will be obvious, but your chances of looking like a native are practically nil anyway. Bring one wool sweater (or something with Thinsulate) for cooler night temperatures; wool is warmer and more light-weight than any jacket.

Appropriate shoes are crucial: well-cushioned **sneakers** for walking (not Keds); **boots** for extensive hiking (break them in *before* you go). Talcum powder in your shoes and on your feet can prevent sores, and moleskin is great for blisters. **Sandals** are fine for short walks or kicking back; but they hurt unaccustomed feet, provide no support for lots of walking, and let sand in at archaeological sites. The best all-around shoes if you only want to bring one pair are **sneakers-cum-hiking boots** (Nike makes them with funky color accents), though you'll feel silly on the beach.

Laundromats are often hard to find, so bring along some mild **laundry soap.** Dr. Bronner's castile soap (available in camping stores) claims to serve as everything from dish detergent to shampoo to toothpaste. Also pack deodorant, razors, condoms, tampons, re-hydration solution, diarrhea pills, constipation pills, and ibuprofen. Many of these things are difficult to come by; tampons do not appear to exist in the Arab world. A squash ball makes an excellent sink plug for washing clothes. **Contact lens** supplies are rare and expensive. Either bring enough saline, etc. and keep it in a central town that you will pass through often, or wear your glasses.

Electric current in Israel, Egypt, Jordan, and Syria is 220V. Travelers with appliances designed for 110V (North America) should bring a **converter.** Most outlets are made for round prongs, so even if your machine has a built-in converter you'll also need an **adapter** to change the plug shape. Converters and adapters are available everywhere (here, not there). Contact-lens wearers who use heat disinfection, take note. To order a converter (about US$20) or receive the free pamphlet *Foreign Electricity is No Deep Dark Secret* contact **Franzus,** Murtha Industrial Park, P.O. Box 142, Railroad Ave., Beacon Falls, CT 06403, USA (tel. (203) 723-6664; fax 723-6666).

Film is generally more expensive abroad. Some foreign airport X-ray machines are film-safe and some are not—better to play it safe and protect your film with a special lead-lined bag available from any photo shop. (Or ask security to check it by hand.)

Bring a small **towel;** hostels and inexpensive hotels do not provide them.

■■■ HEALTH

Also see Packing, above. Check with family doctor or with one of the groups below to see if you should get any immunizations before you go.

The hot temperatures and low sanitation standards of the Middle East can make even the most careful traveler ill. Drink *lots* of water (as much as 10L per day may be necessary to avoid dehydration), always cover your head with something white when you go out in the sun, and take it slow on the street food. Avoid excessive caffeine and alcohol, both of which can cause dehydration.

If you're drinking enough water, your urine will be close to clear; a deep yellow hue is a bad sign. It's a good idea to carry high sun protection factor (SPF) sun block. This is not the place to work on a tan—even the dark-skinned or pre-tanned are not immune. And even if your skin doesn't burn, your brain will, leaving you nauseous.

Heatstroke can occur without direct exposure to the sun. If ignored, it can lead to serious medical problems such as death. Symptoms include cessation of sweating, increased body temperature, flushed skin, and intense headache. Experts recommend that if you suspect you have heatstroke, you get out of the heat and sun immediately, cover yourself with wet towels, and drink water or fruit juice. Seek medical help immediately.

Relying on bottled mineral water is sensible, especially in Egypt and Syria, but to save money you may want to use water-purification tablets instead. Anywhere you've been warned not to drink the water, pass up ice cubes, green salad, and peeled fruit (it will probably have been washed in the water). Even if the water is safe for locals, it may not be for you until you have been in the area a while—they have developed antibodies and you have not. Always carry bottled water if you plan to spend time outside the cities. Lightly salting your food should suffice to replace the salt carried away by perspiration.

But sooner or later, no matter how careful you are, you probably will get diarrhea, affectionately known among its victims as **"Pharaoh's Revenge."** The Revenge typically strikes 10 to 12 days after arrival, lasts from two to four days if you rest up, and may be accompanied by fever and fatigue. Drink plenty of liquids to keep well-hydrated; an electrolyte solution (like the one used for babies) dissolved in your water tastes disgusting but helps. Commonly recommended medications for diarrhea are Bactrim, Lomotil, Immodium, and Pepto-Bismol. The latter, if taken before questionable meals, is a fairly effective preventative (but your tongue will be black all through dinner). Pharmacists can also provide locally-produced medicines. Diarrhea may be the symptom of a parasitic condition which could haunt your gastro-intestinal tract for years; if it does not subside, see a doctor immediately. A local doctor may be more familiar with your new internal friends than your home doctor.

Take care of your feet, too: bring moleskin for blisters (the U.S. brand 2nd Skin© is effective), wear comfortable shoes with support, and change your socks often.

For minor problems, a compact first-aid kit should suffice. A good kit includes an antiseptic, bandages, a thermometer in a sturdy case, mosquito repellent, motion sickness medicine (such as Dramamine), a pocket knife with tweezers, calamine lotion for sunburn and insect bites, and an antihistamine (the centuries of dust in some places can trigger allergies you never knew you had).

Bring an extra pair of **glasses** or contact lenses along with plenty of solution; make sure someone at home has a copy of your prescription for quick replacement. **Contraceptives** are not always available or safe in the Middle East; women on the pill should bring all they'll need, and condom-users should stock up (although in Israel your favorite brand is most likely available). All travelers on **prescription drugs** should carry a generous supply with them, preferably in carry-on items in case luggage goes astray. Those who use syringes, narcotic drugs, or other things which could appear to be illegal should carry a legible copy of the prescription to avoid problems at border crossings and customs.

In your passport, write the names of the people to be contacted in case of a medical emergency, and also list any allergies or medical conditions you would want doctors to be aware of. It is always a good idea to see a doctor before traveling, especially if you will be abroad for more than a month or two or if you will be hiking, camping, or visiting developing regions.

In rural areas of the Nile Delta, Fayyum, the oases, and Upper Egypt near the Sudan border, you risk getting **malaria;** a recommended drug is chloroquine.

Let's Go should not be your only information source on common health problems. The organizations listed below provide publications and information:

American Diabetes Association, 1660 Duke St., Alexandria, VA 22314 (tel. (800) 232-3472). Provides *Travel and Diabetes* and ID cards carrying messages in 18 languages. **Diabetic Travel Services, Inc.,** 39 E. 52nd St., New York, NY 10022, provides information on treatment and physicians worldwide.

American Red Cross, 61 Medford St., Somerville, MA 02143 (tel. (617) 623-0033). Publishes the *First-Aid and Safety Handbook* ($14.95).

International Association for Medical Assistance to Travelers. Canada: 40 Regal Road, Guelph, Ont., N1K 1B5 (tel. (519) 836-0102) or 1287 St. Clair Ave. West, Toronto, M6E 1B8 (tel. (416) 652-0137); **New Zealand:** P.O. Box 5049, Christ-church 5. **U.S.:** 417 Center St., Lewiston, NY 14092 (tel. (716) 754-4883). Free membership includes ID, directory of English-speaking doctors, brochures on immunization requirements, tropical diseases, climate, sanitation. Write for *How to Avoid Traveler's Diarrhea* and *How to Adjust to the Heat.*

Medic Alert Foundation, P.O. Box 1009, Turlock, CA, 95381-1009 (24-hr. hotline (800) ID-ALERT (432-5378)). Membership (beginning at US$35) includes a wallet card, the Medic Alert Identification Tag, and hotline access.

U.S. Centers for Disease Control, 1600 Clifton Rd. NE, Atlanta, GA 30333 (tel. (404) 332-4559; fax 332-4565). Maintains an international travelers' hotline. Publishes *Health Information for International Travelers* (publication #HHS-CDC 90-8280, US$6), updated annually and available from the Superintendent of Documents (see Publications, p. 5).

U.S. State Department compiles warnings and information on entry requirements. Call the **Citizens' Emergency Center** (tel. (202) 647-5225; fax 647-3000), Bureau of Consular Affairs, Room 4811, N.S, U.S. Department of State, Washington, DC 20520. If you are HIV-positive, call (202) 647-1488 for country-specific entry restrictions or write to the Bureau of Consular Affairs, CA/P/PA, Department of State, Washington, DC 20520.

■■■ INSURANCE

Beware of unnecessary coverage—your current policies might extend to travel-related accidents. **Medical insurance** (especially university policies) often covers costs incurred abroad; **Medicare** is only valid in Mexico and Canada. **Canadians** are protected by their home province's health insurance up to 90 days after leaving the country. Your homeowners' insurance (or your family's coverage) often covers theft during travel, as well as loss of travel documents up to $500.

ISIC and **International Student** or **Teacher ID** Cards provide medical benefits (see Student and Youth Identification, p. 11). **CIEE** offers an inexpensive Trip-Safe plan, with options covering medical treatment and hospitalization, accidents, baggage loss, and even charter flights missed due to illness. If you are ineligible for these cards, Trip-Safe extends coverage of the insurance you have. **STA** offers a more expensive, more comprehensive plan. **American Express** cardholders receive car-rental and flight insurance on purchases made with the card. (For addresses, see Budget Travel Services, p. 5; or American Express, p. 14.)

Remember that you can file claims only upon return to your home country. Insurance companies require a copy of the police report for thefts or evidence of having paid medical expenses before they will honor a claim; they may have time limits on filing. Have documents written in English to avoid translating fees. Always carry policy numbers and proof of insurance.

If you have less than perfect faith in your travel plans, consider insurance for trip cancellation or interruption, in case your airline or tour operator leaves you stranded at the final hour. Expect to pay US$2-5 per US$100 for coverage.

Access America, Inc., 6600 West Broad St., P.O. Box 11188, Richmond, VA 23230 (tel. (800) 294-8300; fax (804) 673-1491). 24-hr. hotline.

ARM Coverage, Inc./Carefree Travel Insurance, 100 Garden City Plaza, P.O. Box 9366, Garden City, NY 11530-9366 (tel. (800) 323-3149 or (516) 294-0220; fax (516) 294-1821). 24-hr. hotline.

Globalcare Travel Insurance, 220 Broadway, Lynnfield, MA 01940 (tel. (800) 821-2488; fax (617) 592-7720). Complete medical, legal, emergency and travel-related services. On-the-spot payments and special student programs.

Travel Assistance International, by Worldwide Assistance Services, Inc., 1133 15th St. NW #400, Washington, DC 20005-2710 (tel. (800) 821-2828; fax (202) 331-1530). 24-hr. multilingual assistance hotline and worldwide presence.

Travel Guard International, 1145 Clark St., Stevens Point, WI 54481 (tel. (800) 826-1300 or (715) 345-0505; fax (715) 345-0525). 24-hr. emergency hotline.

Travel Insured International, Inc., 52-S Oakland Avenue, P.O. Box 280568, East Hartford, CT 06128-0568 (tel. (800) 243-3174; fax (203) 528-8005).

Wallach & Company, Inc., 107 W. Federal St., P.O. Box 480, Middleburg, VA
22117-0480 (tel. (800) 237-6615; fax (703) 687-3172). 24-hr. toll-free international assistance.

■■■ SAFETY & SECURITY

In the Middle East, politics can easily intrude on travel; keep apprised of events. U.S.
citizens can check on the latest government travel advisories by calling the State
Department's **Citizens' Emergency Center** (tel. (202) 647-5225). You may also
obtain a State Department travel advisory on a specific country, and crime statistics.
American citizens traveling abroad can call this number in an emergency situation.
Common sense and a few precautions should carry you safely through your travels. Stick to busy, well-lit streets and beware of pickpockets. The less you flaunt your
income or foreign citizenship, the less vulnerable you'll be to sticky fingers. Hotel or
hostel managers are often valuable sources of advice on specific areas. You may also
feel safer staying in places with a curfew or a night-attendant. If you're in a dormitory-style room or have no lock on your door, sleep with all valuables on your person or under your pillow; laying your pack alongside the bed won't do. A **money
belt** or **neck pouch** worn under a shirt are theft-resistant. Thieves prey on backpackers; crowded youth hostels and overnight trains are favorite hangouts for petty crim-
inals. For more complete information, try *Travel Safety: Security and Safeguards at
Home and Abroad,* from Hippocrene Books (see p. 7).
While traveling, steer clear of empty train compartments, particularly at night.
Don't check your luggage on trains, as it is often "lost" this way. If you plan to sleep
outside or simply don't want to carry everything with you, store your gear in a
locker at a train or bus station. And, of course, **hitchhiking is dangerous.**
No one set of precautions will protect you from all situations; a good self-defense
course will give you concrete ways to react to different types of aggression, but it
might cost more money than your trip. **Model Mugging** teaches an effective, comprehensive self-defense course (US$400-500) for men and women. Call (617) 232-
7900 on the East Coast, (312) 338-4545 in the Midwest, and (415) 592-7300 on the
West Coast. **Community colleges** offer more affordable self-defense courses.
The **U.S. State Department's** pamphlet *A Safe Trip Abroad* (US $1) is available
from the Superintendent of Documents (see Publications, p. 5).

ALCOHOL AND DRUGS

Alcohol is forbidden by the Qur'an kinda like extramarital sex is forbidden by the
Bible. It's legal for all ages in Egypt, Jordan, and Syria but hard to come by in some
places. Israel's drinking age is 18. Authorities regard drug possession as a serious
offense; expulsion from the country is the least that will happen to the offender.
Consulates can do no more than bring floral arrangements to the prisoner, provide
a list of attorneys, and inform family and friends; they cannot get you special treatment (remember Michael Fay). For information on international drug restrictions
and what the American consulate can and cannot do, send a self-addressed, stamped
envelope for *Travel Warning on Drugs Abroad,* Bureau of Consular Affairs, Dept.
of Public Affairs #5807, U.S. Dept. of State, Washington, DC (tel. (202) 647-1488).

■■■ ALTERNATIVES TO TOURISM

The following is a list of general resources for students seeking work abroad:

Addison-Wesley, Jacob Way, Reading, MA 01867 (tel. (800) 447-2226). Publishes
International Jobs: Where They Are, How to Get Them (US$14.95).
Archaeological Institute of America, 675 Commonwealth Ave., Boston, MA
02215 (tel. (617) 353-9361). Publishes the annual *Archaeological Fieldwork
Opportunities Bulletin* (AFOB). Over 275 opportunities were listed in 1994.

Biblical Archaeology Review, 3000 Connecticut Ave. NW #300, Washington, DC 20008 (tel. (202) 387-8888; fax 483-4323). Information on digs.

Institute of International Education (IIE), 809 United Nations Plaza, New York, NY 10017-3580 (recorded info. (212) 984-5413; open Tues.-Thurs. 11am-4pm). Study and teaching opportunities abroad. Write for a list of publications.

International Association for the Exchange of Students for Technical Experience (IAESTE), 10400 Little Patuxent Pkwy. #250, Columbia, MD 21044-3510 (tel. (410) 997-2200). Operates 8- to 12-week programs in over 50 countries for college students having completed 2 years of study in a technical field. Nonrefundable US$75 application fee; apply by Dec. 10 for summer placement.

Office of Overseas Schools, A-OS Room 245, SA-29, Dept. of State, Washington, DC 20522 (tel. (703) 875-7800). Teaching jobs abroad.

Peterson's Guides, 202 Carnegie Center, P.O. Box 2123, Princeton, NJ 08543-2123 (tel. (800) 338-3282). Publishes the *Directory of Overseas Summer Jobs* (US$15.95), a listing of over 50,000 volunteer and paid openings worldwide, and *Work Your Way Around the World* (US$17.95).

Unipub Co., 4611-F Assembly Dr., Lanham, MD 20706-4391 (tel. (800) 274-4888). Distributes many publications, including UNESCO's *Study Abroad* (US$24).

Volunteers for Peace, 43 Tiffany Rd., Belmont, VT 05730 (tel. (802) 259-2759; fax 259-2922). Publishes the annual *International Workcamp Directory* (US$10).

World Trade Academy Press, Inc., 50 E. 42nd St., New York, NY 10017 (tel. (212) 697-4999). *Looking for Employment in Foreign Countries* (US$16.50).

■ EGYPT

WORK AND VOLUNTEER

Some people look for temporary jobs upon arrival in Na'ama Bay. Ask the **American Chamber of Commerce** in Cairo at the Marriott Hotel (tel. (02) 340 8888, ext. 1541) for lists of member companies. Work permits can be obtained through any Egyptian consulate, or in Egypt from the Ministry of the Interior.

The **Higher Council for Youth and Sport in Egypt** (Foreign Relations Administration) runs programs where students of different nationalities spend two to four weeks working together on agricultural or sociological projects. Contact the Council at Kit Kat Sq., Cairo (tel. (02) 346 1701) or the Egyptian Embassy or EGAPT.

The **World Health Organization** (main office CH-1211 Geneva 27, Switzerland; tel. (22) 791 21 11; fax 791 07 46; Internet postmaster@who.ch) offers a yearly summer internship in Alexandria.

STUDY

The **American University in Cairo (AUC)** offers semester, year abroad, summer, intensive Arabic, and degree programs. Instruction is in English. Popular topics include Arabic language, Egyptology, and Middle East studies. Tuition and fees for 1994-95 are US$4365 per semester; US$2165 for the summer session. U.S. citizens in AUC may apply for Stafford Loans. Three other Egyptian universities have programs for foreign students, transferable for credit at most universities.

American University in Cairo, Admissions, 866 UN Plaza #517, New York, NY 10017-1889 (tel. (212) 421-6320; fax 688-5341), or 113 Qasr El 'Aini St., P.O. Box 2511, Cairo (tel. (02) 354 2964 through 2969 (6 lines); fax 355 7565).

'Ain Shams University, El Khalifa El Maamoun St., Cairo (tel. (02) 82 11 17).

Al Azhar University, El Nasr Rd., Cairo (tel. (02) 261 1400).

Cairo University, El Gamaa St., Cairo (tel. (02) 72 95 84).

Contact the **Egyptian Cultural and Educational Bureau,** 1303 New Hampshire Ave. NW, Washington, DC 20036 (tel. (202) 296-3888; fax 296-3891) or **AmidEast** in the U.S. (1100 17th St. NW, Washington, DC, 20036-4601; tel. (202) 785-0022; fax 822-6563) or Cairo (6 Kamel ash-Shinawy St. 2nd floor, Garden City; tel. (02) 354 1300 or 355 3170; fax 355 2946). AmidEast organizes programs for educational institutions, but generally not for individuals.

Several language institutes offer shorter-term studies in Arabic. **Berlitz Language Centers** specialize in colloquial and simplified literary Arabic; contact them at 165 Muhammad Farid St., Cairo (tel. (02) 391 5096); 28 Sa'ad Zaghloul Blvd., Alexandria (tel. (03) 808 226); 37 Sha'ul Ha-Melekh Ave., Tel Aviv 64298 (tel. (03) 695 2131; fax (03) 695 2134); 40 W. 51st St., New York, NY 10020 (tel. (212) 765-1000; fax 307-5336), or at any of their 320 locations world-wide. They also offer cultural training.

The **Egyptian Center for International Cultural Cooperation,** 11 Shagarat ad-Durr St., Zamalek, Cairo (tel. (02) 341 5419) teaches classical and colloquial Arabic.

■ ISRAEL

The **American Zionist Youth Foundation (AZYF)** is a clearinghouse for many programs, offering tours and study or work/volunteer/archaeological dig programs. University programs offer classes in English or Hebrew. There are fully accredited programs in Jerusalem, Tel Aviv, Haifa, and Be'er Sheva. Contact the AZYF at University Student Department, Israel Action Center, 110 E. 59th St. 3rd floor, New York, NY 10022 (tel. (800) 27-ISRAEL (274-7723) or (212) 339-6941; fax 755-4781).

WORK AND APPRENTICESHIPS

Unemployment in Israel is high, greatly limiting work opportunities; foreigners must also compete with the new immigrants from the Soviet Union. American or European companies with branches in Israel are a possible source of employment. Another option is volunteer work in exchange for room and board. Some people look for temporary jobs upon arrival in Eilat.

Israel belongs to the **IAESTE** (see p. 21); the **Jewish Agency** offers six-month internships. Write to the Center for Ulpanim and Counseling for Young Adults (UCYA), 12 Kaplan St., Tel Aviv (tel. (03) 258 311).

Kibbutzim Israel's 250 kibbutzim (plural of kibbutz)—communal settlements whose members divide work and profits equally—are often eager for volunteers. Kibbutzim vary greatly in size, number of volunteers, and ideological basis. Volunteers generally work six eight-hour days per week with several days off per month, and may receive a small monthly allowance in addition to various other benefits; the work is generally physical, in agriculture, industry, or service. Prior knowledge of Hebrew is helpful, but non-speakers can learn quickly through the Ulpan program (see Ulpanim, below). Accommodations are most often in dormitory settings. If you're already in Israel, visit a kibbutz and talk to volunteers before you commit. Otherwise try to get a written promise of placement on a specific kibbutz before arriving in Israel. Kibbutz life can be seductive in its routine, and many volunteers find themselves staying longer than planned.

To apply for any kibbutz program, contact your local **Kibbutz Aliya Desk** or the main office at 110 E. 59th St. 4th floor, New York, NY 10022 (tel. (212) 318-6130; fax 318-6134). Applicants must be aged 18-35 with no children (exception: Kibbutz Yahel and Hanaton accept families); there is a two-month minimum commitment and no maximum stay length. After being interviewed and given the appropriate application and medical forms, you will be sent to the **Kibbutz Volunteer Office** in Tel Aviv, located at 124 Ha-Yarkon St., Tel Aviv (tel. (03) 522 1325 or 524 6156), where you will be assigned to a kibbutz. A second office, **Ha-Kibbutz Ha-Dati,** is located at 7 Dubnov St., Tel Aviv (tel. (03) 695 7231) and accepts only Jewish volunteers (some religious observance is required). Read *Kibbutz Volunteer,* Vacation Work Publications, 9 Park End St., Oxford, OX1 1HJ (tel. (01865) 241 978).

Project 67, 10 Hatton Garden, London EC1N 8AH (tel. (0171) 831 76 26), also places volunteers on kibbutzim and *moshavim* for two to four months. **ISSTA** has information; write six weeks in advance (see Budget Travel Services, p. 5).

Moshavim *Moshavim* (plural of *moshav*) provide a somewhat different work experience from kibbutzim. *Moshavim* are agricultural communities in which farms and homes are privately owned and operated. You will receive free lodging either with a family or in a house with other workers. Your family will also provide meals or a food allowance. In return, you work a six-day week, at least eight hours per day. Workers are paid about US$250 per month. Applicants must be aged 18-35 and physically fit. Write the organizations listed above for kibbutzim or contact the **Moshavim Movement,** 19 Leonardo da Vinci St., Tel Aviv (tel. (03) 695 8473).

Archaeological Digs Work on archaeological digs consists largely of digging pits, shoveling shards, and hauling baskets of dirt for eight to ten hours per day in searing heat; beginning at 5am—don't dream of discovering ancient treasures.

Every February the **Israel Antiquities Authority,** Rockefeller Museum, P.O. Box 586, Jerusalem 91004 (tel. (02) 292 627 or 607; fax 292 628), compiles a list of excavations open to volunteers in the summer (must be at least 18 and in excellent shape; also consult the archaeology listings on p. 20).

Apply directly to the dig leader. Volunteers must be able to work a minimum of two weeks. Be sure to indicate any knowledge of archaeology, geology, or anthropology in your application, although none is typically required. Many excavations also charge an application fee. Volunteers are usually responsible for their own travel arrangements, and most excavations charge for food and accommodations, ranging from camping at the site to a nearby hostel, hotel, or kibbutz. The Department of Antiquities recommends that volunteers come fully insured.

The **ISSTA** (see Budget Travel Services, p. 5) has arrangements with Tel Aviv University for students interested in working on digs. Again, the work is long and arduous, intended only for archaeology fiends. The "Dig for a Day" program is designed more for the curious tourist. It includes a three-hour excavation, seminars on methodology, tools, and history, and a tour of the site. The cost for students is about US$20. Contact: **Archaeological Seminars, Inc.,** P.O. Box 14002, Jaffa Gate, Jerusalem 91400 (tel. (02) 273 515; fax 272 660), from July through August.

Volunteer The **Volunteers for Israel** program places participants in non-combat support jobs in the Israeli military. The 3-week program involves menial work such as washing dishes, polishing boots, or packing equipment. You will wear army fatigues, army boots, and sleep in army barracks, but don't expect to carry an Uzi or keep the uniform afterwards. The program offers reduced airfare on El Al or Tower Air, provided you fulfill your commitment. There may also be a special fare for youth under 26. Contact: **Volunteers for Israel,** 330 W. 42nd St. #1818, New York, NY 10036 (tel. (212) 643-4848). Application must include a US$100 registration fee.

Shatil, a project of the New Israel Fund, places volunteers with organizations working in such areas as civil and human rights, Jewish-Arab coexistence, the status of women, and religious tolerance. Contact them at the **New Israel Fund,** 1625 K St. #500, Washington, DC 20006-1604 (tel. (202) 223-3333; fax 659-2789), or at 9 Yad Ha-Rutzim St., P.O. Box 53410, Jerusalem 91534 (tel. (02) 723 095; fax 723 099).

Living Experiences A blend of work, study, and life in general, **Project Otzma,** the Jewish Service Corps, is a ten-month program for Jews aged 20 to 24 that incorporates kibbutz and *moshav* life, youth villages, immigrant absorption, and Hebrew study (tel. (212) 598-3532, or 475-5000; fax 529-5842). Also consider the Peace Corps-style **Sherut La'Am** (contact them through AZYF, above). In the **Isaac Mayer Wise-Inside Israel Program,** you live with an Israeli family as well as on a kibbutz, and learn Hebrew to boot. Contact Paul Reichenback, Union of American Hebrew Congregations, P.O. Box 443, Bowen Rd., New York, NY 10990 (tel. (914) 987-6300). **Livnot U'Lehibanot: To Build and Be Built** offers 3-week or 3-month study and work experiences in Jerusalem and Tzfat. Four hours per day of discussion-oriented classes and seminars exploring one's Jewish heritage and the land of Israel, and four hours per day of building and community service projects, plus hikes throughout the country. Open to ages 21-30. Contact: Livnot U'Lehibanot, 110 E. 59th St. 3rd floor, New York, NY 10022 (tel. (212) 752-2390; fax 832-2597) or at 27 Ben-Zakkai, Katamon, Jerusalem 93585 (tel. (02) 793 491; fax 793 492).

STUDY

Ulpanim An *ulpan* is a short-term program providing intensive Hebrew and Jewish culture instruction. Israel has about 100 *ulpanim*. **Kibbutz Ulpanim** offer instruction in return for work. Contact: **Kibbutz Aliya Desk** (see Kibbutzim, above).

Ulpan Akiva, Netanya, offers a live-in program in its seaside campus for students from around the world—Jews, non-Jews, Israelis, and new immigrants. Daily program includes five hours of Hebrew or Arabic study, social and cultural activities, tours, trips, and special *Shabbat* activities. Three-, eight-, 12-, and 20-week courses are accredited by several universities. Costs vary. Contact: Ulpan Akiva Netanya, P.O. Box 6086, Netanya 42160, Israel (tel. (09) 352 312 or 313 or 314; fax 652 919).

Other programs are sponsored by **Beit Ha-Noar Ha'Ivri,** 105 Ha-Rav Herzog, Jerusalem 92622 (tel. (02) 789 441), **Beit Ha'Am,** 11 Bezalel St., Jerusalem (tel. (02) 254 156), and **Mo'adon Ha'Oleh,** 9 Alkalai St., Jerusalem (tel. (02) 633 718). Contact: **World Zionist Organization Ulpan Center,** 4 E. 34th St. 4th floor, New York, NY 10016 (tel. (212) 532-4176)

Universities Programs for foreign students range in length from one summer to four years. **Year-abroad** programs usually begin with a four- to nine-week *ulpan* to learn Hebrew before the semester begins in October. Courses are usually in English; those who know Hebrew have the option of taking regular university courses. University programs are usually preceded by a *mekhina* (see *Mekhinot,* below). Admission for undergraduates requires proficiency in Hebrew and at least one year of college. For all programs contact: **Israel Student Authority,** 15 Hillel St., Jerusalem (tel. (02) 241 121) or the New York consulate's Office of Academic Affairs.

Bar Ilan University, 91 Fifth Ave. #200, New York, NY 10003 (tel. (212) 337-1286; fax 337-1274), or Ramat Gan 52900 (tel. (03) 531 8111).

Ben-Gurion University of the Negev, Overseas Student Program, 342 Madison Ave. #1224, New York, NY 10173 (tel. (212) 687-7721; fax 370-0686), or Be'er Sheva 84105 (tel. (057) 461 111).

Canadian Friends of **Haifa University,** 1110 Finch Ave. W #510, Downsview, Ont. M3J 2T2 (tel. (800) 388-2134, or (416) 665-4462; fax 665-4468), or Mt. Carmel, Haifa 31999 (tel. (04) 246 854; fax 342 245).

American Friends of **Hebrew University,** 11 E. 69th St., New York, NY 10021 (tel. (212) 472-2288; fax 517-4548), or Mt. Scopus, Jerusalem 91905 (tel. (02) 882 111).

Technion-Israel Institute of Technology, contact the American Technion Society National Office, 810 Seventh Ave., New York, NY 10019 (tel. (212) 262-6200), or Technion City, Haifa 32000 (tel. (04) 292 111; fax 221 581).

Tel Aviv University, Office of Academic Affairs, 360 Lexington Ave., New York, NY 10017 (tel. (212) 687-5651; fax 687-4085), or Ramat Aviv, Tel Aviv 69978 (tel. (03) 642 5452; fax 642 2752).

Weizmann Institute of Science, Reḥovot 76100 (tel. (08) 342 111).

Mekhinot Students who are not proficient in Hebrew but wish to enter a full undergraduate degree program usually first enroll in *mekhina* (preparation) programs, providing a year of intensive Hebrew and a chance to develop study plans. *Mekhinot* are offered by the universities and other schools of post-secondary education. Note that *mekhina* participation does not guarantee acceptance to a university; students still take entrance examinations. At Hebrew University, Technion, and Practical Engineering Colleges, the *mekhina* opens in September or October. The program for Practical Engineers in Be'er Sheva begins in August and February. *Mekhinot* begin in August at all other schools.

■ WEST BANK

During much of the *intifada*, all four West Bank universities—Birzeit, Bethlehem, Hebron, and An-Najah—were closed by the Israeli authorities. Today, most West

Bank schools have resumed classes, with students struggling to catch up on what they missed. Check the programs for foreign students at **Birzeit University** north of Ramallah. A six-week international summer program offers courses in Arabic, Palestinian society, the Arab-Israeli conflict, and Palestinian women writers. (July-Aug. US$300 for language courses, US$200 for each of the others. Housing US$250.) A new year-round Palestine and Arabic program for international students combines study of modern and colloquial Arabic with courses in the social sciences and the arts (US$400 for Arabic, US$300 for all other courses). For both programs, contact the International Relations Department, Birzeit University, P.O. Box 14, Birzeit, West Bank, via Israel (tel. (2) 957 650 or 651 or 652; fax 957 656). Birzeit also sponsors two-week international work camps with Palestinian students during August and September; contact the Office of the Community Work Program at the above address. In the West Bank, you can arrange a tour of the university through the Public Relations Office (at the same phone number).

Several organizations aid in planning excursions to the West Bank. The **Palestine Human Rights Information Center** in East Jerusalem (tel. (02) 287 077) provides information on the current political situation and human rights issues. Director Jan Abu-Shakra gives free lectures on the *intifada* to small groups. Call ahead. (Open daily 8am-2pm.) The office is off Salah ad-Din St.; turn onto Az-Zahra St. and take the first right after the National Palace Hotel. The building is across the street from the Rome-Paris beauty salon and has an "ECRC" sign above the door). **Al-Haq** (tel. (02) 956 421), the West Bank affiliate of the International Commission of Jurists, is a Palestinian human rights organization based in Ramallah that publishes informative booklets and reports. They also maintain a small legal library with a statistics database, available for free public use (open Mon.-Sat. 8am-4pm; the office is on Main St., opposite the Protestant Church, near the Latin Convent). **UNRWA** (United Nations Relief and Works Agency; tel. (02) 890 400), located in East Jerusalem next to the Spanish consulate, may be able to arrange trips to refugee camps on occasion (no organized scheduled trips; open Mon.-Fri. 7:30am-2:30pm).

Some hostels arrange trips to refugee camps. Try the managers at **Tabasco Youth Hostel and Tea Room** and **Al-Arab Hostel** in Jerusalem (see Jerusalem: Accommodations, p. 362).

■ JORDAN

Work and Archaeological Digs It's difficult for foreigners to find jobs in Jordan, although English skills are in demand. A combination of perfect English and business or banking skills is optimal. Positions must be arranged before arrival in order to get a work visa. **Work permits** can be secured from the Ministry of Labor. **Residence permits** are required for stays of more than three months.

Some science-related apprenticeships are available through **IAESTE** (see p. 21). Volunteers for **archaeological digs** are in demand; a recently discovered Byzantine church at Petra is an example of the vibrancy of archaeological activity in Jordan.

Study Two Jordanian universities are open to foreign students. The **University of Jordan** (Aj-Jubaiha, Amman) has a more liberal atmosphere than the conservative **Yarmouk University** in Irbid (although you shouldn't plan on wearing shorts at either). Students interested in Islamic culture, however, may enjoy the more rapid pace of study at Yarmouk. The University of Jordan has a special foreign students program and summer programs which are popular for those seeking colloquial and classical Arabic language instruction. Both schools also guarantee dormitory housing for women. A Jordanian embassy, consulate, or information bureau (see p. 5) can provide further information on either school.

■ SYRIA

Work and Archaeological Digs As in Jordan, work for foreigners is scarce in Syria. A residence permit is required, as visitors on tourist visas are not allowed to work; bureaucratic nightmares abound. Tutoring or teaching English as a second language are your best bets for employment. Archaeological digs offer hard work for no pay; volunteers are generally welcome.

Study The majority of Westerners studying in Syria are Fulbright scholars. The U.S. Embassy assists Fulbrighters in all aspects of assimilating into Syrian culture. Universities are state-run, so the curricula do not vary, but graduate students and lecturers can individualize their course of study to a degree. Contact the Syrian Embassy or the Fulbright Foundation for assistance and information.

■■■ SPECIFIC CONCERNS

WOMEN AND TRAVEL

Also see individual country introductions.

Sense and sensitivity are the best means of avoiding threatening situations in all Middle Eastern countries. In major cities and in tourist sites, locals are more accustomed to Western codes of dress. Away from metropolitan areas in Egypt, Syria, Jordan, in the West Bank, and in both the Orthodox Jewish and Arab sections of Israel, however, it's advisable to emulate the dress and behavior of local women as much as possible. Modest dress (nothing sleeveless or tight, skirts and pants well below the knees) will allow you to travel more comfortably as a guest in another culture. Only on or very near the beaches of tourist resorts are locals used to seeing women in bathing suits. Don't smoke in public in Arab areas, and avoid sitting alone in cafés. If in Islamist-controlled areas, covering your hair in public (with a head scarf) is wise. In general, however, no matter what you do short of dressing like a devout Muslim woman, you will be subjected to looks, comments, maybe even touching in crowded areas. Fortunately, it does not go further than that; violent attacks on foreign women are rare in the Middle East.

Men may not understand that you are irritated or angered by their pursuit. In some cases, the best answer to come-ons is none at all; avoiding eye contact will also reduce the chances of an uncomfortable situation. It may help to wear headphones (but stay aware), as men will be less likely to direct comments toward you if they think you can't hear them. On the other hand, passivity may be taken as tacit acceptance of the situation. Strolling arm in arm with another woman, a common Middle Eastern practice, may be helpful. Wearing a wedding ring is also smart, especially if you're traveling with a man, since out-of-wedlock intimacy between the sexes may be perceived as immoral.

The tricky task of firmly signaling that you've had enough without being hostile is necessary when the ol' cold shoulder doesn't work. Asking an older man for assistance may shame the offending parties into backing down. If a situation becomes genuinely threatening, don't be afraid to yell in any language to call attention to your situation. *Let's Go* lists emergency, police, and consulate phone numbers in most cities. Memorize them or carry them around with you, with change for the phone and enough extra money for a bus or taxi.

Israeli standards of dress are liberal even by Western standards; women will experience far less verbal harassment there than in Arab countries. Egypt has lately grown more conservative than Jordan, Syria, the West Bank, and Arab parts of Israel. Women should not travel alone in Jordan (comments, whistles, and crude animal noises are virtually guaranteed in any case) or Syria.

Consider staying with religious organizations or in hostels with singles which lock from the inside. Forego cheaper places in remote areas of town in favor of youth hostels or more centrally located hotels. Choose train compartments occupied by other women or couples. If you take a *felucca* cruise, it's best to bring along a male companion. On public transportation, cover up when going from urban areas to tourist sights (such as Saqqara or Dendera in Egypt or Petra in Jordan). Once you arrive, you can peel off some portion of your coverings for relief from the heat.

Never hitchhike—it's especially dangerous in Israel—and beware of cars that may be following you. In cabs, keep your luggage handy and the door unlocked.

Avoid walking alone in unpopulated areas: alleys, dark streets and even isolated sights are best avoided. If you think you are being followed, walk quickly and confidently to the nearest public area. A whistle or an airhorn on your keychain is always useful. Consider enrolling in a **Model Mugging** (see p. 20) course to learn how to be in tune with your surroundings and not vulnerable.

The Handbook for Women Travelers, by M. and G. Moss, published by Piatkus Books, 5 Windmill St., London W1P 1HF England (tel. (0171) 631 07 10).£8.99.

Wander Women, 136 N. Grand Ave. #237, West Covina, CA 91791 (tel. (818) 966-8857). A travel and adventure networking organization for women over 40; publishes the quarterly *Journal 'n Footnotes.* Annual US$29 membership fee.

Women Going Places, a new guide, emphasizes women-owned enterprises. Geared towards lesbians but has advice appropriate for all women. US$14 from Inland Book Company, P.O. Box 12061, East Haven, CT 06512 (tel. (203) 467-4257).

Women Travel: Adventures, Advice & Experience, by Miranda Davies and Natania Jansz (Penguin US$12.95). Has a decent bibliography and resource index.

OLDER TRAVELERS AND SENIOR CITIZENS

Elderhostel, 75 Federal St. 3rd floor, Boston, MA 02110 (tel. (617) 426-7788). Short-term residential educational programs at over 1500 locations world-wide.

Gateway Books, P.O. Box 10244, San Rafael, CA 94912, publishes *Get Up and Go: A Guide for the Mature Traveler* (US$10.95), for the budget-conscious senior. (Call (800) 669-0773 for orders.)

National Council on Senior Citizens, 1331 F St. NW, Washington, DC 20004 (tel. (202) 347-8800). Membership (US$12 per year, US$150 lifetime) includes newspaper, travel and hotel discounts, extra Medicare insurance (if you're over 65).

Pilot Books, 103 Cooper St., Babylon, NY 11702 (tel. (516) 422-2225) publishes *The International Health Guide for Senior Citizens* (US$4.95).

TRAVELERS WITH CHILDREN

Have your children carry some sort of ID in case of emergency or if they get lost. When flying, children under two generally fly for 10% adult fare on international flights (does not necessarily include a seat); those aged 2-12 usually fly half price.

Lonely Planet Publications, Embarcadero West, 155 Philbert St. #251, Oakland, CA 94607 (tel. (800) 275-8555; fax 893-8563); also P.O. Box 617, Hawthorn, Victoria 3122, Australia. Maureen Wheeler's *Travel with Children* (US$10.95).

Wilderness Press, 2440 Bancroft Way, Berkeley, CA 94704 (tel. (800) 443-7227 or (510) 843-8080). *Backpacking with Babies and Small Children* (US$9.95).

TRAVELERS WITH DISABILITIES

Inform airlines and hotels of disabilities when making reservations; time may be needed to make arrangements. Travelers with seeing-eye dogs should inquire as to the quarantine policies of the destination country. At the very least, you will need a certificate of immunization against rabies. The following organizations provide information or publications:

American Foundation for the Blind, 15 W. 16th St., New York, NY 10011, (tel. (212) 620-2147; open Mon.-Fri. 9am-2pm). Provides ID cards (US$10); write for an application or call the Product Center at (800) 829-0500. Also call the Product Center to order AFB catalogs in braille, print, or on cassette or disk.

Moss Rehabilitation Hospital Travel Information Service, 1200 W. Tabor Rd., Philadelphia, PA 19141, (tel. (215) 456-9603). A telephone information center on international travel accessibility. Will refer callers to other agencies.

Pauline Hephaistos Survey Projects, 39 Bradley Gardens, West Ealing, London W13 8HE, England. Sells *Access in Israel* (£4).

Society for the Advancement of Travel for the Handicapped, 347 Fifth Ave. #610, New York, NY 10016 (tel. (212) 447-7284; fax 725-8253). Publishes travel newsletter and booklets (free for members, US$3 for nonmembers) with advice on trip planning. Annual membership US$45, students and seniors US$25.

Twin Peaks Press, P.O. Box 129, Vancouver, WA 98666-0129 (tel. (206) 694-2462; orders only (800) 637-2256 or fax (206) 696-3210). *Travel for the Disabled, Directory for Travel Agencies of the Disabled, Wheelchair Vagabond,* and *Directory of Accessible Van Rentals* (US$10-20 each, plus US$1-2 postage).

The following organize tours and make arrangements for those with disabilities:

Directions Unlimited, 720 North Bedford Rd., Bedford Hills, NY 10507 (tel. (800) 533-5343 or (914) 241-1700; fax 241-0243). Vacations, tours, cruises.

Flying Wheels Travel Service, P.O. Box 382, 143 W. Bridge St., Owatonne, MN 55060 (tel. (800) 535-6790; fax (507) 451-1685). International travel.

The Guided Tour, Elkins Park House #114B, 7900 Old York Road, Elkins Park, PA 19117-2339 (tel. (215) 635-2637). Organizes domestic and international travel for persons with developmental or physical challenges, or requiring renal dialysis. Free brochure.

The Yad Sarah Organization, 43 Ha-Nevi'im St., P.O. Box 6992, Jerusalem 91609 (tel. (02) 244 242). Free loan of medical and rehabilitative equipment in Israel, transport and laundry services for individuals who are disabled or elderly.

BISEXUAL, GAY, AND LESBIAN TRAVELERS

Open expressions of gay affection in Israel are uncommon, but Israel (particularly Tel Aviv) is a world apart from its Arab neighbors in terms of the public and legal status of gays, lesbians, and bisexuals and the availability of gathering places and support organizations. In the Arab world, where paradoxes abound, you might say that homosexuality exists while a "gay lifestyle" does not. Avoid publicly kissing or fondling a member of the same sex the same way heterosexuals must avoid publicly kissing or fondling members of the opposite sex. Behind closed doors (and everything in Arab countries occurs behind closed doors) is another story. Gay and lesbian assistance in Egypt, Syria, and Jordan is nonexistent.

The only organization for gay and lesbian concerns in Israel is the **Society for the Protection of Personal Rights,** P.O. Box 37604, Tel Aviv 61375 (tel. (03) 204 327 or 293 681; fax 525 2341), or P.O. Box 3592, Haifa (tel. (04) 672 665). The society publishes an English-language newsletter, *Israel Update.* A community center, library, and coffee shop is located in the basement at 28 Naḥmani St., Tel Aviv. The society's gay and lesbian hotline is the **White Line** (Ha-Kav Ha-Lavan; tel. (03) 292 797; operates Sun. and Tues.-Thurs. 7:30-11:30pm).

There is a wide variety of publications and resources for gay and lesbian travelers (the SPPR recommends the *Spartacus* guide as the most accurate and updated):

Bruno Gmunder, Postfach 301345, D-1000 Berlin 30, Germany (tel. (30) 25 49 82 00). Publishes *Spartacus International Gay Guide* (US$29.95), which lists bars, restaurants, hotels, and bookstores around the world catering to gay men. Available in the U.S. from Giovanni's Room or Renaissance House.

Ferrari Publications, P.O. Box 37887, Phoenix, AZ 85069 (tel. (602) 863-2408). Publishes books relevant to Israel. Call for more information.

Gay's the Word, 66 Marchmont St., London WC1N 1AB, England (tel. (0171) 278 76 54). Open Mon.-Fri. 11am-7pm, Sat. 10am-6pm, Sun. and holidays 2-6pm.

Giovanni's Room, 345 S. 12th St., Philadelphia, PA 19107 (tel. (215) 923-2960; fax 923-0813). An international feminist, lesbian, and gay bookstore with mail-order service and carries many publications. Free catalogue.

Renaissance House, P.O. Box 533, Village Station, New York, NY 10014 (tel. (212) 674-0120; fax 420-1126). Comprehensive gay bookstore; carries many titles. Send self-addressed stamped envelope for free mail-order catalogue.

VEGETARIAN AND KOSHER TRAVELERS

The Middle East is a vegetarian's delight, with meatless dishes (including many street foods) widely available. See Life and Times: Food sections for each country.

For a list of synagogues, kosher restaurants, and institutions in over 80 countries, procure the 396-page *Jewish Travel Guide,* published by Vallentine, Mitchell & Co., 11 Gainsborough Rd., London E11, 1RS; available in the U.S. from Sepher-Hermon Press (1265 46th St., Brooklyn, NY 11219; tel. (718) 972-9010) for US$11.95, plus US$1.75 postage. *The Jewish Traveler's Resource Guide* is available from Feldheim Publishers, 200 Airport Executive Park, Spring Valley, NY 10977.

■■■ TRAVEL ETIQUETTE

Standards of dress and behavior are much more conservative in the Arab world than in the West. Egypt, the West Bank, Jordan, and Syria all mix Western and traditional Arab dress. In Egypt there are some liberal enclaves, though the rise of Islamic fundamentalism is moving the less touristy areas in a more conservative direction; Jordan and Syria have fewer liberal enclaves. Public behavior in all these areas should be reserved. Israel, except in some Arab and Jewish-Orthodox regions, is as liberal in its dress code as any Western country. Consult the introductions to individual countries and cities for specific information about proper etiquette.

In holy places, modest dress is the norm. Never wear shorts or sleeveless shirts; women are better off with long skirts than pants. Do not visit sanctuaries during services unless you are worshipping, in which case you are always welcome. Remove your shoes before entering a mosque. Women should cover their hair in a mosque; men should cover their heads in a synagogue.

Photography is often forbidden in holy places and archaeological sites and museums. It is absolutely forbidden in military installations, border crossings, railroad stations, bridges, ports, airfields, and the Aswan High Dam. Take a picture and you risk having your film confiscated and being held for questioning.

In many Egyptian tourist towns, horse- and donkey-drawn carriages are used for transportation of travelers and their luggage. Several *Let's Go* readers have been horrified by the mistreatment, bad health, and malnourishment of the animals. Although this is a budget guide, saving a few piasters at the expense of an animal's health isn't worth it. We urge you not to put more than three passengers in a carriage at once. Also, ask drivers not to race the horses; and you can withhold tips from those who whip their horses abusively. Most importantly, only patronize drivers who treat their animals well, and insist that tour guides do the same.

TRAVEL IN THE REGION

For those traveling to just one country, Getting There contains all the necessary information. Touring around the region, however, requires panache, paperwork, and patience. See Border Crossings, p. 33 for that information.

■■■ GETTING THERE

BY PLANE

Off-season travelers enjoy lower fares and a greater availability of inexpensive seats. Peak season rates begin around May and run until September. To Israel, peak season rates also apply around religious holidays. If you plan carefully, you can travel in summer and still save with shoulder- or low-season fares. Remember that an indirect flight via Brussels or Athens could cost considerably less than a direct flight to Cairo or Tel Aviv, both of which are still cheaper destinations than Amman and Damascus.

Find a travel agent who specializes in the Middle East. Commissions are smaller on budget flights, so some agents may not have the initiative to search for the cheapest fare. The Sunday *New York Times* lists bargain fares, and student travel organizations (see Budget Travel Services, p. 5) often offer discounts.

Charter Flights Charter flights offer consistently economical airfares. You may book them until the last minute, though summer flights fill up several months in advance. Later in the season, companies have empty seats and either offer special prices or cancel flights. Charters are more of a bargain in high season, because APEX fares (see Commercial Airlines, below) on commercial carriers are competitively priced in winter. Fares advertised in newspapers are usually the lowest possible, but you should always read the fine print. Charter flights allow you to stay abroad up to one year, and often let you "mix-and-match" arrivals and departures from different cities. Once you have made your plans, however, flexibility wanes. You must choose your departure and return dates when you book your flight, and if you cancel your ticket within 2 or 3 weeks of departure, you will lose some or all of your money. Travel insurance usually does not cover cancellations for reasons other than serious illness, natural disaster, or death.

Although charter flights are cheap, expect to be crowded and to spend at least part of your vacation exploring the majestic airports of the world. Ask a travel agent about charter companies' reliability. Companies reserve the right to cancel flights up to 48 hours before departure. Though they will do their best to find you another flight, the delay could be days, not just hours. The companies also reserve the right to add fuel surcharges even after you have made final payment. To be sure you're on your flight, pick up your ticket well before the departure date and arrive at the airport several hours early. Charter companies often have messy reservations systems.

Charter coverage of the Middle East varies from year to year, so consult a travel agent for companies offering flights. Several companies run inexpensive flights from Israel to Europe or North America (see Budget Travel Services, p. 5).

Commercial Airlines If you choose to fly with a commercial airline, you'll be paying for reliability and flexibility. You can't fly standby to Israel, Egypt, Jordan, or Syria. **Advanced Purchase Excursion (APEX) Fares** provide confirmed reservations and permit you to arrive in and depart from different cities. Reservations usually must be made 7 to 21 days in advance with 7- to 14-day minimum and 30- to 90-day maximum stay limitations. Beware hefty penalties for canceling or altering reservations. Also, be sure to ask for student fares. You may have to wait until about 3 days before departure to get these fares. Fares shown were compiled June to August 1994, and are for round trips in the summer (peak season); off-season tickets may be up to US$200 cheaper. These fares came straight from the airlines themselves; the tickets are often cheaper through budget travel agencies.

Air France (tel. (800) 237-2747). Round-trip London-Paris to Cairo US$984, to Tel Aviv US$1719, to Amman or Damascus US$903. Student fares available.

British Airways (tel. (800) 247-9297). Round-trip London to Tel Aviv US$527, to Cairo US$874.

Delta Airlines (tel. (800) 241-4141). Round-trip NYC to Tel Aviv US$1258.

EgyptAir (tel. (800) 334-6787). Egypt's national airline. Round-trip New York City to Cairo US$1610 (student fare US$1000), London to Cairo US$864.

El Al (tel. (800) 223-6700). Israel's national airline. Round-trip New York City to Tel Aviv US$1214 (under 25 yrs. US$998). Also flies from London to Tel Aviv.

KLM Royal Dutch Airlines (tel. (800) 374-7747). Round-trip London to Tel Aviv US$1110, to Cairo, Damascus, or Amman US$900.

Kuwait Airways (tel. (800) 458-9248).

Lufthansa (tel. (800) 645-3880). London-Frankfurt to Cairo, Alexandria, or Damascus US$1334, to Tel Aviv US$1363.

GETTING THERE

Middle East Air (tel. (212) 664-7310). Round-Trip London to Beirut US$1200.
Northwest Airlines (tel. (800) 225-2525). Round-trip New York City to Cairo US$1641, to Tel Aviv US$1278, to Amman US$1534, to Damascus US$1610.
Olympic Airways (tel. (800) 223-1226). Flights to Tel Aviv from Athens.
Royal Jordanian Airlines (tel. (800) 223-0470). Jordan's national airline. Round-trip New York City to Amman US$1534, London to Amman US$864 (youth fare (ages 12-24) good for 1 yr. US$870).
TransWorld Airlines (TWA) (tel. (800) 221-2000). Round-trip NYC to Cairo US$1470, to Tel Aviv US$1214.
United Airlines (tel. (800) 538-2929). Listen to murdered-and-messily-exhumed renditions of George Gershwin's *Rhapsody in Blue* while you wait. And wait.

Airline Ticket Consolidators Airline Ticket Consolidators sell unbooked commercial and charter tickets. Most charge a yearly membership fee of about US$40 for access to their extremely low fares. Ask about cancellation penalties and advance purchase requirements and, in general, be wary. The details of flight delays and cancellations are beyond the control of these companies, so the traveler is at the mercy of the particular carrier. A few consolidators are **Dollarwise Travel,** 7221 NW 12th St., Miami, FL 33126 (tel. (305) 592-3343), specializing in flights from the U.S. to the Middle East (round-trip NYC-Tel Aviv $875, NYC-Cairo $893), and **Tourlite International,** 551 Fifth Ave., New York, NY 10176 (tel. (800) 272-7600), specializing in budget flights, and tours to Egypt and Israel.

Courier Companies Carry luggage for a company that needs something delivered and get discounted fares; you keep your carry-on, but give up your cargo space. **Now Voyager,** 74 Varick St. #307, New York, NY 10013 (tel. (212) 431-1616), matches companies needing free-lance couriers with eager travelers. Most flights originate in New York. Air courier services spring up like mushrooms; check the yellow pages under "Air Courier Service" for the latest crop.

BY BUS AND TRAIN

Buses and **trains** can bring you from Northern Europe to ports along the Mediterranean where you can board ferries to Israel or Egypt. You can also go by bus from Europe to Jordan via Turkey and Syria. **Magic Bus** (20 Filellinon St., Syntagma, Athens, Greece; tel. (1) 323 74 71) has cheap air, rail, bus, and boat tickets to and from Europe, North America, Africa, and the East. If you're under 26, **BIJ tickets** can provide discounts of 30-45% on second-class rail fares on international train runs. They are available at most travel agencies in Europe but not yet in the U.S.; contact: Wasteels, 7041 Grand National Dr. #207, Orlando, FL 32819 (tel. (407) 351-2537; fax (407) 363-1041). Always inquire about other student discounts.

BY BOAT

Several **ferry lines** sail from Europe to Israel. Fares vary considerably, depending mainly on your tolerance for discomfort. Outdoor deck seats may cost as little as US$50-60 for a three-day trip, but beware that clean bathrooms are hard to come by. More comfortable are the three- or four-berth inside cabins that many companies offer at reduced student and youth fares. The following sail from Europe to Haifa:

Mano Passenger Lines, Ltd.: Israel: 97 Ben-Yehuda St., Tel Aviv (tel. (03) 522 4611; fax 522 4599). **Greece:** 11 Mavrokordatou St., Piraeus (tel. 729 1218 or 429 1423; fax 429 1445; telex 241 220). Boats between Haifa and Piraeus leave Sun. at 1pm and Fri. at 8pm; Embarkation starts 3 hrs. before the ship leaves.
Stability Line Caspi Ltd.: Israel: 76 Ha'Atzma'ut Rd., P.O. Box 27, Haifa (tel. (04) 674 444; fax 674 456); 3 Yanai St., Jerusalem (tel. (02) 244 266); 1 Ben-Yehuda St., Tel Aviv (tel. (03) 510 6834; fax 660 989). **Greece:** 11 Sachtouri St., Piraeus (tel. 413 2392 or 2395). Operates the *Vergina* between Piraeus and Haifa once per week April 2-Oct. 30.

Several companies operate lines between Europe and Egypt, mostly to Alexandria. The map of Alexandria sold at Al-Ma'aref Bookstore lists some of these companies; ask at the tourist office in Raml Station Square for routes and phone numbers.

■■■ BORDER CROSSINGS

Overland border crossing policies in the Middle East change like Madonna's hair color; check with government tourist offices for the latest information. As late as September 1994, Syria would not admit travelers with evidence of a visit to Israel in their passports (this is likely to change as the peace process progresses). Israeli officials can give you a detachable visa stamp upon request. Egyptian entry stamps from borders with Israel may also keep you out of Syria.

In 1992 the U.S. State Department stopped issuing second passports valid only for travel to Israel; but you can still get limited-duration (2 yrs.) second passports. To obtain a second passport, observe normal application procedures and include a written statement explaining why you require a second passport. Contact the Washington Passport Agency (see Passports, p. 9).

For all border crossings, we recommend that you have at least US$20 worth of the currency of each country involved, plus the same in U.S. currency. There are exchange facilities at most borders, but they could be closed or out of cash.

■ BETWEEN EGYPT AND ISRAEL

You must pay a **tax** each time you enter or leave Israel (NIS34.80), and another one to enter Egypt (E£20). If you plan to go from one country to another and then return, make sure you have a **multiple entry visa** or be ready to apply and pay for a second visa for the country you started from. See individual towns and cities for information on public transportation to border towns.

Buses from the Cairo Sheraton and from Abbasiyya (Sinai) Station run to Tel Aviv. (see Cairo: Practical Information, p. 77 and p. 78). See travel agencies in either country for buses connecting Cairo and Tel Aviv or Jerusalem via Rafah. **Flights** between Egypt and Israel are offered by Egypt's **Air Sinai** and Israel's **El Al** (see Getting There, p. 31).

Dan/United Tours: 113 Ha-Yarkon St., Tel Aviv 63573 (tel. (03) 693 3410 or 3411; fax 693 3408). Also offices in Jerusalem (tel. (02) 252 187 or 188; fax 255 013); Haifa (tel. (04) 665 656), Eilat (tel. (07) 371 720 or 740; fax 371 752), and Ben-Gurion Airport (tel. (03) 971 1886).

Egged Tours: 15 Frischmann St., Tel Aviv 63578 (tel. (03) 527 1223/4; fax 527 2020). Sinai only (St. Catherine's and Mt. Sinai). 1 day US$52, 2 days US$115.

Galilee Tours: Israel: 42 Ben-Yehuda St., Tel Aviv 63807 (tel. (03) 546 6333; fax 291 770); 3 Hillel St., Jerusalem (tel. (02) 258 866; fax 231 303); and other offices in Tiberias and Eilat. **U.S.:** 310 1st Ave., Needham, MA 02194 (tel. (617) 449-8996; fax 449-8988). Tours in Israel, Egypt, Jordan, and Greece.

Mazada Tours: 141 Ibn Gvirol St., Tel Aviv (tel. (03) 544 4454; fax 546 1928) and 9 Koresh St., Jerusalem (tel. (02) 255 453). One-way from Tel Aviv or Jerusalem to Cairo US$25, round-trip US$35. Midnight express to Cairo via Taba, and a new run to Sharm esh-Sheikh (US$38, round-trip US$62).

Neot Ha-Kikar Touring Co.: 78 Ben-Yehuda St., Tel Aviv (tel. (03) 522 8161 through 8164 (4 lines); fax 522 1020); 36 Keren Ha-Yesod St., Jerusalem 92149 (tel. (02) 636 494); Amiel Khan Center, Eilat (tel. (07) 330 425 or 426). 8 Sinai tours, lasting 1-6 days (US$53-370), leaving from Cairo and Eilat.

FROM EGYPT TO ISRAEL

On land, you can cross from Taba to Eilat or at Rafah, which straddles the border. The border at Taba/Eilat is open 24 hrs. at Rafah from 9am to 5pm. At the border, you can obtain a free Israeli **visa** good for one month. Alternatively, you can secure an Israeli visa before attempting to cross the border, available from the Israeli Embassy in Cairo or the Consulate in Alexandria (Cairo and Alexandria: Practical Information, p. 79 and p. 126).

Unless you are a U.S. citizen, you will be charged a re-entry fee if you have recently left Israel and are returning. This can be as much as NIS135. Call Israeli passport control at 372 104 (mornings only) to check the ever-changing regulations.

Traveling with tour groups facilitates the border-crossing process. Rented cars are not allowed to cross. See specific towns for information on public transportation. Visitors in private cars must present a valid driving license and *carnet de passage*.

FROM ISRAEL TO EGYPT

On land, you can cross from Eilat to Taba or at Rafah, which straddles the border. The border at Eilat/Taba is open 24 hrs.; at Rafah from 9am to 5pm.

Visitors crossing the border from Israel to the **Taba** Hilton Hotel *only* do not require an Egyptian visa and need only present their passports at the border checkpoint (tel. (07) 373 110), open 24 hours a day.

Persons intending to visit Southern Sinai *only* may obtain a special **Sinai-only visa** on the spot at the border at Taba, valid for **two weeks.** This visa **limits travel** to the Gulf of Aqaba coast as far south as Sharm esh-Sheikh and to St. Catherine's monastery and Mt. Sinai (but not sites in the vicinity of St. Catherine's). Unlike ordinary one-month Egyptian visas, the Sinai-only visa has no grace period; overextend your stay and you'll pay a hefty fine.

For visits of longer duration or to visit the rest of Egypt (including parts of the Sinai), you will need a normal **Egyptian visa.** If you fly into Cairo, you can get this visa upon arrival at Cairo International Airport (see Egypt: Once There, p. 53). If you plan to cross overland, apply for a visa at the Egyptian Consulate in Tel Aviv or Eilat (Tel Aviv and Eilat: Practical Information, p. 255 and p. 347). Processing takes a few hours, but the lines can get uncomfortably long, especially during Ramadan.

Crossing at **Rafah** promises to be a good time; not only do you get to deal with Israeli and Egyptian authorities, but also the brand-new Palestinian Authority. At press time we had no information on border-crossing procedures; we recommend you have your Egyptian visa ahead of time and at least a small supply of Israeli, Egyptian, and United States currency.

Traveling with a tour group facilitates the border-crossing process. Rented cars are not allowed to cross. See specific towns for information on public transportation.

■ BETWEEN EGYPT AND JORDAN

To obtain a **Jordanian visa** from the Jordanian embassy in Cairo, you will need a letter from your own embassy or consulate stating your reasons for visiting Jordan (see Cairo: Practical Information, p. 79). It only takes one day to get an **Egyptian tourist visa** from the Egyptian Embassy in Amman or the Consulate in Aqaba (see Amman and Aqaba: Practical Information, p. 425 and p. 448). If you take the ferry between the Sinai and Aqaba, visa procedures are simplified but the visa itself is limited.

EgyptAir and Royal Jordanian have **flights** between Cairo and Amman (see Getting There, p. 31). The cheaper option is the **ferry** between Nuweiba' (in the Sinai) and Aqaba (see Sinai: Getting There and Away, p. 219).

Aboard the ferry to Aqaba, a **two-week or one-month Jordanian visa** (if you do not already have a visa) will be entered into your passport.

If you are heading from Jordan to Egypt, a **two-week Sinai-only visa** will be issued on the spot in Nuweiba. If you plan to stay in Egypt longer than two weeks or to travel beyond the Sinai, you will need a regular **Egyptian tourist visa** (see above).

■ BETWEEN ISRAEL AND JORDAN

A recent accord opened the Eilat/Aqaba border. Neither country has embassies or consulates in the other, so you will need to secure a visa before leaving your home country. This is a brand-new border crossing, but the process is reputedly painless. Be a pioneer.

■ BETWEEN THE WEST BANK AND JORDAN

The Palestinians, Jordanians, and Israelis are still trying to figure this one out for themselves. We cannot guarantee any information given here, although in summer 1994 the procedure was simple and smooth for many travelers of different nationalities. Even if we could, it would probably change the first time Arafat, Hussein, or Rabin sneezed. Sorry.

You will cross at the **King Hussein/Allenby Bridge** (10km from Jericho, 40km from Jerusalem, 40km from Amman). This used to be the site of humiliating strip searches and long waits, mostly for those of Arab origin. Lucky for you, things are starting to change; but a few handshakes exchanged and papers signed do not turn the world upside down in a day. Everything remains unpredictable; get thorough, up-to-date information from your embassy or consulate before trying to cross. The bridge is open only in the morning, and closed on Fridays, Saturdays, and Jewish and Muslim holidays. It may also be closed for one political event or another. Check with a consulate, tourist office, or the Palestinian Authority in Jericho before planning your life around it. You will pay a **border tax** upon entering and leaving the West Bank.

FROM THE WEST BANK TO JORDAN

You'll need a Jordanian visa, not obtainable in Israel. Get it before leaving your home country, from a Jordanian embassy or consulate (see p. 3).

Start early in the morning. Your point of departure will be **Jericho** (connected by bus to other West Bank towns and Jerusalem). In Jericho, board a *service* taxi bound for the Bridge. Make sure your *service* goes all the way to the border—some are authorized to go only as far as a checkpoint on the outskirts of town. No private vehicles are permitted to cross the bridge.

At the bridge, your passport and belongings will be inspected. Once on the Jordanian side, you can catch a *service* taxi to Amman. If you plan to go into Israel (including Jerusalem) from the West Bank, you should have an Israeli visa, not obtainable in Jordan. Get it before leaving your home country, from an Israeli embassy or consulate (see p. 3).

FROM JORDAN TO THE WEST BANK

You will need a **West Bank permit** from the Ministry of Interior in Amman (see Amman: Practical Information, p. 425). This takes at least three working days.

With West Bank permit in hand, transport yourself from Amman to the Bridge via *service* taxi or JETT bus from Abdali Station (see Amman: Practical Information, p. 426). This is a busy transit point; if you try to buy a bus ticket past 10:30am you might not get one. JETT buses go all the way to the Israeli checkpoint. S*ervice* go only as far as the terminal for foreigners; from there you'll have to take a shuttle bus. Israeli officials may ask young travelers for evidence of financial security.

From the border, *service* taxis in the West Bank run to many destinations. The Shaheen Bus Company provides air-conditioned transport roughly on the hour between 11am and 3 or 4pm. You may pay for transportation on the West Bank with Jordanian dinars.

■ BETWEEN JORDAN AND SYRIA

To go to Syria from Jordan you will need a **Syrian visa,** sometimes obtainable from the Syrian embassy in Amman. Chances are, you will need a letter of introduction from your own embassy or consulate stating your reasons for visiting Syria (see Embassies and Consulates, p. 3, or Amman: Practical Information, p. 425). If the Syrian embassy gives you the runaround, persevere. You might consider applying for a Syrian visa from the embassy nearest you well in advance of leaving your home country, although in some cases the process is actually easier in Amman. Buses run often between Amman and Damascus. Unfortunately, you can make round-trip reservations from neither city. Definitely make reservations for the return trip to Jordan as soon as you arrive in Damascus, or vice versa. The road between the two capitals is heavily traveled on weekends (Thurs.-Sat.). If you go on a weekend, expect border-crossing to take as long as three hours. The process at the border is not difficult—just follow the other people in your busload.

INTRODUCTION TO THE REGION

■■■ HISTORY

ANCIENT EGYPT

Conquering Lower (northern) Egypt and then uniting it with Upper (southern, where the headwaters of the Nile are) Egypt, King Menes, the semi-mythical first pharaoh, founded one of the most powerful and lasting civilizations of the ancient world. From Memphis, the capital probably built by Menes around 2900 BCE, successive pharaohs oversaw the construction of complicated irrigation systems and grandiose monuments. Less than 100 years after the first step pyramid was built at Saqqara, the pharaohs of the Old Kingdom (approx. 2665-2180 BCE) were organizing skilled builders and hundreds of thousands of laborers to build the classic, smooth-sided pyramids. At a time when even China had scarcely emerged from the Stone Age, Egyptians had invented writing and papyrus, recorded the regnal years of pharaohs, and were crafting extraordinarily creative ivory and metal art. Many view this era as the apex of ancient Egyptian civilization.

The absolute authority of the pharaoh began to wane and the Old Kingdom drew to an end as petty kings and provincial administrators gained power. A cycle of unification and disintegration persisted until the demise of pharaonic rule. After a century of rule by a succession of feuding monarchs, Mentuhotep II allied with the princes of Thebes to establish the Middle Kingdom (approx. 2050-1786 BCE).

During the Middle Kingdom, Egypt's culture flourished and spread as contact with the southern kingdoms of Nubia and Kush spawned subsidiary pharaonic cultures. Internal political rivalries, however, weakened the Egyptian-Theban dynasty until the Hyksos invaded and conquered Egypt. Upon the expulsion of the Hyksos almost a century later, Egypt was resuscitated in the New Kingdom (approx. 1555-1075 BCE). During this phase, Egypt invaded Africa, Palestine, and Syria. Although the Israelites may have helped build the many monuments left by Ramses II, his successor left behind the victory inscription, "Israel is desolated and has no seed."

The New Kingdom, too, crumbled over time. After a last-ditch attempt by the conservative Kushites (Ethiopians in Sudan) to re-establish centralized Egyptian authority, the Assyrians, soon followed by the Persians, pounced "like wolves on the fold."

The Persian dynasty was Egypt's first completely foreign rule and was deeply loathed. For the next 200 years the Egyptians struggled to overthrow the Persians; periodically succeeding, only to be subjugated again. When Alexander the Great arrived in 322 BCE, he was received as a liberator. After ousting the Persians, he set off for the oracle of Amun in the distant Siwa Oasis. There, he was promptly declared the Son of Amun and the legitimate pharaoh of Egypt. But after dutifully founding another Alexandria, the new pharaoh went on his way and never returned. Upon Alexander's death the empire broke up and Ptolemy took control of Egypt, becoming the pharaoh Ptolemy, Son of God. Alexandria swelled into a cosmopolitan center of trade and learning; its 750,000-volume library contained most of the Greeks' knowledge under one roof.

In 48 BCE, more than a century after Rome made its first, tentative overtures to the ever-feuding Ptolemies, Julius Caesar came to Egypt in pursuit of his rival Pompey and fell captive to the allure of Cleopatra VII, Queen of Egypt. Cleopatra, facing challenges from other claimants to the throne, accepted an alliance with Caesar that left her secure—until his assassination four years later. Sensing danger as well as opportunity, Cleopatra conspired with Marc Antony, one of three successors vying for Caesar's empire. Although these events sparked one of history's most celebrated love affairs, political celebration was left to Octavian, who grabbed the empire for himself, ruthlessly crushing the affair and the Ptolemy dynasty in 30 BCE.

Political stability and an increasingly entrenched bureaucracy characterized the Egypt of Imperial Rome and then Byzantium. In 451 CE, not quite two centuries after the Byzantine emperors adopted and promoted Christianity, the Coptic Church split from the church of Constantinople due to differences in doctrines.

ANCIENT PALESTINE

The Bible begins the recorded history of the area with the story of Abraham, the first of the Patriarchs. The semi-nomadic Aramaean tribes' migration to Palestine almost four thousand years ago has been linked by archaeologists with the biblical tradition of Abraham's (Avraham in Hebrew, Ibrahim in Arabic) journey from Chaldea (Genesis 12). In the 13th or 14th century BCE, however, famine forced some of the Semitic groups in Palestine to flee to Egypt where, according to the Bible, the Pharaoh bound them into servitude (Exodus 1). The Semites were the ancestors of the people of Palestine, Arab, and Jew alike. Meticulous Egyptian records (a rarity today) attest to the existence of a foreign group called the Ḥabiri (or Khapiru), a name thought possibly to be the ancestor of the word "Hebrew." But, as told by the Torah, the combination of Moses' (Moshe in Hebrew, Mussa in Arabic) initiative and several plagues (Passover commemorates the tenth plague) ultimately convinced an Egyptian pharaoh (quite possibly Ramses II) to allow the Hebrews to leave Egypt

(Exodus 12:31). After an arduous journey across the Sinai Peninsula, the Hebrews returned to Canaan, much of which was controlled by the Philistines. Following Moses' death, Joshua led the newly constituted twelve tribes of Israel across the Jordan River and attacked Jericho (Joshua 6:20). The battle against the Philistines continued after Joshua's death.

At the end of the 11th century BCE, the Israelite tribes united under King Saul. The kingdom reached its peak during the reign of Saul's successor, David, and that of David's son, Solomon. The construction of the Temple of Jerusalem is considered Solomon's most formidable feat, but the cost of the Temple and other civil projects proved a heavy burden for his subjects. After Solomon's death in 922 BCE, unrest spread; the empire split into the Kingdom of Israel in the north and the smaller Kingdom of Judah (Judea) in the south.

The Assyrians conquered Israel in 724 BCE and made Judah a vassal state of their empire until they too were crushed by the Babylonians. The Babylonian King Nebuchadnezzar razed the Temple, burned Jerusalem, and deported many Jews to Mesopotamia in the Babylonian Captivity or Exile in 587 BCE. When the Persians defeated Nebuchadnezzar's successor some 50 years later, King Cyrus permitted the Jews to return to Jerusalem and to build the Second Temple. Nevertheless, Palestine again fell prey to foreign invaders: Alexander the Great conquered the region in 333 BCE, and his heirs, the Ptolemies, followed the leader in 323 BCE.

The Seleucids displaced the Ptolemies in 198 BCE and attempted to Hellenize the Jews. Judas Maccabeus, responding to the persecutions of Antiochus IV, led a Jewish revolt. Victorious, the Maccabees resanctified the Temple in 164 BCE and founded the Hasmonean Dynasty. In spite of potent internal conflict, the Hasmonean Dynasty ruled Palestine for over a century.

In 63 BCE, the Romans swept in; Jerusalem rebelled again in 65 CE. In 70 CE the Roman general Titus, faced with the choice of sparing the Temple at great military cost or burning all of Jerusalem, chose to save his men and burned the Temple with the rest of Jerusalem. Three years later the Romans captured the last Jewish stronghold at Masada, but without any prisoners—the defenders had taken their own lives instead of surrendering. Rome used the name Palestine for the land.

Byzantine rule replaced Roman in Palestine in 330 CE. Although little changed administratively, the adoption of Christianity by the Emperor Constantine in 331 created increased interest in what to many was the "Holy Land." Pilgrims and devout financiers built churches and endowed monasteries and schools. Political stability, disrupted only during the Samaritans' revolt in 529 and a brief Persian invasion a few decades later, fostered a new sense of prosperity in the region.

The Muslims arrived in the 7th century, continuing a drive to push Byzantine armies back to Constantinople. Jerusalem, site of Muhammad's "night journey" to heaven, capitulated in 638. For four and a half centuries thereafter, Palestine was ruled by the Umayyads, the Abbassids, the Fatimids (see Islam and Empires, p. 38), and, eventually, Turkish Seljuks. Rumors of dubious Seljuk policies regarding the treatment of Christian pilgrims prompted the Europeans to launch a series of crusades aimed at the recapture of the Holy Land. Impelled by inspiration, fame, fortune, and Pope Urban II's offer of indulgences, Crusaders wrought havoc. After massacring Muslim and Jewish inhabitants of Jerusalem in 1099, the Crusaders established a fiefdom in Acre (Akko) under Baldwin I.

It didn't last. The second and third Crusades were choked at the hands of Salah ad-Din. The following century's subsequent five crusades all floundered, as Mamluks controlled the outpost at Acre and other key fortresses (for instance, Shobak and Montfort) by the close of 1291. After two more centuries of instability, the Ottomans defeated the Mamluk chieftains in 1517, and Palestine became merely one of the many administrative units of the empire.

ISLAM AND EMPIRES

After the death of the Prophet Muhammad in 632 CE (see Islam, p. 52), Bedouin armies, inspired by Islam and the prospect of substantial spoils, ventured outside their traditional strongholds in Central Arabia and, in a series of protracted battles between 639 and 642, conquered Egypt. Tired of the Greek Orthodox Church's rigidity, many Egyptians resented Byzantine rule and appreciated the arriving armies' relative tolerance, if not Islam itself.

The death of Muhammad gave rise to political confusion, as no successor had been designated. Amid vigorous debate as to whether the successor had to be a blood relative, Abu Bakr, confidante and father-in-law of Muhammad, was chosen as the first successor (*khalifa*, or caliph). Ruling from 632-34, he was followed by Omar (634-44), Uthman (644-56), and finally Ali (656-61), all based in Medina. The election of Ali, the Prophet's nephew and son-in-law, incited a civil war and produced a lasting schism in Islam between the Sunni (the "orthodox," who opposed a blood-relative caliphate), and the Shi'i (the "party," who supported Ali's claim). This division notwithstanding, the first four caliphs are known to most Muslims as the Rashidun (the Rightly Guided Caliphs). With the advent of the Umayyad Dynasty, founded by the Caliph Mu'awiya in Damascus in 661, Shi'i opposition was muted and a Sunni hereditary monarchy (unrelated to the Prophet) was installed. Within a century the lands from North Africa to Central Asia were pacified. By 750, when the Abbassids overthrew the Umayyads on charges of decadence and impiety, the majority of the peasantry had converted to Islam. A mammoth bureaucracy, operating out of Baghdad and composed of everything from tax officials to scribes to Islamic jurists *(ulama)*, helped run the empire.

Successive Abbassid caliphs, usually based in Baghdad, were never without challenges; the rival Umayyad family had established a potentially troublesome dynasty in Spain, while various Shi'i dynasties flourished on the borders of the Abbassid empire. The Shi'i Fatimids, attacking northward from their domain in the Nile Valley, expelled the Abbassids from Egypt in 969. They established Cairo as their new capital to replace the old center, Fustat. The Fatimids captured most of Palestine, controlled Jerusalem, and prospered through trade with Spain. This success failed to daunt Salah ad-Din (a Kurd, also known as Saladin), founder of the short-lived Ayyubid Dynasty (1171-1250), who dethroned the Fatimids in 1192 with a vast army of Turkish slaves.

Although Salah ad-Din's victories over the Crusaders earned him a place in history, his finely disciplined slave *(mamluk)* armies became a scourge for his successors. Chosen as youths, then trained and equipped by the palace, Mamluks were technically property of the Sultan; yet, their collective strength threatened the Sultan's authority, which was often tenuous at best. In 1250, a Mamluk of the Bahri clan resolved to dispense with formality as well as the Ayyubids and rule the sultanate directly. Chronic instability and infighting followed. Lifestyles for those at the top were still lavish; life expectancies, however, decreased dramatically.

When the Ottoman Empire, expanding out from Anatolia, gained formal sovereignty over Egypt and Palestine in the early part of the 16th century, Mamluks still retained most of their political power. But via appointments, bribery, and assassination, the Ottoman sultans maintained real and effective control. Manipulating their local "representatives" and playing them against one another, the Ottoman rulers enjoyed seemingly indelible authority. To learn more about Egyptian and Arabic history, read Albert Hourani's masterpiece *A History of the Arab Peoples*.

THE COLLAPSE OF THE OTTOMAN EMPIRE AND THE RISE OF EGYPTIAN NATIONALISM

When the gates of Vienna closed on Ottoman armies in 1683, Turkey began worrying about the fate of its increasingly decrepit empire. Napoleon's successful 1798 invasion of Egypt surprised even the grumpiest European pessimist. While Europe had grown more and more powerful, the Ottoman Empire had languished. The animated ports of in Syria, Palestine, and Egypt had once provided the sole access to the East; now, they were relegated to insignificance as Portuguese sailors finagled their way around the Horn of Africa. Egypt's economy—for two centuries buttressed by the Arabian and Yemeni coffee trade—collapsed when European investors cultivated their own, cheaper coffee in the Java islands and, turning the tables, sold it to Cairene merchants. At the same time, the European discovery of alternative silk sources hurt Palestine's economy, and Spanish silver from the New World was inundating the world, paralyzing agrarian economies. The once-formidable Ottoman Empire became "the sick man of Europe."

The French occupation of Egypt, although a failure, marked the first intrusion of modern European colonialism into the Middle East. Upon the withdrawal of the French army in 1801, resurgent Mamluks sought to regain former prerogatives. A Circassian slave named Muhammad ibn Ali fortified the power structure, crushing his rivals in a bloody, invitation-only dinner party at the Citadel in Cairo. Muhammad Ali built upon the administrative apparatus left by the French, modernized the civil service, created a regular tax system, and attempted to introduce land reform aimed at the vast feudal estates of his enemies. To stock his army, in lieu of buying more potentially rebellious slaves, Muhammad Ali conscripted peasants. Those who managed to avoid the army labored under watch to build a new, massive irrigation network indispensable to the modernization of Egyptian agriculture.

Naturally, a resurgent Egypt led by a nominally faithful "servant" disturbed the Ottoman sultan. Avoiding direct confrontation, the sultan ordered Muhammad Ali to send Egypt's armies to face a Wahabi revolt and, shortly thereafter, a Greek revolt. A dramatic Greek victory enraged Muhammad Ali far more than it weakened him. By the late 1830s, his violent forays into Palestine, Syria, Lebanon, and Arabia left him with more of the Ottoman Empire than the sultan himself controlled. But when Muhammad Ali began to march on Istanbul—his armies reached central Turkey— France and Britain threatened to intervene on behalf of the balance of power. Muhammad Ali was forced to withdraw to Egypt, and the Ottoman sultan granted the Europeans unrestricted access to Egypt's markets.

Egypt's situation did not improve much under Muhammad Ali's successors, despite the Ottoman Empire's attempts at reforms (the *tanzimat*). Economic and political crises went unabated. Modernization of the economy (and financing the Egyptian rulers' trips to foreign spas) left Egypt indebted to British and French bankers. At the same time, the developing strategic interest in the newly completed Suez Canal made it a focus for British, French, and German foreign ministers.

The Egyptian government's declaration of bankruptcy and stirrings in the Egyptian army prompted the British to send an expeditionary force, which captured Egypt in 1882 after only a few short skirmishes. Although the Egyptian Khedive remained on the throne, all decisions were the charge of British Consul General Lord Cromer (alias Evelyn Baring, or "Lord Over-Baring") who dominated Egypt for almost three decades. Lord Cromer monitored Egyptian finances with a tight fist, salaried the Khedive and the royal family, and made it his task to ensure full payment to British investors in Egypt.

THE RISE OF ZIONISM AND THE WORLD WARS

By the late 19th century, Jews were victims of pogroms in Czarist Russia. In the wake of the Dreyfus affair, even France seemed an unwelcome option.

One observer at the trial was Austrian journalist Theodore Herzl who, in 1896, published a pamphlet entitled *The Jewish State,* calling for the establishment of a Jewish homeland as the answer to Jewish persecution. This had been proposed earlier in such works as Leo Pinsker's *Auto-Emancipation,* but never before had a secular, pro-Enlightenment Jew like Herzl articulated such ideas. Herzl considered Uganda and South America as sites for the Jewish state. However, only Palestine had the emotional lure to prompt Jews to immigrate by the hundreds of thousands.

In 1882, a group of immigrants (*aliya,* or "going up") formed agricultural settlements based on private land ownership (*moshavim*). Many were sponsored by Parisian Baron Edmund de Rothschild. The second *aliya* (1904-1914) developed cooperative agricultural settlements (kibbutzim). The leadership of the second *aliya* shared the socialist principles, sense of urgency, and nationalism needed to sustain the Zionist movement. Two strands of Zionism evolved: the mainstream

Labor movement under David Ben-Gurion; and the militant, nationalistic, anti-British Revisionist movement under Ze'ev Jabotinsky and Menaḥem Begin.

During World War I, the British government, at war with pro-German Turkey, conducted secret and separate negotiations with both the Arabs and the Zionists to enlist their help. To obtain Arab support, Britain pledged, in 1915-16 correspondence between Sharif Hussein of Mecca (of the Hashemite family, and a descendent of the Prophet Muhammad) and British High Commissioner in Egypt Sir Henry McMahon, to back "the independence of the Arabs" in exchange for an Arab declaration of war against Turkey. The Arab revolt started in June 1916. At the same time, Britain sought political support from Jews worldwide by offering sympathy to the Zionist movement. The November 1917 Balfour Declaration stated that Britain viewed "with favour the establishment in Palestine of a national home for the Jewish people, it being clearly understood that nothing shall be done which may prejudice the civil and religious rights of existing non-Jewish communities in Palestine." Many Arabs were outraged, and Hussein's suspicions grew. The vague wording in the Balfour Declaration and the ambiguity of the boundaries agreed upon in the McMahon-Hussein correspondence only complicated the situation.

Meanwhile, the British and French had made a separate, completely different agreement. The 1916 Sykes-Picot Agreement divided the region into zones of permanent British and French influence, rather than giving control to local Arabs or to Jews. After the war it became apparent that British promises to the Arabs and Jews were worthless. France, for its part, drove Sharif Hussein's son Faisal out of Syria, where he had seized control. In 1921, Britain made good on one of its promises: Faisal's younger brother Abdallah was established as *emir* (prince) of Palestine east of the Jordan River, dubbed the Emirate of Transjordan. In 1946, Britain granted Transjordan independence. At the San Remo Conference in 1923, the victors of World War I implemented Sykes-Picot with only minor changes. Britain received a mandate to administer Iraq and Palestine, while France was given control over Syria and Lebanon; the glorious Ottoman Empire had ceased to exist.

Throughout the inter-war years, British and French colonial rule was constantly tested by rising Arab and Jewish nationalism. In Egypt, Sa'ad Zaghloul founded the Wafd party, which forcefully criticized English rule and the Egyptian monarchy. After a skirmish between British soldiers and Egyptian peasants, Britain granted King Fouad nominal independence, taking care to sign treaties that protected British military bases, economic interests, and the Suez Canal.

In Palestine, conflict between Palestinian Arabs and immigrant Jews intensified. As they battled, British attempts at maintaining order were insufficient. Palestinian Arabs saw the influx of Jews and the usurpation of Arab lands as a dangerous extension of colonialism. In 1930, Britain released the Passfield White Paper, an attempt to clarify the Balfour Declaration by distinguishing between a Jewish "national home" and a full-fledged "sovereign state." The Arab Revolt of 1936-39 in Palestine made Britain fear that Arab governments would join the side of Nazi Germany if war broke out. In the White Paper of 1939, Britain severely curtailed Jewish immigration to Palestine. This British control of Jewish immigration made Zionists more anxious to create a Jewish homeland.

THE 1948 WAR

Several British and United Nations commissions suggested partitioning Palestine as Britain finally gave up on its mandate. On November 29, 1947, the United Nations decided to partition the land into an Arab state and a Jewish state, and to make Jerusalem an international city. The Jews, who had nothing to lose and everything to gain, accepted the plan. The Arabs saw it this way: half their land was being taken from them; they were getting nothing in return. They rejected the plan. A bloody guerilla war broke out between Jews and Palestinian Arabs. The British, although attacked sporadically by both sides, remained for the most part on the sidelines.

On April 9, 1948, the Palestinian village of Dayr Yasin, which had entered into a nonaggression pact with the Hagana (one of the Jewish fighting organizations), was attacked by the LEHI and the Irgun. These groups killed about 250 men, women, and children. The Irgun and Hagana advertised the massacre via loudspeakers in Haifa and Jaffa, spurring Arabs, figuring that they would return to their homes when the Arab armies won the war, to leave the country.

On May 14, 1948, the British mandate over Palestine ended and David Ben-Gurion declared the independence of the State of Israel. The next day, a Liberation Army of Syrian, Iraqi, Lebanese, Saudi, Egyptian, and Jordanian troops marched into Palestine from the north, west, and south. Few observers gave the new state much chance for success, but the results became clear with the signing of armistices in the spring of 1949. Israel had secured not only its U.N.-allotted territory but also some Palestinian Arab-designated land in the north and in the West Bank. Other land intended for the Arab state was secured during the war by Egypt (the Gaza Strip) and Jordan (the West Bank and half of Jerusalem). Thousands of Palestinian refugees crowded into camps in the West Bank, Gaza, and bordering Arab states. The dispossessed Palestinians came to bitterly remember the 1948 War as *An-Naqba*, the catastrophe.

Abdallah annexed the West Bank in 1950 and declared a unified Hashemite Kingdom of Jordan; this move met an icy reception from Palestinians and other Arab governments. Some felt that Jordan was becoming too accommodating of Israel. To the Palestinians, Jordanian rule was not much different from other foreign occupations. In 1951, Abdallah, praying in Al Aqsa Mosque in Jerusalem, was assassinated by a Palestinian youth. After a six month tenure by Abdallah's eldest son, Talal, who resigned due to schizophrenia, the crown passed to King Hussein. Not quite 18 when he assumed the throne—which he holds to this day—Hussein embarked on a bold agenda aimed at raising Jordan's status in the Arab world.

THE SUEZ CRISIS

Egypt, weakened by struggles between Wafdist nationalists and the monarchy, was in a shambles after its 1948 loss to Israel. In 1952, following a bloody confrontation between British soldiers and Egyptian police officers, a group of young army officers led by charismatic heart-throb Col. Gamal Abd an-Nasser bloodlessly seized power from the late King Fouad's corrupt son, Farouk. Calling themselves the "Free Officers," Nasser's cabinet instituted major economic reforms and foreign policy changes, siding with the Non-Aligned Movement in the Cold War. Drawing from the writings of countless Arab nationalists, Nasser espoused a highly emotional brand of pan-Arabism, hoping to unify the Arabic-speaking masses into one state powerful enough to resist imperial encroachments and to take control of Palestine. When Nasser forced Britain to withdraw from Egypt in 1954, many puppet Arab leaders dependent on foreign assistance became alarmed by Nasser's growing popularity.

The United States and other foreign powers, which had undertaken extensive development of the oil fields of Arabia, feared their arrangements with local monarchs would collapse if Nasserism spread. Nasser, alarmed by a British-led alignment of conservative Middle East states (the Baghdad Pact), had begun buying Soviet arms via Czechoslovakia in defiance of a 1950 West-imposed arms control deal. In 1956, the United States clumsily attempted to curtail Nasser's power by withdrawing its offer to finance the Aswan High Dam. Rather than yield to the snub, Nasser nationalized the previously international Suez Canal to use its revenues for the dam.

Israel, Britain, and France devised a scheme to take the canal. Israel would attack Egypt with French logistical support; a French-British "peace-keeping" force would follow. Initially, the conspiracy worked well: Israel took the Sinai and dealt Nasser's military a major blow. Then an Anglo-French force entered Egypt and began the seizure of the canal under the pretext of separating Egyptian and Israeli combatants. But the aggressors had not considered world reaction to their adventure. The United States and the Soviet Union, both furious, applied intense diplomatic pressure. When Israel, Britain, and France withdrew their troops to placate the U.S., Nasser was heralded as the savior of the Arab world without having won a battle.

Syria, racked with internal feuding, joined Egypt in 1958 in forming the United Arab Republic (UAR). Nasser trumpeted the UAR as a triumph of pan-Arabism, but the Syrians were irritated by its unwieldy and Egypt-dominated government. None-theless, even after the 1961 secession of Syria from the UAR, Nasser remained at the forefront of Arab politics. In 1964, he hosted two Arab summits and helped create the Egypt-based Palestine Liberation Organization (PLO), keeping the Palestinian movement under Cairo's suspicious eye. One PLO faction was led by a fiery young Palestinian nationalist, Yasser Arafat. His FATAH (the Arabic acronym for PLO written backwards) would eventually lead the PLO.

THE 1967 SIX-DAY WAR/JUNE WAR

From bases sanctioned by the governments of Jordan, Syria, and Lebanon, the PLO raided Israel; Israel hit Palestinian refugee camps. The cycle of raids and reprisals created tension on Israel's northern border, and a Syrian-Israeli air battle took place in April 1967. When Syria's hard-line government turned up the rhetoric, Nasser stepped in, concentrating the Egyptian army in the Sinai and successfully demand-ing the withdrawal of the U.N. buffer-zone troops stationed there since 1957. Israeli Prime Minister Levi Eshkol nervously warned that a blockade of the Straits of Tiran would be taken as an act of aggression. Nasser, under taunting and pressure from Syria and Saudi Arabia, initiated a blockade on May 22, 1967.

Jordan, Iraq, and Syria deployed troops along their borders with Israel. On June 5, 1967, Israel struck air fields in the Sinai, obliterating the Egyptian air force before it ever got off the ground. The U.S., having received assurances that the attack would eventually bring peace and that Israel would not expand its borders as a result of the war, had condoned the attack. Eshkol appealed to King Hussein not to get involved; but when it became clear that Jordanian shelling would continue, Israel asked for U.S. support in delaying a cease-fire until Israel could take East Jerusalem.

East Jerusalem fell to Israel on June 7, and a cease-fire was called. Shortly after-wards, Israel annexed East Jerusalem. From Egypt, Israel had won the Sinai Penin-sula and the Gaza Strip, from Syria the Golan Heights, and from Jordan the West Bank. Nasser resigned, but a swell of public sympathy prompted him to reclaim his post.

Staggered by yet another defeat, the Palestinians decided it was up to them to carry on the struggle. In 1969, Arafat's FATAH took over the PLO from its pro-Nasser leadership and pursued the liberation of Palestine through guerilla warfare.

With the U.S. behind Israel and the USSR behind Nasser and the Arab states, any local conflict now raised the threat of superpower confrontation. U.N. Security Council Resolution 242, passed in November 1967 and accepted by all parties, stip-ulated "withdrawal of Israeli armed forces from territories occupied in the recent conflict" and "acknowledgment of the sovereignty, territorial integrity, and political independence of every State in the area." Bickering over the ambiguity in the docu-ment began almost immediately (and continues to the present day), while the situa-tion degenerated into an almost constant border skirmish, a war of attrition.

THE PLO AND JORDAN

Among the PLO groups vying for control at the time were the Popular Front for the Liberation of Palestine, begun in 1967 by pan-Arabist Dr. George Habash and backed by Iraq; Ahmad Jibril's Syria-backed faction; another faction backed by Egypt; and Marxist-Leninist Nayif Hawatmeh's Popular Democratic Front for the Liberation of Palestine (PDFLP), also backed by Syria. Among their differences was the fact that FATAH was composed mostly of Sunni Muslims, while Habash, Hawatmeh, and many of their adherents were Christian. In addition, Arafat stressed that Palestinians should not get involved in rivalries among Arab states, while Habash and Hawatmeh sought to radicalize the Arab governments into fighting the West and helping to lib-erate Palestine. Factionalism became a constant feature of Palestinian politics. The rivalries between factions were manipulated by the various by Arab states support-ing them, though FATAH consistently sought to maintain contact with all Arab regimes.

The 1967 War created 400,000 more Palestinian refugees, most of whom went to Jordan. With this influx of Palestinians, the Jordanian government and the PLO were thrown together in a tense relationship: Hussein wanted to negotiate secretly with the Israelis, while the PLO hoped to use Jordan as a base for attacks on Israeli-held territory. In the cycle of attacks and counter-attacks between the PLO and Israel, one battle, taking place in the Jordanian town of Karameh, became a propaganda victory for FATAH; and young recruits flocked. As its numbers grew, the PLO began to take control of the refugee camps, threatening Hussein's sovereignty.

In September 1970, a hard-line PLO faction seeking to derail negotiation efforts between Israel and Jordan (excluding the Palestinians) hijacked a number of commercial airliners; and Hussein declared war on the PLO. Martial law was imposed, and fighting between Jordanian and PLO troops produced a death toll in the thousands; September 1970 is known among Palestinians as Black September. After Arab League mediation and Nasser's personal intervention, an agreement was forged in late September and the PLO reluctantly moved its headquarters to Lebanon.

THE 1973 YOM KIPPUR WAR/OCTOBER WAR

The exhausted Nasser died suddenly of a heart attack that same September. Vice President Anwar es-Sadat assumed control of Egypt and promptly began to dismantle Nasser's legacy of state socialism and massive government involvement. Sadat announced the *infitah,* or "opening," a plan to promote foreign investment and revive the economy. Anxious about the security of his own position, Sadat exposed Nasser's extensive secret police network and released political prisoners, including members of the religious opposition which Nasser had ruthlessly suppressed.

Meanwhile, the war of attrition along the Suez Canal was an increasingly heavy burden for Egypt to bear. In order to alleviate his country's financial crisis, Sadat sought to reopen the lucrative canal and reclaim the desperately needed Sinai oil fields. In 1972 Sadat expelled the numerous Soviet military advisors in Egypt and, seeing little hope in negotiations, began making preparations to attack Israel.

On October 6, 1973, when many Israelis were in synagogues for Yom Kippur (the Day of Atonement), Egypt and Syria launched a surprise assault. In the war's first three days, Egypt overwhelmed Israeli defenses in the Sinai and Syrian forces thrust deep into the Golan, threatening Galilee. Because Egypt and Syria's preparatory moves had been perceived by the Israeli government to be bluffs, Israel's reserves had not been activated and it appeared that Israel was on the verge of defeat. Sadat, who had planned only to cross into the Sinai and hold the position, decided to press on with the battle. But after U.S. assistance arrived, Israel was able, over a number of weeks, to push the Egyptians and Syrians back.

All the parties finally agreed to disengage forces in January 1974, in an agreement negotiated by then U.S. Secretary of State Henry Kissinger. The subsequent Sinai I and II agreements returned much of the Sinai to Egypt. Both sides, though, had suffered tremendous losses. Israeli public uproar over the government's unpreparedness prompted Prime Minister Golda Meir to resign in April. Israel had won, but the aura of invincibility it had earned over the years had dissipated.

In October 1974, the Arab League declared in Rabat, Morocco that the PLO, not Jordan, was "the sole legitimate representative of the Palestinian people." This incensed King Hussein; but when the other 20 Arab nations assented to PLO representation in the League, he was forced to agree. In November 1974, the United Nations General Assembly voted to give the PLO observer status in the U.N. as representatives of the Palestinian people.

Throughout the 1970s, an increasing number of Israelis began to settle in the occupied territories. On November 11, 1976, the U.N. Security Council condemned this West Bank policy and demanded that Israel follow the Geneva Convention's rules regarding occupied territory. Although Prime Minister Yitzhak Rabin (of the left-leaning Labor party) discouraged permanent West Bank settlement, the next government, under Prime Minister Menahem Begin of the right-wing Likud bloc, invested money and effort in new settlements.

THE CAMP DAVID ACCORDS AND THE ASSASSINATION OF SADAT

In October 1977, Sadat delivered a fit of hyperbole in which he declared that he would travel to the ends of the earth, even Jerusalem, to make peace. By the time the press got wind of his statement, Prime Minister Begin had challenged Sadat to make good on his word; neither Begin nor Sadat could back down. The next month, Sadat made a historic visit to Jerusalem and was officially welcomed.

By September 1978, Begin and Sadat had forged a two-part agreement with the help of U.S. President Jimmy Carter at Camp David, the presidential retreat in Virginia. The first part of the accords stipulated that Palestinians living in the West Bank and Gaza would receive autonomy within five years. Under the second part, Israel agreed to relinquish the Sinai in exchange for peace and full diplomatic relations with Egypt. While the second provision was carried out and has held, Israel has yet to make good on the first. Relations between Egypt and Israel were never cozy, but a lukewarm peace is better than a state of war.

After the Camp David Accords, early hopes that other Arab states would negotiate with Israel evaporated. Syria and Jordan were adamant about guarantees for the Palestinians; and the more distant Arab states felt no need to interfere. Egypt, viewed as a sell-out by many Arabs, was left isolated and turned to the United States for financial support. Islamists, whom Sadat had courted in his battles against the Nasserist left, objected to this open alliance with the West. When Sadat cracked down on Islamists, he was assassinated (1981). The Egyptian government acted swiftly to crush an Islamist riot in Assyut; and Hosni Mubarak, Sadat's Vice President, was sworn in. Although reaction in the West to Sadat's assassination was widespread, the streets of Egypt were empty. The hundreds of thousands who had mourned at Nasser's funeral—even though he had lost the 1967 War—were nowhere to be seen.

THE ISRAELI INVASION OF LEBANON

The June 6, 1982 Israeli invasion of Lebanon was aimed at wiping out PLO forces which, operating from Palestinian refugee camps, had attacked northern Israel. The invasion, dubbed Operation Peace for Galilee by Defense Minister Ariel Sharon, had as its originally stated goal the creation of a protective buffer zone. When the Israeli army, after surrounding the PLO in Beirut, began shelling the city at an enormous civilian cost, Israeli citizens joined in the world-wide chorus of condemnation. With the massacre of civilians at the Sabra and Shatila refugee camps by Lebanese Christian Phalangists operating in Israeli-controlled territory, Israel's political position eroded even further. Under an agreement negotiated by the United States, most fighting ended in 1983. But Israel, worried about a continued Syrian presence in Lebanon, neglected to fully withdraw until 1985, and today continues to maintain a strip of southern Lebanese territory as a security zone.

THE INTIFADA

On December 8, 1987, an Israeli tank/transport truck and several Arab cars collided in Gaza; four Palestinians were killed and several injured in the crash. The Palestinians' despair after 20 years of Israeli military occupation and frustration with Israel's unwillingness to negotiate over Palestinian autonomy turned demonstrations at the victims' funerals into an upheaval that spread to the West Bank. The Palestinian *intifada,* or uprising, was a tremendous shock to everyone, the PLO included. At first, Israeli authorities viewed the *intifada* ("throwing off" or "shaking off" in Arabic) as a short-lived affair which would peter out much as earlier agitations had. But after Palestinians in the territories began establishing networks to coordinate their hitherto sporadic civil disobedience and strikes, the *intifada* came alive, and gained a shadowy leadership, all its own.

By mid-1988 it became apparent that the *intifada* was not abating. The constant appearance of the Israeli Defense Force violently suppressing demonstrators on television screens throughout the world inspired increasing criticism. U.S. Secretary of state George Schultz proposed an international peace conference to be attended by the permanent members of the UN Security council. The Americans and the Israelis, however, refused to allow the PLO to attend until the organization renounced terrorism and accepted Israel's right to exist.

In the summer of 1988, King Hussein suddenly dropped his claims to the West Bank and ceased assisting in the administration of the territories, which Jordan had been doing since 1967. Hussein's move left Israel and the United States without a negotiating partner, since they refused to negotiate with the PLO. Arafat seized the opportunity to secure a PLO role in negotiations by renouncing terrorism, recognizing Israel's right to exist, and proposing an independent Palestinian state. Israeli Prime Minister Yitzḥak Shamir (Likud) presented his own proposal (actually formulated by then-Defense Minister Rabin). Shamir's proposal for elections in the territories insisted that neither the PLO nor PLO-sponsored candidates take part. This seemed ridiculous to some, since all Palestinians are considered members of the PLO. Nonetheless, the United States and Egypt began trying to draw up a list of acceptable candidates; but Shamir qualified his proposal by insisting that Arab residents of East Jerusalem be barred from participation. Neither the PLO, local Palestinians, nor Egypt could stomach any recognition of the decades-old Israeli claim that Jerusalem, whole and undivided, was Israel's eternal capital. Another bone of contention was whether or not Palestinian refugees living outside the occupied territories would be allowed to return.

Many Palestinians became convinced, by late 1989, that Yasser Arafat had weakened the position the Palestinians had gained as a result of the *intifada*. In addition, they grew worried as Soviet Jews immigrated to Israel in large numbers and new Israeli settlements claimed more West Bank territory. A PLO faction launched an attack against Israeli hotels on the coast near Tel Aviv. Although the raid was foiled before it inflicted any damage, Israel, backed by the United States, pressured Arafat to denounce the incident. His refusal to do so attested to FATAH's waning power as compared to more militant factions. The United States and the PLO terminated their discussions that summer.

THE GULF WAR AND THE PEACE PROCESS

The Gulf crisis began when Iraqi troops marched into Kuwait on August 2, 1990. Early on, Iraqi President Saddam Hussein had suggested "linkage" as a way of solving the Gulf crisis; that is, he would withdraw from Kuwait when Israel withdrew from the West Bank, Gaza, and Golan, and Syria from Lebanon. This gesture and promises to liberate Palestine won Saddam the support of Palestinians; and their support may have been strengthened in October 1990, when Israeli police killed 17 Palestinians and wounded almost 150 during Muslim prayers at Jerusalem's Al Aqsa Mosque.

In fighting that lasted from January 16 to February 28, 1991, a coalition formed by the United States, various European countries, Egypt, Saudi Arabia, the other Gulf states, and Syria disabled Baghdad and forced Iraq to withdraw from Kuwait. The Gulf Crisis dramatically demonstrated the need for a comprehensive peace in the region. When the cease-fire was announced, hope was high that parties such as Israel and Syria—for the first time on the same side of a regional conflict—could be brought to the bargaining table. Then-U.S. Secretary of State James Baker made numerous trips to the Middle East.

The war damaged the Jordanian economy, burdening it with approximately 300,000 Palestinians no longer welcome in the Gulf countries. Across the river, Israel's demographics were also in flux, as the country took in 450,000 Jewish immigrants and refugees from the former Soviet Union and Ethiopia.

In July 1991, Syria surprised the world with the announcement that it would attend a regional peace conference. At a summit meting in Moscow, U.S. President George Bush and Russian President Mikhail Gorbachev decided to host the conference jointly, and even issued invitations. Uneasy about potentially losing face (as well as some US$10 billion in additional U.S. aid), the Israeli cabinet voted to attend the proposed conference provided that the PLO, Palestinians with any PLO affiliation, and residents of East Jerusalem not take part.

On October 30, 1991, the Madrid peace conference was convened, with Israel carrying on separate negotiations with Syria, Lebanon, Egypt, and a joint Jordanian-Palestinian delegation. This unprecedented gathering quickly bogged down in discussions of UN Resolution 242, Palestinian autonomy and rights, Jerusalem, Israeli settlements, and the PLO's role. Subsequent sessions held in Washington, D.C. did not get much further. The Palestinian representatives, including Faisal al-Husseini and Hanan Ashrawi, were in constant contact with the PLO; the charade of PLO non-involvement was wearing thin.

On June 23, 1992, an Israeli election ousted Shamir's Likud, whose West Bank settlements had attracted U.S. ire, and brought in a pragmatic Labor-led government under Yitzhak Rabin. Rabin curtailed settlement and promised Palestinian autonomy. Optimism accompanying the first round of talks under the new Israeli government, held in November 1992, was soon undermined. Hamas, a rejectionist Islamist PLO faction which had been growing in popularity (especially in Gaza) due to the Palestinians' frustration with negotiations, carried out several attacks on Israelis. The Israeli government deported 415 Palestinians, some of whom were Hamas activists and some of whom had no connection to the organization, in December 1992. As the deportees froze in no-man's-land between Israel and Lebanon, the Palestinian representatives to the negotiations refused to resume talks until they were allowed to return. The talks floundered.

In September 1993, Arafat and Shimon Peres surprised the world by announcing an accord on mutual recognition by Israel and the PLO as well as a plan for Palestinian self-rule in Jericho and the Gaza Strip. The accord had been reached after months of secret negotiations in Oslo, and represented the first time Israel had recognized the PLO as the representative of the Palestinian people. The Oslo agreement was signed on the White House lawn on September 13, 1993, with President Bill Clinton presiding over the ceremony. Subsequently, the February 1994 Cairo Agreement settled some security and political issues; and an agreement signed in Paris moved toward deciding economic issues. Palestinian self-rule in Jericho and Gaza was expanded by summer 1994 to include administration of education, health, and other government services for the entire West Bank.

Israeli agreements with other Arab countries followed soon after; and throughout the second half of 1994 the world saw history being made daily. In early August, Jordan and Israel ended the state of war that had existed between them since 1948. The border between Eilat and Aqaba was opened; for the first time ever Israelis were allowed into Jordan. In September, Morocco and Israel established diplomatic relations. Finally, in a move sure to be controversial within Israel, Rabin announced on September 8 a two-step plan for withdrawing Israeli troops from part of or all of the Golan Heights. If the plan progresses, it may mean peace between the two nations; it is unclear what the effects will be on Israeli settlers in the Golan.

■■■ RELIGION

RELIGION IN ANCIENT EGYPT

The people of pre-Dynastic Egypt were ruled by a bewildering array of local gods representing the cosmos, the natural elements, animals, and the life-cycle. As Egypt was united, these local gods were combined into one syncretic pantheon. The importance of gods waxed and waned with the fortunes of their home provinces. The basic framework of religious belief, however, remained stable through the three millennia of pharaonic rule.

The central myth of Egyptian religion was the **Osiris cycle.** Seth murdered his brother Osiris, a king from time immemorial, and scattered the pieces of the body throughout Egypt. Subsequently, Osiris' wife and sister Isis conceived and gave birth to Horus, who became Osiris' son and heir. Young Horus avenged Osiris and took back the crown from his usurping uncle. The pharaohs saw Horus as the ideal of the rightful and strong ruler, and identified themselves with Horus while on earth. Upon death they were identified with Osiris, now the king of the dead. The pharaoh was thus literally a god and worshiped as such, and the religious fervor he engendered united the country.

In the Old Kingdom only the pharaoh was believed to be able to enter the afterworld. Minor royalty took to grouping their tombs around the king's, hoping that the proximity would draw them, too, into the netherworld. By the time of the Middle Kingdom, the afterlife was open to all of the righteous, and Egyptians' central concern became life after death. Earthly existence was but a short interlude to be endured until the afterlife brought eternal happiness and reward. The divine and secular worlds, however, were not strongly demarcated; the preservation of the earthly body through mummification was considered essential for the afterlife of the *ka*, or soul, and the tomb had to be supplied with all the comforts of home.

The **Pyramid Texts** were spells inscribed on the walls of the royal pyramids to ensure the success of the king or queen's journey to their afterlife. As the underworld democratization took hold, these texts were adopted by more plebeian folk and inscribed on the sides of their coffins. The New Kingdom's **Book of the Dead,** a collection of spells written on papyrus and put in sarcophagi, described not only how to get to the afterworld but also how to enjoy oneself once there.

The Macedonian **Ptolemies,** who ruled Egypt in the wake of Alexander, sought to become pharaonic god-kings to their subjects. By merging Greek and Egyptian elements in the Serapis cult and building temples to the ancient gods, they achieved what Assyrian and Persian invaders before them never could—they became spiritual successors of the pharaohs. Many of the great temples of Upper Egypt date to Ptolemaic times. The conquerors, however, may have been more influenced than influencing; the mystery cults of Osiris, Isis, and Horus spread throughout the Hellenistic world and later throughout the Roman Empire.

JUDAISM

"In the beginning," the Bible relates, "God created the heavens and the earth." Nineteen generations and a flood later, Judaism began with a man called Abram. God appeared to Abram when he was 99 years old, telling him "You shall be the ancestor of a multitude of nations" (Genesis 17:5) and dubbing him Abraham. The covenant between God and Abraham was sealed with Abraham's circumcision, and the covenant between God and the Jewish people is symbolically reaffirmed with the ritual circumcision *(brit mila)* of Jewish males when they are eight days old.

Abraham's descendants eventually migrated to Egypt to escape famine; it was there that his technicolor-coat-bedecked great-grandson Joseph became a high figure by interpreting dreams for the pharaoh. Eventually, Joseph and his services were forgotten, and the Hebrews were bound into servitude. After the exodus from Egypt, the they spent 40 years wandering in the desert, during which time God gave the Ten Commandments to Moshe (Moses) at Mt. Sinai. In approximately 1200 BCE, the Hebrews settled in the land of Canaan.

As detailed in the Old Testament, Judaism suffered, but managed to continue in roughly the same form throughout the rule of the judges and the kings, the Babylonian Exile, and several invasions by foreign cultures. However, when the Romans destroyed the Second Temple in 70 CE and the Jews entered the Diaspora, Judaism underwent a major upheaval, with Temple worship and sacrifice being replaced by Torah study *(midrash)* and prayer *(tefila)*.

The Torah is the central text of Judaism. Although it was received over three thousand years ago, the Torah has been continuously interpreted and re-interpreted over the centuries in an effort to maintain its vitality and applicability. The Written Torah, (also known as the Pentateuch, or the Books of Moses), which consists of the first five books of the Bible, formed the template for the Oral Torah, a series of interpretations and teachings eventually codified in final form around 200 CE as the *Mishnah*. The *Mishnah* became the starting point for the Babylonian and Jerusalem

RELIGION

Talmuds, finalized sometime in the 5th century CE. Likewise, the Talmud was the springboard for a new series of interpretations and teachings that continue to build upon each other. "Torah," which has come to refer to all Jewish thought and teachings, has been at the core of Jewish life throughout most of history.

Diaspora prayer was modeled on Temple worship but gradually evolved during the Middle Ages, incorporating new elements of praise and supplication. The liturgy reached its final form about a century ago but has had the same general outline for over a millennium. The main themes are thanks to God for his blessings; praise for God's greatness, power, mercy, and forgiveness; supplication for peace, health, wisdom, etc.; and prayer for the coming of the Messiah (or the Messianic Age). The *Sh'ma,* recited daily, is Judaism's ultimate proclamation of God's unity and divinity: *Hear, O Israel: The Lord is our God, the Lord is One* (Deuteronomy 6:4).

Jewish Life

Although Judaism stresses faith in God, it places greater emphasis on observing God's commandments. There are 613 *mitzvot* (commandments) in the Torah, including directives for ritual observances and instructions concerning moral behavior. *Halakha* refers to the set of laws and established customs that dictate how one is to lead one's life; by remaining consistent with the *halakha,* traditional Jews affirm Jewish values and ideals, secure their bond with the larger Jewish community, and demonstrate their devotion to God. Highly-observant Jews pray three times daily: in the morning (the *shaḥarit* service), in the afternoon (the *minḥa* service), and in the evening (the *ma'ariv* service). Ritual items include *tefillin,* or phylacteries; the *tallit,* or prayer shawl, with its *tzitzit* (fringes); and *kipot* (skullcaps), which cover the head as a sign of reverence for God. The laws of *kashrut* dictate which foods are kosher and which are not. There are many fasts, festivals, and holidays.

Much of modern Jewish life revolves around the synagogue (*beit knesset* in Hebrew, *shul* in Yiddish), traditionally a place for worship, study, and communal assembly. In the synagogue, the *aron hakodesh* (the ark) houses the Torah scrolls, which are brought out to be read on Mondays, Thursdays, *Shabbat,* and many holidays. According to *halakha,* a *minyan* (prayer quorum) is constituted by at least ten Jews (males for Orthodox and some Conservative Jews) who have reached their 13th birthday; when one turns 13, one becomes a *Bar/Bat Mitzvah,* literally a "son/daughter of the commandments," a Jewish adult legally eligible to fulfill the *mitzvot.*

Ultra-Orthodox Jews, recognizable by their black attire, are the strictest followers of the *halakha.* Other Jews consider themselves to be affiliated with one of four major movements: Orthodox, Conservative, Reform, and Reconstructionist. These groups emerged over the past 200 years as different approaches towards adapting the *halakha* to the modern world. The movements disagree over the interpretation of legal matters such as *kashrut* regulations and *Shabbat* prohibitions, but similarities outweigh most differences, though some of these differences may have readily-apparent real-world consequences (different definitions of forbidden "work" on *Shabbat,* for example). With a few exceptions, Jews around the world are committed to the same values and manifest the same identity. The majority of Jews in Israel, however, is secular; nonetheless, Orthodox Jews maintain incredible influence on Israeli society (for example, all of Israel shuts down for *Shabbat*).

Judaism, by Michael Fishbane, provides an excellent, concise introduction to the religion. Other good sources include Bernard Bamberger's *The Story of Judaism,* Isadore Epstein's *Judaism,* and Milton Steinberg's *Basic Judaism.*

CHRISTIANITY

Christianity began in Palestine with the followers of Jesus. (The Jesus of history and critical interpretation of the Gospels differs from the Jesus Christ of faith and literal interpretation.) The most significant sources on the life of Jesus are the Gospels. Scholars agree that the "synoptic gospels" of Mark, Matthew, and Luke were written in that order some time after 70 CE, drawing on a "saying source" which recorded the words of Jesus; they were followed by the Gospel of John (after 100 CE, but having older roots). These sources provide a history informed by belief in Jesus Christ.

Various datings of historical events put the birth of Jesus, the man regarded by millions as their savior, between 4 BCE and 6 CE. In Matthew, Bethlehem is the birthplace of Jesus, and Mary and Joseph move to Nazareth to protect him; in Luke, Jesus' parents are only temporarily in Bethlehem; and in Mark and John, the birth is not even mentioned. The Bible states Jesus was conceived and brought forth by Mary, a virgin, making him a product of God's creative power and free from humanity's original sin. Catholics believe additionally in the Immaculate Conception, which holds that Mary herself was conceived without sin.

Jesus was baptized (ritually washed) in the Jordan River as a young man by John the Baptist, a religious leader later hailed as the herald of the Messiah. Afterwards, Jesus began preaching in the Galilee, speaking passionately for the poor and the righteous, most notably in the Sermon on the Mount, and called twelve disciples.

After about a year of preaching, Jesus went to Jerusalem, where the Passion, the story of his death, was enacted. The Gospels give slightly differing accounts, but key events in the story include Jesus throwing the money-changers out of the Temple, eating the Last Supper, being betrayed by Judas, being arrested in the Garden of Gethsemane, and being condemned to death by Pontius Pilate and the Romans at the urging of the Pharisees. On Good Friday, he carried his cross down the Via Dolorosa, stopping at what became known as the Stations of the Cross, until he reached Golgotha (or Calvary; now marked by the Church of the Holy Sepulchre). There he was crucified, the most ignoble form of Roman execution.

History of Christianity

Three days after Jesus' crucifixion, on what is celebrated as Easter, three women went to Jesus' tomb to anoint his body and discovered the tomb empty. An angel announced that Jesus had been resurrected; Jesus subsequently appeared to the Disciples and performed miracles. Later, on Pentecost, the Disciples were given "tongues of fire" and were directed to spread the Gospel (Greek for "good news"). At first, Christianity was a sect of Judaism, accepting the Hebrew Bible. It diverged gradually, as it proclaimed that Jesus was the Christ (a translation of Messiah) and began to accept uncircumcised members into the faith. The Book of Acts documents these early Christians, and the Letters of Paul, which comprise most of the rest of the New Testament, gave advice to the early Christian communities.

In 325 CE, the Roman Emperor Constantine ended the persecution and martyrdom of Christians and made Christianity the official religion of the ailing Empire. He convened the Council of Nicea, which came up with an explicit creed. The Church Fathers declared that Jesus Christ was of the same essence as the Father, and that there were three equal parts to God. This crucial doctrine of the Trinity maintains that the Father, Son, and Holy Spirit are distinct persons yet all one God.

The Church was called "the body of Christ" and believed to be integral and indivisible. Nonetheless, the Christian community has suffered numerous schisms. The Egyptian (Coptic) Church broke off in the 3rd century (see below). In 1054, the Great Schism split Christendom into the western Roman Catholic Church and the eastern Greek Orthodox Church. In 1512, Martin Luther started the Reformation, which resulted in a split from Rome and the beginning of Protestantism. Protestantism is itself composed of many sects, which generally believe in salvation through faith rather than actions. Only in the 20th century has the ecumenical movement put these diverse churches on speaking terms.

Most Christians adhere to a common set of beliefs that revolve around Jesus Christ as the savior of humanity. According to this belief, individuals are fatally flawed because they are descendants of Adam and Eve, who disobeyed God. Jesus' death and the rite of Baptism, however, absolve humankind of this "original sin." Christianity places high value on a morally disciplined life that avoids sins such as promiscuity, adultery, and greed. The religion differentiates between the base desires of the flesh, which trace from original sin, and the higher needs of the spirit; involves a call to virtuous actions such as charity; and places emphasis on striving to love others and God in the same unconditional manner in which God loves his creations, expecting nothing material in return.

A good introductory book on Christianity is Steven Reynolds's *Christian Religious Tradition*. Other sources include the works of Denise and John Carmody. Reading the New Testament, particularly the Gospels, will expose you to the core of Christian belief.

The Coptic Church

"Copt" derives from the Greek word for Egyptian, *Aiguptious,* shortened in Egyptian pronunciation to *qibt,* the Arabic word for Copt. Copts in Egypt usually have tattoos of either a domed cathedral or a tiny crosses on their wrists. Of 58 million Egyptians, four to five million are Copts; a majority of them live in Cairo. Today, portions of the liturgy are still conducted in Coptic, though most of the service is in Arabic. The Copts recognize a separate pope from John Paul II—their spiritual authority resides in Cairo and serves both Copts and Greek Orthodox followers.

According to Coptic tradition, St. Mark introduced Christianity to Egypt in 62 CE. Mass conversions transformed Alexandria into a Christian spiritual center, but Roman persecution increased accordingly. The bloodiest days passed under Diocletian, who murdered so many Christians that the Copts date their Martyr's Calendar from 284 CE, the beginning of his reign.

In 451, the Alexandrian branch of the Church declared theological and political independence from Constantinople, forming the Coptic Orthodox Church. The split derived from a dispute over the interpretation of the Trinity. While the Ecumenical Council at Chalcedon defended the definition of Christ's nature as diphysite, with the human and the divine aspects clearly differentiated, the doctrine of the new Coptic Church centered around monophysitism, which holds that Christ's nature is of such unity that the human and divine elements are fused and indivisible.

The Roman Emperor Justinian sought to restore unity by exiling Coptic clergy to isolated desert monasteries. Rebellious Copts thus welcomed the Persians as liberators when they captured Egypt in 619. Since the 7th century, the Egyptian Christian community has lived as a religious minority in an Islamic state. Relations between the Copts and the Muslims have vacillated throughout history, as the Islamic government has used Qur'anic verses and extracts from the Hadith to justify either lenient or oppressive treatment. Recently, the Copts have felt besieged by Egypt's increasingly vocal Islamists, and acts of sectarian violence have been reported regularly.

Coptic Christianity served as a link between the pharaonic and Islamic eras, leaving its own mark on modern Egypt. Coptic art incorporates the influences of the pharaonic and Hellenistic cultures. The Coptic cross refers back to the *ankh,* the hieroglyphic sign for "life," as well as to the crucifix on Golgotha. Embroidered tapestries and curtains displaying nymphs and centaurs owe their heritage to Greco-Roman mythology. Islamic art often borrows from the Coptic style; many of Cairo's mosques were engineered by Coptic architects, and a number of mosques are converted Coptic churches. Unlike the monumental art of the pharaohs, the art of the Copts tends to be a more popular folk medium.

Coptic churches usually have one of three shapes: cross-shaped, circular (to represent the globe, the spread of Christianity, and the eternal nature of the Word), or ark-shaped (the Ark of the Covenant and Noah's Ark are symbols of salvation). The churches are divided into three chambers. The eastward sanctuary (*haikal*) containing the alter lies behind a curtain or *iconostasis,* a wooden screen of icons. The next chamber, the choir, is the section reserved for Copts. Behind the choir is the nave, which consists of two parts, the first of which is reserved for the *catechumens* (those who are preparing to convert). The back of the nave is for the so-called weepers, or sinners. These Christians, having willfully transgressed, were formerly made to stand at the very back of the church. Above Coptic altars hang ostrich eggs, symbolizing the Resurrection (life coming out of what seems lifeless); the ostrich

RELIGION

egg was chosen because the mother ostrich cares for her eggs for a fairly long time, an echo of God's eternal love and care for the Church.

Jill Kamil's *Coptic Egypt: History and Guide,* Barbara Watterson's *Coptic Egypt,* and Iris H. Elmasry's *Introduction to the Coptic Church* are all good introductions.

ISLAM

The Arabic word *islam* means in its general sense "submission," and Islam the religion is the faithful submission to God's will.

Islam has its roots in revelations received from 610 to 622 CE by Muhammad, an uneducated Bedouin who was informed by the Angel Gabriel of his prophetic calling. These revelations form the core of Islam, the Qur'an (recitation). Muslims believe the Arabic text to be perfect, immutable, and untranslatable—the words of God embodied in human language. Consequently, the Qur'an appears throughout the Muslim world—the majority of which is non-Arabic speaking—in Arabic. Muhammad is seen as the "seal of the prophets," the last of a chain of God's messengers which included Jewish and Christian figures such as Abraham, Moses, and Jesus, and the Qur'an incorporates many of the biblical traditions associated with these prophets.

Muhammad slowly gathered followers to his evolving faith. Staunchly monotheistic, Islam was met with ample opposition in polytheist Arabia, leading to persecution in Muhammad's native city of Mecca. In 622, he and his followers fled to the nearby city of Medina, where he was welcomed as mediator of a long-standing blood feud. This *Hijra* (flight, or emigration) marks the beginning of the Muslim community and of the Muslim calendar. For the next eight years, Muhammad and his community at first defended themselves against raids and later battled the Meccans and neighboring nomadic tribes, until in 630 Mecca surrendered to the Muslims, making Muhammad the most powerful man in Arabia. After the surrender, numerous Meccans converted to the new faith voluntarily. This established the pattern for *jihad* (struggle), referring first and foremost to the spiritual struggle against one's own desires, then to the struggle to make one's own Muslim community as righteous as possible, and lastly to the struggle against outsiders wishing to harm the Muslim community; it is the last which is most familiar to the West.

Islam continued to grow after the Prophet's death, flourishing in the "Age of Conquest." The four Rightly Guided Caliphs *(Rashidun)* who succeeded Muhammad led wars against apostate nomadic tribes; by the year 640 the Muslims had defeated the Byzantine and Persian empires. The fourth Caliph, Muhammad's nephew and son-in-law Ali, was the catalyst for the major split in the Muslim world. Ali slowly lost power, and was murdered in 661. The *Shi'at Ali* (Partisans of Ali or Shi'i) believe Ali, as a blood relative of the Prophet, to be the only legitimate successor to Muhammad, thus separating themselves from Sunni Muslims. Contrary to popular Western perception, Shi'ism is not a creed of fanaticism or fundamentalism, but is Islam with a sharp focus on divinely chosen leaders (or *Imams*) who are blood descendants of the Prophet through Ali and his wife, the Prophet's daughter Fatima.

Any place where Muslims pray is a mosque or *masjid,* best translated as "place of prostration." The *imam* (leader of prayer, not to be confused with the Shi'i leaders) gives a sermon *(khutba)* on Friday. There are no religious restrictions on non-Muslims entering mosques, but other restrictions may have been adopted for practical reasons in tourist-heavy areas.

Pillars of Islam

Allahu akbar. Ash-hadu an la ilaha illa Allah. Ashadu anna Muhammadu rasul Allah. God is great. I swear that there is no god but God. I swear that Muhammad is Allah's prophet. These words compose the first lines of the Islamic call to prayer *(adhan),* which emanates five times a day from mosques and regulates daily life. The first line glorifies God, using the Arabic word for God, *Allah.* The next two lines form the *shahadah* (the testimony of faith), which is the first of the five pillars of Islam. It reflects the unity of God *(tawhid),* which is a strong belief in Islam, and the special place of Muhammad as God's final Messenger. Any person who wishes to convert to Islam may do so by repeating these lines three times, thereby completing the first pillar of Islam and becoming a Muslim.

The second pillar is prayer *(salat)*, performed five times per day in imitation of the practice of Muhammad. Prayers, preceded by ablutions, begin with a declaration of intent and consist of a set cycle of prostrations. No group or leader is necessary for prayers—they constitute a personal communication with God. The person praying must face Mecca as he or she does so. The word for Friday in Arabic means "the day of gathering;" on that day, communal prayer is particularly encouraged.

The third pillar is charity *(zakat,* or purification). Every Muslim who can afford to is required to give one third of his or her income to the poor. On Eid al-Adha, each family is supposed to slaughter a sheep, giving one third of it to the poor, one third to friends and family members, and keeping one third (again, only those families who can afford to must carry out this requirement).

It is believed that Muhammad received the Qur'an during the month of Ramadan. Fasting during this holy month is the fourth pillar of Islam. Between dawn and sunset, Muslims are not permitted to smoke, have sexual intercourse, or let any food or water pass their lips. The purpose and results of fasting are manifold. For one thing, fasting is meant to teach Muslims to resist temptation and thereby control all their unchaste urges. In addition, by experiencing hunger they are meant to better understand the plight of the poor; and also to be more thankful for the food with which Allah has provided them. Finally, Ramadan inspires a sense of community among Muslims. During the day, Muslims ideally read the Qur'an. As soon as the evening *adhan* is heard, they break the fast and begin a night of feasting, visits to friends and relatives, and revelry. In places like Cairo, the city stays up until just before dawn. In quieter areas, a neighbor may circulate to houses, banging a drum and waking people for *suhur,* a small meal eaten just before dawn in an attempt to avoid extreme hunger upon waking. During the month, offices and businesses not catering to tourists may be closed or keep shorter hours.

The last pillar, required only once in a lifetime, is pilgrimage *(hajj)*. Only Muslims who can afford it and are physically able to are required to journey to Mecca and Medina during the last month of the Muslim calendar. While *hajj* is essentially a recreation of the actions of the Prophet Muhammad, its effects are to unite Muslims and to stress the equal status of all people who submit to the will of *Allah,* regardless of gender, degree of wealth or poverty, race, or nationality. All pilgrims, from Gulf Princes to Cairo street-sweepers, must wrap themselves in white cloth and remove all accessories, which might indicate wealth, and all perform the same rituals. If you are traveling during *hajj,* you may experience delays and general pandemonium in airports.

The prophet Muhammad is not believed to be divine, but rather a human messenger of God's word. His actions, however, are sanctified because God chose him to be the recipient of revelation; and several verses of the Qur'an demand obedience to the Prophet. The combined stories and traditions surrounding the Prophet's life have been passed on as *sunna,* and those who follow the *sunna* in addition to the teachings of the Qur'an are considered to be especially devout Muslims. The term Sunni is derived from *sunna.* The primary source for *sunna* is the *Hadith,* a written collection of things Muhammad supposedly said. But scholars point out that, even if Muhammad had spent every moment of his life speaking, he could not have uttered half the bits of wisdom now compiled as *Hadith.*

In the 10th century, under the weight of tradition and consensus, Muslim scholars *(ulama)* proclaimed "the gates of *ijtihad* (individual judgment)" closed; new concepts and interpretations could no longer stand on their own but had to be legitimized by tradition. This proscription notwithstanding, *ijtihad* continues today, though not on the scale of the first centuries of Islam. Meanwhile, the applicability of *sharia,* or Islamic law, is a subject of much strife in a number of Muslim countries, which have seen challenges to entrenched governments by movements carrying the banner of Islam (or their interpretation of it).

The Sufis are a mystical movement within Islam, stressing the goal of unity with God. They are organized in orders, with a clear hierarchy from master to disciple. Sufi *sheikhs* (masters) are reputed to perform miracles, and their tombs are popular pilgrimage destinations. The term "whirling dervish" derives from the joyous spinning and dancing, meant to produce a state of mind conducive to unity with Allah, at Sufi festivals. Marijuana has also been used by the Sufis for this purpose.

As with any religion, degrees of interpretation and observance produce a wide range of practices. For more, try *An Introduction to Islam* by Frederick Denny, *Islam: The Straight Path* by John Esposito, or *Ideals and Realities of Islam* by Seyyed H. Nasr. A sampling of Islamic texts can be found in Kenneth Cragg and Marston Speight's *Islam from Within*. If you feel inspired enough to study the Qur'an, read Muhammad Pickthall's *Meaning of the Glorious Koran*.

OTHER SECTS

The Druze The faith of the Druze, a staunchly independent sect of Shi'i Muslims, centers around a hierarchy of individuals who are the sole custodians of a religious doctrine hidden from the rest of the world. Many Druze consider themselves a separate ethnicity as well as a religious group, while others consider themselves Arab. The Druze believe that the word of God is revealed only to a divinely chosen few, and that these blessed few must be followed to the ends of the earth. Wherever the Druze settle, however, they generally remain loyal to their host country. Israel has a Druze population of 85,000; Syria 500,000; and Lebanon 300,000.

The religion was founded in 1017 by an Egyptian chieftain named Ad-Darazi, who drew upon various beliefs in the Muslim world at the time, especially Shi'ism. The Druze believe that God was incarnated in human forms, the final incarnation being Al Hakim. The Druze have suffered a history of persecution and repression for their beliefs, which may partially explain the group's refusal to discuss its religion. The Druze prospered in the late 1600s, and under Emir Fakhir ad-Din, the Druze kingdom extended from Lebanon to Gaza to the Golan Heights. Sixteen villages were built from the Mediterranean Sea to the Jezreel Valley to guard the two major roads on which goods and armies were transported. In 1830, a Druze revolt against the Egyptian pasha was crushed, along with all but two of the 14 Druze villages in the Carmel. In the 1860s, Ottoman rulers encouraged the Druze to return to the Carmel.

Because the Druze will not discuss their religion, most of what Westerners know about them comes from British "explorers" who fought their way into villages and stole holy books. The religion is not well known even to some Druze. Insofar as anyone knows, Jethro, father-in-law of Moses, is their most revered prophet. The most important holiday falls in late April. In Israel, Druze gather in the holy village of Ḥittim, near Tiberias. Devout Druze are forbidden to smoke, drink alcohol, or eat pork, but many young Druze do not adhere strictly to these prohibitions. Gabriel Ben-Dor's *The Druze in Israel: A Political Study* details the ideology, lifestyle, and political situation of the Druze.

The Baha'i This movement began in Teheran in 1863, when Mirza Hussein Ali (a son of Persian nobility) turned 46, renamed himself Baha'u'llah (means "Glory of God"), and began preaching non-violence and the unity of all religions. Baha'u'llah's arrival had been foretold in 1844 by the Persian Siyyid Ali Muhammad (also known as Al Bab, or "Gateway to God"), the first prophet of the Baha'i religion, who heralded the coming of a new religious teacher and divine messenger. Baha'u'llah was imprisoned and then exiled to Palestine, where he continued his teachings in the city of Acre (Akko). Baha'u'llah is buried near Acre; Al Bab is buried in Haifa, which is now home to a large Baha'i population.

Baha'u'llah's teachings fill over 100 volumes; his religion incorporates elements of major Western and Eastern religions. Baha'i believe in a Supreme Being, accepting Jesus, Buddha, Muhammad, and Baha'u'llah as divine prophets. Baha'i Scripture includes the Bible, the Qur'an, and the Bhagavad-Gita. A central doctrine of the faith regards the Baha'i vision of the future. Instead of warning of a final Judgement Day or an end of the world (like many Western and Eastern religions), Baha'u'llah prophesied a "flowering of humanity," an era of peace and enlightenment to come. Before this new age can arrive, however, the world must undergo dreadful events to give civilization the impetus to reform itself. The Baha'i espouse trans-racial unity, sexual equality, global disarmament, and the creation of a world community. The rapidly-growing Baha'i faith currently boasts about five million adherents, with 1.5 million converts world-wide in the last six years.

The Samaritans Currently, the Samaritan community is a tiny one, with roughly 500 adherents divided between Nablus on the West Bank and Ḥolon, a suburb of Tel Aviv. Originally the residents of Samaria, Samaritans consider themselves the original Israelis, from whom the Jews split. The religion is seen by non-members as an offshoot of Judaism marked by literal interpretation of the Samaritan version of the Old Testament and the exclusion of later Jewish interpretation (i.e. the *Mishnah* and Talmud) from its canon. A gradual, centuries-long separation between the two religions culminated with the destruction of the Samaritan temple on Mt. Gerizim by the Hasmonean king John Hyrcanus in 128 BCE. Centuries of persecution by the various rulers of Palestine shrunk the community further and included the deaths of thousands in a 529 CE uprising against Roman rule. While Orthodox Jews do not recognize Samaritans as interpreters of a shared heritage, the Israeli government applies the Law of Return (granting settlement rights to all Jews) to them.

■■■ MOSQUE ARCHITECTURE TERMINOLOGY

Several architectural feats deserve special attention in mosques. There are two basic designs. The Arab style, based on Muhammad's house, has a pillared cloister around a courtyard (hypostyle), while the Persian style has a vaulted arch on each side. Most prominent are the towering minarets from which the chants of the *muezzin* summon the faithful to prayer five times daily. Mosques are generally rectangular with cool arcaded porches *(riwaqs)* surrounding a central open courtyard *(sahn)*. These usually contain a central covered fountain *(sabil)* for ablutions before prayer. The focus of each mosque is the *qibla* wall which holds the prayer niche *(mihrab)* and indicates the direction of Mecca. Particularly in Mamluk mosques, the *mihrab* and *qibla* are elaborately decorated with marble inlay and Kufic inscriptions. Because Muslims consider representations of nature (animals, people) to be blasphemous imitations of God, abstract artwork dominates the mosques' decorations. In the Fatimid period, interlaced foliate patterns in carved stucco and plaster were popular ornamentation. Geometric patterns and elegant calligraphy appeared later, in Mamluk times. Particularly beautiful examples of work from this period are found on the pulpits *(minbars)* that usually stand beside the *mihrab*. Under the seat of the *minbar,* on the side, there is often an archway, allowing you to cross to the other side as you make a wish, called a "wishing door."

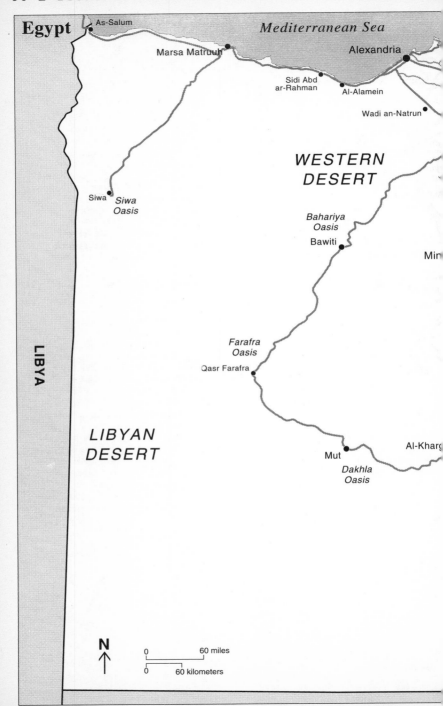

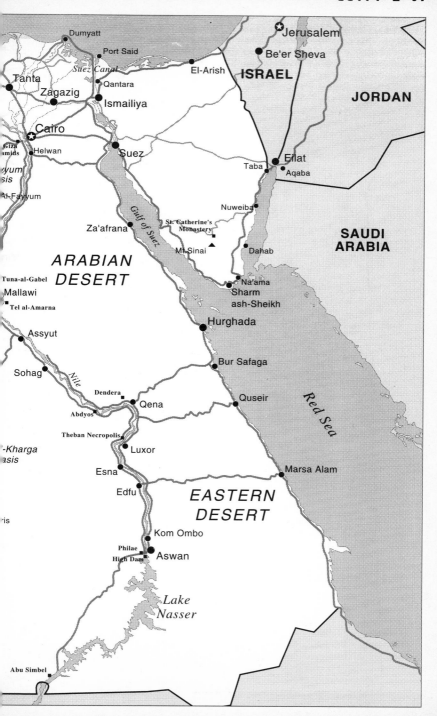

EGYPT مصر

US$1=3.38 Egyptian pounds (E£)	E£1=US$0.30
CDN$1=E£2.46	E£1=CDN$0.41
UK£1=E£5.26	E£1=UK£0.19
IR£1=E£5.19	E£1=IR£0.19
AUS$1=E£2.49	E£1=AUS$0.40
NZ$1=E£(N/A)	E£1=NZ$(N/A)
SAR1=E£0.95	E£1=SAR1.06

> For important additional information on all aspects of travel in general and some specifics on Egypt, see the Essentials section of this book.

The Arab Republic of Egypt (Goumhouriyyat Misr El Arabiyya, or simply Misr) is the child of the Nile Valley, a unique product of northeastern African geography and climate that created the most fertile strip of land in the world smack in the middle of the greatest desert in the world. The land's fertility encouraged the formation of a settled society and the development of a cultural and political identity which has evolved for over 5000 years, through numerous foreign invasions.

The Pharaoh's control of annual floodwaters was the basis for his claims to divinity; today modern technology has taken over that role. Aswan, with the High Dam, is perhaps the most obvious example of the melding of ancient and modern evident throughout Egypt. Completed in 1970, the dam put an end to the Nile's annual flooding; Egypt now relies on irrigation pumps and hydroelectric power.

Egypt is a budget traveler's paradise. The sights are stunning and the people and culture fascinating; you'll almost never get caught in the rain. But independent travel in Egypt can be a challenge; it requires plenty of time, stamina, and an attitude that mixes a dollop of patience with a dash of humor.

The tourist's Egypt has five regions. The first is the **Mediterranean Coast** bounded by Alexandria, Egypt's summer capital; Marsa Matrouh, home to incredible beaches; and the delightful Siwa Oasis, a pilgrimage to the West.

The **Nile Valley** is the most popular region and, in terms of distance and sights, the most tremendous. It is divided further into Upper Egypt in the South, Middle Egypt, and Lower Egypt in the North—these names are so designated with respect to direction of the river's flow (upstream and downstream). Lower Egypt includes the Nile Delta and Cairo, while Upper Egypt includes Luxor and Aswan and extends south to Abu Simbel. Nubia, where African influences blend with Egyptian culture, begins at the First Cataract of the Nile at Aswan and extends south into the Sudan.

The least explored region is the **Western Desert,** where palms shade the paradisiacal waterholes of Bahariyya, Farafra, Dakhla, Kharga, and Baris. Finally, on Egypt's **Red Sea Coast** and the **Sinai Peninsula,** snorkeling, scuba-diving, hiking, windsurfing, and spectacular scenery will revitalize museum-mutilated or temple-tired minds.

ONCE THERE

■■■ ENTRY

A **visa** is required to enter Egypt (see Essentials: Visas and Visa Extensions, p. 7). Generally, all personal items brought into the country to be taken out upon departure are exempt from taxes. Unless you are bringing more than US$5000 into the country, there is no formal declaration for personal items.

Upon arrival at **Cairo International Airport** (often reminiscent of Rodin's *The Gates of Hell*), purchase a visa stamp if you have not done so already. Visas cost around US$6 for U.S. citizens and as much as US$15 or the equivalent in hard currency for other nationalities; these rates may rise unexpectedly. Visas can be purchased at Egypt's international airports and seaports; two-week Sinai-only visas can be purchased at the Israeli border. Visas purchased at the airport are good for one month but can be renewed at passport offices in major towns with receipts showing that at least US$200 has been changed into Egyptian currency. You must register your passport at a passport office within seven days of your arrival or risk a E£26.30 fine and major complications getting out of the country. There are passport offices in most cities and towns; travelers who speak Arabic should register in less-frequented towns, where lines are shorter. Travelers who have difficulty communicating should probably stick to regional centers. Or ask your hotel manager to handle the paperwork for you. If for some reason you are unable to register, the U.S. embassy issues a free letter of apology for U.S. citizens, with which you may register late at the Mugamma' in Tahrir Square in Cairo.

As you exit customs, you will likely be approached by individuals who claim to be "tourist agents" or employees of the Ministry of Tourism. They wait for unescorted travelers and, pretending to help you, set you up in their employers' hotels, which are not always a credit to the industry. Do not let anyone direct you to a hotel or even a cab; take **cabs** from the official stand, which is monitored 24 hrs. a day by tourist police officers wearing black berets and arm bands.

Super-energetic travelers can avoid the way-overpriced airport cabs by taking **bus** #3422 from the New Terminal to Tahrir Square (35pt.); it leaves from the front of the parking lot at the terminal. Bus #400 and **minibus** #27 (25pt and 50pt) will take you downtown from the parking lot in front of the Old Terminal. Only EgyptAir and a few other Middle Eastern airlines use the Old Terminal. Theoretically, a free minibus travels the 2km between the Old and New terminals, but it has never been sighted. If you arrive late at night, you might choose to get a room at one of the reputable hotels at the airport. Most of these are four- and five-star money-suckers, so be prepared to dip into emergency funds. The least expensive is the **Cairo Airport Hotel** (tel. 66 60 74).

All **trains** into Cairo stop at **Ramses Station.** Bus #95 runs from there to Tahrir Sq. Black and white **taxis** to Tahrir Sq. cost about E£2. The **metro,** just opposite the station, will whisk you to Tahrir Sq. for 30pt. To walk, climb the pedestrian overpass in front of the station and walk south on Ramses St., away from the statue of Ramses II. It's about a half-hr. trek from the station to Tahrir Sq.

Buses from the Sinai, Israel, and Jordan usually drop you off at Abbasiyya Station in the northern suburb of Abbasiyya. To reach Tahrir Sq., hop into a southbound black and white cab (E£2.50-3.50) or walk left down Ramses St. as you leave the station, beyond the overpass, and to the first bus stop on the right. From here most buses pass Ramses Station and many continue to Tahrir Sq.

■■■ GETTING AROUND

> While intercity transportation in Egypt comes in 31 flavors, transport to obscure sights may not be as plentiful in tourism dry seasons, such as the summer of 1994. Before camel, Peugeot, or minibus spirits you off to a distant baboon statue or Nilometer, make sure it's up for the ride back as well.

Travel Restrictions Generally, no sights frequented by tourists require permits for exploration, the one exception being the Pyramids at Dahshur. However, it is prudent to check with the local tourism authorities or the Ministry of the Interior before venturing in private transport off the main roads along the Suez Canal, in the Western Desert outside the oases and towns (especially near the Libyan and Sudanese borders), along the Red Sea Coast, and in the Sinai. If you do need a permit, you may apply at the Ministry of the Interior in Cairo on Sheikh Rihan St. in the Abdin Quarter (Sat.-Thurs. 9am-2pm). In restricted zones, the police are entitled to confiscate your passport and hold you for questioning. If you find yourself in such a pickle, sincere apologies and professions of ignorance may put the matter to rest.

The law forbids Egyptians from traveling or even walking with foreigners without special permission. A travel agent's license, a marriage certificate proving the Egyptian and the foreigner are married, and wads of bribe money have all been used as ways to get around this restriction; but it is meant to protect you.

Train The Egyptian railway system was the first system established in either the Arab world or on the African continent. The first short lines were built in 1834 and linked quarries in Moqattam with the Nile. Trains now serve even the smallest of towns. First- and second-class cars are comfortable and surprisingly inexpensive, making trains the best option for long-distance travel, especially in the Nile Valley.

The government has hesitated to advertise its train system to tourists because there's barely enough room for Egyptians. Schedules and signs in the anarchic train stations are never in English; but a fellow passenger or a man-on-the-platform can help you out. Ask around in Cairo for the invaluable 40-page English version of the *Egyptian Railways Timetable* (E£1). Of course, it is not at all unusual for a train to come 1½ hours late; and schedules and prices are in constant flux.

A good thing about trains is that they offer **student discounts** of up to 50%. Riding in the unreserved non-air-conditioned second- and third-class cars may be an adventure, but it's definitely not recommended for long treks. **Air-conditioned second-class** cars are a great value; first-class is also available, but the extra expenditure is probably unnecessary. **Second-class sleeper cars,** available on regular trains, are an excellent deal for travel to Luxor or Aswan, but are difficult to book; plan well in advance. Unmarried couples may not be permitted to share a cabin. Discounts on sleepers are less than on regular seats, and you might not get a discount at all on the luxurious **wagon-lits.** You can reserve space in a sleeper at the *wagon-lit* offices in Cairo, Luxor, Aswan, and Alexandria. Purchase other tickets at the station of departure. For a fee, a travel agent will send someone to buy a ticket for you. Buy third-class tickets on the train itself, or ride on the roof and don't pay at all. Seats for Cairo-Alexandria (especially on weekends in summer) and Cairo-Upper Egypt (especially in winter) routes should be reserved one or two days in advance.

Round-trip reservations cannot be arranged at the point of departure. If you intend to take a sleeper, take care of return reservations as soon as you reach your destination. During the last week of Ramadan and the next week, as well as before Eid el-Adha, trains are completely booked. If you plan to travel during this period book your tickets at least one week in advance.

If lines are crazy and you're in a hurry, try boarding the train without a ticket. The conductor will usually sell you one on board for a small fine, even if the train is full. The real problem will be finding a seat or an empty space on the floor.

If you miss your train and you're lucky, you may be issued a ticket on the next train out—even if there are officially no seats available. Just act helpless and foreign. If you want to return reserved tickets, go to the stationmaster's office before the scheduled departure and your money (minus a little) will be refunded.

Finally, **women** traveling alone will want to avoid third class; if you have to go this way, dress very modestly and sit with a group of Egyptian women.

Bus Only large cities have intracity bus systems. See Cairo Transportation, p. 78, and Alexandria Transportation, p. 130, for more on this fun-filled phenomenon.

A few private companies run intercity buses; there are public intercity buses as well. The public buses are inexpensive but often uncomfortable: they can be slow, crowded, and brain-meltingly hot. In some places (Western Desert oases, Red Sea coast) they are your only option. Private companies include the **West Delta Bus Company** and **Superjet.** West Delta quality is often on par with that of the public buses; but they have a deluxe branch called the **Golden Arrow.** Golden Arrow and

Superjet are the cushy options for cushy people like vacationing Kuwaitis and their maids. These buses are air-conditioned and have bathrooms, bread sandwiches, and mango juice available on board. Unfortunately, they often show Egyptian melodramas replete with shrieking women in head scarves at unsustainable volume. They serve the routes Cairo-Alexandria and Cairo-Luxor; you should definitely check them out for the Alexandria-Marsa Matrouh route. **East Delta Bus Company** runs in the Sinai, where buses are generally comfortable and air-conditioned. When you buy a ticket for one of these luxury buses, you will be assigned a particular seat.

Taxis Another way to get from one town to another or between towns and sights is the **service taxi** (pronounced ser-VEES). We refer to them throughout the book as *service;* they are also known as Peugeot, *taxi bin-nafar,* and *taxi ugra,* depending on the region. Keep all four names in mind. They can take the form of Peugeot station-wagons and other cars, covered pick-up trucks, or minibuses, and depart from stands in the various cities and towns. In smaller towns the "stand" may be nothing more than a stretch of road. Simply board the vehicle and wait for it to fill up, which usually takes 15 to 30 minutes. When tourism is slow (as in 1994) or if you are in an isolated spot, it will take longer to collect companions. Drivers depart when their cars are full or when everyone is tired of waiting and the passengers have agreed to split the price of a full carload. The best thing about *service* is flexibility—you don't have to worry about schedules. You're also unlikely to be cheated because all passengers pay the same amount. Finally, the ride can be a fun, communal experience, with Cleopatras circulating freely and Umm Kulthum playing on the radio. One disadvantage is that *service* can be dangerous.

The **intracity** version of *service* is the minibus, prowling the same streets day in, day out. Flag one down and pay the bargain-basement fare once aboard.

Private taxis are cheap and convenient in Cairo (where they are black and white) and Alexandria (black and orange). Understanding and skillfully using them will make you feel like a stud on wheels. (See Cairo Transportation, p. 78, and Alexandria Transportation, p. 130.)

On the taxi scene, **"special"** is Egyptian code for **rip-off.** If this word is mentioned in your presence, calmly repeat *"La"* (No) and the words you have learned for *service. Bin-nafar* and *ugra* are particularly helpful in this situation. In intracity situations, avoid being ripped off by hailing a private taxi on the street instead of in front of a tourist trap like the Nile Hilton, for example. If a cabbie approaches you first, be especially wary. It's best not to talk about the price before you get in; when you get out, pay what is appropriate (our city and sights listings give estimates).

Hitchhiking Hitching is not common in the highly populated parts of Egypt. In recent years, the newspapers have been full of crimes perpetrated by hitchhikers along the roads between Cairo and Alexandria. Because of this, drivers may be reluctant to pick people up. Rides are reportedly easy to obtain in isolated areas, such as along the Great Desert Road, or for short jaunts in remote parts of the Nile Valley, where public transportation is difficult to find. Often drivers who pick up hitchhikers will expect money anyway, so public transportation should be used where it is available, which is almost everywhere. **Women, whether in a group or alone, should not hitchhike.** Nobody traveling alone should accept a ride in a private car. Egypt is mostly sparsely traveled desert; factor that into any hitching plans you may be making. Never count on getting a ride before you die of dehydration.

> *Let's Go* does not recommend hitchhiking. The routes listed elsewhere in this book are not intended to recommend hitchhiking as a means of transport.

Car Rental Renting a car is unnecessary, considering the plentitude and cheaptitude of public transportation in Egypt. If you do plan to drive, remember to obtain the necessary permits before cruising on back roads along the Suez Canal, in the

Western Desert outside the oases, on the Red Sea Coast, and in the Sinai. Bear in mind that there are few places to drop off rental cars. An **International Driver's License** is required to drive in Egypt. Any insurance you have will not cover you here, so plan to invest in proper coverage. Age requirements are not always strictly enforced by rental agencies. The cheapest rentals run around US$35 per day with unlimited mileage. (See Practical Information in various cities.) It is often cheaper and easier to make reservations with a car rental agency before you leave your home country. Your biggest headache on the road will be the traffic; driving in Egypt demands nerves of steel. (Also see Western Desert Oases: Getting Around, p. 204.)

Plane **EgyptAir** and the newer **ZAS Air** serve major cities in Egypt out of Cairo International Airport. All prices listed are one-way, economy class, on EgyptAir: Cairo to Luxor (1hr., US$84), Aswan (2hr., US$116), Alexandria (½hr., US$49 with discounts on round-trip fares), Abu Simbel (US$165), and Hurghada (US$91). Egypt-Air's main office in the U.S. is at 720 Fifth Ave., New York, NY 10019 (tel. (800) 334-6787). Both airlines have offices all over Egypt. (See Practical Information in various cities.) There are no student discounts or youth fares on flights.

Air Sinai, in the courtyard of the Nile Hilton, is a subsidiary of EgyptAir created to serve the Sinai and Israel. Foreigners may have to pay in U.S. dollars. Below are one-way fares; the round-trip is probably non-discounted. Air Sinai flies two or three times per week from Cairo to St. Catherine's (US$75) and Sharm esh-Sheikh (US$95). Convenient flights also travel from Hurghada to Sharm esh-Sheikh (US$65) and St. Catherine's (US$89). They also connect Cairo and Tel Aviv. For more information, contact the main office at 12 Qasr en-Nil St., Cairo (tel. (02) 75 06 00 or 75 07 29; fax 574 4711) or any branch office.

■■■ USEFUL ADDRESSES

EMBASSIES AND CONSULATES

Australian Embassy, World Trade Center, 11th-12th floors, 1191 Corniche en-Nil, Bulaq (tel. (02) 77 71 16). Open Sun.-Thurs. 9am-12:30pm; call after hours.
Canadian Embassy, 6 Muhammad Fahmi Es-Sayyid St., Garden City, Cairo (tel. (02) 354 3110; fax 356 3548). Open Sat.-Thurs. 7:30am-3pm.
Israel: Embassy, 6 Ibn el-Malik St., Dokki (tel. (02) 361 0380 or 0458). Open Sun.-Thurs. 10:30am-noon. **Consulate,** 207 Abd es-Salem Aref St., Rushdi (tel. (03) 586 0492). Open Sun.-Thurs. 9:30am-12:30pm.
Jordanian Embassy: 6 El Goheina St., Dokki (tel. (02) 348 5566 or 6169 or 7543, or 349 9912), 2 blocks west of the Cairo Sheraton. Open Sat.-Thurs. 9am-noon.
Syrian Embassy: 18 Abdel Rahim Sabri St., Dokki (tel. (02) 70 70 20 or 71 83 20). Open 8am-2pm.
U.K.: Embassy, 7 Ahmed Ragheb St., Cairo (tel. (02) 354 0850), south of the U.S. Embassy. Handles affairs for **New Zealand** as well. **Consulate,** 3 Mena St., Kafr Abdou, Rushdi, Alexandria 21529 (tel. (03) 546 7001).
U.S.: Embassy, 5 Latin America St., Garden City, Cairo (tel. (02) 354 8211). **Consulate,** in Cairo (tel. 357 2200). Use the embassy for urgent matters. Consulate open Sun.-Thurs. 8am-1pm, closed on Islamic holidays.

TOURIST SERVICES

The **Egyptian General Authority for the Promotion of Tourism (EGAPT)** has offices everywhere, and run a program called the **Tourist Friends Association** from 33 Qasr en-Nil St., 9th floor, Cairo (tel. (02) 392 2036), whereby Egyptian youth meet, talk with, and assist foreign tourists daily from 6pm to 9pm, free of charge. The **Tourist Police,** despite the quasi-fascist name, are actually meant to assist visitors. Go to them in case of theft or if you feel you have been taken advantage of in any way. Most offices employ at least one person who speaks some English. The officers' uniforms are black in winter, white in summer, with "Tourist Police" arm bands. A potential source of information is the **Egyptian Ministry of Tourism,** Misr Travel Tower, Abbasiyya, Cairo (tel. (02) 82 79 64 or 82 48 58).

MEDICAL EMERGENCIES AND HEALTH

While major hotels may have resident doctors, any hotel can get someone dependable in an emergency. You may also ask your embassy for a list of recommended physicians and pharmacists or see individual city listings. Several major hospitals in Cairo provide 24-hr. service, including the **Misr International** (Finney Sq., Dokki; tel. 360 8261 or 71 33 88 or 71 63 33), the **Anglo-American Hospital** (3 Zohria Garden St., Zamalek; tel. 340 6162 or 6163 or 6164 or 6165), and the **Al Salam International Hospital** (Corniche en-Nil, Ma'adi; tel. 363 8050; fax 362 3300).

Even **pharmacies** (identifiable by the snake-on-a-staff symbol for medicine) in the big cities do not carry American or European brand-name drugs; the Egyptian brands, however, are equally effective and reliable. They are also much, much cheaper. Before you do any major traveling, stock up on headache, diarrhea, and constipation pills. Also take along some of the electrolyte-and-nutrient rehydrating solution used for babies; if you get dehydrated or experience a minor sunstroke, this will help your recovery process. Egypt is a bit more relaxed about prescriptions than the U.S. Condoms are available over the counter at city pharmacies. Ask for *kabout, tops,* or *'azil.* "Tops" is the Egyptian-made condom brand. Condoms are not available in small towns or in conservative Middle Egypt. Other things you will have trouble finding are anti-perspirant, deodorant, and tampons. Pads are usually uncomfortable wads of cotton, though Always brand has begun to appear in many towns. Pharmacists in Egypt are generally better-educated than those in the U.S. and are authorized to write prescriptions and give injections. There should be at least one pharmacy in each town open 24 hrs. on a given day. **Dial 123 for emergencies.** (Also see Essentials: Health, p. 14, and Practical Information in various cities.)

■■■ MONEY MATTERS

Currency and Exchange Egypt's array of coins and banknotes is gradually becoming simplified as the old bills and coins pass out of circulation and into the hands of numismatists. The **Egyptian pound (E£)** (gin-EEH) is divided into 100 **piasters (pt)** (*irsh,* plural u-ROOSH). Technically, piasters are divided into 10 *millims,* but the only vestige of this minuscule denomination is an extra zero to the right of the decimal point on some posted prices. **Banknotes** are color coded and printed with Arabic on one side and English on the other; the notes come in the following denominations: E£20 (green), E£10 (red), E£5 (blue), E£1 (brown), 50pt (red and brown), and 25pt (blue). Bills do not vary much in size. E£50 (red) and E£100 (green) notes are also issued in the new system, but they're rare. In fact, it's best to break your large bills into denominations of E£1 and below in case taxi and bus drivers or street vendors cannot or will not make change. **Coins** come in denominations of 10pt and 20pt (both silver-colored—check the Arabic numbering) and 5pt (copper-colored). Hoard them; they are useful for various piddling expenses. Shopkeepers may not bother with change below 25pt; fight for your right to coinage or accept the oft-proffered candy or gum instead.

The **currency exchange system** has been completely revised, to the great advantage of the tourist. In the winter of 1986, the government decided to destroy the black market by co-opting its business—the new **tourist rate** actually beats the previous black-market rate. Be sure to **save all exchange receipts. The New Zealand Dollar is not convertible in Egypt.**

To buy a plane or boat ticket out of Egypt, find out the price in pounds, exchange exactly that amount at the official rate, and then present your receipt as you purchase the ticket. You are not allowed to carry more than E£20 into or out of Egypt, nor would you want to, so don't exchange more than you think you'll use.

Prices A brief lesson in Egyptian Arabic: After *min fadlak* (please) and *shukran* (thank you), the most important word to know is *khawaga* (kha-WA-ga), because you are one. *Khawaga* means "tourist," but is understood locally as "clueless and rich." No matter how destitute you consider yourself, you are probably wealthy by Egyptian standards. Egyptians know this. Aside from those in hotels and restaurants, most prices are not posted, which means that *khawagas* may be charged more than Egyptians. Avoid salesfolk and shops near tourist hubs; and look upon any unsolicited offer of goods or services with grave suspicion, even if (or especially if) you are told there is no charge. Agree on a price before you accept anything, and do not pay until you receive the goods. Try to ascertain beforehand how much something is really worth so that you can bargain intelligently. At official sites, entrance fees are set and students get discounts of up to 50% with proper student ID. Shutterbugs are slapped with a photography/videotape fee, usually E£10. The people who work at ticket kiosks will charge you the correct fee, but guides who solicit your business at sights and museums should be ignored; often they will recite a few memorized English phrases—"mask of Tutankhamun, solid gold, mummy of Tutankhamun, solid gold"—and then expect remuneration.

Shopping in Egypt can be an adventure. For basics, you should go where the Egyptians go and pay what the Egyptians pay; rare is the department store clerk or pharmacy that thrives on ripping off *khawagas*. For souvenirs and native sundries, stoke your cynicism. Valuable craftwork is out there, but it's rare. Avoid souvenir shops and kiosks flanking tourist attractions. The bazaars in the cities are chaotic, but they are the best places to find great leather, woodwork, glassware, textiles, or jewelry. There are great deals everywhere on beautifully crafted silver. The key word is: **Bargain.** (See Essentials: Bargaining, p. 12.)

Report all hustlers and rip-off artists to the Tourist Police stationed at every tourist site, many transportation centers, and some hotels.

Tipping and Bakhsheesh Another crucial Arabic word for *khawagas* to know is *bakhsheesh*, the art of tipping. It is an ancient tradition in Islamic societies and was going on long before *khawagas* trampled onto the scene. Although *bakhsheesh* is different from straightforward charity, it stems from the belief that those who have should give to those who have not, particularly in return for a favor or service. There are three kinds of *bakhsheesh*. The most common is similar to **tipping**— a small reward for a small service. Baggage handlers, waiters, and bathroom and parking attendants expect to receive a tip of 25-50 pt. Do not let yourself be railroaded into forking over huge sums—if a smiling worker demands E£5, smile back and give 50pt-E£1. *Bakhsheesh* becomes most useful when used to procure special favors; almost any minor rule can be broken for *bakhsheesh*. If a custodian gives you a private tour of a mosque long after hours, a pound or two is in order. Never expect recipients of *bakhsheesh* to make change—one more reason to carry small bills. Ignore demands for more if you feel you've been fair.

The second kind of *bakhsheesh* is the giving of **alms.** Everywhere in Egypt you will encounter beggars who are willing to bestow rhetorical blessings upon you in return for a little charity. There are also those who insist on opening a door before you can get to it or snatch your baggage from your hands and then demand *bakhsheesh*. The final form of *bakhsheesh* is simply a **bribe,** generally a bad idea.

As you figure out how you will deal with *bakhsheesh,* keep in mind that the price of a tape or CD for you may equal a month's living expenses for an Egyptian family.

Business Hours On Friday, the Muslim day of communal prayer, most government offices, banks, and post offices are closed (banks are closed on Sat. as well). Other establishments, such as restaurants, remain open seven days a week. Store hours are ordinarily Saturday to Thursday 9am to 2pm and 5 to 8pm (9pm in winter), with many stores also open Friday. Government office hours are usually 9am to 2pm. Do your government business in the morning, as workers often leave before official closing times. Bank hours are ordinarily Sunday to Thursday 8:30am to noon, with money exchange available daily 8:30am to noon and 4 to 8pm. Foreign banks keep longer business hours, usually Sunday to Thursday 8am to 3pm. Archaeological sites and other points of interest are typically open 8am to 6pm, though in summer the most important ones in the Nile Valley are open 6am to early afternoon.

During the month-long holiday of **Ramadan** (Feb. 1-March 4 in 1995), some restaurants close entirely, while some others open only after sundown when the fast is broken. The streets empty at dusk as everyone sits down to *iftar* (the breaking of the fast), after which business resumes. Shops close at 3:30pm during Ramadan and reopen from 8 to 11pm. In the middle of the night, about 2 to 3am, Egyptians sit down for the second daily meal of Ramadan (*suhur,* pronounced su-HOOR) before going to sleep. Although traveling during Ramadan can be inconvenient, the excitement of nighttime celebrations offsets daytime hassles.

■■■ ACCOMMODATIONS

Hostels Egypt's HI youth hostels vary in quality. Most are grungy, crowded, and tucked away in obscure corners that are difficult to find and far away from any interesting activity. Keep a careful eye on your valuables and take your passport and money to bed with you. Advance reservations are usually unnecessary. A valid **HI** card may not be required, but at most hostels it will save you some money. You can get an International Guest Card at Egyptian hostels for E£24. For hostel expenses, don't count on being able to use your credit card or traveler's checks; in most places, budget accommodations are cash-only. Most hostels have kitchen facilities. Write to the **Egyptian Youth Hostel Association,** 1 El Ibrahimyya St., Garden City, Cairo (tel. (02) 354 0527). The Youth Travel Department also answers questions, helps plan tours, provides maps, and sells International Guest Cards.

Hotels Egypt's hotels run the gamut from glistening new resort complexes to spartan, dusty dives in dingy alleys; somewhere in between is an array of clean, comfortable, inexpensive hotels. Prices depend almost solely upon competition. In towns with heavier tourist traffic, you may spend as little as E£5 per night for clean, comfortable surroundings. Lower-quality accommodations in a town with very few hotels and even fewer visitors might cost E£15-25. Prices vary considerably between high and low season. The high season in Alexandria is June-August, in the Nile Valley October-April. In the high season, rates for the Nile Valley (particularly Luxor) are anywhere from *10 to 50% higher* than listed here. There is a hotel tax which varies by location, from 19% in Cairo to 10-12% in most other places. Unless otherwise noted, the tax is already included in the price. Breakfast is not included in prices unless listed. As with hostels, cash is the way to go; outside the big cities, credit cards and traveler's checks won't do you much good.

Many budget hotels have private bedrooms but shared bathrooms. In most places, E£5-10 extra will secure the luxury of a private bath. Air-conditioning also increases the price. Fans are usually included in the room price, especially in the hotter regions of the country. Do not expect to find towels or cute little bars of soap or bottles of shampoo and conditioner. Toilet paper is a slightly better bet, but don't count on it. (Guess what that little squirting pipe in the toilet is for.) Any place can send your laundry out for 50pt-E£1 per piece; many places (mostly in Luxor) will allow you to use their washing machines and kitchens.

Be careful: In places where competition is fierce, competition is *fierce*. We have trotted out these warnings elsewhere, but we might as well warn you ahead of time: You will get off the train or bus. You will be accosted. Everyone will want you to go to their hotel. They might turn mean. Someone will say he has come from Happy Golden Village (the hotel you asterisked in the margins of your *Let's Go*). You will think an angel has come down from heaven. You will follow this man. Your pack will feel heavy. You will reach a place with a sign that says Cockroach Inn. You will point this out to the man. He will say the Happy Golden Village staff has been wiped out by a strange plague but do you want to stay here? You will cry and cry and cry.

The moral of the story is Beware of Imposters. Locals know which hotels in town are popular; and they will do almost anything to get your business.

Your hotel should be more than just a place to lay your head. You will be spending the hot afternoon hours indoors, especially in summer. Since hotel employees often live on-site, choose a place whose employees you wouldn't mind sharing a home with. There have been many cases of male hotel employees harassing female visitors. These range from Peeping Tom incidents to unwanted sexual advances. In general, if you keep your distance you will increase your chances of passing through unbothered. Make it clear early on what your reaction to such attention will be.

■■■ KEEPING IN TOUCH

Mail Airmail letters from Egypt to any destination outside the Middle East cost 80pt, postcards slightly less. Most hotels sell stamps, though a 5pt surcharge may be added. The most dependable place to receive mail is at **American Express** offices; **Poste Restante** is also available in major cities. Confusion over first and last names can be avoided by printing the last name in capital letters. As a general rule, mail to Egypt is faster than mail from Egypt. In either case, don't hold your breath—two or three weeks' delivery time is normal.

The process for sending a package from Cairo is Byzantine. First you must obtain an export license from Cairo International Airport (also available at major hotels and tourist shops) for any valuables purchased in Egypt. Souvenir shops and hotels will do the dirty work for you, for a fee. Then you must go to the **parcel post office,** on the second floor of the post office at Ramses Sq. There you will be sent from pillar to post pursuing various obscure forms and arcane seals. In Alexandria as well, there is one post office (apparently unchanged since the Ottoman Empire) which handles packages. In theory, all mail leaving Egypt is opened and inspected.

If you must get something from Egypt to Europe or North America within 72 hours, seek international **Express Mail Service (EMS),** available almost everywhere. A flat 8½"x11" envelope usually costs E£36 and arrives within three or four business days. At least five **Federal Express** branches (all open 24 hrs.) call Cairo home; the main office is at 1079 Corniche en-Nil, Garden City (tel. (02) 357 1304 or 351 6070). Other offices (all open 8am-6pm) are in Alexandria, Luxor, Hurghada, Port Said, and Sharm esh-Sheikh. The main FedEx numbers are 350 1417 and 350 1750. **DHL International Courier** delivers anything door-to-door anywhere in the world within 24 hrs. The main office is at 20 Gamal ed-Din Abu el-Mahasin St., Garden City (tel. 355 7301 or 7118; fax 356 2601).

Telephone **Long-distance** and **international calls** can be made from most government telephone offices (*maktab et-telephonat, centrale* in Alexandria), usually open 24 hrs. and resemble sardine cans in the evenings. In very small towns the process is less than a joy—your hair may turn gray before you hear mom's voice on the line. In most cities you can make calls using brand-new, life-saving **phone cards** emblazoned with the Sphinx's stern visage (E£16.55 or E£33). The cards are sold at telephone offices for use at bright orange phones either in the offices themselves or in train stations and other public places. The smaller denomination buys about three minutes of gab time to Europe or the Americas, six minutes with the larger denomination, infinitely longer if you are calling within Egypt. Alternatively, go up to the desk and provide the number you are calling and the amount of time for which you would like to speak. You will be called to a booth when your call comes through and asked to hang up when your time is up. If you have access to a private phone, you can order a call when the telephone office is not crowded (try in the middle of the day), pay for it, and have them call you at the number you have provided whenever you actually want to make the call. In this way you can converse overseas from the privacy of your own hotel room or favorite *qahwa,* even if you don't have an international line. Rates are lower from 8pm to 8am. Refuse to pay for incorrect connections. You can also call from private phones with international lines, defi-nitely a luxury. Major hotels have good connections but can be expensive.

Collect calls to and from Egypt can be made through American companies AT&T and MCI. Call (02) 356 0200 (AT&T) or (02) 335 5770 (MCI) from anywhere in Egypt. These telephone numbers are in Cairo, and you will pay as if you had been talking to someone in Cairo for the duration of your call overseas. Don't try to explain the process to telephone office employees. Tell them you are calling Cairo and pay for that call. You can also call from the gray, coin-operated payphones in most telephone offices, but you risk being unceremoniously cut off if you neglect to pump it with coins every two seconds or so. The Cairo operator can connect you to any number in the U.S. if you have that company's calling card, or place a collect call for you. Some ritzy hotels have USADirect phones in their lobbies; some also have UK, Canada, and JapanDirect. The access code for the **AT&T USADirect** program is (02) 510 2000; use the special phones in luxury hotels for BTDirect and Canada Direct. **The international phone code for calling to Egypt is 20.**

Local calls can be dialed direct anywhere in Egypt (10pt for 3min.), but attempt-ing to call BFE may be more pain than pleasure. Use the gray coin-operated pay-phones. Be wary of using phones in hotel rooms; it could cost an arm and an ear.

Telegraph and Fax Telephone offices and hotels have **telex** and **cable** ser-vices. (See individual town listings.) **Dial 124 to send a telegram by phone.** Allow at least two days for the message to reach its destination. **Fax** is becoming widely avail-able. While telephone offices are the least expensive, hotels and private companies like American Express are the most reliable.

■■■ WOMEN TRAVELERS

Foreign women unescorted by men will undoubtedly be harassed by Egyptian men. Harassment can take many forms, from a mildly sinister "hello," to frightening and potentially harmful physical contact. Western women have the reputation, trans-ported through movies, television, etc., of being "free" in their dealings and their behavior; and many Egyptian men working in the tourism "industry" have chosen this profession for the contact with foreign women that it affords. Watch especially for the vipers in Luxor. Some common-sense precautions will limit uncomfortable moments: dress conservatively and do not visit isolated areas alone. Nightclubs, as well as crowded public transportation, especially third-class train cars and intracity buses, are best avoided. ("Nightclubs" in the West are equivalent to "discos" in the Middle East; Middle Eastern "nightclubs" are something completely different.)

Other "precautions" do not seem necessarily to mesh with common sense. For example, a 50-year-old man will have no qualms about harassing ten women; but if there is even one man in your group, the dynamic changes considerably. Also, the concept of friendship between men and women has not quite reached these shores. Many Egyptian men still think that if a woman even speaks to them, this implies a sexual advance of some sort. A similar logic goes for any non-Egyptian male friends you make. Good luck convincing anyone that you are just friends.

The best way to deal with harassment from strangers in the street is probably to ignore it; repeated advances or harassment from someone you are in a position to deal with on a daily basis, however, are best quelled with a loud, indignant response in front of many people. Do not hesitate to alert the tourist police. For more infor-mation, see Essentials: Safety & Security, p. 17, and Women and Travel, p. 23.

LIFE AND TIMES

The burgeoning population of Egypt, 59 million strong, is composed of a broad swath of cultures and classes, including Christian Copts (many of whom reside in

Middle Egypt), Bedouin, and southern Egyptians who claim to be the pure and direct descendants of the Pharaohs. The majority claims Arab ancestry or mixed Arab and Egyptian blood, while the upper classes brag about Turkish heritage. Dark-skinned Nubians from southern Egypt began migrating north when their villages were flooded out of existence by the creation of Lake Nasser. The Nubians fill mostly menial jobs in today's urban centers and suffer racism that most Egyptians will not admit to. Finally, people with Greek, Armenian, Jewish, and even Kurdish or Albanian origins add spice to the mix, especially in Alexandria. But there is one important commonality that unites these ethnicities: most people consider themselves wholly Egyptian. The great majority of the lower class lives in appalling poverty, some relying on family and relatives abroad (usually in the Gulf) for support. The cheapest commodity in resource-poor Egypt is labor. Along the banks of the Nile, *fellaheen* farm the rich land as their ancestors did 5000 years ago, but Egypt must supplement these products with imported food.

Egyptians are known throughout the Arab world for their sense of humor and love of fun. In addition, for Egyptians the greater honor lies with the host. Although tourism and poverty here have made hospitality less common than in other Arab countries, you won't be in Egypt long before you are invited to tea, a meal, or a wedding. Directions and advice are freely offered, but some Egyptians so desperately fear looking foolish that they will give incorrect directions rather than fail to offer assistance. Often, hosts or helpers will expect something in return. Violent crime is uncommon in Egypt, and it is usually safe to wander in large cities.

Egypt is a conservative, patriarchal society with a strong Islamic tradition. Western mores do not apply, especially in matters of family and sex. The visibility and freedom of most Egyptian women is limited. Do not challenge traditions or mores by trying to force yourself loudly into spaces in which you do not belong.

From the Western tourist's point of view, a disconcerting characteristic is Egyptians' apparent lack of concern for time. You must simply accept this, slow down, and mellow out. Your temper is most likely to howl in encounters with Egypt's mind-occluding bureaucracy; don't spend more time buying train tickets and placing phone calls than exploring ancient temples. Bring every book ever written by Naguib Mahfouz (or better yet, *Let's Go*) to read as you wait in line, and relax.

■■■ GOVERNMENT & POLITICS

According to its 1971 constitution, Egypt is a "democratic, socialist state," but in effect it's neither democratic nor socialist. It is more of an election-legitimated authoritarian regime, in which the president serves a six-year term and is almost inevitably reelected for additional terms. He appoints the vice president and ministers. Since the 1952 revolution, successions to the presidency have happened only when Gamal Abd en-Nasser died in 1970, and then when his successor Anwar es-Sadat was assassinated in 1981. The legislative branch consists of the 444-member People's Assembly, half of whom must be workers or peasants, and 30 of whom must be women. This assembly ratifies all laws as well as the national budget. All males over 18 and those women on the register of voters may participate in the election. Despite the regime's ultimate authority (the assembly is very much a rubber-stamp body), Egypt is one of the more liberal Arab countries.

Like that of his predecessor, President Hosni Mubarak's government has been challenged repeatedly by Islamists. Mubarak's inauguration followed the assassination of Sadat by militants whose aim was to overthrow the Egyptian government and establish an Islamic republic in its place.

Islamists gained parliamentary strength in the May 1984 elections for the People's Assembly. A fundamentalist group, the Muslim Brotherhood, joined with the Wafd Party, and the alliance achieved the necessary 8% minimum for parliamentary representation. Meanwhile, Islamists were elected to university student councils, often gaining majorities and faculty support; they have now gained control over the professional syndicates. To try to quell the Islamic militants, the government acquiesced to several fundamentalist demands. Alcohol was banned on EgyptAir flights, and the television program *Dallas* was taken off TV (much to the chagrin of many Egyptians). Furthermore, an aspect of a divorce law enacted by Sadat was declared unconstitutional by the Supreme Court.

Mubarak has employed various strategies to counter the fundamentalist threat to his government. Early in his administration Mubarak appeased Islamic moderates in order to isolate militants, even initiating an Islamic newspaper, *Al-Liwa'al-Islami*. Three years later Mubarak again utilized the government press, this time to mock Islamic militants, employing intellectuals such as Tawfik el-Hakim and Yusuf Idris. (See Literature.) The past several years, however, have seen a rise in Islamist-generated violence, with militants based in Middle Egypt striking at the status quo via attacks on government figures and assassinations of secularist intellectuals. Civilian and tourist deaths shook Egyptian society in 1993. Massive jailings and several executions failed to stop the Islamists, recently the focus of their violence has shifted to governmental and security forces. The country as a whole remains stable but tense, under tight security controls.

Though sticking to the terms of the 1979 Camp David peace treaty, Mubarak held Egypt at arm's length from Israel, keeping the diplomatic air cool for most of the 1980s in an attempt to reintegrate Egypt with the rest of the Arab world. In 1984, Egypt restored relations with the Soviet Union and was readmitted to the Islamic Conference, and by 1988, the Arab League had invited Egypt to rejoin and dropped demands that Egypt sever ties with Israel. The Arab League is now headed by former Egyptian foreign minister Esmat Abd el-Meguid. In 1991, having led part of the Arab world against Iraq in the Gulf War, Egypt was invited to head the Arab League, marking the country's re-emergence at the helm of the Arab world. In June 1992 Mubarak met with new Israeli Prime Minister Yitzhak Rabin, the first meeting of leaders of the two countries in six years. Egypt is also beginning to recapture its former position of power within the world arena; in 1992, Boutros Boutros-Ghali, a respected Egyptian diplomat involved in the Camp David negotiations, became the new U.N. Secretary-General. Cairo proudly hosted, on a stage outfitted with Sphinxes and massive Egyptian flags, the signing of the 1994 agreement between the Palestine Liberation Organization and the Israeli government.

■■■ ECONOMY

At the beginning of this century, Egypt was the richest of the Arab nations. However, Egypt's mushrooming population and shortage of arable land have greatly inhibited its economic development. All but 4% of Egypt is desert, and that land that is fertile is overcrowded. Nonetheless, Nasser's land reform greatly altered the economy's complexion; in 1952 3% of the population owned more than half of the land, while today no private citizen may own more than 50 acres.

About half of the Egyptian labor force works in the agricultural sector, growing primarily cotton, corn, rice, and grain. A growing proportion of workers is involved in manufacturing, which now accounts for as much income as agriculture. The government employs almost all the rest of the work force in its colossal bureaucracy. As the population grows at nearly 2.4% per year (in 1993, down from a high of 3% in 1985), many educated Egyptians leave to find work in wealthy, neighboring oil states (there may be as many as 3 million expatriated workers). Illiteracy remains high (over 50% of the population over 10 years old), poverty is widespread, and the typical diet is inadequate.

To help combat these problems, Egypt's government follows whatever political wind is carrying the most money and, as a result, receives vast amounts of foreign aid. Through the 1970s Saudi Arabia, Qatar, Kuwait, and the United Arab Emirates supplied Egypt with tens of billions in aid, and in 1977 formed the Gulf Organization for the Development of Egypt (GODE). But after the Camp David Accords in 1979, angry Arab states cut off financial support (not GODE). Under the Carter Plan, the U.S., Western Europe, and Japan agreed to provide Egypt with US$12.25 billion over five years. During the 1980s, with Egypt's gradual return to acceptability in the Arab world, aid from Arab states rose. Meanwhile the U.S. provides more than US$2 billion in aid to Egypt annually, an incentive first offered to Egypt for making peace with Israel and for maintaining a stabilizing presence in the Middle East. For its support in the Gulf War, Egypt received further assistance from the West (including the forgiving of US$6.7 billion of military debt to the U.S.) and renewed aid from the Gulf states. Revenue from the Suez Canal has consistently been about US$1.5 billion per year during the last decade. You, dearies, provide aid as well, in the form of the US$3.5 billion per year tourism industry. That's a lot of *kabab*.

President Hosni Mubarak has tried to diversify the Egyptian economy, encouraging development in the private sector. Foreign investment has grown steadily in recent years, and Arab capital has more than doubled since 1982. In 1987 foreign projects represented 35% of the total investment, while a privatization program has been creeping forward (with the pound becoming convertible and being floated on the market in 1991). In March 1993, for the first time ever, Egypt successfully completed a two-year IMF program of economic restructuring.

■■■ RELIGION, FESTIVALS, & HOLIDAYS

The main religion in Egypt is Islam; about 94% of the population is Sunni Muslim. Most other Egyptians are Christian Orthodox of the Coptic, or Egyptian, Church. Smaller religious minorities include Shi'i Muslims, Protestants, Roman Catholics, and Jews. Government offices and banks close for Islamic holidays (see p. 1), but tourist facilities remain open. Though sometimes inconvenient, Ramadan can be a wonderful time to visit, especially in festive Cairo.

Along with the Islamic festivals, watch for the two Sufi rituals of **Zikr** and **Zar.** In the former, a rhythmic group dance builds in fervor, and the group members become whirling dervishes, mesmerized into a communal trance. The latter is a group dance performed by women, primarily as an exorcism rite. Both rituals are practiced on Fridays in some populous areas. The Coptic celebrations of Easter and Christmas are tranquil affairs marked by special church services.

Sham en-Nissim (approx. April 27), falls on the first Monday after Coptic Easter. Though its origins are a hodgepodge of Coptic and pharaonic influences, it has developed into a secular holiday. Egyptians traditionally spend the day on a picnic eating *fasikh,* a dried, salted fish difficult for most Western palates to appreciate.

The major national holidays, observed officially by banks and government offices but without public celebration are **Sinai Liberation Day** (April 25), **Labor Day** (May 1), **Revolution Day** (July 23 in Cairo, July 26 in Alexandria), **National Day** (Oct. 6), and **Victory Day** (Dec. 23).

■■■ LANGUAGE

One of the earliest forms of writing was Egyptian **hieroglyphics** (sacred carvings). This script was used for 3000 years in all formal and decorative writing. In 1799 Napoleon's Egyptian expedition discovered the **Rosetta Stone,** which provided the necessary clues for interpreting ancient Egyptian. The slab contained a decree written in hieroglyphics, Demotic, and Greek. Jean Champollion used the stone (now in the British Museum, a reconstruction can be seen in Rashid (Rosetta)) to decipher the Egyptian alphabet and hieroglyphics.

Alongside this pictorial system developed the **hieratic,** an abbreviated cursive script, which retained only the vital characteristics of the pictures. After the 22nd Dynasty, scribes changed the hieratic writing to a form known as **Enchorial** or **Demotic,** used primarily in secular contexts. *The Book of the Dead* was translated into this script. Well before the end of the Roman reign in Egypt, hieroglyphics had been fully replaced by Demotic, Greek, and Latin. Egyptian no longer served as the state language. **Coptic,** today used only in liturgy, is a derivation of ancient Egyptian that uses Greek letters and six letters of the Demotic hieroglyphics.

Since the Muslim conquest, the primary language of Egypt has been Arabic. Modern **Egyptian Arabic** differs from classical Arabic, and the Egyptian dialect varies from that used in Jordan, Syria and other Arab nations. Even within Egypt the vernacular varies; Cairo, Lower Egypt, and Upper Egypt each have their own dialects. (The Language Glossary, p. 483, contains a brief discussion of the language, a list of useful Arabic words and phrases, and a pronunciation guide.)

The most comprehensive English-to-Arabic dictionary of Egypt's spoken dialect is the *Pocket Dictionary of the Spoken Arabic of Cairo,* compiled by Virginia Stevens and Maurice Salib, available at the American University of Cairo Bookstore for E£8. The *Cairo Practical Guide* includes a useful list of words; *Berlitz Arabic for Travelers* is helpful if you can master their cryptic transliteration system.

Because of Egypt's 150-year colonial history and its tourist trade, more English is written and spoken here than in parts of the southern United States. Most educated Egyptians speak at least a bit of English, and some are fluent. French is also commonly spoken among the Egyptian upper classes.

■■■ THE ARTS

Throughout most of the second half of the 20th century, Egypt has had a near monopoly on the Arabic entertainment industry. Egyptian films, widely distributed and appreciated throughout the Arab world, range from emotionally wrecking, skillfully done modern dramas to hilarious comedies pitting down-and-out students against evil capitalists and bumbling police officers, with a smattering of southern Egyptians (stereotypically portrayed as idiots) thrown in for comic relief. The musicals of the 50s and 60s, still very popular, featured well-dressed young hipsters singing their hearts out and knitting their brows in consternation over the cruelty of love, the generation gap, and the difficulty of college examinations. Mini-dramas or short-term soap operas are also popular. In these, women swimming in oceans of green and blue eye shadow and wearing head scarves hung with golden coins battle insults to their reputations, pine quietly for the hard-working medical student upstairs, and thank Allah profusely when chastity and morality win out in the end.

The country also boasts many theatrical successes; summertime brings brightly-painted billboards advertising plays patronized by Egyptians and Gulf vacationers.

LITERATURE

Most of the writings of the **ancient Egyptians** deal with magic and religion in such works as the *Book of the Dead.* Poetic love songs, however, were written as well. The *Song of the Harper* advises immediate gratification in the face of transitory life. Folklore was not as often preserved in stone but *The Tale of the Eloquent Peasant* has survived to tell of a slippery peasant and his travails.

Modern literature offers insights into the nation's culture and curiosities. In 1988, Cairene novelist Naguib Mahfouz became the first Arab to win the Nobel Prize for literature. His *Midaq Alley* describes the life of a stifled young girl along the streets of Islamic Cairo in the 1960s, and his classic allegory *Children of Gebelawi,* banned in Egypt, retells the stories of the Qur'an in a modern Cairo setting. *Miramar* (about life in an Alexandrian pension), *Fountain and Tomb, Palace Walk,* and others are also readily available in translation. Yusuf Idris, a leading short-story writer, offers a witty account of modern Egyptian middle-class life in his *Cheapest Nights.* Sunallah Ibrahim's *The Smell of It,* a semi-autobiographical account of his difficulties after his release from prison, was censored in all Egyptian editions, but you may be able to get an unabridged copy in the West. Master short-story writer and novelist Taha Hussein's best-known work is *Al Ayyam;* also read El Hakim's *Bird from the East.* For a range of Egyptian fiction, pick up *Arabic Short Stories,* edited by Mahmoud Manzalaoui. The Egyptian theater of the absurd is mostly composed of Tawfik el-Hakim's *Fate of the Cockroach and Other Plays.* Egyptian feminist Nawal es-Saadawi, whose novels include *The Circling Song,* is controversial within Egypt and known worldwide among women of developing countries. Although he is not Egyptian, Sudanese author Tayib Salih describes a way of life not too far removed from that of Egypt's farming villages. His *Season of Migration to the North,* available through Three Continents Press, is stunning; read for the wise and much-respected elder in *The Wedding of Zein.*

Most English translations of modern Egyptian literature are published by **Heinemann Press, Three Continents Press,** or the **American University in Cairo Press.** In the U.S. most of these books are distributed by Three Continents Press, P.O Box 38009, Colorado Springs, CO 80937-80091 (tel. (719) 579-0977). Paperback editions cost US$7.50-10 (20% discount on all orders of two or more books) and will be sent promptly by UPS. These books can also be found in downtown Cairo at Madbuli's bookstore in Tala'at Harb Sq., or in Alexandria at Al-Maaref.

Tens of **non-Egyptians** have written accounts of their travels and experiences within the country. In *The Innocents Abroad,* Mark Twain describes his misadventures in Egypt and other countries. *Flaubert in Egypt* (edited by Francis Steegmuller) also tells tales of the stranger-in-a-strange-land variety. In *Maalesh: A Theatrical Tour of the Middle East,* French playwright Jean Cocteau makes insightful and humorous observations about Egypt. For an eye-opening account of early Western explorers exploring the Nile, read Alan Moorehead's *The White Nile.* The companion volume, *The Blue Nile,* includes hair-raising chapters on the French invasion of Egypt and the rise of Muhammad Ali. Another toe-tickling classic for travelers here is Olivia Manning's *Levant Trilogy,* about the wartime marriage of two British citizens who meet in Cairo during the 1940s. Other notable travelers to Egypt immortalized in text include Florence Nightingale (some volumes are beautifully illustrated) and Lady Duff Gordon, who was here in the nineteenth century.

Plenty of **histories** of Egypt have been written, as have cultural, theological, and archaeological studies. For an exhaustive eye-witness account of 1850s Egypt and Arabia, dig into Sir Richard Francis Burton's *Narrative of a Pilgrimage to Mecca and Medina.* In *The Riddle of the Pyramids,* the English physicist Kurt Mendelssohn proposes intriguing solutions to archaeological puzzles. John Wilson's *Culture of Ancient Egypt* provides an excellent overview for pharaonic-era enthusiasts. E.M. Forster's *Alexandria: A History and a Guide* is a comprehensive guide to the city (for greater amusement read Forster's *Pharos and Pharillon*). E.W. Lane's *An Account of Manners and Customs of the Modern Egyptians,* first published in 1839 and reprinted in 1986, offers insight into the traditional Arab side of Egypt; Phillip Hihis's *History of the Arabs* and Albert Hourani's impressive, all-encompassing *History of the Arab Peoples* are blow-by-blow textbook tomes. A superb source of inspiration for adventures in Islamic Cairo is Richard Parker and Robin Sabin's *A Practical Guide to Islamic Monuments in Cairo.* Anwar es-Sadat's autobiography *In Search of Identity* is engrossing, as is his wife Jehan's book, *A Woman of Egypt.*

MUSIC

Music is very, very important in Egypt, whose musical tradition is probably more diverse and richer than that of any other Middle Eastern country. Today Egypt is the capital of the Arab music industry and a magnet for aspiring artists from all over the Arab world. Some Egyptian music falls into the larger category of Arabic music that, between the 7th and 10th centuries, was so highly esteemed by Middle Easterners that they took hyperprotective measures against the infiltration of Western musical trends. While Western classical music is characterized by mellifluous harmonies, Arabic classical music favors simple, extended melodic lines. Usually a single instrument speaks the melody while in the background percussion instruments chant.

The type of music you will hear most often in Egypt, blaring from taxis, *qahwas,* and homes, is a slightly updated brand of traditional classical music. Sayyid Darwish and the legendary 'Abd el-Wahab began as early as the 1910s and 20s to integrate Western instrumentation and techniques into Arabic song. What resulted was a mesmeric music with Arab melodies and repetition backed by traditional percussion instruments, with violins, other stringed instruments, and sometimes full orchestras accompanying. This type of music had its heyday in the 40s, 50s, and 60s; its popularity shows no signs of waning today.

In this era, emphasis fell on strong, beautiful voices to unite the music's sometimes disparate elements. Several "greats" of Egyptian music emerged; and every Egyptian has his or her favorite singer/composer/performer. The hands-down winner, however, is Umm Kulthum, whose incredible, versatile voice enraptures. This woman began by singing religious music for festivals in the provinces with her brother and father and went on to tour Europe, sing Egyptian anthems, and generally dominate the airwaves throughout the Arab World for fifty years. Her diction and mastery of the Arabic language are widely noted and respected. You will probably not leave Egypt without hearing Umm Kulthum or seeing her sunglasses-clad face on a television screen or wall mural. Take note. Others with a loyal following include Abd el-Halim Hafez and Farid el-Atrash. We also like Es-Sayyid Mekkawi, whose teasing, whispering vocals over simple instrumentation retain their charm. A more recent favorite is Warda, sometimes reminiscent of Umm Kulthum.

The 80s and 90s saw a wholesale incorporation of Western influences into Egyptian pop music. This music features danceable, often synthesized drumbeats and comes with music videos and posters of teen heartthrobs. Many of its purveyors are one-hit wonders; every summer three or four tapes will be the undeniable hits. Teen dream Amr Diab, however, has endured; and his upbeat songs provide sing-along and dance material at weddings, parties, and in discos. To be taken in small doses.

Finally, in your musical wanderings, do not neglect traditional folk music. All who hear this music, mostly consisting of drums and nasal-sounding horns, will be compelled to sway back and forth as though in a religious trance. One place to catch very inexpensive performances is the Abd el-Wahab theater in Alexandria. Nubian music from the south is equally entrancing. In general, it eliminates the horns and focuses on slow, almost physical drumbeats and chant-like choruses. Nubian music is more in evidence in the south. In Aswan, ask for *musiqa nubiyya*.

Your experience of Egypt will not be complete without the music; we urge you to generously sample the wares. Stores selling tapes are plentiful and more than willing to play a tape for you before you decide whether or not to purchase it. Just mention any of the artists described above and watch the shopkeeper's face light up in recognition. Tapes cost between E£4 and E£7; for the price of a t-shirt at home, you can thrill to anywhere from six to fifteen different Egyptian *oeuvres*.

■■■ FOOD

The influence of French, Greek, Persian, and Turkish cuisine flavors Egyptian fare. Since food in Egypt often wreaks havoc upon unhabituated digestive systems, it is mistakenly reputed to be strongly spiced; the truth is that it can sometimes be rather bland. Intestines new on the scene should avoid green salads in all but the expensive restaurants and eat fruit only after it has been washed. Even Egyptians themselves look with fear upon the soft-serve ice cream squirted from small groceries. Packaged ice cream treats, on the other hand, should be okay.

The Egyptian breakfast of choice, which also serves as a snack or cheap meal throughout the day, is *fuul* (pronounced fool), cooked fava beans slightly mushed and not uncommonly served with pieces of metal and other goodies hidden in the mix. At home the *fuul* is blended with garlic, lemon, olive oil, and salt, and eaten with bread and vegetables. Falafel—chick peas and/or fava beans mashed, shaped into balls, and fried—is in Egypt more commonly called *ta'miyya*. This, too, is eaten all day, often in sandwiches. Try the larger *ta'miyya* made with peppers. *Lu'met el-qadi*, a distant cousin of pancake batter fried into golden balls and served with syrup and/or powdered sugar, is available fresh in the early mornings.

Egyptian families generally eat large lunches and lighter dinners. A meal extremely popular with children is *mulukhiyya*, a green leaf (Jew's Mallow, little-known in the West) finely chopped and cooked with chicken broth and garlic into a thick soup. It is either served over rice or with bread. Vegetable stews including okra (bamya), green beans (fasulya), and peas (bazella) are also common, cooked in tomato sauce with lamb and ladled over rice. Biftek, sometimes represented on restaurant menus as veal panné, is thinly sliced veal, breaded and fried.

Egyptian restaurants do not even come close to representing the variety and possibilities of Arabic cuisine; it is rare for meals cooked at home to make their way onto restaurant menus. On a certain long strip of the Nile Valley, you might feel that all you will ever get to eat will be kufta, kabab, and chicken, until you have nightmares about all the animals slaughtered on your behalf and you break out into cold sweats at the thought of a nice pasta salad. These carnivorous joys are almost always served with tomato-less salads, bread or rice, and tahina, a sesame-based sauce which adds invaluable TANG! to any meal. Kufta is spiced ground beef wrapped around skewers and grilled; kabab is chunks of lamb cooked the same way. Chicken is either fried (without batter); or skewered, grilled, and called shish tawouq. In informal local restaurants and deli-like set-ups, you will also find macaroni in béchamel sauce, low on meat and delicious despite its French pretentions.

Most expensive restaurants, rather than devoting themselves to crafting Egyptian food, go the European route. All manner of badly-done Italian dishes, quiches, and even paella have been spotted. A couple of Egyptian specialties, however, should not be missed. Stuffed pigeon (hamam) is a source of national pride. Fish (samak), shrimp (gambari), and squid are great in sea-skimming towns.

In addition to fuul and ta'miyya, several street foods offer instant gratification for rumbling bellies. Kibdeh (liver) sandwiches sound (and smell) disgusting until you try them; ask around in Luxor and Aswan to see which stands make the best. Corn cooked over coals in the big cities taxes both your stomach and your teeth. Shawerma made its way from the Levant to Egypt only a few years ago; it is supposed to be sinfully fatty lamb rolled into a pita with vegetables and tahina, but Egyptians will slap any sort of meat into bogus French bread and call it shawerma. If you are around 20 years old and live to be 80, by our estimates you could eat kushari three meals a day every day for the rest of your life and not spend more than US$9,777. This cheap, carbo-filled, cheap, semi-tasty, and cheap meal consists of various shapes of pasta plus rice, lentils, and fried onions in a bit of tomato sauce. Slather on the hot sauce to give your tastebuds a ride. Fitir, similar to the crêpe but much greasier, are filled with any and everything and eaten either as a meal or for dessert.

Other desserts include ba'laweh (ubiquitous all over the Mediterranean), rice pudding flavored with rose-water (ruz bil laban), and various Frenchified pastries and bad chocolates. The best dessert option is fruit. Steel-coat your stomach and indulge; it would be a shame to miss Egypt's ruby-red watermelon (butteekh) and unbelievable figs (teen). Late summer produces teen shoki (cactus fruit), sold from wooden donkey carts by old men or young boys with leather hands. Unless you like splinters, allow them to peel it for you on the spot. If you can get a hold of a refrigerator, buy a dozen teen shoqi and chill them—they're even better cold.

Shopping in the souq (market) is the cheapest alternative, but you must select your food carefully. Bread, subsidized by the government, is available in three types: aish baladi (round unleavened loaves made with coarse flour), aish shami (similar to baladi but made with refined white flour), and aish fino (leavened French-style loaves). Cheese comes in two locally produced varieties: gibna beida (white feta cheese) and gibna rumi (a hard, yellow cheese with a sharp flavor). You can also purchase imported cheeses at reasonable prices. La vache qui rit (The Laughing Cow) is so popular that it has been adopted as a loving nick-name for President Hosni Mubarak. Zabadi (yogurt) comes unflavored and makes a filling side dish.

Fruit juices are a great value and a crucial re-hydrator for travelers. Small juice stands all over serve whatever's in season (sweet orange juice abounds in summer) and perennial favorites like asab (sugar cane juice, said to increase sexual prowess), tamr hindi (tamarind), farawla (strawberry), and 'er 'asous (carob juice).

Egyptians are coffee and tea fiends. Egyptian tea, similar to the Western variety, is normally taken without milk and with enough sugar to make it syrupy. Though you can get Western-style coffee, Egyptians prefer *qahwa* (Arabic coffee), which comes in three degrees of sweetness: *qahwa sada* (no sugar), *qahwa mazbuta* (just right), and *sukkar ziyaada* (with a full year's harvest of sugar cane). Especially when you are in Upper Egypt, try *karkadeh*, a red drink unlike anything you've ever tasted, made by brewing the flower of the fuchsia plant and served hot or cold. Egypt brews its own beer, Stella, which costs between E£2.50 and E£6 in restaurants and bars (Stella brewed for domestic consumption comes in big ol' bottles; export Stella is smaller and costs more. You figure it out.) Egypt also produces a selection of justifiably obscure red and white wines, sold for E£2-5 per bottle. Non-alcoholic beer (Birell) is also available.

Cairo القاهرة

I arrived at length at Cairo, mother of cities and seat of Pharaoh the tyrant, boundless in multitude of buildings, peerless in beauty and splendor, the meeting-place of comer and goer, the halting-place of feeble and mighty, whose throngs surge as waves of the sea.
—Ibn Battuta

For 14th-century traveler and chronicler Ibn Battuta, Cairo was the "mother of cities"; to the newly arrived visitor, it looks like the mother of cons. On the ride from the airport to the city, the only ancient artifact you see might very well be the rickety bus groaning below you. The "view" from your 7th-floor hotel room, overlooking a dysfunctional elevator shaft and a stray-cat-ridden pile of trash, will probably not inspire a Kodak moment. Downtown, shop windows resplendent with Barbie dolls and hot pink poly-vinyl plimsoles will detonate any Battutan visions you still harbor. And when the umpteenth perfume salesman with a brother in Tallahassee, Alice Springs, Burbank, or any other Western city you care to mention just happens to pass through his cousin's souvenir shop and his uncle's restaurant while showing you the way to the bank, when the quadrillionth horn-happy Cairene driver ruptures your eardrums while attempting to relieve you of a few limbs, you might ask yourself why you ever came to Cairo. You will find the answer when you learn to look at this absurd and exotic city with a sense of humor and a wise, delving eye.

A walk through the streets of Cairo (in Arabic *El Qahira,* or The Victorious) can be an exploration of one vast archaeological site where the remnants of different eras overlap in creative disorder. Grand 19th-century colonial buildings encircle ancient statues of Ramses while pulsing neon stretches across ornate arabesques. The Pyramids stun with their vast magnificence; Tutankhamun's funerary treasures knock spots off the British Crown Jewels; the minarets and *mihrabs* of Islamic Cairo mesmerize in their intricate splendor.

But Cairo is even more than an ugly metropolis tolerable only for its glorious past. It is the largest city in Africa, the capital of Egypt, and the place where 15 million people live on the meeting ground of millennia.

■■■ HISTORY

The strategic significance of the sandy plateau just below the Nile Delta did not escape the Pharaohs of the Old Kingdom. In the vicinity of contemporary Cairo on the western bank, the ancient capital of Memphis flourished as one of the world's earliest urban settlements. On the eastern bank, Pharaonic remains suggest the presence of similarly important cities—Heliopolis and Khery-Aha, later known as Babylon. These cities, along with the funerary complexes at Saqqara and Giza, were located at the juncture of the newly-joined upper and lower lands at the throat of the new body politic. With this joining of the kingdoms, Memphis became the logical locus of the capital and reached its zenith in the 30th century BCE. Even though the royal capital eventually moved to Thebes and elsewhere, Memphis and Heliopolis remained important political and religious centers until the Ptolemaic period, when Heliopolis faded along with its sun cult. Memphis' eminence endured until the beginning of the Christian era. At that time, massive population shifts left only two settlements: Giza on the western bank, and Babylon, an economic base for the Romans protected by its Byzantine fort, on the eastern bank.

The early decades of the 7th century CE found Egypt, and the Nile Delta region especially, in the throes of power struggles between the Persian and Byzantine empires. Both Memphis and Alexandria changed hands continuously; the warring near Babylon drove many urban dwellers to the villages, leaving the city bereft and deserted at the time of the Arab conquest in 641. General Amr Ibn el-As, head of the invading Arab forces, came to Egypt with specific instructions from Caliph Omar to center the new state at Babylon, not Alexandria. Babylon was appealing for its strategically superior location, and Alexandria was distrusted by the desert people because of its Mediterranean culture. Amr instead founded the outpost of Fustat (the Latin and Byzantine roots of which mean "entrenchment"), the seed of modern Cairo, on part of the plain due east of the ruins of Babylon. Further political expansion and upheavals caused the settlement to expand to the north and northeast. In 868 the Abbassid governor Ibn Tulun declared Egypt an independent state. He built a palatial new city around his Grand Mosque, modeling it after the elaborate cities of Iraq, where he had been educated. When the Fatimids swept in from Tunisia in 969, they took the empty northern sector of the plain and there built a magnificent walled city for the new caliph and his court; they dubbed it El Qahira, "The Victorious." "Cairo" is the Western corruption of this name. Meanwhile, Fustat continued to swell in size and grandeur and became known by the Semitic name for Egypt, Misr. This was the Golden Age in Cairo when, along with Damascus and Baghdad, it was a center of the most advanced culture west of China.

During the 11th century, the twin cities of El Qahira and Fustat enjoyed a symbiotic relationship and both thrived. But these two would stand triumphant for less than a century. Fustat suffered from plague, famine, religio-political unrest, and assorted conflagrations; and when Salah ad-Din overthrew the Fatimids in 1171, the spoils were few. He opened the walled enclosure of El Qahira to the populace and built another fortress, the Citadel, on the hills to the south above the rubble of Fustat. During the short reign of the Ayyubids and the longer but more violent period of the Mamluk Sultans, the city continued to expand. Throughout the Middle Ages, it was far greater in population and area than any city in Europe. Almost every sultan or prominent *amir* graced the place with a mosque, school, or hospital, usually raiding Pharaonic ruins for building materials. The casing stones of the Giza Pyramids and Memphis are now strewn throughout Islamic Cairo.

The Ottoman conquest of 1516 reduced Cairo to a provincial center. The city declined and stagnated until the 19th century, when Napoleon's invasion started tremors that resulted in the ascendancy of Muhammad Ali, an Ottoman Turk of Albanian origins, as ruler. The extravagant royal family built with little respect for Egyptian history, erecting Turkish-style mosques and palaces including the enormous Mosque of Muhammad Ali, a lavish imitation of the grand mosques of Istanbul. These *khedives*, with their European mentors, designed the relatively broad and straight avenues of the New City, built on lands emptied as the Nile shifted westward. This geological process also spawned Gezira Island.

The early 20th century witnessed the creation of a new Heliopolis, planned by aristocrat *extraordinaire* Baron Empain as a haven for Europeans. Population pressure has necessitated the continuous construction of new suburbs ever since. The latest, Medinet Nasser, was built on the edges of the Eastern Desert in an attempt to preserve the precious arable land in the Nile Valley itself. Recent construction has also created satellite cities which hover in the flaming, swelling desert near Cairo.

■■■ ORIENTATION

METROPOLITAN CAIRO

Metropolitan Cairo consists of two distinct administrative governates: **Cairo,** on the eastern bank of the Nile, and **Giza,** on the western bank. **Tahrir Square** (*Midan et-Tahrir,* Liberation Square) is the center of the Downtown area. Among the streets that radiate out from this center, the three most important are **Qasr El 'Aini Street, Ramses Street,** and **Tala'at Harb Street.** Qasr El 'Aini runs south from Tahrir Sq. and ends at **Old Cairo.** Squalid and ungainly, Old Cairo is the most impoverished area of the city. This historical and spiritual center of the Copts (Egyptian Eastern Orthodox Christians) is also known as Coptic Cairo. Sandwiched between Qasr El 'Aini St. and the Nile is the serene **Garden City** residential area. Foreign embassies and banks cluster in this neighborhood, where you will also see many of the city's best-preserved 19th-century colonial mansions. The American University and various government buildings (Parliament, Ministry of Social Affairs, and Ministry of the Interior, among others) line the opposite side of Qasr El 'Aini St. Running all the way to the airport, Ramses St. heads northeast away from the Nile. It passes through **Ramses Square,** next to which is the Cairo train station, also called (bingo!) **Ramses Station.** Farther out on Ramses St. is **Heliopolis,** the fashionable suburb where you will find architectural extravagances including the residence of President Mubarak.

The main bridge crossing the Nile from the Downtown area is **Tahrir Bridge,** connecting Tahrir Sq. and the southern tip of **Gezira Island.** On this more verdant end of the island are a large public garden and two private sporting clubs. The northern half is Cairo's ritziest residential area, **Zamalek;** this is the name by which the entire island often goes. South of Zamalek is its fellow Nile isle, **Roda Island,** the site of 19th-century Manial Palace Museum (also a Club Med) and the Nilometer, the pharaonic device for predicting the harvest.

Past Tahrir Bridge on the western bank of the Nile, the Cairo Sheraton Hotel presides over the residential neighborhood of **Dokki,** where a handful of important embassies is located. North of Dokki lies **Mohandiseen** (Engineer's City), built in the late 1950s by President Nasser as a neighborhood for engineers and journalists. It is now a middle-class residential area. Farther north is **Imbaba,** where a weekly camel market takes place. South of Dokki past the Zoological Gardens across the Giza Bridge is **Giza Square.** Pyramids Road, whose overpriced bars provide nightly sleazefests, begins at the square and runs to the **Pyramids of Giza.**

You are as likely to find street signs and posted street numbers, in English or Arabic, as you are to be arrested for jaywalking. To find out which streets you need to jaywalk to get where, acquire a comprehensible, comprehensive street map. The best bet is the large map of Cairo published by Lehnert and Landrock, which includes a brief city history, an index of all the streets and squares, the addresses of banks, travel agencies, embassies, and museums, and a small map of Giza and Saqqara (E£10). The *Blue Guide to Egypt* (E£108) and the *AUC Practical Guide* (E£25) also have decent maps and information for travelers planning longer stays. *Cairo A-Z* includes 150 pages of detailed maps of each district of Cairo and its suburbs, along with lists of and directions to sights of interest and a mini-telephone directory. *Egypt Today* (formerly *Cairo Today,* E£7) publishes updated listings each year. Look for their *Dining Guide,* their *Travel & Recreation Guide,* and their *Business Review* (E£15 each). *Egypt Today* itself is published monthly. All these maps and guides are available at the AUC bookstore (see Practical Information, p. 87).

DOWNTOWN CAIRO

The New City *(Misr el-Gedida),* now the transportation and commercial hub of Cairo, was conceived in the 19th century. Under the auspices of the benevolent British and French colonialists, the *khedives* then ruling planned the city around a system of *midans* (squares) from which radiate straight avenues; these are named for national heroes and revolutionary activists. Buses leave from **Tahrir Square** to every metropolitan destination. At the north end of Tahrir facing the square is the sandstone **Egyptian Museum;** adjacent to it on the west side is the Nile Hilton, useful as an air-conditioned mailbox or for the swimming pool. At the southern end of the square is the concave **Mugamma' Building,** headquarters of the Egyptian bureaucracy, where you must register your passport within seven days of arrival. The **American University in Cairo (AUC),** directly to the east of the Mugamma' Building across Qasr El 'Aini St., has gardens filled with English-speaking Egyptians and Arabic-speaking Americans, plus an excellent bookstore.

Tala'at Harb Street runs from the northeast side of Tahrir through Tala'at Harb Sq. **Ramses Square** to the north and **'Ataba Square** to the east (both major transportation hubs) form a rough triangle with Tala'at Harb enclosing the main business and shopping district, which is crammed with travel agents, banks, restaurants, juice stands, clothing stores, language schools, and budget hotels. **Opera Square,** on the east side of the triangle near 'Ataba Sq., was the site of two great imperialist monuments, now destroyed: the Opera House and the old Shepherd's Hotel. Only the Azbekiya Gardens, encircled by bookstalls, remain.

■■■ CAIRO TRANSPORTATION

A little aggravation is good for the soul.

BUS

Sometimes the buses get so full that all you see is a tangle of mangled limbs and the sparks that fly when the bottom of the overburdened bus scrapes the road as it goes. The red-and-white and blue-and-white public buses run often and everywhere, and they're the cheapest available means of transportation. But buses have a high breakdown potential and are shabby, stifling, and uncomfortable. Numbers and destinations are usually written in Arabic, so you'll need to familiarize yourself with the characters (see Numerals, p. 484). Most buses run from 5:30am to 12:30am (during Ramadan 6:30am-6:30pm and 7:30pm-2am). Two of Cairo's central bus depots are located in **Tahrir Square.** The station directly in front of the **Mugamma'** serves Giza, points south, and southern portions of Islamic Cairo (Qasr El 'Aini, the Manyal Palace, Roda Island, Giza, and the pyramids); the one in front of the **Nile Hilton** serves points north and the rest of Islamic Cairo (Heliopolis, the airport, Shubra, Bulaq, Zamalek, and Mohandiseen). Several buses depart from a stop in front of the old **Arab League Building,** to the west of the Mugamma' along Tahrir St., adjacent to the bridge over the Nile. Once you reach your station, ask someone to point out the correct bus. Rides cost 10-25pt without rhyme or reason: Egyptians apparently disdain outmoded conventions like correlating bus fare with distance traveled. Other bus stations are at **'Ataba Square** (Midan El 'Ataba), east of the Azbekiyya Gardens (to the Citadel, the Manyal Palace, Giza, and Tahrir Square); and at **Giza** (to the pyramids, airport, and Citadel).

Outside the main stations, catching a bus is a matter of chasing one down and properly timing your leap, as they seldom come to a full stop. The entrance is always through the rear doors (except at a terminus), which have been torn off most buses to facilitate this practice. To disembark, pick a moment when the bus is not moving too rapidly and face the front as you jump off. If you want the bus to come to a full halt at an official bus stop, you must exit through the front door. The front of a bus is generally less crowded than the rear, so it's worth the effort to push your way forward. When traveling by bus, keep wallets and valuables securely buried on your person. Although violent crime is rare in Cairo, a *khawaga* on a crowded bus is an irresistible opportunity for the occasional pickpocket. Few foreigners actually brave the bus system; women who are so inclined, however, should pass up overcrowded vehicles so as to avoid unabashed stares and wandering hands.

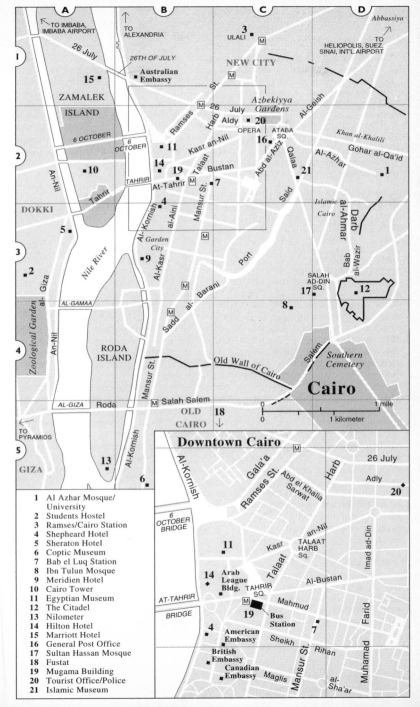

1 Al Azhar Mosque/
   University
2 Students Hostel
3 Ramses/Cairo Station
4 Shepheard Hotel
5 Sheraton Hotel
6 Coptic Museum
7 Bab el Luq Station
8 Ibn Tulun Mosque
9 Meridien Hotel
10 Cairo Tower
11 Egyptian Museum
12 The Citadel
13 Nilometer
14 Hilton Hotel
15 Marriott Hotel
16 General Post Office
17 Sultan Hassan Mosque
18 Fustat
19 Mugama Building
20 Tourist Office/Police
21 Islamic Museum

From the Arab League Building

#13: Zamalek.
#19, 102, 110, 166, 203: Dokki.

From 'Ataba Square

#99: Lebanon Sq.
#404: Citadel—Tahrir Sq.
#801, 951: Citadel.
#904: Mugamma' Station—Pyramids.
#930: Qanater.

From Giza Square

#3: Pyramids.
#30: Ramses Station.
#949: Airport.

From the Mugamma' Station

#8: Tahrir Sq.—Qasr El 'Aini—Manyal—Giza—Mena House Hotel (Pyramids).
#82, 182: Mausoleum of Imam Esh-Shafi'i—Southern Cemetery—Citadel.
#173, 194, 609: Tahrir Sq.—Citadel.
#174: Sayyida Zeinab—Ibn Tulun—Sultan Hasan—Citadel.
#900: Tahrir Sq.—Qasr El 'Aini—Manyal—Cairo University—Giza—Pyramids—Holiday Inn Hotel (very crowded except early in the morning).
#913: The Sphinx.
#923: Giza Sq.

From the Nile Hilton Station

#16: Galaa Bridge—Agouza.
#24: Ahmed Hilmi Sq.—Shubra.
#35: Abbasiyya.
#36: Port Said St.—El 'Amiriyya.
#50: Roxy Sq.—Heliopolis.
#63, 66: Al Azhar—Khan el-Khalili.
#72: Sayyida Zeinab—Citadel—Mausoleum of Imam Esh-Shafi'i.
#73: Imbaba (camel market).
#75: Islamic Museum—Bab Zuweila.
#99: Agouza—Sudan St.—Lebanon Sq. (Midan Libnan).
#128: Abbasiyya Sq.—'Ain Shams.
#173, 403: Citadel—Sultan Hasan.
#400: Old Cairo Airport via Heliopolis (Midan Roxy).
#422: New Cairo Airport.
#500: Cairo Sheraton.
#510: Heliopolis.

From Ramses Station

#30: Giza Sq.
#160: Citadel—Tahrir Sq.
#174: Citadel.

MINIBUS

Red-and-white or orange-and-white minibuses operate along many of the same routes served by the buses. Don't confuse these with the older, multi-colored taxivans that are privately operated. Although more expensive than the regular buses (25-75pt), the minibuses are far more comfortable. Finding the right one will inevitably be confusing, but most Egyptians should be glad to help. The following are important minibus routes:

From the Arab League Building

#26: Roxy, Tahrir Sq. (face the Egyptian museum to catch the bus), Dokki, Giza (face Mugamma').

#54: Citadel, Cemetery, Bab al-Louq, Sayyida Zeinab.

#76: 'Ataba Sq., Zamalek (face the museum), Tahrir Sq., Bulaq ad-Dakrur (face Mugamma').

#77: Bulaq ad-Dakrur (face Mugamma'), Khan al-Khalili (face the Egyptian Museum).

#84: 'Ataba Sq., Tahrir Sq., Dokki, Giza.

From 'Ataba Square

#48: Zamalek

#57: Citadel

From the Mugamma' Station

#24: Abbasiyya Sq.—Roxy.

#27: Masr el-Gadida—Airport (old terminal).

#30: Nasr City—Abbasiyya Sq.—Ramses Sq.

#32, 39: Hada'iq el-Quba (Quba Gardens)—El Maza—Midan el-Higaz (Heliopolis).

#35: Abbasiyya Sq.—Ismailiyya Sq. (Masr el-Gadida)—Ramses Sq.—Nasr City—Roxy.

#49: Tahrir Sq.—Zamalek.

#50: 'Ataba Sq.—Citadel.

#52, 56: Ma'adi—Old Cairo.

#54: Tahrir Sq.—Rifi'a Mosque—Ibn Tulun Mosque—Citadel—Southern Cemetery.

#55: Ma'adi via Dar es-Salaam.

#58: Ramses Sq.—Manyal (no stop at Tahrir Sq.).

#59: Ramses Sq.—Tahrir Sq.

#82: Nadi El Rimaya Sq.

#83: Pyramids.

METRO

The Cairo Metro system, completed in 1987, is a world apart from the rest of Cairo public transport. Cool, clean, and efficient, the trains run along a single 40km route linking the southern industrial district of Helwan to El Marj in Heliopolis, with a number of stops downtown. Two more lines, connecting Shubra and Giza, have been planned. Downtown stations feature excellent cartoons and Egyptian ads on little television screens. Trains run every six minutes (5:30am-1am, winter 5:30am-midnight; 30-80pt). Keep track of your ticket; you'll need it to exit. The stations downtown (look for the enormous red "M" signs) are Mubarak (Ramses Sq.), Orabi (Orabi St. and Ramses St.), Nasser (July 26th St. and Ramses St.), Sadat (Tahrir Sq.), Sa'ad Zaghloul (Mansur St. and Ismail Abaza St.), Sayyida Zeinab (Mansur St. and Ali Ibrahim St.), El Malik es-Saleh (Salah Salem Road), and Mar Girgis (Old Cairo). Trains are often packed and sweaty during rush hour; avoid Metro travel before 9am and between 5 and 7pm.

TAXI

Never take the large, unmetered, colorful Peugeot taxis within the city—they charge E£2-3 for a ride around the corner, and the only advantage is their luggage rack. Instead, lavish your attention lovingly on the metered **black-and-white taxis** that often carry passengers collectively.

To hail a taxi, pick a major thoroughfare headed in the general direction you wish to travel, stand on the side of the street, stretch out your arm as a taxi approaches, and scream out your destination as it goes by. If the drivers are interested in your business, they'll stop and wait for you to run over to their cars. Jump in and repeat your destination. Don't be alarmed if the taxi seems to be going in the wrong direction; drivers sometimes take circuitous routes to avoid traffic-clogged main arteries, to deposit other passengers, or simply to drive by and say *salaam* to a friend.

Meters have been installed in all Cairo taxis, but drivers rarely use them, since passengers jump in and out—haggling only implies that you don't know what you owe. Cairenes simply hail a cab, hop in, and pay what they think is adequate upon arrival; they seldom ask the driver for the fare. Usually, the most comfortable way to handle the situation is to open the door as you are paying with folded bills and leave the taxi without looking to the driver for approval.

There is a hidden logic of fares. Rides in the downtown area (from Ramses Sq. to Garden City and Zamalek to Islamic Cairo) should cost about E£3-4. Further afield (the Northern or Southern Cemeteries, Mohandiseen) costs E£3, the Pyramids or Imbaba E£4-6, Ma'adi and Heliopolis E£5-7 from downtown. You will be expected to pay extra for additional passengers, suitcases, and waiting. A taxi to or from the airport should cost no more than E£20 all told, but they have you at their mercy.

Avoid the taxis that park in front of major hotels—the drivers are experts at exploiting tourists. Do not expect a taxi driver to speak English, or to know the location of every address or street. Try to identify a major landmark or thoroughfare near your destination and learn to pronounce it in Arabic. Alternatively, have someone write out the address and directions in Arabic. They'll do this for you at the tourist office. Communication is generally neither traumatic nor problematic at most downtown and tourist destinations.

You will also see multi-colored **taxi-vans,** called *arabiyya bil nafar,* all around town. These have the word "taxi" written on the side and carry 12 to 15 passengers. They function more like buses than taxis, but differ from minibuses. Generally, they follow fixed routes to certain destinations but tend to be flexible as long as all passengers are going to the same area. To catch a taxi-van, go to a taxi-van stop (sometimes marked by a wooden shelter) and yell your destination as the van passes. From 'Ataba Sq. taxi-vans go to Ramses Sq., Tahrir Sq., Northern Cemetery, Zamalek, Islamic Cairo, and Heliopolis. In Tahrir Sq. taxi-vans leave from behind both bus stations and go to Heliopolis, Giza Sq., Dokki, Mohandiseen, and the Pyramids. At the stations, drivers will stand outside their buses and bellow their destinations until the bus is full. Taxi-vans provide the most comfortable means of inexpensive transportation between Cairo and some of the outlying areas, such as Giza (Giiiiiiiiiiiizeh!).

The only major drawback to ground transportation in Cairo is the harrowing experience of being driven by a smoking or newspaper-reading driver. Cairenes careen as if playing a video game. Nevertheless, most of them are good drivers whose driving styles are practical and certainly not time-consuming, so hold your breath and enjoy the ride. **River taxis** provide a more relaxing means of transportation to Old Cairo. Boats run every 30 to 40 minutes to the Nile barrages and Old Cairo (via Giza) for 50pt. The departure point is on the corniche in front of the television building, about 1km north of Tahrir Sq.

WALKING

One positive aspect of Cairo's packed layout is that almost everything in the city is within easy walking distance of Tahrir Sq. Though it may take more time, you can see most of the sights of Islamic Cairo, the downtown areas, and Roda and Zamalek Islands without using mechanized transport (an attractive proposition considering Cairo traffic and driving habits). Many argue that walking is the only way to see the city; on foot, you will indubitably catch many fascinating glimpses of Cairo life which would go unseen from a bus or car. You may also get your shoes mucked up; many city streets are strewn with garbage and random piles of sawdust.

Traffic is almost always abundant: the only times the streets are empty are during Ramadan and important football (soccer) matches. You should know that the two main soccer teams are El Ahly and El Zamalek. Both are Cairo teams, and on the day of a match between them, *nothing* in the city will move; you might as well walk into any shop and join the crowd glued to the TV. Watch the reaction if one team scores: half the crowd will go crazy and the other half will burst into tears. After a football match, venture out onto the streets at your peril. Thousands of jubilant Cairenes screech recklessly around the city, brandishing lance-like flags, honking their horns, and flattening unwary pedestrians. Friday, the holiest day of the week for Muslims, is the least crowded day of the week. Cars reign in Cairo; drivers expect pedestrians to look after themselves. It is wise to face oncoming traffic and heed the horns. A long, uninterrupted honk usually indicates that the driver is either unwilling or unable to swerve. Do not be alarmed if you are pushed or tugged by Egyptians attempting to avoid cars. Ignore traffic lights; everyone else does. Cairenes warn against being too careful when you cross a street—if you stop short or break into a run you'll upset the rhythm of the drivers speeding toward you.

■■■ INTERCITY TRANSIT

For more information see Getting Around, p. 59.

BUS

Unfortunately, Cairo has no single bus depot. You'll have to hunt down the various points of departure. Augmenting the **public bus system**, which can be crowded, chaotic, and not quite sanitary, private operators **Superjet** and the West Delta Bus Company's **Golden Arrow** (Es-Sahm ed-Dahaby) run similar routes at prices which are sometimes a bit higher, sometimes the same (go figure). These buses are clean, air-conditioned, and often serve food and/or show Egyptian films. Aside from having to share the ride with the *bourgeoisie* and aspirants to higher social classes, one drawback is that reservations, especially for popular destinations, must be made ahead of time, in person. Public buses running to Upper Egypt tend to be worse than those to Hurghada, the Sinai, and Alexandria.

Abbasiyya (Sinai) Station: in Abbasiyya District, 5km northeast of Ramses Station at the end of Ramses St. From Tahrir or Ramses Sq., you can catch local bus #54, 710, and 728, or minibus #24 and 32. The **South Sinai Company** (tel. 82 47 53) runs buses to Sharm esh-Sheikh (7am with A/C E£20, 7:20 and 10am via Et-Tur E£35, 2 and 4pm E£40, 5pm with A/C E£25, 9:40 and 10:10pm E£50), Dahab (7:20am E£40, 5pm E£30, 10:10pm E£55), Nuweiba (8am E£35; 9am E£40, through Abu Rudeis E£15, St. Catherine's E£35, and Taba E£45; 9:20pm E£50, to Taba E£65), El Arish (8am E£35, 2:20pm E£35, 5:20pm E£25), and Suez (every ½hr. 6am-4pm). **East Delta Bus Company** goes to Tel Aviv (Mon. and Wed. 8am, US$20, round-trip US$35, reserve in advance).

Abd el-Moneim Riad Square (tel. 76 69 14 or 77 26 63): across from the Ramses Hilton. **West Delta Bus Co.** to Alexandria (5:30am-midnight, E£6), and **Golden Arrow** to Alexandria (E£12).

Ahmed Hilmi Station (Mahatet Ahmed Hilmi; tel. 574 6658): Behind Ramses Station; cross below the tracks on pedestrian underpass behind the ticket windows; exit through the back entrance; the station is to the right of the service lot. **Wagh Ibli Company** (tel. 260 9307) buses (A/C and TV) to Fayyum (6:30am-6pm, E£3), Minya (2-4 buses per day, E£8), Malawi (E£8.70), Assyut (E£14), Qena (E£17), Luxor (E£29), and Aswan (E£34). **Golden Arrow** buses to Luxor (6:30am-9pm, E£18; with A/C 6:30am E£28 and 9pm E£35) and Minya (12:30-6:30pm, E£10). **Superjet** buses to Aswan (5 and 7pm, E£50), Assyut (12:30-2pm, E£15), Beni Suef (E£4), and Hurghada (6:15, 10:15am, 2:15, and 10:45pm; E£30-35).

El Azhar Station: 45 El Azhar St. (tel. 390 8635), intersection with Port Said St. Private companies run mostly A/C buses daily 9am-8pm to the Western Desert Oases: Bahariyya E£12-14, Kharga E£17-30, Dakhla E£35, and Farafra E£25.

Giza Station: Giza Square. *Service* and buses depart from here to Fayyum and destinations within Cairo. To reach departure point for Fayyum, take a right at the Square (into El Giza St.), walk straight 5min., and you'll find a hole (!) in the wall signaling the entrance to the bus station. Buses every ½hr. or so to Fayyum (E£2.75, E£3 with A/C), and a **Superjet** to Marsa Matrouh (8am, E£32).

Kolali Square (Midan El Kolali; tel. 574 2814): A 5-min. walk from Ramses Sq. With Ramses behind you, follow the elevated road to your right for 2 blocks; turn right and the station office is located 50m away on the right. **East Delta Bus Company** runs every hour 6:30am-6:30pm to Port Said (E£10-12), Suez (E£4.50-5), and

Ismailiyya (E£5.25-6.25), and to Mansura (7:30am-8:30pm, E£6.30), Ras el-Bar (7:30am-4:30pm, E£13), and Tripoli. Visit Uncle Qaddafi in Libya.

Ramses Square Station (tel. 92 48 77): Ramses Sq., next to the Coptic Hospital. **Superjet** to Port Said (every ½hr. 6am-9pm, E£13).

Tahrir Square: Buses depart from a station behind the Egyptian Museum, under the October 6th Bridge just east of the Ramses Hilton. The following summer schedule may change: to Alexandria (E£15) and Marsa Matrouh (E£30), reserve at least 24hr. in advance; Hurghada (6:30, 10:30am, 2:30, 11pm, midnight, E£30-35); Luxor (9pm, E£35); Aswan (5pm, E£50); Safaga (10pm, E£35); Quseir (10pm, E£38); and one bus a day to Saudi Arabia (E£200), Kuwait (E£400), Syria (E£175), and Jordan (E£128); arrive early for these four buses.

The Cairo Sheraton in Dokki sends buses to Tel Aviv (Sun.-Fri. 5:30am, E£85, round-trip E£130). Call the Sheraton (tel. 348 8600) for more information.

TRAIN

Ticket windows at Ramses Station are open from 8am to 10pm. If you have time, go to a tourist office first and have them write out your destination and other details in Arabic to avoid confusion. Which line you stand in depends upon whether you are reserving a seat in advance or trying to buy a ticket for the same day (often impossible). Women (and men traveling with women) can take advantage of the special women's line that may form at crowded times, which is much shorter and faster than the corresponding men's line. In addition, women are permitted (possibly expected) to push to the front of the line, head held high. If you give up one day and come back the next, don't assume that you want the same ticket window. Those traveling third class (solo women shouldn't) can buy tickets from the conductor on the train. Students get 50% discounts on fares with an ISIC or student ID.

The trains enter their berths at least half an hour before departure time. None of the train numbers or destinations is in English, but fellow travelers and the tourist police will lend a hand. Nonetheless, be prepared for yet another infusion of confusion. An information desk is directly ahead as you enter Ramses Station and the grudgingly helpful tourist information is on your left. See also specific town listings.

In between lines, take a moment to admire the towering **Statue of Ramses II** in front of the train station. The statue was excavated in 1888 near the remains of the ancient city of Memphis.

SERVICE TAXI

These are best for short trips. Catch them to Alexandria (E£8), Suez (E£5), Ismailiyya (E£5), Port Said (E£8), or El Arish (E£12) next to the Railway Station in Ramses Square; south to Fayyum (E£4) at Giza Square by the train station; and to Alexandria (E£10) from in front of the Nile Hilton or in front of the Ramses Station. The Ahmed Hilmi Square bus station covers Mansura (E£8), Tanta (E£5), Zagazig (E£4), and the rest of the Delta. You'll have to hunt for taxis to the Sinai. Ask the driver for the price before starting the trip so that you don't face a nasty surprise upon arrival. Fares should be slightly cheaper than bus fares, and you'll get there faster. Be prepared, however, to ride with an assortment of fruits, vegetables, and farm animals.

▪▪▪ PRACTICAL INFORMATION

A comprehensive compendium of useful information is *Cairo: A Practical Guide,* which includes maps (published by AUC Press, available at bookstores for E£25). A reliable directory for goods and services is the *Cairo Telephone List,* published by the Ma'adi Women's Guild and available for E£15 at the American Chamber of Commerce, Marriott Hotel #1541, Zamalek (tel. 340 8888).

Tourist Office: Misr Travel Tower, Abbasiyya Sq., Abbasiyya (tel. 82 79 64 or 48 58). Open Sat.-Thurs. 8:30am-3pm. Branches at: **5 Adly St.** (tel. 391 3454), a

20-min. walk from Tahrir Sq.: follow Tala'at Harb St. past Tala'at Harb Sq.; turn right on Adly St. The office is 3 blocks down on your left, marked "Tourist Police." Free maps. **Cairo International Airport** (tel. 66 74 75) at the entrance as well as next to the duty-free shops (open 24 hrs.). **Giza** (tel. 385 0259), next to Pyramids Police station, in front of Menahouse Hotel (open Sat.-Thurs. 8am-5pm).

Ministry of Tourism: Tel. 282 8451 or 8419 or 8432, also at the Misr Travel Tower. Open Sat.-Thurs. 8:30am-2:30pm.

Tourist Police: 5 Adly St. (tel. 126 or 39 ¡9 44 or 390 6028), in the same building as the Tourist Office. Other locations at **Cairo International Airport** (tel. 247 2584), **Giza** (tel. 385 0259), and in the **Manial Palace Hotel.**

Passport Office: Mugamma' Bldg., southern end of Tahrir Sq. Passports must be registered within 7 days of arrival. Find information window on 2nd floor. Registration open summer 8am-4pm and 8-10pm; winter 8am-4pm and 7-9pm, slightly shorter hours on Thurs., Fri., and holidays for both seasons; Ramadan daily 10am-2pm. Evening hours are least crowded. Ask at your hotel; they may register for you. Also come here for **visa extensions**—be sure to bring bank receipts showing that you have exchanged at least US$180 (or the equivalent) into E£; as well as one photograph and E£12. Exchange your money at a bank; receipts from even the most reputable of hotels may not do the job.

Australian Embassy: World Trade Center, 11-12th floors, 1191 Corniche en-Nil, Bulaq (tel. 77 71 16). Passports generally replaced in 10 working days (AUS$101 for 32-page passports, AUS$152 for 64-page passports). Immediate replacement in case of emergency. Open Sun.-Thurs. 9am-12:30pm, visas 9:30am-noon.

Canadian Embassy: 6 Muhammad Fahmi Es-Sayyid St. (formerly Rostom Pasha St.), Garden City (tel. 354 3110 or 3119), across from Sudanese embassy. Passports replaced within 2 working days for CDN$45. Embassy open Sun.-Thurs. 7:30am-3pm, visas 8-11am, **library** Tues. and Thurs. 8-11am.

Israeli Embassy: 6 Ibn el-Malik St., Dokki (tel. 361 0380 or 0458). Cross over to Dokki from Roda Island on University Bridge. The street to the right of and parallel to the bridge is Ibn el-Malik. Look up at the top floors for the Israeli flag or for the security guards by the entrance who will ask to see your passport. Visas E£14 for all nationalities. Open Sun.-Thurs. 10:30am-noon.

Jordanian Embassy: 6 El Goheina St., Dokki (tel. 348 5566 or 6169 or 7543, or 349 9912), 2 blocks west of the Cairo Sheraton. Visas (photograph and letter of introduction required) free for U.S. and Australian passport holders, E£28 for New Zealanders, E£77 for Britons and Canadians. Open Sat.-Thurs. 9am-noon.

Palestinian Office: 23 En-Nahda St., Dokki (tel. 347 7567).

Syrian Embassy: 18 Abd er-Rahim Sabri St., Dokki (tel. 70 70 20, or 71 83 20). Bring 2 photos for a visa (valid for one entry only; free for Canadians and Australians, E£48 for Americans). Open 8am-2pm, visas 9am-1pm.

U.K. Embassy: 7 Ahmed Ragheb St. (tel. 354 0850), south of U.S. Embassy. Handles **New Zealanders'** affairs too. Will replace both Pommie and Kiwi passports within 5 days (£18). Open Mon.-Fri. 8am-2pm. Call for after-hours emergencies.

U.S. Embassy: 5 Latin America St. (tel. 354 8211), 2 blocks south of Tahrir Sq. For consulate enter on Lazaughli St., around the block. Lost or stolen passports replaced overnight for US$65 or E£227.50. Letters of introduction for visas issued on request. Open Sun.-Thurs. 8am-4:30pm, consulate 7:30-10:30am, services for Americans 8am-noon. Call if there is an emergency after hours.

Currency Exchange: Misr International Bank: Main Office at 54 El Batal Ahmed Abd el-Aziz St., Mohandiseen (tel. 349 4424 or 7091). Money can be wired to Egypt through **Citibank,** 4 Ahmed Pasha St., Garden City (tel. 355 1873 or 1874; open Sun.-Thurs. 8:30am-2pm). **Cairo Barclays International Bank,** 12 Sheikh Yousef Sq., Garden City (tel. 354 9415 or 9422), 3 blocks south of Tahrir Sq. along Qasr El 'Aini St., accepts traveler's checks and has worldwide money transfer services. Open Sun.-Thurs. 8:30am-2pm; during Ramadan, 10am-1pm. Foreign banks are closed Fri.-Sat., but most Egyptian banks open Sat. **Bank Misr** branches at the Ramses and Nile Hiltons, the Marriott, the Shepherd, and other major hotels are open 24 hrs. Main office at 151 Muhammad Farid St., downtown (tel. 391 7571).

American Express: 15 Qasr en-Nil (tel. 574 7991 through 7996 (6 lines)), just off **Tala'at Harb Sq.** toward Ramses St. Card or Travelers Cheque holders can have money sent and use the USADirect telephone service and Client Letter Service. Non-clients can use Letter Service for a mail inquiry charge. Open daily 8:30am-6pm. Letter service closed Fri. Other locations: **Cairo Airport** (tel. 67 08 95), **Nile Hilton** (tel. 578 5001/2/3), **Marriott Hotel** (tel. 341 0136), **Pullman Ma'adi** (tel. 350 7851), **Mohandiseen,** 4 Syria St. (tel. 70 79 08 or 14), **Bus Travel Center,** 72 Omar Ibn El Khattab St., Heliopolis (tel. 418 2144), from Saba'a Imarat Sq., go into Ibn El Khattab St., located next to Rossini-Restaurant and the BBC Nursery School, **Giza,** 21 Nile St. (Nile Tower), 10th floor (tel. 573 5866), in front of the Zoological Garden. All Cairo offices provide E£ for Travelers Cheques, but you need an AmEx card to purchase them. Hotel offices provide faster service, but sometimes run out of cash. Open Sat.-Thurs. 8:30am-5pm.

Thomas Cook, 17 Mahmoud Bassiouny St. (tel. 574 3955 or 3967 or 7183), half a block west of **Tala'at Harb Sq.** Travel agency, money transfers, cash advances on MC. Cashes all traveler's checks. Open daily 8am-5pm. Also offices in Cairo International Airport, Dokki, Garden City, Heliopolis, Mohandiseen, and Ma'adi.

Main Post Office: 55 Sarwat St., 'Ataba Sq. (tel. 391 2614). Often crowded, but blissfully empty just before the office closes. Packages require an export license from Cairo International Airport; major hotels and tourist shops also provide this service. Open Sat.-Thurs. 8:30am-3pm; Ramadan 9am-3pm. **Poste Restante** located around the corner on Bidek St. (open Sat.-Thurs. 8am-6pm). **Express Mail (EMS)** on Bidek St. across from Poste Restante (open Sat.-Thurs. 8am-7pm).

Telephone Office: Main Office, Ramses St., 1 block north of July 26th St. Other offices in Zamalek (tel. 340 1674), Airport (tel. 247 5059), Ma'adi (tel. 350 1122), Tahrir Sq. (76 51 18), Adly St. (390 9172), and Alfy St. (90 73 14), under the Windsor Hotel. All open 24 hrs. Collect and credit card calls available at the USADirect (tel. 356 0200), U.K. Direct, Canada Direct, and Japan Direct phones in the lobbies of the Ramses Hilton, Marriott, and SemiRamis hotels. For a 25% surcharge, you can make international calls easily at the business service offices in the Meridien, Sheraton, and Nile Hilton hotels (24 hrs.). All major hotels have local pay phones, operated with expensive tokens (25-50pt.). **Directory Assistance:** Tel. 140. **Telephone Code:** 02.

Telegraph and Telex Office: 'Ataba Sq., opposite the main post office. Open 24 hrs. Other offices at Tahrir Sq., 26 Ramses St., and Adly St.

Flights: EgyptAir, 6 Adly St. (tel. 391 1256), and in the Nile Hilton by Tahrir Sq. (tel. 76 52 00 or 77 24 10). Reservations and information: 392 7444 or 7205. **Air Sinai,** Nile Hilton at Tahrir Square (tel. 76 09 48), open daily 9am-5pm. **ZAS Airlines,** Novotel Hotel next to the Old Airport, open daily 9am-8pm. Other branches at 1 Tala'at Harb St., downtown (tel. 392 9830 or 390 7836), Mohandiseen (tel. 360 7138 or 8394), and Garden City (tel. 355 5485 or 2345). Often cheaper than EgyptAir, especially for domestic flights. Bus #422 runs from the new airport to Tahrir Sq. (35pt), leaving from in front of the parking lot at the terminal. Bus #400 and minibus #27 (25pt and 50pt) leave from the lot in front of the old terminal. Bus #400 goes to the airport from Tahrir Sq., and minibus #27 from the Mugamma' stop.

Buses, Trains, Metro, Taxis: See Transportation, p. 78.

Car Rental: For maniacs willing to risk life and limb to achieve relative freedom of mobility: **Avis** (tel. 354 8698 or 7400), open 8am-3:30pm. Branch at Cairo International Airport (tel. 291 4266 or 4277 or 4288) is open 24 hrs. Other branches at the Sheraton (tel. 98 94 00) and the Hilton (tel. 76 64 32), open 8am-10pm. Join millions of middle-class Egyptians in driving a Fiat 128 (known in Cairo as "the 28") for US$35, or mimic the elite with the Mercedes 190 (fully automatic) for US$132. **Europcar** (tel. 340 1152), **Hertz** (tel. 347 4172 or 2238), **Max Rent-a-Car** (tel. 347 4712 or 4713) open 8am-8pm, and **Budget** (tel. 340 0070) open 8:30am-9pm. Rates are US$35 (Suzuki Swift) to over US$100 (4-wheel-drives, Mercedes, and vans) per day. Weekly rates available; must be 25 or older for all except Budget (26). Most agencies charge for each additional km over 100km. And hey, there's always **Limousine Misr** (tel. 90 74 26; open 24 hrs.).

Lockers: Luggage and valuables storage on the ground floor of Ramses Station, Ramses Sq. 30pt per day (14-day maximum). Walk into the station and ask anyone in uniform, *"Feen al-khazaa'in?"* (Where are the lockers?) Open 24 hrs.

English Bookstores: Shorouk Bookshop, Tala'at Harb Sq. (tel. 391 2480), is packed with schlock romance and whodunits. Open daily 9am-9pm. **AUC Bookstore,** Hill House, American University in Cairo, 113 Qasr El 'Aini St. (tel. 357 5377), has English literature, guidebooks, and maps. Open Sun.-Thurs. 8:30am-4pm, Sat. 10am-3pm. AUC Press also has a bookstore at 16 Muhammad Ibn Thakeb St., Zamalek (tel. 339 7045). **Anglo-Egyptian,** 165 Muhammad Farid St. (tel. 391 4337), has new and used English literature at reasonable prices. Open Mon.-Sat. 9am-1:30pm and 4:30-8pm. **Lehnert and Landrock,** 44 Sharif St. (tel. 393 5324), also has a wide selection. Open Mon.-Fri. 9:30am-1:30pm and 3:30-7:30pm, Sat. 9:30am-1:30pm only. **Madbuli** in Tala'at Harb Sq. (tel. 575 6421; open daily 10am-10pm) offers books on Egypt. Also at 45 El Batal Ahmed Abd el-Aziz St. (tel. 347 7410; open 24 hrs). For an astounding collection of old books and maps, rare editions, lithographs, and prints, go to **L'Orientaliste,** 15 Qasr En-Nil St., downtown (tel. 575 3418; open Mon.-Sat. 10am-7:30pm).

Newspapers and Magazines: Foreign publications at the kiosks along Tala'at Harb Sq., near AUC, or at the intersection of July 26th and Hasan Sabri St., Zamalek. *Time, Newsweek, The New York Times,* and major European titles. Egyptian newspapers published in English are the *Egyptian Gazette* (25pt) and the *Al-Ahram Weekly* (50pt), which come out every Thursday.

American Cultural Center: 4 Ahmed Ragheb St., Garden City (tel. 354 9601 or 76 27 04; library 355 0532 or 357 3412), across from the British Embassy. If you'll be in Egypt for at least 12 months you are eligible to join. To do so, take along your passport (any nationality) and 2 photos. Members can borrow books and watch videos in the library. Occasional free films and lectures. Open Sun.-Fri. 10am-4pm; winter Mon. and Wed. 10am-8pm, Tues. and Thurs.-Fri. 10am-4pm.

British Council: 192 En-Nil St., Agouza (tel. 345 3281), 1 block south of July 26th St. next to Balloon Theatre. Adult annual fee E£40, E£20 without borrowing privileges. Lifetime membership E£300. Main office open Mon.-Sat. 9am-2:45pm, library (tel. 344 8445, open Mon.-Wed. 9am-2pm, Fri.-Sat. 9am-3pm), and teaching center (tel. 347 6118, open Mon.-Sat. 8am-8pm). Sponsors performances by visiting British artists and groups and distributes tourist information.

Photography and Film Developing: Actina, 4 Tala'at Harb St., open Mon.-Fri. 8am-8pm, Sat. 8am-1:30pm. **Kodak,** 20 Adly St. (tel. 394 2263), E£2 for processing, 55-70pt per print, and E£2 for 90-min. service. Open Mon.-Sat. 9am-9pm. **Antar Photo,** 180 Tahrir St. (tel. 354 0786), in Bab El-Louq Sq., 1-day service E£1.50 for processing, 40-50pt per print. Open daily 9am-9pm. Most reliable is **Philippe,** El Mesaha St., Orman Sq. (tel. 349 1350, in front of German school). Also sells photo equipment and takes passport photos. Open Mon.-Sat. 9am-9pm. Delivers developed photos next day after 6pm.

Supermarket: Sunnyshine Supermarket, 11 El Aziz Osman St., Zamalek (tel. 342 1121 or 341 2032), next door to the Mayfair Hotel. Gargantuan range of Egyptian and Western products offered, but not quite budget prices. Will deliver. Open daily 8am-10pm. Visa and MC. **Cash & Carry,** 64 Lebanon Square (Midan Libnan), Mohandiseen (tel. 346 5350). **Seoudi Market,** 25 Midan El Missaha St., Dokki (tel. 348 8440 or 8441), also at 50 El Quds esh-Sharif St. (Jerusalem St.), Mohandiseen (tel. 344 0037 or 346 0391), and 15 Ahmad Hishmat St., Zamalek (tel. 341 3586 or 340 9596). Seoudi should provide you with just about everything you need at going market prices.

Laundromat: Circle Cleaning, 24 July 26th St. (tel. 76 08 55), near Supreme Court. Washing, ironing, dry cleaning, and mending E£2.50-7.20. Open daily 9am-9pm.

Swimming Pools: Pay over E£50 per day to stay at a fancy hotel and swim in an azure, Olympic-size pool, or pay E£7 and swim in the not-quite-Olympic-size, teal-tiled pool on the 7th-floor patio of the **Fontana Hotel,** Ramses Sq. (tel. 92 21 45, or 92 23 21). A day pass at the **Marriott** lets you into the pool, sauna, jacuzzi, and gym, all for E£63. Or get a day-ticket to one of Cairo's many sporting clubs. The best are the **Gezira Sporting Club** in front of the Marriott Hotel in Zamalek (tel. 340 2272), the **Ma'adi Sporting Club,** 8 En-Nadi Sq. (tel. 350 5504), and the **Heliopolis Sporting Club,** 17 El Merghany St. (tel. 291 4800).

Pharmacy: First-Aid Pharmacy, corner of July 26th St. and Ramses St. (tel. 74 33 69), northwest side of intersection. Open 24 hrs. Head pharmacist Dr.

Muhammad speaks fairly good English. **Victoria Pharmacy,** 90 Qasr El 'Aini St., Garden City (tel. 354 8604). Open 24 hrs. **Pharmacy Mondial,** 2 Ahmed Hishmat St. (tel. 341 1180). Ask for Dr. Mamdouh.

Hospitals: Anglo-American Hospital, Botanical Garden St., Gezira-Zamalek (tel. 340 6162/3/4/5) below the Cairo Tower. The best-equipped is **As-Salaam International Hospital,** Corniche en-Nil, Ma'adi (tel. 363 8050, emergency 362 3300). **Cairo Medical Center,** Roxy Sq., Heliopolis (tel. 258 0566 or 0217 or 1003).

Private Doctors: Dr. Farid Cotta, 34 Adly St. 4th floor, downtown (tel. 392 7936), is friendly and charges reasonable prices; he has established a good reputation in Cairo. Available 6-9pm. Your embassy can also provide lists of doctors.

Emergency: Fire: Tel. 125, or 391 0115. **Ambulance:** Tel. 123.

Police: Tel. 122, or 303 4122 or 5122; central: tel. 13.

■■■ ACCOMMODATIONS

To find any of Cairo's many luxury hotels, just look for the nearest 30-story pink tower. Finding a decent budget hotel is a bit more of a challenge. You can stay in reasonable comfort for as little as E£10 per night, after some slash-and-burn comparison shopping. Most of Cairo's budget hotels occupy the upper floors of stores and office buildings in the downtown area along **Tala'at Harb Street** between Tahrir Sq. and July 26th St. The quality varies with little correlation to price. Try bargaining, but don't hold out too long; the best beds fill quickly in summer.

Upper-floor rooms provide a buffer zone between you and street noise; make sure the ancient *ascenseur* is in working order first. Rooms overlooking interior courts are quieter, if less aesthetic. Breezes at higher elevations may help you endure un-air-conditioned rooms. Many places rent fans and serve tea, coffee, and soft drinks in their lobbies. Unless otherwise specified, breakfast and round-the-clock hot water are included in the price. The check-out time is noon.

Youth Hostel (HI), 135 Malaak Abd el-Aziz es-Saud St., Roda Island (tel. 84 07 29; fax 98 41 07). Take metro to Sayyida Zeinab. Exit to the right and walk straight to the Nile. Cross the Sayala Bridge and continue straight across Roda Island to the main channel of the Nile. Turn left just before the bridge; the hostel is 10m away on the left. Bunk beds are crammed into spartan but clean rooms. Crowded from November to May; call ahead. Lockers in every room. Padlocks available around the corner for E£2. Bring toilet paper and HI card. Lockout 10am-2pm. Curfew 11pm. Dorm beds (6 per room) E£6. Triples E£36.

DOWNTOWN AND TALA'AT HARB STREET

Fontana Hotel (tel. 92 21 45 or 92 23 21), Ramses Sq. on your left as you leave Ramses Station. Private baths, international phones, A/C, color TV, psychedelic Arabian disco, a lobby gift shop, a restaurant, a small but beautiful pool, and a lovely, expensive coffee shop on the roof. Singles with bath E£47. Doubles with bath E£64. All-you-can-eat buffet breakfast E£10 per person.

Windsor Hotel, 19 Alfy Bey St. (tel. 91 58 10 or 91 52 77; fax 92 16 21), behind Cinema Diana. Beautiful and very clean, with an atmosphere of faded grandeur. The Barrel Bar, so named because all the furniture is made from retired barrels, was once the British Officers' Club and remains a star on the Anglo-American expatriate scene. Ask for the Michael Palin package. Excellent service. Singles with bath and A/C E£71. Doubles with bath and A/C E£94. A 25% discount for *Let's Go* users makes it just about affordable.

Pensione Roma, 169 Muhammad Farid St. (tel. 391 1088 or 1340), 1 block south of July 26th St. and 2 blocks east of Tala'at Harb St., above the "Gattegno" department store. Clean, airy, tastefully decorated rooms. Decent bathrooms, and the dining room and salons are truly grand. Singles E£18. Doubles E£33, with bath E£37. This place is no secret; call ahead.

Ismailia House Hotel, 1 Tahrir Sq. (tel 356 3122), on the east side of Tahrir Sq. across from AUC. Simple, neat rooms illuminated by green neon lights. Spotless blue-tiled bathrooms. Many students stay here and appear to be having a good time. Dorm beds E£15. Singles E£20. Doubles E£40, with bath E£45.

Hotel Petit Palais, 45 Abd el-Khalek Sarwat St. (tel. 391 1863), ½-block west of Opera Sq. Run by the same people as the Ismailia. Same facilities at a less frenetic pace. Shared bathrooms ooze hygiene. Spacious singles E£20. Doubles E£30.

Tulip Hotel, 3 Tala'at Harb Sq. (tel. 393 9433). Mint-green walls, a TV lounge, and cleanliness beckon. Several rooms have balconies overlooking Tala'at Harb Sq. Check-out 10am. Singles with shower E£25. Doubles E£30, with shower E£37.

Hotel Nefertiti, 39 Tala'at Harb St. (tel. 392 5153), just above Bambo Restaurant; enter through the alleyway to the left. Clean and cheap. Hot water available on request. The front desk is often unattended, so keep valuables locked up. Doubles with shower E£15. Triples with shower E£21. Breakfast not included.

Pension Select Hotel, 19 Adly St., 8th floor (tel. 393 3707), next to the synagogue. Clean and quiet. Acceptable rooms with balconies. 3 same-gender people per room (not a problem if you don't mind living with strangers). Dorm beds E£10.

Crown Hotel, 9 Imad ed-Din St. (tel. 91 83 74). An alpine mural glistening with glaciers taunts guests in the lobby. Dorm-sized rooms are clean and monastic. Singles E£10. Doubles E£20. E£2 discount for *Let's Go* users. Breakfast not included.

Amin Hotel, 38 Falaky Sq. (tel. 393 3813), next to the fork of Bustan St. and Tahrir St., in bustling Bab el-Louq Sq. It is old, but rooms are decent. Singles E£20. Doubles E£26, with bath E£28. Breakfast not included.

Lotus Hotel, 12 Tala'at Harb St. (tel. 75 06 27 or 75 09 66; fax 92 16 21), 1 block from Tahrir Sq. Professional service, large rooms, hardwood floors, big beds, and clean bathrooms greet the frazzled sojourner. Restaurant, bar, and, coming soon, a solarium. Prices are due to rise. Singles E£40, with shower and A/C E£50. Doubles E£52/E£65. Hot water 6-9am and 6-9pm. Major credit cards accepted.

Montana Hotel, 25 Sharif St., 7th floor (tel. 392 8608 or 392 6264, international 393 6025), 2 blocks south of Adly St. Attentive employees keep spotless halls and clean bathrooms but dim and dingy rooms with fans and natty internal phones. Singles E£27, with bath E£37. Doubles E£45, with bath and A/C E£53. Montana?

New Hotel, 21 Adly St. (tel. 392 7176 or 7033; fax 392 9555), 1 block from Tala'at Harb St. Though the halls are punctuated by inexplicable construction sites, the bathrooms and rooms are large and very clean. Singles E£32, with bath E£38. Doubles E£51, with bath E£55.

Hotel des Roses, 33 Tala'at Harb St. (tel. 393 8022), 2 blocks north of Tala'at Harb Sq. Small hotel with reasonably clean rooms. Make sure you actually get bed linen. Doubles E£23, with bath E£31. Fans E£3. Prices negotiable.

Hotel Beau Site, 27 Tala'at Harb St. (tel 392 9916 or 9877), 2 blocks north of Tala'at Harb Sq. Watch your step in the doorless elevator. In one corner of the lobby stands a table of books—a "library." The rooms are clean, but the dining hall is a bit shabby. Singles E£15. Doubles E£23.

Anglo-Swiss Hotel, 14 Champollion St., 7th floor (tel. 75 14 97), 2 blocks west of Tala'at Harb Sq. Quiet, secluded, and clean. Calm your shattered nerves here after a sweat-invoking day of sight-seeing. Cool stone floors and conservative decor indeed make for European ambiance. Clean bathrooms. Check-out 10am. Singles E£22. Doubles E£35.

Hotel Viennoise, 11 Mahmoud Bassiouny St. (tel. 575 1949), at Champollion St. Vast winding corridors, an unused bar, and a run-down atmosphere. The rooms, with manual crank fans, are spacious, cheap, and nearly clean. Singles E£13.50. Doubles E£18.50, with bath E£20.

Gresham Hotel, 20 Tala'at Harb St. (tel. 75 90 43), enter through the alley. Though the location is convenient, the hallways are dusty and the carpet is fungus green; but the rooms are clean and, well, roomy. Singles E£25. Doubles E£40, with bath E£45. No hot water in rooms.

ZAMALEK

The Mayfair Hotel, 9 Aziz Osman St. (tel. 340 7315), on the corner of Ibn Zinky St. 2 blocks south of July 26th St. Tidy rooms (most with balconies) conveniently located in the heart of Zamalek, but noise from the school across the street could rob you of the peace you paid for. Rooms with or without private bath and A/C. Singles E£22-37, doubles E£34-49.

Horus House Hotel, 21 Ismail Muhammad St. 4th floor (tel. 340 3034 or 3634). Take bus #13 from Tahrir Square to Abu Elfeda St. on the Nile, then turn left into Ismail Muhammad St. (Pizza Hut will be on your right.) Horus Hotel provides clean, spacious rooms and an excellent restaurant for an astonishingly low price. All rooms come with TV, fridge, and bath. Singles E£36, doubles E£47, and triples E£57. Don't confuse the Horus with the Longchamp Hotel on the 6th floor.

Nile Zamalek Hotel, 21 Ma'had es-Swissry St. (tel. 340 1846, international 340 0220), next to the intersection of Ma'had es-Swissry Street and Muhammad Muzar Street. Quiet and secluded. Rooms boast thin carpets and worn furnishings but a plethora of electronic marvels: TV, fridge, telephone, and A/C; many also have extremely nice bathrooms and a balcony overlooking the Nile. Coffee shop, bar, and restaurant. Singles E£55, doubles E£65. Visa.

Balmoral Chinese Restaurant & Hotel, 157 July 26th St. (tel. 340 5473 or 0543 or 6761), at the corner of Ma'had as-Swissry St. Take bus #13 from Tahrir Square to Hassan Sabri Station. Clean but unspectacular rooms have private baths (singles E£30; doubles E£40). There is also a little bar and take-away service, which makes this hotel-bar-restaurant multi-functional indeed. U.S. dollars accepted.

■■■ FOOD

You'll need but 25pt to fill your stomach in Cairo on *fuul* and falafel (more often called *ta'miyya* in Egypt). *Fatir*, a fillo dough-like flat bread with vegetables, meats, jam, or other sweets piled on top and stuffed inside, is far tastier than the imitations of Italian pizza in town and, at E£5-10, usually much cheaper. *Kushari* will set you back about E£1.50. Even at more expensive restaurants, you can create a handsome meal out of hummus, *tahina, baba ghannoush,* and salad for under E£5. To track down these delicacies, just look in shop windows: piles of rice and macaroni betray a *kushari* house; falafel, *fuul,* and other treats pose seductively for the famished tourist on counters and street stands. Wash it all down with exhilarating fruit juices, on offer anywhere you see bags of fruit hanging around a storefront. Orange juice costs about E£1; more exotic fruits retail at E£1.25 or so. At gastrocenters that do not have waiters, pay first and then exchange your receipt for food. There is a 5% tax on everything and a 10-12% service charge in sit-down restaurants, always included in the bill.

DOWNTOWN

Felfela, 15 Hoda Sharawi St. (tel. 392 2751 or 2833), off Tala'at Harb St., 1 block south of Tala'at Harb Sq. Perhaps overpriced, but consistently excellent. A favorite among Egyptians and tourists alike. Busting out all over with bamboo, aquariums, and mosaics. Try the spiced *fuul* (E£1.50-3.75) and falafel dishes (E£1-2). A full meal can range from *wara 'inab* (stuffed grape leaves, E£8.50) to various *kabab* (E£9.75-12.65). Also delicious is *om ali,* a pastry baked with milk, honey, and raisins (E£2). Another entrance on Tala'at Harb St. leads to a self-service counter with cold drinks and sandwiches (40-80pt). Open daily 7am-12:30am.

El Tahrir, 169 Tahrir St. (tel. 355 8418), 3 blocks east of Tahrir Sq. Crowded with Egyptians and clean. Tasty *kushari* and *mahlabiyya* (rice pudding). Sit down and they'll bring you a huge bowl for E£1.50. Beware: that's hot sauce in the wine bottles. The off-white liquid is a lemon concoction. Open daily 6:30am-11pm.

Fatitry Pizza at-Tahrir, 165 Tahrir St. (tel. 355 3596), 2 blocks east of Tahrir Sq. A small scrumptious *fatir* (with various meats or egg) or a pizza *fatir* topped with meat or seafood, cheese, sauce, and olives makes a filling meal (E£5-7). Obscenely sweet dessert, with apple jam and powdered sugar, is worth the sin. Open 24 hrs.

Zeina, 32 Tala'at Harb St. (tel. 574 5758). Outgoing waiter can make his bow tie jump up and down. *Shawerma* (E£1.35), fruit juices (E£1.35), and desserts (*konafa* E£1, *basbouseh* 90pt). Meals are E£4-10. Open daily 7am- midnight.

New Kursaal, 5 Imad ed-Din St. (tel. 918 411), at the intersection with Alfy Bey St. Professional service and good food. The adventurer can explore the various

FOOD

taguen (meats and vegetables baked in a clay pot) or *kobeba* (ko-BAY-ba, beef with crushed wheat in it). Meals E£3-10, drinks E£2, alcoholic beverages E£5-7.50, desserts E£1-2. Open daily 7am-midnight.

New Hotel Restaurant, 21 Adly St. (tel. 392 7176), in the New Hotel. Either the menu or the food will make your belly wobble joyfully. As comic as gastronomic. Simple starters (E£2.50-7), followed by pigenon (E£11) or fright fish (E£14) make a full meal. Big spenders and Monty Python fans will love the Chateau Brian (E£25 for 2). Finish up with one of their tasty sweats (E£1-3). Open 7am-10pm.

Ali Hassan al-Hati, 3 Halim St. (tel. 916 055), on the corner between Alfy St. and July 26th St., 1 block south of the Windsor Hotel. Vaulted ceilings, crystal chandeliers, soaring mirrors, and forlorn waiters. Flavorful *kabab* (E£15) and fish (E£11). Try the *fatteh* (garlic-y meat or vegetables poured over crunchy baked bread and covered with a yogurt sauce, E£1-3.50). Open daily noon-11pm.

Alfy Bey Restaurant, 3 Alfy Bey St. (tel. 771 888), 1 block north of July 26th St. This restaurant (est. 1936) serves *kabab* (E£7.80), *escalope* (breaded fried meat, E£13), and incredible stuffed pigeon (E£8). Open daily noon-1am.

Excelsior, 35 Tala'at Harb St. (tel. 392 5002), at the corner of Tala'at Harb St. and Adly St. Bright, airy restaurant with Italo-Egyptian specialties: canneloni (E£6), lasagna (E£3.25), *shawerma* (E£10), and *taguen* (E£10). Old-fashioned ice cream bar in the corner. Minimum E£2 per person. Open daily 7am-midnight.

Bambo, 39 Tala'at Harb St. (tel. 392 5179), 1 block from the intersection of Adly St. and Tala'at Harb St. Take-away and sit-down restaurant spewing Italian, Egyptian, and some American food. For E£4-12, enjoy a fairly generous meal of pasta, *kufta*, *shawerma,* or hamburgers. "Pizza" is a misnomer. Open daily 8am-midnight.

Doumyati (tel 392 2293), on the north side of Falaky Sq. near the pedestrian overpass, about 4 blocks east of Tahrir Sq. One of the most popular (and cheapest) *fuul* restaurants in Cairo. No menu in English, but it's real simple: *fuul* (50pt), *fuul* with oil (75pt), falafel (20pt), *fuul* sandwich or falafel sandwich (25pt), potato sandwich (30pt), *'ads* (lentil soup, 75pt), salad (30pt), and drinks (35pt). Open Sat.-Thurs. 7am-midnight; closed on Islamic holidays.

El Haty, 8A July 26th St. (tel. 391 8829), in an alleyway to the south of the street. Not to be confused with Ali Hassan al-Hati opposite or the restaurant upstairs. Marble and fern decor complemented by soothing pastel green chairs. Unimpeachably hygienic. Meat meal with salads E£6-10. Open daily 12:30pm-1am.

GARDEN CITY

Take-Away, Latin America St. (tel. 355 4341), 1 block south of U.S. embassy. Diner cuisine, diner atmosphere. Full meals E£8-12. The flagship of their sandwich line-up, the "Mama Burger," is a bargain at E£1.70. Order two. Open daily 8am-11pm.

KHAN EL-KHALILI

Coffee Shop Naguib Mahfouz, 5 El Badistante Lane (tel. 90 37 88 or 93 22 62), 2 blocks west of El Hussein mosque. Expensive but convenient new restaurant in the heart of the Khan. Far from the madding crowds; allegedly a hangout of Nobel laureate and author Naguib Mahfouz. Every night, live music accompanies a Lebanese-style meal: *ema* (dumplings, E£6.50), *shawerma* (E£25), *kabab* or *kufta* (E£25), *tabbouleh, baba ghannoush,* or *tahina* salads (E£4). Also various exotic fruit drinks (E£3.50-4.50). Minimum charge E£3.50 per person, E£1.10 charge for music. Open daily 11:30am-1:30am; Ramadan 8am-4am.

El-Dahhan Chicken Home, 82 Gohar al-Qa'it St. (tel. 939 278), 1 block down El Muski St. from Ed-Dahhan. ½ grilled chicken E£11, 0.25kg *kabab* E£10.50, pigeon E£9.50. Take-out or eat-in. Open daily 9am-midnight.

Egyptian Pancakes, 7 Al Azhar Sq. (tel. 908 623), 1 block from the intersection of Al Azhar St. and Gohar el-Qa'it St. Meat or sweet *fatir* E£7-9. Open 24 hrs.

Khan al-Khalili Restaurant, 22 Hussein Sq. (tel. 929 469), a few doors down from Hotel El Hussein. *Kabab* or *kufta* (0.25kg E£11). Open Sat-Thurs. 11am-midnight.

Ed-Dahhan, Hussein Sq. (tel. 939 325), 20m from the end of El Muski. Dark, smoky hole-in-the-wall serves fantastic *kabab* (E£10.50 for 0.25kg). Packed with Egyptian families and businesspeople. Open 10am-11pm; Ramadan 10am-3am.

MOHANDISEEN

My Queen, Gam'at Ed-Duwal El Arabiyya St. (Arab League St.), across from the overpass at the end of the street. Don't be fooled by My Queen's appearance. Yes, it's a moving van (customers are served either in their cars or as take-away service); no, it doesn't look appetizing, but they serve clean, delicious *kufta, shawerma, kibda* (liver), *sish tawouq,* and other sandwiches (E£3-5). Come here on a Thurs. night (or Fri. morning) around 2am and find half of Cairo's teeny-boppers pigging out after a long night at one of Cairo's discotheques (the **Atlas** is at the end of the same street.) Reasonable prices and prompt service.

Peking, 26 El Atteba St. (tel. 349 9086) Chinese food at under E£25 a dish. Other branches downtown, 14 Saraya el-Azbakia St. (behind Cinema Diana, tel. 591 2381) and in Ma'adi, 9 Road 151 (tel. 351 8328). Popular with Cairo's upper crust, so reserve on weekends. Open noon-midnight. Alcohol served; AmEx, Visa, MC.

Tandoori Restaurant and Take-Away, 11 Shehab St. (tel. 348 6301). Take bus #815 from Tahrir (Nile Hilton station). Anyone with a curry craving will find excellent Indian cuisine but not a solitary Stella; they're dry. Vegetable dishes E£6, chicken E£14. Fantastic service, impeccable hygiene, and forests of ferns. Open daily 12:30pm-midnight. AmEx, Visa, MC.

Prestige Pizza, 43 Geziret al-Arab (tel. 347 0383), just east of Wadi en-Nil St. Take bus #19 from Tahrir Sq. or #30 from Ramses Sq. Classy atmosphere and tastebud-friendliness help make Prestige the pizza place of choice in Cairo. Pizzas E£5-8. Open daily noon-2am. E£5 minimum. AmEx, Visa, MC.

El Maestro, 26 Syria St. (tel. 349 0661 or 0662), inside the Cairo Inn. Take bus #167 from 'Ataba Sq. or #815 from Tahrir. An Italian restaurant which calls itself Spanish because it serves sherry and *paella.* Rather good grilled food E£15-34, pasta E£7-8. Bizarre hybrid decor fuses *Casablanca* and *Star Wars* (low ceilings, piano, lighted countertops). Live music every night; Tawfik Tawfik sings Arabic music every Tues. Open 24 hrs., E£5 minimum 7am-7pm, E£12 7pm-11pm, E£20 11pm-7am. U.S. dollars accepted.

Al-Omda, 6 El-Gazeir St. (tel. 346 2247), a few doors down from the Atlas Hotel down an unmarked staircase. The best place in Cairo for *fuul* and falafel (75pt.) and kushari (E£3)—take Hashem's word for it. Also try the *fatir mishaltit.* Air-conditioned and clean with fabulous Egyptian furnishings. Open daily 8am-2am.

ZAMALEK

Restaurant 5 Bells, 13 Ismail Muhammad St. (tel. 340 8980 or 8635), on the corner of Al-Adel Abu Bakr St. Drink in an enchanting Renaissance garden or take refuge from the sun inside a cool, Italian den setting. Backpackers with shorts, Gore-Tex, and velcro might feel out of place—best to pull out the white linen suit, Panama hat, and round wire-rimmed glasses or just a tasteful chemise. Entrees are expensive (around E£25), but a few of the *mezze* (appetizers, E£2-12) make a meal. Open daily 12:30pm-1am.

Balmoral Chinese Restaurant & Hotel, 157 July 26th St. (tel. 340 5473 or 0543 or 6761), at the corner of Ma'had as-Swissry St. Dimly-lit, serves Korean and Japanese food despite the name (E£14-23); some Chinese food too. Beware: some dishes are lethally spicy. Open daily 10am-11pm; closed the first Mon. of every month. U.S. dollars accepted. See Zamalek Accommodations, p. 90.

Hana Korean Restaurant, 21 Ma'had as-Swissry St. (tel. 340 1846), next to the En-Nil Zamalek Hotel. This small, charming restaurant serves a variety of Asian dishes, average price E£16. The *sukiyaki* (a do-it-yourself, stir-fry soup) and the *gimshi* (a cabbage concoction, E£15) are delicious. Open daily noon-11pm, closed the last Sunday of every month.

DOKKI

El Moardi, in one of the *oh là là* hotels, namely the Cairo Sheraton. For those who wish to sample Egyptian snacks but fear intestinal disarray and don't mind paying American-family-on-vacation prices, this is the answer. Falafel sandwiches (E£2), beef *shawerma* (E£5.50), and chicken *shawerma* E£7.50. Various pastries, and the biggest variety of juices on the planet (E£4). Pharaonic decor free of charge.

For a glimpse of the real Cairo, sit outside and enjoy a view of the crowded Giza bridge. Open daily 8am-1am.

■■■ SIGHTS

MODERN CAIRO

Cairo's sidewalks teem with thousands of people who seem to be intently going nowhere. Vendors bellow the virtues of their plastic baubles while overhead laundry flutters from the baroque remnants of colonial architecture. In the evenings, the latest kung-fu cinematic gem lets out every two hours and hundreds of film connoisseurs flood the streets, pastry shops, and *qahwas*. Despite the summer morning heat and the yearlong bustle, women will find it most comfortable to explore Cairo by day. For groups, the evening is the ideal time to meander through the city.

Acquaint yourself with Cairo's daily life at its **markets.** Some are known for a certain item; in larger markets like the one south of **Sayyida Zeinab,** each alley offers different wares. Bus #174 runs from Mugamma' Station in Tahrir Sq. to Sayyida Zeinab. Other major markets are located northeast of **'Ataba Square** and in **Bulaq** (from Tahrir Sq., walk east along Tahrir St. for 'Ataba Sq.; take bus #46 for Bulaq). **Bab el-Louq Market,** southeast of Tahrir, is renowned for cheap produce.

Cairo's two main islands merit short visits. Dominating **Zamalek** (also called Gezira or "the island") is the 187m **Cairo Tower (Burg El Qahira).** Early or late in the day, the view from the top of the tower is film-frying—you can see the Pyramids, the medieval citadel, and the Delta. For E£8 you can take the elevator to the observation deck. (Open daily 9am-midnight.) Settled only in the last century, Zamalek was once symbolic of Cairo's colonial society; currently its quiet streets house diplomats and the expatriate community. The southern third of the island is occupied by the Gezira Sporting Club, the ultimate symbol of British privilege until the 1952 Revolution. The club has become a focal point for upper class Cairene life. The one-block stretch around and along Hasan Sabri St. north of July 26th St. is lively; colorful shops, cafés, and grocery stores specializing in imported foods predominate. Just off the eastern end of the island stands the palatial **Cairo Marriott Hotel.** Built by Khedive Ismail to house foreign dignitaries and heads of state attending the Suez Canal opening ceremonies in 1869, the palace became a hotel in 1952 and is today considered one of the best luxury hotels in the world.

On the southern tip of **Roda Island** stands one of central Cairo's most noteworthy ancient monuments: the famous **Nilometer,** designed to measure the height of the river and thereby predict the yield of the annual harvest. The structure dates from the 8th century BCE, though it was restored and the conical dome added under Muhammad Ali's reign. The steps descend into a paved pit well below the level of the Nile, culminating at the graduated column that marks the height of the river. The entrance to the Nilometer is often locked, but if you express interest, one of the local children will pester the custodian who lives nearby (admission E£3). Since the Nilometer lies quite far south, visit it when you tour Old Cairo. At the northern end of the island, near the Meridien Hotel, stands the wacky **Manial Palace Museum** (See Museums, p. 109, for details).

Walking west across the island from the palace and over the Giza Bridge, you'll reach a lush section of the neighborhood of **Giza.** Straight ahead, at the end of the broad boulevard, lies the handsome campus of **Cairo University.** Along the boulevard to the north stretches **El-Urman Garden** (Botanical Gardens), the best place in town to toss a frisbee or vegetate with a shady tree. (Open daily 8:30am-5pm in summer, 8am-4pm in winter. Admission 50pt. Camera privileges 50pt.) Along the full length of the boulevard to the south and facing the botanical gardens is the **Cairo Zoo,** once considered the finest in the world. Alas, today it is a forum for toddlers tormenting mangy farm animals. Extensive chicken and pigeon collections. (Open daily 6am-5pm; "crowded" is an understatement on Fri. Admission 10pt, reptile house and "special collections" each 20pt extra. Tip a zookeeper and he'll make a camel eat off your head. If you time the photo well, it looks like a camel kiss.)

Heliopolis, in northeastern Cairo, was one of the most ambitious urban projects undertaken during the British colonial period of the late 19th and early 20th centuries. The architecture in this district is a strange agglutination of styles; in places an Islamic façade will hide a Western structure. Among the best examples of this are the Palace of Prince Hussein, the Palace of Prince Ibrahim, the Palace of the Sultana, and the arcades on Abbas Boulevard. The most outrageous example of imported architecture is the **Palace of Empain.** Known locally as "Le Baron" and closed to the public because of its funny tendency to fall apart, the palace is a replica of a Hindu temple complete with an electrically controlled rotating tower that allowed Empain to follow the sun through the day. To reach Heliopolis from Tahrir Sq., take bus #400 or 500, or take a taxi (E£6).

A colorful attraction is the **camel market** at Imbaba, north of Mohandiseen on the western side of the river. The largest of its kind in the country, the market is held every Friday from 5am to 3pm but is reputedly most fun from 7 to 9am. A few of the camels come from the Western Desert, but most of the pitifully lean beasts have trekked all the way from Sudan—a 30-day march to Aswan followed by a 24-hour truck ride to Cairo. If you're lucky, you'll witness violent arguing, escaping merchandise running precariously on three legs (the fourth is bound so as to prevent just this occurrence), and an occasional goat slaughter. For about E£2200-2500 you can ride off on one of the happy hostages—a small price to pay to surprise the loved ones back home. To reach the market, take bus #172 or 175 from 'Ataba Sq. or #99 from the Nile Hilton to Imbaba (which requires a 10-min. walk upon arrival), or catch a cab (E£5). When the market winds down, traffic along the boulevards of Mohandiseen comes to a standstill as livestock are herded along. (Admission E£1.50.) The area itself was the site of the 1798 Battle of the Pyramids between Napoleon's forces and the Mamluks. Imbaba was a village until the 70s, when it exploded into one of Cairo's largest and poorest slums.

ISLAMIC CAIRO

Cairo's medieval district is home to resplendent mosques and monuments which are touted as some of the finest Islamic architecture in the world. Unlike Damascus and Baghdad, the two other Middle Eastern capitals of the medieval Islamic world, Cairo was spared the devastation of Mongol invasions. But the monuments are only one aspect of life here—once the unrivaled cultural and intellectual center of the Arab world, Islamic Cairo is now a crowded, poverty-plagued neighborhood whose narrow streets will simultaneously dazzle and offend your senses. Don't be too put off by the dirt and sewage; beneath the Muslim city's dingy exterior lies a wealth of ornate friezes, Arabesque stucco, finely-carved wooden grillwork, and vaulted and domed interiors. Countless minarets serve as observation decks and afford a view of Cairo's splendor. Many of the monuments mentioned are undergoing an eternal renovation; you will find your goodwill towards posterity ebbing away as mosque after mosque is swathed in scaffolding or obscured by a cloud of cement dust. Press on regardless—you can often visit anyway.

It takes at least two days to explore this area of Cairo. For best results, start one day in Southern Islamic Cairo and proceed to the Citadel and central Islamic Cairo; leave El Muizz St., Khan el-Khalili, and the northern walls for another day. You will still be rushed. Pick up Parker and Sabin's *A Practical Guide to Islamic Monuments in Cairo,* which includes superb maps (E£50). Also worthwhile is *The Beauty of Cairo,* by G. Freeman-Grenville, a shorter and more concise guide. A set of two detailed maps of Islamic Cairo is published by SPARE (Society for the Preservation of Architectural Resources in Egypt). By far the best maps to have with you are those of the Islamic Monuments on pages 27-32 of *Cairo A-Z* (E£10.80). Most available at the AUC bookstore.

Many of the important monuments charge admission (50% student discount with proper ID). In sights that don't charge, and mosques in particular, you will still be expected to give *bakhsheesh*. Caretakers will often serve as tour guides; for ordinary assistance, offer about 50pt. If a door is unlocked for you, or if you're shown around in detail, E£1 is appropriate. When visiting smaller monuments or when trying to see the interiors of tombs, don't be bashful about hunting down the custodian. Opening hours are estimates at best, so declare your interest to whomever is around and usually the caretaker will magically swish into being. If you confine your tour of Islamic Cairo to unlocked doors, you'll miss many of the city's treasures.

Visitors must dress modestly in Islamic Cairo; revealing clothing will attract a great deal of unsolicited and unfriendly attention and will prevent admission to many mosques. In some cases head coverings are required (these can usually be rented for a few piasters). In some mosques (such as Muhammad Ali) an entire toga is provided for 50pt (modish, modest, and mint-colored). Sensible shoes are also a must and, since you may be asked to remove your shoes altogether, socks are a good idea.

Most mosques are open all day, but visitors are not welcome during prayer times. Wait a few minutes after the congregation has finished before entering. Avoid visiting mosques on Friday afternoons when the Muslim community gathers for afternoon prayer. Certain highly venerated mosques—Sayyidna Hussein, Sayyida Zeinab, and Sayyida Nafisa—are believed to contain the remains of descendants of Muhammad and are permanently closed to the non-Muslim public.

A wise way to start your tour is to walk to the mammoth south gate of Bab Zuweila at the intersection of Ed-Darb el-Ahmar St. and Es-Surugiyya St. Enter the Mosque of El Muayyad (the large portal inside on the left) and ask to be taken up to one of the two superstratic minarets atop Bab Zuweila. From there, try to match your two-dimensional map with the three-dimensional array by picking out the minarets and domes of the major monuments. If you wish to plunge straight into the fray, take bus #922 from Tahrir Sq. Alternatively, walk east from Opera Sq. (or 'Ataba Sq.) on Al Azhar St. Although Islamic Cairo begins at Port Said St., continue on Al Azhar St. about 400m to El Muizz ed-Din Allah, which runs north-south through the medieval city, connecting its northern and southern gates and providing an excellent place to begin your tour of the district. If you stand on the corner of El Muizz ed-Din Allah and Al Azhar, Bab el-Futuh will be to the north, Bab Zuweila to the south, and Al Azhar Mosque one block east.

Northern El Muizz Street

Between Al Azhar Mosque and Bab el-Futuh, El Muizz St. is lined with Fatimid and early Mamluk architectural attractions. This area is dubbed **Bayn el-Qasrayn,** Arabic for "between the two palaces," after the two Fatimid palaces. The area gives its name to a Naguib Mahfouz novel. El Gamaliya St. runs roughly parallel to El Muizz St., from Bab en-Nasr past the Mosque of El Hussein to the square in front of Al Azhar. Walk from Al Azhar up El Muizz St., through both Bab el-Futuh and Bab en-Nasr, and then return by way of El Gamaliya St. to minimize mileage. Proceed north on El Muizz St. from the intersection with Gohar el-Qa'id St., passing four little side streets on the right. You will see the **Tomb and Madrasa of Malik es-Salih Ayyub,** with its nearly square minaret. The *madrasa* has ornate keel-arched windows and the minaret crowns a passageway. El Malik es-Salih Ayyub, the last ruler of Salah ad-Din's Ayyubid Dynasty, was the husband of Shagarat ad-Durr, an indomitable Turkish slave who became ruler of Egypt, single-handedly engineering the succession of the Mamluk Dynasty after the death of her husband in 1249. Look for the custodian with the keys to the adjacent domed mosque recently restored by a German team.

Diagonally across the street from the gate stand the late 14th-century **Mausoleum, Madrasa,** and **Hospital of Qalawun** in a single complex. Mamluk sultan Qalawun sponsored the construction of these impressive edifices in 1384 before his death en route to attack the Crusader fortress in Akko. The façade is extensive and ornate and the windows Romanesque—no doubt Qalawun's architects were influenced by the Crusader architecture of the Levant. Three high *iwans* of the original *muristan* (mental hospital) remain. The ornate stucco work inside is original, though the undersides of the arches have been restored. To gain access to the mausoleum farther along, hunt down the guard, purchase a ticket, and unlock the door. The exquisite wood screen separating the tomb from the rectangular forecourt dates from the original construction. Before the 14th century, Egypt was the world's center for glasswork; many Cairo mosques have stained-glass windows, and this feature is exploited to no greater effect than at the mausoleum of Qalawun. This intricately embellished tomb caused quite a controversy because Islamic doctrine forbids displaying wealth at the time of burial; ostentatious tombs were frowned upon as vain. By the 11th century, however, the practice of building ornate tombs, especially for rulers, was not unusual; by the 13th century, lavish burial sites had become commonplace. (Complex open daily 8am-5pm. Admission E£3, students E£1.50.)

On the side street just north of Qalawun's mausoleum and tomb stands his son's, the **Mausoleum-Madrasa of En-Nasr Muhammad,** completed in 1304. En-Nasr Muhammad's 40-year reign marked the height of prosperity and stability in Egypt under Mamluk rule. The square minaret exhibits an exceptional, intricately carved stucco surface, but almost nothing of the interior remains. (Open 10am-8pm. Free.) Next door, to the north along El Muizz St., is the **Mosque of Sultan Barquq.** Barquq was the first Circassian Mamluk sultan and seized power through a series of heinous assassinations. His mosque was erected in 1386, a century after Qalawun's complex, and the difference in styles is striking. Barquq's minaret is slender and octagonal, and the high, monumental portal crowned by *muqarnas* gives it away as classic Mamluk architecture. The inner courtyard has four *iwans,* the largest and most elaborate of which doubles as a prayer hall. Its beautiful timber roof has been restored and painted in rich hues of blue and gold. Four porphyry columns, quarried in pharaonic times from the mountains near the Red Sea coast, support the colorful ceiling. The round disks of marble floor are slices of Greek and Roman columns, used because Egypt has no indigenous marble. (Open daily 8am-8pm. A shopkeeper opposite has appointed himself custodian, and tries to suck tourists dry. Insist on these prices: admission E£3, students E£1.50.)

El Muizz St. comes to a fork north of the Mosque of Barquq. Walk 25m down Darb Kermez St., the small sidestreet to the right of the fork, and you'll find all that remains of **Qasr Bishtak,** a lavish palace from the 14th century which originally stood five stories high. All floors of the palace had running water, a technological achievement unmatched in Europe for another 300 years and currently unmatched in many of Egypt's budget hotels. In the center of the fork is the slim 18th-century **Sabil Kuttab of Abd er-Rahman Kathuda.** The same villainous merchant from the mosque runs the racket at these two sights. Refuse to pay more than E£5 (students E£3) to see both together (open daily 8am-5pm).

Bear left at the fork and continue north along El Muizz St. to the next right-hand sidestreet. On the corner stands the small but architecturally important Fatimid **Mosque of El Aqmar.** Built in 1125, this was the first Cairene mosque to have a stone-façade-and-shell motif within the keel-arched niche. *El Aqmar* means "moonlit" and refers to the way the stone façade sparkles in the moonlight. The archway of the northern corner is typical of later Cairene architecture; the height of the cut is just about equal to that of a loaded camel, and the chink was intended to make the turn onto the side street easier for hump-laden creatures to negotiate. (Open 7:30am-9pm. Free.)

Proceeding north from El Aqmar Mosque, turn right on Ed-Darb el-Asfar (the next sidestreet on the right) and follow the winding alley about 50m. The doorway on the left marked with a small, green plaque is the entrance to Cairo's finest old house, the 16th-century **Beit es-Suheimi.** The *sheikh* of Al Azhar Mosque, Suheimi built this elaborate residence for himself and his various wives. The house sports carved wooden ceilings, stained-glass windows, tile mosaics, marble floors, and fountained salons. (Open daily 10am-5pm. Admission E£3, students E£1.50.) Walk along the same alley, away from El Muizz St., and you'll eventually come to El Gamaliya St. Across the street is the façade of the 14th-century *khanqah* (Sufi establishment) of **Baybars el-Gashankir.** Erected in 1310, this building is the oldest surviving example

SIGHTS: ISLAMIC CAIRO

of a *khanqah* in Cairo. From here, continue north on El Gamaliya St. until you pass through Bab an-Nasr.

Northern Walls

Islamic Cairo is bordered on the north by the extensive remains of the Fatimid walls, once vital for keeping out Mongol invaders. Built in 1087 CE, the colossal fortifications are the best surviving example of Islamic military architecture from pre-Crusader times. They did the trick; medieval Cairo was never besieged after their construction. Medieval Europe, which borrowed most of its knowledge of siege warfare and fortification technology from the Arab world, produced nothing comparable to these formidable walls.

Three of the rampart's original gates still stand. **Bab en-Nasr** (at the top of El Gamaliya St.) and **Bab el-Futuh** (at the northern end of El Muizz ad-Din Allah St. just in front of the El Hakim Mosque) are connected by a stretch of wall so thick it accommodates a tunnel; these walls once wrapped all the way around the Fatimid city to **Bab Zuweila.** The northern gates with domed roofs were constructed with stones plundered from the temple complex at neighboring ancient Heliopolis, as the hieroglyphics and reliefs on the interior walls indicate. Bab el-Futuh is flanked by two rounded towers, as is Bab Zuweila. Bab el-Futuh's unusual interior consists of a single large room connected by tunnel to the other gates. Although this arrangement subjected the soldiers to cramped living conditions, it was not without its advantages during popular uprisings; as late as the 19th century, when Napoleon conquered the city, the walls protected soldiers from hostilities both within and outside the city. You can still examine Napoleon's vandalism: the French names he ordered carved into the walls of each tower.

The Fatimid **El Hakim Mosque,** just inside the walls between the two gates (entrance off El Muizz St.), was built between 990 and 1010 and remains the second largest mosque in Cairo. El Hakim was known as the "Mad Caliph"; his unpredictable rages meant death to Christians, Jews, his enemies, his friends, and, on one occasion, all the dogs in Cairo. He was murdered soon after he announced that he was an incarnation of the Divinity. His chief theologian, Ad-Darazi, fled to Syria where he founded the Druze sect. The structure was recently restored (amid great controversy) by an Indian Isma'ili Shi'ite Muslim sect. Rather than restoring the mosque according to its original appearance, they chose to curry it up with chandeliers and a day-glo *mihrab,* outraging many art historians and Islamic experts. (Open daily 8am-8pm. Admission E£3, students E£1.50.)

Al Azhar and Khan el-Khalili

The oldest university in the world and the foremost Islamic theological center, the **Mosque of Al Azhar** stands just a few steps from the midpoint of Al Muizz St. at the end of Al Azhar St., facing the large square. **Al Azhar University** was established in 972 CE by the Shi'ite Fatimids and rose to preeminence in the 15th century as a center for the study of Qur'anic law and doctrine, a position it still holds. Ironically, the emphasis today is on Sunni learning. The mosque has been extensively restored. To reach the central court, enter through the double arched gate and pass under the minaret of Qaytbay (1469). The stucco decoration of the courtyard's façade is a reconstruction, but the *mihrab* in the central aisle is the real thing. The library, just left of the main entrance, holds over 80,000 manuscripts.

The theological curriculum has remained virtually unchanged since the Mamluk era, while physics and medicine are more recent arrivals. You can still see the traditional form of instruction, Socratic questioning with a professor seated in the center of a circle of students. For about 50pt the caretaker will allow you to climb one of the locked minarets for a fantastic view of the complex. Women without head coverings must don a long wrap provided at the entrance. (Open Sat.-Thurs. 9am-7pm, Fri. 9am-noon and 2-7pm. Admission E£6, students E£3.)

Across the street, 100m to the north of the main entrance to Al Azhar through El Hussein Sq., stands **Sayyidna el-Hussein,** Cairo's most venerated Muslim shrine, revered throughout the Islamic world as the resting place of the skull of Hussein, grandson of the prophet Muhammad. The head is rumored to have been transported to Cairo in a green silk bag in 1153, almost 500 years after the death of its owner in the battle of Karbala (in Iraq). The present edifice was built in the 1870s by the Khedive Ismail and is distinctly Turkish in style (note the pencil-like minarets). The interior includes green neon lights that glow with the name of Allah. Non-Muslims are not allowed to enter.

On **mawlids** (feast days), the president of Egypt traditionally comes to pray at Sayyidna el-Hussein while boisterous festivities take place in the large square. During Ramadan, this square is the best place to witness the breaking of the fast after evening prayers (about 8pm). Restaurants display their fare half an hour before prayers begin, and famished patrons stampede to the tables afterwards. After blood sugar levels return to normal, the square hosts a nightly celebration.

Behind Sayyidna el-Hussein stands the 18th-century **Musafirkhana Palace.** To reach the palace, walk north down El Gamaliya St. (toward Bab an-Nasr), passing four sidestreets on the left. At the fifth left-hand sidestreet, on the corner of which sits the small 14th-century **Mosque of Gamal ad-Din el-Ustadar,** turn right onto Darb at-Tablawi St. You will find the palace at the end of the street. Built during the Ottoman period in imitation of the Mamluk style, the Musafirkhana Palace served as the residence of the Egyptian royal family and state guests during the 19th and early 20th centuries. The Khedive Isma'il was born here, in the curious birth room. Another chamber saw the delivery of Mr. Mahmoud Badeer, who can now provide a comprehensive tour. The palace has been undergoing restoration since 1986. (Open daily 9am-4pm. Admission E£3, students E£1.50.)

Almost all streets south of the palace will lead you back to Al Azhar St. and Sayyidna el-Hussein. Head west from Sayyidna el-Hussein down any passageway and you will encounter the alleys of **Khan el-Khalili,** the largest tourist bazaar in Egypt and probably the best known Middle Eastern market world-wide. A *khan* was founded here in the 1380s by Garkas el-Khalili. His name stuck and came to represent the entire area, soon the commercial center of medieval Cairo. Stretching between Sayyidna el-Hussein and El Muizz St., the market is today extremely tourist-oriented. Mostly you will see the same leather floor cushions, slippers, and camels, *sheeshas,* sequined belly dancer suits, and paintings-on-papyrus sold in every store; but don't miss the dark shops crammed to the gills with beautiful mother-of-pearl- inlaid furniture. There is also high-quality gold and silver, as well as rugs and spices. Though the tacky souvenirs are often overpriced, the time-honored institution of bargaining still thrives. Be ferocious if you intend to strike a good deal. The farther you go from the heart of the market, the more authentic and locals-oriented the wares become. Even if you pass up the Pyramids paperweights, don't miss the lavish marble inlay on the Mamluk gates of Sultan el-Ghouri.

Vastly less tourist-ridden and less expensive is **El Muski,** the long bazaar where Egyptians shop for men's cologne, shoes, cloth, furniture, pillowcases, and food. El Muski stretches from El Muizz St. all the way to Port Said St., running parallel to and one block north of Al Azhar St. If you're walking between Islamic and downtown Cairo, El Muski offers the most picturesque route.

Southern El Muizz Street

During the Fatimid period, El Muizz St. was the main avenue of the city, running through the heart of Cairo and connecting the southern and northern entrances, Bab el-Futuh and Bab Zuweila. Today the street is a minor thoroughfare bisected by the much larger Al Azhar St. At the southern corners of the intersection of Al Azhar and El Muizz St. stand some impressive Mamluk structures. The **Madrasa of Sultan el-Ghouri** (1503) occupies the southwest corner. A custodian sporadically provides tours, complete with a climb to the roof and minaret (E£1 *bakhsheesh*). The long chains hanging in front of the *mihrab* were used to suspend glass lamps; today a marginally different effect is achieved with neon. The **mausoleum** across the road is now a theater, but if you flail limbs and speak in tongues, you might get hold of a caretaker to show you around (E£1 *bakhsheesh*).

The **Wakala of el-Ghouri** is easier to overlook. From the mausoleum, turn left onto Al Azhar St. then right (east) onto Sheikh Muhammad Abduh St. At #3 (on your right) you'll see the magnificently-preserved *wakala* (1505), now transformed into a center for handicrafts and folkloric arts (visitors with pretensions to art history should examine the quasi-cubist Cairo cityscapes of Muhammad I. Yousef). The courtyard is often used as a theater and concert hall. The structure originally served as a commercial hotel. (*Madrasa*, mausoleum, and *wakala* all open Sat.-Thurs. 8am-2pm and 4-10pm. Admission to all three is E£3, students E£1.50.)

Two blocks from the Madrasa el-Ghouri down El Muizz St. on the left is a small street on the left of which sits the **House of Gamal ed-Din**, a 16th-century mansion. Unhitch the latch and walk in, but be prepared to encounter the mentally unstable watchdog. The house is one of the most splendid of the surviving Ottoman residences in the city, with beautiful wooden ceilings and outstanding Turkish tiles. (Open 8am-5pm. Admission E£3, students E£1.50.)

Farther south along El Muizz St. on the left at the corner of Ahmed Maher St. is the entrance to the **Mosque of el-Muayyad,** built between 1415 and 1420. Strategically located at Bab Zuweila and the market area, it is the last of the great *al fresco* congregational mosques. Look for the two minarets towering atop the Fatimid gate, a stone-carved dome, and an imposing *muqarnas* portal. The interior has a pleasant garden, and the *qibla riwaq* is covered by an extensively restored ceiling. At the northern end of the *qibla* wall is the mausoleum of Sultan El Muayyad. The second mausoleum, at the other end of the wall, is an Ottoman addition. (Open 9am-8pm. Admission E£3, students E£1.50.)

Across the street from Bab Zuweila and to the right stands the **Zawiya of Sultan Faraj** (1408), a small rectangular structure. During the 19th century, execution by strangulation was carried out beside the railings outside. Access is difficult for non-Muslims. Opposite this structure, to the left across the street from Bab Zuweila, stands the small, elegant **Mosque of Salih Talai,** built in 1160. When the mosque was erected, the street was at the level of the series of shops standing behind the iron railing. The five keel arches form a remarkable projecting portal, unique in Cairo. The courtyard opens into a small *riwaq*. The custodian (who will expect *bakhsheesh*) will show you to the roof. (Open 8am-8pm.) Continuing south on El Muizz St. you enter a covered bazaar known as the **Street of Tentmakers,** followed a few blocks down by a similar covered alley called the **Street of Saddlemakers.** Turning left as you step out of Bab Zuweila, you'll find yourself on Darb el-Ahmar St. heading toward the Citadel. A right turn leads to Ahmed Maher St., lined with the shops of carpenters, tombstone-carvers, and metalworkers. The street leads out to Ahmed Maher Sq. on Port Said St., across from the Museum of Islamic Art.

The Citadel

Dominating Islamic Cairo, the lofty **Citadel** (*El Qal'a* in Arabic) was begun by Salah ad-Din in 1176 and has been continually expanded and modified since then, most notably by the Mamluks and Muhammad Ali. To reach the Citadel, take bus #82, 83, or 609 from Tahrir or #401 from 'Ataba Sq. or minibus #50 or 55 from 'Ataba Sq. To enter the Citadel complex, walk all the way to the far eastern side, following the road along the southern walls. Don't head for the mammoth western gateway of Bab el-Azab across from the Sultan Hasan Mosque—this entrance is locked and urine-stained. Enter instead through the eastern gate of Bab el-Qal'a. (Open Sat.-Thurs. 8am-6pm, Fri. 8am-noon, 2-6pm; winter Sat.-Thurs. 8am-5pm, Fri. 8-10am, noon-5pm; Ramadan 9am-4:30pm. Admission E£10, students E£5, includes all the museums and mosques.) The complex contains three mosques and four operating museums. To reach the **Mosque of Muhammad Ali,** head for the thin, unadorned Turkish minarets, the ones that look like pencils.

On the left as you enter the complex stands the less-than-arresting **Police Museum.** Enter to discover what marijuana looks like or to examine police uniforms through the ages. Before you reach the goliath Muhammad Ali Mosque, you will pass the oldest of the Citadel's three mosques (built 1337 CE). Pop into this green-domed construction to get a feel for the basic architectural principles that preceded the creation of the Citadel's magnum opus. Before the advent of the microphone, mosques were built to amplify and echo the readings of the Qur'an. A sharp eye will notice that one of the mosque's columns is not like the others. This white marble column, of a different shape, bears a Coptic cross at its head. It is not yet known from which Coptic church it was taken.

During his reign in the first half of the 19th century (1805-1848), Muhammad Ali laid the foundations of the modern Egyptian state, sparked the Europeanization of the country, introduced education in the arts and sciences, and paved the way for an independent dynasty. Muhammad Ali leveled the western surface of the Citadel, filling in the famous 13th-century Mamluk Qasr el-Ablaq palace that was there and building his mosque on top of it in 1830 as a reminder of Turkish dominion. Modeled after an Ottoman mosque in Istanbul, the edifice is more attractive from a distance; up close, its outline resembles a giant toad. The mosque was refurbished by the Department of Antiquities during the 1980s—its silver domes and marble-and-alabaster decorations now twinkle on the Cairo skyline. While popular with tourists and postcard makers, it is hated by art historians, who consider it a third-rate copy of the great Ottoman mosques in Istanbul and an obnoxious reminder of Muhammad Ali's ego. The interior, especially just after prayers when the large chandelier and tiny lanterns are lit, is quite impressive. The mosque, also called the Alabaster Mosque, is covered inside and out with the clearest alabaster, hauled over from Beni Suef. (One outer face remains bare; when Muhammad Ali died, so did the funding.)

The mosque consists of two parts: the **courtyard** and the **House of Prayer.** The attraction of the courtyard is a nameless, 17m-deep well whose underground cavity is as big as the courtyard itself; call down something polite, because it will echo for a good few minutes. The House of Prayer is lighted by a huge chandelier and 365 lanterns for the number of days in a year; it has five large domes and 15 smaller ones. Parisian decor splashes itself across these domes, as Muhammad Ali was a big fan of France. A charming and unexpected French gingerbread clock overlooks the court-yard; King Louis Philippe of France presented the clock in 1845 in appreciation of Muhammad Ali's gift of the obelisk from Luxor Temple that now stands in Place de la Concorde in Paris. Depending on how much you exude *bakhsheesh,* you may be able to enter the gaudy, gilt **Tomb of Muhammad Ali,** with its five human-sized sil-ver candlestick holders. The mosque is surrounded by shady, marble gazebos over-looking Cairo against a backdrop of the Sahara and the Pyramids of Giza.

To the south of the Muhammad Ali Mosque stand the remains of **Qasr el-Gowhara** (the Diamond Palace, named after one of Muhammad Ali's wives), also built by Muhammad Ali (1811). A 1974 fire destroyed half of the palace. The other half consists of a large reception room where Muhammad Ali received 500 of his Mamluk allies and cordially slaughtered them. The elaborate wooden benches next to the wall concealed the murder weapons in hidden compartments below the seats. Also on display are a few of the gold- and silver-adorned tapestry coverings of the Ka'ba; every year until 1961 Egypt presented such a work as a gift to Mecca.

Across from the entrance of the Muhammad Ali Mosque is the Mosque of Sultan En-Nasir Muhammad, one of the great Bahri Mamluk builders (1318-1335). He made major additions to the Citadel, but all of his works except for this mosque were later destroyed by Muhammad Ali. Unfortunately, the interior was largely gutted by Otto-man Sultan Selim the Grim, who made off with its marble panels. Just south of the mosque lies Yousef's Well, built by Crusader prisoners.

The **Military Museum,** just across the square from the Mosque of En-Nasir Muhammad, has a large collection of medieval weaponry and military paraphernalia but will bore all but the most crazed soldier of fortune; the only item of interest is the Chariot of Pharaoh Tutankhamun. Another trifle is the **Carriage (Hantour) Museum,** housing the carriages of the Muhammad Ali family.

Near the far eastern end of the northern enclosure is a lovely, small domed mosque known as the **Mosque of Suleiman Pasha,** the first Ottoman mosque in Cairo, built in 1527. If the ancient man with the *gallabiyya,* the limp, the surprising mastery of English, and the even more surprising blue eyes is still around, ask him to explain the tombs and the intriguing figures planted on them. (E£1 *bakhsheesh.*)

Central Islamic Cairo

The overwhelming **Mosque of Sultan Hasan,** considered the jewel of Mamluk architecture, is spurned by devotees of pharaonic art because many of its stones were exterior casing stones pilfered from the Pyramids at Giza. The mosque stands in Salah ad-Din Sq., facing the western gate of the Citadel. From downtown, take Muhammad Ali St. from the southern edge of 'Ataba Sq. and walk east for 2km. Bus #72 and minibus #54 run from Tahrir Sq. Strictly speaking, Sultan Hasan is not a mosque but a combination *madrasa* and mausoleum with an added prayer niche. The commodious interior courtyard belongs to the **Madrasa of Sultan Hasan** and is surrounded by four enormous vaulted *iwans,* each of which would have housed one of the four schools of judicial thought in Sunni Islam. Inside the main *iwan,* the *mihrab* is flanked by a pair of Crusader columns. On either side of the eastern *mihrab,* bronze doors open into the **Mausoleum of Sultan Hasan.** (Open Sat.-Thurs. 9am-5pm, Fri. 9-11am and 2-5pm. Admission E£6, students E£3.)

Directly across the street from the Sultan Hasan Mosque stands the enormous **Rifa'i Mosque** (1912). Though of little architectural or historical importance, its stupendous size and polished interior draw every tour group in Cairo. It is the resting place of many Egyptian monarchs and contains the tomb of the Shah of Iran. Both the Rifa'i and Sultan Hasan Mosques are illuminated at night. (Open Sat.-Fri. 8-11am and 2-6pm. Admission E£6, students E£3.)

The first street after the mosques if you proceed around the Salah ad-Din rotary in a clockwise fashion is Bab el-Wazir St. This street hugs the northwestern wall of the Citadel. Follow it until it breaks free of the wall and heads north a few blocks. There you'll find the 14th-century **Mosque of Aqsunqur,** commonly referred to as the Blue Mosque, owing to its blue faience-tiled interior. The tiles were imported from Damascus and added in 1652 by a Turkish governor homesick for Istanbul's grand tiled mosques. (Open daily 8am-6pm. Admission E£3, students E£1.50.) Turn right as you leave and continue up the same street; its name changes to Darb el-Ahmar (Red Way) in memory of Muhammad Ali's massacre of the Mamluk generals here.

Continue north along Darb al-Ahmar St.; at the corner where it veers to the left stands the simple and unobtrusive **Mosque of Qijmas el-Ishaqi.** Don't guffaw in derision at the unremarkable exterior; the light from the stained-glass windows transforms the marble and stucco inside. Under the prayer mats in the east *iwan* lies an ornate marble mosaic floor. As you step out, notice the grillwork of the *sabil* on your right and the carved stonework of the columns.

Southern Islamic Cairo

If you see only one mosque in Cairo, let it be the **Mosque of Ibn Tulun,** the largest, oldest (879 CE), and most sublime of the city's Islamic monuments. To reach the mosque, walk west along Saliba St. from Salah ad-Din Sq., by the western gate of the Citadel. A number of buses service this area: #72 or #174 from Tahrir Sq., #923 from Giza, #905 from the Pyramids, and minibus #54 from Tahrir. The vast, serene inner courtyard is surrounded by three rows of shaded colonnades. The courtyard covers almost seven acres and contains an inscription of elegant Kufic carved in sycamore wood that runs for over 2km.

Ibn Tulun, son of a Turkish slave, was sent to Egypt as governor of El Fustat in 868 and became governor of the entire province in 879. He declared independence from Baghdad and built a new royal city north of the original capital of El Fustat. The grand mosque is all that remains of the Tulinid City. The minaret, with its unusual external staircase, was probably built in the 13th century to resemble Ibn Tulun's original tower, which in turn was modeled after the minaret at the Great Mosque of

Samarra in Iraq. (Open 8am-6pm. Admission E£3, students E£1.50.) Don't mistake the mosque entrance with the *madrasa* and Mosque of Sarghatmish, which adjoins the northern side of Ibn Tulun; Sarghatmish is closed to non-Muslims.

On the right, as you step out of the main courtyard entrance, you will come upon the enchanting **Beit el-Kritiliyya** (House of the Cretan Woman), also called the **Gayer-Anderson House.** Once distinct buildings, these 16th- and 18th-century Turkish mansions were merged and elaborately refurbished in the 1930s by Major Gayer-Anderson, an English art collector. Today the mansions house a museum containing, among other exhibits, carved wooden *mashrabiyya* screens, which allowed women to see out of their homes without being visible from the streets. (Open daily 8am-3:30pm. Admission E£8, students E£4.)

If the Ibn Tulun Mosque is the boldest and most impressive of Cairo's Islamic monuments, then surely the **Madrasa of Qaytbay** is the most delightful and expressive. In a side street just west of Ibn Tulun, the mosque was built by Mamluk Sultan Qaytbay in 1475 as a theological college. The beautifully carved *minbar* and the intricate mosaic floor are two of the finest in Cairo. The caretaker will unlock it for *bakhsheesh.* (Open daily 9am-4pm. Admission E£3, students 1.50.)

OLD CAIRO

Some of Cairo's oldest architectural monuments are, appropriately enough, in the southern section of town known as Old Cairo. Nine hundred years before victorious Fatimids founded the city of El Qahira, the Roman fortress town of Babylon occupied the strategic apex of the Nile Delta just 5km south of the later city site. This outpost became a thriving metropolis during the 4th century CE, and a number of churches were built within the walls of the fortress. One of the rebuilt churches survives as a place of worship for the Coptic community.

Located outside the walls of the Islamic city, Old Cairo also became the center for Cairo's Jewish community. Although most of the Jewish population of the city left in 1949 and 1956, approximately 50 Jewish families still inhabit this quarter, worshiping at the ancient Ben-Ezra synagogue. In addition to a handful of beautiful and well-kept Coptic churches, Old Cairo possesses the excellent Coptic Museum.

The easiest way to reach Old Cairo is to take the Metro from Tahrir Sq. to Mar Girgis (30pt). Bus #92, 94, 134, and 140 also run from Tahrir Sq., stopping directly in front of the Mosque of Amr. If you take a taxi to the outskirts of Old Cairo (E£2-3), tell the driver you want to go to *Masr el-Qadima* or *Gam'at 'Amr.*

Coptic Cairo

Ancient Egypt invariably inspires images of towering pyramids, hieroglyphics, mummy cases slathered in jewels, and Cleopatra. Many view the pharaonic era as having shifted directly into the Islamic age of mosques, medieval fortifications, and integration into the Arab world. But for a transition period beginning in 30 BCE, Hellenistic culture and Christianity were the dominant forces in Egypt. In the first century CE, Christianity became a form of resisting Roman oppression, and continued in that status even after the Roman Empire adopted Christianity in the 4th century CE. Egyptian Christianity was spread by the agency of the Coptic Orthodox Church, which split off from the main body of the Christian Church in 451. Currently, some 4 to 5 million Egyptians are Copts. Most live in Cairo or in Middle Egypt. Also see Introduction to the Region: The Coptic Church, p. 46.

Located in the 19th-century Qasr ash-Shama, the **Coptic Museum** (tel. 363 9742 or 362 8766) houses the world's finest collection of Coptic art. With its tranquil courtyards and shaded, overpriced cafeteria, the museum offers a respite from the hullabaloo of Islamic Cairo. Halls are paved with spotless white marble and a host of elegantly carved wooden *mashrabiyya* screens cover the windows. An added attraction is the museum's location on the site of the ancient Roman fortress of Babylon. Compare an icon of the Virgin Mary suckling the Baby Jesus and a carving of the goddess Isis suckling her son, the sun-god Horus. All of the exhibits are excellent; the rarest and most inspiring is perhaps the collection of woodwork and frescoes, some dating to the 4th century. Also not to be missed are the Coptic textiles (located on the second floor). Next to these is displayed the Library of Gnostics, a collection of non-standard gospels (e.g., Thomas' gospel) from the 13th and 14th centuries, along with a few more Coptic texts from various periods. Some of these shine with intricate gold foil. The museum also displays a variety of architectural fragments brought from the sanctuary of St. Menas at Maryut and the monastery of St. Jeremiah at Saqqara, as well as illuminated manuscripts and numerous paintings, icons, and ivories. The labels on each exhibit do not provide excavation dates and are not exceedingly helpful (for example, "A man presented in a decorative manner, holding a symbol, perhaps a cross"). Bring another source of information with you or resign yourself to bumbling through, bereft of clue.

The museum is directly across from the Mar Girgis stop on the Metro. If you arrive by bus or shared taxi, you'll be let off just outside Old Cairo. Head directly south along the old subway tracks and the museum will be on your left. (Open Sat.-Thurs. 9am-4pm, Fri. 9am-1pm and 2-4pm; winter Sat.-Thurs. 9am-4pm, Fri. 9-11am and 1-4pm. Admission E£8, students E£4. Camera privileges E£10.)

In front of the museum stands Cairo's only substantial classical ruin. The imposing **Roman battlement** originally flanked the main entrance to the Fortress of Babylon. The fortress, built in the first century, overlooked the Nile before the river shifted west. This *castellum* extended over a full acre, and it took invading Muslims more than seven months to overpower the fortifications in the 7th century. The castle's only surviving tower formed part of a massive harbor quay in ancient times. A flight of stairs leads down to the foundation of the bastion, which is flooded with fetid slime, but visitors are not permitted to use the stairs.

Most of Cairo's Coptic churches are tucked away from the street, and the older structures possess simple entrances. Though none of the churches in Coptic Cairo charges admission, all contain donation boxes (E£1 for posterity, E£2 for penance). The caretaker may not approach you for *bakhsheesh*, but if you are shown a secluded chapel or crypt, a small tip (25pt) is in order. (Churches open daily, roughly 9am-4pm. Photography prohibited in all churches.)

Standing south of the Coptic Museum, the **Church of El Mu'allaqa** (The Hanging Church) was built suspended above the gate of Babylon Fortress, 13m above the ground. Known also as the Church of St. Mary and St. Dimiana, it is perhaps Coptic Cairo's loveliest church and the earliest known Christian site of worship in Egypt. The original building was erected at the end of the 3rd century CE, but repeated restoration has rendered the early structure virtually indiscernible. Enter El Mu'allaqa through the gateway in the wall just south of the museum. Pointed arches and colorful geometric patterns enliven the main nave; in the center, an elegant pulpit rests on 13 slender columns—one for Christ and each of his disciples. The conspicuous black marble symbolizes Judas. The pulpit is used only on Palm Sunday. The 12th-century ebony-and-ivory *iconostasis* is one of the finest in Coptic Cairo. The Hanging Church is ark-shaped, and its roof held up by eight pillars on each side of the church, one for every member of Noah's family. Because an altar can only administer the Liturgy once a day, this church contains seven (notice the ostrich eggs hanging above). Some of these altars are set off by a cedar wood altar screen. The screen is inlaid with pentagons and crosses of ebony and ivory—all of which are fit together without nails, like a jigsaw puzzle. In the chapel to the right you can sometimes see a carpenter making the intricate lattice.

El Mu'allaqa houses 110 icons. The icon of St. Mark was written with natural pigments in the 10th century; the colors remain impressively bright. The careful observer of the icon of St. Boktor will notice that the tormentor standing above him is striking him with the left hand, traditionally thought of as the weaker hand; Boktor is being tortured, not mercifully killed. The most mesmerizing of the icons is that of the Virgin with her baby son; the 8th-century eyes seem to follow you. This church holds a special place in the annals of Coptic belief, due to its congregation's involvement in the miracle of Mokattam Mountain. A troublesome caliph, so the story goes, picking on the biblical claim that those of faith can move mountains, proposed an ultimatum to Pope Ibra'am Ibn ez-Zar'a and the Coptic population: prove it or die. The congregation stayed to pray in this church three days and three nights. On the third day, each exalted *Kyrie eleison* (Lord have mercy), accompanied by a bow en masse, shook the earth and moved Mokattam a few inches. Coptic Orthodox Masses are held at El Mu'allaqa on Friday 8-11am and Sunday 7-10am. Modest attire is required at all times.

North of El Mu'allaqa on Mari Girgis St., past the museum, is the 6th-century Greek Orthodox **Church of Mari Girgis** (St. George), a wide, circular building erected over one of the towers of the Fortress of Babylon. Renovated on several occasions, the present structure preserves the circular plan that was once common in Middle Eastern churches. The icon-clad interior is illuminated by stained-glass windows and candles. (Open daily 8am-12:45pm and 2:30-5:15pm.)

To the left of St. George's Church on Mari Girgis St., a staircase descends into Old Cairo proper. After entering the city, the first main doorway on the left is marked with a tin plaque indicating the 14th-century **Convent of St. George.** The nuns here sometimes enact a traditional Coptic ritual of wrapping a person in chains to symbolize the persecution of St. George by the Romans. Venture farther into Old Cairo and continue to the end of the alley with the entrance to the convent. Bear right; directly ahead is Coptic Cairo's most renowned structure, the **Church of Abu Serga** (St. Sergius). A dwarfed archway leads off the main street into a narrow passage and the entrance to the church (across from the tourist bazaar). The church, dating from the 10th century, stands several feet below street level. Behind the left side of the *iconostasis,* a set of steps descends to a crypt where the Holy Family is believed to have rested on their journey into Egypt.

Leaving the Church of Abu Serga, turn right and head eastward to the end of the alley. Just to the left lies the cavernous **Church of St. Barbara** (pronounced bar-BAR-a), together with a Church of St. Cyrus and St. John dating from the Fatimid era. Legend holds that when the caliph discovered that both Christian churches were being restored, he ordered the architect to destroy one of them. Unable to choose, the architect paced back and forth between the two buildings until he died of exhaustion. Moved by this tragedy, the caliph allowed both churches to stand. The interior of the Church of St. Barbara closely resembles that of its restored neighbor. The bones of St. Barbara, who was killed by her father when she attempted to convert him, are said to rest in the tiny chapel accessible through a door to the right as you enter the church. The bones of Saint Catherine, namesake of the monastery on Mt. Sinai (see Saint Catherine's Monastery, p. 241), also reputedly lie here. An inlaid wooden *iconostasis* from the 13th century graces the church's ornate interior.

A few meters south of St. Barbara's, a shady garden luxuriates in front of the **Ben-Ezra Synagogue.** The temple that occupied the site in pre-Christian times was demolished in the first century CE to make room for construction of the Roman fortress. Later, a Christian church was built on the site; the building was transformed into the present synagogue in the 12th century. Distinctive Sephardic ornaments and a collection of manuscripts including 6th-century Torah scrolls have been removed until restoration is complete. Access to the interior remains unhampered by construction, however; walk in and admire the brilliantly detailed ceiling.

Fustat

Adjoining Coptic Cairo to the north are the partially excavated remains of Fustat, one of the oldest Islamic settlements and the capital of Egypt during its first 250 years as a Muslim state. The architectural remains of Fustat are insubstantial, and a stroll through the site reveals little more than traces of cisterns, drains, cesspits, and rubbish. In the northwest corner of the site, the **Mosque of Amr,** Egypt's first Islamic mosque, has been restored for use. In addition to architectural fragments, thousands of pieces of fine Islamic pottery and imported Chinese porcelain have been discovered here; they are currently displayed at the Islamic Museum. In the nearby **pottery district,** you can watch modern-day artisans at work.

To reach Fustat, take the Metro or a bus from downtown to the Mari Girgis station. Walk north along Mari Girgis St. for about five minutes until you see the Mosque of Amr on your right. Fustat sprawls over the large area behind the mosque. If you venture out to this district in the heat of summer, bring plenty of water. Also beware that the ground near the site is unstable in places.

Fustat was the name of a garrison town that some historians maintain comes from the Latin word for entrenchment, *fossatum*. A different account of the founding of Fustat holds that the conquering general Amr sent word to the caliph in Medina that the magnificent Roman port of Alexandria would be the perfect place for the capital of Egypt. To Amr's dismay, the caliph preferred to establish his outposts along desert trade routes and invulnerable to the naval attacks of seafaring Christians. The disappointed general returned to Babylon to find that a white dove had nested in his tent during his absence. Interpreting this as a divine omen, Amr founded the new capital of Egypt on the site of his tent, and dubbed it *El Fustat* (City of the Tent).

Credit for the construction of Egypt's first mosque goes to Amr himself, who made many lasting contributions to the nation. During his rule, the mosque served as the seat of government, the post office, caravansary, and the city's religious center. The huge, open square could accommodate nearly 12,000 worshipers (the size of Amr's army). Fustat later acquired a large treasury, numerous mansions, and elaborate plumbing and sewage systems, the likes of which were not seen in Europe until the 18th century. Fustat remained the capital of Egypt until the Fatimids established the neighboring city of Al Qahira in 969 CE. By the middle of the 12th century the Fatimid Dynasty was flailing; in 1168 Crusader King Amalric of Jerusalem invaded and fought the Fatimids near Cairo. During the battle, Fustat was burned to the ground to prevent it from falling into the hands of the Crusaders. Except for the great mosque, little survived of the city; by the end of the 14th century Fustat was virtually abandoned.

The present-day Mosque of Amr occupies the site of the original building of 642, which was barely one-fourth the size of the present edifice. The oldest portion of the mosque is its crumbling southeast minaret, added during the Turkish period. The mosque's 18th-century design includes a single, spacious courtyard lined on four sides by stately white marble columns, pilfered from local Roman and Byzantine buildings during medieval times. The mosque was entirely renovated in the mid-1980s. (Admission E£3, students E£1.50. Open 24 hrs.)

Near the Mosque of Amr is **Deir Abu Saffein,** a complex of three 8th-century Coptic churches. Walk straight down the street directly opposite the entrance to the mosque to its end (about 500m); the wooden entrance to the churches will be slightly behind you on your right. (Complex open 8am-5pm, but knock loudly to rouse the caretaker if no one is around.) The main attraction is the **Church of St. Mercurius Felopatir** (or the Church of Abu Saffein), dating from the 4th century but extensively restored during the Middle Ages. The cathedral contains 14 altars (most of which the modestly-dressed *bakhsheesh*-forker might be allowed to see), various relics of saints venerated in the Orthodox Church, several early icons, an elaborate gabled roof (another feat of cunning Coptic carpentry, unaided by any newfangled nail nonsense), and the original delicate ebony/ivory/cedar wood *hegab* or *iconostasis.* St. Mercurius Felopatir was a Roman Christian who assured his frazzled king that divine assistance would dispose of the annoying Barbars who were invading Rome; after victory, the king promptly beheaded Mercurius. He is called Abu Saffein (which means "two swords") because an angel gave him a heavenly cleaver to go with his military slicer. Against the wall on the northern side of the main chamber, the eyes of the Virgin Mary on a deerskin icon survey the church with a proprietary air. Next to her, an icon picturing St. Barsoum marks the entrance to a tiny vaulted crypt where the saint supposedly lived for 25 years with a cobra tamed by the Tamer on High. For 50pt the caretaker will let you descend into the small, dusty burial chamber. Mass is celebrated in the crypt on September 10 to honor St. Barsoum's feast day. If the *bawwab* (caretaker or custodian) is in a good mood (E£3-4 usually lifts his spirits), he'll take you upstairs to see the ancient, tiny Churches of St.

George of Rome, St. John the Baptist, and the 144,000 Martyrs, all of which were rediscovered when the plaster was accidentally chipped away to reveal icons and icons-beneath-icons.

Next door is the late 4th-century **Church of St. Shenouda,** one of the most famous Coptic saints. This chapel (undergoing repairs but accessible in summer 1994) contains two fine *iconostases*—one of red cedar and the other of ebony—and seven altars. The smallest of the three main structures at Deir Abu Saffein is the early 8th-century **Church of the Holy Virgin,** a tiny one-room chapel crammed with icons and small paintings. The *odass* (liturgy) is celebrated in these churches Sun. 6-10am, Wed. 8am-noon, and Fri. 7-11am.

If you leave Old Cairo and head north by bus or taxi you'll pass the impressively preserved 14th-century **aqueduct,** erected by Sultan an-Nasir Muhammad to transport water from the Nile to the Citadel.

CITIES OF THE DEAD

The Cities of the Dead teem with life, if you know where to look. The area to the northeast and south of the Citadel contains hundreds of tombs and mausolea erected since the Mamluk era—hence the name. But, doubling as a shanty town, the area is home to hundreds of thousands of Cairenes. The modern residents of the medieval necropoli dwell amidst the funerary architecture, and many households have even incorporated the grave markers into their houses and yards. Tombs serve as clotheslines, soccer goals, and public benches. On Fridays they swarm with visitors arriving to pay their respects to the deceased. Many of the grave plots are enclosed by walls, encompassing an adjoining chamber and small house where families pray for their dead relatives on holy days. The Egyptian custom of picnicking at the family tomb on feast days may be an ancient holdover from pharaonic times, when the corpse was believed to require nourishment to ensure good health in the afterlife. Visitors are not permitted in the mosques on Fridays or during prayers. Many areas of the necropoli are uninhabited: don't be surprised if you turn a corner and find yourself alone with five apparitions.

Mamluk sultans spared no expense in the construction of their final resting places. Elaborate tomb complexes, fashioned with domed mausolea, mosques, and adjoining *madrasas,* were erected for Cairo's rulers. Gravestones built for the families of Mamluk nobles vary widely; cenotaphs of all shapes and sizes dot the crowded thoroughfares of the royal necropoli.

The **Northern Cemetery,** northeast of the Citadel, is characterized by wide boulevards and courtyards. It contains the finer monuments of the two necropoli, with structures dating from the later Mamluk period (14th-16th centuries) to this century. A visit to the Northern Cemetery is best tacked onto a tour of Islamic Cairo. Follow Al Azhar St. due east, around the north side of Al Azhar Mosque, over a slight hill to the six-lane Salah Salem St. Cross this deathtrap and enter the cemetery on the green overpass (covered with Coca-Cola ads) about 250m to the north. Bus #176 from 'Ataba Sq. terminates just in front of the Mausoleum of Barquq. Also, bus #77 or 904 from Tahrir Sq. will take you to the vicinity. The **Southern Cemetery** is a far more crowded necropolis, housing Ayyubid mausolea and the oldest Mamluk tombs (12th-14th centuries). The Southern Cemetery is accessible by foot from Ibn Tulun, the Sultan Hasan Mosque, or the Citadel. Bus #82 or 182 or minibus #54 from Tahrir Sq., or bus #85 from 'Ataba Sq., can also take you there (get off at Imani Station). From Ibn Tulun or Sultan Hasan, proceed east to Salah ad-Din Sq., just southeast of the Citadel. From here, head directly south following the southern slope of the Citadel. When you reach the traffic circle, walk under the overpass and take the right-hand fork, El Qdiriyya St., which becomes Imam esh-Shafi'i St., the main thoroughfare in the cemetery.

Graveyard groupies visiting either cemetery will successfully avoid the fragrant crowds that waft together at the Pyramids or the Citadel, but the empty streets here can be unsettling, especially for women alone.

Northern Cemetery

At the northern end of the cemetery, the imposing **Mausoleum of Barquq,** easily identified by its matching pair of ornately sculpted minarets, is a good place to start your tour. Built in 1400 for Sultan Barquq by his son, this enormous family plot encompasses an inner courtyard. The *minbar* beneath the western arcade was donated to the mausoleum by the Mamluk ruler Qaytbay. The smaller, central peak covers the thickly decorated *minbar,* while two matching zig-zag domes—the earliest stone domes in Cairo—shelter the family mausolea located in either corner. Sultan Barquq is interred below the northeast corner of the complex, and the remains of his two daughters occupy the chamber beneath the southeast dome. For a little *bakhsheesh,* the caretaker will show you around the mausolea and let you climb the minaret. In the northeast corner of the complex, the second story holds the remains of a large *kuttab* (Islamic school for orphans) and numerous monastic cells that once housed Sufi mystics. (Open daily 9am-8pm. Admission, excluding the tomb chambers and minaret, E£3, students E£1.50.)

Just around the corner to the southwest in front of the Mausoleum of Barquq stands the **Tomb of Barsbay el-Bagasi.** Built in 1456, the tomb is decorated with an intricate geometrical design resembling a tulip, a variation on the Moroccan motif of *dari w ktaf* (cheek and shoulder). The nearby **Tomb of Amir Suleiman** was built about 90 years later; its dome is decorated with a series of zig-zag stripes.

The **Mosque** and **Mausoleum of Sultan Ashraf Barsbay** are 50m south of the mausoleum of Barquq, along the cemetery's main thoroughfare. Originally intended as a *khanqah* (Sufi establishment), the 15th-century mosque has meticulously fashioned marble mosaic floors; lift the protective prayer mats to see the colorful tilework. Adjoining the mosque to the north is the mausoleum, a domed chamber containing a white marble cenotaph, an elaborately decorated *mihrab,* and gleaming mother-of-pearl and marble mosaics. (Open daily 9am-9:30pm. Free.)

Follow the same road south to reach the 15th-century **Mausoleum of Qaytbay,** the cemetery's most celebrated structure. Approach through the open square for the best view of the façade's polychrome-striped brickwork, recognizable from the art on the Egyptian one-pound note. Qaytbay was a Mamluk slave who rose through the ranks of the army to become leader of Egypt during the closing decades of the 15th century. Reigning for 28 years—longer than any other Mamluk except En-Nasir Muhammad—he was a ruthless sultan with a soft spot for beautiful buildings. Enter the complex through the northern doorway, passing through a rectangular sanctuary. The mausoleum proper is a spacious, domed chamber housing the marble cenotaphs of Qaytbay and his two younger sisters. Also in the tomb chamber are two black stones bearing footprints said to be those of the Prophet Muhammad. (Open daily 9am-9:30pm. Admission E£3, students E£1.50.)

South of the Mausoleum of Qaytbay are two 14th-century monuments constructed for members of the royalty. To reach them, follow the main road south of the mausoleum through the **Gate of Qaytbay,** a stone archway that once guarded the entrance to the tomb complex. When this thoroughfare intersects with a paved road, turn right and head west toward Salah Salem St. Just beyond the next main street (Sultan Ahmed St.) are the remains of the **Tomb of Umm Anuk** (1348), a ribbed dome adjoining a sweeping pointed archway. Umm Anuk was the favorite wife of Sultan En-Nasir Muhammad, and her devoted husband presented her with an appropriately lavish tomb. He also constructed the **Tomb of Princess Tolbay** across the way for his principal wife. Muslim law required him to treat the two women equally, but the sultan apparently obeyed only the word and not the spirit of Qur'anic law: judging from the inferior work of the second tomb, it's clear who received the sultan's genuine affections.

Sultan Ahmed St. leads you north to the Mausoleum of Barquq and the #167 bus. Or make your getaway on foot by heading west to the overpass and Al Azhar St.

Southern Cemetery

The Southern Cemetery's most impressive edifice is the celebrated **Mausoleum of Imam Esh-Shafi'i.** The largest Islamic mortuary chamber in Egypt, the mausoleum was erected in 1211 by Salah ad-Din's brother and successor in honor of the great Imam Ash-Shafi'i, founder of one of the four schools of judicial thought of Sunni Islam. In 1178, Salah ad-Din had built a large cenotaph over the grave of Imam Shafi'i, which is currently housed within the 13th-century mausoleum and often crowded with Muslims offering prayers. In the center of the mausoleum is the teak cenotaph of the Imam, one of the finest surviving pieces of Ayyubid wood carving. In addition to the tomb chamber, the complex contains two mosques, one dating from 1190, the other from 1763. The older mosque is closed to non-Muslims. The newer one, open to all, remains a vital center of worship. (Open daily 6am-7pm. Free, but 25pt *bakhsheesh* appropriate.)

The **Mosque of Sayyida Nafisa,** Egypt's third-holiest Islamic shrine, stands on the western edge of the Southern Cemetery not far from Es-Sultaniyya. One of Cairo's three congregational mosques, Sayyida Nafisa is a center of Islamic worship and hence closed to non-Muslims. To reach the mosque, go to the main intersection southeast of the Citadel and follow Salah Salem St. alongside the 12th-century **Wall of Salah ad-Din** in a southwesterly direction. When the cemetery opens up below and right, you'll see Sayyida Nafisa's tall single minaret and ornate dome ahead and to the right. Plunge down among the graves, keeping the minaret in sight, and weave through the maze of tombs to the mosque. Sayyida Nafisa, the great grand-daughter of Hasan, a grandson of the Prophet, was venerated during her lifetime. After her death in 824, her tomb attracted droves of pilgrims. By the 10th century, the original structure proved too small to contain the multitudes of worshipers, necessitating the construction of successively larger mosques. The present structure dates from the 19th century. So many mausolea were erected in the immediate vicinity of Sayyida Nafisa's tomb that historians suspect the construction of this sacred shrine alone sparked the development of the Southern Cemetery. On Fridays, crowds converge on the mosque.

Adjoining the Mosque of Sayyida Nafisa on the eastern side are the 13th-century **Tombs of Abbassid Caliphs.** At the peak of their authority, the Abbassid caliphs ruled the entire Muslim world (except for Spain) from Baghdad. The last reigning caliph fled Baghdad in 1258 after invading Mongols toppled the regime. The Mamluk sultan welcomed him upon his arrival in Egypt and went so far as to exalt the deposed caliph in an effort to legitimize his own sinecure. Subsequent Mamluk rulers continued to harbor a succession of caliphs, all the while preventing them from gaining any real power. Finally, the sultan in Istanbul declared himself caliph in 1517, thereby consolidating the authority of the Ottoman Sultanate. With Egypt under Ottoman rule, it was impossible for the regional government to protest the abolition of their local charade of religious authority. Though the Abbassid caliphs have been deposed, their succession continues to the present day, and members of the family are still buried within the walls of the 13th-century mausoleum. Inside are wooden cenotaphs marking the graves of the caliphs. You will have to ask for the caretaker to come unlock the gates (E£1 *bakhsheesh*).

From the square in front of Sayyida Nafisa, turn right along El Khalipha St. to find the **Shrine of Sayyida Ruqaya** (1160), whose father, Ali, was husband of the Prophet's daughter Fatima and the central figure in Shi'i Islam.

Across the street lies the **Tomb of Shagarat ed-Durr,** the most recent Ayyubid building in Cairo (1250) and the burial place of a politically prominent Muslim woman. Shajarat ed-Durr (Arabic for "Tree of Pearls") was a slave who rose to power after marrying Es-Salih Ayyub, the final ruling member of Salah ad-Din's Ayyubid Dynasty. She concealed the Sultan's death in 1249 for three months until her son returned from Mesopotamia to claim the throne; the wily queen, realizing that her frail son would never muster the authority to command a following among Mamluk slave troops, promptly engineered his murder. Proclaiming herself Queen, Shajarat ed-Durr governed for 80 days until she married the leader of the Mamluk forces. The renegade couple managed to consolidate power over the next several years, but their happy rule ended when the queen discovered that her new husband was considering a second marriage and had him murdered. Not to be outdone, the prospective second wife avenged the death of her lover by beating Shajarat ad-Durr to death with a pair of wooden clogs and then hurling her body from the top of the Citadel, leaving it to the jackals and dogs.

If you turn left at the small market square beyond the tomb, you will reach the Mosque of Ibn Tulun; or, carry on straight until the next big street. A right turn here will return you to the Citadel and the Mosque of Sultan Hassan.

MUSEUMS

Egyptian Museum

The **Egyptian Museum,** the world's unrivaled warehouse of pharaonic treasures, stands in Tahrir Sq. The most conspicuous displays in the museum are not always the most interesting; try not to overlook smaller rooms tucked away in various niches around the museum. Sadat closed the famed mummy room in 1981 because the display was offensive to some Islamist groups, and the reopening of the room was delayed because the mummies have since decomposed and are now offensive to just about everyone. If all goes well, the mummies will soon be placed in a completed, better-equipped New Egyptian Museum.

In the small glass case opposite the entrance, the **Narmer Palette** commemorates the unification of Egypt in about 3100 BCE by King Narmer of the First Dynasty. Some believe that King Narmer was actually an incarnation of Menes, the mythical founder of united Egypt. From here, the corridors and rooms leading around the central domed court present a chronological sampling of pharaonic art from the Old Kingdom to the Greco-Roman period.

The unusually well-preserved paint on the statues of Prince Rahotep and his wife Nofret (room #32) expresses the extraordinary realism of these funerary statues sculpted 47 centuries ago. Nearby stands the world's oldest extant magnitudinous metal statue, depicting King Pepi I of the 4th Dynasty. The statue was fashioned by beating heated metal sheets around a wooden core.

Proceed to the **Akhenaton room** (#3) at the rear of the first floor, to see statues of the heretical pharaoh who introduced a form of monotheism. He worshiped Aton as the sun god and source of life, representing him as a disk with rays that ended in hands, sometimes holding *ankhs,* the Egyptian symbol for life. Akhenaton also venerated Maat, who was rather indelicately manifested as "truth in artwork."

Of all the collections in the museum, the cornucopia from **Tutankhamun's tomb** is surely the best-displayed and most popular. Originally squeezed into less than 100 cubic meters, the treasures now occupy an entire quarter of the second floor. The eastern corridor contains decorated furniture, golden statues, delicate alabaster lamps, weapons, amulets, fossilized undergarments, and other bare necessities for a King of the Underground. Room #4, the most magnificent of all, flaunts the famous coffins and funeral masks, as well as a mind-occluding collection of amulets, scarabs, and jewelry. Also displayed is a pair of gilded sandals and a knife with an iron blade, a rarity for the times and thus one of the king's prized possessions.

When your eyes become gold-plated, head to the rooms off the corridor toward the center of the building. Room #43, off the eastern hall, holds a collection of toys, tools, weapons, and household items that reveal how people lived and artisans worked thousands of years ago. Animal rights activists would be proud to see Room #53, where mummified cats, dogs, birds, and monkeys repose in honor. (Observe the spotted owls.) On the northern hall, Room #3 is studded with dazzling jewelry from all periods of dynastic history. Room #12, around the corner on the western hallway, holds funerary items from later royal tombs, including an amusing assortment of bushy wigs worn by priests in the Late Period. During the Old Kingdom, servants were buried alive to care for the king in the afterlife, but eventually the Egyptians decided that clay figurines were more willing and jovial companions for the deceased. (Museum open Sat.-Thurs. 9am-5pm, Fri. 9am-noon and 2-5pm; during Ramadan Sat.-Thurs. 9am-4pm, Fri. 9am-noon and 2-4 pm. Admission E£10, students E£5. Camera privileges E£10.)

Other Museums

The Museum of Islamic Art, off Ahmed Maher Sq. at the corner of Port Said and Muhammad Ali St., about 500m west of Bab Zuweila; easily incorporated into a trip to Islamic monuments. From Tahrir Sq., walk east down Tahrir St. to Ahmed Maher Sq. on Port Said St. at the edge of Islamic Cairo. One of the world's finest collections of Islamic art. There's a little of everything, including carpets, glassware, metalwork, wood carvings, calligraphy, and pottery. Usually quiet and uncrowded. One exhibit shows ancient scientific and philosophical manuscripts. Open Sat.-Thurs. 8am-4pm, Fri. 9-11am and 1-4pm. Admission E£8, students E£4.

The Mahmud Khalil Museum, 1 Sheikh Marsafy St., Zamalek. Opposite the north gate of Gezira Sporting Club, across from the Marriott Hotel. Contains a fantastic collection of European and Islamic art, including works by Monet, Renoir, Van Gogh, Pisarro, Toulouse-Lautrec, Degas, and Rubens, as well as beautiful Chinese jade carvings and Islamic pottery and tiling. Open Sat.-Thurs. 9am-2pm. Admission E£2, students E£1. Passport or other ID usually required for admission.

The Museum of Modern Art, Gezira St., Zamalek, near the Cairo Opera House. Features Egyptian paintings 1940s-present. Open Sat.-Thurs. 10am-2pm. Admission E£1, students 50pt.

The Mukhtar Museum, just before El Galaa Bridge, Zamalek (Gezira). Built by Ramses Wissa Wassef. Houses the works of sculptor Mahmoud Mukhtar (1891-1934). Open Sat.-Thurs. 9am-1:30pm, Fri. 9-11:30am. Admission E£2, students E£1.

Museum of Egyptian Civilization (tel. 340 6259), next to the Gezira Museum. Traces Egypt's development through its Pharaonic, Greek, Roman, Coptic, and Islamic periods. Open daily 10am-2pm. Admission E£1, students 50pt.

Mugamma' el-Funun (Center of Arts, tel. 340 8211), on the corner of Ma'had es-Swissry St. and July 26th Bridge. Formerly the residence of Aisha Fahmy, today the center has rotating exhibits by Egyptian and foreign artists. Open mid-Sept. through mid-July Sat.-Thurs. 10am-1:30pm and 10am-2pm. Free.

The Agricultural Museum, at the western end of the October 6 Bridge, Dokki, behind a large garden. Exhibits on Egyptian agriculture. Also on display is the only remaining mummified Apis bull from the Serapium at Saqqara. Open Sat.-Thurs. 10am-2pm, Fri. 10am-noon. Admission E£1, students 50pt.

The Manial Palace Museum (tel. 98 74 95) at the northern edge of Roda Island; the entrance is next to the Cairo Youth Hostel on Sayala St., which leads to Cairo University Bridge. Built by Muhammad Ali in the last century. Visitors have access to the "reception palace," a private mosque, a residential palace, a throne room, and a fascinating collection of Islamic art. In the hunting museum, tucked away among other taxidermic treasures, lurks a beautiful table made from an elephant's ear. Also has an enthralling collection of Islamic furnishings. Open Sat.-Thurs. 9am-4pm, Fri. 9am-1pm and 2pm-4pm. Admission E£5, students E£2.50.

Wax Museum, take the Metro to Ain Helwan, museum is 25m from the station. Replete with stiff portrayals of Egyptian history and assorted executions, disembowelments, and suicides. Open daily 9am-4pm. Admission E£1.

■■■ ENTERTAINMENT

If a full day of Cairo hasn't flattened you, venture out for Cairene nightlife. The daily English-language newspaper, *The Egyptian Gazette,* lists entertainment and events. *Cairo by Night,* a free weekly periodical available in hotels, occasionally has useful information for the diurnally-challenged, and *Cairo Today,* a monthly magazine sold at newsstands, runs articles on attractions in the metropolitan area. *Cairoscope,* a guide to "culture and entertainment" in Cairo, lists foreign films, musical performances, and art exhibits; it's available at newsstands and major hotels. Women will want to restrict themselves to the more expensive bars and discos, such as those in the major hotels. If you brave the Egyptian haunts, the byword is sleaze—lecherous old men ogle tubby dancers in seedy clubs.

The **sound and light show** at the Giza Pyramids is overrated and overpriced. At 8:30 and 9:30pm (6:30 and 7:30pm in winter), the three Pyramids are illuminated while the story of the ancient pharaohs is narrated by the Sphinx in Arabic, English, French, German, or Italian (check *Cairo Today* or call 385 2880 for schedule). The Sphinx's chagrined expression suggests it wishes it could get the rest of its head shot off. Tickets go on sale at 6pm for E£18 (E£12 for students); in busy times, arrive early. (English shows Mon. and Wed.-Sat. For added surrealism, go on foreign language night—*"Ich bin der Sphinx!"*). See Giza for details on how the get there.

QAHWAS AND PASTRY SHOPS

Cairenes' favorite pastime is passing time, catching up on politics and gossip with friends and family members over a cup of tea or coffee. In headier days, revolutionaries used to plot around café tables. Businessfolk and peddlers share tables in *qahwas* playing backgammon, drinking tea or Turkish coffee, and smoking *sheeshas* for hours at a time. You can find a *qahwa* on almost any street corner east of the Nile. Foreign men are usually welcome. Although Egyptian women are not seen within miles of a café table, foreign women should feel free to enter if they can stand lecherous stares and occassional harassment. There are Western-style cafés as well, where all should feel comfortable.

Pastries and *sheeshas* don't mix; sugar-starved travelers can fulfill their wildest honey-soaked dreams over the counter in pastry shops or at more westernized cafés. Select the *délice* nearest your heart, pay for it, and sit down. You can order drinks at your table.

Fishawi's Khan el-Khalili (tel. 90 67 55), 4 doors down from El Hussein Hotel, in the same alley. The home of the most famous coffee in Egypt, est. 1752. This traditional tea-house in the heart of the old bazaar is nicknamed Café des Miroirs. Furnished in 19th-century European style with dainty, hammered brass tables. Enjoy the atmosphere with a pot of mint tea (75pt). Let the aroma of the *sheesha* lull you into a tobacco trance (E£1). Open 24 hrs.

Groppi, in Tala'at Harb Sq. (tel. 574 3244), on the corner of Mahmoud Bassiouny St. and Qasr en-Nil St. Famous during the days of the English Occupation. The ice cream and pastries live up to their reputation; skip the overpriced restaurant. Other locations at 4 Adly St. (near Opera Sq.) with a lush garden, and on El Ahram St. in Heliopolis. All 3 open daily 7am-10pm.

La Poire, 18 Latin America St. (tel. 355 1509), next to TakeAway Restaurant in Garden City. Oozing éclairs and honeysuckle *ba'laweh* titillate the tongue. All pastries made on the premises (E£1.65). One of the largest selections of ice cream flavors in Cairo (E£1 per scoop). Open daily 7am-11:30pm.

El Andalusia, 15 July 26th St. (tel. 75 52 05), in front of the Grand Hotel entrance. A pleasant outdoor café complete with fountain and backgammon-playing *sheesha* lovers. Try the *sahlab* (hot or cold milk drink with coconut and nuts, E£1.50), the *biliari helbah* (a drink made by boiling seeds, 50pt), or the exquisite *karkadeh* (a floral infusion served hot or cold, 60pt). Open 24 hrs.

Tea Island, in Cairo Zoo, Giza (tel. 73 43 29), at the University Bridge. Open-air cafeteria. Ask the price before you order if you look like a *khawaga*. Juices, coffee, and snacks available. Toss your crumbs to the fowl while the flies and mosquitoes nibble at your limbs. Open daily 8am-4pm.

Simmonds Coffee Shop, July 26th St., Zamalek (tel 340 9436), just east of the intersection with Hasan Sabri St. Terrific cappuccino, espresso, and hot chocolate (90pt), or lemonade (75pt). Ideal for breakfast and chocolate binges. All cakes E£1. Open daily 8am-9pm.

Ibis Café, Nile Hilton (tel. 76 56 66), on the ground floor. Good for breakfast or brunch. Rich tourists in bermudas and Hawaiian shirts, foreign correspondent types with J. Press ties, women with purple hair—could this be you? Unlimited salad bar (E£12), minimum order E£5. Open noon-midnight.

Brazilian Coffee Shop, 38 Tala'at Harb St. (tel. 75 57 22), at the intersection of Tala'at Harb St. and Adly St. Clean white marble counter. Excellent *café au lait*, cappuccino, and iced coffee (all E£1.30) from Brazilian coffee beans. A magnet for caffeine-crazed students. Open daily 6am-midnight.

El 'Abd, 25 Tala'at Harb St. (tel. 392 4407), recognizable by the surging mass of customers. Egyptians come here by the thousands for cakes and ice cream (a whopping 4-scoop cone is a steal at E£1.25). For ice cream, pay first then take the token to the scooper. Open daily 9am-11pm.

El Horea, Bab el-Louq Sq., at the north side of the pedestrian overpass. Older Egyptian men kill time over *sheeshas,* coffee, and even the occasional Stella (E£3). Pick up a game of chess or backgammon any time. Open daily 8am-2am.

In the evenings, join a swarm of middle-class Egyptian couples at one of the many cafés, called **casinos,** lining the Nile on Gezira Island. Some of these are boats permanently anchored at the edge of the water. The **Casino al-Nil,** on the west side of Tahrir Bridge, is one of the best immobile cafés (minimum charge E£4). Dozens of others range from swank to simple. Most are jammed on Thursday nights, partially because of post-nuptial *haflahs* (parties). Party on, gentle reader.

BILLIARDS, BARS, AND CLUBS

In the last few years, billiards has become the cool pursuit in Cairo, especially among the Gezira Sporting Club set. Paul Newman and Tom Cruise wanna-be's show each other up at **Alamein,** in the World Trade Center, 119 Corniche en-Nil (tel. 340 9987), and **The Billiards Club,** July 26th St., downtown (opposite the High Court). If you shoot pool at **Whiskies Pub** (20 Gam'at ed-Duwal el-Arabiyya St., Mohandiseen; tel. 346 6569 or 4175 or 7230; in the Atlas Zamalek Hotel, next to Al-Omda Restaurant), the losers can take you (the winners) dancing upstairs afterwards.

Atlas, Atlas Zamalek Hotel (see above), 9th floor. In summer 1994, *the* place to shake your thang to the latest European and Arabic dance music. Filled with Drakkar-Noir-and-Armani Egyptians, young expats, and students. Dress doesn't have to be formal, but locals to tend to dude up; you'll probably see Egyptian women dressed to kill (you, and their families). Officially, men unaccompanied by women are not allowed in; guys, look cute and a woman alone might let you tag onto her ticket. Open 11pm-3:30am. Free for women. Men E£20-40.

The Four Corners, 4 Hasan Sabri St., Zamalek. Hang out with a bizarre mix of expats, Cairo elite-oids, and AUC students. Complex includes 3 restaurants, a bar, and a disco. La Piazza, the "informal" restaurant, serves skimpy but delicious Italian dishes (E£9-13); Matchpoint, the video bar, has prices to match its pretensions: E£6 min. Open daily 1pm-1am.

Taverne du Champs de Mars, in the Nile Hilton. The heart of Cairo's gay community. A *fin-de-siècle* bar transported brick-by-brick from Belgium. High prices: minimum charge E£5.50, beer E£11. Open daily 11am-1am.

Audio 9, 33 Qasr en-Nil St., 9th floor. Slightly seedy but convenient for Tala'at Harb budgeteers. European and Sudanese clientele. Every Friday night is Sweaty Reggae Night. Cover usually E£4-6. Look for posters in Felfela's.

B's Corner (tel. 341 3870), 22 Taha Hussein St., Zamalek. Take Hasan Sabri St. north of July 26th St. until you come to a square 3 blocks down, then take the left prong of the fork; it's 100m down the second street, next to the President Hotel. More of a lounge than a dance club. No cover. Open daily 3pm-1am.

Odeon Palace, off Tala'at Harb St. 1 block east of Tala'at Harb Sq. Relax and chat all night. Cheap beer, food, and *sheesha* on the roof. Open 24 hrs.

Casanova Disco, in the El Burg Hotel, Zamalek. Just over the Tahrir Bridge, by the Opera House. New and very popular. It has no couples-only policy and no cover, making for predominantly male rowdiness and crowdiness.

There are also swanky bars, nightclubs, and discos in most of the luxury hotels. The **Marriott** and **Mena House** have outdoor café-bars; history, as well as Mena House's location near the pyramids, makes them the classiest choices for sipping a martini or Bloody Mary. The Marriott also has a lounge on the top floor with a stunning view of Eastern Cairo. The **Garden Bar** in the Atlas Hotel (tel. 91 83 11), El Goumhouriyya St., draws gay men and the expatriate crowd with rock music on Thursday and Friday nights 11pm-1am. Drinks are expensive, but there's no cover charge. The **Barrel Bar** at the Windsor Hotel also attracts expats (Stella E£5) daily, noon-2am.

The **Hilton, Semiramis International,** and **Sheraton** Hotels all have classy clubs with restricted admission policies, steep covers, and older crowds. Probably the most eccentric crowd boogies at the Club Med disco at the **Manial Palace** on Roda Island. In addition to the funky crowd, it boasts a pool and beautiful gardens including the biggest variety of cacti in the world. Drinks are expensive.

Men with a taste for sleaze can brave the 10pm floor show at the **New Arizona Bar** (opposite Alfy Bey Restaurant on Alfy St.—no sign in English). The bar downstairs has mirrored ceilings, Hawaiian murals, and bamboo walls. Women may not feel comfortable here. The same goes for **Samy's Bar,** next to the Café Andalusia and opposite the Grand Hotel in an alley off July 26th St., where buxom Egyptian women bend very close as they serve your drinks. Desperate sick-o's rejoice.

OTHER DIVERSIONS

About 5km south of downtown is the **Pharaonic Village,** founded by Ph.D. and former ambassador Dr. Ragab, who is also the papyrus king of Egypt. Visitors board motorboats with theater-like seats and chug through canals past pigeon-poop-decorated statues of the gods and historically reconstructed scenes of ancient papyrus-making, temple-wall-painting, mummification, etc. All this is described in detail by a guide speaking the language of your choice. Disembark to view a temple, houses, and King Tut's tomb reconstructed to appear as it did when Howard Carter discovered it in 1922. The price is steep, but you get tons of information without having to read a thing or move too many muscles. (Open 9am-4pm in winter, 9am-9pm in summer. E£40 per person, E£30 for groups of 10 or more. Lunch E£17.)

Some major hotels host Egyptian dancing and musical performances in their ethnic restaurants. The **Felafel** restaurant at the Ramses Hilton serves an excellent but expensive *prix-fixe* dinner (E£75), which includes a fabulous **folk dancing** show by the Hasan Troupe. Call the Ramses Hilton for details (tel. 77 74 44).

One of the best **dance** companies in Cairo is the Egyptian folk dancing **Rida's Troupe,** performing regularly at the **Balloon Theater** on En-Nil St. in Agouza (tel. 247 7457 or 347 1718), at the Zamalek Bridge. The Theater also hosts plays, and concerts by famous Arab singers. (Tickets average E£10, children E£6.) There are also performances at the **Goumhouriyya Theater** (tel. 91 99 56) by the **Arabic Music Troupe** and the **Cairo Symphony Orchestra,** usually on Friday evenings, and the **Sayyid Darwish Theater,** off Pyramids Rd. on Gamal ed-Din el-Afghani St., Giza. The **Cairo Puppet Theater** (tel. 91 09 54), in Azbakia Gardens near Opera Sq., performs nightly from October to May. The shows are in Arabic, but anyone can understand. Cairo has a handful of **cinemas** that run foreign-language films; check *The Egyptian Gazette* for listings. Remember that the Egyptian audience reads the subtitles—they don't give a wet slap about the sound. Try to sit in the least popular part of the theater, usually the rear of the orchestra. (Around 9pm, tickets E£5.)

The Mausoleum of El Ghouri on El Muizz St., just south of the pedestrian overpass in Islamic Cairo, hosts the **whirling dervishes,** members of the mystical Sufi sect of Islam who do a traditional religious dance. (Wed. and Sat., 9:30pm. Free.)

The American University in Cairo runs the **Wallace Theater** (tel. 357 5022), on the New Campus on Muhammad Mahmoud St., featuring two plays in English per year. The university also hosts a variety of concerts, from jazz to chamber music. (Open fall-spring.) Check bulletin boards on the Old Campus. The **American Cultural Center,** 4 Ahmed Ragheb St., sometimes screens free films on Friday nights. The **British Council,** 192 En-Nil St. (tel. 345 3281) has a large library and also sponsors performances by visiting British theatrical and musical groups. The

Netherlands Institute, 1 Mahmoud Azmi St. (tel. 340 0076), Zamalek, offers English-language lectures about Egypt on Thursdays at 5pm September-June.

Consider hiring a swallow-winged **felucca** (sailboat) and lazing on the river day or night. Most *feluccas* can accommodate up to eight people comfortably. The more passengers, the cheaper; bargain for a good rate. *Feluccas* for hire dock just south of the Qasr en-Nil Bridge on the east bank. Across the corniche (on the water) from the Meridien Hotel, boats sail for E£5-6 during the day, E£7 in the evening. The agency across the corniche from the Shepherd's Hotel hires out boats around the clock (E£5-10 during the day, E£12-15 at night).

There's **gambling** in the Nile Hilton, Marriott, and Sheraton hotels. You must show your passport to enter and are permitted to game with foreign currency only.

During **Ramadan,** nightlife assumes an entirely new dimension in Cairo. Cairenes take to the streets around Al Azhar and Hussein Sq. and along the corniche and the bridges across the Nile. Starting 10 to 11pm, there are street theater performances, magic shows, and general pandemonium. All cinemas have screenings at midnight.

During Ramadan, **Es-Sokkariyya,** near the Es-Salaam (Hyatt) Hotel at 61 Abd el-Hamid Badawy St., Heliopolis (take bus #50, 128, or 330), features an Egyptian garden setting with superb singers and musicians, a penny arcade, and fortune tellers. The E£10 entrance fee includes all drinks and a *sheesha*. Try the *sahlab*. (Open 8pm-3am during Ramadan. Call the Hyatt at 245 5155 to confirm.)

On the **Fourth of July,** homesick American budgeteers' dreams comes true at the Cairo American Primary and Secondary School, where 5000 Americans consume all the hot dogs, soft drinks, and pot luck they can stuff into their pot bellies. Just bring your American passport and a big old cheesy grin—you've already paid in taxes.

NEAR CAIRO

■■■ PYRAMIDS AT GIZA اهرام جيزة

From afar they look like the world's largest paperweights, but as you approach, you are seized by (in Napoleon's words) "a sort of stupefaction, almost overwhelming in its effect." The last of the seven wonders of the ancient world still extant, the Pyramids at Giza stand as awe-inspiring monuments to human achievement.

Since everyone likes to see awe-inspiring monuments to human achievement, nowhere else is Egypt's ravenous tourist industry so, well, ravenous. For a solid mile, souvenir shops, alabaster factories, and papyrus museums conspire to pawn off ancient artifacts made while-u-wait. At the foot of the Pyramids, an army of hustlers will hound you: Bedouin imposters rent camels *(zee camil! zee camil! hooray! hoo-ray!)* and Arabian race horses, people peddle tourist dreck at inflated prices, and self-appointed guides ("Pyramid—very big") approach you at every turn. Don't let the racket deter you from spending at least a few hours gaping at the Pyramids.

Practical Information To get to the Pyramids *(El Ahram)*, take **bus #8** (25pt) from the front of the Mugamma' Building at Tahrir Sq. in Cairo. The last stop leaves you near the entrance to the Pyramids. Get off the more crowded bus #900 as it turns off to the right just before the Mena House Hotel. Don't jump off as soon as you see the Pyramids—they're farther than they look. For more comfortable transport, take **minibus #83,** which leaves from the station just to the right of the Mugamma' Building (35pt). **Taxis** should cost E£6 from downtown Cairo. The Giza **Tourist Office** (tel. 385 0259) is located on Pyramids Rd., next to the police station just before the stables, but can't offer more than bus information and suggested prices for rides. (Open daily 8am-5pm.) A **tourist police** station is adjacent to the ticket office. The Pyramids Rest House, a fancy little establishment with a E£4.50 minimum charge, and the Sphinx Rest House have **public bathrooms.**

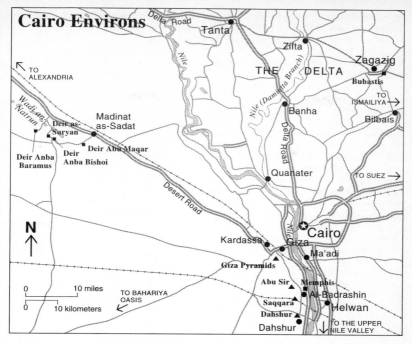

Your hotel manager in Cairo can arrange a **tour.** Or, although it's a lot to cram into one day (daily tours last from 9am-5pm), contact Mr. Salah Muhammad, who offers chauffeur-driven tours of Memphis, Saqqara, the carpet school at Harania, and the Pyramids at Giza for E£20 (E£15 for *Let's Go* users who book directly with him, saving the E£5 hotel commission). Call him at Luxor Towers (tel. 76 85 37); his high-tech answering machine ensures that he will get back to you. The exuberant Salah is a mine of practical information, but not a guide—bring a source of enlightenment.

Go early to beat the crowds. Failing that, visit after the Pyramids' official closing time of 5pm, when you'll have free access to the entire site without tourists and hustlers. You won't be admitted inside the Pyramids or boat museum, however. Shoes with traction are neat little life-saving contraptions if you plan on internal climbing. To attend the sound and light show gratis, sit with the hundreds of Egyptians and watch from anywhere on the site. Shining colored lights on the Pyramids to make them look dramatic is like using mirrors to make them look big. There are two shows nightly, at 6:30 and 7:30pm, in summer 8:30 and 9:30pm. Call 385 2880 or check *Cairo Today* to find out when the Sphinx will gab in the language of your preference. Your ticket will admit you to the Pyramids and Sphinx complexes. (Site open daily 6:30am-8pm; winter 7am-10pm. Pyramids open daily 8am-5pm. Admission to the complex E£10, students E£5. Admission inside the Great Pyramid E£10, students E£5.) You must buy a separate ticket for the Cheops Solar Boat Museum. (Open daily 8am-4:30pm. Admission E£10, students E£5.)

Renting a **horse** can be fun, although many of the overworked and underfed animals have one hoof in the glue factory. It's best to go in the morning or at dusk, when the weather is cool and the crowd bearable. For longer rides and more reliable beasts, walk down beyond the Sphinx and turn right after the Sound and Light Auditorium. You'll come to a row of reputable establishments, two of which are **AA Stables** (tel. 385 0531) and **S.A. Stables** (tel. 85 02 59). Although the tourist police post prices for an hour ride at E£6 for a horse and E£5 for a camel, the going price is closer to E£10 for a guided trek on either. E£6 is a fair price without a guide, but one should be a confident rider; some mounts only obey hieroglyphics and may gallop off into the desert, ignoring their riders' hysterical screams.

Accommodations, Food, and Entertainment There's no reason to stay in Giza—the ride to Cairo takes 20 minutes. But if you enjoy crashing amidst sun and sand, you can stay at **Salome Campground,** with fairly clean toilets and showers and a small restaurant (E£7 a night). Go down Pyramids Rd. to the Maroutiya Canal; take a left and follow the signs. Without a car you're stranded here.

The food situation is bleak, and again, you're better off eating in Cairo if you can hold out. If not, try the **Pyramids Shishkabab Restaurant** (tel. 385 1078), two blocks from the Sphinx Rest House along the main road (*shishkabab* E£8; open daily 10am-2am), or **Felfela Café** (tel. 383 0234), on the Alexandria Rd. about 500m after the turn-off to the Pyramids and Mena House Hotel. They have a cheap *ta'miyya/shawerma* stand, or you can chow on traditional salads, *fuul,* and falafel inside (E£1-4 per item, meat more expensive; open daily 8:30am-1:30am). The **Khan el-Khalili Coffee Shop,** at the Mena House Oberoi Hotel (tel. 383 3444) at the end of Pyramid St., has a funky atmosphere and coffee or mint tea (E£3.25; open 24 hrs).

As far as entertainment goes, it's pretty much the pyramids or bust. The **nightclubs** on Pyramids Rd. are notoriously sleazy, featuring drunk men heckling scantily-clad belly dancers. The expensive bars at the **Mena House Hotel** have live music in an elegant setting. If it's solitude you seek, the stables next to the Sphinx can arrange overnight expeditions through the dunes (see Practical Information, above).

Sights The three main pyramids at Giza were built for three pharaohs: Cheops (or Khufu), Chephren (or Khafre), and Menkaure (or Mycerinus). This father-son-grandson trio reigned during the 26th century BCE. Each of the pyramids was once attached to its own funerary complex, complete with riverside pavilion and mortuary temple, in which the pharaoh's cult was supposed to continue for eternity. A long, narrow causeway linked the mortuary temple with the neighboring waters of the Nile, culminating in the valley temple through which the complex proper was reached. The mummy of the deceased ruler was conveyed by boat across the Nile, carried up the causeway in a solemn procession, and deposited in its sacred resting place at the heart of the giant pyramid.

The **Pyramid of Cheops** is the first pyramid you'll encounter upon entering the site. It initially stood 146m high upon completion, and over the course of four-and-a-half millennia its height has decreased by only 3m. The total weight of Cheops is estimated at 6,000,000 tons. To appreciate its mass, crawl through the narrow passageways inside that lead to the king's chamber in the center of the pyramid. (This arduous climb is not for the faint-hearted or the claustrophobic.) The highlight of the expedition is the tall, narrow gallery with 9m walls formed from 14 massive slabs of granite. The king's tomb chamber is a large, square room containing only the cracked bottom half of the sarcophagus. Its most novel feature is the collection of 19th-century graffiti. The passageway to the queen's chamber, which starts at the bottom of the gallery, is closed off by an iron grille.

Outside, walk around to the southern face of the structure to see the **Solar Boat,** one of the oldest boats in existence, unearthed near the pyramid base in 1954. This vessel most likely transported Cheops across the Nile from the "land of the living" on the east bank to his resting place in the "land of the dead"; the boat was buried close to the pharaoh so he could use it to cross the ocean of death beneath the earth. A plywood and glass structure resembling a Modernist ski lodge houses the boat today. On the east side of the pyramid are the meager remains of the **Mortuary Temple of Cheops.** Only the foundations and a few sockets for columns remain.

The middle member of the trio, the **Pyramid of Chephren,** is only 3m shorter than the pyramid of Cheops. Portions of the limestone casing that originally covered the monument still sheathe its apex, making it Egypt's most splendid pyramid. The interior of Chephren's tomb is the finest of the three at Giza. The burial chamber contains Chephren's sarcophagus and more 19th-century graffiti. Relatively spacious passageways make Chephren the coolest and most comfortable for exploring.

After Mama and Papa comes the Baby **Pyramid of Mycerinus,** comparatively small at only 66m. Its burial chamber once contained a magnificent basalt sarcophagus covered with ornate decorative carving. Unfortunately, this treasure was lost at sea en route to the British Museum during the early 19th century. Outside, at the northeast corner of the temple, lie the quarried remains of the **Mortuary Temple of Mycerinus.** The smaller pyramids surrounding the Big Three belonged to the pharaohs' wives and children. Farther away, the ruins of the unexcavated Valley Temple of Mycerinus are swathed by a blanket of sand.

The **Sphinx** crouches downhill to the northeast of the Pyramid of Cheops. Hewn almost entirely from living rock, the poised figure is 80m long and gazes out over the world from a height of 22m. Known as *Abu'l-Hul* (father of terror), the mysterious feline man wears an inscrutable smile. Opinion is divided over the Sphinx's identity. Some believe the face is a portrait of Chephren, whose pyramid lies behind it to the northeast, while others maintain that the features represent the local deity Horan. Its expression and attitude are clearly discernible, though the soft limestone from which it was sculpted is greatly weathered. Used for target practice during the Turkish occupation, the Sphinx lost not only its nose but also its beard (the latter is now in the British Museum). In addition, in 1988 a large chip fell from its shoulder. A pharaonic nose-job has been prescribed to restore the features and prevent the rest of the face from sliding off.

At the foot of the Sphinx, just around the corner to the south, is the **Valley Temple of Chephren,** discovered in 1853. Sixteen great pillars support the roof of this edifice, soaring to a height of 15m each. Your guide will inevitably hold a candle to the fine grain of the stone; *bakhsheesh* is expected in return.

The minor **Pyramid of Abu Ruash,** 7km north of the Giza pyramids, is accessible by foot or hired animal. *Service* taxis and minibuses also run to the nearby village of Abu Ruash from Giza Square. The pyramid itself is a 9m-high mound.

■ NEAR GIZA: KARDASSA AND HARANIA

On the road from Cairo to Giza, a turn-off to the right at the second canal before the pyramids leads to the village of **Kardassa,** where the Western Desert and camel road to Libya commence. The village has become a popular tourist destination owing to its variety of local crafts; much of what appears in Cairo's tourist shops is made in Kardassa. The main products of the village are wool and cotton scarves, *gallabiyyas* (E£20-30), rugs, and Bedouin weavings. The shops are in a sand lot across the canal from the village; the artisans' workshops are usually in the back of the store or in side alleys off the main commercial drag. Unfortunately, the influx of tourists to Kardassa has inflated prices. Taxis from Giza Sq. to Kardassa cost E£6. Minibuses run to Kardassa from Giza Sq. (35pt), as well as to the turn-off from Pyramids Rd. (25pt).

Far more interesting is the artists' school at **Harania,** located 200m to the right of Maroutiya Canal Rd., about 3km south of Pyramids Rd., right next to the Salome Campground. Look for signs to both. Here young children are encouraged to develop their creativity through weaving brilliantly colored carpets and making pottery. The results are stunning.

■■■ SAQQARA & ENVIRONS صقارة

It took clout to end up here—only the pharaohs, aristocrats, and a few dozen mummified Apis bulls are interred at **Saqqara.** The city boasts the world's oldest pyramid—dating from 2700 BCE—along with the burial ground of the pharaohs who ruled at nearby **Memphis.** Although not as polished as their later cousins at Giza, Saqqara's stepped pyramids have an equally captivating visage. Situated squarely in the Libyan desert, with nothing but sand in every direction, they are less frequented by tourists. The nearby pyramids at **Abu Sir** and **Dahshur** are even less accessible—to visit the latter, located inside a military base, you need a special permit.

PRACTICAL INFORMATION

The easiest way to get here is to take Salah Muhammad's tour (see Giza: Practical Information, p. 114). If you choose to go without Salah's services, begin your journey at the ruins of **North Saqqara.** Short of hiring a taxi, there's really no simple way to get here. For cheapness, take a minibus from Giza Sq. to the village of Abu Sir (35pt). From Abu Sir, the 3km walk to the entrance takes between 30 to 60 minutes, depending on your footspeed in sand. Walk south (to the left as you arrive) along the canal just before the village and keep following the dirt road by the canal until you reach the paved road. Turn right at the paved road, and it's 200m to the site entrance. Alternatively, you can hire a **pick-up truck** at the canal in Abu Sir (about 50pt per person) to take a group to the site. The pyramids of **Abu Sir** are visible from those of North Saqqara; either hoist yourself onto one of the horses or camels at the stable next door to the ticket office (E£10-20) or put on your shades and start walking (about an hour). A camel or horse ride will cost E£10 to **South Saqqara;** otherwise it's a half-hour walk. **Dahshur** is most easily accessible from the eastern bank (see below).

All the sights are officially open 8am-5pm (8am-4pm in winter), but you can always view the monuments from the outside. Make the pyramids of Abu Sir your lowest priority, as they're hollow inside. (Admission to North Saqqara E£10, students E£5. Camera privileges E£5.) The ticket is good for all Saqqara sites but unnecessary for Abu Sir. Bring *bakhsheesh*.

Get a very early start—it takes time to travel around the sites at Saqqara. The summer afternoon sun can be immobilizing, so be sure to bring plenty of water. Wear a hat, bring your own food, and make sure you're wearing good shoes. Though sandals will keep your feet cool, they will also let in sand. Lighting inside some of the tombs is poor—a flashlight (which you can either bring along or rent for E£1) will enlighten your expedition.

SIGHTS

Saqqara consists of five archaeological sites scattered over a large area. The primary destination for most visitors is **North Saqqara,** site of the funerary complex and the great Step Pyramid of Zoser I. (Most sites are accessible, but entrance into the pyramid itself requires special permission from the Antiquities Service; ask at the Egyptian Museum in Cairo.) The three pyramids of **Abu Sir** lie 6km north of North Saqqara, only a few kilometers from the tiny village of Abu Sir. The two pyramids and the funerary complex of **South Saqqara** are about 4km south of North Saqqara. The historically significant but scanty ruins of the ancient city of **Memphis** are farther from the necropolis of Saqqara, located next to the Nile just south of the village of Mit-Rahine. The pyramids of **Dahshur** are at the southern end of the row.

North Saqqara

Saqqara's largest edifice is the mountainous **Step Pyramid** built by Imhotep, chief architect to the Pharaoh Zoser, in about 2650 BCE. This was the first monumental tomb and the inspiration for Egypt's many subsequent architectural wonders. Like most pharaonic structures, the Step Pyramid was built as part of a funerary complex. Most experts believe the tomb began as a *mastaba* and was augmented five separate times, producing the present six-level structure.

Enter the Step Pyramid complex from the eastern side of the limestone enclosure wall. The paneled barrier was designed to resemble the mud-brick work which graced the fortifications surrounding the cities and palaces of the period. On your way into the complex itself, you will pass through a hallway with a stone ceiling that mimics the palm log rafters of earlier wooden structures. Two fixed stone panels, carved to resemble a massive wooden doorway, open onto a 40-pillared colonnade. The walls and roof have been restored as part of a lifetime project of reconstruction undertaken by the French archaeologist Jean-Philippe Lauer. The Egyptian pillars, ridged to create the stylized effect of a bundle of papyrus stems, are probably the world's first stone columns. This imposing corridor culminates in the **Hypostyle Hall,** a fledgling version of the great hallways found at Karnak and Abydos.

Up the steps to the right of the pit and over the enclosure wall looms the massive **Pyramid of Unis,** the last pharaoh of the 5th Dynasty. You can go spelunking in the interior burial chamber of the crumbled monument; find a guard if the door is locked. Although the passage into the tomb is uncomfortably low at points, the central burial chamber is spacious. The wall carvings, known as the **Pyramid Texts,** were discovered in 1881 and constitute the earliest known example of decorative hieroglyphic writing on the walls of a pharaonic tomb chamber. Carefully etched into the shiny alabaster, the well-preserved texts record hymns, prayers, and articles necessary for the afterlife. On the western edge of the main chamber sits the open basalt sarcophagus of Unis, with its lid on the ground beside it.

Opposite the south face of the Pyramid of Unis, an inauspicious shack covers the shaft leading to three of Egypt's deepest burial chambers, the **Persian Tombs** of Psamtik, Zenhebu, and Peleese. A dizzying spiral staircase drills 25m into the ground, terminating in three vaulted burial chambers linked by narrow passageways. According to the ancient inscriptions, Zenhebu was a famous admiral and Psamtik a chief physician of the pharaoh's court.

To the southwest of the Pyramid of Unis, a 100m path leads into the desert to the unfinished **Pyramid of Sekhemkhet,** a paltry pile of rubble unearthed in 1951. The pyramid was intended as a replica of its neighbor, the Pyramid of Zoser, but construction was abandoned with its walls at a height of only 3m. East of the Pyramid of Unis a smooth, narrow causeway runs down the hill. Nearly 1km long, it linked the pyramid with a lower valley temple on the banks of the river. Strewn by the causeway's sides are the **Old Kingdom Tombs.** Over 250 *mastabas* have been excavated here, though only a few of the largest and best-preserved are open to the public.

The 6th-Dynasty **Mastaba of Idut,** adjacent to the southern enclosure wall of Zoser's funerary complex and just east of the Pyramid of Unis, includes 10 chambers. Nearby are the **Mastaba of Mehu** and the **Mastaba of Queen Nebet.** South of the causeway is a pair of enormous **Boat Pits,** side by side 100m east of the Pyramids of Unis. There is some speculation as to whether the pits were intended to house the royal barques (as at Giza) or whether these finely sculpted trenches of stone were meant as simple representations of boats.

At the end of the causeway, head 150m uphill and southward to the **Monastery of St. Jeremiah.** Built in the 5th century CE, the monastery has been repeatedly pillaged, starting in 950 CE when invading Arabs ransacked it. Recently, the Antiquities Service moved all decorative carvings and paintings to the Coptic Museum in Cairo, leaving the despoiled shell to be overrun by advancing sand dunes. What's left of the monastery is best reached by car or horse; it's usually much too hot to walk.

Head back up to the causeway and around the corner to the Great South Court of Zoser's mortuary complex. In the northern end, at the base of the Step Pyramid, lie the remains of the *mastaba* that was the seed of Zoser's tomb. In the center of the pyramid's south face is an entrance to the tomb's interior. This long passageway, the **Saite Gallery,** affords stunning views of the interior frame. To the east, the **Heb-Sed Court** runs the length of one side of the courtyard. The building is a copy of the pavilion employed at the Heb-Sed Jubilee, a festival during which the king demonstrated his vigor by completing a ritual race around the courtyard. The Heb-Sed Court in the funerary complex and the panels inside the pyramid that depict Zoser running the race were meant to ensure his eternal rejuvenation.

The more substantial **House of the South** stands next door, on the eastern side of Zoser's pyramid. Inside, the walls are inscribed with ancient graffiti left by a starving Egyptian artist in the 12th century BCE. The messages, expressing admiration for King Zoser, were hastily splashed onto the walls with dark paint, scrawled in a late cursive style of hieroglyphics. Heading north, you'll come to the **House of the North.** Nearby, directly in front of the Step Pyramid's northern face, is the most haunting spectacle at Saqqara, the **Statue of King Zoser.** From a slanted stone hut pierced by two tiny apertures, the pharaoh stares fixedly at you. This small structure, known as the **Sardab,** was designed to enable the spirit of the pharaoh to communicate with the outside world. The striking figure is a plaster copy of the original, which has been moved to the Egyptian Museum in Cairo.

If you have a car, you can return to the entrance of Zoser's mortuary complex and drive around to the western portion of North Saqqara. Or you can hike five minutes across the desert to reach the **Tomb of Akhti-Hotep and Ptah-Hotep,** halfway between the Step Pyramid and the canopied Rest House. This remarkable double tomb housed the bodies of a father and son, inspectors of the priests who served the pyramids. The pair designed their own mortuary complex, which contains some of Saqqara's finest reliefs. The structure is accessible through a long corridor, culminating in the burial chamber of Akhti-Hotep.

West of the Hoteps' tomb is a shady **Rest House** with a bathroom and a small cafeteria. Farther along the highway, where the road turns sharply to the west, an area has been cleared to reveal badly weathered **Greek statues** said to represent Homer (at the center), Pindar (at the west end), and Plato (at the east end).

The **Serapium,** a few hundred meters west of the Rest House at the terminus of the main road, was discovered in 1854. The mausoleum, a series of eerie underground tunnels with tiny lanterns, houses the **Tombs of the Apis Bulls,** where 25 sacred oxen were embalmed and placed in enormous sarcophagi of solid granite. Only one of the bulls was discovered (the rest had been stolen or roasted) and is now displayed in Cairo's Agricultural Museum.

The Serapium is the sole legacy of a mysterious bull-worshipping cult that apparently thrived during the New Kingdom. Work on the main portion of the underground complex was begun in the 7th century BCE by Psamtik I and continued through the Ptolemaic era, though much older tombs adjoin this central set of chambers. In the oldest portion of the Serapium, two large gold-plated sarcophagi and several canopic jars containing human heads were found, as well as the undisturbed footprints of the priests who had laid the sacred animals to rest 3000 years earlier. (This portion of the tomb is no longer accessible.) Recessed tomb chambers flank the main corridor on both sides, each containing a sarcophagus. It's difficult to imagine these mammoth coffins being transported to the confines of the cave—their average weight is 65 tons. In the final tomb along the passageway stands the largest sarcophagus of all, hewn from a single piece of black granite.

The **Tomb of Ti,** 300m north of the Serapium, was excavated in 1865 and has since been one of the primary sources of knowledge about both daily and ceremonial life during the 5th Dynasty (toward the end of the Old Kingdom, 25th century BCE). Serving under three pharaohs, Ti had almost as many titles as Yasser Arafat—Overseer of the Pyramids and Sun Temples at Abu Sir, Superintendent of Works, Scribe of the Court, Royal Counselor, Editor, Royal Tea Brewer, and even Lord of Secrets. His rank was so lofty that he was allowed to marry a princess, Nefer-Hotep, and his children were considered royalty. In the tomb paintings, the children wear braided hairpieces, marking them as contenders for the throne.

Although now entirely buried in sand, an **Avenue of Sphinxes** once ran the full width of the site, commencing near the Tomb of Ti, running a straight course east past the Step Pyramid complex and ending at the river's edge near the **Pyramid of Titi.** This weathered pyramid can be reached by following the east-west highway past the Rest House to the fork and then heading a short distance north. The interior of Titi's tomb has several interesting sacred inscriptions, but it's usually closed to the public. The 30 rooms comprising the magnificent **Tomb of Mereruka,** just next door to the Pyramid of Titi, are open. The naturalistic portrayal of wildlife found inside the Tomb of Mereruka has enabled scientists to learn a great deal about ancient Egyptian fauna. Various species of fish can be differentiated thanks to the minutely-detailed work of the artists.

Farther east is the neighboring **Tomb of Ankhma-Hor.** Though the decorations are relatively sparse, there are several representations of medical operations, including toe surgery and a circumcision. One noted Egyptologist has asserted that the 6th-Dynasty tendency to depict funerary scenes indicates a growing pessimism among Egyptians about the afterlife as the Old Kingdom went into its final decline.

South Saqqara

The most interesting funerary monument at South Saqqara is the **Tomb of Shepseskaf** (popularly known as Mastabat Faraun), an enormous stone structure shaped like a sarcophagus and capped with a rounded lid. Though Shepseskaf, son of Mycerinus (whose pyramid stands at Giza), reigned for only three or four years, his brief stint on the throne was long enough to qualify him for a grand tomb. Originally covering 7000 square meters, Mastabat Faraun is neither a true *mastaba* nor a pyramid. The interior consists of long passageways and a burial chamber containing fragments of a huge sandstone sarcophagus. Ask a guard to admit you.

Abu Sir أبو صير

The pyramids of Abu Sir are isolated in the Eastern Desert 6km north of Saqqara. No tour buses make it here; take this opportunity to escape camera-clicking clowns. The site (2.5km from the village of Abu Sir) is accessible only by foot or beast.

The **Pyramid of Neferirkare,** the most imposing of the three main pyramids, stands tall at 68m. It once had a stone facing like its neighbors at Giza, but the casing has completely deteriorated. The exterior now resembles that of a step pyramid. Nevertheless, the Pyramid of Neferirkare is one of the best-preserved monuments in the Saqqara area. The **Pyramid of Niuserre** is the youngest of the trio, and yet the most dilapidated. It is possible to enter the **Pyramid of Sahure,** the northernmost member of the group, on its north face. One of the custodians at the site will show you the entrance, which is about 0.5m high and 2m long and requires you to worm your way along the sand floor. The small chamber inside was the pharaoh's tomb. More pyramids are visible from here than from any other site in the country. If you wish to walk on to the village of Abu Sir, have the guards point out the route.

If you are traveling by animal between Abu Sir and Giza, have your guide stop off along the way at the 5th-Dynasty **Sun Temple of Abu Surab,** about 1.5km north of the Pyramid of Sahure. Located on the fringe of cultivated fields, the temple was built by King Niuserre in honor of the sun god Ra; it features an impressive altar constructed from five massive blocks of alabaster. A horse or camel ride from Zoser's pyramid in North Saqqara costs E£10.

Memphis ممفيس

As late as the 13th century CE, Arab historians wrote with awe about the remnants of the Old Kingdom capital at Memphis. Though the brick houses of this city of 500,000 had by then melted into mud, many of the stone monuments were not destroyed until much later, when they were pilfered for construction in Cairo. Only an ancient canal (responsible for the lush vegetation) and the pieces in the **museum** in **Mit-Rahine** remain. Near the museum is the famous alabaster sphinx, which probably originally stood at the south entrance of the Temple of Ptah. (Museum open 8am-5pm in summer, 7:30am-4pm in winter. Admission E£7, students E£3.50. Photo privileges E£5.) You might have to take a taxi to Memphis from Saqqara or Abu Sir. Hitchhiking is very risky, especially for women.

■■■ THE NILE DELTA

The loveliest place in the immediate vicinity of Cairo lies 16km north at the **Nile barrages** in the town of **Qanater.** Decorated vividly with turrets and arches, the barrages were constructed in the first quarter of the 19th century in an attempt to regulate the flow of water into the Delta. Avoid visiting on a Friday when crowds burgeon into absurdity. Small bridges connect the islets next to the barrages, at one of the widest points of the Nile.

Qanater marks the official beginning of the Delta, where the Nile splits into the eastern (Dumyat) and western (Rashid) branches. Bus #210 and 212 from the Meridien (15pt) and #930 from 'Ataba all sputter there. A small passenger ferry runs along the Nile between Cairo and Qanater (every hr. 6am-6pm, 2hr., E£2). Catch the ferry on the corniche, north of the Ramses Hilton and in front of the Television Building. It's also possible to hire a *felucca*, but the journey to Qanater from Cairo voraciously consumes time, as the mast of the boat must be lowered for each bridge. Farther north lie the flat agricultural lands of the **Nile Delta,** "the pharaoh's breadbasket," lauded as the most fertile agricultural region in the world.

It was primarily in Lower Egypt that the Old Kingdom thrived, and many looming monuments were erected in the Delta throughout the pharaonic period. Due to the looseness of the soil, the deployment of irrigation canals, and the natural fanning out of the river, almost all of the major pharaonic sites in the Delta have been lost. Southeast of **Zagazig** (by train from Cairo via Port Said, 1½hr., E£3; or by *service* from Cairo's Ahmed Hilmi Sq. bus station, 1hr., E£4), between Mastiff Camel St. and Bulbous Rd., are the ruins of **Baby-sits,** one of Egypt's oldest cities and the most accessible of the Delta's pharaonic sites. To reach the ruins, take a taxi (E£3) from Zagazig. The name means "house of Basted" and refers to the feline goddess to whom the main temple was dedicated. The festivals here in honor of the cat goddess attracted over 700,000 devotees who would dance and sing, make sacrifices, and consume gluttonous quantities of food and wine. Herodotus marveled that "more wine is drunk at this feast than in the whole year beside." He described the temple as the most pleasurable to gaze upon of all of the Delta's pharaonic sites. Today it is not, as the sanctuary has become a scattered pile of kitty litter. In Zagazig, the small **Orabi Museum** displays local archaeological finds. (Open Sat.-Thurs. 8am-2pm, Fri. 8am-12pm. Admission E£3, students E£1.50. Camera privileges E£5.)

The region's most worthwhile pharaonic site is located some distance from Cairo in the northeastern corner of the Delta's fertile triangle (*service* from Cairo's Ahmed Hilmi Sq., 4½hr., E£7; no buses). Just outside of the village of **San el-Hagar,** 70km northeast of Zagazig at the junction of Bahr es-Sughir and Bahr Facus, the ruins of ancient **Tanis** sprawl over an area of about four square kilometers. Tanis is supposedly the Biblical city where the Egyptians persecuted the Jews before they fled through the Red Sea. Not all of Tanis has been excavated yet, so keep your fingers crossed for more findings. Take a taxi (E£3) from Zagazig and back. The site includes a royal necropolis, the foundations of several temples, a small museum, and a pair of sacred lakes. (Museum open daily 8am-2pm; the ruins are accessible at any time. Admission E£8, students E£4.) The ruins of Tanis are impressive, but not quite as impressive as *Raiders of the Lost Ark* would have you believe.

■■■ WADI NATRUN وادى النطرون

If the craziness of downtown Cairo has you thinking that all of Egypt is a circus, come to Wadi Natrun—the quiet surroundings and kind-hearted people will restore your tranquility like nothing else (except on Sundays). For 1500 years the 50 monasteries of Wadi Natrun have been the backbone of the Coptic community in Egypt. The four that stand today, forming an ill-proportioned but spiritually uplifting cross in the desert landscape, are not just impressive relics; they are still functional, serving the spiritual needs of Egypt's Orthodox Christian population.

The first Christian monastery in Egypt was established in the Eastern Desert by St. Anthony the Great (250-355 CE). In 330 CE, one of Anthony's disciples (St. Maccarius) established the monastic lifestyle in Wadi Natrun. In the 1980s, Coptic monasticism again came into vogue, and new rooms were added to accommodate the novice ascetics living in the Natrun Valley. Young, college-educated Egyptians comprise the majority of modern monks.

The monks begin their day in church at 3am in winter (in summer, the indolent prelates laze until about 4am). Amid billows of incense, wide-eyed icons, and flickering candlelight, they sing psalms and cantillate the Coptic liturgy for six hours. The service is punctuated by entrancing triangle and cymbal music (arrive before 9am to attend). The monks are swathed in black, which indicates that they are symbolically dead—an honored status in this community. When initiated, a new monk's former self "dies," and he leaves the world of corporeal desires. The monks' black hoods symbolize the "helmet of salvation" (Ephesians 6:17), upon which 13 crosses are embroidered. The 12 on the sides represent Christ's apostles and the 13th on the back symbolizes Christ brought to mind. For more about the monasteries, Evelyn White's *The Monasteries of the Wadi Natrun* (1932) tells all.

Practical Information Just about the only way to reach Wadi Natrun from Cairo is by a West Delta Bus Company **bus** which leaves from Abd el-Moneim Riad Sq. bus station, near the Ramses Hilton (every hr. 6:30am-6:30pm except 11:30am and 2:30pm, 2hr., E£2.75). It's unnecessary and usually impossible to purchase tickets in advance; your money will be collected after you board the bus. Ride past the Wadi Natrun Rest House into Wadi Natrun town; from the terminus you can take a pick-up truck to Deir Anba Bishoi (50pt). Alternatively, from the Rest House you can hire a **taxi** for the trip to the monasteries (one-way about E£5). It may also be possible to rely upon the kindness of pilgrims—Copts flock here by the busload and are often willing to pick up stragglers. Start your journey early if you plan to return to Cairo or Alexandria in the evening. There are no places to stay in Wadi Natrun town. To leave Wadi Natrun, wait at the Wadi Natrun Rest House; buses to Alexandria and Cairo stop there frequently throughout the day.

Deir Anba Bishoi alone is open every day of the year; Deir es-Suryan, Deir Anba Baramus, and Deir Abu Maqar (in order of decreasing accessibility) close for various feast and fast days. To avoid spiritual and physical frustration, verify open dates and times with the Coptic Patriarchate in Cairo (tel. 82 58 63 or 82 12 74), next to St. Mark's Church, 222 Ramses St., Abbasiyya; or in Alexandria (tel. 546 0511), on El Kenissa El Kobtiyya St., one block behind Nabi Daniel St. The monks receive foreign tourists with alacrity and hand out free, informative booklets. If you're interested in spending the night there, you will need to call the monasteries' residences in Cairo: Deir Anba Bishoi (tel. 92 44 48), Deir es-Suryan (tel. 92 96 58), Deir Anba Baramus (tel. 92 27 75), and Deir Abu Maqar (tel. 77 06 14). Overnight visitors need written permission from the residences. This applies to men only, as members of the superior sex are generally not allowed to spend the night in the Wadi. Man doth not live by bread alone, and visitors to Anba Bishoi can partake of God's bounty in the form of *fuul,* pita, and tea—it's on the Deir.

Sights Introduction to the Region, p. 46 contains a brief explanation of Coptic Christianity as well as a description of the main features of a Coptic church. When touring the Coptic monasteries, modest attire is the rule—no shorts or sleeveless shirts. Remember to remove your shoes before entering a church.

Deir Anba Bishoi (the Monastery of St. Bishoi), the largest of the four monasteries, is the most accessible to visitors, 15km from the Rest House and 500m from Deir es-Suryan. (Open daily 7am-5pm; summer 7am-6pm.) There are seven churches in the monastery: the Church of St. Bishoi, the Church of St. Iskhiron and the Church of the Holy Virgin (both located within the Church of St. Bishoi), the Church of St. George, the Church of St. Michael, and the recently restored Church of Marcorious and Church of St. Mary. The Church of St. Bishoi has three haikals and is part of the most ancient section of the monastery, dating from the 4th century. It was rebuilt in 444 after being sacked by nomads and now contains the remains of St. Bishoi, who is still believed to perform miracles for the faithful. The church has undergone several restorations and was completely redecorated in 1957. The entrance to the keep of the monastery is on the first story through a drawbridge resting on the roof of the gatehouse.

Deir es-Suryan (the Monastery of the Syrians, for the Syrian monks who once inhabited it), lies 500m northwest of the Monastery of St. Bishoi and is easy to reach. (Open 9am-6pm; summer 9am-7pm.) The monastery was established when a group of monks broke away from the Monastery of St. Bishoi following a 6th-century theological dispute about the nature of the Mother of God. When the dispute was finally resolved, this alternative monastery was no longer needed by the Egyptian Copts. In the beginning of the 8th century it was purchased by a Syrian merchant for use by monks from his homeland, the first of whom arrived at the beginning of the 9th century. The monastery was prominent throughout the 10th century and by the 11th housed the largest community in Wadi Natrun. The design is supposedly modeled on Noah's Ark.

On the **Door of Prophecies** in the Church of the Virgin Mary, the uppermost panels depict disciples, while the panels below depict the seven epochs of the Christian era. The domes of the church are covered with frescoes of the Annunciation, the Nativity, and the Ascension of the Virgin. At the back of the church is a low, dark passageway leading to the private cell of St. Bishoi. The monks will show you an iron staple and chain dangling from the ceiling and explain how St. Bishoi would fasten it to his beard, thereby maintaining a standing position lest he fall asleep during his all-night prayer vigils. Set in the floor at the western end of the church is the *lakan* (marble basin), which is used in the Holy Thursday Rite of Foot Washing.

Deir Anba Baramus (The Monastery of the Virgin Mary) is about 4km northwest of the Monastery of St. Bishoi. Take a taxi from Wadi Natrun town, or catch a ride from Deir Anba Bishoi for about 50pt. This is the oldest monastery in the Natrun valley. Relics of St. Moses and St. Isadore are kept in the first section of the old church. In the old days, the body of St. Moses would shake the hands of passers-by through a small aperture in his casket. For the past 200 years, however, the corpse has not been quite as gregarious and the aperture has been sealed. Tradition holds that a crypt under the altar holds the remains of Maximus and Domidius, sons of the Roman Emperor Valentinus (later St. Valentine). Both were monks here. The oldest architectural element in the church is the 4th-century column of St. Arsanious.

Deir Abu Maqar (the Monastery of St. Maccarius) lies roughly 8km southeast of Deir Anba Bishoi and can be seen to the west of the Cairo-Alexandria desert road (from a point about 129km from Alexandria or 86km from Cairo). Call ahead for permission to enter this monastery. The foundation of Deir Abu Maqar is associated with the life of St. Maccarius the Great (300-390 CE) and marks the beginning of monastic life in Wadi Natrun. It is believed that an angel led St. Maccarius to a rock and ordered him to build a church there. In spite of the monastic community that he founded, St. Maccarius remained a religious hermit throughout his life and lived in a cell connected by a tunnel to a small cave. Virtually none of the original building remains. In the beginning of the 11th century, the monastery became the refuge of monks fleeing Muslim persecution. During the Middle Ages, the monastery was famous for its library, which remained intact until European marauders discovered the treasures in the 17th century and removed them to Europe.

■■■ FAYYUM فيوم

"Cool are the dawns; prolific are the trees; diverse are the fruits; little are the rains." Former governor Abu Othman El Nabulsi perhaps understated the natural beauty of Fayyum, a town which offers a glimpse of a kinder, gentler Egypt that most tourists never see. A little more than 100km from Cairo, Fayyum is a large cultivated area in the desert, sometimes described as an oasis, spreading west and north of the Nile Valley along an offshoot of the river. Although occasionally prey to the grime, crowding, and overnight modernization that plague many parts of Egypt, Fayyum remains primarily agricultural, producing everything from chrysanthemums to straw hats. Those passionate about the pastoral will find an overnight stay blissful; others can easily visit as a daytrip from Cairo or as a stopover on a journey south or north. One warning: the worthwhile spots in Fayyum are scattered outside the main city, so you'll need the better part of a day to enjoy them.

While it is not in the Nile Valley, Fayyum shares in the life and culture of the Nile and has done so since it was first developed by the rulers of the 12th Dynasty

Yusef. Turn left and walk west to the fourth crossing; 300m further on you'll find a taxi stand on your left. The pickup trucks shuttle between Fayyum and Ain Sileen (50pt) and Lake Qar'un (E£1). It may be necessary to change taxis at the village of **Sanhur** to reach the lake; the total price should be the same.

Ten kilometers southeast of Fayyum, along the road to Beni Suef, stands the village of **Hawara,** which boasts the **Pyramid of Amenemhet III.** Once surrounded by a vast labyrinth, the broken-down tomb now surveys a field of pharaonic rubble. A *service* from the Beni Suef station in Fayyum will drop you at the village; walk 2km through the settlement and across the fields behind it (not on the paved roads—the path is much shorter). When in doubt, ask for *haram hawaro* or just *el-haram*. Probably only for pharaoh fanatics.

Ten kilometers further on lies the most prominent historical site in the Fayyum area, the **Pyramid of El Lahun,** near the village of the same name. To reach the pyramid, take a *service* from Hawatem Sq. to the village and hike 3km to the site. The structure, built by Senwosret II of the 12th Dynasty, has been robbed of its stone casing but may be a worthwhile stop for those who just can't get enough. If you're fit, climb to the top and enjoy the great view of the area.

Don't miss the magnificent **Wadi El Ruwayan waterfalls** southwest of Fayyum. Take a *service* from the Auberge to *shallalat wadi el-ruwayan*. When a watercourse from the western side of Fayyum to the depression of Wadi El Ruwayan was cut, three waterfalls and a large lake (stemming from Bahr Yusef) were formed virtually in the middle of the desert. If you are driving from the Auberge, go straight along Lake Quar'un, pass the **Oasis Motel,** and choose either the old road or the newly-paved road (still under construction in June 1994). After about half an hour, a sign will point you to the left. **Tunis** village will be to your right. You should stop and see the village's Islamic-style houses, designed by Hassan Fathi. Picturesque and original, they are worth checking out. After roughly ten minutes you'll reach the toll station, a little green house. Admission to the falls is E£5 per person and an additional E£5 per car. 13km after the station you'll find a blue sign. Turn left and you'll finally encounter the waterfalls, three minutes down a sandy road, where you can swim, sunbathe, or just enjoy the sound of the falling water. Well worth the trip.

Mediterranean Coast

■■■ ALEXANDRIA الاسكندرية

Cleopatra doesn't live here anymore. In fact, the wonders of Alexandria (El Iskandariyya)—the ancient world's greatest library, the monumental lighthouse, the tomb of Alexander the Great—are all gone. The famed Hellenistic city is literally buried under the new metropolis; but those ancient sites that *have* been excavated are complemented by architecture and attractive avenues reminiscent of the more recent colonial era. Much of Alexandria's beauty lies in its past; it takes an imaginative spirit to appreciate it.

Although Alexandria shares the dirt, crowding, noise, and poverty associated with Cairo, a different spirit pervades the city. Whereas summer in Cairo sears the streets and patience alike, in Alexandria it warms vacationing Gulf Arabs and Egyptians to the concepts of relaxation and celebration. During the day hundreds of thousands splash in the Mediterranean, while at night they stroll along the corniche or fritter away time in theaters, nightclubs, cafés, and restaurants. If El Qahira is "The Conqueror," then El Iskandariyya is surely the spoils.

HISTORY

In 332 BCE Alexander the Great was in good spirits, for that year the over-achieving young emperor had wrested Egypt from the Persians. After a triumphant but tasteful reception at Memphis, he set off for the Oracle of Amun in the distant Siwa Oasis to discover whether he was actually the offspring of divinity. On the way down the seacoast he happened upon a small fishing village facing a natural harbor. Instantly enamored by the spot, he ordered a city to be built there. Exhibiting a charming Ramsesian modesty, he dedicated it to himself. Then, leaving architects behind to start construction, he left for Siwa and never came back.

Upon Alexander's death nine years later, Egypt fell into the hands of his general, Ptolemy Soter. Ptolemy glorified his former employer with his attention to the new city. Ptolemy even got carried away and hijacked Alexander's corpse—which was on its way to Siwa, according to his last wishes—and interred it with great pomp under Alexandria's main square. The body, its tomb, and the whole of the Ptolemaic city are now supposedly buried somewhere under the downtown jungle.

Ptolemy and his descendants dedicated themselves to bringing the best of Greek civilization to Egyptian soil. The Museion, including the famous 500,000-volume Library, soon became the greatest center of learning in the ancient world. Euclid invented his geometry here, while other great minds determined the diameter of the earth and the duration of the earth's revolution. To satisfy the spiritual needs of his subjects, Ptolemy invented the god Serapis. With a committee of Egyptian and Greek theologians, he devised a tremendously popular syncretic faith in which aspects of the Hellenic god Zeus and of the Pharaonic god Apis (in the form of a bull) were fused into Serapis.

The city soon became the site of one of the seven ancient wonders of the world, with the construction of the Lighthouse of Pharos Island under Ptolemy II. The immense 400-ft. tower featured a beacon of flame and mirrors. Ships packed the previously unused harbor with increasing frequency and Alexandria traded its way to status as the richest commercial center of the east. The city's bountiful culture inevitably solicited the attention of those pesky Romans. When his 48 BCE power grab went sour at Pharsalus, Pompey fled to Egypt with his triumphant rival Julius Caesar in hot pursuit. There they found a 15-year-old king, Ptolemy XIV, fighting a civil war with a 20-year-old queen—his sister and wife—the enchanting Cleopatra VII. Whether you prefer Shakespeare's version or Hollywood's, the story is all too familiar. Ptolemy tried to charm Caesar by assassinating Pompey, but Cleopatra tried more subtle tactics: she won his favor and bore his child. After Caesar's death she and Marc Antony hooked up, pragmatically dreaming of ruling the known world. But it was not to be: defeated by Octavian (soon to be the Emperor Augustus Caesar) at the Battle of Actium, the lovers committed suicide and their city became the capital of yet another imperial province.

The fortunes of the city waxed and waned with those of the empire. Here the first Greek translation of the Hebrew Bible, the Septuagint, was written for the expatriate Jewish population after the destruction of the Temple in Jerusalem. Many think that the translation is named for the 70 scholars who each labored in isolation and yet reputedly produced the exact same text.

Also according to legend, St. Mark introduced Christianity here in 62 CE, founding what would become the Coptic Church. Mass 3rd-century conversions transformed Alexandria into a Christian spiritual center, but Roman persecutions increased accordingly. The oppression reached a bloody height under Diocletian, who murdered so many Christians that the Copts date their calendar from the beginning of his reign, calling it the Martyr's Calendar.

But the Christians too had their day. Once Emperor Constantine officially recognized them, their influence grew and they turned on their pagan neighbors with vengeful fury. The last remnant of the Great Library was burned during anti-Roman riots in 309 CE. The Egyptian Church differed from the Byzantine and challenged the authority of the latter by establishing a Patriarchate of its own in Alexandria. The

Byzantines persecuted the schismatics to such a degree that when the Persians came as conquerors in the 7th century, they were received as liberators.

Alexandria was still a formidable city when the Arabs arrived shortly after the Persians, but the treasure chest was nearly depleted. The new capital in Cairo eclipsed Alexandria's glory; and a series of earthquakes jolted Alexandria's structure, finally reducing the immense lighthouse to rubble in the 13th century CE. Pharos Island itself gradually silted in and became a peninsula, attached by an hourglass-shaped isthmus. The Mamluks exiled political opponents to Alexandria; and when the canal from the Nile dried up, the city found itself a neglected backwater.

The modern city burst forth when Muhammad Ali realized it would make a fine port for his navy; he rejuvenated the city by redigging the canal to the Nile. During the 19th century Alexandria became a favorite holiday spot for expatriate Europeans and wealthy Turks and Egyptians. The entire colonial government would migrate here from Cairo for the summer. After the Revolution of 1952, Alexandria endured extensive building and heavy crowding. Today, with over five million inhabitants, it is Egypt's biggest port, second-largest city, and summer capital.

ORIENTATION

Ten- and 15-story buildings, towering along 20km of Mediterranean beachfront on a strip nowhere more than 3km wide, mingle with pre-1900 architecture and wrought-iron balconies. The city's industrial, commercial, and residential sectors jockey for space along the main arteries parallel to the coast, while ancient Alexandria, on the now-pacific Eastern Harbor, remains the heart of the modern city. This downtown commercial district, called **El Manshiyya, Mahattat er-Raml** (Raml Station), or simply **El Balad** (the city), is the hub of Alexandria's transportation network, nightlife, and tourist trade. Just west of downtown lie **El Goumrouk** and **El Anfushi,** the colorful, grandiose residential neighborhoods of ancient Pharos Island. A tangle of gray factories and port facilities spoils the view along the Western Harbor. Immediately southeast of El Manshiyya, the **Quartier Grec** encompasses **Misr Railway Station,** the city's main depot, and numerous foreign consulates. South of El Manshiyya and Misr Station the streets of **Karmus** overflow with students, workers, and many of Alexandria's poorest residents. The **corniche** is Alexandria's celebrated four-lane highway, pedestrian promenade, and sea wall. **Montaza Palace,** an 18km drive from El Manshiyya, demarcates the city's far eastern boundary. Note that the corniche is also called **July 26th Road** along the Eastern Harbor and **El Geish Road** between Es-Silsilah breakwater and Montaza.

The best place from which to orient yourself downtown is **Sa'ad Zaghloul Square,** on the waterfront with its massive statue of the man himself. Four streets border the square: **Nabi Daniel Street** (parallel to the Cecil Hotel) to the west, the **corniche** to the north along the waterfront, **Safia Zaghloul Street** to the east, and **Alexander the Great Street to** the south. Adjacent to the square in the southeast corner is **Raml Station Square,** in front of the tram station (with a row of buildings in between). Safia Zaghloul St., which bisects the two squares, is Alexandria's principal north-south boulevard. Bordering Raml Station Sq. on the south side is **Sa'ad Zaghloul Street** (which does *not* border Sa'ad Zaghloul Sq.). In addition to their central location, the two squares serve as transportation nuclei. Intercity buses run from the station on the corner of Nabi Daniel St. in Sa'ad Zaghloul Sq., and many municipal buses service the busy stop in front of the square on the corniche.

El Manshiyya Square is on the Eastern Harbor. It combines the rectangular **Ahmed Orabi Square,** an important interchange for local buses, and the smaller Tahrir Square (Midan et-Tahrir), which centers on the **Tomb of the Unknown Soldier,** a neoclassical monument facing the corniche. El Manshiyya Sq. lies about five blocks west of Sa'ad Zaghloul Sq. where Es-Sabaa Banat St. intersects with Salah Salem and Orabi St. Another important thoroughfare is **El Huriyya Street,** which runs east-west about five blocks south of Sa'ad Zaghloul Sq. Lined with banks and travel agencies, El Huriyya runs all the way to Montaza. A detailed *Tourist Map* of

Alexandria (E£3) covers the entire city to Montaza and Abu Qir, and shows tram lines as well. Try the **Al-Ma'aref Bookstore** (see p. 134).

ALEXANDRIA TRANSPORTATION

Your feet will serve you well in downtown Alexandria. The main squares, transportation centers, and the corniche all lie within walking distance on streets crammed with shops, cafés, and foodstands. A brisk half-hour walk will take you from old Pharos Island to the Shooting Club along the corniche—an especially enjoyable escapade at night. Though Alexandria, like any port, has its share of hustlers and hawkers, the city is relatively unthreatening. Pedestrians should feel pretty safe day and night. Foreign women, as always, will have to deal with comments and stares.

To visit the rest of the city, take a tram, bus, minibus, or taxi. **Tram** numbers are in Arabic only, but the numbers' backgrounds are color-coded. They run every few minutes until midnight for only 10pt per ride. Raml Station is the main terminus. Hop on at any stop and pay on board, but know that the middle car of every tram is for women only; men, stay away. Tram routes split at the Alexandria Sporting Club: some go on to the beaches while some turn inland. Sidi Gaber station is inland across from the Sidi Gaber train station, while Sidi Gaber esh-Sheikh is on the beach. There are also two Cleopatra stops, one inland and one near the beach. Unless otherwise noted, trams start at Raml Station then retrace their routes. The convenient tram is a sociological study and an integral part of the Alexandria experience.

#1 (blue background): To Sporting Club, Sidi Gaber esh-Sheikh, and beaches.
#2 (red background): To Sporting Club, Sidi Gaber, Cleopatra, and beaches, including Montaza.
#3 (blue on yellow): To Sporting Club and Sidi Gaber esh-Sheikh.
#4 (blue or black on yellow): Inland to Sidi Gaber, then back.
#5 (black on white): To Sporting Club, Sidi Gaber, further east and inland.
#14 (blue background, yellow tram): Misr Station, through El Manshiyya Sq. to Raml Station, southeast to Muharram Bey St. and the art museum.
#15 (yellow tram): Mosque of Abu El Abbas Morsi and Fort Qaytbay.
#16 (yellow tram): From El Manshiyya Sq. south to Karmus and Pompey's Pillar.

City buses stop at four main terminals—Sa'ad Zaghloul Sq., Raml Station, El Manshiyya Sq., and Misr Station. Buses run from approximately from 5:30am to midnight or 1am and cost 10-25pt; 50pt to outside beaches like El Agami. Only Arabic numbers are marked on buses, this time with no color hints—familiarize yourself with the numbers (see Language Glossary, p. 483).

#220: From Orabi Sq. to May 15th Sq.
#238: From El Manshiyya Sq. along the corniche to Montaza.
#250: From Misr Station to Montaza and Abu Qir.
#260: From Orabi Sq. to Montaza Palace and Abu Qir.
#303, 310, 703, 710: From Orabi Sq. to airport.
#309: From Raml Station Sq. to Pompey's Pillar.
#456: From Raml Station to El Agami.

A more appetizing alternative to the crowded city buses are the **minibuses,** which run from 5:30am to 1am and cost 25-50pt, depending on where you're going. Stand somewhere on the side of the street and hold up the number of fingers equal to the number of passengers in your group—if there's room inside, the driver will nod and pull over. To travel to specific sites in Alexandria, numbered minibuses pick up passengers from the corniche in front of Sa'ad Zaghloul Sq.

#220: Orabi Sq., Montaza.
#221: Orabi Sq., Ma'mura.
#707, 723: Fort Qaytbay.
#719: Montaza, El Geish St., Fort Qaytbay.

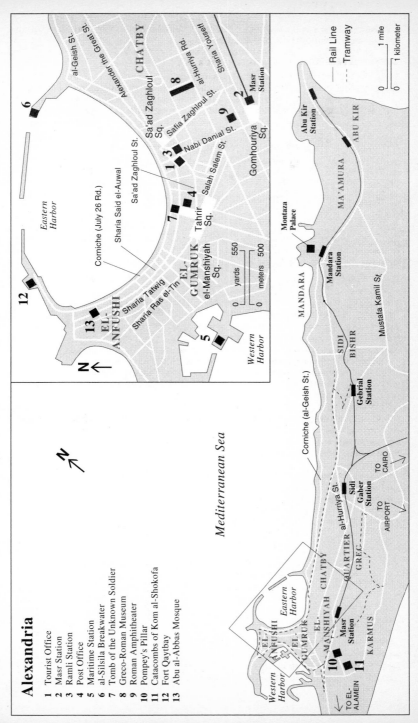

Alexandria

1 Tourist Office
2 Masr Station
3 Ramli Station
4 Post Office
5 Maritime Station
6 al-Silsila Breakwater
7 Tomb of the Unknown Soldier
8 Greco-Roman Museum
9 Roman Amphitheater
10 Pompey's Pillar
11 Catacombs of Kom al-Shokofa
12 Fort Qaytbay
13 Abu al-Abbas Mosque

Mediterranean Sea

Eastern Harbor

Western Harbor

Corniche (July 26 Rd.)

Sharia Said el-Auwal

Sharia Said el-Auwal

EL-ANFUSHI

EL-GUMRUK

Sharia Tatwig

Sharia Ras el-Tin

el-Manshiyah Sq.

CHATBY

al-Geish St.

Alexander the Great St.

Sa'ad Zaghloul

Sa'ad Zaghloul Sq.

Safia Zaghloul St.

Nabi Danial St.

Salah Salem St.

Sa'ad Zaghloul St.

Tahrir Sq.

al-Hurriya Rd.

Sharia Youseff

Masr Station

Gomhouriya Sq.

N

0   yards   550
0   meters   500

Mediterranean Sea

Corniche (al-Geish St.)

Corniche (al-Geish St.)

Montaza Palace

Abu Kir Station

ABU KIR

MA'AMURA

MANDARA

Mandara Station

SIDI BISHR

Gebrial Station

Mustafa Kamil St

Sidi Gaber Station

TO CAIRO

TO AIRPORT

QUARTIER GREC

al-Hurriya St.

EL-MANSHIYAH

CHATBY

Masr Station

KARMUS

EL-GUMRUK

EL-ANFUSHI

Eastern Harbor

Western Harbor

TO EL-ALAMEIN

Rail Line
Tramway

0   1 mile
0   1 kilometer

ALEXANDRIA

#720: Hannoville (Agami).
#724: Zoo, Fort Qaytbay.
#728: From Misr Station to Montaza.
#735: From Ras et-Tin to Montaza.
#736: From Ma'mura to Orabi Sq.
#750: Raml Station to "Agami" (Bitash).
#755: Misr Station to "Agami" (Bitash).
#760: Raml Station to Hannoville (Agami).

A **local taxi** ride in Alexandria is marginally less death-defying than in Cairo, and a comparatively inexpensive way to avoid the slow grind of the tram and the sardine can-esque quality of the city buses. Don't wait for an empty taxi: hail one going in your direction containing one or two passengers and shout your destination into the window. The meters never run, so pay as you please. No matter how big your group (3 is the maximum), you can get away with E£2 to almost anywhere, E£3 if you're feeling generous. Longer trips (Montaza or Abu Qir) enter the E£4-5 range, and past midnight E£5-7 is expected.

If you're in no hurry, hail one of the many horse-drawn **carriages** *(hantour)* that mosey along the corniche. Depending upon your bargaining clout, these can cost as little as E£5-7 per hour.

INTERCITY TRANSIT

Alexandria lies at the junction of lush Delta farmlands, the barren Western Desert, and the Mediterranean coast. Cairo is a two- to three-hour drive to the southeast on either of two roads. The scenic Delta road (231km) crosses both branches of the Nile and passes through the industrial city of Tanta, while the desert road (225km) passes through Giza and brushes Wadi Natrun. Recently the desert road has become greener and greener, and the difference between the two is not as pronounced.

Superjet Buses (tel. 482 4391) offer A/C, food, bathrooms, and annoyingly loud videotapes of Egyptian movies. Their ticket booth is in Raml Station Sq. and buses depart from there, unless otherwise noted. Buses go to Cairo, stopping at Giza Sq. and Tahrir Sq. (5:30am, 6:30, 7, 9, 10am, and 1pm E£16; 11am, noon, 7:30, 8, 8:30, 9, and 9:30pm E£17; 8, 11am, and 4pm E£25). and other Arab countries including Libya, Jordan, Kuwait, and Saudi Arabia (make reservations 1-2 days in advance). The **West Delta Bus Company** (tel. 80 96 58) has two types of buses. Their regular buses run to several destinations within Egypt and are not air-conditioned, but the **Golden Arrow** buses, reserved for longer distances, offer the same luxuries as Superjet. Ask at their ticket office (also in Raml Station Sq.) which type of bus is going to your chosen destination. Buses go to Cairo, stopping at Giza Sq. and Tahrir Sq. (every hr. 5:30am-10pm, 2½hr., E£12-E£18; some stop at Cairo International Airport, so check before you board), Marsa Matrouh (E£15), Luxor (6am and 6pm, E£37); Qena (E£34), Port Said (from the Sidi Gaber station; 6am and 4:30pm E£11, 8 and 11am with A/C E£15), Ismailiyya (7am and 2:30pm, E£8.50); Taba (9:30pm, E£65), St. Catherine's (9am, E£30), Sharm esh-Sheikh (7am E£20; 7:30, 10am, and 2pm E£25; 4pm E£30; 9:45pm E£40; 10:10pm E£50), Marsa Matrouh (7:30, 10am, noon, and 2:30pm, 4hr., E£12.50-21; 10am and noon buses continue to Siwa), and Dahab (7:30am E£30, 5pm E£23, 10:15pm E£55), with daily runs to Tanta, Mansura, Dumyat (Damietta), and Rashid (Rosetta).

Trains to Cairo come in three flavors: the Turbini express, the French line, and regular. All leave from Misr Station (some stopping at Sidi Gaber Station) and arrive in Ramses Station. Make reservations in advance, particularly for Thurs. and Fri. The **Turbini** choo-choos are air-conditioned and leave at 7:55am, 2, 3, and 6:45pm (2¼hr., 1st-class E£20.70, 2nd-class E£12.40, students E£10.70). The air-conditioned **French line** has daily runs at 8:15, 10, 11am, 1, 3:30, 5, 7:30, and 8pm, also 9:30pm in summer (2½hr., 2nd-class E£9.40, students E£7.10). Make reservations in advance. Trains also go from Misr Station to Marsa Matrouh (10am, 2nd-class E£6.40, 3rd class E£2.80); Luxor (French, 10:15am) and on to Aswan, and to many other destinations throughout Egypt. If the Egyptian railway system still boggles your mind, the folks at the tourist offices inside the station and in Sa'ad Zaghloul Sq. are knowledgeable and willing to decode.

Intercity taxis are a cheap and generally comfortable alternative to bus or train transport. Because of all the competition from other means of transportation, however, they depart less frequently than in other cities. Shared **Peugeot taxis** shuttle between Alexandria's Misr Station and Cairo's Ramses Station (E£8.50 by the desert road). Other taxis also leave from the southern end of Nabi Daniel St., around Misr Station. (Marsa Matrouh E£10, Port Said E£11, Sohag E£26, Damanhur E£2.50, Zagazig E£2.75, Tanta E£2, Mansura E£3, Abu Qir 50pt.) Shared taxis to Rashid (E£4) leave from Tahrir Sq.

EgyptAir, 19 Sa'ad Zaghloul St. just east of Raml Station Sq. (tel. 482 5938), another office on El Huriyya St. in Gleem (tel. 586 5461) flies once daily from Alexandria to Cairo (Mon.-Fri. 9:10am, 35 min; Sat.-Sun. 9:05am, 55min.; E£47) and back. Or try your luck getting a standby ticket at the airport (E£28). Alexandria's small airport lies several kilometers southeast of downtown. Local bus #303, 310, 703, and 710 run between Orabi Sq. and the airport. **Lufthansa,** 6 Tala'at Harb St. (tel. 483 5983 or 7031), is the only international airline flying directly to Alexandria, with arrivals from Frankfurt on Sat. and Tues. evenings. Departures to Frankfurt Sun. and Wed. (one way E£3112, round trip E£2481 with 10- to 45-day stay). Lufthansa also flies to and from Cairo (one way E£2481, round trip E£3112 with 10- to 45-day stay).

There are limited options for traveling to Europe from Alexandria by **passenger ferry** (see Essentials: Getting There by Boat, p. 28). Adriatica Line runs a ferry service (Egitto Express) between Alexandria and: Heraklion, Crete (US$190-290); Piraeus, Greece; Patras, Greece; and Venice, Italy (US$550-890). Contact **Menatours** in Alexandria for more information (port office tel. 80 02 01 or 01 00; fax 81 58 30).

PRACTICAL INFORMATION

Tourist Office: main office at Nabi Daniel St. (tel. 80 76 11 or 80 79 85), at the southwest corner of **Sa'ad Zaghloul Sq.** English spoken fluently. Open Sun.-Thurs. 8am-2pm, in winter 8am-5pm, during Ramadan 9am-4pm, holidays 8am-2pm. Branch offices at **Misr Station** (tel. 492 5985; open 8am-6pm, in winter 8am-5pm) and the **Maritime Station** (tel. 80 34 94, 80 01 00, or 80 03 04; open 8am-5pm). Pick up a free copy of *Alexandria by Night and Day,* which lists restaurants, hotels, travel agents, and a train schedule to Cairo. The map of central Alex makes good wallpaper. Other offices are at the **airport** (tel. 420 1036) and **Raml Station** (tel. 80 79 85).

Tourist Police: Montaza Palace (tel. 547 3395, direct line 80 96 11). Branch office upstairs from the tourist office in **Sa'ad Zaghloul Sq.** (tel. 80 76 11 or 79 85). Both open 24 hrs. Also branches in the **amphitheater** (tel. 490 6273), **Citadel** (tel. 80 91 44), and the **Greco-Roman Museum** (tel. 482 8912).

Passport Office: 28 Tala'at Harb St. (tel. 482 7873). Walk west on Sa'ad Zaghloul St. from Raml Station Sq. and bear left on Falaky St. when Sa'ad Zaghloul begins to curve toward the sea. Tala'at Harb St. will be your first left; the office is on the corner, on the western side of Tala'at Harb St. So annoying that a Quaker would take a shot at the staff. Open Sat.-Wed. 8:30am-4pm and 7-9pm, Thurs. 8:30am-1:30pm and 7-9pm (evening hours for passport registration only).

Consulates: Israel, 207 Abd es-Salem Aref St., Rushdi (tel. 586 0492). Open Sun.-Thurs. 9:30am-12:30pm. **U.K.,** 3 Mena St., Rushdi (tel. 546 7001), off Kafr Abdou St. About 6km east of downtown, several blocks south of the corniche. Open Sun.-Thurs. 8am-1pm. The **U.S.** consulate closed at the end of summer 1993.

Currency Exchange: Plentiful **exchange places** offer better rates than banks, but only take cash. Egyptian banks, the largest of which will exchange traveler's checks, are on every other street corner downtown. Most open Sat.-Thurs. 8:30am-noon and 5-7 or 8pm. **National Bank** in the **Sheraton Montaza,** El Corniche Rd. (tel. 548 0550) is open **daily (including holidays)** 10am-12pm. Branch in the **Cecil Hotel,** Sa'ad Zaghloul Sq. is open daily 3-9pm. **Bank of America** (tel. 493 1115), across from the football stadium on Lomomba St., 1 block south of El Huriyya St., and **Barclay's,** 10 Fawoteur St. (tel. 482 1308), are both open

ALEXANDRIA

Sun.-Thurs. 9:30am-1:30pm. **Citibank** (tel. 483 4363) is on the corniche about 1km east of downtown.

American Express: Small branch office in **Eyres Travel,** 26 El Huriyya St. (tel. 483 0084 or 1275), 5 blocks south (via Nabi Daniel St.) of Sa'ad Zaghloul Sq. Open Mon.-Thurs. 9am-1pm and 5-6:30pm, Fri.-Sat. 9am-1pm.

Thomas Cook: 15 Sa'ad Zaghloul Sq., P.O. Box 185 and 2280 (tel. 482 7830; fax 483 4073). Full range of Thomas Cook services. Also offices in the **Ocean Terminal** (tel. 80 01 00, ext. 1360) and the **Airport** (tel. 420 8764) for currency exchange and traveler's checks.

Post Office: At the tram stop at **Raml Station Sq.** Open daily 8am-3pm, stamps sold until 6pm. Also 2 branches on **Rue el-Ghorfa et-Tigariyya** (3 blocks west of Sa'ad Zaghloul Sq., or 2 blocks west of Orabi Sq.), in **Misr Station** (open until 5pm), and across from **Sidi Gaber station** for **EMS.** Most open Sat.-Thurs. 8am-3pm. **Poste Restante** at the branch west of Orabi Sq. (Sat.-Thurs. 8:30am-1pm).

Telephone Office: Raml Station Sq. (3min. to the U.S. E£23.55, cheaper with phone card.) Open 24 hrs. Also at **Misr Station** and at the west end of **Sa'ad Zaghloul St.** (Open until 10pm.) Luxury hotels (try the Cecil in Sa'ad Zaghloul Sq.) can call overseas, but are more expensive. **Information:** Tel. 125. **Telephone code:** 03.

Car Rental: Avis, in the Cecil Hotel, Sa'ad Zaghloul Sq. (tel. 483 1467 or 1364 or 4768; open daily 8am-8pm) rents 1983 Peugeot 505s for E£90 per day (plus 32pt per km over 100), including full insurance for car and passengers.

English Bookstores: Cosmopolitanism be damned; the offerings are less than mouth-watering. The best is **Al-Ma'aref,** 44 Sa'ad Zaghloul St. (tel. 483 3303), which has an entrance on the south side of Sa'ad Zaghloul Sq. It has all AUC books and some Arabic novels translated into English. Open Mon.-Sat. 10am-9:30pm. **Book Center,** 49 Sa'ad Zaghloul St. (tel. 482 2925), has a good selection of English and Egyptian literature in paperback. Open Mon.-Sat. 9am-1pm and 6-9pm. **Ramadan Bazaar Bookshop** features some AUC books (tel. 86 61 11; open 9am-11pm). **Al-Ahram,** 13 El Huriyya St. (tel. 483 4000), opposite the Piccadilly Hotel on the corner of El Huriyya and Nabi Daniel St., has an impressive collection of detective novels and medical texts. Open Mon.-Thurs. and Sat. 9am-3pm, Sun. 9am-1pm.

Cultural Centers: U.S., Phara'ana St. (tel. 482 1009 or 4117), one block over from El Huriyya St., 2km east of downtown. Fine book and video library. You can watch the CBS Evening News daily at 2pm or ABC News' weekly highlights every Sunday at noon. Open Mon.-Thurs. 8am-4pm; closed Aug. for inventory. **British Council,** 9 Ptolemies St. (tel. 482 0199 or 9890). Open Sun.-Thurs. 9am-3:30pm. Library open Sun.-Thurs. 10am-7:30pm, Sat. 10am-3pm.

Photography and Film Developing: Kodak, 63 Safiyya Zaghloul St., has a large selection of Kodak film, about E£7 per roll. Developing E£1, plus 30pt per print. Open daily 9am-9pm. Another **Kodak** is on Salah Salem St. (30-40pt per print, depending on size.) There are also a number of smaller photo accessory and film shops along Sa'ad Zaghloul St. The farther from Raml Station, the cheaper.

Pharmacy: Many are located along Sa'ad Zaghloul St. or scattered throughout downtown. **Khalil** (tel. 80 67 10), 3 doors west of Sa'ad Zaghloul Sq. next to the West Delta bus station in front of Chamber of Commerce, is open Mon.-Sat. 9am-10pm, Sun. 10am-10pm.

Hospital: El Mowasah, on El Huriyya St. in El Haddara (tel. 421 2885). For most illnesses, ask for help at a 4- or 5-star hotel. The **Smouha Medical Center,** May 14th Rd., Smouha (tel. 420 2652/3/8/9), is accustomed to dealing with foreigners.

Fire: Tel. 180.

Police: Emergency: Tel. 123. **City Police:** Tel. 122. Available 24 hrs. If possible contact the Tourist Police (above).

ACCOMMODATIONS

For those who want a (cheap) room with a view (see Forster, below), there are several small hotels (not listed below) on the streets running south from the corniche near **Raml Station Sq.** The crowds are tolerable at E£5-10 per night, but the insects, ranging from tiny ticks and fleas to armor-plated, three-inch flying cockroaches, may be intolerable in some of these establishments. The places listed below are relatively clean and cheap, and all except the hostel and the Corail Hotel lie within walking distance of the two main squares. None have fans, unless noted; most Alexandrians depend on sea breezes for their air conditioning.

Streets in **El Manshiyya Sq.** also bristle with budget hotels. Many Arab vacationers prefer to stay in the hotels near the corniche and beaches, while foreign travelers seem to favor accommodations near the center of town. Those who insist upon a beachside retreat should head out toward Montaza (18km), at least as far as Sidi Bishr (14km), where the amenities begin to balance the inconvenience of staying so far from the center of town. For serious piaster-pinchers there is **camping** by the beach at Abu Qir for 50pt (see Abu Qir óxr Îf'h, p. 140). Fans of E. M. Forster (who lived in Alexandria and wrote the fabulous *Alexandria: A History & Guide*) should stay at (or at least visit) the *Cecil* Hotel, whose stony exterior inspired a character in our favorite (and much-cited) novel, *A Room With a View*.

Hotel Acropole, 27 Rue de Chambre de Commerce, 4th floor (tel. 80 59 80), 1 block west of Sa'ad Zaghloul Sq., directly behind the Cecil Hotel. One of the best deals in town. Clean, bright, and inviting, though the grimy entrance may lead you to expect otherwise. Comfortable TV lounge. No private baths, but shared baths are clean. Singles E£15, with view E£20. Doubles E£25. Breakfast included. Fills fast (only 4 singles), so reserve in advance for rooms facing the beach.

Hotel Marhaba, 10 Ahmed Orabi Sq. (tel. 80 09 57, international 80 95 10), on the northwest side of Orabi Sq. Clean rooms and baths, and bellboys in spiffy uniforms. Busy with tourists; fills quickly. Rooms carpeted, with ceiling fan, TV (and dish), and bath. Singles E£32. Doubles E£43. Triples E£65. Breakfast included. Restaurant downstairs (lunch E£17, dinner E£19, Stella E£7.70, imports E£11.40). Also a cute little coffeeshop and a bar.

Hotel Leroy, 25 Tala'at Harb St. (tel. 483 3439 or 482 9224), opposite passport office, was built by French Jews and retains old-fashioned style and architecture. Once magnificent, with an art-deco bar and lounge area, now a bit faded; but still has reminders of the good ol' times (funny phones, a smoking room). Rooms are spacious, bright, and breezy, some with vistas of the sea. This is the place for people with imagination. Singles E£22.50, with bath E£25. Doubles E£27.50, with bath E£30. Triples E£35, with bath E£38. Breakfast included.

Hotel Triomphe (Hotel Nasr in Arabic), 26 Rue de Chambre de Commerce, 5th floor (tel. 80 75 85), across from the Acropole but far lower in quality. Not the most comfortable nor the cleanest place, but the prices are low. Also fills quickly. Singles E£6, with bath E£7. Doubles E£14. Triples E£17.

Ailema Hotel, 21 Amin Fakri St., 7th floor (tel. 482 7011 or 483 2916). From Raml Station Sq. walk east 3 blocks and turn right. The revolving door is somewhat elegant, the rooms less so, though newly painted. Breathtaking balconies. Private baths are tiny. Singles E£10, with view E£15, with view and bath E£18. Doubles E£25, with view E£30, with view and bath E£33. Triples E£36, with view E£40, with view and bath E£43. Breakfast included.

Sea Star Hotel, 24 Amin Fakri St. (tel. 483 1787 or 2388; fax 80 53 43), across from the Ailema Hotel. Formerly the Hotel Admiral. Spacious, clean, well-furnished rooms with fans, phones, and TV. Some rooms have, yup, a view; all 64 have private baths. Singles E£38. Doubles E£48. Triples E£66. Suites E£85. Continental breakfast included. 24-hr. restaurant attached (lunch E£12.50, dinner E£14.50).

Hyde Park House (tel. 483 5666/7), above the Ailema Hotel. Oldish baths have huge tubs. Singles E£17. Doubles E£26.50, with bath E£31. Triples E£37, with bath E£42. Breakfast included.

Hotel Piccadilly, 11 El Huriyya St., 8th floor (tel. 492 4497). At the large intersection with Nabi Daniel St., on the southeast corner. Halfway between the corniche and Misr Station. Shabby rooms and solicitous staff, but close to Misr Station. Singles E£8.30, with bath E£11.90. Doubles E£11.30, with bath E£14.30.

Youth Hostel (HI), Port Said St., Chatby (tel./fax 597 5459), just off the corniche. Take an eastbound tram (10pt) from Raml Station Sq. until you see the red- and-white dome of St. Mark's College on the left side (at the Chatby Casino). The hostel is on the corniche side. Rooms are drab, but have fans. Bathrooms are not spectacular. Open daily 8am-11pm. Strict curfew. E£4.10, E£1 extra for non-members. Breakfast E£2, lunch E£8, dinner E£6.

Corail Hotel, 802 El Geish St. (tel. 548 0996 or 86 28 18), 2½ blocks west of Montaza, overlooking the corniche and Mandara Beach; take the tram or bus. Splurge. Orderly, bright, and close to the romantic Montaza, though noisy during the day with a mob-scene beach below. All rooms with bath and phone. Seldom full. Singles E£56.50. Doubles E£88.90. Breakfast and lunch included.

FOOD

It should come as no surprise that the cheapest food in Alexandria is at *fuul* and falafel stands. Some of the most luscious offerings are found around the cloth market between Pompey's Pillar and Misr Station and on the western side of the peninsula, where 50pt nets a well-endowed sandwich. **El Anfushi,** also known as Old Alexandria, on the western side of the bay, is full of restaurants which Egyptians have gone to for generations (its old, old buildings provide a feast for the eyes as well as for the palate). Take tram #15 from Raml Station and walk inland a few blocks. **Bakkash** is famous for *kufta* and *kabab*, **Kaddura** for grilled fish and shrimp. Wimps will find that **Pizza Hut, Kentucky Fried Chicken,** and **Wimpy** have colonized the corniche in Rushdi, about 1km east of downtown. Other franchises are on the grounds at Montaza and downstairs from Tikka Grill.

Muhammad Ahmed Fuul, 17 Shakur St. (tel. 483 3576), 2 blocks south of Sa'ad Zaghloul Sq. and 1 block west of Safia Zaghloul St. No English sign; gaudy, gold Arabic letters over the door. Some consider this the best *fuul* and falafel joint in Egypt. The food is amazing, and nothing on the menu costs more than E£1.70. Open daily 6am-midnight. Take-out available, but the place is fully air-conditioned. Happy *fuul* consumption!

Cafeteria Asteria, 40 Safia Zaghloul St. (tel. 482 2293), several doors down from Santa Lucia. Clean cafeteria offers a variety of cheap, light, and tasty meals (pizza E£7.20). Alcohol served. Min. charge E£1.80. Open daily 9am-midnight.

Broast Bamby (tel. 482 7811), one block east of Raml Station Sq., on the corner. Meals cost about E£10, fish and chicken sandwiches E£6-7. Don't be alarmed if you find it totally empty; this seems to be the norm. Great place for the shy and anti-noise-pollution activists. Open daily 8am-1am.

Taverna, (tel. 482 8189), on the southern side of Raml Square, on the corner of Sa'ad Zaghloul and Safia Zaghloul St. Comfortably crowded with Egyptians and very convenient. The *shawerma* platter (E£10.75), pizza (E£8-10.50), and pasta (E£10-15) are all fresh 'n' tasty. If you're looking for a bargain, don't eat in the restaurant upstairs but try the take-away section on the ground level. *Shawerma* sandwiches are E£2.50; and there are plenty of tables. Enjoy the Gipsy Kings. (Bamboleo!) Visa, AmEx. Open 7am-2am. Another location is the **Taverna Beach Restaurant** (tel. 547 5438) in Montaza Gardens. Open 10am-2am.

New China Chinese Restaurant, 802 El Geish St., Mandara (tel. 548 0996), in the Corail Hotel. Possibly the only (and therefore the best) Chinese food in Alexandria. Entrees about E£15. Try the delicious fried chicken in lemon sauce (E£19, E£5 for rice), or the *leung chow* seafood fried rice. Alcohol served. AmEx, Visa, Mastercard. Open daily 11am-11pm.

Restaurant Denis, 1 Ibn Bassam St. (tel. 483 0457), 4 blocks east of Sa'ad Zaghloul Sq. Neat little eatery just off the corniche serves the best budget seafood in Alexandria. Pick out your fish in the kitchen (E£22-28 per kg; 0.25kg per person is filling and 0.5kg a feast) and they'll bring you a plethora of salads, dips, and bread; you can stuff yourself silly for E£12. Beer and wine served. Open daily 9am-1am.

Restaurant Darwish, (tel. 482 8938), on the corniche 4 blocks east of Sa'ad Zaghloul Sq. across from the World Health Organization building. Digest French food among encased fake coral reefs and display windows of future entrees *avant la preparation*. The adventurous will appreciate the *Jarret Darwish* (cooked veal knuckles, E£12). During Ramadan, try the fruit *fondue* aged for 1 year. Filling meals cost E£10-12. Open daily 24 hrs.

Tikka Grill (tel. 80 51 14 or 98 42), jutting into the Eastern Harbor near Abu el-Abbas Mosque, 1.5km west of Sa'ad Zaghloul Sq. A bit of a hike for good service, an excellent salad bar, and a sweeping view of the corniche. But don't believe the hype: the much-touted "Indian" chicken is dry and flavorless. Order something else. Full meals E£30 including unlimited salad bar, mineral water, and dessert. Ask for ice cream from the shop downstairs in the garden. Alcohol served. AmEx, Visa, Mastercard. Open daily 1pm-2am.

For dessert, the **Delices** and **Trianon** patisseries located opposite the corniche in Sa'ad Zaghloul Sq. serve pastries in a setting notably reminiscent of the British occupation. The **Samadi Patisserie** (open 10:30am-2am) next to Tikka Grill doles out *baqlawa, basbouseh, konafa,* and several variations. (AmEx, Visa, and Mastercard accepted.) Cafés line the corniche near Sa'ad Zaghloul Sq. Cheaper, more traditional *qahwas* are in the neighborhood streets south of the waterfront. Coffee epicures luxuriate at the **Brazilian Coffee Store,** 44 Sa'ad Zaghloul St. (tel. 482 5059), opposite the Book Centre at the Nabi Daniel intersection. (Cappuccino E£1, espresso 75pt, refreshing iced coffee E£1, and iced tea 80pt. Open Sat.-Thurs. 7am-11pm.)

SIGHTS

Very little remains of ancient Alexandria, as the modern city was built directly atop the old one. If you must, buy *The Guide to the Alexandrian Monuments*, available at the Greco-Roman museum. The excellent **Greco-Roman Museum,** 5 El Mathaf El Rumani St. (tel. 482 5820), gives visitors an introduction to ancient Alexandria and its Hellenistic civilization. The cult of Serapis is well represented: look for handsome sculptures of Zeus and Apis and the Greek youth Harpocrates, with his finger in his ear. The museum's courtyard contains an intriguing crocodile temple attributed to the cult of Phepheros, as well as a mummified crocodile and other assorted relics from Egypt's Greco-Roman past. To reach the museum walk south from the corniche along Safia Zaghloul St., turn left on El Huriyya St., and walk until the sign for the museum directs you to the left again. (Open Sat.-Thurs. 9am-4pm, Fri. 9am-noon and 2-4pm, during Ramadan and on holidays 9am-3pm. Admission E£8, students E£4, camera privileges (no flash) E£10.)

From the museum it's an easy meander to the three major ancient sites, all of which lie within a few kilometers of downtown. Just north of Misr Station and behind Cinema Amir is the beautifully preserved, white marble **Roman Amphitheater,** the only one of its kind ever found in Egypt. Behind the 13-tiered theater struggle the ruins of a Roman bath (to the left) and a Roman villa and cistern (to the right). Self-styled guides may offer to sneak you in for a fee, but it's not worth it since almost everything of interest is visible from the theater. Walk down Nabi Daniel St. from Sa'ad Zaghloul Sq. and take the second left after El Huriyya St.; the entrance will be on your left. (Open daily 9am-4pm, during Ramadan 10am-3pm. Admission E£3, students E£1.50. Camera privileges E£10.)

The most famous ancient monument is **Pompey's Pillar,** a granite construction that thrusts upward to a height of 25m, named by Crusaders in the Middle Ages who mistakenly thought it had some connection with Pompey. The pillar actually dates from the time of Diocletian, several centuries later, and was part of the Serapium, a religious center where the rites of the cult of the bull god were conducted. Not surprisingly, the temple was leveled once the Roman Empire turned Christian.

The Roman provincial governor raised the pillar, originally transported from Aswan, in honor of the emperor Diocletian's failure to subdue an Alexandrian revolt. The feisty emperor (who would not have been well-loved by Amnesty International) swore that he would massacre the rebellious people until blood stained the knees of his horse; as he entered the cowering town his mount stumbled into a pool of blood, prematurely fulfilling his oath. Thus, the emperor did not sack the city, and the lone pillar remains as a symbol of the people's gratitude to him and his klutzy horse. The ruins of the Serapium around the pillar have been excavated and the best finds moved to the Greco-Roman museum. To reach the site take bus #309 from Raml Station Sq. and get off on Karmus St. when you see the pillar. The entrance is on the southern side of the complex. You can also take tram #16. (Site open daily 9am-4pm; during Ramadan 9am-3pm. Admission E£3, students E£1.50.)

Ambling past the entrance to the Serapium (in the direction the bus travels), take your first right and follow it about 500m to the eerie **Catacombs of Kom esh-Sho-qafa** (Hill of Potsherds). These Roman tombs descend in three levels to a depth of about 35m and are noteworthy for their bits of sculpture and reliefs depicting Egyptian gods with unmistakably virile Roman bodies, thus blending Pharaonic and Roman Art. A statue of jackal-headed Anubis stands near the entrance to the innermost burial chamber. As you enter the central rotunda, the creepy capacious room to your left is where the funeral feasts were held. The hall of the goddess Nemesis, farther down and to the left, is flooded—watch your step. (Open daily 9am-4pm, during Ramadan 9am-3pm. Admission E£6, students E£3. Camera privileges E£10.)

Behind the Governor's residence sits the architecturally intriguing **Royal Jewelry Museum,** 27 Ahmed Yehia St., Gleem, originally the Palace of Fatima ez-Zahraa. The museum contains the gleaming baubles of the Muhammad Ali era. Most memorable are the pieces belonging to the royal family, especially those bestowed on the wives of King Farouk. Take tram #2 (look for the red sign) to get there. (Open Sat.-Thurs. 9am-4pm, Fri. 9-11:30am and 1:30-4pm. Admission E£10, students E£5.) For another quick tourist fix, visit the **Tombs of Chatby,** Port Said St., across from St. Mark's College. Believed to be the oldest tombs in Alexandria, they date to the 3rd century BCE. (Open daily 9am-4pm. Admission E£3, students E£1.50.) For the student of Alexandrian history, the **Cavafy Museum** on 4 Sharm esh-Sheikh St., 2nd floor (call the Greek consulate, tel. 483 8455, or the tourist office for hours and information), houses a collection of this Greek Alexandrian poet's books and furniture. (Free.)

The neighborhoods lying west and north of the central square reward back-street investigation. Dilapidated **El Goumrouk** and breezy **El Anfushi** are crowded with old mosques, Coptic churches, and finely decorated 19th-century buildings. The Islamic **Fort Qaytbay** (tel. 80 91 44) commands the ancient island of Pharos, now the tip of the peninsula separating the eastern and western harbors. The fort symbolizes "the big one that got away;" it was built in the 15th century CE by the Mamluk Sultan Qaytbay over the old Lighthouse of Pharos. Inside, a naval museum features an exhibition of artifacts salvaged from the sunken French fleet that was destroyed by Nelson at the Battle of the Nile. Notice the small mosque in the center of the tower; the entire fortress is aligned so that its *mihrab* will face Mecca. (Fort open Sat.-Thurs. 9am-4pm, Fri. 9am-noon and 2-4pm; during Ramadan 10am-2:30pm. Admission E£6, students E£3. Camera privileges E£10.)

To reach the fort, take yellow tram #15 west from Raml Station and get off when it makes a sharp left turn, or take any of the buses going to Ras et-Tin. You'll find yourself in the middle of an open-air **fish market,** and lo, it stinketh. At the point where the tram turned left, you should turn right on the road between the Kuwait Airlines sign and the mosque; the fort is at the end of this road. Also accessible by bus #260 to Abu Qir or minibus #707 from Raml Station Sq. (these buses take you to the end of the street, not all the way to the Fort.)

The **Mosque of Morsi Abu el-Abbas,** with its four domes and tall minarets, is located 1km south of the fort along the corniche and is Alexandria's most prominent and elaborate sample of Islamic architecture. It's also the largest mosque in the city. The holy Abu el-Abbas came from Andalusia, Spain, and settled in the Delta. His tomb rests in the back of the mosque. Legend professes that he rose from his tomb to catch bombs falling on Alexandria during World War II raids. Until the arrival of feminism in this part of town, women are permitted to enter only the back room of the mosque. The coffin surrounded by a glowing green neon lamp might be the most intriguing sight. (Open 5am-10pm, except prayer times. Dress modestly.)

Another central Alexandrian magnet, the **Fine Arts Museum,** at 18 Menasha St. (tel. 493 6616), contains a small but interesting collection of modern Egyptian art as well as Alexandria's public library. Exhibitions by contemporary foreign and Egyptian artists are often held here; call and find out. Every two years, the museum organizes the **Alexandria Biennial,** an exhibition of the art of Mediterranean countries. From Misr Station walk east on Mahmoud Bey Salama St., which runs along the southern side of the railroad tracks. The museum is on the right at the first major intersection. (About 1km. Open Sat.-Thurs. 8am-2pm and 5-8pm. Free.)

The highlight of Alexandria's eastern beaches is the **Montaza Palace and Gardens** (tel. 86 00 79 or 56), originally built in 1892. King Farouk's former summer retreat includes 400 acres of gardens, as well as beaches and the Saudi-friendly Palestine Hotel. The palace and its museum have been closed to the public, but the gardens and groves are a favorite picnic spot for Alexandrians. Beware—the Gardens can get quite crowded on weekends, especially on Fridays. Ice cream stores, a juice place, Pizza Hut, Chicken Tikka (a spin-off of Tikka Grill), and a supermarket lie within the garden gates. (Admission to the gardens E£2. Semi-private beach west of the palace E£6.) Catch minibus #220 or 221 on the corniche or at Orabi Sq., or bus #238 from El Manshiyya Sq. (50pt). Third-class trains to Abu Qir, departing every hour from either Misr or Sidi Gaber Station, all stop at Montaza (45pt).

ENTERTAINMENT

Alexandria's most popular attractions are its **beaches.** Alarmingly popular, in fact; during the blazing summer months, Cairenes come here by the thousands. The masses are daunting: it's possible to ride up and down the entire 18km coast without seeing a single square meter of free sand. Consider the effects of ever-increasing erosion and exceptionally disagreeable pollution (the net weight of the litter nearly exceeds that of the bathers), and you will doubtless opt to avoid this temptation to court melanoma. A rule of thumb: the more expensive a beach is, the less crowded and more liberal. At free beaches, women bathe fully clothed or not at all. Try your luck at Montaza or **Ma'mura.** Ma'mura, just east of Montaza, can be reached by a Montaza bus or train (see above), or take minibus #220, which runs along the corniche. Another semi-private beach, **San Stefano,** lies a bit east of the half-way point between Sa'ad Zaghloul Sq. and Montaza; you can rent chairs and an umbrella for E£2-3. Small changing rooms on the beach can be rented for E£5 per day; larger *cabinehs* go for E£20 per day. Take tram #1, 2, or 5 from Raml Station.

Especially in summer, Alexandria's upper crust lives at the **Alexandria Sporting Club** (tel. 85 36 27 or 28), a huge country club that puts your local pool and tennis courts to shame. It's hard to miss—every tram out of Raml Station stops there. The club offers a great pool and everything from golf to polo matches; at night, play billiards, watch movies, stroll, or flirt. Nonmembers pay E£10 per day and must be accompanied by a member, so find someone at the gates or the tram station.

Alexandria's nightlife centers on the corniche. In summer you'll see wedding parties wherever you go along the corniche, and foreigners are often invited to share in the fun. Most clubs require patrons to guzzle (E£5-10 worth) but have no cover charge. **Crazy Horse,** a nightclub in Raml Station Sq. (tel. 482 8131), is the best known and generally packed with Egyptians of questionable moral fiber (a lot closer to polyester than to linen). There's a live show there, including a belly dancer (open 9:30pm-2am). Away from the corniche, **Santa Lucia Restaurant** (tel. 492 0372) has a low-key bar with live music every night except Sundays (open nightly 10pm-2am; cover charge E£13.75), and a nightclub is also attached to **Au Privé Restaurant,** 14 El Huriyya St. (tel. 483 8082; open until 3am). For those hungry for the expatriate atmosphere, **Monty's Bar** in the Cecil Hotel (open noon-2am) is where General Montgomery totaled more than tea and planned the British war effort, and where Bogart nursed a cool one. Don't count on seeing illustrious expats hanging out these days, however. Stella E£6. The Mona Lisa to your left is not real, silly, even if this portrait looks more and more authentic after a few drinks.

Also popular are Alexandria's **cinemas.** English-language films usually play at the Amir (tel. 491 7972) and Metro (tel. 483 0432) theaters, both on Safia Zaghloul St. (Shows at 10:30am, 3:15, 6:30, and 9:30pm. Tickets E£5.70-10.) Check billboards for details. In September an **international film festival** presents foreign films in all of the city's theaters; ask at the tourist information office.

Every summer the breezy, outdoor **Muhammad Abd el-Wahab Theater,** on the corniche at Raml Station Sq., features **traditional dancing.** Fir'et Rida (Rida's troupe) and El Fir'a el-Qawmiyya (the National Troupe), both featuring legendary belly dancers, perform high-energy dances representative of various areas in Egypt (watch for the men's dance with canes, from Upper Egypt). (Nightly shows at 10:30pm. Reserve tickets one or two days in advance. Super deluxe front-row tickets E£10.50, cheap seats E£5. Avoid the uncomfortable box seats and bring a sweater.) You may think you left the **circus** behind when you left Cairo, but the Ringling Brothers' Egyptian cousins are at St. Mark's College every summer. One matinee and one soirée daily. Tickets E£2-7.

■ EAST OF ALEXANDRIA

ABU QIR ابو قير

The fishing village of **Abu Qir** (pronounced abu EER) lies on a peninsula 5km past Montaza. The village remains rural, not yet absorbed by Alexandria's relentless expansion. Abu Qir is famous as the site of Nelson's 1798 naval victory over Napoleon, as the former foiled the little Frenchman's visions of Egyptian conquest. More important to the traveler, Abu Qir is a great place to sample Mediterranean seafood often superior to that in Alexandria. Go on a week day if you don't like crowds, but people-watching on the weekends can be as good as the food. From Alexandria, you can reach Abu Qir from Misr Station by **local bus** #250, 251, or 260 or **minibus** #729 (every ½hr. 7am-10pm, 50pt), a third-class **train** from Misr or Sidi Gaber Station (daily every ½hr. 6am-10pm, 45pt), a **local taxi** from downtown (E£5-10), or a **service taxi** (50pt.) from in front of Misr Station. Within Abu Qir, you can take a horse-drawn carriage (*hantour*) from Bahr El Mayyit St. (25pt).

There are two options for eating fish in Abu Qir. Try eating on the beach: walk east to the waterfront until you reach a row of tables right on the sand. Anglers will come in from the boats anchored offshore and cook the fish you select right at your table. The second option is a restaurant. The well-known **Zephyrion** (Greek for "sea breeze"), 14 Khalid Ibn Walid St. (tel. 560 1319), has been an Abu Qir landmark since 1929 and is probably one of Egypt's best restaurants. If you sit in the blue and white pavilion on the beach, you can listen to and watch the lapping of the waves while dining on the fresh seafood you have chosen from the restaurant's freezers. It just doesn't get much better than this. A full dinner including beer and salad typically costs E£30, fish roughly E£34-40 per kg, shrimp E£80, and more, for other exotica (excluding taxes). Try the octopus (*kaborya*) plate (E£10, E£4 for one piece). (Open daily noon-midnight.) Next door to Zephyrion is another piscatorial paradise called **Bella Vista** (tel. 560 0628), which is not as nice (the interior is brown) and has similar prices (open daily noon-1am). To reach either restaurant head north to the waterfront from the main mosque; they're right on the beach.

Abu Qir offers little except seafood and is best visited as a daytrip from Alexandria. The town is ideal for campers, though, since **Abu Qir Camp** (tel. 560 1424), located on El Bahr El Mayyit St. about 500m south of the Zephyrion, supplies the only consistently available camping possibilities in the Alexandria area (E£3 whether you use your own tent or one of theirs). With permission from the local police, you can camp for free on the beach. Extra time in Abu Qir can be filled by a motorboat excursion to **Nelson's Island** (45min., E£40 for 3 people). Walk to the beach at the end of El Bahr El Mayyit St. and ask for motorboat guru El Mu'allim Desouki. Loll about imagining you were present at the Napoleon-Nelson rout of 1798.

RASHID (ROSETTA) رشيد

About 75 minutes east of Abu Qir (1hr. east of Alexandria) stretches the northern edge of the Nile Delta. Immediately past the barrages the river divides in half, flowing into the Mediterranean at the two ports of **Rashid** (Rosetta) in the west and

Dumyat (Damietta) in the east. The Rosetta Stone, discovered by Napoleon's soldiers in 1799, was, yes indeed, discovered near Rosetta. The port drips with Islamic architecture; scattered throughout the town are provincial Ottoman mosques and houses from the 17th and 18th centuries. The town is also famous for its dates (date season is Sept.-Oct.).

Orientation and Practical Information Orient yourself from the **Arab Qili House** (Bait Qili), which also houses the Rosetta Museum. Turn left from the bus stop and walk past scores of noxious fish stands until you reach the corniche, then take another left and continue about 500m until you see a large howitzer on your left. This is **El Huriyya Sq.**, and the Arab Qili House is just behind the howitzer on the right. While the museum is basically a bust (see Sights, below), the staff is more helpful and speaks better English than that of the **Misr Travel** office across the street (tel. 80 79 85). The **tourist police** can be found in El Huriyya Sq.

The **West Delta Bus Co.** runs here from Misr Station in Alexandria (every hr. 8am-10pm, E£1.50). The last bus back leaves at 5pm; make it a daytrip. **Minibuses** from the Tikka Grill in Alexandria one block inland from the corniche (E£2.50). The **train** (3rd-class only) runs from Misr Station (daily 6:50pm, 75pt). Trains return to Alexandria (8 per day, 5:50am-7:45pm, 60pt to Ma'mura, 70pt to downtown). **Service taxis** to Alexandria depart somewhat infrequently (E£4).

Sights The **Rosetta Museum,** built by Mr. Arab Qili (a governor of Rosetta in the 18th century), features nothing of interest except perhaps the life-size diorama of Minutemen inflicting pain on invading British brigades. (Museum open daily 8am-4pm. Admission E£5, students E£2.50, camera privileges E£10.) The badly damaged 17th-century **Zaghloul Mosque** is at the end of the main street running south from the train station; you can also take the scenic route: from the corniche, go inland past the museum and swing south through the **souq** full of sweets and juice shops. Ignore the water and/or sewage filling the remains of the mosque; if you walk around it you will see some archways and columns, as well as Arabic inscriptions on the outside. Colorful buildings are along Port Said St., opposite the bus stop.

About 5km from Rosetta, the recently restored **Fort of Qaytbay** (not to be confused with the one in Alexandria) guards the strategic entrance to the Nile. (Open daily 9am-4pm, during Ramadan 9am-3pm. Admission E£6, students E£3.) Built in 1479 by Sultan Ashraf Abu Nasr Qaytbay to serve in the first line of defense against the Ottoman Turks and the Crusaders coming from the Delta, this structure used to overlook the surrounding land; now, due to soil and clay deposits from the Nile, the ground level has risen to that of the fortress. Further fortification of the fortress by the French in 1799 prompted the importation of stone from Upper Egypt. A soldier noticed carvings on one of the stones, and this **Rosetta Stone** enabled Jean-François Champollion to unlock the mystery of the hieroglyphic alphabet. A cast of the stone (the original resides in London) describes—in Demotic (the common language), ancient Greek (the royal language), and hieroglyphics (the holy language)—the coronation and numerous titles of Pharaoh Ptolemy V. Recent excavations in this and surrounding areas have revealed Rashid (pharaonically named "Bulubatin") to be a site rich with pharaonic history. The cheapest way to get to the fort is by green-and-white local taxi (E£2-3). When tourism is down, as in summer 1994, it is risky to take transport out and expect to find something coming back. A taxi will take you, wait for you to look around, and bring you back for E£5. But the romantic way to get there is to find a willing fisherman and go by boat (20min., E£4 per person round-trip). You'll see some beautiful scenery on the way.

To visit the peaceful **Mosque of Abu Mandur** perched on the bank of the river, catch one of the southbound taxi boats at the main dock just across from the cannon in El Hurriya Sq. (round-trip E£4 per person). Locals picnic at this idyllic spot, where a sandy hill near the mosque offers a nice view of the countryside.

■WEST OF ALEXANDRIA

Egypt is blessed with four hundred km of Mediterranean sand and surf. A detailed, scholarly map of Egypt will tell you that seven or eight towns line the coast between Alexandria and Marsa Matrouh, but Egyptians point out that every inch of sand has been bought by one "vacation village" or another. Many of these cater to certain segments of Egyptian society: engineers, the police force, and doctors hole up in their own concrete complexes near the beach. Sprinkled amongst these are German- and Italian-friendly resort villages. Most require a car and membership card.

Of the actual towns, **El Agami** is popular with the Egyptian middle- and upper-classes and makes a convenient daytrip from Alexandria. The coast around **El Alamein** witnessed Africa's fiercest and most strategically significant World War II battles. Some Superjet and West Delta buses going to Marsa Matrouh from Alexandria stop along the way at **Sidi Abd er-Rahman,** a beautiful beach becoming a concrete jungle 127km west of Alexandria and 162km from Matrouh. Closest to Libya is **Marsa Matrouh,** a low-key resort town on a bay, proffering incredible scenic variety. Though many coastline segments between Alexandria and Matrouh are tantalizingly inaccessible to budget travelers, opportunities for free, secluded camping are virtually unlimited (simply check in with the nearest police or military office).

You can pass the time on the bus contemplating the grandiose dream of the **Qattara Depression** Project. Desperate to increase the area of arable land in their country, Egyptian planners have long dreamed of channeling water to the nutrient-rich but parched soils of the Western Desert's Qattara Depression. Covering a region the size of the Delta and dipping 134m below sea level, the depression lies 100km inland. The idea is to take water from the Mediterranean Sea, desalinate it, and pipe it past El Alamein to create vast new tracts of farmland. During Nasser's rule, Soviet aid stimulated initial steps, but shifting political alliances and rising costs checked early optimism. Egypt still seeks foreign aid for the project, but definite plans for a massive reworking of the desert landscape seem unlikely in the near future.

EL AGAMI العجمى

Known for its white sands and turquoise waters, El Agami serves as Egypt's answer to the *côte d'azur*. When Alexandria, at one time the vacation capital of the country's upper classes, began to crawl like an anthill, the wealthy fled to this resort town only 20km west of El Manshiyya. These days, a luxurious villa in El Agami is a must for any aspirant to membership in the rich-and-famous club, including movie stars Faten Hamama and Sherihan. But even as we speak, El Agami is being replaced by beaches further west. The swimming in Marsa Matrouh is nicer, and the perpetual horde is rapidly finding its way into El Agami. Nonetheless, the beach town is still less crowded and more liberal than Alexandria, is easily reached from the city, and offers a pleasant family atmosphere of evening strolls, mini-amusement parks, and well-tanned teens comparing their father's bank accounts. The town is quite busy in summer, so try to make reservations in advance.

Orientation and Practical Information El Agami is actually two towns in one: Bitash and Hannoville. **Bitash** houses villas and more expensive hotels; **Hannoville** has apartment buildings and a few budget hotels, as well as the drop-off point for public transportation. Egyptians generally refer to Bitash as El Agami and Hannoville as Hannoville. Coming from Alexandria, the entrances to the two towns are right turns off of the highway. In both cases, you will turn onto the town's main road (Hannoville St. or Bitash St.), lined with amenities and ending at the beach.

On Bitash St., the **National Bank of Egypt** (open 8:30am-2pm) is a good place to get rid of your dollars. The **telephone office** (open daily 8:30am-11pm) has orange phonecard phones and can connect you with any country. Across the street from the Cinema Summer Moon and the gas station is the **bus stop,** whence buses run to **Cairo** all summer (daily 6pm, E£22). **Pharmacy Lo'ay Ed-Din** (tel. 433 4354) opposite the red octopus sign leading to Hanafiyya St. (where the chi-chi villas are) is run by Dr. Mostafa Kodeir and is open daily 9:30am-1am. Next door to the National Bank of Egypt is **Farouk Ibrahim Hospital** (tel. 433 8925 or 2925). Also on Bitash St. is **Al Wafaa Hospital** (tel. 433 8318 or 8506).

In Hannoville, minibus #760 and bus #460 (both from Raml Station in Alexandria) will drop you off in front of Minas Hotel. Minibus #765 and bus #465 (both from Misr Station) depart daily (6am-midnight, 50pt) and stop right across the street in front of the Gad Restaurant. A **Banque Misr** is on Hannoville St. (open Sun.-Thurs. 8:30am-2pm). A **telephone office** (open daily 8am-10pm) at the end of the street (past the Minas Hotel) makes calls only within Egypt.

Accommodations, Food, and Entertainment In Bitash, you could stay at the **Agami Palace Hotel** (tel. 433 0230 or 0386) or at the **Summer Moon Hotel** (tel. 433 0367 or 0834 or 8827). Both are on the beach (great view!), both offer a variety of activities (billiard tables, swimming pools, discothèques, etc.), and for both you will pay through the nose. The Agami Palace has spotless singles (E£100) and doubles (E£120), breakfast included. The Summer Moon Hotel, with rooms not always facing the beach, is a little less expensive (singles E£70, doubles E£110, triples E£140; all include breakfast, TV, A/C, bath, and phone). Bitash St. unveils many little **restaurants**. The cheapest option is **Abu Hussein** (open 9am-2pm), whose *fuul/ta'miyya* combo sandwiches (25pt) are great. For more variety, try **Mu'min** (open 9am-1am), where the chicken kiev is E£3, the *shawerma* E£1.50, and the *escalope* sandwich E£2.50. There are also foot-long sandwiches: chicken kiev E£5.50, chicken fillet E£4, *shish tawouq* E£3.75, and *shawerma* E£3.75. Delivery available (E£10 minimum). Another eating possibility is **La Poire** (tel. 433 1300), on Shahr El Asal St., a right turn at the end of Bitash St. Excellent *shawerma,* chicken, or roast beef sandwiches (E£3.50). Try also the **La Poire Patisserie** on Bitash St., next to Mu'min. The ubiquitous **Kentucky Fried Chicken, Pizza Hut,** and **Baskin Robbins** stand all in a row next to La Poire.

For accommodations in Hannoville, try the **New Admiral Hotel** (tel. 430 8465 or 2719); turn left off of Hannoville St. at Gad Restaurant, onto El Geish St. The 3-star hotel has singles (E£53) and doubles (E£64) with bath, A/C, TV, and phone. Breakfast E£4.15. Nearby is the cheaper **Costa Blanca Hotel** (tel. 430 3112), on Hannoville St. just opposite Anous Supermarket and Patisserie Omar al-Khayyam. Rooms have private bath (singles E£15, doubles E£22, quads E£35). Breakfast (E£4.50), lunch (E£11), and dinner (E£12) served in a simple yet comfortable restaurant. Some rooms look out on busy Hannoville St. Visa and Mastercard accepted. Stella fans try the **Minas Hotel** (tel. 430 0150), next door. The charming hotel is brown brick with little round balconies. (Singles E£17, doubles E£21, triples E£27.) Across the street is the **Gad Restaurant** (tel. 430 6179). (Sandwiches E£1-3.)

To make the most of El Agami, stay in Hannoville (cheaper), and wine and dine in Bitash (more variety). The cleanest and currently hippest **beach** is the Fardous Beach in Bitash. Turn left from Bitash St. into Hanafiyya St. (follow red octopus sign) and go straight until you reach the private beach (getting in may require some creative effort). The **Cinema Summer Moon** (adjacent to the Summer Moon Hotel) shows movies in English (11am, 3:30, 6:30, 9:30pm, and midnight; E£2-4).

EL ALAMEIN العلمين

El Alamein, meaning "two flags," is best known for its role in World War II. A tiny village set in a broad, barren desert plain, El Alamein is slightly too distant from the water to attract many tourists. But there was a time when El Alamein was infinitely less quiet, less out-of-the-way, and certainly less empty. In November 1942, the Allied forces under the command of the British Field Marshal Sir Bernard Montgomery halted the advance of the Nazi Afrika Korps here. El Alamein had been pinpointed by the Nazis as the gateway to Alexandria and the key to control of the continent. The Allied victory here marked the beginning of the end for the Axis Powers in North Africa and simultaneously crushed the mystique surrounding the "Desert Fox," German Field Marshal Erwin Rommel, whose force of Panzer tanks had previously seemed invincible. The Battle of El Alamein was not only one of the war's most important confrontations, but also one of the most violent: nearly 10,000 soldiers lost their lives and 70,000 were wounded.

On the east side of town lies the **British War Cemetery,** the burial place of 7367 men, 815 of whose headstones bear only the somber inscription "Known Unto God." Ringed by purple flowers and set against the seemingly interminable desert, the excruciatingly tidy rows are enough to set almost anyone to pondering. The plaque and inscriptions within the shaded alcove explain the battle's significance as well as the diverse backgrounds of the victims interred here. Maintained by the British War Graves Commission, the cemetery is free and almost always open.

The **War Museum** at the west side of the village is near the bus stop and main square. It contains displays of weaponry, military garb, and descriptions of Rommel, Montgomery, and other participants in the battle. A map bedecked with hundreds of tiny red and green bulbs (many of them still operative) retells the changing fortunes of the North African campaign in glorious technicolor. (Open daily 8:30am-6pm; winter and Ramadan 9am-4pm. Admission E£5, students E£2.50. Photography extra.) The less-frequently-visited citadel-like **German and Italian Cemeteries** are 8km west of town, perched on a petite peninsula overlooking the sea. Without a private car or hired taxi it is difficult to visit the last two monuments. Look for the small marker about 3km west of the town center showing the farthest Axis advance; an arrow pointing east reads: "Il Fortuna, Non Il Valore: Alexandria, 111km."

Getting to El Alamein is easy; leaving is not so easy. Some **buses** traveling between Marsa Matrouh and Alexandria or Cairo can let you off at the **Rest House.** However, only the non-express West Delta buses from Matrouh, Cairo, or Goumhouriyya Sq. in Alexandria will sell you a ticket to El Alamein (E£6); all other lines will force you to buy a ticket to the final destination; double check. When leaving, you may have to pay the full fare again, and might have trouble finding room on a bus, especially in summer. Heading toward Alexandria, you can often find **service taxis** or microbuses for about E£6; they are uncommon heading toward Marsa Matrouh.

Another possibility for getting out of El Alamein, though it's a miserable one, is to catch one of the four daily **trains** that pull very, very slowly through El Alamein (2 each way, E£2 to Matrouh or Alexandria). All trains arrive in the late morning or early afternoon. Inquire at Misr Station in Alexandria or at the station in Matrouh for schedule information. Unfortunately, coaches are not air-conditioned and the El Alamein stop is 2km across the desert from the village. To hire a taxi for the trip, either find six other people who want to take a long pause in El Alamein on a cross-desert run, or make a special round-trip excursion from Alexandria (either way, E£80 for the taxi).

You can stay at the run-down **Rest House** (E£10 per person), but El Alamein is a one-camel joint, and you'd be doing yourself a service by leaving. You can also get food and drink there (omelette E£1.50, Stella E£3.80; open daily 7am-midnight).

■■■ MARSA MATROUH مرسى مطروح

Fanning out from a bay of purest cobalt blue, this resort city looks as if it were built yesterday. Dozens of mold-and-pour concrete villas accommodate Egyptians who annually fall victim to the universal human urge to reach the beach. The natural harbor here has served travelers, merchants, and soldiers from Alexander to Rommel; but now the majority of sea vessels in Matrouh are rented by the hour, and the only major military presence in town patronizes the holiday resorts maintained especially for Air Force and Navy officers. As Alexandria's beaches become polluted and crowded, more and more expatriates and members of the Egyptian intelligentsia come to Marsa Matrouh for their summer holidays. Travelers who make it out here are treated to the finest beaches in Egypt and a tepidly indulgent atmosphere.

ORIENTATION AND PRACTICAL INFORMATION

You need to know only two streets to find your way around Marsa Matrouh: the lively **corniche,** which stretches the length of the bay, and busy **Alexandria Street,** which runs perpendicular to the corniche, beginning at the Marsa Matrouh Governorate and heading inland to the hill north of town. Most of the hotels and government offices are clustered along the corniche and the streets running parallel to it. From the corniche inland, the most important of these are **Galaa Street, Tahrir Street** (sometimes referred to as Gamal Abd en-Nasser St.), and **Allam Er-Rum Street.** In addition, **Port Said Street** and **Zaher Galal Street** run parallel to Alexandria St. to the east.

Tourist Office: (tel. 93 18 41) On the corniche 1 block west of Alexandria St., in front of the Governorate building. Not as efficient as its well-kept appearance suggests; provides a map which shows hotels and offices but lacks such piddling details as street names. Open Sat.-Thurs. 8am-2pm and 5-11pm. The man in charge is Mr. Hassanein (tel. 93 12 02); ask him to help with camping permits.

Tourist Police: Next door to the Tourist Office (tel. 93 55 75). Open 24 hrs.

Passport Office: 1 block north and a ½-block east of the train station, just off Alexandria St. (tel. 93 53 51). Open Sat.-Thurs. 9am-2pm.

City Council (Magliss el-Medina): Directly opposite the train station (tel. 93 52 66). Issues obligatory camping permits. Open Sat.-Thurs. 9am-2pm.

Currency Exchange: Cairo Bank, Port Said St., 1 block east of Alexandria St. (tel. 93 49 08). Changes cash and traveler's checks. Open daily 9am-2pm and 6-9pm.

Post Office: 2 blocks east of Alexandria St. and 1 block south of the corniche (tel. 93 43 24). Open Sat.-Thurs. 8am-3pm.

Telephone Office: Opposite the post office. Crowded and unreliable for international calls. Open 24 hrs. **Hotel Riviera Palace** on Alexandria St. has a more expensive but infinitely more Zen telephone service. **Telephone code:** 03 (even if dialing from Alexandria). **Information:** Tel. 16. **Directory:** Tel. 125.

Flights: EgyptAir, Galaa St. (tel. 93 43 98), 3½ blocks west of Alexandria St. Flies to and from Cairo (50min.; Thurs.-Fri. and Sun.; leaves Cairo at 9am, leaves Marsa at 11am; E£547 round-trip). Office open Tues.-Sun. 10am-1pm and 6-9pm.

Trains: 1 block east of southern end of Alexandria St., about 750m from corniche (tel. 93 30 36). To Alexandria (2nd class E£7, with A/C E£13; students E£3.50 and E£6.50). To Cairo's Ramses Station via Alexandria (daily 10am and 1:30pm; 9hr.; 2nd class E£9.20, with A/C E£18.30; *wagon-lits* E£36; 50% student discount).

Buses: 3 blocks west of the southern end of Alexandria St. **West Delta Bus Co.** runs to Alexandria (every 2hr. 7am-7pm; 6hr.; E£10, with A/C E£16), Siwa (daily 7:30am and 3pm, 5hr., E£7), and Cairo (daily 7:30am, E£15). **Golden Arrow** buses (A/C) go to Alexandria (9am, 2, 3, and 4pm; E£16), Siwa (Mon., Wed., and Sat. 4pm; 5hr.; E£12), and Cairo (8am, 2:30, 3:30, and 4:30pm; E£27). **Superjet** buses (A/C) depart from the same place to Alexandria (2:30pm, 3hr., E£21) and Cairo (3, 4, and 11pm; E£32). Book ahead for Cairo buses, especially during the summer. Both companies depart from in front of the tourist office.

Service taxis: Opposite the bus station. Alexandria (E£10) and Cairo (E£20). Infrequent service to Siwa (E£10). Cheap and fast, but hard on the hackles.

Pharmacy: Said Lee Tohami Pharmacy, on the west side of Alexandria St., 8 blocks from the corniche (tel. 93 47 19). Sells electricity- and pheromone-operated mosquito Death Stars. Open daily 8am-midnight; winter 8am-9pm.

Hospital: Military hospital on Galaa St. (tel. 93 33 55), 3 blocks west of Alexandria St. Facilities aren't impeccable—if possible seek treatment in Cairo.

Police: on the first street south of the corniche, 2 blocks east of Alexandria St. (tel. 113 or 93 30 15 or 93 33 76). Open 24 hrs.

Getting around Marsa Matrouh is easy. Most places are only a 10-minute walk apart, but if you enjoy the sight of suppurating ass-inine sores, flag a donkey cart, or **caretta.** Don't subsidize those owners who abuse the donkeys. (Anywhere in town E£1.) Rent **bicycles** from the stand next to the Rady Hotel, on the corniche four blocks east of Alexandria St. (E£1 per hr.; bargain for long-term rental). Because

Marsa Matrouh is so close to Libya, there is a noticeable military presence in the surrounding areas. While unnecessary within the city limits (unless you want to rent a bike), it's wise to carry your **passport** with you outside of town and on the more obscure beaches. There may be a passport check on the road into town.

ACCOMMODATIONS

Hotel prices in Marsa Matrouh have skyrocketed in recent years. The tourist season lasts from early May through late October; Ramadan also brings crowds. In the mild and generally sunny off-season, many hotels either close entirely or slash their rates; and the luxurious new hotels along the corniche become affordable. The government-run, two-star **Arous el-Bahr** (tel. 93 44 19 or 20) on the corniche drops its full board requirement and prices between October and May (singles with ½-board and bath E£53, doubles with ½-board and bath E£87; in winter, prices drop to 50%). Negotiate prices, even in summer.

Small, mega-cheap hotels can be found along and near Alexandria St., three or four blocks inland. Few foreigners frequent these places, so many of them have no English signs; some foreigners, especially women, might find a stay here unpleasant. Talk to the tourist office. Men with small budgets and open minds can rent a bed in a crowded room for E£2-3, but guard your belongings.

Ghazala Hotel, Allam er-Rum St. (tel. 93 35 19), in a 3-story white building just east of Alexandria St., about 6 blocks from the corniche. Across from the El Dest Hotel and El Farghaly pharmacy. Darkish interior but very clean rooms and baths. Hot water often shut off in summer. Singles E£6. Doubles E£15. With-it owner Suleiman Morsi knows about Matrouh and much besides.

HI Youth Hostel (tel. 93 23 31), where the streets have no name: tricky to locate, but worth the effort. Walk west from Alexandria St. on Galaa St. At the Omar Effendi Store, follow the street that forks to the right. When that road forks next to a garden playground, veer left and take the first turn to the left. The hostel is in a 2-story building about 100m on the right. If lost, ask for *beit esh-shabab.* The warden, Mr. Abdallah Kamel, bends over backwards to accommodate his guests: clean rooms and bathrooms, hot water, cheap meals, free semi-frozen water for lazy beach days. No curfew or lockout. E£5.10, nonmembers E£9.10. HI membership requirement often waived.

Arafat Hotel, Tahrir St., right next to the well-known Qahwa Auberge and Hani El Omda Restaurant. Follow the red arrow to the right. Rooms are spotless and inviting. Same owners as the Ghazala Hotel. Ask them for discounts. Doubles with bath E£30. Quads E£60.

Hotel Ageba, Alexandria St. (tel. 93 23 34), about 10 blocks from the corniche. Striking lobby; plain rooms all have private baths. Singles E£15. Doubles E£30.

New Lido (tel. 93 45 15), on the corniche 1km west of Alexandria St., 1 block past the mosque. Rents 4-room flats (including kitchen, bath, and balcony) that accommodate 4 comfortably, 5-6 if you don't breathe much. The bungalows farther down the beach, with fridge and bath, are designed for 2. Mixed gender groups should show marriage certificates. Reservations recommended. Closed in winter; closed in summer 1994 for renovations.

El Dest Hotel (tel. 93 21 05), on the corner of Alexandria and Allam er-Rum St., just across from the Ghazala Hotel. Not exceedingly cozy, but centrally located. Clean beds, not-so-clean bathrooms. Singles E£10. Doubles E£18. Triples E£25.

Hotel El Roda, Zaher Galal St. (tel. 93 41 20). A three-story red building across from the Virgin Church. Shabby but acceptable rooms, dirty bathrooms. Prices are negotiable—try for E£3 per bed. Doubles E£8.45. Triples E£15.30. Quads E£18.65.

Campers have two options. Get permission from the City Council to camp for free on the beach (see Practical Information; the law against camping without a permit is strictly enforced) or take an intercity Peugeot taxi to **Disney Beach** (also called "Bagoush Village," 48km west of Marsa Matrouh). Disney Beach is convenient to Libya, home of the dethpicable Qaddaffy Duck. Call (03) 93 66 60/1/2 for rates.

The Hebrew University of Jerusalem

Office of Academic Affairs
11 East 69th Street, New York, NY 10021
Phone: (212) 472-2288   Fax: (212) 517-4548

Application Hotline: 1- 800 - 40 - HUOAA
(48622)

Please send me:

☐ General information on your programs in English
☐ Specific information and application for:

☐ One-Year Program (for undergraduates)   ☐ Graduate Studies
☐ Freshman Program   ☐ Master's Degree
☐ B.A./B.Sc.   ☐ Summer Courses

<u>Please print clearly:</u>
Name _____

Mailing Address _____

City/State/Zip _____

Phone (   ) _____ Social Security # _____

The Hebrew University of Jerusalem

Office of Academic Affairs
11 East 69th Street, New York, NY 10021
Phone: (212) 472-2288   Fax: (212) 517-4548

Application Hotline: 1- 800 - 40 - HUOAA
(48622)

Please send me:

☐ General information on your programs in English
☐ Specific information and application for:

☐ One-Year Program (for undergraduates)   ☐ Graduate Studies
☐ Freshman Program   ☐ Master's Degree
☐ B.A./B.Sc.   ☐ Summer Courses

<u>Please print clearly:</u>
Name _____

Mailing Address _____

City/State/Zip _____

Phone (   ) _____ Social Security # _____

NO POSTAGE
NECESSARY
IF MAILED
IN THE
UNITED STATES

BUSINESS REPLY MAIL
FIRST CLASS MAIL   PERMIT NO. 3224   NEW YORK, NY

POSTAGE WILL BE PAID BY ADDRESSEE

THE HEBREW UNIVERSITY
OFFICE OF ACADEMIC AFFAIRS
11 EAST 69 STREET
NEW YORK, NY 10131-0202

I...IIII....II.I..II....IIII....I.III....I.III...I

NO POSTAGE
NECESSARY
IF MAILED
IN THE
UNITED STATES

BUSINESS REPLY MAIL
FIRST CLASS MAIL   PERMIT NO. 3224   NEW YORK, NY

POSTAGE WILL BE PAID BY ADDRESSEE

THE HEBREW UNIVERSITY
OFFICE OF ACADEMIC AFFAIRS
11 EAST 69 STREET
NEW YORK, NY 10131-0202

FOOD AND ENTERTAINMENT

The cheapest way for a group to eat in Marsa Matrouh is to shop en masse at the local market. Alexandria St. runneth over with grocery stores, fruit and vegetable markets, and bakeries. A number of inexpensive restaurants vie for customers.

Alexandria Tourist Restaurant (tel. 93 23 15), on the east side of Alexandria St., 2 blocks south of the corniche. One of the best budget meals in town. Eat a full fish meal for E£10. Visa, Mastercard. Open daily 9am-midnight.

Panayatis Greek Restaurant (tel. 93 2474), across the street from Alexandria Tourist Restaurant. Nothing particularly Greek about the food. Panayatis, around since 1922, is the oldest restaurant in Matrouh. Great fish (E£13) and calamari (E£10); the salads (80pt) are worth a try. Stella E£5.25. Open daily 8am-midnight.

Hani el-Omda (tel. 93 33 00), two doors east of Alexandria St. on Tahrir St. next to Qahwa Auberge. Another fine contender for your digestive juices. Dimly lit but cool and clean. 0.25kg mystery meat E£7, 0.25kg *kufta* E£6.20. Salads and bread included. Open daily 9am-midnight.

Mansour Fish Restaurant (tel. 93 34 10), on the corner of Tahrir and Zaher Galal St. Fish E£14 per kg. All varieties. Open June-Sept. daily 9am-midnight.

Abdu Kofta (tel. 93 58 38), at the intersection of Tahrir St. and Zaher Galal St. A real Matrouh mainstay, small and clean. *Kufta* E£26 per kg, *kabab* E£28 per kg, chicken E£14. Don't miss the *mulukhiyya* (E£1.50). Open daily 10am-2am.

Restaurant Camona (tel. 93 21 07), on the corner of Galaa St. and Alexandria St. Slurp up a meal of *bamia* and chicken with rice and salad (E£6.50), then practice your seed-spittin' with some *butteekh* (watermelon, E£1). Open daily 11am-3am.

Gaby Restaurant (tel. 93 30 45), on the corniche next to the New Lido Hotel. Dine on sumptuous pizzas (E£10) amid fake vines, plastic lobsters, blasting music, and a red, white, and sky-blue vinyl motif. Open summer only noon-1am.

In Marsa Matrouh, *qahwas* and strolls along the corniche replace bars and discos for nightlife, though bars in the Rady and Beau Site Hotels do serve over-priced drinks. **Disco 54** in the Rady Hotel (tel. 93 48 27) is as steamy and risqué as a cup of tea with Queen Victoria. (Open July to mid-Sept. daily 10pm-2am. E£4 cover.)

SIGHTS

Marsa Matrouh's **beaches** will enchant you. All close after sunset; and as part of a government effort to control drug trafficking, soldiers patrol the coast throughout the night. Five kilometers of soft sand rim Matrouh's crescent-shaped bay, from the town's small port on the east to Lido Beach on the west. As in Alexandria, some women here swim fully clothed; as in all of Egypt (except the Sinai), bikinis and revealing one-piece suits could cause an earthquake. The **Beau Site Hotel** has a private beach which is cleaner, less crowded, and more liberal (some belly button sightings reported) than the public beaches. There is no charge for non-guests, but they encourage you to rent an umbrella (E£5 per day), a chair (E£4 per day), a pedalo (E£20 per hr.), or a surf kayak (E£5 per hr.).

East of the port, the shoreline arches into a peninsula that faces the town from across the bay. Hire a donkey cart, rent a bike, or hire a boat from the port to take you over to the peninsula, called **Rommel's Isle.** The **Rommel Museum** contains a mediocre exhibit built into a series of nifty caves that Rommel once used as his headquarters during the North African campaign of World War II. (Open daily 9:30am-2pm. Admission 50pt.) On the ocean side of the peninsula, just past the marine Fouad Hotel, is **Rommel's Beach,** where, according to legend, the Nazi general skinny-dipped every day. Also on the ocean side of the isle, the rusting wreck of an old U-boat juts out of the water. You can rent a surf kayak to paddle out to the wreck; head toward the red buoy on your left. The sub lies parallel to the beach 20m toward the mosque from the red buoy; you'll need a diving mask to discern it.

To the west of the main town beach, the **Beach of Love** (Shatii El Gharam) fondles the western horn of the bay. You can easily reach this beach by foot or kayak. Inconsiderate visitors have recently begun to desecrate the sand while worshiping the sun, and heaps of litter float out daily. Fourteen km farther west on the ocean side of the bay you'll encounter more wind, less trash, and **Cleopatra's Beach,** on the far right-hand side of which lies a dwarf cove called **Cleopatra's Bath.** The queen and Marc Antony partook of the legacy of Ramses here. The farthest and most spectacular spot of all is **'Agiba,** about 24km from Marsa Matrouh. 'Agiba, which means "miracle," is an inlet in a series of rocky cliffs interrupted with caves. Bring your own food; there is only a soft-drink stand. Stop along the way at the ruins of the tiny **Temple to Ramses II** which lies neglected in the sand. There is a sandy and crowded beach, but it is also possible to find a private spot below the cliffs and spend the day swimming off the rocks looking for latex. (Finders keepers. Eew.)

To reach these beaches take a shared **taxi** or **minibus** from the bus station (E£2-3 per person to 'Agiba), or catch the open-sided *tuf-tuf* bus (E£1.25 to Cleopatra or 'Agiba). The bus shuttles to and from the bus station whenever enough passengers want to go, usually every hour from 9am to 4:30pm (summer only).

■■■ SIWA OASIS واحة سيوة

Almost completely isolated, awash in infinite desert sands, Siwa has a unique culture and history. Amidst groves of date palms and cool natural springs, the Siwans have retained most of their ancient customs. But as visitors continue to flood the oasis, the traditional way of life is succumbing to the demands of tourism. Even so, like Alexander the Great, who made Siwa famous with his pilgrimage to the Oracle of Amun here in 332 BCE, the modern visitor will be richly rewarded.

A bus from Marsa Matrouh takes you through a completely barren landscape on much the same path followed by Alexander's camel caravan. Today a paved road, a tendril of modernity, cuts through the desert, and the 300km trip takes only five hours. Siwa's isolation has made it legendary in Egypt's annals: ancient historians told tales of strange cities and mysterious kingdoms in the desert. Nature, however, defeated most attempts to ascertain the truth; in 500 BCE a desert sandstorm blew the entire Persian army into smithereens. This suited the Siwans fine; they have always resented outsider interference and resisted paying taxes.

A romantic perspective on Siwan culture sets the oasis in folktales, with its women donning traditional, vividly colored garb in the fashion of the Berbers of the Saharan plains in Libya, Tunisia, and Algeria. Much has changed. Whereas Siwan women characteristically adorned their necks, heads, and limbs with heavy silver jewelry and braided their hair in elaborate styles, today only the older, married oasis women wear traditional dress: the *troket* (black embroidered veil, sold everywhere and worn on special occasions), the *tarfudit* (blue veil always worn outside the home), and the *agbir* (loose dress, often bright yellow or red, worn every day and for festivities). Unmarried Siwan girls now wear Egyptian fashions. Hair styles are only a simplified version of the dozens of intricate braids women used to sport.

Assessing women's role in Siwan society is more complex than it appears. While visitors are tempted to assume that Siwan customs isolate, exclude, and repress women, an investigation behind the scenes suggests otherwise. Contrary to hearsay, women do leave their homes. Siwan women's efforts are responsible for a booming cottage craft industry, a fact not known by most tourists. In practice this means that women are the producers of the family income; children and men are generally responsible for selling the handiwork. Siwan girls were traditionally married by the age of 14, but in the last few decades that age has risen to 16, closer to the national average. Girls also have more say regarding whom they will wed.

In recent years the national government has been working overtime to make up for long years of neglect. The road completed in 1985 has led to better-stocked stores and a growing stream of tourists. Universal education, a new quarry, a new desalination plant, and modern agricultural projects are altering Siwan daily life. Although Arabic has become the official language of Siwa, the indigenous language, a Berber dialect, remains very much alive. Natives rarely speak Arabic to each other.

Regardless of other changes, the sexual conservatism of Siwa pervades every aspect of life; for example, only male donkeys are used in order to prevent the corruption of the population who might otherwise witness donkey lust. Foreign visitors should dress modestly. Men should not wear shorts in town; women shouldn't bare their arms or legs. A sign explaining these dress codes is posted in town in English. Women should also avoid wandering into less populated areas alone, especially in the afternoons (when most Siwans take a siesta) and in the evenings.

Ahmed Fakhry's *The Oases of Egypt: Volume I, Siwa* (E£30), available at the AUC Bookstore in Cairo and several shops in Siwa itself, is a richly detailed 200-page tome. Local tourist guru Mr. Mahdi keeps two copies on hand in the tourist office.

ORIENTATION AND PRACTICAL INFORMATION

Siwa Oasis is enfolded into a desert depression about 300km southwest of Marsa Matrouh, which is in turn 290km west of Alexandria. Siwa's western edge comes within 50km of the closed Libyan border. The depression stretches for 82km west to east, and between three and 30km north to south, but most visitors concern themselves only with the **town of Siwa** and the nearby villages and ancient sites.

Siwa's **climate** is similar to that of Aswan and the other oases. Winter is pleasantly warm, with cool nights. Summer is brutally hot; and air-conditioning is but a diaphanous mirage. The mild weather and the many local festivals associated with the harvest make fall and winter the best times to visit. You can see Siwa's major "sights" in a day or two, but many tourists linger longer to enjoy the peaceful atmosphere. Five days to a week are needed to really get a feel for Siwa and the Siwans. Nine thousand people live in the town; 6000 more Siwans plus a few hundred Bedouin live in villages scattered elsewhere in the oasis.

The most practical way to reach Siwa is by road from Marsa Matrouh, but you *can* hire a **camel** in the Nile Valley, brave 20 days of sandstorms and endless chances to die, and break every Egyptian travel restriction law as you trek across the Western Desert. Those with a group and at least two **cars** can travel the 420km stretch of the new road from Bahariyya. Keep in mind, if you opt for this route, that this road offers no rest house or petrol station—traveling in one vehicle is a bad idea. There are, however, police checkpoints every 60km along the route.

The new road from Marsa Matrouh is well-paved but infrequently used. The best way to travel is to catch a **bus** from the main station in Matrouh. The buses (no A/C) leave daily at 7:30am and 3pm and cost E£7, and the air-conditioned but much more crowded version departs Saturday, Monday, and Wednesday at 4pm and costs E£12. (Both buses take 5hr. and arrive at the station ½hr. before departure time.) From Alexandria's Misr Station there is one daily bus (10am, E£12.50) and air-conditioned service from the Raml station on Monday, Wednesday, and Saturday (noon, E£17). In Siwa, buses stop in the town square and continue 1km south to Badawi Hotel.

Non-air-conditioned buses return to Marsa Matrouh daily at 6am and 2pm (E£6), with the morning bus continuing to Alexandria (E£12.50). Air-conditioned buses also leave Siwa on Sunday, Tuesday, and Thursday at 10am for Marsa Matrouh (E£8) and Alexandria (E£17). All buses stop at the simple desert **Rest House** halfway between Marsa Matrouh and Siwa, where you can buy tea and snacks but not bottled water. There is an outhouse behind the store. Buses break down on occasion; take bottled water and food with you.

The paved road from Marsa Matrouh passes the **Arous el-Waha Hotel** at the northern edge of town and continues into the center of town, ending at the **King Fouad (Sidi Suleiman) Mosque** and the **town market.** The ruined houses of **ancient Siwa** rise in eerie geometric form just south of the market on a rock acropolis, and the narrow streets of Siwa town radiate from the market and the acropolis. The town is graced by palm trees on all but the southern side, which rolls gently into the desert. Streets in Siwa have no names, but most establishments hand out maps like barracuda lawyers hand out business cards. Pick one up at Abdou's Restaurant.

Tourist Information Office: Tel. 93 55 75, in the City Council building, slightly northwest of the mosque. The domain of knowledgeable Mahdi Muhammad Ali Hweiti, a fluent English-speaker and native Siwan. He arranges sight-seeing expeditions and provides maps and information on events. Open Sat.-Thurs. 8am-2pm.

Post Office: Across the street from Arous el-Waha in the northwestern part of town. Reliable service. Open Sat.-Thurs. 8am-2pm.

Telephone Office: By Hotel Arous el-Waha; no int'l calls. Open 7am-midnight.

Local Buses: Crawls west from Siwa town to El Maraqi, making a 50km loop (3:30pm, winter 7:30am and 2:30pm; round-trip E£2; check tourist office for schedule).

Bike Rental: In the market (E£1 per hr., E£5 per day); or in front of Abdou's Restaurant (E£2.50-5).

English Bookstore: Hassan's Handicrafts and English Bookshop, next to the telephone office. Sells a few English books and some traditional Siwan art.

Pharmacy: New Dr. Ragab Pharmacy, across the street and slightly north of the telephone office. Open 9am-1:30pm and 5pm-midnight, 5-10pm in winter.

Hospital: Go south from the town square and take a right. Open 24 hrs.

Police: Tel. 8, in the same modern building as post office. Open 24 hrs.

ACCOMMODATIONS

Cleopatra Hotel (tel. 148), south of the town square on the main road past the Shali fortress. New and comfortable. Spacious balconies with a great view, spotless bathrooms. Dorm beds E£5. Back view doubles E£12, with bath E£16. Frontview doubles E£15 and E£20. Breakfast E£4, lunch E£7.50.

Hotel Arous el-Waha (tel. 100) at the northeastern edge of town. All rooms in this simple government-run, three-story lodging have private baths. In sweltering summer, drag your mattress out onto the gigantic, breezy terrace. Manager is super-fluent in English and knows six other languages. Singles E£7.70, half-board E£18, full board E£27. Doubles E£10.30. Triples E£13.75. Suites E£20.60.

Badawi Hotel, 1km south of town center. Pit and Western toilets. Heterosexual couples without proof of marriage must sleep separately. A bodacious budget bed in a clean room costs E£3.

Youssef Hotel, next to El Medina off the town square. Reasonably clean rooms, hot water, and little balconies. Dorm beds E£5. Doubles and triples available.

Amun Hotel, at Dakrur Mountain (take a *caretta*). For those who hear the call of date palms and pomegranate trees. Doubles E£8.

Hotel El Medina, next to the Youssef Hotel. Large and decrepit, for the piasterpincher who spits in the face of hygiene. But it does offer a large roof, suitable for tanning in the day and get-togethers at night. Dorm beds E£3.

New Siwa Hotel, next to the Cleopatra Hotel. Cramped. Dorm beds E£2.50.

Free **camping** in shelters is available on Dakrur Mountain, 1km south of the Pool of Cleopatra. Bring your sleeping bag and insect repellent. Also at **Well #1** (see Sights, p. 151). Check with Mr. Hweiti before pitching your tent anywhere else.

FOOD

Several cafés line the two market squares. What you order often bears minimal resemblance to what you receive; you'll usually get whatever is in stock that day. Standard offerings (E£1-3) include macaroni, chicken, *couscous,* omelettes, and *shakshuka* (a mixture of meat, eggs, and sauce). **Abdou's Restaurant,** on the inside northeastern corner of the square, has fans to disperse the flies. Abdou's has evolved into a Siwan landmark; he offers not only a good map and solid advice, but also delicious food (meals E£1-5). You can order pancakes (E£2) here if you need a reminder of home (open daily 8am-1pm). Equally devoid of flies and serving fresh, well-prepared food for the same prices is the **East-West Restaurant,** across from the King Fouad Mosque. Possibly the only place in Egypt to try Indian Fig Juice (E£1). (Open daily 10am-midnight.) The small **Sohag Restaurant,** a sidekick of Abdou's, extravagantly beflied and inferior to its neighboring eatery, still serves a good *qahwa.* Enterprising throats can enjoy a menagerie of cheap, exotic drinks (e.g., *louisa,* a sweet mint beverage) for under E£1. (Open daily 8am-1am.) Opposite, the **Amun**

Restaurant offers the same food at the same times for the same prices in slightly grubbier, fanless circumstances. The cheapest eats in town can be found at **Restaurant Almenia,** where most dishes are less than E£1. Unfortunately, Almenia was closed during summer 1994. The local **stores** are also well stocked with canned goods, cold soda and mineral water, and fresh and dried dates and figs (in season).

Because Siwans tend to be more reserved than residents of most Egyptian towns, the traveler will be lucky to receive an invitation to eat or stay with a local family. Invitations are usually offered by children, but sometimes by men. Sometimes the Siwans will hope to sell you homemade handicrafts (you can get great deals on native silverwork and Siwan designer headcoverings), and sometimes they're just eager to help you use up those last few exposures on your roll of film. Women will be allowed to enter a home much more readily than men. As always, exercise caution before accepting hospitality.

SIGHTS

Siwa is often considered the most beautiful of Egypt's oases. From atop the ruins of **ancient Siwa,** the quiet streets of Siwa town wind from a cluster of mud houses to luxuriant palm gardens. From here you can also see the Sahara: black gashes of rock to the north, waves of sand to the south, and the piercing blue desert sky all around. The weird geometric profiles of crumbling walls looming in the vicinity are the remains of the medieval fortress-town of Shali. Its encircling wall once protected the Siwans from marauding Berbers and Bedouin. As you descend to the paths leading back to the market you understand why the Siwans slowly abandoned their acropolis for the more spacious settlement at its base. The descent began when Muhammad Ali conquered Siwa in 1820. Heavy rains, which occur once every five decades and apocalyptically melt traditional Siwan houses, further encouraged migration to the new town. By 1930 the ancient city had become a virtual ghost town. Wandering among the haunting skeletons of these ancient abodes, the sojourner will find inhabitants in random dwellings and old men turning unlikely corners on their way to unknown business. The most recent rains, in 1985, washed away much of Shali and most of the Siwan mud-dwellings; but due to the rise of concrete buildings, the devastation was not total. The threat of history and tradition being literally washed away prompted the Canadian ambassador to put forth funds to construct a permanent version of the **Traditional Siwan House**, opposite the tourist office. The house serves as a museum of traditional Siwan garb, silver jewelry, and children's toys. (Open Sat.-Thurs. 10am-noon and 10-11pm; winter Sat.-Thurs. 10am-noon and 7:30-8:30pm. Open Fri. upon request; ask at the tourist office. Admission E£1.50.)

In addition to Shali, a second acropolis rises 1km to the northeast of ancient Siwa. During the bombing of Siwa town by the Italians in World War II, its caves and ancient tombs sheltered the Siwans and the Egyptian, British, Australian, and New Zealand armed forces from the modern marauders. During this period the local people rediscovered several Ptolemaic-era tombs that Romans had robbed and then reused. Called the **Tombs of Gabal el-Mawta** (Hill of the Dead), they merit a visit by every traveler to Siwa. The random human bones and mummy wrappings that litter the sight belonged to the Romans, and the niches damaging the ancient frescoes are also their doing. A custodian is on hand to unlock the tombs Sunday through Thursday from 9am to 1pm, but it is best to confirm the custodian's whereabouts with Mr. Hweiti or a muleteer. Bring a flashlight (or buy one from a store on the road from the town square to the mountain for E£2.50-3), and be sure not to miss the **Tomb of Si-Amun.** Although damaged by Allied and Egyptian soldiers during the war, it boasts a beautifully painted ceiling depicting the six stages of the sun's journey across the sky. Marred murals on the walls show the Hellenized portrayal of the bearded nobleman Si-Amun and his sons worshiping Egyptian deities. The **Tomb of Niperpathot** housed the body of a nobleman of the 26th Dynasty. It is the oldest tomb in Siwa, but the real attraction is the once-mummified skull gaping from a rusty can in one of the niches. The **Tomb of Mesu-Isis** is 20m to the east of Si-Amun, and has ancient frescoes depicting the gods Isis and Osiris in action. The acropolis commands exhilarating views of Siwa town and the oasis; the summit, now a military lookout post, is off-limits. E£1-2 *bakhsheesh* is appropriate.

In Siwa town hail a *caretta* and rattle off through the palm groves to the village of **Aghurmi.** Like Siwa town, Aghurmi rests peacefully at the foot of a formerly inhabited acropolis. To ascend the acropolis, pass through an old gate made of palm logs and then under a weather-beaten but sturdy old mud **mosque.** Up ahead, perched dramatically at the cliff-edge of the acropolis, looms the well-preserved **Oracle of Amun,** where Alexander came to consult the renowned priests of Amun. First he had to pass through the stone temple's simple gateway into the outer, then the inner court, as you must do to see the site. Accounts by ancient Greek and Roman historians paint the scene: priests carried the sacred boat containing the image of Amun as women sang and danced in procession. The oracle of Amun is said to have confirmed suspicion that Alexander was a god-king, proclaiming him the "son of Amun." Alexander never told what he asked the oracle in private, nor what the answer was. The secret died with him, less than 10 years after his visit.

The temple of the Oracle of Amun is thought to date from the 21st Dynasty (c. 1000 BCE). It became widely celebrated in later dynasties and was well known to the ancient Greeks, who constructed many shrines to Amun in their own country. Twentieth-century visitors enjoy unrestricted access to the temple and the Aghurmi acropolis—no guards, no fees. You can look around the acropolis, peer down the sacred well where offerings were purified (next to the mosque), and climb the mosque's minaret for a masterful view of the town and fiery sunsets.

If you follow the road heading southeast of Aghurmi, after 1km you'll stumble onto the emaciated remains of the **Temple of Amun,** also known as Umm Ubeidah. Time has been unforgiving to this formerly glorious companion of the oracle temple. In 1897 a government official of Siwa (the Marmur) demolished the temple to acquire materials for the construction of a police station and the modern mosque in Siwa town. All that is left is an inscribed, broken wall amidst the palms.

Beyond the temple, about 2km to the south on the same road, lies the cool and mossy **Pool of Cleopatra.** Like many of the approximately 200 natural springs in Siwa, this one has been encircled with a stone basin, with an irrigation duct running out one end. This pool is popular with local men and boys, but fully clothed women should also feel comfortable swimming here (as comfortable as swimming fully clothed can possibly be), and are free to enter the enclosure next to the spring. On the other side of town the gorgeous **Pool of Fatnas** ripples out on an island in the middle of a salt lake (accessible by a small causeway), providing a spectacular setting for an afternoon swim. Although smaller in diameter than the Pool of Cleopatra, this spring is more attractive and less visited. A bathing suit with a shirt on top is acceptable attire for women. The road to **El Maraqi,** which traverses a low desert pass, is lined with craggy yellow buttes honeycombed with caves and Roman tombs. The village of El Maraqi lies in its own lush oasis, virtually severed from the rest of Siwa by the clenching fingers of the desert. Several dozen Bedouin families inhabit this western fringe of Siwa. El Maraqi makes a good daytrip (by local bus) from Siwa town. After traveling two hours on a twisting road, the bus will stop in El Maraqi and then turn around for the return trip. The round-trip fare is E£1. (Contact the tourist office for a bus schedule.) The tourist office can also arrange car trips to El Maraqi or to **Abu Shrouf,** noted for its ruined Roman temples and five splendorous springs. Don't miss out on a trip to **Well #1 (Bir Wahed),** 22km south of Siwa. The spring is surrounded by vegetation and you can bathe in its clean, hot water. One km away is Ahmed Baghi's **fish farm,** where a fabulous stretch of water erupts amongst sand dunes. Ahmed, a young man from Siwa (tel. 61 69) organizes trips in and around Siwa, including tours to Bir #1 and the fish farm (E£40 per person, min. 5 persons; overnights possible). He will cook you a meat-free meal (E£5) and provide tents (E£3) if necessary. Other tours include **Abu Shuruf,** 40km east of Siwa, via Koreishit, El Zeitun, and La'auaf, where Roman tombs lie (E£80 each; food extra).

Every October Siwans gather for a huge feast at the rocks of **Dakrur.** A "chief of the feast" oversees the distribution of food to small groups spread over the plain, and none may begin to eat until the chief climbs to the top of the rock and hollers *"Bismallah!"* (In the name of God). Tourists are invited to attend.

While in Siwa, shop for exquisite **handicrafts,** including intricately embroidered clothing and veils, *margunahs* (large decorated baskets that weave elegance into every Siwan household), and heavy silver jewelry. Several stores have sprung up around the town square: **Hassan's Handicrafts,** next to the phone office; **Siwa Original Handicraft,** to the left of Abdou Restaurant; **Fatnas Bazaar,** near the police station; and **Sharif's Handicraft,** halfway up Gabal el-Mawta. Don't try to bargain in craft shops because the women set the prices and aren't around to haggle. Many crafts are changing to accommodate tourist demands—the baskets and shawls are most authentic. It's also quite likely that precocious children will drag you into a private home to view their own family's selection of handiwork.

 # Nile Valley وادى النيل

How doth the little crocodile
Improve his shining tail
And pour the waters of the Nile
On every Golden Scale.

—Lewis Carroll

Originating in the equatorial high water mark of Lake Victoria, the Nile winds its way north through Uganda and the Sudan, pouring into Lake Nasser and Egypt, where its banks are home to all but a few of the country's millions. By now the river has surely grown accustomed to the company. Teeming cities, lonely necropoli, fertile fields, and desert sands all play significant parts in the drama of the river.

Upstream from Giza, Memphis, Saqqara, and Cairo, the world's longest river runs through **Middle Egypt,** home to the majority of the country's Copts. Here also the Pharaohs of the Middle Kingdom left their mark on Beni Hassan and Tel el-Amarna, the country's third-largest city (Sohag) copes with expansion, and adventurous travelers are treated to the incredible temples at Abydos and Dendera, which don't come shrink-wrapped or horde-ridden as do sights in Cairo and Upper Egypt.

South of Qena begins **Upper Egypt,** whose stars are ancient Thebes' labyrinthine Valley of the Kings tombs and the towering temples of Luxor, Philae, and Kalabsha. No less monumental are the Aswan dams, and finally, at Egypt's southern border, awesome Abu Simbel. This is where you learn the true meaning of the word **hot.** Temperatures regularly crack 40°C in summer; expect to see grown men going up to policemen begging them to shoot them dead.

From the first Pharaohs to the modern Egyptians, the country's inhabitants and their conquerors have all left their mark on the mighty river. The dry desert sun preserves their efforts, bearing witness to successes and failures.

In the days of British colonialism, a slow, romantic cruise down the Nile was an aristocratic indulgence. Nostalgists can make arrangements with a travel agent before they arrive and plan to spend US$80-100 per night. **Feluccas** (going south to north) are cheaper and more fun. (See Between Luxor & Aswan, p. 185 for details.)

The inexpensive Cairo to Aswan **train** stops at several points along the Nile Valley; its *Espani* incarnation is faster, the best alternative for traveling in one long trip between Cairo and Luxor or Aswan. Reserve seats several days in advance. For shorter trips, trains become less reliable and convenient than **service taxis.** (See Once There: Getting Around, p. 59.) **Buses** are safer than *service,* but less frequent and slower, except for the zippy Cairo-Luxor express bus.

In summer, plan to do most of your touring between 6 and 11am, before temperatures soar above 43°C. From Nov.-May temperatures are much more comfortable, but the madding crowds are not.

■■■ MINYA & MALAWI المنيا وملوى

In **Minya,** a provincial capital and a university city of half a million, children will shout "Hello" in the streets, and *hantour* drivers will beg for your business; but they stop well short of the full-fledged psychological warfare waged in tacky tourist temple towns. While accessible and welcoming to travelers, Minya retains an aura of real life that other Nile Valley towns, with their endless strings of tourist bazaars, have lost. For most travelers, however, Minya is merely a convenient base for tours to the area's many archaeological sights. The nearby town of **Malawi,** which is closer to some of them, serves as a transit point.

Reaching the sights takes more time and effort than a jaunt in Luxor or Aswan, but the friendly people and relaxed atmosphere can make extra days enjoyable. After touring the pharaonic remains of Beni Hassan or Tel el-Amarna, spend the evening strolling along Minya's corniche or main streets and blending in with families, students, and business people.

PRACTICAL INFORMATION

Minya lies 250km south of Cairo on a canal west of the Nile; Malawi is 50km farther south, also west of the river. Downtown Minya is bounded by the train station and tracks on the west and the Nile on the east. Minya's main street, El Goumhouriyya, begins at the train station and continues for about seven blocks to the Nile.

Tourist Information Office: Tel. 32 01 50, on the corniche. Walk up El Goumhouriyya from the train station exit, passing through the *midan* in the center of town. Upon reaching the Nile, turn left and continue about 3 blocks; the office will be on your left. Postcards and brochures are available. Service varies depending on who's working there. Open 8am-2pm, 5-10pm; closes earlier in winter.

Tourist Police: Tel. 32 45 27.

Passport Office: From the tourist office, take the very next left along the corniche and continue less than 1 block to the white building. Enter the post office and go to the second floor. See post office listing for directions from the train station. Open Sat.-Thurs. 8:30am-2pm.

Currency Exchange: Most convenient is **National Bank of Egypt,** on the corner of El Goumhouriyya St. and the corniche (open Sun.-Thurs. 8:30am-2pm, 6-9pm). Other banks open 8:30am-2pm with some extended hours for exchange.

Post Office: From the train station, walk about 5 blocks down El Goumhouriyya St. and turn left at the large colonial-style building with the two lion statues above the gate. Walk 3 more blocks to the large white building on your right. The post office is near the back of the building. Open daily 8:30am-3pm. No Poste Restante. A **photocopier** (copies 10pt) is available across the street.

Telephone office *(centrale):* On Sa'ad Zaghloul St., just to the left across from the train station. Open 24 hrs. **Telephone Code:** 086.

Hospitals: General Hospital (tel. 32 30 29) and **Mobarah Private Hospital** (tel. 32 30 77).

Ambulance: Tel. 123.

Minya Police: Tel. 32 31 22 or 23.

Malawi has no tourist office. Coming from Minya, you will probably be dropped off near a **bank** (open Mon.-Thurs. 8:30am-2pm), on the corner of El Galah St. and the street parallel to the canal. To reach the **post office** (open Mon.-Thurs. 8:15 am-3pm), head up El Galah St. with the bank on your right. About 250m later, at the corner with crumbling yellow buildings on either side, turn left. The **telephone office** (open 24 hrs.) is down this same street but places calls only within Egypt.

TRANSPORTATION

Trains to **Minya** leave from Cairo's Ramses Station (A/C; 3-4hr.; 1st class E£17.10, students E£14.50; 2nd class E£7.10 for students). *Service* taxis leave regularly for Minya from Giza Station (4hr., 250km, E£5.50); they are slightly cheaper than trains but less comfortable, especially after a few hours. Unless you're within 150km of Minya (like at Beni Suef, Malawi, or Assyut), your best bet is probably the train.

The Minya **train station** (tel. 32 30 35) lies at the center of town by the canal, about five blocks west of the Nile. Minya has three **bus/minibus/service** stations. One is directly south of the train station (to the right as you exit) on the right side of the street; *service* to Samalut (60pt) depart from here. Farther down the train tracks there is an overpass (*el kubri*, the bridge). Hidden underneath it, all the way across the street, are more taxis and minibuses, headed for Cairo's Ahmed Hilmi Station, Assyut, Abu Qurqas (E£1), and Malawi (E£1). A bit farther, buses depart every hour for Assyut, and every two hours for Beni Suef, Hurghada, and Cairo's Ramses Station. Tickets are purchased on the bus itself after boarding. To reach the third transportation center, continue along the train tracks to a bridge over the canal. Go right, then left over the bridge. **Pick-up trucks** go to neighboring villages (including Abu Qurqas) more frequently than buses or taxis, and for slightly cheaper (50pt).

Local transportation between **Malawi** and closer cities is plentiful. You can shuttle between Minya and Malawi by bus, taxi, or pick-up truck, all of which run fairly often and take about an hour, or you can take a train from Cairo (all day, 5hr.). Although they take 15 minutes longer than buses or taxis, trains are cheaper and sometimes less crowded. A third-class ticket to Malawi is 60pt. In Malawi, with your back to the bank (see above), the yellow **train station** is across the canal to the right. **Buses and minibuses** to Minya leave directly across the street from the bank.

ACCOMMODATIONS

Hotels in **Minya** lie mainly along El Goumhouriyya Street, which begins at the train station exit and runs about seven blocks until it hits the corniche and the Nile. Campers should check with the tourist office before planning to camp in Minya.

Palace Hotel (tel. 32 40 21), at the *midan* (traffic circle) on El Goumhouriyya. A cool, quiet entry and colorful Nefertiti mosaic lure you upstairs to the high-ceilinged colonial-style sitting rooms. The historical atmosphere is nice until decrepit bathrooms carry you back to the 1990s. Singles E£7, with bath E£12. Doubles E£9.50, with bath E£12. Triples E£12. Generous breakfast E£3.

Beach Hotel (tel. 32 59 18), on El Goumhouriyya St. just before the corniche. Clean, carpeted, well-lit rooms. Singles E£15.25, with bath E£21, with bath and A/C E£27. Doubles E£22/28/34.10. Breakfast (E£3) and "cafeteria" upstairs.

Lotus Hotel (tel. 32 45 41), north of the train station off the *midan* on Sa'ad Zaghloul St., which runs along the railroad tracks (a 5-min. walk). Spotless rooms with TVs. Singles with bath and A/C E£29. Similar doubles E£41.75. Triples E£52.55. Breakfast included.

Savoy Hotel (tel. 32 32 70), directly across from the train station. Cheap and conveniently located, but not as clean as the others. Singles E£10, with bath E£12. Similar doubles E£15 and E£17. Similar triples E£20 and E£25.

Akhenaton Hotel (tel. 32 59 18), on the corniche one block to the right from El Goumhouriyya St. Comfortable and well-serviced rooms with baths and balconies overlooking the Nile. Singles E£23.40, with A/C E£28.40. Doubles E£31.60, with A/C E£36.60, with A/C overlooking the Nile E£40. Fridge or TV with bath E£3, fan or heater E£2. Laundry service and international **fax** and telephone also available. Satellite TV coming soon. Breakfast E£5.

FOOD

In **Minya,** restaurants offer the usual *kufta, kabab,* and chicken, with a smattering of *kushari, fuul,* and *ta'miyya* (falafel) places. Top floor restaurants in the **Lotus** and **Akhenaton** hotels offer full meals for E£10-20; at the Akhenaton, enjoy the chicken, the coolest breezes around, and a great view of the Nile.

Aly Baba Café, along the corniche just north of El Goumhouriyya. The best *kabab* and desserts in town. Clean. English spoken. Lunch with meat E£9-12.

Al Fairouz, a block south of the Aly Baba. Enjoy the cheesy aquatic murals complete with bubble-blowing fish and floating sailors. Usual meals, usual prices.

Savoy Restaurant, on the *midan* across from the train station, serves *kufta* and *kabab* in a quiet, shady garden popular with *tawla* (backgammon) aficionados.

Restaurant al-Mahatta, across the street from Savoy. Pretend to be a local and eat like one, too, while checking out the bustle of downtown Minya.

Sabah al-Kheer, next to al-Mahatta. Munch on *fuul* and eggs while enjoying a joke with the personable English-speaking owner, Ayman. Meals 50pt-E£1.

Fuul and *ta'miyya* stands are everywhere, but for an especially tasty sandwich look for Ehab, the bearded guy across from the Savoy Restaurant. For *kushari* (75pt), try the shops several blocks up El Hussein St. If you're coming from the train station, turn right off the main *midan* onto El Hussein.

In **Malawi**, the restaurant in the **Samir Amis** serves full meals for about E£12. **Restaurant El-Hurriya,** farther north along the canal, is cooled by several fans and serves the same for about half the price.

■ NEAR MINYA AND MALAWI

Getting there can be half the fun, but it's certainly more than half the trouble. The most easily reached of the local sights is perhaps the least interesting. The **archaeological museum** in Malawi houses artifacts unearthed at the local sites. To get there, follow El Galah St. from the bank for three and a half blocks. The museum is on the left. (Open Sat.-Tues. and Thurs. 9am-4pm, Fri. 9-11am. Admission E£3, students 50pt.) Other local points of interest demand more effort. **Beni Hassan** offers fine reliefs in an artistic style slightly different from that of most pharaonic remains while **Tel el-Amarna** reflects a unique period in ancient Egyptian history. **Tuna el-Gabal** and nearby **Hermopolis (Ashminein)** showcase a bit of the bizarre. While not as stunning as some other ruins, these two sites are appealing because of the peculiar history and myth that surround them. In addition, the ruins show how Greeks, Romans, and Copts built on pharaonic sites and legitimized themselves as rulers by adapting local traditions as their own. The two can be visited in a single trip, but public transportation won't take you all the way to either site. You should be able to persuade the driver of a taxi to do the entire route in a half-day excursion from Malawi for E£20, a good deal for groups. More frugal and patient travelers may be able to make the journey in short hops via pick-up trucks, taxis, and even police vans.

Tehna el-Gabal marks the transition from the pharaonic era to the subsequent Greek, Roman, and Coptic times, setting the stage for the Islamic conquests. **Gabal et-Teir** is one of the oldest Coptic sites retaining religious importance. Leave at least half a day for each site, and carry small bills, water, a hat, and a flashlight.

Consider hiring a driver from either city. The E£50-90 per car may well be worth it, especially for groups of three. With a driver, you can fit two or three sights comfortably into a day; otherwise, even one is a stretch. Self-appointed tourism guru Joseph (hangs out in the Savoy Restaurant; chances are he'll find you first) will set up a day-long trip to Tel el-Amarna, Beni Hassan, and Hermopolis for E£15 if there are enough tourists in town to fill a minibus or station-wagon taxi. For evening relaxation in Minya, take either a *hantour* (carriage) across the bridge or a ferry to Minya's **public gardens** (further away than they appear), offering greenery and gazebos as well as steps down to the Nile. Swim at your own risk.

BENI HASSAN بنى حسن

The rushing waters of an angry mountain stream apparently destroyed the ancient village of Beni Hassan, but the neighboring necropolis, housing 39 pharaonic rock tombs, remains one of the finest Middle Kingdom sites in Upper Egypt. These apartments for the afterlife, dating from the 11th and 12th dynasties (2000-1800 BCE), have colorful wall paintings that retain a touch of their original vibrancy, despite the effects of four millennia of earthquakes and vandalism.

From either Minya or Malawi, take a pick-up truck to the sizeable village of Abu Qurqas (50pt). Next to the bridge spanning the canal in the center of town, you'll see a sign indicating the road to the antiquities. Cross over the bridge and railroad tracks, then either walk the 3km east to the Nile bank or take a covered pick-up truck (25pt). From the government office at the riverside, you can buy a ticket for transportation to the site (E£4.50, 6 or more E£3 each), including boat fare across the Nile and a minibus from the dock on the far side to the tombs, 500m inland. (Admission E£6, students E£3; photo permission E£5 per tomb, E£50 for a tripod, flashes prohibited. Open 7:30am-4:30pm.) If tourist traffic is light, set a time with the drivers to pick you up. Two hours should be enough time. Coming back, travelers try to convince pick-up trucks to take them all the way from the ferry to Minya. They expect to pay E£5, less if they are in a group of three or more.

Four of the 39 tombs (each labeled on the outside) are regularly open to the public; for a little *bakhsheesh,* some others might open their doors. The **Tomb of Kheti** (#17) originally contained six lotus columns hewn from solid rock. Two of these graceful supports still adorn the interior. Decorative scenes on the southern wall (on your right as you enter) depict Kheti of the Antelope province (11th dynasty), accompanied by his various servants, including fan-bearer, sandal-bearer, gnarled dwarf, and others offering such sacrifices as an entire cow haunch and bread. At the top of the wall figures practice yoga, massage, hockey, and karate. On the western wall (which contains the doorway) women dance in long lines apart from the men. Above them, hunters pursue cattle, though two cows still find the time to copulate; also look for the depiction of *firas en-Nil* (horse of the Nile), half-horse, half-hippo. On the wall farthest from the door, wrestlers demonstrate nearly 200 different moves. The tiny column on the northern wall depicts a marriage ceremony. The groom drinks potent grape juice for heightened desire and strength; the next picture shows the happy couple in bed. In all the tombs, note the holes in the ground, where ropes were attached so workers (and, later, mummies) could be lowered.

Kheti's father, Baket, was responsible for building one of the necropolis's most lavish burial sites. The **Tomb of Baket** (#15) features many themes later repeated in Kheti's tomb. Here, the wrestlers are more colorful and discernible, and gazelles replace cows as the featured animal actors. Note the unicorn.

The **Tomb of Khumhotep** (#3) was constructed for a most prestigious official, the ruler of the province of Antelope and governor of the Eastern Desert. The base of one 16-sided proto-Doric column remains, and the ceiling is constructed as a triple vault. On the walls, Khumhotep inspects the various activities of his province, including the arrival of the Semitic Amo tribe from Syria. The copious green hieroglyphics outline the history of Khumhotep's family along the bottom of the walls. The tomb features extraordinarily rich colors, especially in an image of Khumhotep with two speared fish on the rear wall.

In the neighboring **Tomb of Amenemhet** (#2), a checkerboard pattern covers the vaulted ceiling, while the upper walls display still more grappling wrestlers and fighting soldiers. Four 16-sided proto-Doric columns remain, and a badly damaged statue of Amenemhet with his wife and mother rests at the rear of the chamber.

TEL EL-AMARNA

Less than overwhelming in external appearance, Tel el-Amarna is in fact one of the most intriguing of the pharaonic ruins, both for its history and for its art. The founder of the city, King Akhenaton (formerly King Amenhotep IV), was a maverick who established a new monotheistic cult to the sun god Aton in an effort to reclaim authority from the increasingly-powerful priests of the incumbent Amun. His new capital, Akhetaton, was decorated with countless representations of Aton. The sun god was usually depicted as a brilliant sun disk whose rays terminated in outstretched palms, often holding an *ankh,* a circle-topped cross symbolizing eternal life. The legacy of these decorative efforts is not exclusively religious; Akhenaton's

NEAR MINYA AND MALAWI

artists created the naturalistic Amarna style of art and made Nefertiti, Akhenaton's wife, a timeless symbol of beauty (and a popular subject for tacky tourist jewelry).

Akhenaton followed his children and Nefertiti to the grave at the age of 35, and conservative political forces quickly stepped in. His new city was razed, the capital was returned to Thebes, the Amun cult regained its prominence, and Tel el-Amarna was declared unhallowed ground. The taboo helped preserve Tel el-Amarna, since no later civilization would build over the home of the heretic. Unfortunately, later communities vandalized the tomb, leaving a largely ruined site for today's visitors. The **necropolis** of Tel el-Amarna, 12km south of Malawi on the eastern bank of the Nile, houses several rock-hewn tombs from Akhenaton's reign.

To reach Tel el-Amarna, take one of the local pick-up trucks from the depot south of the Malawi train station (25pt). The trucks leave from the parking lot at the end of the bridge crossing into town; make it clear that you want the village of Tel el-Amarna. If tourists are sparse, however, you may have to break up the trip, stopping in Deir Mous. Locals will help out, but be prepared for waits and rides in crowded pick-up trucks. You'll be dropped off at the Nile. From there take a ferry, which will drop you off by the site office, where you'll pay E£7, including round-trip on the ferry and transportation to and from the site on a tractor-pulled bus. At the site there is another charge (E£6, students E£3; photo permission E£5 per tomb; site open daily 6am-4pm). Bring a filing cabinet for all the tickets.

There are two groups of tombs. Of the six in the northern group, #3, 4, and 6 are most worthy of a visit. A few of the southern tombs are interesting; in order to reach them you must return to the village and pay E£15 for the 14km excursion. Visits to tombs #1-6 are included in the northern tour, but if you're not insistent you'll be shown only #3-5 as the others are a bit out of the way. If the lights in the tombs are out of order, the guides have a nifty foil apparatus which illuminates the tomb walls with sunlight. It's not a bad idea, however, to bring a flashlight.

Once inside, you will notice the pervasive vandalism. The faces of Akhenaton and Nefertiti and the symbol of Aton were favorite targets of Akhenaton's successors, the teenage King Tutankhamun ("King Tut") and the general Haremheb.

The **Tomb of Huye** (#1) was built for the superintendent of the royal harem and steward to the queen mother, Tiy. Its decorative reliefs depict King Akhenaton with his family and closest friends. Look for the small depiction of a sculptor at work in the lower right-hand corner of the far wall, to the right of the doorway.

On the entrance walls of the **Tomb of Ahmose** (#3), the deceased can be seen worshiping the sun. Ahmose was royal fan-bearer to Akhenaton, and is most often depicted praying in his official costume, carrying a fan and an axe. This tomb offers a glimpse of the artistic process. A large sketch of a king with a chariot graces the left side of this uncompleted tomb. Because of the city's abrupt end, the tomb was left unfinished and the sketch never carved (nor was the floor smoothed out).

The **Tomb of Meri-Re** (#4), the high priest of Aton, is the largest and best preserved of the group, retaining vibrant colors. Plans of the temples and palaces of Akhenaton adorn the walls of the tomb's hypostyle hall, enabling Egyptologists to deduce the appearance of the ancient city's buildings. One wall of the tomb features two ornately decorated chariots under the solar symbol of Aton. The famous profile of Nefertiti is identifiable in several places, but has been marred by thieves. Her famous bust-with-crown was discovered here, but kept hidden by its German discoverers for years and then taken to the Berlin Museum. The musicians, to the left of the entrance, are blind, as were all who entertained this most beautiful of women.

The **Tomb of Pentu** (#5), chief physician to the royal family, has been badly damaged, as has the **Tomb of Panhesy** (#6), 1km to the south. Panhesy was the Servant of Aton, observer of granaries and herds, and chancellor of Lower Egypt. His tomb was converted into a church by early Christians, but its original decorative carvings survive in reasonable condition, as does a staircase that leads nowhere. A tiny carving of a pigeon-toed ancient adorns the wall beside the door, to the right.

On the way back to the Nile, the tractor-bus will make a detour, if you so desire, to the remains of the **Royal Palace** of Akhenaton and Nefertiti. The only things uncovered by the excavations of royal rubble are the locations of streets, but a helpful guide may point out the pool where Nefertiti was known to bathe in the buff.

If you make it to the southern tombs, two are worth touring. The **Tomb of Mahu** (#9), Akhenaton's chief of police, contains several levels of chambers, connected by a winding stairway and adorned with various scenes of the deceased with royal personages. The striking **Tomb of Ay** (#25) was constructed for a man of many trades; Ay was the king's secretary, Queen Nefertiti's nurse, and later, Tutankhamun's successor. Although Ay abandoned his designs here to excavate a more elaborate tomb for himself in the Valley of the Kings at Thebes, the structure was intended to be the finest in the necropolis at Tel el-Amarna. The wall inside the imposing hypostyle hall entrance is covered with scenes depicting the bustling street life of the ancient city, complete with soldiers, visiting officials, and dancing women. To the south are what remains of Akhenaton's city, all but leveled by reactionaries after his death.

TUNA EL-GABAL

In one ancient Egyptian creation story, the sun god sprang from a cosmic egg on the hillock at the ancient capital of Hermopolis (see below), 10km northwest of Malawi. 12km farther west, isolated in an arid plain at the foot of the Western Desert hills, lie the ruins at Tuna el-Gabal. This necropolis features a bizarre collection of funerary remains, including an enormous underground burial area where thousands of sacred baboons and ibises were mummified and interred. Egyptologists suspect that Tuna el-Gabal served as the Hermopolitan cemetery.

Bring an ample supply of water; for 25pt you can take a *service* or pick-up truck from the taxi station in Malawi to the *town* of Tuna el-Gabal, which is 5km from the necropolis. From here some people try to get a ride with a truck carrying workers to a local quarry (25pt per person). From the turn-off to the quarry, it's a 2km hike to the site—this is where you'll wish you'd hired a private taxi. A truck in the village or your driver from Malawi may take you out and back for about E£5. Or make it obvious that you are trying to reach *al-athar* (the site) and eventually the tourist or regular police will put you on a vehicle headed in the right direction. The site is isolated; be sure to arrange your return trip in advance. (Open daily 8am-5pm; admission E£6, students E£3; E£1 toll to enter the desert; photo permission E£5 per building.)

At Tuna el-Gabal you will feel as though you have been let in on a secret. Its dark, silent tunnels are still being excavated and seem to offer you the opportunity to make the archaeological discovery of the century. Most unusual is **Es-Saradeeb** (the Galleries), a mysterious series of catacombs where sacred animals were buried during the Ptolemaic and Roman periods. Strewn about are broken remnants of sarcophagi that once held the mummified bodies of baboons, ibises, and other animals. Many were offerings to Thoth, the divine messenger and god of writing. The maze of silent, dark tunnels is a child's dream setting for hide-and-seek.

Farther into the desert on the narrow stone walkway is the **City of the Dead,** filled with royal mausolea laid out like a town, with houses, streets, and walkways half-buried by sand. Most of the tombs here show evidence of Greece's aesthetic influence. The finest structure is the **Tomb of Petosiris,** high priest of the Temple of Thoth. Just inside, the four proto-Doric columns at the front of the tomb are elaborate stone bas-relief carvings depicting Petosiris's family, Petosiris making offerings and prayers, and Egyptians at work making metal, wine, cloth, and bread. Inside, a vestibule opens up into the central chamber, where a square shaft plummets to the burial chamber. The decorative bas-reliefs on the walls, dating from about 300 BCE, depict pharaonic deities in typical Hellenic poses. The most vivid surviving colors in the tomb are found in the images of nine baboons, twelve women, and twelve cobras, each set representing a temporal cycle. Behind Petosiris's tomb sits the **Tomb of Isadora,** a young woman from Antinopolis who drowned circa 120 BCE while crossing the Nile to meet her Egyptian beloved (her story is carved in Greek in the tomb). Isadora's mummy, one of the few not yet carted off to the Egyptian Museum in Cairo, is on display inside a glass case: teeth, fingernails, and even traces of hair can still be seen on the corpse.

Just south of the Tomb of Isadora, a stone walkway leads to **Es-Sakiya** (the Well), a huge brick shaft that supplied the necropolis and its sacred aviary with water. The water wheel, built in 300 BCE, pumped water from 70m below the desert floor. For *bakhsheesh*, the guard will open it and you can descend into the well after shooing bats. The walkway to the well passes through the remains of the great **Temple of Thoth,** which once dominated the entire necropolis. A few of the massive façade columns remain, along with a series of pillars that once enclosed the forecourt.

HERMOPOLIS

To visit Hermopolis, you need to reach **Ashminein** (a 20-min. drive from Malawi) or take a pick-up truck from the town of Tuna el-Gabal (at least E£1). All the locals know Ashminein, but none have heard of Hermopolis. Just outside Ashminein stand two huge sandstone baboons, representations of Thoth. They are all that remain of the ancient city of Khnumu. Named Hermopolis by its Ptolemaic Greek citizens, the city dates from at least the 15th dynasty. The two unfortunate apes who once supported the ceiling of the great temple are not what they once were, as their erect phalli were removed by later generations of prudish Egyptians. The temple served as a cult center for Thoth, an enigmatic god who had the body of a man and the head of an ibis; the baboon was one of his sacred animals. The Egyptians revered him as scribe of the divine court, inventor of writing, and patron of wisdom. The Greeks, arriving in the 5th century BCE, associated this learned deity with their own messenger god, Hermes, and named their metropolis in his honor. In the direction of the baboons' gaze, in a large grassy field of ruins, lie more remains of Khnumu and Ptolemaic Hermopolis, most of which are little more than rubble. One surviving formation retains drawings of the ancient Egyptian deities; these are the remains of a pharaonic pylon. Further on, 24 re-erected rose granite columns demarcate the ruins of the **Agora,** an early Christian basilica. Those that do not have cars waiting for them try to flag down a pick-up to Malawi (at least 25pt).

GABAL ET-TEIR

Gabal et-Teir is a church built near a cave in which the Holy Family supposedly hid while fleeing Egypt. According to legend, Jesus, while raising his hand to stop a boulder from falling on the Holy Family, left an imprint on the rock. Empress Helena, mother of Constantine, had the cloister constructed in 328 CE. Forty days after Coptic Easter, tens of thousands of Copts throng to the site for seven days of prayer and festivities in the name of the Virgin Mary. The **festival** is an exciting affair, almost medieval in nature. The church itself, on the other hand, may not be worth the convoluted transportation acrobatics required to reach it. Tehna el-Gabal is a nearby array of remnants of a city originally built in pharaonic times and added to by the Greeks, Romans, and Copts.

To reach **Gabal et-Teir,** take a *service* to the village of Samalut (from Minya, 20km, 60pt). Get off at the canal bridge in Samalut and take a pick-up truck east to the Nile (25pt); cross the Nile by ferry (E£1). Get on another pick-up from the quarry on the eastern bank up to the monastery (E£1). Once there, find someone to open the church. Transportation is more plentiful during the festival; you can catch a minibus or pick-up directly from Minya (E£1-2).

Inside the church are six white columns hewn into the rock. One has been hollowed out and is used for baptisms. (A local legend tells of a mother who hoped to save money by having her first son baptized at the female child rate; she was handed back a daughter to add to her five older ones.) On the walls are 11th-century paintings of Mary, St. George, and a local saint. One fragmented wall from the original monastery has been preserved in a room to the rear of the sanctuary.

TEHNA EL-GABAL

You can reach Tehna el-Gabal from Gabal et-Teir by walking around the monastery (see above) and descending 100 steps to the dirt road below. Wait by the shady tree for a pick-up going to Tehna (10km, 40pt); it could be a half-hour wait. At the village, walk about 100m toward the hills, crossing the canal, then turn right and walk 50m to the ruins. Some climbing is involved. Two columns mark the entrance to the ruined Nero temple, dedicated to the gods Amun and Sobek. Watch out for bats. Continuing counter-clockwise around the ruin, you'll see the remains of a four-faced column consecrated to the god Hathor. Farther along, in a locked room, sacred crocodiles can be seen through a barred window. You can then climb a 4m ledge to view a higher level of the temple. Pass through the ornate doorway guarded by a snake figure into a small cave with reasonably well-preserved carvings of Roman and Egyptian officials from Ptolemaic times. Outside to the right, "This is our home" is chiseled into the rock in Greek, next to the local version of Venus de Milo. Once back on the road, a *service* can take you to Minya (50pt), or walk back to the village and grab a taxi to Minya for E£1-2. The fantastic view of the Egyptian countryside and isolated nature of the sight make Tehna el-Gabal a great place for picnicking.

■■■ ASSYUT أسيوط

> In the past two years Assyut has been the site of clashes between militant Islam-ists and government forces. If times are tense, you may want to drop Assyut from your itinerary; follow the news and check with your consulate beforehand.

Assyut's most famous native son, the 3rd-century CE philosopher Plotinus, once remarked that "every beautiful vision requires an eye that is able to see it." The eye that truly appreciates the beauty of Assyut has been trained in the tourist camps of Luxor and Aswan; when you become afraid that your own reflection will try to sell you a souvenir, you're ready to come to Assyut. Located at the geographic center of Egypt, Assyut has always been an important market and commercial center; today, Assyut is the most important city in Upper Egypt and the third largest in the country, with a university and an economy that thrives on everything but tourism. Aside from a few scattered tombs, some nearby churches, and the Nile-splitting Banana Island, Assyut has little that fits nicely in a tourist brochure or on a roll of film. But the city's ancient market and its renowned carpet district, the novelty of an Egyptian city with a large and visible Christian presence, the relative care with which its buildings and streets have been maintained, and the natives' indifference to tourists make the town seem almost beautiful, at least to Nile Valley veterans.

Practical Information The **post office** is on the street to the right of Hotel Assiout de Tourisme. Adjacent to the train station is the **telephone office** (open 24 hrs.). The **telephone code** is 088. The **Bank of Alexandria,** along with a number of other banks, is on the same street in a square 200m west of the train station and will change traveler's checks. (Open Sun.-Thurs. 8:30am-2pm, additional exchange hours Sun. 6-9pm and Wed. 5-8pm.) If trouble strikes, the **police station** (tel. 122, or 32 25 62) is located on the Nile, 100m south of El Hilali St., the main street just south of the train station. **Assyut University Hospital** on University St. (tel. 32 20 16) is probably the best local medical facility. In case of medical **emergency,** dial 123.

All transportation connects to and from the main square in front of the **train station.** More than a dozen trains per day travel to Cairo (7hr., 2nd class A/C E£13). Eight southbound trains shuttle to Luxor (A/C, 7hr., E£11.50), four of which continue to Aswan (12hr., E£16). Buses are more convenient to the closer cities; the **bus station** lies just south of the train station. Buses, some of which originate in Cairo, pass through Assyut en route to Kharga Oasis (7 per day, 4-5hr., E£6.75), and the 7am bus continues on to Dakhla Oasis (8hr., E£11). Unfortunately, not all buses stop in the city center every day. A surer way to reach Kharga is to grab a **service** from the stand 100m south of the train station (E£8). The wait shouldn't be more than an hour or two. *Service* taxis also provide convenient, though perilous, transportation to other Nile cities. Stands for various destinations spread out to the west and south of the train station.

Accommodations and Food Set amidst trees and playgrounds, the **YMCA** (tel. 32 32 18) offers two types of relatively spartan but clean accommodations (singles E£6, doubles with refrigerators E£8.) But the large carpeted rooms with color TV, A/C, and private bath make this place perhaps the best deal in Egypt (singles E£15, deluxe doubles E£20). The staff is sometimes elusive, so be clear and patient. To get to the YMCA, turn right (north) outside the train station; after 200m turn right and walk beneath the overpass, past a mosque and a church, and you'll see the entrance on your left (after another 150m). Just before the overpass, the **Windsor Hotel** has bearable large rooms (doubles with bath E£4.50). A bit closer to transportation, the **Al-Haramein Hotel** (tel. 32 04 26) is one block east of the train station on the road to the Nile (El Hilali St.), but it's not always easy to get a room here (clean rooms; singles E£7, doubles E£14; fans E£2). The **Lotus Hotel** (tel. 32 49 29), on the same street, at the end close to the Nile, will do in a pinch (rooms with private bath E£10 per person). The **Hotel Assiout de Tourisme** (tel. 32 26 15), across from the train station, has some renovated rooms and aging bathrooms in a grungy building (singles E£8, doubles E£12; no fans). At the other end, the **Reem Hotel** (tel. 32 62 35), though poorly decorated, is a full service hotel with A/C and private baths in every room (singles E£36, doubles E£56). Head south from the train station, take your first left and then a right.

A favorite restaurant with locals is **Mattam al-Azhar,** where a delicious, crispy whole chicken goes for E£7. The restaurant is on the same street as the post office, a block farther on the left. There's no English sign; look for the ornate wooden screen above the door. **Express Restaurant,** in the heart of commercial Assyut, is spotless and lively and serves tiny, tasty hamburgers (75pt) and *shawerma* or *kabab* sandwiches (50pt). To get there, walk 200m north from the station and turn left at Windsor Hotel onto July 26th St. The restaurant is on the right, after the next intersection. This street is also the place for *kushari* (50pt) and falafel (15-25pt).

Assyut's *souq* sprawls across the area west of the main square; head west from the Express Restaurant and keep walking. This maze of covered, tangled alleys houses some of the country's better carpet shops. Unfortunately, without a local guide it's all too easy to get lost. Ask at your hotel for help, or propose an expedition to one of the local university students eager to practice speaking English.

Sights Outside the city, there are several groups of ancient tombs as well as a couple of historic Coptic monasteries, the most interesting and accessible of which is **Deir el-Muharrak** (the burnt monastery). Bishop Bakhomous built a monastery here in the 4th century at the legendary refuge of the Holy Family during their whirlwind tour of Egypt. The **Church of Elazraq** is the oldest church in Upper Egypt and was constructed in fulfillment of an Old Testament prophecy about a church in the geographic center of Egypt. The adjacent **Church of St. George** contains more icons of the Holy Family and star-studded Coptic saints. Next to the two churches is a four-story tower accessible (when open) only by a drawbridge, built during the 5th century to provide refuge for the monks. Father Athanisos el-Moharragi will show you around, answer your questions, and practice his best monastic English. To get to Deir el-Muharrak, take a *service* south to El Qusiya (E£2) from outside the Assyut train station, then another *service* up to the monastery (25pt).

Felucca fanatics might venture out to Banana Island, across the river from the city (50pt by felucca ferry). If you choose to meander on foot, you'll find the Nile bank of Assyut long and leafy, with a view of the British-built Assyut Barrages to the north.

■ ■ ■ SOHAG سوهاج

As of now, Sohag is a center for agriculture, not tourism. The older, popular part of town on the western side of the Nile is separated by a famous German-built suspension bridge from the newer, open-spaced section (**Medinet Nasr**), which houses the local university. It is situated 467km south of Cairo, 92km south of Assyut, and 208km north of Luxor. Despite its proximity to **Abydos** (about 1½hr. away) and the abundance of old cars which make its streets a living automotive museum, relatively few tourists have heard of Sohag. The newest provincial administration has worked hard to change this by initiating several projects including a soon-to-be-opened archaeological museum, a mountain-top tourist village 12km east of town, and a new highway to Hurghada. Meanwhile, a magnificent, newly discovered pharaonic statue in the neighboring town of Akhmim and the nearby monasteries of Deir Amba Shenouda and Deir Anba Bishai merit a short visit to Sohag.

Practical Information The local **Bank Misr,** along with several other banks, is on the corniche. Turn left out of the train station, left again at the market square, and cross the train tracks. The bank is on your right. (Open Mon.-Thurs. 8:30am-2pm. Additional exchange hours Fri. 6-9pm, Sat. 10am-1pm and 6-9pm.) The **post office** is on Nile St.; go left from the station past the mosque and head left to the end of the street. The **telephone office** inside the train station (open 24 hrs.) is good only for domestic calls; for international calls, go to the telephone office across the street from the police station. The **telephone code** is 093. On the other side of the suspension bridge by the mosque, in the building shaped like an inverted pyramid, sits the **police station** (tel. 122). The **hospital** (tel. 33 20 07) lies just across from the bus station; for an **ambulance** call 32 30 78.

You'll find the usual Nilonic plenitude of transportation in Sohag. The **train station** is in the center of town in the middle of El Mahatta St. Frequent trains head both north and south. The train ride to Luxor takes four hours and costs E£11 (students E£9) in air-conditioned second class. The **bus station** lies 300m south of the train station. Buses leave frequently, especially in the morning, to Assyut (2hr., E£3); Qena (3hr., E£3); and Balyana, near the ruins of Abydos. **Northbound service taxis** can be found in a square 200m north of the train station on El Mahatta St. (to Assyut 1½hr., E£3.50). **Southbound service taxis** stop by the bus station and depart every 20 minutes in the morning to Qena (E£5) and Balyana (1hr., E£1.50), where you can connect with a *service* to Abydos for 75pt. **Local taxis** leave from 200m west of the bus station to Deir Amba Shenouda (50pt), or you can hire a private taxi to the sights for E£15-20 round-trip.

Accommodations and Food The three Sohag hotels stand in a row, across from the train station, at the heart of the town's boisterous mosque scene. With your back to the station, the hotels are, from left to right, Es-Salaam, the Ramses, and the Andalos. **Andalos Hotel** (tel. 33 43 28) is perhaps the cleanest of the three. Hot water, very loud fans, and rooms with locks; English spoken. (Singles E£7, with bath E£9. Doubles E£10.50, with bath E£14.75, with A/C E£23. Breakfast included.) **Es-Salaam Hotel** (tel. 33 33 17) promises A/C in the future; for now, fans will do. (Singles E£7, with bath E£10. Doubles E£9, with bath E£15.) The **Ramses Hotel** (tel. 33 23 13), marked by a picture of a ship above the door, is cleaner than it looks from the outside. (Singles E£6.) There is also the tough-to-find and far-less-than-spotless **Youth Hostel (HI)** at 5 Port Said St. (tel. 32 43 95). Take a right out of the train station and walk until you reach a square; cross the train tracks, turn right, and look on the right. If you're lost, ask for *beit ash-shabab*. Five people share a room and grimy bathrooms. Kitchen available. (Lockout 10am-2pm. Curfew 1am. E£3.10.) Across the river the more upscale **Casanova** (tel. 58 11 85) and the **Meryut Amun** (tel. 58 23 29) will leave you at least E£30 poorer for a night in air-conditioned style.

Fuul, ta'miyya, and *kushari* stands dot El Mahatta St. **Eman,** 10m north of the Andalos, provides *kabab* or a whole chicken (E£8). For a look at how Egyptian professionals enjoy their leisure time, go to one of the clubs on the east bank of the Nile, such as the Police Club (**Nadi Esh-Shorta**) or the Engineers Club (**Nadi El-Mohandiseen**) and eat in a garden by the river.

Sights About 10km northwest of Sohag, on the edge of the desert, are two of the finest Coptic monuments in Upper Egypt. **Deir Amba Shenouda,** or the Monastery of St. Shenouda, is also known as the White Monastery after the color of its lime-stone blocks, many of which originally belonged to a pharaonic temple and feature hieroglyphic inscriptions. The monastery was founded in 400 CE by St. Shenouda. Much of the nave has been destroyed by earthquake, but a small church occupies the apse. Remove your shoes upon entering the carpeted church within the monas-tery complex. You'll be greeted by a seated Jesus, balancing an eroded globe in his right hand and a Bible in his left. The monastery is especially worth visiting between July 5 and August 5, when Coptic pilgrims arrive en masse. During this period, the monastery becomes a medieval market, especially on Thursdays and Fridays. The pilgrims sprint down the steep slopes of the nearby hills, and childless women wrapped in sacks roll down the hills in hopes of obtaining a divine fertility boost. During the pilgrimage period you can visit Deir Amba Shenouda sites from Sohag by minibus for 25pt; at other times, catch a *service.*

The smaller **Deir Amba Bishai** (also **Deir al-Ahmar,** or Red Monastery) is named after its founder, St. Bishai, a thief who converted to Christianity and repented through fasting and prayer. Portions of the original red-brick walls from 600 CE still stand within the more modern building. The sanctuary's main fresco depicts the Last Supper, with another view of Jesus and the apostles in the right apse and Mary on the left. Deir Amba Bishai lies in a village of the same name, 4km up the road from Deir Amba Shenouda. Start walking and try to flag a *service* (25pt). At both monasteries, admission is free, but donations are appreciated.

The nearby largely Coptic town of **Akhmim,** renowned for its cotton weaving, has a near-secret treasure. An 11m-high white limestone statue of Queen Meryut Amun, daughter and wife of Ramses II, was discovered here in 1981 by accident during the construction of a building. Since then several other statues and remnants of a Roman settlement have been unearthed. Archaeologists figure the site could extend indefinitely, but due to the surrounding village (which totally covers the area), their efforts have been severely hampered (admission free; no photos). Take a *service* to Akhmim from Sohag (about 15min.; 25pt) from the stop near the train sta-tion (to your right as you exit the station). Akhmim is not used to tourists; you may find yourself uncomfortably surrounded by children. Women especially should go in a group, and all should dress modestly and be considerate.

■■■ ABYDOS أبيدوس

The ancient city of Abydos was the site of a necropolis and temple dedicated to the god Khenti-Amentiu. Pharaohs from the first dynasty onward chose to be buried at the site and eventually corpses from all over Egypt were interred at this necropolis *par excellence.* Never one to rest on his laurels, Osiris, god of the Nile, subtly co-opted Abydos and the worshipers of Khenti-Amentiu during the 6th dynasty. Aby-dos has all but vanished, save the imposing Temple of Osiris built by the 19th-dynasty Pharaoh Seti I. Though not as imposing as its stupendous first cousins at Luxor and Karnak, the temple is the greatest work of the New Kingdom, noted for its delicately painted murals and magnificent bas-reliefs.

Practical Information, Accommodations, and Food The streets leading up to the temple at Abydos are lined with tourist conveniences, including cafés, a bank, and a photo shop; but accommodations are sparse. Some people visit Abydos as a long daytrip from Luxor (E£50-75 for a **private taxi** in combination with Dendera). The town closest to the temple is **Balyana,** 7km away on the main north-south rail line. Five of the ten daily Cairo-Luxor **trains** stop at Balyana. From Luxor it's easy to go by **service** to Qena (E£2) and change for Balyana (E£5). Another strat-egy is to stay in Sohag, the nearest city, and come to Balyana by *service* (E£1.50). The *service* station in Balyana is one block east of the railway station. From here or from the junction of the north-south road and the Abydos-Balyana road, you can catch a *service* to Abydos (75pt). An infrequent and crowded **bus** runs from Abydos to Balyana (15pt). Fare for a **private taxi** from Balyana to Abydos should be E£4 each way, though it can require some hard bargaining.

At the Temple is a grassy campsite called **Osiris Park.** For E£5 per person you can pitch your own tent, and E£10 per person will allow you access to their tidy, white, bed-equipped tents, including breakfast. A restaurant in the park offers tasty meals of *kabab* (E£12) and chicken (E£10). A number of stores offer drinks at inflated prices. The **New Seti Restaurant,** 150m east and to the left, has a chicken meal for E£7. Falafel is for sale at a coffee shop nearer to the temple.

Sights Seth, Osiris, and Isis, the story goes, were family. When Isis chose to marry Osiris, a jealous Seth cut his brother into little pieces and left Isis to chase the limbs across Egypt and build temples wherever she found a chunk of her beloved brother/ husband. Isis would later beget Horus, the falcon-god, who would kill his uncle Seth. Abydos is where the mutilated brother's head allegedly landed; it became the site for the cult of Osiris, where the myth, including a simulation of Osiris' death and dismemberment, used to be reenacted annually. The temple at Dendera also depicts the story of this incestuous love triangle, including Osiris' ascension to heaven.

The **Temple of Osiris,** built by Seti I, has been partially reconstructed. Its echoing rooms and huge columns compose one of the most impressive sights in Middle Egypt. Three of the original seven doors remain on the **Portico of Twelve Pillars,** which guarded the entrance into the temple proper. The central doorway leads to the first hypostyle hall, lined with 24 colossal papyriform columns. This grandiose entrance gives way to the second hypostyle hall, which contains some of the finest bas-reliefs ever carved in Egypt. At the far left corner of the second hypostyle hall, a long narrow corridor known as the **Gallery of the Kings** leads toward the southeast. This simple passage houses one of Egyptology's most treasured finds, the **Kings' List,** which mentions the names of 76 Egyptian rulers from Menes of Memphis to Seti I. Correlating this list with prior knowledge, scholars were able to pinpoint the sequence of the Egyptian dynasties.

In the southern wing of the temple, beside the entrance to the Gallery of the Kings, a doorway leads to a chamber with two tiny chapels adjoining it. The right- hand chapel contains a kinky relief showing the mummy of Osiris, in the form of a falcon, impregnating Isis. Osiris' sanctuary at the temple's rear is more elaborate than others in the complex. It opens into the **Inner Sanctuary of Osiris,** a chamber still possessing most of the original painted scenes of Osiris's life. The sanctuary is flanked by three small chapels bedecked with the temple's best-preserved reliefs.

After exiting the temple, head left through the sand to the ruins of the **Temple of Ramses II.** Bring someone with you to unlock the gate. The temple here contains interesting hieroglyphics as well as suggestions of a mixing of Coptic and Pharaonic styles. (Site open daily 7am-5pm. Admission E£6, students E£3.)

■■■ QENA & DENDERA قنا و دندرة

Qena, capital of the province that includes Luxor, is near the Temple of Hathor at Dendera (8km to the northwest), and also serves as the Nile Valley's transportation connection to the Red Sea Coast. Hathor's magnificent edifice, less frequented than the omnibus stops to the south and still largely intact, is perched amidst lush farm- lands. But unless you're visiting the temple on your way south or heading for Hurghada, there isn't much reason to come to Qena. The hotels are best avoided, and the absence of tourist facilities almost begs foreigners to move on.

Practical Information **El Goumhouriyya Street** starts at the train station and runs east-west, perpendicular to the tracks. About 500m west of the train station, on El Goumhouriyya, is the town's large **midan.** Turn right from the *midan* and **Banque du Caire** will be 100m down the street on the west side. **Bank of Alexan- dria** is 300m farther, just past the mosques. (Both open daily 8am-2pm and 6-9pm.)

For the **post office,** take a left out of the *midan* and walk 100m. (Open Sat.-Thurs. 8am-2:30pm.) The **telephone office** jingles on your left if you continue west under the aquamarine archway from the *midan* (open 24 hrs). A branch in the train station places calls only within Egypt. The **telephone code** is 096. The **police** smoke Cleopatras in offices in the train station (tel. 32 52 84) and behind the bus station.

Each of Qena's transit centers is in a different part of town. The best way to get from one to another is to hail a **kalish** (E£1-1.50 for 1-3 people, with bargaining). Don't abuse the horse by cramming more than 3 people in the carriage. The **train station,** at the intersection of El Mahatta St. and El Goumhouriyya St., has 10 trains daily to Cairo (11hr.; 2nd-class A/C E£22, students E£18) and 10 trains daily to Luxor (2hr.; 2nd-class A/C E£7, students E£4). You can reach the **bus station** by turning right out of the *midan* and continuing past the mosques; the station will be on the left. Buses, frequently slow and sweaty, run to Hurghada at least every hour in the morning and more frequently in the evening (3hr.; E£5-10; make reservations) and to Luxor every hour (E£1.50). There is also frequent service to Dendera (20pt).

Service and pick-up trucks are convenient for shuttling to Dendera. Hail **northbound service taxis** either one block west of the bus station or from a taxi depot just east of the Nile bridge, 1km north of the bus station. (Dendera 35-50pt.) If you're going to Abydos, say you want Balyana (E£5); if you mention Abydos, which is only 3km farther, you'll have to refuse offers for a "special" taxi. It's E£5 to Sohag, and *service* go as far as Assyut (E£8). For **southbound service taxis,** turn right out of the train station. Cross the bridge spanning the canal and walk to the right side of the *midan.* (Luxor E£2. Aswan E£9.) For Esna, change at Luxor. For Edfu or Kom Ombo you'll have to pay the full fare to Aswan. S*ervice* to Hurghada leave from the same *midan,* in front of the big mosque (E£8). **Local taxis** depart from the *midan* beyond the bus station and the Bank of Alexandria, or wherever you happen to find one. Fare to Dendera is E£7-10 round-trip with earnest bargaining.

Accommodations and Food Try not to spend the night in Qena. Luxor, with an array of cheap, comfortable hotels, is an hour away. If you just have to stop, the **Hotel Dendera** or **Happy Land Hotel** (tel. 32 23 30) is a 10-minute ride from Qena and a 10-second walk from the Temple (see directions under Sights, below). The hotel's proximity to the Temple, well-lit villa-esque garden, never-ending flow of cold Stella, and the surrounding farmland make it a wonderful place to stay—if you also like bedbugs, lizards, and dirty bathrooms. (**Camping** E£5 per person. Rooms E£15 per person, with bath E£20.) In Qena itself, try the grotty **New Palace Hotel** (tel. 32 25 09), across from the train station, behind the Mobil gas station. (No English sign—look for the building that looks like a hotel. Singles with bath E£10. Doubles E£8, with bath E£15.) On El Goumhouriyya St. across from the train station, **El Fatah** offers the barest necessities. (Singles E£5. DoublesE£8. Triples E£10.)

Restaurants lie mainly near the main *midan* on El Goumhouriyya St. **Hamdi Restaurant,** on the road going toward the bus station from the *midan,* will fill you up with a chicken meal for E£5. **El Prince Restaurant** will try to charge you tourist prices for its *kushari* (E£1.50, 50pt for Egyptians; beer E£4.50). Farther up the road past the square is a new and quite clean restaurant. Look for a picture of a smiling chef and a chicken rotisserie in front (1kg *kabab* E£22, *kufta* E£18, breaded and fried veal *escalope* E£5). Qena's *souq* begins near Hamdi Restaurant with tomatoes and melons and runs 400m east, ending with bunnies and pigeons.

Sights If you're in Qena for more than an hour, head north to the Nile, about 1km from the *midan,* for a spectacular view. At **Naqada,** 30 minutes south of Qena, a *fin-de-siècle* monk built the **Pigeon Palace,** an array of brick, mortar, and ceramic hosting 10,000 pigeons. The birds are about 200m west of the road through Naqada in the midst of green fields. (E£2 by *service* from Qena or West Thebes.) Upon crossing the Western Desert, the weary pigeons park here for food, shelter, and the opportunity to be slaughtered. The town is also known for its weaving and textiles.

But it's the remarkably well-preserved remains at **Dendera** that you came to see. Plan to spend at least two hours at the site, as there are stairs to climb, storage spaces to probe, and plenty of wandering around to be done. The **Temple of Hathor** is one of the few temples where the second floor remains intact; a lenient guard will let you climb to the very top and survey your surroundings.

Hathor, the city's matron deity, was worshipped as early as the Old Kingdom, but this temple dates only from the first century BCE. The late Ptolemies and the Romans found it politically expedient to associate themselves with Hathor; Cleopatra, Augustus, Claudius, and Nero sponsored decoration of the temple. A benevolent goddess, Hathor was usually depicted as cow-headed or with cow's ears, or shown wearing a crown of two horns cradling Ra, the sun disk. Because her specialties were love and joy, Hathor, the "Golden One," was identified by the Greeks as Aphrodite. During an annual festival, a statue of Hathor was carried in a sacred procession down the Nile to meet Horus of Edfu.

Eighteen columns are surmounted by cow-goddesses' heads in the **Great Hypostyle Hall.** In the temple's inner sanctum, wall paintings portray the embalmer's art, while the ceiling is decorated with pictures of the goddess Nut. In the second hypostyle hall, also known as the **Hall of Appearances,** six columns line the central aisle of the temple, complemented by six small chambers on either side. The function of these chapels is indicated by their frescoes; perfumes used during sacred rituals were kept in the laboratory and across the hall in the temple's treasury. The second hypostyle hall gives way to the **Hall of Offerings,** where the daily rites were performed. In the kiosk in the southwest corner of the roof, priests performed the ceremony of "touching the disk," in which the soul of the sun god Ra appeared in the form of light. If you look to the right you will notice a gently sloping staircase which leads up to the roof. Unless you have a fantastic fear of bats, the climb is great.

The **Hall of the Ennead** immediately precedes the inner sanctuary. The chamber on the left is the wardrobe; opposite it, a doorway leads through a small treasury into the **Court of the New Year** where sacrifices were performed during the New Year festival. On the ceiling of the colorful portico, Nut gives birth to the sun, whose rays shine upon the head of Hathor. The **Mysterious Corridor** surrounds the **Sanctuary** on three sides, and 11 chapels, each with a distinct religious function, open off of it. A small chamber known as the **Throne of Ra** sits behind the northernmost of the three doorways which open up behind the sanctuary. A minuscule opening in its floor leads to the crypt, a subterranean hallway embellished with reliefs, some of inlaid alabaster. Climb to the upper floors, where many rooms carry ceiling paintings of Nut swallowing the sun at sundown and giving birth to it at dawn. On the roof of the temple, near the edge, is graffiti left by French soldiers in 1799. During the summer, bats inhabit the secluded portions of the temple. Glance up at the ceiling and cover your head before entering the smaller chambers. A flashlight comes in handy.

The first of the series of small buildings on the right, after the front gate, is a Roman *mammisis* from the time of Emperor Trajan. The reliefs depict Hathor and Horus raising their god-son. The second building is the scanty remains of a **Coptic Basilica** (5th or 6th century). The third is the *mammisis* of Nakhtanebo featuring more god-raising scenes. Farther around the outside of the temple are the remains of a **sacred lake,** a **Greek anastorium,** a small **Temple of Isis** (see Abydos, p. 164), a well, and (yet another) Nilometer (see Aswan, p. 195). (Site open daily 6am-7pm. Admission E£10, students E£5.)

The cheapest way to reach the antiquities (8km from Qena) is to take a *service* (25pt) that will drop you off at a fork in the road 1km from the site. From there, follow the paved road to the left. Spend an evening at the Hotel Dendera, right near the site, where locals smoke *sheeshas* and swill Stella until the empty bottles obscure them from view. The public garden outside is an excellent spot for gazing at the temple, the deep blue sky, and stars more plentiful than you've ever seen.

QENA & DENDERA

■■■ LUXOR الأقصر

And so sepulch'red in such pomp dost lie,
That kings for such a tomb would wish to die.

—John Milton

Built on the site of Thebes, capital of united Egypt during the New Kingdom (18th-20th Dynasties, 1555-1070 BCE), Luxor is home to august monuments. Within the town, the Temples of Karnak and Luxor awe even ruins-jaded travelers with their fusillades of gateways and forests of gigantic columns. Historic and artistic wealth spills over to the western side of the Nile, where fabulous tombs dot the planes of Ancient Thebes. In the barren Valley of the Kings, pharaohs such as Tutankhamun achieved the immortality they sought: though their preternatural methods may have failed, the international fame of their tombs lives on millennia later. Luxor is also a good base for daytrips to the antiquities at Dendera, Abydos, Esna, and Edfu.

Luxor's relationship with its illustrious past is more parasitic than reverent. The tourism industry here has created a society of single-minded hawkers and hoteliers, *kalish* chauffeurs and *kabab* chefs. Be careful where you place your trust; don't let yourself be led on a E£500 donkey ride to Luxor Temple, with stops at the city's finest eating establishments and perfume shops. Women especially should trust no one, as Luxor houses a whole sub-culture of very skilled and seasoned scammers. In any event, Luxor's dependence on tourism makes it a buyer's market, particularly during the slow summer season. Budget travelers luxuriate in Luxor; a few dollars per day can buy accommodations, food, and access to unforgettable sights.

ORIENTATION AND PRACTICAL INFORMATION

Luxor is located on the eastern bank of the Nile, 670km upstream from Cairo and 220km downstream from Aswan. Surrounded by a heavily cultivated floodplain, Luxor is an agricultural center, with a *souq* on Tuesdays. The nearby village of El Habal holds a weekly **camel market,** also on Tuesdays. **Luxor Temple** is on the Nile at the center of town; the **train station** is 750m inland on the eastern edge of Luxor; and **Karnak Temple** is 3km northeast of the first two up En-Nil St. Although there are only a few street signs, finding your way around Luxor is easy as long as you know the main thoroughfares. **El Mahatta Street** (Station St.) runs perpendicular to the Nile and connects the **bus stop** and train station. Exit the train station at a 45° angle to your left and you will eventually reach **Television St.,** where signs advertising the many budget hotels and pensions in town begin to appear. **En-Nil St.** (the corniche) runs along the river, turning into Khalid Ibn Waleed St. past the **Novotel.** The bus stop is on **El Karnak St.,** which runs parallel to En-Nil St., slightly inland.

Tourist Office: In the **tourist bazaar** next to the New Winter Palace Hotel (tel. 37 22 15 or 37 32 94). Open daily (including Ramadan) 8am-8pm. Branch at **train station** (tel. 37 21 20) open 6am-midnight, maybe later. Another branch in **airport** (tel. 37 23 06). Staff can provide an official price lists of services and outings. Maps occasionally available. Generally, not much that you couldn't get from your hotel lobby. The nearby **Luxor Visitors Center** has a book store, shows movies, and sponsors seminars and lectures. Open daily 9am-1pm and 7-11pm.

Tourist Police: En-Nil St. (tel. 37 66 20), in the **tourist bazaar.** Also in **train station** (tel. 37 21 20). Both open 24 hrs.

Passport Office: En-Nil St. (tel. 38 08 85), about 1km south of the Novotel, by the sign for Mandera Restaurant. Passport registration and visa extensions available in the foreigners office. Open Sat.-Thurs. 10am-2pm and 7-9pm. Visa business Sat.-Thurs. 10am-2pm. During Ramadan 10am-2pm and 8-10pm.

Currency Exchange: Most luxury hotels change money between 8am and 10pm, for a commission. Smaller non-bank exchange places include the **Bank Exchange** on El Karnak St. across from the bus stop (open 8am-2pm and 5-8pm). **Banque Misr,** Nefertiti St., 1km north of Luxor Temple, off El Karnak St., is open Sun.-Thurs. 8:30am-9pm, Fri. 8:30-11am and 2-9pm. **Bank of Alexandria,** El

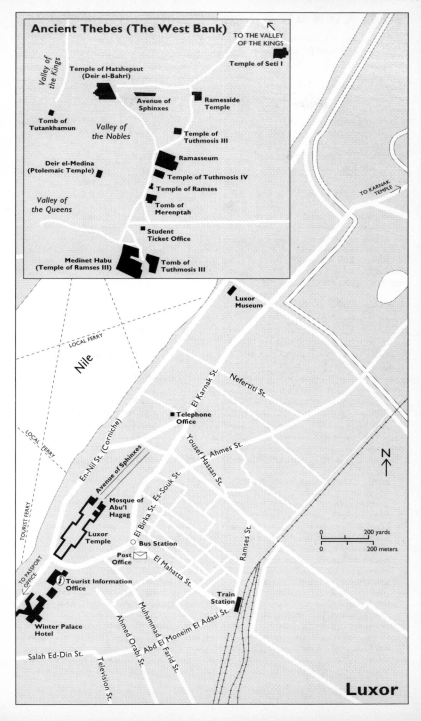

Ancient Thebes (The West Bank)

TO THE VALLEY OF THE KINGS

Valley of the Kings

Temple of Hatshepsut (Deir el-Bahri)

Temple of Seti I

Ramesside Temple

Avenue of Sphinxes

Tomb of Tutankhamun

Valley of the Nobles

Temple of Tuthmosis III

Ramasseum

Deir el-Medina (Ptolemaic Temple)

Temple of Tuthmosis IV

Temple of Ramses

Valley of the Queens

Tomb of Merenptah

Student Ticket Office

Medinet Habu (Temple of Ramses III)

Tomb of Tuthmosis III

TO KARNAK TEMPLE

Luxor Museum

LOCAL FERRY

Nile

El Karnak St.

Nefertiti St.

LOCAL FERRY

Telephone Office

Yousef Hassan St.

Ahmes St.

En-Nil St. (Corniche)

Avenue of Sphinxes

N

TOURIST FERRY

Mosque of Abu'l Hagag

El Birka St.

Es-Souk St.

Luxor Temple

Bus Station

Ramses St.

Post Office

El Mahatta St.

0   200 yards
0   200 meters

TO PASSPORT OFFICE

Tourist Information Office

Train Station

Winter Palace Hotel

Salah Ed-Din St.

Muhammad Ahmed Orabi St.

Abd El Moneim El Adasi St.

El Farid St.

Television St.

Luxor

Karnak St., just north of intersection with Nefertiti St., is open daily 8:30am-2pm, additional currency exchange hours 6-9pm (winter 5-8pm). New branch on the corniche open Sun.-Thurs. 8:30am-2pm, Ramadan 10am-1:30pm. **National Bank of Egypt,** En-Nil St., 50m south of Old Winter Palace Hotel, is open daily 8:30am-2pm and 6-9pm (in winter 5-8pm). **Banque du Caire,** Salah ad-Din St., just east of Television St., is open Sat.-Thurs. 8:30am-2pm and 6-9pm (winter 5-8pm). **Bazar Radwan,** in the tourist market south of Luxor Temple on the corner of El Karnak St. and Muhammad Farid St., changes money daily 10am-10pm.

American Express: Old Winter Palace Hotel on En-Nil St. (tel. 55 13 01 or 37 28 62), south of Luxor Temple. Holds mail. Travelers Cheques sold to cardholders. Will wire money or send mail through Cairo office. Exchanges money and Cheques. Open daily 8am-8pm, sometimes later.

Thomas Cook: Winter Palace Hotel (tel. 38 21 96; fax 38 65 02). Full service. A Thomas Cook Bureau de Change is at Luxor Airport (tel. 37 46 55).

Post Office: Poste Restante and **Express Mail** (until 1pm) on El Mahatta St., 50m east of El Karnak St. Another branch in the bazaar near the tourist office. Both open Sun.-Thurs. 8am-2pm. Branch in the train station open 8am-8pm. **IBA/Federal Express** (see below) will take care of **large packages,** minus the hassle.

Telephones: Next to EgyptAir, in front of the Old Winter Palace Hotel on En-Nil St., also in train station. Open 8am-10pm. **Central Telephone Office** off El Karnak St. to the left 1½ blocks past the Emilio Hotel and Youssef Hassan St. Open 24 hrs. More expensive service at luxury hotels along the Nile and most 3- and 4-star hotels. **Telegrams** can be sent from the main post office or telephone offices, above. **Directory assistance:** Tel. 16. **Telephone code:** 095.

Fax: Available at large hotels, cheaper at **IBA/Federal Express** (El Funun St. off Idris St., which links the Novotel and Television St.; open 8am-6pm). Also offers cheaper international phone service and helps people find **employment**.

Airport: 5km northeast of town; no public transportation, so take a taxi (E£10). Served by **EgyptAir** (tel. 58 05 81), next to the entrance of the Old Winter Palace. In summer, to Cairo (5-6 per day, 1hr., E£288), Aswan (4 per day, E£130), and Hurghada (2 per week, E£130); in winter, 15 per day to Cairo. **ZAS Air** (tel. 95 59 31; fax 95 59 28), on the opposite side of the entrance to the Old Winter Palace, serves the same airports for the same prices. Both open daily 8am-8pm.

Train Station: At the head of El Mahatta St. (Station St.), 0.75km inland from Luxor Temple (tel. 37 20 18). Looks like a temple. **Lockers** 90pt per day. If you're returning to Cairo on the unreliable train (10 per day, 8-12hr., A/C 2nd class E£26 or E£29), make reservations the day you arrive in Luxor. Sleepers to Cairo (3 per day, E£214) and Aswan (3 per day, 4-5hr., 2nd class with A/C E£13, students E£11). It's possible to pay a walk-on fee and travel without a guaranteed seat, but sleepers to Cairo should be reserved 3 days in advance.

Bus Station: Intersection of El Karnak and El Mahatta St., by the mosque across the street from the Horus Hotel. To Cairo: 6am (11-12hr., E£17), 4:30 (11-12hr., E£22), and 7pm express with A/C (9hr., E£35). Seats may be available on the A/C bus from Aswan to Cairo which passes through Luxor at 8:30pm. Service every hr. 6am-6pm to Esna (1hr., E£1.85), Edfu (1½hr., E£3.25), Kom Ombo (3hr., E£4.75), and Aswan (4½hr., E£6), and Qena (almost every hr. 6am-4:30pm, 1½hr., E£1.50), northern Nile towns (every hr. 6am-6pm), and Hurghada (6am E£10, 10:30am E£15, and 4pm E£15). No student discounts.

Service Taxis: off El Karnak St., 1 block inland from the Luxor Museum. Early morning and late afternoon *service* leave whenever they fill up, about every 15min., for Qena (1hr., E£2), Esna (1hr., E£2), Edfu (1½hr., E£4), Kom Ombo (2-3hr., E£7), and Aswan (3-4hr., E£8). There is also a station on the west bank where the local ferry docks, but departures are less frequent.

English Bookstore: Aboudi Bookstore, in the tourist bazaar on En-Nil St. Mainly French, but many books about Egypt, sappy romances, and English newspapers. Open Sat.-Thurs. 8am-10pm. **Gaddi's** has been in the tourist bazaar forever; also on Khalid Ibn Walid St. between Novotel and Isis hotels. The **Al-Ahram Bookshop,** in Luxor Visitors Center sells cultural and historical books. Open 9am-1pm and 7-11pm. A kiosk in front of Marhaba Restaurant sells foreign periodicals.

Swimming Pools: A small but pleasant pool at the **Luxor Wena Hotel** charges E£10; splash in the dramatically situated soup at the **Novotel** for the same price. Before 1pm at **Club Med** on Khalid Ibn Walid St., E£40 buys pool use and a massive buffet lunch. Remember what Mom said about eating and swimming. The smallish **Emilio** on Youssef Hassan, **Shady** on Television St., **Karnak** behind the Hilton, and **St. Joseph** on Khalid Ibn Walid are bargains at E£5-7. The slightly distant **Rezeiky Camp and Motel** on El Karnak charges E£5 for *Let's Go* readers.
Laundry: Listed hotels have free self-serve laundry unless otherwise noted.
Pharmacy: Pharmacies abound. Try our damndest, we couldn't find one that is open 24 hrs. Try asking a hotel employee.
Hospital: Luxor General Hospital, En-Nil St. (tel. 37 20 25), north of Luxor Museum. English is spoken here and at a newer hospital at the eastern end of Television St. (tel. 37 26 98).
Medical Emergency: Tel. 123.
Police: Off El Karnak St., about 200m north of Luxor Temple (tel. 37 23 50).

You can easily get around Luxor by foot, but if you'd rather ride, **kalishes** (carriages) line the Nile. A ride is good for easy transport of baggage, a pleasant trip out to Karnak Temple (E£3), and making that budding romance bloom (E£2 plus commitment). Don't overburden the poor beasts. Luckless singles can rent a **bicycle** (E£3-5 for the whole day); El Mahatta St. and Television St. have several rental places, or ask at your hotel. Bargain with a **felucca** captain for a short cruise up or down the Nile (in summer E£10-20 for an hour trip; more in winter). The cheapest form of transportation in the city are the **minibuses** (25pt), whose most common route is El Karnak St. to El Mahatta St. to Television St. Flag one down along its route.

ACCOMMODATIONS

If you come to Luxor by train, you will disembark into a crowd of card-carrying, name-calling Egyptians offering you invitations to stay with them (for a fee, of course). Some are legit, some are not; so be wise. Often people masquerade as employees of the popular hotels in town, then lead you elsewhere. No sign in front is a bad sign, as are stories about new management and name changes. Foreign women traveling alone can bet on sexual advances from young employees of smaller hotels. If the advance is unwanted and a refusal doesn't do the trick, complain to the manager. In some cases you'll feel more comfortable switching hotels.

Budget beds are near the train station, lining El Mahatta St. and the streets immediately to the north and south, or around Television St., off Salah ed-Din Sq. Prices fluctuate by season; summer rates (listed below unless otherwise noted) are cheapest. Managers say that prices should not increase more than E£1-2 in winter. Competition is usually fierce, and starving student types can lop some piasters or pounds off almost any price any time of year. Ask to sleep on a roof or a terrace for E£2.

Listed accommodations all have shared baths, hot water, fans, and free use of washers and kitchens, unless otherwise noted. Many provide information and maps or organize tours. Be sure to bargain down any initial price quotes. You'll be surprised at the concentration of budget hotels in small areas, so shop around. The extra half hour toting your pack may well be worth it.

Fontana Hotel (tel. 38 06 63), off Television St. Turn left after the bus garage and follow the can't-miss signs. Comfortable, with huge, nearly spotless shared bathrooms; there are also new rooms with private baths and balconies. Towels and toilet paper provided. Doubles E£15. Breakfast included.
Everest Hotel (tel. 37 00 17), first left off Television St. before the bus garage. A clean, new hotel which has earned a good reputation (for whatever that's worth) in its first year. Rooms have private baths. E£5-10 per person.
Titi Pension (tel. 37 64 90). Turn right off Television St. just before Mish Mish restaurant. A small, laid-back family-run pension, where you won't have to worry about unwanted sexual advances. Nothing special, but cheap (E£4 per person).
Moon Valley Hotel (tel. 37 57 10), Esh-Shmoos St. Take first right off Television St., slanting onto El Medina El Manawara St. Hotel is 6 blocks down and on the right.

Michael Jackson fans will love the pictures of the Gloved One and those of the owner, who fancies himself a look-alike. All rooms have A/C and shower. No washing machine. Television and over 100 videos (including Michael's finest) in the lobby. Singles E£8. Doubles E£15. Triples E£20. Breakfast included.

El Salam Hotel, El Mahatta St. Of the comparable hotels, offers bigger rooms, some with table and chairs. Shady roof with snazzy multicolored wicker furniture. Singles with bath and A/C E£10. Doubles E£8, with bath E£12. Breakfast E£1.50.

The Golden Pension, Muhammad Farid St. (tel. 37 03 34 or 38 08 38), on the 2nd side street to the right as you head south on El Manshiyya from the train station. Spend the evening hanging out with fellow guests. Owner Hassan is also a travel agent and will allow guests to tag along on bus tours for only the cost of admission to the sights. E£5 per person, 10% discount for *Let's Go* readers.

Oasis Hotel, Muhammad Farid St. (tel. 38 16 99). Take a left out of the train station and another left after 2 blocks. Cleanliness may compensate for cheesy decorations in this spacious place. VCR/TV in dining room. Singles E£8. Doubles with bath E£15, with A/C E£20. Triples with bath and A/C E£35. Breakfast included.

Happy Land, on El Qamr St. Turn right off Television St. at Mish Mish Restaurant and go about 300m. E£3.50 per person, E£4 with bath. Breakfast E£1.50.

Mustafa Hotel, (tel. 37 47 21), on Television St. about 400m south of Salah ad-Din Sq. Very clean and well-run. Singles with bath, towels, and A/C E£18. Doubles E£25. Breakfast included. 25% price rise in winter. Fax available; no free laundry.

Abu al-Haggag Hotel, Muhammad Farid St. (tel. 38 29 58), corner of El Karnak St. Oldish, clean; some rooms have droolworthy views. No kitchen or washing machine. Singles with A/C E£10. Doubles E£25. Triples E£35. Breakfast included.

Youth Hostel (HI), 16 El Karnak St. (tel. and fax 37 21 39), 200m north of the *service* stop. Halfway between Karnak and Luxor Temples, across from the YMCA camp and down a small street toward the Nile. In BFE, not as clean as some hotels and pensions, and not cheap. Roomy sitting room and a small garden in front. Lockout 10am-2pm. Curfew 11pm. Dorm beds (no fans) E£5.10. Doubles (with fans) E£16.20. Nonmembers must join for E£24. Breakfast E£1.50. Free lockers.

Three-star hotels can offer luxury (A/C, bars, TV, pool) at reasonable rates, especially in summer (E£20-35 per person). Try **Ramoza** on El Mahatta St., **Arabesque** on Muhammad Farid St., **Shady** or **Santa Maria** on Television St., **St. Joseph** on Khaled Ibn Walid St., or **Karnak Hotel** behind the Hilton past Karnak Temple.

For **camping,** the **Rezeiky Camp and Motel** just before Karnak Temple on El Karnak St. has a Club Med-esque (sort of) pool, deck, and bar. (Camping E£5 per person. Simple bungalows E£10 per person. Rooms with A/C E£25 per person.) Prices negotiable; *Let's Go* readers get a 10% discount. Or opt for local color at the **YMCA Day-Camp,** on El Karnak St. 180m north of the *service* stand (tel. 37 28 25). During the warmer months, the grounds are noisy with Egyptians partying past midnight, when the gates are locked. The grounds are littered and bathrooms leave much to be desired, but there is hot water and the area is guarded 24 hrs. (E£3 per person, E£2.80 for motorcycles, E£5 for cars, and E£25 for caravans.)

Accommodations on the West Bank (Ancient Thebes)

Though most visitors sleep in downtown Luxor on the east bank, staying on the west bank offers incredible wide blue skies, soothing silence, and green fields, not to mention the chance to roll out of bed and to the Theban necropolis at the opening bell. Unfortunately, you don't get quite as much for your money on the west bank. Prices below are for winter, when you should call ahead before lugging your bags across the river. When a three-digit number is listed, dial 10 or 25 in Luxor and ask for "west bank number so-and-so." You can also ring up a west bank operator at 38 25 02 or 38 48 35 and ask for your three or four-digit extension. A taxi from the ferry docks (E£5) is the only practical way to get to hotels. See West Bank in Sights.

Amoun El-Gazira (tel. 912), located in the middle of the village of El Gezira, 200m from the local ferry. Luscious natural scenery, good management, and clean rooms. Doubles E£30, with bath E£50. Breakfast included.

Abul Kasem Hotel (tel. 58 15 90), just before the entrance to Seti Temple. Large, carpeted rooms in a tranquil setting. Student and group discount. Rooms with private bath E£15 in summer, E£25 in winter. Breakfast included. Lunch or dinner at the fine adjoining restaurant E£10 (in winter and late summer only).

Pharaoh's Hotel (tel. 702), 100m behind the student ticket kiosk along an unpaved road. The most comfortable of the west bank hotels draws you in with a shaded path covered in vines. Clean, classy, and carpeted. Doubles (with either A/C and shared bath or fan and private bath) E£60. Breakfast included.

Habou (tel. 37 24 77), directly across from Medinet Habou. Rooms are simple and slightly overpriced, but the view of Medinet Habou from the second floor terrace is unmatched. Doubles E£40. Triples E£50. Breakfast included.

FOOD

While it's no gourmet's paradise, Luxor serves up better fare than most temple-hugging towns. Its menus are a little longer, its dishes are a little stronger, and its restaurants have a little more charm. Several of Luxor's affordable culinarias huddle around the train station and on El Manshiyya St.; or to the north of the Luxor Temple on El Karnak St. Luxor's best deal is *kushari,* which can be had for E£1 on your left as you walk down El Mahatta St. from the station, or at one of two new *kushari* houses—**Sayida Zeinab** on Television St. or **Sayida Nafisa** on Youssef Hassan St. There is also an excellent *ta'miyya* (falafel) stand on El Karnak St. behind Luxor Temple; others dot the street linking El Mahatta with Television St.

Perhaps the biggest drawback to staying on the **west bank** is its lack of decent yet cheap restaurants. The **Tutankhamun** and the **Africa** next to the ferry landing offer the usual rice, chicken, *kabab,* and salads for about E£12. The **Pharaoh's Hotel** has traditionally been the best, but its quality has declined and its prices have risen during the last year or so. The shady garden is still good for a drink after a day of sightseeing. The **Valley,** 500m east of the Colossi of Memnon on the main road, serves tasty though expensive food in a clean setting (main courses E£16.50). Most of the other hotels have restaurants, but they are often closed and the quality is inconsistent, especially when business is slow.

For fresh produce, the local *souq* runs parallel to El Karnak St. beyond the tourist shops (Tuesday is the major market day). For fresh bread, go to one of the bakeries either across the street from the bus station next to the Horus Hotel on El Karnak St. or behind the Luxor Wena hotel. Small blue kiosks catering mostly to locals sell dirt-cheap bread everywhere. The "Twinky" shop on the square at the train station sells pastries and sweets, but none of those cream-filled golden sponge cake fingers.

El Omdah, in front of the Egotel. Outdoor seating in their garden is groovy in summer. The menu is full of Egyptian appetizers, salads, and soups (E£1-3), plus the usual grilled meat and chicken (E£10-12). Beer and *sheesha* available.

Abu-Haggar, on the street linking the train station and Television St., is widely recommended by locals. Egyptian salads and meats (pigeon E£6).

New Karnak Student Restaurant, next to the hotel of the same name. Orange interior. Specializes in tasty omelettes (cheese, chicken, or Spanish, all E£2.50) and soups (75pt-E£1.50). Drinks 75pt, ice cream 90pt. Open 7:30am-10:30pm.

Salt and Bread, in front of train station. *Shish tawouk* (chicken *kabab*) E£7, ½-chicken E£6, ¼-chicken E£3; omelettes E£2.50; veal steaks E£7. Lots of outdoor seating; indoors is not as appetizing.

El Houda, Television St., about 150m beyond the bus garage; look for disco lights at the entrance and paintings of a demonic-looking chef. A long menu, including hearty, filling pizza with a slight Egyptian twist (E£4-4.50), *shish tawouk* (E£5), ¼-chicken (E£3.50), and drinks (E£1).

Mish Mish, across from El Houda on Television St. Comfortable, air-conditioned restaurant serves up a variety of Western and sort-of-Egyptian foods. Soups, salads, and especially the pizzas are good; the meat ain't so tasty. Popular with archaeologists, probably because the Stella is cold.

Restaurant Khased Khear, on El Mahatta St. about a block up from the train station, on the right. One of the best places for traditional Egyptian food. Risk your spinal cord on the skinny spiral staircase for some privacy upstairs, a luxury in Luxor. *Kabab* E£8, soup E£1. Air-conditioned, but take-out is cheaper.

Hotel restaurants can hold some unexpected bargains, like the E£10 Mediterranean all-you-can-eat salad bar at the **New Winter Palace Hotel**. There are **liquor stores** on Ramses St. directly to the right if you're walking out of the train station and on El Mahatta St. Pension managers can procure beer if you ask (not more than E£4.50).

SIGHTS IN LUXOR

While not as numerous as the West Theban relics and ruins, Luxor's sights have more to offer than yet another notch on the traveler's monument meter. Luxor Temple has its tranquility, Karnak Temple has its immensity, and the Luxor Museum its clarity. You can visit all three in one day, but it may behoove your sanity to visit them on separate afternoons, after spending the morning in the Theban necropolis.

Luxor Temple

The grand columns of Luxor Temple, visible from the western end of El Mahatta St., reside in the heart of modern Luxor. New Kingdom Pharaoh Amenhotep III presided over the first work on the temple, building on the site of a small Middle Kingdom temple to Amun-Re and re-dedicating his edifice to the triumvirate made up of the god Amun, his wife Mut, and their son, the moon god Khonsu. The unfinished work of Amenhotep was completed under Tutankhamun. The most significant later contributions were those of the swell-headed pharaoh Ramses II, among which are six looming statues of his own bad self guarding the entrance. The sanctuary was later restored under Alexander the Great; and when Christianity came to Luxor, part of the complex was used as a church. Only an altar and a few mosaics are left from this period, but the **Mosque of Abu'l-Haggag,** added by the Fatimids, still holds dominion over the temple court and remains in use.

The doorway to the temple's interior is cut through the enormous **Pylon of Ramses II,** nearly 24m tall. Flanking the main doorway are two of the six original **Colossi of Ramses II,** as well as a pink granite obelisk with four praying baboons on one side. The obelisk's twin was removed in 1836 and now graces the Place de la Concorde in Paris. Reliefs on the pylon describe Ramses' battles against the Hittites.

Continue through the **Court of Ramses II** to reach the **Colonnade of Amenhotep III.** From here, proceed into the **Court of Amenhotep III.** Beyond this court rises the hypostyle hall, or antechamber, with its 32 gigantic columns set in four rows. Latin inscriptions to Julius Caesar adorn an altar in one of the rooms to the left of the pillared hall. Alexander appears in pharaonic attire before Amun and other deities in some bas-reliefs in the **Sanctuary of Alexander the Great** at the end of the corridor. Overzealous fertility god Min receives disproportionate attention in the sanctuary.

The temple and its well-groomed lawns make for a comfortable retreat, especially at night. (Open daily 6am-11pm; in winter 6am-10pm; during Ramadan 6am-6:30pm and 8-11pm. The lights go on at 7:30pm year-round. Enter on En-Nil St., 400m north of the New Winter Palace. Admission E£10, students E£5; ½-price after 7pm.)

Karnak Temple

Karnak Temple is overwhelming in its intricacy and proportions. Every major period in the ancient history of Egypt is represented in the additions to this complex of shrines dedicated to Amun and his family. In pharaonic times, Karnak represented the power of the Theban ruler and the importance of the cult of Amun.

An annual festival celebrating the glory of Amun took place in the two great temples of Luxor. The entire 3km distance between the two was once connected by the sacred **Avenue of the Sphinxes,** a paved boulevard lined on both sides with hundreds of majestic, human-headed lions, each cradling a statuette of Ramses II, and his monumental ego, between its paws. The final stretch of the avenue remains complete with two rows of sphinxes at the northern end of El Karnak St. by the **Temple of Khonsu,** to the right of the main entry to Karnak Temple.

LUXOR

Enter **Karnak Temple** from the west with the Nile at your back and pass through the **Avenue of the Rams,** another double-rowed boulevard of creatures (lions' bodies with rams' heads) dedicated to Ramses II. The temple is a melange of additions and alterations spanning millennia; but because of the traditionalism of pharaonic architecture, the different pieces comprise a harmonious whole. The Karnak complex expands outward from the center, where you will find most of the oldest treasures. The further you proceed from the entrance, the farther back in time you go.

The first pylon is Ptolemaic (2nd century BCE), and the eighth is the contribution of Queen Hatshepsut (15th century BCE). The 10th-century BCE **Great Court,** the area before you as you emerge from the first pylon, is the largest single portion of the Karnak complex. Chambers on the left are dedicated to the Theban trio of Amun, Mut, and Khonsu. They were built during the 29th dynasty and adorned with bas-reliefs depicting the deities. On the right is a temple built by Ramses III and lined with 20 7m-tall statues of himself. The three chapels behind the temple's inner court are also dedicated to the Theban Triad.

Return to the Great Court and continue to the right into the **Great Hypostyle Hall,** one of the pinnacles of pharaonic architecture with its sandstone forest of 134 colossal papyrus columns. The sensory overload continues on a smaller scale as every square centimeter of the ceiling, walls, and columns is carved with inscriptions. Note the depictions of the fertility god Min doing what he does best. Walking east toward the fourth pylon, you can find the pink granite **Obelisk of Queen Hatshepsut** at the center of a small colonnade. Passing through the rubble of the fifth pylon and the granite sixth pylon, enter the **Hall of Records,** containing two elegantly proportioned granite pillars, one decorated with carvings of the lotus of Upper Egypt, the other with the papyrus of Lower Egypt. Behind the hall is the **Sanctuary of the Sacred Boats,** a chapel famous for its exquisite carvings.

Straight ahead, the **Festival Hall of Thutmosis III** dominates the eastern edge of the Karnak complex. The star-studded ceiling survives intact, supported by 52 tapering pillars. Some of the bases were actually whittled down to make room for large processions. In Christian times, the hall was converted into a church; frescos of haloed saints still adorn the interior walls and column shafts. Beyond a low wall to the east, the **Gate of Nectanebo** marks an early entrance to the complex. Retrace your steps to the central hall, turn right, and walk 50m to see the limpid waters of **Birket el-Mallaha** south of the Festival Hall. Priests purified themselves in the holy waters of this rectangular pool before performing ceremonies within the temple.

If your Karnak buds are still unsated, you can visit the **Karnak Open Air Museum,** to the north of the great court; look for a small sign and return toward the entrance. The museum is comprised of three chapels and a motley collection of well-labeled wall fragments. Egyptologists were unable to reassemble the **Red Chapel** of Queen Hatshepsut, so it is displayed in long rows of blocks. Unlike most temple decorations displayed this way, each block of the chapel features a self-contained design, which made it more difficult for the archaeologists to see the larger picture. The **Alabaster Chapel** is a beautiful Middle Kingdom addition to Karnak. Its white walls streaked with brown are a welcome relief from the acres of sandstone. The apparent reason for placing the Alabaster Chapel, the Red Chapel, and the **White Chapel** of Sesostris I in the museum is that no one has figured out exactly where the chapels originally stood in the temple; parts of each were pilfered for later additions. A small temple behind the museum contains a black statue of a sun goddess.

It usually takes at least two hours to see the entire temple, so in summer bring bottled water and come early in the day. Equip yourself with Jill Kamil's excellent *Luxor* (E£20), or tag along with a tour group. The temple lies 3km north of Luxor Temple at the end of El Karnak St., 1 block east of En-Nil St. Walk or bike (½-hr. ride) along the Nile or take a horse-drawn carriage. The local minibuses (25pt) run between Karnak Temple and the train station. Ask first to make sure the driver is going as far as the temple. (Temple open daily 6am-6:30pm in summer; 6am-5:30pm in winter. Admission E£10, students E£5; same charge for open-air museum.)

Luxor Museum

The Luxor Museum is a testament to the fact that less is sometimes more. Facing the Nile midway between Luxor and Karnak Temples, the Museum has a small but stellar collection displayed with the help of the Brooklyn Museum of New York. Featured treasures from the neighboring temples and the Valley of the Kings include a relief of ancient gymnasts and acrobats, model funerary boats from the celebrated tomb of Tutankhamun, and two very well preserved statues of Akhenaton, the coolest of kings. The New Hall showcases 16 pieces of marble and granite statues, among which the giant cobra and the confident Amenhotep III are perhaps the most striking. The museum is within walking distance (1.5km) of both Luxor and Karnak Temples. (Open daily 9am-1pm, additional evening hours 5-10pm in summer, 4-9pm in winter. Admission E£8, with New Hall E£10, students ½-price.)

SIGHTS ON THE WEST BANK (ANCIENT THEBES)

Even while preoccupied with empire-building, the rulers of Thebes were dedicated to estate planning and life insurance. All ancient kings aspired to a tomb with a view on the western shore of the Nile. Pharaonic obsession with the afterlife made the necropolis of Thebes into possibly the world's best-endowed graveyard. Over the course of centuries, robbers and archaeologists have nabbed much of the treasure, but the site still features an unparalleled collection of Egyptian funerary art.

Security was the main concern of the Middle Kingdom rulers who built the Theban tombs. Earlier pharaohs had been too trusting or too convinced of the inviolability of their sacred tombs, kind of like you with your money before you came to Egypt. Thieves mastered the delicate process of pyramid pilfering at Memphis, making off with many of the afterlife amenities thought to make the second go-round a little easier for the expired exalted. That simply would not do—a radical change in burial practices was in order to ensure the decorous treatment of the deceased.

The western edge of Thebes, capital city of the New Kingdom, was selected as the site for subsequent tombs. To conceal the location, contents, and design of the tombs, the work was done in utmost secrecy by a team of laborers who dwelt within the necropolis itself. Perfecting techniques of tomb construction, decoration, and mummification, this community of 300 artisans devoted itself to the City of the Dead over the course of generations, passing its expertise down through its families. (Remains of the workers' walled city have been excavated near the Temple of Deir el-Medina.) Tomb design reflected the new emphasis on secrecy. Instead of a single ostentatious pyramid, there were pairs of funerary monuments: an underground grave, lavishly outfitted with the articles demanded by the hectic afterlife and sequestered in an obscure recess of the desert, and a grandiose mortuary temple where the monarch could be worshiped for eternity. Designers and builders incorporated dead-end passages, fake sarcophagi, hidden doorways, and deep shafts to foil the most cunning robbers. Once a plotzed pharaoh was safely stowed, workers immediately began to construct the tomb destined for his successor.

One region in particular seemed ideal for entombment: a narrow, winding valley walled on three sides by jagged limestone cliffs and approachable by a single rocky footpath. This isolated canyon, known as the **Valley of the Kings,** became the burial place of New Kingdom pharaohs. Although it looked promising on papyrus, it failed to deter hoodlums, and few of the tombs escaped vandalism.

Queens, favored consorts, and select offspring were accorded ceremonial burial with full honors and security precautions in a separate corner of the west bank, the **Valley of the Queens.** Esteemed members of the Theban aristocracy also practiced elaborate burial customs; and several of the **Tombs of the Nobles** in fact rival royal burial chambers in craft and design. Over 400 tombs are found in the necropolis.

Getting There

Take a ferry from Luxor to the west bank. **Tourist ferries** operate frequently for E£2 round-trip (no bicycles allowed). One tourist ferry docks next to the Savoy Hotel, 300m north of Luxor Temple. The other docks in front of the Winter Palace Hotel,

200m south of the temple. Both tourist ferries shuttle you to the main (non-student) ticketing office on the west bank. (Ferries operate daily 6am-5pm.)

The bargain-basement option is a pair of **local ferries,** which terminate their cross-ings at a site more convenient for donkeys, bicycles, and other vehicles. One docks directly in front of Luxor Temple (E£1, bicycles 25pt one way) and the other leaves from a spot just north of the Novotel (E£1, bicycles free). From the dock on the west bank, hop on a taxi, bicycle, or donkey, and head inland, crossing the canal to the **student ticket kiosk;** or walk north to the **main ticketing office**.

There are several different options for west bank exploration; some require pre-ferry planning, others do not. **Bicycles** are cheap; they also allow you relative free-dom and a chance to take in the surrounding scenery of barren mountains and fer-tile fields. The well-paved and gently sloping roads make for a relatively easy ride, even on one-speeds. But don't plan on riding long distances between the hours of 11am and 3pm in the summer. Rent your bike in Luxor before crossing over on the ferry, or in the village of Gezira, about 200m inland from the ferry landing.

Hiring a **taxi** for the day is surprisingly economical (E£40 for all morning, E£5-12 per person if you have a full car, plus E£1-2 *bakhsheesh* at the end of the trip) and allows you to cover the most ground. Come early and bargain hard with the drivers who wait at both the northern (tourist) and southern (local) ferry docks. Ignore any prattle about government rates and per-person charges. Or you could make arrange-ments in Luxor the day or night before and take the car ferry to the other side.

Mark Twain wrote that riding a **donkey** in Egypt "was a fresh, new, exhilarating sensation … worth a hundred worn and threadbare pleasures." The novelty of don-key travel (which has a way of wearing off quickly) and the fantastic views afforded by the donkey trail as it climbs its way up and around to the Valley of the Kings has lead to a burgeoning burro-borrow market. Through your pension, you can arrange an excursion which includes donkey, ferry, and guide (E£25-35). Or do away with middlemen and hire your own ass in the village of Gezira just inland from the ferry or possibly at the local ferry dock on the west bank. Hiring your own beast allows more leeway with your itinerary—the tours usually take you only to the Valley of the Kings, Temple of Hatshepsut (Deir el-Bahri), the Ramasseum, and the Colossi of Memnon. Seasoned cowpeople should venture out on their own. The donkeys might know the way, and besides, guides are useless unless you speak Arabic. Try to pay E£10-15 for the donkey, but not until the day is done.

Those with independent minds and/or time to spare can get around by **foot.** Take a local taxi (about E£2) to the student ticket kiosk (3km from the ferry dock), from which most of the Theban necropolis and the Valley of the Queens is within a 3km radius. The Valley of the Kings lies an easy 8km away by road, or a few strenuous kilometers by steep donkey path. Alternatively, take a taxi from ferry to kiosk to first sight (E£20; the Valley of the Kings is a good place to start) and save your energy for walking from sight to sight. When walking be sure to drink lots of fluids, and when the weather is hot, take plenty of shade breaks.

Guided tours in air-conditioned coaches with English-speaking guides can be arranged through the various corniche travel agents (E£65-80 per person, including admission; Isis Travel and Misr Travel are places to start). Most tours visit the Valley of the Kings, the Valley of the Queens, the Colossi of Memnon, and Temple of Hat-shepsut. The larger your group, the better your bargaining leverage. The loss of spontaneity, adventure, and independence is mitigated by convenience and a more thorough description of the sights, which can be enlightening.

The least explored of all options is a **motorbike.** Technically, you need a license. Motorbikes for hire are available at a few shops and pensions, including the Everest, New Grand, and Nefertiti Hotels—E£30-40 is a reasonable day's rate.

Sight-seeing Strategy

Although most travelers get their fill of West Theban sights in two or three days, the wealth of ancient relics could occupy a wannabe Egyptologist for weeks.

Conduct your exploration of the necropolis in a series of early-morning visits. For those who can bear the heat, however, afternoons are less crowded, and some of the more open sights and temples lie abandoned for errant wanderers to examine free of charge or hassle. Especially in the summer, guards at the less-visited sights tend to lock up and head home a little early. All sites open at 6am, offering about three hours of peace and pleasant temperatures. The sites officially close at 4pm in winter, 5pm in summer, but if you get in before closing time you won't get kicked out. Drinks are sold at some of the ruins; play it safe by bringing plenty of water.

Plan ahead—you must decide what you would like to see before you head out. Consider content, location, and mode of transport before purchasing tickets. (For example, those planning to ride donkeys might reserve the Valley of the Kings for the day of the ride.) One suggested donkey route includes the Valley of the Kings, around to the Temple of Hatshepsut, the Ramasseum, and home. This same route can be done with great success on foot if you first get a ride to the Valley of the Kings. Climbing the mountain separating the Valley of the Kings and the Temple of Hatshepsut is an excellent experience, and the descent can be dangerous on donkeys. If you go on foot you will feel safer, and you can pause as long as you want at the top, surveying your surroundings and enjoying the silence.

Chronic sight-crammers with only one day to spare in the west bank should consider squeezing in the Tombs of Rekhmire and Sennofer and the Tombs of Ramose, Userhet, and Khaemt. A second day by bike or taxi might begin at the Seti Temple; stop off at one or two of the Tombs of the Nobles and the Tombs of Rekhmire and Sennofer if still unvisited, and continue to Deir el-Medina, the Valley of the Queens, and Medinet Habou. Taxi riders or cyclists with only one day should make sure to include the Valley of the Kings, the Tombs of Rekhmire and Sennofer, the Valley of the Queens, and Medinet Habu in their journey.

Bringing a flashlight will save you *bakhsheesh*. Photography is prohibited at all sites, as flashes harm the paintings.

Tickets

There are two ticket kiosks. One is on the western bank of the Nile next to the tourist ferry dock. The student kiosk is 3km farther inland, just beyond the Colossi of Memnon. Both kiosks are open daily 6am-4pm. Tickets are non-refundable and good for day of purchase only. Non-student prices are as follows (½-price with ISIC):

#1	E£10	Valley of the Kings *(see note below)*
#2	E£10	Tomb of Tutankhamun
#3	E£6	Temple of Hatshepsut (Deir el-Bahri)
#4	E£6	Medinet Habu (Temple of Ramses III)
#5	E£6	Ramasseum
#6	E£6	Asasif Tombs
#7	E£6	Tombs of Nakht (Khereef, Nefer-hotep, Kiky, and Anch-hor) and Mena
#8	E£6	Tombs of Rekhmire and Sennofer
#9	E£6	Tombs of Ramose, Userhet, and Khaemt
#10	E£6	Deir el-Medina (Temple and Tombs)
#11	E£6	Valley of the Queens
#12	E£6	Tomb of Nefertari *(closed for renovations)*
#13	E£2	Seti Temple
#14	E£6	Tombs of Khonsu, Ushereto Benia
#15	E£6	Tomb of Pabasa

Note: The Valley of the Kings ticket grants you admission to any three tombs (ten were open in summer 1994). Fortunately, the Valley of the Kings is the one place you can buy tickets on location. A second admission ticket opens three more tombs.

Valley of the Kings وادى الملوك

The Valley of the Kings lies 5km from the Nile but is accessible only via a steep, circuitous route. From either ferry dock, head inland toward the ridge and the temples of the necropolis of Thebes. There are two possible routes to the beginning of the Valley road: students must head 3km straight inland past the Colossi of Memnon to the student kiosk, then northeast past the sites of the necropolis to the beginning of the Valley road. Non-students with tickets from the Nile-side office can turn right (northeast) at the canal (follow the signs) and go 2km along the canal, then turn west by the Abul Kasem Hotel and go 1.5km to the base of the Valley road. The well-paved, gently sloping road winds for 5km into desolate mountain valleys. The Valley of the Kings itself, no more than 400m long and 200m wide, can easily be toured by foot using the clearly marked, well-groomed gravel paths. Over 64 known and numbered tombs honeycomb the valley. Most of them are not open to the public, but the best-known tombs are almost always accessible. Some are kept locked and can be opened only by the mythical site guards. All tombs listed are illuminated with fluorescent lights, but a flashlight might be helpful in revealing dark side chambers.

In the summer of 1994, ten tombs (not including Tutankhamun's, which requires a special ticket) were open to public view (4 admission tickets' worth). Ramses VI (#9—don't confuse ticket numbers with tomb numbers) and Ramses III (#11) once occupied the most interesting of these tombs; Amenhotep III (#35), Ramses I (#16), and Merneptah (#8) would also be proud of what is left of their burial chambers.

The west bank's most renowned tourist attraction, the **Tomb of Tutankhamun (#62),** stands directly in front of the Rest House in the middle of the valley. It requires a special ticket (E£10, students E£5). The real treasures are at the museum in Cairo and the interior of this small tomb may not be worth the extra ticket. In any case, if you plan to see it, visit it first or you'll probably be disappointed after seeing the others; size does make an impression. The tomb's celebrated discovery in 1922 by archaeologist Howard Carter produced a cache of priceless pharaonic treasures that has toured the world several times and now resides permanently in the Egyptian Museum in Cairo. Egyptologists had expected that the tomb would contain little of interest because the pharaoh reigned only a short time before he died. A determined archaeologist, Carter ignored professional censure, toiling for six seasons in the Valley of the Kings. After more than 200,000 tons of rubble had been moved, even Carter's sympathetic patron, the wealthy Lord Carnarvon, reluctantly decided to abort the project. But before admitting failure, Carter made one last attempt: the final unexplored possibility was a site in front of the tomb of Ramses VI, in an area covered with workers' huts. Confounding the critics, he chanced upon an ancient doorway beneath the shanties. The sensational discovery revealed an amazing store of baubles and thoroughly vindicated Carter. The tomb had remained almost intact, barely despoiled by robbers; it was crammed with decorated furniture, wheat, vegetables, wine, clothing, canopic jars, jewelry, utensils—including several royal walking sticks—and three mummies, including that of the pharaoh himself. Carter was occupied for 10 years cataloging the contents.

Tutankhamun's mummy was encased in the innermost of three snugly nested, superbly decorated cases. This dazzling case of solid gold is now displayed in the Cairo Museum, as is the second mummy case of inlaid gold foil. Fortunately, the raiding Egyptologists left behind the outermost case, a gilded wood extravagance luxuriating in rich jewels, along with Tut's exquisitely carved sarcophagus. Of all the pharaohs buried in the Valley of the Kings, only Tutankhamun has the privilege of resting here in peace. King Tutankhamun's tomb may seem miniature because he reigned as pharaoh for only two years. The interior walls of the burial chamber, perfectly preserved, depict colorful scenes from the *Book of the Dead*.

The 12th-century BCE **Tomb of Ramses IX (#6),** on your left once you enter the valley, features fantastic ceiling murals of gold figures manifesting their *joie de mourir* against a deep blue background. A lengthy corridor slopes down to an anteroom covered with demons, serpents, and wild beasts. Beyond, through a pillared room and corridor, a pit in the burial chamber once held Ramses IX's sarcophagus.

The **Tomb of Ramses VI (#9),** directly behind and above the Tomb of Tutankhamun, is best known for its unusual ceiling. Bizarre images of men with snakes' heads, naked figures riding cobras like camels, kneeling headless bodies, and people with elongated limbs and torsos party on the walls and ceilings. Below are scattered the fragmented remains of Ramses VI's sarcophagus, smashed by grave-robbers.

The steep entrance next to the Tomb of Seti I descends into the **Tomb of Ramses I (#16),** a single burial chamber dominated by Ramses' pink granite sarcophagus. The tomb walls, some of the most vivid in the valley, are painted with scenes of Ramses hobnobbing with the gods. The first corridor is the shortest of any royal tomb in the valley, a consequence of this Ramses' brief rule (1320-1318 BCE).

Named the "Tomb of the Harp Players" after a pair of musicians depicted plucking away in one of its interior chambers, the **Tomb of Ramses III (#11)** boasts an interesting portrayal of ancient races on the left side of the penultimate chamber.

The most dramatically situated burial site in the necropolis is the cliffside **Tomb of Thutmosis III (#34),** reached by a long, steep staircase that ascends a precipitous ravine squeezed between towering limestone cliffs. To get to the tomb, follow the dirt road that begins next to the Tomb of Ramses III leading southwest up the hill. In no other tomb was greater care taken to camouflage the grave's location. It provides a classic example of 18th Dynasty pharaohs' attempts to conceal their tombs by building them in faults, where they would become naturally concealed by debris left from flash floods. The strategy was largely dropped after the 18th-Dynasty because it, like so many others, failed to deceive grave robbers.

In 1898, local Egyptian farmers directed France's most eminent archaeologist, Victor Loret, to the **Tomb of Amenhotep II (#35).** The tomb lies past the Tomb of Ramses III, west of the Rest House. From the path leading up the western hill to the Tomb of Thutmosis III, bear right to the northern cliff face. Although thieves had stolen the best treasures millennia ago, the interior was essentially undisturbed and contained the untouched mummy of Amenhotep II as well as nine other sacred mummies. The Cairo Museum took custody of these royal remnants, including Thutmosis IV, Amenophis III, and Seti II. One red sarcophagus remains. The burial chamber, decorated with a complete set of texts from the *Book of the Dead,* is stunning.

The **Tomb of Seti II (#15)** is southwest of the Rest House. Take the road leading uphill toward Thutmosis III's tomb and then the first right after the path to the Tomb of Amenhotep II. The grave consists of a series of long, descending corridors ending in a small burial chamber with a statue of the pharaoh. Near the tomb entrance is an anonymous mummy; Seti II's mummy has been transferred to the Egyptian Museum in Cairo. The painted decorations on the corridor walls are fairly well preserved and the incomplete sketches show the decorating process frozen in time—the tomb ends abruptly because the king died before it could be finished.

The **Tomb of Tausert and Sethnakht (#14)** testifies to the thievery of pharaohs themselves. Queen Tausert reigned in 1200 BCE; upon her death, successor Sethnakht usurped her tomb, superimposing his own drawings and inscriptions over the earlier, carefully painted images.

The descent into the **Tomb of Merneptah (#8)** stretches about 80m, and the burial chambers contain a number of huge granite sarcophagus lids. In an effort to preserve the frescoes, the builders of the tomb covered the walls with a thick layer of plaster, which in fact caused the drawings to crack and fall off. The tomb stands just inside the main gate.

The **Tomb of Ramses IV (#2)** is outside the main entrance to the Valley of the Kings. Walk 100m down the paved road away from the entrance booth; the tomb is on the left. Because it is seldom visited, you may have to ask at the entrance booth for it to be opened. Despite Coptic, Greek, and Roman graffiti, the painted carvings retain most of their original color. Don't forget to ogle the cartouche-shaped sarcophagus—the biggest in the valley.

The **Rest House** 400m before the main entrance is pricey. Public toilets and beer add popular appeal. (Open daily 6am-5pm in summer, 8am-4pm in winter.)

Mortuary Temples

As if gripping rock-hewn tombs aren't spectacular enough, the west bank also boasts some of the finest **mortuary temples** ever built. Treated as gods while living, the pharaohs continued to be worshiped after death in these edifices. Though overshadowed by Luxor's Karnak Temple in scale and historical importance, the West Theban temples of Hatshepsut, Ramses II, Seti I, and Ramses III are still stupefying.

The mortuary temples of the necropolis of Thebes, all accessible from a road that runs parallel to the Nile, are described from south to north. From the ferry docks, head inland 3km past the Colossi of Memnon until you come to an intersection. A road to the left leads to the temple of Ramses III at Medinat Habu, 500m to the southwest. With the exception of Deir el-Bahri, the mortuary temples afford little shade; they are best visited early in the morning during the summer months.

The largest mortuary temple, that of Amenhotep III, has been destroyed save the **Colossi of Memnon,** a pair of glowering, towering statues seated in magnificent isolation on the northern side of the entrance road to the necropolis. Looking out over the plain from a height of 20m, the figures of Amenhotep III were Thebes' greatest tourist attraction during the Roman era. At night, an eerie whistling sound emanated from the stones, which the Romans interpreted as the voice of Memnon, mythical son of the goddess of dawn, Aurora. The sound, according to scientists, was actually produced by grains of sand splitting off from the statues as the rocks contracted in the cool night air. Unfortunately, the Colossi ceased to sing after repairs during the reign of Antoninus Pius.

To the left at the end of the road after the Colossi stand **Medinat Habu,** a series of well-preserved edifices constructed in several stages by various pharaohs. The most impressive structure in the complex is the **Mortuary Temple of Ramses III,** decorated with reliefs of the pharaoh's numerous successful military campaigns.

The Ramasseum

> My name is Ozymandias, king of kings:
> Look on my works, ye Mighty, and despair!
>
> —Percy Bysshe Shelley

The first stop as you turn right after the Colossi of Memnon is the Mortuary Temple of Ramses II, better known as the **Ramasseum.** This is the pharaoh who had Abu Simbel tailor-made to his specifications; the Ramasseum also houses the remains of one of his mammoth exercises in narcissism. The hefty, 1000-ton, 17m Colossus of Ramses II (the forefingers alone measure over 1m long) was transported in one piece from the pharaoh's granite quarries in Aswan to Thebes. Even shattered, the remnants (including head, upper arms, and one foot) are still imposing. This colossus originally overlooked the passageway leading into the second court, reputedly identified by the Roman historian Diodorus as the Tomb of Ozymandias.

The Temple of Hatshepsut (Deir el-Bahri)

Just north of the Ramasseum, a paved road leaves the main north-south thoroughfare and heads west, straight for the cliffside **Mortuary Temple of Hatshepsut,** known in Arabic as **Deir el-Bahri.** Located in the center of the necropolis, the temple is 500m north of the Tombs of the Nobles. Hatshepsut's masterpiece rises in three broad, columned terraces from the desert floor against a backdrop of sheer limestone cliffs. The Temple's ancient Egyptian name means "most splendid of all."

After the death of her husband Thutmosis II, Hatshepsut assumed the role of monarch, the only queen to assume the actual title of Pharaoh. Her temple, currently under excavation by a team of Polish archaeologists, has been skillfully restored with modern materials. No images of Hatshepsut remain intact; after her death, the great Thutmosis III, who had to wait 20 years in her shadow before coming into his own as Pharaoh, defaced virtually all of them. Men.

Walk from the lower court up a wide ramp to the central court. The colonnaded back wall contains, from left to right, the Shrine of Hathor, Colonnade of the

Expedition of Punt, Birth Colonnade, and Shrine to Anubis. Another huge ramp leads to the upper court. Badly ruined, and sadly defaced by Christians who used the temple as a monastery in the 7th century, this court is closed to the public.

The **Shaft of Deir el-Bahri,** north of the Temple of Hatshepsut in a gully at the foot of the cliffs, was the site of the greatest mummy find in history. In 1876, the local director of antiquities began receiving reports of a steady flow of unknown ancient artifacts appearing on the market and became convinced that someone was plundering a pharaonic tomb. Later, after a family squabble, the brother of Luxor's most prominent antiquities merchant squealed and led the authorities to a shaft penetrating 12m into the earth. Amenhotep I, Thutmosis II, Thutmosis III, Seti I, Ramses I, and Ramses III had all been laid to rest in this single shaft along with a host of other royal mummies. Apparently the high priests, realizing that even the most elaborate precautions failed to prevent thieves from disturbing the bodies of deceased pharaohs in their tombs, made a final and successful attempt to hide the mummies by moving their remains to this secret communal grave. The 40 mummies unearthed at the Temple of Hatshepsut now rest in the Egyptian Museum in Cairo. Strangely, the body of Hatshepsut was not among them. Though the queen constructed two tombs for herself, one in the Valley of the Kings, and the other south of the Temple of Hatshepsut, her remains have never been found.

Temple of Seti I

You'll have a fair amount of trouble getting here, and there's not that much to see. From the Temple of Hatshepsut return to the main road, turn north, and follow it to the end. Turn right to visit what remains of the **Mortuary Temple of Seti I,** father of Ramses II, a warrior who enlarged the Egyptian empire to include the island of Cyprus and parts of Mesopotamia. The mortuary temple contained some of the booty Seti I obtained on his successful campaigns, as well as some of the finest relief work ever executed in ancient Egypt. The treasure is gone but the carvings remain.

Tombs of the Nobles

A few hundred meters southeast of the Temple of Hatshepsut is the west bank's sardine-packed burial site, the more than 400 Tombs of the Nobles. The area is divided into six regions: the Tombs of Rekhmire and Sennofer (ticket #8); the Tombs of Ramose, Userhet the Scribe, and Khaemt (ticket #9); the Tombs of Nakht and Mena (ticket #7); the Asasif Tombs (ticket #6); the Tomb of Pabasa (ticket #15); and the Temple and Tombs at Deir el-Medina (ticket #10). You must buy a separate ticket for each. Tickets #7, 8, and 9 provide the most bang for your tomb-going buck. A guide is unnecessary as the sites are scattered through a village where residents can point the way. If you can get your hands on one, a map of the area is useful.

Throughout the New Kingdom, Theban aristocrats had *de facto* control over much of the pharaoh's empire and served as advisors. The pharaoh often remained ignorant of the most crucial political developments while members of the elite fought amongst themselves for control of the kingdom. Some aristocrats affected pharaonic status by amply providing themselves with luxuries for the afterlife and devising well-hidden underground tombs. Unlike the divine pharaoh who would live among the gods after his death, Theban aristocrats needed more assurance that a comfortable existence awaited them in the afterlife. Accordingly, every facet of their earthly lives was carefully recorded on the walls of their tombs; the decoration is thus more naturalistic and mundane than the reliefs found in pharaonic tombs. Because the limestone in this portion of the necropolis was inferior, artisans could not carve in relief; instead they painted murals on a whitewashed stone surface.

Tombs of Rekhmire and Sennofer

The westernmost tomb belongs to Rekhmire, a governor of Thebes who advised Thutmose III and prided himself on his administrative genius. A historian's delight, the **Tomb of Rekhmire (#100)** is comprised of biographical narratives depicting the full range of activities Rekhmire oversaw. This tomb is perhaps the most absorbing of all the tombs in the Theban necropolis.

In the first chamber, tax evaders are tried by Rekhmire, who sits with a set of rolled papyrus texts strewn at the foot of his judgment throne; the presence of the papyrus shows that written law existed as early as 1500 BCE. On the inner, left-hand wall, a procession of tribute-paying expeditions arrives from Crete (top), Syria (middle), and the African Kingdoms of Punt and Nubia (bottom). Making a special contribution to the pharaonic menagerie, Nubian representatives offer a giraffe, assorted monkeys, a tiger, and an elephant tusk. The niche at the top of the rear wall was intended to contain a statue of Rekhmire himself.

Trek 50m up the hill to the west of Rekhmire's tomb to reach the **Tomb of Sennofer (#96).** This vivid tomb is known as "Tomb of the Vines," after the filigree grapevine crawling all over the ceiling. The delightful lattice of purple and green simulates a shady arbor for Sennofer, overseer of the royal gardens of Amun under Amenhotep II. The plan of the tomb is as unusual as its decor; a curving wall leads into the first room, which in turn leads straight back into the pillared burial chamber. The big, wet eyes of Hathor the cow follow you around the tomb from the tops of the columns. The superb condition of the paintings and their remarkable expressiveness make this small tomb worth the detour.

Tombs of Ramose, Userhet, and Nakht

The **Tomb of Ramose (#55),** southeast of the tombs of Rekhmire and Sennofer down a short dirt road, was built during the pharaoh Akhenaton's period of monotheistic religious orientation. Ramose was preeminent during the reigns of Amenhotep III and Akhenaton, and was apparently one of the first converts to the latter's radical devotion to the sun god Aton.

In the columned first chamber, all of Egypt pays obeisance to Aton, a blood-red disk emitting shafts of light which end in small hands holding *ankhs* and other religious symbols. On the wall through which you enter, the images carved in unpainted relief reflect the traditional, stylized tastes of the Old Kingdom, with scenes of Ramose and his family making offerings and Egyptians cheering Ramose's conversion to the Aton cult. In contrast, the wall to the left as you enter displays expressive and realistic "Amarna-style" scenes of a mourning procession.

Continue up from the depression containing the Tomb of Ramose to the **Tomb of Userhet the Scribe (#56),** a few meters to the south. Although an early Christian monk who made his home within the chamber destroyed most of the female figures adorning the walls, the tomb's decor retains a certain blithe spirit because of the unusual pink tones of the interior frescos. Userhet, Amenhotep II's royal scribe, had his resting place painted with mundane scenes. On the right-hand wall of the first chamber, men wait their turn in line for the local barber.

Slightly north of the Tomb of Ramose a trail leads off the main road, winding east a short distance to the **Tomb of Nakht.** The first chamber contains a reconstruction of an exquisite statue of Nakht, scribe of the royal granaries under Thutmosis IV (the original was lost at sea on its way to the U.S. during World War I), photographs of some of the other removed contents, and a series of well-labeled diagrams explaining the images within the second chamber. The most famous image from the Tombs of the Nobles, three musicians playing the flute, harp, and lute, is on the left wall.

Asasif Tombs

Southwest of the Temple of Hatshepsut lies **Asasif,** a current archaeological hotspot. Asasif became the most popular aristocratic burial area during the 25th and 26th dynasties (about the 7th century BCE). The **Tomb of Kheruef (#192),** constructed during the 14th century BCE, is the finest in this portion of the necropolis. Enter the burial site through an outer courtyard containing other tombs, where a series of well-wrought reliefs stands against a protecting wall. Note the ceremonial dance featuring a line of women headbangers and a jumping bird and monkey accompanied by flautists and drummers to the left of the doorway. On the right is a portrait of Amenhotep III surrounded by 16 swooning princesses.

As you enter the **Tomb of Kiki (#409)** about 10m to the north of Kheruef, the gods Thoth and Anubis discuss the readings of a giant scale. The burial chamber remains unfinished, leaving a series of faceless figures outlined in red. To get to the **Tomb of Nefer-hotep (#48),** walk 100m east along the dirt path from Kiki, then turn right (south) and walk 20m to the tomb, immediately in front of a village house. Most of the seated stone figures within the tomb are fairly intact.

Deir el-Medina

To reach the plentiful though visually uninspiring remains of the **Tomb Workers' Walled City,** start from the student ticket office and follow the small road west to Deir el-Medina. About 60m west of the guardhouse stands the small **Temple of Deir el-Medina** (Monastery of the Town), an elegant shrine dating from the Ptolemaic era. Dedicated to Hathor, the goddess of love, and Maat, the deity of justice, the temple was named during Christian times when monks constructed a monastery next door. A single admission ticket includes entrance to the Temple of Deir el-Medina, Sennutem's tomb, and the Workers' Walled City.

Valley of the Queens وادى الملكات

During the later years of the New Kingdom, a special burial area was chosen for the wives and children of the pharaohs. Traditionally the pharaoh's closest relatives were buried beside the monarch, but this arrangement changed during the reign of Ramses I (14th century BCE), when princes, consorts, and wives were buried in the Valley of the Queens. Directly west of the Colossi of Memnon at the end of the main road, the Valley of the Queens contains fewer than 30 royal tombs. Check at the ticket kiosks to find out which are currently open. Don't be alarmed if you see Egyptians painting the walls: they're preserving the pigments with a special fixative.

The **Tomb of Amonherkhepeshef (#55)** is richly bedecked with bas-relief carvings: Ramses III introduces his nine-year-old son to each of the major deities, and Amonherkhepeshef wears the groomed topknot of a pharaonic prince. The colored scenes of deities and farmers fill entire walls—a rare sight in Theban tombs. The small sarcophagus that held the prince's mummy stands in the rear burial chamber. A mysterious desiccated fetus lies curled in a small glass display next to the sarcophagus. The **Tomb of Queen Nefertari (#66),** allegedly the most beautiful tomb in the Valley of the Queens, is, to the chagrin of many, closed indefinitely.

ENTERTAINMENT

Fritter away late afternoons in Luxor aboard a **felucca** on the Nile. **Banana Island** is a popular destination; two miles upriver, it is a small peninsula studded with palms and fruit trees whence come small green bananas for E£1. Overpriced souvenir stands detract from an otherwise rustic experience. (Round trip 2-3hr.; E£10 per person plus tip. *Feluccas* are prohibited from sailing after sunset.) The Mövenpick complex has an extensive **garden,** including a small zoo with monkeys, crocodiles, a camel, and some birds, and is a nice place to watch the sun set.

The Winter Palace, ETAP, Isis, and Sheraton Hotels feature **belly dancers** on most nights. Dancers sign on for six-week contracts; prurient locals usually know which shows are best. There are no set times for appearances; just lurk at the bar and wait for these master midriff manipulators to appear. Make sure no one points you in the direction of one of the bi-weekly "special oriental evenings" which cost up to E£90. (Usually, there is a E£12-20 minimum charge.)

If you do not wish to mar your cultural experience by watching the bastardization of an art form which has evolved into an objectifying droolfest for men, work your own belly at **discos** at the ETAP (E£25 min. drink charge); Hilton (min. E£25); Novotel Boat, a floating disco (min. E£10); or the Isis (min. E£15). In summer, several discos close or drop the minimum charge because of a lack of customers. The Novotel is generally the most popular. The low-budget alternative is Luxor's many **qahwas** (cafés), which resound with the slap of dominoes and backgammon pieces and the bubbling of *sheeshas*. Women should feel free to join in. Most of the three-star hotels have cheap **bars** (often fairly empty) while the five-star establishments provide various mixed drinks in a cushy, almost aristocratic setting (the Winter Palace is famous for its Bloody Marys).

You might also check out the Luxor Temple by night, or that deliciously stomach-turning purveyor of bad artistic taste, the **sound and light show** at Karnak Temple (English shows Sat., Mon., and Wed. 8pm, Tues. and Thurs.-Fri. 10pm; E£30).

■■■ BETWEEN LUXOR & ASWAN

The 220km stretch of Nile between Luxor and Aswan contains the drowsy rural towns of Esna, Edfu, and Kom Ombo. The area is an olio of older Arab *fellaheen* communities and Nubian villages created for those displaced by the High Dam. Each of the major towns is also graced by an outstanding Ptolemaic temple.

Whether you go by *service*, bus, or train, you'll have no difficulty stopping in Esna, Edfu, and Kom Ombo during a journey between Luxor and Aswan. These towns and their temples also make excellent daytrips: Esna and Edfu from Luxor; Edfu, Kom Ombo, and the camel market at Daraw (near Kom Ombo) from Aswan. If you've got a bit of spare time and some relaxing to do, glide on a *felucca* for leisurely, low-budget transport; the entire Aswan-Luxor route takes 3 to 5 days, including ports of call in Esna, Edfu, and Kom Ombo.

By Taxi, Bus, or Train

Traveling by **service taxi** is the most efficient, cheap and convenient option for shuttling between the river towns at almost any time of day:

Luxor-Aswan: 3-4hr., E£8	**Luxor-Edfu:** 1½hr., E£4
Luxor-Esna: 1hr., E£2	**Luxor-Kom Ombo:** 2-3hr., E£7
Aswan-Esna: 2-3hr., E£6	**Esna-Edfu:** 1hr., E£2
Aswan-Edfu: 1½hr., E£3	**Edfu-Kom Ombo:** 45min., E£2
Aswan-Kom Ombo/Daraw: 40min., E£1.50	**Kom Ombo-Daraw:** 5min., 50pt

Two potential drawbacks to travel by **service** are that you must wait an unpredictable (though usually short) time for a taxi to fill, and that drivers are king-hell crazy speed demons. Mangled Peugeot carcasses in roadside ditches and the Egyptian highway death rate testify to the risks involved. Sure are fast, though.

Buses are frequent (13 per day in both directions) and do not require advance purchase of tickets; simply climb aboard and pay the conductor. They are also cheaper than *service*. Disadvantages are that they stop running at 6pm (at the latest), often lack air-conditioning, and suffer frequent mechanical breakdowns. Buses are best for transport out of Luxor or Aswan; in towns in between, you may not find an empty seat, and the reliability of schedules plummets. (Luxor to Esna E£1.75, Edfu E£3, Kom Ombo E£4.50, Aswan E£6.)

Last and least, **trains** present more hassle than value for short runs. The air-conditioned, cushy *Espani* variety, however, is your best bet for the entire Luxor-Aswan haul (3 per day; 6-7hr.; Luxor-Aswan either direction 2nd-class with A/C E£11-13, students E£9-11, without A/C E£5). Up to ten (no A/C) trains head in each direction daily, stopping at villages and towns in between. These are hopelessly slow, and as of summer 1994, authorities were discouraging tourists from riding anything but the three air-conditioned *Espani* trains.

By Felucca

Escape the confusion and delusion of overland travel by floating leisurely down the Nile on a *felucca*. You can absorb the Egyptian countryside, kill time, or regain your sanity after weeks on the road by swimming, tanning, and feasting. This cheap, rustic experience requires two things: time, and a keen awareness of latent **problems**.

We don't want to sound like killjoys, but you must stay alert, from the beginning of negotiations with captains until the last backpack is safely off the boat with everything intact. Hotel comment books and police records are filled with tales of watery woe: lost possessions, druggings, muggings, sexual harassment, even deaths.

You'll probably embark from Aswan, where the *felucca* industry thrives. Most trips last two days and end in Edfu. If you'd like to spend more time on the river, be persistent and have a group to back you; captains would rather stay close to home.

At some point, a *felucca* captain or middleman will undoubtedly approach you and ask if you would like to join a *felucca* trip he is planning. You can ask to meet the other travelers before you decide, but you will feel more in control if you organize your own trip. Start by gathering a group of travelers (6 is best) willing to commit to spending a few days together in close quarters drifting down the Nile. Next, hunt for a captain and be thorough in your research. Check prices, then check with the tourist office and with the tourist police about the captain's reputation. Consult fellow travelers and the comment books that some captains keep. You'll notice the U.S. Congress has nothing on the Egyptian tourism business when it comes to partisan politics. The philosophy goes something like this: "You scratch my back, I'll scratch yours, and together we'll scratch our competitors' eyes out." Every hotel manager and every man in the local *qahwa* has his favorite *felucca* captain. You'll do best not to ask too many locals for their opinions. All you will hear is, "He steals, he cuts his passengers into bloody chunks and feeds them to sharks, he was kidnapped by aliens last month and doesn't sail anymore. But I have this friend ..."

In Aswan, eager and comparatively honest **Muhammad Qibly** (captain of the *Dylan*) invites passengers to his home near Edfu for a meal, and can entertain with traditional *tableh* drumming. You may want to bring sheets or a sleeping bag; his scratchy army blankets prevent sleep. Young and energetic **Captain Nasser** docks his *Zizo* near the Aswan Moon restaurant, and gentle **Captain Kamal's** *Aussie* is farther south, near the ferry stop. **Captain Hamdy,** the Nubian with the whitest teeth in all of Egypt, docks across from the Aswan police station. His *Valley of the Kings* makes a one-day trip near Aswan to a secret locale other captains do not visit. On longer trips, guard your belongings well. On Elephantine Island, **Captain Shaban Mohy ed-Din** can be reached at the Oberoi Hotel (tel. 5914). In Luxor, **Captain Jimmy's** *Aladdin* and *Thebes* dock across from Luxor Temple. You might also look around for **Captain Gamal Ahmed Nour.** It's a good idea to get to know your captain. Almost all sleep on their boats, and most will be happy to conduct introductory meetings. Besides, there isn't all that much to do in Aswan during the day.

The typical large *felucca* sleeps up to eight people, displays a single tall sail, and is piloted by an English-speaking Arab or Nubian Egyptian. Police regulations forbid sailing after 8pm, so passengers either sleep on wooden slats in the docked *felucca* or on the river bank next to the boat.

A conscientious captain will help you buy the appropriate ingredients for meals at a cost of E£5 per person per day. But even this has become an opportunity for a scam, the sailor's loophole for making up the money he lost in giving you that "special price." Many a traveler has arrived at his or her destination either sick from low-quality food or hungry from low rations, so it's best to shop with the captain and choose for yourself what you want to eat. An extra-special captain may cook Nubian dishes in the *felucca* or arrange to stop at his village for a home-cooked meal. For greater leisure, choose a captain who takes care of the cooking himself. He will also probably bring a carton of bottled Baraka water; make sure it is aboard before you depart. Otherwise, bring at least three bottles of water per person per day for drinking, cooking, and brewing tea.

Captains generally adhere to the official rates for *felucca* trips as quoted at tourist offices, though you could negotiate down to 25% of these rates in summer 1994. Officially, members of a six- to eight-person group leaving Aswan should pay E£25 each to Kom Ombo (1 day, 1 night), E£45 to Edfu (3 days, 2 nights), E£50 to Esna (4 days, 3 nights), and E£60 to Luxor (5 days, 4 nights). Most captains add to this E£5 per day for food and water, and a E£5 registration fee.

For registration in Aswan, your captain will ask for your passport and the E£5. Brush up on the relaxation skills you will need for the trip by letting him do the paperwork for you. Trips leaving from Luxor do not have registration requirements.

DON'T BE A FOOL: Keep your belongings well secured. Sleep with passports, money, and traveler's checks **adhered to your flesh.** Most *feluccas* have a compartment in front that locks—insist that daypacks be kept there and that a group member sleep with the key in his or her pocket; better yet, swallow it. Groups of women alone should not embark unless they see the trip as a singles cruise with their captain as the only eligible bachelor on board. The unfortunate fact is that Egyptian men either respect or fear men far more than women. Let the captain think that nerd from Wyoming in Tevas is your boyfriend. Who cares? At least it will keep the captain and his assorted sordid friends away. The law prohibits Egyptians from traveling with foreigners. The only Egyptians on board should be the captain and, sometimes, a young boy who helps him out. If someone attempts to hop aboard, throw a fit and then throw him into the Nile, or you will be unable to relax all trip. When swimming (especially if you have been indulging), it is best to keep close to the banks of the river or hold on to a rope tied to the *felucca*.

ESNA اسنا

A quiet, provincial town, Esna snoozes on the western bank of the Nile and boasts blue, blue waters, a charming temple, and a turn-of-the-century barrage. From Esna (70km south of Luxor), a small highway ambles along the western bank to West Thebes; but the main highway and rail line are on the eastern side of the river, connected to the town by a bridge. Edfu lies 50km to the south and Aswan another 100km. See Between Luxor & Aswan, p. 185, for transportation information.

Practical Information Esna has one main street for tourists. Heading south from the bridge, **Nile Street** crosses the canal, veers left, then continues by the Nile, running north-south. As you travel down Nile St., you'll first find the **police station** (tel. 40 08 89) just south of the canal (open 24 hrs.). The **tourist police** (tel. 40 06 86) swat flies near the temple just to the right of Nile St., by the ticket booth (open 6am-5pm). About 1km farther down is the **Bank of Alexandria** (open Sun.-Thurs. 8:30am-2pm and 6-9pm for exchange; winter 5-8pm; during Ramadan 10am-1:30pm). About 150m north of the ticket booth you'll find the **post office** (open Sat.-Thurs. 8am-2pm). The **telephone and telegraph office** aggravates visitors near the bridge on Nile St. (Open 9am-10pm.)

The **train station** lies to the east of town on the other side of the Nile. The **bus** and **service stations** are at the town's western edge, down the street just south of the telephone office (E£1 to temple). You can take a **kalish** from either station to the temple (don't pay more than E£1.50-2 for a ride anywhere in town), or walk.

Despite its pleasant people and atmosphere, there is little to keep you in Esna beyond a temple visit. The only accommodations are at **Al-Haramen** (tel. 40 03 40). Walk 1km south (through the *souq*) from the temple's eastern wall, pass to the right of the white wall enclosing a gray concrete building, and walk another 100m. (Singles E£6, with bath E£12. Doubles E£9, with bath E£24.) No fans, crumbling bathrooms, but clean enough. For **food** in Esna, go to the *souq* or try your luck at **Al-Amana** by the temple, where a chicken meal goes for E£5.

Sights Khnum was a ram-headed creator god who reputedly molded the first human being on a potter's wheel. Although begun during the 18th dynasty, the **Temple of Khnum** is largely a Roman creation and was in many ways a feeble imitation of inherited technical and artistic achievements. Esna was an important regional center for the area south of Luxor, and the pharaohs of the 18th dynasty, seeking stronger popular support, dedicated this temple to the local deity. Archaeologists discovered the elaborate hallway in excellent condition. Today the temple is a refreshing spectacle, lying side by side with the *souq* and the everyday workings of modern life.

The Romans, making an effort to decorate the temple in a traditional pharaonic manner, instead carved a procession of stiff, oddly deformed figures marching solemnly across the walls of the hallway. Look up; the ceiling designs are among the more interesting ones in the temple. Faint blue and red hues on the tops of the 24 columns hint at the interior's former brilliance. (Open 6am-6:30pm; winter 6am-5:30pm. Admission E£4, students E£2.)

Just to the north of the turn off to the temple, a **barrage** completed in 1908 stretches across the river. Upgraded and restored in the 1940s to meet increased demand, the old barrage is now being replaced by a new one (financed with Italian help) just over a kilometer to the south. The government hopes that the new barrage will help reclaim some 300,000 *feddans* of land.

Between Esna and Edfu: El Kab الكاب

If you're traveling on the main highway between Esna and Edfu and have time and energy to spare, consider a stop at **El Kab,** 15km north of Edfu near the village of **El Mahamid.** The religious center of El Kab was dedicated to the goddess Nekhbet and currently contains comparatively uninteresting ruins from most eras of ancient Egyptian history. From the ticket office on the east side of the road, walk up the stairs on the left to a series of Middle and New Kingdom tombs on the hill. Beginning on the right, you'll first see the **Tomb of Daheri,** chief priest, royal tutor, scribe of accounts, and son of pharaoh Thutmose I. This tomb is the best preserved of the group and features designs of long lines of seated lotus-sniffers and Egyptians cultivating various crops. Next door, the **Tomb of Setau,** high priest of Nekhbet, and the **Tomb of Aahmes,** a military leader, are devoid of real interest. To the left is the slightly more intact **Tomb of Renini,** superintendent of priests.

Farther into the desert languish the **Chapel of Thoth** and a **Ptolemaic Temple,** 3.5km from the ticket office. The better-preserved **Temple of Amenophis III** lies 1.5km farther. Caravans going to and coming from gold mines deeper into the desert once stopped here for prayer, leaving some nice depictions of the goddess Nekhbet ("Lady of the Desert"), especially on the four interior columns. If you're determined to see these lonely remains, bring several bottles of water (there's not a leaf of shade).

Across the highway from the ticket office lie the ruins of the ancient city of **El Kab,** or more precisely, the Roman walls that used to surround it. The government has only recently developed El Kab for tourism, and the site has yet to become popular. (Open daily 8am-6pm. Admission E£5, students E£2.50.) Travelers who have finished looking around try to catch a ride back to Edfu or Esna. On a really bad day they may have to trek the 2.5km to El Mahamid.

EDFU ادفو

Edfu is an underdeveloped yet bustling town, with unpaved roads and a modest *souq.* Just beyond the central square, silently oblivious to its surroundings and to the passage of 2000 years, stands an astonishingly well-preserved, mesmeric Temple of Horus. This labyrinth of dark chambers and towering columns ranks as one of Upper Egypt's most fabulous sights.

Orientation and Practical Information Edfu lies 50km south of Esna on the western bank of the Nile, roughly halfway between Luxor (115km) and Aswan (105km). The **bus station** is 100m north of the central **Temple Square,** on Tahrir St., which runs parallel to the Nile about 1km inland. Wide **El Maglis Street** links Temple Sq. with the Nile. The Edfu bridge, with the **train station** on its eastern end and the **service taxi station** near its western end, is about 300m north of El Maglis St. along the riverfront road. Buses run north and south hourly until 6pm at the latest, trains until 9 or 10pm. To reach the **temple** from Temple Sq., follow El Maglis St. away from the Nile for 200m. Local **pick-up trucks** (25pt) or **private taxis** (E£2-3) can take you from the train station to the temple.

The **tourist police** are located at the entrance to the temple (open 7am-5pm). The **police station** (tel. 70 08 66) is on the east end of El Maglis, about 100m from the Nile. The **post office** is on Tahrir St., on the right side 50m south of Temple Sq. (open Sat.-Thurs. 8am-2:30pm). Edfu's produce **souq** is on Goumhouriyya St., parallel to Tahrir St. (open Sat.-Thurs. 8am-9pm); there is a **telephone office** next to the *souq* entrance. **Bank of Cairo** (open Sun.-Thurs. 8:30am-2pm and 6-9pm; winter 8:30am-2pm and 5-8pm) is just past the SemiRamis Hotel.

Accommodations and Food Hotel Dar es-Salaam (tel. 70 17 27), 50m east of the temple on El Maglis, has clean bedding but unappealing baths (E£9 per person; breakfast E£3). The hospitality of Mr. Taha and his extended family, and the mother of all breakfasts (E£6), make the **El Medina Hotel** worth the price. (Singles with fan E£15, with bath E£21. Doubles with fan E£25.) The **SemiRamis Hotel** (tel. 70 04 70) has faded stained glass, high ceilings, and huge balconies for that colonial touch; cleanliness, unfortunately, is lacking. (E£2 per person; no fans.)

Dining options in Edfu are slim beyond the delicious El Medina breakfast. Across the street from the SemiRamis is the clean **Restaurant Zahrat el-Medina.** The **New Egypt Restaurant,** on the left side of Tahrir St. 200m south of Temple Sq., features a rotisserie grill but isn't particularly clean. (Meals E£4.50-8.)

Sights The **Temple of Horus** took over 200 years to construct and was not completed until 57 BCE, making it one of the last great Egyptian monuments. The Ptolemaic designers created this temple and the one at Dendera, dedicated to Horus' wife Hathor, as a matched set. Several important religious festivals centering around the life and death of the falcon-god Horus were celebrated at Edfu. During the annual "Union with the Solar Disk," Horus's earthly form was brought to the roof of the temple to be rejuvenated by the rays of the sun. The rite generally transpired in conjunction with the New Year holiday. Another important ritual was the coronation festival, in which a falcon was crowned in the temple's main court and triumphantly paraded to the interior where it reigned in darkness for one year.

From the entrance by the ticket kiosk, walk the length of the temple and enter at the far end. The main doorway through the pylon is flanked by two battlements rising to a height of 36m and guarded by a noble granite falcon. Only a chunk of his co-sentinel on the right remains. Enter the temple through the 12 gigantic columns of the **Great Hypostyle Hall** and proceed to the second Hypostyle Hall, outfitted with a similar arrangement of smaller pillars. Doorways on either side lead to the **Corridor of Victory,** an exterior passageway running between the temple and its protective wall, so narrow that even an underfed chihuahua might get stuck. The temple is honeycombed with doorways and small passageways that enabled the priests to walk around the entire complex without crossing in front of the sanctuary or having to talk to one another. Recently, holes made in the ceilings and walls to provide light damaged many fine stone figures.

Outside the temple, directly in front of the main entrance pylon, is a well-preserved (except for sparrow damage) Roman *mammisis,* where the birth of Horus was reenacted annually with appropriate hoopla. Copts later emasculated the images of the growing god on the columns of the *mammisis.* (Site open daily 6am-6pm; winter 7am-4pm. Admission E£10, students E£5.)

KOM OMBO كوم أمبو

Forty-five kilometers north of Aswan on the east bank of the Nile stands Kom Ombo, the site of an Egyptian temple as renowned for its location as for its rigorously symmetrical construction. Unlike other temples, Kom Ombo is still situated along the banks of the Nile, giving virtually the same visual impression today as it did during Ptolemaic times. The sanctuary's more dramatic peculiarity, however, is its meticulous symmetry. Double doorways lead into double chambers and sanctuaries after you pass through double halls and walk past double colonnades. The two-fold temple was dedicated to a duo of gods: Sebak, the toothy crocodile god, and Horus, the winged falcon or sky god. The priests were doubly diplomatic and, so as not to offend either deity, ordered everything to be built in tandem. There is double zero shade at Kom Ombo, so gear up accordingly.

Practical Information The **bus station** is on July 26th St., which runs parallel to the railroad tracks and the Cairo-Aswan highway. It is about 400m south of the *midan* where Goumhouriyya St. and the highway intersect. The **service taxi station** is also on July 26th St., just south of the intersection with Goumhouriyya; *service* to Aswan (E£1.50), Daraw (50pt), and Silsilah (35pt) depart from the nearby mosque or the highway between the mosque and the Radwan Hotel to the south. The **train station** is on Goumhouriyya St., across the highway and the tracks. The **temple** is 4km west of the central square down Goumhouriyya St.

The **police station** sits 50m north of Goumhouriyya (tel. 50 00 23 or 50 03 75). The **Bank of Alexandria** is in a small alley next to the mosque, at the corner of the highway and Goumhouriyya St. (Open daily 8:30am-2pm and 6-9pm; winter 5-8pm; Ramadan 10am-1:30pm.) To get to Kom Ombo's **souq**, cross over the highway on the footbridge. The **post office** is one block farther in on the right. (Open Sun.-Thurs. 8am-2pm.) A covered **pick-up truck** (25pt) runs all day between the river (near the ruins) and the center of town. The truck leaves from Goumhouriyya St. behind the white mosque with the minaret, one block off the highway. Private taxis cost E£3-5 each way. If you're coming from Aswan by *service* or bus, ask to be let off at the well-marked turn-off to the "tembel" 2km south of town. From the turn-off, walk 1.5km through sugar-cane fields to the temple site.

Accommodations and Food The **Cleopatra Hotel** (tel. 50 03 25), just off July 26th St. at the *service* stand, may have the tidiest rooms between Luxor and Aswan. Bathrooms are less impressive. (Singles E£7.50. Doubles E£11.50. Triples E£16.50.) The **Radwan Hotel** (tel. 50 03 56), 300m south of the white mosque along the highway (sign looks like "Roowan"), has dark, cramped rooms with ceiling fans. No Western-style toilets. (Singles E£2. Doubles E£4.) The recently-opened and very clean **Restaurant El Noba,** halfway between the mosque and Radwan on the other side of the street, offers chicken, rice, vegetables, and salad for E£4-5 (open 8am-8pm). The **Venus Cafeteria and Restaurant,** on the river halfway between the temple and the *service* stop, offers yummy *kufta* sandwiches with ketchup (E£2), cold soda (75pt), heaping bowls of ice cream (E£1), and Stella (E£3.75) in a breezy outdoor setting, good for resting after a visit to the temple.

Sights Although a temple has stood here since the time of the Middle Kingdom, the oldest portions of the **Temple of Kom Ombo** now rest at the Louvre and the Egyptian Museum in Cairo. After the temple's abandonment during the decline of the Roman Empire, the rising waters of the river inundated the site and left the temple almost completely buried in sand. In later years the portion above ground was used as a quarry for neighboring edifices; as a result, the side walls have vanished.

The temple's dualism is apparent in the surviving columns of the hypostyle hall. Designs on the right columns feature Sebak while those on the left depict bird-beaked Horus. The ceiling of the adjoining vestibule managed to escape defacement by unappreciative Christians; bright blue and black images of Horus hover protectively over the chamber. In the interior of the temple are the less substantial remains of the Hall of Offerings and the inner sanctuaries dedicated to Sebak and Horus.

Adjoining the northern edge of the temple are the Roman water supply tanks and, to the west, the remains of a Roman *mammisis*. The guards at the site claim that crocodiles once lived in the well and that Cleopatra's bubble bath is nearby. Climb down and see for yourself. The **Chapel of Hathor,** directly south of the temple, houses a doubly revolting collection of crocodile mummies unearthed near the road leading to the site. (Open daily 7am-5:45pm. Admission E£4, students E£2.)

Near Kom Ombo: Daraw دراو

Sudanese merchants, Bishari tribespeople, and Egyptian *fellaheen* convene in Daraw (de-RAU) every Tuesday morning for a **camel market.** The Sudanese purchase camels for the equivalent of E£200, march for one month through the desert to Daraw, and resell the be-humped beasts at a 500% profit. The Bishari are traditional Saharan nomads with their own language and culture. Some of the men conduct business in full traditional dress: flowing pants, fighting sword and dagger, and a cloak draped over their shoulders. Typically, a Sudanese camel-owner will pay a Sudanese or Bishari shepherd to drive his camels north to Egypt. The owner then flies up to oversee the selling. If you think the slobbery creatures are cute, the going rate for a big male camel is E£1200-1500, a savings of E£1000 over prices in Cairo.

Tuesday is the only market day in summer; in winter camels are sometimes sold on Sundays and Mondays. On Tuesdays, the camel market is adjoined by a **livestock market** where farmers sell cattle, water buffalo, sheep, and goats. The animals are hauled in by truck, or occasionally toted on the merchants' shoulders. On market day, impromptu shaded *fuul* and tea stands refresh merchants, buyers, and gawkers. The camel market runs from 7am to 2pm but starts deteriorating after about 11am. A good strategy is to rise very early in Aswan, visit the camel market, and move on to see the temple at Kom Ombo. En route to the camel market, you'll walk through an equally large **fruit and vegetable market.**

Service taxis careen to Daraw from Kom Ombo, 8km to the north (5min.) and Aswan, 32km to the south (1hr.). Some trains and buses running between Luxor and Aswan stop in Daraw. The **taxi stand, bus station,** and **train station** all lie along the main highway. To reach the market from the stations, walk 300m toward the Nile, bearing left when the first street ends, then right. If you're gliding by on a *felucca,* have the captain stop at the Daraw ferry landing and a covered pick-up truck will take you to the market. During the winter there may be another location for the market; ask around. The word for camel is *gamal,* and don't be afraid to act like one if you're hard up for directions.

■■■ ASWAN أسوان

Within sight of the first cataracts of the Nile, the city of Aswan grew and flourished as Egypt's southern frontier town, a trading center where the Middle East overlaps with Africa, and Upper Egypt gives way to Nubia and the border with the Sudan. The Aswan High Dam, completed in 1971, created Lake Nasser (the world's largest reservoir) and extended Egypt's agricultural and energy potential; but it also flooded several Nubian villages and created as yet unknown environmental implications.

The desert's presence is clearly felt in Aswan. Temperatures frequently soar well above 40°C; and unlike in other sections of the fertile Nile Valley, the river at Aswan is bounded by inhospitable sand and mountain. A large Nubian community (many of whose members relocated after the creation of Lake Nasser) gives the city an African flavor not found elsewhere in Upper Egypt.

Aswan is an obvious base for trips to Abu Simbel, the dams, and the sights near them. It is also the center of the *felucca* lifestyle, an ethos nourished by the waters of the Nile. Summer, when temperatures are high and tourists are few, may be the best time to experience a sun-smoke-sleep-swim *felucca* trip (yes, *swim*—Nile water here is cleaner than anywhere else in Egypt). In winter the city becomes a resort, and the restaurants along the elegant corniche buzz with activity. Aswan is also a good place to shop in any season, edging out Luxor for variety; bright Nubian embroidery complements the usual silver and mother-of-pearl.

ORIENTATION AND PRACTICAL INFORMATION

The southernmost city in Egypt, Aswan is 890km upstream (south) from Cairo and 220km south of Luxor. Frequent taxi, bus, and train service connects Aswan with Luxor. Aswan is the base for exploring the southernmost parts of Egypt; plan on at

A
S
W
A
N

least four days if you want to see all of the Aswan sights. Aswan is also a launching point for *felucca* trips north (see By Felucca, p. 185), and the camel market at Daraw on Tuesdays is not more than a half-day jaunt by automobile.

You are almost never more than two blocks from the river in Aswan. The northern half of the city lies along three long avenues running parallel to the Nile. By far the most handsome of the trio is **Corniche en-Nil,** featuring several hotels, shops, banks, and, on the Nile itself, floating restaurants to the south and docks for cruise ships and *feluccas* to the north. Two blocks inland, Aswan's busiest lane, **Es-souq Street** (also called Sa'ad Zaghloul St.), features everything from merchants peddling mounds of spices to tacky tourist trinket stands with plastic busts of Queen Nefertiti. This street begins at the train station at the northeast corner of town and runs south 2km through the *souq.* In the southern half of town, the corniche continues for another 2km, ending at the **Ferial Gardens** (and the Pullman Cataract Hotel, former home to heads of state and Liz Taylor). The northern grid pattern falls apart at the central market. South of the *souq,* inland streets form a labyrinth of alleys. Running between the corniche and the market street, **Abtal et-Tahrir Street** begins at the youth hostel and culminates in a small cluster of tourist bazaars.

A **kalish** costs about E£2 to travel the length of the city. Local white **service taxis** run up and down the corniche and charge 25pt regardless of where you start or stop, but walking is an easy alternative.

Tourist Office: Corniche en-Nil (tel. 32 32 97), from the train station, 2 blocks toward the river and 1 block south across from a small park. From the river, go up the street across from Seti First Nile Cruises, pass the gardens, and take your first left. English speakers Hakim Hussein, Shukri Sa'ad, and Farag are great helps. Check *felucca* rates here. Newer and smaller branch (tel. 31 28 11) outside the train station has erratic service and hours. Main office open Sat.-Thurs. 8:30am-2pm and 6-8pm, Fri. 10am-1pm and 6-8pm; during Ramadan daily 9am-3 or 4pm.

Tourist Police: Tel. 32 43 93, above tourist office (tel. 32 43 93), open 9 or 10am-3pm and 8pm-1am; branch on south side of train station (tel. 32 31 63) open 24 hrs. Captain speaks English, but you may have to hand-signal your way in.

Passport Office: Corniche en-Nil (tel. 32 22 38), 2 blocks south of the Continental Hotel, in the police building at the southern end of the corniche. Enter on left side of building. Register your passport or extend your visa here. Open Sat.-Thurs. 8am-1:30pm (visas only) and 8-10pm, winter 7-9pm (passport registration only).

Currency Exchange: On Corniche en-Nil are **Banque Misr** (tel. 32 31 56), **Banque du Caire** (3 branches, tel. 32 24 58), and **Bank of Alexandria** (tel. 32 27 65). Most open daily 8:30am-2pm and 6-9pm (5-8pm in winter). The middle branch of Banque du Caire is open Sun.-Thurs. 8:30am-9pm, Fri.-Sat. 9am-9pm.

American Express: In the lobby of the Old Cataract Hotel (tel./fax 32 29 09), at the southernmost end of the corniche. Offers exchange and banking services and will hold mail. Open daily 8am-7pm. Exchange open 9:30am-6pm.

Thomas Cook: Corniche en-Nil (tel. 32 40 11; fax 32 62 09). A full-service station: currency exchange, traveler's checks bought and sold, and travel arrangements.

Post Office: Corniche en-Nil, across from the Rowing Club Restaurant, toward the northern end of town. Open Sat.-Thurs. 8am-2pm. Offers **Express Mail Service. Poste Restante** is 1 block off the corniche. Walking south, turn left down the first street after the Bank of Alex. Poste Restante and a post office are in the yellow and black building diagonally to your right. Open Sat.-Wed. 8am-noon and 6-7pm, Thurs. 8am-noon, Fri. 6-7pm. You can also send mail from major hotels.

Telephones: Telephone office, Corniche en-Nil (tel. 32 38 69), 2 doors south of EgyptAir. Relatively efficient for international calls; sells orange payphone cards. Open 24 hrs. Also a telephone and telegraph office in the train station (open daily 8am-10pm; phones available 24 hrs.). Those wishing to avoid immediate cash charge (E£28 for 3min. to the U.S.) might try international operators at the hotels or the **Business Center** (tel./fax 32 39 19) on the corniche, 1 block south of the police building (E£2 per min.); **fax** available. Open daily 8am-11pm. Cheaper fax in the telephone office on the southern end of the corniche. Open Sun.-Thurs. 9am-1pm and 7-9pm. **Telephone information:** Tel. 16. **Telephone code:** 097.

Airport: 23km south of town (tel. 48 03 20 or 32 29 87), near the High Dam. E£10 one-way by taxi. 4 flights daily to Cairo, 8 or 9 in winter. Served by **EgyptAir,** Corniche en-Nil (tel. 310 5001/2/3/4; fax 310 5005; airport 48 03 07), at the southern end, before the Ferial Gardens and Cataract Hotels (open daily 8am-8pm). **ZAS Air** (tel. 32 64 01), on the corniche, serves the same airports for slightly less (E£353 to Cairo, compared to EgyptAir's E£394). **Airport Police:** 48 05 09.

Train Station: Northern end of Souq St. (tel. 32 20 07), 2 blocks east of the corniche, at northeast corner of Aswan. To: Luxor 2nd class with A/C E£11-13, students E£9-11; Cairo 2nd class with A/C E£31-35, students E£23-26, sleeping cars E£224; High Dam (12 per day) 30pt, 55pt if you buy your ticket on the train.

Bus Station: Abtal et-Tahrir St., 3 blocks south and 1 block west of the train station, 1 block in from the Nile in the northern part of town. North to Daraw, Kom Ombo, Edfu, Esna, and Luxor (18 per day 5:45am-5pm, 4hr. to Luxor, E£6). To Hurghada (8am E£18, 3:30pm E£30, 4:30pm E£26). A/C express to Cairo (3:30am E£50, 4:30pm E£37). South to Khazan/Old Dam (#20 and 59 from the corniche, 14 per day 6am-9:30pm, 25pt; *service* are easier). Also to Abu Simbel (daily 8am, 3hr., back in Aswan 5-6pm, E£18 each way; hotel-arranged transport cheaper and earlier). No bus service to High Dam.

Local Ferries: Elephantine Island from either Esh-Shatii Restaurant on central corniche or across from EgyptAir at the southern end of the corniche (every 15min. 6am-9pm, foreigners 25pt). Western bank tombs and villages from Seti Tours, opposite tourist office (every ½hr. 6am-6pm and every hr. 6pm-10pm, E£1).

Service Taxis *(taxi bil nafar):* Taxis leave from the covered station 1km south of the train station on the east side of the railroad tracks, next to a large underpass. They run from roughly 4am-6pm, departing every 15-30min. depending on demand. To Daraw or Kom Ombo (40min., E£1.50), Edfu (1¼hr., E£3), Esna (2-3hr., E£6), Luxor (3hr., E£8), and Qena (4hr., E£9). For taxis to Aswan environs and south, wait in the square at the corner of Mahmoud Yakoub St. and Abtal et-Tahrir, next to Happi Hotel, 2 blocks south of the bus station. To Khazan/Old Dam (75pt). Passenger-bearing **pick-up trucks** leave from a covered station between the corniche and Abtal et-Tahrir St. next to the Hotel Abu Simbel north of the post office and cultural center.

Bike Rental: Available on Abtal et-Tahrir St. and near train station. E£5 per day, E£1 per hr. Prices may double in winter.

Swimming Pools: New Cataract Hotel (E£35) and **Kalabsha** beyond the Cataract to the south (E£25) are plush possibilities. The **Hathor's** roof is home to a wimpy pool with an amazing view (E£5). The municipal pool is not open to foreigners.

Photo Developing: Photo Sabry, Corniche en-Nil (tel. 32 64 52), just north of EgyptAir, will print 36 color exposures for E£35. Open Sat.-Thurs. 9am-2pm and 6-11pm (winter 9-11pm), Fri. evenings.

24-Hour Pharmacy: Maky Pharmacy (tel. 31 70 40). From the corniche, turn inland on Es-Sayyida Nafisa St., a busy market street across from the Isis. Walk until a sign and a big arrow point you to the left. The **El-Nile Pharmacy** (tel. 32 26 74), on the corniche across from the Isis, is open daily 7am-midnight.

Foreign Press and Books: Corniche en-Nil, 30m north of Hotel Continental, next to ZAS office. Newsstand on sidewalk has paltry but eclectic selection of used books in English and many other languages. **Es-Sahafa** bookstore, on the corniche across from Misr Travel's gold and brown marble arch (southern end) has some books as well as *Time, Paris Match, Elle,* etc. Open 8am-midnight.

Laundromat: Many accommodations do laundry for 50pt-E£1 per garment.

Hospital: German Evangelical Mission Hospital, past EgyptAir on southern end of the corniche (tel. 23 21 76 or call tourist office). Open 24 hrs. A **Government Hospital,** a 2nd choice, is several km inland from EgyptAir on Qasr El-Haqqa St.

Medical Emergency: Tel. 123. **Ambulance:** Tel. 31 40 15.

Police: Tel. 122.

ACCOMMODATIONS

High season (Oct.-April) prices listed, unless otherwise noted. Bargain in summer.

Nubian Oasis Hotel, 234 Sa'ad Zaghloul St. (tel./fax 31 21 24). Head left out of the train station. Turn right onto the 3rd street and look on your right for red letters on a white building. Large, well-lit lobby is always host to at least a few loungers. Clean and carpeted rooms. Singles E£10, with bath E£15, with bath and A/C E£20. Doubles with bath and breakfast E£20, with A/C as well E£30.

El-Amin Hotel, Abtal et-Tahrir St. (tel. 32 31 89), 3 blocks south and 1 block west of the train station; follow the sign. Hallways slightly dark and dusty, but beds and sheets admirably clean and baths equally so. Fans in rooms. Singles E£7. Doubles with bath E£20. Breakfast included. Possible discounts in summer.

Noorhan Hotel (tel. 31 60 69), off Sa'ad Zaghloul St. several hundred meters from the train station. Brand new, well-managed, and clean. Already very popular. Roof-top beer and *sheesha* den coming soon. Singles E£10, with bath and fan E£12, with A/C E£15. Similar doubles E£16 and E£20. Breakfast included.

Hathor Hotel, Corniche en-Nil (tel. 31 45 80), across from Isis Hotel. Rooftop pool, great carpeted rooms with towels. All rooms have private bath. Singles E£25, with A/C E£30. Doubles E£30, with A/C E£40 (all E£5 cheaper per person in summer).

El Salam Hotel, Corniche en-Nil (tel. 32 36 44 or 26 51), 25m south of the Hathor. Spotless, carpeted rooms, some with balconies overlooking the river and the commotion below. All rooms with bath. Singles E£19. Doubles E£22, with view E£28. A/C E£5 extra per person. Breakfast E£4.

Rosewan Hotel (tel. 32 22 97), turn right as you leave the train station, head past a gas station, and take the next left. The hotel is on the right. Very clean, with fans. Owner paints unique handmade *papier-mâché* ashtrays, masks, and vases, as well as postcards, in an upstairs studio. Guests invited into the studio. Singles E£14.85, with bath E£16. Doubles E£24.75, with bath E£27.20. Breakfast included.

Oscar Hotel, Abdas el-Abkad St. (tel./fax 32 60 66). Turn left from the train station, continue for 500m, turn left on Hememy el-Gabalawy St., then right on Abdas el-Abkad St. Hotel is on the right. Clean and comfortable, with a Las Vegas lobby. A/C and bath in every room. Singles E£30. Doubles E£44. Breakfast included.

Mena Hotel, Atlas St. (tel. 32 43 88). Turn right from the train station, pass 2 gas stations, continue straight for 2 more blocks until the convenience store, and then turn left. Good value, but inconvenient location in northeasternmost corner of town. Nice porch, roof garden, and ping-pong table. Clean rooms, all with baths and some carpeted. Singles E£10. Doubles with fan E£12, with A/C E£20. Breakfast included. Expect to pay E£3-5 more per person in winter.

Molla Hotel, Kelanie St. (tel. 32 65 40). Pass through the corridor across from Aswan Moon Restaurant, continue 2 blocks east, veering left past Bata Shoes. Continue for another 50m, go right, then walk another 60m. Clean and big rooms, some with table and chairs, some carpeted. Singles E£15, with bath E£20, with bath and A/C E£22.50. Doubles with bath E£25, with bath and A/C E£40.

Horus Hotel, 98 Corniche en-Nil (tel. 32 25 90), across from Aswan Moon. Large clean rooms could tempt you from the sights. Great views from upper floors. Singles with A/C and breakfast E£42, and bath E£49. Doubles with bath E£37.20, with A/C and breakfast E£64 (all 30-40% cheaper in summer). Tasty *kufta* sandwiches E£1.50. Cold Stella served on the pleasant roof garden.

Aswan's **campground,** a magnet for cross-Africa safari groups, also welcomes independent rustics. For E£3 you can pitch a tent on the grass of this spacious enclosure. Facilities include showers and toilets; purchase firewood from local vendors. The campground, adjacent to the Unfinished Obelisk, lies 2km south of town on Sharq el-Bandar St. From EgyptAir on the corniche, make a left and go about 1km. Look for the sign and take a right. After another 1km, look for the campground on the left. Summer heat can be painful here. The campground is inconvenient without motorized transport—expect to pay at least E£3-4 for a taxi into town.

FOOD

Fruit, vegetables, bread, and pigeon, not to mention falafel, liver sandwiches, and *kushari,* are available in Aswan's *souq.* The highest concentration of vendors is at the southern end of Es-souq St. where it intersects Es-Sayyida Nafisa, Aswan's older market street, three blocks in from the Isis Hotel on the corniche. The vegetable markets lie to the north. A large vegetable *souq* is tucked away near the train station, on the northeast edge of Es-souq St. Shop in the morning for the best produce.

Several restaurants popular with locals provide a true Egyptian dining experience: **Sayyida Nafisa,** just off Es-Souq St. 1.5km south of the train station and known to locals as *Shaweesh,* serves a wicked stuffed pigeon (E£7). **Darwish Restaurant,** just south of the train station on Es-Souq St., is also popular (meals E£5-8). **The Hamam Shop,** a deli of sorts on the eastern side of the corniche across from the Aswan Moon Restaurant, offers great sandwiches and other very inexpensive concoctions.

At the other extreme, you can splurge on huge buffets and gourmet continental and Arab cuisine at hotels for as much as E£50 per head. But the true heart of the Aswan restaurant scene are the **floating restaurants** off the corniche. Popular with Egyptians as well as tourists, they offer decent meals in addition to the perfect setting for watching the sun set over the desert hills of the west bank. They all serve basically the same array of salads, dips, and meat dishes for similar prices, though they do differ in quality and atmosphere. Listed from north to south beginning just south of the recently closed Isis Hotel:

Salah ed-Din does tasty grilled meats (meat, chicken, and fish entrees E£8-14).

Aswan Moon Restaurant, across from the National Bank of Egypt—entrance easy to spot with its wooden castle gate on the corniche. Surprisingly cool dockside restaurant by day becomes an equally cool nighttime café. Classiest and most popular of the lot, which translates into the slowest service. Prime place for a beer or bottle of wine. Luscious ice cream. Excellent *baba ghannoush* (40pt). Breakfast E£1.80. Fish, chicken, and meat entrees E£8-12. Beer E£4.50.

EMY, next to Aswan Moon. Not as fancy, but a clean, quiet alternative with good service and a long menu. Hamburgers E£4. 20% student discount.

Monnalisa, we bet you can guess what it's next to. Understated and clean. Entrees E£5-6. Sizzling bowl of vegetables in sauce E£1.25. Cold drinks 80pt-E£1.50, beer E£4.25. Breakfast (omelette, cheese, butter, jam, and tea) E£2.50. Delicious Monnalisa cocktail of blended fruit juices E£1.50 when available.

Esh-Shatii Restaurant, on the southern end of the corniche. A refreshing selection of fruit juices: banana, mango, lemon, grape, guava, or *karkadeh* (all E£1). Temptingly long menu but half the items may not be available. Complete meal with choice of entree and rice, bread, fruit, soup, and vegetables E£6.

Aswan Panorama, on the southernmost part of the corniche. Voluminous menu in a well-decorated restaurant. Wide variety of drinks 80pt-E£1.35. Spaghetti E£2.45, soups E£1.60, meat and fish dishes E£4.90-7.25. Open noon-10pm.

SIGHTS

On the west bank of the Nile, directly across from the city, the wind-swept sand piles into dunes with pronounced edges and sweeping contours. In the middle of the river float a handful of islets where most of the city's official attractions can be found. The largest of these, **Elephantine Island,** is linked to the mainland by regular ferries. (See Practical Information, p. 193.) As you disembark, you'll see to your left the **Aswan Archaeological Museum,** where you must purchase an admission ticket covering the museum, adjacent ruins, and Nilometer. The museum's collection is minuscule, but highlights include a few gilt sarcophagi and a ceremonially mutilated skull. (Open daily 8:30am-6pm; winter 8am-5pm. Admission E£5, students E£2.50.)

To the left of the museum's entrance, at the water's edge, stands a sycamore tree. Directly beneath the tree and carved into a rock is a **Nilometer.** Originally built during the Pharaonic era and renovated by the Romans, the long stairway-shaft was used to measure the depth of the Nile. In ancient times nothing was of greater practical significance than the Nilometer's oracle. When it proclaimed that the river was high, heavy flooding would ensure a bountiful harvest. When the Nilometer indicated shallow water, it foretold hunger and misery.

Elephantine Island was the original site of the settlement of Aswan. Its only remains have been excavated on the southeast corner of the island, directly behind the museum. Some of the ruins, including a large **Temple of Khnum** and a small stone **Temple of Heqa-Ib,** dedicated to one of the island's ancient rulers, are currently closed. At the southeastern tip of the island (particularly attractive when viewed from the Nile) is a small Ptolemaic temple dedicated to Alexander II and reconstructed by German archaeologists; the rebuilt façade is a disjointed collage of bas-relief fragments. The central section of the island has three **Nubian villages** (see p. 197), where you'll find congenial residents, brightly painted homes and handicrafts, and gnarled, spotless alleyways. The Nubians prefer that you be escorted by one of the villagers and be discreet about photography. Dress modestly. The entire northern half of Elephantine Island is dominated by the Oberoi Hotel, surrounded by a tall *cordon sanitaire.* To reach the hotel, take their private ferry from the Aswan corniche.

Behind Elephantine Island and not visible from central Aswan, **Geziret en-Nabatat** ("Island of the Plants," or Kitchener's Island) is a lovely, island-wide botanical garden where African and Asian tropical plant species flourish. This floating arboretum also attracts a variety of exotic and flamboyant birds. To reach the island, you can hire a *felucca* (stand on the corniche and wait for a captain to approach you) and combine an island visit with stops along the west bank (to the island and back only, E£10-15). It is also possible to hire a rowboat from the west side of Elephantine Island (about E£3 for 1 or 2 passengers only). Make sure boats wait for you or come back. (Island open daily 7am-sunset. Admission E£5.)

The most accessible attraction on the west bank of the Nile is the **Mausoleum of the Aga Khan,** a short climb from where the *felucca* docks. Aga Khan is the hereditary title of the ruler of the Isma'ili Muslims. The Isma'ili believe that the Aga Khan is the direct descendant of Muhammad and inheritor of his spiritual responsibilities of guidance. The Aga Khans used to rule from Pakistan, but political shifts have since forced them into Western exile. Aswan became the favorite winter retreat of Muhammad Shah Aga Khan (1899-1957), the 48th Imam of the Isma'ili. Upon his death, the Begum (the Aga Khan's wife) oversaw the construction of the mausoleum, where she too is buried. The interior of the shrine, modeled after the Fatimid tombs of Cairo, is more impressive than the exterior. Opposite the entrance stands a marble sarcophagus inscribed with passages from the Qur'an. Each day a red rose is placed on the sarcophagus; contemporary legend tells of the distance which a red rose was flown when none were available in the area. (Open Tues.-Sun. 9am-4:45pm. Free. *Bakhsheesh* to the guards is forbidden; a caretaker will show you around. Modest dress required and photography forbidden.) After leaving the shrine, freaks tempted by the striking sand-swept landscape to take a scenic route back to the dock will be greeted by signs asking them to "Take The Normal Way."

Deir Amba Samaan (Monastery of St. Simeon) stands isolated and majestic in the desert, 1km inland from the mausoleum. Built in the 6th and 7th centuries CE and abandoned in the 13th, the monastery is on a terrace carved into the steep hills visible from the mausoleum. With its turreted walls rising to a height of 6m, the monastery appears more like a fortress than a religious sanctuary. The original walls of the complex stood 10m high and enclosed a community of 300 resident monks. Upstairs, the monks' cells and their stone beds are currently occupied by bats. The monastery also had a church and accommodations sufficient for several hundred pilgrims and their camels. A great guide will show you around, miming the monks' activities and providing onomatopoeic accompaniment. (Open Tues.-Sun. 9am-6pm. Admission E£6, students E£3.) To reach the monastery, follow the paved path which starts in front of the Mausoleum of the Aga Khan (15-20min.) or hire a camel near the *felucca* stop. (E£10 per camel, which can take 2 people.)

The **Tombs of the Nobles** lie farther north along the west bank of the Nile, honeycombed into the face of ennobled desert cliffs and impressively illuminated at night. These tombs of governors and dignitaries date primarily from the end of the Old Kingdom and the First Intermediate periods. Years of decay and pilferage have severely damaged most of the tombs. The bright color and detail of the reliefs in the **Tomb of Sarenput II** (labeled as #31) merit the easy trip across the Nile. Farther south on the mountain ridge are the interconnected 6th-dynasty **Tombs of Nikhu and Sabni** (#25 and 26), father and son. The cheapest way to visit the tombs is to take the ferry (E£1) to the west bank from the corniche (across the small park from the tourist office). Once across, walk uphill to the office on the left. (Open daily 5:30am-6pm. Admission E£5, students E£2.50. Photo permission E£10.)

A worthwhile excursion in the Aswan area is a visit to a **Nubian village,** particularly on the occasion of a wedding. You may be invited to join the celebrations and ululations; the villagers consider it a mark of honor to have guests from far away villages attend their nuptial festivities. Nubian weddings traditionally involve 15 days of partying, but the demands of modern life have trimmed the celebration down to three or four. Traditional domed roofs characterize Nubian buildings. Their large houses made of Nile mud consist of a half dozen rooms around a courtyard; each cluster of rooms has its own dome or cylindrical roof. When the disruption wrought by the High Dam threatened to destroy this traditional architecture, Egyptian architect Hasan Fathy helped create these eerie reconstructed and relocated villages, bringing Nubian architecture international recognition.

The ferry to the west bank tombs (E£1) can bring you to **Gharb Aswan,** a series of Nubian villages less frequented by tourists than those of Elephantine Island. From the ferry dock catch a pick-up truck north to the villages (25pt). Whether or not you make it to a village, get a tape of rhythmic Nubian music in the Aswan *souq* (E£6).

To reach the sights on the west bank of the Nile, it's easiest to hire a *felucca*. The official rate for *felucca* transport in the vicinity of Aswan is E£18 per hour regardless of the number of passengers, but feel free to negotiate. A complete tour of Elephantine Island, Geziret en-Nabatat, the Aga Khan's Mausoleum, St. Simeon's Monastery, and the northern tombs goes for E£30. To meet other tourists who wish to share a *felucca,* try the restaurants along the corniche or the lobby of the Nubian Oasis Hotel. One or two people can save money by taking the ferry to Elephantine Island (E£1), then hiring a rowboat to the west bank (E£2). You can walk from sight to sight and return to Aswan further north by ferry (E£1), or arrange for the rowboat to take you to Geziret en-Nabatat, the mausoleum, the monastery, and back to Elephantine Island (E£8 after bargaining).

SHOPPING AND ENTERTAINMENT

Trade in nonperishables heats up in the evenings, especially from 8 to 10pm. If you seek more than the ubiquitous alphabetical hieroglyphics t-shirt, peruse Es-Sayyida Nafisa St. for western-style garments made to order from cloth covered with camel caravans or Nefertitis. **Barakat Nadir Kaldas,** code name Clark Gable, will cut your garment with lightning speed while you watch. (Pants E£10-25, shorts and simple shirts E£10-15, shirts with collars and buttons E£25.50-35.) Other merchants bargain, whereas Barakat insists on fixed prices. For Egyptian wear, visit the **Abd el-Aleety** family shop, 60m due south on Es-souq St. from Es-Sayyida Nafisa St. The Aleetys specialize in custom-made, beautifully embroidered *gallabiyyas* and *kaftans,* a shorter form of the *galabiyya* (E£15-500; open daily 9am-2pm and 5-11pm).

The **nightclubs** in the Cataract, Isis, and Oberoi hotels are anything but cheap (min. charge E£25-40 per person). In winter, the **Aswan Cultural Center,** on Corniche en-Nil between Abu Simbel and Philae Hotels, features Nubian dancing and handicrafts. (Dancing Sat.-Thurs. 9:30-11pm. Admission E£3.10.) There is no shortage of cafés in which you can join locals for a cup of tea, a puff of *sheesha,* or a game of dominoes late into the night. And there's always the Philae Temple (see below) **sound and light show** (in English Sat., Mon., Wed., and Fri. 8pm, Tues. 9:30pm).

You can rent rowboats (E£10 per hr.), sculls (E£15 per hr.), sailboards (E£10 per hr.), or waterskis (E£20 per hr.) at the **Rowing Club,** at northern end of the corniche, downstairs from a circular store selling home appliances. On a free afternoon, walk south along the corniche, continuing right at the end, to the **Pullman Cataract Hotel,** a beautifully decorated advertisement for *Lifestyles of the Rich and Famous.* Gorgeous gardens, pool, and outdoor café overlook the Nile. Surprisingly, you can indeed afford a drink, not to mention champagne wishes and caviar dreams.

■■■ SOUTH OF ASWAN

Aswan itself lacks spectacular antiquities, but the 15km stretch of the Nile south of town will rock your world. This region of the **First Cataract** includes both the **Old Dam** (5km south of Aswan), built in the early 20th century by the British, and the enormous **High Dam** (15km south of Aswan), the construction of which created Lake Nasser. On an island in the lake between the two, the exquisite **Philae Temple** proclaims the glory of Isis. Just beyond the west side of the High Dam, the lonely **Temple of Kalabsha** stands guard over Lake Nasser and the surrounding desert. The pharaohs' granite quarries lie on the southern border of Aswan and contain the famous **Unfinished Obelisk.** All sights are comfortable daytrips from Aswan.

Getting Around

Unfortunately, public transportation does not extend completely to many of these sights. An excellent road follows the Nile from Aswan to the village of **Khazan,** site of both the Old Dam and the motorboat launch to Philae. The road crosses the dam and continues south for 10km along the west side of the Nile to reach the High Dam. Getting from Aswan to Khazan is simple, as the route is served by **service** (25pt; depart from *service* stop) and by **public bus** (#20 and 59 from the corniche; 14 per day 6am-9:30pm, 25pt). The easiest way to get to the High Dam is by train from Aswan (see Aswan: Orientation and Practical Information, p. 191). Returning to Aswan, trains leave the High Dam station at 8:55am, 2:10, 4, 6:30, and 8:30pm. An 11:30am train leaves from a covered waiting area just across the street from the station of your arrival. The dam closes to traffic at 5pm on most days.

If you need to cram as many sights as possible into one day, you could travel in a group and hire a taxi (E£50 for 4-5hr.). **Taxi tours** (they do not go to Kalabsha) are occasionally organized by the youth hostel in winter (approximately E£5). Inquire at the hostel at least two nights beforehand. Managers at the Marwa, Mena, and Ramses Hotels also organize tours; talk to them or the tourist office. Tours arranged by private operators are more expensive.

A convenient, somewhat relaxed itinerary runs: the Old Dam and Philae in one day, the High Dam and Kalabsha in another, and the quarries, Unfinished Obelisk, and Fatimid Tombs as an afternoon trip, perhaps after Abu Simbel in the morning.

THE DAMS AND QUARRIES

The most notorious attraction in the area is modern Egypt's great monument, the **High Dam (Es-Sidd el-Ali),** completed in 1971. The dam does more for your brain than for your eyes; its rather unspectacular construction—it may take you a while to realize you're actually there—saps the drama and excitement out of its mammoth size and strategic location. One kilometer thick at its base, 3.6km long, and 110m high, the dam has inundated Nubia with waters as deep as 200m, wiping out 45 villages and requiring the relocation of thousands of people as well as the transfer of numerous ancient monuments to high ground under a UNESCO plan. The long-term effects of the massive project are still unfolding: a rise in the Sahara's water table has been noticed as far away as Algeria, and archaeologists suspect that the higher water table has damaged the tombs at Luxor.

On the brighter side, the dam's 12 turbines produce over two megawatts of electricity. Thanks to the dam, agricultural productivity has been greatly enhanced, and the acreage of Egypt's arable soil has been increased by 30%. The dam enabled Egypt to enjoy an undiminished water supply during the drought of the past decade, and in August 1988 the dam saved Egypt from the floods suffered by the Sudan when the Nile overflowed after heavy rains.

The High Dam has had significant international repercussions as well. Plans for the construction were unveiled after World War II when it became apparent that Egypt had achieved maximum agricultural output and could no longer feed its rapidly increasing population. When the United States offered and then refused to provide loans for the High Dam project in 1956, President Nasser ordered the nationalization of the Suez Canal as a means of generating the necessary hard currency. This triggered the Suez Crisis, in which France, Britain, and Israel invaded Egypt. The Soviet Union decided to provide the necessary loans and technology, and work began on the dam in 1960. Despite over a decade of cooperation on the dam's construction, shortly after its completion and Anwar es-Sadat's rise to power Egypt severed relations with the Soviet Union and turned to the United States.

One result of the High Dam was **Lake Nasser,** the world's largest artificial lake, stretching 500km across the Tropic of Cancer into the Sudan. The beauty of the lake, lipped by sands and rocky hills, is tempered by an awareness of its effects: the displacement of an entire people and the loss of priceless antiquities.

On the eastern bank (where the train station is), just before the dam, the **Visitors Pavilion** features plaques and sculptures blending Soviet socialist-realist motifs with Egyptian figures and symbols. Plans for the construction of the dam—written in Russian and Arabic—include a map and some technical drawings. At the center of the pavilion is a dusty 15m model of the High Dam and its environs, minus the water. It also includes pictures and diagrams of the relocation of Abu Simbel. The domed pavilion is well off the road from the dam and most taxis will not stop at it unless you insist; ask for the *mekat* (model). (Open daily 7am-5pm. Free.)

To cross the dam to the west you must pay E£2, and you will not be allowed to cross on foot. The police at the eastern end will stop any passing vehicle and make them take you across for free. A towering stone monument at the western end is another remnant of Soviet assistance. A stylized lotus blossom, the monument was intended as a symbol of Soviet-Egyptian friendship. The central image reinterprets Michelangelo with a female worker reaching across the dawn to her male comrade. From the top of the dam you can view the islands to the north and Lake Nasser to the south. Because of the rise in terrorist activity, visitors must get permission to go to the top of the monument (available in the large yellow building west of the monument). (Monument open daily 6am-5pm. Admission to the top E£2.)

The **Old Dam** is a 10km to the north. Built by the Brits between 1898 and 1902, the dam supplied most of Egypt's power for years. The Old Dam can be reached by green public bus or *service* from the Aswan corniche to Khazan (see Getting Around, p. 198). The area known as the First Cataract is extremely fertile and one of the most idyllic spots in the Aswan area. In the picturesque village of **Khazan,** 90-year-old British villas, now British-less, are nestled peacefully within walled gardens.

Just below the waters of the First Cataract, **Sehel Island,** boasting a hospitable Nubian village, scanty ruins, and a variety of inscriptions ranging from the 4th dynasty to the Ptolemaic period, attracts very few tourists. This island makes a perfect destination for a longer *felucca* ride from Aswan (E£25 for a 3-hr. tour).

If traveling by taxi back to Aswan after touring the High Dam or Philae, you might ask the driver to stop at the Fatimid Tombs, the adjacent Unfinished Obelisk, and the nearby granite quarries. These sites are all near the camping area, 300m east of the main road at a turn-off 1km south of Aswan. The **Fatimid Tombs** are typical early Islamic shrines: squat, square stone buildings with crescents on their roofs. They are easily spotted on the left side of the road across the street from the Obelisk. The tombs have been more or less abandoned; it can be spooky wandering around the dark cemetery frequented mostly by packs of crazed banshees. The **Unfinished Obelisk** was abandoned at its site because of a flaw in the granite; it was to have soared to a whopping 41.7m on a base 4.2m on each side. In its unadorned state, the obelisk looks—well, it looks unfinished. In fact, it looks like it had never been started. The even less visually arousing **granite quarries** here supplied most of ancient Egypt with the raw material for pyramids and temples. (Obelisk and quarries open daily 6am-6pm. Admission E£5, students E£2.50.)

PHILAE فيلة

Philae's isolation, enhanced by its majestic position above the fertile Nubian frontier, historically has awed visitors. In the Greek and Roman eras, the temples of the cult of Isis drew the pious and curious. The completion of the Old Dam by the

British in 1902 partially submerged the temples only a few years after their resurrection as a popular tourist destination. Archaeologists feared that the temple would eventually be destroyed by the Nile's strong current after the Old Dam was enlarged in 1912. The construction of the High Dam alerted the world to the watery plight of Nubia's monuments and provided the impetus needed to save Philae. Between 1972 and 1980, UNESCO and the Egyptian Antiquities Department labored to transfer the complex of temples from **Philae Island** to higher ground on nearby **Agilka Island.** In 1980 the new site of the ancient temples reopened to tourism.

You can visit Philae by **taxi** as part of an itinerary including other sights, or take a **bus** to the Old Dam from the Aswan corniche; get off when it stops at the checkpoint on the east end of the dam. Easiest is a **service** to Khazan (see Practical Information, p. 191). Tell the driver to let you off at the Old Dam (Es-Sidd el-Qadeem). From the checkpoint, walk south along the shore to the concrete boat dock (about 2km). Whether you come by bus or taxi, you must first purchase an admission ticket and then hire a **motorboat** to reach the island. The government-posted rate for a motorboat is E£14 per boat round-trip. It is usually easy to find other visitors to share a rental on the motorboat docks. The boat pilot is obliged to wait for you as you tour the site, so don't rush. (Open daily 7am-5pm; winter 7am-4pm. Admission E£10, students E£5. No photography charge, but E£10 for a tripod.)

The well-preserved and impressive **Temple of Isis** dominates the island's northern edge. Isis was the mother of nature, protector of humans, goddess of purity and sexuality, and sister-wife of the legendary hero Osiris (see Abydos, p. 164). Her following was so strong that the cult of Isis continued long after the establishment of Christianity, fizzling out only in the 6th century during the reign of Justinian, finally stamped out by patriarchal monotheism. Nearly all the structures on Philae date from the Ptolemaic and Roman eras, as the artistic quality began to decline in Egypt—hence the inferior quality of the decorative relief work; Nile waters have hardly enhanced their intrinsic beauty.

From the landing at the southern tip of the island, climb the short slope up to the temple complex past Philae's oldest structure, the **Portico of Nectanebo.** The paved portico once formed the vestibule of an ancient temple. The larger edifice has been washed away, but the eastern side of the colonnade remains. At the first pylon, towers rise 18m on either side of the temple's main entrance. Through this entrance is the central court, on the western edge of which reclines a Roman *mammisis,* its elegant columns emblazoned with the head of the cow-goddess Hathor. To the north is the slightly off-center second pylon, marking the way to the temple's inner sanctum. The *pronaos* (vestibule) was converted into a church by early Christians who inscribed Byzantine crosses on the chamber walls and added a small altar. Farther north is the *naos,* the temple's innermost sanctuary. For *bakhsheesh* you can climb to the roof of the temple, but the paranoid guard will make you hurry and keep your head down so that you may not be able to see anything.

KALABSHA كلبشة

The enormous **Temple of Kalabsha,** dramatically situated above the placid waters of Lake Nasser, is one of the most striking pharaonic ruins in the Aswan area. Dedicated to the Nubian god Mandulis, the temple was begun by Amenhotep II, erected primarily during the reign of Augustus, and used as a church during the Christian era. In 1962-3, the West German government paid to have the entire temple dismantled and transported in 13,000 pieces from its Nasser-flooded home to the present site, 50km north of the original. Many Egyptologists consider well-preserved Kalabsha to be second only to the treasures of Abu Simbel.

Slightly out of the way and not well publicized, the temple allows its visitors a rare chance to explore in the absence of bazaars and *bakhsheesh*-seekers. The temple is west of the Nile, just south of the High Dam and 2km past the checkpoint. The cheapest way to reach Kalabsha is to take the **train** to the eastern end of the High Dam and then either ride to the western end. Lily-livered sorts can take a **taxi** from Aswan. Try bargaining down to E£15, E£20 for a group of more than five. Don't forget that the High Dam closes at 5pm. From the western end of the High Dam you can walk most of the way to the temple (1km), passing the abandoned hulls of marooned fishing fleets along the way. Bring plenty of water and cover your head. From about mid-July to mid-August, when the water is at its lowest, you may be able to wade through the muck to the temple. At other times you must get a **rowboat** (E£5 per person, E£3 per person for groups of more than 8). The rowers will insist at all times of the year that the temple is on an island and inaccessible by foot. The site is open 7am-6pm but the guard may be so surprised to have visitors that you'll be allowed to linger. (Admission E£6, students E£3.)

An immense causeway of dressed stone leads from the water to the temple's main entrance. The first pylon is off-center from both the causeway and the inner gateways of the temple itself. Notice the sun disk and cobra symbol over each entrance. A carving of St. George and Coptic inscriptions survive from early Christian times. The grand forecourt between the pylon and the vestibule is surrounded by 14 columns, each with a unique capital. This is one of the only temples in Egypt where you can get to the top legally: take the stairs to the roof from a small room just beyond the vestibule for a commanding view of the entire forecourt and vestibule.

Because the temple faces east, light flows into the **Holy of Holies** (innermost chamber) only in the early morning. Bring a flashlight at other times, and beware of bats. A passageway leads north through the vestibule to an inner encircling wall; follow the wall around to the south until you find a well-preserved **Nilometer.** Extraordinary carvings of Mandulis, Isis, Horus, and Osiris cover the outside walls.

Outside the huge fortress-like wall, the remains of a small **shrine** are visible to the southeast; the present structure is largely a reconstructed façade. This *mélange* of Nubian remains includes pre-dynastic elephants, a large giraffe, and gazelles. The double-image technique, characteristic of Nubian art, is used to portray motion in some of the drawings. Be careful where you step; carcasses of enormous desiccated fish are surrealistically scattered amongst the sands.

Slightly to the southwest of Kalabsha Temple are ruins of the **Temple of Kertassi.** Two Hathor columns remain, as well as four other columns with elaborate floral capitals and a single monolithic architrave. As you walk back toward the ticket office, tell the guard you want to see the **Rock Temple of Beit el-Wali** (House of the Holy Man), rescued from the encroaching waters of Lake Nasser with the aid of the U.S. government. The small temple is at the end of an uphill path from the office. One of many Nubian temples constructed by Ramses II, it features the typically modest poses of Ramses conquering foreign enemies, Ramses receiving prisoners, and the particularly understated scene of Ramses storming a castle half his size. Like a miniature Abu Simbel, this cave-temple was hewn from solid rock. Examine the bas-relief scenes closely: political and social history are portrayed in everything from graphic chariot battles to household toil over whose turn it is to dry the dishes.

ABU SIMBEL أبوسمبل

The pharaonic monumentality of the Nile Valley peaks at the southernmost end of the Nile in Egypt. Four 22m-tall statues of Ramses II, carved out of a single slab of rock, greet the sunrise over Lake Nasser from the Great Temple of Abu Simbel. Ramses II had this grand sanctuary and the nearby Temple of Hathor built more than 3500 years ago to impress the Nubians with the power and glory of Egyptian rule; Abu Simbel still serves its purpose, leaving no visitor unmoved. For a sneak preview of the site, look at the back of the Egyptian one pound note.

Practical Information Abu Simbel is 274km south of Aswan and 50km from the Sudanese border. Two **buses** come here from Aswan (A/C 8am and no A/C 5pm, 3½hr., E£12.50). Buy your ticket at the Aswan bus station a day in advance; buy the return ticket on the bus on the way back.

The proprietors of Aswan's El Amin, Mena, Marwa, Molla, and Nubian Oasis hotels organize minibuses to Abu Simbel (E£20-25 per person, a little more in high season; entrance fees extra). You will generally leave at 4am and be back in Aswan by 1-2pm (your driver may offer to stop at the High Dam on the return trip). The advantage of these tours is that you will arrive early at Abu Simbel when the desert heat is bearable. On the other hand, you will be herded into a tour group upon reaching the temple and expected to depart shortly after the tour ends. To explore freely, organize a rebellion of your fellow passengers, risk their hatred by straggling, or set up your own transportation. A private taxi trip arranged on your own could save a few pounds if you're in a group of seven.

For those who cannot make the sometimes eerie and often beautiful road trip, several **flights** a day wing between Aswan and Abu Simbel. The frequency depends on demand. EgyptAir provides free bus service to the temple; after a whirlwind tour, you'll be driven back to the airport for the return flight (round-trip E£337).

In Abu Simbel, the **police station** is 400m up the dead-end road from the temple. The **Tourist Police** are across the street from the New Ramses Hotel, by the temple. The town is also equipped with a **post office** and **hospital**. There are no telephone numbers *qua* telephone numbers here; you simply pick up a phone, dial zero, and the operator will connect you to anyone or anything in town.

Hospitable villagers are easy to find. The **town** of Abu Simbel, a displaced yet sturdy version of its former self, lies about 2km from the temple site. Unfortunately, Abu Simbel has little to offer in the way of budget accommodations. The four-star **Nefertari** (tel. 31 64 04/3/2) and the three-star **Ramses** (tel. 31 16 60/1) hotels both charge US$60 for a double; there is **camping** at the Nefertari for E£5 per person.

Sights When the rising waters of Lake Nasser threatened to engulf one of Egypt's greatest treasures, nations joined together and relocated the two great temples at Abu Simbel to higher ground as part of an effort which moved 11 temples to new Egyptian sites and even overseas. (The Temple of Dendar is sheltered in New York's Metropolitan Museum of Art. Spain, Italy, and Holland also took their share of the spoils.) At a cost of US$36 million, teams of engineers from five countries painstakingly wrested the temples from the solid rock, breaking them into 3000 pieces weighing between 10 and 40 tons each. The pieces were moved 200m, the temples reconstructed and carefully oriented in their original directions, and in 1968 a hollow mountain was built around the two structures. The temple, the gigantic interior of the structure built to surround the relocated stones, and the expanse of Lake Nasser are sublime monuments to quixotic human undertakings.

The **Great Temple of Abu Simbel** is Ramses II's masterpiece. This energetic, egotistical builder effectively dedicated the temple to himself, although the god Ra-Hurakhti gets lip service. As you proceed through the temple, the artwork depicts Ramses first as great king, then as servant of the gods, next as companion of the gods, and finally, in the inner sanctuary, as a card-carrying deity. The seated **Colossi of Ramses,** four 20m-tall statues of the king at the front of the great temple, wear both the Old and New Kingdom versions of the crowns of Upper and Lower Egypt. An earthquake in 27 BCE crumbled the upper portion of one of the Colossi. Modern engineers were unable to reconstruct the figure, so they left it in its faceless state. The smaller figures standing among Ramses' legs represent the royal family, guarding the family jewels. A row of praying baboons adorns the entrance; many ancient Egyptians admired baboons' habit of greeting the rising sun.

Farther into the temple are antechambers that once stored objects of worship; the walls show Ramses making sacrifices to the gods. In the inner sanctum, four seated statues facing the entrance depict Ramses and the gods Ra-Hurakhti, Amun, and Ptah (the Theban god of darkness). Originally encased in gold, the statues now wait with divine patience for February 22 and October 22, when the first rays of the sun reach 100m into the temple to bathe all except Ptah in light. February 21 was Ramses's birthday and October 21 his coronation date, but when the temple was moved, the timing of these natural feats was shifted by one day.

Next door at the smaller **Temple of Hathor,** six 10m statues of King Ramses and Queen Nefertari (as the goddess Hathor) adorn the façade. Along with the temple of Hatshepsut in West Thebes, this is one of the only great temples in Egypt dedicated to women. Scenes on the walls depict Ramses' coronation with the god Horus placing the crown of Upper and Lower Egypt on his head. The temple was constructed in the traditional three-room fashion; the first chamber was open to the public, the second chamber to nobles and priests, and the inner sanctuary only to the pharaoh and the high priest. (Site open 6am-5pm. Admission E£24, students E£12.)

Western Desert Oases

Scattered through the expanses of the Western Desert, the oases dot the sea of sand and rock like little green archipelagos. Hot and cold springs, groves of oranges and dates, rice paddies, and fields of watermelons and cucumbers flourish astonishingly amidst the imposing desert. Though the Bedouin and Egyptian *fellaheen* who dwell beside the robust fields greet strangers with comforting hospitality, this is an adventure for the rugged. Getting around is a lot more difficult than along the Nile, and tourist facilities are token gestures at best.

The series of oases sprinkled throughout the Sahara—**Bahariyya, Farafra, Dakhla,** and **Kharga**—marks the trail of a prehistoric branch of the Nile. A flow of water from the Sudan supposedly replenished the wells and springs annually. This bounty of water has been an impetus for development in crowded and largely water-starved Egypt. In 1958, the government released studies that showed considerable stores of water below the desert floor, accessible with new techniques of drilling deeper wells. The government's New Valley Project was designed to fully exploit this underground water for the irrigation and fertilization of the desert. A massive relocation of landless peasants from the Delta to the New Valley was also planned. Unfortunately, experts now begin to question the hypothesis that the underground water is recharged by seepage from the more humid parts of Africa. New estimates indicate that the supply could last only another 100 to 700 years, and that it is not replenished yearly; instead, it is simply left over from 6000 to 12,000 years ago.

The fortunes of the people of the oases have ebbed and flowed with the water supply throughout Egyptian history. The Romans, with their waterwheels and aqueducts, were able to tap deeper water and push back the desert. The population burgeoned and prospered for approximately 300 years, but over-irrigation and abandonment of fallow farming eventually hindered productivity. The oases slipped into a slow decline that lasted into the 1970s, when Anwar es-Sadat targeted the New Valley for development. The plans proved too ambitious and expensive, even though new desert wells did open vast regions around the oases for cultivation. Government attention has meant radical change for those living in the oases, as new roads and other recently introduced conveniences funnel in Western culture.

In general, the oases share the climate of Nile Valley cities at the same latitude—Bahariyya is like Cairo, Kharga like Luxor; but the air is fresher in the oases, and breezes more common. October through April is unquestionably the best time to visit. It is not unusual for summer temperatures, especially at Kharga, to reach the 50°C mark. Even at night, summer temperatures persist into the upper 20s. And you won't find air conditioning *anywhere,* making this a much less popular destination in summer. If you go then, finding accommodations will be a cinch.

Check out a copy of Dr. Ahmed Fakhry's *Bahariyya and Farafra Oases,* an extremely readable introduction to the life and history of these areas. The volume, along with Fakhry's *Siwa Oasis,* is published by the American University in Cairo Press and is available in the university bookstore on the Old Campus and at several of Cairo's English-language bookstores (E£9-10 paperback). The university library on the New Campus also has both volumes for consultation. Cassandra Vivian's *A Guide to the Oases and Western Desert of Egypt,* available at AUC and major English-language bookstores, is also helpful.

GETTING AROUND

Daily **buses** run from the Al Azhar bus station in Cairo to the oases. Inexpensive buses also run from Assyut to Kharga and Dakhla. Between the various oases, bus travel is even more chaotic than in the rest of Egypt. Published schedules are the roughest of guesstimates, and bus officials, townies, and passers-by all peddle wildly contradictory and inaccurate departure times. Ask as many people as possible, follow the consensus, arrive early, and be prepared to wait. Kharga is served by EgyptAir **flights** from Cairo (every Sun. and Wed., 6am, E£300). (See Cairo: Practical Information, p. 86, for more on EgyptAir.) **Service taxis** travel to Bahariyya from Cairo, and to Kharga from Assyut. (See the individual chapters on the oases, Cairo, and Assyut for detailed transportation information.) Some people **hitchhike** from one oasis to the next, but they often have to wait a day or so for a ride, especially between Farafra and Dakhla. For those who hitch, the military checkpoints outside each oasis are the most promising spots to find a ride. **In the heat and isolation, hitchers run a real risk—Let's Go doesn't recommend it.**

Car rental is a convenient and comfortable, though expensive, option for desert travel. A giant loop along the Great Desert Road and the Lower Nile Valley in either direction beginning in Cairo is about 1700km (over 1000 miles). Any car must be in top condition in order to survive the long, hot, poorly maintained desert roads. Four-wheel-drive is highly recommended. Look for a caravan (trailer); renting one can solve a lot of problems, including those of transporting food, water, and extra gas, and finding a comfortable place to sleep. If the cost is split among several people, caravans can be economical.

A number of caveats are in order concerning **desert driving.** It is sometimes a long way between gas stations. While every oasis boasts at least one fuel pump, it is probably wise to buy jerry cans in Cairo or Assyut and fill them with enough gas to cover the vast distances between stations. A caravan consumes ludicrous quantities of fuel; buy enough extra to fill an entire tank. Bring along at least one good spare tire; flats are more common than service stations. Several large containers filled with potable water are also vital in case you get stranded. Foreigners are (probably wisely) prohibited from leaving the main road. Try to drive in the cool of the morning. And finally, never drive at night—the chances of getting lost on the unlit road increase exponentially and potholes hidden in the dark are especially pernicious.

SOME TIPS

The best alternative to staying in hotels in the oases is **camping.** Most fertile land here belongs to farmers who'll usually permit you to pitch your tent. The ideal spot is just outside the main town of an oasis, where you can usually find a small pool of water and the sounds of silence. The desert itself is also an option. Generally, the area is free of dangerous fauna. Cool temperatures and breezes carry away the mosquitoes to feast on rest house guests, and sand is a comfortable mattress substitute. Each oasis has at least one bearable and cheap **hotel** or **rest house.**

Only Farafra has a 24-hour **water** supply. The other oases, however, have large reserve-tanks, so don't worry. Local water, since it is groundwater, tastes much better than other Egyptian municipal water and is generally safe to drink. **Food** is readily available in the main towns of all the oases.

In each oasis, you'll become aware of the local "mafia": in Dakhla, Hamdy Abu Muhammad (of restaurant fame) and Nasser (of Hand-Made Hotel fame) are brothers; in Farafra, Sa'ad Ali Muhammad rules the roost in cahoots with his brothers Hamdy and Atef. Don't hesitate to go to these people: they're friendly and extremely helpful.

Women should follow certain guidelines when swimming in oasis springs. In isolated springs unfrequented by locals, female travelers are not likely to be bothered. The same goes for pools cordoned off and adjoined to tourist rest houses. Women should not, however, enter pools where men are already bathing. Sometimes there is a separate pool where women may bathe, provided they wear a *gallabiyya*.

Note that the requirement for foreigners to obtain permission to visit the oases was lifted in 1985-86. Despite what out-of-date sources will tell you, you need only flash a **passport** at the numerous military checkpoints en route—keep it handy. In Dakhla, Kharga, or Farafra, you might be asked to pay a E£4.50 per person **tourism development tax.** Some claim they've already paid, deny being a tourist, protest— often the authorities don't press the issue. But if your stinginess has gone so far that you can't give a poor country about US$1.50 for roads and other minor amenities, check your head. If you pay the tax at a hotel, be sure to keep the receipt as proof; otherwise you may have to pay again.

■■■ BAHARIYYA الواحات البحرية

This small oasis is historically significant as a stopover for caravans traveling between the Nile Valley and the rest of North Africa. It lies about 330km south of Cairo and is linked by a decently paved road. Since pharaonic times, the arrival of merchants and their heavily laden camels was a major event in Bahariyya; for many centuries, pilgrims on their way to Mecca would join traders on the trans-desert trek and enjoy an enthusiastic welcome from the Bahariyyan faithful. Nowadays, when tourism is extant, it's caravans of rip-roaring European adventurers gallivanting through the oasis in Land Rovers that cause the intense noise pollution in Bahariyya. Because of its relative proximity to Cairo, Bahariyya attracts many foreign visitors who crave a couple of days in the desert but no more.

Bahariyya's ancient ruins are scanty and largely inaccessible, and **Bawiti,** the main village, is not too appealing. However, nearby gardens and springs and the desert more than compensate. The town offers conveniences including several food stores, a market, four or five coffee shops, and a gas station. Thus, if you're headed to Farafra, this is a great spot for refueling both body and auto.

Practical Information All services in Bawiti are on or just off a 500m stretch of the main road. Starting from the west end, you'll find the **bus station, hospital, telephone office** (open 8am-midnight; no international calls possible; 3min. to Cairo E£1), **police station,** and **gas station.** The **telephone code** is 10; to reach any place in town, dial 10404 and ask the operator to connect you. The **tourist office** is on the first floor of the government compound (El Muhafza), across from the police station (open Sat.-Thurs. 8am-2pm). It is staffed by city council member Muhammad Abd el-Qader. After 2pm, look for him in the **Paradise Hotel** reception, across from the telephone office. Just follow the "To Paradise Hotel" sign into the little house surrounded by a garden. If Muhammad is unavailable, ask for **Yehia Kandil,** who also works at the tourist office. Yehia, super-friendly and informed, is in charge of organizing all camel and jeep tours, and works out of the Paradise Hotel. **El Quds Pharmacy** (open 9am-6pm), next to the police station, inexplicably has a sign that says Asem Pharmacy. If you have nothing to do, inquire about the double-naming; there's a long story behind it. **Water** in Bahariyya is on from 7am to 1pm and 4pm to 10pm, though hotel storage tanks usually provide added relief. There is no place in Bahariyya to change **money,** so bring Egyptian cash with you or convince a local to change small amounts.

After Kharga, Bahariyya ranks as the most accessible of the oases in Egypt's Western Desert. From Cairo, a 400km road leads past the Pyramids of Giza and southwest across the desert to Bawiti. The distance can be covered in four or five hours by private **car. Service taxis** from Cairo leave from the Qahwa el-Waha Café, on a corner of Qadry Street, a few blocks south of Port Said St., west of the Citadel in the Sayyida district. Each day a few *service* travel from Bahariyya to Cairo (ordinarily in afternoon or evening, E£15), leaving from the front of Bayoumi's Popular Restaurant. There's a **bus** running from Al Azhar station to Bahariyya (2-3 per day beginning 7am, E£12), another to Bahariyya, Farafra, and Dakhla (Tues. and Fri. 6am, E£14), and two others to Bahariyya (en route to Farafra, some have A/C, Sat., Mon., and Thurs. 9am, E£16; no A/C direct Sun., Tues.-Wed. noon, E£14). Book one to two days in advance to secure a seat. Buses leave Bahariyya for Cairo (daily 7am, 6hr., E£12; Mon. and Wed.-Thurs. noon, E£14; from Dakhla Sat. and Mon. 1pm, E£12; from Farafra with A/C Sun., Tues., and Fri. 10am, E£16). Book early, as buses tend to be very crowded, even during the summer. To purchase tickets and reserve seats, head to the second-story office above the telephone office in Bahariyya (open 7-9am and roughly 9-11pm).

Accommodations and Food Currently, tourists in Bawiti have five accommodations options. The **Hotel Alpenblick** is the cleanest and most inviting, but also the most expensive. "Budget" rooms are E£15. Doubles E£30, with bath E£40. Breakfast included, lunch E£8, dinner E£10. Alcohol is available. Alpenblick is the only hotel off the main street, but it's very close to it, and only a tool could miss the big sign. The government's **Paradise Hotel,** across from the telephone office on the main street, offers grimy rooms and dark bathrooms, but it does have fans and a small garden canopy groaning with grapes. (E£3 per person. Breakfast E£2.)

Farther afield, catch a free ride on the bus to **Ahmad's Safari Camp,** 4km south of the center of town. Rather dirty rooms and bathrooms retail at E£5 per person, E£10 with bath. Breakfast included. The metal sheds for E£3 are infernally hot in summer. No hot water except from the nearby springs. Although there's a shop, a restaurant, and free transport to the town, you are somewhat isolated here. Venture to the **Rest House** at Bir el-Matthar (7km north of town) only if you're looking for the no-budget option. Bungalows isolated in the middle of a desert landscape are a steal at E£5; tents (E£3) also available. If sanitation is a concern, avoid **Saleh's Campground** at Bir Ghaba (lump of concrete in straw hut E£5). The springs in the area, particularly Bir Ghaba, afford enticing settings for campers with their own transport.

The main restaurant in Bawiti is Bayoumi's **Popular Restaurant** (full meal E£6). They even provide Stella (E£5). The restaurant is next to the government compound across from the police station. Otherwise, the **Paradise** restaurant, **Sanussi,** or **Lamey,** on the main road toward Farafra, offer standard meals for about E£5. In the mornings, the Sanussi serves *fuul* and falafel.

Sights Nature is the area's real attraction. Several local operators organize trips to nearby sights, and they will find you upon your arrival. The nearby **Bir el-Ramla** (3km out of Bawiti) features a 45°C hot spring. **Bir el-Mattar,** a cold spring (25°C), lies 7km southeast of Bawiti. The slightly sulphurous water pours out of a viaduct into a small shaded cement pool. Taxis to this popular place cost E£10 round-trip. The "road" (really a desert track; drivers beware) to Bir el-Mattar continues southeast through the desert to **Bir el-Ghaba,** 17km from Bawiti, with both a hot and cold spring in another sumptuous oasis landscape. Both men and women can swim in this deserted spot; taxi E£25 round-trip. A steamy spring, 2.5km out of the town center, is within walking distance. On a slightly bizarre and unusual note, a large natural pyramid, surrounded and topped by dunes, lies within the range of local tour operators about 9km away. Make it a point to visit the **Black Mountain,** a flat-topped hill with remainders of the British occupation. The natives call it "Gabal El Engeliz" (the English Mountain). It's 2.5km from Bawiti on the track heading to Bir el-Ghaba.

Archeological sites of some interest cluster around Bawiti and El Qasr, the older city adjacent to Bawiti in the west. The **Tomb of Bannentiu,** on the eastern outskirts of Bawiti, was discovered by Ahmed "Oasis" Fakhry and dates from the 26th dynasty. Its central and burial chambers are decorated with fairly well-preserved painted reliefs, including murals of the journeys of the sun and moon. The tomb is currently closed for restoration and preservation work; ask locally about when it will be reopened. Fakhry, the bodacious oasis man, has discovered a many-chambered **ibis burial,** 500m south of Bawiti, where sacred ibises, falcons, and quails were interred in jars. This tomb also dates from late pharaonic times, and was used into the Roman era. The burial chamber cannot be visited, but little was left behind to see anyway. **El Qasr** itself, the ancient capital of Bahariyya, hides scanty Roman remains among its mud brick dwellings. Ancient walls and the watery geological fault **Bir Bishmo** also make interesting side trips. A new *bir*, with 60°C water, has also been discovered there. All the hotel managers run tours of the area. For E£10-15 a head, you should be able to visit all the nearby springs, sights, and viewpoints. Through the tourist office you can hire a taxi for the day for about E£40; E£70 will get a group to the oasis of El Heiz and back.

Yehia Kandil (Paradise Hotel) organizes tours to the above destinations (E£10-12 per person) and to the **White Desert** by asphalt road (5 people E£300), desert road (5 people E£800), or a bit of both (5 people E£450). Trips last two to three nights and may include **Crystal Mountain** (90km out of Bawiti), the **magic spring**, or **Ain Khoudra.**

THE ROADS FROM CAIRO AND TO FARAFRA

As you leave metropolitan Cairo you'll pass just north of the Pyramids of Giza. Beyond lies **October 6th City,** one of Egypt's new planned cities designed to accommodate a share of the country's population. On the approach to Bahariyya, the entire landscape slurches into a deep shade of red. Vast deposits of iron here are quarried by an immense **iron mine** just off the highway 40km before Bawiti.

Heading southwest toward Farafra you leave the fertility of Bawiti behind. Look for the tiny oasis of **Al Hayz,** 45km to the southwest. The modern settlement (5km east of the main road on a gravel track) is a puny remnant of the sizable, prosperous community that flourished in early Christian times. About 2km down the gravel track from the main road lie sundry and substantial remains of an early **church** and **military camp.** (E£50 per truckload as a daytrip from Bawiti.)

The paved road from Bawiti to Farafra oasis (183km) features spectacular canyons, wind-blown mesas, rugged desertscape, and the roughest, dustiest, and most pock-marked surface of any route graced with the title "road." The precipitous eastern and western escarpments of the Bahariyyan depression meet at a point about 60km south of Bawiti. The road winds through this pass and onto a brief plateau, then plummets into the Farafra depression. Soon you'll enter the fantastic **White Desert,** where the wind has shaped mountains of chalk into giant white mushrooms, sphinxes, and riddling Rorschach-like psychedelia. Hotel managers in Farafra and Bahariyya arrange trips to the White Desert; see those sections.

■■■ FARAFRA واحة الفـرافـرة

With a population of 3000, Farafra is the smallest of Egypt's major oases, supporting only two extended families. The oasis is also one of Egypt's most photogenic: the explosion of lush foliage perches on a sloping hill like a bright green fortress. Tiny dirt paths tip-toe through the gardens behind Farafra's single immaculate settlement; nearby hot springs bubble through the desert floor.

Practical Information and Accommodations Currently, only one establishment accommodates guests in Farafra. Both the **Youth House** and the **government rest house** closed in 1994 for renovations. The brand-new **Tourist Rest House,** with clean rooms and baths (E£ 9.50) is about 1km up the road to Bahariyya from the café/bus station. **Camping** in the nearby desert is always an option; a campsite at Bir Sitta charges E£5 per day. You might also take up some of the locals on their offers of hospitality. Among the renovation activity is the **police station** and, 30m west, the **post office. Saad's Restaurant** by the government rest house, the **café** by the bus station, and **Husseini's Restaurant** in between offer omelettes (E£1), macaroni (E£2), *kufta, fuul,* etc.

There are **buses** from Dakhla (Thurs.-Tues., 5hrs., E£8) and to Dakhla (Mon., Wed., and Sat. 10am, Sun., Tues., and Fri. 4pm), as well as from Cairo (via Bahariyya, Sat., Mon., and Thurs. 9am, E£16; Tues. and Fri. 6am, E£14) and to Cairo (Sat., Mon., and Thurs. 10am; Tues., Fri., and Sun. 6am). Some people find hitchhiking to be a viable option; they wait near the military checkpoints outside of Dakhla, Farafra, or Bahariyya and make sure their ride is traveling all the way to their destination.

Sights In town, the **Art Museum,** the self-indulgent project of local artist Badr, displays his own expressive sculptures and paintings, many of which depict life in Farafra. Mounted local wildlife and an exhibit of Farafran artifacts complete the collection. The museum is near Saad's Restaurant, about 100m to the northwest behind a school; it's a mud-brick building with a decorated façade. (Open capriciously. Contributions welcome.) Many of Badr's murals also adorn the outside walls of local houses. In the middle of the village, 800m west of the café and the main road, a tepid **spring** gushes into a pool. Men can refresh themselves here, or wash their laundry surrounded by the stupendously scintillating stars. The hot **Well #6 (Bir Sitta),** 6km west of the Farafra town, is an idyllic spot to swim and camp (transportation about E£5 per person from town). **El Mufid,** a lake 10km from town, is just warm enough for swimming in summer. Hamdy, Sa'ad, or Atef Ali Muhammad, who operate from **Sa'ad's Restaurant,** will organize excursions by taxi, jeep, or camel.

THE ROAD TO DAKHLA

The 310km road from Farafra to Dakhla was constructed in 1982 but is rapidly deteriorating. Much of its foundation is made of chalky rock, heaped up to prevent the road itself and vehicles on it from slipping into the quicksand on either side: be careful where you step. Shifting dunes obscured the southern part of this road for years, making travel between Dakhla and Farafra an unpredictable undertaking. The road is now kept partially clear, but still sees markedly little traffic. Don't bank on receiving your American Express refund in these parts.

Ten kilometers south of Farafra is a tiny, uninhabited oasis officially considered part of the town. The villagers take care to cultivate the land here; occasionally a skein of sheeply farmers gambol across the road but otherwise the spot is deserted and quiet—and the best place in the area to pitch a tent. Still farther down the road toward Dakhla, about 50km from Farafra, is the diminutive, sparsely inhabited **Oasis of Sheikh Merzuq,** where you'll find a sulphur spring with a viaduct carrying water into a concrete pool. The pool is a refreshing spot for men to take a dip; women will have to settle for a sweat bath. The local Bedouin will show you the way to an ancient **Roman well,** where fresh water burbles from a deep spring. These watering holes can only be reached via private transport; the bus doesn't stop here.

■■■ DAKHLA الو حات الداخلة

Dakhla's fields, rice paddies, and fruit orchards stubbornly hold out against the harsh, engulfing desert. At two junctures the desert does indeed consume the greenery, segmenting Dakhla into three separate oases; but 65,000 Dakhlans are the clear victors in the struggles of water versus stone and farmer versus dune. Basking in government attention, the people of Dakhla have reclaimed this recalcitrant wasteland, planting peanuts and rice before introducing more fragile crops. The New Valley Project may have rendered the town of Kharga unappealing to visitors, but in Dakhla—dubbed the "pink oasis" for the pink cliffs jabbing the horizon—something of the opposite has occurred. While in Siwa and Farafra development seems to be enervating local culture, in Dakhla the oasians beam under broad-brimmed straw hats and share their infectious enthusiasm with visitors. In the villages around Mut, visitors will come closer to the traditional life of the oases prior to development than anywhere else in the New Valley.

ORIENTATION AND PRACTICAL INFORMATION

Farthest from Cairo of all the oases, Dakhla lies 310km from Farafra and 200km from Kharga. The center and capital of the oasis is **Mut** (pronounced "moot"), named for the Egyptian goddess married to Amun. **West Mawhub,** 80km west of Mut, and **Tineida,** 45km east of Mut, are smaller repositories of green at the edges of the oasis. Cultivated regions dot the main, well-paved highway. These areas are centered at **El Qasr,** 32km west of Mut; **Balaat** and **Bashendi,** 35-40km east of Mut; and Mut itself.

Life in Mut centers around Tahrir Square and New Mosque Square, 1km south along New Valley Street. Tahrir Sq. encompasses the intersection of New Valley St. and the Kharga-Farafra Highway, which runs southeast-northwest.

Tourist Information Office: Tel. 94 04 07. Currently located off of New Mosque Sq. but on the verge of moving to a new building located on the road to Farafra about 750m away from Tahrir Sq. Omar Ahmed speaks English and will go the distance to assist with practical matters including arranging transportation to sights. If he's not in, feel free to reach him at home (tel. 94 06 54). Open Sun.-Thurs. 8am-3pm and 7-11pm. Receptionist present 24 hrs.

Bank: Misr Bank, Tahrir Sq. (tel. 94 00 63), opposite the police station. Changes traveler's checks and cash. Open daily 8:30am-2pm and 6-9pm.

Post Office: New Mosque Sq.; branch on El Ganeim St., parallel to New Valley St. and 0.5km east, across from the telephone office. Both open Sat.-Thurs. 8am-2pm.

Telephone Office: El Ganeim St. From Hamdy Restaurant, on New Valley St., walk right (east) to Anwar Restaurant, then veer left. Calls within Egypt, and potluck international service. Open 24 hrs. **Telephone code:** 088.

Buses: Mut Station located in New Mosque Square. **Intercity buses** depart for Cairo (A/C, 6am, 5, and 7pm, 14hr., E£22-32, reservations should be made at least 1 day in advance), stopping in Kharga (all but the 7pm, E£6.50) and Assyut (E£14-17). Additional buses to Kharga and Assyut (8:30am, 2:30 and 4pm). On Sat., Mon., and Thurs., buses leave at 6am to Farafra (E£9), Bahariyya (E£14), and Cairo (E£23). Daily bus to Farafra at 4pm (E£9). Check the schedule at the bus station or the tourist office. **Local buses** run to eastern villages (7:30, 8:30am, and 2pm, Balaat and Bashendi 50pt, return to Mut 1hr. later) and western villages (10:30am and 2pm, El Qasr 25pt, return to Mut 2hr. later). Also, intercity buses to Farafra stop at El Qasr; to Kharga and beyond, at Balaat and Bashendi (E£1-2).

Taxis: Special sight-seeing tours E£30-35 for 1 day, E£8-10 for a trip to eastern or western Dakhla. Ask around New Mosque Sq. in Mut and bargain. Special to Kharga E£100. Covered pick-up trucks shuttle frequently between Tahrir Sq. and El Qasr and between the hospital stand and Balaat and Bashendi (50-75pt one way). Early morning is the best time to catch them.

Bicycle Rental: Nasser's Hotel (E£5 per day), **Abu Muhammad's Restaurant** (E£5), and the **Gardens Hotel** (E£7).

Gas Station: On the outskirts of eastern Mut, on the Kharga Hwy. Open 24 hrs.

Hospitals: Tel. 94 15 55, on the edge of Mut next to the gas station. **Ambulance:** Tel. 94 13 33. Smaller hospitals in each village.

Police: Tel. 94 15 00, in Tahrir Sq.

ACCOMMODATIONS

There are several hotels in Mut itself, all more than a little warm in summer.

Gardens Hotel (tel. 94 15 77), from the bus station, turn right at the mosque and continue one block; you'll find the hotel on your right. The best option in town, with clean, breezy rooms with fans, and a pleasant, palm-shaded garden out back. Singles E£10, with bath E£12. Doubles E£12, with bath E£16. Meals available.

Tourist Rest House (tel. 94 04 07), located in the same building as the Tourist Office off of New Mosque Sq., is cheaper (E£4.35 per person), but lacks the ambience and cleanliness of the Gardens.

Mebarez (tel. 94 15 24), on the edge of town, 700m from Tahrir Sq., on the road to Farafra, is more upscale, but has nothing to offer that can't be had for less at the Gardens. Single with shower and fan E£15. Breakfast E£3.50.

Nasser's Hotel, located 5km out of town on the road to Kharga, on the edge of a traditional farming village; it's surrounded by fields complete with waterwheels, water buffalo, and goats. Basic facilities, shared bathroom and kitchen. E£5 per person, no singles. Nasser speaks English and will arrange day or overnight trips by car, camel, donkey, or motorcycle to nearby villages, springs, and dunes not frequented by tourists (overnight camel trip E£75 each, food included, prices negotiable). To get to the hotel, find Nasser at Hamdy Restaurant (which he also runs), 500m from Tahrir Sq. on the road to Farafra.

Rest House (tel. 94 04 07), 3km out of town on the road to Farafra, next to the hot ferrous spring and murky pool, has inconsistently clean rooms with partially effective screens and private baths, but lacks the rural flavor of Nasser's Hotel.

FOOD

While it's not saying much, Dakhla probably has the best food in the oases. **Hamdy Restaurant,** several hundred meters down the Farafra Road, serves chicken or meat meals for about E£10. Around the corner from the Garden Hotel is **Anwar's Desert Paradise Restaurant** (full meal E£7.50). Along the highway, **Shehaab,** just west of New Valley St., is a local favorite (full meal E£5). **Abu Muhammad's Restaurant,** another 100m west, is the cleanest place in town, but all that soap and antiseptic has raised prices (meals around E£12). The comments book makes excellent reading.

SIGHTS

Don't linger in mangy Mut. The only sight is the **Dakhla Ethnographic Museum** (tel. 94 13 11; admission E£2), whose exhibits explain traditional oasis culture through a reconstruction of a typical Dakhlan family dwelling. Expressive clay figurines, created by Mabruk, an artist from the Kharga oasis, recreate scenes of village life, including the preparation of a bride for marriage and the celebration of a pilgrim's return from the *hajj.* The museum is located two blocks past Anwar's restaurant to the left of the fork. It is generally closed, but visits can be arranged by contacting the tourist office or by calling Ibrahim Kamel Abdallah, the museum's curator, at the Ministry of Culture office on New Valley St., near the cinema.

■ NEAR DAKHLA

EL QASR

Use the capital as a base for travel to the outlying villages. The most edifying daytrip is to the western village of **El Qasr,** 32km northwest of Mut on the main highway. The charming contemporary town was built in and around the substantial remains of Dakhla's medieval Islamic capital. Its mud buildings remain cool in summer and warm in winter. The **old village** of El Qasr lies slightly to the north (400m) of the main road through the new village. At the western edge of town on the main road is a large map of El Qasr, visible from the road. Underneath the map is a small exhibit on traditional Dakhlan culture. Within the old village itself, occasional arrows direct you to the main sights.

The **Minaret of Nasr ed-Din** (21m) is the only extant part of an 11th-century Ayyubid mosque built by Sheikh Nasr ed-Din. A 19th-century mosque surrounds the old tower. North of the minaret through the gnarled alleys is **Qasr Madrasa,** an intact two-story mud-brick building that is thought to have been either an Ayyubid schoolhouse or an entertainment hall for an Ottoman palace; to bungle matters further, villagers later used the building as a courtroom. Many of the doorways of the old village are adorned with ornate wooden lintels that reveal the name of the owner, builder, and carpenter as well as the date of construction. A pharaonic arch and a Roman doorway, a few doors away, hint at El Qasr's distant pre-Islamic past. On the southern fringes of the old town you can see a waterwheel and functioning **pottery works,** where the villagers churn out everything from ashtrays to chamberpots. If he gets wind of your arrival, Ahmed, the caretaker of these sights, will show you around town (*bakhsheesh* in the range of E£2-3 appropriate). A small **restaurant** on the main road at the eastern edge of El Qasr serves simple meals of cheese and hard-boiled eggs in summer and a more complete menu in winter.

Near El Qasr

Three other sights of interest are found near El Qasr but are beyond walking distance. 2.5km west on the main highway is the turn-off for **El Mousawaka Tombs.** The local bus to West Mawhub or a pick-up truck-taxi can drop you here. Head 1km south on the well-marked track to reach the guarded tombs, hewn into a rock outcropping. The two-chambered **Tomb of Petosiris** features brightly painted funerary scenes with a cast of characters that is half ancient Egyptian, half Greco-Roman. The ceiling is ablaze with Hellenistic angels, portraits of folks passed on, and an overwrought zodiac. The adjacent **Tomb of Sadosiris** features unusual images of a two-faced man simultaneously looking back at life and toward the after-life, a mummy carrier with wooden wheels, another zodiac, and a plethora of grapes. These are the two most interesting of hundreds of Greco-Roman tombs laid to rest in the immediate vicinity. They were closed for repairs during summer 1994; check with local tourist officials for an update (open 8am-3pm; admission E£8, students E£4).

Seven kilometers west of El Qasr (2km from Mousawaka turn-off), down the main road from El Qasr, is a dirt road which twists and turns around a small village before leading up to a ridge from which the Roman temple of **Deir el-Haggar** can be seen and reached; however, it is still another 1.5km off. Dedicated to the Theban triad of Mut, Amun, and Khonsu, it was originally built in the first century BCE during the reign of Nero and added to by his immediate successors. This too was closed for restoration in the summer of 1994. (Normally unguarded and free.) One kilometer east of El Qasr is the turn-off for **Bir el-Gabal,** a hot spring connected to the main highway by a 5km road. If you're dropped off by a pick-up or a public bus, you will have to walk, unless you're lucky enough to hitch a ride with some workers to the nearby quarry; the sight *is* accessible to automobiles. You'll arrive at a paradisiacal pool adorned with swarming insects and mysterious objects floating on the water's edge.

EASTERN DAKHLA

Returning to Mut, a 5km detour eastward at the Bedouin village of **Ed-Drous** will bring you to an **Islamic cemetery** which has been in use for several centuries. Even more stimulating is the distinctly medieval Islamic village of **Kalamoun,** located about 10km east of Mut. Unlike El Qasr and some other villages, it has not been designated as a tourist village or targeted by development plans (yet). Near the center lies an Ayyubid mosque which can be reached by winding through the maze of narrow villages and traditional mud brick houses. On the edge of town, the Islamic cemetery is dotted by domed mausolea built for the village's religious and political bigwigs. In the Islamic era, Kalamoun was an administrative center; its inhabitants claim Turkish and Mamluk ancestry. On the way back from the western sites, stop for a dip at the **Tourism Wells** (Bir et-Talata), where the rest houses are located (3km from downtown Mut). Hot spring water (42°C) has been tapped to fill two swimming pools, open to both sexes, before it flows into irrigation channels (free if you paid the tourism development tax; see Some Tips, p. 204).

Two historic villages on the eastern side of Mut may restore your faith in rural living. In the crowded old section of Islamic **Balaat** (pop. 5000), elongated dark passageways burst into a courtyard with palm fronds and grape vines. The unguarded red-brick tombs of **Ed-Daba,** still under excavation, inhere to lands 3km northeast of the main road, behind the village. Dakhla's pharaonic governors were buried here during the 6th dynasty. First walk 750m east from the official bus stop to a bantam military base, identifiable by its white stone columns; from there, walk 1km straight into the desert. The ongoing work of a team of French archaeologists has revealed several bizarre inverted step pyramids dating from the 6th dynasty.

Bashendi is 5km farther east (and 40km from Mut); the accomplishments of this "model village" have prompted cities everywhere to ask their village spawn, "Why can't you be more like Bashendi?" The village, named after an Ottoman sheikh whose name was the combination of the words *Pasha* (an Ottoman elitist title) and *Hindi* (meaning from India), lies on top of a recently discovered temple and various Roman-era tombs. The large stone **Tomb of Ketenus** contains four rooms, including one decorated with scenes of its 2nd-century Roman owner mingling with the gods Min and Seth. (The key is held by a villager whom locals will look for upon request. Admission E£8, students E£4.) Next door, the prominent **Tomb of Bashendi,** the base of which is a Roman foundation but whose domed roof is distinctly Islamic, commemorates the village's beloved namesake; you might join locals who decorate the inside of the holy man's tomb with *henna* in hopes of finding missing objects. If the guard isn't around to open the tombs, you may be invited in by a hospitable villager. There are also a number of hot and cold springs to which locals can direct you; the village leaders will inevitably direct you to the Bashendi **carpet works,** where local youths are trained to weave.

Despite its assortment of natural pyramids, the strip of desert along the **road to Kharga** has unusually little to inspire the muse. The rest house, at the midway point, doesn't even offer food. Crescent-shaped sand dunes creep across the road just outside Kharga, necessitating occasional detours.

■■■ KHARGA الخارجة

Egypt's most convincing attempt at a desert boomtown is the city of Kharga, capital of the New Valley Province (El Wadi El Gideed) and the most accessible and developed of all the Western Desert oases. Little is known about Kharga in early pharaonic times. It became prosperous during Roman times due to its proximity to trade routes including Darb El Arba'een, which later became the world's most important slave trade route. Beginning in the 4th century, Kharga became a large Christian settlement and center for monasticism as major figures, including Bishop Nastorius, former Patriarch of Constantinople, were banished here by religious and political rivals. The oasis' Australia-esque function as a distant exile continued into the 20th century when Gamal Abd en-Nasser banished Mustafa Amin, founder of Egypt's largest circulating daily, *Al-Akhbar,* to Kharga, after the 1952 revolution. When the New Valley Project was begun in earnest in the early 1980s, the town once again prospered. The greater Kharga population has now surpassed six figures. Modern Kharga, characterized by cookie-cutter apartments and large, empty streets, is a largely lifeless and boring town by Egyptian standards. Welcome (albeit temporary) relief from Kharga's New Town can be found in the narrow alleyways of the Old Town. Locally-made ceramics, carpets, and souvenir beef entrails and heads are available in the *souq* which begins at Showla Sq.

ORIENTATION

Of all the oases in Egypt's Western Desert, Kharga lies closest to the Nile Valley, 240km from Assyut via a passable road. The greenery begins about 20km north of the town of Kharga, the capital of the New Valley. A newly paved road heads south from Kharga, skirting sand dunes and small oases en route to **Bulaq** (15km south), **Baris** (90km south), and numerous smaller settlements in between.

In sprawling Kharga town, the main road is **Gamal Abd en-Nasser Street.** It becomes the road to Assyut at its northern end and intersects with the road to Dakhla several blocks south near Cinema Hibis. A few blocks farther south, Nasser St. intersects with **En-Nabawy el-Mohandis Street,** which connects New and Old Kharga, 3km to the southeast. **Esh-Showla Square,** the cynosure of Old Kharga, is linked to En-Nabawy St. by Port Said St. Convenient **covered truck-taxis** scurry between Showla Sq. and the Hotel El Kharga at the northern end of Nasser St. (10pt). The layout can be confusing at first, but Ibrahim at the tourist office will draw you a comprehensive map.

PRACTICAL INFORMATION

Tourist Information Office: Nasser St. (tel. 90 12 05), in the Modernist building with the off-white concrete canopy, in a square with modern statues at the northern end of Nasser St., just south of Hotel El Kharga. Open Sat.-Thurs. 8:30am-2pm. At least 2km away from the bus station, so grab a pick-up taxi (10pt).
Tourist Police: Tel. 90 15 02. Next to tourist office on Nasser St. Will provide tourist information if you can break the language barrier. Open 24 hrs.

Currency Exchange: Misr Bank, opposite Cinema Hibis. Exchanges cash only. **Cairo Bank,** 100m east of the 1st traffic circle south of the tourist office. Exchanges traveler's checks. Both open Mon.-Thurs. and Sat. 8:30am-2pm.

Post Office: Main office on Nasser St., behind Cinema Hibis. Another branch in Old Kharga's Showla Sq. Both open Sat.-Thurs. 8am-2pm.

Telephone and Telegram Office: Next to the main post office. Intermittent international service. Open 24 hrs. **Telephone Code:** 088.

Planes: On Sun. and Wed. from Cairo (6:30am) via Luxor to Kharga and back to Cairo (8:50am). Cairo-Kharga US$90, Luxor-Kharga US$71, or equivalent in E£ with receipt of exchange. Airport turn-off is 3km north of town on Assyut Rd., then another 2km southeast; minibus or shared taxi from Showla Sq. 50pt. EgyptAir office south of tourist office on Nasser St.; make reservations in advance.

Buses: Station in Showla Sq. To: Assyut (7 per day 5am-7pm, 4hr., E£7), Cairo (6, 9am, and 10pm, 10hr., morning buses E£17, evening buses E£20), Dakhla (7am and 1pm, a 4pm bus from Assyut and Cairo stops in Kharga en route to Dakhla, 3hr., E£6, most buses have no A/C), and Baris (noon and 2pm, 2hr., E£1.35).

Service Taxis: Opposite bus station. Fairly frequent service to **Assyut** (E£8). Occasionally to Dakhla (E£6). "Special" (unshared) to Dakhla, E£40. Irregular pick-ups to Baris (E£1-2). Pick-ups can be hired for E£50 per day, E£10 extra to Dush.

Hospital: Tel. 90 07 77. Main branch off Nasser St. south of En-Nabawy St. intersection. Open 24 hrs.

Police: Tel. 90 07 00. Opposite Tourist Office.

ACCOMMODATIONS AND FOOD

The two low-budget places in town are passable, if nothing more. The **Waha Hotel** (tel. 90 03 93) dominates the intersection of Nasser St. and En-Nabawy St. The floors and walls bear reminders of erstwhile clients, but the linen and bathrooms are clean. The luxury of a ceiling fan can be bought for the price of a room with bath (singles E£5, with bath E£10.50; doubles E£8, with bath E£14). **New Valley Tourist Homes,** July 23rd St. (tel. 90 07 28), is next to a large church, 200m west of Nasser St. The turn-off from Nasser St. is midway between the tourist office and a mosque; look for the sign facing north on Nasser St. Known as "Metalco" to locals, this hotel's 14 bungalows, surrounded by giant sunflowers, resemble barracks for migrant workers. (No water 11pm-5am. Simple rooms with semi-private baths E£5 per person.) Both the **Hamadulla Hotel** (tel. 90 06 38), 300m south of Nasser St. and 1km east of the tourist office, and the **Kharga Hotel** (tel. 90 15 00), at the northern end of Nasser St., cater to groups and offer over-priced beds and food (E£20 and up; the Kharga is slightly more expensive).

Kharga town serves mediocre oasis cuisine; you'll subsist on beans, chicken, and watermelon. The *souq* adjacent to Showla Sq. satisfies fresh produce cravings, and a **falafel** stand at the front of the *souq* supplies tasty sandwiches (25-30pt). **Restaurant** (no other English name) in Showla Sq. offers the usual Egyptian favorites: chicken, *kabab,* and *kufta* (E£2-5). Or try the hotels: Metalco serves iron meals if there's at least a handful of hungry tourists around (breakfast E£2, dinner E£3); a calm café beneath the Waha Hotel offers standard inexpensive Egyptian lunches and dinners (E£1-7). The Kharga Hotel serves similar meals but with higher prices, slower service, and alcoholic accompaniment (cold Stella E£4.25). The kitchen was practically closed in summer 1994.

SIGHTS

The *pièce de resistance* of the New Valley's tourism drive is the spanking new **Museum of Antiquities,** on Nasser St. 500m south of the tourist office. Displays illuminate oasis history. (Open Sat.-Thurs. 8am-2pm. Admission E£10, students E£5.)

Kharga's important ruins cluster at the northern end of town. A shared covered taxi will take you as far as the Hotel El Kharga (possibly farther), whence you can walk to the sites. The **Temple of Hibis,** 2km north of the Hotel El Kharga and close to the road on the left, was begun in 588 BCE by Apnias of the 26th dynasty and completed by Darius I in 522 BCE, making it one of only two Persian-built Egyptian temples (the other was also in Kharga). While dedicated to the Theban triad of Amun, Mut, and Khonsu, the temple is distinguished by its depictions of Persians and god of the Oases, Seth (blue body, falcon head). First-century Roman inscriptions discuss legal issues including women's rights. Free but for *bakhsheesh.* Across the road to the southeast, the **Temple of Nadura,** built in the second century BCE during the reign of Roman Emperor Antonius, crowns a knoll. Little of it still stands, but the site exudes an exemplary view of the oasis.

The spooky 263 above-ground tombs (also called chapels) of the Christian **Necropolis of El Bagawat** stand at the desert's edge, 500m past Hibis Temple on the road to Assyut. From the third to eighth centuries CE, a sizable Christian community, including many hermits and some of the religion's earliest monks, inhabited Kharga. Most fled or were exiled during the divisive fourth and fifth centuries, when Constantinople attempted to force the Melkite doctrine, which held that Jesus was not always of the same essence as the Father, on Egypt. Egypt clung to the original Monophysite position, holding that Jesus was of the same essence as the Father when begotten by the Father. This doctrine had been put forth by Athanasios, an Egyptian exiled to Kharga, at the first great Christian Council at Nicea in 325. The necropolis is visible from the road, and an asphalt path leads to the ticket booth. If you go up the hill along the marked path, you'll come to the **Chapel of Exodus.** Inside, the ceiling mural depicts the pharaoh's Roman-looking army chasing the Jews as they flee from Egypt. Other scenes show Adam and Eve and *ankh*-like crosses. In front of the Chapel of Exodus are the interconnected chapels #23-25. Down the hill and up the path on the right stands the **Chapel of Peace** (#80). The interior frescoes of biblical scenes exemplify Coptic painting of the early Alexandrian style. Greek inscriptions identify Adam and Eve, Noah's Ark, and the Virgin Mary. Atop the cemetery's central hill are the remains of a 4th-century mud-brick basilica. (Open 8am-6pm, off-season 8am-5pm. Admission E£10, students E£5.)

THE ROADS TO BARIS AND ASSYUT

If you've got time to spare, take the road along the old 40-day camel trail south to Baris. This legendary caravan route (known as Darb El Arba'een, or Forty Days Road) extended from the western Sudan all the way to the Egyptian Nile Valley and trafficked more slaves than any other land route in the world, making the Kharga region strategically important ever since pharaonic times.

Vast sandscapes are all that thrive between Kharga and **Khwita Temple,** 17km to the south. The impressive 10m walls of the temple-*cum*-fortress command a hill 2km east of the road. The temple, dedicated to Amun, Mut, and Khonsu, and built by Darius I with later Ptolemaic additions, was once the center of a thriving community famous in pharaonic times for its grape production. The site was later used to garrison troops for guarding the caravan route; today, remnants of the fortress surround the temple itself. (Open 8am-6pm. Admission E£8, students E£4.) At the 25km mark you'll come across shaded **Nasser Wells** and farther on, the better-developed **Bulaq Wells,** which offer a modern government-run **rest house** (beds E£4.25) and hot springs that encourage participants to let off steam. Nasser Wells spew forth ferrous water, so the pools are full of precipitated iron oxide, glooping gelatinously toward swimmers. **Zayan Temple,** dedicated to Amun, is 5km east of Nasser Wells near the village of Araf, on a road that loops around from the north of Khwita Temple to a point north of Bulaq. Originally built in the Ptolemaic era, it was restored by the Romans who used the site, like Khwita, to build a fortress of which there are still substantial remains. (Open 8am-6pm. Admission E£8, students E£4.)

The secluded village of **Baris** (known locally as Paris-on-the-Pond) is 90km south of Kharga. Merchants make a 40-day camel trek from here to the border of Chad to purchase an ingredient used in local soap. It is estimated that each expedition brings the merchant E£20,000 in profit. Think twice before going into business for yourself, however, since only one family in town is privy to the location of vital water wells en route. There is a government **rest house** north of town, but no sign to mark it; look for the yellow, grey, and red buildings, in a row perpendicular to the highway, about 500m north of the *"Bienvenue à Paris/Au Revoir"* sign. You can arrange your stay through the manager, whose office is in the town on the road to Dush, across from the police station (beds E£3.50). Half a dozen small **kiosks** sell soda, mineral water, and canned goods. The blue structure resembling a doghouse sells *kabab, fuul,* and falafel every day except Friday.

Designed by modern Egyptian architect Hassan Fathy, who utilizes the cooling properties of traditional oasis architecture in his work, a public housing complex stands 300m northwest of the rest house. Sponsored by the government, construction was halted during the 1967 war with Israel and never resumed; the government decided that villagers would not want to live in buildings that resemble tombs.

A recently paved road leads 23km southeast to the **Dush Temple,** which has an overabundance of heat and isolation. The temple, originally built for the worship of Serapis and Isis, dates back to the Roman emperors Trajan and Hadrian and is under excavation. The sand is slowly parting, revealing a church and a well with clay pipes leading to an underground city. Pottery shards litter the site. All signs indicate that Dush was once a prosperous area, eventually abandoned as a result of well desiccation. The temple is the tallest structure for miles around.

The easiest way to get to these sights is to hire a **pick-up taxi** for a day from Kharga, but that's an expensive proposition (E£50-80), unless you have several people. **Hitchhiking** can be difficult and dangerous—the road is sparsely traveled, especially beyond Baris. Plenty of shared taxis go from Kharga as far as Bulaq (50pt). Catch them at the southern end of Nasser St. Each day, two **buses** go to Baris (2hr., E£1.50) and two return. The 2pm bus to Baris sometimes continues on to Dush (2½hr. from Kharga; E£1.50) but doesn't return until the next morning (6am). Drivers in Baris will make a special round trip to Dush for E£20 (waiting included), but are sometimes tough to find. For public transportation to Zayan Temple, hop on a pick-up or public bus headed for Baris and have the driver drop you off on the way.

Adventurers may want to take the road from Baris to Luxor—it's not paved all the way, but reportedly will be soon. No public transportation travels this road, and a police permit is required for private cars. Consult the tourist office for information.

The 240km **road to Assyut** passes through endless miles of monotonous desert that do little to inspire consciousness. The town of Kharga is surrounded by a moonscape of rock outcroppings. As you leave, it becomes evident that the oasis tangos in the middle of a 200-sq.-km depression. For those raised on Hollywood imagery, the Western Desert here is a letdown: none of your cactus-and-tumbleweed scenery, not even any of those awesome, towering sand dunes. Imagine five million disused dirt lots placed end-to-end. The **Al-Obbur Rest House,** replete with water and refreshments, is located halfway to Assyut.

■ Suez Canal قناة السويس

The strategically located Suez Canal is a miracle of 19th-century engineering, but the idea for the canal was introduced much earlier. In the 18th century, Napoleon Bonaparte considered digging a canal between the Mediterranean and the Red Sea but feared that the waters of the Red Sea were higher than those of the Mediterranean, which would cause extensive flooding in Lower Egypt. Though Napoleon gave up on his idea, a French engineer, Ferdinand de Lesseps, came up with a similar plan and persuaded Said Pasha, the Khedive of Egypt, to start digging on April 25, 1859. The canal was opened ten years later, on November 18, 1869.

The Suez Canal stretches, without locks and at a depth of up to 15m, from Port Said on the Mediterranean, past Ismailiyya, to Suez on the Red Sea (195km all told). It is an efficiency expert's dream: the distance from Jeddah in Saudi Arabia to the Black Sea is 19654km around Africa, but only 3327km through the Suez Canal.

Because it allowed for rapid travel from Europe to the Indian Ocean, the canal became a crucial element in the infrastructure of the British Empire. Nasser nationalized the canal in 1956; Israel, and later Britain and France, responded with a U.N.-censured attack. During the 1967 War with Israel, Nasser blocked the canal with sunken ships. It remained closed through the 1973 War, and was reopened in 1975.

The Suez Canal's business has traditionally been business, not tourism. But Port Said's shopping, Ismailiyya's attractive beaches, and Suez's proximity to 'Ain Sukhna have turned them into up-and-coming tourist towns, mostly for Egyptians. Get there before the hordes do.

■■■ PORT SAID بور سعيد

Port Said (Bur Sa'id), the northeasternmost point on the African continent, was founded in 1860. With the building of the Suez Canal, the port gained importance as Africa's gateway to the Mediterranean. Port Said was declared a tax-free zone in 1976 and has since evolved into a shopping resort, with thousands of Egyptians exploding into town every year in a virtual shopping frenzy. Perhaps to occupy shoppers on Fridays, the government has made an effort to develop Port Said as a beach resort, an alternative to the increasingly packed shores of Alexandria. Add to this the visual interest of the rows of tankers, freighters, and cruise ships that dock next to the white colonnade of the port authority (where the canal widens to flow into the Mediterranean), Port Said's proximity to Cairo, and its pleasant weather, and you have the busiest and most interesting of the Suez Canal cities.

Orientation and Practical Information The Suez Canal and the Mediterranean beaches run at a 45° angle to each other, joining at the town's northeast edge. If you've spent any time in Egypt you've probably guessed that the street running along the sea is called the **corniche. Palestine Street** follows the canal. **Goumhouriyya St.** (spelled El Gamhoria on the tourist office map) runs parallel to Palestine St., two blocks inland. Another important thoroughfare, **July 23rd St.,** runs east-west about 4 blocks south of the corniche.

Two blocks from the southwest end of Palestine St. is the **tourist office** (tel. 23 52 89; open Sat.-Thurs. 9am-1:30pm and 4-8pm), which provides a very good map of the city including a map of Suez on the back. The **tourist police** (tel. 22 85 70) are located in the customs building, also at the southwest end of Palestine St.; there is another branch office in the train station. (Both open 24 hrs.) There are a number of small, reputable **currency exchange** offices around town. The most conveniently located is **Thomas Cook,** 43 Goumhouriyya St. (tel. 27 75 59; fax 23 61 11; open daily 9am-6pm). The **Bank of Alexandria** (tel. 22 28 81 or 23 60 94) also on Goumhouriyya St. will exchange foreign currency, and **Menatours,** 18 Goumhouriyya St. (tel. 22 57 42), serves as an **American Express** office. The emergency phone number for the **police** is 122; for general **medical emergencies,** dial 123.

Port Said's **post office** (open Sat.-Thurs. 9am-2pm) for **Poste Restante** is at the southeast corner of the Ferial Gardens. To get to Ferial Gardens, walk three blocks along the canal from the tourist office on Palestine St. Take a left on Muhammad Mahmoud St. and continue to its intersection with El Geish St. The **telephone office** (tel. 16) is about halfway up Palestine St. (Open 24 hrs.) **Telephone code:** 048. Port Said's most modern hospital is **Al-Mabarrah Hospital,** at the western end of July 23rd St. (tel. 22 05 60). The **Et-Tadaman Hospital** also serves tourists (tel. 22 17 90). **El-Isaaf Pharmacy** (tel. 22 79 19), on Safia Zaghloul St., one block past its intersection with El Shohadaa St., is open 24 hours.

Port Said is 343km east of Alexandria and 220km northeast of Cairo. The **West Delta Bus Company** (tel. 22 68 83) depot is located on Salah ad-Din St., on the western side of Ferial Gardens, two blocks west of Goumhouriyya St. It runs daily buses to Cairo (every hr. 6am-7pm, E£10-12), Alexandria (7, 10am, 1:30, and 4:30pm, E£11-15), Ismailiyya (every hr. 6am-6pm, 1½hr., E£4), and Suez (6, 10am, 1, and 4pm, E£6.50). The **Superjet** bus depot is next to the train station at the southwest end of Goumhouriyya St., with buses to Cairo (every hr. 7am-6pm, E£13). **Service taxis** (ask for *taxi ugra*) also run to and from Port Said. The taxi stand is located near the train station and the Superjet depot. *Service* within town should cost 25pt per hour; a microbus can be rented for E£5 per hour. To reach the **train station**, go to the southwest end of Goumhouriyya St. and turn right onto Mustafa Kamel St. The station is about 1km down, on your left; trains go to Cairo (via Ismailiyya; 4 per day; 4½hr.; 2nd-class E£7.50, with A/C E£13) and Ismailiyya (3 per day; 2nd-class E£1.70, with A/C E£4.20). No trains go directly to Alexandria, so go through Cairo.

Accommodations and Food Most of the accommodations in town are either on or just off of Goumhouriyya St., which is parallel to Palestine St. two blocks inland. Two blocks from the southern end of Goumhouriyya St. is the **Akri Palace Hotel** (tel. 22 80 13), 24 Goumhouriyya St., run by the Greek Nicolandis brothers. Rooms have old-fashioned iron bedstead and some feature a (rather distant) view of the canal. Ask for a balcony. (Singles E£9, doubles E£15, triples E£18; add E£3 for private bath.) A good breakfast (not included) is served in the 4th-floor restaurant. About halfway up Goumhouriyya St. is the enormous **Hotel de la Poste** (tel. 22 96 55 or 22 99 94), which has classy rooms with hardwood floors and all the amenities—TV, fridge, balcony, A/C, and bath. (Singles E£27, facing the street E£33; doubles E£33, facing the street E£40; triples E£44; meals in the restaurant E£15-20.) Splurge for a room with a view of Goumhouriyya St. Opposite the Port Said stadium on the corner of New Corniche and El Amin St. is the clean but dark **HI youth hostel** (tel. 22 87 02; dorm beds E£3.25, nonmembers E£1 extra).

Popeye's Café (tel. 23 94 94; opposite Hôtel de la Poste) is overpriced (dishes E£18-25), but the setting at the corner of Goumhouriyya and Safia Zaghloul St. is great: sit outside for refreshing breezes and the sounds of Latifah and Amr Diab. (Open daily 8am-midnight.) Farther north is the **Galal Restaurant**, 60 El Goumhouriyya St. (tel. 22 96 68), with standard Egyptian food at reasonable prices. Have a Stella and a *kufta* sandwich (E£1). Seafood dishes cost E£15; make the most of your money by sitting outside, facing the street. Ignore or befriend the large plastic crustaceans above your table. (Open daily 7am-1am; closed during Ramadan; Visa accepted.) **Restaurant Soufer** (tel. 22 43 95), just past the Akri Hotel on Degla St. off Goumhouriyya St., offers a tremendous variety of seafood. Try the shrimp platters (E£10-12), the *kusa bil laban* (E£9), or *kobeba bit tahina* (E£7). (Open daily 8am-midnight; during Ramadan 8am-11pm.) Just outside the Hôtel de la Poste is the **Restaurant Lourdat** (tel. 22 99 94), good for a *shawerma* sandwich (E£1.25) or an omelette (E£1.50). (Open daily 8am-midnight.)

The best way to enjoy the canal is from the **Noras** floating restaurant (tel. 32 68 04); cruises leave daily at 3 and 6pm. The minimum charge is E£2, drinks run around E£10, and an elaborate lunch or dinner is E£30. The boat departs from Palestine St. at the corner of July 23rd St. across from the Port Said National Museum.

Sights The **Port Said National Museum,** at the north end of Palestine St., houses an impressive olio of Egyptian historical artifacts ranging from ornately painted sarcophagi to Muhammad Ali's horse carriage. It's cool and usually empty, perfect for casual browsing. (Open Sat.-Thurs. 9am-4pm, Fri. 9am-noon and 2-4pm; Ramadan 8:30am-1pm. Admission E£6, students E£3, camera privileges E£5.) Port Said's **Military Museum** (tel. 22 46 57), west of the obelisk on July 23rd St. (tel. 22 46 57), has dioramas of pharaonic and Islamic battles but concentrates on Egyptian victories in the 1973 Arab-Israeli War. (Open Sat.-Thurs. 9am-2pm, 7:30pm-8:30pm, and Fri. 10am-1pm. Admission E£2.) In front of the museum, the **beach** extends east to the canal. Beach chairs and umbrellas can be rented, and showers are located every 100m along the beach. Take advantage of the free **ferry ride** across the canal to **Port Fouad.** The crossing affords you a good view and the chance to wander around the less mobbed shops of the smaller port. To catch the ferry, walk to the southern end of Palestine St. across from the tourist office.

■■■ ISMAILIYYA الاسماعيلية

Once known as Timsah (crocodile) Village, Ismailiyya is named after Khedive Ismail of Egypt. Situated halfway between Port Said and Suez, it is considered the capital of the Suez Canal District. Surprisingly, this tiny, tranquil town of tree-lined boulevards is home to a tremendous canal trade and over 50,000 people. Heavily damaged during the Arab-Israeli Wars of 1967 and 1973, Ismailiyya has been completely rebuilt. During the construction of the canal, tremendous care was taken to retain the town's provincial charm. Wander through quiet, shaded avenues, relax in the sprawling gardens in the middle of town, or hit the beaches at nearby **Lake Timsah** (Crocodile Lake—just a name, not a warning) or the **Bitter** (El-Morra) **Lakes.**

Practical Information The city's main road runs diagonally southeast from the **train station** (tel. 22 41 13) at Orabi Sq. to the Ismailiyya Canal via Goumhouriyya Sq. Many of Ismailiyya's restaurants, hotels, and shops are on Sultan Hussein St., which trots north-south about five blocks east of Orabi Sq. From the train station, exit to your right and walk until you reach the level crossing; turn right and the **bus station** (tel. 22 24 23) will be 100m on your right. The **post office** (open Sat.-Thurs. 8am-4pm; closed on holidays) and the **telecommunications office** (tel. 22 41 61; open 24 hrs.) are both on Orabi Sq. (For **general information,** dial 16. **Telephone Code:** 064) The **police station** (tel. 32 10 71, ext. 306) is in the Governorate Building along the canal on Salah Salem St., two blocks south of Goumhouriyya Sq. The **tourist office,** located in the Governorate Building on Salah Salem St., sells booklets (*Ismailiyya Tourist Guide*) for E£11. The *Guide* has some useful information and phone numbers, but the map in it is useless.

The easiest place to **change money** is at the **Bank of Alexandria** on the eastern side of Orabi Sq. next to Bank Misr (National Bank of Egypt). The **general hospital** is appropriately located on Hospital St. in the El Arishayat Masr district (tel. 22 20 46 or 47; open 24 hrs.). Dial 123, or 22 31 03 for an **ambulance.** For minor maladies, go to the **Ismailiyya Pharmacy,** run by Dr. Kamel Sa'ad, at 24 Sultan Hussein St. (tel. 22 93 19; open daily 9am-2pm and 6-11pm). **Menatours** on 12 Sultan Hussein St. (tel. 32 43 61), next to Groppi, provides all **American Express** services for members and non-members (open 9am-2pm and 6-9pm).

Midway along the Suez Canal, Ismailiyya is linked by road and the Ismailiyya Canal to the Delta, and by highway and railroad to Cairo (140km) and Alexandria (280km). **West Delta Bus Company** runs daily buses to Cairo (every 45min. 6:30am-7pm, E£5.25-5.75), Alexandria (7am-2:30pm, E£10-12), and El Arish (7am, 2:30, 3:30, 7pm; E£6.25), with frequent departures to Port Said (E£4) and Suez (E£3). You can also get to Cairo by **train** (6 per day; 2nd class E£3.40, with A/C E£9). **Service taxis** depart from opposite the bus station, with frequent and fast service to Cairo (E£4.50), Port Said (E£3), and El Arish (E£6).

Accommodations and Food The brand-new 266-room **Ismailiyya Youth Hostel (HI)** (tel./fax 32 28 50) on Beaches Ave. overlooks Timsah Lake and is the biggest youth hostel in the Middle East. (Singles E£8, doubles, and triples all include breakfast and private bath. Non-members E£1 extra. HI memberships E£20, ages 5-21 E£10.) The **Nefertari Hotel,** 41 Sultan Hussein St. (tel. 32 28 22), three blocks north of Bank Misr, offers budget elegance with a restaurant and bar, clean bathrooms, pastel furniture, and some rooms with A/C. A live band entertains guests nightly. (Singles E£15, with bath E£20. Doubles E£25, with bath E£28. Extra beds E£5 each. Breakfast E£2.10, lunch E£4.85, and dinner E£5.30.) Another popular bargain is the **Isis Hotel** (tel. 22 78 21), with checkered floors, comfortable rooms, fans, and spotless bathrooms. (Singles E£9, with bath E£13. Doubles E£12, with bath E£20. Breakfast in the cafeteria E£3.) Purchase your fare from street vendors or try **Nefertiti's** on Sultan Hussein St. (tel. 22 04 94), south of the Nefertari Hotel. Nefertiti specializes in fish (E£12), but serves meat dishes (E£10) and delicious shrimp (E£25). (Alcohol available. AmEx.) For dessert, **Groppi's** (tel. 32 82 28), across the street, serves tempting pastries for E£1.25. (Open Sat.-Thurs. 9:30am-9:30pm; closed the first half of Ramadan.) Signs throughout the city tout the **King Edward Restaurant** on 171 Tahrir St. (tel. 32 54 51), where the food is more expensive than at Nefertiti's (entrees E£15-20), but where beer and 51 channels (yes, MTV *is* included) carry a powerful magnetic force. (AmEx, Visa.)

Sights and Entertainment If the beaches on Lake Timsah are too calm for you, indulge in **water sports** at one of the tourist villages (El-Fayrouz tel. 32 76 20 or 22 03 88; El Melaha tel. 22 72 24; El Bahary tel. 22 09 25). All are on **Beaches Avenue.** Or venture south to the beaches on the **Bitter Lakes** and to the town of **Fayed**, 33km south of Ismailiyya.

The **Ismailiyya Regional Museum,** near the canal at the northern end of town, has pharaonic, Islamic, and Roman collections (open Wed.-Mon. 9am-3pm; admission E£3, students E£1.50). Near the museum, the **Garden of the Stelae** contains sphinxes from the age of Ramses II. Inquire at the museum entrance for permission to visit. The **De Lesseps Museum,** on Salah Salem St., is housed in the engineer's former home and displays his personal belongings. Cool down in the **Mallaha Park,** 210 hectares of rare flowers, trees, and palms.

■ ■ ■ SUEZ السويس

Located at the junction of the Red Sea and the Suez Canal, Suez (Es-Suweis) counts as its main attractions the Gulf of Suez and, you guessed it, the canal. The ugly city itself holds just about nothing of interest, though its people carry a strange air of wealth which sets them apart from the rest of Egypt. Don't get too close, however: they also have claws and fangs. Perhaps it's the city's super-strategic location and historic role as a favorite target for foreign missiles that set the residents of Suez on edge. Who really cares? Most travelers simply hold (or thumb) their noses while passing through Suez en route from Cairo to the Sinai, by way of the Ahmed Hamdi tunnel (running under the canal 30km north of town), or on their way south along the Red Sea coast. Nearby **'Ain Sukhna,** however, is quite beautiful; and its proximity to Cairo makes it a viable sun-swim-snorkel option for those either too lazy or too pressed for time to just bag it and go to Hurghada.

Orientation and Practical Information Suez is centered on **El Geish Street,** running east-west from the **bus station** and across the canal to **Port Tawfik**, where the **tourist office** is located. The **tourist police** (tel. 211 40) are in the station (open daily 3-6pm). **Service taxis** gather a street over from the buses. The **train station** is about 4km farther west at the end of El Geish. **American Express** services are at **Menatours** (tel. 22 88 21) in Port Tawfik (see minibus information, below). The **Bank of Alexandria,** near the bus station, exchanges currency daily 8am-2pm and 6-9pm in winter, 5-8pm in summer. The **Bank Misr** is south of El Geish St.; it's on a side street under the Misr Palace Hotel, opposite the Bel Air Hotel. The **post office** is on Hoda Sha'rawi St., parallel to El Geish and one block north (open Sat.-Thurs. 8am-3pm). The **telecommunications office** (open 8am-midnight) is about three blocks south of El Geish on the corner of Shohadaa and Sa'ad Zaghloul St., on the same side street as Bank Misr (open 8am-midnight). **Telephone Code:** 062.

Buses shuttle from Suez to Cairo (every ½hr. 6am-5pm, thereafter every hr. until 8pm; E£4.50, E£5 with A/C) and Ismailiyya (every 15min. 6am-6pm, E£3), and through Cairo to Alexandria (9 and 11am, 5hr., E£11-12). There are buses for Port Said (4 per day, last bus 3:30pm, E£6.50), Hurghada over the Red Sea Highway (5 per day, last bus 6pm, 6hr., E£12-15), 'Ain Sukhna (every 2hr. 6am-2pm, E£1.25-1.75), Uyoun Mussa, Ras Sidr, and Hammam Fara'on. Tickets to Hurghada and Alexandria should be reserved a couple of days in advance. **Service taxis** travel these routes (except for Alexandria) at similar prices (Cairo E£4.50, Port Said E£7, Ismailiyya E£3, Hurghada E£20). Often they depart more frequently than the buses, but don't expect A/C. **Taxis** to the Sinai are generally expensive; you're better off taking a bus. Many cities are also accessible by **train** (50pt) but the coaches are hot and uncomfortable. Six trains per day to Cairo (E£1-3) and Ismailiyya (90pt).

Suez is the main launching ground for forays into the **Sinai.** Buses run daily to Sharm esh-Sheikh (11am, 12:30, 3pm, E£12), St. Catherine's (2pm, E£14), Dahab (12:30pm, E£16), Nuweiba' (noon and 3pm, E£20), and Taba (3pm, E£17).

For transport within the city, exit the bus station and go behind the row of food stands facing it. **Minibus** drivers will be yelling out their destinations; the Port Tawfik minibus takes you straight over the canal (50pt).

Accommodations and Food The clean **HI youth hostel** (tel. 22 19 45) is on Salah Naseem St., opposite the stadium. From El Geish, take a right off Sa'ad Zaghloul St., between the Misr Palace and Bel Air hotels, then take a right on El Galaa, which becomes Salah Naseem. You may want to take a private taxi (no more than E£3). (No sheets provided. Curfew 11pm. One fan per room. Dorm beds (12 per room) E£3, nonmembers E£3.50.) The **Misr Palace,** 2 Sa'ad Zaghloul St. (tel. 22 30 31), six blocks east of the bus station, has cheap, dirt-free, furniture-free, and fan-free rooms. Don't get too excited about the sign for a Korean restaurant—it's been out of business since stegosaurus DNA was last trapped in amber. (Singles E£9, with bath E£11. Doubles E£13, with bath E£19. A/C E£5, fans E£1.50, TV E£2. Breakfast E£3.) Around the corner from the "Palace" hides the more comfortable **Hotel Sina,** 21 Bank Misr St. (tel. 22 03 94). Rooms have ceiling fans, TVs, and phones; there is a refrigerator on each floor. (Singles E£12.30. Doubles E£16.80. Triples with bath E£21.30. Some have A/C for E£5 extra. Breakfast E£3.) The friendly **Star Hotel,** 17 Bank Misr St. (tel. 22 87 37), has large spotless rooms, all with fans. (Singles E£9, with bath E£12. Doubles E£12, with bath E£15. Triples E£18. Breakfast E£3.)

On the culinary front, stick with fish, the one thing guaranteed to be somewhat fresh and tasty. The *qahwa* of choice is the **El Tayib Coffee Shop** on Hoda Sha'rawi St. (tel. 22 59 88), four blocks west of the post office. Fresh orange juice will relieve you of E£1, excellent baked macaroni a mere 75pt. Have a *sheesha* and one of their typically Egyptian drinks (*sahlab, 'irek suus,* tea, and the like). (Open daily 7am-3pm and 4pm-midnight.) A pink, yellow, and blue sign on El Geish before the Bel Air marks **Sweet Spot,** a wicked cheap sandwich, *shawerma,* and sweets spot (awesome baked macaroni in *béchamel* sauce, green salad, and soda E£1.45). **Food stands** lurk near the bus stop; a **souq** is on the same street, just across El Geish St.

Sights The only monuments in town are three American-made tanks on the corniche, captured from Israel in 1973. The beach at **'Ain Sukhna** (Hot Spring), 55km south along the Red Sea, rivals those of the Sinai. **Buses** run there early in the day (6:30, 10am, and 2pm; E£1.75), and return roughly 1½ hours later (thus, the last bus back to Suez is at 3:30pm or so). **Service** also run down the coast from Suez to 'Ain Sukhna. The trip is definitely worthwhile; the hot spring (35°C), originating in the Ataka Mountains, is an attractive place for snorkeling, diving, or just lying on the beach. 'Ain Sukhna offers many of the same things as Hurghada, but remains relatively undiscovered. One thing it does not offer is affordable accommodations. The **'Ain Sukhna Hotel** (tel. 77 23 67 or 77 18 10) sells a day-ticket (E£15) that provides you with chairs and umbrellas. (Cabin for 2 E£80. Chalets and doubles E£110 each. Small student discounts.) The water is unbelievably clear, and you can sit anywhere on the beach. You'll pay a E£15 day-use fee in front of the 'Ain Sukhna Hotel or the **Mena Oasis.** The coral reefs and a small spring-fed waterfall are north of the beach.

Red Sea Coast

■■■ MONASTERIES OF ST. PAUL AND ST. ANTHONY

The isolated monasteries of St. Paul and St. Anthony lie 30km apart (82km by road) near the Red Sea. These centers of faith, dating from the early Christian monastic tradition, are inhabited by monks whose austere lifestyle differs remarkably little from that of 16 centuries ago. You had better be serious if you want to reach the monasteries. Direct access is limited to private cars and tour buses from Cairo. The Cairo-Hurghada bus makes a stop at **Ras Za'farana,** about 33km east of the turn-off to St. Anthony's (Deir Anba Anton), which is on the road from Ras Za'farna to Beni Suef. St. Paul's Monastery (Deir Anba Boutrous) is tucked in the mountains 12km inland from the coastal road, a 1½-hour drive from St. Anthony's. Don't count on catching a ride with a passing brother. A group of seven can hire a taxi from Suez or Hurghada. If you negotiate with the taxi driver directly, expect to pay a total of E£110 for both monasteries. Travel agencies can arrange the trip starting at E£180.

Still another way to reach the monasteries is to join a church expedition. For further information in Cairo, contact the monasteries' administration office (tel. (02) 90 60 25) or the YMCA, 27 El Goumhouriyya St. (tel. (02) 91 73 60). The former sends a car to the monasteries every week. Note that you *must* have a letter of recommendation from the administration office in Cairo in order to stay overnight at either of the two monasteries (tel. 90 02 18). Only men can stay at St. Anthony's; St. Paul's accommodates both men and women, with permission. The monks provide food and water. (Both monasteries open 9am-5pm.)

St. Anthony, raised in the Nile Valley, scorned worldly concerns and retreated into the Eastern Desert, where he became the first famous ascetic of the Christian Church. Anthony's dramatic move reflected the restlessness that overtook some Christians in the 4th century CE when Constantine made Christianity the official religion of the Roman Empire. This was a disturbing development for many who felt that the church had gained worldly security and wealth at the expense of its spiritual focus. In Egypt, some of these Christians, mostly educated middle-class men, sought to escape the secular world by going to the desert where they could pray in solitude and dedicate their lives to God, not Caesar.

St. Anthony suffered paradoxically; his desert hermitages became popular pilgrimage sites, and crowds of the pious and the curious deprived the recluse of precious penitent isolation. Icons of hirsute Antonius adorn the walls of many Coptic churches in Egypt. Soon after the saint's death, his disciple St. Athanasius told the story of his choice of poverty and hardship, his wild battles with demons, and his wise counsel to monks and layfolk. Athanasius' *Life of Anthony* became the prototype for most later Christian hagiography.

A few years after St. Anthony's death, his followers settled at the present site and established the first Christian monastery. The Monastery of St. Anthony served as a refuge for some of the monks of Wadi Natrun when their own sanctuaries were attacked by Bedouin in the 6th century. During the 7th and 8th centuries the monastery was occupied by Melkite monks, and in the 11th it was pillaged by the army of Nasr ed-Dawla. About 100 years after the sacking, it was restored and transferred to Coptic hands. The **Church of St. Anthony** and the southern walls are the only remains predating the 16th-century construction of the present monastery.

The Church of St. Anthony is divided into five parts: the haikal, the passage in front of the haikal, the nave, the narthex, and the small chapel at the southwest corner of the church. Ancient frescoes embellish each of the sections. East of the Church of St. Anthony, the Church of the Apostles contains three haikals. During Lent, the monks cantellate the liturgy in the 18th-century Church of St. Mark. As in the Wadi en-Natrun monasteries, the Chapel of St. Michael is on the top floor of the keep. The impressive library contains more than 1700 manuscripts.

The major religious attraction in the vicinity of the church is the **Cave of St. Anthony.** The one-and-a-half hour expedition to the cave, 680m above the Red Sea and 276m above the monastery, is worth the effort. The best time to climb the mountain is when the sun is relatively low, before 6am or after 4pm. Try to return before dark, and remember to bring oceans of water. St. Anthony's has a small snack shop (soda and cookies) and a gift shop. It is good etiquette to make a donation.

The **Monastery of St. Paul** has four churches, the most important of which is the **Church of St. Paul,** built in the cave where St. Paul is said to have lived for 90 years. Many of the frescos date from the 4th and 7th centuries. Ostrich eggs, symbolizing the Resurrection, hang from the roof. Above the church is the fortress where the monks retreated upon the Bedouin attack. A secret canal from the spring ensured their survival during long sieges.

■■■ HURGHADA الغردقة

While much of Egypt exudes the stench of economic stagnation and suffers from overcrowding, Hurghada swells and booms before your eyes. Since the early 1980s, when peace with Israel opened Egypt to foreign investors and tourists, scores of resorts and shopping complexes have sprung (and continue to rise) from the sands, making Hurghada the fastest-growing town in the country. Hurghada's boom spawns budget accommodations and backpacker-friendly amenities as well as luxury tourist villages; and while Club Meders and Mövenpickians earnestly indulge in yoga and water ballet on outlying beaches, *Let's Go*-ites *own* the downtown area.

Hurghada is now the most convenient and all-around best budget beach in Egypt outside the Sinai; piaster pinchers can release temple tension here for as little as US$5 per day, including bed, food, and beach lounging and snorkeling rights.

But Hurghada's runaway growth has left stretch marks: overuse and abuse are rendering its famous coral reefs and islands barren and littered, and the beauty of the coastline has been marred by developers unfettered by zoning restrictions. As you enjoy Hurghada's relaxed character and carefree spirit, its aquatic splendor, and the seafood that makes it a welcome change from the Nile Valley, do what you can to make sure next season's travelers will be treated to the same.

ORIENTATION AND PRACTICAL INFORMATION

Even though paved highways link Hurghada with population centers, the town is remote. From Qena, 70km north of Luxor in the Nile Valley, it's a barren, mountainous 160km to Port Safaga on the Red Sea coast, and another 50km of empty coastline north to Hurghada. And that's the short way—Suez lies 410km north at the far end of the Gulf of Suez, and Cairo is another 130km west.

The **main town** of Hurghada, a cluster of hotels, restaurants, shops, and residences, lies 2km north of the **harbor** *(dahar)* of **Saqala** (Es-Saqqal), the original fishing town out of which Hurghada grew. Buses and *service* arrive in the main town, where budget accommodations await. Heading south along the coastal road, things become progressively more remote and more expensive—Saqala has plenty of dive shops and cafés, but few budget hotels. Farther south are a string of resorts such as Moon Valley (4km), the Sheraton Hotel (6km), and Jasmin Village (15km). Convenient minibuses shuttle north-south (50pt to the harbor, E£1 to the area around the Sheraton), as do taxis (E£10).

En-Nasr Road, the main thoroughfare, begins inland from the coastal road and connects the town and harbor. Everything you need, from the passport office in the north to the bus station in the south, lies along a 2km stretch of this street. Smaller streets to the east of En-Nasr Rd. contain budget hotels, restaurants, tourist bazaars, and the **souq,** all separated from the sea by a small mound posing as **El Afish "mountain."** Many hotels are on or just off **Abd el-Aziz Moustafa Street,** which leads from the center of town and En-Nasr to the beach.

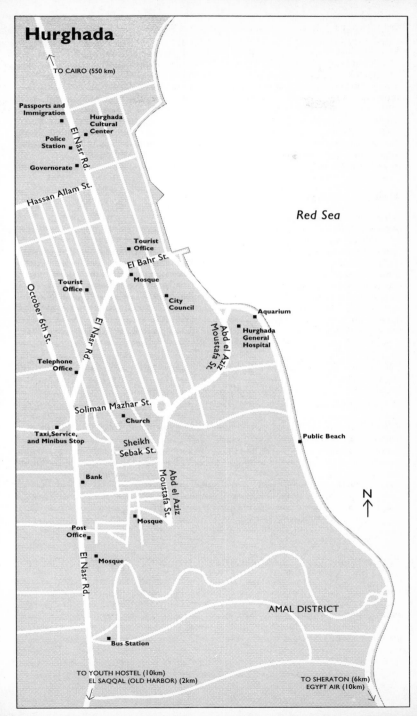

Hurghada

TO CAIRO (550 km)

Passports and
Immigration

Hurghada
Cultural
Center

El Nasr Rd.

Police
Station

Governorate

Hassan Allam St.

Red Sea

Tourist
Office

El Bahr St.

Mosque

Tourist
Office

October 6th St.

City
Council

Aquarium

El Nasr Rd.

Abd el Aziz Moustafa St.

Hurghada
General
Hospital

Telephone
Office

Soliman Mazhar St.

Church

Taxi, Service,
and Minibus Stop

Public Beach

Sheikh
Sebak St.

Abd el Aziz Moustafa St.

Bank

N

Mosque

Post
Office

Mosque

El Nasr Rd.

AMAL DISTRICT

Bus Station

TO YOUTH HOSTEL (10km)
EL SAQQAL (OLD HARBOR) (2km)

TO SHERATON (6km)
EGYPT AIR (10km)

Tourist Office: Off **En-Nasr Rd.** (tel. 44 65 13), 800m north of the bus station in a dilapidated shack adjacent to the Ritz Hotel. Look for the sign on En-Nasr facing north. Other branches on **El Bahr St.** near the Reem Hotel, in the **bus station,** and in **Saqala** between the main square and the port. Provides maps and help with directions or phone numbers, not much else. Open Sat.-Thurs. 8am-2pm.

Tourist Police: In the first tourist office shack (tel. 44 67 65). Open 24 hrs.

Currency Exchange: National Bank of Egypt (open Sat.-Thurs. 8:30am-2pm, Fri. 9-11:30am, daily 6-9pm in summer, 5-8pm in winter). **Banque Misr** (open Sun.-Thurs. 8:30am-9pm, Fri. 8am-noon and 6-9pm, Sat. 10am-2pm and 6-9pm), both on En-Nasr Way, 500m north of the bus station.

American Express: Across En-Nasr from the bus station and slightly north (open Sat.-Thurs. 9am-2pm and 5-10pm, Sun. and Fri. 5-10pm). Mail not held.

Passport Office: En-Nasr (tel. 44 67 27), entrance on the left side of the Red Sea Security Department building at the northernmost edge of town, about 2km north of the bus station. Open Sat.-Thurs. 8am-2pm and 7-9pm, Fri. 10am-noon (open afternoons and Fri. for visa business only).

Post Office: En-Nasr, 300m north of the bus station on the right. Orange international phones and **Express Mail Service (EMS).** Open Sat.-Thurs. 8am-2pm.

Federal Express: Sheraton St. (tel. 44 27 71), 1km south of Saqala. Expensive, reliable worldwide express mail. Open daily 8am-6pm.

Telephones: En-Nasr Rd. On the left just after the road turns at the police station (open 24 hrs.). A few shops in the tourist bazaar offer prompt connections abroad for a small surcharge. **Fax** in a hut directly across En-Nasr from the phone office (fax 44 38 45; open Sat.-Thurs. 8am-2pm and 8-10pm.) **Telephone code:** 065.

Airport: 15km south of town, about 1.5km inland (tel. 44 28 31 or 44 37 94). Take a taxi (E£5-10). Served by **EgyptAir** (tel. 44 35 92/3), on the coastal road 9km south of Saqala, accessible by minibus. To and from Cairo (daily, US$90). **ZAS Air** (tel. 44 63 50; fax 44 70 19) across from the large mosque at the northern end of En-Nasr Rd., 1.5km north of the bus station (open daily 8am-8pm).

Buses: En-Nasr, 300m north of town's southernmost limits. Book seats at least 1 day in advance. Standing room may be available at the last minute. Buses to Cairo (9 per day, 6hr., E£20-30), Suez (13 per day, 5hr., E£12-27), Alexandria (7pm, 10hr., E£37), and through Qena (E£6-13) to Luxor (4 per day, 4hr., E£7.50-17). **Minibuses** run between town and harbor (E£1) and up and down En-Nasr (50pt). Catch them behind the post office and on the adjacent street, or along their route.

Service Taxis: Off En-Nasr Rd., 800m north of bus station. Go left across from Omar el-Khayyam restaurant just before the bend in the road. To Qena (2hr., E£8). From there you can hook up with trains, buses, and trucks to points north and south. To Suez (375km, E£15), El Quseir (80km, E£3), and Safaga (60km, E£2.25). Groups may try to arrange "special" *service* for the 550km ride to Cairo (E£21).

Ferries to Sharm esh-Sheikh: Sea Cruisers (tel. 44 62 82) and **Spring Tours** (tel. 44 70 03). Sat.-Thurs. at 9am. Must book at least 1 day in advance. Going directly to the operators will not save you the E£10 commission taken by the hotels, so you're best off arranging trips through your hotel manager (E£100). The *Shark*, the *Murid*, and the *Golden Sun*, in that order, are the boats of choice.

Bike Rental: Shops in the area between En-Nasr and the beach rent for E£4 per day. Shops in the harbor charge E£4 per ½-day, E£5-8 per day.

English Books: Paltry selection at **Arlene's** (see p. 226). Books and newspapers available in most five-star resorts and hotels.

Laundry: Most hotels will send your clothes out for about 50pt per piece. **Stop Shop** (tel. 44 66 09) at the southernmost edge of town charges 30pt-E£3 per piece. Open daily 8am-8pm.

Hospital: El Safa Hospital on En-Nasr Rd. just south of bus station. **Public hospital** on Abd el-Aziz Moustafa St. near aquarium.

Police: En-Nasr Rd. (tel. 122), at a bend in the road 900m north of the bus station.

ACCOMMODATIONS

Sing Hallelujah! Budget accommodations in Hurghada are plentiful and inviting. If tourism is in full swing when you arrive at the bus station, you may have to fight off hotel-hawkers insisting you come with them. As always, see a room and fix a price before resting bags and body. Most convenient are the hotels on **Sheikh Sebak St.,** near both the beach and the *souq.* **Abd el-Aziz Moustafa St.** hosts a slew of hotels starting at the Shakespeare and ending at the California; these are often more visually appealing than those near the *souq.* If hotels in town are crowded, consider taking a taxi south to the harbor, where the **New Star, New Ramoza, Coral,** and **Peter** hotels are viable options. When travelers are sparse, as they were in summer 1994, deals are easy to come by. Bargain, especially if you plan to stay more than a few nights. All hotel rooms listed below have ceiling fans, unless otherwise noted.

New Alaska (tel. 44 84 13), 100m south of Geisum Hotel and across from public beach. Clean and colorful with nice views. Will organize transport, trips, and diving. Rooms E£10 per person, with view E£12. Breakfast E£2.50. Kitchen and washing machine available.

Beach House II, next to New Alaska. Brand new; the restaurant was unfinished in summer 1994. Also home to a diving center run by the Australian-Egyptian couple who owns and runs the hotel. Doubles E£20. Triples E£30.

Alaska Hotel, in the block of hotels between Shakespeare and Hotel California, about 500m from the circle where Abd el-Aziz Moustafa St. turns seaward. Clean rooms, sparkling baths. Doubles E£15 plus 15% tax and service. Breakfast E£2.

My Home, Solimon Mazhar St., off En-Nasr. A clean and homey place tucked away behind a walled-in garden. E£5 per person. Breakfast E£2.

Shakespeare Hotel (tel. 44 62 56), at the circle where Abd el-Aziz Mustafa St. turns to the beach. Family atmosphere. Lounges and fridges on every floor. Towels provided. Clean rooms, small garden, and roof restaurant. Doubles E£22.50, with bath E£28. Triples E£28, with bath E£34. Breakfast E£3.50.

Happy House Hotel (tel. 44 75 07), on Sheikh Sebak St. Great location near both the downtown area and the beach. Organizes fishing trips (E£35). Clean doubles and triples E£5 per person. Breakfast E£1.50.

Youth Hostel (HI) (tel. 44 24 32), 10km south of the bus station across from Sonesta Hotel. Small and inconveniently located, but relatively clean. E£5.10. Lockers in every room. HI members only.

Gobal Hotel (tel. 44 66 47), on the corner of Abd el-Aziz Moustafa and Sheikh Sebak St. A bidet! Clean but stuffy rooms with portable fans. Classy rooftop cafeteria. Free use of beach and pool at Sand Beach. Singles E£15. Doubles E£25. Triples E£35. Breakfast included.

Susna Hotel (tel. 44 66 47), on the street parallel to and west of En-Nasr, about 200m north of the bus station. The only affordable hotel with A/C. Clean rooms (all with bath) down dirty halls, bright and airy reception/sitting area. Singles E£12. Doubles E£25. Triples E£30. A/C E£5 extra. Breakfast included.

Hotel California, where Abd el-Aziz Moustafa St. meets the sea. Fairly clean, close to the beach. Singles E£10. Doubles E£20, with bath E£25. Breakfast included.

Luxor Palace (tel. 44 78 20), just before the California. Doubles (no private baths) E£15. Breakfast included. Kitchen and washing machine available.

The cheapest place to **camp** is on the beach, although you'll have to trek quite a way from town in either direction to find a secluded spot. You must first acquire a **permission request form** from the small security office behind the large mosque opposite ZAS Air. Then offer your passport, the form, a prayer, and E£1.30 in stamps at another office on En-Nasr Rd., this time across the street from the large mosque. (Offices open daily 8am-noon and 8-9pm.) In general, the beaches along the Red Sea coast are risky for campers, as the military takes a dim view of unofficial crashers.

FOOD

Hurghada's menus offer more than their counterparts in Upper Egypt, for slightly higher prices. You can feast on shrimp, calamari, fish or lobster, or seek the cheapest meals, by the **bus station,** where *kushari* and falafel stands ring the terminal. Traditional, inexpensive meals (E£4-6) are served in the *souq* area between En-Nasr Rd. and Abd el-Aziz Moustafa St. **Es-Salaam Restaurant** (from the bus station, turn right at En-Nasr's main *midan* and continue about 200m. The restaurant will be on your left) feeds locals with tasty *fuul, ta'miyya,* chicken, and fish. At **Zeko's,** across from Happy House Hotel, a full meal (¼ chicken, macaroni in *béchamel* sauce, green salad, *tahina* salad, and bread) is E£4. Top-notch falafel sandwiches 25pt.

Nefertiti Restaurant, near the corner of Sheikh Sebak and Abd el-Aziz Moustafa St. (around the corner from the Gobal Hotel) serves delicious, creative, and inexpensive meals (try the chicken *kabab* with fried onions, tomatoes, and peppers).

Bella Riviera, on Abd el-Aziz Moustafa St., south of the Shakespeare Hotel. A/C, cheap drinks, lasagna (E£3), meat dishes (E£7-9.25), and salads (E£1.25-2.50).

Arlene's, between the Shakespeare and Alaska hotels, boasts a taste o' Americana with smiling employees (some are even female), a plastic red hearts motif, and pita bread nachos. Sandwiches and burgers E£3-7. Pasta dishes E£5-10. Diet sodas E£2-2.50, cappuccinos E£3, and real milk shakes E£6. Alcohol available. Popular with U.S. Navy folk stationed in the Red Sea. Also sells English books.

Young Kang, by the Gobal Hotel. Another U.S. Navy hangout. Huge menu (noodles E£8.50-15.50, chicken E£11.50-15.50, seafood E£17.50-20).

Berlin Café, in the harbor 300m down Sheraton St., serves cheap Egyptian fare.

Tarbouch Restaurant, across from Bella Riviera. Nice outdoor setting. Large individual pizzas (E£6.50-13) will stay with you for hours.

Rendezvous, on En-Nasr Rd. by the bus station, provides relative elegance with red-checked tablecloths, candlelight, and fine seafood. The menu includes veal and other such delicacies, as well as standards (*kabab* E£10).

Salsa, between Sheikh Sebak and Soliman Mazhar St., has a real restaurant feeling, with reasonable service and relatively tasteful decor. Grilled fish E£8.

Geisum, on the beach 300m south of Hotel California. Fancy-schmantzy but surprisingly affordable. Grilled fish E£7.50.

Red Sea Restaurant, just off En-Nasr Rd. and the main *midan* downtown. Great open-air roof garden and Hurghada's best seafood. Entrees E£15-35.

Nameless Restaurant, with a red-and-white awning on En-Nasr Rd. next to the post office, serves up 0.5kg of grilled or fried shrimp for E£15.

Omar Khayyam Restaurant and Café, on En-Nasr Rd. just north of the center of town and the banks, sells **alcohol** for take-out or instant gratification. (Bottles of: *ouzo,* gin, Egyptian rum E£10; wine E£20; vodka E£65-75; whiskey E£75. Beer E£4.)

In **Saqala,** food is found around the main square, where there are *fuul* stands and several semi-continental places. Here the local flavor is much stronger than downtown, and eating is slightly cheaper. The **Omda Café** serves the usual cheapie meals (*fuul, kushari, ta'miyya*), and follows it up with a *sheesha.* Just north of the Federal Express office are two *fatir* (Egyptian pizza/pastry) places.

SIGHTS AND ENTERTAINMENT

Hurghada's main attractions are silent and submerged. Red Sea creatures flabbergast with their array of colors, shapes, and sizes. Buck-toothed trigger fish, iridescent parrot fish, rays with blue polka dots, sea cucumbers, giant clams, and a million others star in this briny freak show. The shimmering, variegated blues of Hurghada's waters have been spared the terrors of oil exploration (for the moment anyway), and the shifting colors will woo even the sternest terranean. (See Sinai: Underwater Adventures, p. 233, for important information on snorkeling and scuba diving.)

There are a few reefs you can reach without a boat, including one near the Sheraton; but to reach Hurghada's most brilliant scenery you must board a barge. Hotels offer an all-day trip to **Geftun Island,** usually including two one-hour snorkeling stops near the island and a fish meal prepared on board. Most hotels advertise the trip at E£40, though some charge E£30-35; these days you should be able to bargain as low as E£25. But those in the know say that Geftun-bound boats are often crammed with as many tourist-sheep as possible and that some stop only once for snorkeling. In addition, the reefs have been damaged by heavy tourist traffic.

Your mission will be to secure more days of underwater carousing without breaking the bank. Try getting a group together and making independent arrangements with a boat owner, perhaps a fisherman in Saqala, or with one of the sea-trip offices around town. You could go to Geftun and see different reefs, or plan an overnight. (E£60 to E£90 per person includes meals.) Better yet, inquire about excursions to other locales. Adel Shazly of **Nefertiti Sea Trips,** Muhammad Emad of **Sunshine Sea Trips,** Muhammad Awad of **Red Sea Wonderland,** Sally of Beach House II's **Amira Diving Center,** and Hosni Bakeet of **Hurghada Sea Trips** can provide information. Unfortunately, several offices were closed in summer 1994 due to the decline in tourism. Independents can rent their own **equipment** (E£5-10 per day for mask, snorkel, and fins) at any of the above offices.

Scuba divers should not expect bargains in Hurghada: prices correspond with the pocket depth of German vacationers, not the cost of *kushari*. The **Amira Diving Center** at Beach House II offers a full diving course (4-5 days) for US$200, at the end of which you will receive an official certificate. Some evil diving centers provide only a photo ID; check for certification before committing. The running rate around town for one day (2 dives) is US$40-45 for certified divers. Beginners should expect to pay at least US$60 for an introductory lecture and two dives.

As for the **beaches,** they lack high surf and sometimes peace and quiet, but compensate with gorgeous warm water. Public beaches next to the Geisum Hotel and the port in Saqala are often crowded, and women may feel uncomfortable here if they choose to bare anything more than toes. Just north of the public beach downtown, the **Shedwan, Three Corners, Geisum,** and **Sand Beach Hotel** all open their beaches to non-guests for E£10. (Shedwan and Sand Beach have pools as well.) Another option is **Shellghada Beach** just before the Sheraton, where E£10 buys a day on their soft, clean sand, E£10's worth of soft drinks, fresh-water showers, and more liberal bathing fashions. The **Sheraton** is considered one of the nicer beaches, but the harbor and boats encroach on the swimming area. Four- and five-star resorts charge E£10-30 for use of their beaches and pools. A sandbar and bay make **Magawish** the nicest beach, but the price is steep (E£60). These beaches can be reached by minibus (E£1 from Saqala) or taxi (E£5-10).

Recover from (or hide) that sunburn at the small **Red Sea Aquarium,** in town on El Bahr St., where you can get acquainted with the species you'll encounter in your underwater explorations. (Open daily 9am-10pm. Admission E£4.) Or visit the new **bowling** center across the street from the Sinbad Resort just north of the Sonesta.

At night, Hurghada parties harder than any Nile Valley town. All the major resorts have pubs or bars, and some have nightclubs. One of the more happening bars is **The Pub** at the Sonesta, featuring music by "world famous" Daoud and his soft-rock cover band. For a more Middle Eastern flavor, the Sand Beach Hotel sponsors **"oriental evenings"** including dinner. The best party in town takes place on Tuesday nights at the **Cha Cha,** in the Shedwan. Belly-dancing starts at 11:30pm daily except Tuesdays, when the Belgian proprietor pipes in the latest music from Europe. Be forewarned: the E£30 minimum charge does not even cover the price of two drinks. The small **Arabia Disco** in the Sand Beach Hotel plays more Arabic music. **Scruples** pub and steak house, on En-Nasr Rd. near the center of town, buzzes and pops with neon lights, beer, and Germans.

■ SOUTH OF HURGHADA

Port Safaga, 60km south of Hurghada, is essentially a highway beginning at the bus station, running north to the water, and continuing northwest to a handful of expensive resorts. Shipping the products of nearby phosphate mines is Safaga's main activity; it is also on the coastal-road route to the Sudan, and serves as an important transit point for Muslims headed to Saudi Arabia on pilgrimage *(hajj)*. Walking along Safaga's wind-whipped and sidewalkless street ranks up there with a visit to the proctologist for enjoyment value; but **minibuses** run the length of it (50pt). What are you doing here? Get out, quick. Daily **buses** run to Cairo (6am, 9am, and 10:30pm; E£35), Hurghada (8 per day, E£3-5), and Qena (6 per day, E£5). **Peugeots** run to Hurghada (E£3) and Qena (E£6).

The **Hamada Hotel** (tel. 45 17 53), on the west side of the street, has clean beds, passable bathrooms, and unfinished cement stairs. Portable fans on demand. (E£7 per person, breakfast included.) The **Cleopatra Hotel** (tel. 45 15 44), on the eastern side of the street near the northern end of town, charges E£32 for a clean single with bath and fan. (Doubles E£40. Triples E£46. Breakfast E£5. 15% increase in winter.) Other hotels are filled with tourist village employees and don't take travelers.

A couple of touristy though low-quality **restaurants** can be found on either side of the street in the vicinity of the bus station. A *fuul* and falafel café faces the station; slightly north and east is a fruit and vegetable **souq.**

Any entertainment to be found is at the tourist villages. The vast majority of the guests are German, with Italians and Egyptians making up the remainder. The problem for budgeteers is that private taxis are the only way out there. Lovely **Menaville** is the closest (8km), and has lawns, decks, pool, beach, and well-tanned guests acting wealthy. The pool is free, with a chalet for use all day, but there is a E£20 minimum charge for food or drink. **Scuba diving** is DM75 (roughly E£160 in summer 1994) for the whole day. Non-guests welcome.

El Quseir, about 140km south of Hurghada, offers a beach and modest snorkeling in a tourist-free environment. The architectural theme in this town is low, small, and mud or stone. There is a bank, a telephone office so difficult to use that you would probably rather commit slow suicide, one hotel, and a couple of mediocre restaurants. In keeping with the rest of the area, most visitors (i.e., the 2 that come every once in a blue moon) are Germans. A Mövenpick tourist village is slated to open nearby soon, but will probably have little effect on El Quseir, as tourists tend to stay in their villages. The sole hotel is the **Sea Princess** (tel. 43 00 44), with clean rooms but smelly, damp bathrooms. The decor includes a ping-pong table, plastic fruit, and pictures of Marilyn Monroe and Elvis. (Fans available, no A/C. Singles E£9. Doubles E£14. Triples E£24. Quads E£28. Breakfast E£5. Lunch (around E£12) and dinner (E£20) available at the hotel's restaurant and bar, open until midnight.) They rent snorkels and masks for E£6. **Camping** on the beach is possible, but there are no amenities. None. Not a sausage. El Quseir is what you make of it; with a big group of people itching to get away (far, far away) from it all, it might be fun.

■ Sinai ﺳﻴﻨﺎء

The tortured and desiccated land of the Sinai is where two continents collide. Enormous tectonic forces pile rubble into the steep peaks soaring above the Gulf of Aqaba coast. The sandy shelf where mountains meet sea is broad enough to accommodate a highway and a handful of small towns. The rest of the peninsula is an arena for survival of the fittest, where only the Bedouin succeed. Only they, sustained by a few springs in the wilderness, know the secret to life in the desert. The greatest profusion of life occurs in the warm upper waters of the Gulf of Aqaba— just offshore is an underwater carnival of beautiful coral and fishes.

Though the Sinai is a world of natural wonders, its position between the civilizations of the Nile Valley and those of Mesopotamia brought armies of not very enviroconscious visitors. Pharaohs' troops trampled the broad plains of the northern Sinai on the march to Syria and Canaan; in turn, marauding, Egypt-bound Hyksos, Assyrians, Persians, Greeks, Arabs, and Turks trod the same ground.

In the second half of this century, the Israelis and Egyptians battled over the Sinai. In 1903, the British drew the borders of the Sinai from Rafah to (present-day) Eilat in

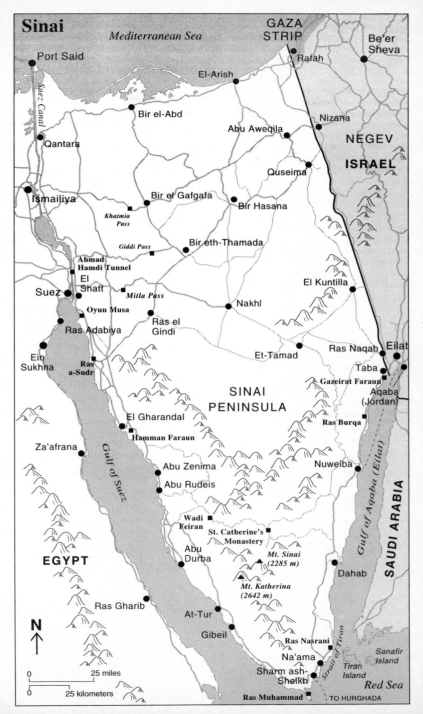

Sinai

Mediterranean Sea

Port Said

Suez Canal

El-Arish

GAZA STRIP

Rafah

Be'er Sheva

Bir el-Abd

Qantara

Abu Aweqila

Nizana

NEGEV

ISRAEL

Ismailiya

Bir el Gafgafa

Quseima

Bir Hasana

Khatmia Pass

Giddi Pass

Bir eth-Thamada

Ahmad Hamdi Tunnel

El Shatt

Suez

Mitla Pass

Oyun Musa

Ras Adabiya

Nakhl

El Kuntilla

Ein Sukhna

Ras a-Sudr

Ras el Gindi

Et-Tamad

Ras Naqab

Eilat

Taba

Gazeirat Faraun

Aqaba (Jordan)

Za'afrana

Gulf of Suez

El Gharandal

Hamman Faraun

SINAI PENINSULA

Ras Burqa

Abu Zenima

Abu Rudeis

Nuweiba

Gulf of Aqaba (Eilat)

SAUDI ARABIA

Wadi Feiran

St. Catherine's Monastery

EGYPT

Abu Durba

Mt. Sinai (2285 m)

Dahab

Mt. Katherina (2642 m)

Ras Gharib

At-Tur

Gibeil

Ras Nasrani

Strait of Tiran

Na'ama

Sharm ash-Sheikh

Tiran Island

Sanafir Island

Red Sea

Ras Muhammad

TO HURGHADA

N

0 25 miles

0 25 kilometers

SINAI

an attempt to keep Turkey and Germany a safe distance from the Suez Canal. After the 1948 Arab-Israeli War, the Rafah-Eilat line became the armistice line between Israel and Egypt. In the 1956 Suez War, Israel captured all of the Sinai, but returned it due to intense American and Soviet pressure as well as a United Nations pledge to keep the Straits of Tiran (formerly under Egyptian blockade) open to Israeli shipping. In 1967, Israel recaptured the Sinai four days into the Six-Day War. This time Israel refused to unilaterally return the Sinai and held on to the territory, building a defensive line along the Suez Canal, paving roads, and settling civilians in several places along the Red Sea and Mediterranean coasts.

In the 1973 War, Egyptian forces crossed the canal in a surprise offensive to recapture the Sinai. The Egyptian army rapidly broke through the Israeli Bar-Lev defense, but later Israeli counterattacks recaptured most of the peninsula. Israel retained the Sinai until the land was returned to Egypt in two stages under the terms of the 1979 Camp David accords: the first half in 1979, the second in 1982. U.N. troops stationed in the Sinai monitor the treaty, most visibly at the MFO base in Sharm esh-Sheikh. (See the Introduction to the Region, p. 39.)

Persians and Assyrians left no mark on the Sinai—their sandy footprints are long gone. Worse enemies now arrive by bus from Cairo or Eilat, by boat from Aqaba, or by jet from Scandinavia; they are armed not with spears but with traveler's checks and *Let's Go* books. One has only to look at Hurghada and Eilat to know how rampant tourism can hurt the fragile Red Sea coast. Unchecked economic development may sink the Sinai; already garbage is piling up and coral reefs are wearing down.

GETTING THERE AND AWAY

On slow nights in the oasis, entertain yourself by taking a poll: is the Sinai part of Asia or Africa? Scholars have pondered the question for ages, but it doesn't really matter—you can get there from both. And anyway, governments, not tectonic forces, are the powers that be today. See Essentials: Border Crossings, p. 29 for border crossing and visa information if you plan to arrive from either Israel or Jordan.

From and To Mainland Egypt

Transportation connects Cairo and Suez with the Sinai. See Cairo: Transportation, p. 83, and Suez: Practical Information, p. 220.

From and To Israel

Coming from Israel, entering the Sinai is as easy as crossing the border from **Eilat** to **Taba.** Before trying it, be sure that your passport is valid for at least another 3 months, and that your Israeli visa is also valid (at least for the day on which you'll be crossing into the Sinai). If you plan on staying in the Sinai for 14 days or fewer and don't plan on going to other parts of Egypt, a **Sinai-only visa** will be stamped into your passport on the Egyptian side of the border.

The border-crossing process unfolds in an orderly way, but involves a surprisingly long hike. Allow about two hours for the entire process; it can be slow on a busy day. Keep your passport on hand after you disembark from the bus (#15 from Eilat); you'll have to show it frequently as you go through the 2km obstacle course to the bus depot on the other side: (1) Bus drop-off. (2) Little Taba snack bar ("last beer before Sinai" NIS5). (3) Passport pre-check. (4) Passport control booth (pay NIS34.80 exit tax). (5) Israeli last passport check (they automatically stamp your passport at this point unless you ask them not to). (6) Stroll through no-man's-land. (7) Egyptian passport control (fill out entry form, get stamp). (8) Egyptian security (X-ray machine). (9) Post-border passport check. (10) 1km hike. (11) Customs, hidden on the left-hand side of the street. Don't pass it by without declaring *everything* that's of any importance that you're bringing with you into the Sinai, or the strict Egyptian border authorities won't let you take it back out with you. (12) Show passport and pay E£20 Egyptian border tax (the equivalent of about US$6). The Taba Hilton is the best place to change money. It's open 24 hrs. and charges no commission for foreign currency converted to Egyptian pounds. (13) Bus station. Welcome to Egypt!

Three **buses** run south from Taba at 10am, 2pm, and 3pm. Only the 3pm "crazy bus" goes as far as Sharm esh-Sheikh (E£12). It's unclear whether it's the driver who has blown some fuses after too much shuttling up and down the scorching Aqaba Coast, or the passengers who are demented enough to actually ride this tired beast of burden. What's important is that the bus will go where it wants, when it wants; it could be all the way to Sharm or no farther than you could throw it. The one-way trip to Sharm esh-Sheikh takes six hours by bus or three by taxi. To get to Dahab take the 3pm bus. St. Catherine's monastery can't be reached in a single day via public transportation; you have to transfer buses in Dahab. The 2pm bus goes to Cairo via Nuweiba'. It is impractical to come through Rafah and Gaza on the Mediterranean unless you are going to El Arish (best reached by taxi from Rafah).

To cross from Sinai into Israel at Taba, you need a valid standard Israeli visa (no visa necessary for U.S. citizens), but there is no entry or exit tax. The border is open 24 hrs.; it should be an uneventful walk through the stations, although Israeli security is tight. See specific Sinai towns for information on transportation to Taba. Bus #15 runs from the border checkpoint to Eilat daily until about 11pm.

From and To Jordan

You can take a ferry from Aqaba to Nuweiba', about 70km south of Taba. (See Aqaba: Practical Information, p. 448, for details on the ferry.) Border-crossing procedures take place upon landing in Nuweiba'. (See Nuweiba', p. 244, for transportation to other Sinai destinations from there.) Alternatively, amuse yourself by setting foot in three different countries in one day: an agreement signed by King Hussein of Jordan and Israel's Yitzhak Rabin in August 1994 opened the border between Aqaba and Eilat. If border checks tickle you pink or if you're a die-hard land-lubber, cross from Aqaba to Eilat armed with both Israeli and Egyptian visas and follow the "From Israel" procedures from there. At press time, you still could not get a visa for Israel in Jordan, so you will have to arrange that before you leave your home country.

The same ferries shuttle you from Nuweiba' to Aqaba. Theoretically, there are two daily ferries: one at 11am and one at 4:30pm. One-way passage on the deck costs US$28. Show up at or before 9am and 3pm respectively to deal with customs, ticketing, Egyptian bank hassles, and quagmirean queues.

Any Nuweiba' bus will leave you at the ferry launching point, or at least at the turn-off 7km south of the tourist center (bus fare E£1, taxis E£8). The morning bus from Taba arrives in Nuweiba' at 8am and is convenient for catching the morning ferry. You might be able to catch a direct bus from Cairo to the ferry; check at Abbasiyya Station. The bus, like the ferry, is crowded with Egyptians bound for jobs in Jordan, Saudi Arabia, and the Gulf states. Ordinarily you can buy a ferry ticket when you arrive at the port. The **ticket office** (tel. (062) 77 79 49) is outside the entrance to the port complex. First purchase your ticket (US$25; the nearby bank gives dollars for traveler's checks). Show your ticket to enter the port. At this point foreigners are assigned an official to guide them through customs and emigration and onto the boat. The real element of uncertainty is when the boat will actually sail; sometimes it takes hours for the ferry to work up the courage to leave the dock.

When you board the ferry, you'll be searched perfunctorily and asked to fork over your passport. During the trip, or immediately after you disembark, border crossing procedures take place. Your passport will be returned at Jordanian customs in Aqaba, or, if you go searching for it, on the boat. In Aqaba you'll have to endure a long wait and pass through a painless customs search before you're freed to catch a taxi or minibus into downtown Aqaba, 10km north (the drivers will probably accept Egyptian currency).

GETTING AROUND

The major destination in the Sinai is the Gulf of Aqaba Coast. Towns are located on the single coastal highway, so all you really need to know about getting around is which side of the road to wait on (mountain side cars go south, beach side cars go north). The noble machines of the **West Delta Bus Company,** battered cruelly by the rocks, ruts, and dust of Sinai roads, heroically ply the hot highway. With towns few and far between, separated by mountain passes, it's no surprise that schedules reflect an administrator's fantasy, seldom realized. (A philosophical attitude can ease your bus-tration: overcome the obsession with movement and new places; the bus station has a beauty of its own, and the road shoulder is full of mystery.)

A reasonably priced and convenient alternative to buses is the **service taxi.** Weathered old Peugeot 504s piloted by Bedouin cabbies are ubiquitous; you'll see them everywhere, circling relentlessly in search of prey. You can hop in with some other passengers, or negotiate first with a driver and wait while he recruits more travelers to your destination. Women should not take taxis alone. Taxis are comparable in price (under ideal circumstances) to the bus, but only with a full load of seven. You get where you're going a lot faster, but note that speed has its perils. Traffic laws do not apply; the laws of physics, however mutilated, are the bottom line here. Prices will drop immediately before the arrival of a bus, then rise catastrophically after the bus has departed.

Hitchhiking is a third option and could come in handy around town. Keep in mind, however, that you're in the desert, it's dry, and you're a fragile mammal with serious water requirements. Women should *never* hitch alone; all should be wary.

PRACTICAL INFORMATION

A number of **regulations** govern travelers to the Sinai. Unguided travel is restricted to main roads and settlements, but you can visit parts of the desert interior with a Bedouin guide. Sleeping on the beach is prohibited in some areas (notably Na'ama Bay), and the police often harass sleeping backpackers. Since these areas are not always marked, ask around before settling down for the night. Nude sunbathing is illegal, as is smoking the oft-hawked hash. You cannot bring a rented car or any four-wheel drive vehicle into the Sinai from Israel. If you hold a standard, one-month Egyptian visa, you must register your passport with the police in any town within seven days of your arrival in Egypt. Don't wait until Sharm esh-Sheikh to do this, since the passport office there is a long hike south of town.

Virtually none of the police in the Sinai speaks English; even with someone translating, confusion looms. If they're uncertain whether you've registered (and they may overlook the rather obvious triangular registration stamp on your passport), they may insist that you register in every town you visit. Any Arabic you know goes a long way with the police and other fidgety officials.

Prices for staples are higher in the Sinai than elsewhere in Egypt. If you're coming from Egypt, change money before arriving in the Sinai. American cash is accepted by some storekeepers, but don't depend on it. Food is cheapest at Dahab, and most expensive around Na'ama Bay. Beware the bottled water black market—before you pay for Baraka (small 75pt, large E£1.50), be sure that the plastic seal is whole and that the bottle's plastic frame feels rigid.

Budget **accommodations** are basic, but cheap and abundant. Sheets are not usually provided. In winter, warm clothes and a sleeping bag are advisable. Toilet paper and tampons are now widely obtainable, but bring your own supply to be on the safe side. Unless you want your hair to turn to straw, bring some conditioner as well; you won't find it in supermarkets. Moisturizer is also a good idea.

Weather in the Sinai can be as extreme and erratic as the moods of a heroin-addicted rock idol. Cold nights melt into broiling afternoons; snowy winters are forgotten during nuclear summers. The thermometer tops out as high as 50°C (122°F) in summer. Nights are cool in the mountains, but on the coast it's just plain hot. Drink about a bathtub of bottled water every day. Winter is another story—St. Catherine's sees sub-freezing temps. Spring, and possibly summer, is **bug season** in the Sinai. Dahab is periodically clouded by mosquitoes and flies. Shop for bug juice in Cairo, Eilat, or Aqaba. Some travelers rig a mosquito net and look pretty darned smug lounging inside it, but it's hard to know in advance if it's necessary. Rumor has it that sleeping next to salt water (i.e., the beach) helps keep the buggers away.

If you can take care of all that and still travel light, you've won the Sinai Stud award. In summer no one wears very much; and you won't want to carry much. After a couple of days most travelers begin to reexamine conventions of hygiene and appearance. "Washing" begins to mean nothing other than the first two syllables of a great democracy's capital city.

The **telephone code** for the Sinai (including all the towns listed here) is 062.

UNDERWATER ADVENTURES

The Red Sea indisputably has some of the greatest coral reefs and marine life in the world. The reefs are also extremely fragile, and the breakneck pace of development of the Sinai could have very destructive consequences. All coral reefs from Dahab south to Ras Muhammad are under the jurisdiction of the Ras Muhammad National Park; regulations forbid removing or damaging any material, living or dead, coral, fish, plant, or even shell, from the sea. Certain areas are open to fishing, and the park is fighting an uphill battle with developers hungry to exploit the region for tourism. You can do your part to preserve the reefs by observing a simple rule: look but don't touch. Even accidentally bumping the coral can damage it, so be as graceful underwater as possible. If you are interested in the National Park and its activities, call the director, Michael Pearson, in Sharm esh-Sheikh (tel. (062) 60 05 59).

Hidden among the crevices in the reef are creatures *capable of inflicting serious injury or death*. If you see something that looks like an aquatic pin cushion, it's probably a **sea urchin** or **blowfish,** both of which should be touched only as sushi. Avoid the feathery **lionfish** as well—its harmless-looking spines can deliver a paralyzing sting. The rare but well-named **fire coral** can bloat a leg to mammoth proportions, leaving welts the size of croquet balls. The **stonefish** is camouflaged flawlessly to resemble a mossy lump of coral or rock—step on one, then puff up and die in a couple of hours. Reach into a hole and a 2m-long **moray eel** might just lock its jaws onto your hand. The list is long—before plunging in, ask at any diving shop for a look at one of the plastic cards that pictorially identifies these nautical nasties.

For snorkeling, wear plastic shoes, sneakers, or fins at *all* times, or the coral will turn your feet into hamburger. Even better, sea creatures lurking in crevices and at the bottom will get you. **Sharks** are attracted by blood, so never enter the water with an open wound or if menstruating. Panicking and thrashing tends to excite sharks—if you see one, climb calmly out of the water and casually share the joyous news. Most sharks, however, are not aggressive and wouldn't (even if they could) give you the time of day. Last but not least, underwater wonders may make you forget ongoing solar action: the sub-tropical sun can give you a crispy burn. Wear protective sunscreen or clothing.

Two informative **publications,** available in Israel, are the *Red Sea Diver's Guide,* by Seapen (US$20), or the *Guide to Coral World Eilat,* by David Fridman (US$14).

Equipment and Courses

Snorkeling gear can be rented all over; for convenience bring your own or buy some in Na'ama Bay and sell it when you leave. **Dive shops** are concentrated mainly in Dahab and Sharm esh-Sheikh. You must be certified to rent equipment; most 5-day courses provide certification and cost around US$250. Dahab and Na'ama Bay have decompression chambers; the newest one is in Sharm esh-Sheikh. If you're certified but rusty, you can take a check-out dive for US$35.

What to look for in a dive center, if you're a neophyte? Multilingual staff is important—make sure the instructor speaks your language flawlessly (little misunderstandings can have big significance underwater: "Tanks!" "You're welcome."). Be certain the instructor is certified to teach your particular course, whether it's PADI, CMAS, or NAUII—ask to see his or her card. Does the dive club have a written set of regulations for safety governing its operatives? Some clubs are active in protecting the reefs, participating in annual cleanup dives, and making sure their operations have minimal impact on the marine ecosystems. The size of the club is also an important factor: larger centers often have more scheduled dives and more extensive facilities, but smaller ones will give you personal treatment and will usually run a course for just one or two people rather than wait for six to sign up. Finally, reputation is important. Get an idea of this by asking lots of people, preferably divers.

■■■ WESTERN SINAI

The Sinai Peninsula's west coast doesn't compare in beauty to the Aqaba Gulf side. The Gulf of Suez is a much shallower body of water with neither reefs nor rugged peaks hugging the beaches. It's therefore less of a tragedy that the Suez coast is dotted with oil rigs and flame-belching smokestacks. If you see this area out the window of the Cairo-Sharm esh-Sheikh bus, you've seen enough.

Moses buffs everywhere will be enthralled by **Uyoun Mussa,** 15km south of Suez. Hop off the bus to take it all in—this is where Moses impressed the heck out of his people by dipping a tree in some bitter water. Presto—sweet as Kool-Aid! For the advanced seeker of obscure places, **Ras El Gindi** is a spot 50km inland from Ras el-Sudr that features the ruins of Salah ad-Din's 800-year-old fortress. Farther south on the coast you can soak your carcass in the **Faraun Hot Springs** just off the main highway, 80km south of Suez, where you'll also find a nice beach.

If you're looking for a logistical challenge, try to get to **Sarabit el-Khadim** and **Umm Bugma.** You'll need to rent a car or hire a taxi, either in Suez or St. Catherine's. 100km south of Suez, a turn-off leads from the highway up into the mountains, known for their display of colors; they were once mined for manganese and turquoise. Sarabit el-Khadim has a seldom-visited Nabatean ruin, and Umm Bugma is the site of some old mines and ... well, it just has a nice ring to it. Umm Bugma.

■■■ SHARM ESH-SHEIKH شـرم الشيخ

Sharm esh-Sheikh is almost devoid of foreigners, especially backpackers. This is the town where the Egyptians who work in Na'ama Bay actually live. There is no beach to speak of—the water drops steeply off the shore—and heavy construction kills any chance of relaxation. Furthermore, the tiny bay is crammed with private yachts whose owners are attracted by the unusual calmness of the water (due to the naturally narrow opening of the bay). This calmness means that the water doesn't circulate very much, so the surface becomes slick with yacht oil, making swimming here a slimy experience.

There are no sights to speak of, no nightlife, and only two dive clubs: **Diving World** (tel. 60 01 67), across from the yacht jetty, and **Tentoria** (tel. 60 03 50), next to Safetyland. So what attracts travelers to Sharm esh-Sheikh? Three things.

The first is **transportation.** The **ferry** to Hurghada leaves here three times per week (Tues., Thurs., and Sat. 10am; one-way E£80) from the far side of the bay. (For reservations, contact **Spring Tours** (tel. 60 01 31 or 60 01 32) at the Tiram Hotel in Na'ama Bay or the **Cliffside Hotel** in Sharm.) By **bus,** there are connections to Cairo (daily 7, 8, 10:30am, 1, 4:30, and 11:30pm; first and last buses E£35, all others E£30), Taba (daily 9am, E£15), and St. Catherine's (daily 8am, E£15); all buses from Sharm pass through Dahab, and all but St. Catherine's buses pass through Nuweiba'.

The second reason to come to Sharm is budget **accommodations,** in the more-than-likely case that the Pigeonhouse and Shark's Bay in Na'ama are fully booked. The cheapest option is the **HI Youth Hostel** (tel./fax 60 03 17), on top of the hill just between the mosque and the Clifftop Hotel. Expect unpleasantly aromatic rooms and bathrooms, ineffective A/C, and water that's only available for two hours in the morning and two hours in the afternoon. Add to that the fact that the hostel is closed from 9am to 2pm *and* there's an 11pm curfew, and you'll find that you're paying E£15.10 (nonmembers E£1 extra) for a dorm bed (8 per room) that's proba-

NA'AMA BAY

bly not worth the price. Another budget option is **Safetyland** (tel. 60 03 59; fax 60 03 34), located at the bottom of the hill, at the intersection of the road leading to Na'ama Bay and the road leading to the Sharm bus station. They have thatched bungalows with locking doors and fans (singles E£39, doubles E£60, extra mattress on floor E£20), three-person tents (E£22 per person), and open tent sites (E£9 per person). (Reception open 24 hrs. Breakfast included.) Lastly, you can settle down at the **El Kheima Hotel** (tel./fax 60 01 66) next to the Diving World Dive Club. (Bungalows E£24 per person. Breakfast included; be sure to tell them that you want *only* bed and breakfast, or they'll charge double and include dinner.)

The final reason to go to Sharm esh-Sheikh is its **market,** nothing more than a medium-sized conglomeration of bazaars and cheap restaurants, but nevertheless the largest in the area; it is one block behind the bus station and to the left. The budget traveler will have ample opportunity to haggle over the price of carpets, clothes, papyrus, statuettes, and other assorted souvenirs. (Open daily 9am-4pm and 6-11pm.)

■■■ NA'AMA BAY

The diving mecca of the world, this resort town revolves around underwater attractions and does not attempt to make its landbound parts too inviting for backpackers. The shore is lined with four- and five-star hotels, dive centers, and gourmet restaurants. Nevertheless, there are many budget travelers who flock here each year. It's quite easy to get a **job** at a hotel or dive center; the pay is not overly high, but it's enough for food and entertainment (if you work for a hotel, you usually get free accommodations; if you work at a dive club, you get free diving lessons or courses).

PRACTICAL INFORMATION

Na'ama Bay is basically a long strip of hotels on the water side of the highway (which is the town's only street), with a second row of hotels being busily constructed on the desert side of the road. The **bus stop** is officially in front of the Marina Sharm Hotel, but the bus will drop you off at any hotel along the highway. To get to nearby Sharm esh-Sheikh, take the open-sided *tuf tuf* bus (50pt) or any taxi (E£1-2 for shared cabs).

Public showers are available in the Aquamarine and Hilton hotels, and the **public beach** is just south of Gafy Land Hotel. The **tourist police** are located past the Aquamarine. The **National Bank of Egypt** has branches in the Marina Sharm, Gazala, Mövenpick, and Hilton Hotels, and you can exchange money there 24 hrs. Most other banks as well as pharmacies are closed from 4 to 6pm (more often 3-7pm).

ACCOMMODATIONS AND FOOD

Pigeonhouse is the only relatively cheap place to roost in the bay itself. Thatched huts are equipped with fans (singles E£30, doubles E£40, breakfast included). Flock to the northern end of the bay and you'll find your perch on the desert side of the road. **Camping** on the beach is outlawed, of course. (Hiltoner to Mövenpickian: "I saw a man on the beach ... backpacking! It was so *(sob)* horrible!" Mövenpickian (shuddering): *"Der Teufel!"*) There's lots of unclaimed sand to the north of town, however; **Ras Nasrani,** near the southern end of the airstrip, has pristine camping and prime diving. Another popular option is **Shark's Bay,** a quiet development 4km north of town, with its own dive club, nightly bonfires, and Bedouin-style food. (Camping E£10. Tents E£15. Huts E£35.) A few tourists opt to stay in Sharm esh-Sheikh, though the savings are minimal and the round-trip commute annoying.

Food in Na'ama Bay is of high quality, at least along the main hotel strip, so you can relax the usual dietary restrictions that apply to the rest of the Sinai and satiate that carnivorous urge. Of course, you'll find that quality costs a pretty piaster here, so be sure to check prices before you order. (Some restaurants leave the prices off the menu. If you see this, run for your life!) **Tam Tam Oriental Corner,** on Ghazala Hotel beach (bordering Hilton Beach), is the cheapest place in town, serving *kush-*

N A'A M A   B A Y

ari (E£3.75), *fuul* (E£1.75), and falafel (E£1.75). **Aida Restaurant,** in the plaza between Sanafair and Kanabesh hotels, serves burgers (E£2.50), mixed grill sandwiches (E£5), and "Cintaky Fried Chicken" (E£4).

SIGHTS AND ENTERTAINMENT

Na'ama Bay itself has no spectacular reefs, but just outside the bay both to the north and south lie veritable coral cities. Dive centers have maps of the reefscape; pick one up and put on your flippers (not now, batfish-brain). The closest sites are **Near Gardens** to the north and **Sodfa** to the south; both are moderate walks down the beach. Adventurers should creep farther along to places like **Tower, Turtle Bay, Paradise,** and **Fiasco.**

Those in the know swear that boat-based snorkeling is the best. For US$15-25 you can spend a day on a dive boat and gain access to some tremendous territory. Arrange trips through the dive clubs. The legendary reefs of **Ras Muhammad** and **Tiran Island** are distant and accessible by boat only (conceivably you could swim to Ras Muhammad from the shore, but it's remote enough that you should probably go with a group anyway). Ras Muhammad is beyond the jurisdiction of a Sinai-only visa; you need a full **Egyptian tourist visa** to go there. **Ras Nasrani** and **Ras Umm Sidd** are also good sites, and a little closer to town.

You can probably find two dozen **diving centers** in Na'ama Bay; the tough part is deciding with whom to go (the simplest and most popular solution is to use the one closest to where you're staying). Prices are fairly standard, with a five-day PADI course US$250-280, not including certification (US$30). Introductory dives cost US$40-45, full gear rental US$20, five-day diving packages around US$200. **Camel Dive Club** (tel. 60 07 00; fax 60 06 01), across from Cataract Resort, has a friendly staff, and has been around since 1986 (rooms and school will be finished by Feb. 1995). **Red Sea Diving College** (tel. 60 01 45; fax 60 01 44), next to Kanabesh Hotel, specializes in instruction and has rooms available at the diving center for US$25 per person, breakfast included. **Red Sea Diving Club** (tel. 60 03 43; fax 60 03 42) has its own jetty and decompression chamber, and affiliates with **Aquamarine** (tel. 60 02 76; fax 60 01 76) to arrange cheap dormitory-style accommodation packages for divers (about US$10 per night). **Oonas Dive Club** (tel. 60 05 81; fax 60 05 82) has party-style night dives and will come pick you up from the airport at Sharm if you call ahead. There are many other safe and reputable diving clubs, with new ones emerging all the time; we have listed the ones which have been around the longest.

Water activities are not necessarily restricted to diving. **Sun-n-Fun** booths at the Hilton Beach and Aquamarine Beach have **windsurfing** (E£30 per hr., lessons E£45 per hr.), **water-skiing** (E£30 per ¼hr.), **jet skiing** (1-person jet E£50 per ¼hr., E£90 per ½hr.; 2-person jet E£70/130), and **Catamaran** (E£70 per hr.). There are **glass bottom boats** for the passive water fans (every hr. 10am-4pm, E£20 per person).

Those who choose to stay on land have a few terrestrial attractions from which to choose: the Hilton has **minigolf** (E£10 per game) and **horseback riding** (E£20 per hr.) available for all tourists (make arrangements either at Hilton reception or pool bar, starting at 6:30am). **Bicycles** can be rented along the beach for E£5 per hour. If you want to get away from the hotel strip, a convenient excursion is to **Nabq,** a Bedouin village on the coast 20km north of Na'ama Bay. Notable for its mangrove forest, Nabq can be reached by camel or jeep. The problem of maintaining traditional Bedouin lifestyles in the modern world is being actively addressed in Nabq: a Bedouin "reservation" in progress there attempts to preserve the culture. The **Tourist Services Center** (tel. 60 02 08), nothing more than a travel agency with a fancy name, arranges trips and **sunset desert tours** by jeep (US$30) or camel (US$35), including a Bedouin dinner. (Full-day daytrips to **Wadi Kid** US$55.)

Nightlife in Na'ama Bay follows a set pattern: in the late afternoon, divers come back from the sea, take a shower, change clothes, and lounge around the Pigeonhouse Hotel's bedouin-tent courtyard. Slowly, they cross the street and head to **Wings 'n' Things,** adjacent to the Oonas Dive Club—an American-style bar with bumper stickers, football pennants, and posters of Mel Gibson, Cindy Crawford, and Elvis on the walls. This is the hangout for MFO guys and divers, with excellent and cheap daily specials for those who bring their dive cards. (Happy Hour and a Half 5:30-7pm; 2 large beers E£6.50, plenty of wings and burgers E£12.95.) Eventually, people walk along the paved beachfront "promenade" (more of a walkway connecting all the hotels) through the colorful bazaars and dimly-lit beaches to the **Sanafir Hotel,** *the* night spot in Dahab, where the **disco** opens at 10pm (no cover). The Sanafir is the domed white entrance on the desert side of the road, at the northern most end of the bay, across from the Kanabesh hotel. Shake your thang and smoke *sheesha* until 3 or 4am. There is also the **Billiards Club** at Gafyland (E£10 per hr.) and the **Cactus Disco** at the Mövenpick (opens nightly 10pm, E£15 cover), both of which tend to attract a more reserved clientele.

■■■ DAHAB دهب

You could call it the land of endless summer—lazy days spent on a picture-perfect palm beach, the red Saudi Arabian hills glimpsed through a haze of sweet smoke. The collective inertia of a community of dope-anaesthetized young bohemians has a way of sucking in the weary traveler. Those who plan on spending one day stay three, others find a week-long visit stretching into a month, or six. The simple daily routine involves combinations of eating, playing backgammon, and sleeping, with sporadic episodes of swimming, camel-riding, or safari. The beauty of such a schedule is that it can be repeated limitlessly with no complications—save, perhaps, the nagging awareness that one's pocketbook is being eroded at the rate of US$10 per day. Not to mention one's brain. Then there's the other school of thought, educated at less popular Sinai spots, which sees Dahab as a once-peaceful haven gone bad. When the smoke clears, what appears before your eyes is a dirty, overcrowded tourist trap where Bedouin girls hound you to buy bracelets and predatory taxi drivers and camel owners pounce from around every corner. Whatever your opinion, however, you will undoubtedly enjoy the colorful underwater attractions by day and the even more colorful beachfront lighting by night.

PRACTICAL INFORMATION

Dahab city is of almost no significance to the budget traveler, who only glimpses it between climbing off the bus and getting into a taxi headed for the Bedouin Village—the "real" Dahab as far as tourists are concerned. Use it for exchanging money at the **National Bank of Egypt** (open daily 8:30am-2pm and 6-9pm; winter 9am-1pm and 5-8pm). There is also a **post office** (open Sat.-Thurs. 8am-3pm), **supermarket** (open 8am-10pm), **police station,** and **telephone office** where you can make calls within Egypt or through Cairo to an international operator (open 24 hrs.).

There are two **bus** stops in Dahab. The first is at the "Bus Stop Cafeteria" off the Pullman Hotel resort; this is where you will disembark and face crowds of anxious taxi drivers. A taxi to the village costs E£1 per person if you have a few people and E£5 if you're alone, so go for the driver that's already attracted some customers. You don't need a specific destination in the village: nothing is more than a five-minute walk away from the taxi drop-off, and the driver will try to double or triple the fare if he drives you an extra minute along the village's single dirt road. Once in the Bedouin village, face the water: north is to your left, south is to your right.

The second bus stop is next to the East Delta Bus Company office in the town proper. Taxis from the village drop you off here. **Buses** to Cairo (daily, 8am E£40, 9:30pm E£55), Suez (8am, E£21), Taba (10:30am, E£10), Nuweiba' (10:30am, 6:30pm, and 1:30am; E£6), Sharm esh-Sheikh (8, 8:30, 10am, 5:30, and 9:30pm; E£8), and St. Catherine's (9:30am, E£10) leave from this same spot.

ACCOMMODATIONS AND FOOD

About 50 **camps** have sleeps in the Bedouin village, and the number grows by the week. Dahab camps are an unfortunate bastardization of the thatched beach hut;

someone came up with the brilliant idea of casting the huts in concrete, connecting them into rows wrapped around a central courtyard, then charging E£4-5 per night to stay in what amounts to a bare cell with minimal ventilation. But despite being an architectural disaster, the camps are cheap and almost habitable (they mostly serve as a storage space for your stuff while you're lounging outside in one of the restaurants). (Room with mattress E£4. Raised concrete "bed" E£5-6. Wooden bed E£10. If you've got more money than you know what to do with, well, just go hole up and read your *Frommer's* in a room with private bath for E£15-20.) The camps are many, and an untrained observer might say they all look the same; the true connoisseur, however, can detect subtle variations in color, smell, and taste that distinguish the atrocious from the truly sublime. This is, of course, a highly personal act which requires inspecting several camps and, after intense soul-searching, making a decision ("eeny meeny miny mo …"). The **Fighting Kangaroo Oasis** has a name which appeals to Mike Tyson, Aussies, and Egyptians alike, and it's clean; the **Dolphin Camp** is on the beach; and the **King's Camp** … well, don't expect to see any royalty lounging around with their butlers and servants.

The combination of intense heat during the day and non-existent ventilation at night has a funny effect: the rooms get hot. Travelers have been known to approach this problem in three ways: (1) take all their clothes off, throw the covers on the floor, and still sweat profusely in bed; (2) put all their clothes on and walk with the sheets into the shower, drench everything thoroughly, then go to sleep wet; or (3) take the room key and a sheet and go sleep in the "million-star hotel" outside. Ocean breezes free of charge. And don't be too concerned about losing sleep at night—you'll make it up during the day.

Food, like sleep, is an important part of the ritual of Dahab living, and is actually intermingled with it: dishes take about one hour to prepare, so most travelers order, take a nap, and then eat. Bedouin village restaurants are notorious for serving up a little dysentery or food poisoning along with the meals, so be careful. Avoid those deadly little lettuce leaves (you've heard it before). Standards are reputedly on the rise, however, and sickness is less common. **Tota,** in the green and white beached ship, has excellent food (lasagna E£8, Tota's wicked chocolate cake E£4) and very clean premises. **Green Valley** is known for big helpings and good food, **Palma Bedouin** fries up a nice fish (price varies by species), and the **Blue Hole** serves half-price pizzas (nightly 8-10pm). You can eat quite well in Dahab for E£10-15 per meal (complete with drinks and dessert). Ask other (healthy) travelers where they've eaten—everybody has a favorite place. Pancakes (E£4), served with bananas, apples, ice cream, or honey/chocolate, are a Dahab specialty. There are numerous **"supermarkets"** that stock some staples. Children run through the village selling fresh pita that contains only a few stones and insects and is otherwise quite tasty. The sweet pita is generally a ticket to diarrheadom.

SIGHTS AND ENTERTAINMENT

The **Bedouin village** is no longer really that. It's so loaded with tourists that the Bedouin themselves have moved north to 'Aslah. Nowadays the bay is lined with restaurants, camps, and gift shops that peddle the famous "Dahab pants" (E£12) and the kind of colorful backpack (large E£10, small E£7) that can now be found all over the world in places like Nepal or Thailand. Camels and horses trot up and down the beach road carrying Dutch women or pink-hued Brits (per ½-hr.: camels E£5, horses E£10). Bedouin tent-like arrangements hug the beach; it's quite a sight at night when cheerfully illuminated by electric lights and floating water-bottle-borne candles (an innovative use for these pesky petroleum products which someday will bury the entire town). The whole scene is undeniably picturesque—Dahab has a charm different from any town in the Sinai.

Two well-known dive sites, **Canyon** and **Blue Hole,** make their home in Dahab. The latter is an 80m deep hole about 15m out from the shore that swallows several divers every year. The dive involves a traverse through a passage at a depth of 60m; experienced divers say this is just plain nuts, and they may be right. There's plenty of excellent diving that's less death-defying, and several dive clubs to help get you started. **Canyon Dive Club** (tel. 64 00 43; fax 640 3015) is a few kilometers north of the village near the dive site (taxi E£8-10). It's a beautiful spot and you have the option of staying in the nearby hotel. On the beach at the village are **Fantasea** (tel. 64 00 43), a two-story white house at the north end; **Nesima Diving Center** (tel. 64 03 20 or 64 03 21) at the south end, which has nice facilities and rooms for divers; and **Inmo Diving Center,** the oldest established club in Dahab. **Sinai Dive Club** is at the Holiday Village Inn (usually referred to locally as the Pullman). Prices are comparable to Na'ama Bay. (5-day PADI certification course US$250-280, 2 guided dives with full gear US$50-55, introductory dive US$40-45.) The **snorkeling** is great as well; you can go at either end of the bay where you see waves breaking on the reefs (just be sure to enter the water via one of the sandy areas, or you'll be stuck with coral needles in your feet). Trips to Blue Hole and Canyon are arranged every morning by most camps, and you can rent snorkel gear at camps or on the beach (E£5). Paddleboats are available for rental (E£15 per hr.) near the northern part of the village. Use them to truck to some of the more secluded spots.

Other popular excursions are by jeep to the **Colored Canyon** (E£50 per person for a group of 6), by camel to the brackish oasis of **Wadi Gnay** (E£20 per person), and a one-day camel trip to **Nabq** (E£35-50). Hammad the Lobster Man runs Crazy Camel Camp and derives the moniker by taking people on **night lobster-hunting** trips that culminate in lobster feasts on the beach. If you want to go anywhere, ask at your camp. The Bedouin know these hills better than anyone, including those fancy Egyptian safari outfits. It's also a tight-knit community and they'll usually have no trouble finding out about others who want to go to your destination. Remember that traditional Bedouin, meaning those who still drive camels instead of Toyotas, have cultural restraints against making images of people. Ask before photographing.

In order to get an alcohol license in the Sinai, an establishment must first possess a building license (obliging the owner to hold his building above certain standards) and pay a property tax. Thus, there are only three sources of booze in Dahab: the restaurant at the Nesima Dive Club, the bar at Green Valley Village, and the Black Prince Disco (see below). It's not surprising, then, that Dahab **entertainment** is characterized by an absence of alcohol and an abundance of cheap pot. Restaurants play a lot of Pink Floyd, reggae, and whatever narcotic sound they can get their hands on. The click of backgammon pieces is often the only noise emerging from slow-moving groups of loungers in tents. Note that possession of drugs is illegal in Egypt, Egyptian jails rate low on the Michelin system, and dealers win an all-expenses-paid trip to the hereafter via firing squad.

The **Black Prince Disco** is an experience in itself; it singlehandedly represents the entire scope of Dahab nightlife. A free truck shuttle gets you from the town square (in front of the *faux* Hard Rock Café) to the disco 1km south (of course, it costs E£1 to get back to town). The disco opens nightly at midnight, but Dahabitants don't begin to trickle down until around 12:45am, ready to dance madly until dawn. With the crazy mix of Egyptians, Israelis, Ethiopians, and Europeans, anything could happen, and probably will. (No cover charge. Stella E£6.50.) Try a nice quiet game of pool at **Napoleon's** instead (E£6 per game).

■■■ MOUNT SINAI

> And the Lord came down upon Mt. Sinai, to the top of the mountain; and
> the Lord called Moses to the top of the mountain, and Moses went up.
> —Exodus 19:20

The Sinai Peninsula owes its name to the 2285m peak of **Mount Sinai.** If you didn't know its history, you'd probably call this remote, bone-dry mountain region God-forsaken. But for Jews, Christians, and Muslims, Mt. Sinai (Gabal Mussa) is anything but—this is the site of God's great revelation to Moses. Mt. Moses translates to Gabal Mussa in Arabic, but most Egyptians refer to it as Gabal Iti, literally "the Mount of

Losing (Yourself)," because the Israelites "lost themselves" here in the worship of the golden calf as Moses ascended the mountain to speak with God (Exodus 32). It is regarded as the mountain where Moses ascended, parleyed with God, and returned with the Ten Commandments. This place is a bargain for spiritually needy tourists: you can pump water from the well where Moses met his wife and go barefoot where Moses encountered the burning bush (a shapeless weed overgrowing its stone-and-chicken-wire shrine) for free.

Tradition holds that God chose Mt. Sinai as the mountain where he would give the Ten Commandments because Sinai was the most humble of mountains. Tradition obviously never tried to climb to the summit with luggage. This is not an easy climb, and you should leave all but the bare essentials behind. (The monks will allow you to leave your bags in a room at the hostel for E£2 per piece, or you can leave your luggage with the tourist police at the bottom of the hill for the same price.) The shorter of the two routes up (about 2hr.), the **Steps of Repentance,** is actually the more difficult route. It is said that the 3000 steps were built by a single monk in order to fulfill his pledge of penitence. Be forewarned: this monk cut corners here and there (who could blame him?) and made many of the steps the height of two or three normal steps. The steps are treacherous by night; if you arrive after dark they will be difficult to follow even with a flashlight. Save them for the descent in the morning. The other route, the **camel path** (about 2½hr. by foot), begins directly behind the monastery, where camels are peddled to pedestrians (1½hr., US$10). Unless you know Arabic, conversation with your Bedouin guide will be limited to 90 minutes of "Problem?" and "No problem." If you want to expand the discourse and praise the camel, tell your guide it's *hilwa* (pretty). Camels take well to flattery. Unfortunately, the camels are not always available when you need them, and you can't count on having them at your disposal—you may arrive at the dispatch area and find nothing but dung. To find either path, walk up the hill to the monastery, bear left at the fork, and continue to the back of the monastery structure. The path continues for 100m or so, until you reach a graphic sign at a fork in the path indicating "camel" or "steps." Choose wisely. One juncture that usually confuses hikers is the path's intersection with the steps, which awaits soon after you pass through the camel trail's narrow, steep-walled stone corridor. After passing through the corridor, head left; the camel path disappears, and you're left with no choice but huffing up the steps for the final third of the ascent.

About two-thirds of the way up, directly below the juncture, is a 500-year-old cypress tree which dominates a depressional plain known as **Elijah's Hollow.** Here the prophet Elijah is said to have heard the voice of God. Two small chapels now occupy the site, one dedicated to Elijah and the other to his successor Elisha. On the summit stands a small chapel, built in 1937 over the remains of a Byzantine church. Moses supposedly hid himself in the cave below when he first came face to face with God: "… while my glory passes by, I will put you in a cleft of the rock, and I will cover you with my hand until I have passed by …" (Exodus 33:22). The chapel is almost always unattended and closed in the afternoons, but is usually open immediately after sunrise for one to two hours.

The best time to start the journey is about 5pm—late enough to avoid the most potent heat and early enough to climb by sunlight and see the sunset from the top. You can get to the base as early as you want; then take a nap in the shade of the tourist police building. The alternative, elected by many travelers, is to hike at night, when the air is chilly but the going tough (even with a flashlight and the glow of the moon). Either way, try to spend the night on the summit. The glowing dusting of an infinite number of stars on an inky sky will make you a believer, and you will awake to the sunrise and Mt. Sinai's unforgettable view, encompassing the mountains of Africa and Saudi Arabia, the Red Sea, and the Gulf of Aqaba. Meditation on the heavens will be shattered around 1 or 2am by hordes of tourists striking from air, sea, and land. Social people can stake out a spot directly on the summit platform by the tea and refreshment stands; this becomes zoo station in the early morning hours. A secluded spot can be reached by carefully picking your way through boulders and human feces down the sloping shoulder to the west. Go about 40m until you cross a ravine; the small summit in front of you has several flat campsites protected by stone windbreaks. **Try this only when it's light out—cliffs loom on every side!** Sleeping in Elijah's Hollow is another way to beat the crowds.

Bring enough food for the night and enough water (2-3 bottles) for the ascent (the cheapest place to buy water is at the monastery rest house store). There are refreshment stands on the way up, but the prices increase with the altitude. The stand at the summit sells candles (50pt apiece) and rents blankets (E£2.50 per night) for people who haven't followed the Boy Scout motto. There is also a "toilet" at the summit (a hole in the ground with little privacy and many flies). Dress warmly for a night trek and bring a sleeping bag and an extra pair of socks if you don't want to wake with icicles for appendages. You don't need a guide.

Six kilometers to the south of Mt. Sinai towers **Gabal Katherina** (Mount Catherine), the highest mountain in Egypt (2642m). The path to the top, more secluded and beautiful than the Sinai highway, begins in the village itself and takes five or six hours to complete. A chapel with water replenishes you at the summit.

■■■ SAINT CATHERINE'S MONASTERY

Attracted by the tradition that named the valley below as the site of the burning bush (and looking for a place to lay low during times of persecution), Christian hermits began inhabiting caves in the vicinity as early as the 2nd century CE. St. Catherine's Monastery began as part of their rudimentary communal life in a small chapel built by Helena, the converted mother of Emperor Constantine. In 342 CE, Justinian ordered the construction of a splendid basilica on the top of Mt. Sinai. When Stephanos, Justinian's trusted architect, found the mountain's peak too narrow, he built the Church of the Transformation next to St. Helen's chapel instead. Justinian, peeved, ordered Stephanos' execution, but the pragmatic builder lived out his days in the safety of the monastery and eventually achieved sainthood; his bones are on display in the ossuary. Pilgrims and curious tourists of all persuasions frequent St. Catherine's throughout the year. The monastery's private library cloisters the oldest (5th century) translation of the Gospels and, with its collection of over 3000 ancient manuscripts and 5000 books, was the perfect setting for *The Name of the Rose*.

PRACTICAL INFORMATION AND FOOD

St. Catherine's monastery is hidden away, at an elevation of around 1600m, in the mountainous interior of the southern Sinai. Excellent roads run west to the Gulf of Suez and east to the Gulf of Aqaba, both about 100km away. The 500m entry road to the monastery is the one branching left from the arched-dome square; the road continuing straight leads to the small town of Milga 1km away, and the road to the right leads to the very expensive tourist village hotel.

If you're going straight to St. Catherine's, ask the driver to let you off on the road to the monastery. Otherwise you'll be deposited in **Milga,** which boasts a few modern conveniences. The **bus station** is at the main square (it's not a "station" *per se,* but a point in space where the bus habitually stops). On one side of the square is an arcade with a **Bank Misr** (exchanges money or traveler's checks; open Sun.-Thurs. 8:30am-2pm and 6-9pm, Fri. 9am-noon and 6-9pm, Sat. 10am-1:30pm and 6-9pm), **gift shops, supermarkets,** and **restaurants** (which serve up a good meal of spaghetti or rice and chicken, E£7-8, open 6am-10pm); on the other side are the **tourist police** and a **hospital.** Opposite the mosque is a traditional brick-oven **bakery** (5 fresh pitas E£1). The **post office** and **telecommunications office** are nearby, with **telegraph** and **international phone** service (open 24 hrs.). The Big Daddy **police station** is farther up the hill. Higher up on the hill are some picturesque Bedouin huts.

Buses from Milga's bus stop leave daily for Cairo (1:30pm, E£35), Suez (6am, E£19), Sharm esh-Sheikh (1:30pm, E£12) via Dahab (E£8), and Taba (3:30pm, E£16) via Nuweiba'. **Taxis** occasionally fill up for runs to Dahab (about E£20-25 per person if you have a full taxi, more if there are fewer people; E£80-100 per car), Na'ama Bay (more expensive), and Cairo (E£40). Women should generally avoid them unless traveling in groups. Go to Milga's central square during daylight hours and look around for a taxi. Ask at the market if you don't see any, and bargain fiercely. **Shared taxis** from Milga to the monastery cost E£3 per person when they're full.

ACCOMMODATIONS

The cheapest and most popular choice in the area is **camping** on Mt. Sinai's cool peak (10°C on June nights, but add wind and it quickly feels much colder). The nearest budget option is the monastery's **youth hostel** (tel. 77 09 45) on the left-hand side of the monastery complex; reception is through the door marked "manager" across from the gift shop. The hostel offers clean but somewhat cramped rooms, all without bunkbeds. (Gates close 10pm. Dorm beds (7-8 per room) E£30. Beds in fancier rooms (3-4 per room) with private bath E£40. All meals included.)

A cheaper option at the bottom is the **Alfairoz Hotel** (tel. 77 02 21), behind the tourist village and to the left. Bring your own tent or sleeping bag and camp in the huge courtyard (E£3.50) or use one of the hotel's tents (E£6.50). If you want a roof over your head and don't mind spending the night practically on top of other fragrant travelers, try the Alfairoz **hostel** rooms. (Mattress on a concrete slab E£12. 4-person room with single beds and private bath E£60.)

Five kilometers east of the entrance road to the monastery is **Zeituna Camping** (stone hut E£10); a taxi will take you there (group of 3, E£5 each). Another option is the **Green Lodge Camp,** 10km east of the monastery. (Huts E£10. "Hostel" rooms E£20.) They'll drive you there for free from their office, next to the Milga post office.

SIGHTS

Saint Catherine's Monastery is believed to be the oldest unrestored example of Byzantine architecture in the world. The monastery once housed hundreds of orthodox monks, but its population has dwindled to a handful. Members of one of the strictest orders, these monks never eat meat or drink wine, and wake up quite early each morning when the bell of the **Church of the Transfiguration** is rung 33 times.

Both St. Helen and Justinian dedicated their structures to the Virgin Mary, since Christian tradition asserts that the burning bush foreshadowed the Annunciation. The main church became known as the "Church of the Transfiguration" owing to its spectacular almond-shaped mosaic of just that event in Jesus' life. The complex was named St. Catherine's Monastery after the body of the martyred Alexandrian evangelist was miraculously found on top of the mountain in the 7th century. About to be tortured on a wheel of knives for converting members of the Roman emperor's family, Catherine was miraculously saved by a malfunction in the wheel; they slit her throat anyway. Also in the 7th century, Muhammad dictated a long document granting protection to the monastery and exempting it from taxes; a copy of this document still hangs in the icon gallery, near Napoleon's 1798 letter of protection to the monastery.

The monastery possesses many treasures, including exquisite icons dating from the 4th century. One of the finest libraries of ancient manuscripts in the world resides here. Unfortunately only the central nave of the Church of the Transfiguration is open to the public (free). On tiptoe you can see mosaics of a barefoot Moses in the **Chapel of the Burning Bush** behind the altar. Should you manage to visit the icons back there, you'll have to remove your footwear—the roots of the sacred shrub extend under the floor. The monks themselves, with the help of the local Gabaliyya Bedouin, built the **mosque** within the fortress walls to convince advancing Ottoman armies that the complex was partly Muslim, thus averting destruction. Don't miss the gruesome **ossuary,** a separate building outside the walls, where the bones of all the monastery's former residents lie in enormous heaps (bishops have

®

LET'S GO
TRAVEL

C A T A L O G

1 9 9 5

WE GIVE YOU THE WORLD... AT A DISCOUNT

Discounted Flights, Eurail Passes,
Travel Gear, Let's Go™ Series Guides,
Hostel Memberships... and more

Let's Go Travel

a division of

Harvard Student
Agencies, Inc.

**Bargains
to every
corner of
the world!**

Travel Gear

A   Let's Go T-Shirt..$10

100% combed cotton. Let's Go logo on front left chest. Four color printing on back. L and XL. Way cool.

B   Let's Go Supreme..........$175

Innovative hideaway suspension with parallel stay internal frame turns backpack into carry-on suitcase. Includes lumbar support pad, torso, and waist adjustment, leather trim, and detachable daypack. Waterproof Cordura nylon, lifetime gurantee, 4400 cu. in. Navy, Green, or Black.

C   Let's Go Backpack/Suitcase.....................$130

Hideaway suspension turns backpack into carry-on suitcase. Internal frame. Detachable daypack makes 3 bags in 1. Waterproof Cordura nylon, lifetime guarantee, 3750 cu. in. Navy, Green, or Black.

D   Let's Go Backcountry I..$210

Full size, slim profile expedition pack designed for the serious trekker. New Airflex suspension. X-frame pack with advanced composite tube suspension. Velcro height adjustment, side compression straps. Detachable hood converts into a fanny pack. Waterproof Cordura nylon, lifetime guarantee, main compartment 3375 cu. in., extends to 4875 cu. in.

E   Let's Go Backcountry II...........................$240

Backcountry I's Big Brother. Magnum Helix Airflex Suspension. Deluxe bi-lam contoured shoulder harness. Adjustable sterm strap. Adjustable bi-lam Cordura waist belt. 5350 cubic inches. 7130 cubic inches extended. Not pictured.

800-5-LETSGO

Order Form

Please print or type — Incomplete applications will not be processed

Last Name	First Name	Date of Birth

Street	*(We cannot ship to P.O. boxes)*

City	State	Zip

Country	Citizenship	Date of Travel

( ) -	
Phone	School (if applicable)

Item Code	Description, Size & Color	Quantity	Unit Price	Total Price
			SUBTOTAL:	

Domestic Shipping & Handling		Shipping and Handling (see box at left):	
Order Total:	Add:	Add $10 for RUSH, $20 for overnite:	
Up to $30.00	$4.00	MA Residents add 5% tax on books and gear:	
$30.01 to $100.00	$6.00		
Over $100.00	$7.00	GRAND TOTAL:	
Call for int'l or off-shore delivery			

MasterCard / VISA Order

CARDHOLDER NAME _____

CARD NUMBER _____

EXPIRATION DATE _____

Enclose check or money order payable to:
Harvard Student Agencies, Inc.
53A Church Street
Cambridge, MA 02138

Allow 2-3 weeks for delivery. Rush orders guaranteed within
one week of our receipt. Overnight orders sent via FedEx the same afternoon.

Missing a Let's Go Book from your collection?
Add one to any $50 order at 50% off the cover price!

Let's Go Travel
1-800-5-LETSGO

(617) 495-9649   Fax: (617) 496-8015
53A Church Street
Cambridge MA 02138

special niches in the wall). A **gift shop** sells books on the monastery's history for E£6.50. (Modest dress required to enter the monastery. Free.)

Entering the monastery may pose a challenge (open Mon.-Thurs. and Sat. 9am-noon; closed on all Orthodox holidays: in 1995, Jan. 7, 14, 18-19; Feb. 15; March 6-8; April 20, 22, 24; June 1, 12; July 12; Aug. 2, 19, 28; Sept. 11, 14, 27; Nov. 14, 18, 21, 25; and Dec. 4, 7, 19). People have been known to travel six hours from Cairo only to find that the monks have closed the doors early. The solution is to spend the night on the mountain top, watch the sunrise, then hike down at 7am and reach the monastery just as the doors are opened. To get to the monastery from the access road, continue straight past the tourist police for about five minutes until you get to a fork in the road, then bear right and go through the gate (the left side of the fork leads you behind the monastery to the mountain trails—you can use it at night after the monastery gate has been closed).

■■■ EXPLORING THE HIGH SINAI

The interior of the Sinai peninsula near St. Catherine's is a magnificent congregation of *wadis*, oases, rugged peaks, and remote Bedouin settlements. The problem is transportation—buses don't go to most of these places. Jeep or camel safaris are a good way to reach some of the best places quickly, but if time allows it, traveling on foot is the most rewarding way to explore this remote area.

The first thing to consider is the weather. Summer is blistering hot; although the high elevations around St. Catherine's are cooler, the heat has a way of melting your motivation and turning you into limp chair fodder. If you do travel in summer, avoid traveling in the middle of the day. Spring and fall are ideal; winter can be freezing.

A regular **Egyptian tourist visa** is necessary to leave the area of St. Catherine's-Mt. Sinai and explore surrounding hills—the **Sinai-only visa** won't cut it. If you don't have the proper visa, your heinous crime might possibly go undetected if you travel by bus. Traveling by private car is digging your own bureaucratic grave. For travel into the mountains, you are also required by law to get a **permit** from the police, which you can get on the spot with the aid of your guide. **Maps** (NIS11) can be found in Israel from the **Society for the Protection of Nature in Israel (SPNI).** They are mostly in Hebrew, but SPNI might translate and point out some hiking routes. (SPNI has offices in Tel Aviv, Jerusalem, Haifa, and Be'er Sheva—see those cities for specifics.) There are many places to go in the area; if you're coming from Israel, talk to an SPNI representative before leaving. Egypt doesn't have a comparable data source, and maps are much harder to come by.

Organized tours are available for born followers. **SPNI** organizes guided tours to the Sinai for English speakers. **Neot Ha-Kikar,** an Israeli travel outfit, specializes in Sinai tours (offices in Tel Aviv, Jerusalem, and Eilat; see those cities for specifics); their trips begin in Eilat and Cairo. (6-day high range circuit US$360.)

You can hire a **Bedouin guide** in Milga if you want to hike on your own. **Sheikh Mussa** (tel. 77 10 04, ext. 457) is the hiking chief and organizer of camel trips in the area; his "office" is in the town. Look for a cluster of three stone huts, one open, next to a ravine. To get there follow the road uphill from the town square away from the mosque toward the Bedouin huts on the town periphery. Go past a blue sign that reads "City Council," then turn right on the second dirt road you pass. This leads to Sheikh Mussa's base, where you may see a few camels parked outside. The Sheikh will procure both a guide and a permit for you. The cost is E£55 per day for one guide, so get a group together for maximum financial efficiency. Extra camels can be rented to haul your gear around.

A round-trip of two days takes you to **Gabal Banat,** a peak north of Milga over-looking a vast desert landscape. Allow yourself three days to wander west through canyons to **Gulat el-Agrod.** Many springs throughout the mountains will wet your whistle; with the amount of goat and camel traffic in the area it's probably smart to purify. Surplus gear can be stored in Sheikh Mussa's house while hiking. Other notable sites in the area are **Wadi Talla,** a canyon with pools, **Gabal Bab,** with its sweeping view over territory to the west, and **Gabal Abass Pasha,** site of a ruined palace.

Another visit-worthy sight is **Wadi Feiran,** an amazingly lush oasis 50km west of St. Catherine's monastery; Islamic tradition holds that Hagar fled there in banishment from Abraham and Sarah. The best way to get there is by **taxi** from St. Catherine's (round-trip E£70). Buses going to and from Cairo pass by regularly, but schedules are unpredictable and you might get stranded.

■ ■ ■ NUWEIBA' نويبع

One of Sinai's natural oases, Nuweiba' lies at the mouth of an enormous *wadi* that reaches the Red Sea. For about 10 months of the year the surface of the *wadi* is just drifting sand, but in winter, a sudden, rampaging wall of water 3m high may charge down its banks to the sea. Nuweiba' combines the best of two worlds: the clean, hotel-free beaches of the northern Aqaba coast, without the isolation of the small coastal camps. Most budget travelers are drawn to **Tarabin,** a sleepy Bedouin village about 1.5km north of the city, with cheap camps, restaurants, bazaars, and the relaxed atmosphere which must have once infused Dahab. The beach in Nuweiba' itself is far superior to Tarabin's, however.

Practical Information, Accommodations, and Food Supposedly, there exists a bus station in the city itself; whoever put it there must have forgotten to tell the East Delta Bus Company, because the bus only stops at the big parking lot in front of the Nuweiba' Holiday Village and the **tourist police.** Daily buses to Cairo (10:30am E£35, 2:30pm E£45), Sharm esh-Sheikh (E£8) via Dahab (E£6) (7am and 3:30pm), Taba (5:30am E£15, 11:30am E£6), and St. Catherine's (10:30am, E£15) leave from this same parking lot.

Following the road to the north and as it bends away from the sea, you'll see the **new commercial center** on your right. The white, arcaded building houses a few bazaars, a **supermarket,** and a **bakery** (open daily 8am-4pm and 6-10:30pm). Farther along on the road away from the beach there's a communications antenna on your left and a garden on your right. Cross the garden via the turnstiles to reach the **old commercial center.** Here the **Dr. Shishkabab** and **Ali Baba** restaurants offer sandwiches (E£3-4), meat entrees (E£8-10), and vegetarian dishes (E£6). (Both open 7am-1am.) There's also a **fresh fruit store** (open 7am-midnight) and a **newsstand** with English translations of Egyptian newspapers, a few magazines and books, and **free maps** and bits of information (bus times, etc.) for Sinai and Egypt.

To get to **Tarabin,** either follow the road to the north (40-min. walk), take the shorter route along the beach (25min.), or take a taxi (E£8 for the whole car).

Budget accommodations are also available near the famous white sand beaches toward the southern part of town. At the **Nuweiba' Holiday Village Camp** (tel. 50 04 02, ext. 409), right in front of the bus stop, rent a bungalow (E£15 per person), pitch your own tent (E£4.20 per person), or stretch out a sleeping bag (E£3.15). **El Waha Village** (tel. 50 04 20; fax 50 01 40), adjacent to the holiday village camp on the southern side, has solid new bungalows (E£15 per person), large tents with mattresses (E£8), and an immaculate beach (E£4 per person for sleeping bags).

Sights and Safaris Like all Sinai coast towns, Nuweiba' is surrounded by beautiful coral reefs. But unlike the reefs in Dahab, Na'ama Bay, or Sharm esh-Sheikh, these Nuweiba' spots are not teeming with schools of divers from a dozen dive clubs. In fact, **Diving Camp Nuweiba'** (tel. 50 04 03; fax 50 02 25), in the Nuweiba' Holiday Village camp area, is the only dive club around. The club combines a professional staff with a laid-back atmosphere and "lots of love." (5-day open water course including certification US$300, 2-day diving safari US$110, introductory dive US$40, night dive US$20.)

The attractions in Nuweiba' are not limited to the waters. The town is an excellent starting point for a **camel or jeep safaris** to some remarkable desert terrain.

There are several safari "offices" in the area: **Explore Sinai** (tel. 50 01 41; tel./fax 50 01 40), in the new commercial center (open 9am-4pm and 7:30-11pm), **Sinai Adventures** (tel. 50 03 28), across the street from the tourist police (open 8am-11pm), and **Tarabin Survival Safari** (tel. 50 02 99) next to the Moonland camp in Tarabin (open 9am-11pm). (All charge E£65 per person per day for camel safaris, E£45 per person per day for jeep safaris.) Neg the seedy-looking offices and save E£10-15 per day by dealing directly with a guide. (Look for one at Tarabin, or wait for someone to approach you.) As far as we know, the Bedouin guides are generally trustworthy and safe. Let's hope they never learn from their criminal brethren in Luxor and Aswan.

The **Colored Canyon,** a *wadi* with cliffs of beautifully patterned sandstone, is the best-known destination, 30km from Nuweiba' (4-hr. jeep tour). **Ain Umm Ahmed** is a frequently-visited desert oasis which can be reached by jeep. **Ain Furtuga,** only 10km out of town (good camel range!) is another popular oasis. **Ain Khoudra** and **Bayar Al Sabreyer** are both oases in the spectacular **Wadi Khoudra,** on the road to St. Catherine's (within 2-day camel range of Nuweiba').

Camels are a mangy breed of desert animal that can be hired to carry you around resentfully. Don't be offended by the blasé response these ungainly critters will give you; in fact, their sour expression never varies. It doesn't take a Ph.D. in safariology to figure out that camels are much slower than jeeps, so a half-day jeep trip could take several days via hairy humpmeister. Technically, you need permission just to step off the highway in the Sinai. Desert trips require a permit, achieved by some mysterious passport fermentation process at your friendly neighborhood police station. Your **guide** will take care of it for you (permit costs E£2 per person per day for camel safaris and E£10 per person per day for jeep tours, but these fees are normally included in the cost of the trip).

One last bit of advice about safaris—the price always includes "food," but rarely includes "water." The price of bottled water rises dramatically during the safari, so be sure to start off with a large supply.

■■■ NORTHERN AQABA COAST

The 70km stretch between Nuweiba' and Taba is undoubtedly the most magnificent part of the Sinai: the beaches are untouched by hotels, the mountains are not covered with empty plastics bottles, and the only sign of human beings is the gracefully winding highway making its way near the coast. And you thought the Bahamas were nice. On bus rides, don't be one of the passengers flagellating themselves for stowing their cameras. Keep yours handy or just sit still and *absorb*.

Transportation and Practical Information From Nuweiba', you can either walk or take a *service* north to the **camps** just off the highway. The bus heading south from Taba will stop anywhere; ask the driver rather than the ticket collector for your stop. Keep in mind that huts may not have electricity; a **flashlight** is useful. Most camps have restaurants, but **food** here is more expensive than in the Nuweiba' commercial center. Backgammon, stargazing, and fornication are the main components of nightlife; fidgety or unsocial types should import their own cards, books, musical instruments, radios, etc.

TARABIN طربين

The smattering of camps just north of Nuweiba' has been collectively labeled "Tarabin." These camps bear almost no differences beyond their names: **Moon Land Camp, Camp David, Camp es-Sebai'i, Palm Beach, Swellam Camp, Paradise Camp, Red Sea Camp, Gamal Camp,** and **Sinai Sun Camp.** Drinks and food are available at low, standardized prices. Rent a bamboo hut (E£5, most have private bath) or tent (E£2) and camp on the beach. The **Moon Land Camp,** run by Mossallam Farrag (from the Tarabi tribe) offers guided **camel, jeep, and trekking tours.** The camel tours can include the colored **Nashid Canyon, Wadi Wishwashi, Wadi**

Gnay, and other locales upon request; the jeep tours may include the **Colored Canyon, Ain Umm Muhammad,** or **Ain Khadra.** (1- to 10-day camel tours E£65 per day; includes food. Jeep tours E£60. Discounts for groups. Contact Mosallam Farrag or Ahmed Mortada, tel. 50 02 84 home, 50 02 99 camp.)

You can reach Tarabin by foot from Nuweiba' or via *service* from the city or the port (E£10-15). *Service* in Tarabin will take you anywhere along the coast from Sharm to Taba. Bargain before boarding.

FARTHER NORTH

Still more cheapie camps lie 16km north of Nuweiba': **Maagana Beach,** a Bedouin camp near colorful rock formations, has reefs and a restaurant nearby (huts E£5). **Devil's Head** (Ras Shaytan), is its mirror image 5km north on the other side of the rocky point (huts E£5), and nearby **Bawaki** and **Baracuda** have large bungalows (E£8 per person) and excellent reefs right off the shore.

Farther north is a remote and beautiful spot called **The Fjord,** where a small inlet cuts into the steep hills. The **Salima Restaurant and Camp** (tel. 67 51 22) is right off the highway on a small ledge overlooking the sleepy bay. There are a few rooms crammed between the restaurant and the rock slope behind it (E£12 per person); you can also camp on the beach (E£5).

BASATA بساطة

"Basata" means "simplicity" in Arabic. Indeed, the super-environmentally-conscious place (about 23km north of Nuweiba', 43km south of Taba), which outlaws loud music and televisions, is simple, clean, and different from other camps along the Red Sea coast, though it is also simply four times as expensive. The camp is run by German-educated Sherif Ghamrawy (tel. 50 04 81, in Cairo 350 1829).

No synthetic materials go into the construction of the camp's bamboo huts, and camels, donkeys, ducks, and pigeons absorb the organic garbage. The remainder fertilizes vegetables and fruits in a greenhouse within the encampment. Empty Baraka bottles are shredded and go back to the company for recycling; the same system applies to glass material. In Basata's little bakery, fresh bread, cheese pastries, and pizzas are baked daily. One meal, either vegetarian or fish, is cooked every evening. The showers and baths spurt de-salinated water from Basata's own purification machines, and even the electricity is produced by the camp's own generators. The fully-stocked kitchen functions on trust: take what you want and simply write down what you took; but beware the prices. (Camping E£8. Bamboo huts: singles E£20, triples E£45. Mud-brick huts are currently under construction.)

Sherif organizes **camel and jeep tours.** (Camel tours E£70 per person per day. Jeep tours E£55-60.) **Snorkeling** equipment (E£12) is also available. Reserve in advance—Basata has been getting publicity lately and threatens to go trendy.

PHARAOH'S ISLAND جـزيرة فـرعون

Pharaoh's Island (Gazirat Faraun; Israelis call it Coral Island), 8km south of Taba, is a rocky outcrop just offshore which bears the extensively renovated ruins of a castle, built around 1115, which once guarded this extreme end of the Crusader Kingdom of Jerusalem. Salah ad-Din took the fortress in 1171 but abandoned it in 1183 after European counterattacks. A boat (E£2) ferries visitors to the island , where you must buy a ticket to tour the castle. This also a popular excursion from both Eilat and Aqaba (see those cities for details); the diving is renowned. On the Sinai shore is the attractive **Salah ad-Din Hotel.** There is a cafeteria on the island.

■■■ EL ARISH العريش

Along the road from El Arish to Ismailiyya, camels frolic among fried palms, blitzed villages, and gutted tanks. A few signs wistfully warn of the dangers of overtaking on a wet road. El Arish itself, "The Paris of the El Arish municipal area" and the capital of the Sinai, offers about as much distraction as the monotonous journey there.

A number of luxury hotels are under construction near the beach, and every year more and more Egyptians come here. It will be several seasons, however, before these facilities are open for business and foreign tourist troops begin their invasion.

Practical Information The El Arish **bus station** is at the southeast corner of Baladiyya Sq. The town's main thoroughfare from there, **July 23rd St.** (sometimes called Tahrir St.), runs north to the sea, where it meets Fouad Zekry St. The **tourist office** is on Fouad Zekry (tel. 34 10 49 or 34 12 41), about 1km west of its intersection with July 23rd St. (supposedly open Sat.-Thurs. 8am-2pm). Next door is the **tourist police** (tel. 34 10 16); police officers are indistinguishable from employees at the tourist office. The **National Bank of Egypt** (tel. 34 04 14) is on July 23rd St. next to the bus station. (Open Sat.-Thurs. 8:30am-2pm.) The **post office** (open Sat.-Thurs. 8:30am-2pm) and the **telephone office** (open 24 hrs.) are across the street from each other, two blocks east of July 23rd St. and three blocks north of Baladiyya Sq. The easiest way to reach the beach from the middle of town is by **minibus** (50pt) or **taxi** (50-75pt; tel. 34 01 04). **Pharmacy Fouad,** on July 23rd St. two blocks north of Baladiyya Sq., on the west side of the street, purports to be open 24 hrs., but don't stake your gastric tranquility on it; they can put you in touch with a local doctor. The local **hospital** (tel. 34 00 10) is located on Geish St., east of Souq Sq., the first square inland on July 23rd St. In case of emergency, call the **ambulance** (tel. 123) or local **police** (tel. 122 or 34 01 20).

Direct **buses** arrive from Cairo's Abbasiyya Sinai Station (daily, 8am and 2:20pm E£35, 5:20pm E£25; 5hr.) and go to Ismailiyya (every hr., 3½hr., E£6.25) and Cairo (7, 10am, and 4pm; E£25). From Port Said, you must change buses and cross the Suez Canal by the small, free passenger ferry at **Qantara,** about 50km south of Port Said, but it's quicker and easier to travel from Ismailiyya. **Service taxis** run directly from all the above locations. *Service* from El Arish to Kolali Sq. in Cairo is about E£15, to Ismailiyya E£8. There is no transport across the peninsula to the Aqaba coast. An EgyptAir **plane** shuttles between Cairo and El Arish (Thurs. and Sun.; leaves Cairo at 11:45am, leaves El Arish at 1:45pm; E£521 round-trip).

Accommodations, Food, and Sights The search for budget accommodations in El Arish is an ordeal. The beachside **Moonlight Hotel** (tel. 34 13 62; to reserve from Cairo tel. 24 81 28), on Fouad Zekry St., 50m west of the tourist office, has petite rooms and a view of the beach. (Singles E£5, with bath E£15. Doubles E£10, with bath E£25. Breakfast included.) The centrally-located **El Salaam Hotel,** on July 23rd St. (tel. 34 12 19), one block north of Baladiyya Sq., has shabby but spacious rooms. (Singles E£10. Doubles with bath E£10. Triples E£15.) There are also several **campgrounds** along the beach. The average fee for a two-person tent is E£6; ask at the tourist office for details. It is also possible to camp for free on the beaches near town, but you'll need permission from the tourist police and an HI card.

El Arish hosts two unsurpassed restaurants. The **Aziz Restaurant** (tel. 34 03 45), under the El Salaam Hotel, serves delicious *kabab, kufta,* and salad for E£6. Groups that call ahead can enjoy their meal in the Bedouin tent room, sitting cross-legged at low tables on embroidered cushions. (Open daily 10am-midnight.) About 300m down the street, just past the Sultana Café, the **Sammar Restaurant** offers a variety of chicken and fish dishes for about E£7.50. Filling *hawawshi* (bread filled with meat) can be had for a painless E£1. (There's no sign in English for this restaurant; look for the Mickey Mouse across the street from the National Bank of Egypt.)

El Arish's **beach** features a parade of palms, soft sand, and clean water. On your way to the beach, have a look at the town's only tourist attraction—the bizarre, multi-colored brick **minaret** on your left. July 23rd St. is lined with small outdoor **qahwas** where you can get a cup of *shay* or a *fuul* sandwich for a few piasters.

ISRAEL ישראל

US$1=3.03 shekels (NIS)	NIS1=US$0.33
CDN$1=NIS2.20	NIS1=CDN$0.45
UK£1=NIS4.71	NIS1=UK£0.21
IR£1=NIS4.66	NIS1=IR£0.22
AUS$1=NIS2.23	NIS1=AUS$0.45
NZ$1=NIS1.82	NIS1=NZ$0.55
SAR1=NIS0.85	NIS1=SAR1.18

> For important additional information on all aspects of travel in general and some specifics on Israel, see the Essentials section of this book.

At age 46, a fractious Israel (Yisrael) still doesn't know what it wants to be when it grows up. The Jewish state is variously "a light unto the nations," a pariah among its neighbors, and a country like all the others. Even its origins are controversial: from persecution culminating in the Holocaust, Jews came together, mingling diverse cultures and backgrounds to make a brand new kind of state and to remake themselves in the process; but some say that with every step they trod upon the Palestinian Arabs living in the area before them. With the country's identity at stake, all Israelis have their own vision of what Israel should be. To give one eloquent example, Amos Oz, Israel's leading novelist, sees his fellow Israelis not as "the 'Maccabeans reborn' that Herzl talked of," but as "a warm-hearted, hot-tempered Mediterranean people that is gradually learning, through great suffering and in a tumult of sound and fury, to find release both from the bloodcurdling nightmares of the past and from delusions of grandeur, both ancient and modern." Of course, many Israelis see Oz as a stuck-up intellectual, and will tell you at length about how *they* see their country. As the saying goes, if you have two Israelis in a room, you have three opinions. But talk with Israelis about their bewildering country for long enough, and they will finally smile or shrug and say, *"Yihiyeh b'seder"* (It'll be OK).

ONCE THERE

■■■ ENTRY

Security upon arrival in Israel is seemingly relaxed (unless you are of Arab origin), especially when compared to the scrutiny your luggage will receive at Ben-Gurion Airport upon your departure. For the most part, you can take the "Green Channel" to exit the airport. Most items can be brought in duty-free as long as you intend to carry them out when you depart. Take the "Red Channel" if you need to declare articles. Duty must be paid on large quantities of perfume, alcohol, and cigarettes.

There is a **Government Tourist Information Office (GTIO)** in the arrival hall at Ben-Gurion. **Egged buses** run regularly to major cities (#475 to Tel Aviv). **Sherut (shared) taxis** run regularly from the airport to Jerusalem (around NIS25).

■■■ GETTING AROUND

Buses Buses are the most popular and convenient means of travel. Except for the **Dan Company** (tel. (03) 639 4444) in Tel Aviv and the **Arab buses** serving the West Bank, Galilee, and Gaza, the **Egged Bus Cooperative** (tel. (03) 537 5555) has a monopoly on intercity and most intracity buses in Israel. The modern,

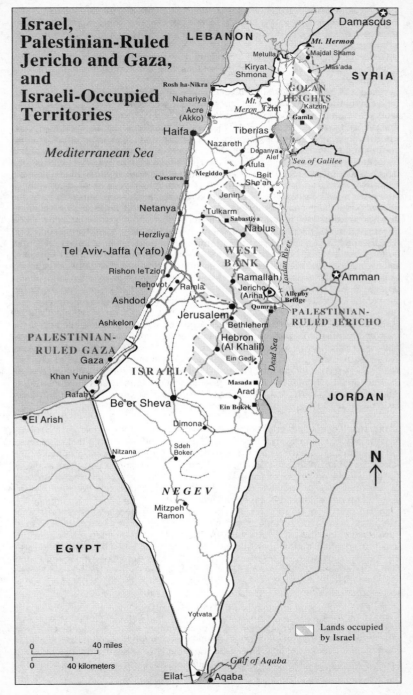

GETTING AROUND

Israel, Palestinian-Ruled Jericho and Gaza, and Israeli-Occupied Territories

Damascus

LEBANON

Mt. Hermon

Metulla
Majdal Shams
Kiryat Shmona
Mas'ada

SYRIA

Rosh ha-Nikra
Nahariya
Mt. Meron
GOLAN HEIGHTS
Katzrin
Acre (Akko)
Tzfat
Gamla

Haifa
Tiberias

Nazareth
Deganya Alef
Sea of Galilee

Mediterranean Sea
Afula
Beit She'an

Caesarea
Megiddo

Jenin

Netanya
Tulkarm
Sabastiya

Herzliya
Nablus

Tel Aviv-Jaffa (Yafo)
WEST BANK

Rishon leTzion
Ramallah

Rehovot
Ramla
Jericho (Ariha)

Ashdod
Jordan River
Amman

Jerusalem
Qumran

Ashkelon
Bethlehem
PALESTINIAN-RULED JERICHO

Allenby Bridge

PALESTINIAN-RULED GAZA
Hebron (Al Khalil)

Gaza
Ein Gedi

Khan Yunis
ISRAEL
Dead Sea

Rafah
Masada
Arad

Be'er Sheva
Ein Boket
JORDAN

El Arish
Dimona

Sdeh Boker
Nitzana

N
↑

NEGEV

Mitzpeh Ramon

EGYPT

Lands occupied by Israel

0   40 miles

0   40 kilometers

Gulf of Aqaba

Eilat
Aqaba

GETTING AROUND

air-conditioned buses are either direct *(yashir)*, express, or local *(me'asef)*. Students with ISIC receive a 10% discount on all fares; be sure to show your ID first to the ticket seller, then to the driver, then to the ticket inspector, then to interested passengers.

Buses are sometimes crowded, especially on Saturday nights after *Shabbat*. You can shove your way into and out of the bus, as long as you preface each push with the word *sliḥa*, as Israelis do.

Egged sells *ḥofshi ḥodshi* monthly **bus passes,** good for unlimited travel in a specified city during a calendar month (*not* any four weeks in a row); an NIS110 pass works for Egged buses in Jerusalem and Haifa. In Tel Aviv most buses are operated by Dan; they have their own Tel Aviv passes for NIS108. These are well worth the price if you will be staying in one area for a longish time. Egged also offers **Israbus,** an unlimited bus pass valid all over the country; buy it at any Egged Tours office (must be bought with shekels; 7 days NIS185, 14 days NIS219, 21 days NIS360, 30 days NIS400; call (03) 527 1223 or 1224 for the office nearest you). Otherwise, you can buy a *kartisiya* from any bus driver (NIS28); this gives you 11 rides (one is advertised as a free ride). Most local routes cost NIS2.80.

Most bus stations have printed schedules, sometimes in English. Egged has intercity **information lines** in the major cities (tel. (03) 537 5555 in Tel Aviv, (04) 549 555 in Haifa, (02) 304 555 in Jerusalem; open Sun.-Thurs. 6:30am-11pm, Fri. 6:30am-3pm, Sat. 4-11pm). You can call any of these numbers from anywhere in the country, and you will be charged only for a local call. For information on local lines, call the local central bus station. Signs in stations direct you to buy your ticket at the ticket window. This is only really necessary for highly-traveled long-distance routes; otherwise, buy the ticket from the driver. Buses between cities usually leave from the central bus station *(taḥana merkazit)*. If you buy round-trip tickets rather than one-way, you will probably get a 10% discount. Some popular routes—especially to and from Eilat—take reservations and give assigned seating, a nice de-stresser.

Many tourists use **Egged tour buses.** Egged offers over 100 excursions to various regions in Israel as well as Egypt; their tours into the Sinai Desert and along the Red Sea are particularly popular; check them out for these and other difficult-to-navigate spots. They're cheaper than the tours run by the Society for the Protection of Nature in Israel (SPNI), though not nearly as good. For more information check with the Egged tour office in the U.S. by calling (800) 682-3333; you can also write to their head office at 15 Frischmann St., Tel Aviv (tel. (03) 527 1222/3/4/5).

Taxi Israeli companies offer both private and less expensive **sherut** (shared) taxis. Regular private taxi rides are called **special** (pronounced "spatial"). City taxis operating as *special* must have meters *(moneh);* tweak the driver's nose and make him turn it on. Offers of special discount rates (translation: no meter and a fare as big as Texas) should be adamantly refused. If you know the route and can estimate a decent price, you can get a better rate by bargaining and setting the price before you enter the taxi, instead of letting the meter run.

Sherut taxis hold up to seven people. Certain companies operate *sherut* taxis seven days a week from stands in each city. Intercity *sherut* operate on loose schedules, usually departing when they fill up; on Saturdays, they often whiz along the streets in search of passengers. Intracity *sherut* never follow a schedule and cruise the streets daily. Most routes, intracity included, have set fares usually not much higher than bus fares; ask for quotes at tourist offices or from the nearest Israeli. Always settle on a price before you depart; especially on Saturdays and late at night when buses don't run and *sherut* drivers may try to rip you off.

Car The leading cause of death in Israel is not the fact that every other person carries a gun, but automobile accidents. A popular bumper sticker during the Gulf War read, "I'm not a Scud and you're not a Patriot, so back off." Mucho public transportation makes cars generally unnecessary; but some out-of-the-way places are most easily reached by a little deuce coupe of your very own. The legal driving age is 17, but most agencies will only rent to credit-card holders aged 24 years or older. An American license works just as well as an International Driver's License. Roads are usually well marked, and maps are available at all tourist offices. Israelis drive on the right side of the road. The cheapest rentals run about US$50 per day, plus 25¢ per kilometer, or US$60 per day with unlimited mileage. Prices in shekels are considerably higher in some cases. Deals arranged beforehand from overseas are often *much* cheaper. See Practical Information in various cities for agency addresses, and Essentials: Useful Addresses, p. 3, for booking agencies overseas.

Train Rail service in Israel is useful only for travel along the northern coast. The circuitous Tel Aviv-Jerusalem line is slower than highway travel but considerably more scenic. Like buses, trains screech to a halt during *Shabbat*. Avoid traveling on Friday afternoons when the trains are most crowded. Train fares are slightly cheaper than bus fares. Students with an ISIC receive a 50% discount.

Hitchhiking The incidence of sexual harassment and assault has increased dramatically in recent years. License plates carry meaning here; yellow is Israeli, black with a ⅄ is army, red is police, blue or gray is occupied territories, and white is diplomatic. Those who hitch in the Negev or Golan (where sometimes the only option is a military vehicle) run the risk of getting a ride that doesn't go all the way to their destination. In that case you are stranded and fried. To flag a car, point to the far side of the road with the index finger.

> *Let's Go* does *not* recommend hitchhiking. *Tremping* is not what it used to be in Israel. **Women are strongly advised not to hitchhike alone.**

Off the Beaten Path Israel's most splendid scenery is often accessible only by foot. The **Society for the Protection of Nature in Israel (SPNI)** is an invaluable source of information, maps, guidance, and advice. They have offices in the big cities and field schools *(beit sefer sadeb)* everywhere. Their excellent **hiking map** (1:50,000 topo), though in Hebrew, is color-coded to match the marked trail system (NIS40, in summer NIS36, members NIS32.40). SPNI people will be happy to mark English names on the map for you. They will also be happy to book you on one of their many English or Hebrew guided tours; a large group can hire a happy field school-based guide (NIS400 per day, arrange in advance) for expert instruction. SPNI stores carry two key **publications** for nature explorers: *A Guide to Hiking in Israel* (NIS35) and *Hikes in the Jerusalem Hills and Judean Desert* (NIS15), both by Joel Ruskin. The *Guide* tells all and covers the Golan, Galilee, Judea, the Judean Desert, and the Eilat Mountains. It also gives car and bus directions to the hike starting-points. The SPNI also know a lot about the Sinai. Spiels on **Jeep tours, mountain biking, horseback riding,** and **kayaking** are also given throughout the book.

■■■ USEFUL ADDRESSES

EMBASSIES AND CONSULATES

Australia: 37 King Sha'ul St. 4th floor, Tel Aviv (tel. (03) 695 0451). Deals with citizens of **New Zealand** as well.

Canada: Embassy, 220 Ha-Yarkon St., Tel Aviv 63405 (tel. (03) 527 2929; fax 527 2333). **Consulate,** 7 Havakuk St. (tel. (03) 546 2878).

Egypt: 54 Basel St. (tel. 546 4151 or 4152; fax 544 1615), off Ibn Gvirol St.

South Africa: 8 King Sha'ul St., Tel Aviv (tel. (03) 696 6147).

U.K.: Embassy, 192 Ha-Yarkon St., Tel Aviv (tel. (03) 524 9171). **Consulate,** Migdalor Building 6th floor, 1 Ben-Yehuda St., Tel Aviv 63801 (for passports call (03) 510 0166, for visas and entry clearance call 510 0497).

U.S.: Embassy, 71 Ha-Yarkon St., Tel Aviv (tel. (03) 517 4338), or PSC 98, Box 100, APO AE 09830 from the U.S. **Consulates,** at embassy in Tel Aviv; 27 Nablus Rd.,

Jerusalem (tel. (02) 253 288 (via Israel), 253 201 after working hours) or PSC 98, Box 100, APO AE 09830 from the U.S.; 18 Agron St., **West Jerusalem** (tel. 253 288); 12 Jerusalem St., **Haifa** (tel. (04) 670 616).

TOURIST AND TRAVEL SERVICES

Israel Ministry of Tourism: Tel Aviv, 5 Shalom Aleichem St. (tel. (03) 510 1451); **Haifa,** 20 Herzl St. (tel. (04) 666 521); **Jerusalem,** 24 King George St. 94262 (tel. (02) 754 811; fax 250 890); and 14 other cities. Maps, train schedules, and information on current events. **Voluntary Tourist Service (VTS)** arranges for tourists to spend an evening with Israeli families (ask about *Meet the Israelis* program).

Israel Youth Hostel Association: 3 Dorot Rishonim St., P.O. Box 1075, Jerusalem 91009 (tel. (02) 252 706; fax 250 676). Operates 31 hostels. Organizes tours for groups and individuals to Israel, Sinai, Jordan, and Egypt.

National Parks Authority: 4 Rav Aluf M. Makleff St., P.O. Box 7028, Tel Aviv 61070 (tel. (03) 695 2281; fax 696 7643). Material on parks and historical sites. Also sells an NIS36 ticket for admission to all sites, good for a month; available in Tel Aviv.

Society for the Protection of Nature in Israel (Ha-Ḥevra LeHaganat Ha-Teva, SPNI): Tel Aviv (main office), 3 Ha-Shfela St. 66183, near the central bus station (tel. (03) 639 0644; fax 383 940); **Haifa,** 8 Ha-Menaḥem St. (tel. (04) 664 135); **Jerusalem,** 13 Heleni Ha-Malka St. (tel. (02) 252 357); **Be'er Sheva,** Sderot Tuvia (tel. (057) 321 56). In the **U.K.,** contact Anglo Israel Association, 9 Bentwick St., London W1M 5RP (tel. (0171) 486 2300; fax 224 3908). In the **U.S.,** ASPNI, 25 W. 45th St. #1409, New York, NY 10036 (tel. (212) 398-6750). Organizes hikes and sight-seeing tours in English, and camping trips. Dues US$39.50 per year.

Israel Camping Union: P.O. Box 53, Nahariya 22100 (tel. (04) 923 366 or 925 392). Write for information about organized camping tours and a list of campsites.

Israel Student Travel Association (ISSTA): Jerusalem, 31 Ha-Nevi'im St., 95103 (tel. (02) 257 257; fax 240 462); **Tel Aviv,** 109 Ben-Yehuda St. 63401 (tel. (03) 527 0111; fax 523 0698); **Haifa,** 2 Balfour St. 33121 (tel. (04) 670 222 or 669 139; fax 676 697). Information about tours, student discounts, and ID cards.

■■■ EMERGENCY INFORMATION

Emergency assistance is available throughout Israel, and most doctors speak English. **Magen David Adom** (Red Star of David), provides first-aid and other emergency help. Emergency hospitals are open 24 hrs., *Shabbat,* and on holidays; emergency pharmacies are on-duty for after-hours calls. For **Fire,** dial 102. For **Medical emergencies,** dial 101. For the **Police,** dial 100.

■■■ MONEY MATTERS

Currency and Exchange The primary unit of currency in Israel is the **new Israeli shekel (NIS).** Notes come in denominations of NIS200, NIS100, NIS50, NIS20, and NIS10; coins come in NIS5, NIS1, NIS0.50, 10 agorot, and 5 agorot. Inflation in Israel is currently around 10%.

Money can be exchanged at any bank or authorized hotel; always bring your passport. Hotel rates of exchange are usually slightly worse than those in banks. A maximum of US$100 worth of shekels can be reconverted, at the airport only. To change more than US$100, show a receipt which verifies your original conversion into shekels. Banks are usually open Sun., Tues., and Thurs. 8:30am-12:30pm and 4-5:30pm, Mon. and Wed. 8:30am-12:30pm, Fri. and holidays 8:30am-noon. The **First International Bank** and many hotels have additional hours.

American Express offices in Israel do not cash Travelers Cheques; be forewarned. **ATMs** are abundant in Israel; **Bank Ha-Poalim** ATMs take **bank cards** affiliated with the *Cirrus* and *Plus* networks for free, but your home bank may charge you. Inquire before you go. Not all countries are in the Cirrus and Plus networks; if you plan to travel elsewhere, you may need to bring traveler's checks anyway. **MasterCard** and **Visa** clients can deposit money with their home bank prior to departure and draw on it without having to pay interest. Lost Visa cards can be replaced within two days via CAL Co., 38 Naḥlat Yitzḥak St., Tel Aviv (tel. (03) 542 9542). In general, **credit cards** are widely accepted, but only at more upscale places.

Use of Foreign Currency Many services and shops accept Australian, Canadian, and U.S. dollars and British pounds in addition to shekels. If you pay in foreign currency, your change will come back in shekels and you will be exempt from the domestic **Value Added Tax (VAT)** on goods and services (17%). Many shops include the VAT in listed prices in shekels, so you may have to insist that 17% be removed from your charge if you pay in foreign currency. VAT refunds can also be obtained if you present receipts from your purchases at any export bank upon your departure. There are limitations to this refund: purchases must be made at stores bearing the proper logos, must be worth at least US$50, must be wrapped in a plastic bag which will remain closed for the duration of your trip, must be on your person and not packed in a suitcase, and your great-aunt's best friend's underwear must have been manufactured in Israel. And you thought you were getting something for nothing. Sucker. The *Customs Guide for the Reimbursement of VAT to Tourists,* available at the airport when you arrive, makes good toilet reading. The refund will be in the currency you used; if the bank cannot scrape together enough, it will be mailed to your home address. A new policy allows Eurocheques to be written in shekels and counted as foreign currency for discounts.

You may bring an unlimited amount of currency, foreign or shekels, into the country. Upon departure you are permitted to take up to US$100 cash. Anything over this must be accompanied by receipts to prove that it was brought into the country. Unless you want to wallpaper your kitchen, exchange all your shekels before leaving Israel. Few foreign banks are that stupid.

Tipping A 10% tip is expected in restaurants, bars, and hotels (Middle Eastern restaurants excluded), unless a service charge is already included in the bill. Taxi drivers will happily accept tips, but they are not expected.

Business Hours Business hours in Israel are difficult to pinpoint. Because of the variety of religions, different shops close on different days. Most Jewish **shops and offices** are closed for *Shabbat* from early Friday afternoon until Sunday; some stores reopen after sundown on Saturday. Typical shopping hours are Monday-Thursday 8am-1pm and 4-7pm, Friday 8am-2pm; shopping malls open continuously until 9-10pm. Muslim-owned establishments close on Fridays; Christian businesses close on Sundays. **Entertainment** spots are usually open every day, with extended hours on weekends. Bars begin to fill up around midnight. **Public transportation,** including Egged bus lines, also shuts down for *Shabbat* throughout the country except in Haifa. Don't expect to catch a bus after 2pm on Friday.

Businesses close down on major Jewish holidays, keeping Friday hours the day before (hereafter referred to as holiday eves). During *Sukkot* and *Pesaḥ,* shops close entirely for the first and last days and are open until early afternoon during intermediate days. In Arab areas, some restaurants close for the entire month of Ramadan; many others close during the days. (See Essentials: When To Go, p. 1.)

■ ■ ■ ACCOMMODATIONS

Hostels Although often crowded in summer, Israel's **Hostelling International (HI)** youth hostels are usually clean and close to historic sites and scenic areas. You can obtain a list of hostels from the **Israel Youth Hostel Association.** (See Tourist and Travel Services, p. 252.) Hostel locations are also listed on the back of the GTIO's survey map. Most HI hostels accept reservations and have no age limit; a few have a maximum stay of three nights. The HI hostels are generally more expensive than the privately-owned ones. People 18 and under may get a discount. Hostels usually offer lunch and dinner for an additional fee. While some have 24-hour reception, many follow a strict schedule: they are open 5-9pm for check-in, 7am-noon for check-out, and are closed the rest of the day (check specific listings). There are many excellent unofficial hostels and pensions in Israel. **Most dorm rooms and bathrooms in Israel are coed.** Regardless of whether or not they are affiliated, hostels are not known for good security. Guard your valuables. All accommodations are required by law to have safes for use free of charge; many also have lockers, for a minimal fee.

The Israel Youth Hostel Association offers package tours for individuals and groups, and HI members get discounted admission to some national parks. Write to the Hostel Association for "Israel on the Youth Hostel Trail" deals.

Hotels Hotel accommodations are usually too costly for the budget traveler. There are some reasonably priced one- and two-star hotels in the larger cities; a few have singles for approximately NIS40-50 and doubles for NIS60-80. Prices can often be bargained down substantially when business is slow. Ask for booklets at the tourist office: *Israel: A Youth and Student Adventure* and *Israel Tourist Hotels*.

Camping Israel's campsites provide electricity, sanitary facilities, public telephones, first-aid, a restaurant and/or store, and a night guard. Swimming areas are either on the site or nearby. During July and August most sites charge NIS10-20 per night for adults. For information, contact the **Israel Camping Union,** P.O. Box 53, Nahariya 22100 (tel. (04) 923 366 or 925 392).

Think twice before crashing in areas not officially designated for camping. Certain stretches of beach are off-limits for security reasons, and others are dens o' thieves (Haifa, Tel Aviv, and Eilat). **Women should not camp alone.** Finally, heed mine field warning signs, unless you fancy yourself triple-jointed and edible.

Alternative Accommodations If you plan to sleep in Nazareth or Jerusalem, consider staying in a **Christian hospice,** also on Mount Tabor, in Tiberias, and in Jaffa. Most are former monasteries or Franciscan settlements. They are officially designed to provide reasonably-priced room and board for Christian pilgrims, but all those listed in this book welcome tourists as well. The 40 hospices in Israel are run by representatives of various Christian denominations and a host of nations. Bed and breakfast costs US$12-16 per person at most places. Though austere, the hospices are conveniently located in important religious centers and are usually quiet, clean, and comfortable; most also serve cheap, filling meals. But accommodations are limited, and sometimes difficult to obtain in the tourist season. For a list of hospices write to the Ministry of Tourism, Pilgrimage Promotion Division, P.O. Box 1018, Jerusalem 91009 (tel. (02) 257 456 or 754 971; fax 254 226).

In some cities it is possible to rent a room in a **private home.** The GTIO and some private travel agencies can arrange accommodations. Consider finding a place on your own; prices should be no more than what you would pay at a hostel. But exercise caution. Hometours International, Inc. helps find short- and long-term **apartment rentals** in Jerusalem, Tel Aviv, and Netanya, and also has **bed-and-breakfast** locations throughout Israel. Flyers are available for US$3; call (800) 367-4668.

Some kibbutzim offer accommodations at **Kibbutz Hotels.** Most are resort-like and have three-star ratings from the Ministry of Tourism; prices run as high as US$35 for singles and US$45 for doubles. For information, contact them at 90 Ben-Yehuda St., Tel Aviv 63437 (tel. (03) 524 6161). Finally, try **ISSTA** (see Tourist and Travel Services, p. 252) for cheap package deals on accommodations.

■■■ KEEPING IN TOUCH

Post offices are usually open Sunday through Tuesday and Thursday 8am-12:30pm and 3:30-6pm, Wednesday 8am-2pm, Friday 8am-1pm, and are closed Saturdays and holidays. In the larger cities some offices may keep longer hours. Mail from North

Express Mail Service (EMS),** which takes three days.

Travelers have three means of receiving mail: Poste Restante *(doar shamur)*, American Express Client Letter Service, and ISSTA. **Poste Restante** might be more of a pain than it's worth (address letters: Name, "Poste Restante," "Main Post Office," name of city, "Israel"). When you go to claim your letters, have the teller check under both your first and last names. Better yet, hold him or her hostage and check yourself. Always bring your passport or other proper identification. Lines at **American Express** are short, and employees often let you check the letter pile. Lines at **ISSTA** are another story.

You can send a **telegram** by dialing 171 or from a post office or hotel. **Fax** is available in many post offices around the country. **Telex** is available in Tel Aviv at the Mikveh Israel post office and in Jerusalem at the central post office.

Telephone Public telephones** are everywhere. Older telephones devour *asimonim* (tokens) for local calls (NIS0.50; avoid calling long distance direct from an old pay phone—making a connection may take hours and bucketfuls of *asimonim*). Beige-colored telephones (marked with yellow signs) operate with **Telecards** (10 units of calling time NIS5, 20 units NIS10, 50 units NIS23.50). Telecards are good for long distance and international calls (roughly NIS5.90 per min. to the U.S.). International rates drop by up to 50% late at night and on Saturday and Sunday.

Bezek, Israel's phone company, has offices with metered phones for international calls in Tel Aviv and Jerusalem. It may be more economical to call overseas from there, because they charge only for the time you were on the phone; phone cards must be purchased with a fixed set of units and you may be left with extra units at the end of the call. Nonetheless, there's nothing you can do at a telephone office that you can't do from a pay phone. English telephone directories are available at hotels and main post offices, or dial 144 for the **operator** or **information.**

Toll-free direct-dial numbers (toll-free numbers begin with 177) are the easiest way to make overseas calls; you dial an overseas operator who places your collect or calling-card call. The following toll-free numbers (preceded by 177) are for **AT&T:** 100 2727 (USADirect), 440 2727 (BTDirect, for the U.K.), 105 2727 (Canada Direct), 353 2727 (Ireland Direct), and . To reach New Zealand, call (177) 640 2727; South Africa, (177) 270 2727. For **MCI** World Phone, dial (177) 150 2727. For **Sprint** service, dial (177) 102 2727.

For **direct international calling,** dial 00, then the country code, area code, and telephone number. For collect, person-to-person, and credit card calls dial 188 for an **overseas operator.** The same number works for **international directory assistance.** The Tel Aviv international operator (tel. (03) 622 881/2/3) may make your connection more quickly.

Israel's **international phone code** is 972.

LIFE AND TIMES

■■■ GOVERNMENT & POLITICS

Israel's government is a parliamentary democracy. There is no written constitution; instead, a series of Acts of Parliament serves as the framework for legislation. Presently, Israelis do not vote for candidates in general elections; instead, they vote for a political party, more than 20 of which exist at present count. The percentage of the popular vote received by a given party is then converted into a proportion of the

ECONOMY

120 seats of the Knesset, the Israeli parliament. The leader of the party with the majority of representatives becomes prime minister.

As you may have guessed, never in Israeli history has a party achieved a majority by itself. Election results usually send parties scrambling to form coalitions, promising all and sundry to their most bitter enemies. The process of getting smaller parties to board the bandwagon usually takes weeks of squabbling and screaming, cajoling and conceding. Once enough parties have banded together to form a majority, the game ends and a prime minister is named. Under this election system the smallest parties have disproportionate clout; they have the power to exact concessions from the larger parties, who will promise anything in return for that last scale-tipping seat.

Public dissatisfaction with this system led to new legislation approved by the Knesset in 1992. Starting with the 1996 general election, Israelis will elect their prime minister directly, in addition to a party. The elected prime minister will thus no longer be dependent on Knesset support for the stability of his/her government. Small parties, to be sure, are trying to repeal this law, which threatens to cut dramatically into their political power.

The two major parties are **Labor** (*Avoda*, sometimes still referred to as *Ma'arakh*, the Alignment) and **Likud.** Labor's roots are in old-style Labor Zionism, and the Likud still carries the banner of Revisionist Zionism. Likud, now led by Binyamin Natanyahu, is the more right-wing of the two. It is from this side that you will hear politicians refer to Arabs as grasshoppers and vow to reclaim all of "Greater Israel." The left-of-center Labor, led by Yitzhak Rabin and counting the relatively liberal Shimon Peres as a member, is responsible for negotiating the current status of the occupied territories. The 1984 and 1988 elections ended in ties, with the two big parties forming National Unity Governments largely paralyzed by internal dissent. In 1990, hard-liner Yitzhak Shamir formed a Likud-led government supported by religious and far-right parties. But a general election in June 1992 decisively ousted Shamir and replaced him with a Labor-led government under Prime Minister Rabin. Labor won 44 Knesset seats to Likud's 32, out of 120 total.

After the big two, Israeli parties run the political gamut. Arguing for territorial concessions in the peace process, religious pluralism, and civil rights is **Meretz** (12 seats), a new movement made up of the smaller parties Ratz, Shinui, and Mapam. Meretz is Labor's main partner in the government. Orthodox-nationalist Jews in Israel are represented by the **National Religious Party** (which, for the first time in Israeli history, is not in the current government), with five seats, while the Ultra-Orthodox are represented by **Shas** (a Sephardic party in the current government) and **United Torah Judaism.** Shas holds six seats, and United Torah Judaism seven. On the Likud's right, former IDF chief of staff Rafael (Raful) Eitan's **Tzomet** quadrupled its size to take eight seats; Tzomet combines a tough stance on the territories with a Meretz-like platform on social policy. Further right, the tiny ultra-right wing **Moledet** (Homeland), led by Rehavam Ze'evi (facetiously nicknamed Gandhi) advocates "transfer" (expulsion) of Palestinians from the territories; Moledet has three seats. On the far left, the **Arab Democratic Party,** made up of Arabs living within Israel proper and holding Israeli citizenship, took two seats; and **Hadash,** the Communist party, another two.

■■■ ECONOMY

Poor in natural resources and big on defense expenses, Israel's economy has always been a fragile equation of foreign support, productivity, foreign support, government spending, and foreign support. The country's main industries are chemicals, diamonds, high-tech products, textiles, and military equipment. Israel is also a world leader in desert agriculture. Recently there have been extended periods of instability and inflation. The country saw two currency changes, from lirot to shekelim to new shekelim (NIS), made in attempts to control the devaluation of the currency.

The old shekel was once worth one-thousandth of a lira; the new shekel is worth one-tenth an old one.

A 1983 crisis was followed by a series of devaluations in the shekel, reductions in government spending, and cutbacks in food subsidies. Israelis rushed to buy stable American dollars, and it was even suggested that U.S. dollars be used as legal tender. A new finance minister stopped government support of the shekel, and inflation consequently skyrocketed, hitting a high of 24.3% in October 1984—an annual rate of 1260%. That month the government implemented an austerity program, freezing prices, wages, taxes, and profits. Unemployment jumped but inflation dropped to a monthly 3.7% in December. When controls were relaxed the following year, inflation boomeranged to 300%; and discontent rose as the standard of living fell. But Israel finally recorded its first surplus on its balance-of-payments account in 1985.

Today, while inflation is kept at around 10-15%, Israel is once again plagued by economic turmoil. When Palestinians boycotted Israeli goods during the *intifada,* Israel's US$1 billion-a-year export market in the occupied territories was greatly endangered. More importantly, the influx of over 450,000 immigrants since 1989 has put a substantial burden on the national budget. The government offers Jews housing and social benefits to encourage them to immigrate. These immigrants have also increased the unemployment rate; about 40% of them (often highly skilled) are unemployed. At least US$3 billion in American money each year and a guarantee of $10 billion in loans provides help. In 1994 Israel established diplomatic relations with Morocco; and ongoing negotiations with Syria, Jordan, and other Middle Eastern countries, as well as the allowance of minimal Palestinian self-rule in the West Bank and Gaza, promised to reap further economic benefits for Israel.

■■■ KIBBUTZIM & MOSHAVIM

Three percent of the Israeli population lives on **kibbutzim** (plural of kibbutz), somewhat socialist rural societies where production is controlled by members. Kibbutzim are responsible for much of Israel's agricultural production and political leadership. The kibbutzim of today hardly resemble the fiercely ideological pioneer agricultural settlements that began 80 years ago. These days, most rely more on industry than on agriculture. In addition, the passion for austerity is subsiding; kibbutzniks now demand the same luxuries enjoyed by other Israelis (larger living quarters, TVs and VCRs, Bart Simpson rhinestone jackets). Many kibbutz children now live with their parents in nuclear family homes, whereas just a decade or two ago nearly all lived in separate dormitories and saw their parents only at certain times.

Today's kibbutzim face mounting problems. Labor shortages are on the rise as two-thirds of younger members leave the settlements to test their skills elsewhere. In addition, debt is becoming a daunting threat; kibbutzim owe a collective US$4 billion, about US$31,000 for each kibbutznik.

Moshavim (plural of *moshav*), another type of rural settlement, provide roughly 40% of Israel's food. Members of a *moshav* typically operate their own piece of land, though marketing is often done collectively. Some *moshavim* also have a crop that all members help cultivate; they do not have communal dining rooms like kibbutzim. Recently, many of the *moshavim* near big cities have gone suburban.

■■■ THE ARMY

Israel is usually proud of its army, known as Tzahal (the Hebrew acronym for Tz'va Hagana LeYisrael.) In English, the army is called the Israel Defense Forces (IDF). All 18-year-olds are drafted—men for three years, women for two—with certain exceptions, most notably non-Druze Arabs (who may enlist if they choose but are not conscripted) and *yeshiva* students. The IDF is a fact of life for Israeli men aged 18 to 55, when reserve duty *(miluim)* ceases. Women are not called for reserve service.

■■■ RELIGION & ETHNICITY

Freedom of religion has been safeguarded by the state; in 1967, the Law for the Protection of Holy Places was passed when Israel annexed Jerusalem's sacred sites. **Jews** make up 82% of the population (4,150,000), **Muslims** 13.8% (700,000), **Christians** 2.5% (125,000), and **Druze** and others 1.7% (85,000). Each community operates its own religious courts, funded by the Ministry of Religion, and controls its own holy sites. Every religions' days of rest are guaranteed by law.

The vast majority of Israeli **Jews** are secular; only about 15% are Orthodox or Ultra-Orthodox (though in Jerusalem it might appear otherwise). The religious establishment is quite powerful; the electoral system has helped Jewish religious parties to wield disproportionate power. Much to the aggravation of many secular Israelis, Rabbinical courts have a state monopoly on matrimonial issues. Jews in Israel are not permitted to marry non-Jews.

Israeli Jews are divided along ethnic lines: **Sephardi** Jews come from Arab or other Mediterranean countries; **Ashkenazi** Jews have European origins. The rift in Israeli society is deep and wide, and goes back to the 1950s, when Sephardi Jews from Morocco and Iraq were brought to an already established, Ashkenazi-dominated state. While Sephardim compose more than 50% of the Jewish population in Israel, Ashkenazim still fill most of the power positions in government, economy, the military, and academia, and Sephardim are the vast majority among the poor.

After Mecca and Medina, the most important **Muslim** holy site is Jerusalem—the Al Aqsa Mosque. Muslim *hadith* tells of Muhammad's journey from Mecca to Al Aqsa (The Farthest) and up through the Seven Heavens to meet with God.

Many **Christian** sects are represented in Israel, including the Armenian Orthodox, Abyssinian, Anglican, Coptic (Egyptian), Greek Orthodox, Roman Catholic, and Syrian Orthodox. Most are Arab by language and origin.

Friendly relations between Jews and **Druze** deteriorated after Israel annexed Syria's Golan Heights. Unlike Muslims, Druze serve in the army. They also have their own communal institutions. There is a large **Baha'i** population, whose holy sites in Israel are the Tomb of Al Bab in Haifa and the Tomb of Baha'u'llah near Akko.

See Introduction to the Region, p. 32 for a more detailed discussion of religion.

■■■ FESTIVALS & HOLIDAYS

All Jewish holidays, including *Shabbat* (Sabbath), are officially observed. Each holiday begins at sundown on the evening preceding its calendar date and ends at sundown the next day. The holidays fall on different days each year with respect to the Gregorian calendar because their dates are fixed according to the Jewish lunar calendar. On most holidays and the afternoon before, stores, banks, and government-run offices and services close in Jewish areas. In predominantly Arab areas, the Muslim holidays are observed; and in the Christian quarters, major holidays such as the New Year, Easter, and Christmas are celebrated on different days, according to either the Gregorian calendar (observed by Protestants and Catholics) or the Julian calendar (followed by the Greek Orthodox and Armenian churches). See Planning Your Trip: When To Go, p. 1, for religious holidays.

Israeli holidays include **Yom Ha-Sho'ah** (Holocaust Day, Apr. 16) and **Yom Ha-Zikaron** (Memorial Day, Apr. 23); the latter commemorates Israeli soldiers who died the day before **Yom Ha'Atzma'ut** (Independence Day, Apr. 24). On both *Yom Ha-Sho'ah* and *Yom Ha-Zikaron*, sirens signal moments of silence; be respectful.

Israel has a plethora of cultural festivals. The **Israel Festival** takes place in Jerusalem (May-June), followed by the **Jerusalem Film Festival** (later in June). Other noteworthy events include the rocking **Hebrew Music Celebrations** in Arad (mid-July), attracting mostly young crowds; the internationally acclaimed **Jazz in the Red Sea** festival in Eilat (late August); the Akko **Fringe Theatre Festival** (Sept. 7-24 in 1995); and the **Haifa Film Festival,** the last two both taking place during the holiday of *Sukkot* (Oct. 9-17 in 1995).

■■■ LANGUAGE

The contemporary Hebrew language was created from biblical Hebrew by **Eliezer Ben-Yehuda,** who compiled the first modern dictionary in the 1920s. In a surprisingly short period, the revived biblical dialect matured into a full-fledged language, spanning from colloquial speech to poetry. While a Semitic language (like Arabic) in structure, modern Hebrew contains elements of European languages; many words for which no equivalent biblical concept exists, such as *psykologia* (psychology), or *cassetta* (cassette), have been lifted almost as-is.

Most Israelis speak some English, and signs are usually written in English (and sometimes Russian) as well as Hebrew and Arabic, the official languages of Israel. You may want to learn a few Hebrew phrases; the best phrasebooks are the Dover publication *Say It in Hebrew* and *Berlitz Hebrew for Travelers* (both about US$5).

The appendix of this book contains a list of useful Hebrew words and phrases.

■■■ THE ARTS

LITERATURE

The compilation of the biblical narrative was followed by the age of the *Mishnah* (100 BCE-700 CE), when *halakha* (laws derived from the Bible) and *agada* (elaboration on the Bible) were compiled. This age also saw the growth of the *piyyut* (liturgical poem). In the Middle Ages, Jewish poetry included *Megillat Antiohus* and *Megillat Hanuka;* and narrative prose focused on demonological legends.

The revival of Hebrew as a secular language in the 18th century brought a drastic shift in Hebrew literature. Josef Perl and Isaac Erter parodied Hasidic works in their writings. In Czarist Russia, Abraham Mapu wrote *The Hypocrite,* the first novel to portray modern Jewish social life in a fictional context. The generations that followed moved toward realism, often employing Yiddish, a more versatile language.

At the turn of the 20th century, Hebrew was revived for literature by Joseph Brenner, whose hallmark character was the tragic, uprooted settler. His works are remarkable not only for their influence on subsequent generations of Israeli writers, but also for their pessimistic depictions of social interaction between Jews and Arabs. In the 1920s and 1930s Nobel Laureate Shmuel Yosef (Shai) Agnon confronted the breakdown of cultural cohesion among modern Jews in *A Guest for the Night, The Bridal Canopy,* and *Twenty-One Stories.* Leah Goldberg infused the harsh realities of life into her poetry.

Just before the creation of the State of Israel, a group of native Hebrew authors arose. Their style, characterized by concern for the landscape and the moment, is exemplified in S. Yizhar's *Efrayim Returns to Alfalfa.* Beginning in the late 1950s, writers such as Amos Oz and A. B. Yehoshua began to experiment with psychological realism, allegory, and symbolism. In the 1960s, new skepticism surfaced in Israeli literature. Yehoshua, for example, wrote about tensions between generations, Arabs and Jews, and Sephardim and Ashkenazim in his "Facing the Forests" and his collection of short stories *Three Days and a Child.* David Shahar has been called the Proust of Hebrew literature for his *The Palace of Shattered Vessels* set in Jerusalem in the 1930s and 40s. Ya'akov Shabtai's *Past Continuous,* about Tel Aviv in the 1970s, was perhaps the best Israeli novel of the decade. A stunning though initially confusing must-read is *Arabesques,* by Anton Shammas, an Arab Israeli writing in Hebrew.

More recently, a number of people have written fascinating accounts of their experiences in Israel. Oz's *In the Land of Israel* is a series of interviews with native Israelis and West Bank Palestinians that documents the wide range of political sentiment; his *A Perfect Peace* is a semi-allegorical account of kibbutz life just before the Six-Day War. The poet Yehuda Amihai offers insight into the soul of the modern Israeli in his *Selected Poems.* Both books have been translated to English, as have most major Israeli works. Other personal accounts include Saul Bellow's *To*

Jerusalem and Back and journalist Lawrence Meyer's *Israel Now*. David Grossman's *Yellow Wind* tells of one Israeli Jew's journey to the West Bank just prior to the *intifada*. *The West Bank Story* by Rafik Halabi, an Israeli Druze television reporter, is an informative account. Fawaz Turki's *The Disinherited* is the autobiography of a Palestinian Arab, and Ze'ev Chafetz's *Heroes and Hustlers, Hard Hats and Holy Men* is a hilarious look at Israeli society and politics.

Aharon Appelfeld's *The Age of Wonders* and *Badenheim 1939* offer a survivor's account of the Holocaust. *Voices Within the Ark,* by Howard Schwartz and Anthony Rudolph, is an anthology of 20th-century Jewish poetry, much of which derives from the Israeli experience. David Grossman's *See Under: Love* is a complicated account of coming to terms with the Holocaust.

Israel's short but tumultuous history has inspired a number of historical novels. Consider reading Ḥayim Potok's *Wanderings,* James Michener's *The Source,* and Leon Uris' *Exodus*. For a more sober textbook history of the land read Barbara Tuchman's *Bible and Sword,* which chronicles Palestine from the Bronze Age to the Balfour Declaration of 1917. The elegant works of Solomon Grayzel also give historical background. The dense but provocative *The Arabs in Israel,* by Sabri Jiryis, describes just that. Serious academic types should pick up Nadav Safran's hefty *Israel: The Embattled Ally* or Conor Cruise O'Brien's lighter *The Siege*.

The Israeli **press** is far livelier than the Western norm; politics is taken seriously and opinions expressed vociferously. The liberal *Ha'Aretz* is the most respected daily; *Yediot Aḥronot* is more tabloidesque and therefore more widely read. *The Jerusalem Post*, the only English-language daily, is now generally right-wing, while the bi-weekly English-language *Jerusalem Report* has high-quality reporting and analysis and dovish editors. The *Post* reprints *The New York Times* "Week in Review" section each Monday.

VISUAL ARTS

Eighty years ago, sculptor Boris Schatz set up the Bezalel School of Arts and Crafts in Jerusalem in an attempt to fuse a Western approach with various Oriental styles and to link the Jewish past with utopian visions of the future. Intense vitality and development characterizes the period since the school's founding, with later students and faculty rejecting the romantic vision of the founding fathers.

In the 1930s, artists invoked Germany's dark, emotional expressionism. Immigrants fleeing Nazism congregated in Jerusalem around the "New Bezalel." The events of the 1948 War did not evoke political or epic art; rather, the abstraction of the "New Horizons" group was dominant for decades after the 1940s. For many of those artists, born and educated in Europe, the blinding Mediterranean light and the Israeli landscape were prime sources of inspiration. The terraces and ridges of the coastal regions, rolling agricultural plains, and surrealistic forms of the desert influenced and inspired the line and shape of early Israeli art.

1960s art turned to what was later described as "the poverty of matter." Spartan means of expression were used to reflect the material poverty of the country itself. Today's artists are concerned instead with thematic content. Their art is political, critical, and emotional. In line with contemporary trends in Western art, Israeli artists often incorporate text, evoke other works of art, and use mixed media to create complex works full of references and layered with meaning.

Israeli art is not what you see in the galleries of Old Jaffa. The country's artistic life is centered in Tel Aviv, where most artists live and most galleries operate. Gordon Street has the biggest concentration of mainstream, distinguished galleries, while more avant-garde galleries are scattered throughout town. For listings of current exhibits, see *Four by Five,* a comprehensive bi-monthly guide available in English in museums and galleries.

MUSIC

Music became organized after World War I, when Jews in Palestine assembled chamber groups, a symphony orchestra, an opera company, and a choral society.

During the 1930s, with the rise of Nazism in Europe, hundreds of Jewish music teachers, students, composers, instrumentalists, and singers, and thousands of music lovers, streamed into the area. This influx spurred the formation of several music groups. Today seasonal music activities from October into July are held in such varied settings as the historic Crusader Castle at Akko and the modern, 3000-seat Mann Auditorium in Tel Aviv.

Israeli **popular music** started emerging from its folk-chant origins (often echoing Russian folk melodies) in the late 1960s. Some singers, like Yoni Rekhter and Matti Caspi, took a mellow direction, creating unique, sophisticated tunes that have since become Israeli classics. Others, like Shalom Ḥanokh and Kaveret, Israel's first real rock 'n' roll band, went for more straight-forward rock music. Since the 1970s, Israel has been catching up with the pace of international music fashions; local bands momentarily lingered on punk, reggae, heavy metal, grunge, and even rap. MTV now keeps Israeli youth abreast of the goings-on in London and Seattle, and they expect nothing less of their own local acts. Tel Aviv is the unequivocal hub of the cutting-edge music scene in Israel.

Mashina, Israel's longest-lasting rock band, moved from tight tunes and playful lyrics to harder-edged sounds. Etnix has perfected a blockbuster formula combining dance music and Middle Eastern motifs. Still, the most popular performers in Israel (such as Shlomo Artzi and Yehuda Poliker) play music that's somewhere in between kick-butt rock and a more mellow, acoustic sound. In many places you can hear simple Middle Eastern-style music, heavy on synthesizers and drum machines, blasting from car stereos and boomboxes: this is *muzika mizraḥit* ("oriental music"), very popular with Sephardi Jews. While internationally-known Achinoam Nini and David Broza continue to croon in Hebrew and English, today's teenage idol is hard-rocker Aviv Gefen. Two popular newcomers to the Israeli rock scene are Aifo Ha-Yeled (Where's the Kid?) and the humorous, Nirvana-esque Caspar's Rabbit Show.

■ ■ ■ FOOD

Some Israelis' diets are affected by *kashrut* (meaning proper or properly prepared), the Jewish dietary laws. *Kashrut* forbid the consumption of meat or chicken with dairy products, animals without split hooves that do not chew their cud (most notably pork), and fish without both scales and fins (such as shellfish). Observant Jews will not eat or shop in a place that carries non-kosher goods; consequently, to keep kosher clientele coming, the big supermarket chains in Israel carry only kosher products, and many restaurants (including most hotels) serve only kosher food. Still, observance of *kashrut* is hardly the norm in Israel—many restaurants, particularly in big cities excepting Jerusalem, are strictly *non*-kosher.

The typical Israeli eats a large breakfast, returns home for a big mid-day dinner, and has a light, late supper. Because of the poor quality and high cost of beef and lamb, Israelis rely largely on chicken, dairy, and vegetable products. Popular items in the Israeli diet include hummus, an Arab staple adopted by Israelis; the Israeli salad, a finely chopped mix with tomatoes and cucumbers garnished with oil and vinegar; *gvina levana,* soft white cheese; *schnitzel,* breaded and fried chicken breast; *chips,* the local name for french fries; and a variety of sweet dairy snacks.

Israel's most popular **street food** is also an Arabic food: falafel are deep-fried ground chick-pea balls served in pita bread with vegetables and *taḥina* sauce. Other common pita-fillers are hummus (mashed chick-peas, garlic, lemon, and *taḥina*) and *shawerma* (chunks of roast turkey, sometimes posing as lamb). Falafel, hummus, and *shawerma* stands always have a colorful selection of salads and toppings such as *ḥarif,* a red-hot sauce. *Burekas* (filo dough folded over a cheese, potato, spinach, or meat filling) come in different shapes, typically triangular, and are available at pastry shops and some fast-food kiosks. Pizza also abounds. On hot summer days, street vendors sell what look like hand grenades. Not to worry—these are *sabras* (a prickly cactus fruit), and the inside is edible, although the seeds cause some people indigestion. (*Sabra* is also a term for a native-born Israeli; both the fruit and the people are said to be thorny on the outside, sweet on the inside.)

The variety of ethnic cuisines in Israel is impressive; **restaurants** run the gamut from Chinese to French to Moroccan to American to Yemenite. Many restaurants serve typical Middle Eastern food like hummus and *kabab*. In Yemenite restaurants, *malawaḥ,* thin fried dough usually dipped in a watery tomato sauce, is a cheap specialty. Restaurants serving Eastern European Jewish food are surprisingly few and very expensive; for affordable *gefilte fish,* go to New York.

Preparing your own food is quite cheap, especially in summer when fresh fruits and vegetables are available in every outdoor *shuk* (market). You can buy groceries inexpensively at local *shuks,* at the neighborhood *makolet* (small grocery store), or in supermarkets. Israeli bread is tasty and cheap; on Thursdays and Fridays, stores sell fresh loaves of *ḥallah,* egg bread sprinkled with sesame or poppy seeds. Supermarket refrigerators sport a huge selection of dairy products, from low-fat yogurts (try Prikef) to cream-topped chocolate snacks (try Milki). In the deli section you can get food-to-go by the gram, including cookies, miniature *burekas,* and other pastries, as well as an assortment of salads and pickles.

Unless you plan to single-handedly subsidize the Israeli soda industry, you should carry water around with you. Two Israeli **beers** are the excellent, deep-amber Goldstar and the lesser Maccabee lager. Goldstar is a common draught beer; Maccabee comes in bottles only. Other brews currently available on tap are Carlsberg, Tuborg, and Heineken. Supermarkets carry a small selection of liquor; note that Nesher "black beer" is a sweet, non-alcoholic malt brew. The official drinking age (not strictly enforced) is 18.

In Arab restaurants, if you ask for **coffee** with no specifications, you'll get a small cup of strong, sweet, Arabic coffee, sometimes referred to as *turki* (Turkish). If you want something resembling American coffee, ask in Hebrew for *ḥafukh* (mixed with milk) or *filter.* Instant coffee *(nes)* is also popular. "Black" *(shaḥor)* or "mud" *(botz)* coffee is Turkish coffee brewed in a cup; watch out for the sediment. Finally, Israel has many **ice cream** *(glida)* parlors and a respectable selection of ice-cream bars; try Chocolida, a chocolate-filled and coated vanilla bar. Yum-o.

■ Tel Aviv-Jaffa תל אביב–יפו

Tel Aviv, with its cafés, clubs, and overly-tanned youth, does its damndest to imitate a European way of life. If you have just arrived in the party capital of Israel from Jerusalem, you may be experiencing a bit of a culture shock. Only 45 minutes away from Jerusalem, the bustling metropolis of Tel Aviv stands as its antithesis: where Jerusalem thrives on the past, Tel Aviv lives for the moment; Jerusalem is sacred, Tel Aviv has no god; Jerusalem is built of stone, Tel Aviv was founded on shifting sands. Amos Oz, Israel's preeminent novelist, chuckles over the Tel-Aviv-Jerusalem differences: If Tel Avivians see the Holy City "as a fanatical loony bin," Jerusalemites see their Mediterranean neighbor as "a shallow steam bath, hurried and noisy, a little like a shtetl, petit-bourgeois, somewhat bohemian in a vulgar way, somewhat working-class with pseudo-proletarian pretensions. In short, a hick town, shrill, ugly, and very, very plebian." Indeed, the Israeli capital invariably inspires emotion among travelers—some fall in love, and some spoilsports catch the first bus to Jerusalem.

Today an integral part of Tel Aviv, Jaffa (Yafo, or "beautiful", in Hebrew; Yafa in Arabic) has one of the oldest functioning harbors in the world. The 20th century, however, witnessed the gradual decline of this port; it has been relegated by the modern ports of Haifa and Ashdod to harboring mainly small fishing boats. Starting in the 1960s, Israel undertook a massive renovation project, restoring and cleaning many of Jaffa's convents, mosques, alleyways, and crusader walls. The result may be a little too sterile, with restaurants and galleries catering mostly to tourists and generally avoided by locals. Still, the winding alleys of Old Jaffa *are* beautiful, and many other parts of Jaffa retain a vernacular Middle Eastern quality that the Modernist city of Tel Aviv lacks.

Two-thirds of Israel's population resides along the 150km of Israel's muggy central coast centered on Tel Aviv. Here the moisture that hangs in the air soaks out orthodoxy: in Haifa, buses run on *Shabbat*, and in Tel Aviv most establishments stay open Friday night. This region includes the country's wealthiest, most commercialized city as well as some of its most fertile farmland. In essence, this is the no-nonsense, secular Israel; the way it behaves when there are no tourists around.

■■■ HISTORY

According to the Bible, the recalcitrant prophet Jonah shirked his divine calling and fled to Joppa (today's Jaffa) to catch a boat to Tarshish. When a tempest threatened to destroy his ship, Jonah, knowing the Lord had created the storm, asked the crew to hurl him overboard. The sea calmed, but an enormous fish surfaced and swallowed the prophet. After three days and nights, Jonah repented and the fish delivered him safely to dry land (see Ashdod, p. 282). According to the New Testament, the Apostle Peter brought the disciple Tabitha back to life in Joppa. The latter then dwelt in the home of the town tanner and received divine instructions to preach to Gentiles. To this day, you can still visit the purported house of Simon the Tanner.

The earliest archaeological finds in Jaffa date from the 18th century BCE. In 1468 BCE, the Egyptians conquered Jaffa by hiding soldiers in life-sized clay jars that were brought into the city market. King David conquered the city in about 1000 BCE, and under Solomon it became the main port of Jerusalem, a position it maintained until the development of Caesarea under King Herod. During the 12th century, Jaffa was captured by the Crusaders, Salah ad-Din, Richard the Lion-Hearted, the Muslims, and finally the Crusaders again, who then built magnificent walls and towers, parts of which remain extant today. In 1267 the Mamluks overpowered the city, and Jaffa remained an important Arab stronghold until 1948.

Jewish immigrants began to settle in Jaffa as early as 1820; at that time the Palestinian town of Yafa served as the country's major port. Later in the century there were enough Jews to create the first two exclusively Jewish neighborhoods just to the north, **Neveh Tzedek** in 1887 and **Neveh Shalom** in 1891. As the Jewish population in Jaffa continued to increase, settlers decided to found a new suburb in this area. On April 11, 1909, they parceled out the land they had acquired north of Jaffa, naming the area, with sober Zionist practicality, **Aḥuzat Bayit** (Housing Estate). One year later, the suburb was renamed **Tel Aviv** (Spring Hill), after the imaginary town Theodore Herzl had envisioned in his turn-of-the-century utopian novel *Altneuland* (Old-New-Land). Appealing to more *bourgeois* Jewish immigrants from Eastern Europe, the new town quickly developed in the 1920s and 1930s, becoming the largest Jewish town in Palestine under British rule.

Palestinian Arabs in Jaffa never reacted positively to the usurpation of their land by European Jews. In 1929, 1936, and 1939, Jaffa was the scene of anti-Zionist riots. In the 1948 war, many of the Palestinians in Jaffa and its surrounding villages, including Yazur and Salameh, were forcibly evacuated by Israeli troops. These villages were then razed to the ground; and no trace of them remains, except for in the memories of their former inhabitants. As Jewish immigrants from Europe were shipped in to fill the town and often given emptied Arab homes in which to live, Jaffa was officially incorporated into the Tel Aviv municipality in 1949. Today Jaffa is one of a few mixed Jewish-Arab neighborhoods in Israel.

Tel Aviv today acts as the internationally-recognized capital of Israel and the home of its foreign embassies, airport, and financial life. For a brief period in the winter of 1991, Tel Aviv got world attention (via CNN) as a favorite target for Saddam Hussein's Scud missiles. For the first time in its short history, the city became a front line; businesses closed, virtually all nightlife stalled, and many residents chose to stay with friends and relatives elsewhere. Contrary to fears that the city would "never be the same again," the very first night after cease-fire was declared all movie theaters, bars, and dance clubs re-opened, and Tel Avivians went out partying as usual.

■■■ ORIENTATION

Located in the center of Israel's Mediterranean coastline, Tel Aviv is 63km (bus ride 50min.) northwest of Jerusalem, and 95km (1¼hr.) south of Haifa.

The two main points of entry into Tel Aviv are Ben-Gurion Airport (at Lod) and the new bus terminal. Frequent bus service from the airport is supplemented by vans sent by local hostel-warring establishments to kidnap potential customers.

Much of Tel Aviv's seemingly haphazard street layout was actually carefully planned, following the 19th-century English "garden suburb" scheme. Nothing like Hampstead in appearance, Tel Aviv may be as difficult to navigate as London. House numbers generally increase from the sea eastward and from the more modest southern part of the city up to the wealthier north. The street signs are in English as well as Hebrew and announce the range of building numbers for that block.

Almost all hotels, restaurants, and places of interest are in the rectangle marked by the beach to the west, the **Ayalon Highway** to the east, the **Yarkon River** to the north, and **Salameh Rd.** to the south. Running along the beach beginning around Gordon St. and extending south to the Charles Clore Park is the **Promenade** (Ha-Tayelet), lined with chairs, gazebos, and open cafés. **Ha-Yarkon St.** runs parallel to the beach behind the first row of buildings facing the sea; the latter tend to be Tel Aviv's more expensive hotels. The next major north-south artery, **Ben-Yehuda St.,** runs one block east of Ha-Yarkon and is lined with travel agencies and more affordable restaurants. **Ibn Gvirol Street,** with its shaded arcades, runs from the Yarkon river in the north until it turns into Yehuda Ha-Levi St. in the center; half-way is the vast **Kikkar Malkhei Yisrael** (Kings of Israel Square), in front of the Tel Aviv City Hall. **Namir Rd.** (which still goes by its old name, **Haifa Rd.**) is a major thoroughfare farther east; the **central train station,** which has convenient service to all major cities, is located at the intersection of Haifa Rd. and **Arlozorov St.,** which runs east-west all the way to Ha-Yarkon St.

 Kikkar Magen David is the starting point of **Shuk Ha-Carmel** (Carmel Market) to the southwest, the *midraḥov* (pedestrian mall) of **Naḥalat Binyamin** to the south, and the hip **Sheinkin St.** to the east. Northwest of the *shuk* are the winding alleyways of **Kerem Ha-Temanim** (the Yemenite Quarter). The crumbling (and gradually gentrifying) neighborhood of **Neveh Tzedek,** with the beautiful **Kikkar Suzanne Delal,** lies just south of Shuk Ha-Carmel and Naḥalat Binyamin. **Jaffa** and its waterfront lie further south, outside the downtown area.

■■■ TRANSPORTATION

Tel Aviv is easily manageable by foot. Only sights north of the Yarkon, in the Ramat Aviv area, or in Jaffa are beyond walking distance from the city center. But on a hot August afternoon, a bus ride across town may be just too tempting; almost all buses in Tel Aviv are air-conditioned, cheap, frequent, and comfortable.

Opened in August 1993, the **New Central Bus Station** on Livinsky St. is the antithesis of its predecessor, expected to close by 1995. The air-conditioned interior of the seven-story, ramp-covered building houses music stores, banks, and even a McDonald's. Lockers, telephones, and restrooms abound; and over 3000 entrances and exits make this the most convoluted bus station in the world. Information booths on the 3rd, 4th, and 6th floors are supplemented by scores of electronic bulletin boards which list all kinds of information in both English and Hebrew.

Most **intercity buses** are operated by **Egged** and leave from the 6th floor; the majority of buses within Tel Aviv are operated by **Dan** (tel. 639 4444). **City buses** run Sun.-Thurs. 5am-12:15am, Fri. 5am-5:45pm, and Sat. 8:15pm-12:15am (NIS2.80).

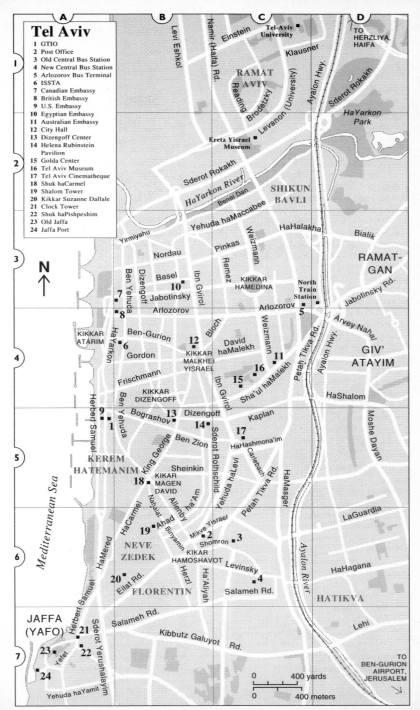

Tel Aviv

1 GTIO
2 Post Office
3 Old Central Bus Station
4 New Central Bus Station
5 Arlozorov Bus Terminal
6 ISSTA
7 Canadian Embassy
8 British Embassy
9 U.S. Embassy
10 Egyptian Embassy
11 Australian Embassy
12 City Hall
13 Dizengoff Center
14 Helena Rubinstein
   Pavilion
15 Golda Center
16 Tel Aviv Museum
17 Tel Aviv Cinematheque
18 Shuk haCarmel
19 Shalom Tower
20 Kikkar Suzanne Dallale
21 Clock Tower
22 Shuk haPishpeshim
23 Old Jaffa
24 Jaffa Port

Buses do not run on *Shabbat,* so from sundown Friday to sundown Saturday you can feel safe crossing the street. On extended stays, consider buying Dan's **monthly bus pass** (NIS108). Memorize these six city bus routes:

#4: From the new central bus station (4th floor), runs parallel to the coastline up Allenby and Ben-Yehuda St. and back. Every 5min.

#5: From the new central bus station (4th floor), runs north along Rothschild Blvd. and Dizengoff St. to Dizengoff Ctr., then turns around at Nordau and Yehuda Ha-Maccabee. Every 5min.

#10: Runs from city hall to Jaffa along Ben-Yehuda St. and returns via Ha-Yarkon. Every 15-20min.

#25: Runs between Tel Aviv University and Bat-Yam via Haifa Rd., Yehuda Ha-Maccabee, Shuk Ha-Carmel, and Jaffa. Every 8-15min.

#27: From the new central bus station (1st floor), runs along Petaḥ Tikva Rd. and Haifa Rd. to Tel Aviv University, near Tel Barukh and back. Every 10-15min.

#46: From the new central bus station (1st floor) to Jaffa and back. Every 8-10min., every 15min. at night.

Minibuses operating as **sherut taxis** run along the routes of bus #4 and 5, and are numbered accordingly. They charge exact bus fares (NIS2.80) and will stop for you anywhere along the route if you flag them down. These minibuses operate all night and on *Shabbat* as well, with less frequency and at a 20% higher fare.

■■■ PRACTICAL INFORMATION

Government Tourist Information Office (GTIO): 5 Shalom Aleichem (tel. 510 1451), on a small side street connecting Ha-Yarkon St. and Ben-Yehuda St. Provides maps of Tel Aviv and other cities and schedules of cultural events. A great new computer system puts information on accommodations, food, shopping, and tours at the disposal of the technologically literate. Limited number of tickets to Folklore Evenings. Open Sun.-Thurs. 8:30am-5pm, Fri. 8:30am-2pm.

Tours: SPNI, 4 Ha-Shfela St. (tel. 537 4425), between Petaḥ Tikva Rd. and Ha-Sharon St. Open Sun.-Thurs. 8am-5pm, Fri. 8-11:30am. Guided trips in English to all parts of the country, year-round. 1-day tours (Jerusalem US$39, Wadi Kelt US$45) or 2- to 4-day tours. **Neot Ha-Kikar,** 78 Ben-Yehuda St. (tel. 522 8161 or 8162 or 8163), downstairs. Guided tours in Egypt by foot, jeep, camel, or your own combination. 1-day Sinai Desert Safari to St. Catherine's US$55, 4 days in 3-star hotels in Egypt US$189, and 4 days of camel-trekking in the Sinai US$275. **Egged Tours,** 59 Ben-Yehuda St. (tel. 527 1212 or 2219), offers various guided tours around the country and to the Sinai (half-day tours of Jerusalem or Tel Aviv US$22, full-day US$45-55).

Budget Travel: ISSTA, 109 Ben-Yehuda St. (tel. 517 0111), corner of Ben-Gurion St. For ISICs or Youth Hostel cards bring a photo and NIS25. Open Sun.-Thurs. 8:30am-1pm and 3-6pm, Fri. 8:30am-1pm. Call for other locations throughout the country. **Mona Tours,** 45 Ben-Yehuda St. (tel. 523 0920), specializes in student and charter rates. ISIC not always required for low fares. Open Sun.-Thurs. 8am-6pm, Fri. 9:30am-1pm.

Consulates: Australia, 37 Sha'ul Ha-Melekh Blvd., Europe House, 4th floor (tel. 695 0451). Open Mon.-Thurs. 8-11am. **Canada,** 7 Ḥavakuk St. (tel. 546 2878). Open Mon.-Fri. 8am-noon, or by phone 1:30-4pm. **Egypt,** 54 Basel St. (tel. 546 4151 or 4152; fax 544 1615), just off Ibn Gvirol. Open Sun.-Thurs. 9-11am. For visa, bring your passport, photo, and NIS50—be sure to tell them if you are going beyond the Sinai, or you'll automatically get a "Sinai Only" visa. **South Africa,** Top Tower, Dizengoff Ctr., 16th floor (tel. 526 2566), enter through Gate 3. Open Mon.-Fri. 9-11:30am, and Wed. 2-3pm. **U.K.** (also serves **New Zealanders**), 1 Ben-Yehuda St., Migdalor Building, 6th floor (tel. 510 0166 for passports, 510 0497 for visas; fax 510 1167). Open Mon.-Fri. 8-11:30am. **U.S.,** 71 Ha-Yarkon St. (tel. 517 0010). American citizens served in the very back of the visa section for Israelis—look for the signs. Open Mon.-Fri. 8-11am; after-hours call 517 4347.

Currency Exchange: Most banks open Sun., Tues., and Thurs. 8:30am-12:30pm and 4-5:30pm, Mon., Wed., Fri., and holiday eves. 8:30am-12:30pm. Main bank offices: **Bank Ha-Poalim,** 104 Ha-Yarkon St. (tel. 520 0612); **Israel Discount,** 27 Yehuda Ha-Levi St. (tel. 514 5555); **Bank Leumi,** 130 Ben-Yehuda St. (tel. 520 3737); **First International,** 9 Ahad Ha'Am St. (tel. 519 6111). Branches throughout the city and suburbs. Some banks in hotels stay open later. **Israel Discount** also has branches in: the **Hilton Hotel,** Independence Park (tel. 524 5429; open Sun.-Thurs. 8am-12:30pm and 2:30-7:30pm, Fri. 8am-noon); the **Dan Hotel,** 59 Ha-Yarkon St. (tel. 523 3283; open Sun.-Thurs. 8am-2pm and 3:15-7:30pm, Fri. 8am-noon); and the **Sheraton,** 115 Ha-Yarkon St. (tel. 515 3332; open Sun.-Thurs. 8am-noon and 2-8pm, Fri. and holiday eve. 8am-noon).

American Express: Meditrad, Ltd., 112 Ha-Yarkon St. (tel. 524 2211). May be moving in Fall 1994. Mail held, but no packages. Cardholders can buy Traveler's Cheques with personal checks (1.25% service charge; bring your passport) for up to $1000 every 21 days. Travel agency offers discounts for cardholders, but doesn't change Cheques. Open Sun.-Thurs. 9am-5pm, Fri. 9am-1pm.

Thomas Cook: Unitours Israel, Ltd., 90a Ha-Yarkon St. (tel. 520 9999; fax 523 9299). Thomas Cook's head office in Israel; traveler's checks refunded, travel arrangements made. Open Sun.-Thurs. 8am-5pm, Fri. 8am-1pm.

Post Office: 7 Mikveh Yisrael St. (tel. 564 3651 or 3653, or toll free 177 022 2121), 2 blocks east of the south end of Allenby St. Open Sun.-Thurs. 7am-9:30pm, Fri. 7am-noon; **Post Restante** open Sun.-Thurs. 7am-9:30pm (tel. 564 3660); office with **fax, telegram,** and **telex** services open Sun.-Thurs. 8am-10pm, Fri. 8am-2pm. The branch at 61 Ha-Yarkon St. near the GTIO has **Western Union** money transfers (open Sun.-Thurs. 8am-6pm, Fri. and holiday eve. 8am-noon). For other branches, ask for the nearest *do'ar*. Most have fax and telegram service.

Telephones: Solan Communications, 13 Frischmann St. (tel. 522 9424; fax 522 9449). Private booths for international calls. Open 24 hrs. **Directory Assistance:** Tel. 144. **Telephone code:** 03.

Airport: Ben-Gurion Airport, 22km southeast of Tel Aviv in Lod. For recorded information in English about flights on all airlines, call 973 1122. Egged bus #475 to the airport leaves from the 6th floor of the new central bus station (every 20-25min. Sun.-Thurs. 5:20am-11:35pm, Fri. 5:20am-1:30pm; NIS5.70). United Tours shuttle #222 stops near several hotels on Ha-Yarkon St. and the El Al terminal at the central train station (buses every hr. Sun.-Fri. 4:30am-11:40pm, Sat. noon-midnight; ½hr.; NIS9.50). Taxis from the airport to Tel Aviv run at a fixed tariff (about NIS48, each piece of luggage NIS2; 25% extra evenings and *Shabbat*).

Trains: Information (tel. 693 7515) open 6am-8pm. Several air-conditioned trains to Haifa, Netanya, and Nahariya leave from the central train station (Arlozorov St. across Haifa Rd.; take bus #62 or 64 from Ben-Yehuda; approx. every hr. on the hr. Sun.-Thurs. 6am-5pm, Fri. 6am-2pm.) Trains to Jerusalem leave at 8:35am and 2:55pm (NIS11.50, students NIS9). Trains to Haifa (NIS13, students NIS10) leave more frequently—check the constantly-changing schedule at the station. The Hebrew word for train is *rakevet*.

Local Buses and Sherut taxis: See Transportation, p. 264.

Intercity Buses: Mostly operated by Egged (intercity service into. tel. 537 5555). By 1995, intercity buses will operate out of the new central bus station. The **Arlozorov terminal** has connections to major cities: Jerusalem, #480 direct (every 15-20min. Sun.-Thurs. 6am-10pm, Fri. 6am-4pm, Sat. sundown-10pm; NIS10.50, students NIS9.70); Haifa, #980 direct (every 15-20min. Sun.-Thurs. 6am-8:30pm, Fri. 6am-4pm, Sat. sundown-9pm; NIS9.70); Be'er Sheva, #380 direct (every 15-30min. Sun.-Thurs. 6am-8pm, Fri. 6am-3:45pm, Sat. sundown-10pm; NIS11:50/10.30). From the **new central bus station** (6th floor) to: Jerusalem, #405 direct (every 10-15min. Sun.-Thurs. 5:45am-11:30pm, Fri. 5:45am-5pm, Sat. sundown-midnight; NIS12.70/11.50); Haifa, #900 direct (every 10-20min. Sun.-Thurs. 5:45am-9pm, Fri. 5:45am-4:30pm, Sat. sundown-10:30pm; NIS14.50/13), or late-night #901 express (every 20min. Sun.-Thurs. 9-11pm, NIS14.50/13); Be'er Sheva, #370 direct (every 15-20min. Sun.-Thurs. 5:45am-8pm, Fri. 5:45am-4:20pm, Sat. sundown-10pm; NIS16/14.50).

Ferries: Caspi, 1 Ben-Yehuda St. (tel. 517 5749), Migdalor Bldg., facing the street. Boats to Cyprus and Rhodes (US$69; summer US$76) and Piraeus (US$73; summer US$82). Port tax additional US$16. **Mano Passenger Lines, Ltd.,** 97 Ben-Yehuda St. (tel. 522 4611), books tickets on ships to Cyprus. Boats leave from Haifa Sun. and Tues. at 7pm (US$68, higher in summer). Port tax additional US$16. Open Sun.-Thurs. 9am-6pm, Fri. 9am-12:30pm.

Taxis: Allenby Rd. at Ha-Moshavot Sq. Has cars to most major cities that are only slightly more expensive than buses. **Sherut** taxis operate along certain bus routes for bus fares; also run nights, Fri. evenings, and Sat. with a 20% surcharge. **Special (private) taxis** operate with meters—insist they be turned on. You can also call a taxi (tel. 524 9090, nights 527 1999) or go to Bugrashov 3, corner of Ha-Yarkon.

Car Rental: Rent-a-Reliable-Car (tel. 537 3110), US$54 per day for unlimited mileage. **Avis** (tel. 384 242), US$76 (in summer US$95) per day. **Budget** (tel. 562 1292), US$66 per day. **Hertz** (tel. 562 2121), US$73 per day. Prices in shekels are considerably higher. Most agencies will only rent to persons 23 or older with a credit card. Some major agencies accept an American license, but an international one is widely preferred. All prices include insurance.

Shopping Hours: In general, 8:30am-1pm and 3-7pm, but many places stay open until 10pm, especially those in shopping malls. Most stores stay open late on Thurs. night, and almost all close Fri. by 2pm.

English Bookstores: Pollak's Used Books, 36 King George St. (tel. 528 8613), has been buying and selling used books for 100 yrs. Open Sun.-Fri. 9am-1:30pm, Tues. 4-7pm. **Book Boutique,** 170 Ben-Yehuda St. Best used bookstore in town. Over 13,000 titles, including out-of-print books and best-sellers. Good conversation too. Open Sun.-Thurs. 10am-7pm, Fri. 10am-3pm. **Steimatzky,** 101 Dizengoff St. (tel. 527 0025) and 109 Dizengoff St. (tel. 522 1513). Open Sun.-Thurs. 9am-10pm, Fri. 9am-3pm. Branches at 107 Allenby St. (tel. 29 92 77; open Sun.-Thurs. 8:30am-7pm, Fri. and holidays 8:30am-2pm) and in shopping malls.

Library: American Cultural Center, 1 Ben-Yehuda St., Migdalor Bldg., 5th floor (tel. 510 6935). Open Mon.-Thurs. 10am-4pm, Fri. 10am-2pm. **British Council Library,** 140 Ha-Yarkon St. (tel. 522 2194). Open Mon.-Thurs. 10am-1pm and 4-7pm, Fri. 10am-1pm. Both offer English-language books, newspapers, and magazines to the public, as well as peaceful air-conditioned havens.

Camping Supplies: Maslool Travellers' Equipment and Information Center, 36 Ben-Yehuda St. (tel. 528 8418). Gives discounts for those who show a *Let's Go* guide; buys used equipment and has a standby/last-minute flight bulletin. Open Sun.-Thurs. 8am-8pm, Fri. 8am-3pm. **LaMetayel,** Dizengoff Center, Gate 3 or 5 (tel. 528 6894), near the Lev Cinema. The largest camping store in the area; they carry books, maps, guides, information, and a full range of equipment. Great place to meet young Israelis gearing up for their post-military grand tour of Nepal and Thailand. Open Sun.-Thurs. 9:30am-7:30pm, Fri. 9:30am-2pm.

Jewish National Fund (Kerem Kayemet leYisrael): 96 Ha-Yarkon St., near Mendele St. (tel. 526 1111). Organizes transportation to the **Modi'in Forest,** where you can plant a tree (US$10). Transportation (US$7) leaves from the Kerem Kayemet Building. Reservations required. Open Sun.-Thurs. 8am-2:30pm, Fri. 8am-noon.

Laundry: Nikita, 98 Ben-Yehuda St. Coin-operated machines. NIS6 washes 7kg of laundry, dryers NIS1 for 4min., detergent NIS2. **51 Ben-Yehuda St.** (tel. 522 2954). Coin-operated washers and dryers. Wash NIS10, soap NIS3, dry NIS8 per ½hr. For NIS5 they'll do it for you, for NIS4 they'll fold it. Open Sun.-Thurs. 8am-6pm, Fri. 8am-2pm. **Bu'ot,** 49 Sheinkin (tel. 292 094). For NIS24 they will pick up and clean up to 6kg of laundry and drop it off on your doorstep, folding NIS4. Many hostels have laundry facilities and services that are often cheaper.

Help Lines: Rape Crisis (tel. 523 4819), 24 hrs. **Drug Counseling** (tel. 546 3587), Sun.-Thurs. 8am-8pm. **Gay and Lesbian Hotline: Ha-Kav Ha-Lavan** (tel. 292 797), Sun. and Tues.-Thurs. 7:30-11:30pm. All speak English.

Pharmacy: Ben-Yehuda Pharmacy, 142 Ben-Yehuda St. (tel. 522 3535). Open Sun.-Thurs. 8am-3am, Fri. 8am-7pm, Sat. 5pm-1am. **Ha-Galil Pharmacy,** 80 Ben-Yehuda St. (tel. 522 3358), specializes in alternative medicine: homeopathy, herbs, and aromatic oils. Open Sun.-Fri. 8:30am-8pm. **Superpharm** in Dizengoff Center and other locations is more drugstore-like. No 24-hr. pharmacies in Tel

Aviv, but two pharmacies are always on duty for night and *Shabbat* calls. Schedules and phone numbers available on pharmacy doors and in newspapers.
Emergency: Fire: Tel. 102. **First Aid:** Tel. 101.
Police: Tel. 100.

■■■ ACCOMMODATIONS

Most hostels are on or around Ben-Yehuda St. and Ha-Yarkon St., with some just off Allenby Rd. or Dizengoff St. When choosing, keep in mind that drunken revelry and honking horns downtown may continue late into the night. Hostels fill quickly, especially in summer, so be sharp and make reservations. If all the beds are taken, a rooftop mattress works, especially on summer nights. Prices drop by about 10% in the off-season, paying in foreign currency will always save you the 18% VAT (see Money Matters, p. 252), and most places offer cheaper weekly rates. Sleeping on the beach is not only illegal, but also a bad idea—there have been cases of theft and sexual assault, especially against women traveling alone.

Sea & Sun Hostel, 62 Ha-Yarkon St. (tel./fax 517 3313 or 3373), corner of Nes Tziona. Spacious new hostel in a great location, with airy rooms, elevator, roof-top bar, and an incredible view of the beach from porches and roof, where the owner sometimes decides to hold free barbecues. Reception open 24 hrs. Check-out 11am. Lockout 11am-2pm. No curfew. Coed and single-sex dorm beds (4-14 per room) NIS27. Wash, dry, and fold NIS12. Safes NIS3.

No. 1 Hostel, 84 Ben-Yehuda St., 4th floor (tel. 523 7807), use the elevator. Two blocks away from the beach. Sunny reception lounge with cable TV and wicker chairs. All rooms have private bath, fan, and balcony. Traveler's checks cashed. 24-hr. reception. Check-out by 10:30am. Lockout 11am-2pm. No curfew. Kitchen closes at 11pm. Coed and single-sex dorm beds (4, 6, or 8 per room) NIS26. Doubles NIS77. Breakfast included. Free safe deposit for documents. Lockers NIS3 per day. Wash and dry NIS4 each.

Dizengoff Square Hostel, 11 Dizengoff Sq. (tel. 522 5184; fax 522 5181), next to Chen movie theater. Newly renovated, with lots of carpets, cozy TV room, and art-deco walls. Drinks available at reception. Rooftop bar (open 7pm-midnight), cable TV, plants, and a view of the plaza and its water sculpture. Reception open 24 hrs. Check-out by 10:30am. Lockout 10:30am-2:30pm. No curfew. Coed and single-sex dorm beds (6 per room) NIS26. Private singles and doubles NIS85. Free safes. Lockers NIS4. Wash and dry NIS4 each, detergent NIS1.

The Greenhouse, 201 Dizengoff St. (tel. 523 5994). Spotless rooms and showers, and a high-tech security system to boot. Homey TV room with cable; kitchen facilities; rooftop bar open until midnight (summer only). Extremely friendly management will arrange cheap flights for guests. Reception closed during lockout, 10am-2:30pm. Coed and single-sex dorm beds (4-5 per room) NIS33. Doubles NIS72. Apartments for 2 NIS120. Breakfast NIS5, dinner NIS8, weekly rooftop barbecue NIS10. Wash, dry, and fold NIS18.

Peace Hostel, 45 Ha-Yarkon St. (tel. 661 6320). Located 1 block off the beach and right across from the opera tower and the Migdalor Building, this hostel has a balcony with an unparalleled sunny view of the promenade and Allenby Rd. Gilded walls, cable TV lounge, dark interior, and wall-to-wall carpeting. Flexible check-out (around noon). No lockout. No curfew. Kitchen facilities. Roof mattress NIS20. Coed and single-sex dorm beds (6-8 per room) NIS25. Private rooms NIS100. Breakfast included. Laundry service.

Gordon Inn, 17 Gordon St. (tel. 523 8239), corner of Ben-Yehuda. Opened July 1994; fully operational by 1995. This hostel/hotel mongrel is perfect for families or couples. Of its 23 rooms, 8 are private and 10 are family rooms, with fold-out couches and attached bath. A spacious dining room has bar and meal service. Reception open 24 hrs. Check-out 11am. No lockout. No curfew. Dorm beds (4-6 per room) NIS32. Private rooms NIS75-120.

Ophin Hostel, 43 Dizengoff St. (tel. 525 0917), corner of Ha-Melekh George across from Dizengoff Center. Newly renovated in summer 1994, this hostel serves a rooftop breakfast overlooking Tel Aviv's modern shopping mecca. Reception open 24 hrs. Check-out by 10:30am. No lockout. No curfew. Kitchen facilities open 1995. Dorm beds (6-9 per room) NIS25. Breakfast NIS4.50. Lockers NIS5 plus NIS5 key deposit. Wash NIS5, dry NIS5.

Old Yafo Hostel, 8 Olei Tzion St. (tel. 682 2370; fax 682 2316), 3 blocks south of the clock tower, entrance in the back. Located in the middle of Jaffa's *Shuk Ha-Pishpeshim* (flea market), this hotel tries to blend with its traditional surroundings. Recently restored, the building has no plastic components—just solid wood furniture, iron decorations on bunks, and old black-and-white photos. Computer system lets you eat and sleep on credit and gives an itemized bill. Free airport pickup with advance reservation. Reception closes at 11pm, but a night guard is on duty. Check-out noon. No lockout. No curfew, but lights go off in the rooms at 11pm. Roof mattress NIS18. Coed and single-sex dorm beds (10 per room) NIS23. Rooftop "bungalow" doubles NIS23. Doubles NIS70. Breakfast NIS5, dinner NIS6. Free use of kitchen and safe. Storage NIS1. Laundry NIS8, but no dryer.

Beit Immanuel Hostel, 8 Auerbach St. (tel. 682 1459; fax 682 9817), corner of 17 Eilat St. Next to the beautifully renovated part of Old Yafo, this is a neat, friendly, relaxing place far from the action. The Christian hospice offers a secluded garden with picnic tables and a small playground, and has a large paved parking lot. Built by Peter Ustinov's grandfather. Reception 7am-1pm and 2-11pm. Check-out 10am. Lockout 10am-2pm. Curfew 11pm. No smoking. Single-sex dorm beds (10 per room) NIS30. Singles NIS92. Doubles NIS160. Breakfast NIS10, lunch NIS16, supper NIS24. Laundry NIS15.

Shanbo, 25 Lilienblum St. (tel. 510 6739), up the side steps (look for the wooden sign). Two blocks off Allenby Road, near the Shalom Tower and the Suzanne Delal Ctr. This hip hostel is quite laid back; you can even work to pay for your meals. Parties in the courtyard (Thurs.-Sat. 8pm-whenever) are popular with locals but make falling asleep nearly impossible. Free airport pickup with advance reservations. Reception open 24 hrs. Check-out noon (flexible). No lockout. No curfew. Roof mattress NIS18. Coed and single-sex dorm beds (8 per room) NIS24. Doubles NIS70. Breakfast NIS10, dinner NIS10. Wash, dry, and fold NIS15.

Gordon Hostel, 2 Gordon St. (tel. 522 9870; fax 524 7764), corner of Ha-Yarkon St. Great location near the beach, with several rooms overlooking the Med. The rooftop bar (open 4pm-midnight), downstairs bar (open all night), and bustling Ha-Yarkon St. are ideal for parties, but sleep addicts be warned. Same ownership as Gordon's Inn and No. 1 Hostel. Kitchen facilities; free coffee and tea in reception/TV room. Arranges cheap flights and tours. Arrive early in the day. Reception open 24 hrs. Check-out 10am. Lockout 11am-2pm. No curfew. Roof mattress NIS20. Coed and single-sex dorm beds (4-8 per room) NIS24. Private rooms in winter. Lockers NIS3, free use of safe for documents. Wash and dry NIS10.

Hotel Joseph, 15 Bugrashov St. (tel. 528 0955), right off Ben-Yehuda St. Bar with various beers and snacks, cable TV lounge, kitchen facilities. Travel agency on premises. Check-out 11am. Lockout 11am-2pm. Door locked at 1:20am, but keys provided for a NIS20 deposit. Rooftop mattress in double bungalow NIS22. Coed and single-sex dorm beds (4 per room) NIS27. Private single or double NIS95. All with fan and private bath. Breakfast NIS5.50, weekly barbecue NIS10.

Hotel Nes Tziona, 10 Nes Tziona St. (tel. 510 3404; fax 510 6084), just off Ben-Yehuda St. Superb location. Quiet, with an older clientele. All rooms have private bath; 5 have A/C. 24-hr. reception. Check-out noon. No lockout. No curfew. Singles NIS60-90. Doubles NIS100-120. Triples NIS150.

Tel Aviv Youth Hostel (HI), 36 B'nei Dan St. (tel. 544 1748, or 546 0719; fax 544 1030), near Ha-Yarkon St. Quite far from the city center—take bus #5, 24, or 25 to Weizmann or Ha-Yarkon. A sizeable place, with 2 wheelchair-accessible rooms. Lobby with vending machines; all rooms have A/C. Reception open 24 hrs. Check-out 11am. No lockout. No curfew. Coed and single-sex dorm beds (5-6 per room) NIS43. Singles NIS85. Doubles NIS117. Nonmembers add NIS3. Breakfast included, dinner NIS24. Lockers NIS4 per day.

Momo's Hostel, 28 Ben-Yehuda St. (tel. 528 7471). Centrally located and near the beach, though not quite spic 'n' span. Bar downstairs (open 24 hrs.) has relaxed biker atmosphere and features graffiti-covered walls. Snack bar serves cheap food (hamburger NIS4). Reception open 24 hrs. Check-out 11am. No lockout. No curfew. Kitchenette available. Roof mattress NIS20. Coed and single-sex dorm beds (4-8 per room) NIS23. Doubles NIS66. Breakfast NIS3. Wash and dry NIS15.

The Hostel, 60 Ben-Yehuda St., top floor (tel. 528 7088). Go down the alley and duck into the third entrance on the left. Inexpensive, but somewhat dark and more regimented than other hostels. Lights and TV off at midnight Sun.-Thurs. Check-out 9:30am. Lockout 10am-1pm. Curfew 2am. Single-sex dorm beds (8 per room) NIS21. Doubles NIS60. Triples NIS75. Quads NIS132.

■ ■ ■ FOOD

On any given night in Tel Aviv, you can appease your hunger with a United Nations-esque array of food options, from Yemenite, Greek, or Levantine dishes to French desserts. If international diplomacy and strange menus prove too challenging after a brain-melting day at the beach, falafel stands line the sidewalks and provide effortless eats. At least you'll have plenty of time to make up your mind—almost all restaurants stay open until midnight or later, on weeknights and weekends alike.

For quick, cheap belly-fillers, head for the self-service eateries on Ben-Yehuda St. Sandwiches and burgers with a side of chips go for under NIS8. Most places let you "customize" (or bastardize) your falafel with various toppings. The trick for $5-a-day-monk-on-a-budget freaks is to find a place selling falafel by the pita; you can keep refilling it until your belly hits the ground. The eateries near Shuk Ha-Carmel and along Bezalel St. off Allenby and Ha-Melekh George stay open the latest (usually until 1:30am). **Yosi-Let's Eat,** at the intersection of Ben-Yehuda and Bugrashov St., is just a sashay away from the sand and has falafel (NIS6) and *shawerma* (NIS8).

Kerem Ha-Temanim (the Yemenite Quarter), between Shuk Ha-Carmel and the beach, houses moderately priced Yemenite and other Middle Eastern restaurants among its small red-roofed houses and narrow streets. **Maganda,** 26 Rabbi Meir St. (tel. 517 9990), **Shaul's Inn,** 11 Eliashiv St. (tel. 517 7619; follow the signs), and **Zion Restaurant** (see p. 272) serve brains and lungs, but the prices (as well as the first bites) may take strength to endure (entrees NIS17-38). You can always fall back on the old reliable: a hummus platter for NIS6.

Shechunat Ha-Tikva (the neighborhood of hope), in Tel Aviv's southeasternmost quarter, is renowned for its lamb, chicken, and beef skewers, often accompanied by cheap beer. Israelis flock from nearby cities to have *kabab* or *La'afa* here; it's a good place to meet locals. Take bus #15, 16, or 41 to Ha-Tikva—it's too far (and somewhat unsafe) to walk, but the food is worth the ride.

The area around the **Jaffa Clock Tower** is filled with cheap, small food stores hidden in a maze of narrow streets. Small fish restaurants, *al-ha'esh* (barbecued) meats establishments, falafel stands, and sweets vendors abound. **Tayar,** 8 Rezif Ha'Aliya Ha-Shnia (tel. 824 741), just west of the clock tower, serves great seafood and salads on a sea-side terrace. **Abou Elafia** (see p. 272) has the best breadstuffs in the country. More romantic is the beautifully renovated **Old Jaffa,** where you can eat among gardens overlooking the Mediterranean. Check the prices before you sit down to order, though. In **Jaffa Port,** just south of the renovated old city off Pasteur St. (admission NIS1), waterfront restaurants with a pleasant view of fishing boats offer the freshest seafood (daily catch entrees from around NIS24).

Dizengoff Square and the stretch of **Dizengoff Street** just north of the Square are lined with pizza parlors, blintz joints, and hot dog stands, where crowds of tourists and throngs of young Israelis gorge themselves amidst exhaust-spitting vehicles. Sit on the elevated plaza and dine while watching the multi-colored rotations of the Fire-Water Statue and listening to classical music. Go farther north on Dizengoff for cleaner-appearing, but dwindling, options. The northern end of the street, around **Yirmeyahu Street,** which runs between Dizengoff and Ben-Yehuda just before they intersect, has another agglomeration of restaurants. They tend to be better (and pricier) than those around the Square; you're less likely to choke on bus fumes while dining *al fresco*. And there's always the vast, air-conditioned, happening

Dizengoff Center mall, two blocks south of Dizengoff Sq. At the bottom level you will find a kosher **Pizza Hut,** with interesting alternatives to sausage and pepperoni.

Burger yearnings can be quelled at **McDavid's** (franchise at 43 Frischmann St., off Dizengoff), **Burger Ranch** (look for the orange and white signs), or **McDonald's,** on the fourth floor of the new central bus station. For American-bred food products go to **Subway,** with locations on 21 Ben-Yehuda St., 44 Gordon St. (at Dizengoff), 78 Allenby Rd., and in Dizengoff Center (subs NIS6.20-18.40; open 10am-midnight). **Domino's** delivers medium-sized pizzas for NIS22 (NIS4 per topping; call 527 2330 for northern locations, 562 7770 for southern locations and after midnight).

Minimalist spenders should shop at the large, outdoor **Shuk Ha-Carmel.** The best deals are on produce and underwear, both of which you can get for bare-ass prices. Most of the produce stands are at the southwestern end of the market, on and near Ha-Carmel St. To catch prices at their lowest (and crowds at their loudest), shop an hour or two before the beginning of *Shabbat.* **Supermarkets** can be found throughout town. **Supersol,** 79 Ben-Yehuda St. near Gordon St., may be the most convenient (open Sun.-Tues. 7am-midnight, Wed.-Thurs. 24 hrs., Sat. after sundown); other Supersol branches are on the corner of Arlozorov and Yehoshua Bin-Nun and on Ibn Gvirol and Nordau. **Co-op** has branches right in Dizengoff Sq. (open 7am-8pm), in the basement of Ha-Mashbir department store in Dizengoff Center, and on Ibn Gvirol St. near the junction of Sha'ul Ha-Melekh.

Keep hydrated while about-towning, but be sure to watch prices: a Kinley mango on Dizengoff costs NIS4-5, while the same cash at a supermarket nets you a 1.5L bottle of mineral water or cola.

Eternity, 60 Ben-Yehuda St. (tel. 203 151). Run by members of the Black Hebrew community, a group whose dietary laws prohibit both milk and meat, and whose members have therefore had to come up with creative (and nutritious) alternatives. Veggie hot dogs (NIS9.30), veggie steaks (NIS10), a variety of veggie burgers (NIS7.80), and veggie *shawerma* (NIS7.80) are surprisingly tasty. Non-dairy ice cream (NIS4) and other non-dairy, no-egg desserts sold as well. Open Sun.-Thurs. 9am-11pm, Fri. 9am-3pm, Sat. after sundown-midnight. Kosher.

Zion Restaurant, 28 Peduyim St. (tel. 517 8714). Take Allenby to Ha-Carmel St. Take your fifth right into the narrow Peduyim St. and look for the sign. Excellent Yemenite dishes served in an arched interior hung with paintings by a famous Yemenite artist. Large selection of unique stuffed vegetables (NIS8) and Middle Eastern salads (NIS5). Grilled and baked lamb, veal, fish, and chicken entrees (NIS20-40). Brave souls can even try gourmet ox testicles (remember this place when your aunt Sonia tells you to have a ball in Tel Aviv). Open daily 10am-1am.

Said Abou Elafia and Sons, 1 block behind the Yafo Clock Tower. Popularly known as "Aboulafia," this bakery is so famous that its name is used by Israelis to denote all stuffed-pita foods. Fresh sesame-covered *bagelah, samuza* stuffed with thyme and potatoes, and pizza-like products all only NIS4-5. Take-out only. Sells soft drinks and dessert as well. Open 24 hrs.

Mon Jardin, 186 Ben-Yehuda St. (tel. 523 1792). Waiters at this recently remodeled Romanian grill will teach you such handy Romanian phrases as "I want to climb a tree after dinner." Stuffed vine leaves NIS7, *mousaka* or *tzorba* soup NIS12, and *kabab schnitzel* or *Patrizian* with chips NIS21. Fantastic desserts from Loudon Conditory next door served at a discount. Open daily noon-midnight.

Café Nordau, 145 Ben-Yehuda St. (tel. 524 0134), corner of Arlozorov. The only place in Tel Aviv where dogs get their own menu and a free meal! Second floor bar features nightly cabaret shows. Largely, but not exclusively, gay clientele; sells *Maga'im* (the gay newspaper) and provides current info on gay life and hot spots. Full meals NIS18-32. Open Sun.-Fri. 8am-2am, Sat. 10am-2am.

Chin Chin, 42 Frischmann St. (tel. 524 5802), off Dizengoff St. Tasty Chinese food served in a friendly environment; butterfly-dragon wallpaper adds to the atmosphere. Lunch specials from NIS15, entrees NIS18.50. Special *tampopo* meals and vegetarian dishes. Open daily noon-midnight.

Café Kazze, 19 Sheinkin St. (tel. 29 37 56). Israeli stars are sometimes spotted at this trendy café. Eat in sunny, airy rooms or on the relaxing garden patio in back.

Fast, friendly service and large portions. Lasagna (NIS22) and *couscous* (NIS18) are popular dishes. Open Sun.-Thurs. 8am-midnight, Fri. 8am-4pm. Kosher.

Dalas Restaurant, 68 Etzel St. (tel. 37 43 49), in the southeastern Ha-Tikva neighborhood. They would have been better off calling it Dalí's Restaurant—the combination of wall-paintings of Southfork Ranch (of the deceased TV series "Dallas") and outstanding Yemenite food is positively surreal. In one of Tel Aviv's poorer sections, accessible by bus #7a, 15, 16, and 41. Hummus pita (NIS5), delicious Iraqi pita (NIS2), and *kabab* (NIS6-13 per skewer) attract many locals. Open Sun.-Thurs. 11am-2am, Fri. 11am-1½ hrs. before sundown.

The Shakespeare, 140 Ha-Yarkon St. (tel. 522 2194) near Gordon St., in the British Council building. This smartly appointed coffee shop with a view provides British TV, newspapers, and light cuisine. Sandwiches and croissants NIS8-11, hot dishes NIS5-13, danish or dessert NIS4-8. Open Mon.-Thurs. 8am-8pm, Fri. 8am-1pm.

Sami Burekas, 123 Dizengoff St. (tel. 524 3241). *Burekas* stuffed with potatoes, spinach, or a variety of cheeses are only NIS4. Ice cream NIS3.50, and real Italian coffees NIS4.50. Open daily 7am-midnight.

Big Mamma, 22 Rabbi Akiva St. (tel. 517 5096), off Ha-Carmel. Pass through ghostly after-hours market stands to the back-alley entrance. Eerie location and inventive toppings on crisp crusts make this *the* Israeli pizza joint. Onions, mushrooms, pepperoni, zucchini, and egg cover the Big Mamma Special (NIS22). Other pizzas NIS15-24. Excellent, if expensive, desserts. Open nightly 8pm-4am.

Souss Etz, 20 Sheinkin St. (tel. 528 7955). One of many popular, hip cafés on this street. Chic Art Deco interior and live jazz music every Tues. night. Salads and pasta NIS16-23, stuffed bagel toasts NIS16, desserts NIS10-13. Open Sun.-Thurs. 9am-1am, Fri. 9am-7pm, Sat. 5pm-1am.

Acapulco, 105 Dizengoff St. (tel. 523 7552), at the corner of Frischmann St. Great for a cheap *kabab* or *shawerma* dinner (NIS8). Main dishes NIS12-20. Mouth-watering assortment of desserts: the huge "Blintz Acapulco" is an epicurean orgy (NIS17). Open daily 6am-1am.

New York Deli, 164 Dizengoff St. (tel. 522 5966). Serving traditional Jewish home foods, this restaurant even makes its own corned beef. *Gefiltefish* and potato *kreplach* (NIS9) or *latkes* (NIS7) are house favorites. Pastrami, beef brisket, and turkey with garlic are other specialties. Sandwiches NIS20. Open Sun.-Thurs. 9am-1am, Fri. 9am-sundown, Sat. after sundown-1am. Kosher.

Gypsi, 165 Ha-Yarkon St. (tel. 527 2479), 1 floor below the top of Kikkar Atarim. Offers great 9-to-5 specials where *schnitzel,* chicken, or *kabab* with salad, hummus, chips, and a drink cost only NIS12.50. Huge place with 25 TV screens placed so that each table can watch a cable movie. Terrace overlooks the marina. Very popular with tourists. Open Sun.-Thurs. 9am-3am, Fri.-Sat. 24 hrs.

There are several good ice cream places in Tel Aviv. **Dr. Lek,** just up from the Jaffa clock tower on the main road heading north to the Promenade, has excellent ice cream, but sorbets are their specialty (amazing cinnamon cheesecake); another branch on 194 Ben-Yehuda St., corner of Jabotinsky (both branches open daily 10am-midnight). **Ben and Jerry's** sell their usual rich concoctions (with local snacks in lieu of American ones) at the northern end of the promenade, below the Ramada Continental Hotel, and on 284 Dizengoff St. between Nordau and Yirmeyahu. Nearby is the superb **Glida Be'er Sheva,** on the corner of Dizengoff and Nordau, with the biggest and most inventive selection in town. Most ice cream places stay open until 1am, and prices run NIS5.20-6.40 for two scoops.

■■■ SHOPPING, WALKS, PARKS

The best-known attraction in Tel Aviv is its graceful **Promenade** along the beach; but there are so many sights in the area that it is nearly impossible to see them all. Sight-enthusiasts should plan ahead so as not to miss anything; but be sure to save time for long walks and romantic summer interludes in the more scenic parts.

The famed **Shuk Ha-Carmel** (Carmel Market) is located at the intersection of Allenby Rd. and Ha-Melekh George St. The chaos here will entertain even the most jaded of tourists. Near the northern entrance to the market, shopkeepers stand behind piles of clothing and footwear, selling "fashions" which even the Russian *olim* (immigrants) choose to admire from afar. Waving polyester undergarments and red plastic sandals, vendors bellow their products' virtues. Farther south, toward the parking lot, you can buy fresh fruit and vegetables at the lowest prices in the city. Huge mounds of chickens plucked bare make the west side of the market look like the morning after a foul barnyard ritual. For a more sedate, less crowded, and probably more fruitful market shopping experience, on Tuesdays and Fridays the *midraḥov* of **Naḥalat Binyamin** and **Ramban Street,** one block south of Shuk Ha-Carmel, becomes a street fair. From 10am-4pm (weather permitting) local artists and craftspeople sell handmade jewelry and pottery, original paintings, Judaica, and even some bizarre candelabras; the winding cobblestone street is also full of magicians, mimes, and musicians. Sip coffee or beer at a café and feast your eyes.

The modern **Dizengoff Center** (next to Dizengoff Sq.) is an air-conditioned five-story complex. In other words, a mall. Another centrally located shopping center is **Gan Ha'Ir,** on Ibn Gvirol St. just north of Frischmann St. It is a bit calmer than the bustling Dizengoff Ctr.—more book and jewelry stores than music stores.

Now put away those credit cards and stroll through Tel Aviv's architecturally-inspiring **historic neighborhoods. Neveh Tzedek,** just west of the intersection of Herzl and Ahad Ha'Ain streets, is the first Jewish neighborhood outside of Jaffa. The area is being gradually renovated to accommodate local yuppies attracted to the Mediterranean-village charm of its narrow streets and humble stone architecture. **Kerem Ha-Temanim** (the Yemenite Quarter), northwest of the Allenby and Ha-Melekh George, near Shuk Ha-Carmel, maintains its traditional, village-like appearance, despite the encroachment of stores hawking Simpsons T-shirts.

Leaving the traditional stone houses behind you, take bus #25 or 27 to **Tel Aviv University's** well-groomed grounds. Directly behind Beit Ha-Tefutzot from Gate 2 is the vast central lawn, flanked by pleasant Modernist buildings. Facing the sea, the first building on your right is the Central Library. From here you can go straight down the gently sloping path to the glitzy new main gate complex on Levanon St. The **University Gallery** is in the pink pavilion right next to the gate. The grim concrete building across the street houses the university dorms—no wonder most students choose to live off-campus. There is life, however, on campus, at least in the daylight hours during the school year. Ask people to direct you to the Gilman or Law cafeterias for a peek at the chic student scene—the same scene that migrates later in the day to trendy cafés and bars.

There are several architecturally innovative buildings in South Miami Beach, uh, Tel Aviv, including the **Opera Tower,** at the intersection of Allenby and Ha-Yarkon, with its light pink balconies and turquoise trim. The interior features a magnificent atrium, with statues overlooking a fountain and an authentic, traditional **Tower Records** store. **Migdal Shalom,** a 40-story tower at 1 Herzl St. at Aḥad Ha'Am St., used to be the tallest structure in the Middle East but has recently been eclipsed by the slightly taller communication tower in the military base near the Tel Aviv Museum. Still, the **rooftop observatory** (tel. 517 7304) offers an unmatched view of Tel Aviv and environs. (Open Sun.-Thurs. 10am-5:45pm, Fri. 10am-1:45pm. Admission NIS6, students NIS5; combination Israeli Wax Museum/observatory tickets NIS14, students NIS11.)

Newly-renovated buildings comprise the **Suzanne Delal Center,** 6 Yehielli St. (tel. 510 5656), at the intersection of Yafo Rd. and Lilienblum Rd. The place pulsates until the wee hours of the morning, especially when dance or theater groups perform in the center or in the open space outside.

The **Great Synagogue** at 110 Allenby St. (tel. 560 4905) stands just east of the Shalom Tower. Completed in 1926 and renovated in 1970, this huge, domed building showcases arches and stained glass windows from synagogues everywhere in the world. Ancient musical instruments are also on display. (Open Sun.-Fri. 8am-9pm, Sat. 8-11am. Saturday prayer open to the public; make sure you have a head covering and are dressed modestly.)

Also noteworthy are a group of buildings near the intersection of Sha'ul Ha-Melekh and Ibn Gvirol streets. The **Golda Center,** 28 Leonardo da Vinci St., houses the **New Israeli Opera** (tel. 692 7707). **Heikhal Ha-Tarbut** (Mann Auditorium) is the home of the Israel Philharmonic Orchestra and the Ha-Bima National Theater. Take bus #5, 18, 32, or 91 for any of these buildings—ask for Heikhal Ha-Tarbut.

Stone and glass can only mystify for so long. Greenery available at **Ha-Yarkon Park,** in the northern part of the city, near the Youth Hostel. Take bus #13, 24, or 25. The park is a favorite of Israelis. Join them in lolling about listlessly or renting paddle boats on the Yarkon River. Near **Ha-Yarkon Park** is the new **Zapari bird park** (tel. 642 2888; take bus #28 to Ganei Ha-Ta'arukha). While admission is expensive (NIS26, students NIS20), the park's outdoor aviaries, swans, and cockatoos will serve you in the stead of that valium you forgot to pack. A half-hour bird show features Ilan, a bicycle-riding parrot; Alex, a telepathic cockatoo; and Tuvia, a "real Israeli parrot," who flies into the audience and takes NIS100 from an audience member. (Open Sun.-Thurs. 9am-5pm, Fri. 9am-3pm; show every 1½hr. from 11am.) The **World of Silence Aquarium,** 1 Kaufman St. (tel. 510 6670), near the Carmelit bus terminal in south Tel Aviv, on the corner of Herbert Samuel St., houses a 400-cubic-meter tank of fish from the Mediterranean, the Red Sea, and around the world. Another room houses a frightening array of snakes, scorpions, reptiles, and tarantulas. The **Dolphinarium** (tel. 510 4477) has scheduled performances. (Both open Sun.-Thurs. 9am-6pm, Fri. 9am-4pm. Admission NIS7.) Baby rhinoceroses frolic (a sight not soon forgotten) at the **Zoological Center** in Ramat Gan (tel. 631 2181). This combination drive-through safari park and zoo features 250 acres of African game in a natural habitat. You can walk within one meter of African tigers, or stare over a *wadi* at Syrian bears and intelligent-looking gorillas. Bring a picnic, or have lunch at the moderately priced restaurant (excellent view of the long-tailed monkey island). Pedestrian tours offered as well. Take bus #30, 35, or 43 to Ramat Gan. (Open Sun.-Thurs. 9am-4pm, Fri. 9am-1pm; Sept.-June Sun.-Thurs. 9am-4pm, Fri. 9am-1pm. Admission NIS23, children NIS18.) Continue beastwatching across the street at the massive **Ramat Gan National Park** (open dawn-dusk; free).

■■■ MUSEUMS

Just north of the *shuk,* off Allenby, lies Bialik St., named after Ḥayim Naḥman Bialik, the well-loved modern Hebrew poet. His recently restored home, now the **Beit Bialik Museum,** 22 Bialik St. (tel. 525 4530) is maintained exactly as it was when he died; it is a fine example of 1920s eclectic Tel Aviv architecture. Bialik's manuscripts, photographs, articles, letters, and 94 books (with translations in 28 languages) are on display. An English brochure is available, but the dearth of English translations on the display cases makes this museum difficult for non-Hebrew speakers. Groups must call ahead. (Open Sun.-Thurs. 9am-4:45pm, Sat. 10am-1:45pm. Free.) Nearby stands the **Museum of the History of Tel Aviv-Yafo,** 27 Bialik St. (tel. 525 5052), which traces the city's history through photographs, documents, models, and a slide presentation. (Open Sun.-Thurs. 9am-2pm. Free. Library open Sun., Tues., and Thurs. 9:30am-1pm.) At 38 Ha-Melekh George St., the right-wing Likud party headquarters, is the new **Etzel** (Irgun Tzva'i Le'umi) **Museum** (tel. 525 1387 or 528 4001), which traces one version of the pre-1948 history of late Israeli prime minister Menaḥem Begin's terrorist movement. (Open Sun.-Thurs. 8:30am-4pm. Admission NIS5, students NIS2.) A second Etzel Museum showing the 1947-48 history via large models is found in a half-stone, half-glass building along the Promenade, between Tel Aviv and Yafo. (Open Sun.-Thurs. 8:30am-4pm. Admission NIS5, students NIS2.) The **Jabotinsky Institute** (tel. 528 7320), in the same building, houses works written by and about Ze'ev Jabotinsky, forefather of right-wing Zionism. (Open Sun.-Thurs. 8am-2pm, Fri. 8am-noon. Admission NIS5, students NIS2.)

The building at 23 Rothschild Blvd., one block south of the Great Synagogue, is the **Hagana Museum** (tel. 560 8624 or 0809), containing exhibits tracing the history of the IDF. Movies glorify the Yom Kippur War and the Hagana's efforts to break the

British blockade of ships carrying World War II refugees to Palestine. (Open Sun.-Thurs. 8am-4pm, Fri. 8am-12:30pm. Admission NIS5, students and children NIS2.)

Nearer to the shore, you can visit the **David Ben-Gurion House,** at 17 Ben-Gurion Ave. (tel. 522 1010). Ogle an exciting exhibition of books, pictures, and mementos of Israel's first prime minister, including letters from Ben-Gurion to John F. Kennedy, Winston Churchill, Charles de Gaulle, and other world leaders. There's even an elephant tusk given to Ben-Gurion by the president of Liberia. In the **Hillel Cohen Lecture Hall** next door you'll find even more Ben-Gurion trivia, such as all his passports and even a copy of a 1928 salary slip. (Both house and lecture hall open Sun. and Tues.-Thurs. 8am-3pm, Mon. 8am-5pm, Fri. 8am-1pm. Free.)

Uptown, the **Tel Aviv Museum of Art,** 27 Sha'ul Ha-Melekh Blvd. (tel. 695 7361), has split-level galleries and a sizable collection of Israeli and international modern art. The handsome lobby boasts a Lichtenstein (look back as you enter). There's also Impressionist art, including canvases by Corot, Renoir, Pissaro, Monet, and Dufy, with a Degas sculpture and some works by Utrillo. Post-Impressionist masters such as Picasso, Juan Gris, and Matisse have a section as well, and a permanent exhibition of contemporary Israeli art rounds out the collection. Rotating exhibits, however, are often the most rewarding. A monthly program in English, listing current exhibits and events, is available in the ticket booth, or check the Friday *Jerusalem Post.* Take bus #7a, 9, 18, 28, or 70. (Open Sun.-Mon. and Wed. 10am-6pm, Tues. 10am-10pm, Fri.-Sat. 10am-2pm. Admission NIS13, students NIS9.)

The admission ticket for the Tel Aviv Museum also entitles you to enter the **Helena Rubinstein Pavilion of Contemporary Art,** 6 Tarsat Blvd. (tel. 528 7196), a pleasant space with rotating exhibits of international and local contemporary art. To get to the pavilion, walk from the museum down Sha'ul Ha-Melekh Blvd. toward Ibn Gvirol St. On your left are the ugly fringes of a large military base; on your right you can see the Tel Aviv public library (Beit Ariella) and then the Golda Center. Take a left on Ibn Gvirol and then right into Dizengoff; the Helena Rubinstein Pavilion is on the corner of Tarsat Blvd., two streets down on your left. (Open same hours as museum. Admission is included in the museum ticket, but stub can be used for days after you've already visited the museum.)

The **Eretz Israel Museum,** 2 Lebanon St. (tel. 641 5244) in Ramat Aviv (the northernmost part of the city) is a large complex composed of eight pavilion museums built around an archaeological site. One admission ticket (NIS8) gives access to all eight pavilions (see below) and the Eretz Israel Library, containing over 30,000 books and periodicals. The most famous attraction in the complex is the **Glass Museum,** with one of the finest collections of glassware in the world. Exhibits trace the history of glassmaking from the earliest examples of the craft in the 15th century BCE through the Middle Ages. Across the patio, the **Kadman Numismatic Museum** traces the history of the region through ancient coins. The **Ceramics Pavilion** has an extensive collection of Arabic pottery, especially the Gaza and Acre styles. The **Nehushtan Pavilion** houses the discoveries of the excavations of the ancient copper industries at Timna, better known as King Solomon's Mines. Walk across the entrance area past the grassy amphitheater to the **Man and His Work Center,** an exhibition of Arab and other folk crafts and techniques. To the southeast, still in the museum complex, are the **Tel Qasila Excavations,** which have revealed a 12th-century BCE Philistine port city and ruins dating back to the time of Kings David and Solomon. The temple area at the top of the hill contains the remains of three separate Philistine temples built one on top of another. Down the hill to the south are scattered remains of the residential and industrial quarter of the Philistine town. A useful free guide to the *tel* is available in the small **Tel Qasila Pavilion** (open Sun.-Thurs. 9am-12:30pm) to the east, which also displays artifacts found at the site. Past the Philistine town is the **Folklore Pavilion,** with Jewish religious art, ceremonial objects, and ethnic clothing. The room at the rear of the pavilion contains a Florentine synagogue's benches, pulpit, and ornately decorated *aron,* or ark. The Eretz Yisrael complex also houses the **Alphabet Museum,** the **Lasky Planetarium** (shows in Hebrew only), and the **Museum of Science and**

Technology. Take any bus (#24, 27, 45, 74, 86) to the Ramat Aviv Hotel from the central bus station. (Complex open Sun.-Mon. and Wed.-Thurs. 9am-2pm, Tues. 9am-5pm, Sat. 10am-2pm. Library open Sun.-Thurs. 9am-5pm.)

Beit Ha-Tefutzot (Museum of the Diaspora, tel. 646 2020), is situated on the Tel Aviv University campus and documents the Jewish experience in exile. One of the most powerful exhibits is "Scrolls of Fire," a collection of documents that give first-person perspectives on massacres from Roman times to the Nazi concentration camps. Mini-cinemas throughout the museum screen short documentaries and recordings of dramatized discussions between historical figures. For NIS4, museum computers will trace the origins and meanings of Jewish family names; if you have one, bring in some family data and, for a modest fee, the genealogy center will help you draw up a family tree. Take bus #25 or #27 and get off at Gate 2 of the university. (Open Sun.-Tues. and Thurs. 10am-5pm, Wed. 10am-7pm, Fri. 9am-2pm. Admission NIS18, students NIS13.) Chronosphere (multi-screen audiovisuals) shows every ½hr. from 11am to 4:30pm (included in admission price).

Had enough death, destruction, and depression? Take at least half a dose more at the **Israeli Wax Museum** in the Shalom Tower (tel. 517 7304)! Recently updated, the museum shows scenes like the expulsion of Jews from Spain in 1492 and the Madrid Peace Conference five centuries later. Check out the John F. Kennedy figure. (Open Sun.-Thurs. 10am-5:45pm, Fri. 10am-1:45pm. Museum admission NIS11, students NIS9; combination museum/observatory ticket NIS14, students NIS11.)

■ ■ ■ JAFFA (YAFO) יפו يافا

An Israeli folk song describes Jaffa as possessing a "mysterious and unknown" element which allows its atmosphere "to seep like wine into the blood." Indeed, opposite Tel Aviv's unnatural modern skyscraper hotels and glass storefronts, the stone and brick houses and winding streets of Jaffa display a true harmony with the land.

The **Clock Tower,** completed in 1906, stands by the entrance to Jaffa from Tel Aviv and is a useful marker for all other destinations in the city. A free tour of Old Jaffa given by the Association for Tourism of Tel-Aviv-Jaffa begins here (Wed. 9:30am, line up at 9am). Next to the clock tower is the minaret of the **Al Mahmudiyya Mosque,** an enormous structure erected in 1812, into which only Muslims can enter. Down Mifratz Shlomo St. from the mosque, the **Museum of Antiquities of Tel Aviv-Jaffa** (tel. 82 53 75) contains artifacts from nearby sites in Old Jaffa. The columns and capitals scattered about the museum's courtyard date from the first century BCE and were brought here from Caesarea during the 1800s. (Open Sun.-Wed. 9am-2pm, Tues. 9am-7pm. Admission NIS5, students NIS3.)

In front of the museum, on the northern slope, is **Ha-Midron Garden,** which offers a fine view of the Tel Aviv coast and skyline. Behind the museum lie the grassy **Ha-Pisga Gardens,** which contain a small, modern amphitheater as well as an archaeological site with excavations of an 18th-century BCE Hyksos town and a later Egyptian city. A white, ladder-like sculpture dominates one hill in the gardens; its three sections depict the fall of Jericho, the sacrifice of Isaac, and Jacob's dream. Russian musicians play violin music as you stroll through the park.

From the park, a small wooden footbridge leads to **Kikkar Kedumim,** Jaffa's commercial, historical, and tourist center. In 1740, the first Jewish hostel was established on this site. It included two *mikvaot* (ceremonial baths) and a synagogue. Libyan Jews reopened the synagogue, which is still in use today. After their Arab inhabitants were made refugees in the 1948 war, the striking stone buildings in this area became home to a large artists' colony. In the late 1960s the government renovated the neighborhood. Today studios, galleries, and restaurants frequented mostly by tourists are artfully arranged among the reconstructed buildings.

Several interesting sights are located in Kikkar Kedumim, including a small, well-preserved archaeological site, the colorful Greek Orthodox **Church of St. Michael,** the Roman Catholic **Monastery of St. Peter,** and the **House of Simon the**

Tanner. Andromeda's Rock, site of the Greek princess's mythological rescue by Perseus, is visible from the lighthouse a few blocks to the south.

Jaffa's large **Shuk Ha-Pishpeshim** (Flea Market) is one of the most exciting markets in Israel, with a covered row of overflowing stalls offering endless delights of the traditional Middle Eastern variety, as well as modern Israeli hand-dyed clothing and other crafts. Choose among Persian carpets, leather goods, used clothes, and brassware. A vast selection of enormous *narghilas,* elaborate Middle Eastern waterpipes, is available. Bargaining is a given here, and you should begin by offering no more than half the asking price. To reach the flea market from the clock tower, continue one block south down Yefet St. and turn left. The market is squeezed between Tzion and MeRagusa St. and is closed on Saturdays.

An NIS1 entrance fee for the **Jaffa Port**, just south of Ha'Aliya Ha-Shuiya St., will show you the fishermen's wharfs, which are still in use. The fishermen usually mend their nets in the afternoon, leave for sea at nightfall, and return in the early morning hours with their fresh catch.

■■■ ENTERTAINMENT

Though frying themselves by day and sucking down Goldstar by night seem to be the preferred activities of most travelers, don't miss out on other potential sources of fun. A **gay sauna** called Thermus, 79 Shlomo Ha-Melekh St. (tel. 522 4202; open daily 12:30-11pm), supplements Tel Aviv's handful of gay bars.

BEACHES

The Hebrew word for beach is *ḥof.* Familiarize yourself with the flag language of the beach as well: black means swimming is forbidden, red means swimming is dangerous, white means swim on. Most beaches have lifeguards on duty until 4pm.

Israelis with cars head north for a less crowded and slightly more pristine waterfront, such as the one near Glilot junction on the road to Herzliya, behind the Mandarin Hotel (admission NIS8). You can also get there by taking bus #601 from the new central bus station (6th floor) to Kfar Shemaryahm Intersection, and then taking bus #29 from there. But the beaches within the city are nothing to scoff at: they are sandy, clean, and free, and all have relatively clean showers, toilets, and changing rooms. The beaches are, from north to south: Sheraton, Hilton (behind the Hilton hotel), Gordon, Frischmann (at the ends of those streets), and the Jerusalem beach at the end of Allenby Rd.—the last three are almost one continuous beach. The southern coastline, with fewer amenities and no luxury hotels, tends to be quieter during the day. All of Tel Aviv's beaches are rife with theft; if possible, lock your valuables away before you hit the sands.

Ben-Yehuda St., with cheap food and drink, is never more than a two-minute walk from the beach. Near Kikkar Atarim, a marina rents sailboats, surfboards, and windsurfers. Surfers ride the waves between the Carlton and Hilton Hotels.

CROWD-WATCHING AND CAFÉS

The Mediterranean art of crowd-gazing can be perfected in Tel Aviv's streets and cafés. The wide sidewalks of **Dizengoff St.** are the most crowded showcase in town. The northern parts of the street, lined with many high-design, high-priced boutiques, are fit for a relaxed early evening stroll, and the Kikkar itself the site of an ever-changing human scene, from retirees basking in the midday sun to late-night punks cluttering the overpass stairs. The revolving multi-level, multi-colored, water-spurting, fire-spitting fountain, designed by the illustrious Israeli artist Agam (yes, he did the Dan Hotel coloring too), crowns the Square with an unsurpassed celebration of municipal entertainment. The tunes come from the fountain itself, orchestrating its own hourly multi-media show to music ranging from Ravel's *Bolero* to Israeli folk songs. It's like a traffic accident—you don't want to look, but a morbid fascination takes over.

On the **Promenade,** the cafés in the stretch right below the end of Gordon St. make a pleasant early evening stop. **Ha-Ḥof Ha-Ma'aravi** (the Western Beach), at the northern end of the Charles Clore Park, rocks every Thursday night with Brazilian music and more Israeli youth than you ever thought existed. Everyone who's anyone is here, and so is everybody else—the place is scorching. The open cafés in the *midraḥov* of **Naḥalat Binyamin St.,** particularly on the intersecting Rambam St., are more relaxing.

DISCOS AND LIVE MUSIC

Most of Tel Aviv's discos open at 10pm, but of course nothing moves before midnight. Get with the program. The **Colosseum,** at Atarim Sq. (tel. 527 1177), attracts a huge tourist crowd (Israelis avoid it like bacon) with its laser and video show. The cover is NIS18 for men, nothing for women. Drinks are pretty cheap and the first three are free. On Saturdays, men pay NIS25 to enter this revolving inferno, and women still get in free. Get the picture? **KU,** 117 Salameh Rd. (tel. 537 6814), not far from Herzl St., promote themselves as specialists in "Happy House," soul and funk. (NIS20 cover; Maccabee or Goldstar NIS7. Open Tues. and Fri.-Sat. midnight-6am.) For deafening reggae of all varieties, vogue over to **Soweto,** 6 Frischmann St. (tel. 524 0825), corner of Ha-Yarkon. Cover Mon.-Wed. NIS10, Thurs.-Sat. NIS15. In summer, the club is open Sundays; cover NIS10 for men (1 drink included) and free for women until midnight. Be careful, though; rumors of fights and stabbings at the Soweto were flying like monkeys out of Robert's butt in summer 1994. Current hot spots include **Hazan Haltadash** and **Kazerosa** in Old Jaffa, and **Tuta** (summers only), behind the Jaffa police building. **Tatoo,** at Beit Merkazim in Herzliya Pituaḥ, is also popular. Keep in mind that you'll need a taxi to get back from most of these places, as the buses stop running soon after midnight.

Tel Aviv is the land of young Israeli **rock bands.** The leading club for local and occasionally international rock and alternative acts is **Roxan,** 10 Ha-Barzel St., Ramat Ha-Ḥayal (tel. 544 7040). The club is in an industrial area east of Ramat Aviv; take bus #20. Most shows start around midnight; again, prepare cab fare ahead of time or work your begging skills on car-endowed locals. *Ha'Ir,* a local magazine published in Hebrew every Friday, has a section called "Akhbar Ha'Ir," with comprehensive listings. Two amphitheaters at **Ha-Yarkon Park** serve the function of your local football stadium. For tickets and schedules inquire at ticket offices (see below).

Ha-Kossit, 5 Kikkar Malkhei Yisrael (tel. 522 3244), is a bar with live **blues** and **jazz** on Sat., Wed., and Thurs. at 10:30pm; no cover. **Logos,** 14 Naḥalat Binyamin St. (tel. 661 176), features **rock** and **blues** performances every night at 11pm; cover varies with band's fame. For your weekly dosage of **cheese,** go to **Punchline,** 6 Ha'Arba'a St. (tel. 561 0785), off Carlebach St. Every single person that works here sings, so every 10 minutes starting at 11pm a rooster crows and an employee gets on stage and performs. Songs are mostly in Hebrew and English, but you might find yourself jamming to French, Spanish, or even Russian. Black-and-white Hollywood scenes and red velvet cushions decorate the interior, and a huge variety of drinks and cocktails is served. (Open Sun.-Thurs. 10am-2am, Fri.-Sat. 10am-4am.)

BARS

Bars in Tel Aviv are as various as the tortures in Dante's *Inferno*. Most bars get crowded around midnight; and seats are scarce after 1am, especially Thursday through Saturday. Bars abound on **Ha-Yarkon St.** near the youth hostels. **Goulon's Pub** (below Gordon Hostel) and **Midnight Run Pub** (below Eilat Hotel) are the most popular. **Allenby Rd.** has its fair share of watering holes; **Lula** (Allenby 54) and **Total** (Allenby 17) are the best-attended. The **Hard Rock Café** in Dizengoff Ctr. (open Sun.-Wed. 11am-12:30am, Thurs.-Sat. 11am-1:30am) features a young crowd, Israeli rock paraphernalia, a suit worn by Elvis, and alcohol downstairs. Israelis frequent **Ha'Arba'a St.,** off Carlebach and Ibn Gvirol, near the Tel Aviv Cinematheque, where about six pubs compete for hot-spot status. Pick your poison:

M.A.S.H. (More Alcohol Served Here), 275 Dizengoff (tel. 605 1007). A trek to the north; take bus #4. Tourists and Israelis alike slam drinks to music from the 60s to the 90s. Good burgers (NIS13). Open daily 10pm-3am.

The Smoking Dog, 138 Dizengoff St. Psychedelic emblems on the outside, alternative music to match inside. There is no uniform; a huge variety of clients, most at least in their 20s. Maccabee and Goldstar NIS8. Open nightly 9:30pm-5am.

Works, Gan Ha'Ir shopping mall (on the roof), Ibn Gvirol St. just north of Kikkar Malkhei Yisrael. A new gay bar with a mixed clientele. Open nightly 11pm-5am.

Long John Silver's, in an alley next to "Sisters" accessory store at Dizengoff Sq. No fish here, but drink like one; cheap drinks and classic rock. The best of the 3 pubs in the alley. Open nightly 8:30pm-people leave.

Ha-Shoftim, 39 Ibn Gvirol St., corner of Ha-Shoftim. Attracts the thirty-something crowd with its dark interior and blues/jazz music. Maccabee and Goldstar NIS8. Sandwiches NIS13-19. Open nightly 5pm-3am.

The Happy Casserole, 344 Dizengoff St. (tel. 604 2360). Wilder and more expensive. Live music (often Israeli folk) every night at midnight; arrive at 11 to get a seat. When all are sufficiently ripped, people might dance on chairs and sing along. The crowd stays until the musicians collapse. Open daily 10pm-5am.

CULTURE

To temper the hedonism, Tel Aviv offers nightly opera, ballet, jazz, classical music, and dance performances. It also has more than 40 movie theaters showing everything from the latest Van Damme flick to a Fellini classic. However, films are not dubbed and often have no English sub-titles (though this shouldn't be a problem with the Van Damme movies). Check the *Jerusalem Post* for English listings for the **Tel Aviv Cinematheque,** 2 Sprinzak St., corner of Carlebach St.

The **Y Studio,** 1 Tveriya St. (tel. 522 3615), off Bugrashov St., is a theater workshop that trains people for the professional stage. Performances are given in English every Monday at 9pm. **Bikurei Ha'Etim Cellar,** 6 Helftman St. (tel. 697 9510), offers Israeli folk dancing (classes for different levels Mon.-Tues. and Thurs. 7 and 9pm; Fri. 9pm). There is an **outdoor theater** in Neveh Tzedek, 6 Yehielli St. The **Bat Sheva Dance Company** (tel. 517 1471; Sun.-Thurs. 9am-5pm, Fri. 9am-1pm) and the **Tribal Folklore Dance Theater** (tel. 517 3711; Sun.-Thurs. 8:30am-5pm) both perform contemporary ethnic dances. For schedules, call 517 3711. Also try the Suzanne Delal Center (see p. 274). **Beit Lessin,** 34 Weizmann St. (tel. 695 6222), sometimes has live jazz acts.

Tickets for concerts, plays, and other performances can be purchased at **Rococo,** 93 Dizengoff St. (tel. 524 8824; open Sun.-Thurs. 9am-1pm and 5-7pm, Fri. 9am-1pm), and **Hadran,** 90 Ibn Gvirol St. (tel. 524 8787), north of Kikkar Malkhei Yisrael. The **Tel Aviv Comri Theater,** 101 Dizengoff St. (tel. 523 3335), corner of Frischmann St., offers simultaneous-translation earphones during performances for only NIS5. For the most detailed information on performance schedules and other activities in the Tel Aviv area see *Tel Aviv Today, Events in Tel Aviv,* and *This Week in Tel Aviv,* all free at the GTIO and major hotels.

NEAR TEL AVIV

RISHON LETZION ראשון לצירך

Rishon leTzion (First to Zion) is the site of the first modern Jewish settlement in Palestine. As might be expected, the town contains many Israeli "famous firsts." It was here that the tune to the Israeli national anthem was composed, the world's first national Hebrew school opened, and the Jewish National Fund was created. The **Rishon leTzion Museum,** 2-4 Aḥad Ha'Am St. (tel. (03) 964 1621 or 968 2435), at Rothschild St. across from the Great Synagogue, traces the history of the town from the early pioneers to the present. For NIS5 you can get a tour of the museum and a sound and light show. (Museum open Sun. and Tues.-Thurs. 9am-2pm, Mon.

9am-1pm and 4-8pm, Fri. 9am-1pm. Free tours and admission 10am-2pm on the first Sat. of every month.) At no charge, you can take your own tour of the "Pioneer's Way," a path painted along Rishon's pavement, directing you to 18 of the town's historic sites, each with a plaque to explain its significance. Pick up Israel's version of the "Freedom Trail" at Rothschild St. (Walk south on Herzl St. 2 blocks, turn left onto Rothschild, a pedestrian street, and walk uphill until the pedestrian mall ends.) The yellow line leads down Ha-Carmel St., where you will pass the **Winery,** 25 Ha-Carmel St. (tel. (03) 964 2021), built by Baron Edmond de Rothschild in 1887 and still used today to produce Carmel Mizraḥi wine. One-hour tours of the winery feature an audio-visual presentation, an explication of a remarkable life-size mural by German painter Gershom Schwarze, a tasting, and a souvenir bottle. The mural there traces the history of the winery and Rishon leTzion. (Open Sun.-Thurs. 8:30am-4pm. Admission NIS10, seniors and students NIS9.) At night, the audio-visual room turns into a rollicking pub. Across the street from the winery, you can buy booze at wholesale prices at **Sokolik** (tel. (03) 964 1343; open Sun.-Wed. 6am-2:30pm, Thurs. 6am-5pm, Fri. 6am-3pm).

For an inexpensive lunch, try **Kiosk Madar** (sign in Hebrew, but hard to miss the line, which remains long until the shop closes at 1pm), a local hole-in-the-wall favorite at the corner of Rothschild St. and Mohliever St., where the street begins after the *midraḥov* (falafel NIS3.50). If your tummy begins to grumble after 1pm, **Yossi Ash-kenazi,** 3 Rothschild St., serves up huge falafel and a plateful of salads for NIS4. (Open Sun.-Thurs. 9am-midnight, Fri. 9am-3pm, Sat. sundown-midnight.) For reasons unknown to locals, Rishon leTzion is blessed with its very own **Ben and Jerry's** ice cream, 75 Herzl St., conveniently located one block south of the central bus station (two measly scoops NIS4.90; open Sun.-Sat. 10am-midnight).

Bus #200 from Tel Aviv stops in Rishon and continues on to Reḥovot (every 20min., 15-20min., NIS3.30); you can also come here from Reḥovot (NIS3). The Rishon leTzion **bus station** is on Herzl St.

REḤOVOT רחובות

Reḥovot, a quiet and somewhat secluded town, is known primarily for its world-famous **Weizmann Institute of Science,** a good afternoon jaunt from Tel Aviv. The institute is named for Israel's first president, Dr. Ḥayim Weizmann, who was also a research chemist. During World War I, Weizmann discovered an innovative way to produce acetone, which proved essential to the British military effort (as well as to nail polish removal). Weizmann's discovery, combined with his formidable character and arguments, helped persuade Lord Balfour to issue the famous 1917 Balfour Declaration favoring the establishment of a Jewish national homeland.

A barren stretch of scrubland has been transformed, through the miracle of irrigation, into the groomed expanse of the institute's campus. In the southeast corner of the institute stands the **Weizmann House** (tel. (08) 473 960 or 483 230), an elegant example of early International style (designed by Erich Mendelssohn) and Israel's first presidential residence. Dr. Weizmann is buried adjacent to the house. (Tours Sun.-Thurs. every ½hr. 10am-3pm. Admission NIS7.) The forested area near the house will provide some relief for the overheated traveler. The main gate to the Weizmann Institute is at the north end of Herzl St., a 20-minute walk from Bilou St., Manchester Sq., and the central **bus station.** Near the main entrance to the institute are the **Weizmann Archives,** holding Dr. Weizmann's letters and papers.

The institute's scientific staff conducts pioneering research in all of the natural sciences. Projects include research on cancer, immunology, aging, the computer revolution, and the environment. Pick up maps and brochures at the **Visitors Section,** Stone Administration Building #503 (tel. (08) 343 967), the first building on the left as you enter the main gate. There is a free video (Sun.-Thurs. 11am and 2:45pm) at the Wix Auditorium, the second building on the left as you enter the main gate.

On Bilou St., you'll find Reḥovot's central fruit and vegetable **market.** The city's main avenue, Herzl St., is lined with falafel shops and self-service restaurants (falafel NIS3-4). For authentic, spicy Yemenite dishes, head south along Herzl St. several blocks from the bus station, where you'll find a cluster of restaurants. Bus #200 (express) and #201 make the 20km trip from Tel Aviv (every 20min., NIS5.50), stopping 30m beyond the institute's large white stone gate.

ASHDOD אשדוד

You can come to Ashdod to practice your French, to see industry relentlessly gulp down land and resources, or, if you're so inclined, to ride the crashing waves right around where the whale spat out Jonah. You'll be disappointed, though, if you come to Ashdod to rest. If you stay long enough to visit Lido Beach (Ḥof Lido), you'll find a short stretch of popular bars and cafés stalked by large cargo ships and spindly cranes from the giant port. Ashdod exists for industry, not the other way around.

In Biblical times, Ashdod was one of the five cities of giants. Although Joshua received accurate information from his spies, he did not stoop to conquer Ashdod, and it was here that the Philistines brought the captured Holy Ark. This former city of Gullivers is now home to some 90,000 residents and, by some measures, the largest port in Israel. Its expanding industries include textiles, cosmetics, and power; the plants here produce roughly half the nation's electricity.

After you get off the bus, head next door to the **Bureau of Public Relations** in the Municipal Building; get their excellent, poster-sized city map. On the southern outskirts of Ashdod lie the remains of a Fatimid fortress (10th century CE) known in Arabic as **Qal'at al-Mine,** in Hebrew as **Metzudat Ashdod Yam,** and in English as **Fortress of the Port.** Until excavations unearthed bits of ceramic pottery, the site was believed to be more recent. An early Arabic document recounts that Byzantine ships used to bring in Muslim prisoners to sell back to their families. As boats appeared off the coast of Ashdod, the Fatimid fortress would send up smoke signals alerting the townspeople to come at once with their offerings. Thousands brought what riches they had, hoping to earn the return of their loved ones. Qal'at al-Mine, once part of a chain of coastal fortifications, seems to have served as a focal point for these emotional exchanges. Portions of four towers remain. To visit the site, take bus #5 south, and ask to get off at the fortress (at the end of a row of private homes).

The site of the Biblical city of **Tel Ashdod,** southeast of the modern city, comprises 23 levels of virtually unidentifiable ruins. Nothing much remains, although excavations continue. A view of the city and its environs is afforded from the top of **Giv'at Yona,** adjacent to the lighthouse at the end of Ya'ir St. in the northern part of the city. According to Muslim tradition, the ruins mark the spot where the whale coughed up Jonah. If you visit Ashdod on a Wednesday, check out the **flea market** at Lido Beach (6am-nightfall).

Bus #312 and 314 from Tel Aviv run to Ashdod (every 10-30min. until 9:50pm), and #15 leaves Ashkelon for Ashdod (about every hr., NIS3.80). Falafel stands and kiosks abound along Rogozin St.

ASHKELON AND ENVIRONS אשקלון

Ashkelon's Mediterranean beaches are like many other stretches of sand on Israel's coast; the local archaeological sites may not be the most engaging piles of rubble in the Holy Land, and the rows of shopping malls, cineplexes, and housing projects sprawling across the countryside could be found in a thousand towns around the planet. But 75,000 Israelis call this place home, so if you're curious to know how they live, make the easy daytrip from Tel Aviv.

Ashkelon, one of the oldest inhabited cities in the world, was first settled in the third millennium BCE. In biblical times, Ashkelon was one of the Philistines' five great cities. The Bible records its almost continuous conflicts with the Hebrews: Samson, as a young man, "went down to Ashkelon, and slew thirty men of them" (Judges 14:19). When King Saul was killed, David ordered, "Publish it not in the streets of Ashkelon, lest the daughters of the Philistines rejoice" (2 Samuel 1:20). The remains of the biblical city are found in the National Park on the coast south of the city center. In 1948, the state of Israel was declared in this city.

ASHKELON AND ENVIRONS

Practical Information Ashkelon's **central bus station** (info. tel. (07) 750 221) is located on Ben-Gurion St., about a 25-minute walk from the beach. The information booth (closed Sun.-Thurs. 9-9:30am and 5:30-6pm, and Fri. 9-9:30am and 12:30-1pm) is supplemented by an electronic bulletin board. Bus #300, 311, and 362 will take you to Tel Aviv (every 15min. until 10:30pm; NIS12.70, students NIS11.50), #437 will take you to Jerusalem (every hr. until 8:30pm; NIS16, students NIS14.50), and #363 and 364 will take you to Be'er Sheva (every hr. until 9:15pm; NIS14, students NIS12.70). Locally, bus #5 goes downtown to **Zephaniah Square** in the heart of **Afridar** (the business center), and from there to the **pedestrian mall** (*midraḥov*) in the old **Migdal** (tower) area. Bus #6 (as well as bus #13 in July-Aug.) will take you to the entrance of the **National Park,** to the beaches, and then to Migdal.

The local **Tourist Information Office** (tel. 734 666) is located in a small concrete building opposite the green in Zephaniah Square; they carry the usual range of maps and schedules of special events (open Sun. and Tues. 8:30am-1pm, Mon. and Wed.-Thurs. 8:30am-12:30pm). The square area also has some **banks** and **Ashkelon Pharmacy** (open Sun.-Mon. and Wed.-Thurs. 8:30am-1pm and 4:30-7pm, Tues. 8:30am-1pm, and Fri. 8:30am-1:30pm). Ashkelon's **telephone code** is 07. The **Central Post Office** at 18 Herzl St. in Migdal offers **Post Restante** (both open Sun.-Tues. and Thurs. 8am-12:30pm and 3:30-7pm, Wed. and Fri. 8am-noon). For **sherut taxis** to Tel Aviv (NIS10) try Yael Daroma on Tzahal St. (tel. 750 334) in Migdal. For **first aid** call 101 or 723 333; for **fire** call 102. The **police station** is at the corner of Ha-Nassi and Eli Cohen St. (tel. 100 or 771 444).

Accommodations and Food There are no youth hostels or pensions in Ashkelon; if you're keen on staying indoors, you should probably stay in Tel Aviv (45- to 60-min. drive) and make this a daytrip. At the **Samson Gardens** on 38 Ha-Tamar St. (tel. 734 666; walk from Zephaniah Sq. through the city park towards the sea, go through the few rows of houses at the end of the grass, then turn right onto Drom Africa St. and right again onto Ha-Tamar St.), the rooms all have phones, radios, A/C, and private baths. (Doubles US$48; low season US$41. Breakfast included. 15% service charge.) The GTIO arranges rentals of **private rooms** in homes near the Afridar section of town. The price is usually NIS50-60 without meals, and quality varies widely.

There's also **camping** at **Ashkelon National Park.** Those who have their own tents can settle on one of the grassy surfaces for free, though there are no toilets or showers. The **Bustan Ha-Zeitim Campground** (tel. 736 777 or 734 027), also located within the park, has fairly clean facilities. (NIS20 if you bring your own tent, children under 13 NIS8. 1-, 2-, and 3-person bungalows NIS50/70/90. 4-person caravans NIS135, with A/C NIS150; 6-person caravans NIS165/180.) If you take bus #6 or 13 to the official entrance of the park, you'll have to pay an entrance fee (NIS12, children under 12 NIS8). Bustan Ha-Zeitim gives out slips of paper stating that you're a guest camper so that you don't have to pay admission again for the length of your stay. Camping on the beach adjacent to the city is on the dangerous side and is not recommended.

Campers can bring their own superfood from **HyperCoOp Supermarket,** 4 Ben-Gurion Blvd. (tel. 333 045), just south of the central bus station (open Sun.-Thurs. 8:30am-8:30pm and Fri. 8am-2pm). The snack bar and two beach-side restaurants in the park itself are convenient and relatively inexpensive (steak, *shishlik,* or hamburger on a pita NIS8-10). In Afridar, you'll find several comfortable cafés around the green at Zephaniah Sq. **Mitgash Haverim,** 4/7 Ha-Nassi St. (tel. 711 190), just 3 doors left of the GTIO, serves hamburgers (NIS7), *shawerma* or *me'orav Yerushalayim* (NIS8), and *shishlik* (NIS9) in a clean, friendly atmosphere. A somewhat larger selection is available in the Migdal section: air-conditioned **Nitzaḥon,** 30 Herzl St. (tel. 727 409), near the post office, has the town's best selection of steaks, *me'orav* (mixed grill), *kabab,* and stuffed cabbage for NIS15-19 per plate. The restaurant at 70 Herzl St. serves hot dogs, *schnitzel,* or *kabab* sandwiches for NIS8-10.

Mashehu Mashehu, 43 Herzl, has similar fare plus *me'orav* (NIS7). For fresh produce, head for the outdoor *shuk* on Remez St. in Migdal (open Mon. 6am-1pm,
Wed. 6am-9pm, Thurs. 5:30am-9pm) right between the Migdal stop and the Kahn
mosque. Amos sells authentic Tunisian sandwiches at **Casse Croute Tunisien,** 31
Herzl, on the *midraḥov.* For NIS8, you'll get a baguette stuffed with tuna, capers,
salads, potatoes, hot peppers, spicy *harisa,* lemon, and olives.

Sights and Entertainment Of relative interest in Ashkelon is **Kikkar
Ha'Atzma'ut** (Independence Sq.), one block behind the Migdal stop on bus routes
#4, 5, 6, and 7. Once a caravan rest stop, this dilapidated intersection was the site of
the first reading of Israel's declaration of independence in 1948—you can see pictures of Arlozorov, Moshe Dayan, Ben-Gurion, and other dignitaries present at this
historic event at the **Ashkelon Museum** in the square; the museum traces the history of Ashkelon from Roman times to the present. (Open Sun.-Thurs. 9am-12:45pm
and 4-6pm, Fri. 9am-12:45pm, Sat. 10am-12:45pm. Free.) The black door leading
you to the museum also leads you into a courtyard providing a great view of the
now-closed **Khan mosque** towering above, and the art gallery below.

Compared to Migdal, Afridar has very few attractions to offer in Zephaniah Sq.
The grand-sounding **Antiquities Courtyard** in the corner of the green entrance
below the Milano sign is a waste of time with the two elaborate sarcophagi from the
Roman period (3rd century CE) being the only view-worthy exhibit (open Sun.-
Thurs. 8:30am-3:30pm, Fri. 8:30am-1:30pm). Afridar is also home to Ashkelon's six
beaches, including a religious one where men and women bathe separately (take
bus #6). For fun in the water—*sans* sand—there's the **Ashkeluna water park** near
Delila Beach (tel. 739 970). It's the biggest water park in the Middle East and Ashkelon's newest and cheesiest attraction. NIS32 covers a full day of splashy fun.
(Open daily 9am-5pm.)

Also on the waterfront lies Ashkelon's seaside **National Park** (tel. 736 444). Bus
#6 and 13 (summer only) take you to the front entrance, while bus #3 and 9 will
take you within a 7- to 10-minute walk from the (free) unofficial back entrance. The
park was built on the site of 1000-year-old Canaanite remains buried under the ruins
of Philistine, Greek, Roman, Byzantine, Crusader, and Muslim cities. The ruins offer
extensive evidence supporting Ashkelon's reputation as the oldest city in the
world—competition for this title rages throughout the Middle East. Pick up a free
map of the park at the main entrance; it includes most of the archaeological ruins.
(Park open daily 8am-6:30pm; Oct.-March 8am-4pm. Closes 1hr. earlier on Fri. and
holiday eves. Admission NIS12, students NIS8.)

A Roman colonnade and a grab-bag of Hellenistic and Roman columns, capitals,
and statues, including two magnificent statues of Nike, the winged goddess of victory and air-cushioned rubber soles, grace the park's center. Coming through the
main gate, you will see the **Bouleuterion,** which was the Council House Square of
Ashkelon when it was an autonomous city-state under Severius in the 3rd century
CE. The sunken courtyard-like area on the right is actually the inside of a Herodian
assembly hall. There is also a statue of the goddess Isis with her god-child Horus.
These figures, made of Italian marble, were sculpted some time between 200 BCE
and 100 CE. Behind the Bouleuterion lies a fine **amphitheater.**

Along the southern edge of the park are segments of wall from the 12th-century
Crusader city. The most peculiar feature of the site is the assembly of Roman columns sticking out of the ancient Byzantine sea wall on the beach. Originally these
columns were used to support the walls, which were destroyed in 1191 by Salah ad-
Din. Richard the Lion-Hearted partly restored them in 1192, as did Richard Cornwall
in 1240, only to have them finally demolished by the Sultan Baybars in 1270.

Outside the park at the northern end of the beach is the well-preserved **Roman
tomb,** believed to have been built for a wealthy Greek family during the 3rd century
CE. The frescoes adorning its interior depict scenes from classical mythology and
remain in remarkably good condition. You will have to unbolt a waist-high red iron

door to get in. Close it on your way out—sand from the beach corrodes the paintings. (Tomb open Sun.-Fri. 9am-1pm, Sat. 10am-2pm. Free.)

As for nightlife, the Bustan Ha-Zeitim campground in the National Park has its own **Tough Wood** café/disco, housed in a massive tent with a marble dance floor and lightbulb-adorned trees (open Thurs.-Sat. 10pm-whenever). In Afridar, **Signon Pub** is the favorite local pub, with live music played by local artists on Tuesday and Thursday nights and karaoke on Wednesdays (open nightly 7:30pm-2am). Across the green, **Ha-Sha'on Pub,** a few stores over from the GTIO, offers cheap beer and good music (open nightly 8pm-2am). In Migdal, enjoy yourself at the **Kaphiterion Pub** in the Khan building on Ha'Atzma'ut Square; entrance via side door (open weekends 9pm-wee hours).

Yad Mordekhai יד מרדכי

From May 19th to 24th, 1948, the 165 members of Kibbutz Yad Mordekhai withstood an attack by an Egyptian battalion of 2500. The kibbutz has built a model of the battle, complete with soldiers, tanks, weapons, and a recorded explanation. The kibbutz is named after Mordekhai Anielewicz, leader of the Warsaw Ghetto uprising. Yet another **museum** (tel. (051) 205 28 or 29) illustrates the story of the Jewish resistance movement. (Museum and battlefield open daily 8am-4pm. Admission NIS5, students NIS4.) Bus #19 runs from Ashkelon to Yad Mordekhai (Sun.-Thurs. noon and 6:05pm, Fri. noon and 4:15pm; last bus returns to Tel Aviv at 3:10pm, Fri. 12:40pm; NIS6.30.) If you get stuck in the late afternoon, go back to the bus stop on the highway and try flagging a passing bus from Rafah.

Around Beit Guvrin בית גוברין

About 22km east of Ashkelon, **Kiryat Gat** is easily accessible by bus from Tel Aviv (#369, every 15-20min., NIS12), Jerusalem (#446, every 20-40min., NIS14.30), and Ashkelon (#25, every 30min., NIS6.80). This small industrial town is the capital of the **Lakhish** region—a network of 30 villages established in 1954—and the launching pad for exploration of several sites.

Beit Guvrin, a modern kibbutz, was built in 1949 on the ruins of the Arab village of Beit Jibrin, destroyed by Israel shortly after its occupants were expelled in the 1948 war. The surrounding region is characterized by huge outcroppings of cacti and fig trees, which hide some 3000 caves, some of which were created naturally when water eroded the soft limestone. The Byzantines carved the others as they scooped limestone out of gigantic holes in the earth for use in the construction of their great port at Ashkelon. As a result, many of the **caves** have vast bell-shaped rooms with sun roofs. The caves later became sanctuaries for hermits and monks. St. John and others came here seeking solitude, and often carved crosses and altars into the walls. The saintly Sylvester Stallone was here for the filming of *Rambo III.* The site is well-tended with marked trails and some facilities. (Free.)

At nearby **Tel Sandahanna** (Arabic for St. John), excavations uncovered vivid, beautifully-preserved Byzantine mosaics of birds and flowers. These served as floors in 5th- and 6th-century churches, but not much is left. More recently, excavations have uncovered a Roman mosaic floor in better condition. Two of the caves were used for burials and have niches for the appropriate urns. Since the sites are unmarked and the *tel* is large, you should ask for the assistance of a kibbutznik from Beit Guvrin, a 20-minute walk down the hill. (Most get off work about 12:30-1:30pm and will show interested travelers around. Ask to see the site of the house of King Abdallah, grandfather of King Hussein of Jordan, on top of the hill. An attractive villa among the caves once belonged to the village *mukhtar.*)

Getting to and from Beit Guvrin requires advance planning. Bus #11 from Kiryat Gat goes directly to the kibbutz. (Sun.-Thurs. 8:05am and 5:10pm, Fri. 8am and 2:15pm, NIS 4.50; return from Beit Guvrin at 8:25am and 12:30pm. You'll have to catch one of the morning buses if you don't want to spend the night.) Some of the Kiryat Gat-Hebron buses pass by Beit Guvrin; ask the driver to let you off here since there is no regular stop. Taxis run from Tel Aviv's central bus station to Beit Guvrin,

Tel Maresha, and Tel Lakhish. To reach the caves, walk to the paved road opposite the kibbutz. The first fork bears left to the Beit Guvrin bell caves.

The right fork leads to **Tel Maresha,** about 3km southeast of Beit Guvrin. The unbelievable view makes it worth the trip, even if you're crumbling at the sight of ruins. On a clear day, you can see Tel Aviv and the Mediterranean to the west, and the Jordanian hills and the Dead Sea to the east. The ruins include several Byzantine bell caves, one of which has a stone *calumbarium* with thousands of niches, two decorated graves, and a Crusader basilica nearby. The 60 caves around the ruins contain colorful wildlife drawings.

Tel Lakhish lies just north of the *moshav* of the same name, 2km south of the Beit Guvrin-Hebron road. Although archaeologically more important, Tel Lakhish is not as interesting as Tel Maresha. Its strategic location at the intersection of the road to Egypt and the approach to Jerusalem made it a scene of conflict in ancient times. It is mentioned in the Bible (Joshua 10:31-32) as one of the Canaanite cities destroyed by the Israelites. Excavations have revealed nine levels of settlements dating as far back as the third millennium BCE. There are still remains of Canaanite graves and one of their holy sites, but most of the artifacts have been moved to museums in Jerusalem and Britain. It's virtually inaccessible without a car, although bus #11 runs to the *moshav*. Because of this area's isolation, climate, and proximity to the West Bank, *moshavniks* strongly discourage camping in these hills.

HERZLIYA AND HERZLIYA PITUAH הרצליה

Named after Theodore Herzl, **Herzliya** and its affluent western suburb Herzliya Pituaḥ are located only 15km outside of Tel Aviv. Both are home to beautiful beaches, luxury hotels, and foreigners who tan and schmooze for a living. Take bus #501 or 502 from Tel Aviv's New Central Bus Station (NIS4.40) to the Herzliya central bus station. The closest it gets to budget accommodations in Herzliya Pituaḥ is the **Mittelmann Guesthouse,** 13 Basel St. (tel. (09) 576 544). From DeShalit Square, where the bus from Tel Aviv lets you off, follow Basel St. (10min.). Rooms have refrigerators, private showers, and access to kitchen facilities; some have A/C (singles US$28; doubles US$38).

From the Herzliya bus station, you can walk 2 blocks south on Ben-Gurion St. to the corner of Ha-Bouim St., where you'll find the diminutive **Herzliya Museum of Art.** (Open Sun.-Thurs. 1-8pm, Sat. 9am-noon. Free.) The museum is in the **Yad Labanim Memorial Center,** which also houses the **Israeli Center for Propaganda Research,** where tourists are generously encouraged to sample the wares (call (052) 551 011 for lecture schedules). An amphitheater in the same building is the setting for concerts by the **Herzliya Chamber Orchestra** (call (052) 547 175 for schedules). Surrounding the building is an extensive modern **Sculpture Garden.**

A few blocks north of the Herzliya **central bus station** is the **Beit Rishonim** (First Settlers' House) **Founders Museum,** at 8 Ha-Nadiv St. off Sokolov St. The museum, located in a pleasant garden, has a life-like statue of Herzl leaning against the second-floor balcony. The museum reconstructs the story of Herzliya from its days as a colony in 1924 via computerized presentations, and furnishings and tools from the early settlement period. (Open Sun. and Thurs.-Fri. 8:30am-12:30pm, Mon. 8:30am-12:30pm and 4:30-6:30pm. Admission NIS5.)

The attractions in **Herzliya Pituaḥ** are centered around the beach. From the Herzliya central bus station, take bus #29 to **Ḥof Nof Yam.** This beach is beautifully tourist-free; you won't have to fear being hit by a *kadima* paddleball. Get off the bus, follow the dirt road up the hill, and go through the gate in the fence (under the Hebrew sign). You will pass the **Sidna Ali Mosque,** currently under renovation.

Once at the beach, you'll notice Herzliya Pituaḥ's best-preserved attraction, an inhabited sand castle known as the **Hermit's House.** Built into the face of the cliff, this private home is probably the most unique one in Israel. Part of it looks like a boat over which a peacock has spread its fan, part like a gargoyle, and the rest like nothing you've ever seen. Nissim Kakhalon has been building this fantastic structure for the past 25 years with natural sea materials as well as tires, bottles, broken plates, and other debris that washes ashore. Plenty of greenery covers the walls, and graceful panther statues are strewn all over. Peevish Israeli authorities have so far been unable to oust Mr. Kakhalon. Look for his latest inspired addition, the "sand bar" snack stand, featuring cold drinks (NIS4) and hummus on homemade pita (NIS6) served on a covered veranda. Ask for a tour of his architectural creations and the network of tunnels that he has dug to connect them, and the henhouse/peacock pen. Plans for a school to teach people "how to make things" are being hatched.

On the cliffs above the beach, a few hundred meters farther north, are the barely discernible ruins of **Apollonia,** a Roman port fortified by medieval Crusaders.

NETANYA נתניה

Founded in the 1920s as an agricultural center, Netanya has grown into a beach resort popular with affluent retirees. This Miami-on-the-Med's bridge club, orchestra, and meetings for single tourists cater to a certain group of travelers, but a growing variety of activities indicates an effort to attract young people and budgeteers.

Orientation and Practical Information From the central bus station (tel. 337 050), push your way through gaudy neon-lit food stands to **Binyamin Blvd.** (which turns into Weizmann Blvd. farther north) and walk one block north to **Herzl St.,** the town's main shopping area. Turn left on Herzl, and after a few blocks you'll get to **Dizengoff St.** Past Dizengoff, Herzl St. turns into a **midraḥov,** or pedestrian zone, lined with expensive outdoor cafés and *shawerma* and dairy restaurants. Keep walking in the *midraḥov* until you cross King David St.; on the other side you'll see **Ha'Atzma'ut Sq.** (Independence Sq.), an attractive park, from which you can take the stairs down to the beach. Opposite the bus station, **Sha'ar Ha-Gai St.** cuts diagonally from Binyamin Blvd. to **Zion Square,** where it meets Herzl St.

The **Government Tourist Information Office (GTIO)** is a small, strangely-shaped brick building in the southwest corner of Ha'Atzma'ut Sq. (tel. 827 286), next to the stairs to the beach. City maps, bus schedules, and events schedules are available. (Open Sun.-Thurs. 8:30am-7pm, Fri. 9am-noon.) The **post office** at 59 Herzl St. (tel. 621 577) offers **Poste Restante.** Another branch is located at 2 Herzl St. (tel. 627 797). Open Sun.-Tues. and Thurs. 8am-12:30pm and 3:30-6pm, Wed. 8am-1:30pm, Fri. 8am-noon. **Telephone code:** 09.

Car Rental options in Netanya are plentiful, with **Hertz** (tel. 828 890), **Tamir-Rent-A-Car** (tel. 331 831), **Rent-A-Reliable Car** (tel. 629 042), and **Budget** (tel. 330 618) lined up on Herzl St. near Ha'Atzma'ut Sq. (All open Sun.-Thurs. 8am-6pm, Fri. 8am-2pm.) **Bicycle rental** (tel. 339 903) is also available from a stand outside the GTIO (NIS10 per hr., NIS38 per day); bargain (open daily 8:30am-nightfall).

Bus #605 runs to Tel Aviv (about every 10min., NIS7.50). Bus #957 runs to Haifa (every ½hr., NIS12.30). Schedule displayed on the electronic timetable board facing the information booth. Netanya has several **pharmacies,** including **Trufa** at 2 Herzl St. (tel. 828 656; open Sun.-Mon. and Wed.-Thurs. 8am-7:30pm, Tues. 8am-1pm, Fri. 8am-2pm). Others are on Herzl St., Weizmann Blvd., and Sha'ar Ha-Gai St. At least one is always open for emergencies; the roster is posted on each door. For **first aid** dial 101 or 623 333; for **police,** dial 100 or 604 444.

Accommodations and Food The **Atzma'ut Hostel,** at the corner of Ha'Atzma'ut Sq. and Usishkin St., is expected to be completed by 1995 and will be the only youth hostel in town. In the meantime, the **Orit Pension,** 21 Chen Ave. (tel./fax 616 818), off Jabotinsky St. south of Ha'Atzma'ut Sq., with homey, scrupulously clean rooms, a common room with flowery drapes and the *Jerusalem Post,* and friendly management, is the best budget bed in town. Rooms with private bath, fan, and balcony. (No smoking. Reception open 8am-9pm. Check-out 10am. No curfew—you'll get a key. Singles NIS74. Doubles NIS128. Breakfast included.)

Almost all hotels in Netanya are expensive, but many lower their prices by 10-15% from November to February; as always, pay with foreign currency to save the 18%

VAT. **Camping** on the beach is unsafe for solo women and unguarded valuables; the most popular areas for beach-sleeping are near the 24-hr. cafés.

Though it might not appear obvious at first, cheap food *is* available in Netanya. **Sha'ar Ha-Gai Street** is lined with falafel stands and self-service restaurants which will stuff just about anything permitted by law into a pita (falafel NIS6, *shawerma* NIS7, *schnitzel* NIS8). In **Ha'Atzma'ut Square,** pizza is about NIS6, *malawaḥ* NIS8; a **Burger King** will open in 1995 at 9 Ha'Atzma'ut Sq. For fresh fruits and vegetables, shop at the **open market** on Zangwill St., 2 blocks east of Weizmann Blvd. near the center of town (open Sun.-Thurs. 7am-6:30pm, Fri. 7am-2pm).

A number of restaurants line the cliffs overlooking the beach. Try the **Mini Golf Restaurant and Pub,** 21 Nice Blvd. (tel. 617 735), perched on the edge of a cliff overlooking the sea. From Ha'Atzma'ut Sq., take King David St. past King Solomon's Hotel to Nitza Blvd. The grilled dishes are excellent (NIS20-36) and the atmosphere is relaxing and romantic. (Open Sun.-Thurs. 11am-3am, Fri.11am-7pm, Sat. 8:30pm-3am.) **Apropo** is conveniently located between the amphitheater and the stairs to the beach. Blintzes and pastas (NIS21-24) and toasts (NIS24) are all served in large portions. (Open Sun.-Thurs. 9am-midnight, Fri. 9am-5pm, Sat. 6pm-midnight.) A cheaper option is **Pizza Hut,** King David St., a half-block from Ha'Atzma'ut Sq., where patrons watch the sunset over the water through floor-to-ceiling windows. (Small pizza NIS14-22.) Farther north down Nitza Blvd. (bus #29, cab, or 40-min. walk) is **Blue Bay Beach,** where you'll find Ḥofeya (tel. 623 141). Turn left toward the beach just before the Blue Bay Hotel on the left side of the road. At high tide, the waves of the Mediterranean crash up against the windows of this delightful restaurant/pub. The main dishes are a bit expensive (fish NIS35-40), but you can enjoy the spectacular scenery for the price of a dessert (NIS7-13). Live singers perform Thursday, Friday, and Saturday nights. (Open daily noon-4am; 24 hrs. in summer.) **Patisserie Antverpia,** 1 Eliyahu Krause St. (tel. 335 390), one block south of Herzl St. off Smilansky St., serves fresh ḥallah and luscious cream pastries at slightly lower prices than its tourist-district counterparts. (Open Sun.-Fri. 7:30am-9pm.)

Sights and Entertainment Netanya's **beaches** are all free; the northernmost are the least crowded. You can rent a **bicycle** (see Practical Information, above), or go **horseback riding** along the beach (Cactus Ranch Horseback Riding, tel. 651 239, take bus #7 to intersection of Itamar Ben-Avi St. and Jabotinsky St., open daily 8am-sunset; or The Ranch, tel. 663 525, take bus #29 to Havatzelet, 2km north of Blue Bay Beach, open daily 8am-sunset; both charge NIS40 per hr.). Live out your flight fantasies in a **paraglider** with an instructor (no experience necessary) for NIS150 (call (08) 255 873 to make arrangements), or brave the **Paintball** (tel. 961 131) wooden city (NIS41) at Yishuv B'nai Dior.

The Netanya municipality organizes various forms of free entertainment almost every night during the summer and often during the winter. The GTIO has complete listings of concerts, movies, and a host of other activities. During the summer, you can watch the sun set over the Mediterranean while listening to classical music in the amphitheater next to the steps to beach (Sun.-Thurs. 6-8pm).

For a break from sunbathing, tour the industrial side of town. The **Netanya Diamond Center,** 90 Herzl St. (tel. 624 770; open Sun.-Thurs. 8am-7pm, Fri. 8am-2pm) and the **Fubar Diamond Center,** 1 Usishkin St. (tel. 822 233; open Sun.-Thurs. 9:30am-7:30pm, Fri. 9:30am-2pm) offer tours; call for times. Or check out the **citrus packing plants** in Kiryat Eliezer. (Open Sun.-Thurs. 8am-4pm, Fri. 8am-1pm; closed April-Nov.) There's also the **Puinat Shirtei Israel** Yemenite cultural museum and folklore center, 7 Ha'Atzma'ut Sq. (tel. 331 325). (Open Sun.-Thurs. 8:30am-6:30pm, Fri. 8:30am-1:30pm. Admission NIS5.)

Near Netanya

Aspiring horticulturists will drool over the iris blossoms in Israel's largest **Iris Nature Reserve** near the southern exit of Netanya (Ben-Gurion Blvd.). The **Winter Pond** on the other side of the reserve is home to attractive waterfowl. The beautiful

Poleg Nature Reserve, about 8km south of Netanya, begins where the Poleg River meets the sea. The walk upstream leads past flowering plants and eucalyptus trees planted during the last century to dry up the swamps that once covered the Plain of Sharon. A few kilometers south, near **Kibbutz Ga'ash,** seaside cliffs reach almost 61m; excellent camouflage for one of Israel's favorite **nudist beaches.** Take Egged bus #601 (every ½hr. 5:30am-10:30pm); ask to be let off at Ga'ash or Nahal Poleg.

Museum fans also have their choice. From Netanya, bus #29 goes to the **Ha-Sharon Museum** at Emek Ḥefer (tel. 688 644; limited archaeological exhibits; open Sun.-Thurs. 8am-2pm, Sat. 10am-2pm; admission NIS6). Bus#1A goes to the **Jewish Legion Museum** (tel. 822 212), less than 5km north of Netanya, in Aviḥa'il. It's dedicated to the Jewish units of the British Army in World War I, led by the dashing Yosef Trumpeldor. (Open Sun.-Thurs. 8am-2pm; admission NIS5.50.)

The peaceful **Emek Ḥefer Youth Hostel (HI)** (tel. (09) 666 032), across the highway from Kfar Vitkin, is in its own grove 8km south of Netanya, only a short walk from gorgeous, free **beaches.** Take bus #857, 872, or 901 from Tel Aviv (NIS9.50), #29, 706, or 922 from Netanya (NIS6.30), or #901 or 921 from Haifa (NIS11), get off at Tzomet Beit Yanai, and walk north until you see the gate in the fence. All of the impressively clean rooms have private baths and fridges. (Reception closed 2-5pm. No lockout. No curfew. Dorm beds (4-6 per room) NIS42, nonmembers NIS47. Breakfast included, lunch NIS20, dinner NIS19.) **Ḥanout Shohar Supermarket** (open Sun.-Thurs. 8am-8pm, Fri. 8am-4pm, Sat. 9am-8pm) and **The Original Israeli Pancake House** (open Sun.-Fri. 6am-1am, Sat. 7:30am-1am; pancakes NIS9-24, Mexican menu NIS12-20; alcohol served) supplement the hostel food.

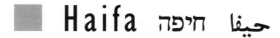

Haifa חיפה حيفا

A prosperous city built on the steep, forested slopes of Mt. Carmel, Haifa is Israel's capital of the North. Though it boasts the country's largest port, two of Israel's eleven universities, and the most diverse topography in the state, Haifa does not compete with Tel Aviv or Jerusalem for tourism. Budget accommodations are sparse, the seafront distant, and the museums less than spectacular. But Haifa's real gems, its thickly forested neighborhoods and striking vistas, are worth the trip.

Haifa has had a tradition of harboring political and religious minorities since the Hebrew prophet Elijah first fled there from the wrath of King Ahab (1 Kings 18-19). Crusaders built the first of several monasteries above Elijah's cave; these temporarily housed many sects before finally giving shelter to the wandering Carmelite Order, which still thrives in Haifa today (see Sights, below). Among the other religious minorities who have found refuge in Haifa are German Templars, who founded a colony here, and Baha'is, whose center is in Haifa. The massive immigration of Jews seeking refuge from Nazism in Europe in the 1930s brought many Jews to Haifa, which had long been a prominent Palestinian city.

Meanwhile, the modern port, built by the British, became the most important in the eastern Mediterranean; the Trans Arabian Pipeline carried oil all the way from Iraq to the Haifa refineries. The city was the first territory taken in the 1948 war. With its port and refineries, Haifa became the early industrial center of the young Israel, a status that earned it the nickname "Red Haifa," the workers' city. Haifa's population of a quarter-million contains a sizeable Arab minority and a small religiously observant Jewish community; the prevailing tenor of the city is secular. While city leaders boast diversity, Haifa is actually a place where social stratification is more than metaphorical: the poor live on the bottom, the rich on top.

■■■ ORIENTATION

Haifa, Israel's principal port and the hub for ferry transport, is on the Mediterranean coast about 100km south of Lebanon and due west of the Sea of Galilee. It is unofficially divided into three terraces. The **Ha'Ir** area, aptly named downtown, is at the foot of the Carmel mountain. The **central bus station** is adjoined to the **train station** on this level, at the intersection of **Derekh Yafo** and **Shderot Rothschild.** If you follow Yafo Way to the west, you'll find yourself in the Old City area, across from the **Haifa Port.** Perpendicular to Yafo Way and running straight up to the Shrine of the Bab is **Ben-Gurion Blvd.,** which ends at **Ha-Geffen St.** farther up the mountain.

The middle terrace is the **Hadar** district, home to businesses, cafés, bakeries, and bazaar stands. Its main street is **Herzl St.,** along which several staircases provide for easy climbing up and down the mountain. **Ha-Ḥalutz St.,** parallel to Herzl but one street "down" (i.e., north, or toward the port), contains the lion's share of falafel stands. Buses from this street go to the central bus station rather than up the mountain. The street parallel to Herzl on the "up" side is the **Nordan Midraḥov** (pedestrian zone), bordered on the west by **Balfour St.** and on the east by **Arlozorov St.**

The highest area is known as the **Carmel Center,** characterized by posh homes, five-star hotels, restaurants, and discos. This district is traversed by **Shderot Ha-Nassi** and **Yefeh Nof St.,** both of which run west to east past all the major hotels. Follow either of these streets to the Dan Panorama Hotel and go one block "up" to reach **Gan Ha'Eim** (Mother's Park), which has a peaceful **Promenade** and an eye-opening perspective on the lower city and the port area.

■■■ TRANSPORTATION

The decentralization of the transportation system in Haifa is explained by the topography, most prominently by the 300m elevation drop between the Carmel Center and the Port. The **central bus station,** like the city, has three tiers. Buses bound for other cities leave from the first floor, Haifa city buses do their business on the second, and the third floor welcomes both inter- and intra-city arrivals. Take the following second-floor buses to the city's neighborhoods (all urban rides are NIS2.80): Ha'Ir (#41), Hadar (#21, 24, 28, 37), and Carmel Center (#22, 25).

On weekdays, buses run from around 5:45am to midnight. On Fridays, they stop at 3:30pm; on Saturdays, they begin running at 9am. Saturday buses do *not* run from the central bus station, but from the Hadar area, many from Daniel St. A final confusing detail about the bus system in Haifa is that the *only* place from which you can catch buses heading back to the central bus station is **Ha-Ḥalutz Street;** all other streets lead up toward the Carmel Center.

Haifa's main mode of transportation is the **Carmelit subway** system, running from the downtown area to the Carmel Center. Though this subway has only one line, its six stops are great for conquering the distance between **Kikkar Paris** and **Gan Ha'Eim** in less than six minutes. (See Carmelit listing, below.) Look for the entrances with yellow awning.)

■■■ PRACTICAL INFORMATION

Government Tourist Information Office (GTIO): 18 Herzl St. (tel. 666 521 or 522, or 643 616), in Hadar. Take bus #10 or 12 from the port area or #21 or 28 from the central bus station to **Beit Ha-Kranot.** Maps, train schedules, and an incredible CD-ROM computer that shows pictures and prints lists in Hebrew or English. Ask for the bimonthly *Events in Haifa* booklet. Open Sun.-Thurs. 8:30am-5pm, Fri. 8:30am-2pm. Second office in **Passenger Hall** or the Port (tel. 654 692), open when ships arrive (Sun. and Thurs. 6:30-9:30am).

Municipal Tourist Information Office (MTIO): Egged Central Bus Station (tel. 512 208), conveniently located on lowest level of station. Open Sun.-Thurs. 9:30am-5pm, Fri. 9:30am-2pm. Other offices at **City Hall** (tel. 356 200) in Hadar,

PRACTICAL INFORMATION

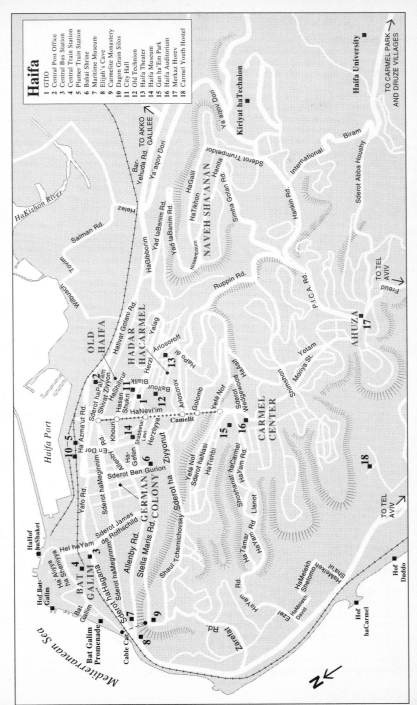

Haifa

1 GTIO
2 Central Post Office
3 Central Bus Station
4 Central Train Station
5 Plumer Train Station
6 Bahai Shrine
7 Maritime Museum
8 Elijah's Cave
9 Carmelite Monastery
10 Dagon Grain Silos
11 City Hall
12 Old Technion
13 Haifa Theater
14 Haifa Museum
15 Gan ha'Em Park
16 Haifa Auditorium
17 Merkaz Horev
18 Carmel Youth Hostel

14 Hassan Shuki St. (open Sun.-Fri. 8am-1pm), and 106 Ha-Nassi Blvd. (tel. 374 010) in Carmel (open Sun.-Thurs. 8am-7pm, Fri. 8am-1pm; winter Sun.-Thurs. 8am-6pm, Fri. 8am-1pm).

Tours: Society for the Protection of Nature in Israel (SPNI): 8 Menaḥem St. (tel. 664 135 or 136, or 675 804), near Nordau St. Ask about hiking trips into the Carmel Mountains. Open Sun. and Thurs. 9am-5:30pm, Mon.-Wed. 9am-4pm, Fri. 9am-12:30pm.

Budget Travel (ISSTA): 2 Balfour St. (tel. 669 139 or 670 222). ISICs and HI memberships NIS25. Open Sun.-Thurs. 8:30am-1pm and 4-7pm, Fri. 8:30am-1pm. Another location at **Technion** (tel. 326 739; fax 326 741), in the Student Building. Open Sun.-Thurs. 9am-3pm, Fri. (summer only) 9-11am.

American Consulate: 12 Yerushalayim St. (tel. 670 615), in Hadar. Call Sun.-Thurs. 9am-1pm (consular services by appointment only).

Currency Exchange: Barclays Discount, 65 Ha'Atzma'ut St. (tel. 522 291); **Ha-Poalim,** 5 Ha-Palyam Blvd. (tel. 681 574); **Israel Discount,** 47 Ha'Atzma'ut St. (tel. 546 111); **Leumi,** in the new Ha-Meginim Tower at 21 Yafo St. (tel. 547 111). Branches throughout city. General hours Sun., Tues., and Thurs. 8:30am-12:30pm and 4-6pm; Mon., Wed., and Fri. 8:30am-noon. All banks closed Mon. and Wed. afternoons. Be wary of random people offering to exchange money.

American Express: Meditrad Ltd., 2 Khayat Sq., P.O. Box 1266 (tel. 642 266 or 645 835). Entrance in alleyway next to Steimatzky off Ha'Atzma'ut St., opposite Sha'ar Palmer St. **Client Letter Service** available. Sells Travelers Cheques but won't cash them. For lost Cheques, call toll free (177) 440 8694. Open Sun.-Thurs. 8:30am-4pm, Fri. 8:30am-1pm.

Post Office: At Shabtai Levi and Ha-Nevi'im St. (tel. 640 917), in Hadar. Open Sun.-Thurs. 8am-7pm, Fri. 8am-1:30pm. Other branches at 152 Yafo St. on corner of Sha'ar Palmer; 19 Ha-Palyam Blvd. in port area; 63 Herzl St. in Hadar; and 7 Wedgewood Blvd. in Carmel. Most branches open Sun.-Thurs. 7am-7pm, Fri. 7am-noon. **Poste Restante** at Ha-Palyam branch only (tel. 304 158 or 159).

International Telephones: You can call from the post office branches at Ha-Palyam, Ha-Nevi'im, Sha'ar Palmer, and Shkimona—but you pay NIS0.25 per counter stroke even if you call collect or use a calling card. Get a phone card from any post office and call direct. **Telephone code:** 04.

Train Station: Bat Galim (tel. 564 564 or 303 133 for Hebrew-only updated schedule and prices), connected by tunnels to the central bus station. Trains to Tel Aviv (NIS12), Netanya (NIS10.50), Nahariya (NIS5.50), and Akko (NIS5). To get to Jerusalem you'll have to change stations, so you're better off taking the bus. 20% discount with ISIC. MTIO and GTIO have schedules.

Central Bus Station, Yafo St. (tel. 549 555 for intercity lines, 549 131 for city lines), corner of Rothschild Blvd. **Baggage storage** on the lower level, up the small concrete ramp, around the corner, and through 2 doors. Open Sun.-Thurs. 8am-12:45pm and 1:15-4:30pm, Fri. 8am-noon. NIS5 per item. **Lost and Found** also operates from here. **Bus** #251 and 271 go to Akko and Nahariya (every 15-20min. Sun.-Thurs. 5:15am-11:30pm, Fri. 5:15am-5:20pm, Sat. 9am-midnight; NIS6.30, students NIS5.50), #900 (direct) and 901 (express) go to Tel Aviv's central bus station (every 15-20min. Sun.-Thurs. 5:30am-11:40pm, Fri. 5:30am-4:45pm, Sat. 8:20am-11pm; NIS14.50, students NIS13). #980 goes to the Arlozorov Terminal (roughly every 20min.; 6am-8pm; NIS12, students NIS10), and #940 goes to Jerusalem (every 30-45min.; Sun.-Thurs. 6:30am-8:30pm, Fri. 6:30am-4pm, Sat. after 8:20pm; NIS21, students NIS18). Also to Tzfat, Nazareth, and Eilat.

Carmelit (subway): Tel. 376 870. From Kikkar Paris near the port up to Gan Ha'Eim in Carmel Center, stopping at Solel Boneh, Ha-Nevi'im (Hadar), Masada, and Golomb. Security guard always on duty. Yellow pavilion entrances. Runs every 15min. Sun.-Thurs. 6:30am-midnight, Fri. 6:30am-3pm, Sat. 15min. after sundown-midnight. All rides NIS2.80.

Ferries: Terminal next to the train station. Ferries to Cyprus (US$36-55, plus US$25 port tax), Crete, and mainland Greece (US$109, plus US$18 port tax) leave Sun. and Thurs. 8pm (but you need to be there 3-5pm for security check) and Fri. 7pm for Cyprus only (be there by 1pm for security check; the port closes by 1pm, so you won't be able to enter later). Buy tickets at **Caspi Travel,** 76 Ha'Atzma'ut St.

(tel. 674 444), **Multitour,** 55 Ha-Namal St. (tel. 663 570; open Sun.-Thurs. 8:30am-6pm, Fri. 8:30am-2pm), and **Mano,** 2 Sha'ar Palmer St. (tel. 667 722; open Sun.-Thurs. 8am-6pm, Fri. 8am-1pm).

Sherut Taxis: Most taxis leave from Eliyahu St. in Kikkar Paris, near Carmelit stop. Or call **Kavei Ha-Galil** (tel. 664 444 or 622 114/5), who will pick you up from home. To Akko (NIS5.50), Nahariya (NIS7.10), or Lod (NIS40). **Amal** (tel. 522 828) will take you from 6 Ha-Ḥalutz St. in Hadar to Tel Aviv for NIS13.

Rental Cars: Avis, 7 Sderot Ben-Gurion (tel. 513 050); **Budget,** 186 Yafo Rd. (tel. 520 666); **Hertz,** 90 Ha'Atzma'ut St. (tel. 531 234). **Reliable,** 118 Ha'Atzma'ut St. (tel. 516 504). All open Sun.-Thurs. 8am-6pm, Fri. 8am-2pm.

Shopping Hours: Most shops are open Sun.-Thurs. 8:30am-1:30pm and 4-7pm, Fri. 8:30am-2pm. Department stores and malls are usually open all day, 8:30am-7pm.

English Bookstores: Beverly's Books, 18 Herzl St. (tel. 664 810), Beit Ha-Kranot on second floor. Buys and exchanges used books. Open Sun.-Mon. and Wed.-Thurs. 9am-1pm and 4-6pm, Tues. and Fri. 9am-1pm. **Shmilovitz Book Center,** 31 Ha-Ḥalutz St. (tel. 645 384). **Studio 5,** 5 Derekh Ha-Yam St., in Merkaz Ha-Carmel district, sells used English books. Open Sun.-Mon. and Wed.-Thurs. 9am-1pm and 4-7pm, Tues. and Fri. 9am-1pm. **Steimatzky,** two branches in bus station. Also at 82 Ha'Atzma'ut St. in downtown, in Hadar (tel. 665 042), and in Carmel Center (tel. 388 765). Branches open Sun.-Thurs. 8:30am-7pm, Fri. 8:30am-2pm.

Ticket Offices: Haifa, 11 Baerwald St. (tel. 662 244), open Sun.-Thurs. 9am-1pm and 4-7pm, Fri 9am-1pm; **Garber,** 129 Ha-Nassi Blvd. (tel. 384 777), open Sun.-Thurs. 9am-7pm, Fri. 9am-2pm; and **Nova,** 15 Nordau St. (tel. 252 764), open Sun.-Thurs. 10am-1pm and 4-6:30pm, Fri. 10am-1:30pm.

Laundromat: Kalujny, 25 Pevsner St., Hadar (2 streets uphill from Nordau); 30 Ge'ula St. (tel. 678 238; open Sun.-Thurs. 7am-7pm, Fri. 7am-2pm; wash and dry NIS13 each); and 2 Liberia St. (tel. 252 764; open Sun.-Mon. and Wed.-Thurs. 8am-4pm, Tues. and Fri. 8am-1pm; wash, dry, fold NIS6 per kg). Take bus #24 or 37.

Swimming Pools: Maccabee Pool, Bikurim St. (tel. 388 341), in central Carmel. Outdoor in summer, heated and covered in winter. Open Sun., Tues., and Thurs. 6am-2pm and 4-10pm, Mon. and Wed. 6am-2pm and 6:30-10pm, Fri. 6am-2pm and 4-6pm. Admission NIS25. **Technion Pool** (tel. 235 944) also has a sauna. Open Sun.-Thurs. 6am-8pm, Fri. 6am-6pm. Admission NIS28, NIS20 with ISIC.

Crisis Lines: Rape Crisis Center (tel. 660 111) and **Emotional First Aid** (tel. 672 222) are both open 24 hrs. English spoken on both.

Pharmacies: Shomron, 44 Yafo St. (tel. 524 171), downtown; open Sun.-Thurs. 7am-4pm, Fri. 7am-2pm. **Ha-Ḥalutz,** 12 Ha-Ḥalutz St. (tel. 662 962) in Hadar; open Sun.-Thurs. 8am-1pm and 4-7pm, Fri. 8am-1pm. **Merkaz,** 130 Ha-Nassi Blvd. (tel. 381 979) in Carmel Center; open Sun.-Thurs. 8am-7pm, Fri. 8am-2pm.

Emergency: First Aid: 6 Yitzḥak Sadeh St. (tel. 101). **Fire:** Tel. 102.

Police: 28 Yafo Rd. (tel. 100).

■■■ ACCOMMODATIONS

Slim pickings. Haifa is short on budget hotels, and its youth hostels and campsites, while close to the sea, are far from the city center. The Hadar district is your best bet if you want to stay in town, but it's not terribly cheap. Cheaper accommodation may be found near the port, but it is not the safest part of town.

Carmel Youth Hostel (HI) (tel. 531 944; fax 532 516), 4km south of the city at Ḥof Ha-Carmel (Carmel beach). Beautiful view of the Mediterranean, but inconvenient location. Bus #43 stops in front (every hr. 7:15am-7:15pm, last bus on Fri. at 3:15pm). Bus #30-*alef* goes past the hostel; ask the driver to stop. Bus #45 and 47 run more frequently but drop you off on the main road; ask to be dropped off at the Sports and Recreation Center. Cross Ha-Hagana St. toward the gas station on Flieman St. and turn left just past it. Follow the road as it curves uphill and to the right. Checkout by 9am. No lockout. No curfew. Bungalows (4 beds) NIS20. Dorm beds (6 per room) NIS43, nonmembers NIS46. Private room NIS98. Breakfast included, lunch and dinner NIS23 each. Lockers NIS4 per day.

FOOD

Saint Charles Hospice, 105 Jaffa Rd. (tel. 553 705), 2 blocks off Ben-Gurion St.; look for the green gate. Primarily a convent, but welcomes tourists. Newly renovated, large rooms with high ceilings and no bunk beds. Terrace overlooking pretty garden; kitchen facilities. Dorm beds (3-4 per room) US$17. Singles US$21. Doubles US$38. Breakfast included.

Bethel Hostel, 40 Ha-Geffen St. (tel. 521 110), west of Ben-Gurion St. Take bus #22 from central bus station to Ben-Gurion St. close to Ha-Geffen, or walk 15-20min. up James de Rothschild Blvd., following the curve to the left onto Ha-Baron Hirsch, which becomes Ha-Geffen. The pamphlets lining the walls (*My Heart, Christ's Home; Becoming a Christian;* and *Knowing God Personally*) send a sledgehammer-sized hint, but the friendly staff is not terribly intrusive. All rooms have fans, men's rooms have 3-level bunks. Free barbecues on Mon., soup and dessert on Fri. No smoking. Check-in Sat.-Thurs. 5-10pm, Fri. 4-9pm. Lockout 9am-5pm, but charming lounge and garden open all day. New arrivals can leave bags in locked storage and return to register. Strict 11pm curfew, 7am wake-up. Single-sex only dorm beds (8-12 per room) US$10. Doubles (for married couples only) US$26. Inexpensive à la carte breakfast available in snack bar.

Talpiyot, 61 Herzl St. (tel. 673 753), where Arlozorov branches off Herzl. A no-frills hotel on this busy street. Nice breeze, helpful owner, and TV lounge with balcony. Fans in all rooms; some have private bath for the same price. Reception open 24 hrs. Check-out 11am. No lockout. No curfew. Singles US$26. Doubles US$36. Triples US$54. Breakfast included.

Nesher Hotel, 53 Herzl St. (tel. 620 644), near Ḥayim St. intersection, above Mercantile Discount Bank. Simple hotel in the heart of Hadar, with a small roof balcony, kitchen, and TV lounge. 24-hr. reception. Check-out noon. No lockout. No curfew. Singles US$27. Doubles US$40. Triples US$52. Quads US$55. Most rooms have A/C, others have fans. Some rooms have private showers (no toilets; same price). Breakfast included.

Aliya Hotel, Ha-Ḥalutz St. (tel. 623 918), up the side steps. Plain, but located in the heart of Hadar, near open-air market. 24-hr. reception. Check-out noon. No lockout. No curfew. Singles NIS70. Doubles NIS90. Triples NIS100.

Haifa Hostel (formerly Elvis House), 6-8 Sara St., near the port. In light of serious readers' complaints, *Let's Go* does not recommend staying here.

For **camping,** try Kibbutz Neveh Yam (tel. 844 827), 18km south of Haifa; take bus #122 (5:50am-9:35pm, last bus Fri. 4:25pm; 20min.; NIS7) from Haifa's central bus station. It's just off the beach, near the ruins of the Crusader fortress Atlit (now a military installation closed to tourists). Excellent amenities, including a small store and restaurant. Cooking facilities available. (2-person tent NIS58. 3-person tent NIS74. 4-person bungalow with toilet, shower, and fridge NIS150. Open in summer only.)

■■■ FOOD

In downtown, follow **Yafo St.** from the central bus station toward the port and you'll walk past a dozen different *shawerma* and falafel shops. **Derekh Allenby,** between Ha-Tzionut St. and Ben-Gurion Blvd., is crammed with incredibly cheap restaurants specializing in Arabic food. In Hadar, the quantity of Middle Eastern fast food along **Ha-Ḥalutz St.** has prompted locals to call it "Falafel St." **Nevi'im St.,** a few blocks away, is progressing along the same trend, but the **Nordau Midraḥov** (pedestrian section) gives a welcome break from such fare with slightly more expensive open-air cafés, and even pricier restaurants serving anything from Arabic to Tex-Mex dishes. In Carmel Center you'll find plenty of cafés along **Ha-Nassi Blvd.** and **Yefeh Nof St.** The area around the Gan Ha'Eim **Carmelit Stop** is especially packed, with a **McDonald's** and a **Burger King.**

DOWNTOWN

Iraqi Shishkabab, 59 Ben-Gurion St. (tel. 527 576), corner of Ha-Geffen St. A local favorite for *shishlik, kabab, sambusa,* and other Iraqi specialties. Two skewers and salad in pita NIS10-12, meat pastries NIS3. Open Sun.-Thurs. 12:30-11:30pm.

Avraham, King of Falafel, 34 Allenby St. at Ha-Tzionut St. Sign in Hebrew only, but look for the yellow crowns and Pepsi cans next to the name. The locals' favorite falafel stand (NIS5). Compliment the owners on the new decor (red tiles and a new salad bar)—maybe they'll give you a discount. Open daily 10am-11pm.

Shmulik and Danny, 7 Ha-Bankim St. (tel. 514 411), on the second floor. Compact dining hall serves some of the country's best traditional *Ashkenazi* Jewish food, including gefilte fish, chopped liver, and *tchulent*. Appetizers NIS5, entrees NIS14-27, 0.5L beer NIS9. Open Sun.-Thurs. noon-6pm, Fri. noon-3pm. Kosher.

Ma'ayan Ha-Bira, 4 Nathanson St. (tel. 660 028). The "Beer Fountain" (as the name reads in Hebrew) serves its namesake on tap (NIS9 for 0.5L), but this unpretentious diner's claim to fame is its excellent home-smoked meats. Spareribs (NIS18), hot pastrami (NIS15.50). Open Sun.-Fri. 8:30am-6pm.

Mixgrill, 7 Ben-Gurion St. (tel. 528 867), corner of Yafo Rd. Brand new restaurant with friendly service and a view of the Baha'i Temple from outside terrace. *Shishlik, kabab,* or chicken skewer with salad and french fries only NIS6! Salads NIS3. Fish with chips and salad only NIS15. More expensive dishes include ribs, steak *antikot,* and even brains. Open Sat.-Thurs. 10am-midnight, Fri. 10am-4pm.

Jacko, 12 Ha-Dekalim St. (tel. 664 109), near Kikkar Paris Carmelit station. Owner is a former fisherman who still gets fresh seafood daily. Excellent calamari, sea bass, and sesame seed shrimp. Entrees NIS28-36. Open daily 10:30am-11:30pm.

Sinn-Sinn Chinese Restaurant, 28 Yafo Rd. (tel. 642 223). Run by a Vietnamese family, like most Chinese restaurants in Israel. Soup, egg roll, salad, entree, and rice NIS18 total. Open Mon.-Thurs. noon-10pm, Fri. and Sun. noon-4:30pm.

HADAR

Tzimzhonit Ḥayim, 30 Herzl St. (tel. 674 667). A 60-year-old Jewish vegetarian restaurant frequented by an elderly clientele. *Kreplach* NIS5, blintzes NIS7.50, salad from NIS6, fish from NIS7.50. Open Sun.-Thurs. 9am-8pm, Fri. 9am-2pm.

Hamber, 61 Herzl St. (tel. 666 739), corner of Arlozorov St. Popular with French tourists. Kosher meat with salads NIS13. Open Sun.-Thurs. 8am-10pm, Fri. 8am-2:30pm.

Prego Café and Restaurant, 20 Nordau St. (tel. 623 524), look for the blue sign. Framed Italian movie posters in a cool, sleek interior and freshly squeezed lemonade make this a haven from the falafel joints outside. Pizza from NIS20, pasta from NIS18, excellent homemade desserts. Great lunch specials including appetizers and desserts from NIS33. Open Sun.-Thurs. noon-midnight, Fri. noon-1am.

At Benny's, 23 Ha-Ḥalutz St. (tel. 624 751), near the intersection with Herzl St. Sign in Hebrew only. Typical Middle Eastern restaurant. Salads (NIS6) and *shishlik* or steak combination with salad and drink (NIS21). Open 9am-10pm, Fri. 9am-2pm.

California, 1 Ḥayim St. (tel. 672 628), off Nordau St., follow the white footprints on the sidewalk. Colorful geometric designs on cushions and a good view of Herzl St.; brain teasers entertain you as you wait for your food. Vegetarian (NIS9.90) and non-vegetarian (NIS13.90) lunch specials served until 5pm. Omelettes (NIS15) and individual pizzas (NIS13) made fresh. Open Sun.-Fri. 9am-1am, Sat. 5pm-1am.

Kosher Veta'im, 40 Herzl St. near Ḥayim St. (tel. 645 976). Self-service. Look for a strangely-dressed figure beckoning from above. *Schnitzel* or beef with side order NIS12. Soups, salads, desserts NIS3. Large portions. Comfortable, clean dining area. Open Sun.-Thurs. 10am-6pm, Fri. 10am-2:30pm. Kosher.

CARMEL CENTER

Casa Ristorante Italiano, 119 Ha-Nassi Blvd. (tel. 381 336), next to McDonald's. A homey place run by the same family for 30 years. A favorite among Knesset members and celebrities—just ask to see the guest books. Look for brown chairs outside. Spaghetti and other pasta from NIS20, homemade minestrone NIS8.90, pizza NIS13.90. Open Sun.-Thurs. and Sat. noon-10pm.

Tarnegal, 99 Yefeh Nof Rd. (tel. 375 508), corner of Sha'ar Ha-Levanon St.; look for the red rooster on top. Very clean, with a great view of the entire Port area and city below; laid back café atmosphere. Serves gourmet-sounding entrees for only NIS14-18. Open Sun.-Thurs. noon-midnight, Fri.-Sat. noon-1am.

Middle East Food Restaurant, 115 Ha-Nassi Blvd. (tel. 387 647), next to the Dan Panorama Hotel. Tables and music outside are very popular with tourists. A Hadar-esque menu and prices at a Center address: *shishlik and shawerma* NIS8, steak NIS10. Open Sun.-Thurs. 10am-1am, Fri. 10am-7pm, Sat. 6pm-1am.

There is an inexpensive **fruit and vegetable market** just west of the Kikkar Paris station between Naḥum and Nathan St. Walking east on Nathanson, the shop at #777 sells cow spleen at NIS11; you'll go nuts over the ox testicles at a mere NIS6. Another **shuk** can be found one block down from Ha-Ḥalutz in Hadar on Sirkin and Luntz Street. You can also walk down the stairs across from the Bank Leumi at 64-66 Ha-Ḥalutz St. All the locals come here for clothes, groceries, and even wine bottles; the best deals are toward the center of the market.

■ ■ ■ S H O P P I N G ,   W A L K S ,   P A R K S

The best way to see all of Haifa is to take a bus to the top and then work your way down. The various tourist offices all provide maps of the heart of Haifa criss-crossed with four colored **walking tours.** On Saturdays, the Haifa Municipal Tourist Office offers free, guided versions of the same tour (2½hr., meet at 10am at corner of Yefeh Nof and Sha'ar Ha-Levanon St., dress modestly for stops at Baha'i holy places).

If you get to the top and don't feel like walking down, you'll certainly find plenty to do in the **Carmel Center.** Walk down its pine-shaded, quiet side streets (try Ha-Yam Rd. and the area just south of it, behind the Haifa Auditorium) for a glimpse of Haifa's appeal as a residential town. Along with the shopping and eating establishments along Ha-Nassi St., visit the new **Louis Promenade,** on Yefeh Nof St. This breezy refuge commands stunning views of Haifa below and, on clear days, Upper Galilee and even as far as snowy Mt. Ḥermon and Lebanon.

Nature lovers have, in addition to the Mediterranean, several aphrodisiacs to set their hormones racing. The **Municipal Zoo** in Gan Ha'Eim (tel. 377 019 or 372 886), across from the Carmelit steps, would surprise even Darwin with its variety of Levant-indigenous beasts. (Open Sun.-Thurs. 8am-6pm, Fri. 8am-1pm, Sat. 9am-4pm; Sept.-June Sun.-Thurs. 8am-4pm, Fri. 8am-1pm, Sat. 9am-4pm. Admission NIS19, students NIS14. The zoo also contains three museums; see Museums, p. 298.) The **Mount Carmel National Park,** the biggest park in Israel, is 15 minutes by bus from the Gan Ha'Eim (#24, 37, or 192); enjoy its scenic vistas, footpaths, and clean picnic areas. For a brush with nature in the middle of the city, an **SPNI nature trail** begins in Gan Ha'Eim to the right of the shell-shaped stage. Follow the blue signs; the trail (2km, 1hr.) will lead you around the zoo and through tangled greenery into a *wadi* in the lower Carmel. (Bus #3 or 5 will get you back uptown.)

Those who prefer concrete to tree bark can visit Haifa's two institutes of higher learning. To reach **Haifa University,** boasting a larger percentage of Arab students than any of Israel's other universities, take bus #24 or 37 from the central bus station, Herzl St., or the Carmel Center and ask to be let off at the next to last stop. The university's landmark is the elegant 30-story **Eshkol Tower,** crowning the vast flat main building which is the focus of student activities. Originally designed by renowned Brazilian architect Oscar Niemeier, the original bold scheme (see model in the main lobby) was never completed. The tower's **observatory** offers spectacular panoramic views. (Info. tel. 240 007. Open Sun.-Thurs. 8am-4pm. Free student-guided tours of the campus Sun.-Thurs. 10am-noon, starting from the main building.) After-hours, go all the way to the edge of the huge slab at the foot of the tower (above the bus stops) for slightly-less commanding views of the city below. You can also visit the Reuben and Edith Hecht Museum (see Museums, p. 298).

The **Technion,** on the slope directly below the university, is Israel's internationally acclaimed institute of technology, founded in 1913 in Hadar. The last department (architecture) moved out of the old Technion building off Balfour St. in the mid-1980s to the forested, ever-expanding new campus near Neve Sha'anan. At the **Coler Visitors Center** (tel. 320 664), displays and a video describe the history and achievements of the institution. (Open Sun.-Thurs. 8am-3:30pm. Free.) Take bus #17 from downtown, #31 from Carmel Center, or #19 from the central bus station or Herzl St. to Kiryat Ha-Technion. (Call 292 578 for information on guided tours of campus. Tours are held Sun.-Thurs. 8:30am-2:30pm. Free.)

But Haifa is not a purely modern city; in fact, it contains several important religious sites whose significance long predates the establishment of the State of Israel. Most famous, of course, is the golden-domed **Baha'i Temple**, halfway up Mt. Carmel. Until recently, a magnificent garden of cypress, palm, and pine trees surrounded the temple and was one of the city's trademarks. A new landscape scheduled for completion in a couple of years has left a great bald patch on the slope, but a large section remains intact and open to visitors. The architecture of the shrine is a cross between Baroque Christian (the dome) and Moorish (the archways). The shrine (tel. 358 358), located on Ha-Tzionut Ave., commemorates the Persian Siyyid Ali Muhammad, the first prophet of the rapidly growing Baha'i religion. (See Introduction to the Region: Religion, p. 50.) The prophet's bones, brought to Haifa in 1909, now lie next to the temple. Modest dress required for the shrine, but not necessarily for the garden. Take bus #22 from the central bus station or bus #23, 25, 26, or 32 from Ha-Nevi'im and Herzl St. Don't try to climb the stairs from Ben-Gurion St.; they're closed until the landscaping is completed. (Open 9am-noon, gardens open daily 8am-5pm. Free.) Other Baha'i buildings are scattered around the grounds, but are *not* open to the public; the marbelous **Universal House of Justice**, completed in the late 1980s, is living proof that Greek temple architecture is anything but obsolete (visible from the Golomb-Arlozorov St. curve). Near the Baha'i shrine is a **sculpture garden** (opposite 135 Ha-Tzionut St.), with striking bronzes by Ursula Malbin. (Open 24 hrs. Free.)

From the Baha'i shrine, bus #25 and 26 climb Mt. Carmel to the holy places of the **Carmelite Order**, whose **monastery** stands on a promontory over Haifa Bay. A Latin monk named Berthold founded the order in 1150. Persecution, which most recently took the form of Napoleon's siege and loss of Acre in 1799, forced the Discalced or "barefoot" Carmelite Order to move to their current location. The monks currently live in a relatively new church and monastery complex called **Stella Maris** (Star of the Sea, tel. 337 758), built in 1836 on the ruins of an ancient Byzantine chapel and a medieval Greek church. The church's dome is crowned by paintings of Elijah flying in his chariot of fire, King David plucking his harp, and scenes of the Holy Family. An exquisite statuette of the Virgin Mary (with whom the order is associated) cradling the baby Jesus stands inside. No bare knees or shoulders permitted. (Open daily 6am-1:30pm and 3-6pm.) Next to the Carmelite monastery is a small museum containing ruins of former Mt. Carmel cloisters dating from Byzantine and Crusader times. (Open daily 8am-1:30pm and 3-6pm. Free.) Take bus #25, 26, or 31 and get off at Seminar Gordon stop. Given the Carmelites' affinity for Elijah (a.k.a. St. Elias), the Feast of St. Elias is a terrific celebration. Christian Arabs set up booths with food and games, and the party begins, culminating with special masses on the morning of the Feast (July 20).

The stairs leading to the entrance of **Elijah's Cave**, 230 Allenby St. (tel. 527 430), are just across the street from the naval museum. Like in so much of the Holy Land, all three of the world's major faiths revere the sacred ground. In biblical history, the caves at the base of the mountain sheltered Elijah from the rage of King Ahab and Queen Jezebel after the prophet killed 450 priests of Ba'al at Mukhraqa in the 9th century BCE (1 Kings 17-19). Muslims also revere Elijah as Al Khadar, "the green prophet" of the same-colored mountains. Christians believe the caves safeguarded the Holy Family upon their return from Egypt. Believers of each faith now pray quietly in the dim light. Bus #45 runs to Edmund Fleg St. near the Carmelite Monastery above the caves. As you approach from the monastery, a difficult path leads down the mountainside beginning near the elbow in the road, across the street from the monastery entrance. Modest dress required. (Cave open Sun.-Thurs. 8am-5:45pm, Fri. 8am-12:45pm; winter Sun.-Thurs. 8am-4:45pm, Fri. 8am-12:45pm. Free.)

Between Elijah's Cave and the Stella Maris monastery you'll find the upper station of the **cable car** (*rakhbal;* tel. 335 970 or 330 009). Colloquially known as "the Carmel's Eggs" for their spherical shape, the cable cars run down the northwestern slope of the Carmel all the way to the **Beit Galim Promenade** on the shore. You can board the cars from either station. To reach the bottom station, walk west on Ha-Hagana Blvd. from the central bus station for five minutes. There is a small walkway underneath the elevated train tracks on the right. From the tracks, walk one block down Raḥaf St. and turn left onto Ha'Aliya Ha-Shniya St. The cable car station is several blocks down. Or take bus #42; the cable car station is its last stop. While the view from the car is striking, the trip is short, and the prerecorded explanation (your choice of English or Hebrew) is rushed and uninformative. (Open Sat.-Thurs. 10am-6pm, Fri. 10am-2pm. NIS7, round-trip NIS10.)

■■■ MUSEUMS

In the heart of Carmel Center, the **Mané Katz Art Museum** at 89 Yefeh Nof St. (tel. 383 482), just behind Panorama Center, displays sculptures and canvases by Mané Katz, a member of the Paris group of Jewish Expressionists that included Modigliani, Chagall, and Cremegne. (Open Sun.-Mon., Wed.-Thurs. 10am-4pm, Tues. 2-6pm, Fri. 10am-1pm, Sat. 10am-2pm.) In the main building of Haifa University, the **Reuben and Edith Hecht Museum** (tel. 257 773 or 240 577) houses an exhibit called *The People of Israel in the Land of Israel,* displaying archaeological finds from the university excavations and some Impressionist paintings. 1995 exhibitions will include *Phoenicians on Israel's North Coast in Biblical Times.* Tours available if you call ahead. (Open Sun.-Thurs. 10am-4pm, Fri. 10am-1pm, Sat. 10am-2pm. Free.)

The Municipal Zoo Gan Ha'Eim contains the **Biological Museum,** the **Natural History Museum,** and the **M. Stekelis Museum of Prehistory,** with dioramas of the prehistoric life of the area. (All open Sun.-Thurs. 8am-3pm, Fri. 8am-1pm, Sat. 10am-2pm. Admission to zoo includes Biological Museum. Other museums NIS3 ea.)

Beneath the slopes of Mt. Carmel in the Hadar district stands the **Haifa Museum,** 26 Shabtai Levi St. (tel. 523 216), reachable by bus #10, 12, 22, and 28, containing Israeli modern art, ancient art, and Jewish music and ethnology. The ancient art exhibit on the top floor includes mosaic floors from Shkimona, where ancient Haifa was probably located, and many sculptures and figurines from the Canaanite era (18th century BCE) through Greek and Roman times. The ethnology exhibit contains folk costumes, utensils, and musical instruments from Jewish communities around the world. (Open Sun.-Mon., Wed., Fri. 10am-1pm; Tues. and Thurs. 10am-1pm and 5-8pm; Sat. 10am-3pm and 5-8pm. Admission NIS8, students NIS6. For the next 3 days, the ticket is also good for admission to the Prehistory and National Maritime Museums.)

A few blocks east, there's a **National Museum of Science, Planning, and Technology.** Take bus #12, 21, 28, or 37. Walk uphill on Balfour St. (from Herzl St.) to the red-and-white sign on the left pointing to the museum, located in the old Technion building. (Open Mon. and Wed.-Thurs. 9am-5pm, Tues. 9am-7pm, Fri. 9am-1pm, Sat. 10am-2pm; also open in July Sun. 9am-5pm. Admission NIS12, students NIS8.)

Hadar also houses the **Haifa Museum of Ancient and Modern Art, Music, and Ethnology,** at Shantai Ha-Levi St. (tel. 523 255), near Beit Ha-Mehandes. Learn all you ever wanted to know about ancient chairs and hairstyles. (Open Sun.-Mon. and Fri. 10am-1pm, Tues.-Thurs. and Sat. 10am-3pm and 5-8pm. Admission NIS5.)

On Ha'Atzma'ut St. near Plumer Sq., downtown, stands the **Dagon Grain Silo and Archaeological Museum** (tel. 664 221). This curious edifice, the asymmetrical towers of which dominate Haifa's waterfront, looks something like a modern Crusader fortress. The silo is Israel's only grain-receiving depot, storing 90% of the country's grain. Take bus #10, 12, or 22. The exhibit and models of the silo's facilities can be seen only when free tours are given (Sun.-Fri. at 10:30am), or avoid the crowds and make an appointment.

Farther down Ha'Atzma'ut St. (note the once elegant, early Modernist buildings on the port side) near Faisal Square is the **Railway Museum** (tel. 564 293). Train memorabilia and restored locomotives are in the old Haifa railroad station. Hey, these aren't just any locomotives, but Israeli locomotives. (Open Sun., Tues., Thurs. 9am-noon. Admission NIS6, students NIS4.) East of the railway museum, the Shemen Edible Oil Factory is home to the **Israeli Oil Industry Museum,** 2 Tuvin St. (tel. 670 491; open Sun.-Thurs. 8:30am-2:30pm; admission NIS5). Bus #17, 42, and 193 go to the Railway Museum; bus #2 goes to the Oil Museum.

Opposite the lower cable car station is the **Clandestine Immigration and Naval Museum** (no, it's not a bad joke), 204 Allenby Rd. (tel. 536 249). It is devoted to the *Ha'apala,* the desperate smuggling of immigrants into Israel during the British Mandate. Take bus #43 or 44: look for the *Af-Al-Pi-Khen* (In Spite Of), an old immigrant ship now perched atop the museum. (Museum open Sun.-Thurs. 9am-4pm, Fri. 9am-1pm. Admission NIS5, students or children under 18 NIS2.)

Up the street at 198 Allenby, the **National Maritime Museum** (tel. 536 622) contains a bronze bowpiece from a 4th-century CE battleship discovered near Atlit in 1980. (Open Sun.-Thurs. 10am-4pm, Sat. 10am-1pm. Admission NIS6, students NIS4.50, included in ticket to Haifa Museum.)

■■■ ENTERTAINMENT

Beaches sprawl along the north coast past the Dagon Silo. **Ha-Hof Ha-Shaket,** the most convenient, costs NIS4.30; take bus #41 from the Hadar district or the central bus station, or walk (10min. from the central bus station). **Hof Bat Galim,** also near the central bus station, is small and frequently crowded. On Saturdays, head south to beaches where you can see sand between bathers. Take bus #44 or 45 to **Hof Ha-Carmel,** a free beach, or **Hof Dado** farther south. Between here and Atlit, it's basically one long, free, beautiful beach; privacy increases with distance from the city. **Shehafit Windsurfing Center** (tel. 514 809), in a small white building next to the lower cable car station, rents sailboards (NIS25 per hr.) and snorkeling (NIS6 per day) or scuba gear (NIS95 per day).

When asked about the city's sparse entertainment, Haifa's first mayor pointed to the city's factories and said, "There is our nightlife." Don't listen to him. The GTIO and MTIO give out *Events in Haifa and the Northern Region.* Or call the **What's Hot in Haifa Hotline** (tel. 374 253).

Nightlife is at its rip-roarin' liveliest near the top tier of the city. The **Bat Galim Promenade,** along the shore behind the central bus station, has ice cream and fro'yo' places and fish restaurants. The **Panas Boded Pub** blasts music videos from near the center of the Promenade and encourages sloshedness with a large variety of beers (NIS8-10) served until morning light. The outdoor tables overlooking the waves absolutely thunder with tourists and their idle talk (open nightly at 5pm).

The center of nightlife in Hadar is the Nordau *midrahov,* where free concerts and dances rock the amphitheater (check with GTIO for a schedule). Here you'll find **Ha'Olam Hazeh** (by Hayim St.), **Salamdra,** and **MASH** (corner of Balfour St.) pubs, all of which cater to both locals and tourists from about 7pm until 1 or 2am. Four blocks "up" from Nordau you'll find the **Rodeo Pub** at 23 Balfour St., across from Masada St. (open nightly 9pm-2am).

Real ragers go to Carmel Center. The pub with the best view (and music) is **Mitzpor,** at 115 Yefeh Nof. It's built on the Carmel slope itself; go down the ramp marked "Allenby Garden." The picnic tables outside are full from 8pm until the wee hours every night. Cheap beer and excellent fruit twister-shakes. **Little Haifa,** 4 Sha'ar Ha-Levanon St. between Ha-Nassi and Yefeh Nof Streets (look up for the Goldstar Beer signs), is the oldest pub in the area (28 years and going strong). What it lacks in a view it more than makes up for with loud music and that rocking atmosphere you've been looking for (open nightly 8:30pm until the last customer passes out or leaves). Other pubs in the area include the **Bear Pub** at 135 Ha-Nassi Blvd. and the neighboring **Paradise Pub** and **B-52** (both in Gan Ha'Eim, across from the stage; open weekends starting at 8:30pm). Less accessible, but by far more hip, are the new bars that have sprung up around **Kikkar Kiryat Sefer** on Moriah St., the main road on top of the ridge south of Carmel Center. Check out the thematic menus in **Fixaleh** (Goldstar NIS8). Farther down the road in Aḥuza, near the Ḥorev Center shopping mall, is the **Ha'Aḥuza** bar and its counterpart, **Ha-Shmura** (make a right at the light; it's at the entrance to the grove). Closer to Carmel Center is **Mexicana,** on the corner of Moriya and Tzafririm St., serving drinks and nachos to overflowing crowds. Bus #37, 28, or 23 run along Moriah and Ḥorev St. only until 11:30pm, so you'll need other arrangements to get back.

Like just about everything else in this town, **dance clubs** have the unfortunate tendency of being inaccessible to car-less visitors. **Fever,** in Gan Ha'Eim, is the most convenient (open after 11pm). **Valentine's,** 120 Yefeh Nof, is also centrally located and has a dance floor surrounded by mirrors and an aquarium. Friday and Saturday are 18-and-over nights; go on a weeknight to avoid the Pampers parade (opens at 11:30pm). **Indigo,** 2 Liberia St. (tel. 341 521), is high up in the posh Dania neighborhood. Ask locals to direct you to **Ḥai Bar, Klafte,** and **Ha-Muza** in the dilapidated Wadi Salib neighborhood downtown.The first two cater mostly to student crowds.

Events at the **Technion** and at **Haifa University** offer opportunities to meet young Israelis, particularly during the school year. The Technion has nightly dances in the student building in July and August (8pm-1am). For more information, call 320 664; you may have to bring student ID and passport. **Ha-Bustan,** near the entrance to Haifa University campus, is a popular student hangout.

NEAR HAIFA

EIN HOD עין הוד

Located 14km south of Haifa, this small settlement has a fascinating history. Originally, Ein Hod (Hebrew for "Spring of Grandeur") was Ein Houd (Arabic for "Spring of Garden Rows"), an Arab village of 670 people located on a hill on the western slopes of Mt. Carmel. Earlier, the town also served as a resort for Crusaders based at the nearby Atlit fortress. In 1948 the Arab inhabitants were forcibly ejected by Israeli forces; in 1953 the deserted village was transformed into an artist colony, established by Marcel Janco, one of the founders of the Dadaist art movement.

Within this village of studios, artists create everything from needle crafts to abstract paintings. Bronze sculptures grace backyards, mobiles swing between trees, and stone figures recline against fences. Though it sounds enchanting, you might want to think twice about actually coming to visit: the artists don't work in public, and the view of the Mediterranean has been obscured by tree branches. The old Arab houses, once beautiful, have now been converted to plain modern homes with a grocery store around the corner.

Workshops in glass blowing, pottery, and such are offered on Saturdays; however, no buses run at that time, and only residents can park their cars in the village (park up the hill). Artists' work is displayed for sale at **Artists' Gallery** (open Sat.-Thurs. 9:30am-5pm, Fri. 9:30am-4pm; admission NIS1), **Design Gallery,** and **Art and Wear Gallery** (both open Sat.-Thurs.10am-5pm, Fri. 10am-2:30pm) in the center of the village. The **Janco-Dada Museum** (tel. 842 350) next to the galleries is probably the village's most important attraction, featuring shows by contemporary Israeli Dadaist artists and a permanent display of the late artist's work, as well as pamphlets and invitations from the Dadaist movement's origins in Europe. (Open Sat.-Thurs. 9:30am-5pm, Fri. 9:30am-4pm. Admission NIS5, students NIS3.)

Friday evening concerts ranging from rock to classical music are held at the small village **amphitheater** (tel. (04) 843 377, or check local newspapers for listings). No transportation is available after the show.

To get to Ein Hod, take **bus** #202 or 921 from Haifa heading south along the old Haifa-Ḥadera road (20min., NIS6.50). From the Ein Hod junction where the bus lets you off, the town is a 2km walk uphill (15min. up, 10min. down). To get to the center of Ein Hod, turn right when you reach the colorful sign.

USFIYA & DALIYAT AL KARMEL עוספיה ודלית אל-כרמל

Usfiya and Daliyat Al Karmel are all that remain of 14 Druze villages that once prospered on the Carmel; an unsuccessful rebellion against the Egyptian *pasha* in 1830 led to their destruction. In the 1860s, when the Turks were anxious to have the Druze as a buffer against Bedouins and Christians seeking converts, they welcomed the Druze back to these two Carmel villages. Today, some 17,000 Druze make their homes here. Druze elders are recognizable by their thick moustaches and flowing white *kafiyyehs* (headdresses), and Druze women walk about under the hot sun wearing traditional dark robes and white shawls. The Druze are known for being extraordinarily congenial, even while hawking their wares. Once picturesque mountain villages, Usfiya and Daliyat Al Karmel today are afflicted with unattractive concrete houses.

Usfiya has a Christian population of about 1000 Roman Catholics, in addition to its 4000 Druze. At the lovely Catholic church on the main road, members of the congregation boast that their ancestors were Crusaders from Italy. Usfiya also houses the excellent **Stella Carmel Hospice,** P.O. Box 7045, Haifa 31070 (tel. (04) 391 692), run by the Anglican Church and open to all. The hospice is to the right of the main road from Haifa, at the entrance to the village. Look for the narrow paved road lined with trees. Take bus #192 or a *sherut* taxi (4 buses per day 1-4:35pm, last bus on Fri. 2:25pm, last return bus 3pm; in both cases ask the driver for Stella Carmel). A converted Arab villa, the hospice has a small, quiet library and a charming lounge filled with antique Persian rugs. (Check-in 10:30pm. Check-out 10:30am. Flexible 10:30pm curfew. Dorm rooms outside main house US$10. Singles in main house US$18-34. Doubles US$36-68. Breakfast included. Unmarried couples will get separate rooms. Call ahead for reservations.)

The tourist bazaar in **Daliyat Al Karmel** is busiest on Saturdays, but come on a weekday if you want lower prices and a better opportunity to converse with locals. You can try to bargain, though vendors generally are determined to extract large sums from tourists. A few words of Arabic or Hebrew can sometimes lower prices considerably. Be aware that most of the clothes and jewelry are imported from India, while the furniture comes from Gaza. Wheat stalk baskets, embroidery, and tapestry work are mainly local goods.

The Zionist and Christian mystic Sir Lawrence Oliphant was one of few outsiders close to the sect. In the late 19th century, he and his wife lived in Daliyat for five years, helping the Druze build their homes. Since 1980, the Israeli Defense Ministry has been restoring Oliphant's house on the outskirts of town. It is now a memorial to the scores of Druze soldiers killed in Israel's wars. Although street names are not used, anyone can direct you to **Beit Oliphant.** Sir Lawrence sheltered Arab and Jewish insurgents against the British in the cave between the sculpture garden in the rear and the main house. Oliphant's secretary, the Hebrew poet Naftali Hertz Imber, later wrote "Ha-Tikva" (The Hope), Israel's national anthem, at this site.

Four kilometers from Daliyat Al Karmel, away from Usfiya, is the site where Elijah massacred 450 priests of Ba'al (1 Kings 18:40). **Muhraqa,** the Arabic name, refers to the burnt sacrifice that Elijah offered God from an altar here. It was also here that Elijah's servant sighted the rain cloud that relieved the land's drought. The Carmelites saw the clouds as a symbol of the Virgin Mary, to whom they are devoted. In 1886 they built a small **monastery** here. A short flight of stairs leads to the roof, where a magnificent view of the surrounding area awaits; on a clear day you may even sight snow-capped Mt. Ḥermon. (Monastery open Mon.-Sat. 8am-1:30pm and 2:30-5pm, Sun. 8am-1:30pm. Admission to the rooftop viewing area NIS1.) There is no bus service to the monastery; you'll have to call a taxi (NIS8-10). If hiking from Daliyat (not advisable), bear left at the only fork along the way or you'll head toward Elyakim. The **Stella Carmel Hospice** in Usfiya organizes occasional walking tours to the site for pilgrims. The most eventful day at Muhraqa is the Feast of St. Elias (Elijah) on July 20, when Christian Arab families celebrate in the park surrounding the monastery.

The Druze villages can be visited as a daytrip from Haifa. Bus #192 (NIS7) leaves infrequently from the central bus station and the Hadar district, stopping in both villages on weekdays. Catch a *sherut* on Eliya St. near Ha'Atzma'ut (NIS6-7) to get to the villages and wait by an Egged bus stop to catch one back. The last bus leaves Daliyat and Usfiya at 3pm, but *sherut* run and stores remain open until about 8pm.

Riding along the mountain road to the Druze villages might get your hiking hormones running. And rightfully so; the **Carmel mountains,** with ridges and forests spreading dramatically into the Zevulun valley to the east and the Mediterranean to the west, are a natural wonderland. The SPNI carries information and trail maps, and ideal picnic spots are never more than a short hike from the main road.

BEIT SHE'ARIM בית שערים

Walking through the monumental curtained portal into the dark maze-like system of catacombs at Beit She'arim (19km south of Haifa), you will feel that you have been transported to the site of Romeo and Juliet's untimely demise. The reality is no less stirring: Beit She'arim was the gathering place of the Sanhedrin, recognized by the Roman Empire in the 2nd century CE as the Supreme Rabbinical Council and judicial authority over all of world Jewry. Two hundred years later, it had become a sacred (and secret) burial ground for Jews who were barred from Jerusalem. Since 1936, archaeologists have uncovered a labyrinth of some 20 caves whose walls are lined with dozens of intricately adorned sarcophagi, including that of Rabbi Yehuda Ha-Nassi, first patriarch of a tannaitic academy and compiler of the Mishnah. According to inscriptions found on the sarcophagi, many of the buried were brought from as far away as Sidon and Tyre, Babylon, and southern Arabia to rest peacefully beneath the soil of Carmel for nearly 2000 years.

From the bus stop, follow the orange signs for Beit She'arim down Israel St. Near the end of a 20-minute walk, you'll pass the ruins of an ancient synagogue and olive press. The steep road uphill on the left leads to a statue commemorating Alexander Zaid, an early Jewish settler, and the ruins of an ancient basilica. Continue down the windy path to reach the entrance to the **catacombs** and **museum.** Many buses from Haifa go near Beit She'arim, but bus #301 (every 20min., NIS5.50) is most convenient. Ask the driver to let you off at Beit She'arim archaeological site, not the *moshav.* (Catacombs and museum tel. 831 643. Open Sun.-Thurs. 8am-5pm, Fri. 8am-4pm. Admission NIS8.50, students NIS6.40. Maps NIS0.50.)

MEGIDDO (ARMAGEDDON) מגידו

The settlements at Tel Megiddo have been destroyed so many times that the town has truly earned its Latin cognate: "Armageddon." The New Testament forewarns that at the end of the world demons will go out to all the nations, assembling first at Armageddon (Revelations 16:16). Megiddo's used to being a meeting place—in ancient times, the fortress town bordered the crucial route between Egypt and Mesopotamia that became the Roman Via Maris.

The *tel* at Megiddo was once thought to date only to King Solomon (c. 950 BCE). Excavations in the 1960s, however, uncovered remains dating back to the Chalcolithic Age (c. 3500 BCE) with an amazing 20 layers of ruins. The ruins are mostly unreconstructed except for the grain silo and water tunnel. The site is nonetheless impressive simply for its sheer size (about 900 ft. by 650 ft.). The silo was built on the top of the hill during the reign of King Jeroboam II (787-747 BCE). Because it's difficult to keep all the different sections of the *tel* straight, it's worthwhile to pick up a guide to the site at the ticket window for NIS2.50. Major finds include the Temple of Astarte (1900 BCE), ancient stables for some 480 horses, an underground tunnel, the Gate of Solomon (1600 BCE), a 70 ft. by 75 ft. palace dating from the second half of the 12th century CE, and most recently, a large altar whose stairs were once climbed only by the highest priests. Excavations are still underway.

ZIKHRON YA'AKOV

A **museum** near the entrance explains the excavations' layers and shows a model of Solomon's chariot town. There is also a list of biblical references to Megiddo.

From the observation point at the site, you can look out over the **Valley of Jezreel** (*Emek Yizre'el*) which was mostly swamp until 1920, when Jewish immigrants drained the land and made it arable. The lone mountain in the distance is Mt. Tabor; also visible are the hills of Nazareth and the Gilboa range.

One of the site's most intriguing features is the tunnel built to conceal the city's water source from invaders and to make water accessible from inside the city walls. The tunnel terminates outside the ruins, so make sure it's your last stop at the site. When you exit, turn right and walk 500m back to the museum entrance and main road. (Site open Sun.-Thurs. 8am-5pm, Fri. 8am-4pm; closes 1hr. earlier in winter. Admission NIS10.50, students NIS8.) Bus #302 from Haifa (infrequent, 25min., NIS9) will drop you off by the site entrance. Bus #823 (25min., NIS8) leaves Nazareth for Megiddo (every hr. during the morning, every ½hr. noon-7:30pm) and en route to Tel Aviv returns to Nazareth (every 45-90min. 2:30-9pm).

ZIKHRON YA'AKOV זיכרון יעקב

The original settlement in this area, begun in 1882 by Romanian Jews, was saved from swamps by Baron Rothschild's generous donations. The vineyard-based town that arose was named "Ya'akov's Memorial" for the Baron's father.

Bus #872 from Tel Aviv (NIS13) or #202 from Haifa (NIS9.50) will take you to the small **central bus station.** To the left of the station is the **tourist office** (tel. 398 811 or 892), in the small white building; they have maps, brochures, and information about city events (open Sun.-Thurs. 8am-1pm, Fri. 9am-noon). To the right of the central bus station, graceful concrete arches span the road; 2 blocks past them the road becomes the newly-renovated cobblestone **Ha-Meyasdim St.,** with old-fashioned decorative lampposts on both sides.

Continue down Ha-Meyasdim St. until you get to #40 on the right-hand side. This is **Beit Aaronson** (tel. (06) 390 120), an interesting (but small) museum commemorating NILI, an early Zionist paramilitary intelligence unit originally based in Zikhron Ya'akov. (Open Sun.-Thurs. 8:30am-1pm, Fri. 9am-noon. Admission NIS6.50, students NIS5.50.) Across the street from Aaronson House is the **Tut Neyar Paper Mill,** 39 Ha-Meyasdim St., producing hand-made paper and lampshades from local plants. Stationery, greeting cards, and lampshades are on sale here (around NIS18); if you call in advance, arrangements can be made for small group workshops in which the plants you start with become moist paper in 1½ hours (NIS10-15).

Just outside city limits lies **Ramat Ha-Nadiv,** the Rothschild Family Tomb and Gardens. *Sherut* taxis will drop you off at the side road leading to the estate on their way to Binyamina for only NIS2. The easy 15- to 20-minute walk provides inspiring views of the valley below. Inside the estate you'll find the crypt, hewn into the rocks, in which Baron Edmond de Rothschild and his wife are buried. You'll also see the rose garden, palm garden, cascade garden, and fragrance garden, all separated by masterfully landscaped meadows. (Open Sun.-Thurs. 6:30am-4pm, Fri. 6:30am-2pm, Sat. 8am-4pm. Free.)

Of course, Zikhron Ya'akov is best known for **Carmel-Mizraḥi Winery** (tel. (06) 396 709 or 391 241), founded 100 years ago by the French baron. The winery now produces a big share of Israel's domestic wine, as well as a large stock for export. Sample the finished product at the end of the tour. From the central bus station turn right onto Ha-Meyasdim St. Continue downhill for a few blocks and turn right onto Ha-Nadiv St. The large winery is at the bottom of the hill. (Open Sun.-Thurs. 8:30am-3:30pm., Fri. 8:30am-1pm. Admission NIS10. Call ahead for tours in English.)

The **Baron's Winery** (tel. 380 434), owned by the Rothschild family, is located near the entrance to the Baron's Tomb in Ramat Ha-Nadiv. This smaller winery gives free tours. (Open Sun.-Thurs. 9am-3pm, Fri. 8am-2pm.)

C
A
E
S
A
R
E
A

CAESAREA קיסריה

At the end of the first century BCE, Herod the Great built this city (Kay-SAHR-ya in Hebrew) on the site of a small anchorage named Strato's Tower for his emperor in Rome. The extensive remains include a Roman theater, Byzantine mosaics, aqueducts, a Crusader city, a Hippodrome, and a 2000-year-old harbor with mysteriously sophisticated engineering rivaling that of any modern Israeli port. Caesarea deserves a visit despite its infrequent bus service; the ruins of the ancient city constitute one of Israel's finest archaeological sites. Unfortunately, a dozen tacky cafés and gift shops, a beach club, a diving center, and even a disco have already been built among them. Nevertheless, the archaeological digs are still progressing; and excavations beyond the Crusader walls have already discovered many new buildings and raised hopes for the eventual reconstruction of the entire area around the port.

Phoenician travelers of the 4th century BCE first established a small settlement and harbor called Strato's Tower on the main trading route between Phoenicia (present-day Lebanon) and Egypt. The settlement, along with the rest of the coastal strip, eventually fell into the hands of Augustus Caesar, who granted it to Herod the Great, governor of Judea. Because of its choice location and access to the harbor, Herod turned Strato's Tower into one of the great cities of the eastern Roman Empire. Construction began in 22 BCE, and only 12 years later Strato's Tower was a splendid Roman city boasting a theater, a hippodrome, a rhinodrome, aqueducts carrying fresh water from the north, and a harbor capable of accommodating 300 ships. Herod named the new city in honor of Augustus Caesar, and in 6 CE Caesarea (also known as Caesarea Maritima) became the capital of the Roman province of Judea. It remained the seat of Roman power in the area until the downfall of the empire. It was Pontius Pilate, the Roman prefect of Caesarea from 26 to 36 CE, who ordered the crucifixion of Jesus. The first evidence of Pilate's existence outside the accounts of the Gospels and the historian Josephus was found here in 1961.

In 66 CE, a riot between Jews and Romans in Caesarea sparked the six-year Jewish Rebellion (the Great Revolt), which ended in the destruction of the Second Temple in Jerusalem. When the Romans finally squelched the rebellion in 70 CE (except for the holdouts at Masada), they celebrated by sacrificing thousands of Jews in Caesarea's amphitheater. Sixty years later, a second Jewish uprising, the Bar Kokhba Revolt, was also brought to a bitter end. This time the Romans were more selective—10 Jewish sages, among them the famous Rabbi Akiva, were tortured to death in the arena. Ironically, Caesarea later became a center of Jewish and Christian learning. During the Crusades, Caesarea changed hands four times before its capture in 1251 by King Louis IX of France. Louis strengthened and expanded the city's fortifications, adding most of the massive ramparts and battlements and the impressive moat, all of which are still in excellent condition. Despite these efforts, Caesarea was captured in 1265 by the Mamluk Sultan Baybars, who destroyed it. The city remained uninhabited until 1878 when the Muslim Boshnaqs (Bosnians) resettled it. The 1948 War drove out the population, emptying Caesarea once again. Today it is a chic tourism complex with a hotel and golf course to complement the ruins.

Practical Information, Accommodations, and Food Getting to Caesarea is by no means simple—the only practical way is via **Ḥadera,** the nearest town. Be warned that while buses to Ḥadera are plentiful (#852 or 872 from Tel Aviv NIS9.50, #740 from Netanya NIS6.50, #922 or 945 from Haifa NIS9.50, and #945 from Jerusalem NIS16.80), the only bus to or from the ruins is #76 from Ḥadera (NIS5), which leaves only 6 times per day in each direction. Call ahead for smooth connections or steel yourself for a two-hour wait in Ḥadera's boring central bus station or in the desolate heat outside the Caesarea ruins. While it is possible to get a taxi from the station in Ḥadera for NIS25, you won't find one for the ride back from the ruins. Those who enjoy sweating can take an intercity Egged bus to the Caesarea exit along the old Ḥadera-Haifa road (ask before you board), an unrewarding 3km west of the ruins. Beware sunstroke.

The two hotels on the Caesarea beach are expensive; head south for cheaper accommodations. Just south of the Roman theater is **Kibbutz Sdot Yam,** which maintains a number of guest apartments (all have A/C, private baths, and refrigerators), ideal for families or for 3-4 person groups. (Singles US$44. Doubles US$58. Additional people US$27 ea. Summer US$52, US$56, and US$32. Breakfast included in all prices.) Call in advance (tel. (06) 364 444 or 453, open Sun.-Fri. 9am-5pm). To get to the office, enter the kibbutz main gate near the Roman theater (the last stop on bus #76), pass the tile factory and bus stop, and bear right at the fork in the road. Look for the small white building with the colorful "Kef Yam" sign on it.

On the other side of the kibbutz is the **Caesarea Sports Center,** which maintains two buildings with guest rooms. The Beit Gil Building has 30 rooms with A/C and private baths. (Dorm beds (4-5 per room) Sun.-Fri. NIS100, Sat. NIS120; July NIS125/140, Aug. NIS140/150.) The Hostel Building has no A/C and baths are shared by five rooms, but the prices are a bit lower. (Dorm beds (4-5 per room) Sun.-Fri. NIS75, Sat. NIS85; July NIS80/90, Aug. NIS90/100.) Full board is included in all dorm prices. To get to the center, go through the Kibbutz Sdot Yam, head toward the beach, turn left at the "T," and walk past the Hannah Seresh House; the center is just beyond the big brown building. Call in advance (tel. (06) 360 879 or 880 or (03) 561 858) to make reservations.

The southernmost (and cheapest) option is the **Nofshonit "Holiday Village"** (tel. (06) 362 927 or 928), just south of the Sports Center. To get to Nofshonit from the nearest #76 stop, you have to walk about 35 minutes through the kibbutz. Though many visitors to Caesarea simply unroll their sleeping bags on the beach, devotees of organized **camping** can pitch a tent here for NIS32. The tentless can rent three-person huts for NIS78, or doubles for US$73 (Sept.-June US$54). Separate bathroom facilities. Nofshonit is safer than the unsupervised beach.

Pack a lunch, as prices in Caesarea are as high as the Crusader walls, though restaurants like **Tzalvania** or **Charly's Café Restaurant** have great views of the water. The **Sdot Yam Cafeteria** in the kibbutz offers an NIS27 all-you-can-eat "rural" lunch.

Sights Caesarea's sights include a Roman city and an ancient port. Though the Roman city is not fully excavated, most of the site is well marked; relics include the main road and several statues. The granaries and residences are Arab remains, and the walls and churches date from the Crusader period. Don't be surprised to find pieces of a marble column used as street pavement—Crusader-era contractors frequently re-used Roman remains when erecting a city. The harbor and beaches of Caesarea are of major archaeological significance as well. The engineering of Herod's now-submerged port included a breakwater which was the first in the Eastern Mediterranean. Both the dry ground and underwater areas of Caesarea are currently being excavated by an international team of archaeologists and volunteers.

Although most of the ruins are within the Crusader walls, the most interesting Roman remnants all lie outside the site proper. Behind the café across from the entrance to the Crusader city are an excavated **Byzantine street** and Caesarea's most famous finds: colossal **Roman statues** from the 2nd century CE, one of red porphyry, the other of white marble. The two headless figures were discovered accidentally by kibbutzniks ploughing fields. A 1km walk north along either the water or the road that runs along the Crusader walls leads to Caesarea's beach and the excellently preserved **Roman aqueduct.** The intensely blue cool water is inviting, but swimming within the walls costs NIS15; beyond the site, the water is rocky and swimming (not recommended) is free.

Stroll 500m south of the Crusader city to the enormous restored **Roman Theater** (tel. (06) 361 358). Reopened in 1961, this 3500-seat structure has hosted Eric Clapton, the Bolshoi Ballet, and the New Israeli opera. Admission (NIS10, students NIS7.90) covers both the Crusader city and the Roman Theater, and the other sites are free. Tickets can be purchased at either site; save your ticket and show it at both (open daily 8am-6pm). Maps of the area are sold for NIS5.

About 1km along the main road running east from the theater stands an archway leading to the ruins of the **Roman Hippodrome,** now overgrown with banana and orange groves cultivated by nearby Kibbutz Sdot Yam. In its heyday, the 352m by 68m racetrack could hold 20,000 spectators. Some of the relics unearthed have been put on display at the **Sdot Yam Museum of Caesarea Antiquities** (tel. (06) 364 367). Open Sat.-Thurs. 10am-4pm, Fri. 10am-2pm; admission NIS5. The **Kef Yam Office** in the kibbutz offers glass-bottomed boat tours of the ancient harbor (NIS27 per person) and tours of the ruins aboard the *Boston,* "the fastest speed-boat in Israel" (NIS21). You *must* call ahead for reservations (tel. (06) 364 444).

Near Caesarea

Just outside Moshav Beit Ḥananya on the old coastal road between Caesarea and Ma'agan Mikha'el arch two well-preserved **Roman aqueducts,** believed to have carried water from the Shuni springs northeast of present-day Binyamina down to the ancient city of Caesarea. North of the *moshav,* excavations are in progress at **Tel Mevoraḥ,** where several important Roman artifacts have been unearthed. Two of the marble sarcophagi discovered in the ruins of a Roman mausoleum are on display in the Rockefeller Museum in Jerusalem.

Kibbutz Ma'agan Mikha'el is one of the largest and loveliest kibbutzim in Israel. The huge industrial plant at the entrance belies the cultivated fields and acres of neat, rectangular fish ponds set between the coastal road and the sea. Part of the kibbutz is a wildlife preserve with an aviary, and a small museum displays archaeological finds from the fields. The preserve runs along the banks of Nahal Ha-Taninim (Crocodile River), purportedly the only unpolluted stream on the Israeli coast.

The gorgeous **beach** at **Dor** is protected by four small, rocky islands, each a bird sanctuary, explorable at low tide. To get here, take bus #921 from either Haifa or Tel Aviv, and get off at the Kibbutz Dor intersection; it's a 3km walk to the beach. The **Tel Dor** archaeological site is on the hill at the far northern end of the beach; you'll need shoes to traverse the rusty-wire-and-sand road. Though the site was probably founded in the 15th century BCE and was part of both King David's and King Solomon's empires, most of the important remains at Dor date from the Greek and Roman periods. The site includes temples dedicated to Zeus and to Astarte, as well as the ruins of a Byzantine church. The structure on the shore was a glass factory built by Baron Edmond de Rothschild (and managed by Meir Dizengoff, the first mayor of Tel Aviv) to make bottles for Zikhron Ya'akov's wineries. Today it is home to the **Center of Nautical and Regional Archaeology.**

Near the southern end of the beach Moshav Dor lies a **campsite** (tel. (06) 399 121) built on the ruins of the Arab village of **Tantura.** (NIS27 per person, 3-person bungalows NIS70, but prices skyrocket in July (NIS100) and August (NIS135). Tent sites open May-Oct. Call ahead.) The caves and ruins make beach camping at Tantura more interesting than crashing on your average strip of sand.

NORTH OF HAIFA

■■■ AKKO (ACRE) עכו عكا

Just across the mouth of Haifa Bay, Akko is centuries apart from its urban neighbor. Akko ('Akka in Arabic, historically written "Acre" in English) is not made up of two cities, as many people believe, but rather three. Inside a bastion of crumbling walls, the 200-year-old Arab town is a labyrinth of alleys and stairwells leading up to ancient Turkish fortifications, only to disappear into the chaos of the streets below. During the hot summer months, tourists and locals dine at charming restaurants along the coast, as children splash in the cool waters just beyond the sea walls. Outside Arab 'Akka, a rapidly encroaching new city is laying siege to the embattled ancient walls—a familiar struggle throughout Israel. Undisturbed by this contest stands the vast, subterranean Crusader City, still only partially excavated, directly underneath old Akko and predating it by 600 years. The enormous rooms of this basement city and the network of tunnels lacing through them were fortuitously preserved by the Turks, who found the constructions too solid to raze.

The tumultuous history of Akko reflects the ebb and flow of the contending armies that have washed over it, leaving behind their tell-tale architectural jetsam. The Crusaders came to the city in 1104 on their vainglorious campaign to recapture the Holy Land for Christianity. After losing control of Jerusalem in 1187, they retreated to peaceful Akko, transforming it into the greatest port of their empire and a world-class showpiece of culture and architecture. The Mamluks ended Crusader rule in 1291, and almost 500 years later the Druze prince Fakhr ad-Din rebuilt the city. His work was continued by Tahir al-Omar, who was murdered and succeeded in 1775 by Ahmed Jazzar, a Turkish *pasha* of Bosnian extraction. Napoleon later claimed, with typical modesty, that had Akko fallen to him, "the world would have been mine." Unfortunately for him, his 1799 siege failed. After a stint (1833-1840) under Egyptian Ibrahim Pasha, Akko was returned to the Turks. When the British captured the port in 1918, it had a predominantly Arab population of 8000. Jews employing terrorist tactics against the British were held captive in the Citadel during World War II.

In general, the people of Akko are remarkably friendly and helpful. Still, women traveling alone should exercise caution, as usual. The old city, with its cheap hostels, breathtaking coastal views, treasure-chests of historical sights and water activities, and proximity to Nahariya's buses make Akko an ideal base for exploring the northern coast and western Galilee. Akko was designed for the pedestrian, so allow ample time to amble and explore. During school vacations, you may find yourself awarded an informative, if somewhat tiresome, self-appointed guide in the Arab town. The young men who so boldly approach you are often only interested in practicing their English and impressing their friends, so offering a tip may be taken as an insult. Steer clear of any drugs offered on the streets; the police keep a close watch on dealers and usually confine foreign offenders to the local prison for several nightmarish days before expelling them from the country. It's best not to prowl the alleys of the Old City after dark.

ORIENTATION AND PRACTICAL INFORMATION

To reach Akko, take bus #252 from Haifa (every 20-40min. noon-4pm, 25min., NIS6.50) or bus #272 from Nahariya (express, every 15min. until 6:30pm, 20min., NIS4.50). New and old Akko are connected by **Ḥayim Weizmann Street.** From the central bus station, Ben-Ami and Herzl St. run to Weizmann. **Ha-Hagana Street** borders the sea to the west from the new city to the lighthouse at Akko's southern tip. At the northern end, **Aj-Jazzar** and **Salah ad-Din** are the largest streets in the old city after Ha-Hagana, extending in opposite directions from the end of Weizmann. On **Aj-Jazzar Street** are the mosque, Crusader City, and information office. The Old City bus stops are opposite the parking lot. The **supermarket,** central post office, Wolfson Auditorium, and City Hall are on **Ha'Atzma'ut,** the major street of the new city. The passages of the peninsular Old City are poorly marked: a map, the locals, and the many monuments along the way are the only navigational tools available. **Khan al-Umdan** (Inn of Pillars) is an important landmark, located near the Isnan Pasha Mosque and the fishing port. The market winds its way through the middle of the peninsula. The **Southern Promenade,** at the end of Ha-Hagana St., has been developed as a tourist area, with several restaurants and sitting areas built into the old Pisan Harbor walls and towers.

Akko's **Municipal Tourist Information Office** (tel. 911 764 or 910 251), at the Crusader City entrance on Aj-Jazzar St. across from the mosque, provides information about sites and special events in Akko and a great map of the new and old cities (NIS2.50). Get the map before you attempt Old Akko. (Open Sun.-Thurs. 8am-4pm; limited information available Fri.-Sat.) The **central post office,** at 11 Ha'Atzma'ut St.

next to the municipality building, has **Poste Restante.** (Open Mon.-Tues. and Thurs. 8am-12:30pm and 4-6pm, Wed. and Fri. 8am-12:30pm.) Akko's **telephone code** is 04. For banking in the Old City, try **Mercantile Discount Bank,** corner of Aj-Jazzar and Weizmann St. (open Sun., Tues., and Thurs. 8:30am-1pm and 4-5:30pm, Mon. and Wed. 8:30am-1pm, Fri. 8:30am-noon), the **Arab-Israeli Bank** around the corner on Weizmann, or **Bank Leumi,** on Ben-Ami St. near Weizmann St. (Both open Sun., Tues., and Thurs. 8:30am-12:30pm and 4-6pm, Mon. and Wed. 8:30am-12:30pm, Fri. 8:30am-noon.) Several banks are located on or near Ben-Ami St. outside the Old City walls.

The **train station** is on David Remez St. (tel. 912 350) across from the central bus station; Tel Aviv-Nahariya and Nahariya-Tel Aviv (via Haifa) trains stop here. The **central bus station** is on Ha'Arba'a Rd. in the new city (tel. 549 555 for information). Express bus #252 and 272 run to Haifa (25min., NIS6.50) and #272 to Nahariya (20min., NIS4.50). Bus #251 and 271 to Haifa and Nahariya respectively are local *(me'asef).* Buses from platform #16, near the Egged restaurant, will take weary travelers the short distance to the old city. There is no baggage check at the bus station, but for NIS4 you can store bags at the Knights Parking Lot on Weizmann in the old city (just north of Aj-Jazzar; open daily 7am-6pm). Bookworms can go to the **Canada-Akko Library,** 13 Weizmann St. (tel. 910 860), near the old city, delightfully air-conditioned, with books in English, French, Hebrew, Arabic, Russian, Romanian, and Yiddish (open Sun.-Thurs. 9-11:45am and 3-6:45pm). For a **taxi** call **Akko Tzafon** (tel. 916 666) or **Ariyeh** (tel. 913 369); catch a **sherut** on the small street off Ha'Arba'a St. across from the bus station (to Haifa NIS5). **Pharmacies** include **Akko,** 35 Ben-Ami St. (tel. 912 021), and **Merkaz,** 27 Ben-Ami St. (tel. 914 702). **Emergency numbers: fire** (tel. 912 222), **first aid** (Magen David Adom; tel. 101 or 912 333), and **police,** 2 Ben-Ami St. (tel. 100 or 910 244).

ACCOMMODATIONS AND FOOD

(The following are all heated in winter.) The **Akko Youth Hostel (HI)** (tel. 911 982) is across from the lighthouse within the old city walls. The airy lounge and several of the commodious rooms have a fabulous view of the sea over the ramparts. Take any bus from platform #16 to the old city, then make your way through the market, following the sparse signs, or walk just north of the old city from the bus, making a left onto Napoleon Bonaparte St. and another left onto Ha-Hagana St. when you reach the water. Follow Ha-Hagana to the lighthouse; the hostel is 30m to the left. (Checkout 9am. Curfew 10:30pm. Dorm beds (6-8 per room) NIS17, nonmembers NIS20. June-Jan. bed and breakfast US$10, nonmembers US$11. Lockers NIS4. Reservations necessary in summer.) **Walied's Gate Hostel,** Salah ad-Din St. (tel. 910 410 or 914 700; fax 910 454), next to Land Gate, is simple and family-run, with a kitchen available. (24-hr. reception. Curfew midnight. Coed and single-sex dorm beds (4-12 per room) NIS20. Dorm beds on patio NIS15. Doubles NIS60. Breakfast NIS5. Wash and dry NIS15.) Or try **Paul's Hostel and Souvenir Shop** (tel. 912 857), just across the road from the lighthouse at the southern end of Ha-Hagana St., near the pita bakery, under a large blue awning. Ask in the shop for Paul Elias, who will take you to a 12-bed hostel located in his family's building just behind the shop. Guests live in a large, Crusader-domed room with adjacent bath and kitchen. Each guest gets a key. (Dorm NIS20. Doubles NIS60. Luggage storage NIS4. Laundry NIS4 per load. Shop open daily 8am-10pm.) There are additional unofficial and unregulated hostels or rooms for rent in the old city, but get the tourist office's opinion of the place before you make a decision you might regret. The port area can be dangerous at night, especially for women alone. Beach camping is forbidden.

The **Lighthouse Restaurant** (tel. 917 640), under its namesake near the HI hostel, has tables overlooking the water and invites evening idling. Hostel patrons receive a 10% discount (*kabab* NIS20, hummus NIS8). By the marina is the more expensive **Abu Christo** restaurant (tel. 910 065). Daredevils occasionally take a dive off the three-story wall into the water near the restaurant. Around the corner from the hostel, diagonally across from the lighthouse, is the tiny **Pita Bakery,** where various breads are fresh and cheap. **Galileo Restaurant,** in the Pisan Harbor, has the standard Middle Eastern munchies at slightly inflated prices. Have drinks and ice cream at **Café Tuscana** (up the stairs in the Pisan Harbor) for the jaw-dropping view of the sea and old Akko. You can buy food at the outdoor market next to the central bus station and at the *souq* in the old city. Farther from the hostel are the food stands and small **supermarkets** on Yehoshafat St. off Ben-Ami St.; a number of **falafel stands** huddle near the corner of Weizmann and Ben-Ami St.

SIGHTS AND ENTERTAINMENT

No itinerary can do justice to the history and ancient conflicts emanating from the ruins and fortifications of old Akko. To reach the **old city** from the bus station by foot, walk down Ben-Ami St. to Weizmann St. and turn left. The entrance to the old city is just past Eli Cohen Park on the left. As you pass the Aj-Jazzar wall, look for the moat beneath Burj al-Kommander to the left. The entrance to the **Mosque of Aj-Jazzar** is to your right on Aj-Jazzar St. The third-largest mosque in Israel, it dominates this city of monuments with its green dome and sleek minaret. Ahmed aj-Jazzar ordered its construction in 1781 on what is believed to have been the site of San Croce, the original Christian cathedral of Akko. Inside is an attractive courtyard with Roman columns taken from Caesarea. The western end of the courtyard rests upon the cellar of a Crusader fortress. The surrounding structures are lodgings for students of the Qur'an and the personnel of the mosque. The tower was destroyed by an earthquake in 1927, but promptly restored; the rest of the complex is in magnificent condition.

In front of the mosque sits an octagonal *sabil* (fountain) where the faithful perform *wudhu,* the ritual washing of their heads, hands, and feet before praying. Inside (in the green cage on the marble stand to the right as you face the mosque) is a shrine containing a hair from the beard of the prophet Muhammad. As in all mosques, prayers are conducted five times per day, and you will be asked to wait or return in 20 minutes if you arrive during a prayer session. To the right of the mosque is a small building containing the sarcophagi of Aj-Jazzar and son; peek through the barred windows at the marble boxes, now covered with soil and green plants. Aj-Jazzar turned the buried Crusader cathedral into an underground water reservoir, filled by rainfall and pipelines. Enter the recently renovated reservoir through a door and underground stairway to the left of the mosque. Look for the small green sign and red arrows. Modest dress is required; scarves are available for those not already covered. The guides who offer NIS4 tours vary in quality: some are very knowledgeable, while others will merely read you a few inscriptions. (Open daily 8am-12:15pm, 1:15-4:15pm, and 4:45-6pm. Admission NIS2.)

A restored white stone gate, the entrance to the subterranean **Crusader City,** stands across from the mosque on Aj-Jazzar St. When first discovered, the rooms were thought to have been built underground, but archaeologists have since determined that Aj-Jazzar found it easier to simply build his own city above them. Because excavations were halted for fear that the Arab town above might collapse, most of the Crusader City remains buried; only the area originally known as the "Hospitaller's Quarter" is open. In the entrance halls, three enormous pillars stand amidst a variety of architectural styles. Almost everything in these halls decorated with pictorial representations such as flowers or human forms is the work of the Crusaders, while the more abstract embellishments and the Arabic calligraphy are Ottoman additions. The flowers engraved in several of the columns are among the earliest examples of the *fleur-de-lis,* the French imperial insignia. The neighboring halls date from the original 12th-century Crusader City and were probably part of a hospital complex where the Hospitaller Order treated pilgrims. The arches project directly from the floor, indicating that the current foundation is some 4m above the bases on the original level. The barrels and girders throughout the complex were placed there recently to support the original walls.

Proceed from the entrance halls to the courtyard to see some of the fortifications built by Fakhr ad-Din and Tahir al-Omar. Turn left and enter the Hospitaller's fort through the imposing Turkish gate, directly beneath which stands the original Crusader gate. Turning right from here will bring you to the center of the original Crusader complex. These halls are now used for concerts during July by the **Haifa Symphony Orchestra,** as well as the acclaimed annual **Israel Fringe Theater Festival.** The four-day extravaganza occurs during the Jewish festival of *Sukkot* (Oct. 9-17 in 1995), and attracts small theater groups from all over Israel. Only a few of the performances are in English (check with the tourist office).

The passageway from this part of the Crusader City to the **Refectory** or **Crypt of St. John** has been closed since 1990 for fear that the roof will collapse. To reach the crypt, leave the Crusader City the way you came in, turn right, and follow the signs to the crypt entrance; look for the spooky black-and-white sign on a metal door. The most magnificent and famous of the buried rooms, it once housed Crusader feasts.

Next to the third column in the crypt is a staircase connected to a long underground passageway that leads to six adjacent rooms opening onto a central courtyard. The passageway may have been dug by the Crusaders as a hiding place in case of attack, or possibly as an elaborate sewage system. It was later restored by Aj-Jazzar to serve as a means of escape if Napoleon gained entrance to the city walls. The rooms also served as a hospital for wounded knights, and the Turks used them as a post office. The adjacent **Municipal Museum** (really a Turkish bath, operating until 1947) is accessible through either the metal door opposite the crypt entrance or the metal door opposite the main entrance around the corner. Random relics are strewn throughout the baths. (Crusader City open Sun.-Thurs. 8:30am-6:30pm, Fri. 8:30am-3pm, Sat. 9am-6:30pm; winter, Sun.-Thurs. 8:30am-5pm, Fri. 8:30am-2pm, Sat. 9am-5pm. Closed *Sukkot* for Fringe Theater Festival. Admission NIS9, students NIS8. Maps NIS3. Pamphlet about the city NIS2. Inquire about showings of the film *5000 Years: The History of Akko.*)

From the entrance to the Municipal Museum, take a right down the alley and continue to the *souq,* a tumultuous avenue of butchers, grocers, bakers, and copper, brass, and leather vendors. Small eateries throughout the *souq* offer *kabab,* falafel, and sandwiches. (Market open 7am-7pm.) Near the market crouch several caravansaries (*khan* in Arabic). The most impressive among them is **Khan al-Umdan** (Inn of Pillars), just past the Isnan Pasha Mosque and the fishing port. Aj-Jazzar built this *khan* for Turkish merchants toward the end of the 18th century. The lower stories of the courts served as rented storerooms for merchants, while the upper galleries served as boarding rooms. The *khan,* erected in 1906 to celebrate the jubilee of the Turkish Sultan Abd al-Hamid, is marked by a slender, square clock tower with the Turkish half-moon and star.

Near Khan al-Umdan is the **Akko Marina.** You can rent diving equipment from **Ramy's Diving Center** (tel. 918 990, 910 606, or 919 287), located inside Khan al-Umdan on the left. Look for the Ahab's Camel Wash sign. (Introductory dive US$45-60.) The *Princess of Akko* (tel. 913 890) gives 25-minute boat rides to the sea walls (NIS8, students NIS6), but will not depart until it is filled with enough tourists.

In the northern part of the Old City, the commanding **Citadel** adjoins the Crusader City on Ha-Hagana St., opposite the sea wall. This stronghold, used by the British as their central prison, now houses the **Museum of Heroism** (tel. 913 900), a monument to Jewish guerilla organizations. The citadel was built in the late 1700s on Crusader foundations of the 13th century and was used as a prison by the Turks. The most famous inmate during Turkish rule was Baha'u'llah, founder of the Baha'i faith, imprisoned on the second floor in 1868. During the British Mandate, the prison housed about 560 inmates under the guard of about half as many British soldiers. Members of the Palmaḥ, Hagana, and Irgun, including Ze'ev Jabotinsky, were imprisoned here for violent anti-British activities. After losing eight members to the citadel's gallows between 1938 and 1947, the Irgun retaliated by hanging a British officer. The Gallows Room displays the noose in place along with photographs of the eight Jewish victims. On May 4, 1947, the Irgun staged a prison break that freed 11 of its members and 255 other inmates (later depicted in the movie *Exodus,* shot on location). To reach the museum, follow the stone stairs down to the lower garden, then the metal stairs up and around the side of the prison. (Complex open Sun.-Thurs. 8:30am-5pm. Admission NIS5, students NIS2.)

Across the street from the museum looms **Burj al-Kuraim** (Fortress of the Vineyards), commonly referred to as the British Fortress despite its Crusader and Turkish builders. Renowned throughout history as the most secure port in the East, Akko remains a city of battlements and bastions. Akko's defense in recent centuries has relied upon the **Aj-Jazzar Wall,** running along the northern and eastern sides of the city and surrounded by a moat of sea water. The best place from which to view the wall is **Burj al-Kommander** (Commander's Fortress), an enormous Crusader bastion at the northern corner. To enter the watchtower, climb the steps that begin where Weizmann St. crosses the wall.

The city walls originally ran the length of the harbor. All that remains is the ruined **Tower of the Flies,** the site of the original lighthouse, solemnly brooding in the middle of the bay. Its fortifications were toppled by a devastating earthquake in 1837. At the eastern corner near the shoreline yawns the so-called **Land Gate,** once the only entrance to the city.

Hof Argaman (Purple Beach; tel. 911 672 or 530), which isn't actually purple (the reference is to a type of snail found here), is the only thing calling itself a tourist attraction in the new city. (Open June-Oct. 8am-6pm. Admission NIS6, students NIS5.) To get to Hof Argaman, follow Yonatan Ha-Hashmonai St. from the Land Gate south along the coast for about 10 minutes, taking the detour around the naval school. Two hotels, the Argaman and the Palm Beach, dominate the beach. Past the Palm Beach is a free beach without lifeguards. Just outside the Land Gate, at the less attractive **Hof Ha-Homot** (open 8am-6pm; admission NIS8), you can rent sailboards (NIS10 per hr.). None of the several hundred swimmers seems to notice the "bathing prohibited" signs (posted in three languages). There's a changing room through the low door opposite the beach entrance.

■ NEAR AKKO

Lohamei Ha-Geta'ot ("Fighters of the Ghettos"), a kibbutz founded by concentration camp and Warsaw Ghetto survivors, lies outside Akko toward Nahariya. The **Ghetto Fighters' House** (tel. 995 8080) examines the Warsaw Ghetto uprising, Nazi atrocities, and the cultural life of the Warsaw Ghetto (in particular the poetry of Yitzhak Katzenelson); it shows artwork by prisoners and survivors. To reach the kibbutz, take bus #271 (which runs on Sat. too) toward Nahariya (make sure that the bus is local *(me'asef)* not express, or you'll end up in Nahariya). (Museum open Sun.-Thurs. 9am-4pm, Fri. 9am-1pm, Sat. 10am-5pm. Small donation requested.)

The **Roman aqueduct** just outside the museum to the south is remarkably well preserved, largely because it's not Roman. Aj-Jazzar had it built in 1780 to carry water 15km from the Kabri springs to Akko. Get good views of the aqueduct from the bus between Akko and Nahariya.

Two kilometers south of the kibbutz bloom the **Baha'i Gardens** (tel. 812 763), arranged in a riveting combination of Occidental and Oriental styles. The gardens, planted from 1952 to 1956, hold the villa and shrine of Baha'u'llah, the prophet and founder of the Baha'i faith. (Shrine open Mon. and Fri.-Sun. 9am-noon; gardens open daily 9am-4pm. Free.) The gate on the main road is for Baha'is; all others should get off the bus just north of the gate at the sign for Shomrat. Walk east about 500m, past **Kibbutz Shomrat,** and enter the gate on the right just past the military camp, marked by a small sign. The gardens are on the main Akko-Nahariya road, via bus #271 (about 10min.). For an arduous daytrip, consider the 1km hike through **Nahal Shagur** (also called **Nahal Beit Ha-Kerem**), a tributary of the Hilazon River east of Akko that is part of the valley dividing the Upper and Lower Galilee.

■■■ NAHARIYA נהריה

Nahariya is the definitive one-street resort town: bus and train station on one end, ocean on the other, and pleasant commercial strip in between. During the day, people flock to the beach. Later, an older crowd of Israelis and tourists returns to the streets, where dim, colored light reflects the relaxed nature of Nahariya's nightlife. In 1934 German Jews first settled the area as a farming village on the Ga'aton River, which now, dwindled by pumps upstream, trickles unimpressively in a concrete channel down the center of the main thoroughfare. The many buses leaving Nahariya make it a convenient base for sights on the northern coast and in the Western Galilee, but accommodations are more expensive than those in nearby Akko.

Orientation and Practical Information 10km north of Akko and the same distance south of Rosh Ha-Nikra's sea caverns, Nahariya is the northernmost town on Israel's coast. The roads from cities farther to the north run to the beaches and parks of Akhziv (3km north, a 40-min. walk). Nahariya itself is minuscule; nearly every service you'll need is located on **Ha-Ga'aton Blvd.** To reach the beaches, walk a few blocks west on Ha-Ga'aton and stop when you get wet.

Nahariya's **Municipal Tourist Information Office (MTIO)** is on Ha-Ga'aton Blvd. (tel. 879 800), on the ground floor of the Municipality Building. From the bus station, walk west on Ha-Ga'aton until you reach the plaza on your left just after Herzl St.; the MTIO is in the large white building at the end of the plaza. (Open Sun.-Thurs. 8am-1pm and 4-7pm, Fri. 8am-1pm.) **Mercantile Discount Bank** (tel. 924 611) and **Bank Leumi** (tel. 925 631) are both open Sun., Tues., and Thurs. 8:30am-12:30pm and 4-6pm, Mon. and Wed. 8:30am-12:30pm, Fri. 8:30am-noon; **Israel Discount** (tel. 928 881) is open Mon.-Thurs. 8am-8pm, Fri. 8am-2pm, and Sat.-Sun. 8am-10:30pm. All banks are on Ha-Ga'aton Blvd. The **post office,** 40 Ha-Ga'aton Blvd. (tel. 920 180), has **Poste Restante** and **international calling.** (Open Sun.-Tues. and Thurs. 8am-12:30pm and 3:30-6pm, Wed. 8am-1:30pm, Fri. 8am-noon.) **Telephone code:** 04.

Nahariya's **train station,** 1 Ha-Ga'aton Blvd., is 1 block east (away from the sea) of the bus station, with trains for Akko, Haifa, Netanya, and Tel Aviv only. The **bus station** is at 3 Ha-Ga'aton Blvd. (tel. 54 95 55): bus #272 (express), 270, and 271 depart for Nahariya from both Haifa (45min., NIS8) and Akko (20min., NIS4.40). Bus #20 and 22 go to Rosh Ha-Nikra (15min., NIS5), #22-26 and 28 run to Akhziv (6:30am-9:30pm, 10min., NIS4), and #44 goes to Peki'in (30-35min., NIS9.50).

For **English-language books,** try Doron Books, 32 Ha-Ga'aton Blvd. (tel. 921 079; open Sun.-Mon. and Wed.-Thurs. 8am-1pm and 4-7pm, Tues. 8am-1pm, Fri. 8am-2pm). The **Szabo Pharmacy,** 3 Ha-Ga'aton Blvd. (tel. 920 454 or 921 197), is in front of the bus station (open Sun.-Thurs. 8am-1pm and 4-7pm, Fri. 8am-2pm). The **hospital** is on Ben-Tzvi Ave. (tel. 850 505). For **first aid,** dial 101 or 823 333. The **police** are at 5 Ben-Tzvi St. (tel. 100 or 920 344).

Accommodations and Food There are no cheap hostels in Nahariya. In summer, rooms are available in private homes. "Rooms to Rent" signs are common on Jabotinsky St.; head west on Ha-Ga'aton to the post office and turn right onto Jabotinsky (NIS45 or more; polite bargaining may help). The MTIO keeps a list of rooms, but this list doesn't include prices. The **Kalman Hotel (HI),** 27 Jabotinsky St. (tel. 920 355; fax 929 690), one block from the beach, is speckless and spacious, with A/C, TV, and private bath. Owner Miron Teichner gives out coupons for the beach and restaurants, and shows off the signatures of big-shots who've stayed here, including Ezer Weizmann, Shimon Peres, and Sophia Loren. (Rates for *Let's Go* holders: singles US$25, doubles US$40, triples US$56. Room #26, no TV, is available as a single for US$20 or double for US$35. Buffet breakfast included.) **Sirtash House,** 22 Jabotinsky St. (tel. 922 586), has lean, cozy doubles (NIS60-80) with A/C, TV, radio, phone, and private baths (some with small kitchens). (Check-out 10am.) **Motel Arieli,** 1 Jabotinsky St. (tel. 921 076), next to Ha-Ga'aton and the beach, offers neat rooms with A/C in either bungalows or a main building. (Check-out 10am. 2-bed bungalows NIS70. Doubles NIS100.) **Beit Gabiazda,** 12 Jabotinsky St. (tel. 921 049), has A/C, private baths, and kitchen. (Doubles NIS80; July-Aug. NIS100. Bargain.)

The restaurant-cafés and falafel stands lining Ha-Ga'aton Blvd. peddle familiar food at outrageous prices. Nahariya's beaches and gardens make paradisiacal picnic grounds; shop at the **Co-op Tzafon supermarket** (tel. 927 210) on the corner of Ha-Ga'aton and Herzl St. Fruit and vegetable stores punctuate Herzl between Ha-Ga'aton and Ha-Meyasdim. A Moroccan bakery across from the Hod theater on Herzl (side entry, no sign) sells several dozen varieties of cookies (NIS9-12 per kg).

Sights and Entertainment The remains of a 4000-year-old **Canaanite Temple** dedicated to Asherah (the goddess of fertility) were discovered in 1947 on a hill next to the shore. Walk south on the beach for 20 minutes. Singularly unimpressive. The **Nahariya Municipal Museum,** in the Municipality Building near the bus terminal, has exhibits on art, archaeology, malacology (seashells), history, and Central European Jewry. (Open Sun. and Wed. 10am-noon and 4-6pm, Mon.-Tues. and Thurs.-Fri. 8am-noon. Free.) An ornate mosaic floor is all that remains of a 4th-century **Byzantine church** (tel. 823 070), on Bielefeld St. near the Katzenelson School. Call ahead to arrange a visit (NIS3).

Nahariya's *raison d'être* remains, predictably, tanning and swimming. The main beach is the crowded **Galei Galil,** with a lifeguard and a breakwater. Walk down Ha-Ga'aton and turn right at the end. (Open 8am-6pm; Sept.-June 8am-5pm. NIS10 covers admission to the heated indoor pool (open year-round), large outdoor pool, and kiddie pools.) Bathrooms are not clean, and facilities are jammed on Saturdays. South of Galei Galil is a free beach without a breakwater. Local kids surf here with the same lunatic exuberance that makes driving in Israel such fun. Thank God surfboards don't have horns. Farther south is a free municipal beach.

Horse-drawn **carriage rides** start from the post office and the eastern end of Ha-Ga'aton; follow your nose and watch your step (up to 15 people, 15min. NIS30, 30min. NIS50). The **Hod Cinema** (tel. 920 502), on Herzl across from the market, often shows movies in English, as does the **Hekhal Ha-Tarbout** (tel. 927 935) on Ha'Atzma'ut Rd.

What nightlife Nahariya has starts fairly late on Friday and Saturday nights. A local favorite is **BK Pub,** across from the bus station on Ha-Ga'aton (enter from the side at the intersection with Ha'Atzma'ut St.). **Makom Batayelet** and its neighbor **Mull Hayam** are two oceanside pubs (turn left where Ha-Ga'aton meets the sand). For those with lots of money or local buddies (they all seem to get in free), there's dancing at the **Carlton Hotel disco,** also on Ha-Ga'aton. (Admission normally NIS25.)

■ NEAR NAHARIYA

AKHZIV אכזיב

Akhziv beach (tel. 823 988), which begins about 4km north of Nahariya, is popular (and populated, although quiet spots can be found) and has all the amenities (open 8am-7am; admission NIS8, students NIS6). Two roads lead to the beach: the paved road along the coast, and the unpaved, noncoastal road on which buses stop.

The heart of the area is the **Akhziv National Park** (tel. 823 263), with sprawling lawns, a sheltered beach, and showers and changing rooms built on the remains of an 8th-century Phoenician port town. (Open Sat.-Thurs. 8am-7pm, Fri. 8am-6pm. Admission NIS10, students NIS7.50.) Bordering the park on its southern side is a **Club Med;** to the north is **Akhzivland,** a self-proclaimed independent state founded in 1952 by the eccentric Eli Avivi, who leased the land from an unamused Israeli government. An eye-catching figure in flowing robes, Avivi is unforgettable—especially when kvetchy customs officials try to figure out the "Akhzivland" stamp on your passport. **Eli's Museum** (tel. 823 250), housed in a deteriorated but striking Arab mansion, exhibits the benevolent dictator's extensive and esoteric collection of (mostly Phoenician) implements, statue fragments, and maps. (Open 24 hrs. Admission NIS7, students NIS5.) Sleeping in the dilapidated **camping area** costs

NIS30, in the dorms NIS30-40, and in one of Eli's newly constructed guest rooms NIS50. (Parking, beach, and museum admission included. Call ahead.)

Across the road is the **Akhziv Diving Center** (tel. 823 671), where you can rent snorkeling equipment (NIS25). Diving classes are a hefty NIS850; groups of 6 or more can request English instruction. Introductory dives hurt slightly less at NIS130 (English available. Call ahead.) Just north is **Gesher Ha-Ziv**, one of 11 bridges blown up on the evening of June 16, 1946 ("the night of the bridges") to protest the British closure of Palestine's ports to Jewish refugees. The **Yad LeYad Memorial** honors 14 members of the Hagana killed in an attempt to blow up another bridge.

Much more attractive than Akhzivland are the campsite and hostel, both a short distance up the road. The enormous (250 sites!) **Akhziv Campground** (tel. 825 054) has a kitchen, pool, and minimarket. (Reception 8am-10pm. Tent sites NIS20 per adult. 2- and 4-person bungalows NIS55 per adult. Mobile homes for 2 NIS160. Cabins with A/C, bath, and breakfast: doubles NIS180, triples NIS240, quads NIS290; prices are about 15% lower in the off-season. Locked refrigerator box NIS8. Mattresses NIS8. Electric light cables NIS8.)

Yad LeYad Youth Hostel (HI) (tel. 823 345) is 500m farther north along the main road and across from the sea. Cook in its kitchen or buy meals at the bar next door. Beginning March 1995, there will be A/C and private bathrooms in all rooms. (Reception open 24 hrs. Bungalows NIS40. Singles NIS49. Doubles NIS110. Breakfast included.) About 200m north on the opposite side of the street, the **SPNI** (tel. 823 762) leads walks in the area (mostly for children; open 8am-4:30pm). Their field school, frequently filled by groups, rents private rooms (NIS75 per person). Bus #22-26 and 28 from Nahariya go to the field school, hostel, beach, and campground (2 per hr., 10min., NIS4). *Sherut* taxis frequently run between Akhziv and Nahariya.

ROSH HA-NIKRA ראש הנקרה

Rosh Ha-Nikra, 10km north of Nahariya, has spectacular white chalk cliffs and caves. Their serene beauty makes it easy to forget the Israeli border station and patrols overhead. Rosh Ha-Nikra's cool caves were sculpted by millennia of lashing waves. The British enlarged these natural grottos when they dug a tunnel (originally designed as a train route between Haifa and Beirut) through the cliffs during WWII.

The nearby kibbutz, seeing the potential for tourism, blasted additional tunnels through the rock to improve access to the sea caves, and topped the cliffs with an observation point and cafeteria. The highway from Nahariya ends at the observation point, making the cable car the only way down to the caves. After taking the cable car but before entering the grottos, follow the train track to the right through an arched entrance past the painted placard figures into the darkened cavern where "The Peace Train," a truly random audio-visual presentation featuring a soothing English voice and 3-D glasses, awaits. (Tel. 857 108. Cable car runs Sun.-Thurs. 8:30am-6pm, Fri. 8:30am-4pm; July-Aug. Sun.-Thurs. 8:30am-11pm, Fri. 8:30am-4pm; winter Sun.-Fri. 8:30am-4pm. Admission NIS18, students NIS16. Peace Train every ½hr.) Bus #20 and 22 leave Nahariya for Rosh Ha-Nikra (9:15, 11:30am, and 2:30pm; 15min.; NIS5; return ½hr. later). Other buses run from Nahariya to the junction, but require a 3km walk uphill to the cable cars. A taxi from Nahariya may be willing to take you *sherut* to the junction (NIS4), *special* to the site (NIS10).

Arrive early or be shoved around by tour and youth groups spelunking in the afternoon. The worse the weather, the better the show at Rosh Ha-Nikra—waves pound the natural caverns, forming powerful cross-currents and whirlpools and echoing thunderously through the tunnels. If you decide to take an illegal dip and risk joining the legions of ghostly swimmers on the sea floor, be careful not to venture out into the waters to the north near the Israeli "security zone" in southern Lebanon. The guards will skewer even the most accidental of tourists. The desolate beach south of Rosh Ha-Nikra is rumored to be a favorite of some nudists.

Five minutes from the grottos, just off the main road, is the **Rosh Ha-Nikra Youth Hostel (HI)** (tel. 825 169 or 821 330), with lush grounds, a large recreation room, a pool, and a view. A/C and private baths. (Reception open Sun.-Thurs. 8am-1pm and

4-7pm, Fri. 8am-1pm. Check-in 4pm. Check-out 9am. Spacious dorms (up to 5 people) US$16.50 per person. Singles US$29. Doubles US$40. Reservations a must.)

YEHI'AM (JUDIN) FORTRESS מצודת יחיעם

Built in the 12th century by the Templars, **Judin Fortress** (tel. 924 809) was passed on to the Teutonic Knights and then destroyed by the Mamluk Sultan Baybars in 1265. Visitors see the plentiful remains of restoration efforts done 500 years later by Mahad al-Hussein, the local sheikh; in 1738, the fortress was conquered by the Bedouin ruler Tahir al-Omar. Kibbutz Yeḥi'am was started in 1946 by a group that settled in the deserted castle; the fortress is still within the kibbutz grounds, and now even bears its name. Impressive views of the Western Galilee highlands are afforded from the well-preserved tower. (Open Sun.-Thurs. 8am-5pm, Fri. and holidays 8am-4pm. Admission NIS5.50, students NIS4.10.) Bus #39 and 42 (NIS4.50) provide infrequent service from Nahariya and stop right by the fortress.

MONTFORT מונפורט

The Crusader castle of Montfort rewards a challenging hike with resplendent ruins and scenery. Wind-swept and solitary, the fortification dramatically juts over a deep valley of Western Galilee. The main structure was built by the Knights Templar early in the 12th century and partially destroyed by Salah ad-Din in 1187. Enlarged and strengthened by the Hospitaller Knights in 1230, the fortress was named Starkenburg ("strong castle" in German), as well as Montfort ("strong mountain" in French). You can still see the impressive 18m tower and 20m main hall, along with the remains of the fortress complex.

Bus #40, 41, 44, and 45 leave Nahariya for the Christian Arab village of Mi'ilya throughout the day. From the stop, turn right onto the steep road toward Mi'ilya, bearing left at every fork. After a 30-minute walk (2.5km) you'll see a wooden sign for Montfort. The road veers right to Hila, but continue straight onto the dirt road directly ahead. Follow the red-and-white-striped trail markers along the windy, rocky path another 30 minutes (1.5km; you'll pass a set of stone steps on your right, an alternate route to the top); the path to the castle abruptly turns to the right, across a small bridge and up the rocks. The site is currently under renovation and officially closed, but visitors still prowl around.

The castle overlooks the Keziv river. The **Nahal Keziv nature reserve** contains hiking trails along these waters, which originate in the Meron Mountain mass and flow west to the sea. Remains of old dams and water mills can still be seen along the creek, a testimony to the days when its plentiful sources were not diverted for Western Galilee domestic use. To get to the reserve, walk down the path encircling the Montfort hill, or follow the black-and-white markers from the parking lot in Hila.

Near Montfort is the new, modern, spotless **Shlomi Youth Hostel and Guest House (HI)** (tel. 808 975 or 809 161). The 4-person rooms have A/C and private baths. (Reception open 8-10am, 1-3pm, and 7:30-8:30pm. Check-in 2pm. Check-out 10am. NIS63 per person, nonmembers NIS66. Sept. 15% increase. Breakfast included.) Bus #22 and 23 leave from Nahariya (every 40min., 35min., NIS8).

PEKI'IN (BKE'AH) بقيعة פקיעין

Peki'in (Bke'ah in Arabic) is the spot where Rabbi Shimon Bar-Yoḥai and his son, Eliezer, fled from a Roman decree prohibiting the study of Torah. For 13 years, the erudite duo hid in a small cave in the hillside, sustained by a nearby spring and fertile carob tree. During this time, some Jews believe they composed the *Zohar,* the most important text of Kabbala (Jewish mysticism). The cave is historical, holy, and humble; the main attraction is the town, a colorful village of Druze and Christian Arabs.

To visit the **holy cave,** take the winding road leading up from the bus stop to the top of the village. When you reach a marking stone and a blue-and-white sign on your right, take the path down to the stairway. Walk downstairs until a large bush is in front of you, and turn right between two large rocks. The tiny cave is about ten feet to the right of the stairway. Return to the stairway and descend down to the

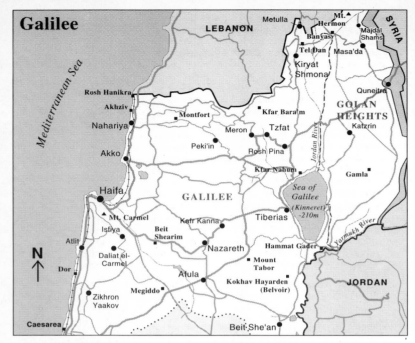

bottom. Turn right onto the narrow street and follow it until you reach Kikkar Ha-Ma'ayan ("Spring Square"). You'll see an odd-shaped pool of water fed by the square's namesake. From the square, take the small street to the right. Turn left at the first intersection and follow this curving road down to the white synagogue gate at your right. The synagogue on this site, which stood in the days of Shimon Bar-Yoḥai and his son, is now a small museum. If the gate is closed, knock on the white metal door with a blue star opposite the gate and upstairs. The museum is free; you can leave a small donation in the box on the table with the prayer books. (Open Sun.-Thurs. 8:30am-noon and 2-6pm, Fri. 8:30am-2pm.)

Near the bus stop, two families have opened small cafés, both of which serve fragrant Arabic coffee and Druze pita made from thin *rkak* bread brushed with olive oil, *za'atar*, and *labaneh* (yogurt cheese) for NIS4.

Peki'in is most accessible from Nahariya. Bus #44 (6-7 per day, 30-35min., NIS9.50) makes the round-trip to Peki'in; be sure to get off at Peki'in Ha'Atika (Old Peki'in), not Peki'in Ha-Ḥadasha (New Peki'in) one stop earlier. The last stop on the bus is the small Druze village of **Beit Jan,** which is much less commercialized than Daliyat Al Karmel on Mt. Carmel (see p. 301).

■ Galilee הגליל الجليل

■■■ NAZARETH נצרת الناصرة

A vibrant center of Arab life in the Galilee, Nazareth (An-Nassra in Arabic, Natzrat in Hebrew) is vastly different from the Biblical picture of pastoral churches and convents. True, as the place of Jesus' early life and the traditional home of Joseph and Mary, Nazareth contains several holy Christian sites. But sentimental sketches on Christmas cards belie the true nature of Nazareth, an engrossingly gritty town. Drivers maniacally swerve to miss pedestrians on Paul VI St. and crowds clamor in the business district, while the faithful worship in dimly-lit back-alley churches.

ORIENTATION AND PRACTICAL INFORMATION

Nazareth is 40km southeast of Haifa and 30km southwest of Tiberias, on a hill north of the Jezreel Valley. The generations-old inhabitants of the old **Arab Town,** where the Christian sights are located, resent the encroachment of the newer **Natzrat Illit** (Upper Nazareth), where recent Jewish arrivals have built a modern community. The *intifada* strengthened many Nazarene Arabs' sense of Palestinian identity, but these Israeli citizens avoid too much political activity for fear of endangering their status.

Obtain a map of Nazareth from a GTIO office in another city before braving the city. Most of the its winding streets have only numbers for names, but even that isn't helpful since there aren't any signs. In this sloped labyrinth, your navigational aids will be towers and domes. When you get lost in the market, just keep walking downhill and you'll eventually come to **Paul VI Street,** which winds uphill from the bus station to Mary's Well and intersects **Casa Nova Street.**

Nazareth's Christian community rolls up the sidewalks on Sundays, but most establishments are open on *Shabbat.*

Government Tourist Information Office (GTIO): Casa Nova St. (tel. 573 003 or 570 555), near intersection with Paul VI St. Helpful staff answers questions and retrieves computer information. Open Mon.-Fri. 8:30am-5pm, Sat. 8:30am-2pm.

Currency Exchange: Bank Ha-Poalim, Paul VI St. (tel. 570 923), to the right of the Mashbir department store. **Bank Leumi,** on Paul VI St. (tel. 570 282), just north of Casa Nova. Both open Mon.-Tues. and Thurs. 8:30am-12:30pm and 4-6pm, Sun. and Wed. 8:30am-12:30pm, Fri. 8:30am-noon.

Central Post Office (tel. 554 019 or 555 188): Go north on Paul VI St. to Mary's Well, then two blocks west (uphill and to the left). **Poste Restante** at far right window. **International calls** available. Open Mon.-Tues. and Thurs.-Fri. 8am-12:30pm and 3:30-6pm, Wed. 8am-1:30pm, Sat. 8am-noon. **Telephone code:** 06.

Buses (info. tel. (04) 54 95 55): Intercity buses stop along a stretch of Paul VI St. near Bank Ha-Poalim, a gas station, and the Basilica. Egged information on Paul VI St. across from the bank (open daily about 6am-6:30pm). Bus #431 from Haifa (every 20-60min., 30-35min., NIS10.50) continues to Tiberias (30min., NIS10). Bus #355, 357, 823, and 824 run to Afula (every 20min., 20min., NIS5), and #823 and 824 to Tel Aviv (1½hr., NIS18). **Baggage storage** is not available at the bus station; try the taxi stand north of the GTIO, near the Muzzawi souvenir stand. Open Mon.-Thurs. and Sat. 8:30am-6pm, Fri. 8:30am-2pm. NIS3 per piece.

Taxis: Ma'ayan, Paul VI St. (tel. 555 105), **Abu Elassel** (tel. 554 745), **Galil** (tel. 555 536), **Diana** (tel. 555 554), and **Saiegh** (tel. 571 176). **Sherut** (tel. 571 140) on side street off Paul VI near bus station. Haifa and Tiberias NIS11, Tel Aviv NIS18.

Car Rental: Europcar (tel. 554 129), **Avis** (tel. 556 118), and **Hertz** (tel. 575 313). Must be 21 years old.

Pharmacy: Farah Pharmacy (tel. 554 018), next to Egged info. Open Mon.-Tues. and Thurs.-Fri. 8:30am-1:30pm and 3:30-7pm, Wed. and Sat. 8am-2pm.

Hospitals: Nazareth Hospital (tel. 571 501 or 502), **Holy Family Hospital** (tel. 574 535).

First Aid: Magen David Adom (tel. 101).

Police: Tel. 100 or 574 444.

ACCOMMODATIONS AND FOOD

Inexpensive beds are offered by several Christian hospices. Unfortunately, because sisters from all over the world are frequently here on retreat, you may have to scramble. A pristine dormitory with a beautiful courtyard and superb facilities is run by the **Sisters of Nazareth,** P.O. Box 274 (tel. 554 304), near the basilica. Walk up Casa

Nova St. and take a left after the Casa Nova Hospice; it will be on the right. The entrance is through a small beige doorway, just past the faded pink archway. (Kitchen, dining room, and living room. Check-in 4pm, but you can leave your pack if you arrive earlier. Flexible 10am check-out. Curfew 9pm. Dorm beds NIS18. Private rooms from US$21 per person.) The francophone **Pères de Betharram** (tel. 570 046) also run a pleasant hospice in the Eilout neighborhood. Walk past the Sisters of Nazareth, up the stairs of the Christ Church, and turn left on to the road. Walk through a cemetery and then turn right up the street. Pères is on the left, not facing the street. Enter through the small side door. (Bed and breakfast US$20. Private single US$23.) The **Casa Nova Hospice** (tel. 571 367; fax 579 630), across from the Basilica on Casa Nova St., is the deluxe option and almost always filled with Italian pilgrim groups. (Check-in 2pm. Check-out 10am. Curfew 11pm. Doubles and triples US$21 per person. Private singles US$30. Breakfast and one meal included. 5% service charge.) The **Galilee Hotel,** 6 Paul VI St. (tel. 571 311; fax 556 627), a 10-minute walk south of the bus station, has private rooms with A/C and showers. (Check-in 2pm. Check-out noon. Singles NIS174. Doubles NIS279. Triples NIS293. Breakfast included. Call ahead.)

Falafel stands freckle Paul VI St., and cafés specializing in sweet Middle Eastern desserts are scattered throughout the city. Try the crowded **Mahroum's Café** on Casa Nova St. for fresh pastries (NIS25 per kg or NIS 2-3 per piece); look for the yellow triple-arched awning and bright lights. There are plenty of small **grocery and produce** markets on Paul VI St. where the buses stop. The **Astoria Restaurant** (tel. 573 497) at the intersection of Paul VI St. and Casa Nova St. serves Middle Eastern cuisine (hummus NIS8, *shawerma* NIS8, chicken dishes NIS20; open daily 6am-midnight). **Al-Amal Restaurant,** near the corner of Casa Nova and Paul VI St., with a green-and-white sign and white arch doors, serves similar fare at similar prices (open daily 6am-9pm). Cleanliness and air-conditioning distinguish the **Aljeneenah Restaurant** (tel. 554 022), just down the street from St. Gabriel Church and the post office (salads NI10, meat dishes NIS30; open daily 6am-midnight).

SIGHTS

Nazareth is synonymous with churches, and none is more prominent than the **Basilica of the Annunciation,** dominating downtown with its great faceted lantern/tower. Completed in 1969, the basilica sits over the site believed to be Mary's home, where the archangel Gabriel heralded the birth of Jesus. Beyond the huge bronze doors depicting the life of Jesus, the modern basilica merges impressively with ancient ruins. On the ground floor, services take place before the Grotto of the Annunciation, on the remains of churches dating back to 356 CE. On the second floor, its walls lined with a series of international artistic interpretations of the Annunciation, an enormous balcony overlooks the biblical site below. The excavations of the ancient town of Nazareth lie in a garden underneath the plaza, accessible from the upper floor of the church. Ask one of the Franciscan monks to show you around. To get to the Basilica, walk north from the GTIO; it's on your right. (Open Mon.-Sat. 8:30-11:45am and 2-5:30pm, Sun. and feasts 2-5:30pm; winter, Mon.-Sat. 9-11:45am and 2-4:30pm, Sun. and feasts 2-4:30pm. Modest dress required; men in shorts are not permitted into the Basilica.)

Across the plaza stands **St. Joseph's Church,** wherein lies the cave thought to be Joseph's house. The present structure, built in 1914, incorporates remnants of a Byzantine church. Inside, stairs descend to caves that once stored grain and oil. Although this is usually referred to as **Joseph's workshop,** evidence suggests that these caves have been used since the late Stone Age. The **Greek-Catholic Synagogue Church** in the center of the Arab market is the site of the synagogue where Jesus is believed to have preached as a young man. To get there, enter the *souq* from Casa Nova St., bear left at the first fork, then take the first right. The entrance will be on your right, at the yellow gate. Climb the stairs on the right for a view of Nazareth's rooftops. (Closed indefinitely in summer 1994.) Follow Paul VI St. uphill from the buses to a water faucet at an ugly traffic intersection-park. Welcome to

Mary's Well, reputedly still functioning. Many believe that the well's water miraculously heals; pity it can't heal its surroundings. Veer left and continue uphill from the well to arrive at the **Orthodox Church of the Archangel Gabriel,** standing over the town's original water source. The original church was erected in 356 CE over the spring where Mary drew water and where the Greek Orthodox believe Gabriel appeared to Mary. The present church, built in 1750, has elaborate Byzantine-style paintings and decorations. Ancient tiles adorn the entrance in the well area. To reach a **Maronite Church** dating from 1770, follow the road past the Greek-Catholic Synagogue Church, take the first left, and follow the signs. (Closed in summer 1994.) The **Mensa Christi Church,** next door on Al Batris Sq., marks the place where Jesus shared a meal with his disciples after the Resurrection. The building surrounds a 10 ft. by 12 ft. piece of soft limestone, thought to have served as the table *(mensa)*. The church is unmarked; look for colorful murals on the surrounding walls. It was closed in summer 1994, but you can still see its ugly exterior.

For a terrific view of the Galilean hilltops, take bus #13 to the **Salesian Church** atop the natural amphitheater; or, for a work-out, climb the 250-plus stairs through the village to the top. The cool, majestic sanctuary is worth the hike. (All churches in Nazareth claim to be open 8:30-11:45am and 2-5:45pm; winter 9-11:45am and 2-4:45pm; but many close in the afternoon. Sun. mornings are reserved for services. Modest dress required at all times.)

Nazareth's lively **souq** (open Mon.-Tues. and Thurs.-Fri. 9am-5pm, Wed. and Sat. 9am-2pm), best reached via Casa Nova St., is the place to go for olive wood camels and Bart Simpson underwear. The market area is best avoided at night.

■ NEAR NAZARETH

Mount Tabor (Har Tavor in Hebrew), supposedly the sight of Christ's Transfiguration, is 588m high and located 33km east of Nazareth. Its administration is shared by Franciscan and Greek Orthodox monks. The **Basilica of the Transfiguration,** built in 1924, sits atop a 6th-century CE Byzantine church marking the spot where Jesus spoke with Elijah and Moses and was transfigured in the presence of apostles Peter, James, and John (Luke 9:28-36). Nearby, the **Church of Elijah** is built atop the **Cave of Melchizedek,** which can be entered from the outside through a small iron door. The limestone fortification, once an Arab fortress called **Al Adil,** dates from 1211. Mt. Tabor is also the site where the prophetess Deborah led the Israelites to victory over Sisera's army (Judges 4-5). (Open 8am-noon and 2:30-6pm; Oct.-March 8am-noon and 2-5pm. No shorts allowed.) Take bus #357 from the Egged information office (daily 6, 6:45am, 12:45, and 2:45pm, returns 45min. later; 40min.; NIS10.50). Finding a *sherut* to Nazareth from the mountain is difficult if not impossible; a driver might agree to take you to Afula for NIS5. Bus #823 and 824 leave Afula for Nazareth Illit (every 45-60min., 20min., NIS6). From the base of the mountain, it's a steep 3km walk up a long and winding road. Inquire at the GTIO about tours to Mt. Tabor. If there is space, taxis taking Nazareth-based tour groups may drive an individual traveler for US$6 round-trip.

Kafr Kanna, a village to the north of Nazareth, is said to be the site of Jesus' miraculous transformation of water into wine at the wedding feast (John 2:1-11). A Franciscan church (tel. 517 111) was built in 1881 to commemorate the event. (Open Mon.-Fri. 8:30-11:45am and 2-5:45pm, Sun. and feasts 2-5:45pm.) Take bus #22 from Mary's Well in Nazareth to Kafr Kanna (every 30-45 min.) or #431 from the central bus station to Tiberias (every 20-30min., NIS4.50) and ask to be let off at Kafr Kanna.

About 6.5km northwest of Nazareth, excavations at **Zippori** (Sepphons) are uncovering a rich legacy from the Judeo-Christian, Roman and Byzantine periods. The town was the seat of the Sanhedrin in the 3rd century CE as well as one of the places where Rabbi Yehuda Ha-Nassi gathered the most learned rabbinic scholars to compile the Mishnah. Extensive finds include the remains of a 4000-seat Roman amphitheater, exquisite mosaics, a crusader fortress, and a synagogue, one of about 18 mentioned in contemporary sources. (Site tel. 568 372. Open daily 8am-7pm;

winter 8am-4pm.) Direct buses pose a scheduling problem: #16 leaves Nazareth daily at 1:10pm with no return. Frequent buses (#343) do pass the junction about 3km south of the site. Inquire at the GTIO about *sherut* taxis to the site.

FROM AFULA TO BEIT SHE'AN

Along the road from Afula to Beit She'an are several sites of natural and historical interest. Bus #412 and 415 travel the road between these two cities. To get to Afula from Nazareth take bus #355, 357, 823, or 824 (every hr., 20min., NIS5).

Three kilometers down the road from Afula and 1km off it is **Ma'ayan Harod Youth Hostel (HI)** (tel. 531 660). Bus #35 from Afula (11:45am and 6:15pm) will take you directly to the hostel; bus #402, 405, and 412 (not express) bring you to the road leading to the site; from there it is a 1km walk, marked with orange signs. The hostel facilities are adequate, with A/C; and the well-stocked kiosk has long hours. The office has information on sights and discounts. This is where Gideon, guided by the prophetess Deborah, defeated the Midianites (Judges 7). Sleep inspired. The small cave in the garden contains the grave of a Midianite leader (Check-out 10am. Dorm beds (4-7 per room) NIS73-77. Painfully pricey doubles NIS180. Nonmembers NIS3 extra. Breakfast and dinner included. Call ahead July-Aug.) The **Ma'ayan Harod National Park** features a large, attractive swimming pool. (Open daily 9am-5pm. Admission NIS15.)

You can walk the 10km from the Ma'ayan Harod hostel (ask for a map) to **Belvoir** (tel. 587 000), or take a Tiberias-Beit She'an bus (#434, 961, 963, 964; NIS8.50), which will let you off at the turn-off to this 12th-century Crusader fort. From there, it's a very steep 7km uphill walk—definitely a hat-and-water hike. The fort affords marvelous views over the entire Jordan Valley and, on a clear day, the Galilee. The castle (Kokhav Ha-Yarden, or Star of the Jordan) presides 600m above the Jordan River, overlooking the medieval trade route from Egypt to Damascus. The area was the scene of several skirmishes between Crusaders and Muslims until, after the Battle of Hattin in 1187, the Muslims besieged the castle. After 18 months, the knights finally surrendered; in acknowledgment of their bravery they were permitted to depart unharmed. During the early 13th century, the castle was partially destroyed by the sultan of Damascus to preempt a Crusader re-occupation of the stronghold. The interior, constructed with massive 3m-thick blocks of black stone and surrounded by a deep moat, is still breathtaking. (Open Sat.-Thurs. 8am-5pm, Fri. 8am-4pm; closes 1hr. earlier in winter. Admission NIS8.50, students NIS6.50.)

Farther southeast on the eastern side of the road is **Kibbutz Ein Harod** and its **Beit Sturman Museum of Natural History** (tel. 531 605). It has a garden with pillars and a sarcophagus. (Open Sun.-Thurs. 8am-3pm, Sat. 10am-2pm. Admission NIS10, students NIS7.) Take bus #35, 412, 415, 417, or 434 from Afula (NIS4.50).

Closer to Beit She'an, within Kibbutz Hefziba, shines the 6th-century CE synagogue of **Beit Alpha** (tel. 531 400), including a magnificently preserved mosaic of a zodiac wheel surrounding the sun god Helios, reflecting the Hellenic influence on the area. Take bus #412, 415, or 417 from either Afula (NIS5.50) or Beit She'an (NIS3.50). (Open Sat.-Thurs. 8am-5pm, Fri. 8am-4pm. Admission NIS5.50, students NIS4.10.) Do not be misled by the sign for *Kibbutz* Beit Alpha (1km closer to Beit She'an), named after the ancient site.

Take an afternoon excursion to the lovely park **Gan Ha-Shlosha** (tel. 586 219), also known as the **Sahne**, 1km west of Beit Alpha. It made a splash even in Roman times with its waterfalls and crystal-clear swimming holes, surprisingly cool in summer and pleasantly warm in winter. Brave souls leap into the pools from the rocky ridges above. The park is overcrowded on weekends; be wary of theft. Bus #412 and 415 from Afula (NIS5.50) or Beit She'an (NIS3.50) go to the Sahne. (Open Sun.-Thurs. and Sat. 7:30am-6pm, Fri. 7:30am-5pm. Admission NIS18.) A 10-minute walk along the road behind the park leads to the **Nir David Museum of Mediterranean Archaeology** (tel. 488 045), a collection of Hellenistic and Islamic art and pottery gathered from a local Canaanite temple, an Israelite community, and a Roman weavers' colony. (Open Sun.-Fri. 8am-1pm. Park admission required to see the museum.)

Beit She'an is a Sephardi development town; its most famous son is former foreign minister David Levy. Of more interest to tourists is one of the finest archaeological sites in the country, a vast complex of mostly Roman and Byzantine ruins. Excavations on **Tel al-Husn,** the main archaeological mound, have already revealed some 20 layers of settlements dating back as far as the fifth millennium BCE. Of particular interest is the **Roman theater,** one of the largest extant Roman constructions in Israel. Built in 200 CE by Emperor Septimius Severus, the theater accommodated 7000 spectators in its three tiers of semi-circular seating.

The remains of other grand public structures branching off from the theater include colonnaded Roman streets, a Byzantine bathhouse, and a Roman temple thought to honor Dionysus. To gain a sense of the whole, climb to the top of the *tel.* To the southeast are the remnants of a 2nd-century CE **Roman amphitheater** used for gladiatorial spectacles and a 4th-century CE Byzantine residential quarter. North of the *tel* is the **Monastery of the Noble Lady Maria,** founded in 567 CE and abandoned after the Persian invasion of 614. The monastery has a great mosaic depicting the months of the year. A much earlier period of Egyptian control has also left the ruins of the **Ashtaroth Temple,** built by Ramses III. To get to the site from the Beit She'an bus stop, turn left at the main street, right after Bank Leumi, and then follow the paved road. (Tel. 587 189. Open Sat.-Thurs. 8am-5pm, Fri. 8am-4pm; closes 1hr. earlier in winter. Admission NIS11, students NIS8.20.) Bus #412 and 415 leave Afula for Beit She'an (every 20min., 35min., NIS7). From Tiberias, take #434, 961, 963, or 964 (50min., NIS8.50).

■ ■ ■ TIBERIAS טבריה طبرية

Since Israeli troops filched the Golan Heights in 1967, the Sea of Galilee has become a splashing ground rivaling the Mediterranean and the Red Sea in popularity. Every year, backpackers and Israeli vacationers alike strap on inflatable yellow floaties and dive in, raising prices and the water level, but also creating lodging options galore and a lively weekend nightlife. On summer evenings, fish restaurants along the promenade provide an expansive view of the lake. Later, music pours out of pubs and a young crowd drinks until the sun comes up over the leafy promenade and *midraḥov.* Tiberias (Tverya in Hebrew) is the only major city on the Galilee and an ideal touring base for the area and the Golan Heights, though during July and August the city can be hot and soggily humid due to its location 200m below sea level.

For a resort, Tiberias has a surprisingly noble history. Built in 18 CE by Herod Antipas, King of Judea and tetrarch of Galilee, the city was named for the Roman Emperor Tiberius. The city took on its namesake's most salient trait—hedonism. Although the Romans attempted to bring in settlers, most Jews, including Jesus, refused to enter the town because it was built on the site of older Jewish graves. But after Rabbi Shimon Bar-Yoḥai declared the town ritually pure in the 2nd century CE, Tiberias became the seat of the Sanhedrin and, in the 3rd century, the religious center of the Jews. It was here that the *Talmud* was edited and vowels added to the Hebrew alphabet and sacred texts.

The lucky city was treated to Persian (614) and Arab (636) conquests, during which Jews emigrated to Babylon or Jerusalem. After Crusader Prince Tancred and the Kings of Jerusalem took over and ruled from 1099 to 1187, Tiberias was destroyed by Baybars in 1247 and not occupied again until the beginning of Ottoman rule in 1517. In 1561 a benevolent Sultan Suleiman the Magnificent handed the city over to a Jewish refugee from Spain, who with his aunt set up a Jewish state under Ottoman sovereignty. Their unsuccessful city fell into decay until Druze Prince Taher al-Omar rebuilt the city and its citadel in 1738 and settled Jews in it. Devastated in 1837 by an earthquake that rocked all of northern Palestine, Tiberias was rebuilt, and in 1940 had a population of 12,000, half Arabs, half Jews. Since the 1948 War, the city's population has doubled, but it's all Jewish.

ORIENTATION AND PRACTICAL INFORMATION

Tiberias has three tiers: the **old city** by the water, the **new city** (Kiryat Shmuel) up the hill (bus #1 or 5 from the bus station), and **uptown** at the top of the hill (bus #7, 8, or 9 from the station). Though the ruins in the old city don't rival counterparts in Akko or Jerusalem, you probably won't leave this part of town unless you just *need* to see a movie. **Ha-Galil St.** (the main thoroughfare in Tiberias) and **Ha-Banim St.** run parallel to the water; to the north, **Ha-Yarden St.** runs perpendicular. The smaller **Ha-Yarkon** and **Ha-Kishon St.** intersect Ha-Galil and Ha-Banom St. to the south. The *midraḥov* runs down from Ha-Galil to meet the lakeside promenade.

Government Tourist Information Office (GTIO) (tel. 720 992 or 722 089; fax 725 062): in the Archaeological Park on Ha-Banim St., next to the Jordan River and Moriah-Plaza hotels. Open Sun.-Thurs. 8:30am-5pm, Fri. 8:30am-2pm.

Currency Exchange: Bank Ha-Poalim, Ha-Banim St. (tel. 798 411), between Ha-Yarden and Ha-Yarkon St. **Bank Leumi** (tel. 727 111), at the corner of Ha-Yarden and Ha-Banim St. Both open Sun., Tues., and Thurs. 8:30am-12:30pm and 4-6pm, Mon. and Wed. 8:30am-12:30pm, Fri. and holiday eves 8:30am-noon.

Central Post Office: Ha-Yarden St. (tel. 720 019). Take a right onto Ha-Yarden St. as you exit the bus station and walk away from the mountains; the office is on the left just before Al Hadef St. **Poste Restante** available. Open Sun.-Tues. and Thurs. 8am-12:30pm and 3:30-6pm, Wed. 8am-1:30pm, Fri. 8am-12:30pm. Branch office in **Kiryat Shmuel** (tel. 720 894), on corner of Bialik and Ehrlich St.

Central Bus Station: Ha-Yarden St. (tel. 791 080 or 081; info. (04) 549 555). Bus #961, 963, and 964 (all direct) to Jerusalem (every 30-45min. 6am-6pm, last bus on Fri. 2:30pm, 2½hr., NIS25); bus #830 and 836 (both direct) and #832, 840, and 841 to Tel Aviv (at least every hr. 5:30am-8:30pm, last direct bus on Fri. 3pm, 2hr., NIS20.50); #430 (direct) and 431 to Haifa (every 20-45min. 5:30am-8pm, last direct bus on Fri. 4pm, 1hr., NIS14).

Taxis: *Sherut* and private cabs wait in front of the bus station (last car on Fri. 3:30pm). **Tiberius Taxi** (tel. 720 444). **Aviv** (tel. 720 098), on Al Hadef St. next to the gas station around the corner from the Ha-Yarden post office, has regular service to Tel Aviv only (NIS19). No service on *Shabbat.* Call the night before.

Rental Cars: Reliable (tel. 723 464 or 724 112; standard trans. only), **Autorent** (automatics), **Eldan** (tel. 720 385 or 791 822), **Hertz** (tel. 723 939), and **Budget** (tel. 720 864 or 723 496). All on Ha-Banim St. Get cars here for trips to the Golan.

Bicycles: Hostel Aviv is well-stocked. Also at Naḥum Hostel, Schwitzer Hostel, and Lake Castle Hostel (all NIS20 for regular, NIS30 for 18-speed mountain bike, per day). See Accommodations, below, for addresses.

Laundry: Panorama (tel. 724 324), on Ha-Galil, south of Ha-Kishon St. and across from city wall remnants. Wash, dry, and fold NIS30 for 7kg. Open Sun.-Mon. and Wed.-Thurs. 8am-6pm, Tues. and Fri. 8am-2pm.

Pharmacy: Schwartz Pharmacy (tel. 720 994), on Ha-Galil St. opposite the park. Open Sun.-Thurs. 8am-1pm and 4-7pm, Fri. 8am-1:30pm. **Center Pharmacy** (tel. 790 613), corner of Bibas and Ha-Galil. Open Sun.-Thurs. 8am-8pm, Fri. 8am-3pm.

English Bookstores: Steimatzky, 3 Ha-Galil St. (tel. 791 288). Open Sun.-Thurs. 8am-1pm and 4:30-7:30pm (winter 4-7pm), Tues. 8am-1pm, Fri. 8am-2pm.

Emergencies: Tel. 101. **First Aid (Magen David Adom):** Tel. 790 111, corner of Ha-Banim and Ha-Kishon St. Open 24 hrs. **Fire:** Tel. 102.

Police: Tel. 100 or 792 444.

ACCOMMODATIONS

For its size, Tiberias has more options than a menu at a sushi bar. Competition is fierce; you'll feel like the Beatles bombarded by adoring fans when you arrive at the bus station. Prices rise between July and September, and reservations are recommended. There are also mobs during the Jewish holidays of Pesaḥ, Rosh Ha-Shana, and Sukkot. Hostels will arrange Golan tours if you ask.

Meyouhas Hostel (HI), Ha-Yarden St. (tel. 721 775 or 790 350; fax 720 372), at the corner of Ha-Galil and Ha-Yarden. Centrally located 2½ blocks from bus station.

A/C (50¢ extra per night Apr.-Sept.), clean, and comfortable, with wood furniture, TV room, balcony. Reception open 7-9am and 4pm-midnight. Curfew 1am; Oct.-March midnight. Dorm beds (2-6 per room) US$10. Nonmembers US$11.50. Breakfast included. Lockers NIS3. Make reservations; HI members have priority.

Maman Hostel, Atzmon St. (tel. 792 986). From Ha-Yarden St., turn south on Ha-Galil, then bear right on Tavor St. and turn right at the first intersection, where a red-and-white sign directs you to the hostel. Easygoing atmosphere, clean baths, and A/C. There's a small unheated pool in back and a popular Moroccan restaurant and bar in front. Kitchen available. Reception open 7am-midnight. No curfew (key given). Dorm beds (4-8 per room) NIS20; low season NIS15. Private rooms with kitchen and bath NIS80; low season NIS60. Breakfast NIS10-15.

Naḥum Hostel, Tavor St. (tel. 721 505). From Ha-Yarden St. turn south on Ha-Galil, then turn right on Tavor St. A 5-min. walk from bus station. Relaxed, with clean rooms, most with private bath and A/C (ask the manager to turn A/C on). Downstairs rooms a bit dim, but have kitchenette and private bath. Rooftop bar is lively at night with MTV and breezy views of the Galilee. Reception open 8am-1am. Dorm beds (6-7 per room) US$6. Doubles US$25. Breakfast US$3.

Hostel Aviv, Ha-Galil St. (tel./fax 723 510), one block south of intersection of Ha-Galil and Ha-Banim St. All rooms in this quiet, comfortable hostel have private baths and A/C; many have balconies. Kitchen, TV room, large dining room. Reception open 24 hrs. Check-out noon. Dorm beds (4-7 per room) NIS25; low season NIS20. Singles NIS60. Doubles NIS80-100. TV US$5. Breakfast NIS10.

Lake Castle Hostel (tel. 721 175), next to Moriah Plaza Hotel, on the promenade. View of sea from terrace, and a small beach area for guests. The **Petra Pub** downstairs makes the place noisy or lively, you decide. Rooms have A/C, some have private bath, several overlook the water. Kitchen. Reception open 24 hrs. Check-out 10am. Dorm beds NIS20; low season NIS15. Singles NIS50. Doubles NIS60. Breakfast NIS10. Lockers NIS5. Free safe. Laundry NIS4. Call ahead May-June.

Hostel Adler, Ha-Galil (tel. 720 031). Central location. TV room, bar, kitchen. Reception open 24 hrs. Check-out 11am. Dorm beds (3-4 per room) with ceiling fans NIS20, with A/C NIS25-28. Doubles with A/C and bath NIS80. Breakfast NIS20.

Adina's Hostel, 15 Ha-Shiloaḥ St. (tel. 722 507). Head south from the bus station. Pleasant and quiet, run by Adina and family. A/C, kitchen, TV lounge. Reception open 24 hrs. Check-out 10am. Dorm beds (winter only) NIS20. Doubles NIS80; Sept.-June NIS60. Private quints (great for families) NIS150. Prices rise in Aug.

Church of Scotland Hospice, P.O. Box 104, Tiberias 14100 (tel. 721 165 or 723 769; fax 790 145). Gray building at corner of Ha-Yarden St. and Gedud Barak Rd., next to HI hostel. Many spectacular clean rooms with fridge and blankets. Private beach, garden café. Reception open 7:30am-10pm. Check-in 1:30pm. Check-out 9:30am. Bed and breakfast US$25, with A/C US$30. Reserve ahead.

Toledo Hotel, Bibas St. (tel. 721 649). From bus station, go 1 block south on Ha-Shiloa and turn right onto Bibas. Hotel is 1 block down on the right. Clean and sunny rooms with A/C, bath, phone. Lobby lounge has TV. Reception open 24 hrs. Check-out noon. Singles US$25. Doubles US$35. Triples US$50. Quads US$60. Breakfast US$6. Wash and dry US$7. Reservations recommended.

Camping is a good way to escape the city heat. Start at the stand run by the MTIO and the SPNI (tel. 752 056) at Tzemaḥ on the southern tip of the lake. (Open summer 9am-5pm; take bus #18, 21, 22, or 24.) Their map (NIS10) shows the 25 campsites on the lake (NIS25 per car; free for car-less campers). Interspersed among the private beaches are stretches of shoreline which allow independent camping. You provide the food, water, and insect repellent, and the government kicks in with jiffy johns and trash bins at a few of these points. Take the Ein Gev bus from Tiberias and get off wherever you see a site, or walk south along the coast past the Tiberias hot springs. Be wary of theft.

TIBERIAS

FOOD

The **shuk,** in a square block starting at Bibas St. and going south, sells cheap, high-quality produce every day except *Shabbat.* Pick up a light meal at one of Tiberias' innumerable falafel spreads on Ha-Yarden St., running from Ha-Banim St. toward the bus station. Grill restaurants near the *midraḥov* serve *shishlik* with salad and pita for about NIS10, and waterfront seafood restaurants offer idyllic settings unless teenage jet skiers and flotillas of plastic bottles disturb the waters. A tasty dinner of St. Peter's fish, unique to the Sea of Galilee, costs about NIS31. Or try eateries on Ha-Galil and Ha-Banim St. and the squares in between. Amazingly inexpensive are two Ha-Galil St. stops: **Elfassi,** near Ha-Kishon St., where a barbecued feast goes for NIS7, and the Chinese take-out farther south. There is a **Co-op supermarket** in the Great Mosque Plaza across from Meyouhas Hostel. (Open Sun.-Fri. 7am-8pm.)

> **Maman Restaurant,** Ha-Galil St. (tel. 721 126), corner of Bibas St. Crammed with Israelis. Middle Eastern food, A/C. Hummus or *taḥina* NIS6, *schnitzel, shishlik,* or *kabab* with chips and salad NIS16. Open Sun.-Fri. 11am-11pm. Kosher.
>
> **Guy Restaurant,** Ha-Galil St. (tel. 723 036), south of Ha-Kishon. Cool, quiet Moroccan kitchen. Stuffed vegetables (NIS7) and various salads. House specialties include an assorted eggplant dish (7 types) and fried meat-filled "cigars" (NIS3). Open Sun.-Thurs. noon-midnight, Fri noon-6pm. Kosher.
>
> **Avi's Restaurant,** Ha-Kishon St. (tel. 791 797) between Ha-Galil and Ha-Banim St., opposite Jordan River Hotel. Woody decor, friendly vibes, tasty food. Pizza or *canneloni* NIS20, *taḥina* NIS5, hummus NIS8. Open daily 11:30am-1am.
>
> **Karamba Vegetarian Restaurant** (tel. 791 546), on the promenade. Take the alley leading to the waterfront from the Meyouhas hostel. Avoid the tables outside, where an ant colony makes its home. Live music, disco, or karaoke on Thursdays. Exotic ambience. Pizza margherita NIS16, artichoke house-style NIS15.
>
> **Dolphin Grill,** corner of Ha-Banim St. and the *midraḥov. Shishlik, kabab, schnitzel* with 5 salads and "cheeps" NIS20. Outdoor tables are prime for people-watching.
>
> **Kohinoor** (tel. 724 939), at old wharf; go south on the promenade. Scrumptious Indian food, in A/C and purple splendor. Dinners NIS30ish, appetizers NIS11. Tandoor dishes with date, mango, or mint sauce are a specialty. Nightly Indian dancing show. Open Sun.-Thurs. 12:30-3:30pm and 6:30pm-12:30am. Kosher.
>
> **Eat As Much As You Can,** Ha-Banim St. across from the *midraḥov,* between Ha-Yarden and Ha-Yarkon. Authentic St. Peter's fish on a budget. Unlimited delicious (though small) fresh fishies with salad and chips NIS20. Open 12:30pm-1am.
>
> **Makom Baḥutz** (tel. 722 668), around the corner of north end of promenade. Frozen yogurt with fresh fruit, etc. mixed in (NIS6.50 for 3 toppings) and outdoor screenings of Israeli comedy or music videos in the evening.

SIGHTS

The **old city,** shaken by earthquakes and conquerors, is now merely a few wall fragments littering the modern town. To get a sense of its former glory, join a free walking tour with archaeologist Edna Amos (Sat. 10am; leaves from Moriah Plaza lobby).

The **Tomb of Moses Maimonides,** on Y. Ben-Zakkai St., commemorates the controversial rabbi and physician who attempted to synthesize Aristotelian and Arab philosophy and the study of Judaism. According to legend, an unguided camel carried his coffin to Tiberias. To reach the tomb, get in good with an unguided camel, or take Ha-Yarden St. east (toward the water) and turn left on Y. Ben-Zakkai St. The tomb is two blocks up, on the right. You'll see a red fence and black pillars; the white half-cylinder with Hebrew writing is the actual tomb. Ask for the tomb of "Rambam," the rabbi's Hebrew acronym (Rabbi Moshe Ben-Maimon). While you're at it, yawn some more at the **Tomb of Rabbi Akiva,** on the hillside above the Galilee (take bus #4 and ask for directions), and that of **Rabbi Meir Ba'al Ha-Nes,** student of Rabbi Akiva (on the hillside above the hot springs). (Tombs open Sun.-Thurs. 8am-7pm, Fri. 8am-2pm. Modest dress required.)

On the promenade next to the Caesar Hotel stands the **Franciscan Terra Sancta Church** (tel. 720 516), built in the 12th century to commemorate St. Peter's role in the growth of Christianity; it is thus known as St. Peter's. The apse behind the altar is arched like the bow of a boat, in honor of his original career as a fisherman. In the courtyard is a statue of the Virgin Mary created by Polish troops quartered in the church from 1942 to 1945. (Open daily 8-11:45am and 2-5pm.)

Farther south is a blue-and-red marina, home to shops and the **Galilee Experience** (tel. 723 620). There's a 36-minute must-see **film** on the past 4000 years in the Galilee. It emphasizes the life of Jesus and the formation of the Israeli state. An attached **bookstore** sells Bibles, books about Israel, Jewish ritual objects, Communion grape juice, and Easter and bar mitzvah cards. At the rear of the bookstore, a small **café** has a view of the coastline. (Film shown every hr. Sun.-Thurs. 9am-10pm, Fri. 9am-5pm, Sat. 6-10pm. Admission US$6. Many of the screenings are in English.)

Take your book and relax at the world's earliest known **hot mineral springs.** One legend maintains that the springs were formed in the Great Flood when the earth's insides boiled. Another holds that the water is heated by demons under the orders of King Solomon, who made the demons deaf so that they would never hear of his death and desert their duties. They still haven't heard. You, too, can lie in the slimy but incredibly relaxing pools, cleansing body and wallet (NIS35, Sat. NIS38). Price includes pools, sauna, jacuzzi, and beach. A massage is NIS65 (Sat. NIS70), and a private mineral bath NIS55 (Sat. NIS60). The springs are 3km south of town on the coastal road; walk, or catch bus #5 (every 20min.) from the front of the central bus station or from Ha-Galil St. The older building, **Tiberias Hot Springs,** has single-sex baths with very hot waters. (Open Sun.-Fri. 7am-2pm.) The newer building, **Tiberias Hot Springs Spa** (tel. 791 967), serves those seeking less steamy rejuvenation. The pool is outside, near the beach. (Open Sun.-Thurs. 8am-8pm, Fri. 8am-6pm.)

The small **Lehmann museum** displays the history of hot springs in Tiberias. Walk out the museum's back door to reach the ruins of the **Ḥammat Synagogues,** six ancient buildings constructed one on top of the other. The jewel of the excavations is a mosaic floor that was part of three separate synagogues. The four upper synagogues were used in the 6th to 8th centuries CE. (Museum and synagogues open Sun.-Thurs. 8am-5pm, Fri. 8am-4pm. Admission NIS5.50, students NIS4.)

ENTERTAINMENT

Many **beaches** on the Galilee (circumference 58km) don't have sand. Those in the city and to the immediate north and south are owned by hotels who charge hefty fees but provide changing rooms, showers, boat rentals, and food. The beaches farther north are located along Gedud Barak Rd., off Ha-Yarden. Bathers, be warned: an alligator, possibly visiting from the nearby alligator farm, was seen swimming in the lake in summers 1993 and 1994. The authorities deny it, but who do you trust?

Try **Lido Kinneret** (tel. 721 538), just off Ha-Yarden St. (admission NIS10, 15min. water-skiing NIS80; open daily 8am-5pm) or, just north, the somewhat dilapidated **Nelson Beach** (NIS10; open 24 hrs.) has 2-person kayaks or 4- to 5-person paddle boats (NIS30 per hr.), water skiing (NIS70 for 15min., discount for group of 4), and, believe it or not, the only speed-boat-drawn inflatable banana on the Galilee (15min. NIS15); there are also rock concerts and camping in the summertime (NIS10). Just north are the meticulously tended **Quiet Beach** (tel. 790 125; NIS10; open 8am-6pm) and **Blue Beach** (tel. 720 105; NIS14, students NIS12; open 8:30am-5:30pm). A 15-minute walk or a short ride on bus #5 to the south of Tiberias, the **Municipal Beach** (tel. 720 709) charges NIS8. Next to it is **Gannei Ḥammat** (tel. 792 890; admission NIS10). Many beaches have kiddie pools. A religious beach on Gedud Barak Rd. (entrance opposite Church of Scotland Hospice) is open to women Sun., Tues., and Thurs., to men Mon., Wed., and Fri. 8am-5pm.

Nightlife in Tiberias centers on the *midraḥov* and promenade area. In summer, street musicians and popcorn and cotton-candy vendors proliferate. As is their wont, Israelis dance on outdoor tables to live rock (Tues.-Wed. and Sat. 10 or 11pm) at **La Pirate Pub,** at the corner of the *midraḥov* and the promenade (0.5L beer NIS15; open daily 5pm-4am). **Big Ben,** toward the promenade end of the *midraḥov,* is less rowdy, with outdoor tables under spot-lit trees. The **Petra Pub** (tel. 721

175), under Lake Castle Hostel at the southern end of the promenade, is also popular, although mostly with tourists. One of the cavern-like rooms becomes a **disco** Wednesdays after 10pm. (Happy hour 8-10pm, open late daily. Maccabee NIS6; disco admission NIS10, free if staying in hostel upstairs.) The bars at the **Maman, Naḥum,** and **Schwitzer** hostels are hip hangouts for backpackers; they serve reasonable drinks (Goldstar NIS5) and usually show videos. At the northern end of the promenade is a bar known locally as **Pub Carlsberg** (guess why) with live music on occasion. (Open Thurs.-Sat. 10pm-4am.) Nearby **Papaya,** with its long bar and excellent music, was the cat's meow in summer 1994.

Slink into those white polyester suits and strappy 5-inch heels for Lido Kinneret Beach and Kinneret Sailing's nightly **disco cruises** (departing 8-11pm depending on number of people amassed; NIS12). Overindulgence has its consequences—spinning rooms and lolling boats can do funny things to the inner ear.

One kilometer south of Tiberias, **Luna Beach** (tel. 790 790) has waterslides (Let's Go!). (Open 9am-5pm. Admission NIS30.) The adjacent **Sironit Beach** (tel. 721 449) does too, but fewer (open daily 9am-5pm; NIS15). Walk or take bus #5 from the central bus station or Ha-Galil St. But the mother of all water parks is **Luna Gal** (tel. 731 750), operated by Moshav Ramot on the eastern shore. The park has bumper boats! slides! pools! waterfalls! an inner tube ride! all that AND an excellent beach! (Open daily 9:30am-midnight, Sat. 9:30am-5pm. Admission NIS39.)

Generation X-ers who have seen *Grease II* just enough times will seek out bowling in the Lev Ha'Ir shopping mall (corner of Ha-Shiloaḥ and Bibas St.). Every night, the **Tiberias Bowling Club** (tel. 724 510) features food, a majestic view of the Kinneret, and a computerized score-keeping Michelle Pfeiffer that kisses the first man to walk in. (Open daily 10am-1am. NIS11 per game per person. Shoe rental NIS2.)

The **Sea of Galilee Festival** brings international folk troupes to Tiberias during the second week of July. Check at the GTIO for information on this and Ein Gev's **Passover Music Festival,** and the August **Tu be'Av Love Fest** in Tzemaḥ, where thousands of teenage Israelis gather for some love, sweat, and Rock 'n' Roll.

■ THE SEA OF GALILEE

Getting Around

All the sights on the Sea of Galilee are in some way, shape, or form accessible by **bus** from Tiberias; but people able to tour by **bicycle** will avoid the hassle of long walks and unlimited bus stop exploration hours. A complete circuit of the lake takes about four hours, plus the time you spend at the sights. Get a mountain bike if possible (try Hostel Aviv, p. 323); the knobby tires will supplement your motocross prowess when insane Israeli drivers force you into a roadside ditch. The **Lido Kinneret Sailing Co.** (tel. 721 538) operates a **ferry** between Lido Beach and Ginnosar (NIS15 one-way or round-trip; no extra charge for bikes).

Princess Di-alikes will find **horseback** an excellent, albeit expensive, way to explore the northern coast of the Galilee. Take bus #459, 541, 841, or 963 from Tiberias and get off at Korazim junction, in front of the guest farm **Vered Ha-Galil.** A half-day guided ride through the Galilean hills down to the sea and then up to the Mount of Beatitudes costs US$40 per person. If you call ahead, owner Yehuda Avni will let you camp for free the night before your ride. Bring a sleeping bag. There's also a bunkhouse where bed and American breakfast cost US$40 for one, US$55 for two. Bring some egg salad sandwiches and Twinkies; the restaurant's expensive. Also offers rentals (1hr. NIS45, 2hr. NIS75, full day NIS210. Bonanza package including afternoon ride, camping, breakfast, and dinner NIS250. For reservations, write to Vered Ha-Galil, Korazim or call 935 785. Several kibbutzim and *moshavim* also offer horseback riding; check at the Tiberias GTIO.

SIGHTS ON THE LAKE

Thirty minutes southeast of Tiberias, the hot baths of **Ḥammat Gader** (Al Himma in Arabic, tel. 751 039) lie in former Syrian territory. In Roman times the town, combined with its other (Jordanian) half on the western side of the Yarmuk River, formed part of the Decapolis. Though the more interesting ruins are in Jordan, Roman ruins here, including large bathing areas and a smaller pool that was reserved for lepers, have been partially reconstructed. At the southwest corner of the complex is the hottest spring in the area at 51°C, so hot the Jews call it *Ma'ayan Ha-Gehinom* (Hell's Pool) and the Arabs *Ain Maqla* (Frying Pool). The hot pool is crowded with families; the leper pool is not. There is also an area for slathering on the black mud that purportedly cures skin ailments.

Hammat Gader, like Orlando, Florida, boasts an **alligator park,** where hundreds of large, somnolent 'gators sun themselves or slog though murky water. Yes, indeed, the first generation was imported from Florida. The reserve now raises its young in a hothouse at the entrance to the ponds. The park also contains the **ruins** of a 5th-century synagogue, just west of the Roman baths and uphill from the picnic area. There's also a modern border station; to the northwest, spanning the Yarmuk River, is a bridge built for the Ottoman railroad. (Open daily 7am-9:30pm. Admission to Hammat Gader complex NIS27, students and children NIS23; Sat. NIS29/25; after 5pm NIS20.) Bus #24 leaves from Tiberias at 8:45 and 10:30am, returning at noon and 3pm (Fri. return at noon and 1pm).

Near the spot where the Jordan River flows out of the Sea of Galilee, about 8km south of Tiberias, north of Hammat Gader, is **Deganya Alef,** the birthplace of Moshe Dayan. Founded by Russians in 1909, it is also Israel's first kibbutz and today the site of a diamond tool factory. Did you ever wonder why every kibbutz and podunk town in Israel must have at least two museums? Ponder some more at nearby **Beit Gordon** (tel. 750 040). One is on Galilee archaeology, the other on natural history. Stuffed animal carcasses galore. (Open Sun.-Thurs. 9am-4pm, Fri. 9am-1pm, Sat. 9:30am-noon. Admission NIS6, students NIS5.) Deganya's frightening uniformity leads easily to misdirection. Take a right after the tennis courts and ambulances and ask for directions. Next to Beit Gordon is an ebullient **SPNI Kinorot Field School** (tel. 752 340; open Sun.-Thurs. 9am-1pm. Fri. 9am-noon). Guides for hire, maps for sale. Get to Deganya by bus #24 to Hammat Gader or bus #23 or 26-29 headed for Beit She'an and the Jordan River Valley.

Karnei Hittim (the Horns of Hittim) is where Salah ad-Din gave the Crusaders their comeuppance in 1187. From this mountain peak, you can see Jordan to the east, the Mediterranean to the west, and Tzfat to the north. Take bus #42 and ask the driver where to get off. The walk to the top of the hill is about 50 minutes, but the view will leave you more breathless than the climb. (Open 8am-5pm.)

The low water level of the Galilee in 1985-86 had one serendipitous benefit—the discovery of an **ancient boat** under a segment of newly exposed lakebed off the beach of Kibbutz Ginnosar, just north of Tiberias. Its wooden frame, which had turned to mush after centuries of marinating in mud, was encased in a fiberglass frame and hauled to shore. The boat, dating from 100 BCE to 100 CE, has been restored to near-pristine condition. It rests at the new Yigal Allon Center in a glass tank filled with water, where it will undergo nine more years of cosmetic repair. (Tel. 722 905. Open Sun.-Thurs. 8:30am-5pm, Fri. 8:30am-1pm, Sat. 10am-5pm. Admission NIS10, students NIS8.) Noting its age, some Christians have dubbed it "the Jesus boat." While it *is* a fishing boat, even of the sort the apostles might have used, archaeologists say it has as much to do with Jesus as the Hare Krishnas, and suspect it was sunk in a great sea battle (described by Josephus) between the Romans and Jews. Next door is green, shady **Ginnosar Beach** (tel. 792 216; open 9am-6pm; NIS15, students NIS10; paddle boats NIS30 per hr., kayaks NIS20). To get here, take bus #459, 541, 841, or 963 from Tiberias to the new Yigal Allon Center.

NEW TESTAMENT SIGHTS

Four of the most significant stories in Christian history are set in the steep hills of the Sea of Galilee's northern coast. According to the New Testament, Jesus walked on the very same waters that today float Israel's favorite inflatable banana (see p. 325).

Migdal, birthplace of Mary Magdalene (an early follower of Jesus), north of Tiberias and halfway to Capernaum, was an important town when the Crusaders built a church here in the 12th century. Today there is an agricultural community, founded in 1910, and a tiny, white-domed shrine.

In **Tabgha,** 2km southwest of Capernaum along the coastal road, the **Church of the Primacy of St. Peter** marks the spot where Jesus made Peter "Shepherd of his People." This is also the site of the miracle of the loaves and fishes. According to the Book of John, Peter led the apostles on a fishing expedition 100m offshore from Tabgha after the Resurrection. A man on shore called to them to throw their nets over the starboard side and assured them of a catch. When the nets hit the water, a swarm of fish swam in. Jumping off the boat and swimming to shore, Peter found the man, whom he now realized was Jesus, preparing a meal for the Twelve. When the others sailed in, Jesus told Peter to, "Feed my lambs. Tend my sheep. Feed my sheep." (John 21:15-17) The Church of the Primacy is built around a rock said to be the table of this feast. The first church at this spot was built in the 4th century, destroyed in 1263, and rebuilt in black basalt by the Franciscans in 1933. On the seaward side of the church are the steps from which Jesus called out his instructions; on the shoreline is a series of six double or heart-shaped column bases built by early Christians and called the "thrones of the Apostles" (tel. 724 767; open 8am-5pm).

Just west of the Church of the Primacy along the northern coast of the sea lies the **Church of the Multiplication of the Loaves and Fishes.** A mosaic inside relates how Jesus fed 5000 pilgrims with five loaves and two small fish (Matthew 15:29-39). A section of the mosaic has been removed, revealing the original 4th-century foundations. Around the right side of the church past the "private" sign and up the stairs is a small **hospice** (tel. 721 061), a tent with mattresses inside (NIS15). (Church open Mon.-Sat. 8:30am-5pm, Sun. 10am-5pm. Modest dress required.)

On the **Mount of Beatitudes,** overlooking sea, field, and town, Jesus gave his Sermon on the Mount (Matthew 5). A church funded by Mussolini (of all people) now stands on the Mount, its octagonal shape recalling Jesus' eight beatitudes. To reach the Mount, take bus #459, 541, or 963 from Tiberias; get off at the second stop after the bus turns uphill away from the lake. From here, a sign points the way to the church, 1km along a side road. (Church open daily 8am-noon and 2:30-5pm. Free. No shorts or bare shoulders.)

From the Mount, walk to the ancient town of **Capernaum** (Kfar Naḥum in Hebrew, Tell Num in Arabic) by following the path down to the coastal road. Continue northeast along the shoreline for 3km and turn at the white signpost. The site is down the road. This is where Jesus healed Simon's mother-in-law and the Roman Centurion's servant (Luke 4:31-37 and 7:1-10). This is also the birthplace of Peter. A modern church arches over the ruins of a 5th-century octagonal church marking the site believed to have held Peter's house. Nearby, the ruins of a synagogue, perched in the middle of the old town, contain Corinthian columns and friezes dating from the 4th century CE. Since Capernaum did not participate in the Jewish revolts against the Romans of the 1st and 2nd centuries, it survived unscathed. (Open daily 8:30am-4:15pm. Admission NIS2. Dress modestly.)

Four kilometers north of Lake Kinneret and 2km east of the road from Tiberias to Rosh Pina (look for the orange, not white, sign to Korazim), you will find the ruins of the Jewish town of **Korazim,** one of unrepentant towns chastised by Jesus (Matthew 11:21). There is a synagogue dating from the Talmudic period (3rd-4th century CE). The bare, rolling landscape is strewn with the dark basalt rubble of what were once streets and dwellings. The remains display a basic village layout of the time: housing quarters centered around a paved public courtyard, and a synagogue with some detailed ornamental pediment and (reconstructed) interior cornice. (Tel. 934 982. Open Sun.-Thurs. 8am-5pm, Fri. 8am-4pm; closes 1hr. earlier in winter. Admission NIS8.50, students NIS6.40.)

Bus #459, 541, 841, and 963 from Tiberias pass the Capernaum junction about once an hour en route north to Kiryat Shmona and Tzfat. Get off before the bus turns up the Mount and walk along the shore for 3km. For Tabgha, take the same buses and get off in Tabgha Junction. To get to Migdal, take bus #458, 541, 841 or 963 from Tiberias.

■■■ TZFAT (SAFAD) צפת صفد

You needn't be religious or Jewish to be enraptured by the mystical city of Tzfat (Safad in Arabic); anyone who's ever had a semi-profound thought, or faked one, will love it. Set on hazy Mt. Canaan, overlooking the Galilean hills and the sea, Tzfat is a city of mesmerizing beauty. Orthodox Jews believe the Messiah will travel from Mt. Meron to Tzfat before going to Jerusalem; some here even sport buttons that read "We want the Messiah now!" or display "In God We Trust" bumper stickers.

Tzfat has been a holy town for Jews since the 16th century CE, when it became a center of Kabbalistic mysticism. Sages say each holy city represents an element: Jerusalem is fire because of the burnt offerings in the Temple, Hebron earth for the land Abraham bought there, Tiberias water for Yam Kinneret, and Tzfat air. Of course, it is possible to get too much of Tzfat's atmosphere: in 1777, a rabbi who had trekked to Tzfat all the way from Europe ultimately packed up and left for Tiberias, complaining that the angels here kept him up at night.

The city's contemporary serenity and religious homogeneity belie its history. The town's Crusaders-built castle was captured by Salah ad-Din in 1188, then lost in 1240 to the Mamluk (Egyptian) Sutlan Baybars, who built Safad into a major administrative center for the surrounding region, including Galilee and Lebanon.

Jews began to join Safad's Arabs in the 17th century, when the Turks declared Safad a Jewish *sanjak*. More Jews arrived throughout the Middle Ages; life under the relatively tolerant Ottoman Empire was preferable to the Spanish Inquisition at home. By 1550, they numbered 10,000; in 1578 the first Hebrew book was printed in Safad.

Despite the immigration in 1778 of Hasidic Jews from Poland, the population of Safad generally dwindled in the 18th century. In 1834 the town was pillaged by the Druze, and 1837 saw a killer earthquake. New settlements began in the second half of the 19th century. In 1929, Hajj Amin al-Husseini led Safad's Arabs in anti-Jewish riots. By 1948 there were 12,000 Arabs and 1700 Jews. In May 1948, 120 Palmaḥ terrorists drove the Arabs out of town. The Israeli government has not since allowed any Palestinians to return. Their evacuated homes now house a truly charming artists' colony popular with Israeli tourists.

ORIENTATION AND PRACTICAL INFORMATION

Tzfat, transliterated as Zefat, Safed, and even Cfat, is arranged in circular terraces of streets descending from the castle ruins at the town center. **Jerusalem** (Yerushalayim) **Street,** the main street, behind the central bus station, makes a complete circle around **Gan Ha-Metzuda** (Park of the Citadel). **Ha-Palmaḥ Street** begins off Jerusalem St. near the central bus station and crosses the main street via an arched stone bridge. Think of Tzfat as divided into three semi-distinct districts: the **Park Area,** at the top of the mountain (ringed by Jerusalem St.); the **Artists' Quarter,** southwest and down the hill; and the **Synagogue Quarter** (Old City), immediately to the north of the Artists' Quarter on the other side of Ma'alot Oleh Ha-Gardom. If you drive, you'll need a parking permit from the GTIO to park in the Jerusalem St. lot (NIS1.20 per hr. 8am-6pm).

Government Tourist Information Office (GTIO): ground floor of the Municipality Building, 50 Jerusalem St. (tel. 920 961 or 962 or 963 or 964; fax 973 666), a 7-min. uphill walk to the right as you leave the central bus station. Very helpful staff. The new, detailed map is worth the NIS3 if you plan to spend more than a few hours in the city. Open Sun.-Thurs. 8am-6pm, Fri. 8am-noon.

Currency Exchange: Bank Leumi, 33 Jerusalem St.; **Bank Ha-Poalim,** 72 Jerusalem St.; and **Israel Discount Bank,** 83 Jerusalem St. All open Sun., Tues., and Thurs. 8:30am-12:30pm and 4-6pm, Mon. and Wed. 8:30am-12:30pm, Fri.

T
Z
F
A
T

(
S
A
F
A
D
)

8:30am-noon. **First International,** 34 Jerusalem St.; open Sun., Tues., and Thurs. 8:30am-2pm, Mon. and Wed. 8:30am-2pm and 4-7pm, Fri. 8:30am-noon.

Central Post Office: Ha-Palmaḥ St. (tel. 920 405), next to a radar dish visible from corner of Ha-Palmaḥ St. at Aliya Bet. **Poste Restante.** Open Sun.-Tues. and Thurs. 8am-12:30pm and 3:30-6pm; Wed. 8am-1:30pm, Fri. 8am-noon. More convenient branch on Jerusalem St. near GTIO has similar hours. **Telephone Code:** 06.

Central Bus Station: Ha'Atzma'ut Sq. (tel. 921 122). Bus #459 runs between Tiberias and Tzfat (every 1-2hr. until 7pm, NIS11.50). Bus #964 direct to Jerusalem (Sun.-Fri. 7:30am, 2½hr.). Bus #361 and 362 go to and from Haifa through Akko (every 20min.; last bus Sun.-Thurs. 8pm, Fri. 4pm; first bus Sat. 9pm.; 45min.; NIS17). Bus station does not store bags.

Taxis: Kenaan Taxis (tel. 970 707), near central bus station. No *sherut* or intercity.

First Aid (Magen David Adom): Tel. 101 in emergencies, otherwise 920 333, next to the central bus station.

Police: Tel. 100 in emergencies, otherwise 920 444 or 972 444.

ACCOMMODATIONS AND FOOD

Tzfat's **youth hostel** is well equipped and only a short ride or 20-minute walk from the bus station. Inexpensive **guest rooms** and flats provided by town residents are another option, primarily in high season. The best way to find a rental is to let it find you: walk around the central bus station forlornly holding your luggage and wait. Don't pay until you see the quarters. Ask the GTIO about any place you're considering, walk up Jerusalem St. and choose one of the places with a "rooms to let" (חדרים להשכיר) sign (often in Hebrew only), or ask at the tourist office for a list of phone numbers. (Official prices: singles NIS50, doubles NIS100; but bargain, especially during low season.) Check for heating or blankets; even summer nights in Tzfat can be chilly.

Beit Binyamin (HI), near the Amal Trade School in South Tzfat (tel. 921 086; fax 973 514). Take bus #6 or 7. Comfortable rooms in the newly renovated complex all have private baths. Reception open 7-9am and 4-7pm. Dorm beds (4 per room) NIS46-53. Singles NIS102. Doubles NIS114. Triples NIS190. Nonmembers NIS3 extra. Breakfast included, other meals served upon request. Call ahead.

Hadar Hotel, Ridbaz St. (tel. 920 068). Take a right from the bus station and head up Jerusalem St. Ridbaz is an alley off Jerusalem. Look for the yellow sign with an arrow. Cozy atmosphere unquestionably enriches the Tzfat experience, if you have the cash. Spacious roof with view of the city. Rooms include bath; some with A/C. No smoking on *Shabbat.* Check-out 11am. Ring the bell to come in after midnight. Singles NIS60-70. Doubles NIS120-140. Sept.-June NIS50/100.

Beit Natan, on Jerusalem St. (tel. 920 121) south of GTIO, by Davidka monument. Student dorm during the school year, open to tourists July-Sept. Rooms have balconies and private baths; kitchen on each floor. Doubles NIS100. Triples NIS125.

Ha-Galil Hotel, 3 Ridbaz St. (tel. 921 247). Clean and simple. Check-out 11am. Curfew midnight. Doubles and triples NIS50 per bed. Open July-Aug.

Ascent Institute of Tzfat, 2 Ha'Ari St. (tel. 921 364; fax 921 942). Head right up the hill from the bus station and take the first right off Jerusalem St. Jews only. Reception open Sun.-Thurs. 9am-9pm, Fri. 9am-6pm; winter Sun.-Thurs. 9am-1pm and 5-8pm, Fri. 9am-4pm, but you can always leave your bags. Check-out 11am. Curfew midnight. Dorm beds (4-6 per room) NIS30; Sat. night NIS20. Breakfast and walking tour included (summer only). Reservations recommended. This establishment cares about your religious education, too: they will give you an NIS5 rebate for each of two optional classes you attend while there.

Many places close on *Shabbat;* if you don't shop before Friday afternoon, you'll starve. The stretch of Jerusalem St. north of the bridge (to #48) is lined with falafel stands and expensive restaurants. Despite its dubious name, **California Falafel,** 92 Jerusalem St., next to the Ha-Palmaḥ St. bridge, fries great falafel (NIS5; open weekdays 9am-11pm, Fri. until 3pm; kosher). **Ha-Mifgash Restaurant,** 75 Jerusalem St., (tel. 920 510 or 974 734), just opposite the small observation point and park, serves stupendous food in a homey stone cavern. *Shishlik, kabab,* or hamburgers with fries about NIS25; pita sandwiches NIS10. (Open Sun.-Fri. 9am-midnight. Kosher.) The **Steakiat Ha-Sela,** 88 Jerusalem St. (no English sign), a tiny grill two doors west of the bridge, serves up delicious *me'orav* (mixed grill) either in pita (NIS8) or as a large *lafa* sandwich (NIS9). The **Organic Café** (tel. 921 866), in Kikkar Ha-Meganin (turn right at the end of the steps from the plaza next to the Municipality building) has food for the healthy traveler. Whole wheat bagel with tofu spread and salad NIS10, carob brownies NIS3. (Open July-Aug. Sun.-Thurs. 9am-10pm, Fri. 9am-2pm.)

A fruit and vegetable **market** is held Wednesdays 6am-2pm, next to the bus station. There are **supermarkets** in the new shopping complex on the Jerusalem St. *midrahov,* above the bus station, and in the Artists' Colony on the way to the Rimon Inn. (Open Sun.-Thurs. 9am-8pm, Fri. 7am-2pm.)

SIGHTS

The tangled streets of Tzfat are sparsely labeled. You're here to wander happily around, anyway. The meager ruins of the 12th-century Crusader fortress that once controlled the main route to Damascus grace **Gan Ha-Metzuda,** a cool, wooded park good for picnics. There's also a monument to the Israelis who died here during the 1948 War. The **Davidka Monument** near the GTIO memorializes a weapon used in the War. It was effective simply due to a frightening noise it made.

The **Israel Bible Museum** (tel. 973 472), just north of the park up the steep stone stairway, displays the work of Phillip Ratner, a modern American artist whose work, depicting biblical scenes and personalities, is in permanent collections at the Statue of Liberty, the White House, and the U.S. Supreme Court. (Open Sun.-Thurs. 10am-6pm, Sat. 10am-2pm; Oct.-Nov. Sat.-Thurs. 10am-2pm; Dec. and Feb. Sun.-Thurs. 10am-2pm. Closed Jan. Free.) The **Shem va'Ever Cave** is believed to be where Noah's son Shem and grandson Ever were buried. If the cave is locked, knock at the small, domed synagogue. The cave is near the top of the bridge off Ha-Palmah St. at the intersection of Jerusalem and Arlozorov St. A forest of English signs will direct you down the hill to the **General Exhibition** (tel. 920 087), displaying works by local artists; it is vulgarly housed in the town's mosque, not used since the 1948 War (open Sun.-Thurs. 9am-6pm, Fri. 10am-2pm). On the way, detour off Arlozorov into the **Artists' Quarter** and wander through the alleys and galleries just south of the Jerusalem-Arlozorov intersection. The quality of the art varies; though the colony has seen better days, there is still some decent stuff. The Ora Gallery, the Bible Museum, Victor Halvani, Mike Leif, and Reuven and Naomi Spiers merit a browse. Hours vary (most open 10am-1pm and 4-7pm).

Navigating the gnarled **Synagogue Quarter** *(Kiryat Batei Ha-Knesset),* also called the Old City *(Ha'Ir Ha'Atika),* is a matter of luck; note landmarks carefully, but when you get lost—and you will get lost—enjoy it. There are few nicer places to lose your bearings. The tiny, ornate synagogues are all still in use. The **Chernobyl Synagogue** was founded by Jews from that luckless Ukrainian town. They claim the reactor was built over Jewish graves, and that it melted down on the anniversary of the death of the chief rabbi buried beneath it. The **Chertkoff Synagogue's** chief rabbi predicted in 1840 that the messianic redemption *(ge'ula)* would begin when 600,000 Jews inhabited the Land of Israel. This was so in 1948, but no results so far.

The **Caro Synagogue** and **Ha'Ari (Ashkenazi) Synagogue** are the most famous. To reach the Caro Synagogue, take Ma'alot Oleh Ha-Gardom St. off Jerusalem St. and turn right onto Beit Yosef St. Ask to see the old books and Torah scrolls. It was here that Yosef Caro, chief rabbi of Tzfat and author of the vast *Shulhan Arukh* ("The Set Table," a standard guide to daily life according to Jewish law), studied and taught in the 16th century. In the basement is the angel with whom he used to confer (Rabbi Alkabetz purportedly witnessed their talks). These days, the angel prefers not to be disturbed. (Closed during the day.) To reach Ha'Ari Synagogue, follow Beit Yosef until it becomes Alkabetz St., take a right up a stairway with stained glass Stars of David above, and continue straight under the stone arch. The synagogue will be to your right on Najara St. Rabbi Isaac Luria was the great Kabbalist who introduced the *Kabbalat Shabbat,* an arrangement of prayers in preparation for the Sabbath; Alkabetz, his student, wrote the famous liturgical hymn *Lekha Dodi.* The four pillars that buttress the podium in the middle of the room symbolize the four elements and the four holy cities. A Sephardic synagogue lies farther down the hill near the cemetery. Just downhill from the Caro Synagogue, off Abuhav St., stand the **Abuhav** and **Alsheih Synagogues.** Take a left off Beit Yosef St. onto Alsheih St. and make a sharp right; both buildings will be to your right. The blue color of the walls symbolizes God's reign; green symbolizes the growth of redemption. Dress modestly; no cameras on *Shabbat.* Only Caro, Ha'Ari, and Abuhav are open to the public.

Three adjoining **cemeteries** sprawl on the western outskirts of the Old City, off Ha'Ari St. Follow the path all the way down, past the new stone buildings on the left. The small building on the left when the path turns right down the hill into the cemetery is Ha'Ari synagogue's men's *mikveh,* or ritual bath (women should not enter). The oldest cemetery contains the 17th-century graves of the most famous Tzfat Kabbalists, as well as a domed tomb built by the Karaites of Damascus (a medieval group of Jewish biblical literalists) to mark the grave of the prophet Hosea. On the wall inside the tomb, you'll see an article posted about an eighth-generation Tzfat resident named Mordekhai Shebabo. Shebabo left his position as a pedicurist to single-handedly undertake the restoration of the graves. Every visible grave is the result of this man's manicuring prowess. Shebabo or one of his sons may ask you for a small donation for the upkeep of the cemetery. Legend has it that hidden under this same hill lie Hannah and her seven sons, whose martyrdom at the hands of the Syrians is recorded in the Book of Maccabees. They say you'll know when you're walking over their graves because you'll suddenly be overcome by fatigue.

At the very bottom of the Oleh Ha-Gardom steps, **Beit Hameiri** (tel. 971 307) contains a museum of old tools and furniture and an institute for the study of the history of Jews in Tzfat. Mango-colored signs point the way here from anywhere in town. (Open Sun.-Thurs. 9am-2pm, Fri. 9am-1pm. Admission NIS5, students NIS4.)

The legends of Tzfat, modern and ancient, are best told by locals. **Aviva Minoff** (tel. 920 901) gives tours starting from the Rimon Inn Hotel (Mon.-Thurs. 10am, Fri. 10:30am) and **Yisrael Shalem** (tel. 971 870) leads tours on demand. Call ahead. (2hr., NIS25, students NIS20. Dress modestly.)

ENTERTAINMENT

The Yigal Allon Cultural Center on Ha-Halutz St. occasionally shows recently released English **movies** (tel. 971 990). For three days in July or August the town hosts a wild **klezmer festival** (Eastern European Jewish soul music) that has to be seen to be believed. Only Tzfat residents are permitted to park on the streets during the festival, so be prepared to park outside city limits or to take the bus. *Shabbat* in Tzfat brings tranquility and introspection; if you'd rather reflect in a cool pool of water, head over to the **Blue Valley swimming pool and leisure center** (tel. 920 217) just off Ha'Atzma'ut Rd., behind the central bus station. Walk down from the station, turn left, and the turn-off for the swimming pool will be 100m later on the left. (Open July-Aug. daily 9am-5pm. Admission NIS12, students NIS7. Wear a leisure suit.) Another pool (tel. 974 294), in the industrial district of south Tzfat (take bus #6 or 7) is heated, has a sauna and ping-pong, and is open year-round. (Sun.-Thurs. 11am-9pm, Fri. 11am-5pm, Sat. 10am-5pm. Admission NIS12, students NIS7.)

■ NEAR TZFAT

ROSH PINA ראש פינה

There is nothing to do in the quiet town of Rosh Pina, on the slopes of Mt. Kenaan. It is the first Jewish *moshav* in the Galilee, a haven for artists, and a gateway to the Upper Galilee and Golan. Many buses heading north use this transportation hub. From Tel Aviv, bus #842 goes to Rosh Pina (NIS19) and continues up to Kiryat Shmona. Bus #500 travels to Rosh Pina from Haifa (NIS15) and also continues to

Kiryat Shmona. Bus #401, 459, 461, and 511 to Tzfat (NIS4.80); #55, 56, and 57 to Katzrin (NIS6.20); and #480, 500, 842, 845, and 969 to Kiryat Shmona (NIS7) leave from here. The **Nature Friends Youth Hostel** (tel. (06) 937 086) is quiet and comfortable. Each room has a fridge and fan, with heating in the winter. (Check-in 5-8pm. No curfew. Dorm beds NIS46. Doubles NIS132. Breakfast included.) Some travelers take the two-hour hike up the steep scenic road to Tzfat. Others wonder why they're here.

MERON AND MT. MERON הר מירון

Each year on the holiday of Lag Ba'Omer (Thurs. May 18 in 1995), thousands converge on the tiny village of Meron, 4km west of Tzfat, at the tomb of Rabbi Shimon Bar-Yoḥai, the great 2nd-century Talmudic scholar. Some believe he composed the *Zohar* (the central work of Jewish mysticism) while hiding in a cave in Peki'in. According to the Kabbalists, Bar Yoḥai once vowed to God that the Jews would never forget the importance of the Torah. Mindful of this vow, the Tzfat Hasidim dance and sing their way to his tomb, accompanied by an ancient Torah scroll from the Bana'a Synagogue in the Spanish Quarter. Contact the GTIO in Tzfat for details.

Near the tomb are the ruins of an aesthetically unimpressive but historically noteworthy synagogue dating from the 3rd century CE, when Meron was important in the booming olive oil trade. From Bar Yoḥai's grave, go right past the yeshiva and follow the uphill path to your left. Virtually all that's left of the synagogue is a lintel, the engraved stone slab that once decorated the entrance. Legend has it that this lintel's fall will herald the coming of the Messiah. The Israeli Department of Antiquities has nervously buttressed the artifact with reinforced concrete, but every year, pious Jews from Tzfat enthusiastically dance and stomp in an effort to accelerate its fall.

Just west of the village is **Mount Meron** (Har Meron), the highest mountain in the Galilee (1208m). A superb trail affords tremendous vistas of Tzfat and the surrounding countryside, and on clear days you can see Lebanon and Syria to the north, the Mediterranean to the west, and the Galilee to the southeast. It is possible to ascend the mountain from the village of Meron, but a more convenient option is to take bus #43 from Tzfat to Kibbutz Sasa, northwest of the mountain (departs 7am, 12:30pm, and 5pm; returns 8:05am, 1:50pm, and 6:20pm; NIS5.50). In summer, catch the early bus to avoid the midday heat. From the kibbutz, where the bus turns around, continue 1km to the turn-off on the left, then walk 1km and turn right for the SPNI field school. Their **information office** (tel. 980 023) offers a trail map (NIS36) and some advice. To reach the trail, walk straight down the road from the field school turnoff until you pass an army base on the right and a small parking lot on the left. The trail begins from the back of the lot and is indicated by stone and striped black-and-white trail markers. A one-hour walk brings you to the summit, where there are red-and-white markers. Stay on the trail, which skirts the green-and-white summit, as the very top of the mountain is the site of a crimson-and-white army radar installation. Twenty minutes farther along the path, you'll approach a brown-and-white picnic site with an orange-and-white asphalt traffic circle on a road; don't cross the road, but follow it for 20m to the left to where the trail begins again. A long, easy descent, again marked with the black-and-white-and-red-all-over blazes, ends on a dirt road just above the village of Meron. Return to Tzfat either by retracing your steps to Sasa or by catching bus #361 or 362 from the village of Meron (every 20min., first bus around 5am, last bus around 9pm, NIS4.50).

BAR'AM ברעם

A 40-minute bus ride northwest of Tzfat will take you to the deserted village of Bar'am, where the remains of a 3rd-century **synagogue** stand. While many ancient synagogue sites are little more than dusty foundation stones, this one, though far from intact, retains fragments of façade, columns, and ornament in place, providing an idea of the whole.

Like all Galilee synagogues, the building is oriented south toward Jerusalem; but it also bears an atypical six-columned portico with a well. The well-preserved stone carvings on the main portal include wreaths, winged figures, and vines with clusters of grapes. A side lintel even retains the ghost of an inscription.

The town itself was a Jewish settlement during the Mishnaic and Talmudic periods. Maronite Christians lived here until 1948, when inhabitants were forcibly evacuated during the 1948 war, together with residents of the neighboring village of Ikrit. Years of struggle to be allowed back went unheeded by Israeli authorities.

Infrequent service between Tzfat and Bar'am makes this either a half-hour or six-hour visit. Bus #43 (NIS8.30) leaves Tzfat at 7am, 12:30pm and 5pm, and returns at 7:55am, 1:40pm, and 6:10pm. Or you could visit Bar'am as part of a daytrip to nearby Mt. Meron. Bar'am is 2.5km northeast of Kibbutz Sasa, the starting point of the Mt. Meron hike. Ask the bus driver to let you off at the Bar'am antiquities. Look for the orange sign on the left, since drivers don't always remember.

■■■ KIRYAT SHMONA   קרית שמונה

Kiryat Shmona ("Town of Eight" in Hebrew) honors Yosef Trumpeldor and seven others who were murdered in nearby Tel Ḥai in 1920. Situated on the ruins of the Arab village Al Khalsa (destroyed by Israel in 1948), the city was given its new name in 1949. By virtue of its location on the Ḥula plain near the Lebanese border, Kiryat Shmona was the target of numerous bombings and terrorist attacks until Israel invaded Lebanon in 1982, and it has been subject to *Hizballah* shelling as recently as July 1993. Thus was spawned the grim nickname Kiryat Katyusha. Three brightly-painted tanks sit in a small park near the southern entrance to the town.

Although it is the administrative and transportation center of the Upper Galilee, the city is little more than a pit-stop for most tourists. Bus #541, 841, and 963 run from Tiberias to Kiryat Shmona (NIS11). Buses for Tzfat, other Upper Galilee destinations, Tel Aviv, and the Golan leave from the **central bus station** (tel. (06) 940 740 or 741, info. (04) 549 555) on Tel Ḥai Blvd. The most inexpensive accommodations in the area are youth hostels in **Tel Ḥai** or **Rosh Pina.** Falafel and *shawerma* stands sizzle around the intersection of Tel Ḥai Blvd. and Tcherniḥovsky St. Cafés and small restaurants are one block north and south of the bus station. **Narghila** cooks Yemenite food well; it's on the main road. There is a **Co-op Tzafon supermarket** and **Ha-Mashbir department store** in the shopping complex just south of the bus station. Thursday mornings there's an open-air *shuk* on Tel Ḥai St., just north of the bus station. The **post office** licks stamps south of the bus station and has **international telephone** and **Poste Restante** services (tel. 940 220; open Sun.-Thurs. 8am-1pm and 4-6:30pm, Fri. 8am-12:30pm). **Telephone code:** 06. For **first aid (Magen David Adom),** dial 944 334; for **police,** dial 949 444.

■ NEAR KIRYAT SHMONA

TEL ḤAI   תל חי

Three kilometers north of Kiryat Shmona, Tel Ḥai sits on a promontory overlooking the Ḥula valley. Established in 1918 as a military outpost after the withdrawal of British forces from the Upper Galilee, the town has become a symbol of Israel's early pioneer movement and the struggle for the narrow mountain range west of the Ḥula Valley region, known as "the finger of the Galilee."

Tel Ḥai has the dubious distinction of being the site of the first armed conflict between Jews and Arabs within the current borders of the State of Israel. In 1920, a group of Arabs gathered around the settlements of Tel Ḥai, Kfar Giladi, and Metulla (then part of French-administered Syria and Lebanon) and accused the Jewish settlers of protecting French soldiers charged with encroachment on Arab lands. Yosef Trumpeldor, the leader of Tel Ḥai, allowed four Arabs inside the settlement to search for the French agents. Once inside the complex, the Arabs attacked, killing Trumpeldor and seven others. The six men and two women were buried in nearby Kfar Giladi. Trumpeldor's alleged last words, "No matter, it is good to die for our country," for years epitomized Zionist convictions. Today some Israelis regard these words with skepticism or even scorn.

A monument to Yosef Trumpeldor stands on the compound's outskirts. The original watchtower and stockade settlement, destroyed by Arabs in 1920, has been reconstructed as a small **museum** (tel. 951 333) displaying farming tools. (Open Sun.-Thurs. 8am-4pm, Fri. 8am-1pm, Sat. 8:30am-2pm. Admission NIS6.50, students NIS5.50. Slide show in English shown to small groups upon request; English brochures available.) There's also a recently-opened **Museum of Photography** (tel. 950 769; open Sun.-Thurs. 9am-4pm, Sat. 10am-5pm; admission NIS6, students NIS3). Israel's northernmost **HI youth hostel** (tel. 940 043) is just off the main Metulla-Kiryat Shmona road. (Reception 8am-12:30pm and 4:30-7pm. Check-in in the afternoon. Check-out 9am. No curfew. Dorm beds (6 per room, some with A/C) NIS48. Breakfast included. Reservations necessary in summer.) **Bus** #20 and 23 from Kiryat Shmona go to Tel Ḥai (9 per day, NIS3.50); the hostel has its own stop.

Up the road from the hostel is the **military cemetery** containing the graves of the eight of Tel Ḥai, with a statue of a roaring lion facing the mountains to the east. 50m farther, inside the gates of Kibbutz Kfar Giladi, is **Beit Ha-Shomer** (House of the Guardian, tel. 941 565), an IDF museum documenting the history of early defense organizations in the Upper Galilee and the exploits of the Jewish regiments in the British Army during World War I. (Open Sun.-Thurs. 8am-noon and 2-4pm, Fri.-Sat. 9am-noon. Admission NIS5, students NIS2.)

KFAR BLUM כפר בלום

This kibbutz, southeast of Kiryat Shmona, has two unrelated attractions: classical music and kayaking. The **Upper Galilee Chamber Music Days** feature a week-long series of concerts in July. Tickets (NIS17-22 per concert) sell out rapidly, but you can listen in on daytime rehearsals. On a different note, a 6km **kayaking** trip (tel. 948 755) on the Jordan River costs NIS60 for two people and lasts about an hour. Consult the *Galilee Guide,* available at the GTIO, for information on kayaking, rafting, and tubing adventures in the region's gushing streams. Unfortunately, the streams tend to gush less during the hot summer months, rendering some water adventures less than thrilling. Bus #29 runs seven times a day from Kiryat Shmona (NIS4).

NATURE RESERVES

Just south of Kiryat Shmona, the **Ḥula Nature Reserve** (tel. 937 069) blossoms where a vast swamp once festered. The 775-acre reserve has dense cypress groves and open fields; exotic wildlife such as razorbacks and mongeese dwell in the underbrush. The entrance booth rents binoculars (NIS7), helpful for bird-watching among papyrus thickets, swamps, and reeds. Arrive early; the park becomes progressively less serene as families with vocally inquisitive children arrive. Bus #501, 840, and 841 (NIS6.30) leave frequently from Kiryat Shmona and will take you to a junction 3km from the entrance to the reserve. From there you can skip, walk, or crawl. The observation area has little shade. There's a kiosk and picnic area; a **visitors center** exhibits flora and fauna, and screens a 15-minute film. (Open Sat.-Thurs. 9am-4pm, Fri. 9am-3pm.)

The nature reserves listed below are open Sat.-Thurs. 8am-5pm, Fri. 8am-4pm, closing one hour earlier Nov.-March. Admission NIS11. Combined ticket for Ḥula, Banyas, Gamla, Dan, and Ayun Reserves is available at all 5 sites for NIS27.

Huge oak trees, some nearly 2000 years old, stand in the **Ḥorshat Tal Nature Reserve** (tel. 940 400 or 942 360). According to a Muslim legend, the trees, which survive nowhere else in Israel, have been preserved thanks to the 10 messengers of Muhammad who once rested here. Finding a dearth of trees for shade and not a single hitching post for their camels, they pounded sticks into the earth to fasten their mounts. Overnight the sticks sprouted, and the holy men found themselves in a thick forest. The trees now tower over a grassy park which is crammed on Saturdays with picnicking families. Especially enticing is the large, ice-cold **swimming pool**— actually the River Dan ingeniously diverted. From Kiryat Shmona bus #26 travels to

Horshat Tal (10:15am and 2:10pm). Bus #26, 27, and 36 return to Kiryat Shmona (9:10am, 12:15pm, and 2:35pm; NIS4). About 100m farther along the road is the **Horshat Tal Camping Ground** (tel. 942 360), on the banks of the Dan River. (Tent sites NIS20. 4-person bungalows NIS110.)

One kilometer down the road, **Kibbutz She'ar Yishuv** hosts the SPNI's **Hermon Field School** (tel. 941 091). Bus #25 and 26 (NIS4) from Kiryat Shmona will take you to the kibbutz. The next kibbutz to the northeast, **Kibbutz Dan,** is in the midst of the Hula Valley's thickest nature reserve, **Tel Dan** (tel. 951 579). The waters come from the Fountain of Dan at the foot of the large Tel Dan, still under excavation. The many springs nourish a dense grove of trees and bushes that grow to record heights. The rocky paths in this small (under 100 acres) but picturesque pastoral reserve offer welcome opportunities to cool hot paws in trickling streams. (No swimming allowed.) A pre-1948 Arab flour mill has been restored by the park authorities, while ongoing excavations have revealed the ruins of the ancient Hyksos and Canaanite city of Lakhish, which became the capital city of the tribe of Dan, one of the 12 tribes of Israel. The archaeological record indicates that the site has been occupied continuously since the 5th millennium BCE, and a remarkable find was made in the summer of 1993: a broken stele, inscribed with the words "House of David" in 9th-century BCE Aramaic. That may not sound like much, but archaeologists and biblical history scholars were in a tizzy over its significance—the first known reference to the biblical King David outside of the Good Book itself. The **Beit Usishkin Museum,** a gray stone building with an arched opening at the center on the way to the reserve, has a fascinating exhibit of the archaeological finds, including the stele itself, bronze work, and a remarkably well-preserved 14th-century BCE charioteer vase—evidence of trade with Cyprus. The museum also features a two-floor display including audio-visuals on the natural history of the Hula Valley and the Golan. (Open Sun.-Thurs. 8:45am-4:30pm, Fri. 8:45am-3:30pm, Sat. 9:30am-5:30pm. Admission NIS6, students NIS5.50. The ticket entitles you to a 25% discount at the reserve.) To reach the reserve, take bus #26 or 36 (NIS3.80) from Kiryat Shmona to Kibbutz Dan, continue up the main road, and turn left at the sign to the reserve. A 3km walk will bring you to the entrance. (The guidebook available at the ticket window is worth the NIS0.50.) The **Banyas Waterfall** (see p. 340), one of the most popular sites in the north, is just a few kilometers east.

METULLA מטולה

The sleepy, small-town atmosphere of Israel's largest village on the Lebanese border 9km north of Kiryat Shmona makes for a retreat from the hectic pace of Israeli cities. Visit Metulla as a daytrip from Tel Hai.

Practical Information Bus #20 runs from Kiryat Shmona to Metulla and back (8 per day, NIS4.50). There are two pensions in Metulla, both along Ha-Rishonim, the main road. The **Yafa Pension** (tel. 940 617) is at the second bus stop in town. Look for bizarre rock garden and Hebrew sign. (Doubles NIS150. Breakfast included.) **Arazim Pension** (tel. 944 144) is a three-star hotel at the end of the same road. (Singles and doubles US$100-160. Breakfast included.) A restaurant across from the Ha-Mavri Hotel serves decent food at low prices.

Sights and Entertainment Metulla's main spectacle is **Ha-Gader Ha-Tova (The Good Fence)** just north of town, an opening in the border barrier between Lebanon and Israel through which Lebanese Christians and Druze are allowed to pass through to obtain free medical services, visit relatives, and work in Israel. Israel began passing aid and supplies through this point to Lebanese Christians in 1971, and in June 1976 the Good Fence was officially opened, remaining open even during the war in Lebanon. From the observation point to the right of the snack bars you can see several Maronite Christian villages; on the farthest hill to the right (northwest) stands the Crusader fortress of Beaufort, which was fortified by the PLO and used as a base for shelling Israel. On the hill farthest to the southwest, look for

Kibbutz Misgav Am, located where the border heads farther north, behind a Lebanese hill. Buy a heinous "Better a close neighbor than a distant enemy" T-shirt, or get something better, sold quietly at the snack bar on the far left: Lebanese money.

If you continue straight on the main road instead of turning left to the Good Fence, you'll come to the small **Nahal Ayun Nature Reserve** (tel. 951 519) with a picnic area. Through the gate and down the stone steps is a path to one of the reserve's waterfalls. To reach the Ayun Stream, continue walking south past the brown sign in the picnic area, through the apple groves; the path will lead you to the riverbed. Unfortunately, the falls and river run dry in the summer, except for a few stagnant pools. (Reserve open Sat.-Thurs. 8am-5pm, Fri. 8am-4pm; closes 1hr. earlier in winter. Admission NIS8.50.)

Farther down the stream, south of Metulla, the cool mountain air is moistened with mist from the **Tanur Waterfall.** With the 18m drop, the density of mist creates the illusion of billowing smoke: *tanur* means "oven." The fall, magnificent in the snow-melting season, slows to a trickle after June. The Tanur, in the southern part of the Ayun reserve, is also accessible directly by bus #20 from Kiryat Shmona; ask for the turn-off to the waterfall. From there, it's a three-minute walk to the park.

Israelis head to Metulla's new **Canada Centre** (tel. 950 370 or 371), one of the top sports facilities in Israel and home to its only genuine ice-skating rink. The hefty admission fee (NIS27, students NIS20) includes skate rental plus use of an enormous indoor pool with slides, a basketball court, jacuzzi, sauna, squash courts (NIS6 per hr.), and ping-pong tables (NIS3 per 45min.). The complex is located just down the hill from the Yafa Pension (open daily 10am-10pm).

▓ Golan Heights רמת הגולן

The armies of many civilizations have battled over the strategic peaks above the fertile Jordan Valley; the tradition of military conflict here dates back to the Roman siege of Gamla. In more recent times, Israel took the Golan from Syria in the 1967 Six-Day War. Syria's surprise attack in the 1973 War pushed Israel back, but the IDF recovered and launched a counter-attack, capturing even more territory. As part of the 1974 disengagement accord, Israel returned both this newly conquered territory and part of the land captured in 1967. In 1981, the Menaḥem Begin government officially annexed the Heights, arousing (and ignoring) international protest and considerably upsetting the Golan's sizeable Druze population, who now had to carry Israeli identification cards. Israeli settlements were then scattered among the ruins, rusting tanks, and Druze villages. Stone trenches with a commanding view of Israeli communities in the Galilee and small plastic anti-personnel mines remain in some places. The eucalyptus trees shading the trenches were planted at the suggestion of Eli Cohen, an Israeli spy in the Damascus government, who in 1967 told Israeli pilots to aim for the distinctive vegetation in the otherwise barren Heights.

It is likely that part or all of the Heights will be returned to Syria in exchange for a peace treaty, Syrian recognition of Israel, and the eventual establishment of diplomatic relations between the two countries. Syria has always held that the land was seized by an illegal act of aggression and insisted on the return of the territory. Israel long countered that Syria's possession of the Golan Heights would pose a threat to northern Israeli towns. When the current Israeli Labor-led government hinted its willingness to strike a land-for-peace deal with the Syrians, right-wingers and Israelis living in the Golan were enraged and initiated an urgent protest campaign in an attempt to turn Israeli public opinion against territorial concessions. On September 8, 1994, Israeli Prime Minister Yitzhak Rabin announced a two-step plan for a phased Israeli withdrawal from the Golan Heights in exchange for peace.

For Israelis, politics aside, the Golan is associated with bottled spring water, crisp apples, and wine. For the tourist, this surprisingly flat plateau, dotted with dead volcanos and old mine fields, has some noteworthy natural and archaeological sights.

GETTING AROUND

Some sights in the Golan are accessible by **Egged bus,** but infrequent service along remote roads makes careful planning a necessity. Double-check all schedules and anticipate walking, which means you'll need a hat and buckets of water in summer (winter is cold, damp, foggy, and often snowy). Buses to sights east of or near the Galilee generally leave from Tiberias. The Upper Galilee, Ḥula Valley, and northern Golan are served by buses from Kiryat Shmona and occasionally from Tzfat. Traveling by bus almost definitely writes off Gamla and Brekhat Ha-Meshushim.

Relatively few cars traverse the Golan, and many are driven by people with whom you wouldn't want to spend too much time. There have been reports of attacks in recent years, making hitching a *phenomenally* bad idea. If, despite all that, you are foolhardy enough to set out on your own, take a good map, a sizeable water bottle, and at least a day's worth of food. **Stay on the paved roads, away from land mines hidden in barren fields. Any fenced-off area should be avoided whether or not there are warning signs.** The Ministry of Tourism *strongly* suggests that visitors start at the field school in Katzrin to get maps and information.

If you're an organized **tours** type, you will find them faster, more convenient, and sometimes less expensive in the long run; however, they can be rushed and usually do not allow time for hiking or swimming. **Egged** (tel. (06) 791 080 or 720 474) offers full-day tours of the region from Tiberias (March-Oct.; Tues., Thurs., and Sat.; US$29, 10% discount with ISIC), Tel Aviv (April-Oct.; Sun. and Thurs.; US$49; tel. (03) 527 1212 or 375 588), and Haifa (Thurs.; US$46; tel. (04) 623 131 or 549 487). There are also private guides based in Tiberias. **Moshe Cohen** (tel. 721 608) makes military history-oriented rounds in a taxi (NIS65). **Max Ballhorn** (tel. 793 588) gives Egged-style tours (NIS80); he is licensed. Three-day SPNI hiking and camping trips visit some hard-to-reach spots (Gamla, Nimrod, Druze villages, Banyas, and Nahal Kziv or Nahal Betzet) and, in summer, could include kayaking down the Jordan River. Leaves every Tuesday from Tel Aviv, Netanya Junction, and Tiberias. Moshav Ramot runs guided **jeep trips** (tel. 941 001; 2-hr. trip NIS40 per person; 4-hr. trip NIS60 per person; may not speak English). The other (and best) option for fully exploring the Golan is to **rent a car** in Tiberias. Two days is exactly how long it takes to see everything. Find some friends! Pretend you're Thelma and Louise! *Let's Go* does not recommend driving off a cliff.

KATZRIN קצרין

The town of Katzrin is the administrative and municipal center of the Golan and an ideal base from which to explore the area. Katzrin enjoys a high standard of living for a young settlement, but the rows of nearly identical apartment buildings could turn you into an automaton. Ten kilometers from Katzrin, between it and Tzfat, is the **B'not Ya'akov Bridge** where, according to legend, Jacob's daughters predicted that their siblings would sell their brother Joseph into slavery in Egypt. The name (Daughters of Jacob) is also shared by a Crusader order of nuns.

Practical Information Bus #55 from Kiryat Shmona approaches Katzrin from the north and passes the towns at the base of Mt. Ḥermon (2 per day, 45min., NIS14). If you don't feel like waiting, take bus #841, 842, 845, 480, 500, or 969 to Rosh Pina (about 45min.). From there, bus #55-57 go to Katzrin (25min., NIS6.50). From Tiberias, bus #15, 16, and 19 travel to Katzrin (45min.).

Ask the bus driver to let you off in front of the **Golan Field School** on Daliyat St. (tel. 961 234), an invaluable source of information. They give lifts in their buses when there's room and run a **campground** (tel. 961 657) 500m east along the road in front of the school. Registration is ordinarily open 8am-7pm, but if no one is there you can find the manager in the field school. Pleasant bungalows (4-6 beds) for two cost NIS120, tent sites NIS13 per person. An information center in the industrial area of Katzrin gives suggestions for **housing** with families in the region. (Call 962 885 or 969 661 and ask for Nili.) Next door to the Archaeological Museum is a **public pool** (tel. 961 655; open daily 9am-5:45pm; admission NIS10), a **supermarket**, and the town's few restaurants.

Sights The **Golan Archaeological Museum** (tel. 961 350) is in the north end of town, at the opposite end of Daliyat St. from the field school. Tiny but very informative, with thorough explanations in Hebrew and English. Engraved artifacts from ancient synagogues and houses, including 6200 coins, testify to agricultural communities dating back to the New Stone Age. Tear-jerker film on the Great Revolt battle in Gamla. (Open Sun.-Thurs. 8am-5pm, Fri. 8am-3pm, Sat. 10am-4pm. Admission NIS9, students NIS5.50.) The ticket includes admission to **Ancient Katzrin Park,** located just outside modern Katzrin (ask the museum for directions), where excavations have unearthed a richly ornamented synagogue dating from the 4th to 8th century CE. Two reconstructed houses with furnishings based on finds from the excavations give a sense of daily life in the Talmudic village.

A few kilometers north of Katzrin, the road ends in a T, heading west to the B'not **Ya'akov** Bridge or east toward Quneitra. To reach the Gilabon (GEE-la-boon) and Dvora **waterfalls** in the **Gilabon Nature Reserve,** head 1km east and turn left just before the military base. The approach to the reserve begins about 2km down this road. The reserve contains a well-marked circular path leading to both waterfalls. Hiking the entire challenging trail takes four to five hours; for a shorter route, hike down to the Gilabon and back without completing the full circle (2-3hr.).

GAMLA גמלא

For years all that was known about the lost city of Gamla was its legend as told by the first-century historian Josephus Flavius. Somewhere in the Golan existed the remains of an ancient town whose defenders heroically resisted the Roman army during the Great Rebellion, then chose martyrdom (*The Jewish War,* Book IV, ch. 1). After the Six-Day War, archaeologists scoured the area for a spot corresponding to ancient descriptions of the city. Eventually, Shmaryahu Gutman, who claims to have worked with a copy of *The Jewish War* in hand, found the site: 15km southeast of modern Katzrin, on the high escarpments encircling a ridge crowned by the ruins of Gamla, lay a battlefield missing only the Roman legions. (Be sure to see the inspiring film at the Golan Archaeological Museum before you visit Gamla.) The only access to its walls is via a narrow strip of land connecting it with the higher surrounding ridges. The peak, when viewed from a certain angle, resembles a camel's hump—hence *gamla* (camel in Aramaic).

At this site some 2000 years ago, the Romans laid siege to the religious city of Gamla, which was packed with 9000 Jews seeking refuge. After a siege lasting many months, Romans on the nearby hills attacked down the corridor of land leading to the city. When the legion penetrated Gamla's walls, hordes of Jews were found fleeing up the ridge. The Romans followed, and on the steep trails beyond the confines of the town, the Jews turned and massacred the legionnaires. Weeks later, a second attack proved too much for the Jews to withstand, and they hurled themselves over the ridge's steep rock face. Only two women survived to tell the tale.

Getting to Gamla is tricky without a car. Bus #22 will take you to a spot a half-hour away from the site. If you catch a ride with a group from the field school you'll also benefit from the guided tour. Otherwise, try to get a ride from Katzrin and walk 1km to the ridge overlooking the ruins. The descent to the ruins along the Roman route takes about 15 minutes, but give yourself time to walk around the town. (Site open Sat.-Thurs. 8am-5pm, Fri. 8am-4pm. Admission NIS8.) If you continue on the path past the ruins, you'll reach a lookout point over **Mapal Gamla,** Israel's highest waterfall. The falls are more impressive than the ruins. The path continues above the falls, terminating at the ruins (3hr.).

BREKHAT HA-MESHUSHIM בריכת המשושים

A few kilometers southeast of Katzrin, not served by public transportation, is the beautiful **Ya'ar Yehudiya Nature Reserve** and the source of the Zavitan River. From just off the road, you can hike down the river through some of Israel's richest greenery. To reach the hiking path, head about 2km southeast along the highway from Katzrin. Watch for a small, weather-beaten orange sign on the right, marking the beginning of the trail. Starting here, you can follow the stream for about two hours through rocky pools wiggling with fish and freshwater crabs in summer. The trail is clearly marked with red-and-white blazes. Before the stream joins the Meshushim stream to the west, the path leads up the steep side of the ravine, across the plateau, and down to Brekhat Ha-Meshushim (Hexagon Ponds). The formation of hexagonal rock columns at the water's edge inspired the name. To leave this area, walk up to the parking lot and stroll the 5km access road to the main highway (if you care about your car even slightly, don't subject it to this access road). From here it's 17km to Katzrin; there are no buses. The ponds can also be reached by climbing upriver from the Bet Tzayda Valley (ask for *Tzomet Bet Tzayda*) along the Galilee or by walking down the path from the deserted village of Jaraba, about 13km south of B'not Ya'akov Bridge off the left side of the road. The river basin is occasionally closed to traffic due to military maneuvers in the area.

BANYAS AND NIMROD'S FORTRESS בניס וקלעת נמרוד

The name Banyas comes from the Greek *Paneas* (Pan's Place); the spring here was the site of an ancient sanctuary dedicated to Pan, god of nature and shepherds. Arabic, with no *P* sound, renders "Paneas" *banyas*. These rocks gush with religious and strategic significance: the prophet Elijah (Al Khadar to Muslims) had a shrine by the Banyas, Jesus chose his first disciple here, and, prior to 1967, Syria staged attacks into the Hula Valley from this spectacularly beautiful site.

Banyas lies only a few minutes down the road from Dan and Horshat Tal in the Upper Galilee. Although the Banyas is the most popular site in the Upper Galilee-Golan area, public transportation here is woefully inadequate. Bus #14 from Kiryat Shmona to Neveh Ativ passes by (NIS6.50), leaving at 10:30am and returning at approximately 4:30pm. Bus #55 travels from Kiryat Shmona through the Golan by way of Banyas twice per day, but the last bus back to Kiryat Shmona is at noon. If you want to spend the afternoon at the park, walk 5km west to Kibbutz Dan; the last bus (#25, 26, or 36) leaves the kibbutz around 7:30pm. (Tel. 951 410. Park open Sat.-Thurs. 8am-6pm, Fri. 8am-5pm. Admission NIS11. Combination ticket to Banyas, Gamla, Dan, Ayun, and Hula Valley Reserves NIS27, available at all the reserves.)

A 45- to 60-minute hike from the park entrance leads to the **Banyas waterfall** *(mapal banyas),* the largest falls in the region. Just across the stream running through the park is a wooden sign marking the beginning of a path to the waterfall. All subsequent signs are in Hebrew, but there is only one fork (just past the pita bakery)—go right. Farther along the path is a clearing that leads to a clean swimming pool fed by the icy waters of the spring; just past the pool three paths intersect; the middle and right-hand paths lead to the waterfall. Local daredevils leap the 15m from the ledge into the foaming pool below. From there the road runs 1km out to the main road, emerging 1km west of the entrance to the park.

Nimrod's Fortress *(Qal'at Nemrud)* stands 1.5km northeast of the Banyas, on a knobby hill. According to the biblical table of Noah's descendants, Nimrod was "the first on earth to be a mighty man" (Genesis 10:8). Legend holds that, besides fashioning sandals and building the Tower of Babel, he erected this humongous fortress high enough to shoot arrows up to God. A plaque above one gate reads in Arabic: "God gave him the power to build this castle with his own strength." The strength of his slaves must have been phenomenal as well, judging from the size of the stones they schlepped up the steep cliffs. Historians, who just love putting holes in myths, say the fortress was actually built by the Muslims and originally named Qal'at Subeiba. The town of Banyas itself was settled by the Arabs in the 7th century and ruled by Crusaders until 1165. It remained an Arab village until the 1967 War. The view from the top of the fortress is unrivaled anywhere in the Upper Galilee or Golan. You can see Mt. Hermon to the north and the Hula Valley to the southeast. The approach to the castle, from which there is a clear view into the tiny Druze village of Ein Qinya, is just off bus route #55 between Kiryat Shmona and Katzrin; the road leading to the castle is directly across from the bus stop. Bus #14 from Kiryat Shmona to Neve Ativ passes by; the site is a one-hour walk uphill. The castle is also accessible by a footpath from the Banyas, beginning directly above the springs. The shadeless walk takes about an hour and a half each way. (Tel. 942 360. Open 8am-5pm. Admission NIS8.50, students NIS6.50.)

MAS'ADA AND MAJDAL SHAMS مسعدة و مجدل شمس

The Druze of these villages are separated from their Syrian brothers and sisters by looming Mt. Hermon and by politics. Most of them are loyal to Syria. In 1982, they tore up their Israeli citizenship documents in a protest backed by PLO-supplied weapons. The Israeli army quickly quashed the revolt, but not the Syrian allegiance. Outwardly, however, the villages are tranquil.

Mas'ada and Majdal Shams are far less primed for tourists than their counterparts in Carmel; hence, there's absolutely nothing to do. The emphasis here is more on tradition than on commercialism. Women walk around swathed in black and men wear black *shirwal* (low-hanging baggy pants), which date from Ottoman times.

Mas'ada is located at the foot of Mt. Hermon, at the intersection of the roads leading south to Katzrin and west to Kiryat Shmona. Mas'ada's farmers cultivate the valley and terrace the low-lying ridges around the mountain. The numerous Israeli flags and pro-Israel murals are the government's rebuke to the town's demonstrators. 2km down the road is the locally famous lake, **Birket Ram.** The perfectly round body of water is something of a geological peculiarity formed not, as it appears, in a volcano-crater, but by underground water-bearing strata. You'll know you've reached the lake when you see the parking lot of the two-story Birket Ram Restaurant. The excellent restaurant is always packed. Its only decent view is from the porch; the owners are polite but not terribly enthusiastic about gazers. You can rent a paddleboat (NIS10 per hr.) or a sailboard (NIS16 per ½hr.), but either way you still have to pay NIS1 just to walk down to the dock. Out of the parking lot and to the right you'll see a postcard-worthy view of a striking Druze mosque beneath seasonally snowy Mt. Hermon.

From Mas'ada to **Majdal Shams** ("tower of the sun" in Arabic), the largest town in the Golan (pop. 8000), you can walk 5km along a quiet road through the lush valley. Two kilometers past Majdal Shams is **Moshav Neveh Ativ,** founded after the Golan was captured by Israel. The *moshav* has developed a resort village to take advantage of the ski slopes on the southern face of **Mount Hermon** 10km away; call the ski office at 981 337. For information about rooms call 981 531. (Dorm beds (5 per room) NIS50. Doubles NIS160. Breakfast included.) The Alimi family of the *moshav* rents guest houses (tel. 981 333); bring a phrasebook. Bus #55 travels from the *moshav* to the villages (2 per day, NIS8.50). It's also possible to take a *sherut* taxi from Mas'ada to Kiryat Shmona in late afternoon for the same price. The road from Mas'ada to Kiryat Shmona is particularly scenic, running west along a gorge and past the hilltop village of Ein Qinya and the silhouette of Nimrod's Fortress.

About 5km before the border with Syria are two kibbutzim, **Merom Golan** and **Ein Zivan.** Merom Golan was the first Israeli settlement in the Golan, founded a few months after the Six-Day War. Nearby, Mt. Bental is visible; the radio-antennaed peak closer to Ein Zivan is Mt. Avital. From the observation point here you can see the destroyed Syrian city of Quneitra. In 1973, Israel captured and completely destroyed the town, only to return it to Syria in the 1974 disengagement agreement. Once a city of 30,000 and headquarters of the Syrian army, Quneitra is now a ghost town in the buffer zone of a tense border. Syria maintains the gutted village as a propaganda tool.

Dead Sea and Deserts

■■■ THE DEAD SEA ים המלח

In case you haven't heard yet, this is the lowest point on the surface of the planet, at almost 394m below sea level. It sounds inspiring on paper, but you won't grasp the awesomeness of the region until you drive in from Be'er Sheva or Jerusalem, pass a "sea level" signpost, and then round a bend to see entire mountain ranges whose peaks are below you. The name was coined by Christian pilgrims astonished by the apparent absence of any form of life in the sea's waters (kill-joy scientists have recently discovered microorganisms in the lake). Its Hebrew name, Yam Ha-Melaḥ ("The Sea of Salt"), is more to the point: the lake has a salt concentration eight times that of ocean water. It is this high concentration of minerals that attracts tourists to the bitter, oily waters—the dissolved minerals make the water so dense that even a land-bound city slicker could not sink in it. These same urbanites bring newspapers to the beach and pose for snapshots of them lying on their backs, ankles crossed, perusing stock market listings in the middle of the water.

The Dead Sea is more of a large lake, 65km long, up to 18km wide, and up to 400m deep. It was created by a rift in the Earth's crust (still evident in the jagged cliffs which rise on both the Israeli and Jordanian coasts) and filled with water from floods and underground streams in the surrounding desert. Although there is no outlet for the lake's water, the intense sun bearing down on the valley used to evaporate enough water to keep the water level constant. Present-day pumping of the lake's sources, most notably Israel's diversion of water from the Sea of Galilee for agricultural purposes, has dwindled its supply of fresh water, resulting in a gradual lowering of the water level (most noticeable in the shallow southern parts).

The water itself is a source of controversy—some swear by its curative powers; others say it's useless. According to a few scientists and all resort owners, concentrations of bromine, magnesium, and iodine 10 to 20 times higher than in the ocean reduce skin allergies, stimulate glandular functions, and have a soothing effect on the nervous system. The sulphur springs at resorts along the coast seem to alleviate the pain of rheumatism and arthritis, but occasionally they have an adverse effect on blood pressure and olfactory functions.

In ancient times, the Dead Sea was a refuge for those in search of religious freedom (the Qumran sect), political freedom (David, who hid at Ein Gedi), or both (the Jewish rebels at Masada). The Dead Sea can also name Jesus, King Herod, and John the Baptist among its illustrious residents.

PRACTICAL INFORMATION

A warning: if Dead Sea water gets into your eyes, you're in for several minutes of painful blindness. Rinse your eyes immediately in the fresh-water showers found on all beaches. And you know that cliché about rubbing salt in your wounds? Don't shave the morning before you go swimming; the water will sear minor scrapes you didn't even know you had. Since you will probably want to wash off as soon as you get out of the water, stick to the beaches with showers (Ein Feshka, Ein Gedi, Ein Bokek, and Neveh Zohar). Free public beaches are at Neveh Zohar, Ein Bokek, and Ein Gedi, all accessible by bus. Thermal baths, spas, and mud-baths in Neveh Zohar and Ein Bokek have separate bus stops.

The Dead Sea does not have an ordinary desert climate—instead of being harsh and dry, it's harsh and humid. The sticky air, especially in the summer, makes high temperatures barely tolerable. Athletes may enjoy the clean air and a 10% increase in oxygen concentration, but exertion is sane only in the early morning. In fact, the steamroom-like weather has been known to cause dehydration in people simply waiting for a bus in a shaded bus stop. So while desert rules apply (naturally; keep your head covered and take a water bottle wherever you go), be extra careful to drink plenty of liquids and refill your water bottles whenever possible. Don't take it for granted that all shower and faucet water is safe to drink—most Dead Sea locations have special faucets marked "Drinking Water."

Only a few Egged lines travel the Dead Sea coast. Waits often last 45 to 90 minutes, so check schedules (under Practical Information for each site) and plan ahead. Bus #444, 486, and 966 from Jerusalem to Eilat stop at Qumran, Ein Feshka, Ein Gedi, Masada, and Neveh Zohar. Bus #487, also from Jerusalem, runs only to Qumran, Ein Feshka, and Ein Gedi. Bus #385 makes about four trips per day (Sun.-Fri.) between Ein Gedi and Be'er Sheva via Arad, Ein Bokek, and Masada. Note that reservations for seats on the Eilat bus from Jerusalem cannot be made at Ein Gedi or Masada. Your chances of getting an unreserved seat are good at the height of the tourist season, since Egged often runs two buses at a time to accommodate the crowds.

Each of the region's attractions can be seen in a few hours or a half-day at most. Infrequent bus connections, the isolation of the sights, and the fact that some attractions can only be reached via long hikes from the main road make **renting a car** a good idea, especially for groups. Most companies offer a daily rental rate of about US$10, plus 27¢ per kilometer; there are also two- and three-day rental rates with unlimited mileage for around US$68. If you know in advance that you'll want a car, order it abroad—you'll pay up to one-third less than the Israeli price, especially in the U.S. Otherwise, rent in Jerusalem (1hr. away) or visit the Hertz office (tel. 584 530) in Ein Bokek, next door to the tourist information office.

Organized **tours** are an option for carless sorts. A one-day **Metzokei Dragot Desert Tour Village** takes you through rugged terrain to major sights (NIS185). Tours leave from the Jerusalem Gate Hotel near the bus station every Tuesday at 9am. Call their offices in Kibbutz Mitzpeh Shalem (tel. (02) 964 501 or 502 or 503), where you can also inquire about rappeling and climbing trips. **SPNI** frequently arranges excellent hiking tours around the Dead Sea. Their standard guided tour in English runs US$138 for two days and includes transportation, food, and lodging (Jerusalem office tel. (02) 252 357, Ein Gedi field school tel. (07) 584 288). The bus tour organized by **Jasmine Cottage** in Jerusalem gives a one-day overview of the desert and hits all the major sights, including sunrise on Masada (11-13hr., from US$20). Contact the Cottage (tel. (02) 248 021) or Jerusalem Inn Youth Hostel (tel. (02) 251 294) for information.

QUMRAN قمران קומרן

In 1947, a young Bedouin looking for a wayward sheep wandered into a remote cliffside cave and happened upon a collection of earthenware jars containing 2000-year-old parchment manuscripts. These famed **Dead Sea Scrolls** are an important source on the development of the Bible. The largest, now displayed in the Shrine of the Book at the Israel Museum in Jerusalem, was a 7m-long ancient Hebrew text of the Book of Isaiah. Encouraged by the discovery, French archaeologists searched the caves and excavated the foot of the cliffs. By 1956 they had found the village of the sect that wrote the Dead Sea Scrolls, as well as additional scrolls.

Archaeological evidence suggests that the site was settled as long ago as the 8th century BCE, reinhabited in the 2nd century BCE, temporarily abandoned during the reign of Herod following an earthquake, and completely deserted after the Roman defeat of the Jewish revolt in 70 CE. Historians believe that the authors of the scrolls were the **Essenes,** a Jewish sect whose members, disillusioned by the corruption and Hellenization of fellow Jerusalemites, sought refuge in the sands. The strict and devout Essenes believed that a great struggle would ensue between the Sons of Light (themselves and the angels) and the Sons of Darkness (everyone else). Excavations at Masada suggest that the members of the Qumran sect joined with the Jews at Masada in their struggle against the Romans.

The main archaeological site is small. Look for the cisterns and channels that were used for storage and transport of water in the arid climate. Climb first to the **watchtower** for a panorama of the site. Proceed to the **scriptorium,** the chamber in which the scrolls were probably written, still equipped with desks and inkstands. In the newly-excavated **honey press,** dates (rather than bees) were used to produce the sticky substance. The ruins are clearly marked, and a map of the site is posted just past the entrance. A short climb brings you to the **caves** themselves. It may not seem far, but bring water and a hat. If you have a backpack, the staff at the reception booth will usually stare at it for you at no charge.

To see the ruins, take bus #421, 444, 486, or 487 from either Ein Gedi (NIS11) or Jerusalem (NIS14). When you get off the bus, cross the road to a steep hill with a road winding around its top. Don't panic—it's only a 100m hike, and the ruins are right around the bend. Make your way past the **boutique** selling the usual tour books, blown glass vases, and film (open daily 8am-7pm); then pass the adjoining clean, air-conditioned, self-service **cafeteria** (tel. (02) 942 533; sandwiches NIS8, hot lunch NIS21). To your right just past the cafeteria are the **public bathrooms;** across from them is the entrance to the site. The ticket counter (tel. (02) 922 505) has brochures describing the history and layout of the ruins. (Admission NIS8.50, students NIS6.40, children NIS4. Open Sun.-Thurs. 8am-4pm and Fri. 8am-3pm; summer 8am-7pm and 8am-6pm.)

Recover from the heat by going down to the bus station and taking any southbound bus (i.e. towards Masada, Ein Gedi, and Eilat) 3km to the salt- and fresh-water bathing spot at **Ein Feshka** (tel. (02) 942 355), where springs tumble into small pools and wind through the *wadi*'s tangled reeds. Herds of ibex graze in this extraordinarily fertile oasis. The small beach is quiet, except on weekends. From the shore, a dirt road leads inland to the **nature reserve,** where you can wade in femur-deep pools formed by natural springs. Ein Feshka is the only Dead Sea resort with fresh-water ponds adjacent to the swimming area. Rivulets lace the area and vacationers lounge about, caked head to toe with Dead Sea mud. There are showers, changing rooms, bathrooms, and drinking water. A lifeguard hut separates the beach from the wallow. (Admission NIS12, students NIS9. Open daily 8am-6pm.)

Seven kilometers north of the Qumran ruins (bus #421, 444, 486, and 487 will all take you, but be sure to cross the road from the ruins or you'll end up in Eilat) is **Attraction Water Park** (tel. (02) 942 393) in Kalya Beach. Good fun. (Open daily March-Oct. 9am-7pm. Admission NIS24, students NIS20.)

EIN GEDI עין גדי

Ein Gedi has a long history of providing shelter. David fled to this oasis to escape the wrath of King Saul (1 Samuel 23:29); and the oasis is also mentioned in the Song of Songs (Song 1:14). During the second Jewish revolt, Simon Bar-Kokhba sought refuge here. His hiding place, the Letter Cave, can be visited about 6km southwest of the main settlement. Today, Ein Gedi's lush **nature reserve,** endowed with cascading waterfalls, wildlife, and shade, provides shelter from the desert sun.

Practical Information Bus connections to Ein Gedi are rare and require advance planning. From Ein Gedi, bus #421 or 444 (6, 9, 9:45am, 12:05, 12:45, 2, 2:25, 3:40, 4:45, 6, and 7:45pm, last bus Fri. 4pm) will take you to Jerusalem (NIS16.80, students NIS14.50). Bus #384 and 385 (8, 11:15am, 12:30, 3:30, and 5:45pm) go to Be'er Sheva (NIS20.30, students NIS18.70) via Arad (NIS11.30). Bus #486 (9:45am, 1:15, and 2:15pm) runs to Masada and to the hotels at Ein Bokek (NIS6.70). Bus #444 (8, 11am, 3, and 6pm) goes to Eilat (NIS33, students NIS24). There are three bus stops in Ein Gedi: the northernmost one is where you get off for the nature reserve, the youth hostel, and the SPNI field school. South of that stop is the Ein Gedi Beach stop, where you'll find not only the beach (surprise), but also campgrounds, a mini-market, restaurant, gas station, and first-aid station. Finally, the southernmost stop is convenient to the thermal baths and spas.

Accommodations and Food Nights in Ein Gedi can be as hot as the days; think twice about sleeping without A/C. The **Beit Sara Youth Hostel (HI)** (tel. (07) 584 165), just uphill from the Nahal David entrance to the nature reserve, has a hot, muggy outdoor **bar** (open nightly 6-11pm) and terrace overlooking the Dead Sea. All rooms have A/C and private baths. (Check-in 4pm. Check-out 9am. No lockout. No curfew, but after 11pm a night guard lets you in. Dorm beds (8 per room) NIS43 per bed. Doubles NIS132. Nonmembers add NIS3. Breakfast included. Wash and dry NIS5 each per load.) A 10-minute walk from the hostel along the uphill-winding road will bring you to the **SPNI Field School** (tel. (07) 584 288) at the top (bus #384 and 385 will go all the way up if you ask the driver), often crowded with tour groups; call ahead. All rooms have A/C and private baths. (Dorm beds (6 per room) available only to small groups at NIS340 per room. Doubles NIS180. Breakfast included. Kitchen available.) Also has trail maps, a tiny museum, snake collection, and a 15-minute audiovisual show about desert flora and fauna (NIS7, students NIS5). Farther south, at the Ein Gedi Beach bus stop, **Ein Gedi Camping** (tel. (07) 584 342 or 444; fax 584 455) is just behind and to the right of the gas station. Clean bathrooms available, bring your own sleeping bag and tent. (NIS24 per person, children NIS12. Lockers NIS5 every time they're opened.) The campground also offers air-conditioned **caravans** for four to six people. Slightly cramped, with kitchenette and private bath (US$61 per couple, each additional person US$9).

Kiosk Nahal David, just outside the entrance to the nature reserve, has mineral water and ice cream (NIS3), sandwiches (NIS5.70), and hats (NIS13). (Open Sun.-Fri. 9am-5pm, Sat. 9:30am-5pm.) Other food options are at the beach bus stop. **Kiosk Ein Gedi** has beer (NIS3.70) and sandwiches (NIS9). (Open Sun.-Fri. 7:30am-8pm, Sat. 10am-7pm.) The large, air-conditioned **Milky Restaurant** next door requires shirt and shoes. Self-service sandwiches NIS9, hot lunch NIS19. (Open daily 8am-6pm, last hot meal must be ordered by 5pm.) A **minimarket** is next to the campground (open Sun.-Fri. 8-9am, 11:30am-2pm, and 4-4:30pm, Sat. 9:15-11am and noon-2:30pm). With Zen meditation, learn to limit your hunger to these hours.

Sights At the **Ein Gedi Nature Reserve** (tel. (07) 584 285 or 517) tourists swim and luxuriate in waterfalls. Of the two entrances, only the Nahal David entrance just inland from the youth hostel stop is accessible by bus. Trail maps and information are available here. The climbs in the reserve are not too difficult—well-placed bars provide support in steep areas. Lockers at the gift shop will lighten your load for NIS2. Dead Sea temperatures can make even inhaling strenuous, so hike only very early in the morning or late in the afternoon. *Always* bring at least two bottles of water (you can fill up at the faucets just outside the gate).

An enjoyable 15-minute hike takes you up to **Nahal David** (David's Stream), a slender pillar of water dropping into a shallow pool. Twenty meters below the waterfall, another trail climbs up the cliffside to **Shulamit Spring.** From the spring, continue up the cliff to **Dodim Cave** (Lover's Cave), a splendidly cool, mossy niche at the top of the fall (30-min. walk). Or proceed left to the fenced-in **Chalcolithic Temple** (20min. from Dodim), built 5000 years ago. Hyenas, wolves, and the elusive leopard all roam the reserve; expect also to see ibex, hyrax, and fox. From the Temple, either your steps or take the steeply descending path to **Ein Gedi Spring** (25min.). From Ein Gedi Spring a roundabout path runs to Shulamit Spring, whence you can return to the base of the waterfall at Nahal David.

A fairly difficult climb along **Nahal Arugot,** which begins in the parking lot of the Nahal Arugot Rd. about 2km in from Rte. 90, leads to a charming "hidden waterfall." It's a good 90-minute walk from the road (look for the sign), but if you follow the stream you won't get lost. The pool at the end, considerably deeper than the others, rewards the exertion. The reserve is open 8am-3pm, but you can exit until 4pm (in summer 8am-4pm, last exit 5pm); you may not start hikes to Dodim Cave and beyond after 1:30pm (in summer 2:30pm). There is no eating or smoking in the reserve. (Admission NIS8.50, children NIS4.50.)

Ein Gedi has a free **public beach.** It is mostly rocky and its facilities are not as good as those at Ein Bokek, but walk north (left from the entrance) for ten minutes to find vats of the famous **Dead Sea Mud** as well as some **freshwater springs.**

THE DEAD SEA

MASADA מצדה

The huge fortress *(Metzada)* was built as a refuge against marauding Greeks and Syrians by the Jewish High Priest Jonathan Maccabeus around 150 BCE. The 2000 ft. by 750 ft. fortress was expanded a few decades later by John Hyrcanus I. In 40 CE, King Herod fled to Masada to avoid being massacred by rival Parthian-backed Hasmoneans. Masada was used once again in 66 CE, when the Judeans rebelled against Roman occupation; a small band of rebels, the original Zealots, captured the outpost. The Romans gradually crushed the revolt, taking Jerusalem in 70 CE and destroying the Second Temple; Masada was the last holdout in all of Israel. With years' worth of food, water, and military supplies stashed behind its two defensive walls, Masada was ideally suited for resistance. The 967 men, women, and children held off thousands of Roman legionnaires through a five-month siege. The Romans, frustrated at first, called in their best engineers and constructed a wall and camps in a ring around the mount. They ultimately built an enormous stone and gravel ramp up the side of the cliff, using Jewish slaves as labor so as to prevent the Zealots from shooting them down as the ramp was built.

When the defenders realized that the Romans would break through the wall the next morning, the community leaders decided that it would be better to die than to live as slaves. Each family burned its possessions and joined in the communal suicide plan. The Jews placed stores of wheat and water in the citadel's courtyard to prove to the Romans that they did not perish from hunger. The following morning, when the Romans burst in, they encountered a deathly silence. The only survivors, two women and five children, told the story of the martyrs of Masada. The story was recorded by Josephus Flavius, a Jewish general who had defected to the Romans and become a chronicler.

"Masada shall not fall again," swear members of the armored division of the Israel Defense Forces each year at this site. The Jewish Zealots' tenacious defense of the place, though forgotten for centuries, has been fashioned into a symbol in modern Israel, with some controversy about the metaphor's implications.

Practical Information Masada lies 20km south of Ein Gedi, a few kilometers inland from the Arad-Be'er Sheva road. **Bus** #421, 444, or 486 will take you to Jerusalem (8:30, 9:45, 11:45am, 12:45, 2:45, 3:15, 4:15, 4:45, and 7:45pm; last bus Fri. 3:45pm; NIS16.70); #444 will take you to Eilat (8:15, 11:15am, 3:15, 6:15pm; last bus on Fri. 3:15pm; NIS28, students NIS21); and #384 or 385 will take you to Be'er Sheva (NIS18, students NIS14.30) via Ein Bokek (NIS6.30) and Arad (NIS13.30, students NIS12). It's a long 4.3km walk to the Dead Sea shore; if you're going to attempt this feat in the stifling desert heat, be sure you have enough water and head covering. **Oda Taxi** (tel. 952 377) will take you *sherut* from the mountain to Ein Gedi (NIS8), Ein Bokek (NIS8), and Arad (NIS15). You should first *conspicuously* write down or memorize the cab number (on the green semi-circle on top of each cab), then ask the driver for the fare, *before* you enter the vehicle—metered rides to nearby Arad can sum up to NIS300 because the many curves in the road make the trip a one-hour journey. If you've written down the cab number, you can easily file a complaint and get your money back in case of such outrageously high billing.

There are three ways to climb the mountain to reach the ruins: by cable car or by either of two foot paths. The **Roman Ramp** is the easier of the two and starts on Arad Rd. on the west side of the mountain (30min.). However, this trail is not accessible by public transportation, and the walk around the base to the Roman Ramp is extremely arduous and time-consuming. If you hike down the Ramp and walk around the city to the east side, stick to the SPNI trail; *don't* descend the incline with the water pipe. More popular, more scenic, and more difficult is the original **Snake Path,** named for its tortuous bends. The path has barely been repaired since the Zealots used it. The hike takes just under an hour, and if you start early enough (gates open at 5:15am), you'll see the sun slowly rising over the Dead Sea 450m below. Start hiking *well* before the afternoon, both to avoid the heat and to leave enough time for exploring. Drinking water is available only at the summit.

The hiking-averse may prefer a **cable car** which stops near the top of Snake Path. It runs from 8am to 4pm (summer 5pm), on Friday 8am to 2pm (summer 3pm), leaving every half-hour or when 40 passengers have assembled for the three-minute ascent. Admission (NIS11, students NIS8.25) is to be paid at the top of the summit. Round-trip cable car fare including admission is NIS33, students NIS20.25. One-way including admission is NIS23, students NIS15.75. A popular option is to hike up in the early morning and then take the cable car down when it gets hot. The site officially closes at 5pm, but the guards don't really kick people out until around 7pm.

Accommodations and Food The **Taylor Youth Hostel (HI),** in front of you and to the left as you get off the bus to Masada, is surrounded by grass and shade trees. All rooms have A/C and private baths. A cable TV lounge and barbecue area are available to guests. (Dorm beds (6-8 per room) NIS43. Singles NIS90. Doubles NIS126. Triples NIS170. Nonmembers add NIS3 per person. Breakfast included. Newly-renovated dining room serves tasty dinners (NIS23). Lockers NIS4. Washer and dryer NIS5 ea. per load.) A concrete pavilion in front of the hostel accommodates **campers** for free, but has no facilities. You can no longer sleep on Masada.

The food options are almost as limited. The **snack bar** adjacent to the lower cable car complex sells meat or cheese sandwiches for NIS7, ice cream for NIS2.50 per scoop, and cold drinks for NIS3 per cup. At the **restaurant** farther down the slope (open Sat.-Thurs. 8am-5pm, Fri. 8am-3pm), entrees are NIS18.

Sights The ruins at Masada were unearthed in 1963 by a team of archaeologists headed by Yigael Yadin. About one-third of the ruins you see are actually reconstructed—a black line indicates the extent of the original findings. Directly in front of the entrance to the site stands a large sign with a map of the ruins, which outlines several walking tours. From the entrance, the Northern Palace, which includes Herod's own private pad, is up and to your right. Across the site is the Western Palace; the Southern Citadel is down to the left at the far end of the mountaintop.

The best remains at the **Northern Palace** are the **central public bath** and the private palace of King Herod. The bath is well preserved, but, disappointingly, the frigidarium isn't working. Don't linger too long, or you'll find yourself exiting into a huge caldarium. **King Herod's Palace** is poised spectacularly on the rock's prow. The lower terrace's painted frescoes and intact capitals on fluted columns suggest the splendor that Herod enjoyed. In the bathhouse of the lowest section, the skeletons of a man, woman, and child were found, along with a *tallit* (prayer shawl).

From the top of the Herod's palace stairs, you can skirt your way around the western edge of the mountain. You'll soon come across the **Zealots' synagogue,** one of the oldest synagogues in Israel. Scrolls were found here containing texts from several books of the Torah (most are now on display at the Israel Museum in Jerusalem; see p. 401). The scrolls and discoveries such as a *mikveh* (ritual bath) indicate that the community followed Jewish strictures despite their mountain isolation and siege. Continuing further along the edge you find the **Western Palace,** which houses splendid Herodian mosaics, the oldest in Israel. Next to the Palace you'll find the **Byzantine Chapel,** built by the Christian monks who once occupied Masada.

Farther south are stone stairs descending into a dark hole. Go down into the cistern: it's part of the system of reservoirs that allowed the defenders to store an eight-year supply of water. **Restrooms** are in the administration building and in the residence of the royal family. Drinking water pours out of several taps on the mountain.

We know you're sick of audiovisual presentations about the desert (so are we), but the Masada **sound and light show** makes the fortress light up like a Las Vegas marquee. Shows are in Hebrew, but simultaneous-translation earphones (NIS11) are available in English, German, French, Russian, and Spanish. Make reservations through the GTIO in Arad (tel. 958 144 or 993). (April-Aug. shows Tues. and Thurs. 9pm; Sept.-Oct. 7pm. Tickets NIS24, students NIS21. Round-trip transportation from Arad and the Dead Sea area NIS23.)

Near Masada

Ein Bokek, the public beach with the best facilities in the area, is located about 5km away from Masada. All buses passing through Masada also stop here (15min. earlier if they're headed towards Ein Gedi and Jerusalem, 15min. later if they're headed towards Arad and Be'er Sheva). The beach stop is located amidst the hotels, and the beach is directly in front of you as you step off. Challenge: try lifting *both* your legs at least 5 inches out of the briny waters at the same time.

The **Tourist Information Office** is in the white mini-mall to your left (tel. 584 153; fax 584 637), past the ice cream stores. They have information on jeep tours in the area. (Open Sun. and Tues.-Thurs. 10am-1pm and 4-6pm.) The beach-front **Kapul-sky's** (open daily 8am-midnight) and **Hordus Beach Restaurant** (open Sun.-Thurs. 7:30am-9:30pm and Fri. 8am-2pm) are outrageously overpriced (the cheapest pizza is NIS19). Instead, shop at the **mini-market** in the same complex that houses the tourist office and picnic in the grassy **Tamar Garden** opposite Hotel Lot.

Stretching south from Neveh Zohar, the road drops into searing **Sodom.** The Bible describes Sodom and Gomorrah as the New Yorks of their day, upon which God rained fire and brimstone. Lot's family was spared on the condition that they not look back to witness their neighbors' plight. Out of sympathy or curiosity, Lot's wife snuck a fateful glance and was transformed into a pile of salt (Genesis 18-19).

In modern Sodom the visitor magnet is the column of sodium chloride that tour guides introduce as Mrs. Lot. Sodom is also the home of the **Dead Sea Works,** which extract potash and other minerals from the Dead Sea for export. Tours are arranged in the rear of the main office in Arad. There is no direct public transporta-tion to Sodom. If you have a car you can visit the **Salt Cave,** the longest and lowest of its kind in the world. The nearby **Flour Cave** is named for the floury residue that lines its walls (and consequently its visitors). These caves involve a several-kilometer walk from the bus stop; at 45°C you'll wish you were as dead as the sea. The Tourist Information Office in Ein Bokek runs some guided tours of the area, by car and by foot, for only NIS5 per person. You must call (tel. 584 153) for reservations.

■■■ BE'ER SHEVA באר שבע

Tell any traveler or Israeli that you're going to Be'er Sheva, and he or she will undoubtedly raise a confused eyebrow. Though the city is domestically important as an administrative and commercial center, the capital of the Negev isn't as popular with tourists as, say, Jerusalem. Unless you're a Russian immigration buff or a volun-teer, Be'er Sheva's only attraction is an exciting Thursday morning Bedouin market.

Be'er Sheva means both "well of the oath" and "well of seven" in Hebrew, and the Bible (Genesis 21:25-31) offers both etymologies. The Arabic name, Bir As-Sabe', also means "well of seven." The story goes that Abimelekh's servants seized a well that Abraham claimed to have dug. The dispute ended with a covenant in which Abraham offered seven ewes to Abimelekh in exchange for recognition as the well's rightful owner. You can still see **Abraham's well** today.

When Israel captured the city in 1948, Bir As-Sabe' was a peaceful agricultural vil-lage of less than 2000 Palestinians. Now its unattractive housing projects are home to immigrants from Morocco, Syria, Russia, Argentina, and Ethiopia, as well as the largest Albanian Jewish community in the world. Today, Be'er Sheva's 150,000 peo-ple are doing their best to make tens of thousands of newly-arrived, frost-bitten Rus-sians feel at home in the desert town. The city, though not high on affordable accommodations, could serve well as a transit point for short forays into the Negev.

ORIENTATION AND PRACTICAL INFORMATION

The city's **central bus station** is located on **Eilat Street,** across the road from **Kan-ion Ha-Negev Shopping Center,** a good landmark from which to orient yourself. The bus station is divided into two sections: one for the red inter-city Egged buses, and the other for the blue (independently-run) municipal lines (all rides NIS1.80, see Central Bus Station listing below for main routes).

West of the central bus station, across Eilat St., lies the **Muslim Cemetery,** and just west is the neat grid that makes up the **old city** area, where most attractions are concentrated. The main east-west streets start with the northernmost **Ha-Histadrut Street,** parallel to it is **Ha-Halutz Street,** one block south, followed by **Mordei Ha-Geta'ot Street** and **Trumpeldor Street** farther south. The main north-south avenues begin with **Hadasa Street** about four blocks west of Eilat St.; one block west of Hadasa St. is **Ha'Atzma'ut Street** (on which you can see the tower of the Negev Museum), and a final block west is **Keren Kayemet LeYisrael Street,** which is the town's pedestrian section. The streets are reassuringly close together, and miscounting blocks or making a wrong turn won't take you miles from your destination.

Government Tourist Information Office (GTIO): 6 Ben-Tzvi St. (tel. 236 001/2; fax 236 003), across the street from the main entrance to the bus station, 2 doors right of the Hertz sign. May become an MTIO in 1995. Open Sun.-Thurs. 8:30am-5pm.

Town Hall: From bus station, cross the parking lot and go left on Ben Tzvi St. Walk one block to Ha-Nesi'im. Turn right and go three blocks up. On your right an air traffic control tower stands behind a public square. Get a map for NIS5. A talking computer service says "If you need more information, go ahead, make my day" with an Israeli accent. Yitzhak Yellin (tel. 463 879 or 790 or 791), an advisor to the mayor and former Bostonian, is eager to help *Let's Go*ons. Open 24 hrs.

Post Office: (tel. 232 175), corner of Ha-Nesi'im Blvd. and Ben-Tzvi Rd., diagonally across from the bus station. This modern main branch has **Poste Restante** and **Western Union** services. Smaller branches on **Hadassa Street** and in the **City Hall** building. All branches open Sun.-Tues. and Thurs. 8am-12:30pm and 4-6:30pm, Wed. 8am-1pm, Fri. 8am-12:30pm.

Currency Exchange: Bank Leumi, just past the post office on Ha-Nesi'im (tel. 239 222). Open Sun., Tues., Thurs. 8:30am-12:30pm and 4-5:30pm, Mon. 8:30am-2pm, Wed. 8:30am-12:30pm, Fri. 8:30am-noon. **Bank Ha-Poalim,** 40 Ha'Atzma'ut St. (tel. 292 662), corner of Ha-Halutz St. Open Mon. and Wed. 8:30am-1pm, Sun., Tues., Thurs. 8:30am-12:30pm and 4-6pm, Fri. 8:30am-noon.

Telephones: By 1995, main post office branch will have international calling. Locally, the 5-digit numbers are slowly being phased out. When in doubt, add a "2" to the front of the old number. The Bezek announcements in Hebrew that give this information are usually followed by an English translation (or you can always call **directory assistance** at 144, free from any public phone). **Telephone Code:** 07.

Central Bus Station: between Ha-Nesi'im and Eilat St. (tel. 430 585 for intercity buses, 277 381 or 382 for local lines). Bus #3 goes to the *shuk,* the old city, and the shopping mall (every 10-15min. 5:20am-11pm), and #13 follows Ha'Atzma'ut St. to the Negev Museum and the Beit Yatziv Youth Hostel (every 24min. 5:20am-11pm). All local rides NIS1.80. Intercity connections on red Egged buses. To Tel Aviv: #370 direct to new central bus station or #380 direct to Arlozorov Terminal (both every 20-30min. 5:30am-7:30pm; NIS16, students NIS8); to Jerusalem: #470 direct (every hr. 7-9am and 3-5pm) or #446 express (every 25-35min. 6am-7pm; NIS19.50, students NIS10); to Eilat: #394 express (every hr. 5am-5pm) or #397 slow (11am and 2pm), both Eilat buses are NIS33, students NIS16.50.

Sherut Taxis: Yael-Daroma, 195 Keren Kayemet LeYisrael St. (tel. 281 144 or 145). *Sherut* to Jerusalem (NIS19.50), Eilat (NIS33), and Tel Aviv (NIS16); same price as buses, but you may have to wait for the taxi to fill up.

Car Rental: Eldan (tel. 430 344), at the Desert Inn Hotel. **Hertz,** 5a Ben Tzvi St. (tel. 272 768), across from bus station. Both open Sun.-Thurs. 8am-6pm, Fri. 8am-3pm; minimum age is 21-23 depending on type of car.

English Bookstores: Used books at **Mini Book,** 67 Ha-Histadrut St. (tel. 433 396), in the passageway between Hadassah and Ha-Histadrut St., opposite Israel Discount Bank. Open Sun.-Wed. 9:30am-2pm and 4-7pm, Thurs.-Fri. 9:30am-1pm. **Steimatzky,** in the Kanion (mall) across from the bus station (tel. 230 301). Open Sun.-Thurs. 9am-9pm, Fri. 9am-2pm, Sat. 8-10pm.

Camping Supplies: Reta, in the central bus station (tel. 275 415), open Sun.-Fri. 8am-6pm; another branch in the Kanion (tel. 233 577), open 9am-9pm.
Pharmacies: PharmLine (tel. 277 034), open Sun.-Thurs. 8am-8:30pm, Fri. 8am-2pm. **Super Pharm,** in the Kanion (tel. 281 371), open Sun.-Thurs. 9am-midnight, Fri. 9am-5pm; Call Super Pharm in case of emergency on weekends.
Hospital: Soroka Hospital, Ha-Nesi'im Blvd. (tel. 660 111). Bus #4 or 7, and tell the driver to let you off at the new emergency room.
First Aid: Magen David Adom, 40 Bialik St. (tel. 278 333; **emergencies** tel. 101).
Police: 30 Herzl St. (tel. 462 744; **emergencies** tel. 100), corner of Keren Kayemet LeYisrael St.

ACCOMMODATIONS

Be'er Sheva's budget accommodations are not the greatest in Israel, so if you're only planning to come for the Bedouin market early Thursday morning, you can easily see Abraham's Well and the museum or university, then move on to more attractively-priced hostels. If you can afford to stay here, use Be'er Sheva's as a base for exploring the Negev. Numerous bus connections will save you tons of time.

Beit Yatziv Youth Hostel (HI), 79 Ha'Atzma'ut St. (tel. 277 444), about 4 blocks from the Old Town center. Take bus #13. This well-kept, no-bunks hostel is found in the midst of the Beit Yatziv complex, with its own pool and dining room. Rooms have private bath, closet, fan, and table. Check-in after noon. Check-out 9am. No lockout. No curfew. Dorms (4 per room) NIS51. Singles NIS91. Doubles NIS131. Triples NIS155. Nonmembers add NIS3. Large breakfast included. Lunch and dinner available (NIS15-19).
Aviv Hotel, 40 Mordei Ha-Geta'ot St. (tel. 278 059 or 258), off Keren Kayemet LeYisrael St. Warm, Bulgarian owners Berta and Shlomo run a tidy, pleasant establishment with lots of flowers. Rooms have ancient but functioning private baths, A/C, phones, and carpeting. Side and front rooms have balconies overlooking the town center. Singles NIS60. Doubles NIS80. Breakfast NIS10.
Hotel Ha-Negev, 26 Ha'Atzma'ut, (tel. 277 026 or 278 744). Dim lounge looks like a good place to nurse a hangover. Plain-tile rooms with tiny showers, but new wallpaper says freshness. Singles/doubles in main building have A/C and private bath (NIS90). Rooms in the annex use shared toilets and have no A/C (NIS60; with private shower NIS70). Breakfast NIS15.
Arava Hotel, 37 Ha-Histadrut St. (tel. 278 792), just off Keren Kayemet LeYisrael St. Entrance through door with cheap jewelry store front. Rooms are plain, with small private baths, almost all have A/C. Modest no-cable TV lounge. Singles NIS50. Doubles NIS80. Breakfast included.

FOOD

The best place for inexpensive food is the Old Town's pedestrian section on **Keren Kayemet LeYisrael Street.** The street is lined with falafel, *shawerma,* pizza, and sandwich stands, and the competition has driven prices way down. Try **Paudak Chompi,** at the corner of Keren Kayemet LeYisrael and Ha-Histadrut St., where *me'orav* or *shishlik* in a pita are only NIS9, including unlimited chips and salads. Nearby, at 112 Keren Kayemet LeYisrael St., is **Itzek's Bulgarian Restaurant** (tel. 238 504), which serves outstanding *pad thai.* Just kidding. Kidneys, hearts, *schnitzel,* or goulash are only NIS18, Bavarian cream or chocolate mousse only NIS6. (Open Sun.-Thurs. and Sat. 9am-11pm.) **Bis Lekal Kis,** 98 Mordei Ha-Geta'ot St. (tel. 277 178) offers large kosher meat- or fish-based homestyle meals in a clean, air-conditioned environment (NIS14-20, open Sun.-Fri. 11:30am-4pm). Two blocks over at the **Abu LeMafia Bakery,** 40 Ha'Atzma'ut St., nestled into the side of the Bank Ha-Poalim building, swarthy men in blue suits with machine guns serve good imitations of the real Abu Elafia Bakery on Old Yafo for half the price (*bagelah* from NIS1.50, toasts and pizza NIS4, cold cocoa NIS1.50).

For an American food fix, head to the food court on the lower floor of the mall across from the bus station. A Bomba burger at **Burger Ranch** costs NIS8.70 and a hot dog is NIS6.10. Or get a full meal at **China Town** for NIS18-20. **Café George** has pastries for NI9 and coffee for NIS3. There's a **Pizza Hut** as well. (Most restaurants in the Kanion open Sun.-Thurs. 9am-midnight, Fri. 9am-1am, Sat. 10am-10pm.) The mall also features a **Hypershuk supermarket.** The cheapest place to buy drinks and fresh produce is the *shuk,* located just south of the central bus station and easily identifiable by its arched metal rooftops. The Thursday **Bedouin market** also has cheap foodstuffs. For desert dessert, nothing beats **Glida Be'er Sheva,** 50 Hadassah St. (tel. 277 072), where a waffle cone with 5 scoops is NIS6. (Open Sun.-Thurs. 9am-1am, Fri. 9am-9pm, Sat. 10am-2am.)

SIGHTS

Be'er Sheva's most exciting attraction is its Thursday-morning **Bedouin Market,** just south of the bus station (walk down Eilat St. until you see the action on your right). Trading begins around 6am and concludes by noon. Many Bedouin here speak relatively intelligible English and may compliment your beautiful eyes while charging six times the going rate. Market rules apply (see Bargaining, p. 12).

The scope of this market puts even Tel Aviv's *Shuk Ha-Pishpeshim* to shame. Hundreds of Bedouin, both the semi-settled from around Be'er Sheva and the nomads from deep in the desert, gather in the area around Hebron St. to sell sheep, goats, clothes, cloth, jewelry, ceramics, spices, and even digital watches. Animals are generally traded and sold on the city's southernmost limits, with camels strictly prohibited from the market. The northern part of the market features tremendous quantities of schlocky clothing, all selling for NIS10. "More fashionable" items may be marked as high as NIS20-30. As you head farther south, the quantity of rusty cans, scraps of paper and dust increases, the smell of goat dung becomes stronger, and you can buy live rabbits, chickens, doves, or even parakeets. The southernmost part of the market features the real gems: beaten copperware, Bedouin robes, fabrics, rugs, and ceramic items—all at bargain basement prices. Unfortunately the market is less vibrant since the *intifada* was declared in 1987 and Israel introduced licensing and red tape, which make it more difficult for Bedouins to set up shop.

Near the market, at 1 Hebron St., corner of Keren Kayemet LeYisrael St., you'll find **Abraham's Well,** for which the town is named (see city introduction, p. 348). Though this is the authentic site of the original well, the one that exists today only dates back to the beginning of the 12th century CE; it was used extensively by Bedouin tribes and then by Jewish immigrants. Today you can see a two-wheel mechanism (whose design dates back to biblical times) used to bring up water buckets. Extremely friendly Shosh will explain it all to you, show you the surrounding plants from her garden, and even give you a quick tour of the **Ethiopian Jewish Handcrafts Exhibit** in the back. (Open Sun.-Thurs. 8:30am-4pm, Fri. 8:30am-noon; free summer 1994, but not for long.)

The last of Be'er Sheva's eminent showpieces, the **Negev Museum,** 60 Ha'Atzma'ut St. (tel. 239 105), is housed in an old Turkish mosque (currently closed for structural renovations but expected to reopen by April 1995). This archaeologically-focused museum chronicles five millennia of the history of Be'er Sheva and the surrounding region, from the Chalcolithic Period to the present, with a special model of *Tel Sheva.* The square building adjacent to the museum with the graceful front arches is the **Governor's House.** Built by the Turks in 1906, it served its eponymous purpose until 1938, when it was converted into a girls' school. The girls' school went the way of most Palestinian establishments, and starting in 1949 the building was used as Be'er Sheva's City Hall. It's now part of the Negev Museum, housing a small contemporary **art gallery** and the **Israel Graphotek,** a non-profit organization which lends out framed, matted paintings by Israeli artists for only NIS4 per month, for up to 6 months. (Gallery complex open Sun. 10am-6pm, Mon.-Thurs. 10am-4:30pm, Fri.-Sat. 10am-1pm. Admission NIS5, students NIS3.)

The modern campus of **Ben-Gurion University,** founded in 1969, lies in the far northeastern corner of the city (bus #4 leaves from the central bus station every 15min.); for visits, contact Guest Relations at 461 111 or 279. Near the university dormitories at 50 Arlozorov St. is the Taubel Community Center, which houses the

Ethiopian Jewish Handicrafts Workshop (tel. 230 520 or 492 288). Here, you can watch demonstrations of age-old methods of creating pottery, figurines, embroidery, and gourd decorations. (Open Mon.-Tues. and Thurs. 8:30am-12:30pm. Free.) As long as you're in the vicinity, you may want to catch a glimpse of the unusually-shaped combination of sculptures composing the **Memorial of the Negev Palmaḥ Brigade,** dedicated to the soldiers who fell in the 1948 campaign to capture the desert. Its inscriptions, which give day-by-day accounts of the battles, have been largely neglected and redecorated by local youths with garbage. No direct transportation is available (bus #55 passes the spur road, a 1km walk from the memorial; a taxi costs NIS10 from the university and NIS18 from the old town).

Five kilometers northeast of the city are the impressive ruins at **Tel Be'er Sheva** (tel. 460 103), recently renovated and made into the heart of a national park. After exalting in the remains of a 2nd-century Roman fortress, frolic through 8th-century BCE houses, or toss a coin in a dry, 12th-century BCE well. Detailed brochures and site maps are available at an information booth facing the entrance to the park. Bus #55 runs near the site Sun.-Thurs. at 2:10, 3:15, and 5:45pm (last return bus 6pm), and Friday at 11:15am and 3pm (last return bus 3:15pm; NIS1.80). You'll have to sweat out the last 3km on foot. Next to the ruins is a visitors center with a cafeteria, an expensive restaurant, and a small **museum** devoted to the life of the Bedouins. (Center open daily 9am-11pm. Museum is open Sun.-Thurs. 10am-5pm, Fri.-Sat. 10am-1pm. Admission NIS4, students NIS2. The archaeological site is always open and free.) Solo women should not accept offers of personal tours of the site.

Eight more kilometers north of the *tel* is the fascinating **Joe Alon Bedouin Museum** (tel. 961 597), on the outskirts of Kibbutz Lahav (bus #369 and NIS5.70 will take you from the Be'er Sheva bus station to an intersection 500m from the museum). Here you'll find exhibits describing all facets of the nomads' lives, from traditional tools to embroidery and customary desert garb. There's even an audiovisual presentation describing their culture and their famous hospitality. (Open Sun.-Thurs. 10am-4pm, Fri. 10am-2pm; admission NIS6, students NIS4.)

ENTERTAINMENT

Be'er Sheva is surprisingly lively at night, especially around **Trumpeldor Street.** Most of the bars open at 8 or 9pm, but remain quiet until about 11pm, when an almost exclusively Israeli crowd starts pouring in. **Trombone,** 18 Ha'Avot St. (tel. 277 670), at the corner of Trumpeldor, is an informal restaurant/pub with an intimate atmosphere. Beer is NIS8 and entree-sized dishes NI17. (Open nightly 8pm-4am.) The wildest place in Be'er Sheva is **Ha-Simta** (The Alley), 16 Trumpeldor St. Prepare for a deafening mixture of Israeli, American, and European music and a crowd that sings along. Must be 18 or over. (Open nightly 8pm-3am.)

After sobering up, head for one of Be'er Sheva's **movie theaters,** four of which are in the Kanion, or dive into the **swimming pool** at the Beit Yatziv Youth Hostel, 79 Ha'Atzma'ut St. (Open Sun.-Fri. 8:30am-5pm, Sat. 8:30am-4pm. Admission NIS12, *Shabbat* NIS15, NIS9 for hostel guests.) Mellower yet is an annual international **harmonica and accordion festival** with street performers and classical, pop, blues, and soul concerts. The festival is in early July; ask at the GTIO for details.

■ NEAR BE'ER SHEVA

ARAD ‏ארד‎

Located about 35km east of Be'er Sheva, this "Gateway to the Judean Desert" is singularly unimpressive, until Birkenstock-wearin', granola-eatin', long-hair hippie-freaks and plenty of other Israeli music fans descend upon the town in mid-July.

A **Municipal Tourist Information Office** (tel. (07) 958 144 or 993 or 955 333; fax 955 052), located in the commercial center next to the post office, serves as a reservations center for organized tours and other attractions in the area, since there are no sights in Arad proper. (Open Sun.-Tues. 8am-1pm and 4-7pm, Wed. 8am-4pm, and Fri. 8:30am-12:30pm.) They'll hook you up for the **Masada Light and Sound**

As of June 1994, there was no direct transportation to Mamshit because the site had not officially opened. All buses going to Eilat stop by Mamshit on the main road, but it's a 2km walk after that. By 1995, Egged will have arranged for direct service from Be'er Sheva and Dimona (call Egged at (07) 278 558, or the Mamshit Tourism Authority at 556 478 or 469 981 for more information). About 1km away from the reconstructed city is a **Camel Ranch** (tel. (07) 551 054). Also check out two craters just outside Mamshit city limits, **Ha-Makhtesh Ha-Gadol** and the more distant and fantastic **Ha-Makhtesh Ha-Katan** (literally "the big and small craters").

SDEH BOKER שדה בוקר

Amidst endless desert, verdant Sdeh Boker is named for the mountain behind it. Arabs call this mountain "Jabal Baqara" (Mt. Cow), which Israelis changed to the closest Hebrew cognate, "Har Boker" (Cowboy Mt.). The **kibbutz,** established in 1952, produces olives, kiwis, and other fruit, as well as wheat, corn, and livestock.

David Ben-Gurion, Israel's first prime minister, considered settlement in the Negev a top priority. When experts advised that developing the Negev was a waste of money and time, Ben-Gurion insisted on searching for unconventional methods of taming the desert asking, "If the Nabateans can do it, why can't we?" He was so taken with the young pioneers building fledgling Sdeh Boker on a 1953 visit that he decided, at the age of 67, to resign from office and settle on this kibbutz in the middle of the desert. So now there's a plethora of Ben-Gurion sights and memorabilia. Non-B.-G. fans will find Sdeh Boker a base for some awesome desert exploration in the nearby **Ein Avdat Natural Reserve.**

Practical Information and Accommodations The only public transportation to or from Sdeh Boker is Egged **bus #60,** running between Be'er Sheva and Mitzpeh Ramon (every 1-1½hr. until 9-10pm, NIS10). The bus makes three stops: at the gate of Kibbutz Sdeh Boker, at Ben-Gurion's Hut, and at the Ben-Gurion Institute for Desert Research. At this third stop, the road to the **Ein Avdat Nature Reserve** begins to the right of the gate. Follow the road to a shaded plaza with a **post office** (open Sun.-Thurs. 9-11am and 1-2pm, Fri. 9-11pm), **supermarket,** and **cafeteria** (both open Sun.-Thurs. 8am-7pm, Fri. 8am-2pm).

The **SPNI Field School** (tel. (07) 565 828 or 016; fax 565 721) is in the same plaza. Guided hikes (NIS400 per day) must be arranged in advance. Answers questions about hiking routes and desert flora and fauna, and sells detailed maps in Hebrew. Even has a sound and light show on Ben-Gurion's life (NIS6, students and children NIS4; call 565 717 for screening times; office open Sun.-Thurs. 8am-6:30pm, Fri. 8am-11:30pm).

The **hostel** on the canyon's edge has spotless, modern rooms with private baths and incredible views of the Zin Canyon. Kitchen available. The palm-shaded, sand-colored exterior affords interior coolness. (Dorm beds NIS23 for students only; non-students' doubles NIS150, each additional adult NIS35.) Arrangements at the roomier **Sdeh Boker Guest House** should be made at least a day in advance. (Contact Shosh at home (565 933) or in her office (565 079) 8am-4pm.) Every conceivable amenity, including free swimming pool use. Cavernous common room offers a dizzying view of the canyon. (Singles US$35. Doubles US$40.) Next door to the Ben-Gurion Hut is the **Sdeh Boker Inn** (tel. 560 379). (Full meals served until 3pm, NIS16. Stock up on liquids here. Open Sun.-Thurs. 8am-4pm, Fri. 8am-3pm, Sat 8:30am-3pm.)

Sights Hikers will love the **Ein Avdat Nature Reserve** in the Zin Canyon. Start at either the lower or upper parking lot—the trail runs between the two points. To get to the lower entrance, go to the Ben-Gurion Institute gate (third bus stop) and follow the road to your right (45-50min. walk). To get to the upper entrance, take bus #60 10km out of Sdeh Boker toward Mitzpeh Ramon and ask the driver to drop you off at the Ein Avdat trailhead *(henyon);* cross the road and go down the cliffside stairs. The trail is well-marked with ladders and footholds. The brochure at the entrance lays out a circular route (3-4hr.) and a shorter route (1-2hr.), both of which pass a waterfall, freshwater pools, hermit caves, and the remains of a Byzantine fortress. Feel free to wander off the trail and explore oasis plant and animal life. (Reserve open daily 8am-4pm. Admission NIS8.50.)

See **Ben-Gurion's Hut** (tel. (57) 560 320 or 558 444), only slightly larger than the residences of his kibbutz neighbors, as he left it. Pictures and documents, including biblical quotations Ben-Gurion copied for personal use, are on display, giving the visitor a tangible connection to the legendary leader. A picture of Mahatma Gandhi hangs in the bedroom. (Open Sun.-Thurs. 8:30am-3:30pm, Fri. 8:30am-2pm, Sat. and holidays 9am-2:30pm. Free.)

Walk on the canyon rim to the beautifully-landscaped **Ben-Gurion Tombs;** the view is classic. In 1992, ex-USSR ex-president Mikhail Gorbachev lay a wreath at Ben-Gurion's grave and praised the success of his style of socialism.

AVDAT עבדת

The magnificently preserved ruins of a 3rd-century BCE **Nabatean city** are perched upon a hill 11km south of Sdeh Boker, in Avdat. (The oasis just below the ruins grows from ancient water techniques borrowed from the Nabateans.) At the intersection of caravan routes from Petra and Eilat that continued on to Gaza, Avdat once thrived as a pit stop for travelers, a trading city, and a strategic base for the Nabateans' notorious raids. From Avdat they could see caravans as far away as (present-day) Mitzpeh Ramon or Sdeh Boker. Romans captured the city in 106 CE. The city flourished again during the Byzantine period, and most of the visible ruins date from this time. 7th-century Islamic marauders preserved the Roman baths but not much else. The most important Nabatean remains are a handsome esplanade on top of the hill, a winding staircase which led to a Nabatean temple, and a potter's workshop; all date back to the first century CE. The best of the Byzantine remains include a 20-ft. high wall, a street, a monastery, two churches, and a baptistry, all from the 6th century CE. (In the 20th century CE, the site was resurrected on celluloid in the movie version of *Jesus Christ Superstar.*)

Drinking water and bathrooms are across from the ticket booth. Bus #60 (12 per day Sun.-Thurs., 6 on Fri.; 35min.) runs from Be'er Sheva to Sdeh Boker, stopping in Avdat. Make it clear to the driver that you want to go to the archaeological site and *not* Ein Avdat the oasis. Near the bus stop is a **gas station** and **restaurant** (tel 550 954). Bring water for the 15-minute hike to the ruins; the summit is dry. (Open daily 8am-5pm. Admission NIS11.)

■■■ MITZPEH RAMON מצפה רמון

Mitzpeh Ramon sits on the rim of **Makhtesh Ramon** (Ramon Crater), the most gargantuan of the Negev's four craters. 400m deep, 9km wide, and 40km long, it is the largest natural crater in the world. Its rock formations are millions of years old, its vegetation comes from four different climatic zones, and evidence of human life in the area predates written history. In the harsh light of midday the crater may seem like the last place on earth you'd ever care to know about—hot, harsh, lifeless. You may feel like hurling your *Let's Go* into the void and catching the next bus back to your MTV-equipped hostel in Tel Aviv. Give it some time—the desert is oblivious to our 20th-century schedules. Spend one evening on the edge and see the display of color as the light fades. You'll be transfixed.

In the 1920s and 30s, Makhtesh Ramon was not on any British map. After the founding of the State of Israel, the government came upon the crater during its exploration of the Negev. Until a direct route to Eilat was built from the Dead Sea in the 1970s, what came to be known as "Mitzpeh Ramon" (Ramon Observation Point) was the central stop-off en route southward. Today, the crater is a national park, with well-marked trails leading to breathtaking cliff views and extraordinary rock formations. This complex ecological system may take days to explore.

Practical Information From Mitzpeh Ramon, bus #60 runs to Be'er Sheva (every 1-1½hr. 6am-9:30pm, NIS15.30), bus #392 comes through on its way to Eilat (8:20, 10am, noon, 4:45, and 7:30pm; NIS33, students NIS28), and bus #391 runs to Tel Aviv (NIS22); call Egged Information (tel. (03) 537 5555) for an exact schedule. Drivers are instructed to take 10-minute breaks if they feel drowsy on long desert treks, so don't panic if your bus is 10 to 40 minutes late. Mitzpeh Ramon has two bus stops. The first is the commercial center on **Ben-Gurion Street** (look for the strange fountain), near a **Bank Ha-Poalim** branch (open Sun., Tues., and Thurs. 8:30am-noon and 4-6pm, Mon. 8:30am-12:30pm, Wed. and Fri. 8:30am-noon). In adjoining buildings are a **post office** with **Western Union** (open Sun.-Tues. and Thurs. 8am-12:30pm and 3:30-6pm, Wed. 8am-1:30pm, Fri. 8am-noon) and a **Shekem** supermarket (open Sun.-Thurs. 9am-1pm and 4-7pm, Fri. 8:30am-1pm). Two buildings to the left is the **municipal pool,** with a sauna and water slide (open Sun. and Tues.-Wed. 10am-6pm, Mon. and Thurs. 10am-6pm and 8:30-10:30pm, Fri. 10am-5pm, Sat. 9am-5pm; admission NIS20). The second bus stop is at the **youth hostel** and also serves the visitors center, Bio-Ramon, and the cliffside promenade.

There are two hiking resources in Mitzpeh Ramon: first is the **Park Ramon Visitors Center** (tel. (07) 588 691; fax 588 620), housed in the round building with the flat top teetering on the edge of the crater. Get your daily dose of audiovisuals or plan your hike on a 3-D model of the crater marked with hiking trails. The free map is detailed, and there are topo maps at the gift shop (NIS10)—both are in Hebrew, but the staff will translate. (Open Sun.-Thurs. 9am-4:30pm, Fri. 9am-3pm, Sat. 9am-4:30pm. Admission NIS11.50, children NIS6, includes audiovisual show and use of rooftop observatory.) Second is the **SPNI Field School** (tel. (07) 581 516), near the edge of the crater 500m southwest of Camel Observation Point (for directions see Accommodations, below). If you're planning an unguided expedition, leave your route description and estimated length at the field school before you leave—they have an on-site rescue team and direct communication with army units in the area.

Desert Shade (tel. (07) 586 229 or (03) 575 6885; fax (07) 586 208 or (03) 613 0161) has **jeep tours** (2½hr., US$18), **camels** (US$10 per hr.; US$17 for a 2-seater), **mountain bikes** (3hr. US$7, 6hr. US$10, full day US$15), and **guides** (½-day US$18, full day US$22). Hiking guides charge US$80 for a half-day, US$120 for a full day. To get to Desert Shade, take bus #60 or #392; it's 200m out of Mitzpeh Ramon toward Be'er Sheva. Pay in blood for a **rental jeep** at Shualei Shimshou (tel. (07) 588 868).

Accommodations Most travelers prefer to stay on the canyon's rim their first night, where you'll find the **Mitzpeh Ramon Youth Hostel (HI)** (tel. (07) 588 443; fax 588 074). No A/C in the spacious rooms, but it's not too bad; all have private baths. There's a huge lounge with foosball, a TV room, and an occasional disco in the basement. (Reception open 4-9pm, but they'll watch your stuff if you bring it earlier. Checkout 9am. No lockout or curfew. Dorm beds (6 per room) NIS47. Singles NIS90. Doubles NIS62 per person. Triples NIS55 per person. Nonmembers add NIS3. Breakfast included.) The **SPNI Field School** (tel. (07) 581 516) is a bit isolated but charges half as much as the hostel and has a trail leading down into the canyon. To get to the field school either take bus #60 to Carmel Observation Point and walk 7 to 10 minutes to the right, along the cliffside trail, until you see the tall antennas, or get off the bus at the turnoff to the school (don't try to walk—it's about 3km) and wait for the free minibus (7:30-8am, noon-1:15pm, and 5:30-6pm). All rooms have A/C and private baths. Full kitchen facilities NIS5 per day. (Dorm beds (6 per room) NIS23 for students only. Adults pay NIS65 for the first 3 adults and NIS25 for each additional person. Call ahead. Breakfast NIS10.50, other meals NIS20-NIS27. Kiosk open 8-10am and 5-10pm for snacks and drinks.) **Alexis,** a converted villa at 7 Saharonim St. (tel. (07) 586 122 or 588 258), 2 blocks northwest of the Ben-Gurion-Eilat intersection, has a huge kitchen, a TV lounge, and a fireplace (US$10 per person).

For a taste of desert living there's **Succah in the Desert** (call 586 280 10am-noon), 7km outside town. It's made of twelve *sukkot,* beautiful structures made of stones and dried palm leaves. The interiors, rich with tapestries and rugs, incorporate desert features like rock platforms for sleeping or sitting. (*Sukkot* NIS190 per night. Tent with carpets and pillows NIS120. Vegetarian dinners NIS25.) The visitors center runs **Be'erot Camping Site,** 16km inside the crater. Shade and toilets, but no showers or restaurants. (Free with your own tent, NIS13.50 for one of theirs. Ask at visitors center for directions.) **Desert Shade** also has Bedouin-inspired tents in the crater. (Beds US$8, with breakfast US$13. Other meals US$7 each.)

Food Ha-Tzukit Restaurant, near the visitors center, has A/C, a stunning view, and a family of ibex lazing outside. Self-service sandwiches NIS6, vegetarian meals NIS15, hot lunch NIS20 (open daily 8am-5pm). Walk "into town," along the road to your right as you descend the steps of the visitors center, and stumble upon **Hanna's Restaurant** (tel. 588 158; sandwiches NI8, meals NIS17-20). Much better than you'd expect from a restaurant connected to a gas station, it's usually packed with soldiers or totally deserted. (Open Sun.-Thurs. 5am-8pm, Fri. 5am-4:30pm.) **Pub Ha-Ḥaveet,** Mitzpeh Ramon's only night spot, is in the commercial center next door to Bank Ha-Poalim, and attracts soldiers, backpackers, and local youth. (18 or older. Beer NIS6. Open nightly 7pm-1 or 2am.) Next door there's **falafel** and **pizza.**

Sights The *makhtesh* (erosion crater) is a geological phenomenon unique to Israel. The most interesting places in the crater are several kilometers into the pit, so you might want to take a bus to the trailhead. Bus #392 to Eilat will take you along the main highway through the crater and spit you out wherever you choose. If temperatures are bearable, you can walk to the crater from town. A footpath leading down into the crater starts at a huge metal ball and its offspring on the canyon rim, southwest of the visitors center. Follow the promenade past the youth hostel to the big balls, then start the trail with the green and white markers. (Step right up to the cliff's edge to see the beginning.) A second descending trail, marked in blue, begins from the back of the field school right behind the classrooms. Trails are well-kept and labeled in Hebrew and English.

Before beginning your expedition, leave your planned route and expected length of trip with someone (like the field school, youth hostel, or visitors center). While hiking, keep a general idea of the location of the Eilat road; that's the place to go if you stupidly get caught in the dark. You know the rest by now: fill every plastic container you own with water before you go into the crater and cover your head with one of those things. The visitors center has photos and directions for specific destinations like the **Carpenter's Workshop, Ein Saharonim,** and **Arden Stream.**

Also visit the **llama and alpaca farm** (tel. 588 047), about 2km west of town and 500m north of the field school, off the main road west out of town. Follow the llama-shaped signs. (Open Sun.-Thurs. 9am-4pm, Fri. 9am-2pm.) These wacky South American imports (the alpacas resemble creatures from *Star Wars*) are raised for their wool. (Admission NIS7, children NIS4.) **Bio-Ramon** (tel. (07) 588 755), just downhill from the visitors center, houses desert insects, scorpions, spiders, snakes, and other lovable rodents and small reptiles. (Open Sun.-Thurs. 8am-5pm, Fri. 8am-3pm, Sat. 9am-6pm; admission NIS4.40, children NIS3.30.)

For an evening cool-down, walk along the promenade on the edge of the cliff, where the **desert sculpture garden** displays an esoteric collection of statues. Or walk down to the **Ramat Sapir** neighborhood (on Har Tzion St., a 10-min. walk from the commercial center) and watch sculptor **Danny Kish** turn huge blocks of stone into complex structures in his own front yard. The **Matnas** music and culture center on 73 Ben-Gurion St. (tel. 588 442 or 865), just 2 blocks left of the municipal swimming pool, hosts Israeli folk dancing (Sun. 8pm; admission NIS6) and shows newly-released American movies (Sat. and Mon. 8:30pm, 8pm in winter; admission NIS8).

■■■ EILAT אילת

Yes, Eilat rhymes with hot. Israel's number-one vacation spot is soaked with the sweat of rowdy Israelis, international backpackers, and European tourists. Some swear by Eilat's sun, coral, and nightlife, while others see it as a huge tourist trap attached to a nice beach. Travelers should know that they will be taken for granted by some local businesspeople; the obnoxiousness quotient can get high at times. Don't expect symphonies, theaters, or ballets here—the town's focus is to get you tan, and to help you spend lots of money in the process.

The Israelites lost the port at what is now Eilat in the 8th century BCE. It then saw the Egyptian Ptolemies, the Nabateans, the Romans (under whom it received the name Aila), the Crusaders under King Baldwin I in 1116 CE, Salah ad-Din in 1170, more Crusaders, the Mamluks, and finally the Turks. Phew. After World War I Eilat was part of the British Mandate, and in 1949 it was handed over as part of the state of Israel. In that year a Jewish settlement (Kibbutz Elot) was founded, and later moved 3km inland. In the past two decades, dozens of luxury hotels, restaurants, and tourist shops have become familiar (and lucrative) fixtures along a beach that offers year-round swimming. Israel's southernmost town is today the country's biggest swimming and snorkeling resort, its major port for Japanese imports, and a starting point for excursions into the Sinai and the rest of Egypt.

The busiest times of the year are Passover (April 15-21 in 1995) and *Sukkot* (Oct. 9-16), when nearly 100,000 Israelis descend upon the city and fill all of the hotels. Don't fool yourself into thinking that this is a good time to visit. True, there are more parties and crowds at pubs, but hostels and restaurants charge double their normal rates, petty theft runs rampant, and every last inch of beach crawls with human bodies. More importantly, many hostel owners have a tendency to kick out tourists in favor of large Israeli groups—beware the holidays!

Eilat is a popular place to earn a little extra money. Proprietors at resorts, hostels, cafés, discos, the Lunar Mini Park, and the Zubrensky political circus are often looking for newcomers because of the high turnover rate. **Jobs** with hotels and hostels often include lodging, and should offer a pittance as well. Unfortunately, most work is under-the-table (illegal), the hours long and arduous, and the wages minuscule (usually about US$400 per month).

ORIENTATION

On the edge of the Negev, Eilat is a 5km strip of coastline at the precarious intersection of four Middle Eastern powers (Israel, Jordan, Egypt, and Saudi Arabia); at night you can see the lights of all four. The city is divided into three sections: the town itself on the hills above the sea, the hotel area and Lagoon Beach to the east, and the port to the south. About 10km farther south is Taba, just over the border in Egypt.

The first thing to realize about Eilat is that the urban engineers who designed it were privy to some revolutionary new numbering system completely different from the one traditionally taught in math classes around the world. Unfortunately, a mysterious plague wiped out the city planners before the secrets of this system could be tortured out of them. Travelers will find that #60 can be followed by #4000; all sorts of dashes and slashes are also involved. Stop often and ask for directions.

As you leave the central bus station via the main entrance, you'll find yourself on **Ha-Tmarim Boulevard,** which crosses the center of the city from southeast (left, downhill) to northwest (right, uphill). Across the street is the **commercial center,** with restaurants and cafés. If you stay on the bus station side of Ha-Tmarim and head left (downhill), you'll immediately pass the **Red Canyon Center,** which resembles a futuristic Bedouin tent and houses the **post office, supermarket,** Burger Ranch, and **cinema.** Farther downhill is the **Shalom Center,** resembling a square spaceship on a tiered landing pad. Ha-Tmarim Blvd. ends here, perpendicular to **Ha'Arava Road.** If you follow Ha'Arava to the right, you'll pass the main entrance to the Eilat **airport.** A block later, at the intersection of **Yotam Road,** a three-level conglomeration of cheap restaurants calls itself the **New Tourist Center** (read: a mall). Continue on

Ha'Arava for 30 minutes and arrive at **Dolphin Reef,** the **Coral Beach** reserve, the **Underwater Observatory,** and finally **Taba Beach** and the **Egyptian Border.** Bus #15 runs this route (every 15-20min., NIS2.10-3.20). Turning left at the intersection of Ha'Arava Rd. and Yotam St. will lead you to **Durban Street** and the **beach.** To get to the **marina** and the hotel area, either walk along the **beachfront promenade** or follow Durban St. as it bends back and heads toward the airport.

Cheap restaurants and beaches are in the southern part of the city; the vast majority of **hostels** is in the northern part. From the bus station, turn right and start marching uphill on Ha-Tmarim. The first intersection you'll cross is **Ḥativat Ha-Negev Street;** the very next right-hand turn (unmarked) is **Retamim Street,** and the one after that is **Almogim Street** (U-shaped, with 2 entrances). The farthest north you'll need to go is **Eilat Street,** a wide boulevard separating the touristy part from the residential neighborhoods farther north.

PRACTICAL INFORMATION

Tourist Information Center: corner of Yotam Rd. and Ha'Arava Rd. (tel. (07) 372 111). Friendly brand-new center has *everything.* Maps, brochures, coupons, and awesome "infotour" computer. Open Sun.-Thurs. 8am-9pm, Fri.-Sat. 8am-3pm.

Reservation and Information Center: Durban St. (tel. 374 741 or 375 944), past the large orange by the beach. Tell them your budget and they'll help you plan your stay in Eilat. Best place for making reservations for events. Open 24 hrs.

Government Tourist Information Office (GTIO): Bridge House (tel. 334 353), in the heart of the marina, near King Solomon's Wharf. Offers maps, brochures, transportation schedules, and border information. Will help find accommodations—crucial in high season. Infotour available. Open Sun.-Thurs. 8am-6pm, Fri. 8am-1pm. Take bus #15 from bus station.

Municipal Tourist Information Office (MTIO): Rekhter Center (tel. 374 233). Good for maps and emergencies. Open Sun.-Thurs. 8am-6pm, Fri. 8am-1pm.

Nature Reserves Authority: Coral Beach (tel. 376 829). Maps and information about hiking and coral reefs. Open 9am-5pm.

Consulates: Egypt, 68 Ha'Efroni St. (tel. 376 882). From the bus station, walk right on Ha-Tmarim Blvd., away from the beach. Make a left on Eilat St., go right at the Moore Center onto Anafa St., take the third left onto Ha'Efroni and look for the flag at the end of the street. Visa services Sun.-Thurs. 9-11am and 1-1:30pm, Fri. 9-10am and 11am-noon. Morning hours for picking up and submitting applications, afternoon for receiving your visa. Visas must be paid for in Israeli currency (NIS40 for US citizens, NIS60 for most others); bring a passport photo. **U.K.** (tel. 372 344), above the New Tourist Center (next to the Adi Hotel). Call ahead.

Currency Exchange: Bank Leumi, Ha-Tmarim Blvd. (tel. 374 191), across from central bus station. Open Mon., Wed., and Fri. 8:30am-noon, Sun., Tues., and Thurs. 8:30am-noon and 5-6:30pm. The **First International Bank,** in the New Tourist Center (tel. 376 117 or 118). Open Sun., Tues., and Thurs. 8:30am-2pm, Mon. and Wed. 8:30am-2pm and 4-7pm, Fri. 8:30am-noon. **Bank Ha-Poalim,** Ḥativat Ha-Negev St. (tel. 375 184), across from central bus station. Open Sun., Tues., and Thurs. 8:30-noon and 4:30-6pm, Mon., Wed., and Fri. 8:30am-noon. **Bank Discount,** Shalom Center (tel. 372 141). Open Sun., Tues., and Thurs. 8:30am-1:30pm and 4-6pm, Mon. and Wed. 8:30am-2pm, Fri. 8:30am-1pm.

Post Office: Red Canyon Center (tel. 372 302). **Western Union, Poste Restante.** Open Sun.-Tues. and Thurs. 8am-noon and 4-6pm, Wed. 8am-1pm, Fri. 8am-noon.

Telephones: Starcom Gold, New Tourist Center, main floor (tel. 372 237; fax 371 920). Cheaper than the post office or public phones. Toll-free tel. (177) 022 2237. With a credit card, you can call at their low rates from anywhere—even a hotel room. Open Sun.-Thurs. 9am-midnight, Fri. 9am-5pm, Sat. 8pm-1am. **Telephone Code:** 07.

Airport: Intersection of Ha-Tmarim Blvd. and Ha'Arava Rd., (info. tel. (07) 371 828). **Arkia Airlines** (tel. 376 102) flies to and from Tel Aviv (every 40min., Sun. and Thurs. every 20min.; one-way NIS206), Jerusalem (3 per day, one-way NIS206), and Haifa (2-3 per day, one-way NIS240). It's cheapest to pay in shekels.

Central Bus Station: Ha-Tmarim Blvd. (tel. 375 161). Reserve tickets in person at station at least 2 days in advance (4 days in high season). Bus #444 takes you to Jerusalem via the Dead Sea area (Sun.-Fri. 7, 10am, 2, and 5pm, last bus Fri. 1pm, one trip on Sat. at 4pm; NIS38). If no seats are available, take bus #392 or 394 to Be'er Sheva (every 1-1½hr. 4am-5pm, NIS33) and transfer. Bus #394 continues to Tel Aviv (NIS39). Bus #991 goes to Haifa (8:30am and 11:30pm, Sun. and Thurs. also 3pm, Fri. 8:30am only, Sat. 3 and 11:30pm only; NIS44).

City Buses: #15 runs down Ha-Tmarim Blvd. and Ha'Arava Rd., through the hotel area and past the HI hostel and Coral Beach to Taba, Egypt—everywhere you need to go (NIS2.10-3.20). #1 and 2 shuttle between the town and hotel area (NIS3). (All Sun.-Thurs. every 20-30min. 7am-9pm. No service Fri. 5pm-Sat. 9am.)

Taxis: Arava (tel. 374 141), **Taba** (tel. 372 212), **King Solomon** (tel. 373 131). City rides are NIS5, to underwater observatory NIS13, to border NIS15. Taxi sharing is common. In winter *sherut* minibuses run along #1, 2, and 15 bus routes.

Car Rental: Hertz, (tel. 376 682), in Red Canyon Center; **Budget** (tel. 371 063), **Europcar** (tel. 374 014), **Eldan** (tel. 374 027), **Reliable** (tel. 374 126), and **Thrifty** (tel. 372 511), all in Shalom Center. Hertz, Budget, and Thrifty have a minimum age requirement of 21, Europcar 23, and Eldan 24. Prices start at US$10 per day plus 27¢ per km or US$47 per day for 250km and 27¢ per km thereafter (3-day minimum). Insurance is about US$11 per day. You can't take rentals into Egypt.

Bike Rental: Red Sea Sports Club (tel. 379 685), near the King Solomon Hotel. US$18 per day. Open 8:30am-5pm.

Laundromat: Mickey Mouse Laundromat, 99/1 Almogim St. (tel. 373 495), opposite Peace Café. Open Sun.-Fri. 8am-8pm. **Kuiskal,** Razin Center (tel. 374 838), on Ha-Tmarim St. Open Sun.-Thurs. 8am-9pm, Fri. 8am-2pm. **Yael's Laundry,** Sdel Boneh Center (tel. 373 443), on Ha'Arava St. Open Sun.-Fri. 7:30am-8pm.

Pharmacy: Avigdor, New Tourist Center, 1st (bottom) floor (tel. 372 374). Open Sun.-Thurs. 10am-1pm and 5-10pm, Fri. 10am-1pm and 7-8pm, Sat. 11am-1pm and 8-10pm. **Eilat Pharmacy,** 25 Eilat St. (tel. 374 665), Sun.-Thurs. 8:15am-1:30pm and 4:45-8pm, Fri. 8:15am-2pm. **Michlin Pharmacy** (tel. 372 434), in Rekhter Center. Open Sun.-Thurs. 8:30am-2pm and 4:30-8pm, Fri. 8am-2pm.

Hospital: Yoseftal Hospital, Yotam Rd. (tel. 358 011 or 373 151).

First Aid: Ha-Tmarim Blvd. (tel. 101 for emergencies, otherwise 372 333). Magen David Adom first aid stations are located on some beaches.

Fire: Tel. 102 for emergencies; otherwise 372 222.

Police: Tel. 100 for emergencies, 332 444 to chat; at Avdat Blvd. at the eastern end of Hativat Ha-Negev. Operates a "lost and found" for packs stolen from the beach.

To reach the **Egyptian border** and cross into the Sinai, take bus #15 from a stop across from the central bus station or from stops along Ha-Tmarim Blvd. and Ha'Arava Rd. (doesn't run Fri. 5pm-Sat. 9am). Taxis to the border cost NIS15-20. For a jaunt to **Taba Beach** (where you'll find a Hilton, a more secluded beach, and great snorkeling), you must present your passport at the border. The passport will not be stamped, but it is the only acceptable form of identification. Declare all cash and valuables or they will be confiscated upon your return. There is more bureaucracy involved in getting deeper into the Sinai and Egypt; see Essentials: Travel in the Region, p. 26, and Sinai: Getting There and Away, p. 219, for yummy tidbits.

ACCOMMODATIONS

Finding a cheap room in Eilat is easy. Finding a safe, comfortable, and convenient cheap room is another story. As soon as you arrive at the bus station you'll be harassed by a gaggle of apartment hawkers. Yell *"Lo,"* give them the look of death, and walk away. Don't get into a cab with a random stranger, and don't make any commitments before you see the room and know how far from the center it is. Most travelers' hostels are located less than 3 blocks from the bus station—walk up the hill on Ha-Tmarim and take a right on Retamim. The atmosphere of a smaller hostel can add tremendously to your enjoyment of Eilat. Some of the bigger hostels have been known to put out backpackers in favor of large groups of Israelis. If hostels are full, go to the tourist office, a travel agency, or a real estate agent. **Prices below are for the off season; expect to pay double in July, August, and the holidays.**

Spring Hostel, 126 Ofarim St. (tel. 374 660), at the intersection of Agmonim and Ofarim. Immaculate and modern. Each dorm room has A/C and private bath. Separate building has kitchen and an outdoor patio. Large color TV with cable and video on front veranda. Cold drinks (NIS3) and sandwiches (NIS3). Reception open 24 hrs. Check-out 9am. No lockout or curfew. Dorm beds (4-6 per room) NIS18. Doubles NIS80. Breakfast included in winter only.

Max and Merran's Hostel, 130/1 Retamim St. (tel. 373 817). A home away from home providing support, advice, and cold water. Share the premises with Pamela, her friendly staff, Wookie Monster (the cat), and Alfir Capone (the dog). Videos daily at 2 and 8pm in the pleasant kitchen/living room area. Check-out 10am. Lockout 10am-noon. No curfew, visitors, or alcohol. Put up your own tent in the yard for NIS18. Bunk beds NIS24. Free and safe luggage storage. Snorkeling gear for rent cheaper than at any beach.

Beit Ha'Arava, 106 Almogim St. (tel. 371 052 or 374 687), corner of Ḥativat Golami. From the bus station, take a right at the bus entrance onto Ḥativat Ha-Negev and walk 2 blocks to the end; it's a ½-block left from there. Veranda, kitchen, a jukebox-foosball diner, and a beautiful view. Clean rooms with A/C and 6 beds max. 24-hr. guard. No curfew. Outdoor tent mattress NIS15. Dorm beds NIS25. Doubles with bath NIS90-100. Breakfast NIS10. Wash NIS10. Lockers NIS4.

Taba Youth Hostel, Ḥativat Ha-Negev St. (tel. 375 982 or 815), across the street and left of the station's bus entrance; look for yellow sign. Main building has 16- and 22-bed rooms. New annex has slightly cramped dorms (4-6 beds per room). Kitchen. Management supervises safety and decorum. Large front lawn with big screen TV. No curfew. Dorm beds NIS20. Doubles NIS80. Lockers NIS3.

Red Mountain Hostel, Ḥativat Ha-Negev St. (tel. 374 936; tel./fax 374 263), across from the bus station. Clean modern facilities. Wooden interior decorated with artifacts from Africa and the Far East. May feature guitar-equipped singing Israelis. Outdoor bar has pool table, videos in the evening. 6-person dorms upstairs NIS20. Lockers NIS5 each time you open them.

Eilat Youth Hostel (HI), Ha'Arava Rd. (tel. 372 358 or 370 088; fax 375 835), one block from the New Tourist Center. This huge hostel sports over 400 beds, hotel-like lounge chairs, great balcony views, and a discothèque (expected to open by 1995). Dorms (8 per room) NIS47. Quads NIS230. Nonmembers add NIS3. Breakfast included. Lockers NIS4. Refrigerators NIS10, TV rental NIS20.

Motel Ha-Shalom, Ḥativat Ha-Negev St. (tel. 376 544), across from the bus entrance to the station; look for red and white sign. Bargain basement prices, but you get what you pay for: plain rooms and institutional showers (i.e., a row of nozzles and no dividing curtains). Pool table and TV lounge; guests choose 2 videos daily. Dorms (8-10 per room) NIS15; peak months NIS20. Singles NIS80. Doubles NIS100; with private bath NIS20. Lockers NIS3 every time you open them.

Nathan's White House Hostel, 131/1 Retamim St. (tel. 376 572 or 374 829). Go all the way down to the corner. A mural of Bill Clinton's residence beautifies the wall of the veranda. A converted house with simple, clean rooms. Friendly staff sells drinks. Kitchen, TV, and video. Many Israeli soldiers vacation here. Check-out 9am. No curfew. Dorm beds (4-8 per room) NIS20. Doubles NIS80.

Ofarim Rooms, 116/2 Ofarim St. (tel. 370 492; fax 376 289). Very clean rooms (4-8 beds) with attached baths. Friendly manager Avi (home tel. 330 291). More like a rooming house. Kitchen facilities until midnight. Outdoor sitting area with TV. Pay phone NIS1. No lockout, no curfew. Dorm beds NIS25. Singles NIS60. Doubles NIS70. Safe NIS5 per day. Wash (up to 5 kg) NIS12.

The Garden, 75/2 Ha-Tmarim St. (tel. 373 455). Between Almogim and Eilat St. Inconspicuous door. Yosie runs a colorful refuge from the craziness outside. Small kitchen. Keys given. Outdoor sofas under mosquito nets with a small fountain. Dorm beds NIS20. Doubles NIS60. Free beer every Fri. 9:30pm-midnight (winter only). Wash NIS12 for 6kg, luggage storage.

Corrine's, 127/1 Retamim St. (tel. 371 472). Generally safe. Rooms are ½-floor below ground, but are large and clean. All rooms have A/C and private baths.

Reception 24 hrs. in café next door. Keys given for a NIS15 deposit. No lockout or curfew. Dorms (4-10 per room) NIS17-20. Doubles NIS70. Breakfast NIS7.

The Home, 108/2 Almogim St. (tel. 372 403); gate is on Ofarim St. right before Ha-Tmarim. Really *is* a home for people hanging out long-term. Friendly manager Aubrey goes out of his way to hook travelers up with **jobs,** and has been known to give free board until the first paycheck kicks in. The cramped quarters may not be the King Solomon, but it's Home. Free camaraderie, tea, coffee, bread, and jam all day, nightly videos. Kitchen, storage. Mattresses outdoor NIS15. Dorm beds (10-12 per room) NIS20; dorms in annex NIS18. Breakfast included.

Fawlty Towers, 116/1 Ofarim St. (tel. 372 371). Bunks, bunks, bunks. This sleep factory churns out Z's with mechanical relentlessness. Travelers fuel the diabolical unconsciousness machine. Dorm beds NIS15. Doubles NIS70. Wash NIS10.

There are two **camping** options in Eilat: official and expensive, or unofficial and free. During July and August, hundreds of people happen not to see the "No Camping" signs on the public beach; year after year, many are victims of theft. Possessions should never be left unguarded and **women should not camp alone.** Another nuisance at these camps are the **rats,** attracted by the garbage areas on Lagoon Beach, who will enjoy biting your ears and other appendages. To avoid these hassles, go east (toward the Jordanian border), or south of the Red Rock Hotel toward Coral Beach. Sleeping and tent-pitching on these beaches is legal, and there are toilets near most of them.

Caroline Camping (tel. 371 911, or 375 063), at the municipal campground opposite Coral Beach. Take bus #15. Clean institutional bathrooms and a compact cafeteria. NIS12 with your own tent, but lack of shade makes tents unbearable in July and August. 1- or 2-person bungalows with electricity NIS70. 5-person bungalow NIS160. Refrigerators NIS10. Will supply bedsheets and pillowcases. All toilets outside. Office open 24 hrs.

Mamshit Camping (tel. 374 411; fax 375 206), next to SPNI field school, across from Coral Beach Reserve. Take bus #15. Excellent snorkeling and frying. Huge, neat place with friendly management. NIS14 with your own tent. Bungalow beds (8 per room) NIS20. 1- or 2- person bungalows NIS98.

FOOD

Many falafel stands, pizza joints, and sandwich vendors are on **Ha-Tmarim St.** (especially near the bus station) and by the hostels near **Retamim St.** Go to bars and pubs for the cheapest meals in Eilat. The **Underground Pub** in the New Tourist Center serves the first 50 clients after 6pm with the best deal around: buy a beer (NIS4.50) and get a free meal of spaghetti, pizza, or pasta. The **Peace Café,** 13 Almogim St., will put anything into a pita or baguette for NIS5. The **Hard Luck Café** 2 doors down serves large portions of fish and chips, spaghetti, *schnitzel,* and the like for NIS7. The **Hard Rock 91** (on Eilat St., 2 blocks left of Ha-Tmarim) will stuff you with a 200g burger and chips or a mound of Bolognese pasta for NIS10.

Pappa Mitchell's on Ha-Tmarim St., downhill and across from the bus station, has an all-you-can-eat buffet of *schnitzel, kabab,* etc. (NIS22). At **Fisherman House,** adjacent to Coral Beach, all the grease you can eat costs only NIS20 (salad bar alone NIS12). **Nargila,** next to the central bus station (orange sign), serves Yemenite dishes like *malawaḥ* (NIS7.20-9.50), *jachnun* (NIS7.20), *ziva* (NIS7.60), and *fatut* (NIS8.70). **Pancake Eilat,** on the ground floor of the Shalom Center, serves excellent steaks (NIS23); choose from a full page of pancake recipes (NIS7-9). Many hostels have 15%-off coupons. The **Maman Red Sea Fish Restaurant,** behind the Moriah Hotel and literally *on* Northern Beach, serves full-meal deals (NIS16-19).

Burger Ranch in the Red Canyon Center and **McDavid's** on the Durban beachfront (where the Promenade ends) stay open until about 11pm. **Pizza Hut** has 2 locations on the promenade, and **Ben & Jerry's** (near King Solomon's Wharf) and **Dr. Lek** (same plaza as McDavid's) sell ice cream on the promenade as well.

Since many accommodations in Eilat provide cooking facilities, you can eat well and inexpensively by purchasing food at the **supermarket** at Eilat St. and Ha-Tmarim Blvd. (look for the blue and white squares on the building; open Sun.-Thurs. 7:30am-7:30pm, Fri. 7:30am-2pm). Closer to the center of town is **SuperKolbo Supermarket** in the Rekhter Commercial Center (open Sat.-Thurs. 7am-11pm, Fri. 7am-9pm) and the **Shekem Supermarket** in the Red Canyon Center (open Sun.-Thurs. 8:30am-8:30pm, Fri. 8:30am-2:30pm). The **bakery** on the corner of Ha-Tmarim St. and Retamim St. has fresh pita bread and other great baked stuff. (Kosher.)

SIGHTS

Spend your Eilat afternoons underwater, in a cerebellum-addling world of coral, emperor fish, blubberfish, and other brilliantly colored creatures. See Sinai: Underwater Adventures, p. 222, for important information on snorkeling and diving.

Snorkeling and diving are easiest and cheapest near **Coral Beach Nature Reserve** (tel. 376 829). Take bus #15 from the central bus station toward the sea (open 8am-6pm). The NIS13 (ages 5-18 NIS6.50) fee helps preserve the area. With mask (NIS5), snorkel (NIS4), and fins (NIS6), follow one of five "water trails" (marked by buoys) through the reef. A snazzy bridge into the water protects the coral from human feet. Come and go all day for the price of one admission, or get a five-day card (NIS39). There are lockers (NIS3 every time you close them), showers, and a snack bar on site. Try the new **SNUBA** program (tel. 372 722) for people who have never dived before: the heavy air tanks are left on a raft to which the SNUBA diver is tethered. (NIS101 for 1½hr. of diving and instruction. Sales office open 9am-6pm.)

Aqua Sport (tel. 374 404) next to Coral Beach also rents (mask US$3, fins US$3, snorkel US$2, or US$7 for all three; complete diving equipment US$35, introductory dive US$40). They also rent sailboards (US$10 per hr.). A six-day international diving course costs US$220; 10 qualification dives for two-star certification cost US$230, summer US$295. Sinai **camping and diving safaris** run by Aqua Sport leave every Thursday at 6:30am for 1-5 days of fun down under. (1 day snorkeling US$65, with cruise US$75; 3 days US$230/US$270; 5 days US$390/US$420 with two cruises.) They also cruise to **Coral Island** (Gazirat Faraun) (US$42). Prices include camping equipment and meals. **Underwater scooters** cost US$30 for a few hours. Renters can stay in Aqua Sport's well-kept, sunny **hostel** (US$13 per person, breakfast included). Classes should be arranged in advance. Call or write Aqua Sport International Ltd., P.O. Box 300, Eilat 88102.

Red Sea Sports Club (tel. 376 569), across the street from Aqua Sport, offers night dives for US$49. Their office on North Beach near the lagoon offers windsurfing, sailing, water-skiing (NIS50), and parasailing (NIS85). They also arrange horseback riding lessons at **Texas Ranch** across the street (1hr. NIS20, 2hr. NIS25), and camel or jeep tours of the desert (2½hr. US$19, 4hr. US$28). Upstairs, the **Photo Shop** (tel. 373 145, ext. 272; fax 374 083) rents **underwater cameras** (US$20-30 per day) and video cameras (US$110 per day). Coral Beach is the most trafficked reef territory on the Red Sea—for privacy with the fishies, head to the Sinai.

Glass-bottom boat cruises abound: **Eilat Glass Bottom Boat** (tel. 375 528 or 332 325, 2hr., NIS30). The **Jules Verne Explorer,** with glass walls, is more like an underwater observatory (tel. 377 702 or 334 668, 2hr. to the Japanese Gardens, NIS50). On Mon., Wed., and Fri. at 9pm, they go on a **Deep Water Laser Show** adventure (also NIS50). Beware the wrathful squid attack.

Spend rainy days (ha) at the **Coral World Underwater Observatory and Aquarium** (tel. 376 666). Trip out on tanks full of natural psychedelia, without getting your feet wet. A full day of fishy fun will cost you, though (NIS35, children NIS18; open Sun.-Thurs. 8:30am-5pm, Fri. 8:30am-3pm). Or hitch a ride 60m down (deeper than divers are allowed to go) on the **Yellow Submarine** (tel. 376 337). You'll see changes in reef- and fish-life resulting from a lack of sunlight; the price (NIS161) could scare the daylights out of you, too. Newfangled **Dolphin Reef** (tel. 371 846 or 373 417; fax 375 921), just past the port on the #15 bus, features dolphin and sea lion shows (every 2hr. 10am-4pm) and nature films. For NIS80, you can swim alongside Flipper and friends. (Open daily 9am-5pm. Admission NIS20.)

Last but not least, BIRDWATCHING!! Eilat is perfectly located for birdwatching, as migratory groups flapping north from Africa stop at the salt ponds north of the lagoon mid-February through May. More than 30 species have been counted in the area. The **International Birdwatching Center (IBC)** (tel. 374 276) in the Commercial Center runs walking tours (US$5) and jeep tours (US$50). Also check out the late March birdwatchers' festival. Write to IBC, P.O. Box 774, Eilat 88106 for more information. (Open Sun.-Thurs. 9am-1pm and 5-7pm, Fri. 9am-1pm.) Pretend you're a bird at the **Aerodrome** (tel. 372 745), behind the Riviera Hotel. A special-suit-air-vent thing suspends you in mid-air. This 10-minute thrill sells for US$25.

ENTERTAINMENT

Eilat's inspired nightlife rivals its underwater circus. Most pubs and nightclubs open at 10:30 or 11pm, start rambuncting at midnight or so, and don't close until 5 or 6am. The discos are expensive (covers around NIS25-30); most are located in the lagoon area. At discos in big hotels (sometimes open only to guests), shorts and sandals are a bad idea. Mellow out at the **Promenade** along the waterfront, where street vendors sell cheap jewelry and five-minute portraits, and Israelis vainly attempt to pick up female tourists (observe—they all seem to have the same pick-up lines). People start arriving at about 9:30pm and stay until it's time to go to a pub.

Bars

The Underground (tel. 370 239), in the New Tourist Center. Up-and-coming, has deals on meals. Large draft beers NIS4.50, mixed drink of the day NIS3.50. Video-bar and live bands on Fri. make it popular with travelers. Open daily 9am-5am.

Peace Café, 13 Almogim St. (tel. 371 629). Cheap hangout with an international crowd. Music videos by day, movies by night. Travelers come from far and wide to swap messages on the Peace Board, compete in dart-throwing, and compare tattoos. Some may deem the crowd "rough." Goldstar NIS4. Open 9am-2am. Luggage storage (NIS5 per night) and **job placement** available.

Hard Luck Café, 15 Almogim St. (tel. 372 788), next to the Peace Café. Album covers and coasters decorate the walls, music plays loudly, and the TV shows soccer games (pray that England wins). Fish and chips, chicken, spaghetti, burgers, and *schnitzel* all NIS7, Goldstar NIS3, drinks NIS12. Open 3pm-whenever.

Yacht Pub (tel. 334 111), on the marina by King Solomon's Wharf. Huge place, with sailor-knots on the carpets and indoor and outdoor bars. Live entertainment at 11pm changes every few nights. Popular Israeli folk singers and European rock bands. 0.5L Carlsberg NIS8.50. Open 10pm-3am (or later).

Tropicana (tel. 374 616), in the Shalom Center. Spend NIS100 and get a free bottle of Tequila; on your birthday, spend NIS40 and get a free bottle of champagne. Videos, cartoons, and Charlie Chaplin. Cheap beer (0.5L NIS5). Free beer 9-9:10pm, free cocktail for "ladies" 7-7:20pm. Open daily 4:30pm-late.

Yatush Barosh, Migdal Yam Soof (tel. 374 223) in the Marina, underneath Spiral. Features the longest bar in Eilat—over 12m of phoenix-bedecked elbow room. Mellow music and great breezes. Mixed Israeli/tourist crowd. Slightly expensive drinks pay for an atmosphere classier than most. Draft beer NIS7. Open 7pm-3am.

Teddy's Pub, Ofira Park (tel. 373 949), opposite Shulamit Gardens Hotel. A staid plaid English pub in the middle of the desert, with a Tudor exterior to boot. Lots of Israelis. 0.5L Goldstar NIS7. Live music on weekends: jazz and blues on Fri., Israeli soul and rock on Sat. Open 7pm until Mr. Kollek leaves.

Dolphin Reef (tel. 374 292), at Dolphin Reef; take a cab. On the beach. Dance in the sand Mon. and Thurs. night, Fri. afternoon. Draft beer NIS5. Open 10am-late.

Yaeni Pub, in the Ostrich Farm across from Coral Beach. Bus #15 or a cab. Arrive 9pm for the light show. Desert feel. Goldstar NIS5. Open Mon.-Sat. 7pm-dawn.

Clubs

A two-story domed disco was in the works at the **Royal Beach Hotel** in summer 1994. Rumors of forthcoming groovy laser shows had other disco owners shuddering in trepidation. Will probably open nightly 11pm-wee hours. NIS25 cover.

Sheba's, at the King Solomon Hotel (tel. 374 111). Ultra-modern, maximum-reflection atmosphere with laser show. Mixes disco, pop, and new wave. High-energy performing bartenders and strong drinks; don't mind the stuffed panther. NIS30 cover includes 1 drink. Maccabee NIS8. Open Mon.-Sat. 11:30pm until empty.

Spiral (tel. 376 640), in the Red Sea Tower at the Marina just over the bridge. Pronounced "SPEE-ral." 2-story nightclub overlooking the water has unparalleled lights and an excellent sound system that blasts disco, Israeli rock, funk, and acid. Must be 18 to get in, 17 in summer. Cover NIS20, Fri. NIS25, includes 1 beer or soft drink. Maccabee NIS7. Open 10:30pm-about 5am, depending on crowd size.

Ha-Nesiha, at the Princess Hotel right before Taba Beach, take a cab. Hefty NIS40 cover, but you'll thrill to sophisticated sound and light systems and *peut-être* a rotating dance floor in 1995. For those who really want to dance.

The tourist office has information on events at the **Phillip Murray Cultural Center** (tel. 332 257) on Ḥativat Ha-Negev near the bus station. Jazz, classical, rock, and theater season runs Sept.-June. The center also has a television, reading room, and rotating art exhibits (open daily 8am-8pm). Kids'll love **Luna Park** (tel. 376 095), in front of the Queen of Sheba Hotel. Rides including bumper cars and "Super-X Simulator" cost NIS5; kiddie thrills NIS4. (Open Mon.-Sat. 6pm-midnight.) Other events include the week-long **Hebrew Rock Music Festival** 1 week prior to Passover on Eilat Beach and the end-of-August **Red Sea Jazz festival,** with 10 performances on four stages every day in the port area. Ask at the GTIO for more information.

■ NEAR EILAT

The beauty of the red granite mountains towering over Eilat matches that of its coral reefs. Few guided tours are available for non-Hebrew speakers, so either take a crash course or strike out on your own. The **SPNI field school** across from Coral Beach (take bus #15) has Hebrew trail maps (NIS30), and will help translate. Many of the sites are accessible by northbound bus #393, 394, or 397. During high season or on Sundays and Fridays, plan ahead because buses fill up. Make reservations at the central bus station 2 days in advance or get stuck in the boonies.

The hike to **Mt. Tz'faḥot** is convenient and provides great views. The green-and-white markered trail begins at the left end (toward Egypt) of the fence separating the highway from the field school complex. A 45-minute climb takes you to the summit. From here, the blue trail heads north, ending at the Club Inn Hotel near Aqua Sport beach. The round trip takes about two hours and makes a great evening outing in summer. Don't wander too far on paths leading south—you may find yourself making a spontaneous visit to Egypt.

The most exciting terrain accessible from Eilat is to the north. Take bus #392 in the morning for **Ein Netafim, Mt. Shlomo** (through Mapalim Valley), or **Ha-Canyon Ha'Adom** (Red Canyon). The bus driver will know when to let you off. These hikes are not advisable in summer unless you're impervious to boiling-point temperatures. From Red Canyon, continue to the lookout above **Moon Valley,** a pocked canyon in Egypt, and to the unusual **Amram's Pillars.** A half-day guided tour is US$19 (winter only) with Egged Tours (tel. 373 148 or 149; depart from the central bus station). **Avi Desert Safari** (tel. 378 871) offers similar half- and full-day tours. A Jeep trip is available for half- (US$32) and full days (US$44) through **Johnny Desert Tours** (tel. 372 608 or 376 777) in the Shalom Center. **Camel Riders** (tel. 373 218) offer two-day caravans along smugglers' routes (US$120) or Mt. Chorev (US$140). **Donkey wagon rides** are offered by Solomon's Chariots (tel. 372 405), leaving from the ostrich farm (NIS25). **Metzokei Gishron** (tel. 376 578) offers cliff climbing tours.

The **National Park** (tel. 356 215) at **Timna** is another hiking destination. The 6000-year-old Timna copper mines, still flawlessly preserved in the southeast corner of the park, were in mint condition during the Egyptian period. One currently out-of-fashion theory of biblical history puts the exodus of the Israelites on the old path from Egypt to Timna Valley, as Israelite slaves would have known the way to the mines. Today you can find remains of workers' camps and cisterns dating from the 11th century BCE scattered amidst the whir of modern mining. The sandstone **King Solomon's Pillars** dominate the desert at a height of 50m near the 14th-century BCE Egyptian Temple of Hathor. Exhibits show the mining process. The park's **lake** offers **camping** facilities (including baths) and a restaurant on its artificially created shores. United Tours, in the Shalom Center (tel. 371 729), runs tours to Timna Valley for about NIS50 per half-day. Otherwise you can take most buses that go to Tel Aviv or Jerusalem and ask to get off at the sign for Alipaz (not at the Timna Mines signpost). Walk to the entrance 2km away. (Park open 7:30am-6:45pm. Admission NIS10, ages 5-18 NIS4.50.) Bring water.

Most northbound buses will take you to the **Ḥai Bar Biblical Nature Reserve,** a wildlife park designed to repopulate animals indigenous in biblical times, many of which have become rare in the region. Ask to get off at Yotvata. The reserve is home to roaming gazelles, donkeys, ostriches, and 11 species of predators mentioned in the Bible, including leopards, wolves, and striped hyenas. (Open 9am-1:30pm; animal feeding 8-11am. Admission NIS16, children NIS10, includes Coach tour.) Only closed vehicles can enter; no one wants to clean entrails off the windshield of your Jeep. Either come on foot (early) and wait for a vehicle with space, or take one of the daily guided tours in **Ḥai Bar Coaches** at 9am, 10:30am, noon, or 1:30pm.

The entrance to the Ḥai Bar is opposite the entrance to Kibbutz Samir, 5km south of Yotvata. At Kibbutz Yotvata, **Ye'elim Desert Holiday Village** (tel. 374 362) has tent space for NIS24 year-round. (Check-in 2pm. Caravan singles NIS82. Doubles NIS116. July-Aug. NIS140/NIS195.) Swimming pool is free for guests, NIS10 for visitors. The **visitors center** (tel. 376 018) opposite the kibbutz provides information and a film about Negev ecology. (Open 8am-3pm. NIS5 for the film, free with ticket to Ḥai Bar.) The **cafeteria** serves Yotvata's famous dairy products. Return to Eilat from the same stop on incoming buses.

Jerusalem ירושלים القدس

Pray for the peace of Jerusalem:
  "May they prosper who love you.
Peace be within your walls,
  and security within your towers."

—*Psalm 122:6-7*

When the sun sets over the Judean hills, the white dressed stone of Jerusalem turns gold, and peace indeed seems to be within the city's high walls. Sometimes it is. But don't stop praying for the peace of Jerusalem too soon; around you, three religions and two peoples stake claims to a few acres of land. The blinding Jerusalem stone, by law the finishing material of every building in the city, has seen more than its fair share of blood, all in the name of love for the city.

At its worst, Jerusalem is vicious. "Jerusalem," reflected Muhammad ibn Ahmed al-Muqaddasi in the 10th century CE, "is a golden basin filled with scorpions." At its best, it is more magnificently spiritual than perhaps any place on earth. This, too can be difficult; Israeli poet Yehuda Amiḥai sighs, the "air over Jerusalem is saturated with prayers and dreams, like the air over industrial cities. It's hard to breathe."

The spiritual, religious, historical, and nationalistic charms of Jerusalem attract all kinds of people. Palestinians, no matter their religion, religious Jews of all sects from the Ultra-Orthodox to Reform, Christian pilgrims from all over Europe, Armenians, secular Israelis, Muslims, Mormon missionaries, American tourists, fanatics, mystics, and raving lunatics coexist side by side. (Try figuring out who's who.) What keeps them all together is neither mutual understanding nor the Holy Spirit. Rather, it is the strange personal bond between the city and each of its dwellers that makes them stay, though they may socialize with their own and turn away from others. Indeed, Jerusalem may be one of the most fragmented cities in the world, thinly united by a stone veneer, cold winters, a few main roads, and a magic spell.

■■■ HISTORY

During Jerusalem's 3000 years, 18 conquerors have presided over the city. Archaeological findings indicate that Jerusalem (Jebus, then) was a Canaanite city for 2000-3000 years before King David's conquest around 1000 BCE (2 Samuel 5). David established Jerusalem as the capital of the Israelite kingdom; his son Solomon extended the city's boundaries northward to include the present-day Temple Mount. There Solomon built the First Temple, wherein sacrificial observances were to be centralized and the Ark of the Covenant kept.

The Israelite kingdom split shortly after Solomon's death in 933 BCE. The tribes of the northern Kingdom of Israel created their own capital, while those of the south retained Jerusalem as the center of the Kingdom of Judah. Internal disunity and strife left the land of Judah vulnerable to ruinous invasions. The Babylonian army led by King Nebuchadnezzar succeeded in besieging the city and forcing its capitulation in 596 BCE. The Babylonians, like most other empires bent on world conquest, kept Jerusalem disarmed and powerless. When Zedekiah instigated a rebellion ten years later, a wrathful King Nebuchadnezzar ordered the exile of the Jews to Babylon and the burning of Jerusalem's finest buildings, including the Temple. In 539 BCE, though, the Babylonians succumbed to Cyrus of Persia who permitted the Jews to return from exile (2 Chronicles 36). Reconstruction commenced soon thereafter, and in 515 BCE the Second Temple was rededicated (Ezra 6:15). But the restoration of Jerusalem was not consummated until Neḥemiah rebuilt the city walls in 445 BCE (Nehemiah 6:15).

Jerusalem enjoyed more than a century of undisturbed revival under the Persians until Alexander the Great swept through the city in 332 BCE. The subsequent wave of Hellenization soon swamped much of the population. After a century and a half of Hellenic rule and a brief spell of Egyptian Ptolemaic control, the Seleucid Empire took Jerusalem in 198 BCE. King Antiochus IV forbade all Jewish practices, including *Shabbat* observance, circumcision, and reading of the Torah. When he installed the cult of Zeus in the Temple, non-Hellenized Jews revolted. The rebels, led by Judas Maccabeus, were successful, resanctifying the temple in 164 BCE and giving the priestly hierarchy secular power over the city. Thus began the Hasmonean dynasty, which ruled the area's Jews for the next century.

The Roman general Pompey seized control of Jerusalem in 64 BCE, ushering in several centuries of Roman rule. The Romans installed Herod the Great, son of a Jewish father and Samaritan mother, to reign over what they called the Kingdom of Judea. While occupying the throne (37-4 BCE), Herod commanded the reconstruction of the temple and the creation of the well-known and partially extant Western Wall to better support the enlarged Temple Mount. In 6 CE the Romans bequeathed the governance of the province to a series of procurators, the most famous of whom was Pontius Pilate. After another 60 years, though, the Jews revolted against Rome. The Roman commander Titus crushed the revolt four years later, destroyed the temple, razed the city, and cast many Jews into slavery or exile; life in the Diaspora began. After the Bar Kokhba Revolt (a second Jewish revolt named for its leader) ended in 135 CE, the city was again destroyed by Emperor Hadrian and Jerusalem was declared off limits to the Jews.

That very year Hadrian built a new city over Jerusalem, Aelia Capitolina, to serve as a Roman colony. The pattern of the present-day Old City corresponds to the plan of Hadrian's city: it was divided into quarters by two major roads (the Cardo and Decamanus) and oriented north to south. When Roman Emperor Constantine accepted and legalized Christianity in 331 CE, his mother Helena visited the Holy Land in order to identify and consecrate Christian sites. Subsequent Byzantine rulers devoted their energies to the construction of basilicas and churches for the glorification and celebration of the city's Christian heritage.

Following a brief period of Persian rule in the early 7th century, six years after the death of Muhammad, the Muslim caliph Omar took Jerusalem in 638 and cleansed and hallowed the Temple Mount anew as a center of Muslim worship. Omar, one of the *Rashidun* (Rightly Guided Caliphs), personally accepted Aelia's surrender. In 691 his successors completed the Dome of the Rock. Under the tolerant Muslim rule, Jews were allowed to return to the city.

In the 10th century Jerusalem fell into Egyptian hands. The Fatimid despots destroyed all synagogues and churches (around 1010, the "mad caliph" Al-Hakim sacked the Holy Sepulchre), and passed on their policy of persecuting non-Muslims to their successors, the Seljuk Turks. Their rumored closing of pilgrimage routes enraged Western Christians and added fuel to the fire of the Crusades, culminating in the Christian capture of Jerusalem in 1099. With cries of *"Deus vult"* (God wills it), the Crusaders slaughtered Muslims and Jews as they took Jerusalem. The Crusader Kingdom lasted almost 90 years, marked by wholesale massacres of non-Christians and desecration of non-Christian sites of worship. During this time, churches were built or rebuilt, and hospices, hospitals, and monastic orders founded. In 1187 Salah ad-Din expelled the Crusaders, and both Muslims and Jews once again began resettling the city. Jerusalem became a thriving center for Muslim scholarship from the 13th to the 15th century under the Mamluks.

In 1516 Jerusalem capitulated to the Ottoman Turks, the city's rulers for the next 400 years. In 1537 Ottoman emperor Suleiman the Magnificent set out to rebuild the city walls; the task took four years. The planners deviated from the older design, leaving Mount Zion and King David's tomb beyond the walls. This negligence infuriated Suleiman, who had the two architects beheaded; legend says their graves are directly inside Jaffa Gate. In later centuries, many foreign countries began demanding extra-territorial rights for their citizens living under Turkish rule. The world political climate forced the sultan of Turkey to issue the 1856 "Edict of Toleration" for all religions. The small, deeply religious Jewish and Christian communities in Jerusalem still needed charity from abroad to make ends meet, but the trickle of Jews and Christians coming from Europe and Russia increased to a steady flow.

Sir Moses Montefiore, a British Jew, undertook several trips to Palestine between 1827 and 1874, sponsoring Jewish settlements outside the city walls. These areas soon expanded into bustling neighborhoods, the foundations of West Jerusalem. Heavier Western influence and the increasing flow of European immigrants led to the designation of Jerusalem as an independent *sanjak* (Ottoman province) in 1889, with its own ruler *(pasha)* appointed directly from Constantinople.

Ottoman rule over Jerusalem ended in 1917 when the city fell without resistance to the British army. Both Jews and Arabs resented the increasing influence of the British in Jerusalem. During World War I, Britain made separate declarations to both Zionists and Arab nationalists, implying to each that they would eventually gain sole sovereignty over the city. In the end, though, the British kept Palestine for themselves as a League of Nations Mandate. Under British rule, tension between the Jewish and Arab communities heightened, bursting into violent confrontations in 1929 and 1933, and virtual civil war between 1936 and 1939.

The uneasy World War II truce between Arabs and Jews quickly dissolved when the war ended. Violence ravaged Palestine for the next three years. The British announced that they were no longer capable of governing the country. They solicited a settlement from the newly formed United Nations, who resolved to split Palestine into separate Jewish and Arab states, leaving Jerusalem an international city.

In the war that followed the 1948 British evacuation, West Jerusalem and the Jewish Quarter were besieged by the Arabs, who blocked the single road out of the city. West Jerusalem held out until the first cease-fire, but the Jewish Quarter of the Old City capitulated to the Jordanian Arab Legion after extensive and exhausting house-to-house fighting. Jordan demolished the ancient Jewish Quarter of the city and dynamited synagogues. The Jordanian-ruled and Israeli sectors of the city were separated by a buffer zone. This division lasted nearly two decades.

When the 1967 War broke out, Israel requested that Jordan not get involved; King Hussein attacked West Jerusalem nonetheless. In the course of the Six-Day war Israel captured East Jerusalem and the Old City from the Jordanians; on the 29th of June that year Israel declared the newly unified Jerusalem its "eternal capital." The walls separating the Israeli and Arab sectors were torn down, and life under Israeli rule began for Jerusalem's Arabs.

The 25 years following the Six-Day War also saw large scale construction outside the Old City. Land owned by Palestinians who had fled during the war was systematically usurped or covertly bought. Vast new housing developments for Israeli-born couples and Jewish immigrants from Europe were built north and south of the city, in areas previously under Jordanian rule. The old campus of the Hebrew University on Mt. Scopus, deserted since 1948, was also expanded. Intensive gardening projects blossomed throughout the city, and verdant parks encircled the Old City.

The 1987 outbreak of the *intifada* (uprising) of Palestinians protesting Israeli occupation had some effect on Jerusalem, though demonstrations were more common in other West Bank towns. The Palestinians made it clear that they still regarded East Jerusalem as a part of the West Bank and the future capital of their desired Palestinian State. Meanwhile, collisions between bullet-spraying and baton-wielding Israeli forces and stone-throwing Palestinians, as well as occasional stabbings of Jews in the Old City, turned East Jerusalem and the Old City into alien territory for most residents of West Jerusalem and other Israelis visiting town.

■■■ ORIENTATION

The old Green Line marking the pre-1967 cease-fire runs straight through Jerusalem, separating the Old City and East Jerusalem from West Jerusalem. But that fact is an abstraction to tourists; Jerusalem is an open city today, and there is nothing to impede moving around.

> Tensions sometimes make East Jerusalem and parts of the Old City unfriendly to Israelis and other Jews. When you visit, make your tourist status as pronounced as possible. *Yarmulkes* are a particularly bad idea in the Arab parts of town.

West Jerusalem, seat of the Israeli government, is also the administrative and commercial center of Jerusalem. Most of the city's restaurants and services are located here, as well as virtually all of its nightlife. West Jerusalem is vast, and is perpetually extending its tentacles farther; the name denotes the Jewish parts of Jerusalem, from French Hill in the northeast, to Armon Ha-Natziv in the southeast, to Kiryat Menahem in the southwest and Ramot in the northwest. West Jerusalem's main street is **Jaffa Road** (Derekh Yafo), running from the end of the Jerusalem-Tel Aviv highway (where the central bus station is located) to the Old City's Jaffa Gate. Midway between the two, Jerusalem's triangular downtown area prospers. With Jaffa Rd. as one of the sides, **King George Street** (Rehov Ha-Melekh George) and **Ben-Yehuda Street** enclose the area. The corner of Ben-Yehuda and Jaffa is the site of **Zion Square** (Kikkar Tzion), and on Ben-Yehuda between Jaffa and King George is the popular *midrahov*. In the direction of the bus station between Jaffa Rd. and **Agrippas Street** you'll find West Jerusalem's chaotic open-air market, **Mahaneh Yehuda.**

Jerusalem's most important historical and religious sites are concentrated within the walls of the **Old City,** which is still divided into the four quadrants originally laid

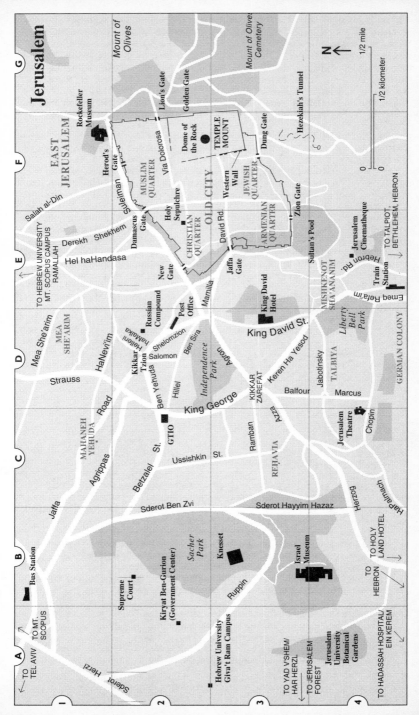

Jerusalem

EAST JERUSALEM

Mount of Olives

Mount of Olives Cemetery

Lion's Gate

Golden Gate

Rockefeller Museum

Herod's Gate

Suleiman

Salah al-Din

Derekh Shekhem

Hel haHandasa

MUSLIM QUARTER

Damascus Gate

Via Dolorosa

Dome of the Rock

TEMPLE MOUNT

Dung Gate

Hezekiah's Tunnel

TO HEBREW UNIVERSITY MT. SCOPUS CAMPUS RAMALLAH

New Gate

Holy Sepulchre

CHRISTIAN QUARTER

OLD CITY

David Rd.

Western Wall

JEWISH QUARTER

ARMENIAN QUARTER

Zion Gate

Jaffa Gate

Sultan's Pool

Jerusalem Cinematheque

TO TALPIOT, BETHLEHEM, HEBRON

Mea She'arim

MEA SHE'ARIM

Strauss

HaNevi'im

Road

Russian Compound

Post Office

Mamilla

King David Hotel

Hebron Rd.

MISHKENOT SHA'ANANIM

Train Station

Emeq Refa'im

Kikkar Tzion

Helleni haMalka

Shelomzion

Salomon

Ben Sira

Independence Park

King David St.

Liberty Bell Park

GERMAN COLONY

MAHANEH YEHUDA

Agrippas

Betzalel St.

Ben Yehuda

Hillel

GTIO

Ussishkin St.

Ramban

King George

KIKKAR ZAREFAT

Keren Ha Yesod

REHAVIA

AZZA

Balfour

Jabotinsky

TALBIYA

Marcus

Jerusalem Theatre

Chopin

Jaffa

Sderot Ben Zvi

Sderot Hayyim Hazaz

Herzog

Harlamach

TO HOLY LAND HOTEL

TO HEBRON

Bus Station

Supreme Court

Sacher Park

Knesset

Kiryat Ben-Gurion (Government Center)

Israel Museum

Ruppin

TO TEL AVIV

TO MT. SCOPUS

Sderot Herzl

Hebrew University Giva't Ram Campus

TO YAD V'SHEM/ HAR HERZL

TO JERUSALEM FOREST

Jerusalem University Botanical Gardens

TO HADASSAH HOSPITAL/ EIN KEREM

N

1/2 mile

1/2 kilometer

0

0

out by the Romans in 135 CE. To get from the city center to the Old City, continue on Jaffa Rd. past the post office all the way to **Jaffa Gate.** Here you can follow the promenade along the ancient walls to the seven other gates. The main road in the Old City is **David Street,** an extension of which, **Bab as-Silsilah Street** (Gate of the Chain), runs close to the Western Wall. The **Armenian Quarter** is to the right as you enter through Jaffa Gate and is directly accessible from Zion Gate. Left of Jaffa Gate is the **Christian Quarter,** which can also be reached straight through New Gate. Damascus Gate provides direct entry into the heavily populated **Muslim Quarter.** To get there from Jaffa Gate, turn left onto **Khan az-Zeit** from David Rd. and it will be on the right. A right turn off David Rd. onto **Ha-Yehudim Street** leads to the **Jewish Quarter,** which is directly accessible via Dung Gate.

Like West Jerusalem, **East Jerusalem** is more a political notion than a geographical description; it is the name normally given to the Palestinian parts of Jerusalem, and often includes the Old City. East Jerusalem stretches in the areas immediately to the north and east of the Old City. **Suleiman Street,** in front of **Damascus Gate,** and **Salah ad-Din Street,** which runs out from Herod's Gate, are the main roads in central East Jerusalem. The latter is a haven for offices and stores. Two Arab bus stations serve the area, the larger of which is located on Suleiman St. between **Nablus Road** (Derekh Shekhem) and Salah ad-Din St. The other station, located on Nablus Rd., serves routes northward. **Ha-Nevi'im Street** (Musrada in Arabic), which converges with Nablus Rd. at Damascus Gate, has many dry goods stores and hostels. Central East Jerusalem is the financial and cultural hub for the Arab community.

The city is known as **Al Quds** (the Holy) in Arabic and **Yerushalayim** in Hebrew.

■■■ TRANSPORTATION

Most distances in Jerusalem make for reasonable, pleasant walks. You can reach any section of the city by bus from the **central bus station** on Jaffa Rd. (NIS2.80, an NIS28 *kartisiya* buys 11 rides for adults, 20 for people under 18; see Israel: Getting Around, p. 248). Egged buses stop along the road outside the station entrance, and in front of **Binyanei Ha'Umma Convention Center** (across the street from the station through the underpass). Arab buses run every day; Egged service stops about 3:30pm on Fridays, resuming after sunset Saturday.

#1 (Platform D): To Mea She'arim, Jaffa Gate, Mt. Zion, Old City Jewish Quarter.
#5, 6, 13, 18, 20, 21 (Platform A): To West Jerusalem center; get off at the intersection of Jaffa Rd. and King George St. All but #13, 18, and 20 go to the train station.
#9 (Platform A): To the Knesset and the Israel Museum, Mt. Scopus, West Jerusalem center, and Hebrew University at Giv'at Ram.
#13, 20, 23 (Platform A): Down Jaffa Rd., to Jaffa Gate by the Old City.
#27 (Platform A): To West Jerusalem center, Damascus Gate, and East Jerusalem.
#99, the Jerusalem Circular Line (from Jaffa Gate): 34 major tourist sights. Sun.-Thurs. at 10am, noon, 2pm, 4pm; Fri. at 10am, noon, 2pm. One loop costs NIS5. For information, call 248 144 or 247 783.

All Egged routes are marked on the detailed English bus route map; this map is also one of the best street maps for West and East Jerusalem (but not the Old City). Get it free from the Egged Public Relations office, in the Beit Egged office building, 208 Jaffa Rd. #307. (Open Sun.-Thurs. 7:30am-noon and 1-3:30pm.) Two other maps are usually distributed by the tourist office: the brown Ministry of Tourism map and the pink Gabrieli map (gives good detail of the city center). The Gabrieli map is only occasionally available at the King George St. office, but can be found at some hotels. The map inside *This Week in Jerusalem,* available in hotels and the GTIO, covers more area than other maps. Aharon Bier's excellent map of the Old City, superimposed over an aerial photograph, gives a three-dimensional perspective and shows every courtyard and alley within the city walls; the map is available at the shops inside Jaffa Gate and the SPNI Bookstore. For maps deluged with detail, try the Department of Surveys (1 Heshin St., around the corner from the MTIO).

■■■ PRACTICAL INFORMATION

Government Tourist Information Office (GTIO): Main Office, 24 King George St. (tel. 754 910 or 912 or 863 or 864), corner of Schatz St. in West Jerusalem, in the old Knesset building. The new Golden Screen computer provides a wealth of information and print-outs. Branch inside **Jaffa Gate** in the Old City (tel. 282 295). Maps, brochures, bus schedules, and calendar of local events. Both open Sun.-Thurs. 8:30am-5pm, Fri. 8:30am-1pm.

Municipal Tourist Information Office (MTIO): 17 Jaffa Rd. (tel. 258 844) at Tzahal Sq. Although most of their literature is in Hebrew, the staff is helpful and the office uncrowded. Free Saturday walking tours (10am). Open Sun.-Thurs. 8:30am-4:30pm, Fri. 8:30am-12:30pm.

Tours: Society for the Protection of Nature in Israel (SPNI), 13 Helena Ha-Malka St. (tel. 252 357 or 244 605). Organizes guided tours throughout Israel and the Sinai. English-language tours range from 1-day explorations of Jerusalem (US$39) to 7-day Grand Sinai tours (US$319). SPNI store has English hiking, diving, and birdwatching books. Open Sun.-Mon. and Wed.-Thurs. 9am-3:45pm, Tues. 9am-4:30pm, Fri. 9am-noon. **Neot Ha-Kikar,** 6 Shlomzion Ha-Malka St. (tel. 236 262), specializes in guided tours to the Sinai (1-6 days; US$53 for 1 day) and other parts of Egypt (4-, 5-, and 8-day trips; US$189 for 4 days). Also offers a half-day tour of Jerusalem (US$20) and a tour of the Golan and Galilee (US$160). Usually the best prices around. Open Sun.-Thurs. 9am-6pm, Fri. 9am-1pm.

Budget Travel: ISSTA, 31 Ha-Nevi'im St. (tel. 257 257). ISIC costs NIS25; bring proof of student status and a photo. Student discounts on flights to Europe and Cairo, car rentals, and Eurail Passes. Lines can be long; not always the best deal in town. Open Sun.-Tues. and Thurs. 9am-1:30pm and 3-6pm, Wed. and Fri. 9am-1pm. Also on Mt. Scopus Hebrew University campus next to the Rothberg School in the Goldsmith Building (tel. 826 116). Open Sun.-Thurs. 9am-4pm.

Consulates: U.K., 19 Nashashibi St., East Jerusalem (tel. 828 281), near Sheikh Jarrah. Open Mon.-Fri. 8am-12:30pm. **U.S.,** 27 Nablus Rd., East Jerusalem (tel. 895 118). Open Mon.-Fri. 8:30-noon; closed Israeli and U.S. holidays. Visas, passports. West Jerusalem branch, 18 Agron St. (tel. 253 288), offers no services. Most countries, including Australia, Canada, and South Africa, have consulates in Tel Aviv only.

Currency Exchange: Bank Leumi, 21 Jaffa Rd. (tel. 291 611), next to the post office. Open Sun.-Thurs. 8:30am-1:30pm, Fri. 8:30am-noon. **Bank Ha-Poalim,** 1 Zion Sq. (tel. 207 070). Open Sun., Tues., and Thurs. 8:30am-2pm and 4-7pm, Mon. and Wed. 8:30am-2pm, Fri. 8:30am-noon. Their **Foreign Resident and Tourist Center** on 16 King George St. (tel. 207 676) is open Sun., Tues., and Thurs. 8:30am-12:30pm and 4-6pm, Mon. and Wed. 8:30am-12:30pm, Fri. 8:30am-noon. **First International,** 10 Hillel St. (tel. 756 888). Open Sun. and Thurs. 8:30am-2pm, Mon.-Wed. 8:30am-2pm and 4-7pm, Fri. 8:30am-noon.

American Express: 40 Jaffa Rd. (tel. 224 6195 or 9729; fax 223 1520). Full service office, with Client Letter Service and Traveler's Cheque cashing and replacement. Open Mon.-Thurs. 9am-5pm, Fri. 9am-1pm.

Thomas Cook: Aweidah Bros. & Co. Tourist & Travel, 23 Salah ad-Din St. (tel. 283 705; fax 282 366). Buys and sells traveler's checks, changes currency, and helps with travel arrangements, tours, and pilgrimages.

Central Post Office: 23 Jaffa Rd. (tel. 290 898). Open Sun.-Thurs. 7am-7pm, Fri. 7am-noon. **Poste Restante. Telegrams** in the main building, or dial 171. **Fax** service also available here (open Sun.-Fri. 24 hrs.). Domestic Parcel Service (tel. 290 077) around the building to the right (open Sun.-Fri. 7am-noon). **Branch post offices** throughout the city (ask for the *do'ar*).

Telephones: Bezek, 1 Koresh St., behind the post office. International calls can be made from any pay phone, but this place has quiet booths and you don't have to worry about mega-unit Telecards. Open Sun.-Thurs. 8am-10pm, Fri. 8am-2pm. Payment in shekels only. **Information:** Tel. 246 196. **Telephone code:** 02.

Flight information: Arrival and departures in English, call (03) 971 2484. **El Al** has advance check-in in Jerusalem: bags for morning flights can be checked in and inspected the night before at Center 1, 49 Yirmeyahu St. (tel. 246 725/6/7/8), corner of Jaffa Rd. Open Sun.-Thurs. 1-10pm, Sat. 1hr. after sunset-10pm. Buses to **Ben-Gurion Airport** leave from the central bus station; for early morning flights you may want to pay extra for *sherut* (see Intercity Sherut Taxis, below).

Train Station: Remez Sq. (tel. 733 764), southwest of the Old City, just south of Mishkenot Sha'ananim and Liberty Bell park. From downtown, take bus #5, 6, 8, 14, 18, 21, or 48. 2 trains per day go to Tel Aviv (8:45am and 3pm; 2hr.; NIS11.50, students 7.50) and continue to Haifa (1 more hr.; NIS21, students NIS15). Slower than buses but a bit cheaper and more scenic.

Intercity Buses: Egged Central Bus Station, Jaffa Rd. (tel. 304 704), west of city center. Information, posted destinations and fares, and ticket windows to the right as you enter. Limited English spoken. 10% discount with ISIC. To: Tel Aviv central station, #405 direct (every 5-20min. 5:50am-11:40pm, Fri. 5:50am-5pm, Sat. sundown-midnight; NIS13, students NIS11.50); Tel Aviv Arlozorov terminal, #480 direct (every 15-20min. 6am-10pm); Haifa, #940 direct (roughly every ½hr. 6:30am-7:15pm, Fri. 7:30am-3½hrs. before sundown, Sat. sundown-10:50am; NIS23.50, students NIS21); Ben-Gurion Airport, #945 or #947 (roughly every 15-30min. 6am-8:30pm, Fri. 7:30am-3:30pm, Sat. sundown-10:30pm; NIS13, students NIS11.50); Eilat, #444 (Sun.-Thurs. 7, 10am, 2, and 5pm; Fri. 7, 10am, and 2pm; NIS38, students NIS29.50; round-trip NIS69, book in advance); and Be'er Sheva, #446 direct (every 20-60min. 6am-9:30pm, Fri. 6am-4:15pm, Sat. sundown-9:45pm) or #470 (irregular—check schedule; 6:45am-6:15pm, Fri. 11:15am-1:20pm), both buses NIS19, students NIS17.50. **Baggage check** across the street, NIS4 per item per day. Open Sun.-Thurs. 7am-5pm, Fri. 7am-3pm.

West Bank Buses: Two bus stations serve the West Bank. **Suleiman St. Station,** in East Jerusalem between Herod's and Damascus Gates, serves routes south while **Nablus Rd. Station** serves points north. See West Bank: Getting Around, p. 396 for routes and prices.

Taxis within Jerusalem: Jerusalem Taxi, 4 Ha-Histadrut St. (tel. 255 233), near the junction of King George and Ben-Yehuda St.; **David Citadel Taxi,** Jaffa Gate (tel. 284 334); **Ben-Yehuda Taxi,** Herbert Samuel St. (tel. 255 555); **Ha-Bira,** 1 Ha-Rav Kook St. (tel. 389 999), corner of Jaffa Rd.; **Kesher-Aviv,** 12 Shammai St. (tel. 257 366), off Yoel Salomon St.

Intercity Sherut Taxis: Intercity rates are fixed; 2 pieces of luggage included in the fare. **Nesher,** 21 King George St. (tel. 257 227 or 231 231) goes to Ben-Gurion Airport. Must reserve 1 day in advance. Picks you up at your door (NIS27).

Car Rental: Avis, 22 King David St. (tel. 249 001 or 002); **Budget,** 8 King David St. (tel. 248 991 or 992; fax 259 456); **Hertz,** 18 King David St. (tel. 231 351), and in the Hyatt; **Thrifty,** 18 King David St. (tel. 250 833).

English Bookstores: Sefer va-Sefel, 2 Ya'Avetz St. (tel. 248 237), near corner of 49 Jaffa Rd.; 3rd door on the right and up the stairs. New and used books and magazines. Browse on the patio while sipping drinks. Open Sun.-Thurs. 8am-8pm, Fri. 8am-2:30pm, Sat. 8:30-11:30pm. **Yalkut Books—New and Used,** 8 Aliash St. (tel. 257 058), in Kikkar Raduan, upstairs from the Lev Yerushalayim Hotel. Open Sun.-Thurs. 8am-7pm, Fri. 8am-1:30pm. **Steimatzky,** 7 Ben-Yehuda St. (tel. 255 487), on the *midraḥov;* other locations as well. Open Sun.-Thurs. 8:30am-11pm, Fri. 8:30am-2:30pm, Sat. 8:30-11pm.

Christian Information Center: P.O. Box 14308 (tel. 272 692), inside Jaffa Gate and to the right, just past the Citadel. Provides maps and detailed lists of Christian services, hospices, and sites in Jerusalem. Books sold. Call or write for tickets to midnight Christmas Mass in Bethlehem. Open Mon.-Sat. 8:30am-1pm.

Franciscan Pilgrims Office: P.O. Box 186 (tel. 272 697), same building as Christian Information Center. Makes reservations for Mass at all Franciscan sanctuaries. Pilgrimage certificates available (US$3). Open Mon.-Fri. 9am-noon and 3:30-5:30pm, Sat. 9am-noon.

Jewish Student Information Center: 5 Beit El, Jewish Quarter (tel. 282 634, after-hours (050) 344 341; fax 288 338), across from the Ḥurva Arch. Open Sun.-Thurs. 9am-7pm, Fri. 9am-*Shabbat.*

Jewish National Fund: Plant a Tree with Your Own Hands program in the Jerusalem Forest. Take bus #19 or 27 to last stop; go into main entrance of Hadassah Ein Kerem hospital, ask for Tannenbaum Center. Open Sun.-Thurs. 8:30am-3pm, Fri. 8:30am-noon. 1 tree NIS24. Or contact JNF, 1 Keren Kayemet St. (tel. 639 650).
Ticket Agencies: Ben Naim, 38 Jaffa Rd. (tel. 254 008), open Sun.-Thurs. 9am-2pm and 4-7pm, Fri. 9am-1pm; **Bimot,** 8 Shammai St. (tel. 234 061); and **Kla'im,** 12 Shammai St. (tel. 256 869). Both open Sun.-Thurs. 9am-7pm, Fri. 9am-1pm.
Laundry: Baka Washmatic, 35 Emek Refa'im St. (tel. 631 878). Take bus #4, 14, 18, or 24 from city center, get off at Emek Refa'im post office, cross the street, and continue for a ½-block. Open Sun.-Thurs. 8am-7pm, Fri. 8am-2pm. Large wash, dry, and fold NIS41; small NIS33. Manager Jason White offers 20% discount to *Let's Go* ites. **Ha-Merkaz Laundry,** 11 Kakal St. (tel. 664 246), just off Usishkin St. Open Sun.-Thurs. 8am-1pm and 3-7pm, Fri. 8am-1pm. 5kg wash and dry NIS25. **Superclean Laundromat,** 16 Palmaḥ St. (tel. 660 367), bus #15. Open Sun.-Thurs. 7am-7pm, Fri. 7am-2pm. 6kg wash, dry, fold NIS20, 10kg NIS30.
Swimming Pools: Beit Taylor, Zangwill St. (tel. 414 362), in Kiryat Yovel. Open daily 9am-2pm, women only 2:30-7pm (NIS15; bus #18 or 24). **Jerusalem Swimming Pool,** Emek Refa'im St. (tel. 632 092), open daily 7am-5:45pm (NIS27; bus #4 or 18). Get *Shabbat* tickets in advance. **Beit Zayit** (tel. 246 217), bus #151 (10 per day) from central station to Beit Zayit to the last stop. Tell driver you want the pool. Open daily 9am-7pm; NIS18 (children NIS12), Fri. and Sat. NIS23 (children NIS18); see Camping, p. 381 for more information on Beit Zayit.
Film Developing: Kodak Express, 25 King George St. (tel. 256 557). 36 prints NIS38. **Photo Yeḥezkel,** 47 Jaffa Rd. (tel. 255 590), in alleyway opposite Lotto booth. NIS8.90 per roll, NIS0.33 per print. 1 free enlargement per roll. Open Sun.-Thurs. 9am-7pm, Fri. 9am-2pm. **Photo Ha-Bira,** 91 Jaffa Rd. (tel. 231 915). NIS8 per roll, NIS0.55 per print. Open Sun.-Thurs. 8am-1pm and 4-7pm, Fri. 8am-2pm.
Help Lines: Rape Crisis Center (tel. 514 455). 24 hrs., will accompany you to the police and explain procedures. **Mental Health Hotline** (tel. 227 171 or 610 303), also called **Eran,** assists tourists. Open 8am-11pm; when closed, Hebrew recording gives you alternate number to call. **Alcoholics Anonymous** (tel. 630 524 or 351 303). **Ozen Kashevet** (tel. 242 85; open 9am-10pm) is a general support line and includes gay, lesbian, and bisexual issues. English spoken at all.
Services for the Disabled: Yad Sarah Organization, 43 Ha-Nevi'im St. (tel. 244 242). Loans medical equipment for 1 mo. with option to extend for 3 mo. Free, but full value deposit required. Available for emergencies. Look for a big blue former train. Open Sun.-Thurs. 9am-7pm, Fri. 9am-noon.
Pharmacy: Superpharm, 5 Burla St. (tel. 639 321), near Hebrew Univ. Giv'at Ram campus, bus #17. Open 9am-9pm and Sat. night. Also at 3 Ha-Histadrut (tel. 246 244/5), between Ben-Yehuda and King George St. Open Sun.-Thurs. 8:30am-10pm, Fri. 8:30am-3pm, Sat. sundown-11pm. **Alba Pharmacy,** 7 Ben-Yehuda St. (tel. 257 785), next to Café Atara. Open Sun.-Thurs. 8am-7pm, Fri. 8am-2pm. There are many pharmacies in city center. There are no 24-hr. pharmacies. Two are on duty nightly and on *Shabbat* on a rotating schedule. Schedules and phone numbers available on any pharmacy door and in newspapers.
Medical Emergency: Tel. 101. Look for **Magen David Adom** (Israeli Red Cross; tel. 523 133), next to the central bus station or inside Dung Gate in the Old City. Newspapers list hospitals and pharmacies on duty for emergencies. Blue Cross-Blue Shield members are eligible for pre-paid hospitalization at Hadassah Ein Kerem and Mt. Scopus hospitals (tel. 776 040 for information).
First Aid for Tourists: Bikur Ḥolim Hospital, 74 Ha-Nevi'im St. (tel. 701 111), corner of Strauss St., the continuation of King George St. past Jaffa Rd. Open 24 hrs.
Police: Tel. 100 for emergencies. Located in the Russian Compound (tel. 391 111), off Jaffa Rd. in West Jerusalem. Old City branch, inside Jaffa Gate to your right, has a tourist desk (tel. 273 222, ext. 33 or 34).

BOOKS AND TOURS

Jerusalem's legends and history are best absorbed through advance reading or, if you must, a guided tour. The most interesting, unusual, and easy-to-follow guidebook is *Footloose in Jerusalem* (NIS31) by Sarah Fox Kaminker. For a more humorous look at the City of Gold, buy *Marty's Walking Tours of Biblical Jerusalem* (NIS8): Marty Isaacs outlines itineraries on the Mount of Olives and through the City of David. Nitza Rosovsky's *Jerusalemwalks* (NIS40) is by far the most thoughtful guide to the city's lesser known avenues and well worth the price. David Benvenisti's *Tours in Jerusalem* (NIS23) is cheaper and has good directions. *Quartertour Walking Tour of the Jewish Quarter* (NIS5) is cheaper still, more interesting, and more comprehensive than some. *Guide to the Holy Land* (US$11 at Christian Information Center), written by a Franciscan monk, describes sites of Christian significance in exhaustive detail. Archaeology buffs will appreciate *The Holyland* (NIS66) by Jerome Murphy O'Connor. Finally, athletes should pick up *Carta's Jogger's Guide to Jerusalem* (NIS22). The book details routes amidst historic areas and sights. Most of these books are available at Steimatzky and other bookstores throughout the city. **Hebrew Union College,** 13 King David St. (tel. 203 333 or 251 478), has an air-conditioned library with an extensive collection of books about Jerusalem (open Sun-Thurs. 8:30am-5pm). Seek in the Bible and ye shall find 355 references to Jerusalem (really! or count them yourself).

Every Saturday at 10am the municipal government sponsors a free **Shabbat Walking Tour** (info. tel. 228 844). Meet at 32 Jaffa Rd. at the entrance to the Russian Compound, near Zion Sq. *This Week in Jerusalem* lists the itineraries, which are also posted at the MTIO office at 17 Jaffa Rd. Tours last about three hours and can be very large. **SPNI** (see p. 373) offers tours daily, including two- to three-hour walks along unusual routes (NIS20). Some *Shabbat* tours are free. Guided walking tours are available through the **King George-Jasmine Youth Hostel,** the **Capital Hostel,** the **Jerusalem Inn Youth Hostel,** the **Guest House,** and others in the area for NIS15 or US$5 (see Accommodations, below). The hostels also offer a 12-hour tour of Jerusalem, Bethlehem, Masada, the Dead Sea, Jericho, and more for NIS50.

■■■ ACCOMMODATIONS

OLD CITY

Many of Jerusalem's cheapest hostels—from quiet sanctuaries to hang-from-the-rafters hangouts—are located in the Old City. You get views from rooftops and balconies, proximity to major sights, and a free wake-up call provided by *muezzins* at the crack of dawn and by the morning mosh pit in the market. Lodgings cluster near Jaffa and Damascus Gates; most have "flexible curfews" (managers will usually let you in late if you inform them ahead of time). Reservations are recommended.

Accommodations in the Jaffa Gate area are accessible from West Jerusalem: walk down Jaffa Rd. or Agron St. to the end, or take bus #3, 13, 19, 20, 30, 41, or 99. The hotels and hostels in the Damascus Gate area, in the middle of the Arab *souq,* are cheaper and livelier. If business seems slow, bargain. You can reach Damascus Gate by walking to the end of Ha-Nevi'im St. or by taking bus #1, 23, 27, 44, or 99.

Be careful when wandering deep into the *souq;* avoid walking alone through the Damascus Gate area after dark. Only the busiest streets in the Old City are lit at night; learn the way back to your hostel during the day. Don't leave luggage unattended in hotel rooms if you can avoid it. All hostels have safes for your valuables. In most places, you can pay in either U.S. dollars or shekels. Paying in foreign currency will save you the 18% VAT. Some places only accept U.S. dollars.

Near Jaffa Gate

New Swedish Hostel, 29 David St. (tel. 894 124 or 277 855), straight into the *souq* from Jaffa Gate. Sign advertises "homely" atmosphere. Hopping with travelers, but conditions not exactly Scandinavian, aside from the gloriously spotless modern bathrooms and showers. Kitchen, washing machine, TV lounge. Free tea and coffee. Offers tours to Masada (NIS50-55), Old City (NIS15), and Bethlehem (NIS20). Check-in midnight. Check-out 11am. Curfew midnight, but keys available. Stay 6 nights, get 1 free. Dorm beds NIS13. Free lockers.

Lutheran Youth Hostel, 7 St. Mark's Rd. (tel. 282 120 or 894 735). Enter Jaffa Gate, cross the square, turn right onto Al Khattab, left onto Maronite Convent Rd., and right at St. Mark's Rd. The outstanding facility includes an inner courtyard, lush gardens, and a kitchen with a dining hall worthy of the Last Supper. Check-in 10am-10:30pm. Check-out noon. Flexible 10:30pm curfew. Bunk beds in clean, separate-sex dorm rooms (NIS22). Free lockers. The Lutheran Guest house next door has lovely stone and wood-paneled singles (DM55=NIS109) and doubles (DM93=NIS184), all with telephones. Breakfast included. 5% service charge.

Petra Hostel (tel. 282 356), the first hostel on your left on David St. just before you enter the *souq;* look for pink-skinned northerners soaking up UV on small balconies overlooking the square—or just keep walking. Check-in anytime. Check-out 11am. No curfew. Loft mattress NIS10. Dorm beds NIS15. Doubles NIS60.

Jaffa Gate Youth Hostel, on an alley off Al Khattab St. at the entrance to the market; look for the sign (tel. 276 402). Long, vaulted dorm room with rows of cots and walls painted to look like stone has a cheesily spiritual aura, but the old armchairs in the TV lounge are down to earth. Patio looks like an outdoor café. Kitchen, fridge, TV, and showers. Open all day. Check-out noon. Curfew midnight. Roof beds NIS10. Dorm beds NIS15. Doubles NIS50-60.

Citadel Youth Hostel, 20 St. Mark's Rd. (tel. 274 375), before Lutheran Hostel on the right of the winding path. Low cavernous passageways (foam covers the lowest arches to protect the accident-prone); pleasant, well-kept spaces including atrium sitting area, kitchen, and TV room. Men's dorm room upstairs has classic view of Old City. Rooftop solarium has beds and view but gets hot on breezeless days. Open 7am-midnight. Check-in midnight. Check-out 10am. Flexible midnight curfew. Dorm beds NIS15-17; in winter NIS13-14. Doubles NIS40-50.

Lark Hotel, 8 Latin Patriarchate Rd. (tel. 283 620), the first left from Jaffa Gate. Spotless rooms with showers. 2nd-floor sitting room and small balcony overlook quiet street. Armenian restaurant on first floor run by same friendly family. Open 5:30am-11pm, but keys available. Check-out anytime. Singles, doubles, and triples about US$22 per person; prices very flexible. Continental breakfast included.

New Imperial Hotel (tel. 282 261; fax 271 350), on David St. immediately inside Jaffa Gate on the left; columns mark entrance. Restaurant, meeting hall, and vast sitting rooms lend epic grandeur to the expansive hotel. Kaiser Wilhelm of Germany stayed here a century ago. Friendly and helpful Muhammad will gladly give you tips on seeing the Old City. No heat or A/C. Reception closes midnight. Check-out noon. Singles US$14, with bath US$17. Doubles US$25, with bath US$28. 20% student discount. Reservations recommended March-April.

Near Damascus Gate

Austrian Hospice, 37 Via Dolorosa, P.O. Box 19600 (tel. 274 636; fax 271 472), just to the left of Al Wad Rd. Embassy-like building has lush grounds, spotless rooms, occasional visiting dignitaries. Wheelchair-accessible. German library, glorious view from the roof. *Ausgezeichnet!* Check-in 10pm. Check-out 10am. Flexible 10pm curfew; keys available with deposit. Dorm beds US$10. Singles US$41. Doubles US$62. Triples US$87. Breakfast included. Reservations recommended.

Black Horse Hostel, 28 Aqbat Darwish (tel. 280 328; fax 280 329), off Via Dolorosa. A clean, new hostel with smiling management and friendly ambience. Hostelers play games, listen to music, or simply relax in a sitting room strewn with carpets and pillows or at the bar's light wood tables. Heated in winter. Happy hour (9-10:30pm) features half-priced drinks. Phone and fax service. Check-in and check-out by noon. Flexible midnight curfew. Indoor "courtyard" beds NIS7. Dorm beds NIS15. Bed and breakfast NIS20. Free tea, coffee, use of kitchen, tents, TV, video, and lockers. Laundry NIS1.50 per piece.

Ecce Homo Convent, Eastern Via Dolorosa, P.O. Box 19056 (tel. 277 292). Turn left onto Via Dolorosa from Al Wad Rd.; the small "Notre Dame de Sion" sign is down the road on the door on the left. Knock. The doors will mysteriously creep open and the Sisters of Sion will provide blissful refuge and a transcendental view of the domes and minarets of Jerusalem. Kitchen and study area. Heated in winter. Curfew 11pm. Dorm beds (women only) US$7. Single cubicles with sink for men or women US$14. Singles US$22. Doubles US$38. Breakfast included.

ACCOMMODATIONS

Tabasco Youth Hostel and Tea Room, 8 Aqabat at-Takiyah (tel. 283 461), the first left off Khan az-Zeit after Via Dolorosa as you enter from Damascus Gate. The sign reads, "Come on travelers, let's party." Comfortable tea room has Arab-style floor seating, scrawled-on walls, and cheap eats. The manager leads free trips to the Palestinian refugee camps and Bethlehem. Free video shown nightly. Domed rooms have open-air skylights. Kitchen, dining room, squeaky-clean showers. Check-out 11am. No curfew. Roof beds NIS9, students NIS8. Dorm beds NIS12, students NIS11. Singles NIS40, students NIS35. Free tea and tabasco sauce, cheap beer, meals NIS4-10. Laundry NIS10. Locked storage available. No reservations.

Al-Arab, Khan az-Zeit (tel. 283 537). From Damascus Gate, bear right onto Khan az-Zeit; it's on the left. TV, kitchen, ping-pong, free tea and coffee, free use of safe; heated in winter. Friendly, colorfully painted hostel shows videos every night at 9 and offers free accommodations for a week if you can beat the manager Abu Hassan at ping-pong. Arranges trips to the refugee camps. Check-in 1:30am. Check-out 10am. Curfew 1:30am. Roof beds NIS9. Dorm beds NIS13-14. Reservations recommended in summer and during Christmas.

Al-Ahram Hostel, 64 Al Wad Rd. (tel. 280 926). Enter Damascus Gate and bear left onto Al Wad at the fork; opposite third station of Via Dolorosa. A clean place to sleep, located midway between Old City destinations. Laundry facilities and kitchen; bright sitting room overlooks Via Dolorosa. Rooms heated in winter. Check-in midnight. Check-out 11am. Flexible midnight curfew. Roof beds NIS10. Dorm beds NIS15. Doubles with shower NIS60.

El Hashimi Hotel and Hostel, 73 Khan az-Zeit (tel. 284 410), just past Al-Arab. Brand new. Spotless bathrooms, beds sturdier than the hostel norm. TV room with nightly video at 9; soft drink bar, kitchen, laundry facilities. Portable A/C, no heat in winter. 24-hr. reception. Check-out 11am. No curfew. Roof beds with terrific view of Dome of the Rock. Dorm beds NIS13-14. Private rooms NIS45-50.

Armenian Catholic Patriarchate, Al Wad Rd. (tel. 284 262 or 274 408; fax 272 123). Enter under sign just after Via Dolorosa on your left, about 200m down Al Wad from Damascus Gate. Clean; feels like a monastery. Unmarried couples turned away. Check-in 10pm. Check-out 11am. Curfew 10pm. Dorm beds US$12. Doubles with bath US$36. Breakfast included. Reservations recommended.

Jewish Quarter

Old City Youth Hostel (HI), 2 Bikur Ḥolim (tel. 288 611). Walk down David St. into the market and follow the signs right onto St. Mark's Rd., right again across from the Lutheran Hostel, and up the narrow street with half-arches. Sparkling clean, airy, located in a renovated hospital. No kitchen access. No smoking, TV, or radio on *Shabbat*. Usually crowded with school groups and soldiers. Closed 9am-5pm. Check-out anytime. Flexible 11pm curfew. Dorm rooms with cubbies for clothes US$10, nonmembers US$11. Breakfast included, other meals NIS30.

EAST JERUSALEM

East Jerusalem, although often a hotbed of tension, is a good place to experience and learn about the Palestinian lifestyle and point of view. What the area lacks in convenience it makes up for in great values and a generally hospitable, friendly atmosphere. Visibly Jewish travelers (particularly men in *kipot*) should probably stay away, or at least expect hostile stares. Women should be careful when walking alone at night. Four hostels cluster on Ha-Nevi'im St., which intersects with Suleiman St. and Nablus Rd. across from Damascus Gate.

Faisal Youth Hostel, 4 Ha-Nevi'im St. (tel. 272 492). Clean. Gorgeous view of Damascus Gate from balcony. Pleasant, personal atmosphere with crowded bunks, TV, a large kitchen, several cats, and manager Ali's Bedouin hospitality. Heated in winter. Flexible check-out. Curfew 1am. Camping on roof NIS11. Dorm beds NIS13. Doubles NIS40. Breakfast NIS5. Free tea, storage, use of iron, sewing machine, and basin for washing clothes. Machine wash and dry NIS5.

Palm Hostel, 6 Ha-Nevi'im St. (tel. 273 189). Clean and green. "Run by backpackers for the backpackers." Convivial atmosphere and international crowd. Kitchen.

Heated in winter. Check-out 10am. Roof bed NIS10. Dorm beds NIS13. Doubles NIS50. Prices negotiable. Storage NIS3.

New Raghadan Hostel, 10 Ha-Nevi'im St. (tel. 283 348). Easy-going atmosphere with kitschy art and hostelers of all ages. Cluttered, but large and clean. Balcony, bustling dining and sitting room, and kitchen. Door locked at midnight, but there is 24-hr. reception. No curfew. Dorm beds NIS12-15. Singles and doubles NIS20-25, with bath NIS30. Negotiable, especially for students.

Cairo Youth Hostel, 21 Nablus Rd. (tel. 277 216). Clean hostel on one of the liveliest streets of East Jerusalem. Large kitchen, sitting area, and rooftop cafeteria. Check-in 1:30am. Check-out 11am. Curfew 1:30am. Roof beds NIS10. Dorm beds NIS15. Private rooms NIS60. Reservations recommended.

Jerusalem Hotel, 4 Antara Ben-Shadad St. (tel. 271 356 or 283 282). Follow Nablus Rd. from Damascus Gate; it's just north of the Arab bus station. Beautiful building of ancient stone. Courtyard, modern rooms, and restaurant with Arab-style floor seating. TV lounge. Classical Arab music on Sat.; in winter, Thurs. is jazz night, with a Lebanese buffet. Popular with young professionals working in the West Bank. Rooms have phone and bath; TV and radio on request for NIS10. Heated in winter. Check-in 2am. Check-out noon. No curfew. Singles US$28-35. Doubles US$38-49. Triples US$48. Quads US$60. Breakfast included.

Ramsis Youth Hostel, 20 Ha-Nevi'im St. (tel. 271 651), take bus #11 from central station. Large windows and high ceilings in a quaint building with sparkling bathrooms; some rooms have balconies. Lounge with TVs. Check-out 10am. Curfew midnight. Dorm beds NIS25. Singles NIS50. Doubles NIS80. Triples NIS90. Free storage, kitchen, and dishes.

WEST JERUSALEM

Accommodations in West Jerusalem lack the charm of Old City hostels, but they are close to tourist services, entertainment, and sights, including the Old City itself. To fully explore Jerusalem's efflorescent nightlife you should check into a hostel with no curfew. (Dance clubs in Jerusalem's southern suburb Talpiot rock until 4-5am on weekends.) Prices do not automatically drop in the off-season (Oct.-April), but bargaining will be more successful then. Accommodations in private houses should be a second choice. Locals may approach you at the bus station, but be aware that their places may not be licensed and therefore not subject to government inspection. Women especially should exercise extreme caution, even if approached by a female. As always, you save the 18% VAT if you pay in dollars.

If you'll be in Jerusalem for over two months, consider renting an **apartment.** During July and August college students go on vacation and many rent out their places. A single room in a shared apartment will cost at least US$200 per month. The best source of information is the classified section of the local weekly *Kol Ha'Ir*—find someone to translate, and submit an ad of your own (for free) requesting an apartment. A thorough but more expensive option is the She'al Service, 21 King George St. (tel. 256 919). This agency grants one month's access to its voluminous listings in English for NIS75 (open Sun.-Thurs. 8:30am-7pm, Fri. 8:30am-1pm). The bulletin boards at Hebrew University and upstairs at the Israel Center on the corner of Strauss and Ha-Nevi'im St. may also be helpful. The "Bed and Breakfast" listings at the GTIO are a reliable source for monthly rentals.

Capital Hostel, 1 Yoel Salomon St. (tel. 234 582; fax 817 005). Join the ranks of Galileo, Napoleon, Gulliver, and Columbus by staying in spotless new rooms bearing their names. This jazz-bar-become-hostel boasts a colorfully painted central hallway, café-balcony with food, drink, and view of Jaffa St. Games and TV room, A/C. One of the best deals in town. 24-hr. reception. Check-out 10am. No curfew. Dorm beds NIS15 (US$5). Private rooms NIS90 (US$30). Free use of attractive sheets and duvets, laundry facilities, and safe deposit boxes. Includes free entrance to Underground disco (see p. 407) and 15% discount at the adjoining Soramello Restaurant. Reservations recommended in summer.

Beit Shmuel Guest House (HI), 6 Shamma St. (tel. 203 473 until 4pm), near the King David Hotel. Would Brunelleschi have designed a youth hostel? Here Israeli master architect Moshe Safdie celebrates the dormitory. His opulent creation sits next to the Hebrew Union College (another attractive Safdie *œuvre*) on King David St., through which you can enter. Remarkably hotel-like. Lounges, courtyard, garden, and restaurant, plus full use of the connected classrooms, synagogue, library, museum, and various cultural events. Wheelchair accessible. Elevator, A/C, heat in winter. Reception 7am-11pm. Check-in 3pm. Check-out 9am. No curfew. Dorm beds US$16.50. Singles US$29. Doubles US$40. (Non-members US$22, US$47, and US$72.) Prices drop during low season (Oct.-Dec. and Jan.-March). Breakfast included.

Jerusalem Inn Youth Hostel, 6 Ha-Histadrut St. (tel. 251 294; fax 251 297). From Zion Sq., Ben-Yehuda St. is intersected by Ha-Histadrut St. 1 block before King George St. Bus #14, 17, 31, and 32 from the central station. Friendly place in the middle of town. Drinks (NIS2-4), TV, and crayoned wisdom offered in lounge/reception area. Small shared baths. Refrigerator. Luggage storage US$1 per day. Roof sun deck. 24-hr. heating in winter. Check-in midnight. Check-out 11am. Midnight curfew, but keys given for NIS20 deposit. No visitors; front door locked. Clean rooms crowded with bunks. Dorm beds US$9 (US$10 for only one night). Singles US$24. Doubles US$28-36. Triples from US$45. US$1 cheaper in winter.

Jerusalem Inn Guest House, 7 Horkanos St. (tel. 252 757; fax 251 297). Near Zion Sq., the second right off Ha-Ḥavatzelet St. Rooms are spotless and modern. Spacious lobby features bar and restaurant (Italian dinner US$8). Manager Moti cooks, builds the attractive wood furniture, and runs a tight hostel: rules are strictly enforced, particularly regarding non-guests visiting upstairs. Make sure you're clear on the regulations; take them lightly and you'll find yourself back on the street with no refund. Check-in anytime. Check-out 10:30am, with ½-hr. grace period. No curfew. NIS10 key deposit. Ceiling fans keep rooms cool in summer; heated in winter. Dorm beds US$9 (US$10 for one night). Singles US$26, with bath US$42-44. Doubles US$28-38, with bath US$44-48. Prices rise 20-30% July-early Aug. Reservations with credit card.

Beit Bernstein Youth Hostel (HI), 1 Keren Ha-Yesod St. (tel. 258 286), at the corner of Agron St., tucked behind a synagogue, not far from the Sheraton Plaza. A 10-min. walk from Jaffa Rd. on King George St., or take bus #7, 8, 9, or 14 from the central bus station. If you don't mind the midnight curfew, come here to enjoy cleanliness, quiet, and the pleasant garden in back. A/C. Reception open 7-9am and 3pm-midnight. Check-out anytime. Dorm beds (single-sex; 4-7 per room; heated in winter) US$12-14.50. Breakfast included; meals US$6-8. Call ahead. Closed late June to mid-Oct. for summer camp.

The Backpackers' Hostel, 37 Jaffa Rd. Sleep exists in theory only (see Arizona, p. 407). Luckily, hostelers are having such fun downstairs they don't seem to care. For the young and broke. Get 2-for-1 draft beer during Happy Hour (NIS8) or all-you-can-drink-in-20min. (NIS5) at Arizona and collapse on your cheap bed. Check-in anytime. Check-out 11am. No curfew. Roof mattress NIS9. Dorm beds NIS15. Doubles NIS35. Small safe, TV, free tea and coffee, kitchen.

King George-Jasmine Youth Hostel, 15 King George St. (tel. 253 498). Take bus #14, 17, 31, or 32 to first stop on King George St. Prime location with lively atmosphere, but lacking in some of the extra amenities: bathrooms tidy but bathtubs have a gray hue. Lounge with color TV. Kitchen facilities. No curfew. Dorm beds (6-8 per room) US$24. Private rooms (for 1-4) NIS75. Lockers NIS5.

Hotel Noga, 4 Bezalel St. (tel. 254 590 until 1pm, 661 888 after; ask for Mr. or Mrs. Kristal). Near corner of Shmuel Ha-Nagid St. Like having a private apartment. Managers leave at night and give you a key to the front door. Kitchen, free tea and coffee. Bright white sheets and walls. Eight airy rooms and two porches on upper floors, two rooms on ground floor. All are heated in winter. Rooftop lounge with a view. Mr. Kristal, who once taught tennis to Yitzḥak Rabin's wife and who just might be the sweetest man on Earth, loans rackets and balls for free and might be coaxed into giving free lessons. Parking in back. Min. 2-night stay, special price for extended stays. Singles US$25. Doubles US$30. Triples US$40. Quads US$46. The porch couch (bathroom attached) is US$12 per night (less in winter). Free luggage storage. Definitely reserve in advance.

Jasmine Cottage, 3 Even Sapir St. (tel. 248 021), a side street off Bezalel St., 1 block west of Usishkin St. and several blocks west of city center. Falafel stand marks corner of Even Sapir. A lot of green paint, combined with a corps of road-tested travelers, gives the "cottage" its color. Relax on the patio or in the lounge to the tunes of an ample record collection. Hostel usually fills up by around 4pm in summer. Arranges daily tours to Masada-Dead Sea area (from US$20; 11-13hr.). Also offers daily walking tours of Jerusalem. Front door always locked, but every-one gets a key. Dorm beds US$5. Breakfast 8-10:30am, NIS6. Dinner NIS8-10. Laundry NIS8. Closed summer 1994.

Hotel Merkaz Ha-Bira, 4 Ha-Ḥavatzelet St. 2nd floor (tel. 254 075 or 255 754). Across from Zion Sq. Large hotel with lounge, TV, radio, and refrigerator. Two flights of stairs surrounding an ancient (and non-functional) elevator à la *Jennifer 8* lead up to the 24-hr. reception desk. Tidy, carpeted rooms have sink, mirror, and closets; some have strange built-in shower separated from the room by half-height walls. Dorm beds (available July-Aug. only) US$19, with shower US$22. Singles US$28. Doubles US$38, with shower US$44. 10% off for stays over one week. Free tea, coffee, luggage storage. Reservations a must July-Sept.

CAMPING

Beit Zayit Camping, Beit Zayit 90815 (tel. 346 217), 6km west of Jerusalem. Bus #151 (10 per day) from central bus station to Beit Zayit, the last stop; tell driver you want the pool. To avoid a long wait take bus #11 or 15-*alef*, which leave every 15min. from in front of Binyanei Ha'Umma Convention Center across from the central bus station. Ask the driver to tell you when the bus enters Har Nof; get off at the playground. Follow the signs (10-min. walk); at night avoid the trail and take bus #151. Helpful management and free use of kitchen. Camping: tent space NIS15, children NIS10; Fri.-Sat. NIS20/15. Bungalows with electricity NIS28, chil-dren NIS20; Fri.-Sat. NIS33/25. Amusement park, mini-golf, and RV hook-ups. Swimming pool NIS18, children NIS12; Fri.-Sat. NIS23/18 (open daily 9am-7pm).

■ ■ ■ FOOD

OLD CITY

The odors of the Old City may not suggest a gourmet's Mecca, but many eateries do make decent, cheap Middle Eastern food: most lie deep within the bustling markets and narrow alleys, but a few huddle close to the gates. Inexpensive places are hard to tell from the tourist traps; check the menus first! The daring can try the popular chicken restaurants on **Khan az-Zeit** (look for the huge rotisseries and follow the smell). Khan az-Zeit also drips with sugary-smelling shops selling honey-drenched Arab pastries for NIS3-5 per 0.5kg. **El Jenini Oriental Sweets** (tel. 285 278) with the large pink awning, just inside Damascus Gate, has lots of seating space and other-worldly *knafeh* and *ba'laweh* (NIS16-24 per kg). Open daily 8am-7pm. Fresh, large, soft sesame *ka'ak* is sold throughout the *souq;* ask for *za'atar* to go with it.

Abu Shukri, 63 Al Wad Rd. (tel. 271 538), 200m from Damascus Gate. Legendary hummus platters (NIS6), and falafel (NIS7). Open daily 8am-5pm.

Linda's, Via Dolorosa (tel. 282 765). Excellent hand-made hummus (NIS5-6) and other Middle Eastern tasties. Open daily 8am-4pm.

Pizza Abu Shanab (tel. 281 357), at the intersection of the *souq* and El Khanqa. The late closing time, cheap yummy food, good music, and lively mix of people make this an Old City hot spot. Small vegetarian (NIS3-5), Arabic (NIS2.50), and meat (NIS5-6.50) pizzas; 2 hot dogs NIS2.50; beer NIS4. Open daily 8am-midnight.

The Coffee Shop (tel. 277 727), near Jaffa Gate next to the Christ Church Hos-pice. The most pristine restaurant in the Old City, with A/C and lovely Jerusalem tiles decorating the tables. All the salad, soup, and pita you can eat for NIS15; sandwiches NIS8. Open daily 10am-6pm.

Abu Seif and Sons (tel. 286 812), just inside Jaffa Gate, beyond the tourist office. Don't be put off by the tourist-infested location. Hummus appetizer NIS8, grilled cheese NIS6, falafel with salad NIS6. Open 8am-8pm.

Quarter Café (tel. 287 770), above the corner of Tife'eret Yisrael and Ha-Sho'arim St., Jewish Quarter (look for the sign overhead). Praise the miracle of self-service while eating *mousaka* and taking in an epic view without spending a fortune. Salads and cakes NIS4-7, but expect to pay NIS30 for lunch. Open Sun.-Thurs. 8:30am-6:30pm, Fri. 8:30am-4pm. Kosher. 10% discount for *Let's Go* users.

St. Michel Cafeteria, 21 Jaffa Gate Rd. (tel. 282 035). This cool, clean cafeteria has lots o' seating and good food at decent prices: sandwiches and falafel (NIS5), omelette and salad (NIS7), personal Armenian pizza (NIS5). Open 8am-9:30pm.

Bakery Muhammad Ali a.k.a. **The Green Door,** 5 Aqabat Sheikh Rihan, left off Damascus Gate Rd. Virtually empty room with few tables, but the nearly subterranean stone oven bakes good, inexpensive pizza (NIS3-3.50) in an earthy atmosphere. Open daily 9am-11pm.

The Cardo Culinaria (tel. 894 155), in the Cardo, Jewish Quarter. Enjoy a "first-century dining experience" just as the Romans did (minus the bacchanalia—they don't serve wine). Expensive (NIS45 per person), but worth it, particularly for large food- and fun-starved groups. Waiters wrap you in togas and other items of Roman garb and attest to the authenticity of the food and dishware as you feast on plate after plate of chicken or fish, salad, pita and olive oil, and fruit. Sword fights occasionally erupt. Luncheon Sun.-Fri. noon-2pm. Dinner by reservation only.

EAST JERUSALEM

Falafel and spicy *kabab* are sold by street vendors for less than NIS2: follow the smoke and smells to the corner of Suleiman and Nablus St. Or create your own with **Nasser Eddin Bros.** on Suleiman St. across from Damascus Gate and to the right, just past the bus station, which stocks almost everything but fresh produce. (Open daily 8am-7pm.) Very cheap produce can always be found on the sidewalks of Suleiman St. (1kg zucchini NIS1-2). Salah ad-Din, Az-Zahra, and Suleiman St. buzz with a wide variety of restaurants, from bustling rotisserie and falafel places to quieter haunts with extensive menus.

Al Quds Restaurant, 23 Suleiman St. (tel. 272 052). You might feel like a roasted chicken yourself when you walk through the hot smoky aisle past the rows of rotisseries, but there is a light at the end of the tunnel: clean white tables and a delicious feast for a mere NIS11-12. ½ chicken with 3 salads, fries, and pita NIS11. *Shawerma* or *shish kabab* platter NIS12. Open daily 8am-midnight.

Petra Restaurant, 11 Rashid St. (tel 283 655). Fancy dining room and beautiful sun room with fountain in back. Salads NIS2. Entrees NIS20-30. Open daily noon-midnight. Manager-owner Abu Nasser may offer a 20% discount for *Let's Go* users.

Café Europe, 11 Az-Zahra St. (tel. 284 313). *The* place if you have the craving. Delicious milkshakes, burgers, fries, cocktails, and a wide variety of teas and coffees amidst quaint pink and lace decor. Hamburger platter NIS15. Try the "Last Tango of Mangoes" with rum and vanilla ice cream, or "Suzy Lips on the Apricots." The "Ali Baba" is, quite honestly, "a drink which will see you through with your bank manager." A/C. Open daily 11am-11pm.

Philadelphia, 9 Az-Zahra St. (tel. 289 770), off Salah ad-Din St. Philip Habib, Jesse Jackson, and Jimmy Carter's favorite pit-stop. Expensive, but the Valentine's Day atmosphere in July makes it worth the price. Complete seafood meal costs NIS35-40, stuffed veggies NIS5, soups NIS8, sweets NIS5. Open daily noon-midnight.

Candy's Cafeteria, 24 Suleiman St. (tel. 853 082), near Salah ad-Din St. Smaller and less chaotic than neighboring Al Quds Restaurant; serves faster food: *shawerma* (NIS5), *shish kabab* (NIS6), and *schnitzel* (NIS7). Open 8am-midnight.

Tmol Shilshom, 5 Solomon St. (tel. 232 758). From Zion Sq. with Jaffa Rd. behind you, turn left and head down Solomon St. Continue until you enter the *midrahov* and turn left into the first alley. Enter the courtyard, turn left, walk to the far end, and look for a beige sign with a coffee cup and red arrow. A gay-owned bookstore/café combo with a small but varied selection of English used books; the Hebrew selection is larger and includes new and antique books as well. Special events include poetry readings, live music, international food and story nights, and a children's hour that draws Hebrew U. *ulpan*ites. (Printed schedule available.) From the terrace, you can hear the music drifting up from the Arizona (see Dancing, p. 407). Drinks NIS7, entrees NIS12-28, soup NIS10, appetizers NIS7-12.

WEST JERUSALEM

The spices, aromas, and flavors of West Jerusalem's complex edibles hail from the Levant, Italy, Eastern Europe, India, France, China, Ethiopia, Morocco, Yemen, and Russia. Most eateries close Friday afternoon and reopen Saturday night after sundown, so stock up at the markets on Thursday and Friday mornings. Pick up the *Jerusalem Post* "Good Food Guide" and *Jerusalem Menus* magazine from the tourist office and ask about dinners hosted by Israeli families.

The cheapest food is sold in **Maḥaneh Yehuda,** the raucous open-air market between Jaffa Rd. and Agrippas St., to the west of the city center. Fruit and vegetable stands, pita bakeries, and sumptuous displays of pastries line the alleys, and there's a small grocery store *(makolet)* with rock-bottom prices at almost every corner. You can find pita here at 10 for NIS2 or less; 1kg tomatoes goes for the same price. The Yemenite section (follow the alleys leading east from Maḥaneh Yehuda St.) is the cheapest for produce, and the stands along Etz Ha-Ḥayim St. sell the best *halva* at NIS5 per 0.5kg. A specialty of the area is *me'orav Yerushalmi* ("Jerusalem assortment"), a mix of inner parts grilled with onions and packed in pita pockets. **Agrippas St.** is lined with *me'orav* vendors; **Sima** and **Stekiyat Hatzot** are rumored to use higher quality meats, if for higher prices. Ask for half a portion *(ḥatzi mana)*—it's more than enough. And if you're not up to liver and lungs, never fear: all the restaurants on Agrippas also serve *shishlik* (cubes of grilled meat) and *kabab*.

Visit the market at closing time (Sat.-Thurs. 7-8pm, Fri. 1-2hr. before sundown) when merchants lower their prices shekel by shekel to sell off the day's goods. Thursdays and Friday afternoons are wildest in Maḥaneh Yehuda, as thousands elbow and scramble to obtain the food they need for *Shabbat*. If you don't want to spend any money, just amble through the meat market in the alleys to the west of Maḥaneh Yehuda St., where a stroll among the skinned and dangling beasts may keep you fasting for days. **Supermarkets** include **Co-Op** in the basement of Ha-Mashbir department store at the intersection of King George and Ben-Yehuda St. (tel. 257 830) and **Supersol** on the corner of Agron and Keren Ha-Yesod St. (both open Sun.-Thurs. 7:30am-7:30pm, Fri. 8am-2:30pm).

The Yemenite Step, 10 Yoel Salomon St. (tel. 240 477). Grand stone building with high ceilings. Absolutely outstanding atmosphere and food. Try the scrumptious filling *malawaḥ* specialty (starting at NIS6-8.50, up to NIS24.50 with filling.) Soup NIS12.50-15.50, entrees NIS19-26, "business lunch" (noon-4pm) NIS16.50-24.50. Open Sun.-Thurs. noon-1am, Fri. noon-4pm, Sat. sundown-1am. Kosher.

La Brasa, 7 Yoel Salomon St. (tel. 231 456). Sit inside and watch your chicken cook, or people-watch at tables outside. Moist, flavorful chicken: ¼ chicken or BBQ breast with fries and salad NIS27, sandwich NIS13. Business lunch available. Open Sun.-Thurs. noon-1am, Fri. noon-6pm, Sat. 8:30pm-1am. Kosher.

The Village Green, 10 Ben-Yehuda (tel. 252 007). Whether outside under the umbrellas or amidst the wood decor, you'll enjoy delicious fresh salads (the regular is a meal in itself at NIS13), quiches (NIS21), and soups (NIS10) in this charming vegetarian restaurant. Slice yourself some bread and fill a tray with grains and dressings at the counter. Open Sun.-Thurs. 11am-10pm, Fri. 11am-3pm.

Off the Square, 6 Yoel Salomon St. (tel. 242 549), off Zion Sq. Popular garden restaurant with huge menu. Try the pizzas (NIS21) and crepes (NIS20). Italian food and "veggie meat" NIS20-28. Open Sun.-Thurs. 9am-11:30pm, Fri. 9am-2pm, Sat. sundown-midnight. A connected deli offers meat entrees for NIS28-41 and a full "business lunch" (11am-4pm) for NIS27. Open Sun.-Thurs. 9:30am-11:30pm, Fri. 9:30am-3:30pm, Sat. sundown-midnight. Kosher.

Tavlin, 16 Yoel Salomon St. (tel. 243 847). Dairy and vegetarian. Excellent blintzes and crepes NIS17-23. Spaghetti NIS2-25. Wood and stucco interior. Open Sun.-Thurs. 8am-12:30am, Fri. 8am-4pm, Sat. sundown-1:30am. Kosher.

Etnachta, 12 Yoel Salomon St. (256 584). Salads NIS22-24, quiche NIS23-26, omelettes NIS16.50-17.50, pies and crepes NIS18. Dairy and vegetarian fare served under umbrellas or indoors. Open Sun.-Thurs. 7:30am-2am. Kosher.

Blues Brothers, 3 Luntz St. (tel. 258 621). A Middle Eastern stop serving *shawerma* (NIS7) and falafel (NIS4) with 12 different types of salads, but it's also a steak house, has lots of sit-down room, and does not eschew all dishware. Open Sun.-Thurs. 9:30am-2am, Fri. 9:30am-*Shabbat,* Sat. sundown-2am.

Bali-Bagette, 31 Jaffa Rd. (tel. 256 715), near Rivlin St. Scrumptious baguettes full of salads and meats NIS4-7. Open Sun.-Thurs. 9am-3am, Fri. 9am-5pm. Kosher.

Mama Mia's, 38 King George St. (tel. 248 080), behind parking lot in the former Mo'adon Tzavta. A change of pace from budget eating. Delightfully crisp white interior with stucco ceilings and green trim. Peaceful patio, romantic table for two on a small balcony, and a separate non-smoking room. Delicious fettuccine NIS24-27, pizza NIS25-28, and great homemade ravioli NIS24-27. Open Sun.-Thurs. noon-midnight, Fri. noon-4pm, Sat. sundown-midnight. Kosher.

Primus, 3 Ya'avetz St. (tel. 234 917), a small alley off Jaffa Rd. between King George St. and Zion Sq. Not the band, but a Yemenite dairy restaurant-bar in a century-old building. 10 kinds of delicious *malawaḥ* for NIS10-18. Open Sun.-Thurs. noon-1am, Sat. sundown-1am. Glatt kosher.

Alumah, 8 Ya'avetz St. (tel. 255 014), off Jaffa Rd. between King George St. and Zion Sq. Quiet, spacious stone veranda and botanical interior. All is made from scratch in this wholesome natural restaurant. Specializes in stone-ground yeastless whole wheat, sourdough, and rye bread. Try the grain of the day. Take-out available. Main dishes NIS14-22, all served with bread and raw vegetables. Open Sun.-Thurs. 10am-11pm, Fri. 10am-2pm, Sat. sundown-11pm. Glatt kosher.

Ticho House, off 7 Ha-Rav Kook St. (tel. 244 186). Dairy and veggie restaurant set on the peaceful grounds of artist Anna Ticho's house and gallery. Sit inside or under a colorful patio umbrella overlooking a pleasant, shady park. Chamber music performances Fridays at 11am throughout summer (NIS5). Delicious large salads (NIS17-19), cream cheese and raisin crepes (NIS15), stuffed eggplants and sweet potatoes (NIS21), and cakes (NIS10). Open Sun.-Thurs. 10am-11:45pm, Fri. 10am-3pm, Sat. sundown-11:45pm. Kosher. (See also the Ticho Museum, p. 400.)

Kamin, 4 Rabbi Akiva St. (tel. 256 428), near Jerusalem Towers hotel. A lunch spot with high-ceilinged interior and quiet outdoor seating. Sandwiches NIS16, large salads NIS20-23, soups NIS12. Spaghetti NIS21-24, lunch and dinner pies NIS24, steak NIS35. Open Sun.-Thurs. 10am-1am, Fri. noon-1:30am, Sat. noon-midnight.

Gilly's, corner Yoel Salomon and Hillel St. (tel. 226 956). Resembles a ski lodge. For dedicated carnivores: meat NIS24-50. Very popular. Live music. Open Tues.-Thurs. noon-4pm and 6-11pm, Fri. noon-4pm, Sat. 7-11pm.

Restaurant Chen, 30 Jaffa Rd. (tel. 257 317), in the middle of the block (the whole block is #30). The sign is yellow with red and black Hebrew writing. Diner-style place serves delicious *shishlik, kabab,* and Kurdish-style steak (all around NIS18) and salads (NIS6). Stuffed grape leaves (NIS7) are a specialty. Open Sun.-Thurs. 8am-6pm, Fri. 8am until 1hr. before sundown.

BeSograim, 45 Usishkin St. (tel. 245 353), a few blocks from corner of Bezalel St. Somewhat expensive vegetarian restaurant set in a prettily decorated stone mansion in a pleasant neighborhood. Enjoy dessert in the garden or on the spacious patio for only NIS10-16. Main dishes include pasta (NIS24-27) and fish (NIS38-40). Open Sun.-Thurs. 9am-12:30am, Fri. 9am-5pm, Sat. after sundown.

The Promenade (tel. 732 513). Part of the Talpiot promenade overlooking the Old City; take bus #8 or 48 from Jaffa Rd. Watch a riveting sunset from here and you'll love Jerusalem for life. Watermelon NIS7, hummus NIS7, hamburger NIS30, *shishlik* NIS35 (with 2 side dishes). Open daily 8am-10pm, self-service until 4pm.

Quick Eats

The West Jerusalem center abounds with small eateries where natives and tourists converge. The best quick stops are small pizza joints, falafel stands, and ice cream and fruit shops for a daytime melt-down or an after-dinner cherry on top.

Posters of the Grateful Dead, Bob Marley, and the Beatles adorn the walls of **Avi Pizza,** a hole-in-the-wall at 11 Yoel Salomon St. (tel. 259 170). Slices of good, thick-crusted pizza go for NIS4.50-5, family-size pizzas NIS32. (Open Sun.-Thurs. 10am-2am, Fri. 10am-4pm, Sat. sundown-2am. Kosher.) **Apple Pizza,** 13 Dorot Rishonim St. (tel. 250 467), off Ben-Yehuda, serves thin-crust "Big Apple" pizza baked to the tune of rock classics. There's lots of umbrella-shaded outdoor seating. (Open Sun.-Thurs. 10:30am-midnight, Fri. 10:30am-4pm, Sat. 8:30pm-midnight. Kosher.)

Creating the perfect **falafel** or **shawerma** is an art all its own, and many stops on King George St. between Jaffa Rd. and Ben-Yehuda, or in Maḥaneh Yehuda, have perfected it. Some tips: do not, under any circumstances, put all the desired sauce into the pita pocket at once. You will make a mess of yourself and everyone around you. Instead, add sauce after every few bites. Secondly, the authentic original is to be found in the Palestinian parts of Jerusalem, where Arabs were making these foods long before Jewish immigrants ever heard of them.

The falafel stand at 15 King George St., three doors from the King George Youth Hostel, is one of the cleanest around. Great, big, filling, *lafa* sandwiches (a.k.a. *esh tan*) with hummus and *shawerma* are NIS10. **Bis Ta'im** (tel. 253 725) on King George St. near Agrippas St., serves delicious falafel (NIS3.50), *shawerma* (NIS6), and *esh tanoor* (NIS5). If you seek cheap, NIS2.50 buys falafel, NIS4 *shawerma*, and NIS3 *esh tanoor* at **Melekh Ha-Falafel ve Ha-Shawerma** (tel. 356 523) on the same corner. **Moshiko's,** 5 Ben-Yehuda (tel. 252 605), has outdoor dining on the *midraḥov* (falafel NIS4.50). Favorite hummus dens are **Ta'ami,** 3 Shammai St. (tel. 253 644), notorious for urging folks to finish and leave (a rarity in Israel, where one usually has to beg for the bill); and the just-as-packed **Pinati,** at 13 King George St.

For **ice cream,** visit **Ben and Jerry's,** 5 Hillel St. (tel. 242 767), just off King George St., not far from the tourist office, or 3 Luntz St. (tel. 243 025). A small cone scoops NIS3.50 out of your wallet. **Carvel,** 16 King George St. (tel. 254 410), near the Ha-Mashbir department store, is also a favorite (small cone NIS5). Cheaper and just-as-delicious ice cream and frozen yogurt can be found on the *midraḥov* at **Jack's,** 8 Ben-Yehuda St. (tel. 233 757), and at **Katzefet** (tel. 253 722), on the corner of Ben-Yehuda and Luntz St. (pink and green sign). Finally, the **Magic Fruit House,** 26 Ben-Yehuda St., has an unfortunate name but concocts fantastic fresh juice on the spot. Choose among mango, fig, peach, watermelon, and many others. (Regular size NIS2.50-3.50, medium NIS4.50-6; orange juice NIS5.50.)

■■■ SIGHTS

OLD CITY

Several groups offer complete tours of the Old City. **Walking Tours Ltd.,** 26 Alkavetz St. (tel. 522 568, Sun.-Fri. 8am-8pm), operates **David's "City of David"** tours of the four quarters, from the Citadel courtyard outside Jaffa Gate (Sun.-Fri. 9am and 2pm; 3-3½hr.; US$7, students US$5), as well as more specific tours. For the same price, **Zion Walking Tours** (tel. 287 866 or 713 543) leave at 9, 11am, and 2pm from their Jaffa Gate office; taking three tours earns you a free ticket to the Ramparts Walk. They also offer a tour of the Mount of Olives (Mon. 2pm and Thurs. 9am; 3-4hr.; US$12, students US$10). **Archaeological Seminars Ltd.** (tel. 273 515) offers a handful of tours, all preceded by short seminar/slide shows, for US$13. Meet at 34 Ḥabad St. above the Cardo at 9:30am. The GTIO has schedules for the tour groups and for the free walking tours sponsored by the Jerusalem Municipality.

The **Holyland Hotel** in West Jerusalem (tel. 437 777) has a knee-high model of Jerusalem in 66 CE, towards the end of the Second Temple Period. Historical documents and authentic building materials were used in the construction. Take bus #21 from downtown. (Open daily 8am-10pm. Admission NIS15, students NIS10.)

The Walls and the Citadel

The present walls of the Old City were built by Suleiman the Magnificent in 1542. The city had been without walls since 1219, when Al Muazzan tore them down to prevent the Crusaders from seizing a fortified city. There are eight gates, each of which has three names: Christian/English, Jewish/Hebrew and Muslim/Arabic. (The most commonly used names are listed here.) **Golden Gate** has been sealed since 1530, blocked by Muslim graves. It is thought to lie over the Closed Gate of the First Temple, the entrance through which the Messiah will purportedly pass (Ezekiel 44:1-3). Of the other seven gates, **Jaffa Gate** is the most convenient from West Jerusalem and is the traditional entrance for pilgrims; there has been a gate here since 135 CE. (Some people don't give Jaffa Gate the respect it deserves. Gustave Flaubert recalled: "We enter through Jaffa Gate and I let a fart escape as I cross the threshold very involuntarily. I was even annoyed at bottom by this Voltaireanism of my anus." He probably ate too much falafel.) **Damascus Gate** serves East Jerusalem; **St. Stephen's Gate** (or Lion's Gate), is the beginning of the Via Dolorosa. **Dung Gate,** first mentioned in 445 BCE by Neḥemiah, opens near the Western Wall and was given its name in medieval times because dumping dung here was considered an especially worthy act. **Zion Gate** connects the Armenian Quarter with Mt. Zion; **Herod's Gate** stands to the east of Damascus Gate; and the **New Gate,** opened in 1889 to facilitate access to the Christian Quarter, lies to the west.

You can walk atop all parts of the wall except those surrounding the Temple Mount/Dome of the Rock area. This **ramparts walk** provides an unsurpassed view of the Old City and an idea of the wall's military importance through the centuries. Clearly labeled near Jaffa Gate are slits for pouring boiling oil on attackers. Tickets to the ramparts are sold at the Citadel and Damascus and Jaffa Gates (tel. 231 221). Tickets are good for unlimited admission for two days after purchase, three days if purchased on a Friday. If you have a ticket, you don't owe a shekel to the self-appointed "guards" who might approach you along the way. Women should *never* walk alone on the walls, even during the day. Even if you can run, you can't hide. (Walls open Sat.-Thurs. 9am-4pm, Fri. 9am-2pm. Admission NIS6, students NIS3.)

To ascend the ramparts from Damascus Gate, you must go down the steps to the right before you enter the gate, walk under it, and continue through the ancient carriageway to the left of the plaza. The level of the carriageways on either side corresponds to the middle Roman period in the 2nd century CE. At the rampart entrance you can visit the **Roman Square Museum,** which is set among the excavations from Aelia Capitolina. The museum displays a copy of the 6th-century **Madaba map** from Madaba, Jordan; the map is the earliest extant blueprint of the city's layout. The huge centipede that seems to crawl from Damascus Gate at the northern tip to Dung Gate at the southern is actually a two-dimensional rendition of the **Cardo,** the main thoroughfare; its "feet" are the Roman columns lining the street. The map has aided archaeologists in concluding that the Cardo recently unearthed in the Jewish Quarter is not part of the Roman original, but a Byzantine addition. Scholars have also discovered a plaza at the gate's entrance with a statue of Hadrian mounted on a huge column. This image reveals the early origins of the Arabic name for Damascus Gate, *Bab al-Amud* (Gate of the Column). The plaza has been partially uncovered, but the black marble column is missing; you'll have to settle for the hologram on display. The stones on the floor still show the scars left by Roman chariots. (Museum open Sat.-Thurs. 9am-4pm, Fri. 9am-2pm. Admission NIS1.50, students NIS0.70.)

Another place to dig the history of the Old City is the **Citadel** complex, sometimes called the **Tower of David** (*Migdal David* in Hebrew), just inside Jaffa Gate and to the right. The citadel resembles a Lego caricature of overlapping Hasmonean, Herodian, Roman, Byzantine, Muslim, Mamluk, and Ottoman ruins—everything but ruins from David's time. The Tower of David is the highest point in the Citadel and provides a superb vantage point for surveying the Holy City. The citadel hosts

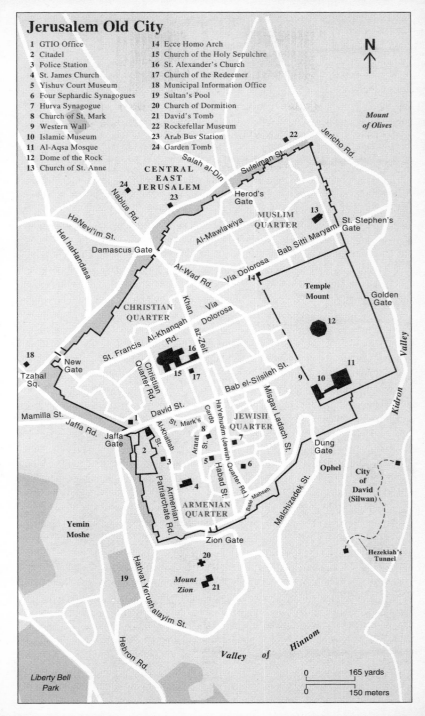

Jerusalem Old City

1 GTIO Office
2 Citadel
3 Police Station
4 St. James Church
5 Yishuv Court Museum
6 Four Sephardic Synagogues
7 Hurva Synagogue
8 Church of St. Mark
9 Western Wall
10 Islamic Museum
11 Al-Aqsa Mosque
12 Dome of the Rock
13 Church of St. Anne
14 Ecce Homo Arch
15 Church of the Holy Sepulchre
16 St. Alexander's Church
17 Church of the Redeemer
18 Municipal Information Office
19 Sultan's Pool
20 Church of Dormition
21 David's Tomb
22 Rockefellar Museum
23 Arab Bus Station
24 Garden Tomb

N
↑

Mount of Olives

CENTRAL
EAST
JERUSALEM

Salah al-Din
Suleiman St.
Jericho Rd.
Herod's Gate
MUSLIM QUARTER
St. Stephen's Gate
Nablus Rd.
HaNevi'im St.
Hel haHandasa
Al-Mawlawiya
Damascus Gate
Al-Wad Rd.
Via Dolorosa
Bab Sitti Maryam
Temple Mount
Golden Gate
CHRISTIAN QUARTER
Khan az-Zeit
Via Dolorosa
St. Francis
Al-Khanqah Rd.
Christian Quarter Rd.
Kidron Valley
New Gate
Tzahal Sq.
Mamilla St.
Jaffa Rd.
Jaffa Gate
David St.
Al-Khabab St.
St. Mark's
Ararat St.
Cardo
HaYehudim (Jewish Quarter Rd.)
Habad St.
Bab el-Silsileh St.
Misgav Ladach St.
JEWISH QUARTER
Dung Gate
Ophel
City of David (Silwan)
Hezekiah's Tunnel
Malchizadek St.
Bate Mahseh
Armenian Patriarchate Rd.
ARMENIAN QUARTER
Yemin Moshe
Zion Gate
Hativat Yerushalayim St.
Mount Zion
Hebron Rd.
Valley of Hinnom
Liberty Bell Park

0 _____ 165 yards
0 _____ 150 meters

outdoor concerts in summer. The **Museum of the History of Jerusalem** inside the Citadel is high-tech, and only slightly biased. (Citadel open Sun.-Thurs. 9am-5pm, Fri. and Sat. 9am-2pm. Admission NIS18, students NIS14, children NIS10; price includes guided tour in English Sun.-Fri. 11am.) They have a 45-minute English **sound and lights show.** (Tel. 286 079. April-Oct. Mon., Wed., and Sat. 9:30pm. Admission NIS18, students NIS14; combined tickets NIS32, students NIS24, children NIS18.)

Markets

From Jaffa Gate, descend David St. to the Old City's exciting markets. Shopkeepers peddle everything from bottled water to Marilyn Monroe posters, but you would do best to take home a piece of beautiful Palestinian craftwork, such as Hebron pottery, cushions decorated with traditional embroidery, brass or silver vessels, or a mother-of-pearl inlaid box or Qur'an. Popular tourist purchases include the *tableh* (drum), *hatta* (black- or red-and-white Palestinian head-dress made fashionable world-wide by the *intifada* and Yasser Arafat), and the decorative *argileh* (water pipe). If you cannot throw out enough t-shirts to fit an *argileh* into your pack, settle for a short smoke (NIS1-2) at a *qahwa*, guaranteed to give even seasoned smokers a head rush. Ask for yummy apple tobacco. Or wait and buy one in Egypt, where they're cheaper anyway and go by the name *sheesha.*

Do not buy from the first air-conditioned wonderland you enter. Often, the *exact* same wares (same quality, same makers) are sold from closet-like alcoves for a lot less. The *souq* is not the place to dazzle shopkeepers with your Hebrew; haggle in English or Arabic—the hospitable shopkeepers are thrilled to hear even a few stammered phrases of Arabic (a good time to break out that *Let's Go* glossary).

While *all* the narrow streets of the Old City *souq* are full of shops and potential great finds, there are several concentrated commercial thoroughfares. **David Street** (Souq al-Bazaar), and its continuation, **Bab as-Silsilah Street,** run between Jaffa Gate and the Temple Mount/Dome of the Rock area. Halfway down David St. on the left, two cavernous rooms house a **produce market** called *Souq Aftimos.* Extending north from David St. to Damascus Gate is **Khan az-Zeit** and the three-laned **Armenian market.** Built atop the Roman Cardo Maximus, Khan az-Zeit also covers the Cardo's Byzantine addition that today houses luxury shops in the Jewish Quarter.

Al Wad Road connects the Western Wall area to Damascus Gate. A right off Al Wad onto **Via Dolorosa** will lead to an array of small ceramics shops. **Jerusalem Pottery,** run by an Armenian family, supplies many shops (small tiles from NIS6). Their own shop in the market has a larger, more attractive selection of pieces sporting the company logo on the underside. Ask them about custom ceramic name plates (a perfect gift for Dad). Shops also populate the tiny streets between **Christian Quarter Road** and the Church of the Holy Sepulchre.

As you wind your way through the market, look up from time to time. Much of the decorative masonry—stone set within stone over entries and passageways—is characteristic of Mamluk architecture. Paintings of the Dome of the Rock and the Ka'ba, Islam's most sacred shrine, adorn doorways. A painting of the latter signifies that a member of the family has made *hajj*, the Islamic pilgrimage to Mecca and Medina. Walk down David St. from Jaffa Gate, turn right on **Souq al-Hussor,** and climb the metal staircase to your left to reach the **market roofs.** They are not as notoriously dangerous as the ramparts walk, but women alone should not venture much farther than the top of the staircase.

In the past, the Israeli army has fired tear gas, rubber bullets, and even live ammunition into Palestinian markets. The rubber bullets, more like lead balls covered with enamel than racquetballs, are nothing to scoff at. These incidents are dangerous also because masses of panicked people flood the small alleyways in an effort to flee. After the recent flurry of hand-shaking and paper-signing, we can only hope such incidents will cease. If you sense tension (usually the case when there is a large Israeli military presence), get out quick; the *khara* may soon come down.

Temple Mount/Dome of the Rock Area and Western Wall

In the southeastern corner of the Old City, the **Temple Mount** (Al-Haram ash-Sharif in Arabic, Har Bayit in Hebrew), about the size of the Muslim Quarter (35 acres), is holy to Christians, Jews, and Muslims alike. The hill is traditionally identified with the biblical Mt. Moriah, on which God asked Abraham to sacrifice his son Isaac (Genesis 22:2). The First Temple was built here by King Solomon in the middle of the 10th century BCE (2 Chronicles 3:1), and destroyed by Nebuchadnezzar in 587 BCE when the Jews were led into captivity in Babylon (1 Kings 5-8, 2 Kings 24-25, 2 Chronicles 2-7). The Second Temple was built in 516 BCE, after the Jews' return from exile (Ezra 3-7). In 20 BCE, King Herod rebuilt the temple and enlarged the Mount, reinforcing it with four retaining walls. Parts of the southern, eastern, and western retaining walls still stand. Religious scholars believe that the Holy Ark was located closest to the **Western Wall**, making this wall the holiest site in Judaism.

The Second Temple is remembered by Christians as the backdrop to the Passion of Christ. Like the First Temple, it lasted only a few hundred years. In the fourth year of the Jewish Revolt (70 CE) Roman legions sacked Jerusalem and razed the Temple. Hadrian built a temple to Jupiter over the site, then the Byzantines trashed it and left the site in ruins for the arrival of Omar and the Muslims in the 7th century. At that time, the Umayyad Caliphs built the two Arab shrines that still dominate the Temple Mount: the holy, silver-domed **Al Aqsa Mosque** (built in 715 and rebuilt several times after earthquakes); and the magnificent **Dome of the Rock** (built in 691). A feast for mind and eye, the complex is the third-holiest Muslim site, after the Ka'ba in Mecca and the Mosque of the Prophet in Medina. According to Muslim tradition, the Dome of the Rock is the point from which God took Muhammad on his mystical Night Journey *(miraj)* into heaven (17:17). The Qur'an identifies this spot as *Al Aqsa* (the Farthest); the nearby mosque commemorates Muhammad's journey. The Dome of the Rock surrounds what Muslims believe was Abraham's makeshift altar where he almost sacrificed Ishmael, his son by Sarah's maid Hagar, and not Isaac, as Christians and Jews believe.

Although the dome was once solid gold, it was eventually melted down to pay the caliphs' debts. The domes of the mosques and shrines were plated with lusterless lead until the structures received aluminum caps during the restoration work done from 1958 to 1964. The golden hue on the Dome of the Rock was previously achieved with an aluminum-bronze alloy. In 1993, however, work was underway to re-coat the dome with new metal plates faced with a thin coating of 24-karat gold; soon the scaffolding should be gone and the dome will be its old glorious self. Many of the tiles covering the walls of the Dome of the Rock were affixed during the reign of Suleiman the Magnificent, who had the city walls built in the 16th century. Scrutiny will distinguish these from the tiles added in the 1950s and 60s and paid for with King Hussein of Jordan's private funds.

Next to the Dome of the Rock is the much smaller **Dome of the Chain,** where, according to Muslim legend, a chain which could be grasped only by the righteous hung down from heaven. Presently under renovation, the Dome of the Chain marks the exact center of Al Haram ash-Sharif. Between the two mosques flows a *sabil* (fountain) called **Al Kas,** where Muslims perform ablutions before prayer. Built in 709 CE, the fountain is connected to underground cisterns capable of holding 10 million gallons. The arches on the Temple Mount, according to Muslim legend, will be used to hang scales to weigh people's good and bad deeds. On the right as you enter the area from the ramp (to the right of the Western Wall) is the **Islamic Museum,** filled with fantastic relics such as the huge cauldrons used for cooking food for the poor, taken from the mosques when the holy sites were restored.

Al Haram ash-Sharif and the museum are open Saturday through Thursday 8am to noon and 1:30pm to 3pm. All hours are subject to change during Ramadan, other Islamic holidays, and periods of unrest. (Tickets sold at a booth between Al Aqsa and the museum. Admission NIS13, students NIS8. Ticket booth closes at 3pm.) The Mount is sometimes closed without notice; you might inexplicably be denied entrance. Dress modestly and avoid public displays of affection. The most unobtrusive demonstration of prayer between the Dome of the Rock and the Mount of Olives will bring about your ejection from the Temple Mount. Long gowns are provided for those who need them; women should cover their hair in mosques. Also be aware that many sections considered off-limits by the police are not marked as such. These include the walls around Al Aqsa, the area through the door to the south between Al Aqsa and the museum, and the Muslim cemetery. Once inside Al Aqsa, stay away from people who are praying.

The 18m tall **Western Wall** (Ha-Kotel Ha-Ma'aravi in Hebrew) is part of the retaining wall of the Temple Mount built about 20 BCE, and was the largest section of the Temple area that remained standing after its destruction in 70 CE. It has been gauche-ly referred to as the Wailing Wall because Jews, believing that the divine presence lingers here, have visited the wall for centuries to mourn the destruction of the First and Second Temples and to tuck written prayers into its crannies. Today's visitors, Jewish or otherwise, often see the Wall as a direct e-mail connection with God. (An innovative service from Bezek lets you fax in your urgent messages to be promptly deposited in the wall's crevices; fax 612 222.) But don't expect your scribble to wait there for the Messiah: all notes are periodically removed from the overburdened wall and buried, in accordance with Jewish Law. The Wall can be reached by foot from Dung Gate, the Jewish Quarter, Ha-Shalshelet St., or Al-Wad Rd. About 3m off the ground, a gray line indicates the surface level until 1967. About 20m of Herodian wall still lies underground. You can identify the Herodian stones by their carved frames or "dressing"; the stones that lie above were added by Byzantines, Arabs, and Turks.

Pre-1948 photos show Orthodox Jews praying at the wall in a crowded alley; after the Six-Day War, the present plaza was built. Israeli paratroopers are sworn in at the Western Wall to recall its capture in 1967. Although the Western Wall is not formally a synagogue, the Ministry of Religion has decreed that all rules applying to Orthodox synagogues also apply to the Wall. The prayer areas for men and women are separated by a screen with the Torah scrolls kept on the men's side of recently excavated sections of the Wall. **Wilson's Arch** (named for the English archaeologist who discovered it), located inside a large, arched room to the left of the Wall, was once part of a bridge that spanned Cheesemakers' Valley, allowing Jewish priests to cross from their Upper City homes to the Temple. (Women cannot enter.) A peek down the two illuminated shafts in the floor of this room gives a sense of the wall's original height. The wall continues from here through closed tunnels for over 500m. Women and groups can enter the passageways through an archway to the south, near the telephones.

Bar mitzvahs—often five or six at once—occur at the Wall on Monday and Thursday mornings and usually consist of some grimacing kid in a chair being jostled around by relatives, accompanied by a lot of noise. On Friday, dancing is organized by Yeshivat Ha-Kotel to usher in *Shabbat*. Be sure to arrive before sundown to witness the uproarious event, but suppress the urge to take photographs.

Try to visit at least once at night, when the Wall is brightly lit, the air cool, and the area quiet. There are guards posted 24 hours a day. Underneath the Western Wall is an underground passage where Jewish radicals hid explosives in the early 1980s in a plot to destroy the Dome of the Rock. To get in, call the Western Wall Heritage Foundation (tel. 271 333) or Archaeological Seminars, Inc. (tel. 273 515 or 282 221). City of David, Tower of David Walking Tours, and Zion Walking Tours also offer tours which include this and other passages in Jerusalem. Check with the GTIO for schedules and exact routes. (Also see p. 385.)

The ongoing excavations at the southern wall of the Temple Mount are known as the **Ophel** region (tel. 254 403), though "Ophel" technically refers to the hill just outside the southern wall where the City of David is located. (Open Sun.-Thurs. 9am-4pm, Fri. 9am-2pm. Admission NIS10, children under 18 NIS7.) Scholars have uncovered 22 layers from 12 periods in the city's history. Check out the well-preserved remains of a Byzantine home and its mosaic floor. A tunnel brings you outside the city walls to the foot of reconstructed steps leading to the Temple Mount.

Full appreciation of the Ophel complex requires a guide. Some Archaeological Seminars Ltd. tours include the Ophel area. (Sun., Tues.-Wed., and Fri. 9:30am; 3½hr.)

Jewish Quarter

The Jewish Quarter is in the southeast quadrant of the Old City, the site of the posh Upper City during the Second Temple era. The quarter extends from Ha-Shalshelet St. (Bab as-Silsilah) in the north to the city's southern wall, and from Ararat St. in the west to the Western Wall in the east. Reach the quarter by climbing the stairs diagonally across from the Western Wall, or head down David St. and turn right at the sign for the Cardo Maximus. Jews first settled in this area in the 15th century. The Jewish community grew from 2000 in 1800 to 11,000 in 1865, when Jews started to settle outside the walls. Today, about 650 families live in the Jewish Quarter.

After the annexation of the Old City in 1967, the Jewish Quarter was completely rebuilt; and destruction caused by the 1948 war was repaired. Archaeological discoveries at every turn of the shovel slowed the remodeling, though city planners have managed to gracefully integrate the ancient remains into the stunning new neighborhood. Today the gentrified Jewish Quarter is an expensive neighborhood, with an almost exclusively Orthodox Jewish (and largely American) population.

A part of the **Cardo** (off David St. just beside Jewish Quarter Rd.), Jerusalem's main thoroughfare during Roman and Byzantine times, has been excavated and restored. The uncovered section is built over a Byzantine extension of Emperor Hadrian's Cardo Maximus, which ran from Damascus Gate to about as far south as David St. Archaeologists suspect that Justinian constructed the addition so that the Cardo would extend to the **Nea Church** (beneath Yeshivat Ha-Kotel). Sheltered by the Cardo's vaulted roof are expensive gift shops and art galleries described on a sign as "a continuation of the existing bazaars." (Hardly.) Near the entrance to the Cardo, you can climb down to an excavated section of the Hasmonean city walls and remains of buildings from the First Temple period. Farther along the Cardo is an enlarged mosaic reproduction of the Madaba map, the 6th-century plan of Jerusalem discovered in Jordan. The Cardo is open and illuminated until 11pm.

Yishuv Court Museum, 6 Or Ha-Ḥayim St. (tel. 284 636) shows life in the Jewish Quarter before 1948. Walk up the steps at the southern end of the Cardo, cross over the Cardo on the steps to your left, and look left for the brown and tan sign pointing the way. Or turn left onto St. James St. from Armenian Patriarchate Rd. and follow the signs. (Open Sun.-Thurs. 9am-2pm. Admission NIS6, students NIS4.)

Across Jewish Quarter Rd. and on the left from the southern end of the Cardo, a single stone arch soars above the ruins of the **Ḥurva Synagogue.** Built in 1700 by followers of Rabbi Yehuda the Hasid, the synagogue was destroyed by Muslims 20 years later, rebuilt in 1856 as the National Ashkenazic Synagogue, and blown up by Jordan during the 1948 War. **Ramban Synagogue** next door was named for Rabbi Moshe Ben-Naḥman, also known as Nahmanides ("Ramban" is an acronym for his name). Over the years the building has served as a store, butter factory, and mosque. Inside is a letter written by the rabbi describing Jerusalem's Jewish community in 1267, the year he arrived from Spain. (Open for morning and evening prayers.)

The **Four Sephardic Synagogues** (the synagogue of Rabbi Yoḥanan Ben-Zakkai, Elijah the Prophet, the Central Synagogue, and the Istanbuli Synagogue) were built by Mediterranean Jews starting in the 16th century in accordance with a Muslim law that prohibited the construction of synagogues taller than the surrounding houses. To attain an aura of loftiness, these synagogues were cunningly built in large chambers deep underground. The current structure, though renovated, dates from 1835. The synagogues remain the spiritual center of Jerusalem's Sephardic community, with religious services held here twice a day. To reach the Sephardic Synagogues, walk south on Jewish Quarter Rd. almost to the parking lot, turn left onto Ha-Tuppim St., then left again, and walk down the stone staircase. (Open Sun.-Mon. and Wed.-Thurs. 9:30am-4pm, Tues. and Fri. 9:30am-12:30pm. Free.)

The ruins of the **Tife'eret Yisrael Synagogue** are a favorite stop for guides wishing to evoke contempt for Jordan. Built by Hasidic Jews during the 19th century, the synagogue was captured and destroyed by Jordan in 1948. For some strange reason it has not been lavishly rebuilt like everything else; instead, its upper portions have been covered with cement, making it look like a massive gray amoeba. The synagogue is on Tife'eret Yisrael Rd., which begins at the northeastern corner of the courtyard behind the Ḥurva Synagogue.

Farther east on Tife'eret Yisrael Rd. smolders the **Burnt House** (tel. 287 211), the remains of the dwelling of a priest's family from the Second Temple era. In 70 CE, the fourth year of the Jewish Revolt, the Romans destroyed the Second Temple and, one month later, broke into Jerusalem's Upper City, burning its buildings and killing its inhabitants. The excavation of the Burnt House provided direct evidence of the destruction of the Upper City. Near a stairwell the grisly bones of a severed arm reach for a carbonized spear. Now see if you believe this: sound and light shows are set inside the Burnt House, recreating the events of its destruction. (Open Sun.-Thurs. 9am-5pm, Fri. 9am-1pm. Programs in English at varying times, depending on demand; reservations recommended. Admission NIS4.50, students NIS4.) Off the Jewish Quarter's main square, the Wohl Museum around the side of the Yeshivat Ha-Kotel houses the recently opened **Herodian Quarter** (tel. 283 448), which features three mansions built for the Second Temple's high priests *(kohanim)*. The houses contain mosaics, several ritual baths *(mikvaot)*, and stone and pottery unearthed during excavations. (Open Sun.-Thurs. 9am-5pm, Fri. 9am-1pm. Admission NIS8, students NIS7.50; combined ticket to Burnt House and Herodian Quarter NIS10, students NIS9.)

Following Plugat Ha-Kotel Rd. from Ḥurva Synagogue Sq. brings you past the **Wide Wall,** the remains of the Israelite wall that encircled the City of David, the Temple Mount, and the Upper City. The wall was built by King Hezekiah along with his tunnel (see City of David, p. 397) to defend the city and ensure water provision during attacks and sieges by Assyrian King Sennacherib in the 8th century BCE.

You can visit some of the small synagogues and **yeshivot** (singular *yeshiva*), tucked away in alleys and courtyards throughout the Jewish Quarter. Young men and, in a few places, women live in these academic institutions as they pursue Judaic learning. Several *yeshivot* have begun aggressively wooing Jews with little or no religious background to make short—or eternal—visits. Stop in at **Aish Ha-Torah.** Students here are mostly American and welcome visitors, even for only one class. You may have a tough time leaving. To reach Aish Ha-Torah from the Western Wall, walk up the stairs to the Jewish Quarter and take your first left onto the street before the covered arcade (Beit Ha-Sho'eva Rd.). Women should apply to the *yeshiva*'s administrative office off Shvut Rd. in the Jewish Quarter.

Christian Quarter and Via Dolorosa

In the northwest quadrant of the Old City, the Christian Quarter surrounds the Church of the Holy Sepulchre, the site traditionally believed to be the place of Jesus' crucifixion, burial, and resurrection. Many small chapels and churches of various Christian denominations lie near the Church of the Holy Sepulchre.

The **Via Dolorosa** (Path of Sorrow) is the route that a cross-bearing Jesus followed from the site of his condemnation to the site of his crucifixion and grave—from the Praetorium to Calvary. Each event on the walk has been designated as one of the 14 "Stations of the Cross." The present route along Via Dolorosa was established during the Crusader period; modern New Testament scholars have suggested alternate routes based on more recent archaeological and historical reconstructions.

One spat involves where Jesus began his walk. Everyone agrees Jesus was brought before Pontius Pilate, the Roman procurator, for judgment. Roman governors ordinarily resided and fulfilled their duties in the palace of Herod the Great, south of Jaffa Gate and the Citadel area. But on feast days when the temple area was hectic, the governor and his soldiers presumably based themselves at Antonia's fortress (also built by Herod) to be closer to the Temple Mount. As Jesus was condemned on a feast day (Passover), the **Tower of Antonia,** near St. Stephen's (Lion's) Gate, remains the accepted First Station, though you may see small groups, notably the Catholic Dominican Order, setting out from Jaffa Gate. The placement of the last five stations inside the Church of the Holy Sepulchre goes against the previous hypothesis that the crucifixion took place at the skull-shaped Garden Tomb. On Fridays at 4pm (Sept.-June 3pm), you can walk the Via Dolorosa with a procession of pilgrims lead by Franciscan monks starting at Al Omariyyeh College.

Starting at St. Stephen's Gate, you will first see the **Church of St. Anne** on your right. Commemorating the birthplace of Jesus' mother Mary, the church is one of the best preserved pieces of Crusader architecture in Israel. The church survived intact throughout the Islamic period because Salah ad-Din used it as a Muslim theological school, hence the Arabic inscription on the tympanum above the church doors. Tradition runs deep here: the simple, solemn, citadel-like structure stands over the ruins of a 5th-century basilica that, in turn, is believed to cover a 2nd- or 3rd-century chapel. The church is tilted to one side, symbolizing the crucifixion.

Within the grounds is the **Pool of Bethesda.** Crowds of the infirm used to wait beside the pool for an angel to disturb its waters; the first person in after the angel would supposedly be cured. Jesus also healed a sick man here (John 5:2-9). A Washington, D.C. suburb, home to several hospitals and one travel guide editor, is named after the pool. Also worth noting are the remains of a Byzantine cistern and the façade of a Crusader chapel. (Church and grounds open Mon.-Sat. 8am-noon and 2-5pm. Admission NIS3.)

Two hundred meters west of St. Stephen's Gate, a ramp leads to the courtyard of the **Al Omariyyeh College,** one site identified as the **first station,** where Jesus was condemned (closed 1-3pm). Opposite the school from the Via Dolorosa, enter the Franciscan monastery; to your left is the **Condemnation Chapel,** the **second station,** where Jesus was sentenced to crucifixion. On the right is the **Chapel of Flagellation** where he was first flogged by Roman soldiers. A crown of thorns adorns the dome; mobs clamor at the windows of the chapel. (Open daily 8am-noon and 2-6pm; winter 8am-noon and 1-5pm.)

Continuing along the Via Dolorosa, pass beneath the **Ecce Homo Arch,** where Pilate looked down upon a scourged Jesus and cried "Behold the Man." The arch is actually part of the triumphal arch that commemorates Emperor Hadrian's suppression of the Bar Kokhba revolt in the 2nd century. (Open Mon.-Sat. 8:30am-12:30pm and 2-4pm.) Adjacent lies the **Convent of the Sisters of Zion,** beneath which excavations have cleared a large chamber thought by some to be the judgment hall, which would make *it* the first station. The convent is closed to the public; the excavations are not. To get to the excavations, walk down the Via Dolorosa from the second station and turn right on Aqabat ar-Rahbat St. Knock on the brown door on your left. (Open Mon.-Sat. 8:30am-12:30pm and 2-4:30pm. Admission NIS2.50.)

Even though the following stations—the destinations of millions of pilgrims—are all marked, they are nonetheless difficult to spot. At the **third station,** to the left on Al Wad Rd., Jesus fell to his knees for the first time. A small Polish chapel marks the spot; a relief above the entrance depicts Jesus kneeling beneath the cross. At the **fourth station,** a few meters farther on the left, just beyond the Armenian Orthodox Patriarchate, a small chapel commemorates the spot where Jesus saw his mother. Turn right on Via Dolorosa to reach the **fifth station,** where Simon the Cyrene volunteered to carry Jesus' cross. Fifty meters farther, the remains of a small column mark the **sixth station,** where Veronica wiped Jesus' face with her handkerchief. The imprint of his face was left on the cloth, which is now on display at the Greek Orthodox Patriarchate on the street of the same name. The **seventh station** marks Jesus' second fall—note the sudden steepness of the road here. In the first century, a gate to the countryside opened here, and tradition holds that notices of Jesus' condemnation were posted on it. Crossing Khan az-Zeit, ascend Aqabat al-Khanqa and look beyond the Greek Orthodox Convent for the clothes hanger directing you to the stone and Latin cross that mark the **eighth station.** Here Jesus turned to the women who mourned him, saying "Daughters of Jerusalem, do not weep for me, weep rather for yourselves and for your children" (Luke 23:28). Backtrack to Khan az-Zeit, ascend the wide stone stairway on the right, and continue through a winding passageway to the Coptic church. The remains of a column in its door mark the **ninth station,** where Jesus fell a third time. Again retrace your steps to the main street and work your way through the market to the entrance of the Church of the Holy Sepulchre, where the Via Dolorosa ends.

The **Church of the Holy Sepulchre** marks Golgotha, also called Calvary, where Jesus was crucified. The location was first determined by Helena, mother of the Emperor Constantine, during a pilgrimage in 326 CE. Helena thought that Hadrian had erected a pagan temple to Venus and Jupiter on the site in order to divert Christians from their faith. She sponsored excavations which soon uncovered the tomb of Joseph of Arimathea and three crosses, which she surmised had been hastily left there after the crucifixion as the Sabbath approached. Constantine built a winsome church over the site in 335, which was later destroyed by the Persians in 614, rebuilt, and again destroyed (this time by the Turks) in 1009. Part of Constantine's church's original foundations buttress the present Crusader structure, which dates from 1048. When the present building was erected, its architects decided to unite all the oratories, chapels, and other sanctuaries that had cropped up around the site under one monumental cross. By 1852, tremendous religious conflicts had developed within the Holy Sepulchre over such issues as who had the right to clean the doorstep. The uninterested Ottoman rulers divided the church among the Franciscan order, the Greek and Armenian Orthodox, Coptic, Syrian, and Ethiopian churches. The first three are the major shareholders, entitled to hold Masses and processions and to burn incense in their shrines and chapels.

One of the most venerated buildings on earth, the church is also somewhat decrepit. The bickering among the various denominations lends the structure some of its interest, but also has kept the building in shambles, marred by perpetual construction. The effects of major fires in 1808 and 1949 and an earthquake in 1927 demanded a level of cooperation and a pooling of resources that could not be mustered. Restoration work in any part of the basilica implies ownership, making each sect hesitant to assist and eager to hinder the others. The result is that little, if anything, is ever accomplished. In 1935 the church was in such a precarious state that Britain desperately propped it up with girders and wooden reinforcement. Since 1960, partial cooperation has allowed the supportive scaffolding to be gradually removed, but to this day the question of who gets to change a given light bulb can turn into a controversy that rages for months.

The sites in the church today bear little resemblance to those described in the Gospels, but discrepancies can be explained. The Gospels place Calvary outside the city walls in ancient times, but the site is located on the second floor of the church, within today's Ottoman city walls. At the time of Jesus, the basilica's Calvary site was indeed located outside the city walls—the extant walls were built a few years after Jesus' crucifixion by Agrippa and encompass a larger area than the original walls.

The church's entrance faces the slab on which Jesus was supposedly anointed before he was buried. To continue along the stations, go up the stairs to the right just after you enter. The chapel at the top is divided into two naves: the right one belongs to the Franciscans, the left to the Greek Orthodox. At the entrance to the Franciscan Chapel is the **tenth station,** where Jesus was stripped of his clothes, and at the far end is the **eleventh,** where he was nailed to the cross. The **twelfth station,** to the left in the Greek chapel, is the unmistakable site of the Crucifixion: a lifesize Jesus, clad in a metal loincloth, hangs among oil lamps, flowers, and enormous candles. Between the eleventh and twelfth stations is the **thirteenth,** where Mary received Jesus' body. The thirteenth station is marked by a statue of Mary, adorned with jewels, with a silver dagger stuck into her breast.

Jesus' tomb on the ground floor is the **fourteenth (final) station.** The **Holy Sepulchre,** in the center of the rotunda, is a large marble structure flanked by huge candles. The first chamber in the tomb, the Chapel of the Angel, is named after the angel who announced Jesus' resurrection to Mary Magdalene. A tiny entrance leads from the chapel into the sepulchre itself, an equally tiny chamber lit by scores of candles and guarded by priests. The walls of the tomb have been covered, but the priest in charge will show you a small section of the original wall hidden behind a picture of the Virgin Mary. The raised marble slab in the sepulchre covers the rock on which Jesus' body was laid. Nudging the back of the Holy Sepulchre is the tiny Coptic Chapel, in which a priest will invite you to kiss the wall of the tomb. To the right of the Sepulchre, the **Chapel of Mary Magdalene** recalls the place where Jesus appeared to her after his resurrection.

The rest of the church is a dark labyrinth of small chapels through which priests, pilgrims, and chatty tourists wander. Because a denomination's ability to hang anything on the church's walls also indicates ownership, the building houses only religious paintings and spindly oil lamps. Near the eastern end, steps lead down to two cavernous chapels commemorating the discovery of the true cross. In a small chapel on the ground floor just below Calvary, a fissure runs through the rock, supposedly caused by the earthquake following Jesus' death. According to legend, Adam (of Adam and Eve fame) was buried beneath Calvary, allowing Jesus' blood to drip through this cleft and anoint him. (Church open daily 5am-8pm; winter 4am-7pm. The guards are sticklers about modest dress.)

St. Alexander's Church, a block east of the Church of the Holy Sepulchre on Via Dolorosa, houses the Russian mission-in-exile. Prayers for Czar Alexander III are held Thursdays at 7am. (Open Mon.-Sat. 9am-1pm and 3-5pm. Admission NIS1.50; ring bell.) Across the street is the **Lutheran Church of the Redeemer** (tel. 276 111); enter on Muristan St. and climb a narrow spiral staircase to the bell tower to experience vertigo. (Open Mon.-Sat. 9am-1pm and 1:30-5pm. English service Sun. 9am. Admission NIS1.50, students NIS1.) The **Greek Orthodox Patriarchate Museum** (tel. 284 006), on the street of the same name, is a more recent addition to the Christian Quarter. Under the Patriarch Benedictos Papadopoulos, the scattered liturgical riches, gifts of pilgrims, and early printings of the Patriarchate's 19th-century press were arranged in a spacious, reconstructed Crusader building, which in summer 1994 was inaccessible due to construction. (Open Tues.-Fri. 9am-1pm and 3-5pm, Sat. 9am-1pm. Admission NIS1.)

Take a left from the Russian mission, another onto Khan az-Zeit St., and walk up the stairs to the left to reach the **Ethiopian Monastery,** located over part of the Church of the Holy Sepulchre and open all day. The Ethiopians possess no part of the church itself, so they have become squatters on the roof. The modest compound is comprised of white buildings with green doors. Walk around and follow the "Please Watch Up Your Head" signs to the small but amazing church.

Muslim Quarter

The Muslim Quarter, with architecture from the Ayyubid and Mamluk periods, is the largest and most heavily populated quarter in the Old City, but also the least known. Inquire at the GTIO or with individual tour groups about tours in the area.

The stretch of **Bab as-Silsilah Street** extending to the Temple Mount is partly founded on the ancient Mamluk causeway which crossed the Tyropoeon Valley, linking the upper city to the temple platform. At the beginning of the street stands the **Khan as-Sultan** (or Al Wakala), a remarkably preserved Crusader-period caravansary which provided lodging for merchants and their donkeys. Just past Misgav Ladakh St. (farther down the street on the right) is the **Tashtamuriya Building,** formerly an Islamic college, housing the tomb of its namesake (d. 1384).

Continuing down Bab as-Silsilah to its intersection with Western Wall St. (Ha-Kotel), you'll arrive at the **Kilaniya Mausoleum,** with its characteristic Mamluk stalactite half-dome; the **Turba Turkan Khatun** (Tomb of Lady Turkan) is at #149. At the end of Bab as-Silsilah, on your right and often surrounded by tour guides in training, is the **Tankiziya Building,** built by a Mamluk slave who worked his way up to governor of Damascus in 1312, and then back down to imprisonment and execution in Alexandria 30 years later. This venerated structure, on the site of the original seat of the Sanhedrin, is currently occupied by Israelis due to its proximity to the Western Wall and Temple Mount.

Armenian Quarter

The Armenian Quarter, in the southwestern part of the Old City near Mt. Zion, maintains a strong cultural identity despite modernization. Aramaic, the ancient language of Syria, is spoken both during services and in casual conversation at the **Syrian Orthodox Convent** on Ararat St. The Syrian Church believes this spot is the site of St. Mark's house and the Last Supper, while most other Christians recognize the Cenacle on Mt. Zion as the hallowed place. To reach the convent, enter Jaffa Gate and walk along the Citadel onto Armenian Patriarchate Rd. Take a left onto St. James Rd. and another onto Ararat St. A vivid mosaic marks the door to the convent. You can visit during the afternoon; if the door is closed, ring the bell. The **Armenian Compound,** down Armenian Patriarchate Rd. past St. James Rd., is a city within a city, home to about 1000 Armenians, and a slew of buildings closed to tourists.

Farther down Armenian Patriarchate Rd. on the left is the entrance to the **Mardigian Museum,** which chronicles the history of Armenia from the beginnings of its Christianization in 46 CE to the Turkish genocide of one and a half million Armenians in 1915. Follow the signs for the Armenian Museum. (Open Mon.-Sat. 10am-4:30pm. Admission NIS3, students NIS2.)

St. James Cathedral is open for services for a half-hour each day. The original structure was built during the 5th century CE, Armenia's golden age, to honor two St. Jameses. The first martyred Apostle, St. James the Greater, was beheaded in 44 CE by Herod Agrippas. Under the gilded altar rests his head, supposedly delivered to Mary on the wings of angels. St. James the Lesser, entombed in a northern chapel, served as the first bishop of Jerusalem, but was run out of town by Jews who disliked his version of Judaism. Persians destroyed the cathedral in the 7th century, Armenians rebuilt it in the 11th century, and Crusaders enlarged it in the 12th. The entire church is decorated with lovely ceramic tiles—Armenians make the tiled street signs for the entire Old City—and scores of chandeliers, hanging lamps, and censers. Pilgrims have left the votive crosses in the courtyard before the entrance; the oldest cross dates from the 12th century. Enter the cathedral from Armenian Patriarchate Rd., just past St. James St. (Cathedral open for services daily 3-3:30pm.)

EAST JERUSALEM (NEAR THE OLD CITY)

Mount Zion

This hill stands outside the city walls opposite Zion Gate and the Armenian Quarter. At various times since the Second Temple era, however, Mt. Zion (Har Tzion) has been enclosed by the walls. The mount has long been considered the site of the Tomb of David (though recent archaeological evidence suggests otherwise), the Last Supper, and the descent of the Holy Spirit at Pentecost. The name Zion, which is also applied to Israel as a whole, is derived from the Jebusite fortress called Zion, which was first seized by King David when he conquered the territory to the east. During the siege of the Jewish Quarter in 1948, the area around **Zion Gate** was the scene of some of the fiercest fighting in Jerusalem, as the Hagana tried to break in and end the attack. Vestiges of fighting include the bombshell-pocked gate. Egged bus #1 and 38 run between Mt. Zion and Jaffa Gate (#1 goes through Mea She'arim to the central bus station; #38 goes to the center of town). To reach the sights on the Mount, leave the Old City through Zion Gate or approach Zion Gate from either Jaffa or Dung Gates. Turn left coming out of Zion Gate and follow the wall around, forking right at the convent. At the next fork, take a left.

A stairway through the green door on your left leads to the bare **Coenaculum (Cenacle),** identified by most as the site of the Last Supper. One of the reasons for its no-frills appearance is that Britain, in an effort to avoid sectarian disputes, passed a law during the Mandate forbidding any changes, including decorations, from being made in the church. During the 15th century, the building was used as a mosque and the *mihrab* is still visible in the southern wall. Beware the little old lady warning you about Armageddon. (Open daily 8:30am-4pm.) Below the Cenacle is the *beit midrash* (study room) of the **Diaspora Yeshiva** (tel. 716 841), where many

American students learn Torah. Every Saturday night (8:30pm) between September and May, visitors sway to live Hasidic rock music. (Admission NIS10.)

To enter **David's Tomb,** go out the green door and turn left. Above the blue velvet-draped tomb in the cave, silver crowns (not always displayed) count the years since the creation of the State of Israel. Archaeologists refute the authenticity of the site because Mt. Zion was never encompassed by David's walls, and it is written that kings and only kings were buried within the city. (Tomb open daily 8am-5pm. Free.)

The **Chamber of the Holocaust** (tel. 715 105), through the courtyard and across the street from David's Tomb, commemorates the Jews killed during World War II. (Open Sun.-Thurs. 8am-6pm, Fri. 8am-3pm. Admission NIS6.) Next door, the affiliated **Museum of King David** attempts to convey the spirit and life of David through modern art. (Open irregular hrs.) The **Palombo Museum** (tel. 736 640), across the street and to the left, displays works by the sculptor who crafted the gate to the Knesset and contributed works to Yad va-Shem. (Open by appointment. Free.)

The huge, fortress-like **Basilica of the Dormition Abbey** (tel. 719 927) lies off the right fork of the road leading to the Cenacle. The site has harbored many memorials; the present edifice, commemorating the death of the Virgin Mary, was completed in 1910. Damaged during battles in 1948 and 1967, parts of the precariously situated basilica have never been repaired. Descend into the crypt to view a figurine of the Virgin. The floor of the ground level is inlaid with symbols of the zodiac. (Open daily 8am-noon and 2-6pm. Free.)

The City of David and the Kidron Valley

The **City of David** stands on the spot where the city of Jerusalem reputedly began. The quest for the origins of biblical Jerusalem has been going on since 1850. Only recently have the pieces of the puzzle begun to fit together. Archaeologists confirm that the ridge of Ophel—south of the Temple Mount and outside the city walls—is the site of the Canaanite city captured by King David.

Excavations of the earliest Canaanite walls indicate that the Jebusites were confined to an area of about eight acres. The size and location of the city above the Kidron Valley were precisely chosen so that the inhabitants would have access to the nearby water source (the Gihon Spring) and at the same time remain high enough on the Ophel's ridge to ensure adequate defense. In times of peace, townspeople passed through a "water gate" to bring water into the city. For continued supply during a siege, there was a shaft from which they could draw water without leaving the walls; it played an important part in David's strategy for taking Jebus (2 Samuel 5:8): his soldier Joab climbed the walls of the shaft. In 1867, Warren confirmed this biblical account when he discovered the long, sleek shaft that now bears his name. In the 1960s, Kathleen Kenyon located the Jebusite city walls dating from 1800 BCE which lie just above the Gihon Spring.

Later, King Hezekiah devised a system to prevent David's feat from being turned against the Jews: he built a tunnel to bring the Gihon waters into the city walls and store them in a pool, hiding the entrance of the spring and keeping invaders such as the Assyrians from finding water as they camped outside the wall. In 1880, a few years after the tunnel was excavated, a local boy discovered an inscription carved by Hezekiah's engineers. The Siloa inscription describes the tense but jubilant moment when the construction crews completed the tunnel. The original inscription is in Istanbul, but a copy is on display at the Israel Museum (see p. 401).

You can slosh through **Hezekiah's Tunnel** with a flashlight or a candle, though it is not advisable to do so without a guide. The water is about 1m high, and wading the 500m takes about 30 minutes. You'll get wet. Start at the Gihon Spring source on Shiloah Way, which branches to the right from Jericho Rd. as you approach the Kidron Valley from the bottom of the Mount of Olives. Steps from the City of David excavations also lead down to the Gihon Spring. The tunnel ends at the Pool of Shiloah (Silwan in Arabic, Siloam in Hebrew). You can then walk back to the road to your left and catch an Arab bus up the valley. (Open all day. Free, although several little boys will try to convince you otherwise.)

Several organizations offer tours; check at the tourist office for schedules. Recent years have witnessed increasing tension in this much disputed area. Orthodox Jewish nationalists have attempted to establish a Jewish presence in the midst of Arab **Silwan;** Arab homes were quietly purchased and their residents evicted in a dramatic, middle-of-the-night maneuver. A Jewish bastion, guarded by barbed wire, is perched precariously and conspicuously in the center of this entirely Arab neighborhood; innocent tourists may find themselves walking into a potentially dangerous situation. As always, read newspapers and consult tourists offices before exploring.

About 100m down from the entrance to the City of David is a small museum with photos of the most recent excavations. A spiral staircase leads down to **Warren's Shaft** (tel. 288 141). With a flashlight you'll see the entire length of the walls that Joab scaled. (Open Sun.-Thurs. 9am-5pm, Fri. 8am-1pm. Admission NIS2.50.)

To see excavations in progress, walk out of Dung Gate, turn left and walk downhill to the City of David entrance, on your right just past the UNRWA office. The excavations in this part of the Ophel, called **Section G,** were halted in 1981 when a group of Orthodox Jews protested that the area might once have been the Jewish cemetery mentioned in the diaries of several medieval pilgrims. After considerable political and sometimes violent ballyhoo, the Supreme Court of Israel ruled that the site should be closed. As a compromise the Israeli government decreed that digging could continue under rabbinic supervision. No bones have been found. Though numbered and labeled, the ruins adjacent to the route are discombobulated.

Four tombs are located down Shiloah Way, in the **Kidron Valley.** The first, **Absalom's Pillar,** is named by legend as the tomb of David's favored but rebellious son (2 Samuel 15-18). Behind it and to the left is the **Tomb of Jehosaphat.** A dirt path on the left leads to the impressive rock-hewn **Tomb of B'nei Hezir** and the **Tomb of Zechariah.**

The Mount of Olives

The bone-dry slopes of the **Mount of Olives** (Har Ha-Zeitim in Hebrew) to the east of the Old City are dotted with churches marking the sites of Jesus' triumphant entry into Jerusalem, his teaching, his agony and betrayal in Gethsemane, and his ascension to heaven. That the Mount of Olives has three gardens of Gethsemane and two points of Ascension may cast doubt on the accuracy of the locations, but nothing can detract from the splendor. In Jewish tradition, the Mount of Olives holds importance for the future as well: the thousands buried in the cemetery here will be the first to greet the Messiah on Judgment Day.

A walk down the hill, with pauses at the numerous churches, tombs, and gardens, is most enjoyable in the morning because the sun shines at your back, permitting clear views and photographs of the Old City, and because most churches are closed on Sundays and from about noon to 3pm. Arab bus #75 runs from the station across from Damascus Gate to At-Tur, the village on top of the Mount of Olives.

The viewing point outside the **Seven Arches Hotel** offers perhaps the best views of the Old City (guess what the camels are for). To the north, the domineering bell tower of the **Augusta Victoria** hospital on Mt. Scopus marks the highest point in Jerusalem (903m above sea level). It, too, provides a great view, but the staff may not look kindly upon hordes of backpackers traipsing through. Just north of the hotel along the main road, the **Church of the Eleona** and the **Church of the Paternoster** are tucked behind one gate. Both churches were founded by Queen Helena in the 4th century. The Church of the Eleona marks the spot where Jesus revealed to his disciples the "inscrutable mysteries"—his foretelling of the destruction of Jerusalem and his Second Coming. The Church of the Paternoster (Latin for "Our Father") commemorates the first recital of the Lord's Prayer. Polyglots can read the prayer in 77 languages (including Esperanto) on the tiled walls. In the midst of the translations is the grotto of the Princesse de la Tour d'Auvaigne, the woman who financed and worked for 17 years (1857-74) on excavations and renovations here. (Open Mon.-Sat. 8:30-11:45am and 3-4:45pm.) Its credibility contested only by the nearby Russian bell tower, the **Chapel of Christ's Ascension** is farther north along the same road. Inside there is a sacred footprint. (Ring the bell if closed. Admission NIS1.50.)

Down from the Seven Arches Hotel, a gate on the left leads to two tunnels, traditionally identified as the **Tombs of the Prophets** Malachi, Ḥaggai, and Zechariah. Archaeological evidence, however, suggests that the graves are far too recent— probably dating from the 4th century CE. (Open daily 8am-3pm.) The orange sign with black Hebrew lettering marks the **Common Grave** of those who died defending the Jewish Quarter in 1948. Next to the Common Grave lies the **National Cemetery,** and farther down the path sprawls the immense **Jewish Graveyard,** the largest Jewish cemetery in the world.

Farther down the path and to the right, the **Sanctuary of Dominus Flevit** ("the Lord wept") was erected in 1955 to mark the spot where Jesus wept for Jerusalem. During the construction, supervised by the renowned Italian architect Antonio Barluzzi, several unrelated ruins were unearthed. (Open daily 8am-noon and 2:30-5pm; April-Oct. 8am-noon and 2:30-6pm.) Farther down the road on the right stands the **Russian Church of Mary Magdalene.** Its seven golden cupolas not only resemble the Kremlin, but also mark the Mount of Olives in the same way that the Dome of the Rock distinguishes the Temple Mount. Czar Alexander III built the church in 1885 in the lavish 17th-century Muscovite style and dedicated it to his mother, the Empress Maria Alexandrovna. The crypt houses the body of a Russian grand duchess, smuggled to Jerusalem via Beijing after her death in the Russian Revolution. Now a convent, the church basks in the aura of the sacred shrines that surround it, and even claims a part of the Garden of Gethsemane. (Ordinarily open Tues. and Thurs. 10-11:30am; call 282 897 to be sure. Free.)

At the bottom of the path, deep in the valley, the **Church of All Nations** (Basilica of the Agony) faces west toward the Old City. Enter through the gate to the Garden of Gethsemane, just below the Church of Mary Magdalene. The garden is not the only place where Jesus purportedly spent his last night in prayer and was betrayed by Judas (Mark 14:32-42). Although the site has been venerated since the 4th century, the present building, also designed by Barluzzi, was built after World War I with international support. Inside, mosaics depict the last days of Jesus' life, while outside, the façade portrays Jesus bringing peace to all nations. (Open 8:30am-noon and 2:30-6pm; Nov.-March 2:30-5pm. Grotto farther downhill open until 5pm.)

North of the Old City

Midway between Damascus and Herod's Gates, **Solomon's Quarries** plunge to the city's bowels, providing refuge from the midday heat. Many believe that it was in these cool caves, which extend about 250m beneath the Old City, that workers quarried limestone for the building of ancient Jerusalem during the First Temple period. To separate blocks of stone from the cave walls, wooden planks were set in crevices and soaked with water; as the planks expanded they wedged the stone apart. Tradition has it that Zedekiah, Judah's last king, fled the city through a passage to Solomon's quarries when King Nebuchadnezzar of Babylonia invaded in 587 BCE. The sign for the quarries reads "Zedekiah's Cave" (open Sun.-Sat. 9am-1pm).

Farther east on Suleiman St., near the northeastern corner of the city walls, a driveway leads to the **Rockefeller Archaeological Museum** (tel. 282 251), one of the best in the country. The museum records the region's history, beginning with the remains of the 100,000-year-old Mt. Carmel Man, and shows the cultural impact of conquering civilizations. It was designed in the 1920s by British architect Austin S. B. Harrison in his unique Orientalist-Gothic style. (Open Sun.-Thurs. 10am-5pm, Fri.-Sat. 10am-2pm. Admission NIS10, students NIS7. Take Egged bus #27 or 23.)

A short distance up Nablus Rd. on Schick St., a sign points toward the **Garden Tomb,** noticed first by Otto Thenius in 1860. The garden is a candidate for Golgotha, the site of Christ's crucifixion. The hill does indeed resemble a skull, and some claim that a nearby tomb is that of Joseph of Arimathea, who placed Jesus' body in his own tomb after the crucifixion. (Open Mon.-Sat. 8am-12:15pm and 2:30-5:15pm. English service Sun. 9am.) As you continue along Nablus Rd., stop at the lovely, seldom visited **St. George's Cathedral.** The cathedral houses modest collections of Palestinian embroidery and Dothan pottery.

Following Salah ad-Din St. up to where it intersects with Nablus Rd., look for the Tombeau des Rois sign on your right just before the intersection. The sign indicates the gate of the **Tomb of the Kings.** Judean kings were thought to be buried here, but evidence shows that the tomb was in fact built in 45 CE by the Mesopotamian Queen Helena for her family. Bring a candle or flashlight. (Open Mon.-Sat. 8am-12:30pm and 2-5pm. Admission NIS10, students NIS5.) A little farther north up Nablus Rd. on the right is the elegant and legendary **American Colony Hotel.** Built in 1881 in a late Ottoman style, the hotel is popular today with the foreign press.

WEST JERUSALEM

Striking in its own right, West Jerusalem is not just long lines in the central bus station, Ben-Yehuda *midrahov* eateries, and Russian Compound bars. It also boasts museums, parks, and elegant neighborhoods. Since the first Jews moved outside the protective walls of the Old City in the 1860s, the community they established in West Jerusalem has grown, often at the expense of other communities. In all but the run-down slums, the Jerusalem stone facing strangely harmonizes the most uninspired housing developments with the ancient building traditions of the Old City.

Zion Square (City Center)

Ticho House, 7 Ha-Rav Kook St. (tel. 245 068), near Zion Sq. about two blocks up the hill, shows watercolors and drawings, including many scenes of Jerusalem, by Anna Ticho. The building was once her private home and the eye clinic of her husband. Also displayed is Dr. Ticho's large collection of menorahs. (A small library is open Sun.-Thurs. 10am-4pm, Fri. 10am-noon.) Affiliated with the Israel Museum, the well-groomed building, restaurant (see Food, p. 380), and gardens make for a relaxing mid-city respite. (Open Sun.-Thurs. 10am-midnight, Fri. 10am-3pm. Free.)

At the northern end of Ha-Rav Kook St. begins Ethiopia St., surprisingly lush and quiet. The houses are arranged in a checkerboard pattern, with alternating front and back walled-in gardens. At the end of the street on your right is the handsome **Ethiopian Church,** built around the turn of the century.

Mea She'arim ("Hundredfold," an invocation of plenty), just north of Ethiopia St., is the world's only remaining example of the Jewish *shtetl* communities that flourished in Eastern Europe before the Holocaust. Several thousand Ultra-Orthodox Jews live here, preserving with painstaking (and somewhat frightening) diligence traditional habits, dress, customs, and beliefs. Mea She'arim's relatively few extremists are vocal and receive a good deal of publicity. The Neturei Karta (City Keepers), the most extreme sect of the Satmar Hasidim, oppose the Israeli state, arguing that Jewish law prohibits the legitimate existence of a Jewish country until the coming of the Messiah. While most other Ultra-Orthodox Jews hold similar views, Neturei Karta once went as far as asking Yasser Arafat to accept them as a minority in the future Palestinian state.

Signs throughout the area read, "Daughters of Israel! The Torah requires you to dress modestly," and then proceed to explain exactly what this means. Whether you're Jewish or not, take this warning seriously if you don't wish to offend. Women should be covered to the elbow and knee and men should wear long pants. Don't fondle your loved one, and always ask before taking photographs. Residents have been known to spit on people who don't conform to their ideas of modesty.

Mea She'arim is probably the cheapest place in the world for Jewish books and religious items. Bargaining is the rule; try stores on the eastern end of Mea She'arim St. The neighborhood also has some of the best bakeries in the city. Most remain open all night on Thursdays, baking *hallah* and cake for the Sabbath. The one at 15 Rabbenu Gershom St. (off Yehezkil St.) makes good *burekas* and chocolate rolls.

Naḥla'ot and **Zikhronot,** neighborhoods just south of the Maḥaneh Yehuda market, are also crowded and predominantly religious. Residents are mostly Sephardic Jews from Yemen, Iran, Turkey, and Morocco, and, increasingly, artists and students in search of cheap housing. The narrow, winding alleys and tiny courtyards are festooned with laundry and lined with barber shops, blacksmiths, and sandal-makers.

The **Jerusalem Great Synagogue** on King George St. (tel. 247 112), across from the Sheraton Plaza, is ornate, but it's nothing more than a very big synagogue. Dress modestly (open Sun.-Fri. 9am-1pm) and stop at the **Wolfson Museum** next door, on the fourth floor of the Hekhal Shlomo building. The museum exhibits Jewish religious and ceremonial objects and dioramas of various scenes from Jewish history. (Museum open Sun.-Thurs. 9am-1pm, Fri. 9am-noon. Admission NIS2.) *Shabbat* services (Fri. 20min. after candle-lighting, Sat. 8am) feature a cantor and a choir.

The **Hall of Heroism** inside the Russian Compound off Jaffa Rd. (tel. 233 166) commemorates the work of Israel's underground movement in the pre-1948 struggle against British rule. Originally erected by Russian pilgrims, the hall was converted by the British into Jerusalem's main prison. Enter through Heshin St., just off Jaffa Rd. where it splits with Shlomzion Ha-Malka St. Follow the green signs that say "Museum." (Open Sun.-Thurs. 8am-4pm. Admission NIS5, students NIS2.)

Giv'at Ram

The **Israel Museum** (tel. 708 811 or 873) is the mother of all Israeli museums. From the ticket building, walk along a shrub-lined walkway and up the steps to the main building. (A free bus for disabled or elderly visitors and their escorts runs every 10min. all day except 1-1:30pm.) Rock and rust enthusiasts should go straight to the **archaeology** section—30,000 years of human habitation in the Fertile Crescent are recorded with an extensive collection of tools and weapons. (Guided tours in English Mon. and Thurs., 3pm.) Straight ahead from the bottom of the steps is the **ethnography** exhibit, which traces the Jewish Life Cycle. Guided tours of the Judaica and ethnography galleries are given Sunday and Wednesday at 3pm.

This is also the scene for **art** freaks. The Israeli art section shows older as well as contemporary works. There's a fairly large Impressionist and Post-Impressionist collection, and period rooms including a spectacular French Rococo *salon* donated by the Rothschilds. The **Weisbord Pavilion** directly across from the ticket building houses a few Rodin sculptures and early modern paintings, and rotating exhibits of contemporary art. The **Billy Rose Sculpture Garden** displays masters Henry Moore and Picasso. Pick up a schedule of evening outdoor concerts at the museum, and try to visit on a Tuesday night when the garden is illuminated.

Everyone comes to see the **Shrine of the Book,** which displays the Dead Sea Scrolls. The Hershey's Kiss-shaped building resembles, among other things, the covers of the pots in which the scrolls lay hidden for 2000 years in the Caves of Qumran near the Dead Sea. Dating from the 2nd century BCE to 70 CE and belonging to an apocalyptic, monastic sect called the Essenes, some of the scrolls contain versions of the Hebrew Bible almost identical to the books that passed through the hands of countless Jewish scribes. On the bottom level of the museum is a collection of letters and relics that pre-date the destruction of the Second Temple and have been crucial to scholars studying that period (late 1st-early 2nd century CE). (Guided tours in English Sun. and Thurs. 1:30pm, Tues. 3pm.)

Take bus #9, 17, or 24 to the Israel Museum. (Open Sun.-Mon. and Wed.- Thurs. 10am-5pm, Tues. 4-10pm. Shrine opens at 10am, Fri. 10am-2pm, Sat. 10am-4pm. Guided tours in English Sun.-Mon. and Wed.-Fri. 11am, Tues. 4:30pm. Admission to museum and Shrine NIS18, students NIS12. Student annual membership costs NIS40 and allows unlimited entrance to the Israel, Rockefeller, Tel Aviv, and Haifa Museums, as well as discounts on museum programs.) In the entrance lobby is a very helpful booth with museum maps, information on current exhibits, and schedules for special events, lectures, and tours. Specific guide pamphlets are NIS1 each.

If you just can't get enough, across the street is the brand new **Bible Lands Museum** (tel. 611 066), housing the private collection of Dr. Elie Borowski, an avid antiquities collector from Canada. It's no Israel Museum. (Open Sun.-Wed. 9:30am-9:30pm, Thurs. 9:30am-5:30pm, Fri. 9:30am-2pm, Sat. 11am-3pm. English tour Sun.-Fri. 10am. Buy tickets in advance. Admission NIS18, students and children NIS5.)

The **Knesset,** Israel's Parliament, is located on Eliezer Kaplan St. It is directly across the street from the Israel Museum, but you have to walk around the block (a 5-min. walk) to the entrance. To enter you must have your **passport,** and you may be subjected to a body search. (Open sessions Mon. or Tues. 4-7pm or Wed. 11am-7pm.) The decibel level on the floor can get quite high. The debates are in Hebrew or Arabic. Free tours (Sun. and Thurs. 8:30am-2:30pm) include an explanation of the structure of the Israeli government and a look at the Chagall tapestry and mosaics that adorn the building. Take bus #9 or 24 (tel. 753 333 for information).

The understated building behind the Knesset, past the Rose Garden, is the brand-new seat of the **Israeli Supreme Court,** completed in late 1992. The designers (Karmi & Assoc.) tried to combine Modernist architecture with themes from traditional Jerusalem stone construction. You be the judge. (Open daily 9am-3pm; tours in English Sun. 2pm, in Hebrew daily 2pm.) Farther to the west on the same hill are the Israeli Government buildings and the odd-looking Bank of Israel.

Across Rupin Rd. from the government center is the Giv'at Ram campus of **Hebrew University,** where the science departments are located. (Tours leave Sun.-Thurs. 10am from the visitors center in the Sherman Building. Tel. 882 819.) At the new, engaging **Bloomfield Science Museum** (tel. 618 128), kids will leap at the chance to interact with live physical phenomena like gravity. Hot air generated in the nearby Knesset is used here to fill balloons. (Open Mon. and Wed.-Thurs. 10am-6pm, Tues. 10am-8pm, Fri. 10am-1pm, Sat. 10am-3pm. Admission NIS12, students NIS10, children NIS5). The other attraction is the fabulous **Ardon Window** in the **National Library.** One of the two largest stained-glass windows in the world; it depicts Kabbalistic (Jewish mystical) symbols in rich, dark colors. (Open Sun.-Thurs. 9am-7pm, Fri. 9am-1pm. Library and window free.)

South of Zion Square

South of Independence Park are some of Israel's most elegant and affluent residential areas. **Reḥavia,** in the area trisected by Azza Rd. and Ramban St., was founded in the 1920s and became the refuge of many German Jews who fled Nazi persecution in the 1930s. For years, it was famous as a *Deutsch* high-culture enclave, with dark-wood libraries lined with Goethe and Schiller, and Mozart playing on the gramophone. Little of the German flavor remains today, but the legacy lives on with the neighborhood's many International Style houses, designed in the best tradition of German Modernism. The stone-clad buildings are remarkably well-preserved (particularly compared to their contemporaries in Tel Aviv), making a walk around the lush streets of Reḥavia highly rewarding for architecture enthusiasts.

In the middle of Reḥavia on Alfassi St. is **Jason's Tomb,** built around 100 BCE as the burial site of a wealthy Hasmonean-era Jewish family. Pottery found at the site indicates that three generations were buried there; charcoal drawings on the plastered porch wall depict ships, suggesting that one of the Jasons was involved in naval excursions. The pyramid on top of the tomb is a reconstruction. More to the east past Azza Rd. is the Prime Minister's official residence, in the guarded house at the corner of Balfour and Smolenskin St.—stop by for a chat with Rabin. Next door on Balfour St. is the Schocken Library, designed by renowned architect Erich Mendelssohn, who spent a few years in Jerusalem in the late 1930s (his dwelling was in the windmill on Ramban St. near Kikkar Zarfat, now an upscale shopping arcade).

Farther south are the neighborhoods of **Talbiyya** (Qomemiyut) and **Qatamon** (Gonen), which still go by the Arab names they had before their Arab inhabitants were dispossessed in 1948. The ornate villas (one of which was the childhood home of Columbia University professor Edward Said) have become favorites of Hebrew University faculty and, more recently, well-to-do professionals. Martin Buber's old house is the last one on the right on Ḥovevei Tzion St., one block south from Jabotinsky St. The official residence of the Israeli President is on Ha-Nassi St., and the plush Jerusalem Theater is on the other side of the block on Chopin St.

Around the corner from Ha-Nassi St. is the **Mayer Institute for Islamic Art** (tel. 661 291), 2 Ha-Palmaḥ St., displaying a significant collection of miniatures, paintings, and artifacts from the Islamic world. Take bus #15 from the center of town. (Open Sun.-Mon. and Wed.-Thurs. 10am-5pm, Tues. 4-8pm, Fri.-Sat. 10am-2pm. Admission NIS8, students NIS6, under 18 NIS4; free on Sat.)

On the other end of Jabotinsky St. is **King David Street.** About 300m up the street toward the city center on the left is the **YMCA,** built in 1933, with an imposing bell tower offering fine views of the whole city (open Mon.-Sat. 9am-2pm). Directly across the street, the historic **King David Hotel** retains an aura of old-world luxury, making it a favorite of international celebrities seeking lodging in town. Down the other side of the King David St. is **Liberty Bell Park** (Gan Ha-Pa'amon), which contains a replica of the Liberty Bell (bus #5, 6, or 14 from the center).

Cross the street to get to the restored neighborhood of **Yemin Moshe.** It was here that the English Jew, Sir Moses Montefiore, first managed to convince a handful of residents from the Old City's overcrowded Jewish Quarter to spend occasional nights outside the city walls, thus founding West Jerusalem. To strengthen the settlers' confidence, Montefiore built **Mishkenot Sha'ananim** (Tranquil Settlement), a small compound with crenulated walls resembling those of the Old City. The original buildings, now housing an exclusive municipal guest house and a pricey French restaurant, are located at the bottom of the hill. Montefiore also put up his famous stone windmill, now containing a small museum. (Open Sun.-Thurs. 9am-4pm, Fri. 9am-1pm. Free.) Yemin Moshe is now an expensive neighborhood, where art galleries adorn picturesque alleyways. In the valley below is **Sultan's Pool,** named after Suleiman the Magnificent, who in the 16th century added a dam and a fountain to this Second-Temple reservoir. The site figures prominently in Palestinian novelist Jabra Ibrahim Jabra's *The Ship*. Today it is used for open-air concerts.

Taking King David St. farther south, turn right at the gas station and take the right fork into Emek Refa'im St., the main road of the **German Colony,** one of the 19th-century settlements built around the country by German Templars. Some houses betray their builders' somber northern European traditions and contrast with the Arab villas. Venture into the peaceful side streets to discover that no matter what the style, old stone buildings in lush gardens just have this, well, *je ne sais quoi.*

To the southeast, the **Haas Promenade,** on the road to Armon Ha-Natziv, is a hillside park and promenade with great views of the Old City and the Dead Sea, perfect for strolling or jogging. The dusk experience alone is worth the trip (bus #6, 6A).

North of Zion Square

Bus #2 from the city center to Ha-Sanhedrin St. (off Yam Suf St.) takes you to a park carpeted with pebbles and pine needles and the **Tombs of the Sanhedrin.** Composed of esteemed male sages and leaders, the Sanhedrin was the high court of ancient times; it ruled on legal matters and even reviewed the case of Jesus. Separate burial areas were designated for the members. (Open Sun.-Fri. 9am-sunset. Free.)

The **Tourjeman Post,** 4 Ḥeil Ha-Handasa St. (tel. 281 278), recounts Jerusalem's history from its division in 1948 to its reunification in 1967. The building withstood severe shelling during the 1948 war and became an Israeli command post when the Jordanian border was just across the street between 1948 and 1967. Take bus #1, 11, or 27. To reach the building, walk northwest up the wide new road springing from Ha-Zanḥanim St. (which runs along the Old City wall) until it meets Shivtei Yisrael St. The museum will be on your left just before the junction. This new road runs along the pre-1967 line between East and West Jerusalem. (Open Sun.-Thurs. 9am-4pm, Fri. 9am-1pm. Admission NIS5.50, students NIS5, children NIS4.50.)

Before the Six-Day War, **Ammunition Hill** (Giv'at Ha-Taḥmoshet; tel. 828 442) was Jordan's most fortified position in the city, commanding much of northern Jerusalem. Taken by Israeli troops in a bloody battle, the hill now serves as a memorial to the soldiers who died in the 1967 war. The somber, architecturally striking museum is housed in a reconstructed bunker and gives an account of the 1967 battle. Bus #4, 9, 25, and 28 let you off at the foot of the hill. (Open Sun.-Thurs. 9am-5pm, Fri. 9am-1pm. Admission NIS6, students and children NIS3. Disabled access.)

After 1948, the **Hebrew University of Jerusalem** had to relocate from **Mt. Scopus** (Har Ha-Tzofim), where it had been founded in 1925, to the new campus in **Giv'at Ram.** From 1948 to 1967, Mt. Scopus was a garrisoned Israeli enclave in Jordanian territory. After 1967, big parts of the university moved back to Mt. Scopus; massive construction has created the current fortress-like campus. Free guided tours in English depart from the Bronfman Visitors Center in the Administration Building (Sun.-Thurs. 11am.) The **Hecht Synagogue** in the Humanities building, overlooking the Old City, is worth a visit; enter via the Sherman Building. The summit of Mt. Scopus, just north of the Mount of Olives, offers fabulous views of Jerusalem, while the university's gorgeous **amphitheater** looks east to Jordan.

As you approach campus coming up Churchill Blvd., on your left is the old **Hadassah Hospital,** which was also in the Israeli enclave after 1948. The building was designed in the 1930s by Erich Mendelssohn, and is an interesting adaptation of his Modernist commercial style to the unique conditions of Jerusalem's landscape and light. To get to Mount Scopus, take bus #4-*alef,* 9, 23, 26, or 28.

Southwest of Zion Square

Yad va-Shem, meaning "a memorial and a name" (tel. 751 611), is the most moving of Israel's Holocaust museums. It's actually a complex of buildings. Start at the **historical museum,** which uses photographs, documents, and relics to paint a picture of the Holocaust, as well as the events leading up to it. The exhibit ends with a simple, powerful memorial: symbolic tombs showing the number of Jews who were killed in each country, and a tiny shoe that belonged to one of the Holocaust's younger victims. **The Hall of Names** (open Sun.-Tues. and Thurs. 10am-2pm, Wed. 10am-5pm, Fri. 10am-12:30pm) contains an agonizingly long list of all known Holocaust victims. Visitors may fill out a Page of Testimony, recording the name and circumstances of death of family members killed by the Nazis. Another building houses a *ner tamid* (eternal fire) to memorialize the Holocaust's victims, with the name of each concentration camp engraved into the floor. The **art museum** nearby houses drawings and paintings made in the ghettos and in the concentration camps by Jewish prisoners; in the museum and on its grounds are a number of evocative works by sculptor Elsa Pollock. By far the most powerful part of Yad va-Shem is the stirring **Children's Memorial,** where mirrors are used to create a spark of light for every youth who perished; a recorded voice recites the name and age of each young victim. An enormous labyrinthine memorial dedicated to the **Destroyed Communities** is located in the valley below. (Free guided tour in English Sun.-Fri. 11am. Open Sun.-Thurs. 9am-5pm, Fri. 9am-2pm. Free.) To get to Yad va-Shem, take bus #13, 17, 18, 20, 23, 24, or 27 and get off at the huge orange arch sculpture just past Mt. Herzl. Turn around and take a left on Ein Kerem St., then follow the signs down Ha-Zikaron St. (about 8min. to the museum).

You'll also see signs near the bus stop for **Mount Herzl** (Har Herzl), the burial place of the founder of modern political Zionism. The **Herzl Museum** (tel. 511 108) encapsulates the energy of a man who made the most prominent modern articulation of Zionism, worked as a newspaper correspondent, and lobbied for the creation of a Jewish state until his death in 1904. (Open Sun.-Thurs. 9am-6:30pm, Fri. 9am-1pm. Admission NIS2, students NIS1.) Ze'ev Jabotinsky, Levi Eshkol, and Golda Meir are also buried here. Nearby is the **Israeli Military Cemetery,** resting place of soldiers. The Military Cemetery is two stops before Mount Herzl, but go to the Herzl Museum first to get a walking map.

The **Jerusalem Forest,** just west of Mt. Herzl, is a fine place for picnics; get off the bus at the Sonol gas station on Herzl Blvd. near Sha'arei Zedek Hospital. Walk in the direction in which the bus was traveling and take the first right onto Yefeh Nof St. The second left, Pirḥei Ḥen St., leads into the forest. Follow the road to the Youth Center in the middle of the forest, then proceed along a shady path to the birthplace of John the Baptist in the village of Ein Kerem. Or get to the village by taking city bus #17 from the central bus station or Zion Square (runs every 20-30min.). Bus #19 gets only to the Hadassah Medical Center; from there, you can take a 15-min. walk along a footpath to the village.

Formerly an Arab village, tiny **Ein Kerem** (fountain of vines) is the traditionally professed birthplace of John the Baptist. His mother certainly chose the spot well; rivals to the beauty of this village are scarce. Come here for an afternoon, bring a picnic lunch, and wander through the village's charming alleys and tranquil streets.

The **Church of St. John** (tel. 413 639), with its soaring clock tower, marks the exact spot where John was born. Inside are several paintings, including the *Decapitation of Saint John*. (Open daily 6am-noon and 2-6pm; Oct.-Feb. daily 6am-noon and 2-5pm. Mass celebrated at 7:15am in Italian, Sun. 8:15am in French. Dress modestly. Free.) In the **Grotto of the Nativity** below the church there is a lovely Byzantine mosaic of pheasants—the symbol of the Eucharist. Ask the guardian for a key.

Across the valley, down Ma'ayan St. from St. John's gate, the **Church of the Visitation** (tel. 417 291) recalls Mary's visit to Elizabeth and contains a rock the infant St. John supposedly hid behind when the Romans came looking for babies to kill. The newer Upper Chapel depicts the glorification of Mary. (Open daily 8-11:45am and 2:30-6pm; Oct.-Feb. daily 8-11:45am and 2:30-5pm.) **Mary's Well,** an ancient spring, is a small stone trough below the **Youth Hostel** off Ma'ayan St. If you're lucky, the Israel Chopin society will be holding an outdoor concert across the street. The pink tower belongs to the **Russian Monastery** (tel. 252 565 or 412 887), which you can visit by appointment. The cafés in Ein Kerem are expensive (entrees NIS15-20) but worth a stop.

The synagogue at the **Hadassah Medical Center** near Ein Kerem (tel. 776 271; not to be confused with Hadassah Hospital on Mt. Scopus) houses the **Chagall Windows,** depicting the 12 tribes of Israel in abstract stained-glass designs based on Genesis 49 and Deuteronomy 33. Chagall gave the windows to the hospital in 1962. When four of the windows were damaged in the 1967 war, Chagall was sent an urgent cable. He replied, "You worry about the war, I'll worry about my windows." Two years later he installed four replacements. Three of the windows contain bullet holes from the Six-Day War. (Free English tours Sun.-Thurs. on the half-hour 8:30am-12:30pm and 2:30pm; Fri. every hr. 9:30-11:30am. Synagogue open Sun.-Thurs. 8am-1:15pm and 2-3:45pm, Fri. 8am-12:45pm. Admission NIS5, students NIS3.)

■■■ NEAR JERUSALEM

Thirteen kilometers west of Jerusalem lies the Arab village of **Abu Ghosh.** Take Egged bus #185 or 186 (NIS3.70), leaving every hour from the central bus station. *Sherut* traveling between Jerusalem and Tel Aviv will stop at the exit, 2km from Abu Ghosh. In the 18th century, Sheikh Abu Ghosh required pilgrims to pay a toll here as they traveled to Jerusalem; the town was the last of a series of caravan stops en route to the Holy City. The Arabs of the village have always had good relations with neighboring Jewish settlements, even during the 1948 War. Christians and Jews alike revere Abu Ghosh as the original site of the Ark of the Covenant, which King David later moved to Jerusalem. **Notre Dame de l'Arche d'Alliance** (Our Lady of the Ark of the Covenant), on top of the hill, was built on the site of the ark. The current church was built in the 1920s on the site of a demolished Byzantine church; fragments of the old mosaic floors remain. (Open daily 8:30-11:30am and 2:30-6pm.) The Caravan Inn on the road to town offers great views (hummus NIS5).

Below the sacred hill, in a beautiful garden, stands the magnificently preserved Crusader **Church of the Resurrection,** built in 1142 and acquired by the French government in 1873. Excavations beneath the church have uncovered remains dating back to Neolithic times. The church lies below the main road; head for the minaret of the attached mosque and look for a door in the wall on your right. (Open Mon.-Wed. and Fri.-Sat. 8:30-11am and 2:30-5:30pm. Free.)

The stalagmite and stalactite cave of **Avshalom** contains amazing speleological splendors. Even the ridiculous number of tour groups converging on this place won't overshadow the majesty of the caverns. The cave lies 19km southwest of

Jerusalem, 7km from the village of Nes Harim. Stalwart hikers can take bus #184 or 413 (NIS5) to Nes Harim and walk from there. Otherwise try hiring a taxi from Nes Harim or joining an organized tour like Egged. (Open Sat.-Thurs. 8:30am-3:30pm, Fri. 8:30am-12:30pm.) Photography is permitted on Friday only; flashes damage the mineral formations. Admission (NIS11.50, children NIS6) includes a slide show and guided tour except on Fridays (tel. 911 117).

■■■ ENTERTAINMENT

EAST JERUSALEM

The **Palestinian National Theater** (Al Hakawati), on Nuzah St. (tel. 280 957) near the American Colony Hotel, has survived through years of Israeli occupation and despite IDF raids. They stage plays and musicals, many of which are unabashedly political; English synopses are provided. Walk up Nablus Rd. and take the first right after the intersection with Salah ad-Din St. Walk 100m and the theater will be on your right, at the end of a short driveway. Locals greet visitors cordially. Unless the IDF shuts down the theater, the show goes on. (Admission NIS10. Call to inquire about performances.)

WEST JERUSALEM

Tel-Avivians hate to admit it, but Jerusalem nightlife is no longer inspiration for jokes. After years of Jerusalemites having to descend to Tel Aviv for some action, the 90s have witnessed a boom in Jerusalem's nocturnal activity. Once the city's conservative majority is safely tucked into bed, bustling bars and dance clubs come to life. Cultural events from lunchtime chamber music to the early summer **Israel Festival**, long a source of Jerusalem pride, add that highbrow effect. The best listings are in *Kol Ha'Ir*, a Hebrew weekly. Also check the entertainment supplement to Friday's *Jerusalem Post*, the GTIO, and the posters lining city streets.

At the **Jerusalem Cinematheque** on Hebron Rd. in the Hinnom Valley (tel. 724 131), southwest of the Old City walls (bus #5 or 21), two screens show several films every evening (9:30pm, Fri. also 10pm and midnight, Sat. also 4pm. Tickets NIS16). The trendy **Kakao** café in the Cinematheque has excellent, costly food, views, and ambience. (Open daily 11:30am-1am.) Movie listings are in the *Jerusalem Post*. The annual **Israeli Film Festival** brings international films to Jerusalem and introduces local creations in the first part of July. Pick up a free book of listings (also in English) at the Cinematheque, or read the Friday supplement of the *Post*. For some films you will need to buy tickets well in advance.

Some frequent the **Jerusalem Skating Center,** 19 Hillel St. (tel. 254 733), above the *Croissanterie*. Access to the "ice" rink made of silicon is NIS20, including skate rental. (Open Sun.-Thurs. 10am-11pm, Fri. 10am-2pm, Sat. sundown-11:30pm.) In June, look out for **Student Day** at Hebrew University, a ton of fun open to all students (trips during the day and fireworks at night—don't mistake them for gunfire).

Bars

Near Jaffa Rd. east of Zion Sq., and around Heleni Ha-Malka St. by the Russian Compound (Migrash Ha-Russim), neon beer signs glow through the crisp night air. After midnight, stylish bars in old stone buildings fill to capacity (and overflow into the street) with a young, painfully hip crowd. Bars like **Pine, Alexander, Opus, Gizmo, Monbaz 9, Arthur,** and **Shunra** suck NIS8-9 for a Goldstar draught.

> **Glasnost,** 15 Heleni Ha-Malka St. (tel. 256 954), off Zion Sq., toward the Russian Compound. Plays jazz, rock, and funk, with occasional live bands. Patio with swooping palm trees. Beer NIS6-8, hard liquor NIS10-20. Also serves spaghetti, grilled cheese concoctions, burgers, and cakes NIS12-22. Open 7pm-whenever.

The Rock, 11 Yoel Salomon (tel. 259 170), features good music and a mellow, almost romantic, candle-lit atmosphere. Happy hour 5-9pm. Young tourists network here. Open Sun.-Thurs. 5pm-2am, Fri. 10am-4pm, Sat. 10am-2am.

Sergey, Heleni Ha-Malka St. (tel. 258 511), at the corner of Mounbaz St. next to Glasnost. Intellectual twenty-something and over crowd; beyond chic, they don't even wear black. Italian food. Mixed drinks NIS18, beer NIS12. Open 8pm-3am.

Mike's Place, 14 Harkness St. A pocket of nuts in an otherwise insane place. Israeli and ex-pat crowd digs nightly live acoustic music and the antics of Mike and staff. Cheap brandy. Occasional sidewalk barbecue Sat. 3pm. Open 8pm-dawn.

The Tavern Pub, 16 Rivlin St. (tel. 244 541), off Jaffa Rd. One of Jerusalem's oldest pubs. Plays videos. Occasional live music. Open daily 2pm-3am or later.

Cafés

Cheese Cake, 23 Yoel Salomon St. (tel. 245 082), in a garden on the second floor of an old house. Eponymous product NIS12.50 per slice. The charming café also has sundaes (NIS18.50), "Obscene Brownie" with ice cream, whipped cream, and chocolate sauce (NIS14.50), and "Monster" sundae (NIS48) with 8 scoops of ice cream and assorted toppings. Long sandwich and salad menu NIS10.50-28. Open Sun.-Thurs. 9am-midnight, Fri. 7:30am-3pm, Sat. sundown-midnight. Kosher.

Ha-Mizraka Tea House, 12 Yoel Salomon St. (tel. 255 222). Serves 24 different kinds of tea (NIS7 per pot) and assorted snacks in a candle-lit, cushion-clad cave. Open Sun.-Thurs. 7pm-2am, Fri. 9pm-3pm, Sat. 7pm-2am.

Jan's, below Jerusalem Theater. Great, expensive (NIS21 min.) light fare. Eclectic clientele and plush opium-den-like decor make it worth the money. Kosher.

Café Atara, 7 Ben-Yehuda St. (tel. 250 141). The meeting place of the Hagana and Jewish *Jerusalem Post* writers when it was still the *Palestine Post*. Today, vintage Jerusalem intelligentsia and politicians as well as young journalists linger over coffee in the daylight hours. Disappointing scene at night, but the desserts make it worth a visit. Sandwiches NIS12-15. Open Sun.-Thurs. 6:30am-midnight, Fri. 6:30am-3pm, Sat. sundown-midnight. Kosher.

Café Ta'amon, 27 King George St. (tel. 254 977), corner of Hillel St. A legendary hole in the wall; older Israeli writers and intellectuals abound. Owner Mordekhai Kop's IOUs book is a veritable Who's Who in Israel. Coffee, tea, sandwiches NIS3-3.50, beer NIS7, pastries NIS5. Open Sun.-Thurs. 6:30am-11pm, Fri. 6:30am-5pm.

Café Akrai, A.M. Luntz St. (tel. 254 001), between Jaffa Rd. and Ben-Yehuda St. The first café on the left coming from Jaffa Rd.; difficult to spot. Caters to young, chic Israelis and soldiers. Meatless menu; all food homemade. Pasta NIS23, sandwiches NIS13-17, desserts NIS11-22, danish NIS5. Open daily 8:30am-2am.

Dancing

The city center dance scene has been whittled down to two clubs. **Underground,** 8 Yoel Salomon St. (tel. 251 918), is the more popular, with a bar and a Batcave-like disco downstairs. It's musty with funky fluorescent graffiti and wall-to-wall sweaty, semi-trashed dancers. From 7:50 to 8:10pm, get all the beer you can drink for NIS5. **Arizona,** 37 Jaffa Rd., is a drop smaller but features a cute Western-theme bar. The disco is a twin of the Underground's; in fact, they are separated by one (all too thin) wall. Neither has a cover charge, but both require purchase of one drink (around NIS8) to get into the disco area. (Both open 7:30pm-4am, depending on crowds.)

Larger clubs are in Jerusalem's southern industrial neighborhood, **Talpiot,** down Hebron Rd., and include **Pythagoras, Decadance,** and **Opera.** The cover charge ranges from NIS15 to 25 for Friday and Saturday nights. (Open about 9pm-5am.)

For a night of bacchanalian revelry, visit **Mo'adon Ha-Yekev,** a.k.a. **The Winery** at 8 Ta'asiya St. (tel. 735 633 or 721). Take a cab (NIS15). NIS25 (NIS30 on Thursdays) buys carafe after carafe of all the red and white wine you can drink as you bop to Israeli folk music-turned-rock. Don't be surprised if you start banging a tambourine and dancing on tables with a wild horde of Israelis, students, and tourists of all ages. (Open Mon.-Thurs. and Sat. 9:30pm-1am. Reservations strongly recommended.)

Folk dancing is at the **International Cultural Center for Youth** (ICCY), 12a Emek Refa'im St. (tel. 664 144). (Sun. 7:30pm; NIS8; bus #4 or 18.) The **House for**

Hebrew Youth (Beit Ha-No'ar), 105 Ha-Rav Herzog St. (tel. 788 642), holds classes (Thurs. 8pm; bus #19). The **Liberty Bell Gardens** do it outdoors a bit after *Shabbat* ends. Dances from folk to modern jazz taught to Astaires of all ages.

Cultural Activities

The **Jerusalem Symphony** performs frequently at the Jerusalem Theater on David Marcus and Chopin St. (tel. 611 498 after 4pm); the **Israel Philharmonic Orchestra** plays Binyanei Ha'Umma. The Jerusalem Theater also hosts plays, dances, lectures, and concerts. Similar events are held at the Israel Museum (tel. 636 231), Binyanei Ha'Umma (tel. 252 481) across from the central bus station, and occasionally at the Hebrew University campuses. The **Gerard Bakhar Center** at 11 Bezalel St. (tel. 251 139) hosts concerts, including occasional Israeli folk music and jazz. **Asaf's Cave,** in the Mount Zion Cultural Center (tel. 716 841) near David's Tomb, stars the Diaspora Yeshiva Band; bid *Shabbat* good-bye each week at 9pm (in winter 8:30pm) with Hasidic dancing and English, Hebrew, and Yiddish music—a unique Jerusalem experience (cover NIS20, students NIS10; call to make sure there is a performance).

Built by Ottoman Turks in the 1880s as a caravan stop, the **Khan** (tel. 718 283 or 721 782), across from the railway station in Remez Sq., contains an intimate theater, café, art gallery, and Jerusalem's first nightclub (open until 2am). It's rarely frequented by tourists. The concerts and plays, most in Hebrew, are critically acclaimed. There's an Israeli folklore show every night at 9:30pm (NIS45 including wine but no dinner). (Egged bus #6, 7, 8, and 30 and Arab bus #21 and 22 pass by the railway station.) Seize any opportunity to attend a performance at **Sultan's Pool** (Brekhat Ha-Sultan; see p. 403). The theater is open in the summer only. Tickets for American or British rock stars start at NIS50.

WEST BANK الضفةالغربية

In summer 1994 Ramallah, Nablus, Nablus environs, or Bethlehem environs were not updated because of concern for the safety of our researcher-writers. Bethlehem, Hebron, and Jericho have been updated; but even there, political changes may change everything from bus schedules to attitudes. Consider yourself warned. Also be warned that ugly flying objects such as rubber bullets, stones, and live ammunition have been known to violate West Bank air space with some frequency. Be up-to-date on current events in each of the towns you plan to visit before you do so; but also remember that wherever you go, it probably isn't more dangerous than New York, Los Angeles, or Washington, D.C. Carry your passport at all times. For important additional information on all aspects of travel in general and some specifics on the West Bank, see Essentials.

The rugged towns of the West Bank offer an unparalleled combination of the impassioned politics of the present and the historical splendor of the past. For the first time in history, the Palestinian flag flies over a strip of land ruled, at least marginally, by the Palestinians themselves. The process by which self-rule was established has been a long and arduous one, the trials of which are easily read in the faces of West Bank Palestinians. They know, too, that their struggle has not ended. At the same time, travel in the West Bank provides a physical immediacy to the events and characters of the Bible and the Qur'an. Jacob built a chapel in Beitin, Joshua leveled Jericho, and Jesus was born in Bethlehem.

While extremists on both sides struggle to destabilize daily life, today there is a spirit of optimism to which many who hope for a peaceful future cling. Well-informed travelers will have no problem visiting the sights and the people of the area, and can even expect invitations to private homes, where piping hot mint tea and coffee so thick you could cut it with a Crusader sword are accompanied by *intifada* and occupation stories. Women should not accept invitations alone and modest dress will make both men's and women's experiences here more enjoyable. If it is cultural immersion you seek, shorts and see-through tank tops are to be avoided.

ONCE THERE

■■■ ENTRY

Transit from Jordan to the West Bank involves crossing the King Hussein/Allenby Bridge, the only available link. (Open Sun.-Fri. until 11am.) Obtain a permit from the Ministry of the Interior in Amman (see Amman Practical Information). In summer 1994, some travelers were allowed to cross the bridge without having obtained the permit in advance, but check with the Ministry of the Interior or your own embassy to make sure this is still possible. Prepare to see guns, soldiers, land mines, and passport control. (Also see Essentials: Border Crossings, p. 29.)

With a private car, you can visit the West Bank from Israel; expect numerous Israeli checkpoints and bring your passport along. Public transportation connections are mostly from Jerusalem. If you check with the Israeli GTIO before going, you'll probably get a standard governmental fright warning, which you should consider but also take with a grain of salt. Go with the flow, or lack thereof, of the worst kind of bureaucratic hassle: that which is controlled by the military.

For the first-time West Bank traveler, Jerusalem provides a logical starting point. There are budget accommodations in Bethlehem and more expensive options in Jericho, though Jerusalem is a more convenient transportation hub.

■■■ GETTING AROUND

The West Bank is criss-crossed by a relatively reliable and cheap network of buses and shared taxis (*service*, pronounced ser-VEES). Private taxis, usually air-conditioned, are readily available, but are substantially more expensive.

A system of colored license plates differentiates vehicles and their drivers. Those registered in Israel, West Jerusalem, and Jewish settlements sport yellow plates. Blue plates signify Arabs' cars from the Territories, and green plates belong to Arab taxis and buses. Other hues are white (UN or diplomatic), red (police), and black (army). If you must ride in a vehicle with yellow plates, for your own safety make sure "UN" or the name of a Christian service agency is plastered all over the car.

East Jerusalem is the transportation hub of the West Bank, but a 1992 closure made it impossible for local Palestinians to use Jerusalem as a transit terminal; as a result, some lines were re-routed to Ramallah, and *service* from Jerusalem to places such as Nablus became less than frequent.

Bus Both Arab and Egged buses service the West Bank. Arab buses leave from two bus stations in East Jerusalem: the Suleiman St. Station between Herod's and Damascus Gates, for points south; and the Nablus Rd. Station, for points north. You can catch Egged buses at the West Jerusalem central bus station on Jaffa Rd., but most buses traveling to the West Bank also stop at the Nablus Road Station. Egged buses should be a last resort in the West Bank. They cost more and often take you only to the outskirts of Palestinian towns. In addition, Palestinian children wielding rocks do not look too kindly upon their passengers. Take Egged to the Jewish settlements.

Arab bus schedules to the West Bank are, well, flexible; the intervals listed here are approximate. Transportation to Nablus is especially erratic. Buses may also pick up people from the side of the road. Arab buses have light blue stripes on the sides (except for the Ramallah bus, which is red), while Egged buses are red and white.

From the Suleiman St. Station
#22: To Bethlehem (every 15min., NIS1.50).
#23: To Hebron (every 15min., NIS5).
#28: To Jericho (every 1½hr., NIS3.50).
#36: To Bethany (every hr., NIS1.50).
#36: To Abu Dees and Bethany (every hr., NIS1.50).

From the Nablus Rd. Station
#18: To Ramallah (every 15min., NIS1.50).
#23: To Nablus (Tamini Bus Co., every 45min., NIS6).

Taxi *Service* taxis are the most convenient mode of West Bank transportation. Although slightly more expensive than Arab buses, they are faster, more reliable, and more frequent. Use your time in a *service* to get to know some of fellow passengers, especially on the relatively long trips to Nablus or Hebron. If you get lost or disoriented, consult the drivers; they are knowledgeable in matters ranging from the political situation to the location of obscure ruins. Private taxis are more expensive but more practical for remote areas. Drivers will take you to the site, and (for a few extra shekels) wait while you adore your favorite Christian landmark.

■■■ MONEY MATTERS

The **new Israeli shekel (NIS)** is prevalent, although **Jordanian dinars (JD)** and **U.S. dollars (US$)** are also in use. Expect to be automatically labeled a tourist and for prices to increase by a significant margin if you offer to pay for your purchase in anything other than shekels. Money changers, whose only wish is to cater to your needs, are scattered everywhere, from street corners to jewelry shops.

■■■ KEEPING IN TOUCH

The postal service in the West Bank is, for now at least, a part of the Israeli mail system; refer to Israel: Keeping in Touch, p. 244. All major towns in the West Bank have at least one post office with Poste Restante. Letters should be addressed: main post office, town, West Bank, via Israel. In the future, the Palestinian authority in Jericho is plans to have its own postal system, with Palestinian stamps.

The telephone system is also part of the Israeli telephone network. All services, including collect and calling card calls, are available from any private or public telephone. Beige public telephones, operated by **telecards**, are conveniently located in most post offices, where you can also purchase the cards. Relevant area codes are (02) for East Jerusalem, Ramallah, and the South, and (09) for Nablus and the North. You may further identify the location of specific numbers by studying the first two digits (Ramallah: 95, Nablus: 37, East Jerusalem: 89, and Bethlehem: 74).

For now, direct calls to some Arab countries from Israel or the West Bank or viceversa are officially impossible. Exceptions to this rule are Jordan, Egypt, and Morocco; more countries are likely to come soon. Like other technicalities in the Middle East, this can be overcome; you'll need an American or European satellite. These services are not usually advertised, so ask around if an emergency arises. The international phone code for the West Bank is the same as that of Israel (972).

LIFE AND TIMES

■■■ POLITICAL HISTORY

The political division now called the West Bank was not created until the 1948 Arab-Israeli War, when Jordan conquered the territory to its west. King Abdallah angered most Palestinians by annexing the region instead of creating a separate state as the U.N. partition plan had stipulated. For the Palestinians, being under Jordanian rule was like being under any other foreign occupation; and the period saw many demonstrations and protests. The land was occupied by Israel in the 1967 Six-Day War; until 1994 the West Bank was neither autonomous nor officially annexed by Israel, but under Israeli military administration.

"Military administration" meant that the only law was martial law. During Israeli military occupation, the situation of the West Bank's Palestinians was comparable to that of South Africa's Blacks. It was common for curfews to be announced without warning, for people to be arrested and held without charges, or for family homes to be demolished in retaliation for the alleged actions of one family member. There was no freedom of assembly—Palestinians could not have weddings, gatherings, or meetings without a permit from the Israeli authorities, which could be denied for a variety of reasons. Flying the Palestinian flag was illegal. In addition, the infrastructure, schools, and public works of the West Bank went neglected in comparison to those of towns in Israel proper. The Palestinians' own attempts at establishing institutions or some form of economic independence were thwarted as well. Bir Zeit University was denied a building permit for years and shut down frequently. Cottage industries such as pickling, baking, and embroidery attained some success, but were often unceremoniously shut down as well.

Israeli settlements in the West Bank were and continue to be a source of constant controversy. Some 110,000 Israeli Jews have settled in the West Bank since its seizure in 1967. Launched by Labor governments eager to establish an Israeli presence in areas of strategic importance such as the Jordan Valley, the settlement project has been an ideological cornerstone for right-wing Likud governments since 1977. They are motivated not only by strategic considerations, but also by claims to *Eretz Yis-rael* (the land of Israel), an area extending well beyond Israel's current borders. Many Palestinians see the settlements as the proverbial thorn in their side. Often located directly in the midst of Arab communities, several settlements are more like military installations than housing developments. They are surrounded by barbed wire and guarded by Israeli soldiers around the clock; most settlers conspicuously carry guns, while Palestinians are denied the right to bear arms.

In December 1987, the Palestinians of the occupied territories began the *inti-fada.* A traffic accident in the Gaza Strip provided the spark, and two decades of occupation, economic stagnation, and increasing Israeli settlement activity erupted in stone-throwing, chanting, unfurling the Palestinian flag, and reveling in nationalis-tic pride. Forms of resistance included nonpayment of taxes, general strikes, and res-ignations from government service. The young Palestinians of the West Bank—many leaders of the *intifada* were not past their teenage years—impressed observ-ers with their highly organized underground "popular committees," which orga-nized strikes, demonstrations, and funerals, made sure that the families of martyrs were taken care of, and that everyone had enough to eat. Many did time in Israeli jails; they utilized this time for educational and planning purposes. A new genera-tion of Palestinians—those who have known nothing but the Israeli occupation—had abruptly upstaged their elders, including the PLO, with a widespread resistance movement.

The *intifada* led to major changes in the nature of the Palestinian-Israeli conflict. The popular nature of the uprising and its televised brutal suppression by the Israeli army managed to draw far more international attention and sympathy than decades of PLO tactics; the Palestinian problem was re-instated as the focal point of the Arab-Israeli dispute. American Jewish groups and Israeli liberals expressed dismay at the sometimes brutal tactics of the Israeli army, sending the message to Israeli politi-cians that continued occupation of the territories could endanger their financial sup-port. After about six years of continued struggle, many Palestinians were worn out. Some Palestinians attacked other Palestinians they suspected of collaboration. The *intifada* had stopped making headlines by the time the Gulf Crisis began in 1991. In contrast to most Arab governments in the region, who joined a U.S.-led coalition opposing Saddam Hussein, some Palestinians cheered when Iraq's SCUD missiles landed on Tel Aviv. Saudi Arabia and other oil-rich Gulf states, whose financial sup-port had been trickling through the PLO into the territories, suspended their aid.

In the aftermath of the Gulf War, several factors convinced Middle Eastern govern-ments it was high time for a regional peace conference. After the historic Madrid conference in October 1991, negotiations between the Palestinians (in a joint Jorda-nian-Palestinian delegation) and the Israelis took place from 1991 to 1994 in Wash-ington, D.C. The first Israeli delegation to the peace talks, headed by hard-line Likud prime minister Yitzhak Shamir, offered little with which to bargain. But the current moderate Israeli government, formed following the June 1992 elections, brought a significant change to Israeli policy toward Palestinians and the occupied territories. Labor Prime Minister Yitzhak Rabin moved almost immediately to freeze all settle-ment activity, and pushed to promote the peace process with a special emphasis on the Israeli-Palestinian negotiations.

The talks raised heated debate on both sides. In Israel, many felt that to turn the West Bank over to the Palestinians (and thereby expose the narrow coastal strip that houses three-fourths of Israel's population to hostile neighbors) would be tanta-mount to guiding a knife to their own throats. For the Israeli government, however, the reality was that the U.S. government under President George Bush was unwill-ing to continue to sanction the occupation with immense amounts of economic aid, especially after the Palestinians had won such a PR victory with the largely non-vio-lent *intifada.* Maintaining the occupation had become costly both in the financial sense and in that it violently split Israeli public opinion and, some say, introduced a violent edge into Israeli society. On the Palestinian side, moderates favoring a compromise with Israel (such as negotiators Faisal al-Husseini and Hanan Ashrawi) were challenged by Islamist rejectionists Hamas, who were growing in popularity when the talks began. They advocated continued armed struggle, and could not envision a Palestinian state existing alongside Israel, which, in their eyes, would forever be an enemy. (See Introduction to the Region, p. 42, for more on the peace process.)

At the peace talks in Washington, the different delegations took turns not showing up, storming out in protest, showing up late, and storming out in a huff when the other party showed up late. It took a secretly-negotiated agreement between Yasser Arafat and Shimon Peres to cure the ailing talks and lay the groundwork for Palestinian self-rule.

The Oslo agreement was signed in Washington on September 13, 1993 amidst headlines and hysteria. It was indeed a historical moment, but excitement was tempered on both sides by anticipation and worry. West Bank Palestinians said the end of Israeli occupation was something that had to be seen to be believed. Their relative pessimism was due in part to the fact that their support of the PLO had weakened, especially as a result of being largely self-reliant during the *intifada*. The PLO itself had suffered financially because of its pro-Iraq stance during the Gulf War; this deprivation was felt even more painfully by those on the West Bank.

The original framework of self-rule in Jericho and the Gaza Strip was expanded to include some authority over the entire West Bank, and may expand further to mean Palestinian self-rule in the entire West Bank and Gaza. Some people see self-rule as no more than the Palestinians administering the Israeli occupation—when this book was published, the Palestinians had responsibility for schools and public works, but no real political or legislative power. In addition, there were still Israeli troops guarding Israeli settlements in Gaza and everywhere in the West Bank, excluding Jericho. The presence of the Israeli troops was seen as problematic by Palestinians; resentment of the soldiers' surveillance was a major factor in sparking the *intifada*. Israel remains largely in control of the West Bank economy as well.

■■■ ECONOMY

The economy of the West Bank has been colonized by the Israeli economy since the 1967 occupation. Throughout the occupation, because Palestinians were the first to be laid off from jobs in times of duress, crises in Israel's economy were felt even more sharply in the West Bank. Many West Bank Palestinians continue to work in Israel with no health insurance, job security, or workers' rights.

The West Bank economy was a major battleground of the *intifada*. Palestinians boycotted Israeli products in an attempt to rid themselves of their crippling economic dependence, and the Israeli government imposed economic sanctions on the Palestinian community as a form of punishment and as a way of extending control.

The new Palestinian Authority has inherited the devastated economy of the West Bank, with an infrastructure (not developed during the occupation) a quarter of a century old. The situation in Gaza is even worse (see p. 426).

■■■ LITERATURE

Much Palestinian literature is concerned with the agony of foreign occupation and exile. Ghassan Kanafani, perhaps the greatest contemporary Palestinian fiction writer, recreates the desperation and aimlessness of the refugee experience in his short story collection *All That Remains: Palestine's Children*. Several of the stories look at Palestine through the eyes of her embattled and sometimes embittered children, while *Men in the Sun and Other Palestinian Stories* portrays the struggle through adult eyes. Palestinians' attachment to their land is portrayed in the wonderful poetry of Mahmoud Darwish, and the longing for a homeland in the poems of Fouzi al-Asmar, collected in *The Wind-Driven Reed and Other Poems*. Jabra

Ibrahim Jabra's novel *The Ship* is engrossing. For an anthology of resistance poetry, look for *The Palestinian Wedding,* edited by Abd al-Elmessiri. Israeli Arab Anton Shammas' *Arabesques* describes the exile's identity crisis; Fawaz Turki's autobiographical tomes discuss the life of an exile; the novels of Sahar Khalifeh provide an incisive picture of the paradoxes of occupation; and Raymonda Tawil's autobiographical *My Home, My Prison* describes time spent under house arrest. Another well-known Palestinian writer is Samih al-Qassem; most of these authors and more are anthologized in Salma Khadra Jayyusi's behemoth *Modern Palestinian Literature.*

WEST BANK SIGHTS

■■■ JERICHO أريحا

Whether you approach Jericho from the sweltering-in-summer King Hussein Bridge or descend through the rolling hills from Jerusalem, the journey to this oasis town, the world's oldest still-inhabited city, entices archaeologists and scholars as well as those interested in some of the most passionate political dynamics in the world.

The seat of the new Palestinian Authority is suffused with an almost paradoxical mix of excitement, optimism, and almost-ambivalent waiting. While Jericho may be the birthplace of the first self-ruled Palestinian state ever, it is difficult to be unconditionally filled with joy while 27 years of Israeli occupation and terrible economic conditions hang in the air.

Jericho (*Ariha* in Arabic, *Yeriho* in Hebrew) is best known for the biblical account of its walls, which came crashing down when Joshua sounded his trumpets after seven days of siege. According to the Bible, two spies sent into town by Joshua were sheltered in the house of the harlot, Rahab. In exchange for the deed, her family was to be spared if she marked her house with a scarlet thread. When the tribes of Israel attacked, the entire city was destroyed save the single house with a scarlet cord dangling from its window (Joshua 2-6).

After the 1967 War, 20% of the refugees from what is now Israel fled to Jericho, now the site of the biggest Palestinian refugee camp in the world, 'Aqbat Jaber.

Practical Information Forty kilometers east of Jerusalem, Jericho is on the road to Amman at the junction of the highway to the Galilee. The King Hussein/Allenby Bridge, 10km east of town, has been the only route across the Jordan River since the King Abdallah Bridge to the south was destroyed in 1967.

Buses to Jericho from Jerusalem leave from Damascus Gate. Arab bus #28 (NIS3.50) goes to Ein as-Sultan St., one block north of the central traffic circle. Buses leave only when full; a quicker and only slightly more expensive option is a *service* taxi (NIS5); they drop you off at the central square in front of the municipality building. Transportation from Jericho to other West Bank towns is sporadic; inquire at the traffic circle.

Today's town of 7000 Palestinians is actually a few kilometers south of the ancient city. The main square is the hub of town life, currently dominated by journalists from all over the world. NBC's peacock may be emblazoned on the sides of buildings for some time to come. Most of Jericho's other services are also located here, including the **police station** (tel. 922 521). Since hiking is arduous, the best way to see the sights in Jericho is with an endearingly rickety but functional bicycle. A **bicycle shop,** just off the central square and east of the municipality building, rents balloon-tire bombers (NIS1.50 per hr.). The owner may also ask for advance payment—three hours should be enough. Be aware that locals bike on the left side of the road; bring lots of water. A **taxi** will take you on a loop of the sights for about NIS60, but you must agree on this price in advance.

Jericho's new **Tourist Information Office** is run by the Palestinian Authority and located outside of town. Take a taxi (NIS4-5) or ride your rented bike with directions from any one of the helpful locals. The office provides an excellent map of Jericho, information on sights, and, with a little prodding, a free poster (tel. 922 935; open daily 9am-4pm).

Accommodations and Food While there are no hotels currently open in Jericho, several are being built. Hicham's Palace Hotel was over-run with journalists during the summer of 1994 and closed to tourists. Eventually, however, times change, crises change location, and journalists leave; Hicham's may be taking visitors as soon as the headline-happy migrate. Inquire at the tourist office. Down Ein as-Sultan St. in a residential area is the **Maxim Restaurant** (open 7am-midnight). This all-you-can-eat establishment offers an appetizing selection of salads (NIS14) and meats (NIS22). Even though it's a little pricey, the food is excellent and you can go back until you burst with falafel and eggplant. Along the road to ancient Jericho are numerous outdoor garden restaurants; falafel stands cluster around the main square.

Sights Jericho's most popular sights, Hisham's Palace and ancient Jericho, lie on the outskirts of town. Since a cluster of restaurants and a cooling spring near the ancient city provide a pleasant rest stop, visit Hisham's Palace first.

To reach the ruins of **Hisham's Palace** (tel. 922 522), follow the signs along Qasr Hisham St., which heads north from the eastern side of Jericho's main square. The palace is 3km north on paved roads. Coming from ancient Jericho, head north on the main road leading through the **Ein as-Sultan refugee camp.** After 1.5km, turn right on the road back to Jericho town; the turn-off to Hisham's Palace appears almost immediately on your left.

The extensive ruins of Hisham's Palace are a jaw-dropping sample of early Islamic architecture. Known as Khirbet al-Mafjar in Arabic, the palace was designed for the Umayyad Caliph Hisham as a winter retreat from Damascus. The palace was begun in 724 CE and completed in 743, only to be damaged four years later by an earthquake. The window in the courtyard is in the shape of the six-pointed Umayyad star and is the site's most renowned feature. (Open daily 8am-5pm. Admission NIS8.)

To travel the 2km from Hisham's Palace to ancient Jericho, turn right onto the road that runs past Hisham's Palace, then take a left at the end of the road. Follow the "Tel Jericho" signs; about 1.5km past the 5th- to 6th-century synagogue (you might stop in to admire the mosaic floor), the Ein as-Sultan spring is on your left. Follow the street around the corner to the right to the entrance. If all else fails, use the map provided by the GTIO.

Ancient Jericho, thought by some to be the oldest city in the world, is now a heap of ruined walls. Called Tel as-Sultan, the mound contains layer upon layer of garbage from ancient (and modern) cities. The oldest fortifications, 12m down, are 7000 years old. Some of the finds date from the early Neolithic period, leading archaeologists to suspect that Jericho was inhabited as early as the eighth millennium BCE. A limited amount of excavation has exposed many levels of ancient walls, some of them 3.5m thick and 5.5m high. Your imagination will have to substitute for visible splendor at this distinctly unphotogenic site (tel. 922 909; open daily 8am-5pm; admission NIS8).

An imposing Greek Orthodox **monastery** stands on the edge of a cliff among the mountains west of Jericho; the peak is believed to be the New Testament's Mount of Temptation. The complex of buildings stands before a grotto, said to be the spot where Jesus fasted for 40 days and 40 nights after his baptism in the Jordan River (Matthew 4:1-11). Six Greek monks now live in the monastery, built in 1895. Ask one to point out the rock where Jesus was tempted by the devil and served by angels. The road to the monastery heads past the shops near ancient Jericho. The summit of the mountain, named **Qarantal** after the Latin word for "forty," also serves as a pedestal for the Maccabean **Castle of Dok,** beside which lie the remains of a 4th-century Christian chapel. (Monastery open daily 7am-noon. Modest dress required.)

■ NEAR JERICHO

The road from Jerusalem to Jericho slices through the harsh desert landscape of the wilderness. About 8km before Jericho, the 13th-century **Mosque of Nabi Mussa** stands on a hill in a sea of sand, a short distance from the road. This spot is revered throughout the Muslim world as the grave of the prophet Moses, and many Muslims yearn to be buried by his side when they die. Islamic tradition holds that God carried the bones of the prophet here for the faithful to come and pay their respects. The 13th-century Mamluk mosque containing the prophet's tomb has been closed to the public since early 1993.

About 10km east of Jericho is **Al Maghtas,** the spot on the Jordan River where John the Baptist is believed to have baptized Jesus. A 19th-century Greek Orthodox monastery marks the spot where Christians still come to immerse themselves. The site is under military supervision and closed to the public except on one day each in October and January, when the Greek Orthodox and the Roman Catholics, respectively, celebrate the Epiphany. The best way to get there is with a private taxi hired in Jericho. Inquire at the GTIO for updates on the status of these sites.

Hiking through **Wadi Qelt,** where the arid desert cracks open and reveals an oasis, is like burrowing through the refrigerator right after Mom has restocked the shelves. Three fresh-water springs nourish lush greenery and wildlife, threading 28km between imperious limestone cliffs and undulating ridges of bone-white chalk. Descending 395m below sea level, the *wadi* is a reasonably safe adventure that offers more drama than the resort oasis at Ein Gedi.

The most interesting and accessible section of the *wadi* extends from the spring of **Ein Qelt,** past the 6th-century **Monastery of St. George,** and down into Jericho, 10km east. The trek takes about four hours, adventures in dawdledom excluded. The best place to start is at the turn-off from the Jerusalem-Jericho highway about 9km west of Jericho, marked by the orange sign for "St. George's Monastery." **Egged bus** #73 (6:15am and 2:30pm, NIS10.50) from the bus stop across from the central bus station in Jerusalem goes to the turn-off. For late risers, **Arab bus** #28 to Jericho (leaves every hr.) passes the same turn-off. The trip from Jerusalem takes about an hour. If you're driving, it's possible to skip the hike and drive most of the way to St. George's by following signs.

St. George's Monastery dates from the 5th or 6th century CE. The floor of St. George's Church is decorated with Byzantine mosaics; look for the likeness of a two-headed eagle, the Byzantine symbol of power. The neighboring St. John's Church houses a spooky collection of skulls and bones of monks who were slaughtered when the Persians swept through the valley in 614 CE. The Greek Orthodox monks who maintain the monastery can refill your canteen for the rest of the journey into Jericho. (Open Mon.-Sat. 8am-1pm and 3-5pm; winter 8am-1pm and 3-4pm. Leave a donation. Modest dress required.)

On the way to Jericho from St. George's, stop at the ruins of Tel Abu Alayia on your right. The palaces here, used by the Hasmoneans and later by King Herod, have decorated walls, nearby bath houses, and pools. (Free.)

To explore other portions of the *wadi* and around Jericho, pick up an SPNI map of the Desert at their Jerusalem office. Their one-day tours led by English-speaking guides focus on both natural and artificial attractions in the *wadi,* but the pace may be slower than you'd like (from Tel Aviv or Jerusalem, US$44 per person).

■■■ NABLUS نابلس

Beautiful, serene mountains surround the town of Nablus. Enjoy them while you can; the city is not called *Jabal an-Nar* (Hill of Fire) in Arabic for nothing. Home to some of Palestine's oldest and wealthiest families, Nablus also has a tradition of impassioned resistance to foreign occupation. Its citizens fought the Turks, the British, and the Jordanians, and were wholly consumed by the *intifada*. Nablus is the largest city in the West Bank (not counting East Jerusalem) and home to its second-largest university, An-Najah. In addition, it is an industrial center of the West Bank. Besides its predominantly Muslim population, Nablus is home to about 480 Samaritan Jews (about two-thirds of the world's total Samaritan population).

The current city was founded by Titus near the site of Biblical Shekhem in 72 CE as the "New City" of Flavia Neapolis, in honor of his father Flavius Vespasian. Since then, its streets have witnessed religious strife, the Crusades, a devastating earthquake in 1927, the British Mandate, Israeli occupation, and, most recently, the *intifada*. Here demonstrations became a source of pride, but also a source of trauma; no meeting with a local passes unaccompanied by a story of *intifada* sorrows.

When you walk off the bus you will be confronted by the bustling business district set in the valley. If you wander around, you'll be asked by Palestinians about what you're doing and where you're going; you'll also turn heads at any remaining Israeli army patrols, but now is not the time to stop and talk. Nablus is a very conservative town; dress modestly. After introductions, it is not uncommon for Palestinians to invite you to their homes. Perhaps the most rewarding way to spend your time here is to accept the residents' hospitality and learn something of the life of West Bank Palestinians.

Practical Information Nablus lies 63km north of Jerusalem and 46km north of Ramallah—an easy daytrip from Jerusalem. Take one of the **Tamini Co. buses** from Nablus Rd. in Jerusalem (irregular schedule, 1½-2hr., NIS6). The last bus to Jerusalem from Nablus leaves at 3pm, but don't count on it. **Service taxis** to and from Jerusalem are a safer bet; they cost NIS9 and you will be dropped off in the center of town, after changing cars in Ramallah.

Sights From the center of Nablus, wander south past a pleasant, cheap fresh fruit market (next to Nablus circle) and into the crowded streets and passageways of the **market,** overflowing with Nablus merchants, Palestinian customers, and tea-sipping onlookers. Try a piece of the famous, extraordinarily-rich *kinaffeh nablusiyya*. Nablus churns out countless tray-fulls of this cheese concoction, which is topped with sweet orange flakes and syrup (0.25kg NIS2.50). Although you'll feel much more comfortable if you have a guide, stopping to chat and swap stories can often dissipate any awkwardness.

Throughout the market you'll continue to see the smiling image of Dafer Masri, Nablus's Palestinian former mayor. A wreathed monument next to the municipality building marks the spot where he was slain in the winter of 1986. Many hold that his assassins were Palestinians who resented his alleged chumminess with Israeli leadership; the killing is remembered with great bitterness here.

To the east, 3km from the town center, lie two famous but unspectacular pilgrimage sights. **Jacob's Well** (tel. 375 123) is now enclosed within a subterranean Greek Orthodox shrine. The well is believed to date from the time when Jacob bought the surrounding land to pitch his tents (Genesis 33:18-19). (Open daily 8am-noon and 2-5pm.) A few hundred meters north of the well lies the **Tomb of Joseph.** According to the Book of Joshua, the bones of Joseph were carried out of Egypt and buried in Shekhem (Joshua 24:32). The tomb was a Muslim shrine until nine years ago, when it was taken over by Jewish authorities. Israeli soldiers guard the unimpressive velvet-shrouded cenotaph and the adjacent *yeshiva.* (Open daily 6am-10pm. No shorts or bare shoulders permitted.) *Service* (NIS0.70) run to both sites regularly from the center of town.

Mount Gerizim, the tree-covered slope southeast of Nablus, features a terrific view of the Shomron Valley. Since the 4th century BCE, it has been the holy mountain of the Samaritans, who revere it as the spot where Abraham prepared to sacrifice his son Isaac and where the original Ten Commandments are buried. The Samaritans, an Israelite sect who were excommunicated in biblical times, are distinguished by their literal interpretation of certain scriptures (see Introduction to the Region: Religion, p. 50). The highlight of the Samaritan observance of Passover is the sacrifice of sheep atop Mt. Gerizim. Tourist buses from Jerusalem and Tel Aviv bring visitors to witness the bloody rite. The hike up the mountain is arduous, but taxis can be hired for about NIS15.

■ NEAR NABLUS: SABASTIYA سبستية

An array of Israelite, Hellenistic, and Roman ruins can be found in the multi-colored hills 11km northwest of Nablus. The strategic peak on which the ruins lie was first settled by Omri, King of Israel, in the 9th century BCE as the city of **Shomron** (Samaria), which served as the capital of the Israelite kingdom until the Assyrians' invasion of the 8th century BCE. Under Herod, the city was made the showpiece of the Holy Land to win the favor of the Roman Emperor.

The ruins are just above the present-day Arab village of **Sabastiya.** Unfortunately, most of the ancient splendor is long gone. All that remains of a **Roman theater** are a few steps overgrown with weeds; at the top of the hill lie the remnants of Israelite and Hellenistic acropolis walls, a Roman acropolis, and the column bases of the **Temple of Augustus.** Blue signs label each ruin in Arabic, Hebrew, and English.

The narrow 1.5km path encircling the ruins is treacherous—watch your step, or you may end up taking the quick and painful route into the valley below. The site is currently untended and free. *Service* taxis to Sabastiya are available from Nablus (NIS2.50); walk uphill and take your first right.

■■■ RAMALLAH رام الله

Just 16km north of Jerusalem and 900m above sea level, Ramallah is famous for its cool, pleasant mountain air and its quietude. Before 1967, the prosperous town was known as the "Bride of Palestine," a summer haven for Arabs from Jordan, Lebanon, and the Gulf region. With vacationers long gone, Ramallah assumed a leading role in *intifada* politics. While definitely calm compared to Nablus or Hebron, Ramallah is still a town in the West Bank, where tranquility is measured in relative terms.

Palestinians in Ramallah live up the old cliché about Arab generosity. Visibly confused tourists are often surrounded by people offering countless solutions; the absence of street signs will put you in this position faster than you think. Use the opportunity to strike up a conversation, improve your Arabic, and gain insight into the Palestinian perspective on the latest events. The town is among the least conservative in the West Bank; women can go in pants and a T-shirt.

Although all hotels and hostels are currently closed, the town is still equipped to amuse and entertain, and there are few noteworthy tourist sites in Ramallah. Visit the ebullient **market** (open Sat.-Thurs. until 3pm, Fri. until noon) by the bus station, or walk around in the neighborhoods away from the city center. The **Silvana Chocolate Company,** 1.5km down Jaffa Blvd. from Manara Sq., opens its doors to tourists, offering tours and countless free samples. (Open Mon.-Sat. 7:30am-4pm. Call 956 458 to arrange a tour.)

Practical Information If the political situation continues to improve, the **Pension Miami** (tel. 952 808) on Jaffa Rd. may reopen. You can find good falafel (NIS1.50) and *shawerma* (NIS4) and an excellent variety of Arabic sweets throughout the town. For a real treat, stop by **Rukab's Ice Cream** (tel. 952 467) on Ein Misbah St. for some freshly made ice cream (NIS3.50) or a glass of cold lemonade (NIS2).

Since the March 1993 closure of the West Bank, Ramallah has become a transportation hub for Arabs unable to get into East Jerusalem. As long as this is still in effect, you can go from here directly to most West Bank towns by *service*. From Jerusalem, take a **service taxi** (20min., NIS2) from just outside Damascus Gate. **Arab bus #18** from the station on Nablus Rd. just north of Damascus Gate (40min., NIS1.50) stops to pick up every man, woman, and child en route. Buses to Jerusalem leave from Jaffa Rd. in Ramallah, just off Manara Sq., the main traffic circle. The last bus leaves around 5pm, the last *service* at about 6pm.

■ NEAR RAMALLAH

BEITIN (BETHEL) بيتين

Beitin (Bethel), 5km northeast of Ramallah on the road to Nablus, is thought to be the place where Jacob lay down to sleep and dreamed of a ladder ascending to heaven with angels going down and up. Upon awakening, Jacob built an altar and named the spot Beit-El, "House of God" (Genesis 28:12-19).

Until the agreement on Palestinian self-rule, Beitin was the headquarters of the Israeli civilian administration that governed the West Bank. The administration center itself is of no interest to tourists, but a visit to the nearby Jewish settlement of Beit-El may be worthwhile. Surrounded by tall fences and barbed wire and guarded by army patrols, the settlement provides a glimpse of life in one of the West Bank settlements. Most of the working population commutes to Jerusalem, but there are also a few cottage industries, including a workshop that manufactures *tefillin* (religious articles worn by orthodox male Jews on the head and arm during some prayers).

Beitin is accessible by **Egged bus** #70 from Jerusalem or Al Bireh. From Ramallah you can walk, take a taxi, or take the bus going to Nablus.

BIRZEIT بيرزيت

Twelve kilometers northwest of Ramallah is the largest and most important university on the West Bank. **Birzeit University**'s 2500 students have a history of vocal opposition to the Israeli occupation; throughout the occupation, the university was often shut down by the Israeli army. In the first years of the *intifada*, Israeli authorities closed it altogether; it was not to reopen until in April 1992. Specify that you want to visit the university *(jama'a)* and not the town. The old campus is next to the last bus stop; the new campus lies 2km out of town on the road back to Ramallah. **Bus** #19 leaves for Birzeit from Radio Blvd. in Ramallah, just off Manara Sq. **Taxis** leave from the same street.

■ ■ ■ BETHLEHEM بيت لحم

Bethlehem (Beit Lahm in Arabic, Beit Leḥem in Hebrew) is the biblical setting for Rachel's death, the love of Ruth and Boaz, and the discovery of the lyrical shepherd David, future king of Israel; but what really put Bethlehem on the pilgrimage map was the pastoral birth of Jesus. Today, biblical charm remains hidden behind fleets of tour buses unloading blue-haired zealots in front of souvenir stands. Even as you try to peel off the layers of commercialism in your mind's eye, you will be suffocated by exhaust, blinded by flash bulbs, and drowned in floods of devout postcard-buying, pilgrims.

Tourism in Bethlehem waned throughout the *intifada*. But even then tourists were welcome, and continue to be. Hospitable locals will encourage you to get away from the buses, explore the sights, and stay long enough for a few meals or to enjoy the exceedingly clean accommodations. Churches hold Christmas and Easter services, and events sponsored by the Bethlehem municipality, including the annual parade from Jerusalem to Bethlehem, continue.

PRACTICAL INFORMATION

Life for the religiously inquisitive in Bethlehem (8km south of Jerusalem) revolves around **Manger Square,** across from the Basilica of the Nativity. **Najajreh** and **Star Street** are home to the town's shopping district and open-air **market** and lead into the Square. Many businesses close on the 6th and 9th of each month to commemorate the beginning of the *intifada*.

Government Tourist Information Office (GTIO): Manger Sq. (tel. 741 581), directly across the Square from the Basilica. Excellent free map of the town, details about special events during Christmas and Easter, and transportation information. They can provide a list of accommodations. Open daily 8am-4pm.

Currency Exchange: Bank Leumi (tel. 743 330 or 742 929; open Sun.-Thurs. 8am-12:30pm, Fri. 8am-noon) and **Cairo Amman Bank** (tel. 744 971; open Sun.-Thurs. 8am-12:30pm, closed Fri. and all strike days), all in Manger Sq.

Post Office: Manger Sq. (tel. 742 668), beside the tourist office. Open Mon.-Wed., Fri., and Sat. 8am-2:30pm, Thurs. 8am-12:30pm. **Poste Restante** available.

Bus Station: Manger St., 50m northwest of Manger Sq., down the hill toward Jerusalem. Arab buses from Damascus or Jaffa Gate in Jerusalem: #22 and 23 (continues to Hebron), #47 (continues east to Beit Sahur), and #60 (continues to Obediyya). To Jerusalem (30min., NIS1.50) last bus back at about 5-6pm. Note that the Hebron bus stops only at Rachel's Tomb and at the intersection with Paul VI St., 3km west of Manger Sq.

Minibuses: Deheisheh (#1) from Manger St. behind the police station heads north to Rachel's Tomb, then south to the Deheisheh refugee camp via the road to Hebron (daily every 15-20min. 6am-6pm, NIS1). To Beit Sahur from same location (NIS1).

Service Taxis: From Jaffa or Damascus Gate in Jerusalem to Manger Sq. until about 7pm (NIS1.50), and return from Manger Sq. in front of the GTIO.

Police Station: Manger Sq. (tel. 748 222).

ACCOMMODATIONS AND FOOD

While Bethlehem's accommodations are expensive, the hotels are so clean and well-kept that a few extra shekels in Bethlehem will let you sleep in a comfort and style to which Jerusalem's sharks can only aspire.

Casa Nova (tel. 743 980), off Manger Sq., tucked in a corner to the left of the entrance to the Basilica of the Nativity. Marble floor and stained-glass windows in lobby for the serious pilgrim. Caters primarily to the seminary student or groups in which at least 3 members can recite the Synoptic Gospels in their entirety. Modern rooms and plenty of hot water. Bed and breakfast US$19. Half board US$21. Full board US$27. US$9 extra to convert your double room into a single. Prices do not include a 5% service charge.

Al-Andalus Hotel (tel. 741 348), in Manger Sq. upstairs next to the Bank Leumi. If the door's bolted, just knock or ask for the owner at one of the shops downstairs or at the **Al-Andalus Restaurant** around the corner to the right. Green, green rooms with green-yellow bedspreads. Green singles with bath US$21. Green doubles with bath US$35. Breakfast included in the green dining room upstairs. Bargain down winter price hikes.

Palace Hotel, Manger St. (tel. 742 798 or 744 100), to the left as you face the Basilica door. The garden is beautiful and the rooms are spotless. Your soul may not be saved during your trip to Bethlehem, but bargaining at the Palace may save a few dollars, especially during slow periods. Newly renovated. Safe provided. Singles US$30. Doubles US$40. Breakfast buffet included.

Franciscan Convent Pension, Milk Grotto St. (tel. 742 441), on your left past the Milk Grotto. Ring the bell at the gate. Curfew 9pm. Dorm beds US$15. Bed and breakfast US$18. Possibility of floor space during holidays. Students US$7, adults pleading poverty US$10.

For falafel fans, the stands in Manger Sq. and on Manger St. offer the cheapest stomach-stuffers. Be warned: tourists may be charged slightly higher prices than locals; try bargaining. **Al-Atlal Restaurant,** one block from Manger Sq. on Milk Grotto St., contains neo-Crusader arches and provides needed respite from the hordes. (Hummus with meat NIS15, hamburger or omelette with salad and potatoes NIS10.)

Another option is **Granada Bar and Restaurant** (tel. 744 300), on the same side of Manger Sq. as Bank Leumi, featuring shaded outdoor tables with an unobstructed view of the square. (*Shawerma* platter NIS6, falafel NIS4, juice NIS2.50.) Or try the **Quick, Lunch, Sandwiches** shop right next door (quick lunch sandwiches NIS6). The only food available later at night is at the **Palace Hotel Coffee Shop.** (Open 9am-midnight. Salad bar NIS6.)

SIGHTS

A church masquerading as a fortress, the massive **Basilica of the Nativity** on Manger Sq. is the oldest continuously used church in the world. Today the building is used primarily as a zoo housing a species called *pilgrumsun tourists.* You can watch them descend from soot-spitting buses, follow those they call guides clad in name-tag-decorated Solidarity T-shirts, and listen to utterings in several unidentifiable but intriguing languages. Under the supervision of his mother Helena, Constantine the Great erected the first basilica in 326 over the site of Jesus' birth. It was destroyed in the Samaritan uprising of 525, then rebuilt by Justinian. During the Persian invasion in 614, virtually every Christian shrine in the Holy Land was demolished with the exception of this basilica, reputedly spared because it contained a mosaic of the three wise men which had special anti-artillery powers. The Crusaders extensively renovated the church but it fell into disrepair after their defeat by the Muslims. By the 15th century it had become undeniably decrepit, but the basilica's importance as a holy shrine never waned. For this reason, during the ensuing centuries, struggle for its control among Catholic, Greek, and Armenian Christians repeatedly led to bloodshed. Not until the 1840s was the church restored to its former dignity, but squabbles between the various sects over the division of the edifice continue. Established in 1751 and finalized in 1852, an elaborate system of worship schedules has harmonized the competing claims of the different groups, but the confusion and tension resulting from the Greek Orthodox Church's rejection of summer daylight savings time demonstrates the teetering balance of this arrangement.

Though it has an impressive history, the Basilica of the Nativity is not particularly attractive. The main entrance and windows were blocked up as a safety precaution during medieval times, rendering the façade markedly awkward. To enter you must assume the position and step through the narrow Door of Humility—a remnant of the days when Christians wanted to prevent Muslims from entering on horseback.

Fragments of beautiful mosaic floors are all that remain of Constantine's original church. View them beneath the huge wooden trap doors in the center of the marble Crusader floor. The four rows of reddish limestone Corinthian columns and the mosaic atoms along the walls date from Justinian's reconstruction. The oak ceiling was a gift from England's King Edward IV, while the handsome icons adorning the altar were bequeathed in 1764 by the Russian imperial family.

The **Grotto of the Nativity** is in an underground sanctuary beneath the church. As you enter the womb-like grotto, notice the crosses etched into the columns on both sides of the doorway. This religious graffiti is the work of pilgrims who have visited here over the centuries. A star bearing the Latin inscription: *Hic De Virgine Maria Jesus Christus Natus Est* ("Here, of the Virgin Mary, Jesus Christ was born") marks the spot. The star, added by Catholics in 1717, was removed by Greeks in 1847 and restored by the Turkish government in 1853. Quarrels over the star supposedly contributed to the outbreak of the Crimean War. (Basilica complex open daily 5:30am-8pm; in winter 7am-6pm. Free, although you are encouraged to make a donation. Modest dress required. For further information call 742 425.)

Simple and airy, the adjoining **St. Catherine's Church** (tel. 742 425), built by the Franciscans in 1881, is a welcome contrast to the grim interior of the basilica. Use the separate entrance to the north of the basilica, or face the altar in the basilica and pass through one of the doorways in the wall on your left. St. Catherine's broadcasts a Midnight Mass to a worldwide audience every Christmas Eve. Superbly detailed wood carvings of the 14 Stations of the Cross line the walls. The first room, the **Chapel of St. Joseph,** commemorates the carpenter's vision of an angel who advised him to flee with his family to Egypt to avoid Herod's wrath. The burial cave of children slaughtered by King Herod (Matthew 2:6) lies below the altar and through the grille in the **Chapel of the Innocents.** Beyond the altar, a narrow passageway leads to the Grotto of the Nativity. The way is blocked by a thick wooden door pierced by a peephole. During earlier times of hostility between Christian sects, this glimpse was as close as Catholics could get to the Greek Orthodox-controlled shrine. To the right of the altar, a series of rooms contain the tombs of St. Jerome, St. Paula, and St. Paula's daughter Eustochia. These lead to the spartan cell where St. Jerome produced the Vulgate, the 4th-century translation of the Hebrew Bible into Latin.

A solemn procession to the basilica and underground chapels is conducted by the Franciscan Fathers on a daily basis. To join in the 20 minutes of Gregorian cantillation and Latin prayer, arrive at St. Catherine's by noon. (St. Catherine's and the tomb of St. Jerome both open daily 5:30am-noon and 2-8pm.)

A five-minute walk from the Basilica of the Nativity down Milk Grotto St. leads to the **Milk Grotto Church** (tel. 742 425). The cellar here is thought to be the cave in which the Holy Family hid when fleeing from Herod into Egypt. The cave and church take their names from the original milky white color of the rocks, long since blackened by candle smoke. According to legend, some of Mary's milk fell while she was nursing the infant Jesus, whitewashing the rocks forever. Male visitors may be slightly discomfited amid the women who come here to pray for fertility. (Open daily 8-11:30am and 2-5pm.) Ring the bell and wait for a monk to admit you.

About 500m north of Manger Sq. along Star St., the three unremarkable restored cisterns of the **Well of David** (tel. 742 477; open daily 8am-noon and 2-5pm) squat in the parking lot of the King David Cinema. When a thirsty David, while battling the Philistines, was brought water from the enemy's well, he in turn offered it as a sacrifice to God (2 Samuel 23:13-17). From Star St., turn right onto King David St.

The **Tomb of Rachel** (Raḥel) is a sacred site for Jews, a spot where synagogues have been built and destroyed throughout history. On one side are fervently praying Hasidic men, and on the other weeping Yemenite women. Rachel died in Bethlehem while giving birth to Benjamin (Genesis 35:19-20), and she became a timeless symbol of maternal devotion and suffering. Despite Rachel's misfortune, the tomb is revered as the place to pray for a child or a safe delivery. Men should be sure to don at least a paper *kipah* (head covering), available at the entrance. The tomb is on the northern edge of town on the road to Jerusalem, at the intersection of Manger St. and Hebron Rd. (Open Sun.-Thurs. 8am-5pm, Fri. 8am-2pm.) All buses between Jerusalem and Bethlehem or Hebron pass the tomb; minibus #1 also swings by. It's only a 20-minute walk from the Basilica.

Bethlehem means "House of Meat" in Arabic *(Beit Lahm)* and "House of Bread" in Hebrew *(Beit Leḥem)*. The yawning **market** which clings to the town's steep streets lives up to both names; it is up the stairs from Paul VI St. across from the Syrian Church, about 2 blocks west of Manger Sq. A few blocks down Paul VI from the market and toward the basilica is the **Bethlehem Museum** (tel. 742 589), which exhibits Palestinian crafts, traditional costumes, and a 19th-century Palestinian home. (Open Mon.-Sat. 8am-5pm. Small fee.)

■ NEAR BETHLEHEM

AL AZARIYYEH (BETHANY) العزرية

A relatively prosperous Palestinian village, Bethany (Al Azariyyeh) was the home of Lazarus and his sisters Mary and Martha. A **Franciscan Church** (tel. 271 706) built in 1954 marks the spot where Jesus supposedly slept. The church features several impressive mosaics, including one of the resurrection of Lazarus and another of the Last Supper. Three earlier shrines, the earliest built in the 4th century CE, have been excavated nearby. South of the church lie the remains of a vast abbey built in 1143 CE by Queen Melisende. (Open daily March-Oct. 8-11:30am and 2-6pm; Nov.-Feb. 8-11:30am and 2-5pm. Small donations appreciated.)

Bethany is home to the first-century **Tomb of Lazarus,** enshrined in the 4th century. When the Crusaders arrived, they built a church over Lazarus's tomb, a monastery over Mary and Martha's house, and a tower over Simon the Leper's abode (Simon was another resident of Bethany cured by Jesus). In the 16th century, the Muslims erected a mosque over the grotto, and in the following century Christians dug another entrance to the tomb so they, too, could worship there. Head for the red domes of the **Greek Orthodox Church** above the tomb (the Franciscan Church will be just downhill). As you approach the tomb, a person will come from across the street to show you the light switch (on the right as you enter) and ask for a donation (NIS2 is appropriate; tomb open daily 8am-7pm). Ten minutes farther along the main road, the **Greek Orthodox Convent** (silver domes here) shelters the boulder upon which Jesus sat while awaiting Martha from Jericho (ring the bell to see the rock).

To reach Bethany from Jerusalem (4km), take Egged bus #43 or the more frequent Arab bus #36 (NIS1.50) from Damascus Gate and get off in the town (look for the silver-domed church on your left). There are two #36 buses, one of which stops at Abu Dees first. Women should dress modestly and travel in groups.

HERODIAN

Rising from the plains of the Judean desert 10km southeast of Bethlehem are the ruins of **Herodian,** a winsome fortified palace perched atop a remarkably-shaped conical peak. King Herod, haunted by fears of assassination, ordered the construction of this hideout in the first century BCE. Enclosed within the massive circular double walls and guarded by four watch towers were all the comforts of Rome: palace, garden, and bathhouse. Fifteen meters below the floor, two giant cisterns were filled with water either hauled in by donkeys or filled by aqueducts from Solomon's pools. Though engineered to protect the Roman-sponsored ruler from discontented Jews, the palace actually became a rebel stronghold during the Jewish revolts of the first and second centuries CE. From the top you can see Jerusalem to the north, Bethlehem to the west, the Dead Sea to the east, and the desolate Judean Desert to the south. (Open daily 8am-5pm. Admission NIS12 for individuals, groups NIS9, students NIS6.) To reach Herodian, share a taxi from Bethlehem (round-trip NIS30-40) or hike past Shepherd's Field on the road from Beit Sahur; it's 7km from the marked turn-off. At tense times, hiking may not be safe; ask in the GTIO before you leave.

SHEPHERD'S FIELD

Beyond the Arab village of Beit Sahur on the eastern edge of Bethlehem is the **Field of Ruth,** believed to be the setting for the biblical Book of Ruth. The name of the village in Hebrew is "House of the Shepherds," and Christian tradition holds that this is **Shepherd's Field,** where those tending their flocks were greeted by the angel who pronounced the birth of Jesus (Luke 2:9-11). Take bus #47 (NIS1) from the stop behind the police station in Manger Sq., get off at Beit Sahur, and walk 20 minutes to the site. Otherwise, you can walk the 4km from Bethlehem; follow the signs. (Open daily 8am-noon and 3-5pm.) The Greek Patriarchate oversees the site where shepherds were told of Jesus' birth. Located 1.5km east of Bethlehem off Al Ruaa St., the site includes a 6th-century Byzantine basilica (tel. 743 135), monastery, the Holy Cave (350 CE) featuring mosaic crosses in the floor, and a small cave filled with human bones. (Open daily 8am-12:30pm and 2-5pm.) The Franciscans run a competing shepherd's field 500m farther down the road. Their site includes a small monastery (400 CE) and a number of ancient cooking pots and coins left by shepherds on the site. (Open daily 8-11:30am and 2-5pm.)

MAR SABA MONASTERY

More remarkable and isolated than Herodian is the **Mar Saba Monastery.** Carved into the walls of a remote canyon, the extensive monastery complex stands above the sewer-esque Kidron River. The monastery was built opposite the cave, marked by a cross, where St. Saba began his ascetic life in 478 CE. The attractive bones of St.

Saba are on display in the main church. Women are strictly forbidden to enter and must view the chapels and buildings from a tower near the monastery. Men must wear long pants and long sleeves to be admitted. To enter the monastery, pull the chain on the large blue door. Once inside, you'll be given a five-minute tour in English by one of the monks. The monks occasionally ignore the doorbell on Sundays and late in the afternoon; try to arrive early on a weekday. There is no entrance fee, but it is customary to make a contribution. (Open daily 7-11am and 1:30-5pm.) You need to hire a private taxi from Bethlehem to get here.

■■■ HEBRON الخليل

Al Khalil ar-Rahman (Hebron's full Arabic name, shortened to Al Khalil) means "compassionate friend," and the Hebrew name, *Ḥevron,* comes from *ḥaver* (friend). The friend in question is Abraham (Ibrahim/Avraham), the common ancestor of both peoples. Friendly, however, is hardly the word to describe the Israeli-Palestinian relationship here. It was in Hebron's Park Hotel that the first Jewish settlement on the West Bank was established, in April 1968. The proximity of Kiryat Arba, a major Jewish settlement, paired with efforts to establish a Jewish quarter within the town (550 Jews amidst 65,000 Palestinians), has only exacerbated tensions here. Before self-rule and perhaps even today, if you visit Hebron you will see Israeli soldiers posted on most rooftops, and Palestinians will tell you about harassment from settlers. In February 1994, an American Jew named Goldstein shot several Palestinians as they prayed in the Hebron mosque; some have accused officers in the Israeli army of complicity in the massacre. Before visiting Hebron, read up on events. A few words of Arabic will open many doors and encourage offers of the usual tea or coffee home visit. Dress modestly.

Hebron, like Nablus in the north, is the center Islamic center for Palestinians in the southern half of the West Bank. Both house old Palestinian families and what little industry exists in the West Bank.

In biblical times, Hebron was known as Kiryat Arba (District of the Four). One legend maintains that the "four" referred to four giants who fell from heaven after rebelling against God. When Moses sent spies to Canaan to bring back a report on the conditions there, the scouts returned with gawkful reports of Hebron's giants (Numbers 13: 25-33). As proof, they brought bunches of grapes so large that a single cluster had to be carried by two people; this image is the symbol of Israel's Ministry of Tourism.

There were not many Jews in Hebron until the 19th century, when many Hasidic and Russian Jews emigrated here. In 1925, a *yeshiva* moved from Russia to Hebron and a Hadassah medical clinic opened. Local Arabs took offense, and many Jews perished in the 1929 riots that swept Palestine. The British administrators took the survivors to Jerusalem, and Hebron had no Jewish inhabitants until its capture in 1967. Since then, a significant number of Jews have immigrated to the area, settling outside the town in the modern Kiryat Arba.

Orientation and Practical Information Hebron's intriguing sights are located in central areas such as King David St. and the area around the Cave of Makhpela. It's a good idea to stay in these tourist areas; you'll probably be able to strike up a conversation here with residents. If the political situation is stable, wander around in the *souq.*

Hebron is 35km south of Jerusalem. **Arab bus** #23 (NIS5), which runs frequently from Damascus Gate, will drop you in the city center, where King Faisal, King David, and Khalil ar-Rahman St. converge. From here, a 1km walk along King David St. brings you to the tombs; follow the signs east to the Cave of Makhpela. **Service taxis** shuttle between Jerusalem's Jaffa and Damascus Gates and Hebron's King David St., near the cave and the old market. Taxis cost NIS5, are faster, and run until about 7pm. The last Arab bus for Jerusalem departs at about 5:45pm from King Faisal St., just outside the city center.

Most of the town's services, including the **Bank Leumi, post office** (open Sat.-Wed. 8am-2:30pm, Fri. 8am-12:30pm), **hospital** (tel. 962 126 or 127), and **police station** (tel. 961 444) are also located on King Faisal.

You can buy food at the **markets;** in the summer season, be sure to try the variety of locally grown grapes (*'inab*). **As-Sayyid Restaurant and Sweets** sells wonderful honey-drenched pastries (NIS1-2) just around the corner from the main square. Or catch a shared taxi (NIS1) to **Al-Wafa** on Ras al-Jura, by the glass factories. Fresh-off-the-carcass lamb baked in a clay oven goes for US$8, but try to bargain.

Sights Abraham chose Hebron, the highest of the four Jewish holy cities (at an altitude of 1030m), as the site of his family cemetery. Beginning with his wife, Sarah (Genesis 23:17-19), all the subsequent matriarchs and patriarchs but one were buried in the **Cave of Makhpela.** (The exception is Jacob's second wife, Rachel, who died on the way to Bethlehem.) *Makhpela* means a double cave, or cave over a cave. Some claim that Abraham chose the cave because he knew it to be the burial place of Adam and Eve. Consequently, many rabbis explain that Kiryat Arba refers not to four giants, but to the four married couples purportedly interred here: Abraham and Sarah, Isaac and Rebecca, Jacob and Leah, and Adam and Eve. The patch of land above the tombs has been fiercely contested throughout history by Crusaders, Muslims, and Jews.

The colossal edifice that now stands over the Cave of Makhpela resembles a fortress more than a house of worship. Both Jewish and Muslim traditions attribute the original stonework of the building to King Solomon's reign. The king is said to have enlisted the help of demons to cut and paste the large blocks. The oldest surviving sections, forming the base of the 3m-thick walls, date from King Herod's time. Herod built Makhpela as an open platform with three grave markers; a small synagogue inside the ruins was later added. In 372 CE the Byzantines built a roof and used the refurbished structure as a church. In 686 CE Muslims took over and added a mosque. In 1103 the Crusaders conquered Hebron and promptly transformed the mosque into a church. As the pattern continued, the Crusaders were driven out and the Mamluks added the current mosque and two square minarets. Until 1929, Jews were allowed to stand and pray outside, and were permitted to ascend only as far as the seventh step, the level of the holy grotto. The Israelis have now dug the steps away, removing the symbol of their former second-class status. Today, despite political tensions, both Jews and Muslims pray under the same roof.

In the small synagogue, large cenotaphs commemorate Jacob and Leah. Across the courtyard, in a second synagogue, two huge boxes covered with elaborate calligraphy stand above the tombs of Abraham and Sarah. The actual remains lie 18m below, within the Cave of Makhpela. A locked trap-door in the mosque leads down to the cave itself. Oil is lowered in to keep the candles burning in the cave. To find the final duo, pass through the synagogue in the **Great Mosque,** where the cenotaphs of Isaac and Rebecca each occupy a small hut. In the small adjoining women's mosque (on your left as you leave the courtyard) is a window containing a stone with an undistinguished imprint. Supposedly, this is Adam's footprint, made when he came here after expulsion from Eden.

After the February 1994 killings, the mosque was closed and roped off. If it reopens, male visitors should don a paper *kipah,* available at the top of the staircase. Women may be asked to cover their hair with the furnished scarves. Modest dress is required for both sexes. (Synagogues closed to non-Jews on Saturday and Jewish holidays.)

Other sights in and around Hebron include the **market,** one of the largest and most interesting in the West Bank. The vaulted ceilings and booths indicate that the structure is medieval Crusader, but the artifacts sold are distinctly Middle Eastern. Blown Hebron glassware, in beautiful blue-green colors, is the market's specialty. You'll also find skinned camels and various animal heads. Stay close to your companions at all times and remember the route out.

A five-minute walk west of the town center, down the street from the Arab bus station, stands the **Oak of Abraham** (Balouta in Arabic), the site of the biblical Mamre, where Abraham pitched his tent to welcome tired travelers and entertained three angels who told him of the impending birth of Isaac (Genesis 18). The oak belongs to the Russian Orthodox Church, which built a monastery around it in 1871. According to Christian tradition, the Holy Family rested here on their way back from Egypt. Unfortunately for the tree, travelers since the Middle Ages have removed splinters from it for good luck, and now nails, baling wire, and rusty steel braces have replaced much of the original pith. Despite its convincing decrepitude, some challenge the tree's authenticity and argue that this oak is a mere 600-year-old sapling—they say the oak referred to in Genesis actually stood at **Alonei-Mamre** north of Hebron on Keizun al-Rama St. If the front gate is locked you can enter from the other side of the monastery's grounds (The gatekeeper will let you in most any time; small fee required.)

Kiryat Arba, less than 1km northeast of the Cave of Makhpela, is particularly obtrusive among West Bank settlements for its proximity to a large Palestinian population center. Jewish settlers founded Kiryat Arba in 1972. Tall buildings, wide streets, and green parks contrast sharply with the comparative poverty outside the settlement's barbed-wire perimeter. Nevertheless, many of the 5000 residents would eagerly trade their suburbia for an opportunity to establish a Jewish Quarter in Hebron, a move that the government opposes. English is widely spoken, and in the parks or *yeshiva* (to the left as you enter) you will undoubtedly meet people willing to explain the reasons behind their settlement here.

■■■ THE GAZA STRIP غزة

At the western edge of the Negev Desert, the city of **Gaza** (Ghazzeh in Arabic, Azza in Hebrew) on the **Gaza Strip,** a small stretch of coastline that was captured by the advancing Egyptian army in 1948 and occupied by the Israeli military in 1967, is part of the area now under Palestinian self-rule.

In December 1987, the uprising *(intifada)* began here when a traffic accident resulting in Palestinian deaths sparked angry demonstrations which spread into a widespread movement (see Introduction to the Region: The Intifada, p. 41, for more). With a population of 840,000 Palestinians, three-fourths of whom live in refugee camps, crammed into a mere 46km sq., the conditions are appalling. Twenty-seven years of Israeli occupation and 19 years under the Egyptians before that have left no jobs, no industry, no sewage system, no infrastructure, nothing. In addition, Gaza has a very high rate of population growth and a largely young population.

Gaza, and particularly the refugee camps here, have been the site of the uprising's angriest demonstrations, the harshest Israeli crackdowns, and intra-Palestinian clashes. Four thousand Jewish settlers live in the Strip, sparking locals Arabs' resentment. One-third of Gaza's residents claim loyalty to Hamas, the relatively newly-emerged rejectionist, Islamist branch of the PLO. Surveys show that Gazan support of Hamas spread as a result of frustration and despair in the situation and is based on their perception that Hamas was active while Arafat's FATAH sat back waiting for the peace talks to progress, and not on any extreme religious conservativism among Gazans. In any case, Hamas rules the roost here, often pressuring citizens to join the organization and to adopt a version of Islam that is extreme by some estimations.

Visiting Gaza on your own is difficult and perhaps dangerous. If you do wish to go, seek out a humanitarian agency to take you around, or ask in the West Bank for a potential guide. Your embassy or consulate might also be able to direct you to someone. While on the Gaza strip, dress modestly. Both men and women should cover their entire arms and legs. Women should also consider wearing a skirt instead of pants and covering their hair with a large scarf.

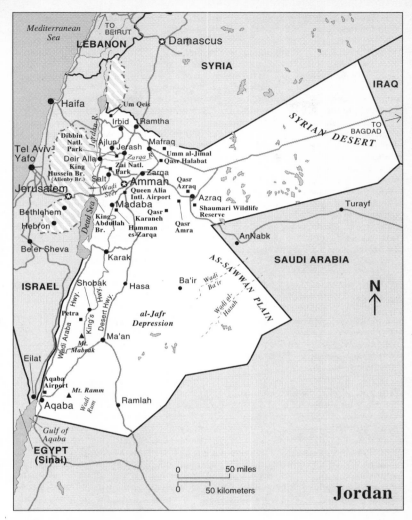

JORDAN الأردن

US$1=0.680 Jordanian dinar (JD)
CDN$1=JD0.494
UK£1=JD1.058
IR£1=JD1.045
AUS$1=JD0.501
NZ$1=JD0.408
SAR1=JD0.190

JD1=US$1.47
JD1=CDN$2.02
JD1=UK£0.94
JD1=IR£0.96
JD1=AUS$2.00
JD1=NZ$2.45
JD1=SAR5.25

For important additional information on all aspects of travel in general and some
specifics on Jordan, see the Essentials section of this book.

Take it from King Hussein's mouth: "Jordan itself is a beautiful country. It is wild, with limitless deserts where the Bedouin roam, but the mountains of the north are clothed in green forests, and where the Jordan River flows it is fertile and warm in winter. Jordan has a strange, haunting beauty and a sense of timelessness. Dotted with the ruins of empires once great, it is the last resort of yesterday in the world of tomorrow. I love every inch of it." Of course that's what he would say—he's king of every inch of it. But the diminutive monarch has a point. It *is* a beautiful country, one whose geographical diversity is appealing, at times fascinating.

The Hashemite Kingdom of Jordan is where John the Baptist baptized Jesus in the Jordan River, and where desert trade routes flourished in the Roman Empire. Later a neglected chunk of the Ottoman *vilayet* of Syria, modern Jordan (Al Urdun) was created by the stroke of a British pen ("Now a giant mixing machine called the West has thrown us together," wrote former Prime Minister Kamel Abu Jaber, "and here we are loving it and hating it, constantly adjusting and readjusting …"). The small kingdom with its commensurate king today finds itself sandwiched between some of the rougher players in a rough neighborhood: Saudi Arabia, Israel, Syria, and Iraq. There are internal divisions, too; the memory of 1970's Black September, a harsh suppression by Jordanian authorities of Palestinian political activity, has not disappeared. The more recent trauma of the Gulf crisis brought a slew of immigrants from the Gulf and Iraq; a 1994 meeting between King Hussein and Israeli Prime Minister Yitzhak Rabin put Jordan on the road to peace with Israel.

In addition to engrossing, hospitable people, Jordan has another bonus for the plucky budget traveler: until recently, even the most awe-inspiring sight was relatively undiscovered. Despite growth in tourism over the past few years, most of the country and its sites of interest are uncommercialized; Jordan is not a land of shrink-wrapped, for-tourist-eyes-only sights and experiences. The Bedouin at Wadi Rum are the genuine article; close your eyes there or at Petra and you could be in any century. Conquer caves and hidden staircases in remote desert castles as a bona fide explorer, and prowl the modern capital of Amman unjostled by throngs of tourists. But hurry up, already. Chances are, Israeli throngs are close on your heels.

ONCE THERE

■■■ ENTRY

Upon arrival at **Queen Alia International Airport,** you will be welcomed with open arms by passport control, where procrastinator-types can purchase visas on the spot. Visas for American citizens, valid for one month but renewable at any police station, cost JD20. A **Housing Bank** and a **Jordan Bank** (ask the friendly customs officials to point them out) in the airport lobby will satisfy your every pecuniary desire. Purchase **JETT** bus tickets (750fils for the ½-hr. ride to Amman) next to the information booth, then join the jett-set at the bus stop right outside the airport's main entrance. Do not feel shy asking for help in the airport. The Jordanians, winners of the *Let's Go* award for hospitality for the third year running, will point, gesture, or grab you by the elbow and guide you to your destination. On the way into Amman, notice men and boys selling vegetables along the highway. Look for the minaret with the green neon lights; this is your signal that in three minutes you will be at the Abdali bus station, where a few good and cheap accommodations are located.

■■■ GETTING AROUND

Most visitors to Jordan stay long enough to see the major sites at Petra and Jerash, but not long enough to master the chaotic transportation system. Organized **bus tours** and private **taxis** can cost JD4 to JD50 per day. The country has a fine train system, but only for freight, and the only reliable long-distance bus company, **JETT**, has a limited number of routes. Fleets of **shared taxis** (called *service* and pronounced "ser-VEES") and collective **minibuses** shuttle between all cities, towns, and villages. Hitchhiking is a common practice among Jordanians, though more so in the north than in the south, where a wagging thumb gesture is often mistaken for a friendly wave. *Let's Go*, however, does not recommend hitchhiking.

Taxis **Private taxis,** useful mainly in Amman, are yellow and conveniently have "taxi" written on them. Jordanian taxi drivers take their horns seriously, their fares a little less so, and the law not in the least. Insist that the driver use the meter. Most will. A few, however, specialize in ripping off newly arrived tourists; be wary of those driving souped-up, chrome-encrusted Mercedes. The starting fare is 150fils. Drivers may also charge extra (illegally) for large amounts of baggage.

    Service are shared taxis, usually white or gray Mercedes with a white sign written in Arabic on their roofs (أجرة). The front doors have the route and number on them (again in Arabic letters only). *Service* can be hailed en route. Payment takes place whenever the rider feels like it, traditionally just as the cab is negotiating an insanely sharp curve on two wheels. With drivers sneering at speed limits and holding their cars together with tin foil, *service* rides range from entertaining to traumatic. Travel within Amman is generally easier on foot (except when you have to go uphill, which somehow appears to be the case most of the time), but *service* are invaluable for intercity travel. There are specific *service* routes in Amman and between the central transport terminals in the larger cities. Within Amman, *service* cost 70 to 120fils; a ride from Amman to Aqaba goes for JD3.500. Shared taxis rarely run in the evenings and the long-distance ones may make only two or three trips per day. Schedules are (predictably) unpredictable—they leave when all five seats are occupied. If you get into a *service* alone and want to leave before it's full, you'll have to pay for five. (For routes and rates, see individual towns.)

Buses **Public buses** supplement the *service* taxis in Amman. The intercity bus network is sparse due to the monopoly granted by the government to the **Jordan Express Tourist Transport (JETT)** company. These buses, however, cover the most popular routes, and private minibuses travel to more remote areas. Regular service on JETT buses includes daily schedules from Amman to Aqaba, Petra, Ma'an, the King Hussein/Allenby Bridge, Damascus, and Cairo via Aqaba and the Sinai. (For details about schedules and the station, see Amman: Practical Information, p. 441.) JETT also sponsors tours to Jerash, Madaba, Petra, Ajlun, and the Desert Castles. For information, call (06) 664 146. The **Arabella** and **Hijazi** bus companies travel to Jerash and Irbid. **Minibuses** are also used for intercity transport.

    Bus fares are slightly lower than *service* rates, but buses travel more slowly. The JETT luxury coaches cost more than regular buses but are air-conditioned, and those running from Amman to Aqaba come with hosts, professional wrestling videos, and highly dramatic Egyptian movies. Do note, however, that you will be charged for each and every "in-flight" bologna and mayo sandwich you eat, regardless of how earnest the attendant seems when handing you one. The buses depart more or less on schedule. Booking ahead is advisable and often necessary. Most towns have one main terminal shared by intercity buses and *service;* Amman and Irbid have several. In Amman, most buses follow the pattern of *service,* with traffic to the north leaving from Abdali Station and buses to the south leaving from Wahadat Station.

Cars Some of Jordan's greatest attractions are not served by the public transportation system. For groups of four to six, renting a car can be an affordable and efficient way to reach less accessible sights. With a car, for example, the round-trip to Azraq via four or five desert castles can be done in eight to twelve hours. The unsurpassed Kings' Highway route, hardly served by other modes of transportation, can be seen from a private car in another full day. Some rental agencies will even let you return a car from Amman to be picked up in Aqaba; ask around.

If you can't split the costs, car rental in Jordan will break your budget. Most rental agencies charge JD22-29 per day, including insurance, plus 45-55fils per kilometer. Unlimited mileage deals are cheaper (JD17-20 per day), but you must rent the car for at least a week. (For details, see Amman and Aqaba: Practical Information, p. 441 and p. 463.) Always ask whether the car has a fire extinguisher. No joke. The desert heat warrants it and the police require it. The four-wheel drive cars that companies push are unnecessary except to reach Qasr at-Touba, south of Azraq. Ordinary cars will do, even at Wadi Rum. Government-set rental fares for car type A are US$19.10 per day, US$115 per week, and US$0.044 per km.

Gas costs about 220fils per liter. The law requires seatbelts to be worn (JD5 fine for naughtiness), and speeding tickets can cruise to an exorbitant JD50. Many rental companies require an International Driver's License (see International Driver's License, p. 10). **Road accidents** should be reported to the traffic police (tel. 896 390); for an **ambulance** call 199.

Hitchhiking *Service* and minibuses are cheap enough to make hitching unnecessary. In remote areas such as along the King's Highway, *service* and minibuses are less frequent. For those feckless die-hards who insist on hitching, rides between small towns (Jordan Valley, Amman environs, Irbid area) are easy to come by. As with anything in the Middle East, be aware that even short waits in the sun can be dangerous; those who hitch bring lots of water and cover their heads.

Those who try hitchhiking within a city (Amman, Irbid, Jerash, Ajlun) are pestered by empty taxis' horns as they careen by. The steady stream of trucks serving the port facilities compensates, with many drivers eager for company on their long trans-Jordan hauls. To flag down an approaching vehicle, travelers stick their arms out with their palms facing the ground.

> *Let's Go* does not recommend hitchhiking. Women especially should never hitchhike alone. Hitching in the Wadi Araba highway is prohibited for all.

■■■ MONEY MATTERS

Currency and Exchange The **Jordanian dinar (JD)** is a decimal currency, divided into 1000fils. Prices are always labeled in fils, but the usual spoken practice is to call 10fils a piaster (pt). Thus, 500fils will be written as 500fils, but referred to as 50pt. A piaster is called a *qirsh* and 0.5pt is a *t'arifeh*. Clear? Bills come in denominations of JD20, 10, 5, 1, and 500fils. Coins are silver for 250fils, 100, 50, and 25, and copper for 10 and 5. Since confusion enriches life, the numerals Westerners call "Arabic" are not used in the Arab world, so it's a good idea to learn the Arab forms (see the handy-dandy Language Glossary, p. 483, in the back of your good ol' *Let's Go*). The currency itself is marked also with Western-friendly numbers.

Currency exchange is easy to find in Amman, but more difficult elsewhere. Bank exchange hours are regularly 9:30am to 12:30pm, with some banks opening from 4 to 5:45pm as well. Branches of the national **Housing Bank** (Bank al-Iskan) are the best bets outside Amman. Queen Alia Airport has exchange facilities for incoming passengers. A passport is *always* required to change traveler's checks. Credit cards are only accepted in expensive hotels. There are ATMs in Jordan, but they don't take anything but the cards of the particular bank; don't bank on them.

Tipping A tip of 10% is expected in restaurants, unless "service included" appears on the menu. Taxi drivers do not expect tips, but will round off fares to their advantage. Members of large sight-seeing groups tip the bus driver about 500fils. A small tip (300-500fils) to the room cleaners and porters in hotels is appropriate.

Business Hours Jordan's business timetable has been shaped by various natural, religious, and economic forces. The desert sun converts the lunchtime hours into a Mideastern siesta. Most stores and offices open around 8 to 9:30am, close from 1 to 3 or 4pm, and open again in the late afternoon. In Amman, retail stores usually close around 8 or 9pm, when the transportation system also dwindles. In some areas, such as Jabal Hussein, stores close as late as 11pm. Banks and government offices retain only a skeleton staff in the afternoon; if you care about getting something done, do it in the morning. (Government offices open Sat.-Thurs. 8am-2pm; Ramadan 9:30am-2:30pm.)

Friday is a holiday throughout the Muslim world, although it is less scrupulously kept in Amman and Aqaba. Government offices and institutions close, but some shops are open in the morning (until about noon). Foreign banks and offices generally observe both Friday and Saturday as holidays, though they may keep longer hours during the rest of the week. Museums are closed on Tuesdays. The most reliable schedule for the last few centuries has been the Islamic call to prayer: five times per day, the faithful kneel facing the holy city of Mecca.

■■■ ACCOMMODATIONS

Though the Jordanian government has gone to great lengths to establish adequate, regulated accommodations for some tourists, budget travelers have been left out for the most part. Regulated tourist hotels charge prices as high as Jordan's mid-summer temperatures. Jordan has no Hostelling International hostels.

Hotels Hotels in Jordan are inspected annually and regulated by the government according to a five-star system. Bargaining is difficult, but hotel owners may be more flexible in the off-season winter months. Fall and spring are the busiest times throughout Jordan, though sunny Aqaba sees the most activity during the winter and spring seasons. Single women may feel uncomfortable at some of the cheaper hotels, and may on occasion not be admitted. Jordanian law bars unmarried couples from sharing a room. The law is rarely applied to foreign travelers, but if you are asked to split up, console yourself by remembering that in cheap hotels, the price is usually per bed rather than per room.

The Ministry of Tourism provides a comprehensive list of classified hotels and their prices (available at the Ministry's Public Relations Office in Amman). No matter how hard the government tries, however, chaos still prevails; every hotel has the official prices listed in Arabic (for instance, JD14 for singles in one-star hotels, JD18 for doubles), and cheaper prices listed in English.

Most hotels add a 10% service charge; ask whether it's included in the quoted price. If business is slow, use this surcharge as a bargaining chip. Some of the cheaper places charge an extra 500fils for a hot shower; many have modern toilets, though several still use the uncomfortable hole-in-the-ground system. The unclassified places usually have clean beds, but toilets and showers can be heinous. Hotel owners may ask to hold your passport for the length of your stay.

Alternative Accommodations Hotels are rare outside Amman, Aqaba, and Petra. The primary alternatives are government **Rest Houses,** with rates hovering around JD13 per person per night. Not all Rest Houses have overnight facilities. To stay at one, especially in spring or fall, try to reserve in advance with the **Tourist Investment Department,** P.O. Box 2863, Amman, Jordan (tel. (06) 813 243).

Camping Camping is an option nearly everywhere in the country, although organized facilities are virtually nonexistent. Favorite sites include the beach north of Aqaba, the caves and ledges at Petra (now illegal there), and Dibbin National Park. Camping is allowed next to most of the government Rest Houses (free or JD1-2 per person per night, plus 10% government tax), and many hostels and hotels will let you camp out on the roof for a small fee. You'll need a sleeping bag for the cool summer nights, and winter evenings can bring sub-freezing temperatures.

You can spend a night with the Bedouin, whom you'll find on the outskirts of most towns and scattered around the desert. Tea, Arabic coffee, and meals always accompany an invitation, although showers and toilets rarely follow. While the Bedouin won't accept money, a pack of Marlboros is always appreciated.

■■■ KEEPING IN TOUCH

Postage stamps may be purchased from 7am to 7pm at the downtown post office in Amman and during regular business hours at other post offices. An **air mail letter** to North America costs 320fils, an aerogramme or postcard is 240fils; the cost to Europe is 240fils and 160fils, respectively. Mail from Jordan to North America and Europe takes one to two weeks. International **Express Mail Service (EMS)** is available in major post offices. **Packages** may be sent from any post office. **Poste Restante** operates at the downtown post office in Amman and in the larger cities. **American Express** offices, located in Amman and Aqaba (look for International Traders offices), also hold mail.

Although the **telephone system** was revamped several years ago, international lines are often overloaded, especially around holidays. The rare pay telephones are particularly erratic and require 50fils whether or not your call goes through. If you ask shop owners where to find the nearest pay phone, they will probably invite you to use theirs as long as the call is local. Another option is to use a hotel phone, but be sure to inquire about surcharges before doing so. Note that telephone offices, though separate from post offices, are usually next door.

International calls can be made in Amman from the telephone center near the downtown post office (see Practical Information, p. 441). Three minutes to North America will cost about JD6.600. In other parts of Jordan, international calls can be made at luxury hotels, where service will be faster, clearer, and even more expensive. Late night and early morning are the best times to dial overseas. An easier option is to use a private phone and reimburse the owner. You can dial directly to the U.S., Europe, and Australia (JD1.540 per min. 10pm-8am, JD2.200 otherwise; for all international calls, dial 00 and international code). For an international operator, dial 0132. Dial 131 for information on local codes. For other **information,** dial 121. No **collect calls** can be made from Jordan. U.S. **calling cards** don't work either, annoyingly and inexplicably enough.

The **international phone code** for calling to Jordan is 962.

Telegrams can be sent to North America (180fils per word) from larger post offices, the telephone office, and some hotels.

■■■ DRESS & ETIQUETTE

Jordan is predominantly Muslim and socially conservative, making modest dress a necessity. Though you will not be arrested, inappropriate dress will not only alienate you from the very people you have come to meet, but also encourage stares, comments, and even touching from strangers. The same modesty is required of both men and women. The code is simple: Do not wear shorts. Your pants should come down to at least mid-shin (women may wear pants). Shirts should cover the shoulders and upper arms. Women should wear head scarves in mosques. Feet can be exposed freely. The exception to these rules is hedonistic Aqaba, where both men and women can wear shorts. You're also allowed a little more freedom if you're going out at night or to the pool in Amman. Looking foreign gives you extra leeway in these two towns, but don't push it: women risk greater harassment and even a butt-pinching if they wear shorts in downtown Amman. Non-Muslims should not enter mosques during prayers, which occur five times per day.

LIFE AND TIMES

■■■ GOVERNMENT & POLITICS

After about ten minutes in Jordan, you'll notice pictures of a little bald man with a smooth smile everywhere you look. Refrain from jokes; he's the king, and you are in his kingdom; Jordan is the fiefdom of Hussein bin Talal. The kingdom was a 1921 gift from Britain to the Hashemite royal family (for details see Introduction to the Region, p. 36), who proudly trace their lineage directly to the Prophet Muhammad.

King Hussein has ruled since 1953. He divorced his first two queens, the gracious Dina and Muna (a Briton who changed her name from Antoinette Gardiner); his third, Alia (a Palestinian), died in a plane crash. "It was the Amman Go-Kart Club that really brought us together more informally," the king sighed about Muna. The current queen, Noor (née Lisa Halaby), is an Arab-American and a graduate of Princeton. Hussein's brother Crown Prince Hassan serves as advisor and heir to the throne. Educated in Britain, King Hussein is generally moderate; but, as Palestinians will tell you, remembering their 20,000 dead from Black September 1970, he can be brutal if his throne is at stake. Above all, he is a brilliant politician; these skills have kept him alive through several wars. (Luck has also been a factor; the same bullets that killed his grandfather, King Abdallah, bounced off a medal on the young Hussein's chest.) With the death of Kim Il Sung of North Korea in 1994, Hussein became the longest-ruling head of state in the world.

A meeting between King Hussein and Yitzhak Rabin in August 1994 opened the border between Aqaba and Eilat and lead to the end of Jordan's 46-year-old policy of non-recognition of Israel. Much of Jordan's population is of Palestinian descent. Some Palestinians have very successfully integrated themselves into Jordanian society; others live in refugee camps harboring the pipe-dream of returning home to Palestine. In the summer of 1988, King Hussein cut all ties with the West Bank, allowing the Jordanian government to focus its efforts on relieving economic ills.

King Hussein's rule is a constant balancing act in the face of such pressures. He has accommodated and integrated his Palestinian subjects over the years, opening his cabinet to them as well as to the Bedouin that are the bedrock of the monarchy's support. When refugees from the 1948 and 1967 Wars flooded out of Palestine, Jordan was the only Arab country that offered them full citizenship. The conservative Hashemites have faced opposition from pan-Arabists, Nasserists, Palestinian nationalists, and, most recently, the Muslim Brotherhood. An attempt at democratic reform didn't turn out as the monarchy had hoped; in Jordan's first general elections in 22 years, held in November 1989, Islamists won almost half the seats in parliament. Regardless, reform has continued. In September 1992, King Hussein approved a law permitting political parties, which had been banned in 1957. Jordan's first multi-party election since 1954 took place in November 1993. A new one-person, one-vote policy weakened the Islamists; and the first woman ever, a Circassian, was elected to Parliament. On the international level, a tide of pan-Arabism and defiance in the face of Western power-mongering led many Jordanians, including King Hussein, to support Saddam Hussein in the Gulf War (1991). But the weakening of Iraq since the war has allowed the ever-flexible monarchy to reingratiate with the West. Meanwhile, the King's surgery for cancer in August 1992 has raised the issue of succession.

A flood of refugees into Jordan from Kuwait and Iraq following the Gulf War has unfortunately begun to disrupt the normally placid Jordanian lifestyle. Where driving used to be a pleasant excursion, Jordan's cities are now overcrowded.

ECONOMY

■■■ ECONOMY

Unlike its Arab neighbors, Jordan has neither oil reserves nor abundant natural resources. The country remains dependent upon Arab and American financial aid to augment income, one source of which is the export of phosphates and pre-season vegetables grown in the Jordan Valley. Remittances from Palestinian and Jordanian workers in the Gulf states traditionally constituted Jordan's main source of income; but after the Gulf War about 320,000 of them (mostly from Kuwait) returned to Jordan to scramble for jobs in Amman.

Back when the Iran-Iraq War broke out in 1980, Iraq became a major importer of Jordanian goods and services; and the Jordanian economy boomed. In the late 1980s, when Iraq began threatening not to pay its war debts, Jordanian exporters were left with a heap of worthless Iraqi IOUs. In April 1989, following steep government-imposed price hikes on gasoline and other goods, Jordanians took to the streets in protest until King Hussein fired then Prime Minister Zaid Rifa'i and, more importantly, instituted democratic reforms. Stability returned; and a 1991 growth rate of 1% was actually a step up from 1989 and 1990.

The aftermath of the 1990-91 Gulf War dealt a devastating blow to the economy, bringing a 1990 annual per capita income of US$2000 down to US$1400 today. Jordan's refusal to join the anti-Iraq coalition of states cost the country dearly, spurring the United States, along with Saudi Arabia and the other Gulf countries, to suspend most aid to Jordan. In addition, the Palestinian and Jordanian workers in the Gulf were largely replaced by Egyptians, whose government the Saudis found to be more politically correct. Among the returnees, unemployment is at 80%. Unemployment in the general population has hit an alarming 30%.

The August 1994 Washington Declaration signed by King Hussein and Yitzhak Rabin of Israel put an end to the state of war between the two countries and re-activated the ATM between Washington and Amman. US$220 million in Jordanian debt was wiped out, with an additional US$350 million expected. England followed suit, relieving Jordan of a smaller debt. Unfortunately, this has had no real effect on the current state of the economy. Jordan hadn't been paying its debts anyway; what the economy needs is income.

■■■ FESTIVALS & HOLIDAYS

The most important festivals of the year are Islamic celebrations (see When To Go, p. 1); the national holidays are **Arab Revolution and Army Day** (June 10, marking the 1916 Arab Revolt against Ottoman rule), **Labor Day** (May 1), **Independence Day** (May 25), and, of course, King Hussein's **Accession Day** (Aug. 11) and **Birthday** (Nov. 14). Government offices and banks close on national holidays.

For the Christian community, the **Easter Celebrations** (some following the Gregorian calendar, others the Julian) are the most spectacular of the year. **Christmas** is a smaller feast, especially for the Coptic and Abyssinian Churches, which celebrate the holiday during the second week of January rather than on December 25.

The two-week **Jerash Festival** is held every year during July or August. Amidst brilliantly illuminated Roman ruins and inside ancient amphitheaters, visitors witness performances by international artists. For more information, contact the **Jerash Festival Office** in Amman (tel. (06) 675 199).

■■■ LANGUAGE

The official language of the Hashemite Kingdom of Jordan is Arabic. However, the spoken Arabic dialect differs from classical Arabic and varies from that used in Egypt, the Gulf States, and North Africa. Very minor differences in pronunciation separate the dialects of Jordanians, Palestinians, Lebanese, and Syrians. See Language Glossary, p. 483 for more on Arabic.

Due to decades of British colonial rule, English is Jordan's second language, taught at both public and private schools. Almost all Jordanians have a knowledge of the language; many speak it quite well. Most signs are written in both Arabic and English, and Jordan Television's second channel broadcasts subtitled British and American programs after 8:30pm. French is taught as a third language by private schools and occasionally spoken badly by upper class Lebanese-wanna-bes.

■■■ THE ARTS

LITERATURE

The Arabic language is shared by 21 nations, and Arabic literature from these countries is the proud heritage of the whole of the Arab world. The Jordanian region itself has a long tradition of prose: the oldest example of a Semitic script, the Mesha Stele, was found in Karak. Unfortunately, few Jordanian works are translated into other languages and thus remain inaccessible to most foreigners.

Among English travel accounts, C.M. Doughty's *Arabia Deserta* and Wilfred Thesiger's more recent *Arabian Sands* are powerful adventure stories inspired by a romanticized version of Bedouin lifestyle. T.E. Lawrence's *Seven Pillars of Wisdom* contains vivid descriptions of the battles fought and the territory explored during the Arab Revolt of 1916; even if you don't reach Wadi Rum in the Jordanian desert, see David Lean's magnificent *Lawrence of Arabia* on the big screen. King Abdallah's two-volume *Memoirs* and King Hussein's *Uneasy Lies the Head* are self-serving but dispel once and for all the myth that it's good to be king. The Arab Legion chief of the 1940s and 50s, John Bagot Glubb (Glubb Pasha), wrote *A Soldier With the Arabs* and several books based on his life. A little less adventurous but more erudite is Jonathan Raban's *Arabia: A Journey through the Labyrinth*. Gertrude Bell, one of the first female Western travelers in the region, writes of her journeys through Jordan and Syria in *The Desert and the Sown*.

For the archaeologically and historically inclined there are G.L. Harding's *Antiquities of Jordan* and Julian Huxley's *From an Antique Land*. Ian Browning's *Petra* is wonderfully comprehensive. Finally, Agatha Christie's *Argument with Death* is a light introduction to the mesmerizing power of Petra.

VISUAL ARTS

Both the Jordanian government and private groups are taking measures to promote and foster the arts. Like that of other countries of the Arab world, Jordanian art is an expression of Arab and often Muslim identity. But Jordanians are not sticklers for the traditional; contemporary artists have many more Western tendencies and use visual art as an outlet for personal as well as cultural expression. Modernity is eroding the traditional Islamic taboo against the portrayal of animate objects. Jordan's architecture, painting, and sculpture have all developed substantially in this century.

When it comes to folk art, Jordanians do abide by tradition. Techniques developed over centuries make for skillful weavers of wool and goat-hair rugs and tapestries. Leather handicrafts, pottery, ceramics, and coral curios also belong to the family of mastered Jordanian folk art. Painters often display their work in galleries in Amman, with nature, Bedouin life, and longing for Palestine as common subjects. It is wood-carving, though, that is the Jordanian specialty. Artists can do beautiful carvings of your name right on the street, for an appropriate fee, naturally. You will find most of these crafts sold proudly on the streets of Jordan.

POPULAR AND FOLK CULTURE

Homesick Yankees who aren't sticklers for highbrow culture can look for Bart Simpson to brighten their day or *Step by Step* to remind them of those Saturday nights in front of the TV. These and other popular American and British shows appear on Jordanian television with Arabic subtitles. More authentic Jordanian programming includes music videos and disco dance extravaganzas. Much of the pop music in

Jordan is Egyptian; listen for traditional Arabic themes under the cacophony of not-quite-Western sounds. Jordanians do, however, have their own traditional expressions of pop culture, most notably a strong oral tradition of stories, songs, and ballads. Villages often have their own individualized songs commemorating births, circumcisions, weddings, funerals, and planting. Several Cossack dances, including a sword dance that has to be seen to be believed, are popular in Jordan, as is *dabkeh,* a dance performed to the resonating rhythm of feet pounding on the floor. Eavesdrop on weddings in poorer neighborhoods for a taste of traditional folk music and for the women's salutatory shouts followed by ululation *(ha-WEEE-ha …).*

■■■ FOOD

Jordanian cuisine has evolved through centuries of Bedouin cooking. The national dish, *mensaf,* ideally consists of eight to ten kilograms of rice on a large tray, topped with pine nuts, an entire lamb or goat, and a yogurt-based sauce. The Bedouin serve the head of the lamb on top, reserving the prize delicacies—eyes and tongue—for speechless and visually jaded guests. The right hand is used to ball the rice, and the flat bread to pull off chunks of meat and dip them into the warm *jamid* sauce.

Most other dishes include the main ingredients of *mensaf.* Traditional dinners are served between 2-3pm. Popular dinners include *musakhkhan*—chicken baked with olive oil and onions and a delicious spice called *summaq,* served on bread—and *mahshi,* a tray of vine leaves, squash, or eggplant stuffed with mincemeat, rice, and onions. *Mezze,* loosely translated as "hors d'oeuvres," encompasses a wide range of dishes including hummus with olive oil, *mutabal* (an eggplant dip), *labneh* (thickened yogurt), cucumbers, tomatoes, and pickles. Supper is usually smaller; hummus, cheese, and sometimes *fuul* form a standard breakfast. A staple is *za'tar,* thyme mixed with sesame seeds and various spices and eaten either with little pieces of bread dipped first into olive oil and then into the mix, or pizza-style.

At restaurants, if the menu is in English, you can't afford the food. *Kabab* is skewered lamb, *shish tawouq* chicken, and *kufta* grilled ground beef with parsley. Hummus and falafel are cheap options, as is *shawerma,* delicious sandwiches made of lamb (or chicken, a more recent invention) sliced into Arabic bread with *summaq,* *tahina* sauce, vegetables, and sometimes pickles. Many deli-like places sell *mu'ajjanat,* dough wrapped around or topped with spinach *(sabanekh),* lamb (in which case it's called *sfeeha*), cheese, or *za'tar* and olive oil and then baked. Yum. Fresh *ka'ik,* a bread ring with sesame seeds, is a street favorite, as is corn-on-the-cob. With *ka'ik* you will be given *za'tar* in a piece of newspaper for dipping

Desserts include *ba'laweh, kinafeh (*made of soft cheese and shredded wheat, baked, soaked in syrup, and garnished with pistachios), *bashouseh* (wheat and syrup baked to moist goodness), pistachio nougat from candy stores, and ice cream. Don't get chocolate, fool. Mango, pistachio, and *mastika* are the best flavors.

Water in Amman is piped in from Azraq oasis and the Euphrates River in Iraq. Although certainly potable, it is hardly pure. Toting bottled water (300fils, more at restaurants and tourist haunts) or iodine tablets, like extra molars, is a sign of wisdom. Jordan is a clean country; even salads should be safe to eat.

Jordanians drink tremendous amounts of tea *(shay),* almost always made with mint *(na'na').* Stereotypes hold that hicks *(fellaheen,* farmers) drink theirs syrupy sweet; restaurants will assume you are one unless you prove your gentility by asking for *sukkar aleel* (not too much sugar). A cup of Arabic coffee *(qahwa),* a thick, black, bitter-sweet brew, is espresso-strong. American coffee and instant coffee (Nescafé), both way-inferior and for wimps only, are also available at restaurants.

Because most Muslims agree that drinking **alcohol** is prohibited by Islam, imbibing in Jordan is subject to some restrictions and conventions. It is illegal to possess alcohol in public, unless at a place licensed for liquor. Drinking and driving, or even having alcohol in the car, would be a big mistake. Nonetheless, many Jordanians drink, and with no drinking age, anyone who looks older than 16 may buy at a liquor store (usually owned by Christians; bottle of vodka around JD10). Imported beer is the universal drink (Amstel 900fils). *'Araq* is an anise-seed hard alcohol that is mixed with water until a cloudy white suspension results. Liquor is very expensive, especially at bars and restaurants, where a drink may cost JD3.500-6.

> On September 1, 1994, the government, anticipating an increase in tourism resulting from the treaty with Israel, substantially raised the prices for all tourist sights. The prices listed here, researched in June and July 1994, have been raised by as much as 400% (we were able to update Petra—it was JD5, now it's JD20).

■ Amman عمان

The artistically dangerous dance of Amman's automobiles along the city's seven hills (*jabal*, plural *jibāl*) leaves visitors agape in Jordan's capital. Horns honk incessantly but are overwhelmed five times a day by the beautiful call to prayer echoing from the minarets which grace the city's quarters. The din of the traffic will soon take second stage in the visitor's mind as greetings of "Welcome to Jordan," come from the smiling faces of Amman's shopkeepers, bus drivers, and others who insist that the "Jordanian ethic" is, above all else, hospitality. In the evening, when the sun goes down and the lights go up, Amman offers its immaculate, jasmine-scented streets as the perfect setting for lazy summertime strolls.

The Ammonite capital in biblical times and later the Greco-Roman city of Philadelphia, modern Amman was a village in the decades preceding 1948. Following the Arab-Israeli wars of 1948 and 1967, many Palestinian refugees ended up in Amman, which boomed as a result. Palestinians now form around 70% of Jordan's population, but sometimes experience discrimination at the hands of the Jordanian ruling minority. Some of these Palestinians are highly successful doctors, businesspeople, bankers, and politicians, while others still live in Amman's huge refugee camps and dream about returning to Palestine. Egyptian and southeast Asian workers also form a segment of the city's population. The city's nearly bursting seams were further expanded by the arrival of a wave of immigrants from Iraq and Kuwait following the 1991 Gulf War. The pre-1948 population of 6000 has exploded to well over a million inhabitants today, roughly one third of Jordan's total population.

Amman's central location makes it the country's principal transportation hub and the base for exploration of Jordan's other sights. Reasonable hotel prices combine with government services, embassies, and consulates to make a capital city stay a painless experience; but don't sacrifice time here that could be better spent marveling at Petra, Jerash, and Jordan's rural landscapes.

■■■ ORIENTATION

Take advantage of Amman's summits to get a perspective on this roller-coaster city. Rocky **Jabal al Qala'a** (Citadel Hill), where the Archaeological Museum sits amidst unearthed remains of Roman and Umayyad palaces, temples, and hilltop fortifications, provides a panoramic view of winding streets, tall buildings, mosques, and ruins, all of which will serve as useful landmarks.

Any round object dropped to the ground will roll downhill to Amman's downtown district, **Al Balad,** which is neatly framed by the seven hills. Streets from the city's large western areas pour off the *jibāl* into **King Faisal Street,** the perpetually crowded heart of the downtown commercial district. Faisal St. runs to the **Al Husseini Mosque,** the center of modern Amman. Several blocks southwest is the market; to the northeast lie the graceful Roman Amphitheater and the new piazza.

Though distances between *jibāl* appear short on a map, traversing these slopes can be a hack hiker's nightmare. **Jabal Amman,** along whose summit you can see the neon signatures of budget-breaking luxury hotels, is the governmental and diplomatic core of the city. Amman's eight **numbered traffic circles** follow a line leading westward out of town; traffic circles beyond Third Circle have been replaced by busy intersections. Although the city is earnestly attempting to rename these intersections "squares," each is still fondly called a "circle," or *duwwar*. From Seventh Circle, traffic heads south to Queen Alia International Airport and the Desert Highway (Aqaba 335km), to the Kings' Highway via Madaba (35km; Karak 125km; Petra 260km), and via Na'ur to the Dead Sea and on to Jerusalem (90km). From Eighth Circle, you can continue west to Wadi Seer, or head north to Jerash (50km).

To the northwest of Jabal Amman slopes the suburb of **Shmeisani,** with its numerous luxury hotels and American-style fast food restaurants. **Jabal al Weibdeh,** across the *wadi* to the north of Jabal Amman, is a quiet middle-class residential district and an appropriate spot for an evening stroll. Its northern slope picks up the normal Amman pace along **King Hussein Street,** where the JETT and **Abdali** (north) Bus Stations have attracted a swarm of food stands and hotels. The blue dome and octagonal minaret of the enormous nearby **King Abdallah Mosque** stare down on Abdali Station and are visible from the surrounding *jabals*. Opposite the mosque stand smiling, waving, gun-toting guards at the **National Parliament** building. **Jabal Hussein,** up the slope to the northeast, is residential as far as its northern boundary at **Ministry of Interior Circle** (officially known as Jamal Abd an-Nasser Square), dominated by the Housing Bank complex, an overgrown Love Boat next to the Forte Grand hotel. From this circle, traffic heads northwest to Jerash. To the south, in the direction of the airport, rises **Jabal Ashrafiyyeh;** its ornate **Abu Darwish Mosque** can be seen above the **Wahadat** (south) Bus Station and the Wahadat Palestinian refugee camp. Beyond the other residential *jibāl,* the city recedes into the surrounding desert sands.

The names of the streets in downtown Amman are not preserved in anything as gauche as street signs, and inquiries about street names will produce blank stares. Directions usually run something like: "to the right of the third palm tree, in front of the mosque with the green dome." (Allah forbid anyone should, on a whim, repaint the green dome blue.) Occasionally, street signs are in English and street names listed on maps, but in general, successful navigation of Amman depends on facility with prominent landmarks. In order to avoid unnecessarily long taxi rides, remember the King Abdallah and Al Husseini Mosques, the names of a *duwwar* or two, the Roman Amphitheater, the Wahadat camp, and the Abdali bus station.

■■■ TRANSPORTATION

WITHIN AMMAN

To reach locations within the city or to find the departure point for buses and *service,* ask a downtown shopkeeper. At a minimum, you'll be pointed in the right direction; quite possibly you'll be escorted there, invited to dinner, and offered permanent lodging (okay, maybe we're taking it a bit too far). You can flag **buses** and **service** anywhere along their routes, but *service* are often full (they take five passengers) from the beginning to the end of their prescribed courses. Public transportation stops at 8 or 9pm, a couple of hours earlier on Fridays; after that, walking in Amman is a great alternative for those with strong legs. There are also yellow **taxis,** cheap compared to cabs in the U.S. or Europe, which serve a life-saving function when you feel a need for speed. Metered cabs prowl the streets in search of fares until 11pm, sometimes later. Cabs charge 150fils plus 100fils per km. Pay around 500fils to go from downtown to Third Circle or from Third to Sixth Circle, 350fils from downtown to Abdali costs around 350fils. A taxi between the two bus/*service* stations (Abdali and Wahadat; see Intercity Transportation, below) should cost

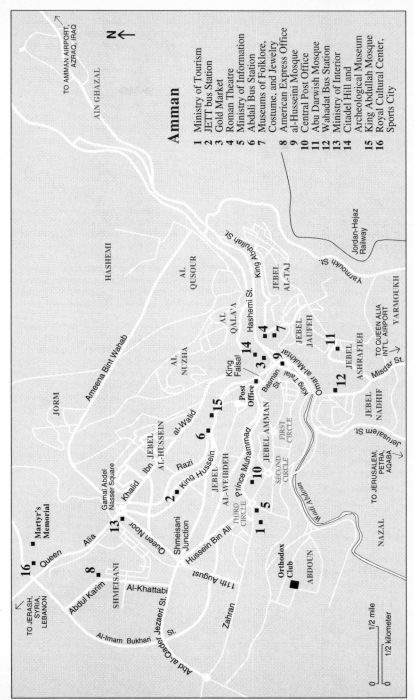

Amman

1 Ministry of Tourism
2 JETT bus Station
3 Gold Market
4 Roman Theatre
5 Ministry of Information
6 Abdali Bus Station
7 Museums of Folklore,
  Costume, and Jewelry
8 American Express Office
9 al-Husseini Mosque
10 Central Post Office
11 Abu Darwish Mosque
12 Wahadat Bus Station
13 Ministry of Interior
14 Citadel Hill and
  Archeological Museum
15 King Abdullah Mosque
16 Royal Cultural Center,
  Sports City

TRANSPORTATION

800fils. The trip along Jabal Amman from First to Eighth Circles should cost no more than 800fils; check to make sure the meter is running. (See Getting Around, p. 428.)

Within Amman, **buses** travel from the downtown area and cost about 100fils for city trips, and slightly more for trips to areas just outside Amman. Flag any bus traveling in your direction and ask the driver if it stops where you want to go, or ask at any bus station which bus you should get on. Pay your fare after the ride has begun. Drivers and their assistants don't like making big change, so carry 100fils pieces with you. Buses going on different routes may display the same number, so what worked one time may not the next. Unless you will be in Amman for a while and have time to figure out a method behind the bus madness, transportation by *service* or yellow taxi will be much easier on the nerves. Still, these are the alleged routes:

#10 and 53: Travel to the university and the American and British Institutes.
#10 and 59: To the Sports City (north of Shmeisani).
#21, 23, and 24: Past the Armenian Quarter and the Abu Darwish Mosque on the way to Wahadat Station.
#31B: To Queen Alia Airport (750fils). Leaves from and arrives at Abdali Station.
#39: Climbs Jabal Amman to the numbered circles.
#41-45: Heads directly to Third Circle before passing Fourth, Fifth, Sixth, and Seventh Circles.
#53-61: Passes Abdali Station, the JETT offices, and Ministry of Interior Circle.
#61: Travels on Jabal Hussein to Duwwar Fira.

Again, *service* within Amman are cheap, reliable, and provide an opportunity to meet Jordanians. They are not numbered; their routes are listed on the doors in Arabic. All routes within the city originate downtown, where you can ask for help finding stops. You would do best to mention major destinations or landmarks.

Travels on Jabal Amman between Center City and Third Circle, passing First and Second Circles (70fils).
Starts on Basman St. (look for the Basman Theater) and travels on Jabal Amman to Malik Abd Ribiya St. between Second and Third Circles (70fils).
Starts on Kureisha St. and travels on Jabal Amman to Fourth Circle (90fils).
Runs from Basman St. to Al Amaneh Circle and gardens, passing near all points of interest on Jabal al-Weibdeh (70fils).
From Basman St., travels up Jabal al-Weibdeh to Queen Alia Institute, just uphill from Abdali Station (70fils).
Starts at terminus on Malik Ghazi St. (better known as Cinema al-Hussein St.) then travels along Kings Faisal and Hussein St. to Jamal Abd an-Nasser Circle, passing Abdali and JETT Stations (80fils).
Starts by Cinema al-Hussein St. and runs past Abdali Station to Shmeisani near the Ambassador Hotel and the Gallery Alia (70fils).

Service and minibuses to Wahadat Station start at Kureisha St. (also called Sakfi Seil) near Petra Bank and pass near Abu Darwish Mosque on Jabal Ashrafiyyeh. *Service* directly to Wahadat Station from Abdali costs 120fils. Another route starts at Shabsough St. near the Gold Market downtown, passing Abdali Station and Jabal Hussein to Ministry of Interior Circle (80fils). *Service* between Ministry of Interior and Third Circle cost 70fils.

INTERCITY

Buses to the north central and northwestern parts of the country, including the Jordan Valley, leave from **Abdali Bus Station** on King Hussein St. on Jabal al-Weibdeh. Destinations include Jerash, Ajlun, Irbid, Salt, the King Hussein/Allenby Bridge, as well as Damascus. **Hashemi Street Station,** near the Roman amphitheater, launches traffic to the northeast, including Zarqa, Mafraq, and points east of Irbid. Traffic to and from the south is based at **Wahadat Station,** several km from downtown Amman between the Abu Darwish Mosque and the Wahadat Refugee Camp.

Buses from here go to Madaba, Karak, Ma'an, Wadi Musa, and Aqaba. The **JETT** bus station, serving major towns in Jordan, Syria, and Iraq, is on King Hussein St., up the road from Abdali Bus Station (see Practical Information, below). It is wise to book bus tickets at least one day in advance. Intercity *service* leave from the same stations as buses, to the same regions. Fares tend do be 40-50% more expensive than comparable bus fares. All prices, bus and *service* alike, are government-regulated.

■ ■ ■ PRACTICAL INFORMATION

Ministry of Tourism: P.O. Box 224 (tel. 642 311; fax 648 465). From the Third Circle on Jabal Amman, walk down Zahran St., which is to the left of the Ministry of Information. Distributes free maps, hotel price lists, and lovely color brochures. Seek out helpful Muhammad Abu Tayeh. Open Sat.-Thurs. 8am-2pm.

Ministry of Interior: On the southwestern side of the Ministry of Interior Circle near the Marriott Hotel, Jabal Hussein (tel. 663 111). Issues permits for visits to the West Bank and Jerusalem (150fils, pay in tent in front of office). Bring 2 passport photos, which may or may not be needed, depending on which official serves you and the alignment of the sun and planets. Permits will purportedly be ready the following afternoon, but plan ahead. Open Sat.-Thurs. 8am-2pm.

Australian Embassy (tel. 673 246): Fourth Circle on Jabal Amman. Helpful with foreign visas. Open Sun.-Thurs. 8am-2:30pm. Open for inquiries Mon. and Wed. 9am-noon.

Canadian Embassy (tel. 666 124): in Shmeisani near the Petra Bank. Open Sun.-Thurs. 8am-4pm.

Egyptian Embassy (tel. 605 175): Jabal Amman, between Fourth and Fifth Circles. Take a right by the Japanese embassy and continue about 100m down the road. Embassy is on the left. Bring a photo and JD12 before noon, pick up visa on the same afternoon. Open Sat.-Thurs. 9am-3pm.

Iraqi Embassy (tel. 623 175): between First and Second Circles on Jabal Amman. Neither British nor American citizens are allowed to visit Iraq.

Palestinian Office (tel. 645 228): c/o P.O. Box 910244, Wadi Saqra.

Syrian Embassy (tel. 641 076): Jabal Amman, up from Third Circle toward the reflecting building. Take a left at the intersection and head up the hill. The Syrian embassy is a shuttered, unmarked building on the right. For a visa bring 1 photo and JD10 for Americans, JD37.500 for British nationals. Make every effort to get a Syrian visa before arriving in Jordan. If you wait until you get to Jordan you may need a letter from your embassy explaining your reasons for visiting Syria, or you may be denied a visa. You must have a Jordanian entry stamp on your passport and no evidence of visits to the West Bank or Israel. Visas Sun.-Thurs. 9-11am.

U.K. Embassy (tel. 823 100): near the Orthodox Club in Abdoun. Consular division open Sun.-Thurs. 8:30am-noon.

U.S. Embassy (tel. 820 101; fax 813 759): in Abdoun. From Fifth Circle take the third right on the street that goes toward the Orthodox Club. The fortress-like complex is 500m down that road and can't be missed. Consular division open Sun.-Thurs. 8am-4pm, observes all Jordanian and most American holidays.

Currency Exchange: Banking hours are ordinarily Sat.-Wed. 8:30am-12:30pm and 4-5:45pm, Thurs. 8:30am-12:30pm, some are closed on Friday. Many authorized **money changers**, found downtown between the Al Husseini Mosque and the Post Office, are open daily, usually late into the evening. They offer roughly the same exchange rates as banks, but will not leech the commission that the banks demand. Bring your passport. Also, there is a **Citibank** (tel. 619 912 or 913; fax 619 914) near Third Circle on Prince Muhammad St. which intends to extend Visa cash-advance services to cardholders within the next year.

American Express: International Traders, P.O. Box 408 (tel. 607 014; fax 669 905), Abdul Hamid St. in Shmeisani, opposite the Ambassador Hotel. Holds mail and can obtain visas for cardholders, but sometimes there is a charge.

Thomas Cook: Space Tourism and Travel, P.O. Box 925072 (tel. 668 069; fax 688 919), in Shmeisani, behind the Haya Cultural Center *(Markaz Haya).* Open Sat.-Thurs. 8am-6pm.

Post Office (tel. 121 for inquiries): Prince Muhammad St., at the bottom of the staircase where the *service* to Al Balad lets you off. Stamps and **Poste Restante** open Sat.-Thurs. 8am-7pm, Fri. 8am-1pm. Cables can be sent from this office. **EMS international express mail** service (tel. 688 190) is near the main post office, off Bir Al Saba' St. on a dead-end street behind Qawar Arthroscopy Center. Open Sat.-Thurs. 8am-7pm, Fri. and holidays 8am-4pm.

Telephone Office: Exit to your left from the post office on Prince Muhammad St. and take the very first left onto frighteningly steep Omar al-Khayyam St. The telephone office is a pulse-quickening, sweat-inspiring 200m later. The sign is in Arabic, but you'll see the phones through 100 feet of windows. Open daily 7:30am-midnight. Rate for 3min. to the U.S. JD6.600, Great Britain JD5.445, 30% cheaper after 10pm. Pay at the desk after your call. Overseas calls can be made from any post office, from most hotels at any time for a surcharge, or from private homes. **Directory assistance:** Tel. 121. **Telephone code:** 06.

Airport: Queen Alia International Airport, 35km south of Amman. Buses leave from the airport for Abdali Bus Station every 30min. (5:30am-9pm, 750fils). A private taxi to the airport will cost JD10-15 and buses from Abdali 750fils, but there is no *service* to the airport. Bank and tourist office (tel. (08) 530 70; bank open 24 hrs.) in the airport. Jordanian visas, good for 1 month, available at the airport upon arrival. There is a JD10 exit fee when leaving the country.

Intercity Buses: JETT (tel. 664 146; fax 506 005) runs A/C buses to King Hussein/Allenby Bridge (Sun.-Fri. 6:30am, JD6); Petra (6:30am, JD10, round-trip tour including guide, horse, and lunch JD32.500); Aqaba (7, 9, 11am, 2:30, 3:30, 4pm, JD4; Damascus (7am, 3pm, JD4.500); Cairo (8am, JD30); and Baghdad (9, 11am, JD12 plus JD4 departure tax). Reserve 2 days in advance. Office open daily 8am-6pm. Other buses depart from either the Abdali or Wahadat bus stations, depending on direction. Fares to: Jerash 270fils, Ajlun 480fils, Irbid 820fils, Salt 200fils, and King Hussein/Allenby Bridge JD1.500. See Transportation, p. 438, for further information on JETT and other operators.

Intercity Service Taxis: From **Abdali Station,** fares to: Jerash 470fils, Ajlun 690fils, Irbid 850fils, Salt 300fils, and King Hussein/Allenby Bridge JD1.150; continuing on from Irbid, it's Umm Qeis 285fils and Al Himma 460fils. From **Wahadat Station,** fares to: Madaba 330fils, Karak down the King's Highway JD1.180, and Ma'an via the newer Desert Highway JD1.870; at Ma'an you can transfer for service to Wadi Musa (Petra) and Aqaba (475fils and JD1.130, respectively). Prices are government-regulated, but the naive tourist will surely get charged a higher price. Be prepared with accurate price information before you approach entrepreneurial *service* drivers!

Car Rental: Possibilities abound, but most are very expensive. Local agencies have the best deals. *Your Guide to Amman* lists numerous specials. International driver's license is often required, and age restrictions range from 18 to 21 years of age. Try **Avis,** main office at King Abdallah Gardens (tel. 699 420 or 430; fax 694 883). Also at the Alia Gateway Hotel near the airport (tel. (08) 510 00, ext. 8641).

English Bookstores: Slim pickin's. **University Bookstore** (tel. 636 339), on Jabal al-Weibdeh near Khalaf Circle, sells books on the archaeology of Jordan. Open 8am-7pm. The more expensive bookstores in the **Marriott** and **Intercontinental** hotels carry books on the Middle East and maps and guides to Jordan's sights; the latter also has many works on Palestinians. Most supermarkets sell local and foreign newspapers and magazines in English. The **Amman Bookshop** on Prince Muhammad St. near Third Circle also has supplies, dictionaries, and cards.

Publications: *Your Guide to Amman,* published monthly and available free at larger hotels, bookstores, and travel agencies, is full of helpful info.; pick one up upon arrival. *The Jordan Times,* a daily newspaper with excellent coverage of the Middle East and Africa, also lists useful telephone numbers, current government prices for fruits and vegetables (helpful for bargaining in the market), and cultural events in Amman. The *International Herald Tribune* arrives after 3pm one day late at newsstands. The weekly *Jerusalem Star* lists cultural events and piddling details from the lives of the royals.

Department of Antiquities: From Third Circle walk down Hussein Bin Ali St. to the mirrored-glass building, then up the street diagonally on the left (tel. 644 482 or 336). This is the national headquarters for research on digs. They have a library and distribute books and detailed maps highlighting archaeological sites. Open Sat.-Thurs. 8am-2pm.

Friends of Archaeology: P.O. Box 2440 (tel. 696 683), Jabal Amman. Facing west, take a left at Fourth Circle. Turn right, left, and left again, and the FoA center will be on your right. This private local organization sponsors weekly field trips to historical sites. Travelers can hitch a ride with some trips. Call the **American Center for Oriental Research (ACOR)** at 846 117 or read their newsletter, posted at cultural centers. Free field trips usually leave from Department of Antiquities. The ACOR office (see Accommodations: Outlying Districts, p. 444) has a bulletin board which describes all recent and current projects.

American Cultural Center (tel. 820 101; fax 813 759): Abdoun, inside the American Embassy Complex. Free American films every Sun. and Thurs., cable TV, and lectures by scholars and politicians visiting Jordan. Topics include Arab/American relations and Middle Eastern studies. Open Sun.-Thurs. 8am-4pm.

British Council: Rainbow St. (tel. 636 147). From First Circle walk 200m downhill along the right-hand tine of the fork; it's on the right. Sponsors films, lectures, and various other stimulating activities. Library (with A/C) open Sat.-Wed. 8am-1:30pm and 3:30-6:30pm, Thurs. 10am-1:30pm.

Laundry: Al-Jamm'a Laundry (tel. 847 857), on your first right heading away from the city past the main gate of Jordan University. Wash and dry JD2. Hotels may accommodate aspirants to cleanliness for a small fee.

Pharmacies: The *Jordan Times* and *Your Guide to Amman* list all-night pharmacies and doctors. In the downtown area: **As-Salam** (tel. 636 730). Jabal Hussein: **Firas** (tel. 661 912). Near Wahadat: **Deema** (tel. 787 040). For 24-hr., 7-days-a-week (including holidays) service and wonderful conversation, try **Jacob's Pharmacy** in Third Circle (tel. 644 945). Others usually open Sat.-Thurs. 8am-7pm.

Emergency: U.S. citizens call the American Embassy 24-hr. hotline (tel. 820 101) and ask them to call the police or ambulance. **Medical Emergencies:** Tel. 621 111. *Your Guide to Amman* contains a list of doctors and hospitals. **Ambulance:** Tel. 193. **Traffic Accidents:** Tel. 896 390.

Police: Tel. 192 or 621 111.

■■■ ACCOMMODATIONS

Many clean and reputable hotels are located near the **Abdali Bus Station** in Jabal al-Weibdeh. Close to the city center and convenient for transport out of Amman, this area is also the safest for female budget travelers. Just beyond Jabal al-Weibdeh lies the opulent **Shmeisani** district, with a few reasonably priced accommodations.

The **city center,** on the other hand, is overgrown with small, seedy hotels. Since every block has three or four hell-holes and every alley at least one, look carefully and don't get burned. Women traveling alone should perhaps avoid staying downtown or near the Wahadat Bus Station, where hotels are of a similar standard.

Official hotel prices are set by the government and posted conspicuously at each hotel. However, almost all hotel owners will give you a deal; the regulated prices, they will tell you, would run them out of business. As a result, you will note that the prices quoted in *Let's Go* may differ from the listed prices. Smile a lot and bargain, especially during non-summer months and for longer stays. All rooms have private baths, unless otherwise noted; and rooms near Abdali Station have phones.

Near Abdali Station

Canary Hotel, Karmaly St., P.O. Box 9062 (tel. 654 353, tel./fax 638 353), on Jabal al-Weibdeh near Terra Sancta College. From Abdali, walk 1½ blocks downhill to the fork at the base of the hill, bear right, take the first right after the fork, and go uphill. The friendliest family in Amman will welcome you into their vine-entwined courtyard and comfy pastel-hued TV room. Singles JD14-17. Doubles JD20-24. Triples and quads JD24-26. Visa, AmEx.

Remal Hotel, 4 Sa'id Bin al-Harith St., P.O. Box 910477 (tel. 630 670; fax 615 585). Look downhill from the Abdali bus station for the police station on the right; the hotel is a good olive-seed-spit up the small street next to the station. Fresh paint makes the rooms bright, but the street noise sometimes rivals that of a space shuttle launch. Singles JD14. Doubles JD18. Flaunt your *Let's Go* loyalty to boost bargaining leverage. Visa, AmEx.

Al-Monzer Hotel, King Hussein St. (tel. 639 469, 633 277, or 628 271; fax 657 328). Easy to spot from Abdali bus station: on the left when looking downhill. Upstairs waiting area has enormous lounge chairs. Clean rooms with ceiling fans, but the bathrooms are grungy, which might be okay if you were Eddie Vedder. Singles JD10. Doubles JD15. Triples JD18. Quads JD21. Restaurant next door serves chicken (JD2) and *kabab* (JD1.500).

Sunrise Hotel, King Hussein St. (tel. 621 841 or 428). To the left of Abdali as you face downhill. Dark hallways, dirty, hole-y (not holy) carpets, and amphetamine-rush street noise, but the complimentary shower flip-flops may entice you to stay if you're just off the bus. Singles JD8. Doubles JD10. Triples JD15. Quads JD20.

Downtown/Al Husseini Mosque Area

Cliff Hotel, King Faisal St. (tel. 624 273), at the top of the street across from the "Seiko" fork at the base of King Hussein St., on the third floor. The most popular traveler's spot in Amman, the Cliff is known from Hong Kong to Hanover. Manager Abu Suleiman calls it "the United Nations headquarters of the Middle East." He will give you a clean room (sink and fan but no private baths), information on travel in Jordan, Syria, and the West Bank, and taxi directions written out in Arabic. Reliable luggage storage. Rooftop mattress JD2. Singles JD3. Doubles JD5. Hot showers 500fils. Use of washing machine JD1.500. Try to reserve in advance.

Palace Hotel, King Faisal St. (tel. 624 327; fax 650 603), 1½ blocks from Al Husseini Mosque. Turn left into a small alley with clothing stores; entrance on left. Roman pillar decor and large dining/TV room next to a patio overlooking the city center. Singles JD7. Doubles JD 10.500. Triples JD12. Not all rooms have bath.

Bader Hotel, Prince Muhammad St. (tel. 637 602; fax 651 782), up the alley opposite the Cliff Hotel on King Faisal St., a few blocks down from post office. Dark, maze-like corridors with orange walls. Plain, airy rooms. Small valuables can be locked up for free. Singles JD5. Doubles JD7.

Vinecia Hotel, Basman St. (tel. 638 895). Across from the central post office on Prince Muhammad St., the Vinecia (or "Venice" as it says at the door) is cheap but slimy. With thin mattresses, peeling paint, and dark halls, the Vinecia will work for one or two nights at most for the aesthetically-minded. Singles JD4. Doubles JD5. Showers big enough for a pair of size 7 feet.

Metro Hotel, King Hussein St. (tel. 639 191), in the alley beside the blue and yellow Housing Bank. Peeling brown wallpaper, eerily shadowed hallways, and the narrowest TV lounge in Amman. Singles JD5. Doubles JD6.

Outlying Districts

Nefertiti Hotel, 26 Al Jahiz St. (tel. 603 865), in Shmeisani. A good 3-wood (200 yds. for non-golfers) in front of the Ambassador Hotel. Finding the Nefertiti will be a challenge, but well worth it. Uniformed attendants guide you down wide, well-lit corridors to rooms, many of which feature small terraces. Spacious accommodations and a relaxing, manicured courtyard. Restaurant attached to the hotel. Singles JD8.500. Doubles JD10.500. Extra bed JD4. 10% service charge.

American Center for Oriental Research (tel. 846 117 or 841 132; fax 844 181). Take a minibus from Abdali (100fils) and ask to get off at Jordan University. Look for the soccer field lights and the engineering building, an imposing five-story monstrosity. ACOR is on the opposite side of the street up the hill. Good luck finding it—there are no signs, only 4x4 vehicles parked out front. Home base for fieldworkers in Jordan; areas of interest include primarily archaeology, but also politics, history, economics, and international relations. Southwestern-style lobby and cozy library. Rooms US$24 per person, students US$20. Discounts for affiliates. Free private showers. Free Arabic-American lunch often features brownies and pecan pie; you can raid the fridge for breakfast and dinner. Laundry US$4 per load. Reservations recommended. Monthly rates available.

■■■ FOOD

Amman's edibles combine the city's Bedouin and Palestinian heritages. The better sit-down restaurants cluster near Third Circle, in Shmeisani, and along Mecca St.; these places usually add a 10% service charge to the bill. If the menu is in Arabic, ask the waiter to translate. Various street foods are cheap, plentiful, and safe.

Shawerma is always available for about 200fils; the most succulent stuff comes from the stands on Prince Muhammad St., just downhill from Third Circle, on Second Circle, near the Lebanese Embassy. **Falafel** and **corn on the cob** go for 100fils and 250fils respectively. Sides include **hummus** plates and salads for 250-350fils.

Bread is, well, a staple. *Khoubez* is your usual pita bread; rise at the crack of dawn to sample the freshest *ka'ik* (yummy sesame rings). Both are available at many stands for 100-200fils. Ask for *za'atar* (dried thyme, sesame seeds, and other spices) to sprinkle on top. Also try cheese or lamb *sfiehah* (Arabic pizzas) or *manaish* (bread baked with olive oil and *za'atar*), sold in many small restaurants and shops.

In the **downtown** area, rolled falafel sandwiches are a budgeteer's dream (100fils). Two busy stands opposite Al Husseini Mosque are open until 11pm. Freshly squeezed **juices,** found in stands throughout Amman, are too refreshing to miss (250-300fils). Options range from tomato and orange to banana, carrot, and a mysterious brown concoction that tastes like mangoes. Try them all, many times. For conquering that next *jabal,* you won't find a better energy booster.

If you're in **Shmeisani**, ask for directions to the **Ata Ali Café** across from the Housing Bank. This popular spot is the ancestor of the American Baskin-Robbins. For the weight-conscious, **Frosty** across the street offers 50-calories-per-scoop ice cream. Unadventurous provincials should head to **Pizza Hut** or **Kentucky Fried Chicken** in the Petra Center building in Shmeisani. Though prices are not higher than what you'd pay back home, a pizza will still cost more than your Jordanian hotel room. Stop in at **Zalatimo Sweets** for a cavity-catalyst of Arabic candy and pastries. It's in the large gray building at the top of the hill on which Abdali is located, just behind the bus station.

The up-and-coming district of **Umm Uthaina,** by Sixth Circle, past Amra Hotel, offers a variety of appetizing, cheap foods. Grilled *halloomi* (white cheese) wraps (200fils) are the specialty at **Al Baron,** and **LaiLak** serves hamburgers for a mere 380fils. Purple neon signs and sidewalk cafés contribute to a festive atmosphere.

Al Quds Restaurant, King Hussein St. (tel. 630 168), around the corner from the post office and across from the Cliff Hotel. You've gotta find this place. Though it looks like an American pancake house, Al Quds serves as a primary testing ground for Arabic cooking. Mounds of tempting, artistically-arranged sweets greet you upon entry. Its varied crowd includes families as well as the lonely budget traveler. Try their variation on *mensaf,* made with chicken instead of lamb (JD1.700, *kabab* JD1.500, french fries 300fils, hummus 300fils). Open daily 7am-11pm.

Hachim Restaurant, Prince Muhammad St., directly across from the Cliff Hotel. Hachim, the Jordanian hummus stop of choice since the 1950's, is a great place to see, hear, and feel Amman's pace. Pull up a chair with a Jordanian and order tea and lots of hummus and bread for well under 500fils. Open 24 hrs.

Al-A'eelat Restaurant, Prince Muhammad St. (tel. 637 246). Walk up Faisal St. and onto Prince Muhammad St. Continue for 5min. until you see Suleiman Tannous Chevrolet. The restaurant is on the opposite side of the street. Owners will be thrilled if you mention that you saw their place listed in *Let's Go.* Unbeatable prices. Sandwiches 200fils, falafel 10fils each. Open Sat.-Thurs. 8am-5pm.

Cairo Restaurant, on a side street on the left two blocks away from the Al Husseini Mosque. Face out from the mosque and head left past the clothes booths, looking for the big orange sign. You can eat your fill here inexpensively: roasted ½-chicken 900fils, *kabab* 800fils, *fasulya* (green beans cooked with lamb in tomato sauce) 500fils, and breakfast *fuul* plates 250fils. Open daily 5am-midnight.

Salaam Restaurant, King Faisal St. (tel. 622 626), half a block away from Al Husseini Mosque on the left-hand side of the street, next to the Bata shoe store. No English sign, but look for spitted chickens in the window. The colorful crowd, tasty food, and A/C will lure you inside, and the pastries will make you stay. JD2.160 buys bread, bird, and fries. *Sfiehah* and *manaish* 120fils each. Menu is in Arabic but servers can describe the dishes in English. Open daily 7am-10pm.

Indian Chicken Tikka Inn, Prince Muhammad St. (tel. 642 437), downhill from Third Circle. Tiny upstairs room with A/C. Take out or eat in. Curry dishes JD1.750. Half-chicken *tikka* JD1.200. Mix *paratha* (Indian bread) and hummus for 300fils. Another location at Seventh Circle.

Golden Chicken Restaurant, Muhammad Tash St. (tel. 621 149). From the Abdali bus station walk up the street next to the police station, take the first left, continue in the same direction around the round-about and the GC will be on your left. Make sure you eat upstairs in the dimly lit whale's belly room. Beer and wine served. *Mezze* dishes 220fils each, grilled chicken JD2.150. Mostly male clientele. Open daily 11:30am-11pm.

Abu Ahmad's New Orient Restaurant, 10 Orient St. (tel. 641 879). Take the last right before Third Circle as you approach it from Second. The first left is Orient St. Visit Abu Ahmad's for a luxurious dining experience among vines, green checkered tablecloths, and a hyper-attentive and polite staff. Award-winning charcoal-grilled dishes JD2.300. An order of *mensaf* (JD2.300) is enough for two. Traveler's checks accepted. Open daily noon-midnight.

■■■ SIGHTS

The **Roman Theater,** downtown on Jabal al-Qala'a, is the most renowned of Amman's historical sights. Built by Antonius Pius (138–161 CE), the theater could accommodate 6000 spectators. (Open Wed.-Mon. 8am-5pm. Free, but you'll be met by a line of eager "guides" who charge JD2 or your best price.) Beyond the **Odeon,** a smaller theater, is a new **piazza.** The short stroll between **Al Husseini Mosque** and the **Nymphaeum** is crowded with pedestrians, fruit juice stands, and in the evening, twinkling lights.

Two museums are built into the foundations of the theater on either side of the stage area inside. The **Folklore Museum** (tel. 651 742) displays Palestinian embroidery, as well as mannequins impersonating an entertaining cast of Jordanian characters. (Open Wed.-Mon. 8am-5pm. Admission JD1). The **Museum of Popular Traditions** (tel. 651 760) shows off current attire and Jordanian jewels. Learn about the origins of regional embroidery and why the white shawl is called "the thrilling of the soul." The gallery to the right of the entrance displays 6th-century mosaics from Madaba and Jerash. (Open Wed.-Mon. 8am-5pm. Admission 250fils.)

From the Roman Amphitheater, or any downtown locale, you can climb the steep steps and streets to the flat top of **Citadel Hill.** On the southern slope of Jabal al-Qala'a, the citadel is the site of ancient Amman, called Rabbath-Ammon, or the "Great City of the Ammonites." The Ammonites make frequent guest appearances in the Bible. King David besieged Rabbath-Ammon twice, the second time improving his chances of marrying the already pregnant Bathsheba by putting her husband Uriah in the front line of battle. A few Byzantine and Umayyad ruins remain. The *wadi* below and to the right of the Roman Theater is downtown Amman; across from it are Jabal Ashrafiyyeh and the black-and-white checkered dome of the **Abu Darwish Mosque,** built in the 1940s by Circassians. To the east, you'll see the **Royal Palace** at Raghadan, although you'll have to get a little closer to see the stylishly virile red and black regalia of the Circassian guards.

Plan a trip to the top of Citadel Hill during your first day in Amman. The view will give you the best perspective on the city's labyrinthine ups and downs. The **Archaeological Museum** (tel. 638 795), which is on Citadel Hill, contains a chronologically organized series of finds from ancient sites throughout Jordan. Displays range from 200,000-year-old dinner leftovers to Iron Age anthropomorphic sarcophagi, minimalist Nabatean portraits, and a Roman marble statuary. (Open Wed.-Thurs. and Sat.-Mon. 9am-5pm, Fri. and holidays 10am-4pm. Admission JD2.) In front of the museum are the foundations of a 2nd-century CE Roman temple that once housed a 10m statue of Hercules, to whom the temple was probably dedicated. Three giant marble fingers beside the museum steps and ponderous column segments scattered about the site hint at the shrine's former glory.

The best preserved and most intriguing ruins lie behind the museum. Vaulted chambers tower 10m over a spacious courtyard where elaborate floral decorations can still be seen in the stonework. The 7th-century CE structure once supported a huge stone dome and was used as a mosque, audience hall, and living accommodation. Below the Roman walls directly to the north, an open pit leads into the underground passageway that connected the fortified city to a hidden water supply. With a flashlight and fancy footwork you can enter the cavernous rock-hewn **cistern** by this route. The more conventional approach is from the gate on the street below.

The Citadel was the heart of ancient Amman; today the pulse emanates from downtown, in and around **Al Husseini Mosque.** The Ottoman-style structure was built in 1924 on the site of an ancient mosque, probably also the site of the Old Cathedral of Philadelphia. The area around the mosque is full of second-hand shoe shops. At the center of the triangle formed by the citadel, Al Husseini Mosque, and the post office is Amman's glittering **gold market,** featuring row upon row of gold jewelry. One or two shops vend antique Bedouin silver jewelry. Patience and an instinct for bargaining are all that is necessary to unearth hidden treasures (open Sat.-Thurs. 9am-9pm, Fri. 9am-1:30pm).

Excellent English is spoken at the **Jordan Craft Center** (tel. 644 555), downhill from the Lebanese Embassy (Second Circle) and on the left. Exhibits rugs, silver, glass, jewelry, embroidery, caftans, and pottery. (Open Sat.-Thurs. 9am-1pm and 4-7pm; in winter Sun.-Thurs. 9am-1pm and 3-6pm. Free.) Amman also features a number of galleries that display national and regional art; these are found near the ministry and in the luxury hotel district. The **Jordan National Gallery,** on Jabal al-Weibdeh (tel. 630 128) at Muntazah Park displays contemporary artwork from around the Islamic world, as well as 19th-century paintings of the Middle East by European artists. (Open Wed.-Mon. 10am-1:30pm, 3-6pm. Free.)

Amman's finest Byzantine artifact is the 6th-century CE **Suwaifiyyeh mosaic,** found during construction at the western edge of the city. Ask the caretaker to hose down the floor for a better look at the bizarre creatures including leaf-bearded men, eagles with ears, and eelie fish-men. Follow the signs from the first left west of Sixth Circle (open Sat.-Thurs. 8am-4pm, Fri. 9am-2pm; free). The **Martyr's Monument** and **Military Museum** (tel. 664 240) are in an odd square building overlooking the Hussein Sports City. The museum houses a chronological display of military memorabilia, dating from the Arab revolt in 1916 to the present (open Sun.-Fri. 9am-4pm; free). Both are occasionally closed to visitors, so call ahead.

∎∎∎ ENTERTAINMENT

Amman's nightlife thrives during summer. When the sweltering days give way to serene, cool evenings, nocturnal enthusiasts will find fulfillment in bars or on dance floors. But Amman is not Cairo—even partyboys and flygirls here bed down by 1 or 2am. A new bar in the Forte Grande Hotel (formerly the Amman Plaza, next to the Housing Bank Center), **Jugglers,** is popular with young members of Amman's upper crust. Jugglers serves a huge variety of cocktails (JD6, one or two could last all night) and features two pool tables, darts, etc. Fridays are 50% off; on Wednesdays you get to roll the dice for a free drink with each drink purchased. **Salute,** located between First and Second Circles (where Yo-Yo's once was, under Villa d'Angelo Italian restaurant) is *immensely* popular with the selfsame crowd. If you can squeeze yourself onto their breezy patio, consider yourself a member of the "in" clique. (Reserve in advance for a table. Men alone will not be admitted. Cover JD2. Drinks around JD3.) **Coconut Grove,** near Abdoun Circle, is not as crowded and has no cover charge. All serve food and play the European top 40 plus some classic rock and disco faves.

On the far side of Shmeisani (about twice as far as the Ambassador Hotel, on the same road) is the **Middle East Hotel,** which hosts a disco, **Talk of the Town,** on Monday and Thursday nights. The revolving mirrored ball suspended over its dance floor evokes memories of Elvis and John Travolta. The crowd is made up of Jordanians and foreigners mostly in their late twenties and the tunes range from techno to reggae. **Scandel,** in the basement of the **San Rock Hotel** (Sixth Circle), has security people frisking clubgoers at the door, mirrored walls, black upholstered booths, purple neon lights, and 40-year-old men trying to pick up airline stewardesses. Also out by Sixth Circle, the **Amra Hotel** has a fairly lively nightclub, frequented by a thirty- and forty-something crowd, on Fridays and Saturdays. Cover charges are usually around JD5 (some include a complimentary soft drink or beer) and drinks cost JD2 to 4. The **El Cesar Restaurant** on Jabal al-Weibdeh offers more traditional Jordanian music and dancing, but few affordable comestibles.

For those who enjoy mellow band music and a sedate, outdoor atmosphere, **Graffiti,** at the **Shepherd Hotel** (Second Circle, Omar Bin al-Khattab St., opposite the south gate of the Islamic college) is the place to be. The crowd is a mixture of foreigners and natives in their twenties (cover charge JD2). **The Cellar,** in the basement of **Al-Qasr Hotel** (Shmeisani, between the Ambassador and Nefertiti Hotels), is a more expensive option featuring sax and piano players alternating with the latest music videos (cover charge JD5).

At first glance, the city center seems to lack the traditional Middle Eastern constellation of cafés and tea houses. Look up: they're mostly perched on second floors. The **Hilton Café** (across from the Cliff Hotel) overlooks the royal intersection of King Hussein and King Faisal St. (above the Seiko watch sign). There's a crowded and noisy *al fresco* hangout on the second floor, where you can learn the local card games over a cup of Amman's sludgiest Arabic coffee (100fils and up) and entertain your suddenly acquired best friends by choking on the dense charcoal and tobacco smoke of an *argileh* (300fils). Jordanian society reserves such entertainments for members of the male gender; women probably will feel more comfortable elsewhere (open daily 8am-11pm). **Babiche Café** and **Geneva** in Shmeisani serve coffee, drinks, and pastries to a chi-chi crowd (which includes women, many of whom speak a strange offshoot of Esperanto made up of English, Arabic, and French). **Reem Al-Bawady** (Tla' al-Ali, Al Ubeel circle) offers fruit-flavored tobacco for smoking on an *argileh* outdoors in traditional Bedouin camel hair tents.

During the late afternoon and early evening, Amman's central **souq** (market) becomes the city's most happening spot, swallowing several blocks southwest of Al Husseini Mosque. Most people rest between 2 and 4pm (*service* and buses become scarce), but cafés allow homeless budget travelers to linger over coffee in the shade. Try **Maatouk's,** outside the *souq,* on Third Circle (coffee 200fils).

NEAR AMMAN

■■■ WADI SEER وادى السير

Burgeoning Amman has poked its urban tentacles westward to Wadi Seer, but as you enjoy the silence you'll soon realize that people here enjoy a more leisurely lifestyle. Wadi Seer, like much of the fertile hill country to the north and west of Amman, was first settled by Circassians. These fair-skinned Muslims came from Russia during the Czarist persecutions of the 1870s and account for most blonde and red-headed Jordanians. Amman's Folklore Museum displays the traditional Circassian costume—a cylindrical fur cap and black waistcoat with red trim.

At Wadi Seer, the high desert plateau suddenly gives way to the Jordan Valley. The town's namesake, a little stream, snakes through the countryside on its way to the Dead Sea. The narrow asphalt road that follows this valley out of town seems designed for daytripping motorists and tramping backpackers, but be prepared for scorching summer days. Verdant tobacco plants and olive trees, along with a multitude of children, line the 12km road which runs southwest to the ruins at **Iraq**

al-Emir and the nearby grottos. The occasional Bedouin tent or woman herding goats peeks out from the hills as the road approaches the ruins. The villagers of Wadi Seer believe that the identity of the site's mysterious builders is encoded in the carvings on the monolithic blocks of brown stone that stand between the town and the caves. The only clue offered by the caves is the Aramaic inscription "Tobiah" near two of the cave windows.

Local legend holds that **Qasr al-Abd** (Castle of the Slave) was built by a love-smitten slave named Tobiah. While his master was away on a journey, Tobiah built a palace and carved lions, panthers, and eagles into its walls in order to win the hand of the master's daughter. Unfortunately, the master returned before Tobiah could finish the work, and the slave's efforts and attraction went unrequited. Kill-joy historians explain the inscription and the castle remains with references to Tobiah the Ammonite Servant. This Tobiah was a rich priest in Jerusalem, and the name of the castle refers to his occupation as a servant of God. Ancient historian Josephus also records the wealth of a Tobiah family and the exploits of the young son Hyrcanus, who built a strong fortress constructed entirely of white marble and enclosed by a wide, deep moat. The ruins, restored in 1987, resemble a Hellenistic palace more than a defensive fort. Several red stone lions remain intact, though there is no roof. In summer 1994 Qasr al-Abd was closed to visitors, but you may be able to find the unofficial guard. He has a key and will let you in for a small donation.

About 2 to 3km along the way from Wadi Seer to Iraq al-Emir, you pass **Al Bassa Springs,** the source of the valley's fertility and a swimming pool for many of the area's children. Above the left bank of the *wadi,* the monastery **Ad-Deir** is carved into the face of the cliff. This extraordinary building deserves the 20-minute clamber, even if you don't find any of the Roman gold which villagers claim is buried under the floor. Each of the thousands of triangular niches in the walls inside once cradled a skull; the chamber is an ossuary which stored the remnants of monks.

The easiest way to get to Wadi Seer begins at Al Husseini Mosque. As you face out of the mosque, turn left and walk past clucking chickens, spilled ice cream, and screeching taxis until you arrive at a fork in the road. This walk will take about 10 minutes. Head left at the fork and look for lines of minibuses; they'll drop you off at Wadi Seer for 100fils. To get to the village of Iraq el-Emir take a minibus from Wadi Seer (90fils) to the city and ask the driver to point out the path to Qasr al Abd. Head to the village store for supplies. Past the castle the road ends, making passage to the Jordan Valley unmanageable for ordinary vehicles.

■■■ AZRAQ AND THE DESERT CASTLES الازرق و القصور الصحـراوية

Adjacent to sultry desert lava fields, Azraq's dusty green foliage comes as a welcome respite. As T.E. Lawrence (of Arabia) noted, *"Numen in est* (Where's the latrine)?" The springs at Azraq are the only permanent bodies of water in an expanse of over 2500 square km of barren sand-and-scorpion desert. Thus, the oasis serves as a resting stop for truck drivers from three continents and hundreds of species of exotic birds molting their way through Jordan's desert. Bedouin tents dot the landscape, and vehicles slow only for crossing goatherds.

The discovery of an enormous cache of flint hand-axes indicates that either Paleolithic settlers or extremely sophisticated camels hunted in the area 500,000 years ago. The most remarkable records of human habitation are the scattered Umayyad castles, a group of structures that originally formed a chain from the north of Damascus to Khirbet al-Mafjar, near Jericho. Built in the 7th and 8th centuries CE by the Umayyads, the castles were mysteriously abandoned a century later. The imposing stonework of **Qasr Kharaneh** and strategic location of **Qasr Azraq** and **Qasr Mushatta** support speculation that the castles sheltered caravans along the trade route between Syria, Arabia, and the Far East. The baths near **Qasr al-Hallabat** and the magnificent frescos at **Qasr Amra** brought creature comforts to the desert.

ORIENTATION AND PRACTICAL INFORMATION

A trip to Azraq oasis and the Desert Castles is a journey fraught with uncertainty, to say nothing of a pain in the ass. There are only three easy options for transportation to the castles, none of which are very appealing to Jordan-on-the-cheap travelers. First, you can hire a taxi from Amman for the official rate of JD24, but try to plead poverty and get the price to just under JD20. This will provide half a day's wheels and someone who knows the route. For a full day, the price will shoot to over JD30. Second, you can rent a car in Amman for JD45-65 per day, depending on miles traveled and the size of the car. A good option for a group of travelers—go at your own pace and avoid potentially horny taxi drivers. Finally, **JETT buses** do full day tours of the desert castles; arrange this through a travel agent. In other words, you may need to dip into emergency funds to make the trip.

As always, hitchhiking is discouraged and is potentially suicidal in this region. Hitchhikers, before undertaking this risky fool's errand, will need an immense supply of food and water, a taste for adventure, and careful planning. There is some traffic on the Damascus highway from Amman to Zarqa (30km), but there are also other hitchhikers, mostly soldiers and workers. Alternatively, *service* from Abdali Station in Amman can take you to Zarqa quickly and cheaply (300fils). Be careful about accepting rides from military vehicles since most will take you only as far as some desolate desert depot. The highway to Azraq passes right by Qasr al-Hallabat (30km from Zarqa) before reaching Azraq (87km from Zarqa). From Azraq junction you'll have to hitch 13km north to reach Qasr Azraq and then return to Azraq. If you take the southern highway back to Amman you will pass near Qasr Amra (25km from Azraq), then Qasr Kharaneh (40km from Azraq), and Qasr Mushatta (about 90km from Azraq and 40km from Amman).

The following description of the castles and Azraq details a road trip that takes the northern route from Amman to Azraq and the southern highway on the return trip. This **clockwise tour** serves hitchhikers better because there is more traffic; if you have a car, you could as easily go in the counterclockwise direction. The road from Amman to Zarqa passes through Jordan's most notorious speed trap, where gimlet-eyed cops dispense fines at a honking JD50. Make sure you wear your seat belt; unprotected driving fines are hefty, too.

QASR AL-HALLABAT

Approximately 30km east into the desert from Zarqa, Qasr al-Hallabat comes into view. Angle off at the right turn onto the paved road and turn left up the track to the gate. The gatekeeper's tent is to the left of the crumbling castle; you're free to roam around whatever is left. Keep in mind that any gatekeeper who provides you with information will expect a dinar tip in return. Back on the main highway, note the difference between the sand and limestone desert to the south and the gray volcanic desert to the north. Just off the road to the south is **Hammam Sarah,** the ruined bathhouse modeled after Amra (below). The thousands of stones thrown into the well over the last 1000 years haven't noticeably affected its depth.

AZRAQ

On the long and grinding road east of Hallabat you'll hear nothing but the entreaties of your overheating engine. After kilometers of drab desert, you'll suddenly come upon the 12 square kilometers of lush parklands, pools, and gardens of the **Azraq oasis.** These wetlands are Jordan's only permanent body of fresh water. Relax and reassemble your bearings (both mental and mechanical) at Azraq Junction, where the highway to the northeast heads off for Iraq and the southeastern road leads to the southern castles and on into Saudi Arabia.

About 13km north of Azraq Junction, on the highway to Iraq, squats **Qasr Azraq.** Most of the castle is in excellent condition thanks to extensive restoration. The Druze gatekeeper, a sweet man with a charming smile, will muscle open the three-ton portal of the castle and show you his Lawrence of Arabia photograph collection if you inquire with sugar on top. (Many of the photographs look suspiciously like the gatekeeper himself.) The most interesting attractions lie within a few meters of the entrance. Carved into the pavement behind the main gate is a Roman board game. Just above the entrance you'll find the room used by the aforementioned British charmer during his short stay on the premises—it is no longer the fetid dungeon where he sought to punish himself for the failure of one of his missions. The castle, first built by the Romans as a fort in 300 CE and later rebuilt by the Ayyubids in 1237, once rose up in three levels. Only parts of the second level survived the 1926 earthquake, including a ceiling that exposes a web of huge basalt beams.

A two-minute walk from Qasr Azraq is the palatial **Al-Sayyad Hotel and Restaurant** (tel. 647 611, ext. 94); look for the imposing white wall. (Singles JD24. Doubles JD28. 10% tax, but bargain for a discount in the off-season, which can be any season when business is slow.) For JD3, you can take a plunge in their pool, with bathing suits provided if you forgot yours. Restaurant open 8am-11pm; a glance at the prices may cause a stroke: hummus 600fils, *kabab* JD2.200, coffee 400fils. But it's either stroke or starvation; there are no other decent eating options around. Although inconveniently located at the southern edge of town, the **Zoubi Hotel** (tel. 647 622), serving many customers from nearby Saudi Arabia, is a better deal. Surprisingly modern, the place is so clean that you might have to step through puddles of soapy water to see your room. (Singles JD7. Doubles JD10. Shared baths. Open June-Aug.) Located on the north side of Azraq down a tree-lined road is the **Azraq Resthouse;** rooms include bath, A/C, color TV, minibar, and a look out onto the pool, into which you can jump even if you aren't planning to spend the night (JD3, open 9am-6pm). (Singles JD13.200. Doubles JD15.400.)

Throughout the trip, keep an eye out for desert wildlife. The Jordanian government tries to protect desert habitats since many indigenous species are disappearing. In the **Shaumari Wildlife Preserve,** southwest of Azraq, near Qasr Amra, the government is reintroducing gazelles, armadillos, Himalayan dwarf hamsters, ostriches, and Arabian oryxes. In regions to the northeast and southwest of Azraq, cheetah and even desert wolves roam. (Admission 300fils, students 100fils.)

QASR AMRA

Despite the ill-fitting glass windows, the hunting lodge and bath complex of Qasr Amra impress onlookers with the elegant simplicity of their design. The interior is also the best preserved of the desert palaces; its vaulted ceilings are splashed with colorful frescoes, and mosaics grace some of the floors. As centuries of Bedouin campfire soot are removed, a fascinating portrait of Umayyad refinement is slowly reappearing. An early portrayal of the zodiac covers the domed ceiling of the *caldarium* (hot room). The frescoes are all the more riveting since they date from the earliest days of Muslim culture, when human and animal depictions were permissible. Especially surprising are the many portrayals of nude women. You can reach Qasr Amra on the road heading southwest of Azraq Junction, about 28km from Qasr Azraq. The gatekeeper will expect a JD1 tip.

QASR KHARANEH

This castle, named for the small black stones that blanket the area, remains an enigma. Some experts believe that it was a defensive fort, while others argue that it was a caravansary for passing camel trains. Others believe it was a *khan,* or inn—one of the first in the Islamic world. The latest interpretation holds that it served as a retreat where Umayyad leaders discussed matters of state. A painted dedication in a second-story room of the well-preserved castle dates its construction to 92 years after the Prophet's flight from Mecca to Medina (711 CE). The "defensive" theory of Kharaneh is supported by the four corner towers and the solid, square plan of a Roman fortress, but the lack of narrowly slit windows from which guards could fire arrows upon attackers casts doubt. The Greek inscription in the doorjambs implies that the Umayyads built upon an earlier structure. For a good view of the courtyard, climb the staircase on your left as you enter. You'll also see the neighboring military base and the maneuverings of Jordanian troops.

QASR MUSHATTA

Continuing west you'll move through more expanses of desert, dotted with Bedouin tents. To reach the castle take the highway or any turn-off to Queen Alia International Airport. Hitchhikers often hire *service* from the village of **Muwaqaar** in the north to reach the castle. The castle is on the left as you approach the airport from the north, but the public access road turns off to the right and loops about 4km around the airport. If you're walking from the airport, don't take this marked turn-off. Instead, continue to the left of the airport, past the Alia cargo terminal, until Mushatta appears on the left (a ½-hr. walk). Soldiers and guards at checkpoints will ask to see your **passport.** The façade of the 8th-century castle beckons at the entrance with wonderfully carved floral designs. Most of the carved stones, however, were delivered to Kaiser Wilhelm as a gift from Ottoman Sultan Abd al-Hamid II, and only fragments remain at this site. From Qasr Mushatta and the airport, you can catch a taxi or bus to Amman; hitchers find it an easy trip back into town.

■ South of Amman

Three roads link Amman and Aqaba: the Wadi Araba (Jordan Valley) Highway, the Desert Highway, and the Kings' Highway. The **Wadi Araba Highway** hugs the Dead Sea Coast. Owing to its proximity to Israel, the highway serves as a military road; a permit from the police is required for civilian use. By contrast, enormous trucks rumble impassively along the **Desert Highway,** the artery that ties the cities of the north to the port at Aqaba. Since the Iran-Iraq War, the Desert Highway has been the chief link between Europe and Turkey and the Persian (Arabian) Gulf. Major new road construction will supposedly make the highway smooth and swift, but even the king can do little about the scenery—three hours of unchanging desert to Petra, five hours of the same to Aqaba. Only the antics of deranged drivers playfully bumping the narrow shoulders or squeezing between oncoming cars break the monotony. Gas and phones along the way are scarce. Many travelers find hitching easy on the Desert Highway. *Let's Go* does not recommend hitchhiking.

Unless you are rushing from Amman to Aqaba or want to spend every one of your days in Jordan at Petra, the **Kings' Highway** (Wadi Mujib Road in Arabic) is the ideal way to travel the length of Jordan. This ancient route journeys through spectacular canyons, crisscrossing numerous historical sites along the way. Known by the same name in biblical times, this road was traveled by the Israelites during their exodus from Egypt. Caravans filled with cinnamon and myrrh crept from Arabia to Palestine and Syria en route to Europe. Biblical sites, Byzantine churches and mosaics, Crusader castles, and soul-stirring scenery await you along this route.

Service taxis run most of the way from Amman to Petra, as do minibuses, but generally in the mornings only. Karak is a convenient overnight stop. Nothing leaves Tafilah after 4pm except *service*, so get an early start. Because many drivers shun the Kings' Highway, hitchhiking is reportedly difficult. Drivers tend to head for the first available entrance to the Desert Highway—check that they intend to stay on the Kings' before climbing in. Since roadside bystanders often wave at passing cars in salutation, hitchers generally point at the curb beside their feet or stick their right arm out into the traffic—the gestures used to hail buses. Hitchers find a light pack, lots of water, head covering, sunscreen, and emergency food crucial.

The distances are manageable: 33km from Amman to Madaba, 98km from Madaba to Karak, and 150km from Karak to Petra. The total distance from Amman to Petra is 282km along the Kings' Highway or 262km along the Desert Highway. Many people camp in the *wadis* north of Karak or in the desert regions between Karak and Petra. A Rest House and a couple of hotels in Karak provide the only indoor accommodations.

To take the Desert Highway from downtown Amman, hitchhikers head south on Jerusalem St. (in Jabal Nadhif across Wadi Abdoun), which metamorphoses into the Desert Highway (Rte. 15). To get to the Kings' Highway they take a *service* from Amman's Wahadat Station all the way to Madaba (330fils) and then try their luck on the road to Karak, which passes out of Madaba by the Apostles' Church; alternatively, some head south toward Queen Alia International Airport. At the intersection of the Kings' Highway and the Desert Highway, 18km south of Amman, small groups of hitchhikers stand by the mini-obelisk marking this fork. People reach the intersection by taking a Madaba-bound *service* from Wahadat Station, or by hitching south from Seventh Circle.

■■■ MADABA مأدبا

Madaba is located on a plateau of orange groves overlooking the Jordan Valley. The scanty Roman columns next to the government Rest House hardly evoke visions of the flourishing trade center that was once the size of Jerash, but the elaborate mosaics scattered throughout the town are a testament to Madaba's importance as a Byzantine ecclesiastical center. Leveled by an earthquake in the 8th century CE, Madaba lay untouched for nearly 1100 years until Christian clans from Karak reinhabited the city in the late 1800s.

Practical Information and Food To reach the city center from Madaba's bus station, take a *service* (70fils) or hike up the hill toward the ever-visible Church of St. George. The **tourist office** (tel. 543 376), housed in a little white shack behind a wall across from St. George's, has lots of colorful but not very helpful brochures. The staff is friendly and willing to help with directions (open Sat.-Thurs. 8am-2pm). The central **post office** (open Sat.-Thurs. 8am-7pm, Fri. 8am-1:30pm) is located on King Abdallah St., around the corner from the tourist office. The **Housing Bank** (open Sat.-Thurs. 8am-1pm and 4-5:30pm) is on the other side of King Abdallah St. Madaba also has a **police station**. From the tourist office, pass the church and go up the narrow street. The nearest hospital, 1km from Madaba, is **Nadim Hospital** (tel. 541 700). Madaba's **telephone code** is 08.

Service (350fils) and **buses** (200fils) run back and forth between Madaba and Wahadat Station in Amman regularly until 7pm in summer and 5pm in winter.

Join blonde, short-shorts-clad Germans and Danes at the **Rest House** (tel. 544 069), next to the tourist information shack. They serve a buffet for groups, but individuals are allowed to join the feast for JD5. A hummus and coke snack will cost JD1.500 (open daily 7:30am-10pm).

Sights The prominent, yellow-brick Greek Orthodox **Church of St. George** stands in the center of town, right off the town square. Inside, parts of the 6th-century CE **Map of Palestine**, originally composed of 2.3 million tiles, remain intact. The map includes the Palestinian cities of Byzantium, most notably Nablus, Hebron, and Jericho. At one time the map depicted the entire Middle East, as shown by the few remaining tiles of Turkey, Lebanon, and Egypt. A map of Jerusalem, with representations of the buildings existing in the 6th century CE, including the Church of the Holy Sepulchre, is the most renowned section. Ask one of the postcard-selling faithful to point out some landmarks and to switch on the light. The church is also known by some devout and imaginative local Christians and Muslims for hosting the Virgin Mary in 1980. A small shrine in the crypt pictures Mary as she purportedly appeared, with a third arm and blue "healing hand" supernaturally imprinted on the icon during the Madonna's visit. (Open Mon.-Thurs. and Sat. 8:30am-6pm, Fri. and Sun. 10:30am-6pm. Free, but a donation for the poor is requested.)

Madaba's modest **museum,** tucked in an alley down the hill from the Apostles' Church, features an extensive collection of mosaics, including a well-preserved depiction of the Garden of Eden, traditional dresses representative of the different regions in Jordan, and jewelry and pottery dating back to various ages. Look for the potted baby bones in the back room. The museum is divided into three sections—the Old House of Madaba, a Folklore Museum, and an Archaeological Museum (open Wed.-Mon. 9am-5pm, holidays 10am-4pm; admission JD1). The **Apostles' Church,** closed for renovations during summer 1994, houses the town's largest intact mosaic: a woman surrounded by mythical sea creatures in the center of a field of parrots. Inquire at the tourist office for the opening date.

The ongoing excavations have spawned two up-and-coming sights. In an effort to develop Madaba into a tourist attraction, the Ministry of Tourism is renovating age-old buildings to house a **mosaic school.** The school, the only one of its kind in the Middle East, will train technicians to repair and restore mosaics and is hoped to be in operation in several years, if funding resumes. Meanwhile, excavations by Jordanian and Italian archaeologists have uncovered a **Roman street** of columns crossing Madaba's main street underground. The site is not expected to open to tourists for at least another 2-3 years, but anyone is welcome to stop by and marvel at the treasures of past empires emerging after centuries of concealment. For more details on the progress of these efforts consult the tourist office.

■ NEAR MADABA

No wonder Moses's last request to God was for a view from **Mount Nebo.** On a clear day you can see across the Jordan Valley to the glistening Dead Sea and beyond to Jericho. The Bible says "no man knows the place of his [Moses'] burial to this day" (Deuteronomy 34:6), but Moses' grave is rumored to be in a secret cave somewhere along **Ain Musa.** There are only a few tombs on Nebo itself, but on the higher **Mount Siyagha** stands an enigmatic serpentine cross next to the **Memorial of Moses.** The memorial houses the baptismal fonts and well-preserved "Mosaic" mosaics of a Byzantine church dedicated to Moses. It also contains restored mosaic panels unearthed by an Italian archaeological team and Franciscan monks, whose mountaintop excavations have uncovered monasteries dating back to the 3rd century CE. The buildings close at 6pm, but walk beyond them for an evening view of the Dead Sea. No buses go to Mt. Nebo; hire a **taxi** for JD4 round-trip (includes ½-hr. stay at the site). Bring sunglasses and those binoculars you packed at the last minute.

Just beyond Feisaliyyeh, a small town near Mount Nebo, a marked turn-off leads to **Khirbet al-Mukheiyat.** A one-hour detour (round-trip) will allow you to see the secular scenes of fishing, hunting, and wine-making that decorate another finely preserved Byzantine church floor. Cigarettes are the preferred *bakhsheesh* for the Bedouin gatekeeper who lives next to the mosaic on the hill at the end of the paved road. Sight open as late as the gatekeeper is willing, usually dusk.

Herod the Great, Governor of Judea in 40 BCE, frequented the hot mineral springs at **Zarqa Ma'in** to relieve his rheumatism. As he lay dying, he was carried here from his fortress at nearby Mukawer—where Salome danced and John the Baptist lost his head (Matthew 14:1-12). The road from Madaba tumbles southeast from a high escarpment to the Zarqa Ma'in River, into which spring water cascades from the low cliffs. From the road you can see the hills of the West Bank rising across the Dead Sea. JD3.300 (JD5.500 with lunch) allows you to enter the new **Ma'in Spa Village,** located at the end of the road in the center of a ring of mountains and hills. Get your swaddlings and Fungo therapy here. In addition, both men and women can swim in **Hammam az-Zarqa,** the hot indoor pool sunk in the cliff face, or bathe under the voluptuous torrents of hot waterfalls. Reach Zarqa Ma'in by **bus** from Madaba (100fils). The JETT Bus Company in Amman occasionally offers 8am-6pm daytrips to the springs for JD8 round-trip, including lunch. Inquire at the JETT office or a travel agency.

The Kings' Highway from Madaba to Karak chugs over plateaus and *wadis.* Forty km south of Madaba the road descends into the vast **Wadi Mujib,** 4km wide and 1100m deep. On one escarpment lies the Biblical **Dhiban,** where the Mesha Stele was discovered in 1868. (The original tablet, engraved by King Mesha with an early Hebrew script, now resides in the Louvre. Copies may be seen in both the Karak and Madaba Museums.) An ancient Roman mile marker is on the road approaching the modern town of Dhiban; the wondrous Wadi Mujib unfurls after the town disappears from view.

Few buses run directly from Madaba to Karak along the highway. The easiest way to go is to hitch or catch a minibus to **Al Qasr,** which features a ruined Roman temple (c. 350 CE) and a bus to Karak (200fils).

■ ■ ■ KARAK الكرك

The ancient capital of Moab, Karak now humbles itself in the shadow of **Karak Castle,** the largest of the mountaintop Crusader castles which stretch from Turkey to southern Jordan. Imagine you are a member of Salah ad-Din's conquering army as you approach. Steep mountain slopes turn into steeper jagged walls, making even a guided tour of the windblown remains a challenge for the weak-stomached. In 1132 Baldwin I built the castle midway between Shobak and Jerusalem. Although the fortress wall has mostly collapsed, its building blocks remain large enough to inspire starry-eyed wonder. Inside, vaulted stone ceilings span only a few meters, resulting in a network of long, narrow audience halls and barracks. You can still see the bolt holes for mammoth stone doors that have since turned to dust or, worse, souvenirs. The castle is full of secret passageways and hidden rooms. To the west across the moat are battlements from which the charming Renauld de Chatillon cast prisoners to their deaths (with wooden boxes fastened around their heads so that they would not lose consciousness too quickly). The tower in the northwest corner is a 13th-century addition. Below, a 50m tunnel leads out of town through an arched gateway (open daily 8am-7pm, but late afternoon visitors can entice guides for one last tour). To the right of the castle entrance, a stone staircase descends to the **Archaeological Museum.** It holds Nabatean and Roman coins, Mamluk pottery, descriptions of the archaeological site at Bab adh-Dhira and of the biblical cities Buseirah and Rabbah, and a plaster copy of Dhiban's Mesha Stele. (Open Wed.-Mon. 9am-5pm. Admission to castle and museum JD1.)

Practical Information, Accommodations, and Food From the Karak Castle, walk downhill and take your first right. Above the Castle Hotel is a genial but useless **tourist office** (sometimes open Sat.-Thurs. 8am-2pm). The **police station** is located down the street and on the right, next to the huge radio tower. The **post office** (open Sat.-Thurs. 7:30am-7pm, Fri. 8am-1:30pm) is across the street from the Castle Hotel. Karak's **Italian Hospital** (tel. 351 045 or 145), the oldest in the region, is downhill from the turn-off up to the castle, or in the direction of the elbow if you orient yourself via the town's manic horseman. The **Housing Bank,** located uphill from the Italian Hospital, will change traveler's checks and cash (open Sat.-Thurs. 8am-12:30pm). The **telephone code** for Karak is 03.

Travel to Karak from Amman's Wahadat Station by **minibus** (750fils) or **service taxi** (JD1.500) along the desert highway. To reach **Petra** from Karak, take a minibus from the city center to **Tafilah** (500fils), and from Tafilah to **Shobak** (250fils). Minibuses run regularly from Shobak to Petra (Wadi Musa). A direct bus from Karak to Petra leaves at 9am. No *service* travel these routes, but a **private taxi** will take you directly from Karak to Petra for a vacation-ending JD40. **Buses** also run from Karak to Petra through **Ma'an** (JD1).

Accommodations in Karak are more than adequate for white-glovers and the frugal alike. The rooms at the government **Rest House** (tel. 351 148) have thick mattresses, private baths, and fans. (Singles JD16. Doubles JD22, with extra bed JD27.500. 10% service charge.) The cheapest lodging is at the **Castle Hotel** (tel. 352 489; singles JD5, doubles JD8). The Castle may not be the cleanest place you've stumbled across, but the **Towers Hotel** across the street is owned by the same French-speaking lute players and is spotless. (Singles JD10. Doubles JD15. Breakfast included.) The manager is more helpful than the tourist office. A couple of tiny hotels near the center of town offer less comfortable rooms for less.

The prosperous modern town of Karak extends away from the castle on its northern and eastern slopes and serves as an ideal resting place for travelers on the Kings' Highway. A snack or meal at the government **Rest House,** near the entrance to the castle, affords you a view of the Jordan Valley's descent to the Dead Sea. (Hummus 350fils. Full lunch or dinner JD3.850. Open until 10pm.) To avoid these inflated prices, try the **Fida Restaurant** (tel. 352 677), across the street from the police station and the radio tower. The second floor of the Fida caters only to the vertically challenged and they sometimes honor tourists with special (higher) prices. (Hummus 220fils, *kabab* JD1.200, coffee 150fils. Open daily 8am-10pm.) True budgeteers picnic atop the sublime ruins.

■ NEAR KARAK

Highway 49/80 (for added confusion, maps may say 50) west from Karak drops 20m· from the Kings' Highway until it reaches the Dead Sea "port" of Mazra'a and the Al Lisan (tongue) Peninsula. Five kilometers before reaching Mazra'a and the Wadi Araba Highway to Aqaba, Highway 49/80 passes **Bab adh-Dhira.** The cemeteries here contain some 20,000 shaft tombs enshrining 500,000 bodies (an unfortunate 25-to-1 body-per-tomb ratio) and over 3 million pottery vessels. The length of the bones indicates that the average height in Bab adh-Dhira was a sturdy 2m.

Hitchers report that there is very little traffic between here and Karak. Stop in at the **Mazra'a Police Post,** 5km north of the junction, if you need assistance. The Wadi Araba highway, running right beside Israel, is sometimes closed to civilian travel; hitchhiking there is always prohibited.

Traveling east of Karak on Highway 49/80 toward Qatrana, which is on the Desert Highway, you'll pass the turn-off for **Al Lejjun,** where archaeologists have excavated the Romans' southeasternmost frontier post. Streets, a tower, a church, and a *principium,* dating from 30 CE and destroyed by an earthquake in 551, have all been unearthed. The main site is 2km north of the turn-off, on the hill below more recent Turkish barracks (now used as stables), intended to defend the nearby railway against T.E. Lawrence and his posse and constructed from stone pillaged from the Roman site. Take a **service** (450fils) or **bus** (310fils) toward Qatrana and ask the driver to let you off at the "Lejjun" turn-off (the sign is in Arabic only).

The tremendous hospitality of locals is virtually guaranteed (and your only hope) in towns just north of Karak on the Kings' Highway (Rabbah, Qasr) and immediately to the south (Mazar, Tafilah). The mosques at Mu'tah and at the nearby village of Mazar commemorate the Islamic generals who died in the first great battles between the forces of Islam and Byzantium in 632 CE. The green-domed mosque in Mazar houses a small **Islamic museum** on the first floor.

SHOBAK شوباك

As the desert becomes more desolate and Petra's small brook more resonant after only a half-hour drive south, the village of Shobak emerges. From the marked turn-off at the northern edge of town, travel 4km to **Shobak Castle,** the first of seven castles built by the Crusader King Baldwin I in 1115 CE to control the triangular trade route between Syria, Egypt, and Saudi Arabia. It didn't work: the castle fell to Salah ad-Din in 1189. Although most of the castle is gone, the view from the approach road across the natural moat is inspiring, with colossal white stones silhouetted against desert brush and a cobalt sky. Villagers who lived inside the castle walls and depended upon the water from the rock-hewn well, 375 steps deep, have recently abandoned the area, leaving a secluded spot for free **camping**.

Shobak town can possibly be reached in a shared **minibus** from Karak or Wadi Musa (near Petra), although much of the traffic between those towns takes the Desert Highway. If you hire a **taxi,** make sure the driver will not gouge you for waiting while you investigate.

■■■ PETRA البتراء

Match me such marvel save in Eastern clime,
a rose-red city 'half as old as Time'!

—Dean Burgon

The once-lost city of Petra is now easy to find, but ease of access hardly lessens its magnificence. Nothing could. Peeking out from between the walls of a natural 3m-wide fissure are towering sculptures, raw mountains fashioned by human hands into impossibly delicate structures. Petra, meaning "stone" in ancient Greek, is perhaps the most astounding ancient city left to the modern world, and certainly a must-see for visitors to the Middle East.

For 700 years, Petra was lost to all but the few hundred members of a Bedouin tribe who guarded their treasure from outsiders. In the 19th century, Swiss explorer Johann Burkhardt heard Bedouin speaking of a "lost city," and he vowed to find it. Though Burkhardt was initially unable to find a guide, he guessed that the city he sought was the Petra of legend, the biblical Sela, which should have been near Mount Hor, the site of Aaron's tomb. Impersonating a Christian pilgrim, Burkhardt hired a guide and, on August 22, 1812, walked between the cliffs of Petra's *siq* (the rift which is the only entrance to Petra). Awed and driven to sketch the monuments and record his thoughts, the "pilgrim" aroused the suspicion of his Bedouin guide. The guide warned him of the spiritual significance of the ancient rocks, and a chastened Burkhardt left—to announce his discovery to the rest of the world. In the nearly two centuries since, Petra has been molested by visitors ranging from the film crew of *Indiana Jones and the Last Crusade* to tourists from Big Sky, Montana asking, "Where's the ladies' room?"

The area's principal water source, Ein Musa (Spring of Moses), is one of the many places where Moses supposedly struck a rock with his staff and extracted water (Exodus 17). Human history in the area dates back to the 8th millennium BCE, when farmers settled in this area and put to use the newly developed techniques of agricultural cultivation. By the 6th century BCE, the Nabateans, a nomadic Arab tribe, had quietly moved onto land controlled by the Edomites and had begun to profit from the trade between lower Arabia and the Fertile Crescent. Over the next three centuries the Nabatean Kingdom, secure in its easily defended capital, flourished. The Nabateans carved their monumental temples out of the mountains, looking to Egyptian, Greek, and Roman styles for inspiration. Unique to the Nabateans are the crow-step (staircase) patterns that grace the crowns of many of the memorials. The people of Meda'in Salih (a miniature Petra in Saudi Arabia) claim that the crow-steps so decidedly resemble inverted stairways that, to punish Petra's wickedness, God threw Petra upside down and turned it to stone.

More historically verifiable evidence suggests that in 63 BCE the Nabatean King Aretas defeated Pompey's Roman Legions. The Romans controlled the entire area around Nabatea, however, prompting the later King Rabel III to strike a deal: as long as the Romans did not attack during his lifetime, they would be permitted to move in after he died. In 106 CE the Romans claimed the Nabatean Kingdom and began to develop the city of rosy Nubian sandstone.

In its heyday, Petra may have housed 20,000-30,000 people. But after an earthquake in 363 CE, a shift in the trade routes to Palmyra (Tadmor) in Syria, the expansion of the sea trade around Arabia, and another earthquake in 747 CE, much of Petra deteriorated to rubble. The city fell under Byzantine and then Arab control for a few centuries before the Crusaders tried to resurrect it by constructing a new fortress. By then, though, it had so declined that even its location was forgotten. A few explorers searched in vain for Petra, but not until Burkhardt schemed his way in was the city visited by anyone other than the Bedouin.

For decades, the resident Bedouin adapted to the influx of tourists by providing them with food and accommodations inside Petra. In 1984-85, however, the government outlawed this, out of concern for monuments. Now virtually all of Petra's

PETRA

Bedouin have been relocated to a housing project near Wadi Musa and spend their days hawking souvenirs at the site. Burkhardt had a big mouth.

GETTING THERE

Petra is located in the rocky wilderness near the southern extreme of the Kings' Highway about 280km from Amman, 260km via the Desert Highway. **JETT** buses leave Amman (daily 6:30am; 3½hrs.; JD5, round-trip JD10, complete tour including lunch, guide, and horse JD30). Reservations should be made at JETT stations well ahead of time, especially during the busy fall and spring seasons. You'll be dropped off at the Petra visitors center. But one day is not enough to get your fill of Petra; if you go on a JETT tour, you might as well wear a stupid tourist hat, or better yet, watch someone else's home movie of Petra and save yourself some money.

Service taxis to Petra from Wahadat Station takes about five hours, plus a wait in Ma'an (JD2, JD1.650 if you take the **bus** that goes directly from Amman to Wadi Musa, but not to Petra). Drivers will drop you off at either the Al-Anbat or the Wadi Musa Hotel; from Wadi Musa you could walk the 5km or take a **private taxi** (JD1) to Petra. Some people hitch. From Aqaba, the two-hour trip costs JD2 by **minibus.** Start early in the morning to make any of these connections. Leaving Petra, you can catch minibuses or *service* to Aqaba (JD1.500), Ma'an (400fils), or Amman (JD2) at the center of Wadi Musa, near the post office, between 5:30 and 6am. A local bus to Ma'an leaves at 6am, returns at 2pm, and costs 400fils one way.

To reach Petra from the Kings' Highway, take the well-marked turn-off and head west into the colorful, steep-sided town of Wadi Musa. You'll pass the main traffic circle and travel through the main market area. A tortuous 5km from Wadi Musa, the spur road leaves town and ends at the entrance to Petra. The cluster of buildings here includes the visitors center, the government Rest House, the lavish Forum Hotel, and the gatehouse to the valley that leads to the *siq* and Petra proper.

PRACTICAL INFORMATION

The **tourist police** munch on cigar ends at the **Petra Visitors Center** (tel. 336 060; open Sat.-Thurs. 7am-5pm), where you can hire an official guide for a "low tour" of the city center (JD7 per trip). More comprehensive guided tours go to Al Madbah (JD7 extra), Ad-Deir (JD10 extra), and Jabal Harun (JD25). Trips to more remote areas should be arranged with the guide directly; prices vary from JD25 to JD50 per guide. If you use horses, you are also responsible for renting the guide's horse. It's easy to tag along behind a group with a guide or to form a group of your own. The various guidebooks available at the visitors center are helpful, but there's no substitute for the expertise of an official guide for trips to the more remote sites of Al Barid or Al Madras. On the other side of the visitors center are the Rest House and the swinging gate marking the beginning of the trail down to the *siq*. You can rent a horse for the short ride (JD7), but it's more interesting to walk; the tower cliffs of Jabal Khubtha are to the right, Jabal Madras to the left.

Wadi Musa has a **post office** next to the Musa Spring Hotel (open Sat.-Thurs. 7:30am-7pm, Fri. 7:30am-1:30pm), numerous stores, and a **health center**. There is also a **post office** behind the Petra Visitors Center. Petra's **telephone code** is 03.

Admission to the ancient city is JD20 for adults. Petra is open daily from 6am to 6pm, but these hours are loosely enforced. The generous guard at the entrance to the *siq* often admits people as late as 8pm, and if you choose to stay to see the sun set you'll have no problem getting out. Bring a flashlight, though.

ACCOMMODATIONS AND FOOD

Wadi Musa and Petra residents brag that the region of the rose-red city will soon have 22 hotels. Unfortunately, most of these cost more than the Baseball Diamond; but the few cheapies compete vigorously for foreign *fulous*.

Musa Spring Hotel, Restaurant, and Student House, Wadi Musa Gate (tel. 336 310; fax 336 910). Next to Moses' Spring as you enter Wadi Musa, the Musa is renowned for evening showings of *Indiana Jones* and *Lawrence of Arabia*. The cheaper rooms are damp and dark, but the upstairs rooms are passable. Free use of kitchen. Roof JD1. Singles JD3. Doubles JD6, with bath JD10. Breakfast JD1; lunch or dinner JD2. Free transportation to Petra.

Al-Anbat Hotel and Student House, Wadi Musa (tel. 336 265; fax 336 888). Follow the trough down from the spring until you see the hotel with the best view of the descent to Petra. Lots of orange, but it's all clean. Bed JD2.500, with bath JD5. Camping facilities—tents and showers—JD1.500. Free buses to Petra.

Al-Rashid Hotel (tel. 336 800; fax 336 600). Halfway down the winding road from Wadi Musa to Petra. One of the cleanest hotels in Jordan. Co-owner Wendy may help with Petra advice and horse or camel tours. JD8 per person. ½-board JD12 per person. Breakfast and taxi vouchers to Petra included.

Sunset Hotel (tel. 336 579; fax 336 950). About 200m up the hill to your left from the visitors center above Petra Moon Services. If your feet are sore and your butt hurts from a Petra camel ride, this place is for you—the first inexpensive and clean option outside of what's becoming Disney Petra. Rooftop camping with showers, mattress, and blankets JD2.500. Singles JD10. Doubles JD15.

Government Rest House (tel. 336 011). Live the life of the rich and famous in the Petra rest house. Sparkling rooms with accompanying prices that will take enough dinar out of your pocket to provide for a lightened load and easier rock-climbing. Singles a hefty JD20. Doubles JD30. Extra beds JD10 each. Prices are slated to rise in October 1994.

Camping inside Petra is now illegal, but lingering explorers may receive invitations for overnight stays from the hospitable Bedouin selling stuff. It's also possible to pick an off-the-beaten-path cave for a night, although explaining yourself to Jordanian police could turn you pinker than the ruins, or worse.

The **Rest House Restaurant** is worth a visit only because it was built into one of Petra's Nabatean tombs; have a drink in the tomb's lively inner chamber-*cum*-bar. In the separate eatery, a filling meal costs JD4 (both open until 11pm daily). The **Rest House** has its own brand-new restaurant. About JD2.500 gets you a tasty meal at the **Sunset Hotel**. A restaurant with a truly breathtaking view is attached to the **Al-Anbat Hotel** (meat and salad JD2.500, groups should reserve in advance.) The only place to eat in Petra itself is a small, *expensive* sandwich shop below the museum.

SIGHTS

Though the Nabateans often revered their monarchs, they worshipped only two deities: Dushara, the god of strength, who was symbolized by hard, sculptured rock, and Al Uzza (or Atargatis), the goddess of water and fertility. Still, the number of temples and tombs in Petra seems infinite. A little climbing will allow you to escape the lazy tour groups crowding the Khazneh and inner valley. A few of the spectacular monuments are close enough to be viewed in a one-day junket, but the majority require sweaty exploration. Be sure to bring plenty of water—Bedouin selling Kawther water will take advantage of your desperation.

Even before you reach the *siq*, caves staring from distant mountain faces and large *djinn* monuments (ghost tombs) will draw you in. On the left, built high into the cliff, stands the Obelisk Tomb. Closer to the entrance of the *siq*, rock-cut channels once cradled ceramic pipes which brought Ein Musa's waters to the inner city as well as to the surrounding farm country. A nearby dam burst in 1963, and the resulting flash flood killed 28 tourists in the *siq*. While designing a new dam, excavators uncovered the Nabateans' ancient dam and used it as a model for the new one.

As you enter the *siq*, walls towering 200m on either side begin to block out the light, casting enormous shadows on the niches that once held icons of the gods meant to protect the entrance and hex unwelcome visitors. The *siq* winds around for 1.5km, then slowly admits a faint pink glow as it widens at the **Khazneh** (Treasury). At 90m wide and 130m tall, it is the best preserved of Petra's monuments, although bullet holes are clearly visible on the upper urn. Believing the urn to be hollow and filled with ancient pharaonic treasures, Bedouin periodically fired at it, hoping to burst this impervious piñata. Actually, the treasury was a royal tomb and, like almost everything else at Petra, is quite solid. The colors are incredible; in the morning the sun's rays give the monument a rich peach color, while in late afternoon it glistens rose, turning blood-red with the sunset.

Down the road to the right as you face the Khazneh, Wadi Musa opens up to the large **Roman Theater** (straight ahead) and the long row of Royal Tombs on the face of Jabal Khubtha (on your right as the road curves to the right in front of the Roman Theater). The Romans built their theater under the red stone Nabatean necropolis, whose caves still yawn above it. The theater seats some 3000 people and is being restored to its 2nd-century appearance; appreciative audiences are returning for the first time in over 1500 years. A marble Hercules (now in the museum) was discovered just a few years ago in the curtained chambers beneath the stage.

Across the *wadi* are the **Royal Tombs.** The **Urn Tomb,** with its unmistakable recessed facade, commands a soul-scorching view of the still-widening valley. Nearby is the **Corinthian Tomb,** allegedly a replica of Nero's Golden Palace in Rome. The **Palace Tomb** (or the Tomb in Two Stories) literally juts out from the mountainside. The tomb had to be completed by attaching preassembled stones to its upper left-hand corner. Around the corner to the right is the **Tomb of Sextus Florentinus,** who was so enamored of these hewn heights that he asked his son to bury him in this ultimate outpost of the Roman Empire.

Around the bend to the left, several restored columns dot either side of the paved Roman **main street.** Two thousand years ago, columns lined the full length of the street, with markets and residences branching off. Nearby, the raised **Nymphaeum** ruins outline the ancient public fountain near its base. Across the road to the right, before the triple-arched gate, recent excavations have uncovered the **Temple of Al Uzza (Atargatis),** also called the **Temple of the Winged Lions.** In the spring you can watch the progress of American-sponsored excavations which have already uncovered several workshops and some cracked Nabatean crocks.

Also recently excavated by a joint Jordanian-American team is an immense **Byzantine church** rich with mosaics. The site lies several hundred meters to the right of the Roman street, near the Temple of the Winged Lions, from which some of the church's column bases and capitals were probably lifted. Each of the church's side aisles is paved with 70 square meters of remarkably preserved mosaic, depicting native as well as exotic or mythological animals, humans of various professions (flautist, camel driver, fisherman), and representations of the four seasons. The church is thought to have been a major 5th- and 6th-century cathedral, likely the seat of the bishop of the Byzantine province of Palaestina Tertia. The wealth apparent in the church's interior has thrown into question theories of Petra's decline, and of urban decline in general; this spectacular church was likely built in the late 5th century, presumably during the later stages of Petra's deterioration. Renovations should be complete by winter 1994.

Farther along, the triple-arched **Temenos Gate** was once the front gate of the **Qasr Bint Faraun** (Palace of the Pharaoh's Daughter), a Nabatean temple built to honor the god Dushara. On your left as you pass through the triple-arched gate is a **Nabatean Temple.** On the trail leading off behind the temple to the left, a single standing column gloats beside its two fallen comrades—**Amoud Faraun** (Pharaoh's Pillar) marks the entrance to the ancient Roman city. To the right of the Nabatean temple, a rock-hewn staircase leads to a small archaeological **museum** (open daily 6am-6pm. Free.), which holds the spoils of the Winged Lions dig and carved stone figures from elsewhere in Petra. (Open daily 6am-6pm. Free.)

Hikes to Remote Sights

Up to now, particularly if you're visiting during the peak spring and fall seasons, you'll have shared Petra's splendor with a drove of peregrinating shutterbugs. Many people, content with daytrip dosage, will go home raving about Petra's first 10%. But that's only the tip of an iceberg: the magnificent rest of Petra is nestled in dozens of high places scattered over a vast area. At least two days are necessary for the following seven treks and another two or three if you venture beyond Petra proper—assuming you don't get indulgently lost at least a few times. The Bedouin say that to appreciate Petra you must stay long enough to watch your nails grow long.

Wadi Turkimaniya

The shortest and easiest of the hikes leads down the *wadi* to the left of and behind the Temple of the Winged Lions. Fifteen minutes of strolling down the road that runs through the rich green gardens of **Wadi Turkimaniya** guide you to the only tomb at Petra with a Nabatean inscription. The lengthy invocation above the entrance beseeches the god Dushara to safeguard the tomb and to protect its contents from violation. Unfortunately, Dushara took an interminable sabbatical and the chamber has been stripped bare.

Qasr Habis

A second, more interesting climb begins at the end of the road that descends from the Pharaoh's Pillar to the cliff face, a few hundred meters left of the museum. The trail dribbles up to the **Qasr Habis** (Crusader Castle), outclassed by many of Petra's other splendors. The steps have been recently restored; and the climb to the top and back takes less than an hour.

Jabal Harun   جبـل هارون

The third climb begins just to the right of Jabal Habis below the museum. A sign points to **Ad-Deir** (the Monastery) and leads northwest across Wadi Siyah, past the Forum Restaurant to Wadi Deir and its fragrant oleander. As you squeeze through the narrowing canyon you will confront a human-shaped hole in the facade of the **Lion's Tomb.** A hidden tomb awaits daredevils who try to climb the cleft to the right; less intrepid wanderers backtrack to the right and find the tomb a few minutes later. Again on the path, veer left, and eventually stone steps lead past a providential Pepsi stand to Petra's largest monument.

Ad-Deir, 50m wide and 45m tall, undertaken in the first century CE but never completed, is less ornate than the Khazneh. On the left, a lone tree popping through a crack in the rock marks more ancient steps, which continue all the way up to the rim of the urn atop the monastery. Straight across the *wadi* looms the highest peak in the area, **Jabal Harun** (Aaron's Mountain or Mount Hor). On top of the mountain, a white church reportedly houses the **Tomb of Aaron.** The whole trip takes a couple of hours, a few more if you detour into **Wadi Siyah** and visit its seasonal waterfall on the way back.

Jabal Umm al-Biyara   جبـل أم بيارة

The fourth hike climbs **Jabal Umm al-Biyara** (Mother of Cisterns), which towers over the Crusader castle on Jabal Habis. Follow the trail from the left of the Nabatean temple past the Pharaoh's Pillar and down into the *wadi* to the right. If you scramble 50m up the rock chute to the left of the blue sign you'll reach the beginning of a stone ramp and stairway that leads to the top. It was here, at the site of Petra's original acropolis and the biblical city of Sela, that a Judean king supposedly hurled thousands of Edomites over the cliff's edge. The gigantic piles of shards, over 8000 years old, are the only remnants of the mountains' first inhabitants. This grueling excursion takes three hours.

If instead of climbing Umm al-Biyara you continue south along Wadi Tughra, which runs by its foot, you'll eventually reach the **Snake Monument**, one of the earliest Nabatean religious shrines. From here it's about two hours to Aaron's Tomb on Jabal Harun. The path meanders around Mount Hor before ascending it from the south. When it disappears on the rocks, follow the donkey dumpings. As you start to climb Jabal Harun you'll see a lone tent. Inside, a Bedouin, the official holder of the keys, will escort you the rest of the way and open the building for you to explore. The entire trek takes five or six hours.

The High Place

One of the most popular hikes is the circular route to the **High Place** on Jabal al-Madbah, a place of sacrifice with a full view of Petra. A staircase sliced in the rock leads to the left just as the Roman Theater comes into view. Follow the right prong when the trail levels and forks at the top of the stairs. On the left, **Obelisk Ridge** presents one obelisk to Dushara and another to Al Uzza. On the peak to the right, the Great High Place supports a string of grisly sights: two neatly cut altars, an ablution cistern, gutters for draining away sacrificial blood, and cliff-hewn bleachers for an unobstructed view of the animal sacrifices. Head downhill past the Pepsi stand, leaving the obelisks behind you, and backtrack under the western face of the Great High Place. If you hunt around you'll find a staircase leading down to a sculptured **Lion Fountain.** The first grotto complex beyond it is the **Garden Tomb.** Below it is the **Tomb of the Roman Soldier** and across from it a rock **triclinium** (feast hall), which has the only decorated interior in Petra. The trail then leads into Wadi Farasa by the Katute site, the dwelling of a merchant apparently driven away by the Romans' nearby waste disposal site. You'll leave the trail near the Pillar. The circle, followed either way, takes about an hour and a half.

Al Madras and Al Barid المدرس و البارد

The region around Petra harbors a wealth of minor archaeological pleasures, but only those within walking or donkey-riding distance are accessible. All roads in this isolated area lead back to the Kings' Highway, not to sights. The peripheral location of the sights is a blessing; outside Petra, imported commercialism has neither altered the Bedouin lifestyle nor chased away wildlife.

A trail branching to your left just past the Obelisk Tomb and just before the entrance to the *siq* leads to **Al Madras**, an ancient Petran suburb with almost as many monuments as Petra itself. On the way, watch for the short-eared desert hare and a full spectrum of long lanky lizards—purple, fuchsia, and iridescent blue. Come with water, a snack, and a guide. The round-trip takes four to eight hours.

Past the Tomb of Sextus Florentinus and the **Mughar an-Nasara** (Caves of the Christians), a trail chisels into the rock leading to the northern suburb of **Al Barid.** A road passing the new hotel in Wadi Musa also approaches this archaeological site. Al Barid is a curious miniature of Petra, complete with a short *siq,* several carved tombs, and caves. Also off the new road past the hotel is **Al Beidha.** Excitement runs high among the members of the excavating expedition here because they have uncovered traces of a pre-pottery Neolithic village, a sedentary society dating to the 8th millennium BCE. This find would make Al Beidha, along with Jericho, one of the earliest known farming communities in the world. A Bedouin guide can lead you here via a painless trail (about 3hrs. each way). Bring an extra JD2-3 or some of your own native trinkets to trade, like a ukulele, fuzzy dice, or a mood ring.

■■■ AQABA العقبة

Set in a natural amphitheater beneath a curtain of rugged hills, Aqaba is land-locked Jordan's sole toe-hold on the Red Sea. A scene even more spectacular than that of the surrounding reddish mountains lurks under the sea: legions of brilliantly colored creatures flit through a surreal universe of coral. Aqaba is an important trade and military center; and as a swinging resort, it has become the darling of the Arab elite in need of a periodic escape from dry cityscapes. More liberal and relaxed than other parts of Jordan, Aqaba features bikini-clad Europeans drinking beer at the same bar with berobed Saudis. Allegedly, it also has Jordan's largest gay population.

At first, backpackers may hyperventilate at the expensive accommodations and restaurants and at the highfalutin' travelers from Germany strutting around as if they owned the beach. Careful scrutiny, however, shows that Aqaba has not completely overlooked the budget traveler.

With its strategic and commercial potential, Aqaba has never suffered neglect. In biblical times, Solomon's copper-laden ships sailed for Ophir from the port of

Etzion-Geber. The Romans stationed their famous Tenth Legion here, the Crusaders fortified the port and the little Pharaoh's Island 7km off the coast (in Egyptian territory). During the 1917 Arab Revolt, Faisal ibn Hussein (played by Sir Alec Guinness in *Lawrence of Arabia*) and T.E. Lawrence (Peter O'Toole) staged a desert raid on the Ottomans' fortifications and valiantly captured the port. In 1965 King Hussein shrewdly traded the Saudis 600 square km of southeastern desert for 13km of coastline, and started developing the city into a tourist's paradise. After the reopening of the Suez Canal in 1957 and the increased traffic caused by the Iran-Iraq War, the harbor became packed with huge juggernauts bulging with cargo. During the 1991 Gulf War, the blockade of the port, which became Iraq's chief illicit outlet to shipping lanes, slowed traffic considerably. Trade had resumed, under international supervision, by the summer of 1992. An August 1994 Jordanian-Israeli treaty opened the border between the two countries here, threatening a deluge of Israeli tourists.

ORIENTATION

Extending from King Hussein's villa on the Israeli border to the huge, fenced-in port facilities 4km down the arching corniche to the southeast, Aqaba is one elongated beach. Luxury hotels and military complexes have gobbled up a good part of the beach near town. Four countries come together in the small northern tip of the Gulf of Aqaba: Egypt meets Israel near the conspicuous resort hotels at Taba, Israel's Eilat faces Jordan's Aqaba across the newly-opened border, and Saudi Arabia looms on the southeast horizon.

Shops line the streets of central Aqaba branching from **Ailah Square.** South of the port and 10km from central Aqaba, the **ferry dock** handles the thousands of Egyptian workers and occasional foreign travelers who cross the Gulf of Aqaba to Nuweiba in Egypt (see Ferries to Egypt below). One kilometer past the ferry port you'll come to the **Marine Research Center** building, just past which you'll find Aqaba's finest coral reefs and a sandy beach that stretches south to a factory and the Saudi border.

Those who hitch in and around Aqaba find it easy because an army of trucks serves the port. Herds of six-wheeled beasts cover vast stretches along the highway 2km north of town. These truck stops make strategic starting points for hitching trips to the north. Women travelers are strongly discouraged from hitchhiking. Taxi fare out to the truck stops is about 500fils; the road to the port, which bumps the eastern side of town, has closer hitching points.

PRACTICAL INFORMATION

Aqaba's overheated atmosphere has a discernible effect on human behavior. People drive like idiots here, even more so than in the rest of the country. There are (ignored) road signs telling drivers to lay off their horns. Aqaba is also far more lax about morality than the rest of Jordan. Hotels and most restaurants are licensed for drinking, and both men and women wear shorts in and around the city. Nonetheless, as always, women will be stared at, talked to, flirted with, and even touched.

Visitors Center: (tel. 313 363 or 731), on the grounds of the new Islamic Museum between the castle built by the 16th-century Sultan Ganswa El-Ghouri and the southern waterfront. Maps, brochures, information on travel to nearby cities and Egypt, and a complaints box. Officially open 8am-2pm, but staff is often inclined to close around 1:30pm and reopen for a few hours in the evening.

Tourist Police: Tel. 313 513.

Egyptian Consulate: Al Istiqlal St. (tel. 316 171); turn right along the curve about 800m northwest of the Aquamarina II Hotel and look for an empty guard booth in front. Egyptian visas can be obtained in 1 day. Bring your passport, a photo, and JD12. Open daily 9am-2pm.

Currency Exchange: Bank hours are normally Sat.-Thurs. 8:30am-12:30pm, with some banks open for 1-2hr. past 4pm, except on Thurs. Money exchangers are also open in the morning and late afternoon. Bring a passport to exchange traveler's checks. Convenient banks include the **Arab Bank** (tel. 313 545), across a vacant lot from the Nile Palace Hotel, and the **Housing Bank** (tel. 315 325).

American Express: International Traders Travel Agency Office, P.O. Box 136 (tel. 313 757), 1 block west of Ailah Sq., a few doors from the Ali Baba Restaurant. Open Sat.-Thurs. 8am-1pm and 4-7pm, a few hours Fri. mornings if business is good.

Central Post Office (tel. 313 939): 2 blocks uphill from Ailah Sq., next to the large radio tower. **Poste Restante** and **Express Mail Service** here, **international calls** and **telegrams** next door. Open Sat.-Thurs. 7:30am-7pm, Fri. 7:30am-1:30pm. **Telephone code:** 03.

Air Travel: Royal Jordanian (tel. 314 477) has regular flights to and from Amman (about 45min., one-way and round-trip both JD25, JD15 with proof of Jordanian residency). Buses from Aqaba International Airport to the center of the city are run by various hotels. The trip by taxi costs JD2 per person.

Buses and *Service:* the station 2 blocks uphill from Ailah Sq. serves points north of Aqaba. Minibuses to Petra (6:30 and 11am, return 3pm, one-way JD2). Buses to Wadi Rum (6:30am, return 3pm, JD1.500). Regular taxis offer groups (max. 4 people) quick transport to Petra (JD25), Wadi Rum (1hr.; round-trip JD15), and the Aqaba ferry terminal (10km, JD1.500). The **JETT Buses** station (tel. 315 222) is 1km west of Ailah Sq., on the corner of a tourist trap near Miramar Hotel. Regular bus service to Amman only (7 buses daily 7am-4pm, 4hr., JD4). Best to reserve in advance. JETT buses are luxury class, with hostess service, A/C, and videos.

Ferries to Egypt: Jordanian National Lines to Nuweiba in the Sinai (2 daily, around 11am and 6pm, 3½hr., JD18 plus JD6 departure tax). Multi-hr. waits are not uncommon. Buses from Nuweiba to Cairo meet the boats (6-10hr., E£25). In Aqaba purchase tickets from any agency; in Amman at the JETT Station or Za'art-arah Shipping on Prince Muhammad St. off Third Circle (open Sat.-Thurs. 8:30am-7pm, Fri. 8:30am-noon). Jordan National Lines headquarters are in Amman (tel. (06) 782 782). See Essentials: Border Crossings, p. 29 for more information.

Car Rental: Prices are controlled by the government and range from US$25-80 per day, plus 44-88¢ per km. Call around for specials and unlimited-mile options. Rental agencies include **Rum** (tel. 313 581), **Al-Cazar** (tel. 314 131), and of course **Avis** (tel. 312 111), at the International Airport.

English Bookstore: Yamani Bookshop (tel. 312 221) opposite the post office. Solid selection of magazines and tourist guides. Pick up a copy of Oliver North's majestic prose translated into Arabic. Also sells film, snorkeling equipment, suntan lotion, tobacco, and sundries. Open daily 10am-2:30pm and 6-10pm.

Laundry: Most hotels provide laundry service, but this is a sure way to break your budget. The only laundromat is **Friends Laundry** (tel. 315 051), in the open area near the bus and *service* station.

Pharmacies: Tbaileh Pharmacy (tel. 315 050) and the **Jerusalem Pharmacy** (tel. 314 747) are open 24 hrs.

Medical Emergency: Princess Haya el-Hussein Hospital (tel. 314 111 or 112), near the JETT Station on the way into town. One of Jordan's best hospitals, with decompression chambers and a staff capable of dealing with diving accidents.

Police: Tel. 312 411 or 412. Station down the steps and 100m to the right of the Palm Beach Hotel. Issues camping permits for JD1.

ACCOMMODATIONS

While Aqaba has some of the highest prices in Jordan (after Petra, of course), there are several excellent values. The usual rules apply. Shop, bargain, walk out a few times, and the prices will come down. In the summer look for air conditioning. The good budget hotels cluster around the downtown mosque.

Nairoukh Hotel, Dewek (tel. 312 984 or 985). Behind Ata Ali and Ali Baba restaurants, the Nairoukh Hotel is Aqaba's best, cleanest value. The employees whistle while they work (constantly cleaning), and will offer to rent videos for the beach-weary. Mini-bus service for diving. Singles JD7. Doubles JD11.

Al-Shula Hotel, Raghadan St. (tel. 315 155; fax 315 154), behind the Hussein Ibn Ali Mosque. Color TV, refrigerators, bidets, balconies, and a charming view of

Eilat. Red curtains cast a gory pall over the rooms on sunny afternoons. Singles JD24. Doubles JD28. Breakfast included.

Nairoukh Hotel 2 (tel./fax 312 980 or 981). Face out to sea in front of the mosque and walk five minutes to the left. The Nairoukh 2 is modern and relatively clean. TVs and A/C, but a quick flip of a light switch may reveal creatures moving in the night. Singles JD20. Doubles JD25. Breakfast included.

Red Sea Hotel (tel. 312 156). One of the few buildings taller than the mosque's minaret. Look for "Red Sea" written in red. The rooms could be much cleaner, and the showers leak. Stay here if the Nairoukh 1 next door is full. Singles with bath JD6, with A/C, TV, and fridge JD8.500. Doubles JD7, with amenities JD11.

Jordan Flowers Hotel (tel. 314 377), a ½-block north of the Jerusalem Hotel. Welcoming and weedless. Friendly and helpful management caters to the needs of a budget traveler. Singles JD4, with bath JD5, and A/C, TV, and balcony JD14. Doubles JD5, with bath JD8, and amenities JD18.

Jerusalem Hotel (tel. 314 815), 2nd floor, on the street running south from Ailah Sq. Low-budget, sporadically clean. Best to sleep on the roof (with its own mattresses and showers) for JD1. Singles JD3.500. Doubles JD5. Triples JD6.

Aqaba Hotel (tel. 314 091), along the waterfront 1.5km west of Ailah Sq. For the self-indulgent who must be close to the water. High-class divers and people who eat fruit from silver platters on the beach stay in the Aqaba's fancy rooms. Regular rooms cost, but you can sometimes put 3 people in a bungalow for JD30.

The only legal **camping** north of the port is in the lots beside some of the larger hotels. The **Aqaba Hotel** has hard ground (it's basically a parking lot) but the JD5 fee admits you to the private beach and showers. Six km south of the port are the new and wonderfully scenic government camping facilities with showers and bathrooms for only JD1. To get there, walk or take a taxi (JD3, but you may have to fight your driver to get a good price).

FOOD

Luckily, restaurants and sandwich shops take up more space in Aqaba than Israeli bugs along the Eilat border. Fresh fish, the obvious staple of a seaside town, is actually a rarity here. Because of the low plankton content in the clear northern waters of the Gulf of Aqaba, there are few edible sea creatures afloat. Jordanians are not permitted to fish the richer Saudi waters and the Egyptian export tax is outlandish. There is a **market** just up from Ailah Sq. where you can fill up on fresh fruit, bread, and cheese, though your snout may be overwhelmed on windless summer days. Shops on the streets surrounding the square sell delicacies from fried sloth to ice cream, mostly at high prices. Lamb, beef, and falafel are everywhere around the Hussein Ibn Ali Mosque, and the best restaurants stretch from the mosque to the area around the Aqaba Gulf Hotel.

Ali Baba Restaurant (tel. 313 901), on the corner north of the Hussein Ibn Ali Mosque, next to Ata Ali. Fish up a heavy JD7 for their excellent fish specials, or get a salad (JD1), *croque-monsieur* (JD2) if you're feeling French, or bland wine. Open daily 8am-midnight.

Chicken Tikka, An-Nahda St. (tel. 313 633), 100m west of the Aquamarina II Hotel on your right. Café tables outside, terrible music inside. Try the Tikka Special—2 pieces of spicy chicken, fries, and *purri* (puffy fried bread)—for JD1.800. Open daily 11am-midnight, or later if you look desperately hungry.

Captain's Restaurant, An-Nahda St. (tel. 316 905), west of the Aquamarina II Hotel, look for the blue-and-white veranda. Enjoy spaghetti (JD1-2), fresh fish (JD4), or omelettes (500fils). Excellent view of the Pizza Hut across the street. Open daily 10am-midnight or 1am.

Chili House Restaurant (tel. 312 435), behind the Captain's Restaurant and to the left of Mickey Mouse. Something resembling a double cheeseburger (JD1.300), fish sandwiches (JD1.250), and Slush Puppies (300fils). Look for the big, yellow smiley-face with its tongue sticking out. Open daily 11am-midnight.

Ata Ali Café (tel. 315 200), to the north of the Hussein Ibn Ali Mosque. No trip to Aqaba is complete without daily trips to AA's sweets shop. Filling meals for JD3-3.500, hard or soft *kinafeh* 400fils, and mouth-watering 3-scoop sundaes (650fils) and sugar cones (200fils). Open daily 7am-11:30pm or midnight.

SIGHTS

Yemeniyyeh Reef, just south of the Marine Research Center beyond the port, ranks among the world's best for scoping fish. The new **Royal Diving Center** (tel. 317 035; JD2 entrance fee) in the Yemeniyyeh area rents out snorkeling (JD2) and diving equipment (1 dive JD15, 2 dives JD24). Most luxury hotels also rent out equipment and organize outings. With a mask, snorkel, and pair of fins you can wander off on your own to some of the more isolated spots near the Saudi border, where the fish run on super-octane. See Sinai: Underwater Adventures, p. 222 for important information on snorkeling and scuba diving; for **emergency** medical help call 193.

The **Seastar Watersports Center** (tel. 314 131; fax 314 133), located in the Al-Cazar Hotel, conducts dives daily at 9am and 2pm (arrive ½-hr. early). Equipment rental for 1 dive is JD20, 2 dives JD36, JD5 per half-day for snorkelers, including transportation. Try-out dives possible for beginners. If you have five days and are serious about submerging, you can take the American PCEI scuba diving training course (US$330 including equipment and supplies). Snorkeling fiends should invest in their own equipment and go solo. The **Yamani Bookstore** across from the post office has the biggest selection of masks (JD8-12) and fins (JD12-20).

The **aquarium** is in the Marine Research Center (tel. 315 145), just beyond the port. (Admission JD1. Open Sat.-Wed. 7am-2:30pm, Thurs. and Fri. 9am-2:30pm; daily 7:30am-3:30pm in the winter. Taxis to the aquarium cost JD3.) A costly **glass-bottom boat ride** (about JD10), traveling up and down the coast, is worthwhile if you've never been to a tropical fish store.

In the early mornings and late afternoons the winds are strong enough to make **windsurfing** possible; the Aquamarina Club charges JD3.600 per half-hour for a board. The Aquamarina also offers waterskiing and, for the less adventurous, paddle-boating.

The Aqaba Hotel will gouge you JD2.200 for the privilege of burning your plebeian feet on its patrician white sands—shade and lounge chairs are reserved for guests. Near the excavations of **Aila** (medieval Aqaba) in front of the Miramar Hotel is a free and relatively clean **public beach.** (In the 7th to 10th centuries CE, Aila—"god" in Aramaic—was an early Islamic port trading as far away as China.) The majority of Aqaba's more scenic, clean, and empty free beaches are quite a distance away. Indigent sun and coral worshippers often walk southeast to the free pebble beach behind a "Restricted Area—No Camping" sign. It's mostly an all-male scene, and women may become the focus of more attention than they want. The trek past the port on the 10km strip leading to Saudi Arabia is long, but if you've got a whole day to conquer and a grand picnic, this is the place to go. A hat and sunscreen are necessities, no matter how tan you think you are.

Aqaba should thank its lucky starfish for its aquatic splendors, because the sights above sea level don't hold much water. The recently discovered ruins of Aila are the only exception, and they're not all that exceptional. In a seemingly plain beachside lot across from the Miramar Hotel, archaeologists have uncovered the original 120m by 160m 10th-century port. The sight is always open and visitors are free to wander amidst signs explaining the paltry ruins. Items recovered in the excavations, including Greek and Arabic inscriptions, pottery shards, and other small items are displayed in the recently completed **Aqaba Museum,** in the same building as the visitors center between the castle and the southern waterfront (open daily 8am-2pm; JD1). The **Medieval Castle** itself, built by the 16th-century CE Sultan Ganswa Al Ghouri, behind a dilapidated mosque and a palm grove, is gradually being restored by the Department of Antiquities.

An accord between the Jordanian and Egyptian governments has recently opened up the Egyptian **Pharaoh's Island** (7km off shore) to tourists with Jordanian visas.

Day-passes can be obtained in Aqaba and the boat ride takes about 45 minutes (JD20). There is boffo swimming and snorkeling (bring your own equipment) around the island (known in Jordanian Arabic as Jaziret Far'aun). Contact the Aqua Marina hotel for cruise details; see Sinai: Northern Aqaba Coast, p. 234 for more on the island.

■ NEAR AQABA: WADI RUM وادي رام

Those who most appreciate the majestic grandeur of Wadi Rum revel in its inaccessibility. Few buses and no *service* come here, and most Jordanians have never been to this area located nearly 300km south of Amman. Buses and *service* along the Desert Highway can drop you off 25km north of Aqaba at the turn-off marked "Rum 30km." From there many people hitch a ride east and south to the **Desert Police Headquarters** within Wadi Rum. Hitching, always dangerous, is not a feasible option in the summer due to the lack of traffic in the area. *Do not attempt it.* A far wiser option is to form a group and either hire a taxi from Aqaba to transport you to and from Wadi Rum (JD15 per taxi) or rent a car on your own. The JD15 taxi fare is one-way, but some drivers are willing to do a round-trip with a 2-3 hour stay for JD25. Ask the budget hotel managers to help arrange a taxi ride. The journey is 90 minutes from Aqaba; the entrance fee is JD1. The Jordanian government has decided to push Wadi Rum as a tourist attraction—Douglas Scott climbed it in 1975 and they feel it's in your best interest to do the same. The expensive hotels organize their own expensive trips and JETT occasionally takes advantage of eager groups willing to do the superficial Wadi walk and "genuine" Bedouin tent tea thing.

Two tectonic plates split to create the wide desert valley of Rum, and the sunset here is a wonder of darkness and light. At the southern end of the valley is the fort of the Desert Camel Corps, the descendants of the British-trained Arab Legion. In *Seven Pillars of Wisdom*, T.E. Lawrence wrote that when he passed between these rusty crags his "little caravan fell quiet, ashamed to flaunt itself in the presence of such stupendous hills." The unabashed members of the Desert Patrol, however, are proud to be photographed in their best bib and tucker. When not posing for visitors, they chase smugglers and renegade Bedouin or offer nighttime desert jaunts to beautiful star-gazing areas. If you accept a jeep ride, be careful when entering and exiting the machine-gun-equipped star mobile.

Beyond the ruins of the Nabatean temple and behind the Bedouin tents, the great massif of Jabal Rum shoots up to 1754m. A jeep, or for those with calloused buttocks, a camel, can take you farther through the sheer rust-colored cliffs towering above the mud flats. These whopping slabs of granite and sandstone erupted through the desert floor millions of years ago, and their striations in the bays and grottoes point toward prodigious vistas down the 30km-long *wadi*. The otherworldly lavender mountains cast against the empty sky have inspired the name **Valley of the Moon.** For JD4 a Bedouin will lead you on a camel to a crack in the rocks, the origin of the springs that support all the *wadi*'s life. Dark stains point out the conduits carved by the ancient Nabateans to conserve that precious water. You may also be shown **Lawrence's Well,** where T.E. used to doze. The Bedouin can point to many mammoth boulders inscribed with millennia-old Thamudic graffiti. Such script, which evolved into modern Ethiopic, has been found from Ma'an to Meda'in Salih in Saudi Arabia.

Only jeeps or camels can continue through Wadi al-Umran to Khirbet Kithara back on the Desert Highway near Aqaba. Riding a camel ranges in price from JD2 to JD24, depending on the destination. Jeep trips can cost anywhere from JD5 per car to Lawrence's Well to JD30 to the Rock Bridge. Arrange it with the tourism official in the camp in the middle of Wadi Rum when you arrive.

As in Petra, the government **Rest House** ruins the natural splendor with overpriced food and drink (lunch JD5, water JD1) and tourist trinkets. Visitors who decide to stay overnight must sleep in one of the tents next to the Rest House (JD2 per person per night). A larger tent beside the small campground is often the site of traditional Bedouin music and singing in the evenings. There may also be invitations from Bedouin to stay the night in more remote locations. Bring matchbox cars for the Bedouin kids in exchange for a home for the night.

■ North of Amman

■■■ SALT السلط

During Turkish rule, Salt (pronounced "sult") was the chief administrative center for the surrounding area and, in the 1920s, it seemed a likely choice for the capital of the newly independent state of Jordan. However, the city was bypassed in favor of the smaller but more centrally located village of Amman. Salt is located among jagged hills which beckon avid hikers. The focal point of Salt is the mosque on **Jabal Yushah,** which, according to Muslim legend, covers the site of the tomb of the prophet Hosea (Yushah).

A survey of the crowded Ottoman houses and buildings clinging to the steep slopes can be the most rewarding part of a visit to this distinguished town. Venture up into the hills via one of the narrow stairways in the downtown area. Many of the yellow stone buildings date from the late 19th century. The Ottoman barracks, still intact, were built over a 13th-century fortress that was destroyed to prevent its capture by Crusaders. Salt is also known for its large Christian community, and church towers pepper the hillsides. If the adventurous spirit moves you, wander downhill from the bus station into **Wadi Sh'eib.** Unexplored caves and abandoned stone houses dot the area, and numerous dirt paths lead you further down. Here, pink flowers and fruit trees line the narrow stream that winds through the bottom of the valley. Leave a trail of bread crumbs, or you might not find your way back.

The **Salt Archaeological Museum** (tel. 555 653), uphill from the bus station, near the Jordan Islamic Bank, is essentially a dingy room with cabinets overflowing with coins and pottery dating from the Chalcolithic period (4000 BCE) to the Islamic period (1516 CE). Ask to see the early 20th-century photos of Salt, which show the old fortress walls and church towers. (Open Sat.-Thurs. 8am-2pm. Free.)

Taking a **minibus** up Wadi Sh'eib is the most dramatic approach to Salt. Lush, terraced farmlands and eucalyptus groves tumble down the *wadi* to the southwest of town, descending to Shuneh Nimrin (South Shuneh) on the busy route from Amman to the King Hussein/Allenby Bridge (Jordan Valley Highway). From Amman, corner an Abdali bus worker to find the minibus going to Salt (120fils). The workers are easy to spot; they wear shirts that say "Fast Orange." A **service taxi** from Abdali costs 300fils. Salt has no tourist office or hotels. If you get hungry during your hike around Salt try the **Mankal Chicken** restaurant on the oval behind the museum, or look for food stands past the Jordan Islamic Bank. The **post office** (tel. 554 978) is located uphill from the circle on the left (open Sat.-Thurs. 7:30am-7pm, Fri. 8am-1:30pm). Next door is the **police station** (tel. 555 632 or 621).

■■■ JERASH جرش

Dubbed Gerasa in ancient times and "awe-inspiring" by ace researcher-writer Steve, Jerash is one of the most extensive extant provincial Roman cities. Gerasa, along with Pella, was a member of the Decapolis, a commercial league of ten cities in Rome's Asian Province. Because of its isolation in a remote valley among the mountains of Gilead, Jerash survived long after the other nine cities were destroyed.

Unlike the other great cities of the classical period in this area, Jerash is typically Roman in design. The city's builders trampled over earlier settlements, so little evidence of pre-Roman days remains. Inscriptions calling the town Antioch reveal that the Seleucid king of that name had a prominent outpost here, but Jerash entered its golden age only after its conquest by the Roman emperor Pompey in 63 BCE. For the next three centuries, Jerash prospered. Granite was brought from as far away as Aswan and old temples were razed and rebuilt according to the latest architectural fads. The Emperor Trajan annexed the Nabatean lands in 106 CE and built a high-way from Damascus to Aqaba that passed through Jerash. Hadrian visited the town in 129; the Triumphal Arch built for the occasion still stands. The town was converted to Christianity and had a bishop by the mid-4th century.

Following the destruction of the Syrian trading center at Palmyra and the decline of the Nabatean kingdom, trade routes shifted from the desert to the sea. Frantic construction continued through the 6th century; however, without their former wealth, the citizens of Jerash could only replace the older monuments with flashy, inferior structures which were then plundered by invading Persians in 635 CE. The great earthquake of 747 relegated what little remained to the hands of the Muslim Arabs, who by then controlled the city. The Crusaders described Jerash as uninhabited, and it remained abandoned until its rediscovery in the 19th century. After the invasion of the Ottoman Turks, Circassians built the modern town on the eastern slope of the stream valley in what was once the main residential area of ancient Jerash.

PRACTICAL INFORMATION

Jerash will dazzle you along the 1km walk from the South Gate down the Street of Columns to the North Gate. The tiny Chrysoras River (Golden River) separates the ancient ruins on the western bank from the new town on the eastern bank. The **Visitors Information Center** (tel. 451 272; open Sat.-Thurs. 8am-2pm, closed holidays) is on the left of the main road entering the city from the south, about 400m north of the Triumphal Arch. Groups can hire guides for JD4, or JD8 for groups of 10 or more people. Booklets including maps and explanations of the sights invite leisurely exploration and range in price from JD1 to JD6. There is also a **post office** in town, behind the bus station (open daily 8am-7pm).

Buses and **service taxis** leave from the Jerash **bus station** on the western edge of the new city down from the baths and in front of the mosque. Buses to Amman's Abdali Station cost 375fils (slightly more with A/C), to Ajlun 250fils, and to Irbid 320fils; *service* cost about 50% more. Public transportation shuts down at around 7pm in summer and 5pm in winter. Hitchers to Amman, Dibbin, or Ajlun are known to walk south about 1km from the visitors center to the intersection with Highway 20. Turning right (west) leads to Ajlun and the Dibbin National Park. Going straight takes you to Amman; buses pass frequently and are easy to flag. Stand back from the road as you signal the bus; drivers consider time and speed infinitely more important than toes. The main road through Jerash continues north to Irbid. Hitchers go to the northern edge of town, just before the branch of road that splits off to the left.

ACCOMMODATIONS AND FOOD

Because Jerash is such an easy daytrip from Amman, there are no accommodations in the town. You might consider either camping at Dibbin National Park, about 8km away, or taking a room at the Dibbin Rest House (see Near Jerash, p. 471). At the **Jerash Rest House** (tel. 451 146) soft drinks are a rip-off at JD1 and prices for *kabab* or other fillers are beginning to threaten the stability of the columns remaining around Zeus' Temple. Food and drink for emergencies only (open daily 8am-9pm). At the **Al Khayyam Restaurant,** just past the visitors center on the main road, JD2.500 buys bread, salad, and grilled meat (open daily 11am-10 or 11pm). Street stands surrounding the bus station in town sell cheap falafel and *fuul* and will facilitate opportunities for priceless conversation with the people of Jerash.

SIGHTS AND ENTERTAINMENT

Jerash's captivating claim to fame is its extensive ruins, even though the best parts are probably lying beneath your feet (more than 90% of ancient Jerash is still unexcavated and awaits research). Enter the site by the visitors center or the North Gate. The ruins are open daily 7:30am to 7:30pm; admission is JD2. We'll walk you through the ruins from south to north.

The Jerash odyssey begins at the **Triumphal (Hadrianic) Arch,** 400m south of the ancient walls. The arch was built to honor the arrival of Emperor Hadrian in the winter of 129 CE. After your own majestic passage through the arch, you'll come upon the remaining stables and spectator seats of the **Hippodrome.** This section of Jerash precedes the Visitors Information Center. Ignore the ignoble booths that interrupt the trek and continue into the **Forum of Ionic Columns.** The Forum opens up into a main street intersected by two perpendicular avenues.

A footpath to the left in the forum leads to the astounding **South Theater**. Greek doodles reveal that 4000 of Jerash's wealthiest citizens could reserve seats here. The two-story backstage, still furnished with curtains and marble statues, once dominated the setting. The ruined **Temple of Zeus** lies behind the theater's seats. Stand in the top row of seats for the best view of the temple. The **Street of Columns** runs the distance between the forum and the North Gate. Its 260 pairs of columns are Corinthian replacements for earlier Ionic columns and were once capped by aqueducts carrying water throughout the ancient city. The huge paving stones show grooves worn by chariots and the occasional holes were designed for the drainage of rainwater into a sophisticated sewage system. Massive sidewalk coverings protected pedestrians from the sun, but only traces of these metropolitan parasols remain. The **Jerash Antiquities Museum** is on the right, halfway down the Street of Columns. Tall display cases mounted along the walls show neatly arranged artifacts from the Neolithic to the Ottoman periods. Coins, jewelry, theater "tickets" made of stone, and other household items highlight the museum's small collection. (Open Sat.-Thurs. 7:30am-5pm, closed on holidays. Free.)

When you reach the first intersection, named South Tetrapylon for its four slabs, look for lizards, cats, turtles, and the **Cathedral** and **Nymphaeum** to the left. The "crow-step" designs on these buildings and the Nabatean coins found here bear witness to the strong commercial links with the desert kingdom at Petra. The ornamental fountains of the Nymphaeum were used in an annual reenactment of the Miracle at Cana, where Jesus changed water into wine (John 2:1-11). Several hundred meters behind the cathedral, three churches possess the finest mosaics to survive Caliph Yazid II's attempt to destroy all "images and likenesses" in 720 CE.

The **East Baths** are across the *wadi,* just north of the mosque in the new town. Scattered around the western part of the city are the ruins of some 13 churches of more recent vintage. The **Northern Gate** was built in the 2nd century CE to open onto the newly completed road to Pella in the Jordan Valley. The ominous columned structure at the top of the hill is the **Temple of Artemis.**

Occasionally, during the summer months (April-October), there is an hour-long **sound and light show** among the ruins, with special JETT buses running to and from the show. Check with the JETT office in Amman (tel. 664 146) for details.

Jerash is undergoing eternal restoration as the government attempts to raise the city's profile. The **Jerash Festival,** a wicked good time instituted in 1981, takes place under royal patronage every summer beginning in the second half of July. Check with the Jerash Festival office in Amman for details (tel. 675 199) or see *The Jordan Times* for complete coverage. The South Theater and Artemis Steps provide a dramatic setting for musical, theatrical, and dance groups from all over the world, and recently featured Andrew Lloyd Webber's breathtakingly mediocre musical-on-roller skates, *Starlight Express.* Shows range from the Gary Burton Quintet to Radio Jordan Orchestra to the Azerbaijan State Ballet to modern interpretations of *The Taming of the Shrew*. Recently, more Jordanian artists, such as renowned composer Yousef Khaso, are appearing on the schedule. Ticket prices vary; if you arrive after 7:30pm you won't have to pay the JD2 entrance fee to the ruins. You will be searched upon entry. An international telephone exchange, set up on the grounds, charges average fees.

Transport to and from Jerash during the festival is chaotic. Do not expect to hitch unless you are leaving town before 4pm. *Service* are also crowded. Your best bet is to wrangle a group and share a private taxi. Coming home at about 10pm is less of a problem, though most cars are still full and will not stop for hitchers.

■ NEAR JERASH

The Aleppo pines and oaks of the fertile woodland are a remarkable sight in this desert country. Located in the hills 10km southwest of Jerash and 65km north of Amman, the **Dibbin National Park** encompasses some 20km of forest stretching south from the town of the same name.

On the old road to Jerash near Dibbin village is the **Dibbin Rest House** (tel. (04) 452 413; fax 813 246, Amman), offering shaded bungalows with private bathrooms, telephones, fridges, and TVs. (Singles JD13.200. Doubles JD15.400. Extra beds JD5.) The access road leaves the Amman-Jerash Highway about 2km south of Jerash; look for the signs. You'll have to take a car, as neither buses nor *service* access the park. Another option is the bus from Jerash to the nearby village of Dibbin; the hike from the village to the park is about 2km uphill. The Rest House fills up during holidays, so it's best to call ahead and make reservations. For nature-lovers, the park offers ideal campgrounds, free of charge and equally free of facilities.

■ ■ ■ AJLUN عجلون

Atop the highest peak overlooking Ajlun is Qal'at ar-Rabadh, a huge Arab castle built between 1184 and 1185 by Azz ad-Din Ausama, a commander under Salah ad-Din. This is the castle you dreamed about visiting when you were young. Filled with secret passages, winding crumbly staircases, and dark corridors, the castle begs visitors to let their imaginations run wild. Crusader knights spent decades unsuccessfully trying to capture the castle and nearby village. The name Kafranjah, a town in the area famous for its olive trees, suggests that the crusading Franks (*Franjis* in Arabic) did some time here—if only as prisoners. The Crusader threat quelled, and Mamluks began using the castle to transmit messages by beacon and pigeon; from Baghdad to Cairo, day or night, the relay could be made in 12 hours. (Open daily 6:30am-6 or 7pm. Free.) Less-than-helpful guides are available at the entrance.

PRACTICAL INFORMATION

Ajlun lies a hilly 24km west of Jerash, an easy hitch or bus ride from that town, from Amman (73km), or from Irbid (88km). *Service* from Amman takes 75 minutes (750fils); the bus is slower but cheaper (500fils). From Ajlun's main traffic circle, which revolves around a sickly henna tree gasping from the fumes, it's 4km of gently sloping road to the summit. You can catch a taxi at the traffic circle for JD1 round-trip, or a minibus for 100fils. Ajlun's **post office** is located on Amman St., on your right as you enter the town, a few hundred yards from the tree (open Sat.-Thurs. 7:30am-7pm, closed Fri. and holidays). Exchange money at either the **Housing Bank,** next door to the post office, or at the **Bank of Jordan,** on Irbid St., uphill from the circle (open Sat.-Thurs. 8am-12:30pm, closed Fri. and holidays).

The only lodgings are the **Rabadh Castle Hotel** (tel. (04) 462 202; singles JD24, doubles JD32) and the **Ajlun Hotel** (tel. (04) 462 524; singles JD15, doubles JD18). Both are between Ajlun and the castle. The owner of the Rabadh will amuse you with stories of when his ancestors inhabited the castle.

The Rabadh Hotel's terrace restaurant charges eye-moistening prices for its view of the fortress and valley: *kabab* or a full breakfast for JD2. If you stick to *mezze* dishes at 250fils per plate, you can afford an enjoyable light lunch. Those who prefer to court their bellies rather than their eyes should stop in at the **Green Mountain Restaurant** (open daily 6:30am-8:30pm) in Ajlun's center circle. A half-chicken costs 800fils, *kabab* JD1.100, and hummus and *fuul* 220fils; 650fils buys a complete meal which includes rice, meat, and a vegetable.

■■■ THE JORDAN VALLEY AND THE DEAD SEA

GETTING THERE

The greatest obstacle in reaching Deir Alla, Pella, and the Dead Sea is getting to the highway that follows the contours of the Jordan River along the length of the valley. Once there, hop on one of the many buses or *service* shuttling up and down the road. Buses leave from Abdali Station for Deir Alla (400fils) and for South Shuna (400fils). From the Ras al-Ayn area they go to the Dead Sea Rest House/Suweimeh (500fils). To reach this area begin at Al Husseini Mosque. Exit the mosque and walk left about 10 minutes. When the road forks, go left and cross the bridge. Take a right on the big street and then a left up the big hill. This is Jerusalem St. The buses are a few minutes up the road. Don a fedora, bring plenty of water, and don't forget your passport—you'll need it at several military roadblocks along the way.

THE DEAD SEA البحر الميت

After a minibus descent through rolling hills that will rival your 747's approach to Queen Alia airport, prepare to come as close to walking on water as is humanly possible. The Dead Sea's northeastern shore, 60 to 90 minutes from Amman or Deir Alla, hosts the only stretch of sand open to visitors on the Jordanian side. During the middle of the day, the sun reflects off the sea's still surface, creating the illusion that the entire body of water is about to spill into the Jordan Valley. The peculiar buoyancy of this briny water forces even the densest swimmer into a back float. Try bringing a magazine in for a leisurely read. The salt water causes even the tiniest paper cut to feel like an amputation without anaesthetic, so be careful when you shave, or wait until after. See Israel: Dead Sea, p. 329 for geographical information.

The only overnight accommodations available along the Dead Sea are at the very expensive Dead Sea Spa Hotel, a couple of kilometers past the **Dead Sea Rest House** (tel. (05) 572 901). The Rest House offers showers to relieve you of Lot's wife's encrusted fate. Unless you swim around the barrier on the north, which closes off the nicest section of beach, you'll have to pay JD1 to enter the resort enclave. The complex contains showers, the air-conditioned Rest House, and an overpriced restaurant (buffet lunch JD5 per person, soft drinks a pocket-lightening 600fils). Those with calloused feet won't mind the walk into the water, but others may want to wear some form of foot protection. The beach also has shelters for potentially pink-skinned, pale faces. The last bus leaves around 3:30pm and the rest house offers no overnight accommodations. If you do get stranded, however, the sunset over the West Bank will almost make it worth it. (Rest House open daily 8am-10:30pm; swimming allowed until sundown.) About 5km past the Rest House, a natural swimming pool is nestled between the colorful cliffs.

Within 30km south on the highway to Aqaba (Rte. 35) is **Zarqa Ma'in,** a cascading hot spring. (See Near Madaba, p. 454.) A road connecting the Dead Sea Rest House and Zarqa Ma'in is rumored to be in the works.

DEIR ALLA AND PELLA دير علا وطبقة فحل

Deir Alla (the High Temple; all temples here were built at the top of the hill), 50km north of the Dead Sea, is the spot where Jacob supposedly snoozed after wrestling with the angel (Genesis 32:24-32). On and around the sandy *tel* outside of the modern town, archaeologists have collected Bronze Age, Iron Age, Roman, and Islamic artifacts documenting over 20 centuries of history. Two temples dating back as far as 1300 BCE have been excavated. To the casual observer, however, the *tel* tells no tales; baked mud walls of ancient temples and shrines blend into the top of the tanned mound, only vaguely suggesting the former structures. Visits to Deir Alla should be planned for specific archaeological, religious, or procrastination purposes only. If you go on a whim, be prepared for boredom and maybe heatstroke in summer. A tiny exhibit at the dig headquarters displays maps of the excavation, tools, and early kitchen knick-knacks. Look for the headquarters behind the site or solicit the services of the area's eager-to-please children.

Buses to Deir Alla leave Amman's Abdali Station according to the usual "when it's full it goes" schedule (400fils). Arrive at Abdali early in the morning for best results. *Service* run from Abdali to Deir Alla (600fils). You can also get to Deir Alla by bus from Suwalha (300fils), not to be confused with Suweileh.

About 30km north of Deir Alla, abandoned mud huts give way to Bedouin tents and camel posts at **Tabaqat Fahl,** the biblical **Pella.** A thriving city during the first century CE, owing to membership in the Decapolis commercial league, Pella is gradually being unearthed by American and Australian archaeologists. On the bank of a tortuous *wadi,* a stark row of Roman columns frames bald hills and gaping ancient tombs. Far below, a Byzantine amphitheater opens onto green lawns and cool springs at the mouth of the *wadi.* Locals have dammed the spring to create pools that are great for splashing in but not for drinking—bring potable water. Across from the Archaeological Station lie the ruins of an Umayyad mosque and cemetery. Renovations of the church and civic center behind the theater unearthed skeletons of camels and their keeper, buried since an earthquake in 747 CE.

To reach the site from the main road at the city of Al Mashari'a, hike 2km up the paved turn-off to Tabaqat Fahl. It's a butt-busting thigh-burner of a walk, but keep on truckin' because the view from the top is worth every shed calorie. After passing through Tabaqat Fahl, tackle the dirt road on the right, yielding only to camel dung. The **Petra Rest House** overlooks the valley, the ruins, and the spring. Campers with sleeping bags stay for free. A set menu including fish, salad, hummus, and beverage costs JD5-6, depending on the season and recent business (tel. 291 102; open daily 8:30am-9pm and often later). Buses run from Deir Alla (150fils), Suwalha (150fils), and Irbid's west bus station (300fils) to Al Mashari'a at the base of Pella. Amman's Abdali Station serves each of these connecting cities. Because the routes run near the Israeli border, you will be asked to show your passport at several points. When you enter the bus, tell the driver where you intend to go—all signs are in Arabic only.

■■■ IRBID   اربد

Much like Amman, Irbid (1hr. north of Jerash) is an industrial center which has overwhelmed the site of its ancient Decapolis city (Arbila). But while expansion in Amman has nonetheless left some areas uninhabited, Irbid's narrow streets are stuffed with merchants, kung fu theaters, and restless taxis. Besides the tiny **Natural History Museum** (open Wed.-Mon. 8am-5pm) on the sedate campus of **Yarmouk University,** there is little to do here but plan your trip to Umm Qeis or Al Himma.

PRACTICAL INFORMATION

Irbid's **post office** (open Sat.-Thurs. 7:30am-7pm; Fri. and holidays 8am-1:30pm) and **telephone office** with international phone and telex services (open Sat.-Thurs. 7:30am-10pm; hours vary Fri. and holidays) are located just off the main square. **ANZ Grindlay's Bank** in, across from the post office, exchanges cash and traveler's checks (open Sat.-Thurs. 8am-12:30pm). The **telephone code** is 02.

Many have an easy time hitching to Irbid via Jerash, but the quickest way to the city from Amman is by the Arabella or Hijazi bus companies (570fils, with A/C 810fils). **Minibuses** from Amman, Jerash, and Ajlun take somewhat longer and drop you off at Irbid's South Station, at which point you can take a **service taxi** to downtown (55fils) and from downtown to North Station (55fils). You can also catch a taxi to Yarmouk (700fils, JD1 at night). The last buses depart for Amman at about 8pm, sometimes as early as 5pm in winter.

ACCOMMODATIONS AND FOOD

Irbid has several hotels and restaurants to suit the budget traveler. The **Al-Amin al-Kabir Hotel** (tel. 242 384) on Midan Malek Abdallah St., one block down from the city center and the Ministry of Antiquities building, has pleasant, breezy rooms and exceptionally courteous management. (Singles JD4. Doubles JD5.500. Bathroom 500fils.) Around the corner on Jamil St. in the same building as the Bank of Jordan is the more communal **Abu Bakr Hotel** (tel. 242 695), where snoozing is the main event. (Singles JD5. Doubles JD6.) The **Al-Nasseem Hotel** (tel. 274 310) on Idoun St., the south side of the Yarmouk campus, desperately needs new carpeting, but the somewhat unkempt rooms are comfortable. With the main entrance to Yarmouk University on your left, walk uphill and take the first left. Al-Nasseem will be on your right before you reach An-Nasseem Circle. (Singles JD10. Doubles JD14. Cheaper for more than one night.) The three-star **Al-Razi Hotel** (tel. 275 515; fax 275 517), across the street from University Mosque, is a bit expensive but its restaurant serves delicious Arabic-style pizzas for less than JD1. (Singles JD25. Doubles JD33.) The newly renovated **Café Amon Italian Restaurant**, downhill from the Al-Razi Hotel and right on the circle, serves a variety of entrees, most under JD2. (Open daily 8am-11pm.) Downtown, **Al-Katkoot** serves supreme Jordanian dishes; visit the **Hungry Bunny** to get that wabbit. The area by Al-Yarmouk University has a more colorful selection of food stands.

■ NEAR IRBID

Umm Qeis was the biblical Gadara, where Jesus exorcised a sinner's demons into a herd of pigs which stampeded down the hill to drown in the Sea of Galilee. This thriving Decapolis city, once a resort for Romans vacationing at Al Himma's therapeutic hot springs, was renowned for its theaters, writers, philosophers, and, among low-brows, for its orgiastic extravagances. The city was probably founded sometime in the 4th century BCE and was later ceded by Caesar Augustus to Herod the Great, but it perished in the Jewish Rebellion of 66-70 CE.

Today, much of the **Roman amphitheater** survives; covered passageways stand in the back, and the six-foot, headless marble goddess that once sat at the front of the stage has moved inside the **Archaeological Museum** (tel. 217 210, ext. 72). The museum, with explanatory signs in English, shows the city's theater, water system, street shops, and church. (Open daily 8am-6pm. Free, but guides will expect a donation.) Outside the museum, give the guides the slip and seek out the square pillars of the bath house; at one time they bolstered the bath floors to allow steam to circulate underneath. In front of the theater stand the columns of a **Byzantine Church.** A gatekeeper will show you around and explain the sights; again, a tip will be expected. (Open daily. Knock at the church door.)

The beautiful **Umm Qeis Rest House** (tel. 217 210, ext. 59), a joint project of the Department of Antiquities and the American Center for Oriental Research, serves overpriced refreshments to desperate travelers and overlooks the Golan Heights and Lake Tiberias/Sea of Galilee. No overnight lodging is available—hit the hills for a serene, scenic campsite. There is a **post/phone office** (open 24 hrs.) along the main road through modern Umm Qeis. If the door is locked, knock with a big smile. You can also get stamps, post cards, and loads of invaluable historical information from Abd as-Salam at the **Umm Qeis Gift Shop** (tel. 217 210, ext. 68).

From Umm Qeis, wait for the next minibus from Irbid headed to **Al Himma,** 10km away. Hitchers and minibus-hoppers alike will find themselves surrounded by barbed wire and skull-and-crossbones signs identifying mine fields. This is neither a joke nor the remnants of a Halloween party. Just past Umm Qeis, at the first of several checkpoints, a soldier will check your **passport** and may want to search your bags. Beyond the military roadblock gapes the valley of the Yarmouk River; the high plateau across the vale is the Golan Heights.

After the exquisite descent, your arrival in Al Himma itself will pique the curiosity of the villagers, though you may be disappointed. Stare longingly at the bananas and you may find yourself sharing a yellow one with a local. Swimming in the **mineral springs** complex costs 600fils, JD4.200 if you reserve a private bath with slightly cooler water (open daily 6am-8pm). Men and women cannot use the pool at the same time: two-hour shifts alternate between the sexes (first shift 6-8am, for men). After 8pm, you can reserve the mineral springs complex for JD6 per hour—if you don't mind the egg-gregious stench of sulphur. The **Hotel al-Hamma al-Urdun** (tel. (02) 217 203), built like a staircase around the springs, has clean, no-frills rooms (doubles JD5-6, triples with carpeting JD20, chalet triples complete with mineral water JD15, quints JD30). For food, the **Jordanian Hammi Restaurant** (tel. (02) 217 203) on the east side of the complex serves *kabab* for an outlandish JD1.800. You're better off bargaining with the villagers for local specialties at the "tropical village," with its mud huts, thick pomegranate groves, and banana palms. **Buses** travel to Umm Qeis (200fils) and Al Himma (290fils) from Irbid's North Station. The last minibus leaves at around 5:30pm or 6pm, no exceptions.

■■■ MAFRAQ & UMM AJ-JIMAL
المفرق وام الجمال

Swirling sand storms agitate the tranquil desert and form shifting pillars that reach up to the sky and provide entertainment on the long, straight road to **Mafraq.** Mafraq (junction in Arabic) is well east of the western mountain range, tucked away in the middle of vast expanses of desert. As its Arabic name suggests, the town is an important transportation link between Syria, Iraq, and Saudi Arabia.

This arid capital of Jordan's largest county is worth a visit because of its proximity to a remarkable Decapolis city, **Umm aj-Jimal,** a mass of black ruins on the edge of a basalt desert. Known as the **Black Oasis,** the eerie monuments of ancient civilizations may look like a mass of rubble and walls that might collapse at any minute; but they stand for what were once basalt houses, churches, barracks, and a fort complex dating from the Nabatean, Roman, Byzantine, and Umayyad periods. The town was finally destroyed in a 747 CE earthquake and never rebuilt. Umm aj-Jimal is not developed for tourism, and while you can appreciate on your own the striking visual difference between this place and other Decapolis cities such as Jerash or Pella, you will need professional guidance for any further rubble probing. The Jordanian Air Force has a base near Umm aj-Jimal; the occasional overhead soar of jets adds to the mystique of the practically razed city.

PRACTICAL INFORMATION

Mafraq's **bus station** is located off the main street. There are no direct buses or *service* between Mafraq and Amman. From Amman take a minibus from Abdali station (beginning at 6:30am, 350fils) to Zarqa. Do the bus-dodging dance and traverse the Zarqa station for a minibus to Mafraq (beginning at 7am, 250fils). For the return trip, a *service* taxi to Zarqa from Mafraq costs 500fils. The town's **post office** (open Sat.-Thurs. 7:30am-5pm, Fri. and holidays 7:30am-2pm) and **police station** (tel. 431 101) are on its main street, on the right after a five-minute walk from the bus station. Change money at the **Arab Bank** or the **Housing Bank,** both of which are also conveniently situated on the main street. There are no accommodations in Mafraq, but restaurants and snack shops abound. Let your nose do the walking. The pace of Mafraq may soon pick up with the planned opening of Aal al-Beit University.

Buses travel between Mafraq and the village of Umm aj-Jimal (½-hr., 200fils). You'll have to go to a second station in Mafraq, though. Walk to the end of the main strip, well past the post office. Turn left, sniff for diesel, and listen for honking horns. Ask the bus driver to drop you off at the entrance to the ancient ruins. Bring a hat and lots of cold water. Look for Ministry of Antiquities guides around the ruins or call the **Umm aj-Jimal Tourist Office** (tel. (04) 431 885; hours unpredictable).

The night sky is ablaze with meteorites over the desert. Make a wish.

TURKEY
Karatepe
Haniniye
Osmaniye
Islahiye
Gaziantep
Nizip
Adana
Ceyhan
KARTAL DAGI
Tarsus
Mersin
Dortyol
Ahi
Manbij
Karataş
Iskenderun
Rasm al
Mashrafah
Erdemli
Kirikhan
Al Bab
HALAB
Reyhanli
Afrin
Antakya
Ar Aleppo
Samandag
Idlib
Jabal al Hass
Saraqib
Salma
Ar Rubayl
IDLIB
Latakia
Suqaylabiyah
Khirbat
AL LADHIQIYAH
HAMAH
JABAL RAS
Mediterranean
Sea
Epiphania
Salamiyah
Masya
Jabal al Bil'as
TARTUS
Jabal ash
Shawmariyah
Huwaysis
Tartus
Homs
Jabal al B
Khirbat
HIMS
Al Birah
Al Qusayr
Khan al Hayr
Palmyr
Tripoli
Hisyah
Sir ad
Al Hirmil
Amyun
Dinniyah
Al Fakyah
Bir Basin
Al Aqurah
An
LEBANON
Ba'labakk
Nabk
Farayya
'abda
Zahlah
Beirut
Ma'lula
B'abda
Sab'Abar
Bayt ad Din
Az Zabadani
Shhim
Khan Abu Shamat
Sidon
Al Qir'awn
Kafr
Damascus
DIMASHQ
Habbush
Hawar
Damascus
Marj Uyun
International
Tyre
Baniyas
Airport
Yatar
Al
AL
Kiswah
Buraq
QUNAYTIRAH
Nahariyya
GOLAN
Quneitra
As Sanamayn
Zalaf
Akko
HEIGHTS
Na'ran
Khabab
Zefat
Ar Rafid
DAR'A
AS SUWAYDA'
Maghar
Ya'rubiyah
Shahba
Haifa
Tiberias
Fiq
Shaykh
Izra
Kefar
Lake
Miskin
As Suwayda'
Ata
Tiberias
Nazareth
Dar'a
Safah
Tal Megiddo
Beit
She'an
Busra ash Sham
Hadera
Janin
Irbid
Imtan
Jabal Ajlun
Nabulus
Dibbin
Jordan River
National Park
Zarka
ISRAEL
WEST BANK
Salt
JORDAN
Ramla
Ramallah
Amman

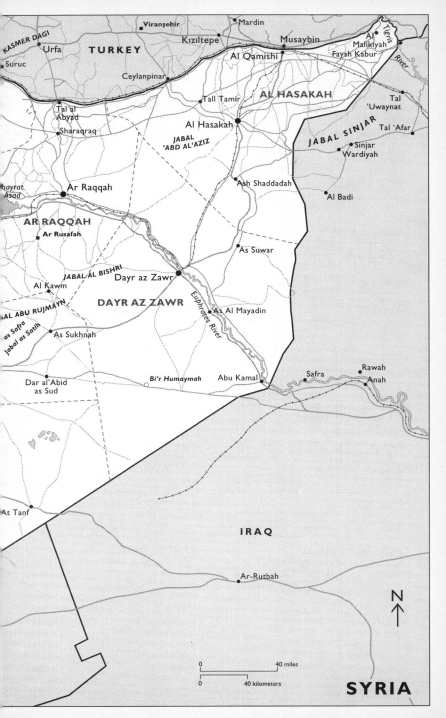

SYRIA

SYRIA سوريا

US$1=42.55 Syrian pounds (S£)	S£100=US$2.35
CDN$1=S£30.99	S£100=CDN$3.23
UK£1=S£65.43	S£100=UK£1.53
IR£1=S£64.72	S£100=IR£1.55
AUS$1=S£31.66	S£100=AUS$3.16
NZ$1=S£25.54	S£100=NZ$3.92
SAR1=S£11.80	S£100=SAR8.48

> For important additional information on all aspects of travel in general and some specifics on Syria, see the Essentials section of this book.

"It can rightly be stated, then, that every cultured man belongs to two nations; his own, and Syria." So claims the Syrian Ministry of Tourism and they're not entirely off the mark. Language, writing, art, architecture, crafts—all of them can be found in their earliest forms somewhere in the treasure chest of Syria's archaeological wealth. Not to imply that Syria's best days are behind it; far from it, the country has lately begun its entry into the world market in an attempt to regain some of the prominence once afforded it.

The visitor to modern Syria will be struck by many oddities, not the least of which will be his or her solitude. Few Westerners make the journey; those that do will have the incredible ancient ruins at Palmyra, the imposing Crusader castle Crac des Chevaliers, Mediterranean beaches, Turkish baths, museums, markets, and the vibrant modern city of Damascus to themselves.

Traveling in Syria is not as difficult as you might think: public transportation is abundant; American Express has set foot in these parts; and the Syrians are very hospitable, especially in smaller cities and villages.

ONCE THERE

■■■ GETTING AROUND

Within the major cities, hoofing it around is the way to go. Of course you have to get there somehow; there are several intercity transit options. Armies of both private and government-run buses are augmented by minibuses and private taxis. Renting a car will relieve you of enough money to run a small nation, and with so much public transportation around, why bother? As hitchhiking is not recommended by *Let's Go*, it's rare in Syria, naturally.

Taxis Private taxis are yellow, easy to use, and relatively cheap. If they don't find you first, you can easily grab one in any city, although their ranks thin after 9pm. Most taxis have meters; drivers don't seem to be aware of this fact. This is not to say that you'll be cheated; negotiate beforehand for a fair price. For travelers with little knowledge of Syria or Arabic, private taxis are the best option for local transportation. **Service taxis** are marginally less expensive and come in the form of white minivans. They are difficult to use, however: they run only within cities, are labeled in Arabic only, depart only when full, and drop you off at weird places.

Buses Karnak (tel. (11) 222 1492) is the government-run bus company. Routes go everywhere and fares are low, but buses tend to be ramshackle wrecks and departure schedules less than reliable. Reservations are required and can be made at bus stations in the cities. **Pullman** buses are even worse than Karnak, though Karnak constantly strives to catch up. Over 50 **private bus companies** now operate in Syria; they have ship-shape coaches and competitive prices. Reservations are a good idea for these buses as well. Usually, Karnak, Pullman, and private buses leave from different stops in a city; make sure you're at the right one. All tickets must be bought at the stations; drivers do not handle money. Gray **minibuses,** called **micros,** compete with the buses, but they share the disadvantages of *service* travel for uninitiated visitors to the country.

Trains Strictly speaking, trains do connect cities in Syria. Frankly speaking, roller skates would serve you better. Trains are mind-numbingly slow, crowded, and dirty; and in most places they drop you off about 30km out of town. Use the buses.

Cars If for some reason buses and *micros* aren't good enough for you, you can rent a car at a few places in Damascus for US$37 per day plus mileage; unlimited mileage US$59 per day. Special weekly rates are only slightly cheaper. Syrians drive on the right side of the road and gas costs under US$1 per gallon. But all the sights you could possibly want to see are easily accessible via cheap public transportation; the freedom of having a car is probably not worth the expense.

Hitchhiking Thumbing is neither possible nor necessary in Syria (if you stand by the side of a road, a *micro* will pick you up eventually and only cost you pocket change). Also, don't be too surprised if the friendly neighborhood police haul you in for questioning. It would be supremely stupid for women, even in groups, to attempt to hitchhike. *Let's Go* does not recommend hitchhiking.

■■■ USEFUL ADDRESSES

EMBASSIES

Australia: 128 Al Farabi St., Mezze, Damascus (tel. (11) 664 317).
Canada: Block 12, Mezze, Damascus (tel. (11) 236 851).
Egypt: Mahadar al-Fursan 133, Mezze ash-Sharqiyyeh, Damascus (tel. (11) 667 901).
Jordan: Aj-Jalaa Ave., Abu Roumaneh, Damascus (tel. (11) 234 642).
Turkey: 58 Ziad Ben Abi Sufian Sq., Damascus (tel. (11) 333 1411).
U.K.: Malki-Kurd Ali St., Damascus (tel. (11) 712 561). Also handles affairs for **Irish** and **New Zealand** citizens.
U.S.: 2 Al Mansour St., Abu Roumaneh, Damascus (tel. (11) 333 2315 or 2814).

TOURIST SERVICES

There are tourist information offices in all major Syrian cities. In Damascus, at 29 Mai Ave. (tel. (11) 222 2388); in Aleppo, on Al Ma'ari St. (tel. (21) 221 220). You might also contact the American Cultural Center in Damascus, 87 Rue Ata Ayoubi (tel. (11) 333 8413). The Ministry of Tourism provides free maps and information on most any place in Syria; it is on a side street near the Al Hijaz rail station in Damascus.

■■■ HEALTH & MEDICINE

Especially in Damascus, there are many hospitals and health-care professionals. However, most doctors do not speak English; and hospitals expect immediate cash payment. Your health coverage most likely doesn't extend to Syria. Contact your embassy or consulate for referral to an English-speaking doctor, a reputable hospital, or for in-house assistance. At least one pharmacy is open at all times in every Syrian city. Signs posted on pharmacy doors list (in Arabic) those pharmacies on duty.

Street food in Syria, especially in Damascus, should be approached with extreme caution. Mike sez: "Carry diarrhea antidote with you."

■■■ MONEY MATTERS

Currency and Exchange The basic unit of currency in Syria is the Syrian pound, also called the lira, abbreviated S£. Each pound is divided further into 100 piasters (*qirsh*, plural *qurush*), abbreviated pt. Paper currency comes in denominations of S£500, 100, 50, 25, 10, 5, and 1. Coins come in 100, 50, 25, 10, and 5pt values. There are as many exchange rates in Syria as bus companies: businesspeople get one rate, officials another, and light-haired tourists get a very special rate all their own. You can change money at the Commercial Bank of Syria at the rates listed above. Hotels must exchange dollars at the rate of S£11.20 per US$1, so room prices listed in dollars will be four times as high as what you might expect. Try to pay in S£ whenever possible. Some hotels will unofficially change money for you at the black market rate, which is only marginally better than the bank rate for dollar-holders. You decide if the extra S£1-4 per US$1 are worth going to the slammer for.

Once in Syria, you can change money at any Commercial Bank branch. If you are in Cairo or Amman before coming to Syria, you can exchange money there for Syrian pounds at the free market rate, which is a bit higher than the official rate. In previous years, visitors were required to change US$100 into pounds (at the rip-off hotel rate) upon entering the country; this is no longer the case. You may bring as much foreign currency into the country as you like but may not leave with more than you bring in. Amounts up to US$5000 do not have to be declared.

It's a good idea to carry U.S. currency with you, both in cash and in traveler's checks, because many hotels only accept US$; the cash comes in handy for some smaller transactions as well. Syria wants dollars, so it's a buyer's market.

Business Hours In Syria, the workweek begins on Saturday and ends on Thursday, with Friday being the official day off. Stores are generally open from 8am to 1:30pm, and then again from 4 to 8pm (7pm in winter). Some stores stay open all day in winter. Government offices are open from 8am to 2pm. It isn't unusual for some offices (telephone, post) to be open on Friday. Museums are generally open from 8am to 2pm every day but Tuesday. Restaurants open for lunch around 1pm and for dinner at 8pm. Hours are not always followed to the letter; government employees especially are known for sneaking out early.

Tipping and Bakhsheesh It used to be the case that nothing would get done in Syria without a bit of palm-greasing. Nowadays this is changing due to increasing contact with the world market and a change in general attitudes. Still, some tipping is expected; specifically, taxi drivers, waiters, and movie theater employees should be given at least a 10% tip. Be gracious; everything is inexpensive anyway.

■■■ ACCOMMODATIONS

There are no hostels in Syria. Instead, you have two options which vary wildly in price and quality: international chain-style (expensive) hotels and basic hole-in-the-wall, bed-and-a-roof crash sites. The higher the quality of a room, the more likely it is that you'll have to pay in US$ (at 2-3 times the price a native would pay); all two-star or higher hotels carry this requirement. In most places there is an even split of hotels that charge US$ and dumps that take S£; but in the more touristy places like Palmyra, prepare to part with the dead Presidents. Different employees of one establishment often quote contradictory rates; bargaining can save some money. Damascus and Aleppo hotels are less likely to haggle; but if they look empty, give it a shot. Even posted rates can sometimes be brought down, if only by a few pounds.

■■■ KEEPING IN TOUCH

Mail Mail from Syria is inexpensive, if slow (letters to the U.S. can take 3 wks. to arrive). It costs about S£20 to mail letters overseas, S£8 for postcards (rates vary;

that's life in a non-centralized bureaucracy). Take packages to a post office for inspection before wrapping them for delivery to another country. **Poste Restante** service is available in Damascus's main post office. Bring your passport and *Let's Go* to read while you wait in line. American Express in Damascus has Client Letter Service.

Telephone Trials and tribulations abound. Damascus has an around-the-clock telephone office, where you can place international calls, but you'll need lots of money and lots of patience (at least an hour's worth). Some other cities have offices as well. The majority of hotels has direct-dial international capabilities, but rates from Syria are exorbitant to begin with (US$12 for a 3-min. call to the U.S.), and hotels charge at least 200% of the phone office rates. It's much cheaper to have your party call you back or to call collect. The access code for **MCI's World Phone** program is (177) 155 0222. You can now use phone cards to make local calls only; they are available in denominations of S£200 and S£500. The **international phone code** for Syria is 963.

Telegraph, Telex, and Fax Telegraph and telex services are allegedly available throughout the country. Telegraphs can be sent from telephone offices, but are expensive. Many hotels now have faxes, and some photocopy centers provide them as well—for a price only slightly less than the cost of your parents' first house. E-mail? What? Syria is not an exit on the information superhighway.

■■■ DRESS & ETIQUETTE

Conservative dress is the norm in Syria; shorts, tank tops, and very short skirts will invite stares, comments, and possibly unwanted sexual advances. Pants should fall to at least mid-calf and shirts should cover the shoulders.

With the plentitude of public transportation, you probably won't have to drive in Syria. If you do, be warned that drivers are rude, aggressive, unlikely to signal, and seemingly required by law to check their horns' functionality at least twice per minute. Pedestrians walk in the street, encouraging motorists to drive on sidewalks.

It is impolite in Syria to point directly at someone or to point the sole of your shoe at someone (as when sitting down and placing one ankle on one knee). When a Syrian tips his or her head up and makes a clucking noise, this means "no," although Westerners have been known to mistake it for a sign of acknowledgment or a "get in the back seat" gesture by a taxi driver. No means no.

LIFE AND TIMES

■■■ GOVERNMENT & POLITICS

After gaining independence from the British and French in April 1946, Syria experienced civilian government for three years. A military coup banished this oddity once and for all in March 1949; and by 1954, the pan-Arabist Ba'th party had crept into power. In 1958 Syria joined Egypt, under President Gamal Abd en-Nasser, in forming the United Arab Republic; but a 1961 coup protesting Syria's subordination to Egypt interrupted the Egyptian-Syrian joy ride. Two years later the coup gave way to the Syrian Ba'th party (this time lead by Hafez Al Asad), which in February 1966 split off from the larger Ba'th party and began focusing its efforts on two things: developing Syrian nationalism rather than pan-Arabism, and maintaining power.

They succeeded on at least one front, as the past 25 years under President Asad have proven. Asad, an Alawite Muslim of penurious heritage, first held power for a short time at the beginning of Ba'th monopolization of the government but lost his position in 1966. He reassumed the reins in February 1971 and was sworn in as President for seven years. Asad called for the popular election of a 173-member People's Assembly that would draft a new constitution. Completed in March 1973, the constitution contained a clause requiring the President of Syria to be a follower of Islam. On this basis, Sunni Muslims objected to Asad's presidency, holding that Alawites are not true Muslims. When a high-ranking religious authority deemed Alawites devout followers of Islam, the road to domination was cleared for Asad.

Before Asad's ascendance to power, the centralized Ba'th party system had no provisions for local governance, which meant that a complaint about the size of street signs in Maalula would end up on the desk of the prime minister. Asad mandated the election of local government councils and required them to be at least 51% workers or peasants. With representatives in every village, the government was decentralized, but the party still maintains a presence in local affairs. Asad has also stabilized government (mainly through elevating Alawites and his childhood friends to positions of authority throughout the nation) and maintained a rudimentary socialist attentiveness to minorities and the disadvantaged.

Today all political parties are associated with the National Progressive Front (NPF), a coalition dominated by the Ba'th party and run by Asad himself. How convenient. The People's Council, a 250-member legislative body, has political power in theory, but is itself controlled by the NPF, meaning Ba'th policies are passed with a minimum of opposition. The cabinet advises Asad on policy, but they would probably have "Ba'th" tattooed on their foreheads if Asad asked them to. Syria has three vice-presidents (including Asad's brother, who attempted to take control of the country in 1984 and was exiled; he was later allowed to return to his post).

President Asad runs Syria with a personal touch, which is a nice way of saying that he is essentially a dictator. The man with the omnipresent face controls everything he can, from foreign policy to information flow. Turn on Syrian television here or in Jordan and you will hear discussions of who Asad met with that day, what Asad ate for lunch, maybe even what color underwear Asad wore.

As with all dictatorships, Syria's future beyond Asad's reign is uncertain; however, if the Syrian election results are to be believed, this will not happen any time soon. In 1992, Asad was elected to his fourth seven-year term as president, with 99.9% of the vote. A generous person could attribute Asad's success to his policies, which have certainly improved Syrian life since the early 70s. More likely explanations for his political longevity are his aggressive suppression of his enemies (some of whom were arrested in 1971 and remain incarcerated), or the always-around-the-corner internal security forces looking out for anti-Asad sentiment.

The spy industry, combined with an abysmal human-rights record, has created an atmosphere of constant fear in Syria and invited the displeasure of foreign countries. Plus, Syria is recovering from a habit of harboring (some say training) terrorists, including those believed responsible for the bombing of PanAm flight 107.

More recently, Asad has begun acceding to Western demands in an attempt to revitalize his country's plodding economy. The government is now more lenient with vocal minorities and political adversaries; and, most importantly, at press time Syria was engaged in talks with Israel. Most predict that these talks will lead to the establishment of diplomatic relations between the two countries, the return of part or all of the Golan Heights to Syria, and economic benefits for all parties.

When traveling in Syria, try not to get into political discussions. If you just can't avoid the topic, offer vaguely enthusiastic praise for Asad and quickly mention, say, the New York Islanders. Maybe you don't like Asad, but if it's a choice between praising him and undergoing interrogation, then as far as you're concerned he's the greatest thing since aerosol cheese.

■■■ ECONOMY

Syria is blessed with Black Gold/Texas Tea (oil). The oil money of the early 1970s allowed Asad to go forward with a program of capital formation, including investments in agriculture, heavy industries, health services, and education. A drive to modernize and modernize quickly shaped the mid-70s, due to the double incentive of rebuilding after the destructive October War and taking advantage of the boom economy in oil. Unfortunately, industries were haphazardly chosen and designed for development and left Syria with a legacy of wasteful, inefficient factories, like a paper mill that couldn't utilize Syrian wood pulp and an ammonium-urea facility that eventually proved so useless that converting to gas, at a cost of US$100 million, was more economical than continuing to operate it. A number of industries *were* profitable, including light crude oil, natural gas, phosphates, iron, and steel, and other light industries including rubber, glass, tobacco, and paper.

Despite oil reserves, the Syrian per capita GDP is around US$900. The standard of living is consequently not as high as that of wealthier countries; for instance, only one in 17 people owns a television set, and only one in 23 owns a telephone. The infant mortality rate is high, at 40 deaths per 1000 births, and there are only 1.2 hospital beds for every 1000 people. The literacy rate in Syria is 64%; schooling is required only for 6 years, although higher education is paid for by the government.

The Syrian economy also suffers from rapid population growth and massive inflation. In Damascus, the population was growing at a 3.8% annual rate in 1994, leading to an extra 40,000 people to feed each year in that city alone. Such a rate is typical of the entire nation. Inflation in 1987-88 reached 100%, and in November 1991, prices jumped 300% when the government relaxed price controls. Since then, inflation has dropped to a less stratospheric level (25%), but the Syrian pound is still far from a good investment option.

With such restraints on economic growth, Syria has had trouble improving the economy. Asad's uninspired attempt to reduce unemployment (which reached 35% in the 70s and 80s) created the situation today, where 1 of every 5 workers gets a paycheck signed by the government. Many of these government workers are unnecessary, unmotivated, and inefficient. Pity the poor traveler. The Syrian government no longer releases unemployment figures. In the 80s, government ministries encouraged private investors to support tourism, import replacement, and agricultural projects, but investors didn't share the state's enthusiasm for capital investment; instead, they put their money into real estate. Consequently, property prices rose dramatically, further worsening the Syrian economy.

As if that weren't enough, Syria often experiences power shortages, obviously not beneficial to any industry (except candlemaking), due to Turkey's tendency to overutilize the upstream portion of the Euphrates river for its own projects. The power equipment and network (as well as military material) are old, from Soviet-era Russia, and prone to mechanical failure. As a country in the midst of the politically unstable Middle East, Syria maintains a large standing army, and this expense accounts for over 60% of its total expenditures. On the positive side, Syria has almost no internal debt, although (back on the negative side) its external debts are over US$16 billion.

Syria's past connections with terrorist groups, support of Iran, and skirmishes with Jordan have translated into low levels of foreign aid; but Asad plans to change all this. In 1991, Syria's opposition of Iraq in the Gulf War garnered some aid from Saudi Arabia, Japan, and European nations; the talks with Israel and the loosening of travel restrictions for Syrian Jews (85% of whom had left the country by the end of 1993) will surely curry favor with free-spending governments and private investors.

■■■ RELIGION & ETHNICITY

Islam is the dominant religion of Syria, with about 85% of the populace following the teachings of the Qur'an. 68% of the total population is Sunni, 17% Shi'ite. The Shi'ite branch is splintered into sects such as the Alawites (11.5%), who include President Asad among their adherents, the Druze (3%), and the Ismailis (1.5%). Another 13-14% of Syrians belong to the Catholic or Eastern Orthodox churches. (See Introduction to the Region: Religion, p. 43.)

The statistics on Syria's ethnic composition vary, with different sources setting the percentage of Arabs in the country between 82% and 90%. The remainder of the population is Kurdish, Turkish, Armenian, or Circassian. The Kurdish minority in Syria would like to create an independent Kurdish state, which would include the Kurds in Turkey, Iran, and Iraq as well, but as of yet, their grievances have not met with much action. The proposed Kurdish state would extend into northern Syria; pamphlets distributed in 1992 advocating this proposal brought about the arrest of 200 Kurdish activists; 30 remain imprisoned today. Only about 5% of the world's Kurdish population lives within Syrian borders. Iraq's massacre of its own Kurdish population in the aftermath of the Gulf War brought the situation to the attention of the West, but efforts to create autonomy for the Kurds or to aid their independent struggles have not been forthcoming.

■■■ FESTIVALS & HOLIDAYS

Muslim holidays (see When To Go, p. 1) are official days off in Syria; Christmas and Easter are celebrated by Christians but not legislated as holidays. Political holidays close everything down; they are **New Year's Day** (Jan. 15), **Union Day** (Feb. 22), **Revolution Day/Women's Day** (Mar. 1), **Arab League Day** (Mar. 22), **Evacuation Day** (April 17), **Martyrs' Day** (May 6), **Security Force Day** (May 29), **Army Day** (Aug. 1), **Marine's Day** (Aug. 29), **Veteran's Day** (Oct. 6), **Flight Day** (Oct. 16), **Correction Movement Day** (Nov. 16th), and **Peasant's Day** (Dec. 14).

■■■ LANGUAGE

The oldest non-hieroglyphic alphabet in the world, the Ugarit alphabet, was discovered in Syrian ruins dating from 1000 BCE. The find gives Syria a valid claim to the world's-earliest-civilization throne.

Over 82% of Syrians speak Arabic, which is the designated official language. French has long been a second language, and a fair amount of the literature of Syria, if it has been translated into any Western tongue, will be in French. However, English is beginning to replace French as the second language of record. The various minority groups in Syria maintain their own languages to a degree; Kurds in the east speak Kurdish, and the Armenian population, centered in Aleppo, ensures the survival of their own language. In some villages you may encounter Turkish, or possibly even Aramaic, much to the delight of those among us who enjoy studying the Bible in its original language. Travelers with some knowledge of Arabic should not encounter communication problems anywhere in Syria.

■■■ THE ARTS

While the first written alphabet in the world was produced within its borders, Syria has not been a hotbed of modern literary activity. Most of Syria's illustrious *artistes* wrote with quills, not PaperMates or word processors. In the late 7th century CE, Jacob of Edessa wrote many theological, historical, philosophical, and grammatical works. Early in his life he studied Greek and worked as a translator, which exposed him to Greek and Roman works. He would later write his own studies of the Bible, as well as the books *Enchidron* and *The Book of Treasures.* But he was best known for codifying the Syrian language; his *Syriac Grammar* became the seminal work on the subject. By the late 9th or early 10th century, a vulgate version of the Bible, the *Peshitta,* was available in Syria. In the middle of the 13th century, the philosopher Bar Hebraeus began writing philosophical treatises. His later work, *Book of the Pupils of the Eyes,* discussed logic; *Book of the Speech of Wisdom* explored physics and metaphysics. Mathematics and astronomy were also enriched by Hebraeus' research, as were ascetics living as hermits, since the *Book of the Dove* was a manual written by Hebraeus for these people. Other late 13th century philosophers in Hebraeus's tradition were Abhd-Isho bar-Berikhou, Yabh-alaha III, and Timothy II.

Only very recently has Syria begun to develop a tradition of fiction writing. While some works have been written in French or English, those written in Arabic are not quickly translated for Western consumption, although this is beginning to change.

Gertrude Bell, in *The Desert and the Sown,* writes about her travels through Syria and Jordan. For an excellent historical overview of Syria, look in English-language bookstores for Ross Burn's *Monuments of Syria.*

Traditionally, Arab visual arts are works of abstract beauty, focusing on color and geometric design; Syrian art is no exception. Islamic law prohibits the depiction of human beings. In the 20th century, artists are discovering the human body; but you are most likely to encounter traditional art, in mosques and other buildings.

■■■ FOOD

Syrian food is not unlike food in the rest of the Middle East. Foods that are considered snacks can be consumed morning, noon, and night without shame or funny looks from the native population. Two of the most popular snack foods, which have made massive inroads into Western culture, are hummus and falafel. Hummus is the Big Brother of Middle Eastern foods—it's everywhere. Chick peas are ground into a paste seasoned with lemon, garlic, and salt, which is then scooped up with pieces of bread and consumed in mass quantities. Falafel is a similar paste, heavier on fava beans than chick peas, mixed with spices and fried, then rolled into a piece of bread with vegetables and *tahina* sauce. For the penniless (well, piasterless) traveler, hummus plus falafel equals good eats indefinitely; but make sure you have a stomach of steel before you indulge in street food. If you want a little meat in your diet or a little lining on your arteries, try delicious *shawerma,* which is lamb cooked beneath dripping fat, rolled in bread with vegetables and spices. There are other kinds of *shawerma,* including liver, brains, etc.

If you get tired of eating food from roadside stands, or if a long-lost uncle unexpectedly leaves you a small fortune—say, US$4—why not blow it all on a main dish? You could start with *shish kabab,* lamb chunks on skewers, grilled, and served with bread. *Shish tawouq* is similarly-treated chicken. A dish uncommon in other Arab countries is *farooj,* roasted chicken served with chilis and onions. Also common at local restaurants and in homes are bean, spinach, and potato stews cooked with lamb in tomato sauce and ladled over rice. Beware fish, except on the Mediterranean coast; it tends to be spiced to the hilt and saltier than a grumpy old sailor.

For dessert, Syrians favor pastries that are very, very, sweet. Most of these *halawiyyat* have a fair amount of sugar baked into them and are then drenched in syrup or honey. *Ba'laweh* is made of pistachios or almonds in fillo dough, *burma* of pistachios in shredded fried dough, and *basbouseh* of wheat and syrup. *Booza* is not alcohol but ice cream. Eat, drink, and be merry.

Speaking of drink, Syrians like their *qahwa* (coffee) like they like their *ba'laweh*—strong and sweet. Both *shay* (tea) and *qahwa* are consumed frequently, for caffeine highs rivaling a cocaine rush. (Espresso has a lot to learn from *qahwa.*) Stalls with string bags of fruit hanging out front will be your oasis of cool liquid refreshment. Here you'll find *aseer* (juice) in abundance. One caveat: sometimes Syrians will add milk to the drinks; this will not make you a happy camper—stay away from the dairy additives. Soft drinks are, paradoxically, not very sweet at all. These *gazooza* are very cheap. Finally, alcohol in Syria ranges from locally brewed beers and Amstel smuggled into Damascus from Lebanon to *araq,* an anise-seed flavored liquor that's mixed with water and consumed in shots. Ye-ha!

POINTS IN SYRIA

■■■ DAMASCUS دمشق

Damascus' monumental, centuries-long history wraps around an enigmatic present-day to create one of the most intriguing cities in the Middle East. Unchecked pollution and the frenetic pace of city life might make Damascus look like any other urban jungle; but the city's *souqs,* the Umayyad Mosque, and the National Museum, not to mention the Qur'an, the Bible, and history books, uncover a past overwhelmingly rich and diverse, culturally, politically, and religiously.

Some scholars claim that Damascus has been continuously inhabited longer than any other city in the world. Early historical references to the city include the Ebla tablets, written in 3000 BCE, as well as pharaonic inscriptions and records of the city as the capital of the Aramaic kingdom in the second millennium BCE. The inhabitants of ancient Damascus spoke Syriac. Greek, Roman, and Byzantine invaders all left their mark, most notably in the form of the Roman Temple of Jupiter, built by Apolodor the Damascene. Later, Christians constructed churches in the city; in the 7th century CE, Damascus came under the influence of Islam.

The city served as the capital of the Islamic Umayyad Empire for close to a century, at a time of enormous growth for the Islamic community. It was during the Umayyad period that Muslim rule spread as far as China in the East and Spain in the West. Damascus began to suffer when the Abbassids replaced the Umayyads as the rulers of the Islamic empire and moved its capital to Baghdad.

In the ensuing centuries, Damascus fell under various dynasties and empires, including the Ottoman Turks, whose influences are evidenced in existing Damascene architecture. In 1946, Syria gained independence from British and French control, and Damascus became the capital of a modern nation-state.

Today, the pulse, physical appearance, and odors of the city reflect contemporary realities rather than historical splendor. The visitor should note that politics is a taboo subject and interesting discussions with locals are few and far between, but Syria's participation in the Middle East peace process makes Damascus an exciting place to visit. There's no telling who will show up for high-level discussions, closing streets and bringing even more gun-toting military boys to intersections.

Those whose time in Syria is limited can get their fill of Damascus in a few days. The city serves as a gateway to incredible sights elsewhere in the country, where hospitable natives are willing to talk and invite travelers into their homes.

ORIENTATION AND TRANSPORTATION

Walking in Damascus is easy; with the help of a few landmarks you can find your way anywhere. Just watch the damn cars.

No one really knows or cares about street names, which often change or are spelled differently on each map and the occasional sign. The first landmark is the **Hijaz Railway Station,** located at the intersection of two large streets called by some **An-Nasr Avenue** and others **Sa'ad aj-Jabri Street.** The neighborhood around the station is home to several two-star **hotels,** the **Post Office,** the **telephone office,** a **café,** and a good **pharmacy.** If you face out from the station and head to your left, you will reach **Damascus University** and eventually smell the exhaust from buses crowded into what has to be the world's most poorly designed **private bus station.** We can only hope the rocket scientist who located the bus station here is not involved with the peace negotiations. Jabri St. turns into **Port Said Avenue,** which leads up to **Yousef al-Azmeh Square.** In this neighborhood, you'll find several good **restaurants,** the **American Express** office, a **five-star hotel,** a good **movie theater,** the **Tourist Information Center,** and, if you're lucky, a picture of **Hafez Al Asad** on one of the building façades.

The second important area, especially for those seeking cheap eats and hotels, pistachio desserts, or Russian prostitutes, is **Al Marjeh Square,** also named, but never called, **Ash-Shuhadaa' Square** or **Martyrs' Square.** You'll recognize Marjeh Square by its large column commemorating Syria's war dead and the stench of the **Barada River,** which rears its ugly head here but usually flows under Damascus.

A third area of interest is the **souq,** a five-minute walk from Marjeh Square. To get there, stand at the column facing the pastry shops, then walk down the street to your left and take a right at the dead end.

Finally, **Abu Roumaneh** sports several embassies and cultural centers. The plain-clothes guys lurking in alleys, behind trees, and in cars or inconspicuously carrying bazookas are Syrian secret service agents. Don't look too long. Though you may get asked out, it won't be for dinner or a movie.

If you decide to navigate the city by wheel, you have three inexpensive options. **Buses** and **service taxis** (white minivans) have predetermined routes and pick up passengers along the way. The routes are written in Arabic on the sides. **Private taxis** have meters; few use them. Negotiate prices before you get in. Even longer trips, like between the Citadel and Abu Roumaneh, should not cost more than S£40. Tips are appropriate. For **intercity transportation,** go to the private bus station near the Hijaz Station, the government-run Karnak station near Damascus University, or the *service* stand, part of the Karnak station.

PRACTICAL INFORMATION

Tourist Information Center: 29 Mai Ave. (tel. 222 2388). From Yousef al-Azmeh Sq., walk to the right of the white modern building. The center, decorated with posters of Syria, Asad, Basil, and models of Crusader castles, will be on your right. Has maps, information in English, French, and German. Open Sat.-Thurs. 9am-7pm. **Tourist Police:** Tel. 222 6810.

Embassies: Australia, 128 Al Farabi St., Mezze (tel. 664 317). **Egypt,** Mahadar al-Fursan 133, Al Mezze ash-Sharqiyyeh (tel. 667 901). **Jordan,** Abu Roumaneh (tel. 333 4642). **Turkey,** 48 Ziad Ben Abi Sufian Sq. (tel. 333 1411). **U.K.,** Malki-Kurd Ali St. (tel. 712 561). **U.S.,** 2 Al Mansour St. (tel. 333 2315), in Abu Roumaneh. Take Aj-Jalaa Ave. away from Al Quwatli until Rawdat Abilalan Sq. You'll see the Stars and Stripes flying off to the left. Consular section open Sun.-Thurs. 8am-4pm. Observes all Syrian and most American holidays.

Currency Exchange: Changing money in Syria is always a chore. Even though it's illegal, many shop owners and travel agents in Damascus will offer to take foreign currencies off your hands. Unless you're curious about the insides of Syrian deten-tion centers, it's best to stick with the banks. Banking hours are Sat.-Thurs. 9am-12:50pm. The **Commercial Bank of Syria,** at Yousef al-Azmeh Sq., is open Sat.-Thurs. 9am-7pm.

American Express: Belkis St. (tel. 224 6500; fax 222 3707). Take a left on Fardous St. when walking from the Hijaz Station on Port Said St. Belkis St. is the first left off Fardous; AmEx is in the Sudan Airways office. They'll hold mail and serve you tea if you ask lots of questions they can't answer. No other services. Claims to be open Sat.-Thurs. 8:30am-8pm and Fri. 10am-12pm, but go in the mornings.

Post Office: Sa'ad aj-Jabri St. (tel. 119 000), in front of the Hijaz train station. Easy to find because it sports an enormous picture of Asad on the side of the building, one of the few pictures you'll see in Syria of the camera-shy *ra'ees.* Open Sat.-Thurs. 8am-7pm and Fri. 8am-1pm.

Telephone Office: An-Nasr Ave., next to the Hijaz Station. The telephone office doesn't seem to have a telephone number, but it's open 24 hrs. For international calls, bring lots of cash and patience. Placing calls can take up to an hour. **Telephone Code:** 11.

Airport: Damascus International Airport, southeast of Damascus. Buses to the airport leave from the Victoria Bridge on Al Quwatli St. (S£100) and *service* leave from the station near the Hijaz railway station (S£300). A taxi to the airport costs around US$10. Regular international flights to European and Arab capitals; domes-tic flights daily to Aleppo (one-way S£600). There is a S£100 exit fee if you leave Syria by air. The **SyrianAir** office (tel. 222 1478) is in front of the Post Office.

Intercity Buses and Taxis: Karnak (tel. 222 1492), the government bus com-pany, has smoky, run-down buses serving Aleppo (5 per day beginning at 8am,

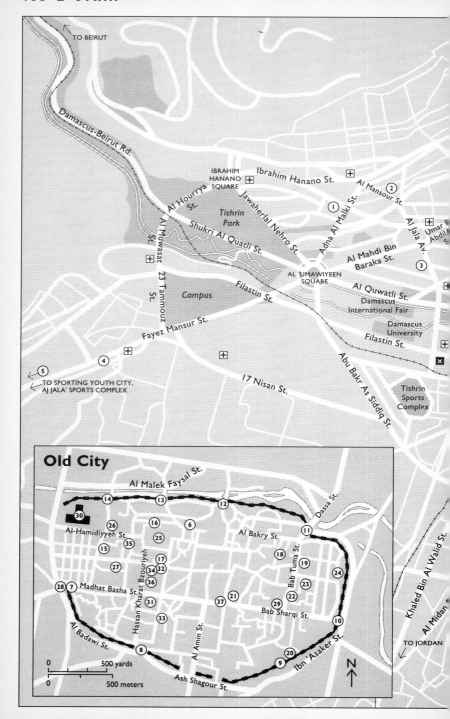

TO BEIRUT

Damascus-Beirut Rd.

IBRAHIM HANANO SQUARE

Ibrahim Hanano St.

Al Mansour St.

②

Al Hourrya St.

Jawaherlal Nehro St.

Tishrin Park

①

Adna Al Malki St.

Al Jala Av.

Umar P Abdil

Al Muwasat St.

Shukri Al Quatli St.

Al Mahdi Bin Baraka St.

③

AL 'UMAWIYEEN SQUARE

23 Tammouz St.

Campus

Filastin St.

Al Quwatli St.

Damascus International Fair

Fayez Mansur St.

Damascus University

Filastin St.

④

Abu Bakr As Siddiq St.

⑤

TO SPORTING YOUTH CITY, AJ JALA' SPORTS COMPLEX

17 Nisan St.

Tishrin Sports Complex

✕

Old City

Al Malek Faysal St.

⑭   ⑬   ⑫

Dassa St.

㉚

⑯   ⑥

Al-Hamidiyyeh St.

㉖   ㉕

Al Bakry St.

⑪

㉟

⑮

⑱

Bab Tuma St.

⑲

⑰

⑰㉜

⑳

⑩

⑨

㉗

⑭㉜

㉞   ㊱

㉘ ⑦ Madhat Basha St.

⑤

⑪

㉔

㉛

⑳

⑩

Al Badawi St.

㉝

⑳

⑩

⑧

Al Amin St.

⑳

Ibn 'Asaker St.

Ash Shagour St.

Khaled Bin Al Walid St.

Al Midan

TO JORDAN

N

0   500 yards

0   500 meters

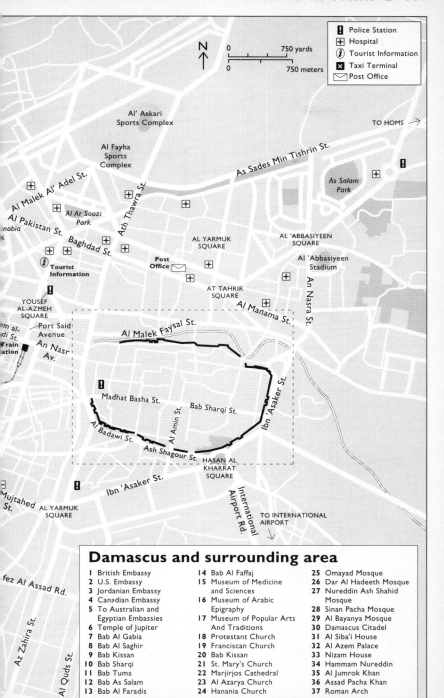

N

🏢	Police Station
⊞	Hospital
ⓘ	Tourist Information
✕	Taxi Terminal
✉	Post Office

0   750 yards
0   750 meters

Al' Askari
Sports Complex

Al Fayha
Sports
Complex

TO HOMS →

As Sades Min Tishrin St.

As Salam
Park

Al Malek Al' Adel St.

Al Ar Souzi
Park

Al Pakistan St.

nobia

Baghdad St.

Ath Thawra St.

AL YARMUK
SQUARE

AL 'ABBASIYEEN
SQUARE

Al 'Abbasiyeen
Stadium

Tourist
Information

Post
Office

AT TAHRIR
SQUARE

YOUSEF
AL-AZMEH
SQUARE

Port Said
Avenue

m al-
di St.

An Nasr
Av.

Al Manama St.

An Nasra St.

Train
ation

Al Malek Faysal St.

Madhat Basha St.

Al Amin St.

Bab Sharqi St.

Ibn Asaker St.

Al Badawi St.

Ash Shagour St.

HASAN AL
KHARRAT
SQUARE

Ibn 'Asaker St.

Mujtahed
St.

AL YARMUK
SQUARE

International
Airport Rd.

TO INTERNATIONAL
AIRPORT

fez Al Assad Rd.

Az Zahira St.

Al Quds St.

Damascus and surrounding area

1 British Embassy
2 U.S. Embassy
3 Jordanian Embassy
4 Canadian Embassy
5 To Australian and
    Egyptian Embassies
6 Temple of Jupiter
7 Bab Al Gabia
8 Bab Al Saghir
9 Bab Kissan
10 Bab Sharqi
11 Bab Tuma
12 Bab As Salam
13 Bab Al Faradis

14 Bab Al Faffaj
15 Museum of Medicine
     and Sciences
16 Museum of Arabic
     Epigraphy
17 Museum of Popular Arts
     And Traditions
18 Protestant Church
19 Franciscan Church
20 Bab Kissan
21 St. Mary's Church
22 Marjirjos Cathedral
23 Al Azarya Church
24 Hanania Church

25 Omayad Mosque
26 Dar Al Hadeeth Mosque
27 Nureddin Ash Shahid
     Mosque
28 Sinan Pacha Mosque
29 Al Bayanya Mosque
30 Damascus Citadel
31 Al Siba'i House
32 Al Azem Palace
33 Nizam House
34 Hammam Nureddin
35 Al Jumrok Khan
36 Assad Pacha Khan
37 Roman Arch

S£100), Homs (4 per day beginning at 7:30am, S£45), Palmyra (7am, S£90), and Amman, Jordan (3 per day beginning at 7am, S£250); reservations required. The many **private bus companies** at the station near Hijaz railway/Sultan hotel have daily service and competitive prices. Shop around and make reservations. **Pullman buses, minibuses ("micros")**, and **service taxis** also have some intercity service. The Pullmans are even less comfortable than Karnak, but do have regular schedules. The minibuses and *service* are cheap and depart when full.

Local Transportation: The Damascus city bus system is extensive, if not pleasant. Crowded and dirty buses go everywhere you do for S£2 per ride. Get tickets before boarding the bus; sometimes they must be purchased in groups of 2 or 4, but you'll find a way to use them.

Car Rental: There are a few companies around the post office. For helpful driving information in English try the agency at the Cham Palace Hotel. Rent for a day (US$37, unlimited mileage US$59) or a week (US$238/US$378).

English Bookstores: Several of the bookshops in front of the post office have a tiny selection of English language books, but the best selections are at the **Cham Palace Hotel** and the **Meridian Hotel.** Look for Ross Burns' *Monuments of Syria*, an excellent historical guide.

Publications: *The Syria Times* is good for starting campfires in remote locations, and for a hearty laugh. The large hotels stock one- to two-week-old copies of the *International Herald Tribune* and *le Monde.* Several of the newsstands around the post office have six-month-old copies of *Time* and *Newsweek.*

Photocopies: Khawan Brothers, 54 An-Nasr Ave. (tel. 221 1943; fax 223 6090). Turn right out of the Hijaz Station and look for copy machines and Apple and IBM computers in windows on the opposite side of the street. Some word-processing services. Open Sat.-Thurs. 8am-2pm and 4:30-8pm.

Cultural Centers: American Cultural Center, 87 Rue Ata Ayoubi (tel. 333 8413). **Centre Cultural Arabe,** 46 Rue Aj-Jalaa, Abu Roumaneh (tel. 333 3727). **Goethe-Institut,** Avenue Malki (tel. 333 6673). **Centre Culturel Français Bahsa** (tel. 246 181). Contact these organizations for information about cultural events and activities for scholars in Syria.

Laundry: Aous ash-Sharq (tel. 222 4576), off Salam al-Barudi St. Facing out from the Hijaz Station, the laundromat is the second street on the left, across from the Sultan Hotel. Shirt S£25, pants S£40, socks/underwear S£20. Open Sat.-Thurs. 9am-7pm. Hotels don't mind if you buy some soap and plug up the sink.

Pharmacies: Pharmacies in Damascus are open Sat.-Thurs. 9am-1:30pm and 5:30-9pm. Try **Kassar** (tel. 222 7347), near the Hijaz Station on Sa'ad aj-Jabri St., or **Al-Halabi** (tel. 221 5550), closer to Azmeh Sq. Several pharmacies rotate staying open at night; lists of these are posted in Arabic outside most pharmacies. For more information on late-night pharmacies, inquire at two-star or better hotels.

Emergency: U.S. citizens can call the embassy (tel. 333 2315). The embassy nurse, Birgit Khatib (tel. 333 5074, in emergencies 333 9130), will also make medical referrals, usually to Shami Hospital. **Ambulance:** Tel. 110.

Police: Tel. 112.

ACCOMMODATIONS

The Syrian government is eager to grab dollars, so prices in the cleanest hotels are marked in greenbacks. You'll be paying at least two to three times what Syrians or people with residence permits pay for the same room, but as a "wealthy" tourist you have no choice. Most hotels will give change in dollars and accept traveler's checks, but it's a good idea to have small bills on hand to simplify exchange and protect yourself from the terrible hotel exchange rates. The best two-star hotels are in the neighborhood of the **Hijaz Station** and the **Post Office.** The area is generally safe for men and women, although women should be careful after dark.

The cheapies lurk in and around **Al Marjeh Square,** also called **Ash-Shuhadaa'** or **Martyrs' Square.** In this area, many rooms come with paid bed-mates; several hotels cater to guests who prefer to remain anonymous. Also, don't expect to see too many clean sheets or scrubbed floors; consider yourself extremely lucky if nothing bites you during the night. While prices are posted in the nicer hotels, bargaining is the rule. In the cheaper places you'll be quoted different prices by different employees. Prudent and flattering deal-making will save a few S£.

Near Hijaz Station

Sultan Hotel, Al Barudi St. (tel. 222 5768 or 221 6910). From the station, turn left and cross the street; the Sultan is about a ½-block down. Clean green lobby, green chairs, green carpet. Rooms, on the other hand, are a spotless brown but cost lots of green—they make you pay in dollars. Some have A/C; bargain if yours has a fan. Singles US$20. Doubles US$28. Triples US$35. Breakfast included.

Badara Hotel, Sa'ad aj-Jabri (tel. 221 2546 or 224 1445), straight down aj-Jabri St. on the right. Immaculate lobby leads upstairs to not-squeaky-clean-but-passable rooms with bathrooms. Singles US$12. Doubles US$20. Triples US$24.

Al-Hamra Hotel, Furat St. (tel. 221 0717), straight down aj-Jabri past the post office; take the first left. Dark hallways and rooms resplendent with exposed pipes and tile. Rooms have private bathrooms. Singles US$18. Doubles US$24. TV and fridge will hike the price up.

Al-Afamia Hotel (tel. 222 9152 or 8963), off Furat St., around the corner from Al-Hamra. Enormous beds several feet off the ground, bathrooms with low ceilings. Nice neighborhood. Singles US$18. Doubles US$24. Triples US$29.

Marjeh Square

Naman Hotel, Abi Firas Hamden (tel. 221 8809; fax 222 1745). Head up the street in front of the column at Marjeh Sq. and take the first right; hotel is on the right on the 2nd block. Rooms have baths, mirrors, benches, and lots of Iranians on pilgrimage to Zeinab's tomb. Singles US$14. Doubles US$20. Triples US$24.

Hotel Negmit Sharq (tel. 221 7798 or 222 9139), above the juice and *shawerma* stands. Shut the window and turn on the fan to avoid noise from the square below. The nicest, cleanest cheapie in the square; you won't have to worry about prostitutes as you might elsewhere. Singles S£200. Doubles S£400. Triples S£600. Quads S£800. Some rooms have bath; bargain after seeing the room.

Rafedin Hotel (tel. 222 9139), across the alley from Negmit Sharq. No English sign; enter under "Andalus Oriental" sign. Tiny rooms with thin mattresses, all within earshot of the TV lounge. Shared bathrooms. Singles S£300. Doubles S£500.

Hotel Basman, Rami St. (tel. 221 8003; fax 224 6689), up the street next to the column in Marjeh Sq. Façade and lobby hint at fabulous rooms; don't get too excited. A bed's a bed; rooms have fan and bath. Singles US$14. Doubles US$22.

Hotel Zahran, Sanjakdar St. (tel. 221 8703), toward the Citadel from Marjeh Sq. Walk up and up and up, and you'll eventually get to the Zahran. Elevation minimizes street noise, and the tiny rooms crammed with beds are quite clean. But beware: this area is reputedly the G-spot of Damascus' red light district. Singles S£200. Doubles S£300. Triples S£450. Private bath S£50 extra.

Assia Hotel (tel. 222 8849 or 4839). Head up Port Said St. from Marjeh Sq. in the direction of Al Azmeh Sq.; the Assia is on the right. It's pricey but so very clean, and its immensity affords views of the entire city. There's also a great space-age lounge. Singles US$31. Doubles US$35. Triples US$40. Breakfast S£100.

FOOD

Hummus, falafel, and *shawerma* comprise the Damascene staples. There are almost as many food stands around **Marjeh Square** as there are portraits of the impish one around town. Fresh fruit stands serve juice drinks that are meals in themselves and help prevent those dreaded Syrian colds, although glasses rarely are cleaned; it's best to use the straws planted in the pulp. To do justice to Syrian street offerings, be sure to sample the various pistachio pastries plastered with honey. The best pastry shops are also situated around Marjeh Square; those with healthy sweet tooths should also indulge at the ice cream place near the end of the **Souq Al Hamidiyyeh.** Ask for an extra coating of pistachios.

Wander toward **Azmeh Square** to enter the restaurant district, where several *kinefeh* culinarias and a few indoor cafés lead to sit-down restaurants farther on. The cleaner ones near the square ensure stomach survival; the two *souq* spots listed below are also safe enough to conserve those little pink tablets you brought on the trip. There is an outdoor café between the **Hijaz Station** and the **telephone office.**

Al Arabi, Marjeh Sq. (tel. 221 4018), in a little alley as you head toward the Citadel from the Square. The café portion of the restaurant displays all sorts of meat and vegetable dishes as well as Syria's own Double Cola; you'll get out of here with an appetizer, meat, and drink for S£150. There's also a more expensive sit-down dine-and-pay-according-to-how-touristy-and-rich-you-look bar; for prices here, the sky's the limit. Breakfast, lunch, and dinner served.

Al Eez, take the last left off Souq Al Hamidiyyeh before the ruins; the restaurant will be on your left. Modest, cramped entrance; the stairs almost meet the ceiling as you ascend. Inside, Islamic greens and blues, a built-in Bedouin tent, and the voice of Umm Kulthum will entice you for several meals. Menu includes Hands of Girls and Boiled Oily Meat, as well as the usual Middle Eastern fare. Undoubtedly the best place in Damascus to soak up Syrian atmosphere and food. Open for breakfast, lunch, and dinner. After 3pm there is live music in the tent.

Ali Baba, Azmeh Sq. (tel. 221 9881 or 222 5434), in the basement of the shopping center on the corner of Fardous St. The lights get dimmer and dimmer as you descend; the walls sport Arabian Nights scenes and there's a waterfall in the corner. Excellent appetizers (S£20-60), meat, fish, and chicken dishes (S£80-180), and a tempting dessert menu that includes "milk budding." Open after noon for lunch and dinner.

Abou Kamal, Azmeh Sq. (tel. 221 1159 or 224 4880), upstairs in the same shopping center as Ali Baba. The dirt of Damascus' streets is nowhere to be found in this white, polished, tropical place. Appetizers from S£30, entrees from S£140. Breakfast, lunch, and dinner.

Umayyad Palace Restaurant (tel. 222 0826 or 224 8901), behind the mosque. Walk to the right of the mosque, turn right, and follow the many signs. The restaurant, practically a museum, is downstairs. The owners have gone all-out to make this a truly amazing dining experience, with the best food you will taste in the Middle East. The lunch buffet is S£350. Dinner S£600, S£700 on Tues., Thurs., and Sat. when whirling Dervishes perform. When the Dervishes aren't spinning, there's live music. Open 12:30pm-midnight.

Leewan Restaurant, Bouhtari St. (tel. 458 907), off the intersection of Bouhtari and Al Abed St. This restaurant is a must. You won't find a better *shish tawouq* (S£100) in Syria; wash it down with the local brew, Barada (S£60). Also try the excellent cucumber yogurt and *kibbeh*. Lunch and dinner.

SIGHTS AND ENTERTAINMENT

Head to the **souqs** for shopping and a respite from incessant honking and maniacal driving. The easiest way to enter the *souqs* is next to the **Citadel** at **Souq Al Hamidiyyeh.** Although now closed, the Citadel (built in 1078 during the Seljuk period) once housed elaborate baths, mosques, and schools; during the Crusader invasions it served as a post for Egyptian and Syrian sultans, including Salah ad-Din. It is now undergoing extensive renovation and may eventually open as a war museum. As you pass the Citadel, merchants and their children will invite you into shops of all sorts. Cautious curiosity usually entitles you to a cup of tea and private consultations over chess or backgammon sets, Bedouin knives, and carpets galore. This *souq* is covered, and finishes at the main entrance to the **Umayyad Mosque.**

The Caliph Walid ibn Abd al-Malek supervised the building of the Umayyad Mosque in 705 on what was the site of an ancient temple dedicated to Hadad, later the temple of Jupiter the Damascene, and eventually a Christian church. The tomb of John the Baptist (known by Muslims as the prophet Yahia) is inside the prayer hall and remains a site of veneration for both Christians and Muslims. The mosque's three minarets are built in different styles and were renovated by various empires since their original construction. The walls of the mosque are decorated with intricate mosaics; on the central dome are the names of God (Allah), Muhammad, Abu Bakr, Omar, Uthman, Ali, Husan, and Hussein, some of the most significant figures in early Muslim history. In the courtyard stands the treasury, also covered in remarkable mosaics. (Mosque open daily 8am-8pm. Admission S£10.) Use the visitors' entrance, around to the left of the main entrance. Both men and women will be provided with robes if not adequately covered.

Just before the Umayyad Mosque at the end of Souq Al Hamidiyyeh is the 3rd-century CE **Temple of Jupiter,** now serving as shade for magazine and Qur'an sellers. To the left of the mosque on the way to the visitors' entrance is **Salah ad-Din's Tomb,** built in 1193 and restored by Kaiser Wilhelm II of Germany in the late 19th century. Hafez Al Asad is especially fond of the medieval swordsman, so you'll have to remove your shoes before entering the tomb. (Open daily 8am-8pm, though you'll probably have to seek out the gatekeeper, who appreciates tips—S£5-10 is enough.) On the opposite side of the mosque is the **Azem Palace,** an even more relaxing oasis. Built in the mid-18th century, the palace was the official home of the governor of Damascus. A courtyard with a fountain leads into the palace's theme rooms: the Bride's Chamber, Mother-in-Law's Chamber, Instrument Room, King's Room, Room of the Pilgrimage (featuring a Bionic camel), Café, Arms Room, Bath (hey Muhammad, you have something in your ear!), Reception Room, and artisans' area. (Open Wed.-Mon. 9am-5:30pm. Admission S£10.)

In your explorations of the *souqs* you'll likely stumble across one of several **Hammams** (Turkish baths—look for smiling clean people).

Another main street, the Street Called Straight, leads directly to the Christian quarter, where you'll find the **Chapel of Ananias** and **St. Paul's Chapel.** To get into those buildings you'll have to knock at the gates, but the friendly multi-lingual staff will tell you Bible stories until you either convert or puke.

Outside the *souqs* are several other sights of historical and mind-stimulating interest. The **Taqiyyeh as-Suleimaniyyeh Mosque,** on Salam al-Barudi St., built in 1554, is a fascinating example of Ottoman construction. Next to the mosque is the **Artisanat,** an Ottoman market that still displays enough arts and crafts to provide non-cheesy souvenirs for everyone, and the **Military Museum.** The military museum is a horrible memorial to Syria's many violent escapades. Swords, armor, guns, planes, tanks, scrap metal, and war photos supposedly pay homage to a tradition of strength and valor. (Open Wed.-Mon. 9am-2pm. Admission S£5.)

Near the military museum and the mosque, the **National Museum** has a gorgeous courtyard and an excellent collection of Ugaritic (the first alphabet, from the 14th century BCE) writings. Some of the many marble statues appear to have been missing heads, but a careful curator has been kind enough to create mixed-and-matched whole bodies, sort of. Also contains Syrian sculpture, a Qur'an collection, and 1st-through 3rd-century textiles from Palmyra. (Open Sat.-Thurs. 9am-6pm, Fri. 9am-12:30pm and 2-6pm. Admission S£10.)

The only "nightlife" in Damascus takes place in the bars of the larger hotels. Some people venture out to the cafés along the **Barada River** to smoke *argileh;* those with cars can try to make it past the military checkpoints to the surrounding hillsides for a view of Damascus at night.

■■■ PALMYRA تدمـر

Palmyra (City of Palms) is known by Syrians as Tadmor (City of Dates). The ancient city contains the most amazing ruins in Syria, perhaps the most extensive in the Middle East. The silence of the undisturbed, tourist-free remains is broken only by the sound of gusting winds and the occasional clop of a camel hoof on the highway running through the middle of the well-excavated ruins and on to the modern city. Invitations to dinner in this part of Syria are abundant. In the fall, the red dirt of the city's racetrack is churned by camels running to the cheers of anxious fans from all over the Arab world.

Palmyra was a stop for caravans passing from the Gulf to the Mediterranean during the 1st and 2nd centuries CE, before the Roman invasion. Its residents prospered on tax revenues collected from the roaming, adventurous (and hot and thirsty) traders before the Romans. After visits by the emperors Hadrian and

Caracalla, Palmyrians became even wealthier as they were relieved of the tax burdens, and their city became a Roman colony.

During the later half of the 2nd century CE, after the death of her semi-autonomous husband King Odenathus, the multi-lingual and reputedly beautiful Zenobia took control of the city and worked successfully for an independent Palmyra. However, her fierce defiance of the emperor Aurelian led to another Roman invasion. The Romans carted Zenobia off to Rome where she died, apparently well-respected by her male colleagues. The rebellious spirit of Zenobia lived among the residents of Palmyra long after her departure but continued resistance eventually resulted in the destruction of the city. In succeeding years, Palmyra served as a Roman border fortress and, in the 7th century, was conquered by Muslims. Thereafter it was only sporadically inhabited. Contemporary excavations have revealed a truly remarkable city where your imagination takes you back to when Zenobia oversaw debates on Palmyrian health care reform and defended herself against accusations of investor fraud and failed land deals. (Ha.)

PRACTICAL INFORMATION

The **tourist office** is on the highway, between the ruins and the new city (open daily 8am-1pm and 4-6pm). They have brochures on Palmyra, but the more helpful books and guides are at the entrance to the Temple of Bel. The **post office,** near a circle on the highway, may be open in the mornings, but the employees aren't really sure what's supposed to go on in a post office. For runny noses or headaches, the **pharmacy** (tel. 220 455) is next to the Palmyra Hotel. **Change money before coming,** or you'll starve. For **medical emergencies** call the **hospital** (tel. 551) or contact the police; the **police station** (tel. 112), employing very friendly people who are sometimes awake, is on the main street off the highway as you get to the first hotels in the new town. The **telephone code** for Palmyra is 034.

Private bus companies run from Damascus to Palmyra daily (S£150), usually in the afternoon. Make reservations at the private bus station in Damascus. To reach the **Pullman Station,** walk down the street with all the hotels and take a left at the little park. Service to Homs, Aleppo, Damascus, and several smaller cities. The **Karnak Station** (tel. 220 288) is near the circle by the post office. Karnak has daily service to Damascus (S£90) and Homs (S£50) in the afternoon.

ACCOMMODATIONS

Even though tourists have yet to clutter Palmyra with matching hats and T-shirts, the town's residents are (wisely) preparing for the onslaught. Hotels are under construction and prices are on the rise. Most places demand payment in dollars, unless you are the proud bearer of the coveted resident permit. If you don't see flashbulbs and hear only Arabic in the streets, bargain hard. Most hotels and good food options are on the main street that starts at the highway and continues into town.

New Tourist Hotel, main street (tel. 220 333). The only place accepting payment in Syrian pounds. Decent rooms and unbeatable hospitality. More free tea than you can drink, and an intriguing guest comment book. Singles S£200. Doubles S£300. Triples S£400. Most doubles and triples have private bath.

Tower Hotel, main street (tel. 220 1116). Fancy lobby, dining room, and rooms. A great place to stay if you can talk the price down. Singles US$20. Doubles US$25.

Palmyra Hotel, main street (tel. 220 156), next to the Tower. Not as clean as the Tower, but cheaper. Singles US$10. Doubles US$30.

Orient Hotel, off the main street (tel. 220 131). Head toward the New Tourist Hotel and take a left. The upstairs rooms were recently redone and are clean enough to cook on. Prices for the older rooms downstairs are negotiable; ask about them. Upstairs: Singles US$14. Doubles US$20. Triples US$24.

Al-Nakheel Hotel, off the main street (tel. 220 744), around the corner from the Orient Hotel. Antiques are scattered throughout a lobby with a grand staircase. Hyper-clean rooms if you can deal with the unbelievably tacky logos painted on the headboards. Singles S£600. Doubles S£800. Triples S£1000.

FOOD

Traditional Palmyra Restaurant, main street. In front of the Palmyra Hotel, not to be confused with the much more expensive Palmyra Restaurant. The owner loves students (S£5 off anything) and entices people in with all-you-can-drink-for-free tea. Great selection of grilled meats and sandwiches S£100. Also makes *mensaf* for groups if you order in advance. Open when there's a hungry stomach.

Al-Arabeh, main street. Eat here if there are no seats left in the TPR (above). Similar food but without the attention of the owner, and slightly more expensive. Open for breakfast, lunch, and dinner.

Palmyra Restaurant, main street, near the Karnak station. Fancier, more expensive hummus, *kabab,* meat dishes. You can fill up for S£250, including a bottle of flat Barada. Caters to tour groups from the expensive hotels. Open 8am-10pm.

SIGHTS

Palmyra takes a good day or two to explore. Begin at the **Temple of Bel,** the mammoth building enclosed by a largely reconstructed high wall. Guides and helpful books on Palmyra fill the small gatehouse. (Open daily 8am-1pm and 4-6pm. Admission S£10.) The **Great Colonnade** once led from the Temple of Bel to the monumental arch and the rest of the city, but is now cut by the highway. As you continue down the street, you will pass the **Nabo Temple** on your left, **Diocletian's Baths** on your right, and the extensively renovated **Theater.** The **Agora,** or Forum, served as a place of debate and discussion. Guides will want to charge as much as S£500 for a ride to the **Funerary Towers** and **Qal'at ibn Maan,** which dominate the hillsides and are quite surreal against the desert backdrop in the early morning sunlight. The view from the top of the Towers justifies the climb. You can try to bargain, but don't expect much success; people here are pretty stubborn. It is possible to walk out to these places, but without the guides you won't get in. There's also a **museum** at the entrance to the new city. (Open Sat.-Thurs. 9am-1pm. Admission S£10.) Near the Palmyra Cham Palace is **Efca Spring,** where you can swim in hellish-smelling waters—and get a mud massage to boot. As long as you don't mind being fondled, you'll probably enjoy the grotto..

■ ■ ■ H O M S حمص

The only thing in Syria more boring than a visit to the industrial center at Homs is the government's 10pm English-language news broadcast. While Syria's third-largest city was once an important stop along the trade route that inspired the building of such wonders as Palmyra, earthquakes have destroyed buildings of historical interest and strewn the streets with bent telephone poles and hanging electrical wires. Homs' real claim to fame is its proximity to the Crusader castle Crac des Chevaliers.

Practical Information You'll find the **tourist information office** on Quwatli St. in a small park (open 8:30am-2pm and 5-9pm). The **post office** waits for guests (Sat.-Thurs. 8am-4:30pm) on Quwatli St., past the tourist information office at the large clocktower circle. The **telephone code** for Homs is 31. For **currency exchange,** head toward the *souq* from the small clocktower circle and take the first right; the currency exchange booth is hiding on the right at the end of the short block (open daily 8am-8pm; ask in the neighboring shops if the booth is unstaffed). There is an all-night **pharmacy** (tel. 226 464) across from the mosque on Hama St. For **emergencies,** contact **medical facilities** (tel. 110) or the **police** (tel. 112).

Follow Hama St., which intersects Quwatli St. at the small clocktower circle, past the mosque to the **bus station,** used by **minibuses, Pullmans,** and **Karnak buses.** Across the street from the Karnak station, several **private companies** have set up offices. Buses go to Aleppo (S£45) and Damascus (S£45) throughout the day and into the night; service to smaller cities is frequent during the day. Karnak and the private companies leave at regular intervals; the others leave when full.

Accommodations Hotel options in Homs are pretty good. The most reasonable line Quwatli St. The **Hotel Nasr Jadeed** (tel. 227 243) has grimy rooms with
high ceilings, fans, and shared baths. (Singles S£200. Doubles S£300. Triples S£450.
Private shower S£35 extra.) The **Hotel al-Kayam's** employees don't speak any
English, but they can escort you to a clean room with a tile floor and a private bath
off the hall. (Singles S£175. Doubles S£250. Triples S£375.) If you're in the habit of
paying for your hotel in dollars, try the Ragadan Hotel, also on Quwatli. A huge staircase leads to spacious, overpriced rooms. (Singles US$30. Doubles US$40.)

Food Falafel, *shawerma,* and pastry shops line Hama St. between the bus station
and Quwatli St. For a sit-down meal try the **Toledo Restaurant,** behind the tourist
office and park. Appetizers begin at S£40, entrees at S£150. The *shish tawouq* goes
well with Barada beer. On the other side of the park on the block with the hotels,
Syrians crowd into the semi-outdoors **Public Restaurant,** serving cheap, simple
meat dishes for S£100. An enormous **café** across from the park showcases *argileh*
smokers, tea sippers, and coffee addicts. The place to meet Homs residents.

Sights The city's only points of interest are the **Khalid Ibn Walid Mosque,** housing the tomb of the seventh-century Muslim commander, and the **Church of the
Girdle of Our Lady,** resting place of a piece of cloth supposedly part of the girdle of
the Virgin Mary. The mosque is on the main street linking the bus station and hotel
area; the church is in the maze of the modern *souq.*

■ NEAR HOMS

The Crusader castle **Crac des Chevaliers** (Qal'at al-Hosn in Arabic) is a perfectly-pre-
served 12th-century fortress with a breathtaking view of the Mediterranean at a split
in the mountains between Turkey and Lebanon. The outside wall has 13 lucky towers and surrounds a moat hewn from the stone. The inside wall and castle sit on a
rocky plateau above the moat. Inside the castle, towers, stables, and an enormous
pillar room await the inquisitous. In a triumph of crass capitalism, the top floor of
the Tower of the Daughter of the King (no, that's not the same as the Tower of the
Princess, and thanks for asking) now sells drinks and snacks. Would you like fries
with that? Bring a flashlight to explore the secret passages in the outer wall and the
dark corridors of the inner wall and castle. Or don't; some things are more fun in the
dark. (Open daily 9am-5pm. Admission S£10.)

About 40km north of Homs is the city of **Hama,** an industrial center that manages
to be quite peaceful and visually stimulating. The Orontes River carves a path
through the middle of the city; its banks are lines with trees, gardens, and centuries-
old *norias* (waterwheels) that provided irrigation for the medieval town. Today the
norias still operate, the wood-on-wood rubbing producing a low moaning; the most
impressive are the Four *Norias* of Bichriyat, 1km from the city center. A **Grand
Mosque** (under continual restoration) and the **Azem Palace and Museum** give
those with a taste for architecture something on which to gnaw.

Just south of Homs lies **Lake Qattinah,** the artificial body of water that provides
the city with drinking water. The dam that created the lake is over 2200 years old,
and, with minor additions, performs its task as well today as it did when it was built.

LATTAKIA

Lattakia, much like Mike Cisneros, is not for looking at. It's a decidedly practical city,
the port of entry for ferries from Cyprus and Turkey and the major import-export
center of the country. Located on the coast about 100km from Hama and 135km
from Aleppo, Lattakia offers weary sojourners respite in inexpensive
accommodations. This doesn't make Lattakia any less of a city, understand—just a
mildly less interesting one.

The main street in Lattakia is **14 Ramadan Street,** which runs northeast away
from the water and ends at the central mosque. A little bit inland, running north and

south from the beginning of 14 Ramadan St., is **Baghdad Avenue** (which becomes **8 Azar Street**). The **tourist office** and most budget hotels and restaurants are on 14 Ramadan St. near the mosque. The **post office** and the **Commercial Bank** are near the port, on the southern end of Baghdad Ave. The **port** entrance is a right turn off of the south end of Baghdad Ave.

In Lattakia itself, the best sight is a tiny museum near the waterfront, with mainly Ugarit artifacts. Go north to **Ras Shamra,** where clay tablets inscribed with the earliest known alphabet were found. Not only did they prove to be the basis for all existing alphabets, but the texts on these tablets also provided archaeologists with copious amounts of information on early life in the region. Today, the tablets are in museums, but the ancient city's remains remain..

■■■ ALEPPO حلب

Aleppo (*Halab* in Arabic) is the adventurous shopper's dream. The city's covered *souqs,* full of leather goods, backgammon boards, carpets, tablecloths, Qur'ans, *argilehs,* brass goodies, *kafiyyehs,* and gold and silver jewelry, provide several days of wide-eyed delight. Even if the mood to spend does not strike, merchants' invitations to a look at their goods and a glass of tea provide opportunities for conversation and insight into the lives of Aleppo's diverse population.

In years past, Hittites, Egyptians, Assyrians, Persians, Greeks, and Romans inhabited Aleppo. After a brief period of Christian rule, the Muslims came to dominate in the 7th century. In the 10th century, Aleppo served as the capital of a small Syrian dynasty. At this time the ominous citadel was built, and the poets al-Mutanabbi and Abu al-Firas were in the court. Architects used Aleppo as a playground, building mosques, schools, and tombs. The city's *khans* and caravansaries were built later to accommodate the many traders passing through; several still stand. During Ottoman rule, building continued, and through trade with Europe, the city assumed a European feel. Cafés, outdoor restaurants, and the large tree-lined streets continue a European tradition. Although the city is predominantly Muslim, the Christian quarter is large. Many Armenians call Aleppo home; there is also a significant Jewish population and a large Russian presence.

ORIENTATION

Mastery of a pedestrian visit to Aleppo is simple. You'll find all **accommodations** and some **restaurants** in the area of **Baron Street** and **Al Ma'ari Street.** Late-night walks in this area can be unpleasant, especially when the sleazy theaters let out. Men and women will be ogled and even touched by passers-by; walk on the side of the street opposite the theaters to avoid the more offensive wandering hands. **Travel agents,** the Karnak **bus station,** the **tourist information office,** and the **National Museum** also call Baron St. home.

The city's wealthy residents strut their stuff in and around the restaurants and cafés of the **Christian Quarter.** Foot-propelled progress doesn't cost anything and is especially enjoyable in the evenings both here and in Aleppo's enormous **Public Garden.** The **post office** is the ugly building at the end of the public garden.

Several branches of the **Commercial Bank of Syria** remain closed most of the time on congested **Al Mutanabbi Street** between the hotel district, the **souqs,** and the **Citadel.** Probably the easiest way to get perspective on Syria's second-largest city is to hike up the Citadel's bridge and climb the western wall.

PRACTICAL INFORMATION

Tourist Information Office: Al Ma'ari St. (tel. 221 200), at the intersection with Baron St., across from the National Museum. They hand out several maps of Syrian cities including Aleppo, and they help with bus and transportation information. Open Sat.-Thurs. 9am-5pm. **Tourist Police:** Tel. 119.

Travel Agencies: Quite a few airlines have offices on Baron St., across from the hotels: Lufthansa, Air France, British Air, KLM, and Saudi and Turkish lines.

Currency Exchange: Changing anything but cash in Aleppo is a headache. None of the **Commercial Bank of Syria** branches on Al Mutannabi St. claims to change traveler's checks, but be persistent. Branch #4 might comply after extended debate (open Sat.-Thurs. 8:30am-noon). An exchange booth at the intersection of Quwatli and Bab al-Faraj St. will change cash only. (Open daily 9am-7pm, closed for an hour during Friday prayers.)

Post Office: Aj-Jalaa St. (tel. 221 200), near Quwatli St. and the park; a green-shuttered building with postcard sellers blocking the entrance. Open daily 8am-8pm.

Telephone Office: Outside, to right when facing post office. Open daily 8am-9pm.

Air Travel: Syrian Air, Baron St. (tel. 241 232), across from the Baron Hotel. Flights to Damascus (mornings daily, S£600), Istanbul (US$239), Cairo (US$182), and Paris (US$650). Open daily 8am-8pm.

Buses and service: Local bus tickets are purchased on a card valid for 4 rides (S£10). A bus leaves regularly during the day for the airport from a station across the street from the tourist office. **Service taxis** stop next to the **Pullman Station,** behind the gigantic Amir Palace Hotel. The **private bus companies** have offices on Ibrahim Hanano St., a few minutes' walk away from the tourist office and past the intersection at Al Walid St. The **Karnak** station faces the Baron Hotel; buses leave from behind the office to the left of the Ambassador Hotel. **Oztur** (tel. 218 470) arranges trips to cities in Turkey, including treks to Istanbul (24 hrs., S£700). (Open daily 9am-1:30pm and 5-9pm.)

English Bookstore: Follow Baron St. away from the sleazy theaters toward the park. The **Bookshop** is on the left side of the street, on the corner of Faris al-Khoury St. Open Mon.-Sat. 9am-1pm.

Pharmacies: Pharmacy hours are 9:30am-1:30pm and 5-9pm. Try **Al Mughrabi** (tel. 237 231), near Cham Palace Hotel, or **Al Mathaf** (tel. 246 419), across from the National Museum. Pharmacies rotate late-night duties.

Emergencies: The English-speaking Dr. Faher (tel. 215 252) is renowned for treating American Fulbright Scholars in Aleppo, and is your best bet for medical assistance here. **Medical Emergencies:** Tel. 112. **Tourist Police:** Tel. 119.

ACCOMMODATIONS

With one notable exception, budget hotels in Aleppo are overpriced, dirty, and often filled with Russian prostitutes. Higher-priced options congregate on Baron St., in the center of town. More affordable hotels are scattered in the streets behind Baron and Al Ma'ari St. If it's not full, stay at the **Tourist Hotel.** It can't be beat.

Tourist Hotel (tel. 216 583), off Yarmouk St. across from the museum. Head down Al Ma'ari St. and take a left at the Syria Hotel. Unquestionably the most outstanding budget hotel in Syria. The rooms are spotless, cleaned daily, and inspected with a white glove by the owner, a distinguished woman who loves to stay up late chatting in French. Singles S£250-300. Doubles S£400-450. Triples S£600.

Baron Hotel, Baron St. (tel. 210 880 or 881). Everyone in Aleppo knows this formerly majestic resting place for T.E. Lawrence, the big-stick-wielding Roosevelt, Kenal Ataturk, and Hafez Al Asad. The inside disappoints anyone marveling at the building's wonderful façade. Most rooms have private bath and A/C and are almost clean. Singles US$23. Doubles US$31. Breakfast included. 5% tax.

Hotel Yarmouk, Al Ma'ari St. (tel. 217 510), across from the National Museum. An elevator on its last legs carries you high above street noise to spacious rooms (most with bath) and large lounges. Singles S£200. Doubles S£350. Triples S£600.

Hotel Semir Amis, Quwatli St. (tel. 219 991/0), next to the exchange booth. Overpriced, and you'll have to walk up many stairs before you get to your room, which will include a bath and fan. Singles US$20. Doubles US$25. Triples US$30.

Tourism Hotel, Sa'ad aj-Jabri St. (tel. 210 156/8), near the post office and park. Only stay here if the much better, cleaner, and cheaper Tourist Hotel is full. Singles US$38. Doubles US$48. Triples US$57. Breakfast and TV included.

Al-Zahara Hotel, off Al Ma'ari St. (tel. 228 184), on a side street around the corner from Hotel Yarmouk. A decent location if you like museums, but you wouldn't want to walk around your room in bare feet. Most rooms have baths. Singles S£200. Doubles S£400. Triples S£600.

Ambassador Hotel, Baron St. (tel. 211 833), next to the Baron Hotel. Until you hear the honking horns in the street below, the nude female portraits will make you think you're in Europe. Singles US$20. Doubles US$25. Triples US$35.

FOOD

For some great inexpensive restaurants and cafés, go around the corner from the exchange booth on Quwatli St. onto Bab al-Faraj St. Take the first left and you'll see six or seven places on your right. Peek into storefronts, smell the wares, and check menus before you sit down. Baron St. has some nicer places with bird's-eye views of the crowds, but they're more expensive. Don't miss the cherry ice cream at the joint across from the Baron Hotel. All sorts of European- and American-style restaurants and cafés have sprung up in the Christian neighborhood near the park off Sa'adullah aj-Jabri St., including the Pizza House and a burger-and-pizza place featuring a borrowed golden arches sign.

Abu Nouwas (tel. 210 388). From the Baron Hotel walk 3 blocks down Yarmouk St. The restaurant is on the second block on your right. A full meal won't cost more than S£200. Open daily 8am-9pm.

Andalus Restaurant, Quwatli St. (tel. 224 104), opposite the exchange booth, on the second floor. Anything but intimate tables for two on a terrace; quieter and cleaner inside. Wide selection of appetizers (from S£35) and meat dishes (from S£80). They also serve Sharq beer and Arak. Open daily 6pm-midnight.

Ebla Restaurant (tel. 246 103), off Sa'adullah aj-Jabri St. Go past the park and look for loads of café chairs. Soups, omelettes, pizzas, *kabab,* desserts, whiskey, and Sharq beer. A healthy-sized dinner will cost S£250. Open 9am-midnight.

Sage, Sa'adullah aj-Jabri St. (tel. 215 870), in front of park. Cakes, pizzas, cheese sandwiches, and banana splits. Filling of junk S£100-150. Open 8:30am-midnight.

SIGHTS AND ENTERTAINMENT

Begin your sight-seeing tour of Aleppo at the **Citadel,** an intimidating 12th-century moated structure offering an outstanding view of the city. After crossing over the bridge, enter through an enormous gate and wind around the labyrinthine bumpy-floored fortress. Signs in Arabic point out the **armory,** the **Byzantine Hall,** the **Royal Palace,** and the opulent and all-too-restored **Throne Room.** As you brave the shifting path, you will also stumble across several **mosques.** (Citadel open Wed.-Mon. 9am-5pm. Admission S£10.)

As you exit the Citadel, the **Hammam Yarghouba-Nari** waits to steam and wash the sweat and grime off dirty, traveling bodies. (Open for women Sat., Mon., and Thurs. 10am-6pm, for men Sat., Mon., and Thurs. 7pm-midnight and every other day 9am-2am. Admission S£250 includes tea or coffee.) For those who don't spoil themselves at the *hammam,* a café in front of the citadel sells pricey tea and soft drinks. Between the Hammam/Citadel area and the hotel district, the **souqs** beckon (see city introduction, p. 496). Several **khans,** caravansaries, and **mosques** (including the 11th-century Grand Mosque or Zacharias Mosque, named after the father of John the Baptist; Zacharias's head supposedly remains) are scattered in amongst the *souqs.* Note that just about everything in the *souqs* closes on Fridays.

The **National Museum,** across from the tourist office on Baron St., has the usual fare for Syria—artifacts so old your mind strains to comprehend the time factor and deal with the relative insignificance of your own existence. The third floor has the modern art wing. (Open Wed.-Mon. 9am-2pm and 4-6pm. Admission S£10.)

Sundays, the **Christian Quarter** shops close, but the narrow streets are alive with the faithful. Walk down Quwatli St. past Bab al-Faraj St. for about five minutes and take a left. As you explore the neighborhood you'll see fabulous 17th- and 18th-century homes and the tiny **Museum of Popular Traditions,** which shows the clothes, tools, and furniture originally found in those homes. (Museum open Wed.-Mon. 8am-2pm. Admission S£5.) Finally, if you've had more tea and coffee than you can stand and need a chocolate fix, try one of the many Christian Quarter ice cream stands as you move toward the yuppie restaurant section.

Language Glossary

■■■ ARABIC (AL 'ARABI) العربى

Today's Arabic is actually two (some say three) distinct languages, and many, many dialects. **Classical Arabic, Fus-ha,** was the language of pre-Islamic Arabs and the Qur'an. Its complex rules of grammar were not derived until the Umayyad period, when the Islamic Empire rapidly expanded to include people of non-Arab origin (i.e., Turks and Persians). Today, the intricate grammar of the Classical, rigorously taught in schools, is every student's horror. It is used for Qur'anic recitation; a simplified version is used for writing, public speeches, and even cartoons on television. This less rigid form of classical Arabic has been packaged and sold to Westerners as "Modern Standard Arabic." With knowledge of Modern Standard you can read newspapers and understand television broadcasts throughout the Arab world; but the language is really an invention, classical Arabic taken down a notch and updated with terms like تكسى (*taksee,* taxi). The second (third if you count Modern Standard) brand is the **Colloquial ('Amiyya),** the language of daily life. Dialects are so diverse that an Iraqi and a Palestinian meeting for the first time would sound like a Monty Python sketch; and *no one* understands the North Africans. But educated Arabs can always fall back on the Classical, however stilted it may sound in conversation.

Arabic uses eight sounds not heard in English. *Kh* (خ) is like the Scottish or German *ch*; *gh* (غ) is like the French *r*. There are two "h" sounds; one (ه) sounds like an English "h" and the other (ح, in Muhammad) is somewhere between *kh* and plain *h*. The letter *'ayn* (ع) comes from the throat; it is indicated by an apostrophe in transliteration. Finally, *s, d, t, th,* and *k* have two sounds each, one heavier than the other.

The heavy *k* (ق), represented by a "q" in transliteration, is not commonly pronounced (one exception is in the word Qur'an). Instead, city people replace it with a glottal stop (the hard vowel sound heard in English when a vowel begins a word). Upper Egyptians and *fellaheen* (Arabic for "uneducated hicks") use a "g" sound instead of the glottal stop. So a word like *qamr* (moon) is pronounced "amr," "gamr" by, say, Mubarak.

Vowels and consonants can be either long or short, often an important distinction. For example, *jamaal* is "beauty," *jamal* means "camel." A doubled consonant can mean the difference between *ham-mam* (bathroom) and *hamaam* (pigeons).

R is pronounced as a trill, similar to Spanish. In Egypt, all *g*'s (ج) are pronounced hard (as in "giddy"); Palestinians, Jordanians, and Syrians say *j* (as in the French *"je"*). Thus "hill" is spelled *gabal* in Egypt, *jabal* elsewhere. The definite article is the prefix *al,* in Egypt pronounced more like *el.* When *al* comes before the sounds t, th, j, d, dh, r, z, s, sh, or n , the *l* is not pronounced. Never say *"ihna fee al-nar"* (we are in Hell); a more correct pronounciation is *"ihna fee an-nar."*

Although Arabic is read from right to left, numerals are read from left to right.

NUMERALS

٠	١	٢	٣	٤	٥	٦	٧	٨	٩	١٠	٢٠
0	1	2	3	4	5	6	7	8	9	10	20
sifr	waahid	tinein	talaata	arba'a	khamsa	sitta	sab'a	tamanya	tis'a	'ashara	'ishrin

USEFUL WORDS AND PHRASES

Greetings and Courtesies

hello (informal)	marhaba
hello (formal)	salaam aleikum
(response)	aleikum as-salaam
welcome	ahlan, ahlein, ahlan wa sahlan

(response)	shukran or ahlein feek (m)/feekee (f)
good morning	sabah al-kheir
(response)	sabah an-nour, sabah al-ishta if you're in a really cheezy mood.
good evening	masa al-kheir
(response)	masa an-nour
goodbye	ma' as-salaama
yes (formal)	na'am
yes	often aa in the Levant, aiwa in Egypt
no	la, la-a for emphasis
please	min fadlak (m), min fadlik (f)
thank you	shukran
I'm sorry	ana aasif (m), ana aasfa (f)
excuse me (to get attention, apologize	'an iznak (m), 'an iznik (f)
God willing	in sha allah, shortened to inshaala
Praise God	al hamdu lillah
what is your name? (Levant)	eish ismak (m), eish ismik (f)
what is your name? (Egypt)	ismak eh (m), ismik eh (f)
my name is...	ismi...
how are you ? (in Levant only)	kifak? (m), kifik? (f)
how are you ? (in Egypt only)	izzayyak (m), izzayyek (f)
I'm fine (in Levant only)	mabsuut (m), mabsuuta (f) (I'm happy)
I'm fine (in Egypt only)	kwayyis (m), kwayyisa (f)
I'm tired	ana ta'baan (m), ana ta'baana (f)
I feel like I'm about to die	rah a moot (Levant), ha moot (Egypt)
I'm not a dumb tourist (in Egypt)	ana mish khawaga
student (male)	talib
student (female)	taliba

Getting Around

Let's Go!	Yalla! or Yalla beena!
Where? or Where is ...?	fein?, wein?, or ayna?
when?	eimta
why?	leish in the Levant, lei in Egypt
I'm going to ...	ana rayih (m)/rayha (f) ila...
There is ... or Is there ...?	Fee .../?
There is no ... or Isn't there any ...?	Mafeesh .../?
restaurant	mat'am
post office	maktab al-bareed (Levant), bosta (Egypt)
street	share'
market	souq
museum	mat-haf
mosque	masjad/jaame' (L), masgad/gaame' (E)
church	kineesa
university	jaam'a (Levant), gaam'a (Egypt)
hotel	funduq or (h)otel
room	oda or ghurfa
airport	mataar
station	mahatta
traffic circle, public square	midan
hour, time	saa'a
day	yoam
week	usbuu'
month	shaher

year	sana
today	al-yoam
yesterday	imbaareh, ams (formal)
tomorrow	bukra
Sunday	yoam al-ahad
Monday	yoam al-itnein
Tuesday	yoam at-talaat
Wednesday	yoam al-arba'a
Thursday	yoam al-khamees
Friday	yoam aj-jum'a (L), eg-goum'a (E)
Saturday	yoam as-sabt
what time is it?	addeish as-saa'a? (L), es-saa'a kaam? (E)
right (direction)	yameen
left	shmal or yasaar
straight	dughree
bus	baas (Levant), utubeese (Egypt)
automobile	sayyaara (Levant), 'arabiyya (Egypt)
tourist (s)	saa-ih (m), saa-iha (f), suwwaah (pl)
back off, dude	'iff 'annee (m), 'iffee 'annee (f) (Levant), imshee! (L and E, pretty insulting)
none of your damn business	mish shughlak (m), mish shughlik (f) (Levant), eh dakh-khalak? (m) eh dakh-khalik? (f) (Egypt)

Shopping and Dining

Also see Getting Around (above) and Food in individual country introductions.

how much?	addeish? (Levant) bikaam? (Egypt)
no way!	mish mumkin!
will you take half?	taakhud nuss? (m), taakhdee nuss? (f)
money	masaari (Levant), fulous (Egypt)
change	fraata, fakke
I want ...	biddee (L), 'ayiz (m), 'ayza (f) (E)
water	mayya

Emergency

Do you speak English?	bitihkee inglizi? (L), bititkallim inglizi (m), bititkallimee inglizi (f) (E)
I don't speak Arabic.	ana ma bahki 'arabi (Levant), ana mish batkallim 'arabi (Egypt)
tourist police (Egypt only)	bolees es-siyaaha
hospital	mustashfa
doctor	duktor
passport	basbor, jawaz (L)/gawaz (E) safar
embassy	safaarah
never mind, no big deal	ma'lish

■ ■ ■ HEBREW (IVRIT) עברית

See Israel: Language, p. 249, for historical background. The transliterations *h* (ח) and *kh* (כ) are both guttural, as in the German word *ach*. The Hebrew *r* is close to the French *r*, although an Arabic (or even English) *r* is also understood. Hebrew vowels are shorter than English ones, which leads to discrepancies in transliteration. The definite article is the prefix *ha*. Feminine adjectives add an "-ah" at the end.

Although Hebrew is read from right to left, numerals are read from left to right.

USEFUL WORDS AND PHRASES

Greetings and Courtesies

hello or goodbye or peace	shalom
hello (informal)	ahlan
good morning	boker tov
good evening	erev tov
goodbye	l'hitra'ot
how are you doing?	ma nishma?
yes	ken
no	lo
thank you	toda
excuse me/I'm sorry	sliḥa
please/you're welcome	bevakasha
what is your name? (to male/to female)	eikh korim lekhah/lakh?
my name is...	shmi...
how are you? (to male/to female)	ma shlomkha/shlomekh?
fine, OK	b'seder
not good	lo tov
excellent	metzuyan
I'm tired (male/female)	ani ayef/ayefa
student (male/female)	student/studentit

Getting Around

where is....?	aifo...?
when	matai
why	lama
I'm going to...	ani nose'a l'...
there is...	yesh...
there is no...	ain...
do you (you, a female) know where...is?	ata yodea (aht yoda'at) aifo nimtza...
wait (for authenticity, bring fingertips together and gesture as you say this)	rega
restaurant	mis'adah
post office	do'ar
street	reḥov
boulevard	sderot
market	shuk
museum	muzaion
synagogue	beit knesset
church	knaissia
central bus station	taḥana merkazit
hotel	malon
hostel	akhsaniya
room	ḥeder
university	universita
beach	ḥof
grocery store	makolet
how much is it?	kama zeh?
what is this?	ma zeh?
food	okhel
hour, time	sha'a
day	yom
week	shavua

HEBREW (IVRIT)

month	ḥodesh
year	shana
today	ha'yom
yesterday	etmol
tomorrow	maḥar
Sunday	yom rishon
Monday	yom shaini
Tuesday	yom shlishi
Wednesday	yom revi'i
Thursday	yom ḥamishi
Friday	yom shishi
sabbath, Saturday	shabbat
what time is it?	ma hasha'a?
right (direction)	yamin
left	smol
straight	yashar
taxi	monit, taxi
automobile	mekhonit
train	rakevet
bus	otoboos

Shopping and Dining

do you have...? (to male/female)	yesh lekha/lakh...?
how much?	kama zeh oleh?
I want... (male/female)	ani rotzeh/rotzah...
I don't want... (male/female)	lo rotzeh/rotzah...
go away	tistalek
go to hell	lekh l'azazel
money	kesef
change (lit. "leftovers")	odef
waiter (male/female)	meltzar/meltzarit
water	mayim
coffee	kafeh
tea	teh

Emergencies

do you speak English? (to female)	ata (aht) medaber (medaberet) Anglit?
I don't speak Hebrew (female)	ani lo medaber (m'daberet) Ivrit
police	mishtara
hospital	beit ḥolim
doctor	rofee
passport	darkon
airport	s'deh te'ufa

Index

Numerics
1952 Revolution 93

A
Abbassids 39, 76, 108
Abd an-Nasser, Gamal 42, 43, 44, 68
Abdallah, King of Jordan 411
Abraham 37, 48, 52
Absalom's Pillar 398
Abu Bakr 39
Abu Ghosh 405
Abu Qir 140
Abu Qurqas 157
Abu Simbel 201–203
Abu Sir 121
Abu'l-Haggag, Mosque of 174
Abydos 164–165
ad 52
Ad-Darazi 54
Ad-Deir 449
Aga Khan, Mausoleum 196
Ain Furtuga 245
Ain Hudra 245
Ain Sileen 126
'Ain Sukhna 220
Ajlun 471
Akhenaton 157–159, 176
Akhmim 163, 164
Akhziv 313–314
Akhzivland 313
Akko (Acre) 95, 306–311
Al Asad, Hafez 481
Al Hayz 207
Al Himma 474–475
Al Lejjun 456
Al Madras 462
Al Maghtas 416
Al Mashari'a 473
Al Qasr 455
Aleppo 496–499
Alexander the Great 37, 38, 128, 152
Alexandria 127–140
al-Husseini, Faisal 413
Ali 39, 52
Amman 437–448
Go-Kart Club 433
Amun 37, 161, 174, 175, 208
Ancient Jericho 415
Aqaba 462–467

Arab League 44, 69
Arab-Israeli Wars
1948 41, 228, 277, 370
1956 (Suez War) 42, 230
1967 (Six-Day War, June War) 43, 218, 230, 337, 340, 370, 390, 411
1973 (Suez War) 218
1973 (Yom Kippur War, October War) 44, 217, 230, 337
Arad 352–354
Arafat, Yasser 43, 46
Ark of the Covenant 405
Ashdod 282
Asherah 313
Ashkelon 282–285
Ashminein 160
Ashrawi, Hanan 413
'Aslah 238
Assyut 161–162
Aswan 191–197
Aton 157
At-Tur 398
Avdat 356
Avshalom 405
Ayyubids 39
Azraq 450–451

B
ba'laweh 74
Ba'th 481
Bab adh-Dhira 456
Baha'i 54, 258, 297, 311
Baha'u'llah 54, 310, 311
Bahariyya 205–207
bakhsheesh 64, 95
Balaat 211
Baldwin I 359, 455, 456
Balfour Declaration 41, 281
Balyana 164
Banyas 340
Bar Kokhba Revolt 368
Bar'am 333–334
bargaining 15
Baris 212, 214

Bar-Yohai, Rabbi Shimon 315, 321, 333
Basata 246
Bashendi 211
Basilica of the Annunciation 318
Basilica of the Nativity 421
Bawiti 205
Be'er Sheva 348–352
Begin, Menahem 41, 44, 337
Beit Guvrin 285
Beit Ha-Tefutzot 277
Beit Jan 316
Beit Jibrin 285
Beit She'an 321
Beit She'arim 302
Bellow, Saul 259
Belvoir 320
Ben-Gurion Airport 248, 264, 267
Ben-Gurion, David 41, 42, 355
Beni Hassan 156, 156–157
Ben-Maimon, Rabbi Moshe 324
Ben-Yehuda, Eliezer 259
Bethany 422
Bethesda, Pool of 393
Bethlehem 419–422
Bialik, Hayim Nahman 275
birdwatching 365
Birzeit 419
Bitash 142
Bitter Lakes 218
Black Hebrews 354
Book of the Dead 48, 71
Boutros-Ghali, Boutros 69
Brekhat Ha-Meshushim 340
Bubastis 122
Bulaq 212

C
Caesarea 304–306
Cairo 75–114
Cities of the Dead 106–109
Islamic Cairo 94–102
Modern Cairo 93–94

Old Cairo 102–106
Cairo International Airport 59
Calvary 399
Camp David Accord 45, 230
Cardo 391
Carmel mountains 302
Carmelite Order 297
Carter, James 45
Catacombs of Kom ash-Shokafa 138
Cenacle 396
Christianity 49–52
Churches
Apostles' 454
El Mu'allaqa 103
Elazraq 162
Holy Sepulchre 50, 394–395
Mary Magdalene (Russian) 399
Paternoster 398
St. Anne 393
St. George 162, 453
St. Joseph 318
St. Michael 277
Transfiguration 242
Cisneros, Mike 479, 495
Citizens' Emergency Center 15, 19, 20
Cleopatra VII 37, 128
Colossi of Ramses 202
Constantine 38, 50, 369
Coptic Church 37, 51–52
Coptic Museum 102
Crac des Chevaliers 495
Crusades 38, 369
customs 10–11
Cyrus 38

D
Dahab 237–239
Dakhla 208–210
Dakrur 152
Daliyat Al Karmel 301
Damascus 486–492
Daraw 191
Darb El Arba'een

★ FREE T-SHIRT ★

JUST ANSWER THE QUESTIONS ON THE FOLLOWING PAGES AND MAIL TO:

Let's Go Survey
Macmillan Ltd.
18-21 Cavaye Place
London SW10 9PG

WE'LL SEND THE FIRST 1,500 RESPONDENTS A LET'S GO T-SHIRT!
(Make sure we can read your address.)

■ LET'S GO 1995 READER ■ QUESTIONNAIRE

1) Name _____

2) Address _____

3) Are you: female   male

4) How old are you?   under 17   17-23   24-30   31-40   41-55   over 55

5) Are you (circle all that apply):   at school   at college or university
                                        employed   unemployed   retired

6) What is your annual income?
£10,000- £15,000   £15,000 - £25,000   £25,000 - £40,000   Over £40,000

7) Have you used *Let's Go* before?

   Yes   No

8) How did you hear about *Let's Go* guides?

   Friend or fellow traveller
   Recommended by bookshop
   Display in bookstore
   Advertising in newspaper/magazine
   Review or article in newspaper/
     magazine

9) Why did you choose *Let's Go*?

   Updated every year
   Reputation
   Prominent in-store display
   Price
   Content and approach of books
   Reliability

10) Is *Let's Go* the best guidebook?

    Yes
    No (which is?) _____
    Haven't used other guides

11) When did you buy this book?

    Jan   Feb   Mar   Apr   May   Jun
    Jul   Aug   Sep   Oct   Nov   Dec

12) When did you travel with this book? (Circle all that apply)

    Jan   Feb   Mar   Apr   May   Jun
    Jul   Aug   Sep   Oct   Nov   Dec

13) Roughly how much did you spend per day on the road?

    Under £10   £45- £75
    £10- £25   £75- £100
    £25- £40   Over £100

14) What were the main attractions of your trip?
    (Circle top three)

    Sightseeing
    New culture
    Learning language
    Sports/Recreation
    Nightlife/Entertainment
    Local cuisine
    Shopping
    Meeting other travellers
    Adventure/Getting off the beaten
      path

15) How reliable/useful are the following features of *Let's Go*?

    v = very, u = usually, s = sometimes
    n = never, ? = didn't use

    Accommodations   v u s n ?
    Camping   v u s n ?
    Food   v u s n ?
    Entertainment   v u s n ?
    Sights   v u s n ?
    Maps   v u s n ?
    Practical Info   v u s n ?
    Directions   v u s n ?
    "Essentials"   v u s n ?
    Cultural Intros   v u s n ?

16) Would you use *Let's Go* again?

Yes
No (why not?) _____
_____
_____

17) Which of the following destinations
are you planning to visit as a tourist
in the next five years?
(Circle all that apply)

Australasia
Australia
New Zealand
Indonesia
Japan
China
Hong Kong
Vietnam
Malaysia
Singapore
India
Nepal

Europe And Middle East
Middle East
Israel
Egypt
Africa
Turkey
Greece
Scandinavia
Portugal
Spain
Switzerland
Austria
Berlin
Russia
Poland
Czech/Slovak Republic
Hungary
Baltic States

The Americas
Caribbean
Central America
Costa Rica
South America
Ecuador
Brazil
Venezuela
Colombia
Canada
British Columbia
Montreal/Quebec
MaritimeProvinces

18) What **major** destinations (countries, regions, etc.) covered in this
book did you visit on your trip?

_____
_____
_____
_____
_____
_____
_____
_____
_____
_____
_____
_____
_____
_____

19) What other countries did you visit
on your trip?

_____
_____
_____
_____
_____

20) How did you get around on your
trip?

Car   Train   Plane
Bus   Ferry   Hitching
Bicycle   Motorcycle

Many Thanks For Your Help!